HOW ASIA GOT RICH

A Pacific Basin Institute Book

THE PACIFIC BASIN INSTITUTE AT POMONA COLLEGE

Now entering its twenty-fifth year of service, the Pacific Basin Institute at Pomona College remains dedicated to its original goal of furthering intelligent communication between the nations of the Pacific Basin and increasing knowledge among Americans of the cultures, politics and economics of the Asia/Pacific countries.

Since moving to Pomona College in 1997, PBI has greatly extended the scope of its activities. Our Pacific Basin Archive of film, video and documentary material, based on the footage used for *The Pacific Century* TV series, has expanded to include more documentary and feature films. PBI's on-going Library of Japan, the first in a planned program of translations from Asian languages, has just published its ninth volume. Maruya Saichi's *Grass for My Pillow,* with two more planned for 2002–2003.

Pacific Basin Institute Books published By M. E. Sharpe

SENSŌ: The Japanese Remember the Pacific War
Letters to the Editor of Asahi Shimbun
Frank B. Gibney, editor
Beth Cary, translator

The Nanjing Massacre
A Japanese Journalist Confronts Japan's National Shame
by Honda Katsuichi
Frank B. Gibney, editor
Karen Sandness, translator

Silk and Insight: A Novel
by Mishima Yukio
Frank B. Gibney, editor
Hiroaki Sato, translator

The Kwangju Uprising
Eyewitness Press Accounts of Korea's Tiananmen
Henry Scott-Stokes and Lee Jai Eui, editors

How Asia Got Rich
Japan, China, and the Asian Miracle
Edith Terry

The Vietnamese War
Revolution and Social Change in the Mekong Delta
David Elliott

HOW ASIA GOT RICH

Japan, China, and the Asian Miracle

EDITH TERRY

Foreword by Chalmers Johnson

An East Gate Book

M.E. Sharpe
Armonk, New York
London, England

An East Gate Book

Library of Congress Cataloging-in-Publication Data

Terry, Edith
    How Asia got rich : Japan, China and the Asian miracle / by Edith Terry.
      p. cm. — (A Pacific Basin Institute book)
    "An East Gate book."
    Includes bibliographical references and index.
    ISBN 0-7656-0355-1 (alk. paper)
    1. Wealth—Asia 2. Japan—Economic conditions—1989– 3. China—Economic
conditions—1976–2000. 4. China—Economic conditions—2000– I. Title. II. Series.

HC415.W4 T47 2001
330.95—dc21   2001034217

Printed in the United States of America

The paper used in this publication meets the minimum requirements of
American National Standard for Information Sciences
Permanence of Paper for Printed Library Materials,
ANSI Z 39.48-1984.

∞

BM (c)   10   9   8   7   6   5   4   3   2   1

For Sarah, Mae, and Charles

We should, even today, make a new start, leave Chinese studies and fencing aside as of secondary importance, and take to the European ways, acquire a number of steam ships, prepare strongholds on the sea and on the land with many big guns which we will make. And in Edo first of all, then in Osaka, Kyoto, Nagasaki, Hakodate and other places, we will have standing armies at all times so that in the event an evil country should come upon us in a lawless manner, we will in all confidence . . . drive them away with our own might. Or, under some circumstances, we may even go out to destroy that evil country. Yet, the whole world will approve our act and not one word of protest will be made. And all the world will look up to the glorious might of this great nation of Japan.

—*Fukuzawa Yukichi,* Tojin Orai *(A primer on foreigners), ca. 1861–63*

Contents

Foreword by Chalmers Johnson   ix
Introduction—Globalization: One Path or Many?   xiii

Part One: How Asia Got Rich

1. Coming Home   3
2. Flying Geese   46
3. Second Invasion   102
4. Tsunami   134
5. Crisis? What Crisis?   218
6. Miracle Makers   238

Part Two: Japan's Lost Decade

7. Legacy   337
8. Sphere of the Sun   370
9. Japan Adrift   419
10. Vortex   504
11. Paradigm Lost   543

Conclusion   559

Acknowledgments   575
Notes   581
Glossary: Acronyms and Terms   625
A Note on Japanese Names   632
Bibliography   635
Index   669

Foreword

Chalmers Johnson

It seems likely that fifty to a hundred years from now, when historians look back on the period we conventionally call the "Cold War," c. 1950 to 1990, and ask what actually happened that was of enduring importance, the answer will be the enrichment of East Asia. At the beginning of that period, groups of Western savants, such as the Council of Rome, argued that Asia's population explosion would soon exhaust the world's food supply and that Asian starvation, illiteracy, and corruption might destabilize the global economy. And yet between 1965 and 1990, seven so-called high-performance Asian economies, joined since the early 1980s by China, achieved the world's highest growth rates and thereby transformed the region's and global balances of power. The leader of this truly unexpected development was Japan, which by 1993 contributed two-thirds of the $6.2 trillion regional economy.

This massive economic growth occurred in a stealthy manner, with the so-called Western nations, particularly the United States, not paying close attention to what was happening and remaining smugly confident that the East Asian achievements merely confirmed the superiority of their own "capitalist" structures. When, during the mid-1980s, they awoke to their hollowed-out industries and discovered that Japan had become the world's leading creditor nation while the United States was the world's bigger debtor, there was nothing for them to do but try to adjust. East Asian growth had become self-sustaining, and Japan's share of it was starting to decline, indicating that East Asian wealth was not just a Japanese phenomenon. By the end of the 1990s, China was the world's fastest growing economy.

These developments have set off one of the most intense intellectual and ideological debates of the second half of the twentieth century: How did Asia get so rich? The answers to that question have enormous implications for the integrity of the "orthodox," Nobel Prize–winning economics as taught in English-speaking countries, for the possibility that there is an Asian model of development, and for the Atlantic world's organizational repositories of punditry and money to help the so-called developing nations, such as the World Bank and the International Monetary Fund. The indefatigable and truly empirical Boswell of this debate, which continues to the present day, is Edith Terry.

I first met Edith Terry in Tokyo on October 26, 1994. I had just given a speech at the Foreign Correspondents' Club of Japan, and she came up afterwards to introduce herself and make a comment or two on what I had said. From 1988 to 1992, she was the East Asian correspondent for the *Globe and Mail*, and in 1993 she received an Abe fellowship from the Japan Foundation to write a book about Japan's strategy toward the other countries of Asia in the wake of the bursting, in the late 1980s, of its economic "bubble." She had already made several discoveries that were more or less unknown to scholars and officials who claimed to follow East Asian economic developments. One of these was that Japanese pressure within the World Bank had led to the Bank's publication in 1993 of its defensive and often contradictory book, *The East Asian Miracle*. In 1994, she also offered to give me a copy of a recent Japanese Economic Planning Agency follow-up study to the World Bank's report, rebutting the Bank's soft-pedaling of the role of governmental "industry policy" in East Asia's high-speed economic growth.

I paid close attention. Terry was doing some of the most original, truly hands-on investigative research on contemporary Japan that I was aware of. I soon received confirmation that she was on to a major story that was going virtually unreported in the dispatches filed by linguistically challenged Western journalists from Japan (Terry reads both Japanese and Chinese). An old friend at Japan's Ministry of International Trade and Industry, Yamada Katsuhisa, who had become head of the Institute of Developing Economics, publicly asserted, "We are not saying that developing countries should imitate Japan. But they do need to study an alternative to neoclassical economic theory" (see William Dawkins, "Pedlars of the Japanese Model to Developing World," *Financial Times*, February 7, 1995). The following month, Terry herself went into print with her revelations that Japan was in open revolt against the World Bank's view of how Asia got rich and was offering a made-in-Japan alternative (see Edith Terry, "Japan Tries Cloning Its Economic Model in Willing Nations," *Christian Science Monitor*, March 24, 1995).

Thus began her major research and writing project that has finally culminated in this important book. The years from 1995 to the present took Terry through the Asian economic crisis of 1997, when she almost abandoned her project, to Japan's economic stagnation and the endless American triumphalism about its own economy. This triumphalism is now somewhat muted in light of the U.S. economic downturn, the unraveling of the "information technology" mania, and the East Asian recovery with its dirigiste orientations strengthened. The emergence of a popular antiglobalization movement in all the advanced democracies except for Japan, and the World Bank's own belated agreement with its East Asian critics—that a market economy under effective governmental supervision produces more growth than either socialist displacement of the market or American-style *laissez-faire*—are also covered in this book.

Terry's project has also taken her back into the past to consider the history of Japan's relations with its natural trading partners, the countries of East Asia, and whether it is possible for Japan ever to overcome its dependency on exports to the United States and to rejoin its neighbors in mutually beneficial economic relations. The result is an insightful book of investigative reporting about some of the cardinal economic, political, and regional issues of the new century for East Asia and the world.

Introduction

Globalization: One Path or Many?

Until the end of the Cold War in 1989, the phrase "economic ideology" to most Westerners referred implicitly to Soviet propaganda. The battle between free-market ideology and Soviet-style collectivism, with its Maoist variant, was the familiar one. Only after the fall of the Berlin Wall did it seem for a few years as though the battle was over and free-market institutions had triumphed.

Then, with the sharp contraction of the Russian economy in the early part of the 1990s, instability in Mexico and Latin America, and ethnic warfare in Africa and the Balkans, the picture grew more complicated. In the mid-1990s, Asia was in the grip of an economic boom that seemed likely to redraw the lines of the global economy. And Japan, which had faced an enormous loss of prestige during the Gulf War, resulting from its own political inertia, suddenly grasped a way to expand its influence among developing countries, starting with the progeny of its wartime Greater East Asia Co-Prosperity Sphere.

These nations could become a critical group of allies in international organizations such as the United Nations as well as alluring venues for Japanese industry, which was being chased abroad with the rapid rise in value of the Japanese yen. Tokyo thus began a quiet but determined campaign to re-enter the treacherous intellectual space where economics plays politics and economic policy becomes a tool of national interest. The campaign wrapped together a newly minted, Japanese approach to development economics, and an old-fashioned appeal to pan-Asian values. Diplomatically, it was accompanied by a sharp tilt to Asia, and a measured downplaying of Japan's relationship with the United States.

The campaign failed in most of the obvious ways, first of all in imprinting the Asian economic model as a distinct and successful alternative to the free market. But it succeeded perhaps, where it was most important—in sustaining a challenge to the reigning ideology of the global economy. Japan became the first of the major powers to attack the convergence theory forcefully championed by the United States in the aftermath of the Cold War. Japan embraced and promoted a theoretical middle ground between the market and centrally planned economies, starkly different from the neoclassical model, which was supposed to work best in the early stages of industrialization, and had been pioneered by the Asian economies. The proof of the Asian model lay in the Asian economic miracle. Until Japan made the link, it was largely an issue for academic economists, not policy makers. In Japanese hands, the Asian model gained strategic and diplomatic traction that ultimately fed into the antiglobalization protests of the late 1990s.

This book is about Japan's challenge to globalization, how it came about, what went wrong, and what went right. Readers who are looking for a litany of Japan's failures, or proof of an imminent comeback, can stop here. The Japan of the 1990s was a study in gray—caught between paradigms, stuck on the horns of a dual economy in which some of its multinationals thundered along while the domestic economy stagnated, crippled by public inertia and political confusion, and yet bearing seeds of a new Japan. Japan might be diminished and humbled in the post–Cold War equation, but amid the gray Japanese were asking questions about core values, seeking the means to engender creativity and entrepreneurialism, and groping for new forms of political and economic leadership. Even its campaign to promote an Asian development model, loaded though it was with propaganda, contained within it a genuine attempt to re-examine the intellectual constructs associated with 150 years of Westernization. Japan lost the decade, but it began to find itself.

In the early stages of the campaign, Tokyo looked for ways to deepen its imprint on Asia. As it evolved, Japan's focus shifted to the premier global institutions of economic management—the World Bank, the International Monetary Fund (IMF), and the World Trade Organization (WTO). Faced with massive dislocation in global financial markets in 1997 and 1998, these institutions responded by abandoning convergence theory and accepting a more pluralistic approach to economic policy. The World Bank, in particular, swiftly got on board a new intellectual platform at least partly to disassociate itself from its past mistakes. Thus the Asian model, that is the Japanese version of it, was embraced by the largest and most influential of the Bretton Woods institutions. This unexpected collateral benefit—economists would call it an externality—served Japan's original purposes as well, strengthening its hand in Asia, and giving it a new platform for dealing with China. By the late 1990s, Japan could no longer hope to contain China's quest for superpower status, or its competing diplomacy within Asia. But it could, through its influence in the World Bank as well as through its own substantial aid program, play a role as mentor and senior partner to the emerging Chinese giant.

Its strategy would be to replace Chinese resentment and hostility with a sense of obligation, bridging a new century in which China would almost certainly become Asia's dominant political and economic power.

The gap between Japanese expectations at the outset of the 1990s and the reality of the early 2000s is so vast that it is difficult to perceive the thread that leads from the strident declarations of Japanese ascendance that breached the decade to Japan's actual accomplishments, overshadowed by the gloom of the era. Not so long ago, in the late 1980s, the West looked with fear and suspicion at an avalanche of Japanese money moving into Asia, together with its diplomatic corollary, as Tokyo launched the process of bridging from economic to political leadership of the region. It was a drum roll without a march, however. Over the next few years, Japan appeared to drop its regional ambitions, stunned not only by a deepening recession but dazed as well by the resurgence of the U.S. economy and China's rapid ascent. But this was not the whole story. Meanwhile, the Japanese financial, economic, and diplomatic bureaucracies were working on the outline of a new, post–Cold War regional structure. Within this new framework, the concept of an Asian model—infused with Japanese bureaucratic practice—was to play a crucial role. It was to serve as a rallying point for Asian economies seeking to fend off market liberalization and band together in defense against global market cataclysms such as the upheavals of 1997–1998. The massive problems of the Japanese economy were no deterrent; for these officials and diplomats, the issue was protecting the legacy of the old paradigm while moving to a new one. By the end of the 1990s, Japan had ensconced itself within a new network of relationships in Asia that were, for the first time, founded on a successfully promoted Japanese idea about managing growth for latecomers to the global economy. And Japan had allies outside Asia as well.

In Tokyo's hands, the contest was subtler than the one between communism and capitalism. Japan's ideas dovetailed with those of many Europeans, the communist states making painful transits to the free market, India, as well as others defending regional practices and local interests against the widening wingspan of the free market. Japan argued the case for economic pluralism and against the champions of convergence, led by the United States. Asian success was used as the leading evidence to prove the point. Here, the world's most populous region, following economic policies inspired by Japan, had achieved wonders by harnessing the market to national interest. Governments collaborated with industry. Rather than strangling the market, Asian governments had succeeded in managing it. Markets free of government interference were not the ultimate goal of economic evolution. At least, in Asia, governments and the market had found a different balance.

The thesis clashed directly with a view that had gone unchallenged during the Cold War, that Asian economies were successful because of their adoption of free market principles and institutions. Flushed with the triumphs of the 1990s, the United States paid scant heed to the debate launched by Japan. But for the Japanese, the effort to promote a Japanese model became increasingly critical to maintaining and expanding its regional and international relationships. Japan at the end of the twentieth century was easing away from its post-war alliance with the United States; at the same time, it lacked a clear view of an alternative structure defining the parameters of the new relationship except for the fact that it would need to be tolerant of Japanese institutions, if not positively embrace them. It had the tools to wield diplomatic influence but little experience in using them. Its most obvious resource was its deep pockets. The country had already built up a position as the leading supplier of development "soft credits" in Asia (financing with lengthy repayment terms and below-market interest rates) and by the late 1980s was expanding its aid program in Latin America and Africa. By the early 1990s, Japan was the world's largest aid donor, primarily through the provision of low-interest loans. International financial institutions such as the World Bank had become increasingly dependent on Japan as the United States pulled back from its obligations.

The stage was thus set for an expansion of Japanese influence going beyond the "yen shock" deals of the late 1980s, when Japanese high rollers plunged into high-priced global real estate and snapped up signature icons of Western capitalism. The implicit questions that Japan raised presented the most fundamental challenge to Western assumptions about growth and governance since Karl Marx. The Asian financial crisis of 1997–98 and the instability it caused added legitimacy to the notion of setting up safety zones outside the stream of globalization, whether for truffle farmers or fragile transitional economies. The Asian crisis may have discredited individual Asian leaders and their cronies, but it reinforced the significance of government as monitor, intermediary go-between, and champion of national interests. Government no longer dared to extract itself from the market, when the market so obviously needed its informational and disciplinary roles in order to function. This was the essence of the Japanese model. The worse the toll of globalization became, the more the Japanese model generated enthusiasm.

The irony was that Asia should become the focus for this debate. Less than a generation earlier, the Council of Rome and other elite punditry shops had engaged in extravagant public lamentations over the fate of Asia's poor. Asia was seen as a black hole for the global economy, a vortex that could suck in all the wealth created by advanced industrial nations. An Asian population explosion would soon exhaust the world's food supply. Asian starvation, illiteracy, and corruption would drag down the global economy and dilute the advances of Western technology. Such was the predominant view of Asia well into the 1970s. Most Asian economies were hard hit by the two oil shocks that occurred during that decade. And then, like a rabbit from a magician's hat, wealthy Asians were suddenly crowding into Western hotels and stock markets; smart Asians were suddenly producing the world's largest semiconductor chips and smallest mobile telephones; and Asian leaders were rudely lecturing their Western counterparts on family values and hard work.

Another peculiarity of the debate is that, in broad outline, the answers were mostly self-evident. How Asia got rich, while Africa, Latin America, and the countries of the old Soviet bloc remained poor, is no mystery. Asia started out with major advantages. Unlike their developing-country counterparts in other regions of the world, nations such as China, Japan, and India—and to a lesser degree Korea, Thailand, and Indonesia—bore a legacy of excellence. Each had experienced periods in which their respective cultures led the world in technological sophistication, the size and splendor of their cities, and depth of learning. Historical pride played a crucial role in negating the psychological and economic damage suffered in the colonial experience. In the post-colonial era after World War Two, fate dealt Asia a handy set of cards through international responses to the triumph of Stalinism in Russia and Maoism in China. First the United States, then Japan, made Asia a large part of its geopolitical strategy, as part of a joint strategy to contain China. Both poured resources into the region, and, in different ways, both opened up their markets to it.

And yet the debate over the sources of Asian wealth has been intense, heated, and fundamental. The real issues behind this success can be gleaned from the recent statistical record covering the period from the mid-1960s to the mid-1990s. During these three decades, the East Asian economies were world champions in the economic growth sweepstakes. Their achievements were called "miracles," and the nations were described as "little dragons" or tigers and their cubs. "Asian tigers" became a familiar figure of speech, conjuring up images of economic prowess to the extent that subtitles were unnecessary in a long series of books about their leaping success and the dilemmas that followed the currency collapse and "Asian crisis" of 1997. China was Dick Wilson's "Big Tiger"; Thailand, Robert Muscat's "Fifth Tiger"; Korea, a "Troubled Tiger" in Mark Clifford's book predating the crisis; after the crisis broke we had Jomo Kwame Sundaram's "Tigers in Trouble" and Robert Garran's "Tigers Tamed." The image prowls and roars and is menacing even in defeat. The ancestral tiger in this tribe was Japan. In the late nineteenth century, Japan overturned the global order established by Western imperialism's quest for wealth and power. In the 1960s, Japan roared again, when it combined tools of state planning and free-market institutions to achieve its second economic miracle. Its immediate neighbors in North-east Asia, Korea, Taiwan, and Hong Kong, took note. By the 1980s, Korea, Taiwan, Hong Kong, and Singapore had worked their own miracles and were dubbed the "four tigers." Finally, in the 1990s, a new litter of tiger "cubs" emerged in Southeast Asia, including Thailand, Malaysia, Indonesia, and the Philippines. The pace accelerated; by the mid-1990s, the transitional states of Indochina were clawing at the door. China loomed as the most formidable "tiger" of all.

At least initially, the debate was about how to interpret the statistics prop-erly. One camp maintained that the Asian economies were successful because they followed the free-market model. The other argued that they had suc-ceeded by adopting the developmental state model pioneered by Japan. The dialogue began mutedly in the mid-1980s, at a time when free-market ideol-ogy seemed unassailable and Japan was so far from promoting an economic ideology of its own that it even lacked any kind of charter or set of guiding principles for proffering its foreign aid. Insiders scoffed at pretensions that Japanese aid was based on any motive other than economic opportunism. Even Japanese aid officials, when pressed, maintained that the basis of their management of the Japanese economy was merely pragmatic, not principled. The origins of the Japanese model were, in fact, very practical. By the late 1980s, Japanese and U.S. interests in Asia, at least in terms of economic policy, diverged sharply. Japan was under pressure from the United States and inter-national financial institutions to fall in line with the free-market policies of the day; these clashed directly with Japan's interest in harnessing the energies of high-growth Asian economies to benefit Japanese business. Tokyo reacted by promoting a Japanese model of development. The "model" was legiti-mized by the obvious success of Japan, the "tigers," and their "cubs"; it was also a tool that Japan could use to deflect the pressures running counter to its emerging economic and diplomatic strategies in Asia.

Japan's first thrust was through elite circles within the World Bank and its own governmental contacts in developing countries. Terms of the debate were polite and gentlemanly. One close student of Japan's strategy within the World Bank, Anne Emig, argued that Tokyo was less interested in producing new litters of tigers around the world than in enhancing its own prestige.[1] By the late 1980s, Japan was already the second largest shareholder in both the World Bank and the IMF yet had little or no impact on lending policy. Fair enough. In 1997 and 1998, however, what had been a hushed argument be-hind boardroom doors suddenly became a loud, bitter dispute in the vortex of a remarkable financial and economic convulsion in the world arena. The latter began with the "Asian financial crisis" of 1997 and segued into the "emerging markets crisis" of 1998. The series of market failures commenced with a speculative attack on the Thai baht that quickly expanded to include all the convertible Southeast Asian currencies, then leaped continents to swamp any unit of exchange that shared certain characteristics with the Asian currencies—U.S. dollar pegs, weakening current account surpluses or deficits, and high interest rates that seemed more a prop to the currency than a means of imposing fiscal discipline. Hedge fund traders yanked support, eventually, from most of the economies that had participated in the investment binge in emerging economies of the mid-1990s. The currency collapse in many economies quickly generated banking crises, and as bank credit evaporated manufacturing ground to a halt.

The 1997–98 crisis raised the specter of global economic collapse, and although markets recovered, the legacy of crisis was a new distrust of market capitalism and a sense that globalization was a tool of the rich economies. The term "globalization" itself came into vogue as an emblem of a runaway process in which the free market expanded at the expense of poor countries, labor, women, children, and the environment—indeed, all but the giant multinational corporations that gradually were assuming the powers traditionally associated with nations. Japan found itself in the swing position. In December 1999, when developing countries—angry at the United States for insisting on the inclusion of environmental and labor standards in the negotiations—scuttled the WTO's launch of the "Seattle Round," Japan allied itself with the cause of the poor countries as well as that of European Greens, who worried that the WTO would open their agricultural markets to imports from lower-cost countries. The failure to launch the Seattle Round was a severe setback to the global trading system. The arguments about economic models were no longer academic; Japan had raised the stakes in the debate far beyond issues of mere prestige.

Except, perhaps, for the term "globalization," the language, counterparties, the tone and tenor of the larger battles in Seattle and beyond were presaged by the rolling financial crisis of 1997–98. Within a matter of months, the Asian crisis transformed a group of countries on the leading edge of globalization into victims of the process. Instead of success as the common denominator of Asian economies, they were linked in catastrophe. The nascent debate over the Japanese and East Asian "model" became swept up into a firestorm of controversy over the reasons for Asia's swift, unexpected, and virtually universal collapse. The Japanese argued that Asian success had been founded on a different relationship between government and the market than the one promoted by "Anglo-American" economics. Western critics swiftly reacted by declaring that the Asian miracle was bogus, and its model had failed. The high growth rates and obvious creation of wealth were based on speculative bubbles and fed by cronyism and corruption. The Asian model had created vast over-capacity and wild spending because it was immune to the discipline of the market. Globalization had not gone far enough. This line of criticism, though serious and substantive, had the unintended side effect of reinforcing the basic premises of the Japanese, that the Asian model was different. Perhaps worse, it helped cement the idea that Asians had flunked globalization's final exam. Globalization and Asia were no longer on the same side. The implication was that if the high-growth economies of East Asia were unable to handle the test, who else could, other than the richest of nations?

Plenty of evidence supported the thesis that the East Asian miracle had failed, not least because of the venality of leaders such as Indonesia's President Suharto and the cowboy banks and real-estate moguls of Jakarta, Bangkok, Seoul, and Tokyo. Also, the Asian economies that weathered the storm exercised more discipline than the "crisis" economies, although the disciplines were not exactly market based. China, Singapore, and Hong Kong sustained perhaps the least damage to their currencies and economies in 1997—China because its capital markets were closed, Hong Kong through swift market intervention when the Hong Kong dollar came under speculative attack that October, and Singapore through preemptive monetary policy that let the air out of its property and stock market bubbles in 1996, a year before the region-wide collapse. In all three economies, governments played a decisive role in mitigating the crisis. Because Hong Kong and Singapore enjoyed the reputation of freewheeling capitalism, their survival seemed to vindicate the "miracle is dead" school. Simultaneously, reform-minded officials throughout the region seized the crisis as an opportunity to push through privatization and deregulation, writing their wish lists into the balance-of-payments agreements with the IMF.

Evidence existed on the other side of the ledger as well, however. Asians felt that they had been the victims of unregulated global capital markets, speculative hedge funds, and imprudent lending practices on the part of international banks, as much as the weaknesses of their leaders and institutions. The sweeping generalizations about Asian corruption as a cause of the crisis seemed unfair, although most senior Asian financial officials agreed upon the need for better banking supervision, functioning bankruptcy laws, and healthy capital markets. Financial liberalization, however, was a tricky business, and many of the weakest Asian banks and credit institutions were a product of textbook capital-market liberalization policies of the early 1990s. In many instances, the same economists and journalists who in 1997 loudly denounced Asian corruption and predicted years of stagnation had been slavish admirers up until the crisis broke. The chameleon behavior of such critics helped reinforce the view that Asia was being treated as a scapegoat, and that globalization was a rigged game favoring those who set the rules.

This bitter feud over who was responsible for Asia's crash was by no means a classic confrontation of East and West. The fundamental issue, which became the basis for the failed negotiations in Seattle two years later, was the management of global capitalism. On one side were those who argued that globalization was inevitable—a force of history—and who viewed the Asian crisis as an event that exposed weaknesses that would have to be resolved before growth could resume. The revisionists, including Japan, believed that the crisis pointed to a need to engineer protective barriers into the system for more fragile economies and social groups. One group perceived globalization in terms of being a sct of universal principles for the creation of wealth. The other saw it as a process that could and must be buffered for the sake of specific communities.

Emergency policies taken to prevent the wide-scale collapse of the Asian banking and financial sectors added another wrinkle to the debate. Rather than discrediting the Asian model, the Asian recovery seemed to give it new life. The crisis shrank the boundaries of private ownership in the financial sector and expanded government control. Post-crisis, Asia's governments essentially owned its banks. Malaysia owned 20 percent of the banking assets in its country, Thailand 30 percent, South Korea 58 percent, and Indonesia a staggering 78 percent. Instead of sinking into a decade of recession in 1999 and 2000, the Asian economies quickly regained their footing as exports soared, assisted by soft currencies and a U.S. economy on warp drive. By 2000, Asia (excluding Japan) was expanding at a 6 percent annual clip.[2] Even as global growth slowed in 2001, led by a stock market crash in the United States, Asian economies remained relatively robust.

The economies leading the post-1997 recovery, particularly Korea and Thailand, had used generous amounts of public money and exports to save their necks. These were "traditional" components of the Japanese model. The IMF, which had presented long lists of economic reforms as conditions to its huge balance-of-payments emergency support loans in 1997 and 1998, by 1999 was suffering an internal overhaul after facing withering criticism for its mismanagement of the crisis, particularly in Indonesia. Korea and Thailand paid back their IMF loans early, and despite the continued support of President Kim Dae Jung and Prime Minister Chuan Leekpai, huge chunks of the IMF programs were tied up in political wrangling. With the resumption of growth came a blunt rejection of reforms in more politically sensitive areas, such as privatization. Success also bred a conviction that the critics had been wrong and the Asian model had been vindicated. In its response to the crisis, the World Bank echoed the Japanese in placing new emphasis on gradualism and good governance. The new mantra emphasized the role of government in managing the market. Privatization, market opening, and financial liberalization occupied lesser positions in the World Bank's pantheon. By another name, the Japanese model guided the Asian recovery.

Success was fragile, however. By late in the year 2000, worrying signs of deflation were appearing as Asian technology stocks tanked, mirroring the collapse of the dot-com boom in the United States, and exports slowed. As the first signs of recession appeared in the U.S. economy, analysts began to worry about the possibility of an "Asian Crisis, Part Two." In January 2001, Ron Bevacqua, chief economist for Commerz Securities in Tokyo, told Michael Zielenziger of the San Jose *Mercury News* that "the Asian nations looked like they got out of trouble, but to some extent it was an illusion driven by the export boom. The only thing that really got Asia out of its crisis was its massive exports to the United States and Europe."[3] A month earlier, Union Bank of Switzerland (UBS) Warburg economists raised the specter that Asian economies might fall into a liquidity trap similar to Japan's: "Does Asia—at least the industrial countries of Korea and Taiwan—risk becoming another Japan? In other words, policy is stimulative but credit growth falters and economic growth stays muted. There is good cause to believe that this may indeed be the base case scenario."[4] Behind such comments were assumptions common to the controversies that boiled out of the financial crisis of 1997. The issues were far from settled.

Against this backdrop, the Japanese campaign to promote an East Asian economic model was like the random shot that eventually leads to war. The battleground was globalization, and in this context, the Asian crisis, Japan's role in it, and Japan's past and future relationship with its geographic neighbors would become episodes in an explosive process reshaping the geopolitical order emerging with the new century. Japan, traveling under the banner of managed growth, would find allies where the free market was too threatening or too painful an alternative for political leaders. Its policies would also alienate its chief ally, the United States, to the extent that Washington continued to prescribe the global agenda. With the new millennium, new pressures were coming to bear that might erode U.S. dominance and not the least of these was the challenge presented by Japan.

Over the course of the 1990s, conventional wisdom dismissed Japanese capitalism as a failure. The Japanese economy had been mired in an on-again, off-again recession, and the nation's foremost economists and business leaders admitted to a loss of a sense of direction. How could Japan promote a model that was so clearly bankrupt? The Japanese, however, continued to believe that Japanese-style *jiritsuteki* (self-reliant) growth offered an alternative with proven results. In their eyes, the search for a new paradigm did not invalidate the one they were leaving behind. So it was with some astonishment that the Japanese viewed the scorn that was heaped on the East Asian model by Western editorial writers after the financial crises of 1997–98. Perhaps even more surprisingly, the West ignored the dotted line connecting the Japanese response to the Asian crisis and its growing collaboration with the World Bank. At least in part because of Japanese influence, the World Bank had undergone an internal revolution reinforced by its analysis of the Asian crisis and aftermath. The change in mind-set had left the World Bank and Japan closely aligned in terms of development policy and practice. This fact would have in turn astonished and dismayed the neoclassical economists who steered the World Bank in the 1980s. Nonetheless, the change was so gradual that, at least in the middle layers of the Bank's bureaucracy, many former neoclassicists joined the ranks of the converted.

How Asia Got Rich traces Japan's leap from an industrial strategy for Asia to crafting an economic ideology for a new century in which globalization aroused as many fears as it does promises of expanded wealth and personal horizons. Moments along this trajectory, particularly Japan's economic "invasion" of Southeast Asia after 1985, have been the subject of numerous works in English, notably Mike Mochizuki's fine *Japan Reorients: The Quest for Wealth and Security in East Asia* and *Asia in Japan's Embrace* by Walter Hatch and Kozo Yamamura. The Asian financial crisis spawned a dozen or more books analyzing its genesis and impact. But Japan's recent Asia policy and its promotion of the Japanese development model have received little attention. To date, the only published works focusing on the change are by the husband-and-wife team Ohno Kenichi and Ohno Izumi. The Ohnos, both development economists, have written about the change in philosophy at the World Bank and development economics from a Japanese perspective in two books published in 2000, *Sekai Ginko: Kaihatsu Enjo Senryaku no Henkaku* (The World Bank: A revolution in development aid strategy) and *Tojo Kuni no Gurobarizeshon: Jiretsuteki Hatten wa Kanoka* (The globalization of developing countries: Is self-reliant development possible?).

I have set Japan's efforts to shape the region in the context of its global goals, although from a Japanese perspective, the former may be more critical to its immediate survival in the stormy waters of post-twentieth-century Asia. In the 1990s, Japan began to focus seriously on future scenarios in which the United States would no longer serve as its protector in the region and an ascendant China might continue to nurture memories of Japanese brutality and take those memories as its cue for conducting future policy. Even the most benign scenario—in which the United States continued to serve as peacekeeper but Japan lost its favored relationship with Washington—was a wake-up call to the Japanese. Japan would need friends in Asia, and it would need them fast.

Initially, I intended to restrict myself to Japan's expanded relationship with Asia after the yen appreciation beginning in 1985. This apparently straightforward assignment rapidly took me in several new directions. Japan's efforts in the late 1980s to implement a regional development plan in Asia led to its effort to influence global economic policy through the premier global development institution, the World Bank. I then saw that in order to understand the intellectual foundations of the Japanese model, I would need to reach back into Japanese efforts at economic engineering within the confines of the Asian empire that had crashed in 1945. This theme led me as well to a different version of the "Japanese model" that saw action in the ideological trenches of the Cold War in the 1950s and 1960s. The Asian financial crisis provided a new context to Japan's intrigues with the World Bank and IMF, making them part of a widening international debate over the consequences and means of globalization.

Finally, Japan's effort to invent a new paradigm in its Asian relationships, coming at the end of the twentieth century, raised haunting echoes of earlier cycles of history when Japan embraced, then rejected, then embraced again the icons of continental influence. In the late nineteenth century, Japanese modernization had been marked by a blanket repudiation of all elements of Chinese and Asian influence. The act established a break in the Japanese psyche that, over time, poisoned its relationship with its own past and made the Japanese more vulnerable to the influence of predatory value systems, whether the militarism of the 1930s or the corporatism of the post-war period. In the context of history, Japan's late-twentieth-century romance with Asia raised the possibility of a more profound reshaping of the Japanese psyche, a healing of the original, self-inflicted wounds of modernization.

While looking back at history, another part of my agenda was to produce a work of journalism, which meant keeping up with the news. In the 1990s, events in Asia seemed particularly fluid and ambiguous. It was a time of transition, when the outline of new relationships first became visible and other possibilities were finally eliminated. I intended to focus on Japan's external policies but inevitably was drawn into a consideration of Japanese domestic issues, adding still another dimension to the narrative. Japan's Asian diplomacy in the 1990s ran counter to the most fundamental of its external paradigms, the U.S.-Japan alliance, still critical to both countries' strength regionally and globally. In order to reshape the alliance structure, it quickly became apparent that Japan would have to revise the domestic institutions that had endured and fossilized under the rubric of the all-important U.S.-Japan relationship. Japan's efforts abroad—whether seeking recognition of its economic model or wooing its neighbors—were external symptoms of a much larger paradigm shift underway within Japan.

I have tried to interpret, and express, the bewildering quagmire that Japan entered at the end of the twentieth century. In terms of national mood, Japan in the arrogant and expansive 1980s, Japan in the confused mid-1990s, and the exhausted Japan of the late 1990s seemed like three different countries. Japanese now refer to the 1990s as their "lost decade." For those tracking Japanese economy and society during this period, signs of drift were equally abundant in Japan's paralyzed politics, its flustered response to domestic crisis, and the mixed messages of its response to the Asian financial crisis.

It was a decade of missed opportunities and incremental change. During this period, two Japanese economies emerged: a successful offshore economy based on Japanese multinationals and a shrinking economy at home. The two were intertwined, and the failure of the political leadership to come to grips with domestic change was echoed in its failure to offer a clear strategy to lead Asian economies out of the crisis of 1997–98. Japan's attempt at regional leadership was constrained by the repeated failures of its political vision, the inability of its post-war economic paradigm to adapt to the fleet-information age, and the resistance of its tribal and closed society to the promise as well as the risks of globalization.

During the Asian crisis, the Japanese economy slid from mere stagnation into deep decline, as the economy contracted for the first time since the oil shocks of the 1970s. Japanese productivity plummeted. In 1999, the Japanese unemployment rate was higher than those of the United States and Great Britain, although this was somewhat misleading because Japan's lowest post-war employment occurred just as the United States and Britain were reaching post-war highs. The 1990s saw Japan wandering in a wilderness of its own making, but also saw unprecedented changes to institutional structures that had been bedrock features of the Japanese economy for almost fifty years.

The changes ranged from new foreign ownership of flagship Japanese auto companies, to elite Japanese graduates flocking to foreign firms, to premier Japanese companies' disregard of the walls between rival *keiretsu*, the giant business combines that took over after World War Two when the U.S. occupation banned holding companies. Auto companies announced they would put subcontracts out to bid, Sakura Bank merged with Sumitomo Bank, and foreign ownership grew in major Japanese companies such as Sony, Rohm, Hitachi, and Mitsubishi Heavy Industries.

Japan's Asia policy was another of these unheralded successes. In the 1990s, Tokyo finally began to break through the persistent myths that had served to retard its diplomacy in the region. One of the most central of these was that Japan had been a victim, not a perpetrator, of World War Two in the Pacific. Closely associated was a second illusion—of Japanese ethnic superiority vis-à-vis other Asians. During the first half of the twentieth century,

Japan's self-assumed civilizing role had played a major part in the propaganda of the Greater East Asian Co-Prosperity Sphere. In the Japan of the 1980s, nothing seemed untoward about the bluster of Ishihara Shintaro, who told *Time* magazine in November 1989 that "Japan's franchise is Asia."[5] The assertion went along both with the determined official position that Japan had completed its official apology to Asians with the war reparations of the 1950s and the unofficial position that the reparations had been a form of tribute to the victor in the conflict. Japanese schoolchildren grew up reading in their textbooks that the Kwantung Army had merely "advanced" in China rather than invaded it, and prejudice against Japan's large ethnic Korean population was not only overlooked but protected by Japanese law. These same Koreans had originally acquired their residence in Japan as a result of the Japanese Occupation of Korea in 1910 and its incorporation into the Japanese Empire. During the colonial period, they had been citizens in an imperial hierarchy founded on the notion that non-Japanese were ethnic inferiors, and the Koreans who remained in Japan after the war's end retained that second-class status.

In the early 1990s, around the time of the fiftieth anniversaries of the beginning and end of the Pacific War in 1991 and 1995, respectively, policy began to change. Japanese official visits to Asian countries, which had been rare, became frequent. Tokyo began managing a web of bilateral summit relationships within the region, which soon developed new geometries. Summits with leaders of the Association of Southeast Asian Nations (ASEAN) began in 1996 and informal trilateral summits with China and South Korea started in 1997. Slowly, painfully, official apologies began flowing as well, beginning in May 1990 with an apology to Korean president Roh Tae Woo during the first official visit to Tokyo by a Korean head of state. The language used in the declaration was so ambiguous that a major diplomatic flap was sparked, but over time, two surprises happened. The apologies became more specific, and Asian leaders began telling Japan they were no longer necessary.

By October 1998, when President Kim Dae Jung made his first official visit to Japan, both rhetoric and body language had sharply improved. Japanese prime minister Obuchi Keizo told Kim that Japan was sorry for the "unbearable pain and damage inflicted on the Korean people" by Japan's 1910 to 1945 colonial rule of the Korean Peninsula. President Kim responded by telling reporters, "We must settle the accounts of the twentieth century . . . as we enter the twenty-first."[6] Meanwhile, Korea and Japan conducted a range of joint activities aimed at building trust. Young scholars participated in a "K-J Shuttle" to participate in frank discussions of bilateral and cultural issues. At the behest of the IMF, Korea removed bans on imports of Japanese-manufactured goods and cultural products. In 1999, the two navies began joint military exercises after North Korea launched a missile across the Sea of Japan.[7] Such gestures came at a political cost, within Japan. More significantly, they marked the gradual attrition of attitudes and ideas associated with Japan's post-war paradigm and their replacement by new behaviors. Like a massive shelf calving icebergs in the throes of a climactic shift, the gestures signaled greater change to come.

Perhaps I should have stuck to my original plan, to write about the flow of Japanese capital into Asia at the end of the 1980s. The business story was remarkable enough: Japan's $100 billion investment transformed Asian economies from labor-intensive resource exploiters to sophisticated manufacturing exporters in less than a decade. Yet, the harder I looked at the subject, the more it seemed to make sense as one stage in the grand sweep of Japan's drive for modernization, as a moment of cultural as well as political and economic change. In the end, what mattered most, at the end of the twentieth century as at the beginning, was how Japan challenged basic presumptions of Western societies, and how that challenge served fundamentally to enrich the world at the same time as unsettling it.

The book is, in some respects, a personal account and family memoir as well as a journalistic and historical narrative. No matter how far we travel, we bring myths with us. They may blind us to reality or encourage us to substitute propaganda for analysis. Our personal myths may also help us to reach a more intimate vision of a place or time. I grew up in Asia, in the Indonesia of Sukarno, the Taiwan of Chiang Kai-shek, the Philippines under Macapagal, the father, and Marcos, the democrat before he turned dictator. As an adult, I had lived in Beijing during the early period of the *kaifang,* or "open door" period of economic reforms, in Tokyo during the apogee of the "bubble economy" and its dire aftermath, and in Singapore and Hong Kong. From my earliest childhood to middle age, I had spent much of my energy seeking a better understanding of Asia. There was a motif in Japan's painful journey through the twentieth century that resonated. All that brilliant energy invested in self-transformation, rejection of an old culture, embrace of the new. I could understand the enterprise and how difficult it was to live with.

E.H. Norman, the Canadian diplomat, growing up in Japan in the 1920s as the child of missionaries, saw the culture in terms of a complex tradition dating from the Meiji period, not only in the introduction of modern institutions but also the maintenance of the Tokugawa order based on feudalism and strict hierarchy. His *Origins of the Modern Japanese State*, published in 1940, argued that Japanese military aggression had deep-seated support in the Japanese elite, a view running counter to later, Cold War propaganda that Japanese aggression was an aberration led by deranged military officers. For the insight, the McCarthyites went after him in the early 1950s, and in 1957 he committed suicide. I like to think that his ideas were shaped by a sense of humanity that was at least partially rooted in Japan, that he developed his theory from long observation.

I, too, have sought to root myself in Asia, in a perspective based on friendships going back to childhood and an education in which Asian teachers and texts were as fundamental to my understanding of the world as the classics of Western tradition. In writing a book about Japan, I hoped to do justice to the humanity of the Japanese, bureaucrats, intellectuals, the *sarariman* at home and abroad, housewives and politicians, who found themselves dealing with circumstances that were to me, at least, oddly familiar.

I have also tried to show how the U.S.-Japan relationship of the immediate post-war period set the terms for Japan's regional strategy for the next half century and beyond. The American and Japanese experiences in Asia are so closely intertwined that neither is fully comprehensible without the other. I grew up in Asia at a time when U.S. power was predominant and the Cold War was at its height. The Vietnam conflict peaked about the time I graduated from high school in Manila. The Philippines, where my family lived through most of the 1960s and 1970s, was a major recreational haunt for military personnel on leave from the war. American soldiers, business, and government were part of the landscape. There was a young, rebellious American community comprising Peace Corps volunteers who wandered back to the big city from the barrios; American military on AWOL, swarming the red-light districts of Ermita, Angeles City, and Olongapo; and high-school kids imitating the hippie movement back home.

My father was a diplomat. His mission was in large part one of economic propaganda. An official with the U.S. Agency for International Development, he labored to persuade Filipinos, Vietnamese, Taiwanese, and Indonesians to embrace American democracy and the free market. We were in the thick of a trans-Pacific current called the Cold War, sucking Americans into the vacuum of post-colonial Asia, changing us and changing them. I am sure that my father believed he could make things better for the Asians he worked with and am equally sure that he was disappointed. I know how much I wanted to re-invent myself as an Asian and how far short I fell of my goal. So I wondered, considering Japan, how its Asian episode would fare, whether it would be short or long, and whether it would change Japan in ways that I myself had been changed.

We long-term expatriates are like sea drift, left behind in the massive tidal shifts of history. In writing this book, I hoped to provide a window for other Americans to see a part of American history in Asia that I had personally experienced. Most of them have never known about this period or forgotten it, a time when the United States busily promoted its economic model in Asia. I was there; I remembered; I could tell the story.

In recent years, it has become popular in Japan to talk about the need for a third "opening"—following the first one by Commodore Matthew Perry in 1853 and the second "opening" by General Douglas MacArthur in 1946. Both these earlier events were based on the use or threat of overwhelming force. Perhaps Japan's third opening will be of a different nature, involving a revolution from within. Its changing relationship with Asia might be an emblem of changes brewing in the Japanese soul, as Japan and the Japanese seek a fresh look at their history, region, identities, and the world.

Hong Kong, April 2002

Notes

1. Anne L. Emig, "Japan's Challenge to the World Bank: An Attempt at Intellectual Leadership" (paper, Columbia University, New York, December 1996), typescript draft.

2. Peter Hartcher, "Recovery Now Looking Fragile," *Australian Financial Review,* June 19, 2000.

3. Michael Zielenziger, "Asia's Export Boom Delays Reforms after 1997 Financial Crisis," San Jose *Mercury News,* January 1, 2001.

4. Quoted in "Deflation Fear Hangs over Recovering Asia," *South China Morning Post,* December 27, 2000.

5. *Time* magazine, November 6, 1989.

6. "Visiting Korean President Kim Dae Jung Gets the 'Heartfelt Apology' He Sought," *Japan Digest,* October 8, 1998.

7. Ralph Cossa, "A Change in Relations: Getting Japan and Korea Past the Past," *Japan Digest,* October 6, 1998.

Part One
How Asia Got Rich

When the white waters fill the spring embankments
Migrating geese each year come winging back.
Gabbling in the swift flow they tug the tender cress,
In flocks they swim along, stirring light ripples,
Or singly drift, chasing a lonely sunbeam.
Hovering above in flight some never come to rest,
While others rise confusedly, ranks yet unformed.
And then with flapping pinions, undulating in the air,
In one grand sweep they all return to their old home.

—*Shen Yue, "Wild Geese on a Lake"*

East Asian policy making is like pharmacology.
A pharmacologist finds the bark of a tree that seems
to shrink tumors in rats. He has no idea how it works.
But thirty years later, somebody gets a Nobel Prize. The
Japanese practitioners have no idea why their policies
worked. They haven't spent their lives giving a pleasing
verisimilitude to their stories; they've just been doing it.

—*John Page, chief economist, Middle East and North Africa,
World Bank, Tokyo*

Yes to Life, No to Debt!
No to Structural Adjustment Programs!

—*Street sign carried by protestors, World Bank/IMF Spring Meetings,
Washington, D.C., April 11, 2000*

1

Coming Home

For much of the 1990s, Japan was like a sumo wrestler on steroids, a spectacular giant, unmindful of its flaws or future retribution. I am gazing at its capital city from the New York Grill, a restaurant and bar fifty floors up in the new and luxurious Park Hyatt Hotel. Its décor includes the exposed racks of a "sky cellar" of 1,600 bottles of imported French and Californian wine. Below is the dense sprawl of west Tokyo. Looming to one side is Shinjuku Station, the world's largest train terminal, spouting department stores and office towers, hung about with video screens, and laced with a reckless variety of transportation ramps, tunnels, and flyovers. There are construction cranes everywhere. The stores boast the latest and best of everything.

The lights are up as night creeps over a reddened Mt. Fuji and its attendant foothills to the west. Tokyo's frenetic residents—the *sararimen* in their dark suits, the office ladies like French poodles in spike heels and the latest Italian and French fashions—pour into the streets in pursuit of a thousand pleasures. At the New Otani Hotel, outlined against the dense black of the Imperial Palace with its moats and shade trees, politicians and celebrities crowd elegantly into a perfect reproduction of the legendary Parisian restaurant, La Tour d'Argent. The New Otani version serves ducklings, pampered according to a French recipe hundreds of years old. Each duckling has a numbered certificate. The luncheon "specials" are $300 a plate.

Beyond the moat, thousands of other Tokyoites are tossing back cold sake in fashionable *izakaya* pubs, crowded with red-faced office workers yelling over the noise. Some will be weary from shopping in eponymous Versace or Armani, Isse Miyake or Yohji Yamamoto boutiques. Others will be fretting over the difficult decisions of where to go next, what to do, what to see. Tokyo is an endless festival. The possibilities seemed limitless, even in the dog days of the 1990s, a time when recession, unemployment, corporate restructuring, and political failures rotted the veneer of Japanese self-confidence. Anxiety entered into the creative cauldron of Tokyo and was reborn in the strained, edgy, volatile Japan of the new century. The sumo wrestler invisibly shifted balance; the decade caught him in the moment just before a lightning lunge. The outcome was as yet uncertain, but the gamble was taken. Japan in the new century would be something new, no longer the Japan of Meiji, Taisho, and Showa eras, no longer the empire or the kingdom of bureaucrats or Japan Inc. It was passing beyond the breakdown and confusion of the 1990s. It was a time of extreme volatility, of heightened risk. The one link with the past was that Japan's fate would drag with it America's future in Asia, because Japan, unlike Vietnam, Thailand, Singapore, the Philippines, or South Korea, was the one indispensable country to American security interests in the region, its island aircraft carrier, its protégé and most brilliant student.

Endangering America, the decade was one in which Japan initiated a revolution in its relationships with its neighbors, particularly with China. Like many other aspects as the nation limped from the 1990s into the 2000s, these new relationships encapsulated polar opposites, generating a nerve-wracking tension, but also muddying events in the eyes of beholders. America saw mainly the ambiguities, overlooking the threat it presented to its own position in the region. At a time when, by most objective measures, Japan had taken on a central role in shaping the Asia-Pacific regional economy and its attendant political and economic institutions, its body language remained that of a peripheral power. As China grew in power and prestige, Japan seemed to shrink inwards, even as it remained Asia's giant in terms of both economic output and international trade. Its bolder geopolitical moves—such as nurturing a strategic dialogue with the Association of Southeast Asian Nations (ASEAN)—were discounted by Washington as feeble and ineffective. And Washington failed to reckon with the threat to the global system as Japan wandered, groping for a new core.

Washington was not alone in its disregard. Many, perhaps most Asians viewed Japan as a diplomatic lightweight in the region. In their view, Japan remained significant only as a proxy for U.S. interests, despite the new post–Cold War reality of reduced U.S. commitment both to Japan and to the region. China shouldered Japan aside with ease in the geopolitical arena, as it grew stronger economically and gradually began to assume the stature of an advanced industrial nation after its acceptance into the World Trade Organization in 2001. Asians accepted Japanese money and financial aid but were quick to criticize its insensitivity to the history of Japanese military aggression in the first half of the twentieth century. Japanese bureaucrats and businesspeople knit together a comprehensive plan to relocate Japanese industry to Asia, while their politicians regularly paid homage to symbols of Japanese militarism. Asians admired and adopted elements of Japan's economic model, yet despaired of Japan's inflexibility and rejected any suggestion that Japan might serve to "orchestrate" Asian growth. Japan's Asian neighbors saw more clearly than Japan that its economic model was obsolete, yet remained intrigued by the concept of an East Asian economic strategy reflecting indigenous solutions to the age-old pursuit of wealth and power.

Japan's evolving relationship with Asia, rich in ambiguities, was at the foundation of Japan's equally complex experience with the pressures of globalization as they intensified at century's end. In order for Japan to perpetuate a pluralistic global regime, against strong pressures for convergence and homogenization, it needed Asia as ally, prize exhibit, and power base. At the beginning of the 1990s, such goals seemed well within Japan's grasp. By the end of the decade, Japan had formally given up the effort to impose a blueprint on the Asian economy, was cutting back its foreign aid drastically, and was falling far behind China's inventive diplomacy.

And yet, the 1990s left behind a tidal mark of profound significance not only for Japan and Asia but also for the world. Japan entered the decade as an outlier in the Asian economy, politically and culturally isolated. It ended the decade, and the century, as a central player in an emerging regional framework aimed at nurturing Chinese growth while deflecting China's potential threat as it rapidly assumed superpower status. In this chrysalis of regional identity, Japan's ideas about growth and development, and even economic coordination on a regional scale, remained potent.

In telling the story of Japan in the 1990s, I have woven together two narratives. The first of these is Japan's diplomatic tilt to Asia, which began formally in the late 1980s with a series of economic initiatives and climaxed with Japan's huge financial outlay in support of the region after the Asian financial crisis. This was far more than a diplomatic juggling act. Japan's abortive Asian courtship was part of an ongoing effort to re-shape the Japanese polity in the aftermath of the Cold War. This required simultaneously jettisoning Cold War baggage and screwing new apparatus in place, analogous to remodeling an aircraft in flight. In the broadest terms, I have tried to show how and why Japan failed in establishing a new Asian economic condominium, yet succeeded in leaving its mark on the globalization debate and in crossing an essential threshold in the Japanese psyche. Japan gave the world a brand new perspective on the nature of the East Asian economic model, which became fundamental to policy and practice in developing nations and the advice provided by international financial institutions. Domestically, Japan's Asian diplomacy represented a rebirth for Japan after a half century in which Japanese political leaders kept their focus firmly on the United States in the service of the war against communism. In pursuing a new set of relationships with its neighbors, Japan aimed not only to revise its alliance structure, but also at cultural and political renaissance. Its success was limited on both fronts, but it succeeded enough to lay the basis for a new regional policy and to begin to awaken the Japanese public to the meaning of global citizenship.

Up until the 1990s, Japan's regional policy faithfully reflected Washington's sanctions and prescriptions. Taking refuge in its pacifist Constitution, Japan refrained from adopting any strategic or security role in the region, while it nurtured Southeast Asia, Korea, and Taiwan as resource suppliers and markets. For the most part, Japan refrained from exploring any new terms and conditions in its relationship with China, continuing to accept the old blueprint for Sino-Japanese relations crafted by the United States at the height of the Cold War. Under U.S. tutelage, Japan was to limit its economic ties with China, substituting U.S.-dominated South Korea and Southeast Asia for the factories and infrastructure of former Manchukuo. Even after the Chinese economic reforms began in 1978, Japanese companies limited their investments, while the Japanese government did little to move beyond the festering psychological residual of Japan's invasion of China in the 1930s. This legacy continued to surface in debates over Japan's officially approved high school textbooks that delivered a whitewashed version of the period, as well as controversies over the treatment of Asian men and women forcibly drafted as soldiers and prostitutes by Japanese occupation forces. Japanese leaders in the 1990s finally moved beyond the ritual tensions of the Cold War and began to inject a new realism into Japan's Asian diplomacy.

The second narrative is the story of the Japanese economic model, and how it became the centerpiece of a national debate whose themes of failure and exhaustion were utterly at odds with the efforts by elite Japanese bureaucrats to franchise out the Asian miracle. I argue that the fundamental failure with Japan's new regional geopolitics was at home, with a domestic social, political, and economic paradigm gone sour. As the model itself was evaporating, Japanese bureaucrats spun an amazing scheme to develop an intellectual and ideological alternative to Western capitalism. Their gaze was turned outward, focused on expanding Japanese influence in the post–Cold War era. They failed to consider the obvious—that few outsiders could believe in a model that was so clearly disintegrating at home. And at an even more basic level, they failed to reckon with the failings of the Japanese people.

Japan's public was woefully ill prepared for the implications of a closer relationship with the rest of Asia, particularly when it came to accepting other Asians into their neighborhoods, companies, and schools. The Cold War had put pressure on Japan to suppress public debate on foreign affairs or defense issues, limiting the degree to which ordinary Japanese gave any thought to global or regional issues. The very word "strategic" fell under a taboo, according to Sassa Atsuyuki, former director of the Cabinet office for National Security Affairs. These limitations came on top of a century in which Japan saw itself as fundamentally a participant in a Western club of nations, superior to any Asian country. At the same time, throughout the twentieth century, Japan's relationship with the West was plagued by ambivalence, caused by the humiliation of its defeat in the Second World War and by a nagging racial resentment.

It was in this context that Japan's Asian tilt marked a dramatic new departure, completing an arc that had begun in the first phase of Japan's modernization with a sharp rejection of its Asian cultural roots. Indeed, it was only as a result of wider changes sweeping Japanese society that Japanese public opinion began to shift toward acceptance and recognition of the geopolitical reality of China's increasing dominance and the need for social as well as political sensitivity toward Japan's neighbors. Thus, however much Japan might resist the tide, globalization has had the effect of helping along a historic reversal of values that set Japan apart from Asia. Japan began the century in alienation from the rest of Asia. It ended with a hesitant reunion.

None of the tension behind these developments is particularly visible on a casual jaunt around Tokyo, which, more than any other Asian city, is settled in its success. Here, in the late 1990s, the East Asian economic model appeared to be in full bloom, delivering a rich, diverse menu of experience to a population that was largely middle class, pleased with itself, and immune to the collapse of the nation's financial and property markets. Few Japanese were investors, and while most owned their own homes, they left property development to speculators, closely allied with gangsters and politicians. Many remained untouched by the collapse of the so-called bubble economy of the late 1980s. *Pia*, a weekly magazine that lists new restaurants, performances, and other Tokyo "events," is thick with entries. On any given afternoon in the big city hotels, middle-class Japanese couples and their children throng the carefully tailored gardens and tearooms, consuming like mad, with no sign of the tremors that were holding back the Japanese economy and foiling attempts at recovery. This was Japan at the end of the century— a nation of "glorious might," wealthy, self-absorbed, unconscious of the fragility of its status in the world and the region.

Yet, beneath the surface glitter, the shoppers and office workers in their pubs and the bureaucrats and politicians in their exclusive *ryotei*—restaurants that serve no food but feature ample privacy and discretion—had just completed an unsettling time. Journalists called it Japan's "lost decade," comparing the period to Latin America in the aftermath of the debt crisis of the early 1980s. Japanese and foreign observers alike began to refer to Japan in terms long reserved for the bargain-basement economies of Africa or the

Caribbean. Creeping disintegration attacked the foundations of society, from the myth of the incorruptible bureaucracy to the paradigm of lifetime employment. The U.S. alliance structure began to unravel at the beginning of the decade with discord over Japan's conduct in the Gulf War; it wobbled, recovered, then wobbled again as Washington instinctively leaned toward China as its principal counterpart in the new, post–Cold War balance of power in East Asia. The foundation never quite collapsed nor was it replaced with anything new. Still, Japan began to change at the margins, accepting new forms of dialogue and a measure of integration with the global economy inconceivable in the 1970s or 1980s and that would drive developments beyond the 1990s and into the 2000s.

In international affairs, Japan aspired to multilateral diplomacy, using economic and technical aid to build confidence regionally and globally. In 1993, the great journalist Funabashi Yoichi, born in China, a veteran correspondent for *Asahi Shimbun* in Beijing, Washington, and Tokyo, wrote wistfully about the world's first "global civilian power,"[1] with Japan propelling a new form of civilization dedicated to economic prosperity rather than territorial aggrandizement. Japan moved toward the first broad public debate of shibboleths of the post-war era, ranging from the merits of Japanese pacifism, written into its Constitution by the Supreme Command of Allied Powers (SCAP) in 1946, to Japanese war crimes, long considered a subject identified with radical leftists and government subversion. In the economy, throughout the 1990s talk was of reform and *ristora* (restructuring). By the end of the decade, the first great mergers across *keiretsu* lines, the first takeovers of flagship Japanese companies by foreign owners, and the rapid expansion of electronic commerce and software boutiques heralded an evolution, if not revolution, in Japan's political economy.

The country finally started to make needed changes, taking the first steps to replace the fortress mentality of its postwar leadership with a more flexible and cosmopolitan outlook. At the same time, evidence mounted of a sharp inward and nationalistic turn on the part of the Japanese public. In 1999, the wartime Japanese imperial flag and national anthem, the Kimigayo, were legally restored after a half-century hiatus. In Spring 2000, Prime Minister Mori Yoshiro created ripples of alarm across Asia by declaring to a Shinto political organization that Japan was *kamigami no kuni* (a divine country with the emperor at its center).[2] Just a few weeks earlier, in his first speech to the Japanese Diet Mori promised to introduce legislation enabling Japanese troops to carry weapons abroad and conduct U.N. peacekeeping operations (UNPKO).

"Contributing to the maintenance of international security is an important task for Japan," Mori said.[3] In another nation, the remark might have seemed innocuous, but in Japan it carried ominous overtones because when all was said and done Article 9 of the Japanese Constitution gave the nation the right to take military action only in self-defense. For most of the post-war period, Article 9 commanded broad public support. Now, it seemed as though the assumption of a more "normal" approach to international security might be coupled with official encouragement of the kind of chauvinism and tribalism once associated with the era of Japanese military aggression.

Thus, Japan entered the new century in a quandary. Was Japan changing? Was it moving slowly towards a new paradigm? Or were the renewed currents of nationalism and xenophobia part of a more broadly based opposition to global trends, a burrowing into the past when Japan successfully maintained its status as a *sakoku,* a closed nation? As long ago as the 1940s, the Canadian historian and diplomat, E.H. Norman, noted the Janus-like quality of political change in Japan.[4] Norman observed that the humanistic impulse was often coupled in Japan with a dark retreat. The same might be said of economic change. Japan's tilt to Asia was linked with a quest for global prestige and expanded autonomy of action within the international arena. It also had elements of autarky. Groping for new paradigms to replace those of the Cold War, Tokyo began to pull away from the United States and its restraining influence. In the 1990s, Japan started to broadcast its differences from Western societies, particularly from those subscribing to the "Anglo-American" economic model. In doing so, Japan limited its own economic future by opting out of the global economy, but also began to map out a composite value structure perhaps more in keeping with Japanese character and tradition.

E.H. Norman might have seen the irony of the way Japan's progressive impulses in these years combined with sinister motifs, in Japan's loud rejection of international demands to restructure its institutions along Western lines, even as its institutions were crumbling. He would have found no joy in Japan's return to some of the cruder themes from its past. On one level, Japan's Asian tilt was pure racism, as though in order to renew themselves, Japanese had to return to the *status quo ante*, of a time before the predominance of the American model, before the German and British ones that had earlier entranced the Japanese elite. On another level, it reflected the *realpolitik* of Japanese leaders in the emerging baby boom generation, convinced that the United States was a waning power, mindful of the deterioration of their own economy, and determined to sustain it by expanding its virtual boundaries to include the high-growth Asian economies. These themes coexisted with the pristine vision of Japan participating in an "Asian renaissance," in Funabashi's hopeful phrase.

Tokyo's attempt to develop a more rounded diplomacy within Asia, to revisit relationships and attitudes toward the region from beyond the Cold War framework, reflected an impulse for survival in the churning geopolitics of the Asia-Pacific in the new century. This positive impulse or motif was revolutionary in nature, ending a century and a half of psychic alienation from the rest of Asia. Embracing a common identity with other Asians signaled a step toward a more general break with the myth of Japanese uniqueness and the cultural habits of exclusion that it fostered.

At the same time, Japan began to construct an Asian sphere of influence, recreating itself as an Asian power and distancing itself from the United States, its Cold War patron and protector. This entailed drafting a detailed economic strategy and campaign to promote "Asian values" reminiscent of Japanese wartime propaganda in its Asian colonies. At the end of the Cold War, new lines of conflict emerged in which "mutual deterrence" was framed in terms of economic strength and industrial strategy. In this new post–Cold War battlefield, Japan's platform would be Asia.

Central to Tokyo's Asian strategy was the attempt to use Asia as a lever to extend Japan's post-war paradigm of export-led growth. In order to persuade other economies to adopt Japanese practices, unlike during the years in which Asia fell under Japanese military control, Tokyo needed to use weapons of persuasion; in doing so, it learned from its own recent history. Japan's Asia policy built on an American protocol. Just as during the Cold War the United States had used Japan as a model for developing countries and transformed its economic blueprint into a tool to promote U.S. interests during, in the ideological free-for-all that followed the end of the Cold War, Japan would use its model as a starting point for economic propaganda.

The two "Japanese models" were, of course, very different. While the United States had sought to portray Japan as a model of capitalist success, the Japanese model created by Japanese officials and intellectuals in the 1990s included institutions foreign to Adam Smith, in which bureaucrats ran "contests" to simulate market interaction and introduced competition, like medicine, in small doses. The Japanese view of economic growth, embodied in the post–Cold War Japanese model, was fundamentally illiberal, and endorsed the visible hand of government intervention over the "invisible hand" of markets. At the same time, the Japanese perspective was evolutionary. Government provided an indispensable platform for economies with scanty infrastructure and information systems. Ideally, over time the role of government would diminish like the Cheshire cat behind its smile. The difficulty lay in fixing the how and when of detachment. Even so, over the course of the 1990s, the global development community, led by the World Bank, gradually adopted the Japanese view until it lay at the center of a new orthodoxy.

Thus, wrapped in paradox and contradiction, Japan's search for a new paradigm was intertwined with a quest for the nation's Asian roots. At the onset of Japan's modernization, it had rejected Asia and embraced the West. In the 1990s, the country began to reinvent itself as an "Asian" nation, establishing its membership in what was then the most buoyant economic community in the world. Echoing the rhetoric of the Meiji Restoration, Japanese policy makers cried for the "revival" of Asia and the "restoration" of Asian values. The two "restorations" were very different, but both used a nostalgic vision of the past to usher in a new order.

The Meiji Restoration came at a time when Japan was facing intense external pressures for change. Western imperial powers were already carving up China in the treaty port system; at home, British and American warships prowled the Japanese coastline. Under the slogan of obedience to a forgotten emperor, rebellious feudal lords marshaled forces to overthrow the central government, charging it with the failure to maintain Japanese defenses. The Japanese imperial family, cloistered in Kyoto during nearly 1,000 years of military rule, was drafted to lead an effort to build Japanese military and industrial strength.

Thus the Meiji Restoration, named after the Meiji emperor, was a political movement that, almost by accident, led to profound social and cultural change. Its initial aim was to break the tenacious hold of the Tokugawa government that had ruled Japan since the sixteenth century. The Tokugawa shoguns had imposed control through an administrative system known as the *bakufu*, a strict hierarchy designed to keep any sector of society, especially the senior feudal lords, or *daimyo*, from mounting a challenge. So stable was the Tokugawa system that it took the rebels fifteen years after the arrival of American Commodore Matthew Perry's "black ships" in 1853 to overthrow the *bakufu* on grounds that it was incompetent in dealing with the foreign threat. With the successful overthrow of the *bakufu* in 1868, however, the new Meiji government transformed Japan into the world's first non-Western industrial and military superpower.

It proved impossible to limit the changes to the factory floor and elite military academies. Japan became the intellectual and cultural center for a larger revolution, where Western ideas fused with Asian experience. It was a crucible for anticolonial liberation movements as well as a foray into the new disciplines of economics and the social sciences. In Japanese woodblock prints from the turn of century, steam locomotives plow through traditional settings of cherry blossoms, and delicate kimono-clad ladies jostle with others in Western gowns. To the Western romantic, such juxtapositions were a sacrilege. To a generation of Asian intellectuals, they were electrifying, a portrait of a future in which Asian societies would throw off the shackles of colonialism and build factories and railway lines.

The Meiji Restoration was about politics and technology. A century later, Japan's Asian "restoration" or renaissance was about culture. It referred nostalgically both to the Meiji Restoration itself—as an example of Japan's success at self-transformation—and to dim antiquity, when medieval Kyoto was among the world's major cities and Japanese commerce and intellectual life stretched west across China and the Silk Road and through the southern seas to the coast of India. It looked back, indeed, to a time when China was the region's paramount power and source of intellectual creativity and technological innovation.

The impulse behind this restoration, or *fukuken*, was a search for greater prestige and recognition. Elite Japanese bureaucrats who were the main spokesmen for the movement were impatient with a global culture dominated by Anglo-American values, including the liberal ideology of neoclassical economics and the free market. The bureaucrats hoped to piece together a rebellion against the dominant global ideology by appealing to Asian nationalism, riding the wave of Asian economic success. This was to be the reverse of the Meiji model, in which political change triggered cultural change. Instead, the promised cultural changes failed to come about, and Japan's Asian restoration fizzled. Even in its failure, however, Japan's Asian "restoration" left a significant wake in the form of new political and diplomatic stances and institutions. The movement—if one can so describe an effort led by a coterie of powerful bureaucrats—was extraordinarily ambitious, and remains a powerful undercurrent in Japanese policy.

If Japan's Asian restoration was a failure as a cultural movement, historically, it was far more than a mere curiosity, completing a 150-year cycle in which Japan had been preoccupied with the task of "catching up" with Western countries. The political and economic structures of modernization had been designed to facilitate this task. Now that Japan had caught up with every other nation but the United States, it began to reassess the values underpinning its modernization effort along with the overall paradigm. Among the most central of these values was a self-conscious separation from Asia, on psychological as well as political and economic planes.

In the late nineteenth century, Meiji intellectuals urged their counterparts to "Reject Asia, and Embrace Europe," under the slogan *Datsu A, Nyu Ou.* The new slogan of the 1990s turned the Meiji slogan on its head: *"Datsu Ou, Nyu A,"* reject the West; embrace Asia. To the ideologues, this meant that Japan was ready to assume leadership of an emerging Asian economic powerhouse that would forcefully imprint its values and ways of doing business on the global system. To idealists, such as Funabashi, the phrase heralded a new Asian renaissance, a return to an era when Asian creativity was unquestioned. To ordinary Japanese, perhaps, it was just another newspaper headline, with little meaning for their daily lives. Even so, in the 1990s, Japan saw much more of Asia on its doorstep, with a vast increase in the number of Asian exchange students and unskilled workers, a growing taste for Asian popular music and movies, the proliferation of Asian eateries, and even the entry of big-time Asian investors such as Hong Kong's Richard Li into the Tokyo property market.

In order to grasp the magnitude of Japan's ambition, it is necessary to recall Japan in the late 1980s, at the height of its "bubble economy," when the nation was steeped in wealth and achievement. To be sure, the rhetoric of *fukuken* was essentially the romantic idiom of pan-Asianism, carrying the chill of the Japanese propaganda campaign that had accompanied its territorial conquests from late in the previous century. The circumstances, however, were far different from those of the colonial era. Fifty years after the collapse of the Greater East Asian Co-Prosperity Sphere, Tokyo operated within a regional framework of fast-growing states that welcomed Japanese influence and which to some degree modeled their economies and political institutions after Japan's.

In the mid-1980s, yen appreciation drove Japan's flagship industries offshore, and the bureaucracy followed. In Asia, Japanese business and officialdom hoped to accomplish what they could not do in Europe or North America—reproduce the managed economy existing in Japan, with its strategic collaboration between government and business aimed at economic growth. Strategically, Japanese policy makers in the latter years of the decade could look out to the horizon and view a frightening scenario in which China would dominate Asia, and the United States would abandon its role as regional police officer. If unchecked, an unfriendly China might threaten Japan both militarily and economically, and without U.S. protection, Tokyo would be vulnerable. Japan's twenty-first-century scenario demanded a new set of options, and so Tokyo began to develop political ties with its former Asian colonies that had hitherto been neglected.

Japan was not alone in touting an "East Asian model" based on Asian economic success. At the beginning of the 1990s, Asians believed that they were about to become the new hub of the global economy. As the largest economy in Asia by far, it was natural that Japan should play a central role as the vision took shape.

The process was interrupted, however, by a major convulsion of global capital markets, beginning in Thailand, ripping through Asian economies, and sweeping across to Brazil and Russia. The emerging markets crisis of 1997 to 1998 caused a general reassessment of globalization. It failed, however, to put an end to the quasi-socialistic, bureaucracy-led model associated with Japanese and East Asian success before the crash. Indeed, one major result was to strengthen the critics of globalization, and Asians began to organize protectively against the next crisis, formulating a web of new organizations and official meetings that in many cases took their cue from Tokyo. The failed cultural revolt against Anglo-American dominance became a successful platform for building something much more important—a new set of institutions linking the Asian economies. The new institutions would increasingly prove useful on a political level.

Most significant of all, Japan lost its outlier status in the Asian system. It began to fit in, even though it had weathered the emerging markets crisis of 1997–98 without distinction. Asians who hoped that Japan would confront the IMF and the United States directly were disappointed. Yet, in the view of many Asians, Japan had played a far more sympathetic role in the crisis than Washington, and in the aftermath, Tokyo moved more confidently within its new Asian networks. Without any direct confrontation with the international financial institutions, Japan put up roughly 80 percent of the $100 billion bailout of the Thai, Indonesian, and Korean economies, far more than any other nation. Moreover, Japan offered its funds unconditionally, in contrast to the elaborate reforms demanded by the IMF, with moral support from the U.S. Treasury Department. For once, Asians were happy to have Japan as a champion, and if they might wish that their champion was more outspoken, at least it had been there to help when the need was greatest. This was a very different game for Japan than during the Cold War years, when Tokyo faithfully served U.S. policy objectives in wars on the Korean Peninsula and in Southeast Asia. The new "Asian" Japan was ready to say no to the United States, and did so with increasing regularity.

To understand the difficulties experienced by Japan as would-be champion of Asia, it is necessary to recapitulate Japan's history as Asian predator and its varied attempts to engage, shape, and otherwise extract benefits from the Asian regional economy. Japan's heavy-handed and often unsuccessful attempts at economic engineering via the Greater East Asian Co-Prosperity Sphere became the foundation for more sophisticated ideas associated with the Asia Pacific Economic Cooperation (APEC) grouping and the ministerial and summitry additions to ASEAN in the late 1990s. The two strategies were linked by a concept called "flying geese," embodying cultural psychology as well as economics. The Japanese thought that Asian economies shared a disciplined nationalism, yoking individual ambition to national goals for economic growth. This history helps to explain why Japanese strategies in Asia were entirely different from those in Europe and North America following the explosion of Japanese capital and investment that occurred in the exchange rate realignments of 1985 to 1987, in the Plaza and Louvre Accords. It also helps to explain why Japan to some extent viewed the Asian financial crisis as an opportunity to strengthen institutions of regional economic integration and deepen its imprint on the regional economy.

The Asian financial crisis threw into turmoil many of the Japanese multinationals based in the crisis countries but also cast a spotlight on the critical importance of Japan's new offshore Asian factories to the domestic economy. Contrary to expectations, Japan's effort to steer Asian growth did not stop with the Asian crisis. Japan's economic interdependence with East Asia and Southeast Asia, in fact, increased. Japan poured billions into shoring up its Asian-based factories and led the bailouts of Thailand, Indonesia, and South Korea. Tokyo's huge rescue effort was aimed in large part at propping up Japanese multinationals in Asia while they sorted out unhedged borrowings in local currencies and coped with the radical contraction of local markets, but it also helped jump-start the economies where its factories were based, by firing up exports and employment. From the perspective of the IMF, the Asian crisis was structural, a result of incomplete liberalization. From the Japanese perspective, it was a liquidity crisis pure and simple, and while it exposed structural problems they were secondary to the issue of managing violent swings in capital flows in developing economies. In addition to its economic implications, the Asian crisis created new pressures on Japan to develop an explicit role in the regional political and security arenas.

In retrospect, the late 1980s and early 1990s represented the last time when Japan could frame an Asian or global policy based solely on economics. Partly because of the magnitude of Japanese intervention, Asians began to view Japan in new ways, not only as a source of aid and investment but as a counterbalancing force to China and the most likely stand-in for the role the United States played in Asia-Pacific during the Cold War. Asians foresaw a new century in which American power would recede, Chinese power advance, and Japan would adopt more complex strategies of balancing than the Cold War games of containment and deterrence. Japan, through the Asian crisis, began the slow but inevitable process of filling in the gaps left by the withering U.S. presence in Asia.

Problems for Japan came from another direction. For the Japanese public, as opposed to elite officials, politicians, and businessmen, the prospect of replacing the United States as regional policeman was horrifying, not least because the post-war paradigm had left it uniquely ill-equipped for a larger role in Asia, let alone the world. In the wake of the Asian financial crisis, successful democratic elections in Thailand, Korea, and Indonesia underlined the failures of the region's autocrats, particularly Indonesia's President Suharto, who had used the pat claims of "Asian values" to legitimize their regimes. The regional trend pointed out the weak link in Japan's plans for Asia, which was that it had never sought broad public support for the policy within Japan. A public consensus for "Asianization" had yet to be built, and politics suddenly mattered. The celebrities of post-Asian crisis democracy in Asia—particularly Korea's president Kim Dae Jung—stood in painful contrast to a succession of weak and bumbling prime ministers in Tokyo. The bureaucracy had not consulted the Japanese people on whether they wanted to re-engage with Asia, and it turned out that for the most part, they did not. A sheer lack of interest in the outside world was among the legacies of Japan's Cold War pact with the United States. Japanese citizens lived in a world where Japan's foreign policy was made halfway around the world, in Washington. But as Japan's domestic problems mounted in the latter part of the decade, the counterpart to Asia's new democratic movements in Japan was a weakening of the social contract underlying bureaucratic governance.

Indeed, if the Cold War left the Japanese public without any sense of connection with the global community, it left Japanese politicians and bureaucrats, let alone corporate executives, without specific mechanisms for reaching out to the Japanese public to build support for policy. The Asianization campaign in many respects floated over the heads of the people. Its propaganda was largely directed to external audiences, particularly in the developing countries of Asia that the government hoped to integrate into a Japanese economic "zone of prosperity."

Historically, Japan had been a peripheral power in Asia. China and India were the two great engines of commerce and civilization. Japan, like Southeast Asia and the tribal empires of the Siberian steppes, figured on the sidelines; all had once been tributary states. Their cultures sprang from the creative ferment of the Tang and Mughal empires. The expansion of Japanese influence in Asia during the twentieth century was a distinct historical anomaly. During the great religious and commercial expansions of Asian history, Japan was the last stop on the Silk Road, craggy islands beyond the civilized centers of the Korean Peninsula, with uncouth rulers just a step away from tribal matriarchy, an abomination to all good Confucians. Beginning in the 1870s, Japan mounted a series of interventions in Asia designed to establish its preeminence. Each ended badly yet left watermarks—cultural recognition, industrial infrastructure, and psychological wounds. Japan had been the only state to control the Asian region under a single political and military mantle, however briefly. Along with the police terror and brutal cultural policies, the period of Japanese territorial expansion, beginning in 1895, left a legacy of central administration and industrial development.

During the imperial period, Japan underwent a geographic transformation from tiny to gigantic. There is a book on my desk chronicling 100 years of Japanese history.[5] One of its statistical tables shows the changing scope of

Japanese territory between 1880 and 1989. Between 1880 and 1895, Japan gained roughly 10 percent in landmass with the annexation of Taiwan and the Penghu Islands. In 1910, with the addition of Korea, Japan suddenly became 50 percent larger. Korea was followed by an explosion of gains, from the Marianas and Marshall Islands in 1920, to Manchukuo in the Chinese northeast in 1932, to the whole of Southeast Asia and China's major cities by the early 1940s. Formally, Republican China, Manchukuo, and the "liberated" republics of the Philippines, Indonesia, Malaysia, and Burma, together with the Thai monarchy, were not Japanese territory but Japanese allies. In fact, they were under the direct control of the Japanese military government.

Even by the narrow definition of "formal territories only," Japan gained 80 percent in size during the years from 1880 to 1940. All of the new territory was under direct Japanese rule and subject to cultural programs installing emperor worship and establishing Japanese as an official language. Such legacies contained both good and bad. In some corners of Japan's former empire, paradoxically, they provided a lingering sense of comfort. In the late 1980s, for many elderly and even middle-aged Taiwanese, Japanese was their only foreign language. I was startled on a trip to Taiwan when both the mayor of Taipei and senior Taiwan executives insisted on speaking Japanese rather than Mandarin Chinese. During one interview, the president of a large manufacturing company ducked out to take a phone call from one of his Tokyo business associates. The conversation was conducted entirely in Japanese.

Lee Teng-hui, former president of Taiwan, is another example of the cosmopolitan qualities of the Japanese Empire. Born under Japanese rule, Lee graduated from Kyoto University and Cornell, and was equally fluent in Japanese and English. Many Taiwanese look back at Japanese rule with nostalgia because the mainland Chinese who assumed power in 1949 treated them more harshly than had their Japanese overlords.

Thus, Japanese rule created at least some conditions favorable to Japan's assumption of a central role in the region's political economy. Even so, Japan's wartime legacy was a continual drag as it sought to enact new policies. In the late 1980s and early 1990s, Tokyo officially issued formal apologies to former colonial states, starting in 1989 with South Korea. So ambiguous were the words, however, that the apologies often did as much harm as good. The gestures left the recipients wondering whether the Japanese were expressing sincere contrition or merely the kind of "regret" one might experience from committing a grievous faux pas. In Japanese society at large, young Asians streaming to Japan to take advantage of educational opportunities in the 1990s often left the country seriously disillusioned. Exposed to verbal abuse and discrimination, Asians experienced the underbelly of a tribal culture that viewed the world as an ethnic hierarchy with other Asians classified as lesser races. Japanese cultural insensitivity remained an important obstacle, both to globalization and simpler forms of regional exchange, such as enticing leading Asian intellectuals and policy makers to accept temporary appointments at Japanese institutions.

Asian Geese

In the fifteen years from 1985 to 2000, Japanese capital and manufacturing investment ignited an economic boom in Asia of historic proportions. Right behind the investors were disciplined teams of Japanese bureaucrats searching for ways to deepen their control of Japan's newly footloose multinationals. Their main strategy was to extend the networks and understandings of Tokyo-led industrial policy to Japan's Asian neighbors. Bureaucrats in the Ministry of Foreign Affairs (MOFA) and the Ministry of International Trade and Industry (MITI) began arguing that Japan should ease away from its symbiotic post-war relationship with the United States and cultivate a new alliance with Asia. Within Asia, Southeast Asia would be Japan's stronghold, the base from which to launch a strategy of containment against China. It was not to be. By the end of the 1990s, Japanese capital was flooding out of Asia, China had managed to charm Southeast Asia and intimidate Washington, the Clinton administration was actively promoting Beijing as its partner of choice in the region, and Japanese influence in the region waned, despite an $80 billion rescue package for the Asian economies during their crisis.

Like a bell curve, Japan's trajectory in Asia during this period seemed to mirror in reverse the extravagant claims of a decade earlier. Nonetheless, the structure of Japan's relationships with Asia and the United States had changed remarkably over ten years. In 1988, Japan exported $77.4 billion to Asia, just over 29 percent of all exports, and imported $55.8 billion, 31 percent of the total.[6] In the 1998 fiscal year, even with the sharp contraction in trade caused by the financial crisis, Japan's exports to Asia represented 34.5 percent of its total exports, at $126 billion, and 37.4 percent of imports, at $97.8 billion, well ahead of Japan's trade with the United States. [7]

In the peak year of 1996, 44 percent of Japan's exports went to Asia and 37 percent of its imports came from there, at $181 billion and $130 billion, respectively. Asia had become Japan's main market, and while one could talk about the need for Japan to lead Asia into recovery after the Asian crisis, equally true was that the loss of $55 billion in exports had seriously interrupted Japan's own efforts to pull itself out of recession. Another measure of increasing linkage was an increase in the practice of billing Japanese imports and exports in yen, reflecting its acceptance as a trade currency. In

1981, only 30 percent of Japanese exports to Asia and 2 percent of imports were invoiced in yen. By 1993, the ratio had increased to 50 percent for exports and 25 percent for imports.[8]

In terms of Japan's total stock of investment in Asia, according to government figures, by 1997 Japan's $111.5 billion was well in excess of the $81 billion in U.S. investment in Asia (excluding U.S. investment in Japan and Australia).[9] Moreover, compared to the United States, Japanese investment had grown from a minuscule base. In 1970, Japan's total cumulative stock of investment in Asia was just $370 million; in 1981, $12.9 billion; in 1988, it reached $32 billion. Counting capital investments of Japanese subsidiaries and affiliates in Asia—roughly $32 billion between 1989 and 1996—the stock of Japanese direct investment to Asia more than quadrupled between 1988 and 1996, to $143 billion. By the middle of the Japanese fiscal year in September 1999, the figure was up to $175 billion.[10]

The rush of Japanese assets to Asia was not driven purely by a quest for profits or even a desire for physical proximity to the Asian market. Japanese businesspeople regularly complained about the high cost of production in developing countries and the difficulty of establishing quality control over locally supplied parts. Japanese companies moved to Asia out of necessity, and the transition was difficult and messy. However, they went through with the expense and the fuss because they understood that the Japanese government would back them up with easy money.

After 1985, when the yen rose sharply in value, Japanese export industries were in serious trouble and should have suffered declines in both cash flow and asset values. Instead, asset values expanded rapidly, creating the "bubble" in stock and asset prices of the late 1980s. This asset bubble was the origin of the Japanese "bubble economy" of the late 1980s. The economist Mikuni Akio argues that the Ministry of Finance (MOF) engineered the bubble purposely by manipulating real-estate values and encouraging rapid credit expansion, using real estate and equity as collateral for loans. Banks understood that they could lend beyond the deposit base because the Bank of Japan would make up any shortfall in liquidity.[11] Japanese banks lent money first, asked questions later. "Markets do exist in Japan, but their primary purpose is to create the illusion that Japan is a market economy," writes Mikuni. As long as asset values continued to grow, good loans and bad ones were relatively easy to repay because their value in current terms was constantly declining. Japanese banks funded Japan's foreign investment spree essentially because borrowers could not use all the money on domestic projects. Japanese investors were able to pour funds into dubious projects in Southeast Asia and elsewhere because of the Japanese government's implicit guarantee.[12]

From the perspective of the Japanese bureaucracy, such investment would accomplish two objectives: Japan would be able to maintain the post-war paradigm, based on exports and guided industrial expansion, and the bureaucrats would remain in charge. "Each important industry started life as a consortium led by MITI, thereby freeing lenders from credit risk," Mikuni explains. When domestic markets were saturated, MITI turned to exports. The post-1985 strategy was a variant of the established pattern. Japan's Asian factories would become a new market for Japanese products, gobbling up high value-added components. At the same time, Asia would become a platform for Japanese exports, taking over production of the commodity end of Japanese consumer manufactures—products such as cameras, videocassette recorders, and air conditioners—that were labor rather than capital intensive. Because of rising production costs, these products had become impractical to make in Japan.

This was the opposite of the strategies employed by Japanese multinationals in Asia during the Cold War. Until the 1980s, the region served as a source of raw materials for Japan, a market for low-end products, and a dumping ground for its polluting industries and cheap consumer goods. The relationship was either exploitative along neocolonial lines, or was a classic example of comparative advantage, depending on one's point of view. The Japanese economist Kojima Kiyoshi argued that Japanese investment in Asia ranged between these two poles, because the relative resource endowments of Japan and its neighbors made possible a more benign and complementary relationship than Western investment, based on maintaining "oligopolistic" advantages.[13] The Japanese strategy of the 1980s was quite different, integrating Asian production bases under the mantle of "made-in-Tokyo" industrial policy. Under the new strategy, Japan could view its entire business in the region as a form of intracompany trade. If returns were weak, profits could always be shifted around to hide the problem. From the perspective of Japanese companies, the system was about maintaining Japanese market share in a global economy. From the perspective of the bureaucrats, it was about maintaining control outside the zone of Japanese territorial sovereignty. Following the example set by the United States a generation earlier, one of the principal tools chosen by the bureaucrats was foreign aid.

Neither the bureaucrats nor Japanese corporations cared as much about profits as they cared about maintaining the cozy relationships of the domestic economic paradigm. Thus, even at its height, Japanese investment in Asia lagged behind the United States's by several key measures without causing any alarm among Japanese investors or officials. By the mid-1990s, depending on the scale of Japanese re-invested earnings, Japanese assets may have outstripped U.S. assets on a stock basis. But in terms of revenues and profits, the United

States was far ahead. In 1996 U.S. multinationals' sales in the region reached $517 billion. Even excluding Australia and Japan, U.S. multinationals rang up $242 billion in sales in the rest of the region that year. The comparable figure for Japan, based on a survey of Japanese multinationals and excluding Australia, was about 40 percent less,[14] about $144 billion, divided half and half between factories in the newly industrialized economies (NIES) of Northeast Asia and Singapore, and the "ASEAN Four"—Thailand, Malaysia, Indonesia, and the Philippines, with another $11.2 billion in China.[15]

Another, even more significant measure was in terms of the profits each country took from its Asian assets. U.S. profits from the region in 1996 were $15.8 billion, excluding Australia and Japan—three times those of the Japanese. Profits of Japanese multinationals peaked in the same year, at $5.1 billion.[16] Finally, the labor productivity of U.S. factories in Asia was clearly much greater, since American companies employed far fewer people than the Japanese—1.8 million people in all of Asia but only about one million excluding Japan and Australia, the two leading targets of U.S. investment. Japanese employment in Asia reached 1.5 million in 1996. Even if Japanese companies were paying their Asian workers less than U.S. companies did, the implication was clear. American companies were making a lot more money in Asia than the Japanese and using their workers more efficiently.[17] That year, U.S. profits of $24.8 billion on investments of $72.4 billion gave American multinationals a return on investment of 34.3 percent, compared to 3.6 percent for Japan, measuring against stock rather than flow. U.S. business had been around in Asia long enough to amortize its investments, and Japan was a newcomer in a period of rapid acceleration of investment. Even so, the gap was extreme.

The productivity gap between Japanese and U.S. investment in Asia reflected at least partially a measure of the fragility and inefficiency of Japanese investments in Asia even before the financial crash of 1997–98 ripped through the structure of the relational loans on which they were based. To be sure, Japanese companies were doing better in Asia than anywhere else in the immediate aftermath of the huge outflow of Japanese investment after 1985. The high profitability of Asian operations was often given by Japanese multinationals in survey questionnaires as a reason for the increasing concentration of Japanese investment in Asia and concomitant decline in their investment in the United States and Europe. Between 1987 and 1996, Asia was the most profitable region in the world for Japanese companies. In 1997, the year of the Asian crisis, Asian profits of Japanese multinationals dropped below that of their factories in the United States but still remained stronger than the income of Japanese operations in Europe.[18]

The Asian crisis predictably dampened Japanese investment in Asia but not by nearly as much as might have been predicted based on the scale of Japanese losses. In 1998, Japanese annual investment in the Asia-Pacific region dropped by nearly half. It went from $11.5 billion in 1997 to $6.1 billion in 1998.[19] Yet, investment returned quickly. In the first half of FY 1999, from April to September, Japanese investment in Asia was $4.1 billion, up 21 percent in yen terms.[20] Japanese investment for the whole year reached $8.3 billion; it declined to $7.9 billion in 1999 and $6.5 billion in 2000, slipping to nearly Latin American levels, while Japanese investment in Europe and North America soared. Still, with the exception of the banking sector, Japanese capital did not flee Asia after the crisis but stayed put.

In fact, in the early period of the Asian recovery, Japanese investment shot up in Hong Kong, Singapore, Korea, and even the Philippines. By mid-1999, Japanese manufacturers were planning to double production and exports to the region. In May, one auto parts executive told the industrial daily, *Nikkan Kogyo*, that he was afraid that the recovery would be all too "impetuous" and that "[i]f we can't make timely delivery of parts to local assembly lines, we will be the loser."[21] Meanwhile, through most of the year, Japanese investors were showing more enthusiasm for the European, Canadian, and North American markets than Asia's. Nonetheless, Japan moved from a role on the margins of the Asian regional economy in the mid-1980s to one substantially larger than that of the United States' in the region by the late 1990s, in just over a decade. Revealingly, as the Asian economies roared back to life, Japan maintained a healthy trade surplus. In FY 1999 through March 31, 2000, Japan exported $169.7 billion to Asia and imported $134.8 billion.[22] Most of the export surge, according to the MOF, was in products such as steel, semiconductors, and optical equipment, all of which were staple inputs for Japanese factories.[23]

While Japanese manufacturers were deepening and expanding their empires in Asia, the Japanese government inched slowly but steadily in the direction recommended by the pro-Asia lobby in the senior government ministries—MOF, MOFA, and MITI. Factions in each agency wanted Japan to cement a new alliance with Asia, utilizing Japanese investment and employment there as a source of political capital. In 1988, Prime Minister Takeshita Noboru presided over the first attempt to frame Japan's "Asianization" policy, announcing that Japan would serve as the spokesman for Asian nations in the Group of Seven (G7) industrial nations. The setting was the G7 economic summit in Toronto, Canada, a coming-out party for a Japan at the height of its bubble. In Toronto, 231 Japanese editors, reporters, and photographers covered the economic summit in exhaustive detail. One network provided eighteen hours of coverage of the three-day meeting.[24] At a press conference with foreign reporters, Takeshita said he was happy to have "contributed toward the further integration of the newly industrialized economies of South Korea, Taiwan, and Singapore with the global economy."[25] Timed to coincide with the summit meeting, Japan announced a new foreign aid plan, doubling the amount of its global spending, from $25 billion in the previous five-year cycle to $50 billion between 1988 and 1993. Most of the money would go to Asia.

In the late 1980s, the Japanese yen appreciated so quickly that Takeshita could have kept his promise almost without raising the underlying foreign aid budget in yen. In fact, Japan completed its $50 billion aid plan several years early. In January 1985, 254 yen bought one U.S. dollar. By November 1988, the ratio had reached 121 yen to the dollar, fell back a bit, then climbed still more, reaching 79 yen to the U.S. dollar in August 1995 before again retrenching. In 1999, it was "normal" for the yen to hover at Yen 100 to the U.S. dollar, and Japanese legislators began talking of introducing parity between the yen and the American dollar by moving the decimal point. Yen appreciation made Japan the world's largest foreign aid donor and gave it the third largest military budget after the United States and the Soviet Union, before the latter dissolved. In its peak periods, the strong yen gave ordinary Japanese a buying power beyond their wildest dreams, making foreign assets cheap and providing a very real sensation of wealth. In Tokyo, in the late 1980s, department stores were setting out $200 coffee and cake "sets" sprinkled with gold leaf.

The strong yen amplified but also had the power to vastly complicate Japan's Asian diplomacy. In Asia, the yen could impose havoc by weakening against the dollar, which would increase the competitiveness of Japanese exports into the American market. The weaker yen of 1996–97, coupled with the 1994 devaluation of the Chinese Renminbi, helped spark the Asian crisis. Post-crisis, Asian central banks began weighting their currencies toward the yen in order to prevent a replay of the collapse of regional currencies, which had been pegged to the U.S. dollar before 1997. Toward the end of the decade, Tokyo was squeezed between U.S. policy to relieve pressure on the yen in order to help it out of its bad-debt problem, and Asian regional pressure to keep the yen high in order to keep the recovery rolling.

In 1988, Japan's G7 partners barely registered Takeshita's ambitious aid offering, let alone the country's self-proclaimed role as spokesman for Asia. Tokyo did not care; it was deep in plans to reshape the Asian economy to meet the needs of an aging, ever more expensive Japan. Much of Takeshita's $50 billion would go to support the Asian program in which Japan would play the role of "brain" at the center of a vibrant regional economy, in a hierarchy based on the dynamic (Japanese economists would always stress the word) comparative advantage of its participants. Takeshita even managed to slip language into the 1988 summit declaration suggesting that such cooperation had the blessing of the G7.[26]

By the end of the 1990s, Japan engaged in regular meetings of its trade and foreign ministers with most of the countries in the region and sponsored meetings of central bank governors with key economies. Tokyo was talking with South Korea about trade deals, with China about defense, and with Vietnam about Japanese-style economic reforms. China, Japan, and South Korea engaged in a new formal relationship with the ASEAN as "ASEAN Plus Three," involving annual summit meetings and preparatory sessions among senior officials. In 1999, at the third session of "ASEAN Plus Three," for the first time the leaders of China, Japan, and South Korea held a separate, formal "summit breakfast," pledging to continue their summits. Korean president Kim Dae Jung, leader of an "East Asian Vision Group" to sort through the implications of the financial crisis, called for an "East Asia Economic Cooperation System" to address an "urgent need" for regional economic cooperation.[27] A decade earlier, when Malaysian prime minister Mahathir bin Mohamad proposed a similar grouping, the East Asian Economic Group (EAEG), later Caucus (EAEC), Japan balked and the United States, led by Secretary of State James Baker, attacked the proposal. The first ASEAN Plus Three summit was entirely lacking in such tension. Preoccupied with the tempestuous Seattle session of the WTO in November to December 1999—the "battle of Seattle"—Washington ignored the Asian meeting. The EAEG was stealing silently back to life, under Japanese direction.[28]

In its low-key way, Tokyo kept working to consolidate its new role as Asian insider. As the only Asian nation with membership in the G8 (Group of Eight) industrial nations (after Russia was added to the former G7 in 1998), the WTO, and Organization of Economic Cooperation and Development (OECD), Japan felt obligated to raise "Asian" issues in these European and American-dominated councils. In terms of news value, the Japanese interventions made little impact. What counted, however, was the process. The annual summits of the G8 became an opportunity for Japan to publicly canvas its Asian counterparts, collecting issues lists and, more important, establishing regular communication channels that, up until the late 1980s, existed only in the UN General Assembly.

As Japan began planning for the G8 summit in the year 2000, when it served as host, officials pitched it as an Asian event. Japan would represent Asia at the table and lost no chance to remind the leaders that they were in Asia. Even the choice of venue, Okinawa, from a Japanese perspective, emphasized Tokyo's connections with the continental culture. Up until 1609, the kings of the Ryukyu Islands had paid tribute to China, and China and

Japan were still disputing ownership through the 1870s. The Ryukyus were formally attached to Japan as Okinawa Prefecture only in 1879. After meeting with his Southeast Asian counterparts in July 1999, Japanese foreign minister Komura Masahiko declared: "As the summit meeting in Japan will be held in the year 2000, a landmark year in Asia, we should like to take that meeting as an opportunity to transmit the voice of Asia to the world even more so than in the past." Responded Surin Pitsuwan, the Thai foreign minister: "It remains to evolve. But I trust and have confidence in Mr. Obuchi [the Japanese prime minister], in fact in Japan, and the Japanese government in general that our views will be solicited, that our concerns will be listened to, and he will make an effort to bring these issues into the process of discussion."[29]

In the late 1990s, the U.S. intelligence community belatedly took note of a new pattern of Japanese foreign policy. "Japan is less confident of its relationship with the United States and its role in the region and the world and fears it is being replaced by China as the most important U.S. strategic partner," observed a memorandum from the National Intelligence Council (NIC) in 1999. "Consequently, it is pursuing a two-track strategy of emphasizing its importance to the United States and shoring up the alliance while hedging its bets by pursuing greater autonomy or independence . . . For the first time, Japan may perceive a true divergence, or at least potential for divergence, in security interests with the United States."[30]

Thus, according to the NIC, anxiety, rather than arrogance, was pushing Japan toward Asia. This was perhaps true in terms of the paranoia that Japan exhibited toward China from the early 1990s, as the latter's economy expanded in the familiar pattern through exports of low-tech goods to the advanced industrial economies. By the late 1990s, China was edging out Japan as the leading supplier of the American trade deficit. China was also the only Asian economy running a surplus with Japan in exports of manufactured goods.

Regardless of the motive, by aligning itself with Asia, Japan introduced a fundamental change in the regional balance of power. In a worst-case scenario, Japanese friction with the United States would undermine the political basis for forward deployment of U.S. troops in Asia. China might then respond belligerently to Japanese defenses that reduced its nuclear edge, such as Theater Missile Defense (TMD). Finally, Japan would be forced to upgrade its offensive capability. This it could do simply by filling in the munitions gaps left by an American pullout. One of the less well-known facts of the U.S.-Japan military alliance was the high degree of interoperability of the U.S. forces with the Japanese "self-defense" army, navy, and air force, which meant that Japan needed only to replace a few pieces in order to change the whole complexion of its military power. This geometry was very much on the minds of Japan's neighbors. When President Kim Dae Jung met with his North Korean counterpart, Kim Jong Il, in June 2000 at their historic first summit in Pyongyang, the South Korean leader said that it was in both Koreas' interests to have U.S. troops stay in Korea even after unification. "We need the presence of the U.S. military on the Korean Peninsula," Kim said, "because if the United States leaves, we will see China and Japan struggling for supremacy. You and I will be in even greater trouble."[31]

In addition to the changes within Asia and Japan, the last decade of the century was a turbulent period in global capital markets. These became increasingly volatile as individual investors poured into mutual funds in the early 1990s, as the mutual funds in turn invested heavily in emerging markets funds in the mid-1990s, and as the on-line trading boom of the mid- to late 1990s took hold. In developing countries, private-sector capital introduced a flood of riches, and in the developed countries, an even greater flood as individuals grew wealthy on speculative capital. Between 1994 and 1996, private lending to emerging markets doubled, from $70 billion to $160 billion, and at the same time mutual funds piled into emerging markets bonds, tripling their assets in just three years from 1993 to 1996. By the latter year, U.S. pension funds alone held more than $50 billion in emerging markets assets, and trade in emerging markets bonds (excluding Brady bonds) was a staggering $658 billion.[32]

By any measure, Asia was the brightest star of the capital market boom of the 1990s. Mutual fund investors had little interest in understanding the economies they invested in and no interest in long-term investment. They were looking for markets that would "bloom and burst," in the words of John Shilling, a World Bank economist tracking the incredible run-up in such investment in East Asia in the mid-1990s. The numbers are still astonishing. In 1970, East Asia attracted $2.2 billion annually out of global capital flows to developing countries of $11.3 billion. In 1980, the number was up to $13.2 billion out of $88.4 billion globally, according to World Bank calculations.[33] In the peak year of 1996, East Asia accounted for fully half of financial flows to developing countries, according to the Institute of International Finance (IIF), $141.8 billion out of $281.3 billion. In the decade after 1985, the flow of capital to East Asia grew ten times over.[34]

Until 1997, there was barely any evidence that the boom might be too much of a good thing. Part of the problem was that only the Bank for International Settlements (BIS) in Basel, Switzerland, followed short-term bank capital movements, presenting the numbers in a manner that was difficult to follow and, in any event, lagging markets by about six months. The World Bank did not look at capital movements of less than one year.

But the main reason was faith in the process of globalization itself. "There was a general tendency to believe that capital flows were good," said Shilling. "In the 1970s, people thought it was wonderful that commercial debt could make up for macroeconomic imbalances in developing countries, and there was a big rush to lend. It was an easy way for [borrowing] governments to avoid making hard decisions."[35] In the 1990s, Shilling said, much the same sensibility lay behind the dramatic increase in portfolio investment in the developing world. The thinking was that capital markets could do no wrong and capital controls would only result in distorted pricing. As it turned out, the markets were not quite as objective in the pricing of risk as theory would lead to believe.

William R. Cline, chief economist at the IIF, argued that commercial banks, caught up in the frenzy of Asian capital markets, ignored market fundamentals in the crazed atmosphere of 1995 to mid-1997. "Spreads," the interest rates that banks charge on loans, fell dramatically for the banks' East Asian clients despite deteriorating current account balances and a sharp slowdown in some of the premier Asian export industries, particularly electronics.[36] While Japanese banks were hard-hit by the catastrophe, much of Japanese investment in Asia was in manufacturing and other productive assets, and was long-term rather than short-term. The Japanese survived the reverse tidal wave of 1997–98 better than most. The problem for manufacturers and other owners of real assets in the Asian crisis was one of liquidity, and while it was difficult to sort out it was preferable to the mess in which owners of un-hedged financial assets found themselves. With the interest-payment clock ticking, owners of financial assets had to seek value by liquidating assets in countries without bankruptcy courts or international accounting standards. They faced a nightmare. Japanese manufacturers and trading companies had it easy by comparison.

A decade before the Asian crisis, Japan was perhaps the first major late industrializing economy to experience the dark side of the globalization of capital. In 1985, when finance ministers of the major industrial economies cobbled together a deal on exchange-rate coordination, under pressure from the United States, it put enormous stress on Japan's export-led growth paradigm. It was intended to destroy it. Washington imagined that its trade deficit with Japan would shrink if a higher yen eroded the competitiveness of Japanese exports. The Plaza Accord of September 1985, coming after months of pressure by the U.S. Treasury Department, saw the yen double in value over a three-year period. The realignment of exchange rates unleashed a historic movement of capital out of Japan. In February 1985, the yen was at its weakest since 1977, briefly hitting a low of Yen 260.24 to the U.S. dollar. By January 1988, there were Yen 127.56 to the dollar, a rise of 104 percent. According to Japan's EPA, the actual *endaka fukyo* (high yen recession), lasted from June 1985 to November 1986.[37] Japanese manufacturers panicked, metaphorically rushing for the door.

Most headed for Europe and North America, where they anticipated governments would soon erect protectionist barriers to Japanese exports, and their strategy was simply to ensure continued access to markets. But Japanese investors also headed for Asia, with an entirely different approach in mind. In the mid-1980s, the Asian regional market held few attractions, and Japanese manufacturers looked instead to their Asian factories to replace export products that could no longer be made economically at home. This strategy implied seeking out economies with infrastructure and human resources as similar as possible to Japan's, and the first surge in Japanese investment to Asia went exclusively to the economies of Northeast Asia—Hong Kong, South Korea, and Taiwan. Japanese investment in these three economies tripled between 1985 and 1986, from $378 million to $1.2 billion.[38]

Meanwhile, Japanese investment in the Southeast Asian "tigers"—Indonesia, Malaysia, the Philippines, and Thailand—fell between 1985 and 1986, from $595 million to $550 million. By 1987, however, Japanese investment in the southern tier began to catch up. By 1991, Japan was investing 40 percent more annually in the Southeast Asian tigers than the Northeast Asian economies. This was partly because rapid growth in the latter resulted in wage and price inflation faster than the Japanese may have reckoned with, and partly because the Southeast Asian economies were cheaper and rapidly putting in the kind of infrastructure that the Japanese needed. Perhaps more than anything else, however, the influx was due to a serendipitous conversion on the part of the governments of Thailand and Malaysia to more open investment regimes. Indonesia and the Philippines proceeded more cautiously but also began to experiment with financial and investment liberalization. The Northeast Asian economies had created special export zones (SEZs) to encourage investment in export industries. The Southeast Asian economies went one better, introducing tax and other incentives, selectively favoring investors in export manufacturing and denying investment privileges to most others.

The parallel between Japan and the globalization "victims" of 1997–98 is far from exact, of course. The crisis that struck Asian economies in Summer and Fall of 1997 hit currency markets first, then spread into the hair-trigger markets for corporate debt and equity. The Asian economies accepted Western reforms that were intended to open up their economies further, at the behest of the IMF and other lenders. Japan learned the opposite lesson from its globalization crisis. It took its yen shock as a cue to spread its social and corporate welfare policies around its geographic neighborhood. Moreover,

Japan took this lesson right through the Asia crisis. If the initial results of the IMF agreements with Asian crisis countries were to make their economies more sensitive to risk and market pricing, partly as a result of Japan's efforts, they also began to seek means to shelter themselves from capital volatility. The countries became more receptive to Japanese arguments to go slow with market liberalization, particularly in the capital account, before monitoring and regulatory institutions were in place—in short, let the bureaucrats set the pace.

Japan's Asia policy flowed in a very direct sense from the need of the bureaucratic elite—first to cushion the social impact of the hollowing out of a large chunk of Japanese export production, as a result of yen appreciation, and secondly, to ensure a warm reception for Japanese investors in Asia in a new arena outside the traditional zones of policy cooperation with the United States. One way to do this was to assert a common identity with other Asians, leading to pronouncements that came as a surprise to many in the region. But coming behind the waves of cash, few Asians found serious reasons to object. And the Japanese, for their part, took pleasure in their new role.

Ten years after the Toronto Summit, Japan launched another aid plan for Asia under far less auspicious circumstances, underlining both how far Japan had come and how far it had yet to go. This was the "New Miyazawa Initiative," a $30 billion "rescue fund" introduced by Miyazawa Kiichi, a Liberal Democratic Party (LDP) stalwart, several times Japan's finance minister and a former prime minister. On the positive side of the ledger, by 1998 Japan was able to present itself as the natural leader of a rescue plan for the economies hit by the Asian financial crisis. The scale of the rescue fund was enormous, and most of it was paid out within six months. By the time that Japan formally shut down the New Miyazawa Initiative in March 2000, Asian economies had rebounded unbelievably from the depths of 1997. Even Indonesia was showing encouraging signs of growth. On the negative side, Japan's own economy remained weak and choked with regulations, designed both to preserve domestic industries and to keep foreigners out. Asians welcomed the New Miyazawa Initiative but not without resentment that Japan did not do more to encourage Asian exports to Japan. Meanwhile, the robust American economy, fueled by a nonstop stock market and with cheap imports helping to restrain inflation, was given full credit for Asia's recovery without policy makers having to do anything other than keep the engine of the U.S. economy purring. With the U.S. economy at full employment, Washington suffered few political repercussions from the Asian crisis and incurred virtually none of the costs.

Like his predecessor, Takeshita, Miyazawa carefully considered the choice of venue for announcing his new initiative. It had to be global, in order to emphasize Japan's chosen role in representing Asia. Miyazawa chose the Fall 1998 meeting of the World Bank and the IMF in Washington, D.C., an event attended by most of the world's finance ministers, hundreds of senior executives, and thousands of journalists. The meeting was cast as a critique of the international financial institutions, particularly the IMF, which had encouraged open capital markets and pushed financial liberalization on Asian economies despite the absence or weakness of monitoring and regulatory institutions. "Capital account flows must not be liberalized too quickly without fully taking into account the circumstances of each country," Miyazawa said, in a statement delivered by a subordinate. He claimed that the region's problems had been caused in part by "over-dependence on the U.S. dollar" and promised to introduce new measures to promote use of the yen as a reserve currency in the region.[39]

Over the next few months, MOF duly began to make funds available to the crisis countries. Asians were grateful. But they also knew the history. A year earlier, in the midst of the crisis, the ministry had quickly backed off a similar, larger plan when the United States opposed it. Asians also knew that Japanese investment and imports from the region had dropped since the crisis and Japanese yen depreciation had also played a role in starting it.

In fact, to many Asians the New Miyazawa Initiative seemed a poor substitute for the hard restructuring that the Japanese economy needed to revive. The latter was in sharp contraction. Just before the Bank Fund meetings, the Japanese EPA had withdrawn its earlier forecast for mild growth in 1998 and replaced it with a negative one. Japanese banks retrenched from Asia—in the FY through March 1999, they pulled back loans by one-fifth. Far from gaining respect for Tokyo, some Asian observers viewed the plan as a measure of how much influence Japan had lost in the region. "Japan hasn't really played much of a role in stabilizing the economies of the region after the crisis," Cheong Mun Kun, head of research at Samsung Economic Research Institute in Seoul, Korea, told the San Jose *Mercury News* that June. "Now our leading trading partner is China."[40]

However much Japanese politicians and bureaucrats might squirm away from it, there was no way around the fact that aligning itself with Asia—let alone assuming leadership—would require real changes in the Japanese economy and society. For most of the 1990s, Tokyo's policy makers behaved as though they believed that Japan's mission was to guide its neighbors in following the same track as Japan had in the high-growth period of the 1960s. No amount of Japanese money could disguise the unreality of the assumptions behind this myth or that the global environment had changed considerably since the era of John Foster Dulles, when the United States was able to exercise unique leverage in using market access as a reward for its allies. After the end of the Cold War, the United States offered no more breaks for developing countries, and Japan could not stand apart and refuse to open its own economy to Asian goods and services. In one of the more extraordinary signs of the breakdown of elite consensus in the years after the Asian financial crisis, the chairman of Toyota Motor Corp., Okuda Hiroshi, returned from a fact-finding tour of Asia in Fall 1998 to sound a blistering attack on the government's Asia policy. Okuda said that Tokyo had unduly restricted Asian imports and immigration of Asian workers; he proposed free-trade agreements with South Korea and Singapore, as well as an open-door policy for Asian workers, particularly to provide services for Japan's aging population. The Okuda Report further declared:

> Japan stands at a major watershed. Ties of interdependency are deepening with Asia and with the world, and resource-poor Japan must further develop its external economic and social relations. Our population is aging, our birth rate is falling, and our population is declining. We must reform old systems, we must move forward rather than back, we must seek new growth and development, and we must be aware that efforts and sacrifices on our part will be required. If we are to continue to grow, we must relax and eliminate regulations and become a country more open to Asia and the world.
>
> It is imperative that we follow up on the "openings" of the Meiji Restoration and the postwar period with a "third opening" now. Opening Japan is urgent to the revitalization of our society and economy, to ensuring that we do not miss the historical trend of globalization. Opening Japan will also enable us to be a true and trusted friend of Asia.[41]

At the turn of the century, even the most committed proponents of a Japanese leadership role in Asia seemed tired. In mid-1999, Kinoshita Toshihiko, one of the most prominent of Japan's Asia hands, former treasurer of its Export-Import Bank (JEXIM), and advisor to the central bank of Indonesia, put it this way to San Jose *Mercury News* correspondent Michael Zielenziger: "Right now the lead goose is fatigued . . . [and] cannot lead the Asian rebound. For a while, Asia will do fine without Japan. But in another four or five years . . . [it] will regain . . . leadership."[42]

"The lead goose is fatigued"—the phrase has a history. For a good part of the century, Japan's vision of its role in Asia was based on a metaphor of flying geese. The idea was that economies learned how to compete internationally by identifying a model, or "lead goose." It came out of the ferment of late Meiji, invented by an economist who mixed ideas freely, borrowing from his travels in the United States and Europe. In the 1920s, Akamatsu Kaname was looking for an explanation for how the Japanese textile indus-

try, initially overwhelmed by British imports, had gotten on its feet and "caught up" with the British industry. Comparative advantage did not tell the story as far as he was concerned. The accomplishment took discipline, concentration, and broad public support. And it took a leadership capable of defining national strategy and goals.

When senior Japanese bureaucrats began piecing together a strategy to elevate Japan's role in Asia in the 1980s, they turned to Akamatsu's metaphor. The image of flying geese is woven through scores of policy white papers from MITI and its offshoot, the Japan External Trade Organization (JETRO), as well as MOFA and occasionally even MOF. The metaphor provided a rationale for Japan's aid program, heavily biased in favor of Asia, including economies that were at or near the point of rising above the per capita income threshold for development. Such economies could help the ones lower down, through trade and investment ties. This was also the way Japanese manufacturers fanned out through Asia, seeking first more sophisticated manufacturing centers and then subcontracting out work to the more primitive economies. Akamatsu's flying geese even crept into the *East Asian Miracle*, an ambitious report published by the World Bank in 1993, exploring the geographical causes of East Asian success.[43]

The Asian financial crisis scattered Akamatsu's geese in all directions. Any aspirations the Japanese might have had at central coordination were dead. Yet, at the end of the 1990s, there were still at least the traces of a flock in motion. By mid-1999, the crisis economies were in the early stages of recovery, and the leaders, South Korea and Thailand, were showing signs of returned health. Even Indonesia, the laggard, was beginning to mend well before the peaceful parliamentary election on June 7, 1999, with rebounds both in its stock market and currency, the rupiah. Economies had struggled back from the brink using two kinds of strategies, one following the IMF's monetary prescriptions but ignoring its fiscal directives, the other adopting Chinese-style currency controls. Both strategies reflected a Japanese inspiration, more or less diluted by neoclassical economic prescriptions. The crisis reinforced the credibility of Japanese prescriptions for gradual market liberalization, coupled with institutional mechanisms to repress consumption, marshal savings, and channel both to productive activity. Some of Japan's Asian faithful continued to pay a more direct form of homage. Vietnam told members of the Okuda Mission that the Japanese advice was "the most suited to conditions in Vietnam of any of the expert recommendations we have received on economic policy from any country or international institution."[44] Even so, by the end of the 1990s, Japan seemed content to subside into the middle of its Asian flock, satisfied with incremental realization of its vision, and turning its back on political and economic leadership.

Invisible Japan

Despite its massive economic size, technological and managerial successes, and despite the huge scope of its Asian investments, Japan in the 1990s was a diplomatic nonentity in its own geographic neighborhood. This was a matter of serious concern among Asian intellectuals and policy makers. "Japan should be at the forefront of all the countries in the region trying to create a sense of Asia-Pacific community," Kishore Mahbubani, Singapore's permanent secretary, later ambassador to the United Nations, said in an interview in 1996. "But I don't see it. Japan has no consistent Asia policy. I have been watching closely, and I just don't see a policy. All I see are economic decisions each one made on its own merits. They could have done so much in the last five to ten years, but they haven't. Everybody treats them with a lot of respect, but in terms of problem solving, we would never look to them. The Australians are more influential."[45]

We were talking while the Asian economies were in the last, feverish stages of the early 1990s boom, before the currency runs and economic catastrophe of 1997, at a time when the World Bank and IMF were collaborating ever more closely with Japan to decipher distinctive Asian strategies for economic development. Japanese money was pouring into Southeast Asia, and Tokyo had just played host to the largest gathering of Asian leaders in Japan since World War Two, at the APEC summit meeting in Osaka in 1995. Even so, Mahbubani described Japan as the weakest of the great powers in Asia, adrift in the geopolitics of the end of the Cold War. He was troubled most by Japan's inability to play an effective role counterbalancing China:

> There are three relationships that define the future of the region—U.S.-China; U.S.-Japan; and China-Japan. Most of the attention goes to the relationships between the United States and China, and the United States-Japan. You don't see much overt tension over China-Japan. But frankly, of the three relationships, the one with the highest level of distrust is China-Japan. No matter how friendly they appear. It comes from the gut, not from the mind, and it comes from both sides. China has suffered a lot of humiliation in the last hundred years, but the most direct and painful was that inflicted by Japan, by their lesser cousin. Whenever Chinese speak of Japan, the underlying theme and premise is that they can't trust those people.
>
> The Japanese, for their part, are lonely in the world. They had this wonderful shield from the Americans, with an almost total convergence of interest. Nakasone [Yasuhiro, Japanese prime minister from 1982 to 1987] called Japan an unsinkable aircraft carrier for the United States. It was a very comfortable, cozy relationship. At the same time, the Japanese economy grew enormously. Those must have been wonderful years. But once the

Cold War ended, Americans began to think they had gotten the wrong end of the bargain. It was foolish of Japan to think they could rely on tension between the United States and China as much as they had on the old Soviet Union. The Soviet Union never had the capability to become stronger than the United States. China does. The United States confronted the Soviet Union when it was at its height, in the 1950s through 1970s. Now the United States doesn't have the same sense of self-assurance about its place in the world. Now they are having a field day, but the degree of preeminence they have had cannot be sustained over the next 20 to 30 years. Japan now has to think the unthinkable. If the Americans suddenly pulled out, they'd be left carrying the can vis-à-vis China. The other problem Japan has is that it has no friends. The Japanese have an enormous pride in the uniqueness of their society, but they are so unique, they have difficulty forming relationships with other societies.

What I'm talking about is, if you look at the relationship between the United States and Canada, as geographic neighbors, there is a high degree of trust and comfort. By contrast, all of Japan's neighbors—the Russians, Chinese, and Koreans—look at Japan with great suspicion. If America abandons Japan, Japan would go nuclear overnight even if it knew the policy would be disastrous. Southeast Asians know that Japan doesn't have the weight to balance China and never will have.[46]

In Singapore, Mahbubani was not alone in his opinion of Japan. In the early 1980s, Singapore had its own episode of "Looking East" by emulating Japanese management practices. By the mid-1990s, the slogan probably meant investing in Batam, an Indonesian island just offshore from Singapore that was going through a policy-induced investment boom. A Singaporean businessman simply shrugged in response to a question about Japan's economic presence in Asia. "Japan," he said, "is finished." About the same time, policy makers in Singapore had begun to worry that their economy was following a course all too similar to that of the Japanese economy in the late 1980s, and were attempting to curb property speculation by hiking interest rates—a strategy that also hit exports by strengthening the Singapore dollar. Elite bureaucrats like Mahbubani, sitting in their gleaming skyscrapers with the world's second largest port at their feet, no longer saw Japan as an attractive model.

In 1996, Singapore itself was basking in the role of economic model for Asian economies making the transition from socialism to the market.[47] That year, Singapore invested $6.9 billion in neighboring Southeast Asian economies, and another $2.2 billion in China. By contrast, in 1996, Japan, an economy roughly forty times Singapore's size, and forty times its population, had invested $14.4 billion in the top four Southeast Asian countries, and $3.6 billion in China.[48] Measured in terms of foreign investment,

Singapore's economic impact on the region was half that of Japan's in 1996, an incredible achievement. Singaporeans felt that they had not only gone beyond the Japanese model but also needed to strip away the remnants of its export-led economy that caused it to resemble Japan too much. In their view, the Japanese model, whatever its allure, had become a liability.

Worse was yet to come. Singapore had seen and heeded the danger signals early. That year, the Monetary Authority of Singapore began raising interest rates in order to take the steam out of the housing market, despite slumping exports of semiconductors and electronics. Other economies were not as skillful in their planning. Thailand, South Korea, Indonesia, Malaysia, and the Philippines headed into crisis. Over the next two years, countless editorials proclaimed the end of the Asian and Japanese models, often using the shorthand "crony capitalism."

Economists had once praised East Asia for the strength of its institutions and value systems, based on Confucian learning and strong families. Now, they held up East Asia as the leading example of how weak institutions could ruin economies. East Asia's world was turned upside down, and Japan was at the bottom.

"Reject Asia, Embrace the West"

The view of Tokyo from the top of the Park Hyatt Hotel in Shinjuku is of a city that never ends. Tokyo melts into its suburbs and the sub-city of Yokohama, a megalopolis of roughly thirty million. Fifty years earlier, the view would have been much different. In 1949, Tokyo was a low-rise city, dusty, pocked with ruins. Today, zoning restrictions still favor the two- and three-story buildings stretching to the foothills of Mt. Fuji in one direction and to Mt. Tsukuba in another, sprawling over into the reclaimed flatlands of Tokyo Bay, to peter out only around Narita Airport, forty-one miles away. The staggered pillars of downtown Tokyo, the aggregations of consumer and business activity around the giant train stations, are jammed with vanity headquarters buildings, bristling with communications towers and gravity-defying architectural forms inspired by Japanese *manga*, or cartoons. The towers punctuate an older landscape in a constant state of churn, renewing itself by the square yard rather than by the larger makeovers of an American city. In-between the skyscrapers, if you know where to look, are entire villages from earlier eras, featuring fading old wooden *sentos*, or bathhouses, and street signs and advertisements from the 1930s.

Somewhere between where I stand, looking out from the Park Hyatt, and the horizon, groups of high school students practice ancient Chinese and Japanese arts of fencing and calligraphy, possibly even writing poetry in classical Chinese. Many wear uniforms of Prussian design that would have seemed at home 100 years ago. All around them, the world of *Pia* and the Nikkei Index surges with ferocious energy. This latter world did not come about by studying Chinese poetry. Japan began the twentieth century forcefully rejecting its Asian identity. Japan committed reckless carnage against its former mentors. Yet, as any abandoned or abandoning lover knows, the afterlife of relationships may linger for years, leaving its imprint even when circumstances and personalities have moved on.

So it was through most of the last century with Japan and Asia. Even during the militarist era, Asia was a weight on the Japanese psyche. When Japanese leaders justified their seizure of China and Southeast Asia on grounds of Japanese ethnic superiority, following the pattern set by British, French, German, and American colonialists, they did so at a cost, which was to deny not only a common identity with other Asians but also their common history. As long as Asia was under the control of the colonial powers, or in the grip of a Cold War dichotomy between capitalism and communism, Tokyo could justify its self-imposed isolation within Asia. With the end of the Cold War, however, the regional environment became more complex. Japan ceased to serve as a proxy for the United States in regional affairs, and although Tokyo maintained and even strengthened its defense relationship with the United States, increasingly Japan was at the mercy of its Asian allies. As soon as the Cold War ended, Tokyo reassessed the regional balance of power in terms that had been familiar for a thousand years before industrialization lifted Western powers to a preeminent position there. Under the new-old calculus with which Japan entered the twenty-first century, once again China was to become Japan's major geopolitical challenge. In meeting that challenge, the heritage of Japan's rejection of Asia was to raise innumerable obstacles to its new policy of rapprochement.

Japan's post–Cold War Asia strategy has shifted course more than once. The accompanying rhetoric has been misleading. Does Japan want to be the leader of Asia or is it merely reassuring the United States that it will continue to "lead" the region the way that Washington wants it to? If Japan wants to take credit for the Asian economic model, is it also responsible for the Asian financial collapse of 1997–98? Does Japan view China as partner or rival? Does talk of an Asian model and an Asian renaissance reflect the genuine birth of a regional sensibility? Or does the rhetoric reflect, instead, the lack of any real connection between Japan and its neighbors?

The ambiguity can be frustrating but serves a purpose—to allow Japan maximum flexibility at a time of profound changes in the global and regional balance of power. The shifts in direction have been reactive and opportunistic, reflecting the emergence of new threats in China and North Korea and overwhelming domestic issues, especially the weakness of the banking sector. Leaving reality aside, the rhetoric has given life to an image of a new regional economic culture in which governments and markets work in tandem, sometimes in corrupt patterns, more often intelligently.

Much of the rhetoric revolves around a nebulous concept of "Asian values"; the fact that it has survived the Asian financial crisis is significant. Even before Michel Camdessus, managing director of the IMF, announced his resignation in November 1999, hosts of critics attacked his medicine for the crisis economies. Before the Asian crisis, Japan was busy laying the groundwork to present itself as the region's mentor and model. The currency collapse, coupled with Japanese banking problems, led many to believe that the Japanese and Asian models were "finished." But by 1999, two years after the crash, the tide had turned again. The region's swift recovery, coupled with dissatisfaction with the IMF—going well beyond its mistakes in the Asia crisis—had led many to the opposite conclusion. Many Asians viewed the crisis entirely differently—as a lesson for economies such as Thailand, South Korea, and Indonesia. These had liberalized their capital markets too quickly, based on Western prescriptions. In the wake of the crisis, Asian economies nationalized their financial sectors rather than sell the assets to foreigners. Asian governments became stronger because of the crash, not weaker.

As Americans, we tend to look at Asia through mental blinders, formed by our own national interest and preoccupations. Washington portrayed the Asian crisis as the last hurrah of Marxist economics, a defeat for the government-led model of development and triumph for the free market. If we look deeper, however, we ought to be able to perceive the outlines of an Asian history in Asian terms. When Americans think of Japan, they tend to think of the country that mounted a challenge to the West, first as a military power, then waging war in that other field of battle known as business. Japan is perceived in black-and-white terms, sometimes as rival, sometimes as paragon, more recently as the sick man of Asia—the purveyor of a "Japanese disease." We tend to look at China similarly, as an evil empire or nation of aspiring capitalists in our own image. Rarely do we look at either nation as we might if America did not exist, as if the only world was Asia.

For most of recorded history, the West has played a negligible role in the affairs of either China or Japan. As the Middle Kingdom, China was the center of East Asian civilization for millennia; Japan was an annoying nation on its periphery, too strong and isolated for conquest. For Japan, China was always a magnet, a source of technology and culture, a challenge to the ambitions of territorially expansive shoguns as well as to the merchant entrepreneurs who raided the China coast for hundreds of years. Only in the modern era did the Middle Kingdom reciprocate Japan's fascination, observing closely its strategies for industrialization and sending generations of students to learn how Japan had mastered Western ways.

Yet Japan shaped China as well. From earliest times, Japanese generals and adventurers represented the greatest of China's threats from overseas. The Japanese had pillaged first the Chinese tributary states on the Korean Peninsula and later plagued Chinese coastal trade. The seclusion decrees imposed by the Ming dynasty in the sixteenth century can be understood as a response to the opportunism of Japanese pirates backed by regional lords. This was a distant drama, however, until the onset of the Industrial Revolution. The latter brought the two into confrontation in a new arena, the quest for economic power.

Beginning with the Opium Wars of the 1840s, Western economic predation against China taught Japan how to take its first steps toward modernization. Japan saw in China the tragic mistakes that it sought to avoid in its own pursuit of wealth and power. An anti-China motif was implicit in the "*Fukoku Kyohei*" (Rich Country, Strong Army) slogan, and it became the intellectual banner of the forces defeating the Tokugawa shogunate, that then went on to "restore" the Meiji emperor in 1868. Nonetheless, the intellectual process is shrouded by which Japan crystallized its rejection of its ancient heritage, conveyed in the slogan, *"Datsu A, Nyu Ou"* (Reject Asia, Embrace Europe). "Take to European ways," and acquire "big guns," wrote Fukuzawa Yukichi in his essay *"Tojin Orai"* (A primer on foreigners).

Datsu A, Nyu Ou, came from the title of a later essay by Fukuzawa. But he claims to have forgotten how and when he first challenged his contemporaries to give up "fencing" and other trappings of a millennium worth of cultural infusion from the Asian continent. "I believe it was in the Bunkyu Era [1861–63]," he said, describing it as a "small piece" that he declined to publish but showed around to friends. The timing and circumstances of that moment leave a certain ambiguity that in retrospect was like the closing of a door on one room, Japan's Asian room, and a stepping onto the threshold of a new and foreign space. From that time on, Fukuzawa, and the Japanese of his generation, divided their world between East and West, regarding the two as polar opposites, one offering modernity and power, the other poverty and disintegration.[49]

The young Fukuzawa undoubtedly wrote his essay in calligraphy, using a sable-tipped brush, his hand steady from years of training. Chinese and Japanese alike had long viewed calligraphy as the premier art form, accessible only to an elite cadre of cultivated gentlemen, administrators, and warriors. Educated Japanese women used only the Japanese *hiragana* alphabet, not considered on a par with the manly forms of Chinese characters. Perhaps the act of writing itself injected an element of cognitive dissonance. Perhaps this is what affected the older Fukuzawa's memory, years later.

Taking to "European ways," from that point forward, the Japanese began to disassociate themselves from Asia in ways large and small. The first steps were modest. Chinese studies, as well as the samurai's art of the sword, were put aside as trappings of an obsolete mind-set. The gesture was aimed clearly at Japanese conservatives, who had placed Confucian learning at the center of their pantheon for more than a thousand years. A mere twenty-two years after the era of *Tojin Orai*, in 1885, Fukuzawa's controversial article, *"Datsu-A ron"* (On leaving Asia) referred more directly to the broader geographic neighborhood. Not only must Japan put traditional culture aside, but also, clear lines must be drawn between itself and the primitive, vulnerable states on its borders. The latter essay foreshadowed a Japan that would spend the next half-century invading, annexing, and pillaging its neighbors. The earlier writing seems to come from an age of innocence, a time when Fukuzawa still understood Japan to be intrinsically Asian to the extent that even the word "foreigner" had lost its original connotation of "Chinese."

A primer on *tojin*, Fukuzawa called it, a "primer on foreigners." The characters for *tojin* translate literally as the "people of Tang," that is, the Tang Dynasty of China. About the time of Rome's final collapse, with Europe in disarray and Byzantium in decline, Japan first discovered the miracle of China by way of the Sinified kingdoms of Korea. Japan's Yamato court had been a loose tribal federation of *uji*, or clans, marrying inside the clan and worshipping their own deities. The language, culture, and theories of governance of the "people of Tang" transformed the primitive village society, transmitting to it a civil bureaucracy and the concept of hierarchy. From the time of Prince Shotoku's "Seventeen-Article Constitution" in 604 until the surrender of the Tokugawa *bakufu* at Edo Castle in 1868, China provided Japan with the constructs for most of its formal institutions.

China, with its Asian tributary states, had traditionally enveloped Japan's world. Later interlopers on the Japanese horizon, such as the Spanish, Portuguese, and Dutch, extended the parameters of reference but were themselves folded into a system designed to extract knowledge, based on manipulations practiced for centuries on Chinese and Koreans. Even Japan's deliberate policy of formal isolation, or *sakoku,* from 1639 to 1854, was patterned after similar prohibitions the Ming Dynasty had imposed on contacts with Japan, designed to restrict its booming piracy trade centered in Kyushu. In 1616, Tokugawa Ieyasu restricted the China trade to Nagasaki, setting the former fishing village on a course to becoming Japan's most cosmopolitan city. When the Dutch were ensconced in a trading station on landfill in Nagasaki harbor, the context of their reception was subsumed within a broader policy to maintain and oversee the far more important trade with China.

Any Japanese reading Fukuzawa's essay in the late nineteenth century would know what he meant. The new *"tojin"* on everybody's mind were Europeans and Americans, who were in the process of toppling Asia's oldest empire and depleting the resources of its satellites. The image of white foreigners in their black ships was predatory and terrifying. The Japanese woman who served as mistress to Townsend Harris, the first American consul general in Shimoda, was pejoratively nicknamed Okichi "Tojin,"[50] "foreign" Okichi. More sinisterly, visiting foreigners and experts on the West, such as Fukuzawa, were subject to attacks and death threats. By choosing the word *tojin*, Fukuzawa hoped to remind his readers of all that Japan had learned from China and in so doing win over ordinary Japanese to his vision of a Westernized state. "It would be fun if I could convert all the old men and women of Edo with the brandishing of my brush!" he wrote playfully. And so he did, as fashionable men and women of Meiji quickly shed their kimonos for bustles and top hats, learned how to commute to work by hanging off straps in trains, and converted their industries from crafts to mass production.

The rejection of traditional culture that began with Fukuzawa went deep and included a determined effort to blot out the psychological and material links between Japan and the Asian continent. Since Fukuzawa's time, Japan has presented itself in geographically antiseptic terms—as a unique case, a country with European discipline and American energy, utterly different from its neighbors. For most of the twentieth century, Japan regarded its Asian neighbors as markets or as sources of raw materials, not as counterparts or equals.

Many Japanese are surprised and disbelieving to learn that Korean artisans designed Japan's first Chinese-styled capital city at Nara. One of Japan's most beautiful and treasured medieval sculptures is clearly Korean in style: the seventh-century Miroku Bosatsu, kept in the ancient Koryu-ji Temple in Kyoto, was probably carved in Silla, the southeastern part of the Korean Peninsula. It is an image of a dreamy young boy, chin propped on his hand, contemplating eternity, in the simple, elongated lines common to Silla sculpture, a contemporary idiom in Buddhist art stretching to the caves of western China. Halfway across the Asian continent, the same visual signature is visible in the ecstatic grotto figurines from the Northern Wei and Sui dynasties in China. For Japan to deny such a heritage is somehow to diminish the Miroku, as if it were an accident rather than the product of genius in an artistic tradition encompassing the known world when Nara was at its height.

For most of the Cold War, erasing history was a matter of formal government policy. High-school history textbooks glossed over the early modern period, and Ministry of Education (MOE) interventions to soften references to Japanese military aggression in Asia provoked frequent complaints and diplomatic rows with China and South Korea. Mainstream Japanese politicians contested such well-documented incidents as the 1937 Nanjing massacre of 100,000 or more Chinese civilians. The high-school history curriculum was weighted toward Japan's early history, beginning with the Jomon and Yayoi periods, from 10,000 B.C. to A.D. 300, when Japan evolved from a primitive hunting and gathering society to bronze and iron age cultures. Frequently teachers skipped the last half-century.

The result has been a memory lapse spanning a generation and takes in most Japanese under the age of sixty. Younger Japanese do not know that Singapore had a Japanese name, Shonan (Light of the South) or that Emperor Hirohito on his white horse ruled an empire from Sakhalin to Burma. If they are aware, the knowledge is carried lightly. That time, that connection with Asia, seems to have nothing to do with Japan in the present.

The Greater East Asian "co-prosperity sphere" was launched in a conference in Tokyo in November 1943 as the *Dai Toa Kaigi*, or Greater East Asia Assembly. For the first and only time, Japan brought together the titular heads of state of its puppet states. A ceremonial photo in front of the Diet building, dated November 6, Showa 16 (1943), displays them flanking Japan's wartime prime minister, Tojo Hideki. Burma's revolutionary leader, Ba Maw, stands proudly in national costume, next to a seated Zhang Jinghui, president of puppet Manchukuo. A young, pale Wang Jinghui, head of the "reorganized" Chinese nationalist government, and the solid-looking Prince Wan Waithayakon of Thailand sit on either side of Tojo, who is posed samurai style, fists on his thighs, legs wide apart.

In the same row appear Jose Paciano Laurel, president of the Philippines, and Subas Chandra Bose, leader of the "provisional government of Free India," the government in exile he had set up in 1940.[51] All are wearing decorations; no smiles crease the faces. The men in the front row tentatively mimic Tojo's traditional posture, sitting with their knees apart also, feet planted firmly on the ground.

One witness, recalling the week of the event, says that the names of these colorful Asian politicians and anticolonial leaders were familiar even to children, "more so than the names of [Japanese] generals."[52] Ba Maw called the gathering a "historic event." Japanese writers painted the meeting as a triumphant celebration of the end of Western colonialism. It may have been this to some of the participants. Certainly, Ba Maw and Subas Chandra Bose accepted the more sentimental gestures of their hosts. Japan had backed their resistance movements with guns and money. At the same time, the episode occasioned profound humiliation, particularly for the Chinese. The *Dai Toa*

Kaigi left a deep-enough stain that it would be nearly fifty years before Japan would dare to host a gathering of Asian leaders, under vastly different circumstances.

Indeed, that next time would be in 1989 to attend the funeral of the man who had inspired and directed Japan's Asian conquests. Rites for the "Showa Emperor," commonly known outside Japan by his personal name of Hirohito, were observed on a cold, damp February day, eight weeks after his death on January 7. The ceremonies went on with barely a hitch. It was Britain's Prince Philip who generated the only controversy: The Duke of Edinburgh barely twitched his head when he took his place in line to pay respects to the departed emperor, enraging both Japanese nationalists (as an instance of lese-majeste) and Britons who criticized him for honoring a former enemy.[53]

With Hirohito's funeral, some taboos were brushed away. In 1994, presidents, prime ministers, and other luminaries showed up once more for the wedding of Crown Prince Naruhito and Owada Masako, a Harvard-trained diplomat. In 1995 in Osaka, Asia-Pacific leaders gathered in Japan again, for the sixth annual ministerial meeting and third leaders' summit of APEC. Each of these events was ceremonial or involved institutions in which Japan was one of many members. As of 2001, Japan had yet to host a meeting of regional leaders in Japan to pursue specifically Japanese diplomatic goals. Yet, in 1997, it had gone as far as extending an invitation, when Prime Minister Hashimoto Ryutaro proposed annual summit meetings between Tokyo and heads of government of ASEAN while touring the region. Initially, he got a cool reception. Only Indonesian president Suharto showed interest. At the time, Dewi Fortuna Anwar, advisor to Suharto's Golkar Party, told Reuters that Hashimoto's proposal was a bad idea. "I don't know if it will be really necessary at the moment, as you are creating a precedent and the United States and China will want (summits too)," Anwar said. "There will be too many summits."[54] Hashimoto's idea prevailed, however, and later in the year, ASEAN convened its first "informal" ASEAN Plus Three summit, with China, Japan, and South Korea in attendance.

The episodes of Japanese "leadership" left deep marks on Asia. Some are benign, such as the *karaoke* fad or Japanese animated cartoons—the inventive, sentimental *anime*—or printed *manga*. Others retain bitter power. When Japan annexed Korea in 1910, the military government razed most of the temples and palaces of old Seoul. The most wounding act was the destruction of the central gateway to the Korean royal palace, the Kyongbokkung and its replacement by a squat, Western-style building that served as the headquarters of Japanese colonial rule. The squat granite block straddled the main artery of the city until 1997, not only blocking the view of Kyongbokkung but also destroying the old Sinified city plan, based on the science of *feng shui*, or wind and water. The symbolism of the main avenue and its squared off streets linked the city, through the ruler at Kyongbokkung to the rocky spires of the Pukan (Northern Han) mountains at his back, an umbilical link with the heavens beyond. In order to impress the permanence and finality of Japanese control on the population, the Japanese symbolically severed the architectural design by physically erecting their headquarters in front of the palace. For many years after Korea's independence, the building housed a museum. When Korea finally removed it in 1997, the demolition progressed brick by brick, starting with the spire. Seated primly on folding chairs with sun umbrellas at hand, at the ceremony marking its demise more than half a century after Japan's defeat, Korean dignitaries wept with joy.

Times change. In 1998 as part of the IMF prescriptions, Korea finally dropped bans on most Japanese imported goods, and by 1999 Seoul and Tokyo were exploring prospects of a free trade agreement modeled after the U.S.-Canada trade deal. In November 1998, on a brilliant, warm fall day in Seoul I visited Kyongbokkung. No trace of the former museum and colonial headquarters could be seen. The broad paving stones had been swept clean. Behind a fence, workers were piecing together a reproduction of the old gate. Under yellow gingko trees and blood-red maples, as photographers turned them this way and that in the sunlight and against the old wall, fashion models in purple lipstick struck poses in magenta-died fur stoles. Old men ambled through the garden. Mothers pulled along children, dressed in padded clothing. The bare branches of a persimmon tree, loaded with fruit, spoke of the richness of harvest, the end of old things, the beginning of new growth after a long interruption.

A rising sensibility stirred in Japan as well, a desire for reconciliation that went beyond the official hyperbole. Yanagihara Toru is a Japanese of the baby-boom generation, born in 1949, a University of Tokyo graduate who was a student radical during the anti-U.S. protests of the 1960s. I had free tickets to a musical, *Ri Koran*, a stylish production put together by Japan's leading theatrical producer, Asari Keita. The theme was the Japanese invasion of China in the 1930s. I invited Toru, a busy economist. It was a return invitation of sorts. Toru had taken me along to various art exhibitions and seminars, as well as helping me with my stories as a correspondent. He was clearly reluctant to accept the invitation. He hated to sit down for long and was impatient with what he considered gratuitous critiques of Japan's war record.

As far as Toru was concerned, World War Two was ancient history. Japan had long since apologized. The effort to paint his country as an unrepentant war criminal was an Anglo-American plot to limit Japanese ambitions, an attitude common to many of his generation. Without direct experience of

World War Two, mostly they wanted to forget it and create a new national identity based on Japan's economic success and constitutionally mandated pacifism.

Nonetheless, he agreed to come. Thus, paired with a reluctant partner, I attended the premiere performance of *Ri Koran* at the Aoyama Theater on a cold winter's night. This lively, Andrew Lloyd Weber–like production was set in Japanese-controlled Manchukuo, in northeastern China. Dark material, indeed, for a musical. A few years earlier, Bernardo Bertolucci's 1987 film, *The Last Emperor*, included a convincing portrayal of Japanese scheming and atrocities. In contrast, *Ri Koran* offered a more nuanced picture of Japanese involvement on the Chinese continent. Its characters included scheming military men and their collaborators but also idealists and other innocents caught up in the era. The story revolved around the main character, Yamaguchi Yoshiko, whose name in Chinese was Ri Koran, or "Fragrant Orchid."

Yamaguchi was a real person who, in the early 1990s, remained very much a presence in Japanese society and politics. She was born in Manchuria in 1920 and had grown up in China in the 1930s. After the end of the war, Yamaguchi became one of Japan's first international film stars, was briefly married to the renowned Japanese-American sculptor Isamu Noguchi, and for many years thereafter was a member of the Japanese House of Councilors, where, among other things, she led the pro-Burma coalition in the LDP. The musical focused on her early career as a film star in China. Yamaguchi's father and grandfather had taught Chinese studies in Japan—the grandfather at his own school in Saga Prefecture in Kyushu. In 1906, Yamaguchi Fumio, Ri Koran's father, moved to Shenyang and got a job teaching Chinese to employees of the South Manchurian Railway. In Chinese fashion, Fumio gave his daughter a Chinese name, Xianglan (Koran in Japanese, meaning "Fragrant Orchid" in both languages). He made sure that she spoke fluent Chinese.[55] As a gesture of friendship, once she was a teenager Fumio entrusted his daughter to the family of a pro-Japanese Chinese general, Li Jichun (whose surname became the Ri of Ri Koran in the Japanese phonetic version of the Chinese characters). Somehow, the Man-Ei Film Co., the Kwantung Army's propaganda arm in Manchukuo, heard of young Ri Koran and recruited her to play in its propaganda films. The Kwantung Army was the Japanese Imperial Army's expeditionary force in China. Koran was sweetly sexy and vulnerable. Her fans, Chinese and Japanese alike, believed that she was Chinese. By the 1940s, Yamaguchi had become a huge star. Most of her roles involved a Chinese woman falling in love with a Japanese soldier.

Ri Koran's fortunes took a downward turn, however, as Mao's troops swept through China in the late 1940s. She stayed behind rather than evacuate to

Japan, and the communists put her on trial for betraying her country. The judge released Ri Koran when he received proof that she was Japanese, and so by definition could not betray China. In the musical, this scene is emotional. A lynch mob of Eighth Route Communist army troops demands the death of Koran and other collaborators: "Kill them, kill them, traitors, they sold their country to hateful Japan, traitors, kill them, kill them, try them, '*Han jian*,' the betrayers," the mob rages. Then Koran announces she is Japanese and produces proof. In an abrupt reversal, the judge forgives her, singing: "Let this unfortunate case be a lesson for future generations, Let's throw away our hatred and think, reciprocate your enmity with virtue."[56]

What was arresting from a Japanese perspective was that the moment was one of forgiveness and redemption, as well as guilt due to Japanese atrocities in China. Much of the plot dealt with the contrast between Koran's idealistic father, a believer in pan-Asian unity, and corrupt, cynical militarists. By the grand finale, as Ri Koran was set free, Toru had tears running down his face. How did he come by such passions, I wondered. Somewhere was a feeling that Japan could be part of a larger tribe. Fukuzawa's legacy was beginning to become undone.

2

Flying Geese

For three-quarters of a century, Japanese economists and officials have used the metaphor of geese in flight to describe the Asian economic model, applying it to industries, economies, and the region as a whole. At different times, in different hands, the metaphor has referred both to a static hierarchical structure in which Japan is assumed to be the "lead goose" and a dynamic model for the developmental state, defined as a state whose political energies are focused on rapid industrialization. In the latter guise, it can be taken for granted that Japan's competitors will catch up and lead the flock as surely as Japan once overtook its Western economic rivals in successive industries.

To describe the history of this trope is to explore Japan's sinuous, contradictory relations with Asia over the course of the twentieth century. The relationship never soared as high as the metaphor suggests. Yet, at heart, there is something to the notion that economic growth depends on focused ambition and striving. No amount of foreign aid or World Bank programs can levitate an economy or a people unless they want growth and are willing to work for it. Japan was the first Asian nation to acquire this wisdom. The Japanese model was not really so much a prescription as a pragmatic lesson in how to get rich. For a time, at least, Asians eagerly adopted the Japanese approach.

I somehow find appropriate that the image binding a century of Japanese intentions in Asia, good and bad, should be identical with the traditional metaphor for homecoming, a flock heading together toward a common destination. At home, I have an old scroll, picked up in a rural antique store; it has no colophon but is from the Kano school, known for its atmospheric effects. Tucked into the middle distance is a flock of geese in its annual migration. A lead goose and a few other champions—delicate apostrophes of black ink—faintly indent a bow-shaped column merging into a line of hills, or perhaps a cloud. The flock of geese is orderly in its chaos, traversing the landscape through instinct and desire.

The image has experienced more than its share of controversy and paradox. Today, one might read it as emblematic of Japan's geopolitical loneliness and isolation as the country seeks to identify itself more closely with its Asian neighbors, yet without being able to shed the rigid views and sociopolitical structures that alienate other Asians more immersed in a freewheeling global culture. Japanese wartime officials used the metaphor to justify turning China and Southeast Asia into outposts of Japanese industry, chaining their economies to the Japanese war effort in the "Greater East Asian Co-Prosperity Sphere." In the 1990s, the image has connoted a longing for tribal belonging, a restoration of an Asian order before the trauma of industrialization, a return to an era when civilization was defined by traditions stretching back millennia. In this guise, it has served mainly to defend authoritarian regimes against the onslaught of liberalism. But it began life, and survives, as one of the fundamental Japanese contributions to economic thought.

The common phrase in Japanese is *ganko keitai,* or the "formation" style economic system. My Japanese-English financial dictionary lists the term in its long form, *gankoteki keizai hatten,* which it translates as the "formation style economic development." The geese, in this phrase, are suggested implicitly. The dictionary further explains that it refers to "neighborhood effects in which the growth of Malaysia, Thailand, and China has been driven by industrial restructuring in Japan, South Korea and Taiwan," and to "intereconomy sequencing in the industrialization process." Finally, a more pedestrian gloss: "The dynamic Asian economies have developed in what is known to the Japanese economists as a 'flying geese formation.'"[1]

To understand the power of the metaphor in post-war Japan, it is necessary to think back before the East Asian financial crash of 1997–98, to the region's thirty years of uninterrupted growth. Before Asia stumbled, it became wealthy, and the wealth was spread widely. Even after the convulsion of the late 1990s, Asian economies remained far more solidly middle class, and far more comfortable than their counterparts in Latin America, Russia and Eastern Europe, Africa, or the Middle East. The great cities of Asia reflected a luxury and dynamism that, even with the setbacks, rivaled Europe and North America. In a 1993 publication, the World Bank noted that there was one chance in ten thousand that success would be so concentrated in a single region.[2]

To the Japanese, no mystery stood behind this observation. The statistical evidence could be summarized: In Asia, the invisible hand was Japan. It saw itself not only as the model for developing countries in East Asia but also as a direct source of change and growth through investment and competition. The geese kept formation because of an overwhelming impulse to overtake the leader. When the leader dropped back, a new one replaced it. The pattern was one in which first Japan, followed by its former colonies, achieved miracles of growth. They left such bastions of U.S. influence as the Philippines in the dust. South Korea, Taiwan, Hong Kong, and Singapore, followed by Thailand, Malaysia, and Indonesia were all members of Japan's flock. Even China took its turn.

Each aspiring competitor added new elements to the mix, and, at the same time, shared a basic paradigm. The flying-geese model combined industrial policy and business cartels at home with robust competition abroad. The strategy was based on results, not just government fiat. In adopting the paradigm, other East Asian economies were able to emulate Japan's success by using similar methods, with government acting as sponsor and referee to a driven private sector. The model—despite its popularity with propagandists—had little to do with ideology. It was about marshaling public and private resources to achieve specific economic goals. Outside Asia, most nations experienced such singularity only in times of war.

In the 1990s, the image of flying geese became interlaced with a determined Japanese challenge to Western economic orthodoxy. Ambitious Japanese bureaucrats cited Asian economic success as empirical proof that the "flying-geese" pattern of economic development worked. Japanese multinationals unrolled "flying-geese" corporate strategies. They differentiated investments by the level of economic growth of the host economy. Their factories in Japan became the lead goose for Asian factories striving to "catch up" by producing goods higher up the technology chain. Flying geese became a barely disguised trope of self-congratulation, ubiquitous in official documents. The suggestion, always just below the surface, was that Japan was responsible for the success of the Asian tigers and dragons.

Who killed neoclassical economics? It may have been Japan's geese. The rise of neoclassical economics occurred in tandem with the fall of communism and a global political shift favoring market economics in the 1980s. By the late 1990s, the pendulum had swung again. Market economics in its more extreme forms had been discredited, the consensus broken.

Not everyone, of course, agreed. In a 1998 bestseller, energy economist and journalist Daniel Yergin proclaimed that the market had seized the "commanding heights" of moral prestige and authority, and, in his view, government was in retreat.[3] Yet, by the end of the decade, government inched back, and a strange malaise seized the erstwhile champions of the free market. A decade after the fall of the Berlin Wall, market economies were more pervasive than at any time since the early part of the century. Socially, politically, and philosophically, however, the free market was in trouble. The high-flown rhetoric of the mid-1980s vanished, victim in part to the rolling financial crisis of the 1990s. In its place was a renewed backlash against the forces of globalization, reminiscent of the 1930s in its arguments and intensity.

Economics is not just about numbers, but about policy and the real world of problems and solutions. It is rich with metaphor, which organizes experience and serves to justify specific actions and strategies. At the heart of liberal economics is an oceanic metaphor, in the "law" of supply and demand. It has never been tested and proven. Yet it gives coherence to huge reefs of theory—perfect markets, the primacy of the consumer, automatic price adjustments, decisions made on the basis of self-interest, and the pull of entropy or "equilibrium" in markets. Corner solutions were consistent with the framework, but liberal economics emphasized internal solutions that it could run through its own black box and come out the other end with neatly packaged answers.[4]

Neoclassical economics took this metaphor one step further, focusing on the mechanics of actual markets for goods, services, and financial assets. It theorized that markets automatically equilibrate, or conduct price adjustments based on supply and demand, and that consumers make decisions based on rational self-interest, operating along a maximum utility curve. Governments were unable to duplicate the function of the market, unless they were somehow to build a computer program that would input every single economic action and actor, and run it as fast as real life. Markets, in short, behaved rationally, while governments were prone to human failure. According to neoclassical theory, governments were assigned a nebulous role in providing "public goods"—a role that shrinks as the market expands. Even public services—such as railroad and bus systems, the postal service, telecommunications, electricity, water, and gas—were eventually to be assumed by the private sector.

If economics is based on metaphor, it also reflects intellectual fashion and politics. In the 1980s, the "neo" in neoclassical economics signified a counterrevolution against the prevailing orthodoxy of the 1970s, especially the *dependencia* movement that began in Latin America. *Dependencia* theory argued that strong government intervention was necessary to counterbalance the structural inequities imposed by dominant players in the global economy. Import substitution in which governments blocked imports in order to foster domestic industries and other forms of industrial policy became popular in the economies embracing the theory. In the early 1980s, industrial policy was a factor in triggering the Latin American debt crisis, then a global commodities slump, crushing growth in second-tier Asian economies, most of which were resource exporters. Southeast Asian economies were among the first to unwind import substitution policies and replace them with incentives for value-added exports and investment. The Southeast Asians pioneered in a strategy of partial liberalization of their economies. They used foreign capital, mostly from Japan, to acquire large-scale export industries. This strategy shifted the focus from domestic market intervention to foreign markets and put them in the vanguard of the neoclassical revolution in Asia.

In the industrial economies, by the late 1970s, huge budget deficits had begun to have a destabilizing effect, exacerbated by commodity-price inflation fanned by two oil shocks. Neoclassical economics offered a way out for governments to cut spending and taxes simultaneously in the name of unleashing market forces. The concept had broad political appeal, and even seemed to work, as the industrial economies pulled out of the recession of the early 1980s. By mid-decade, the free market had become dogma in much of the industrial world and Asia, excluding Japan. The Asian tigers gave free rein to the market, in limited sectors of their economies. Foreign multinationals were able to take 100 percent ownership as long as they used their Asian factories for export. Usually, such arrangements were limited as well to industrial parks, where they could be monitored more easily. Singapore and Hong Kong, which had the reputation of being the most open economies in the world, devoted considerable bureaucratic resources to controlling the market through manipulating asset prices through control of land and large equity positions in local companies. Singapore's largest enterprises were all government-owned companies.

Nonetheless, the Asian economies rocketed through the late 1980s, regularly achieving double-digit growth. Japan, meanwhile, reached an apogee of wealth and influence, as its stock and real estate bubble reached astronomic proportions. Far from being outliers, Asian economies were the superstars of the neoclassical "counterrevolution." As the Soviet Union imploded, Western policy makers pointed to East Asia as proof that market economies had triumphed. When the World Bank talked of an East Asian "miracle," it meant a free-market miracle. The Asian economies had thrown off the shackles of *dependencia* theory, and embraced the discipline of market competition. Even Japan was seen as successful because it adopted neoclassical principles, despite the fortress-like protection surrounding its domestic market. These views of Japan and Asia persisted because market reforms had indeed swept the region. They failed to take into account, however, the degree to which the Asian economies, led by Japan, remained wedded to the very different disciplines of managed economies.

Neoclassical economics placed its faith in open markets, insisting that developing economies were better off with cheap currencies and the free flow of trade and investment, and instructed developed economies to stimulate consumption through lower taxes and interest rates, not through public spending. Yet, there were obvious limits to the theory. In order to function, markets need strong institutions to communicate information about goods and prices. Financial institutions play a major informational role, but so do governments. In the glory days of neoclassical economics in the mid-1980s, the role of government in addressing market imperfections was studiously ignored. The absence of basic mechanisms to communicate market prices in many developing economies was just one such market imperfection that the neoclassicists somehow overlooked. For the most doctrinaire, it was impossible to admit that market failure sometimes implied a need to strengthen government regulation or public institutions.

Indeed, free market advocates argued that strong moral values were enough to hold capitalism together. As long as capitalists behaved ethically, government was unnecessary. One of the odd vignettes of a dying creed occurred during Lady Margaret Thatcher's visit to Tokyo in 1991. Two years earlier, a string of stock market scandals had toppled the government of Takeshita Noboru, contributing to the catastrophic Nikkei stock crash of 1990. Thatcher placed the blame on bad morals, a critique that foreshadowed the barrage of charges of "crony capitalism" against the Asian economies six years later. "We have to practice, not just preach, the ethics of capitalism," she said, in a lecture for which she was paid $750,000.[5] "Popular capitalism is spreading worldwide. More and more people will depend on the integrity of financial institutions. Small and large investors must be given the same treatment. There should be no room in any country in the world for sharp practice."[6]

By the early 1990s, the tide turned against neoclassical economics. A fundamental reason for the failure was that the market grew faster, and more chaotically, than its champions had ever dreamed. Capitalist ethics were not enough as global capital swamped the developing world in the early 1990s. At the same time, the size and frequency of market crises increased as well, concentrated in economies that were in early stages of liberalizing their financial markets. Frequently, governments were left to pick up the pieces, nationalizing insolvent banks and industries. At the popular level, anxiety grew about the competence of market institutions to deal with social problems created as by-products of market efficiency and technological change.

The new counterrevolution had a noisy, human voice. It was led by nongovernmental organizations (NGOs) focusing on human rights, labor, and the environment. It encouraged stronger government, market inefficiency to protect weak players, and the dominance of local over international rules and institutions. And it made strange bedfellows. Developing countries saw the antiglobalization counterrevolution as an excuse for the advanced economies to reinstate protectionism. The Europeans and Japanese, coming from strong traditions of government intervention, saw it as an opportunity to escape U.S. dominance of the global economy. Japan, as we shall see, played a role in fomenting the new movement from inside the leading institutions of global governance.

By the late 1990s, major global financial institutions were quietly making the changeover to a new paradigm. The World Bank, formerly a stronghold of neoclassical economics, began hiring social workers, anthropologists, investment bankers, and area specialists. Until his sudden resignation in December 1999, World Bank Chief Economist Joseph Stiglitz was a fervent proponent of the new wave, building on his own work in information theory. The other Bretton Woods institutions were weakening. In early 1998, the IMF suddenly plunged into the unaccustomed waters of public accountability, vastly upgrading its Web site and dragooning senior Fund staff to conduct question-and-answer sessions in public settings. Chastened by its policy failures to cope with the emerging markets crises of 1997–98, the organization had taken the unusual step of admitting that it could be wrong in a series of internal fact-finding reports carefully leaked to the *New York Times* and other publications. With the resignation of Managing Director Michel Camdessus, the IMF seemed poised for a major overhaul. Similarly, the World Trade Organization began to take more seriously criticism that it was a tool of multinational corporations and developed countries. In Seattle in November and December 1999, environmental, labor, and human rights activists blocked the launch of a new round of global trade negotiations, serving notice on the WTO that it needed to adopt standards other than market efficiency. By the time of the Doha summit in November 2001, the language of social accountability came far more readily to the international bureaucrats gathering at the heavily guarded, intentionally remote conference site in the Gulf state of Qatar.

The conflict between neoclassical economics and forces of antiglobalization reflected inherent strains in the framework of Western ideology, a dialectic going back at least to Socrates and the tension between the rights of the state and the individual. Such a dichotomy had no place within Japanese tradition, tempered by hundreds of years of state Confucianism, the imperial bureaucracy of the war years, and the developmental-state strategies of the post-war era. From the perspective of Japanese bureaucrats in the late 1980s, the government and the marketplace did not do battle. The state and the individual were not in conflict; they collaborated.

Flying Geese: A History

The metaphor of flying geese was central to Japan's campaign to unseat Western economic orthodoxy and is essential to understanding the Japanese "model" and its promotion. Within the group, the leader sets the pace. As the less fleet strive to keep up, they form a V-shaped hierarchy of geese ardently chasing a leader. The image may seem naïve but is sophisticated in its cultural references. Even if Western economists scoffed at it, in Japan, *ganko keitai hattenron*, the "formation" theory of development, captured deep ethical values of the Sino-Japanese tradition in much the same way as scientific rationalism anchored classical economics within the broader sea of Western moral philosophy.

The antecedents of the geese are literary rather than scientific or rational. In poetry, the image dates back to at least the seventh century B.C. to the Chinese *Shi Jing,* the Classic of Songs, familiar to most educated Japanese at least through the war years. In classic Chinese and Japanese literature, the annual migratory flight of geese symbolized heroism, the power of collective action and institutions, and the virtues of nationalism. The first attribute was based on the length of the journey, the second on the geometric formation. The third sprang from loyalty of the birds to their place of origin, returning home each season to a particular marsh or lake.

The manner in which this snatch of poetry came to symbolize the Japanese economic miracle and the strategy behind it is almost as extraordinary as the miracle itself. The idea hovers in the background of Japan's modern debut. Its first iteration was as a theory of the behavioral dynamics of industrial change. It took wing from the eclectic intellectual melange of the Meiji (1868–1912) and Taisho (1912–1926) eras, as an attempt to explain the dynamics of late industrialization in Japanese terms. In the 1930s, the flock was commandeered by militarists who saw it as a neat emblem of Japanese ethnic superiority. In the post-war period, the image of flying geese was revived first as a metaphor for industrial policy, then as a symbol of the Japanese model itself. Along the way, its various uses were never far from propaganda. Yet several generations of Japanese economists and policy makers also believed that the image reflected a genuine Asian reality.

By far the most important Western influence on the concept came from the writings of Friedrich List, an early nineteenth-century German economist who played a large role in shaping the economic theories of National Socialism.[7] Like the German romantic poets and philosophers of the same era, List believed in triumph of human willpower over mere matter. He took particular umbrage at the cool classicism of the Anglo-Saxon school, with its basis in Enlightenment philosophy and claim of universal values. Where the British argued that all economies followed universal principles, List argued that social and political factors affected economic performance as well as resources or the skills set of economic participants. List's Japanese translator, Oshima Sadamasu, observed that the attempt to present economic "universals" was a "device to perpetuate the dominance of the existing economic powers over newly industrializing nations such as Germany and Japan."[8] When List's *National System of Political Economy* was translated into Japanese in the late 1880s, Japanese intellectuals felt that his theories opened room for new ideas and alternatives to the reigning orthodoxy of Adam Smith and David Ricardo. For one thing, List offered hope to Japan, a country with modest natural resources other than timber, fisheries, coal, and gold. For another, his work implied that non-economic factors, such as nationalism, affected economic performance. This element, too, was heartening to Japanese in the late nineteenth century, surrounded as they were on all sides by the evidence of Western technical superiority.

The flying-geese theory incorporated imported ideas, especially the role of the state in development, but added to them fundamentally Japanese observations about political economy and the psychology of developing economies. One of its basic assumptions is a high degree of social consensus about the aims of growth, making it possible for the public to amplify, like a radio tuner, the signals sent out by an empathetic leadership. Unlike any other development theory, the flying-geese theory took into account the burning desire of some economies to achieve growth, as well as the importance of meeting global standards of competition at an early stage.

When Japan's Meiji statesmen decided to catch up with Britain and the United States, the superpowers of the late nineteenth century, they created a national economy to wage war on modern terms. The urgency of the task— they saw foreign imperialists trampling down their doors—meant reversing the pattern of industrialization established by the Western economies, which had developed light industries first, then learned how to use machines to build ships, locomotives, and guns. The Japanese state poured its resources into heavy industries, providing subsidies for strategic products, from iron ships to artillery, which would become the backbone of its conquest of Asia. In doing so, Japan managed to compress a century of European and North American industrialization into a single generation, an achievement that still stuns with its complexity and ambition. The flying-geese theory, and the Japanese model that became synonymous with it, were based on the phenomenal success of Japanese modernization. It sought to explain how government might harness the market to achieve national goals and how, in fact, one particular government managed to do so with brilliant success.

How the geese survived the upheavals of Japan's twentieth-century history is a function of the ambiguity of the image itself. Stripped of history, it remains poetry; take away the poetry, and it remains useful as propaganda. Its longevity reflects as well its un-mysterious appeal to another flock—the bureaucrats who played so large a role in Japan's modernization and postwar reconstruction. It is perhaps no accident that the chief proponents of the flying-geese theory were all members of the Japanese bureaucracy. The image itself is an idealized portrayal of bureaucratic behavior—solid teamwork, loyalty to an organization, devotion to hierarchy. The bureaucratic mind, however, needs clear goals in order to succeed, and becomes rudderless without them.

In 1996, I was lunching with a friend in a tiny, elegant sushi restaurant on an atmospheric back street in the Kanda district of Tokyo. My companion was Imanishi Shojiro, on his way to an assignment as Japanese ambassador to Luxembourg. Imanishi is a patriot, a connoisseur, and a collector of Asian art. He was ecstatic to be leaving Tokyo. "Have you ever seen how a school of fish moves through the water?" he asked with contempt. "The fish have sensors that respond to minute cues from each other's movements. They don't make up their own minds. The school moves as a unit. That's our problem."

Up until the 1990s, however, Japanese bureaucrats displayed an impressive sense of purpose. Their role in Japanese society long predated the flying-geese theory. Indeed, the hierarchical and bureaucratic values implicit in flying geese are among the legacies of a millennium of Confucian influence on Japan. The flying-geese economic theory implicitly assumes a pyramidal structure, with leaders and followers, similar to the Confucian world order.[9] Confucianism placed the emperor on the central axis between heaven and earth and China at the apex of a gaggle of lesser states. Scholar-bureaucrats were at the height of the social order, just below the emperor. In Tokugawa Japan, under Confucian influence, the samurai played a similar role, as administrators but also as conservators of Japanese high culture. In *bushido*, the warrior code, they shared a common idea. Under Meiji and thereafter, officials adopted a new ideology of national growth. For all that, they were still bureaucrats, and they recognized the flying geese as a tribute to their kind.

Confucian echoes exist, too, in the passion for statistics associated with the theory. The economist who coined the term, Akamatsu Kaname, was passionate about data, and embraced the new science of statistics. Such passions, in the Confucian context, could trace their lineage to a Confucian concept, the "rectification of names" or *zhengming*. This argued that government decrees or the "names" for things had to reflect social reality. If they did not, government would fail. Confucian Chinese officials spent huge amounts of time collecting and cataloging local data in order to assure themselves of the correspondence between official rules and the reality of local performance. The approach is one of amassing evidence, rather than testing theory. In Japan, economic policy institutions such as the Institute for Developing Economies (IDE) continued the empirical tradition, maintaining magnificent collections of data on Asian economic performance but conducting little analysis.

(IDE has the odd characteristic of having a quite different name in Japanese, *Ajia Keizai Kenkyujo,* or Asia Economic Research Institute, a name which more faithfully reflects its main function.)

In the post-war period, the flying-geese theory entwined with a major, sustained foreign-policy exercise, as, with U.S. help, Tokyo attempted to build an economic partnership first with Korea, later with Taiwan and Southeast Asia. In Korea and Southeast Asia, Japan attempted to repeat the lessons it learned in northeast China in the pre-war period, offering blueprints for industrialization and Japanese government money to make it happen. Its diplomats used flying geese the way they often had before—as a part of a propaganda campaign to make Japanese economic penetration more palatable.

Back in the home islands, the economic bureaucracy applied the flying-geese model to technological competition and product cycles. The basic theory was that old, tired industries using obsolete technologies should be phased out gently. Some of these tired or "sunset" enterprises, such as forestry or mining, would be allowed a lengthy afterlife on a small scale. The theory was not initially applied to the transfer of Japanese industry outside Japan. Japanese manufacturing strategies in Asia changed radically, however, as Asian economies increased in wealth and wage structures rose. In the first few decades after the war, the main Japanese enterprises in Asia were trading companies, sponging up raw materials for the Japanese industrial machine. Asia served as a market for cheap Japanese manufactures, at a stage when the poor quality of Japanese products limited its exports. In the 1970s, labor-intensive and polluting industries moved out of the country, and the bureaucracy began to link the flying-geese concept with exit strategies for its industry beyond sovereign Japanese territory. Officials envisioned a cycle in which Japan would continually introduce new technology to its domestic factories and flush older ones through a hierarchy of developing economies, mostly in Asia.

The foreign expansion of Japanese multinationals might have followed conventional lines, outsourcing labor-intensive components to low labor-cost economies. The reason it did not was partly because of the reluctance of Japanese bureaucrats to give up control of their prize domestic companies and the strategic emphasis placed by Japanese companies on maintaining reliable supply chains. After Friedrich List, the most enduring foreign influence on the flying-geese strategy was undoubtedly W. Edwards Deming, the American management guru who taught in Japan in the 1950s and inspired the national obsession with total quality control. Without Deming, Japanese investors might not have proceeded as they did, in a broad phalanx of manufacturers and subcontractors, recreating the competitive dynamic of Akamatsu's geese in their own corporate groupings or *keiretsu.* Deming advocated single suppliers for each industrial component, based on a "long-term relationship of loyalty and trust."[10] The bureaucrats came up with plans to ease the pain of industrial relocation by attempting to re-create the domestic environment of government-business collaboration internationally. In Europe or North America, such ideas were impossible to carry out, but investment-hungry Asians were more cooperative.

As metaphor, model, and mantra, the flying-geese concept entered deeply into the psyche and governing institutions of post-war Japan, inspiring regional agreements, foreign aid programs, and the flow of corporate investment in ways compatible with Japanese national interest. The theory was pervasive in Japan's domestic and foreign industrial policies and provided a rationale for foreign policy based on enhancement of the domestic economy. The concept linked the 1938 New Order in East Asia, the Toa Shinchitsujo, with the Greater East Asian Co-Prosperity Sphere of the 1940s and a half-dozen, post-war regional organizations whose intent was to foster regional prosperity, such as the Asia Pacific Economic Cooperation group, or APEC.

How could anyone object to the benign image of earnest, hard-working geese striving to catch up with the leader of the world economy? For most of the first three decades after the end of World War Two, America led the free-market economies, and the metaphor worked as a subtle form of flattery. Only after the breakup of the Soviet Union did Japanese texts assert that Japan was the leader of an Asian flock of geese. From the early 1990s, Japanese writers began using "flying geese" as a synonym for an Asian model that was different and better than the Anglo-American standard. In doing so, they returned to the propaganda norms of the pre-war era.

Indeed, the flying geese had a history as dark, in its way, as the Nazi swastika or Japan's own *hinomaru,* the rising sun flag of the militarists. In the 1930s, Akamatsu himself was drafted into the effort to create a new Asian economy to serve the Japanese Empire, embodying a hierarchy along racial lines. The Japanese race claimed the apex of the formation, and Japanese would resettle the conquered territories and occupy all leadership positions. Such plans were interrupted by Japan's defeat, but the military government prepared for a regime in which Japanese expatriates would repopulate the conquered territories.

One such study, "An Investigation of Global Policy with the Yamato Race as Nucleus," was discovered in a Tokyo bookstore in 1981; it had been a top-secret document when it was released in 1943. "Spelled out in impressive detail here are many of the common assumptions that were expressed cryptically elsewhere, including the rationale behind policies that were actually adopted toward other races and nationalities," writes the historian, John Dower. "At the same time, the researchers had the rare opportunity of offering a long-range vision of Japan's projected global 'new order'—a grand view most harried officials simply had no time to articulate."[11]

The report provides a chilling look at how the flying-geese theory might have been executed if Japan had won the war. It was prepared by the Japanese Ministry of Health and Welfare's Population and Race Section, and went on for 3,217 pages in six volumes. Another two volumes analyzed the potential demographic impact of the war in Asia. The first six volumes were intended as a manual for administrators of the newly conquered regions. One of its key assertions was that nations would assume their "proper place" under Japanese leadership, in close approximation of the flying-geese formation proposed by Akamatsu, then the military's chief Southeast Asian economist, based in Singapore. The authors of the report envisioned Japan's Dai Toa Kyoeiken, or Greater East Asia Co-Prosperity Sphere, as a cooperative body providing alternatives to the chaotic clash of racism, nationalism, and capitalism. Eventually, Japan and its allies would fight until they had no enemies left, and Western society would be annihilated. "The ultimate idea of the Cooperative Body is to place the whole world under one roof and to bring about the existence of a moral, peaceful and rational prosperity in which all peoples of the world assume their proper place," the report stated.[12]

The idea of a hierarchically structured, universal "cooperative body" was Confucian in origin. The Confucian world order was inherently unequal. Members of society performed roles based on their status. Writes Dower: "When it came to proposing concrete policies for the new autarkic bloc, however, the real meaning of 'proper place' became unmistakably clear. It meant division of labor—an international and interracial allocation of tasks, chores, and responsibilities that was based on a gradient of national 'qualities' and 'abilities' determined in Tokyo, and that was so structured economically and politically as to ensure that the relationships of superior and inferior would be perpetuated indefinitely."[13]

The evolution of the flying-geese theory as propaganda was closely linked to Japanese aggression in China. China also provided the first laboratory for creating a Japanese economic satellite that would embody the "flying-geese" norms of competition and strong government. At the turn of the century, the paramount political reality was the disintegration of China. Japan's emergence as a regional power took place on the margins of the collapse of the Qing Dynasty, with few implications beyond the Sea of Japan. In 1895, when Japan annexed Taiwan, explanations had been unnecessary. Taiwan was a spoil of war. Korea was too weak to resist and so isolated that it had no foreign allies when Japan annexed its neighbor in 1910.

By the 1930s, however, Tokyo operated in a more complex international environment and felt pressure to justify its seizures of territory on the Chi-

nese mainland. Under the New Order in East Asia, Japan proclaimed a federal-
style "partnership" with the balkanized China of the 1920 and 1930s, by-
passing weak central government controls. Japan's threat became more
tangible as its civilian government grew weaker. The violent takeover of
Manchuria by the Japanese Kwantung Army—the Imperial Army's expeditionary force in China—and the creation of the Manchukuo puppet state in
1931, caused an international outcry. In 1933, Japan withdrew from the
League of Nations, furious over the findings of the Lytton Commission, which
accused Japan of aggression against China. For a few more years, Tokyo
warily kept lines of communication open with the League—participating
in "peace activities" but not politics—until finally all ties were broken off
in 1938.

Meanwhile, the civilian government had lost control over the Japanese military, particularly the Army. Their disagreements centered on China. The military perceived China as a nation in a state of almost total disintegration that
presented an enormous opportunity for acquisition and control. The Japanese
civilian government, weakened and demoralized, feared the implications of
the Manchurian adventure but realized it was unable to back out. A strategy
developed for Japan to assume control of China as a protectorate. In 1934 a
memorandum drafted by officials of the Army, Navy, and Foreign Ministry
described a framework in which China would be brought into an international
structure with Japan as "nucleus," including Manchukuo.[14] By 1936 formal
diplomacy moved toward treating North China as a "special region."

In the mid-1930s, the Showa Kenkyukai, an elite study group named for
the reign of Emperor Hirohito, wove those threads into a new ideology of
Japanese imperialism: Japanese imperialism was to be "good" imperialism,
based on an impulse toward "partnership" rather than the self-seeking of
Western imperialism. The Showa Kenkyukai's sponsor was the nationalistic
Prince Konoe Fumimaro, prime minister from 1937 to 1939 and again from
1940 to 1941.

Konoe had supported the creation of Manchukuo. He schemed to rid Asia
of Western powers and unite the region under Japanese leadership. The prince
also believed fiercely in the concept of *kokutai*, the body or essence of the
nation, a Japanese equivalent of the "blood and soil" of fascism. The concept
of "partnership" under a beneficent *kokutai* thus took on religious and fanati-
cal overtones. The partnership was in name only. "For practical reasons, this
must be a partnership in which Japan led, resting on an ethic in Japanese
form: on Japan's 'national polity' (*kokutai*), manifested in Japan's 'imperial
way' (*kodo*)," writes W.G. Beasley, a leading historian on Japanese imperialism. "That is to say, the Confucian concept of what was just must be combined with a Japanese idea of how to achieve it (implying that Japan was to

take over China's historical role in Asia, as well as that of the West)."[15]

Manchukuo became the testing ground for applying a set of ideas combining Japanese military control, economic imperialism on the Japanese model, and flying-geese economics. The classic theory of nineteenth-century imperialism, practiced by Western colonial powers, was to repress industrial production in colonies in order to preserve them as markets and protect the comparative advantage of the home state. This pattern of imperialism conformed to Smith-Ricardian criteria for international trade based on comparative advantage. In contrast, the Japanese viewed their colonies quite differently, as extensions of the Japanese economy. Japan's vision for Manchukuo was that it would project Japanese industrial strength by serving as a labor, resource, and manufacturing base. Japanese planners saw the industrialization of Manchukuo as a way of extending Japanese industrial power, as long as the Manchukuo government was passive and did not attempt to impose its own ideas for development.

In fact, many of the post-war institutions associated with "Japan, Inc." had their start in the Japanese industrial laboratory in Manchukuo in northeast China, including the apparatus of government control over industry and five-year plans, as well as the model of state companies. In 1937, Manchukuo became the first East Asian economy to draft a blueprint for economic growth, employing specific production targets that closely resembled Soviet planning methods, down to input-output models for such key commodities as steel, gasoline, petroleum, and salt.[16]

Even earlier, the Kwantung Army created giant joint-stock companies under state control. The government-owned South Manchurian Railway, Mantetsu, founded in 1906 as part of the spoils of the Russo-Japanese War, provided both model and raw materials for the Japanese military government's forays into the market. In the 1920s, the railway had extended Japanese territorial control from the port of Dalian deep into Manchuria. In 1933, the military ordered the creation of an auto company, Nichiman Jidosha Kaisha. In 1934, Mantetsu hived off its mining assets into a new company, the Manshu Kogyo Kaihatsu Kabushiki Kaisha, the Manchurian Mining Development Company. In the same year, General Kunikai Koiso of the Kwantung Army's general staff ordered private electric companies to be combined into a single company, the Manshu Denki Kabushiki Kaisha (the Manchurian Electric Co.), two years before private electricity companies were taken over and nationalized on the home islands.

For all of its production targets and state companies, the Kwantung Army's command economy was not straight socialism. The army intended its state enterprises to adapt to market signals. Writes the historian Ramon H. Myers: "While general tasks were assigned to the special companies, they were given

considerable latitude to organize production. . . . Prices were not administered, and the market still provided the means to allocate labor and goods in
accordance with a firm's willingness and ability to command resources. The
army planners hoped with these semi-official enterprises to combine the most
favorable aspects of capitalist enterprise, such as efficiency, standardization,
and flexibility, with those of a planned economy: the rapid realization of specific tasks and targets, elimination of waste, and full utilization of capacity."[17]

The Japanese government's wartime Five-Year Plan, covering the period
from 1937 to 1941, set targets for steel production in Manchukuo at about
half the level of Japan's, together with targets for the manufacture of weapons, aircraft, automobiles, and rolling stock. "This is not at all the standard
pattern of a colonial economy," Beasley observes.[18] A citizen of empire in
1930s Japan could easily contrast the Japanese, flying-geese approach to the
experience of developing countries under Western imperialism. From a Japanese perspective, Smith-Ricardian comparative advantage seemed little more
than a pretext for restricting industrialization to a handful of privileged nations. In contrast, Japan harnessed regional growth by applying the same
industrialization strategies to Manchukuo that had worked so well within its
borders. All the same, Japan sent out homesteaders to deepen control over its
neighbor through ethnic Japanese colonies. By 1940, Manchukuo had 20,000
Japanese households, mostly drawn from the Army reservists' list, and
2,000,000 Koreans. Over time, Tokyo planned to remake Manchukuo in its
own image. Manchus and Chinese would have become second-class citizens
at best. In the short run, the colony benefited from rapid industrialization,
Japanese-style. After Japan's defeat in 1945, the factories and infrastructure
left behind in northeast China became the heartland of Chinese industry. A
generation later, the trickle-down effect was still evident, in the wealth of
cities such as Dalian and Shenyang and the relative concentration of heavy
industries in the northeastern province of Liaoning, which incorporated most
of Manchukuo after the war.

Japanese industrialization of North China worked in part because their
Chinese collaborators, ostensibly Japan's "partners," shared the Japanese
mind-set vis-à-vis the West. China, too, had attempted to build industries
and railroads using state funds in an attempt to catch up with Western Europe and the United States. The Chinese effort failed because of its weak and
fragmented leadership, but Beijing understood the nature of the task. Southeast Asia was a different story. Although the European powers and the United
States fell quickly before the Japanese onslaught in 1941–42, taking control
of the resource-based economic system proved much more difficult.

Once trade with the West was cut off, Japan was unable to replace markets for such goods as sugar and the roasted tea preferred by Westerners. In

Malaya, the most profitable of Britain's Southeast Asian colonies, the tin and rubber industries quickly collapsed after the Japanese invasion because Japan had little use for either product. Food shortages developed because of the diversion of rice stocks to supply Japanese troops. In the pre-war years, Japanese companies had monopolized the iron-mining industry in Trengganu, Kelantan, and Pahang, in the Unfederated Malay States. Nearly all its product went for export to Japan, and the British administration supported the trade because of the substantial revenues it provided in export duties. But when the Japanese Occupation drew up a five-year plan to develop the Malayan iron, manganese, and bauxite industries, it failed dismally because of the lack of adequate supplies of coking coal, which Britain had imported from outside Malaya. Nippon Steel, Nippon Steel Tube Manufacturing Co., and Osaka Special Steel Co., were assigned the task of building a steel industry in Malaya, and they constructed special blast furnaces in 1944. Mitsubishi was brought in to upgrade facilities at Malaya's only coal mine at Batu Arang in Selangor. However, this plan also fizzled when Batu Arang's coal turned out to be unsuitable for coking coal.[19]

In 1938, Konoe's government brought the concept of a Chinese protectorate to life with the Toa Shinchitsujo. The New Order in East Asia established a condominium government in China: Japanese-controlled local governments would coexist with Chinese governments in Beijing and Nanjing; Japanese troops were to be stationed in China; and Japan would have special rights to mineral extraction in Mongolia and North China. Such moves were only a small step from the annexation of China and the invasion of Southeast Asia. The pro-Axis foreign minister, Matsuoka Yosuke, and other advocates of a drive south to seize European possessions in Southeast Asia began using the phrase "Greater East Asia" (Dai Toa) to indicate that they were ready to advance beyond China's boundaries. In August 1940, just before Vichy France allowed Japanese troops access to French Indochina, Matsuoka proclaimed that "Greater East Asia" would include French Indochina and the Dutch East Indies as well as Japan, China, and Manchukuo.

That August, Foreign Minister Matsuoka also announced the formation of the Dai Toa Kyoeiken, or Greater East Asia Co-Prosperity Sphere, to supersede the Toa Shinchitsujo, the New Order in East Asia. In December, Japan officially decreed the expansion of the China conflict into the Dai Toa Senso, or Greater East Asia War, after the attacks on Pearl Harbor and the British, American, and Dutch colonies in Southeast Asia. The imperial government used the same phrase for the administrative agency it established to run the colonies in 1942. The Dai Toa Sho, the Greater East Asia Ministry, took over responsibilities of the Asia Development Board, created in 1938 to manage the economic affairs of China and Manchukuo.

Dai means "great" and *Toa* is simply "East Asia" in Japanese. But the use and repetition of the phrase Dai Toa had a specific purpose—the words were vague enough that the Japanese were able to redefine continually what they meant as their control expanded in the region. In a logical division of the planet among the Axis powers, Japan might end up with half the world and then that, too, would be Dai Toa, East Asia, unlikely though it may sound today. In the document "An Investigation of Global Policy with the Yamato Race as Nucleus," Japan's conquest of the Asia-Pacific region went through four stages. In the last stage, "Greater East Asia" extended to the coasts of Africa and America.[20]

With such a lineage, it is no wonder that the flying-geese concept has never been wildly popular outside Japan. The export version usually refers to the "Japanese model" rather than to geese or formations. All the more ironic, then, is that Akamatsu Kaname, the originator of the theory, was a genuine product of the liberal and cosmopolitan atmosphere of 1920s Japan.

Flying Geese: The Visionaries

While he may have borrowed the image from classical Chinese poetry, the man who brought flying geese into economics, thereby inventing the Japanese model, was one of the century's great originals. Akamatsu was the son of a rice vendor. He was born in 1896 in northern Kyushu, in a region that for 300 years had been Japan's lifeline to the outside world. By the time of his death in 1974, Akamatsu had played a central role in three broad currents of Japanese intellectual development. This was a man who leapfrogged through the twentieth century. With each leap, Akamatsu gained a new set of public roles so sharply different from the one that came before that his career defies any attempt to impose consistency. Yet, he remained rooted in a pragmatic view of economic behavior in which theory flowed from results, not the other way around.

As a young man, Akamatsu comes across as an intellectual adventurer and explorer of remarkable range, a member of a generation for whom it was de rigueur to scrape together funds to visit Europe and North America and return with the latest books, gadgets, and theories. Akamatsu went beyond mere import of ideas and came up with his own, eclectic vision. The Akamatsu of the war period is a far more ambiguous figure. Occupying one of the most senior positions in the administration of Japan's new colonies in Southeast Asia, Akamatsu played a key role in the attempt to create a new Asia-Pacific economy centered on Japan. Despite his own post-war denials, it is difficult to imagine him as anything but an eager collaborator in the war effort, putting his flying-geese theory to work in the laboratory of occupied Southeast

Asia. In the last part of his career, he was the revered dean of the economics faculty at Hitotsubashi University, a position from which he quietly shaped the Japanese miracle. He did so in company with two friends, the high-profile economic bureaucrat, Okita Saburo, and his foremost student, the indefatigable Kojima Kiyoshi, who helped to redraft his flying-geese theory to conform to the language if not the spirit of liberal economics. These two relationships, more than any other factor, helped raise the flying-geese theory to the level of orthodox ideology.

This elusive figure was the intellectual godfather not only of the Japanese model but also of the Greater East Asia Co-Prosperity Sphere, the "Income-Doubling Plan" of the 1960s, and MITI's techniques of forced industrial growth and planned obsolescence. This extraordinary achievement has been obscured, partly because Akamatsu slips through the cracks not only of neoclassical economics but also between the two major schools of Japanese economics, one Marxist, the other liberal.

To liberal economists, Akamatsu was a primitive trade theorist. His student, Kojima Kiyoshi, was better known and more highly regarded, particularly for his efforts to correlate Akamatsu's ideas with those of such liberal economists as Eli Heckscher, Bertil Ohlin, and Paul Samuelson. Kojima presented Akamatsu as an addition to classic economic liberalism, arguing that trade altered the comparative advantage of nations over time and Japanese investors were more sensitive to these dynamics than Western firms.[21] The Marxists had no use at all for Akamatsu and his friends. Akamatsu may have begun his intellectual career as a passionate Marxist, but he rejected its dogma. He ignored the most basic Marxist precepts. The proletariat had no role in his drama.

Akamatsu began his career in a spirit of impetuous, daredevil eclecticism. He fell in love with German romanticism, Marx, statistics, Friedrich List, and gadgets. A major prize from his intellectual tour of Europe and North America was Japan's first calculating machine. The backdrop to his teens and twenties was the creative ferment of Japan's Taisho Era, from 1912 to 1926, during the short-lived reign of the Meiji emperor's son, the mad Taisho emperor, when the Prussian discipline of Meiji gave way to a liberal interregnum before the militarists took control. This was also the period of the successful Bolshevik Revolution in 1917, when Marxism became fashionable among Japanese students abroad.

Akamatsu understood what it meant to be poor. According to his autobiography, in high school in Kobe he wore his clothes to shreds and finally had to borrow new ones from a friend. Akamatsu's first introduction to economics was through Marx, and at an early stage he decided that there was little to learn from the liberal economics of Smith and Ricardo. For Akamatsu, the economists of the European Enlightenment had proved nothing because their logic rested on deductive reasoning, emphasizing theories and logic rather than evidence and the real world. He felt that scientific rationalism demanded that theory take second place to empirical observation. In this, Akamatsu placed himself at a curious historical juncture between Confucianism and the rising new sciences of statistics, econometrics, and demography. Where Western statisticians, econometricians, and demographers used their tools to define new theories, Japanese economists following in his tradition seemed to look at the acquisition of data as an end in itself.[22]

Akamatsu graduated in 1921 from the Tokyo School of Economics. The institution was founded in 1875 by Japan's first ambassador to the United States just after his return from Washington. One of the earliest of Western-style universities in Japan, the school became Hitotsubashi University in 1949 and is still regarded as the nation's premier university for economics. Ambassador Mori was a radical—he advocated abandoning the Japanese language in favor of English, and his school encouraged the most advanced ideas and intellectual experiments. The rice vendor's son had done well. The Tokyo School of Economics served as the economics think tank for the Meiji reforms and was to emerge as the birthplace of Japanese industrial policy in the 1950s and 1960s. After graduation, Akamatsu got a job in Nagoya as a junior teacher and researcher specializing in commercial and industrial policy at the newly established Nagoya School of Economics, later Nagoya University. A few years later, in 1924, he came up with the money for a two-year tour of Europe and America.

Fifty years after the beginning of Meiji, such trips to the heartland of the industrial revolution were a necessary post-graduate experience for young Japanese intellectuals. Unlike the Japanese of a generation earlier, however, Taisho intellectuals were attentive to the themes of revolution, social injustice, and anticolonialism. In Germany, Akamatsu went to lectures on Hegelian and neo-Kantian philosophy, perfunctorily tucking in a few months at Berlin University studying economics, including List's work. Passing through London in 1926, he raged over Marx's untidy and uncared-for grave, complaining how difficult it was to find.[23] After England, Akamatsu visited the United States for a few months, basing himself at the brand-new Harvard Bureau of Economic Statistics in Cambridge. The Harvard institution pioneered in the brand-new field of quantitative and empirical economics, as well as statistical research, all of which Akamatsu enthusiastically adopted, according to his autobiography. In July 1926, when Akamatsu returned to Nagoya, he brought with him Japan's first mechanical calculator.

By the age of thirty, Akamatsu was ready to deliver his own theories, beginning with an analysis of the Japanese textile industry. The industry was just at the point of becoming a force internationally, and was based in his hometown of Nagoya. In the late nineteenth century, Japan's craft-based textiles had been overwhelmed by British imported textiles, when the Japanese were still producing their goods on hand looms. But the Japanese industry imported mechanical looms and rallied to reclaim the domestic Japanese market, finally emerging as a formidable export force. With the help of his American calculator, Akamatsu thought he detected a broad statistical pattern explaining the nature of the achievement. He used time-series data to graph cycles of the rise and decline of the British and Japanese textile industries, and when the graphs were superimposed on each other, the result reminded him of flying geese.

Akamatsu's concept was disarmingly simple. A "follower" (*koshinkoku*) country is "seduced" into importing goods from *senshinkoku* (advanced) countries. It is then shocked, according to Akamatsu, into producing the goods for itself. Finally, the products become exports to other countries. As a "follower" country moves up the export ladder in stages from nondurable consumer goods to consumer durables and finally capital goods, other "follower" countries begin the same sequence to catch up with it.

The "followers" naturally employ industrial policy, in the form of protection of infant industries and promotion of exports, in order to even the competition with stronger economies. When the lead goose tires, another takes over as head of the formation. The result is a division of labor within a group of economies all striving for the common goal of industrialization. The Nagoya textile industry had become strong by first identifying the preeminent international trade power of its day, Great Britain, researching its strengths, emulating them, and finally beating Britain at its own game. The strategy was dependent on effective policy, not ownership of resources. Nagoya had shown how an economy could beat the law of comparative advantage. It had succeeded in becoming a global textile power despite its lack of natural resources, capital, and labor. If Akamatsu was right, other industries and other economies could do the same.

The flying-geese theory offered an alternative both to nineteenth-century theories of economic imperialism, emphasizing vertical division of labor, and to the liberal economics of Smith and Ricardo, based on a horizontal division of labor across economies. Liberal trade theory in the Smith-Ricardian tradition argued that economies grew by exploiting differences in comparative advantage. The Japanese countered that comparative advantage was effective only as long as economies were at similar levels of development, such as within Europe in Akamatsu's day. The economies flocking together in Akamatsu's pattern moved toward a horizontal division of labor as each upgraded its industrial capacity. Comparative advantage determined each economy's rank vertically, but as comparative advantage changed, so did the economy's status within the hierarchy. This was also a break from the Confucian and Tokugawa legacies of caste-like, fixed vertical hierarchies. The theory was locked firmly around the behavioral insight that competition drives upward mobility through an economic hierarchy, much like Akamatsu's own personal experience.

By the 1930s, Akamatsu's flying-geese theory had caught the eye of the militarists, who reacted primarily to its propaganda value—Great Britain might have been the *senshinkoku* for Japan, but Tokyo would play the leading role for its Asian flock. In 1939, Hitotsubashi University invited Akamatsu back from Nagoya, awarding him a full professorship. In 1940, Akamatsu became the director of research in the East Asian Economic Research Center in Tokyo. Three years later, under military orders, Akamatsu went to Singapore, where he served as the military government's chief economist for all of Southeast Asia. In his autobiography, published in 1967, Akamatsu says it was a relief to go to Singapore because he might otherwise have been assigned to write propaganda for the military government. Whether or not this was the sort of recantation popular after Japan's defeat, there is no question that the militarists made ample use of his ideas.[24]

After the war, the United States command briefly investigated Akamatsu as a war criminal but dropped the charges, partly because the Japanese wartime government had previously investigated him for subversion. The charges were based on a line in Akamatsu's dissertation that read: "the heart of the emperor follows the movements of the hearts of the people." It was supposed to be the other way around, but perhaps Akamatsu's liberal yearnings got the better of him. Ironically, Akamatsu anticipated the formal role that the emperor acquired in Japan's post-war Constitution, as the chief icon of a democratic state. When the U.S. Occupation ended, Hitotsubashi invited Akamatsu back, and in 1953 he became dean of the economics faculty, making him the most influential economist in the nation. From this vantage point, he shaped Japanese economic strategy during the high-growth years of the 1950s and 1960s, together with his student Kojima and his powerful associate Okita.

Flying geese meant something different to Akamatsu, the visionary; Kojima, the economist; and Okita, the urbane bureaucrat. To be sure, for all three men, the concept was more than just a theory. To Akamatsu, the flying-geese model explained Japan's ability to marshal national resources to catch up with the industrialized West, an extraordinary historical event. No other developing country had yet matched Japan's achievement. To Kojima, the flying-geese concept represented an alternative to Western analytical traditions that dominated the economics profession in general, and international trade theory in particular. To Okita, the engineer turned bureaucrat, the motivational aspects of the metaphor loomed large, enhancing its uses as a tool of social and economic engineering.

Two of the three men also had in common that each had seen the metaphor at work in real life, in Japan's wartime economic experiments. Akamatsu and Okita had participated directly in the efforts to integrate the Japanese and Asian economies, Akamatsu in Southeast Asia and Okita in Manchukuo. In Southeast Asia, the plan worked badly. In China, it worked so well that by 1943, the Japanese-controlled northeast China was supplying more than 90 percent of China's steel, almost as much of its pig iron, and more than 80 percent of its electric power.[25] The economy of northeast China under Japanese control was a strange hybrid of National Socialism and market economics, incorporating central planning but also market institutions, such as equity-based capital. Unlike Western colonies, northeast China was integrally part of a regional economy centered on Japan. After 1941, North China, Manchukuo, and Korea were explicitly integrated into Japan's wartime economic mobilization. The Japanese Manchurian Economic Coordinating Committee, formed in 1935, became the model for Japan's post-war Economic Stabilization Board and the national planning authorities of half-a-dozen other Asian economies, practicing an innovative mix of socialism and market economics.

Over time, the flying geese went through numerous script changes. In the 1970s, Akamatsu's student Kojima used the theory to explain that Japanese investment in developing countries was less harmful than the West's because strict heed was paid to comparative advantage. In other words, Japan invested mainly in resources and labor-intensive (often heavily polluting) technologies, areas well removed from Japan's own strong sectors. In the 1980s, flying geese became the catchword for a huge transfer of capital-intensive Japanese industries just behind the curve of cutting-edge technology. In the 1990s, Japanese policy makers and academics used the term synonymously with Asian values and as a uniquely Asian approach to development. By the end of the decade, after the trauma of the Asian financial crisis, the flying-geese metaphor was still only just well enough known outside Japan by Western critics to inspire inside jokes. But the geese had shown phoenix-like qualities in the past. It seemed likely that there would be new sightings.

Other than Akamatsu no individual was more influential in shaping Japan's Asian economic policy than Okita. He was born in Dalian, the son of a news correspondent. He returned to Japan after finishing primary school, yet remained fascinated by the continent. In 1937, Okita took a degree in electrical engineering at the Tokyo Imperial University, and went to work for the Communications Ministry. In 1939, Okita was sent to Beijing to study power-supply issues in North China. When he returned to Japan in 1942, he went into the Research Division of the Ministry of Greater East Asian Affairs.[26]

He switched from engineering to economics after the country's defeat in 1945, simultaneously embracing Akamatsu's "flying-geese" theory, initially as the intellectual model for domestic industrial policy.[27]

A few years later, he was part of a Foreign Ministry advisory group that produced a seminal document for reconstruction of the Japanese economy, with recommendations to reduce military expenditures, improve vocational training, import new technology, introduce economic planning, and provide government with a major role in foreign trade and capital formation. From this committee, Okita went on to head the research section of the Economic Stabilization Board in 1947, where he produced Japan's first economic white paper. Then, after a two-year stint in Bangkok, with the UN Economic Commission for Asia and the Far East, he returned to Tokyo as head of the Planning Bureau of the EPA. In 1958, he began blueprinting Japan's high-growth era with Kojima's help. Thus, Okita shared with Akamatsu a post-war career built around a liberal reinterpretation of wartime institutions of forced regional economic integration and economic planning. Their dream was to reestablish a Japan-centered regional economy without resorting to military force, and for most of the five decades after the war's end circumstances seemed to conspire to help the dream come true.

As EPA Planning Bureau director under Prime Minister Ikeda Hayato, Okita headed a team of 2,000 government officials and economists, mobilized to draft Japan's famous income-doubling plan (*Kokumin shotoku baizo keikaku*) of 1960. It literally created the Japanese "miracle," launching nearly a decade of annual growth rates of 10 percent or more. The plan drastically revised Japan's industrial structure to accommodate rapid growth but created so much political friction that Ikeda's successor, Sato Eisaku, formally abandoned it in 1965. The "income-doubling" era produced horrendous follies of pollution and industrial overcrowding on the already overcrowded archipelago. That did nothing to harm Okita's reputation, however. Japan reached the goal of doubling real national income by 1967. Okita became foreign minister in 1979.

Okita, unlike Akamatsu and Kojima, was well known outside Japan, first as head of Japan's Overseas Economic Cooperation Fund (OECF) in 1973, then in his role as foreign minister. By the late 1980s, he had settled down to life as a spokesman for Japan's international economic policy and behind-the-scenes craftsman of a flying geese–inspired Japanese industrial strategy in Asia. The flying-geese theory provided a conceptual framework not only for dynamic competition among national economies but also among competing industries within a country. Okita found both models useful and made close allies of their authors, pulling both Akamatsu and Kojima onto the team of his income-doubling plan. The younger man, Kojima, became Okita's partner in drafting at least three separate schemes for Asian regional economic integration, reflecting the application of the model to Japan's external economy and foreign relations.

In Okita's hands, the flying-geese theory became the nucleus of an argument that the Asian region was uniquely capable of collective development. In 1985 at a speech at the Fourth Pacific Economic Cooperation Conference in Seoul, he presented this opinion in what quickly became official theology: "Because there is such great variety in the Asian nations' stages of development, natural resource endowments, and cultural, religious and historical heritage, economic integration on the European Economic Community model is clearly out of the question. Yet, it is precisely this diversity which works to facilitate the flying-geese pattern of shared development as each is able to take advantage of its distinctiveness to develop with a supportive division of labor. And this flying-geese pattern in the international division of labor has in turn given rise to North-South relations between the industrialized and the developing nations free from their traditional rigidities."[28]

In the same speech, Okita presented Japan as a model for developing countries, arguing that Japanese investment and technology transfer to its Asian neighbors were secondary to the value of its example: "Japan's most important contribution was to show by its own example that it is possible for an Asian country to achieve industrialization."[29]

If Okita was the political and bureaucratic voice of the flying-geese school, Kojima became its prophet and chief theoretician. Following the Latin American *dependencia* theorists, Kojima presented U.S. investment in the light of "oligopolistic capitalism," out to preserve market dominance by blocking developing economies from entering high-tech industries. Like Akamatsu, Kojima thought that Western economic theory operated as a form of cynical propaganda for Western business, helping to shape the market in ways that gave Western companies an advantage over their non-Western rivals. In this sense, both men saw economic theory as a zone for ideological combat, echoing and amplifying competition in the marketplace, and the Japanese "alternative" had the same cynical propaganda motives that they ascribed to economists of the liberal British and American tradition.

Neither Akamatsu nor any of his followers viewed theory as an innocent exercise devoid of political consequences. Their careers, as they wove in and out of the bureaucracy, suggested otherwise, and the men followed in a tradition in which no room existed for failure. They pursued the theory of Asian economic integration as loyal samurai to a Japan imperiled not only by a lack of resources but also at the mercy of foreign ideas. Their mission was to come up with compelling alternatives, which would similarly serve the interests of Japanese enterprise.

Kojima's main addition to the flying-geese school was an oligopolistic theory of foreign direct investment, based on the supposed differences between Japanese and Western practice. He laid out his ideas in a 1978 book, *Theories of Foreign Investment*,[30] arguing that Western firms pursued a type of investment generally harmful to host countries, that is, "oligopolistic," while Japanese firms were more likely to invest in ways complementary to the host economies. Kojima identified three forms typically Japanese: resource-oriented investment to supply products lacking in the investing country; labor-oriented investment by countries that had lost their comparative advantage because of rising wages; and market-oriented investment due to trade barriers erected by the host country.

Kojima did little to conceal the nationalist motives behind much of his work. In his view, Western economists tended to look at the resource endowment of economies as fixed. Players were stuck with the cards they started out with and could increase their utility only through trade. In contrast, the flying-geese model argued that nations, if not individuals, could modify their resource endowments through strategy. The developmental state could gain an advantage entirely aside from its resource endowment by identifying a model and attempting to capture its success. In doing so, the flock would burst across the sky. Kojima liked to refer to "dynamic" comparative advantage, suggesting both the fluidity of resource endowments and the energy of economies aiming at specific goals.

The Thai economist Pasuk Phongpaichit sees much of Kojima's work as an effort to improve the public relations of Japanese investment in Southeast Asia, much the way Akamatsu's theory had provided a beneficent rationale for Japan's large-scale economic-engineering efforts in Asia in the 1930s. Just a few years before *Theories of Foreign Investment* was published, Japanese prime minister Tanaka Kakuei was humiliated by student demonstrations during a tour of ASEAN countries in January 1974. The riots were encouraged by the governments of Indonesia and Thailand and deeply worried the next four Japanese governments.[31] Prime Minister Miki Takeo proposed an "Asian Marshall Plan," which vanished with his government in 1976 but inspired his successor, Prime Minister Fukuda Takeo, to offer the "Fukuda Doctrine" in August 1977: a pledge of amity and economic and social cooperation with ASEAN, whose centerpiece was a $1 billion program to help ASEAN regional projects. The subsequent governments of Prime Ministers Ohira Masayoshi and Suzuki Zenko in the 1980s made less spectacular, but equally forceful, commitments to ASEAN economic development.[32]

According to Pasuk, Kojima was obsessed with the political psychology of foreign investment; there was something wrong with conventional economic theory because, from a Third World perspective, it inevitably pointed to the market dominance of Western multinationals. Kojima believed, or wanted to believe, that Japanese investment would be more palatable than the European or U.S. varieties. Pasuk writes: "To counter this tendency [to view foreign investment as a tool of rich nations], Kojima asserted that the theory of monopolistic advantage was only one of a range of motivations for foreign investment. He went on to draw a contrast between American investment overseas, which often could be explained in terms of the defense of monopolistic or oligopolistic advantage, and Japanese investments which he claimed were differently motivated and more benignly complementary to the host country's economy."[33]

Akamatsu was ignored by Western and most Japanese economists, paid homage by Japanese bureaucrats in countless official publications, and known only by the image of his orderly geese to business executives who cared to dabble in policy matters. Outside Japan, even the metaphor was virtually unknown. However, a small contingent of economists and social scientists, many of them Asian, took flying-geese theory to heart. Like Kojima, these analysts viewed the model as an alternative to Western theories of development. Some added their own peculiar furbelows.

The economist Watanabe Toshio, at the Tokyo Institute of Technology, saw a "multilayered chase process" in which the four Asian Tigers—South Korea, Taiwan, Hong Kong, and Singapore—chased Japan, and the ASEAN economies chased the Tigers.[34] In an unpublished paper, Ozawa Terutomo, a close associate of Kojima, offered the notion of "tandem economic development." Ozawa said that development could occur in regional "clumps" and "be clustered in a particular region in a cumulative causal manner," triggered by historical and cultural interactions as well as economic forces. "In essence," he wrote, "this paradigm of intra-regionally clustered economic growth captures a phenomenon in which a group of economies, closely interacting in a synergistic manner with one another through the medium of trade and transnational corporations' activities, advance together, led by a predominant economy as the major provider of technology, complementary inputs and markets, followed by progressively less developed economies in a hierarchical pattern." In an avian analogy that bordered on caricature, Ozawa compared Japanese-style technology transfer to a mother bird regurgitating food for its young. According to him, Japan served as the "major translator/processor of technology, as if it were importing 'raw' technology from the West and exporting 'processed or refined—but now largely standardized' technology to the rest of Asia."[35]

Ozawa also claimed that Japan's "technological and organizational capacities to create a vast hierarchy of products" had boosted the process of regional economic integration "in a variety of products and processes across borders" in ways that would have been impossible "without such innovatory contributions made by Japan." He presented a cultural thesis as well, equating the flying-geese model with Asian values. Ozawa argued that cultural affinity gave Asia a special advantage in hosting Japanese technological and industrial transfer in the specific area of "components-intensive, assembly-based industries." Such industries were "business-culture-intensive in producing quality-reliable goods."[36] This was quite different from Okita Saburo's contention that Asian diversity promoted the flying-geese formation. Clearly, the model could lend itself to diverse interpretations.

For flying-geese enthusiasts, the birds got little rest. Edward K.Y. Chen, wrote that Asian states had graduated from competing in V-formation to competing "aerobatically."[37] Moon Chung-In, a political scientist at Seoul's Yonsei University, argued that the Akamatsu model fit Asian circumstances in the 1950s through 1970s but in the 1990s the pattern was one of "swarming sparrows." In his view, all the nations of the region were trying to do the same thing—move into value-added industries while protecting mature ones—without any particular order but mustering a great deal of energy. Moon, perhaps, had the keenest eye. By 1997, the swarming sparrows would be self-destructing as a result, in part, of the combination of overproduction and poorly monitored, overly coddled banking systems.[38]

The Western analysts who took Akamatsu and his flying geese seriously tended to come from such disciplines as political science or anthropology, not economics. Most were highly critical of its use as propaganda for Japan's new "new order" in East Asia, following the tidal wave of Japanese investment in the region in the 1980s and 1990s. Political scientist Walden Bello viewed the flying-geese theory essentially as a propaganda tool to maintain Japanese technological dominance and Asian dependence. Bruce Cumings, an expert on Northeast Asian political economy, saw the "flying geese" model as a "very interesting adaptation of Raymond Vernon's product cycle theories well before Vernon articulated them in the 1960s and 1970s."[39] Kit Machado, a political economist at California State University, wrote, "Inevitably, a Japan-centered regional division of labor will be based almost purely on hierarchy, especially when it crosses Japanese borders. To the extent that it features aspects of community, they are based narrowly on mutual economic interest."[40]

Alice Amsden, an anthropologist by training and a professor of political economy at the Massachusetts Institute of Technology, rejected the flying-geese theory in favor of a state-dominated model. Noting suspiciously that the East Asian geese all "seem to be guided by a similar radar system," she argued that late industrializers develop using nonmarket approaches, using government intervention to boost supply and demand.[41] Richard F. Doner, however, saw that structural changes resulting from very high levels of Japanese investment in Asia had "translated into shifts in comparative advantage consistent with the flying-geese analogy."[42] Danny Unger, another political scientist, claimed that "different actors operating according to disparate logics control Japan's public and private offshore capital flows. Nonetheless, the two processes sometimes work in tandem and complement each other. Nowhere is this more evident than in developing East Asia." One of the few economists to look at the phenomenon, Leon Hollerman, similarly argued that the domestic consensus between Japanese government and business traveled abroad very easily. "Japan's foreign economic policy is essentially an extension or transposition of its domestic industrial policy," he wrote in an article on Japanese investment in Brazil. "Foreign policy attempts to implement the objectives of domestic industrial policy on the international plane. . . . Both industrial policy and foreign economic policy are founded on identical theoretical considerations. Starting from the concept of Japan as a workshop that processes imported raw materials and exports finished goods, both are designed to maximize Japan's comparative advantage in the world economy. Both attempt to do so by arranging a division of labor between Japan and its trade partners that will optimize their complementarity."[43]

When Western economists pondered the question of how much of a role Japan played in regional growth, they tended to look at the issue in terms of demonstration effects or geographical proximity. But the Japanese heirs of Akamatsu insisted that regional economic integration was anything but accidental. And if circumstances did not always go their way, they would help them along. The major product of their collaboration was an Asia Pacific regional organization that aspired to be not just a copy of the European Union or the North American Free Trade Organization, but an incubator for legions of flying geese.

Okita and Kojima, who retired from policy making to a post as professor of International Economics at Hitotsubashi University, worked on the idea together for twenty years. According to the Finnish scholar Pekka Korhonen, Kojima was Okita's "participant, supporter and critic throughout the whole process."[44] Okita was the source of the "political imagination" behind the concept of an Asian regional organization, while Kojima was its "creative theoretician." Okita "skillfully shaped Kojima's ideas into forms that were applicable politically and enjoyed the necessary connections to take these ideas to Japan's top political leadership for consideration."[45]

Thus, close personal and professional ties transformed the idea of Japan's economic integration with Asia into a cross-generational crusade, linking Akamatsu to Okita to Kojima and other Hitotsubashi economists such as Yamazawa Ippei and Ishikawa Shigeru. Part of Akamatsu's legacy was to give importance to Japan's Asian connections. In the post-war period, it was up to Okita, Kojima, and Yamazawa Ippei to keep reminding Tokyo of the importance of its geographic neighborhood. They were more like hobbyists than members of a secret cabal, however. Asia was on the periphery of Japanese interests in the years of defeat and reconstruction. Only when the Asian economies began moving into hyperdrive in the late 1980s and early 1990s did the concept of an Asian economic union, with Japan at its center, begin to command broader attention. By that time, identification with Asia was so widespread among Japanese elite agencies, the business community, and politicians that the vision was no longer a lonely one.

The culmination of these efforts was the establishment of the Asia Pacific Economic Cooperation grouping, or APEC. Historically, APEC was unquestionably Japan's brainchild—the United States was initially a suspicious and reluctant partner. Although the formal proposal came from Australian prime minister Robert Hawke in January 1989, Japan's MITI had long supported the idea of an Asian trade pact and encouraged the prime minister to be Japan's front man.[46]

In 1967, then Foreign Minister Miki Takeo proposed an "Asian Pacific policy" based on an "awareness of common principles," cooperation among the advanced nations in the Pacific area—meaning the United States, Canada, Australia, and New Zealand—and increased levels of Japanese bilateral aid to the region.[47] Kojima wrote the formal paper on which the Miki policy was based, and it was the first draft of ideas that would become the basis for APEC and for Japan's strategy within the organization. No formal proposals issued directly from Miki's proclamation. Instead, Tokyo turned to Okita, who launched a conference series, with Japanese Foreign Ministry support, to examine the idea of regional economic cooperation in Asia.

The series became known as the PAFTAD, the Pacific Trade and Development Conferences. Okita recruited Australian support. The Australian National University and the Japan Economic Research Center, associated with MITI, began publishing research studies on the economies of Australia, Japan, and Western Pacific nations. The first PAFTAD convened in 1968. Participants were academics, mainly economists, senior government advisors, and government officials "in their private capacity." Gradually, Okita upped the ante. In 1976, Okita and Sir John Crawford wrote a report to the governments of Japan and Australia recommending the establishment of an "Organization for Pacific Trade and Development" (OPTAD), modeled after the OECD.[48] In 1978 Prime Minister Ohira Masayoshi put Okita in charge of a special task force to explore the idea of a "Pan Pacific association." In 1980, Okita and Kojima helped to launch the Pacific Economic Cooperation Conference (PECC).

On a parallel course to the academic PAFTAD conferences, the Japanese and Australian business communities put together the foundation for a regional chamber of commerce, the Pacific Basin Economic Council (PBEC). It was little more than a slightly expanded version of the Japan-Australia Business Cooperation Committee, which launched the concept at its first meeting in Tokyo in April 1967. New Zealand joined Japan and Australia, and the United States and Canada boycotted the meeting.[49]

Over two decades, Okita and Kojima drove slowly toward their goal. Each new organization had a little more structure, a little more clout. PECC was in many respects just another talk shop with an expanded membership—inviting business as well as government officials to sit down with the academics. But its formation also spawned a Singapore head office and organizations in participating countries, usually funded by the governments. Okita was not directly involved in the diplomatic foreplay that went into the creation of APEC in Canberra, Australia, in November 1989. He was there in spirit, however, and one of Okita's last official posts before his death in February 1993 was as a member of APEC's Eminent Persons Group, the EPG (his post was taken over by Yamazawa). This individual was supposed to provide philosophical guidance to APEC, although the organization fell apart in 1995 partly because of its aggressive advocacy of trade liberalization under its chair, C. Fred Bergsten, a former U.S. Treasury undersecretary and head of the Institute for International Economics (IIE) in Washington, D.C. Even Okita's death fell under the shadow of his vision of Asian economic integration; he died while on the phone with Bergsten, discussing EPG matters.[50]

The United States was deeply skeptical of Japan's intentions in proposing any form of economic organization in Asia that might compete with its own bilateral relationships and strategy. In 1978, the Congressional Research Service (CRS) commissioned the top U.S. expert on the Japanese economy, Yale University's Hugh Patrick, and Peter Drysdale of ANU to conduct an evaluation of proposals for a Pacific area regional economic association. Despite their sympathetic conclusions, CRS found it necessary to append a blistering attack on the concept by its senior specialist in international economics, Alfred Reifman.

Reifman enumerated the reasons why he did not like the idea, and his rationale became the basis for U.S. policy for at least a decade. The United States, Japan, Canada, Australia, and New Zealand were already members of the OECD, he wrote. "These five countries do not need another forum to talk to one another. Moreover, the OECD is only one of many forums available to these countries. Why do we need to bring these five countries together with a number of Asian middle-income developing countries, an essential part of the proposal for a Pacific Basin OECD?" The organization would compete with the U.S.-sponsored Economic and Social Council for

Asia and the Pacific (ESCAP) and undermine progress on trade liberalization in the General Agreement on Tariffs and Trade (GATT). It represented a countertrend to the "universalist approach" taken by GATT, the IMF, and OECD. "In short," Reifman concluded, "the set of reasons presented for establishing a new regional organization seems considerably short of compelling. The fact that these countries touch on the Pacific Ocean and have a considerable amount of economic relations with each other are not sufficient reasons."[51] He did not state it directly, but the implication was plain that Japan and Australia were steering a course away from U.S. interests. The United States would not participate in talks that it could not control, a reluctance that ultimately reduced its influence over the regional process leading to APEC.

Korhonen, the Finnish scholar, argues that the lineage from PAFTAD to APEC was direct, although after APEC was formed, a grouchy Kojima warned against any premature institutionalization or attempts at policy making. Kojima feared that APEC would become a "structure for predatory industrialized nations to exploit the region," obviously meaning the United States.[52] Despite such caveats, the final push for APEC came from MITI bureaucrats, looking for ways to fend off American interference with their plans to link industrial restructuring in Japan with an expanded Japanese economic presence in Asia, after the sharp yen appreciation of 1985.

In early 1988, Okumura Hirokazu, a MITI official seconded to the JETRO office in Sydney, became alarmed by reports that the United States was planning to push forward with a series of bilateral agreements in the region. This was later formalized as Secretary of State James Baker's "hub and spoke" strategy, in which the United States was at the center of a network of Asia-Pacific alliances.[53] Okumura responded by proposing that Japan work to promote an Asian forum to counter the Baker strategy, using Australia as a front; Prime Minister Takeshita Noboru picked up the theme after a visit to Washington in which he learned that the United States was interested in a free-trade pact with Japan and possibly other Asian countries. Takeshita charged MITI with looking into the matter, and the result was the Sakamoto Report.[54]

The Sakamoto Report was drafted by an Asia-Pacific "trade development study group" led by MITI director-general of the International Economic Affairs Department, Sakamoto Yoshihiro (later vice-minister for international trade). It called on the region to shed its dependency on the United States and adopt a new approach—"development through role-sharing cooperation in the region."[55] This was to be a gradual process, driven by consensus, not rules or legal principles, in contrast to the model of the OECD or GATT, predecessor to the WTO. Japan was to channel foreign investment to the region to support the scheme and open its market to regional imports. Perversely, the bureaucrats believed that the most effective way to contain the United States would be to include it in APEC. "It would perhaps be more effective to combat and contain United States unilateral actions on trade issues if we could include the United States in the forum," MITI Vice-Minister for International Affairs Muraoka Shigeo told Prawiro Radius, cabinet minister to Indonesian president Suharto.[56]

In early 1988, Muraoka traveled through Asia to test out the ideas of the Sakamoto Report. Asians were mystified by the choice of Australia to present the idea. However, according to the brilliant Japanese journalist Funabashi Yoichi, this was not just the product of Japanese timidity. Toyoda Masakazu, the leading author of the report, saw Australia as sharing Japan's anxieties about unilateral trade pressure from the United States.[57] Both countries were also alarmed by the soon-to-be-established EU and NAFTA, which would exclude them despite Australia's ties with Britain and Japan's symbiotic relationship with the United States. The two took refuge in each other. Over the course of 1988, MITI delicately maneuvered Australian prime minister Hawke into place. In January 1989, at a conference of Korean businessmen in Seoul, Hawke launched what he called "my" concept of Asia-Pacific economic cooperation.[58] Hawke's initial proposal was even more MITI than MITI—the new regional entity was to leave out the United States nor did he consult with the United States beforehand. Eventually, Japan prevailed in persuading Australia to include the United States and Canada.

In November, the new organization held its first meeting in Canberrra and acquired the name Asia-Pacific Economic Cooperation. The fact that it sounded like a string of adjectives in search of a noun was intentional. The new organization was supposed to be the opposite of trade bodies with legislative heft, such as GATT, NAFTA, or the EU. Japan argued that the region was too "diverse" to support common trade rules; in fact, Tokyo was determined to use APEC to promote its goals of gradual economic integration according to a Japanese blueprint. For this, it would also need to block any attempt by Washington to use APEC as a tool to write new rules for market liberalization in Japan's backyard. And so Japan resisted calling APEC an "organization," or an "agreement," much less a "union,"and the body limped on with its name that sounded like something was missing. As it limped, however, it grew, from the twelve participants of the original meeting (the six members of ASEAN plus Australia, Canada, Japan, South Korea, New Zealand, and the United States) to an imposing congregation of twenty-one nations, including Russia, most of the countries of Latin America's Pacific coastline, and Vietnam by the year 2000. At the instigation of the United States, in 1993 a summit meeting of the region's leaders to the annual meeting of economic ministers was added, and it quickly became the center-piece of the APEC cycle.

The Akamatsu dynasty has another link to APEC, through Yamazawa Ippei, Kojima's student, also a Hitotsubashi-based economist and Japan's second representative to the Eminent Person's Group (EPG), which comprised senior policy advisors from the APEC economies. Within APEC, Yamazawa became the spokesman for an Akamatsu-derived approach to technology transfer, "south-south" economic cooperation. As Yamazawa explained it, developing countries would help each other to catch up with the more advanced countries in the region, such as Japan, the United States, Canada, and Australia.

At first glance, the approach seemed to take out the controversial element of Japanese planning and direction from the flying-geese pattern. In fact, it corresponded neatly with patterns of Japanese investment in Southeast Asia and China in the early to mid-1990s in which first-tier Japanese subsidiaries in countries such as Taiwan and Singapore increasingly provided the capital for expansion into their less-developed neighbors. The idea that this represented "help" was misleading because the capital movement was based on Japanese multinationals expanding from one country to another. However, it also had strong appeal to economies such as Hong Kong, Korea, and Singapore, which had made large-scale investments in Asia in the course of the late 1980s and 1990s. In the case of Korea and Singapore, governments were also beginning to provide official aid to other Asian economies. Following Tokyo's lead, along with the money often went a lecture on how to spend it in order to achieve the "Singapore model" or the "Korean model" of fast growth and export success.

Another, more subtle aspect of Yamazawa's "south-south" cooperation was that it was designed as a challenge to Western-inspired "shock therapy," calling for sudden and drastic market liberalization. The idea of developing economies helping their juniors move up the ladder might not, on the surface, add up to an argument for gradual market restructuring, but in practice it offered a sharp contrast to policies favored by the United States. In the first place, "south-south" cooperation suggested that developing economies needed to model themselves on economies that were closer to their own experience, rather than to a full-blown Western model. The successful intermediate models in Asia were, for the most part, examples of developmental states with interventionist governments and marked corporatist tendencies. Secondly, "south-south" could also refer to schemes of government financing that essentially ignored the per capita income thresholds for concessionary aid established by the Development Assistance Committee (DAC) of the Organization of Economic Cooperation and Development, the OECD.

The DAC philosophy was that economies should graduate to market-based financing once per capita income exceeded $2,500. Japan struggled with the DAC limit, at times ignoring it, when the constraints interfered with its economic plans in the Asia-Pacific. Philosophically, too, Japan's growth strategy from Meiji on had been not about escaping poverty or exposing its economy to market discipline but about acquiring wealth and power. Given income levels in the industrial economies ten times the DAC threshold, at least some of the countries receiving Japanese aid looked at the DAC limit as a form of punishment for success.

When Japan hosted the November 1995 APEC ministerial and summit meeting in Osaka, it introduced a brand-new agenda for "economic cooperation." The Osaka strategy was to use "economic cooperation" as a precondition for fast-track trade liberalization. Developing countries could wait until they were a little more developed to abandon protection of infant industries and immature markets. The centerpiece of the Japanese proposals, the Partners for Progress scheme, was one in which the Japan International Cooperation Agency (JICA) was to provide seed money for human resource development in the region outside the conventions of the OECD and DAC. In Partners for Progress, Japan brought the idea of Japan as manager of a regional industrial hierarchy up to date.

This was seen by some observers as a Trojan horse for Japanese concessionary aid to jump the DAC limits, partly as a result of Yamazawa's theorizing, which presented an obvious detour around them. As Tokyo defined it, economic cooperation entailed channeling technology and capital transfers in a planned, orderly, strategic manner throughout the region, not explicitly guided but certainly paid for by Japan. In Osaka, a $100 million fund under the rubric "Partners for Progress" was established by Japan to provide funding for research and programs relating to economic cooperation.[59] The amount was about thirty times the budget of the APEC Secretariat in Singapore at the time, which allowed the secretariat to maintain a substantial slush fund for projects and clearly challenged the United States. Although the United States only gave up using APEC as a vehicle to liberalize Asian markets in 1998, after the disastrous Kuala Lumpur APEC summit three years later, after Osaka, Japanese officials boasted that they had succeeded in giving an "East Asian" thrust to the organization.

The Osaka meeting marked for the country both an anniversary and a rite of passage. The anniversary was Japan's defeat in World War Two, fifty years earlier. As a coming-of-age ceremony, its organizers hoped that the symbolism would be equally direct. Japan's Asian neighbors were ready to forget and forgive Tokyo's rampage through the region in the first half of the century. Japan, after a long interruption, was ready to share the perspective of its neighbors. If this amounted to ganging up on the Western club within APEC—the United States, Canada, Australia, New Zealand, and perhaps Mexico and Chile—so be it.

On television screens and in newspaper and wire reports, the proceedings maintained a pristine, Shinto-like calm. The conference site itself was strictly cordoned off, unlike previous APEC meetings. For the week of the ministerial gatherings and summit, Osaka citizens were unable to enter the large park girdled by the moat of Osaka Castle. To get into the hotel where the actual meetings took place, official visitors needed two separate passes. Security guards carefully checked bags and identification. There were no shouted questions to leaders. They posed for pictures in yet another site behind walls, a Japanese-style teahouse specially built for the purpose at the base of the castle.

Backstage in Osaka, hundreds of Japanese officials from dozens of government ministries pushed paper in hotel rooms in the Osaka New Otani, strung with cable and littered with bags of dried squid, coffee cups, and laptop computers representing every major Japanese manufacturer. The positioning of agency enclaves in the main operations center, in the hotel's White Crane Room, was so complex that hand-drawn maps were posted on temporary room dividers. Besides the Ministry of Foreign Affairs (MOFA) and MITI, which had battled for control of APEC from the beginning, dozens of other agencies showed up, anxious to defend their interests. The young officials who did most of the work—all but a handful were in their late twenties—worked from early in the morning until 2:00 or 3:00 A.M. every day for weeks before the meeting.

As an advisor to the Japanese Foreign Ministry, I was with the young officials, helping to draft documents. The job had come my way through my old friend, Imanishi Shojiro, later the Japanese ambassador to Luxembourg, who was then executive director of the APEC Secretariat in Singapore, a job that rotated among the countries hosting the ministerial and summit. I had an ant's-eye view of the proceedings. I would spot Mickey Kantor, the U.S. trade representative, rushing through the hotel with his entourage; overhear comments of those coming from the drafting room, pick up the gist of clashing debates from documents that were revised repeatedly.

At one point, a young official came to me for advice. Sone Kenko puzzled for three days over a document that the Foreign Ministry used for press guidance. At issue was an English word that had become a subject of argument among senior officials of the various APEC delegations—"flexibility." Outside the Japanese delegation, suspicions arose that the Japanese would use the word to undermine attempts to introduce specific, binding commitments to APEC, in the manner of the GATT or its successor, the WTO. It was up to

Sone to finesse the introduction of this suddenly explosive term into the language of the ministerial declaration, through a set of guidelines for his senior colleagues on how to present the Japanese position on flexibility.

This presented a serious intellectual challenge of how best to obfuscate the issue. First he tried, "Japan will avoid any indications that it is abandoning the Bogor declaration timeframe [which set specific target dates for trade and investment liberalization, a diplomatic triumph for the United States]." This left a loophole, after he thought about it. Somebody might ask one of the diplomats a more direct question about "flexibility." Finally, Sone settled upon, "in discussions with the press, we will not mention that the principle of flexibility relates to the Bogor declaration time frame." In other words, just don't talk about it.

Sone's dilemma, as that of the Japanese government as a whole, was how to get its way without staking out clear positions, particularly any that might engender conflict with the United States. The problem was not new. Yet, at the Osaka APEC, Japan moved closer to the open break which would become apparent three years later, at the APEC summit in Kuala Lumpur. The issue revealed the depth to which Japan was committed to Akamatsu's vision of an Asian regional economy based on orderly competition among countries at different stages of development, rather than the free-market model espoused by the United States. Japan regarded APEC's market-opening aims, inaugurated at the 1994 APEC summit in Bogor, Indonesia, as a transparent exercise by Washington to gain better trade terms for U.S. businesses. So, as it turned out, did at least some other Asians. Japan found allies in Malaysia, China, and Indonesia, despite its sponsorship of the Bogor declaration. Japan's allies were all developing countries with highly interventionist governments. To these countries, Japan's theme of focusing on region-wide plans to develop infrastructure and improve skills was attractive, especially since it meant putting off less palatable tasks, such as reducing trade barriers.

But some of Asia's more successful economies, which had thrived in free-market regimes—Singapore, Hong Kong, Taiwan, South Korea, even the Philippines, and Thailand—were dubious about Japan's "Partners for Progress" plan and its idea of supplanting tariff-reduction goals with "economic cooperation." In the end, Tokyo postponed confrontation with the United States for another few years. At the summit's conclusion, Japanese officials trumpeted the successful adoption of an "Action Agenda" for market liberalization while privately boasting that they had blocked the American onslaught.

As Japanese officials prepared for Osaka, history was an ever-present companion. The last time Japan had organized such a meeting was in November 1943, when leaders of the five puppet governments of Japan's wartime Greater

East Asia Co-Prosperity Sphere gathered in Tokyo for that short-lived organization's first and only summit. Since then, Asian leaders had come to Tokyo on three occasions—for the funeral of Akihito's father, Emperor Hirohito; Akihito's coronation ceremony; and the wedding of Akihito's oldest son to Owada Masako. But the APEC meeting was something special, a trial run for Japanese leadership in Asia, and Tokyo did everything in its power to prevent any mishaps and to make the meeting a success.

One strategy was to seduce the press, particularly the Asian press. The Japanese Foreign Ministry went to unusual lengths to encourage positive reporting. It provided all-expenses paid tours of Japan for visiting APEC-country journalists, including their own interpreters, cars, per diems, and first-class hotels at government expense. Among the prominent Asian journalists invited by the Japanese government to explore the country in advance of APEC were Amando Doronila, editorial writer for the *Philippine Inquirer*, and Hong Kong's Frank Ching, author of an influential column on Asian affairs in the *Far Eastern Economic Review (FEER)*. Doronila roomed in the Hotel Okura, the premier hotel for visiting finance ministers and heads of stock exchanges; Ching was set up in the New Otani, a favorite of big-name entertainment artists and celebrity athletes.

From a public relations standpoint, Japan's APEC was a failure. Publicly, Tokyo proclaimed that it had delivered a bold and progressive "Action Agenda." But what came out of Osaka was, in fact, an ambiguous document. While it preserved a formal commitment to the free market, the declaration's language fundamentally undermined the concept. In addition to "flexibility," the Osaka APEC introduced the phrase, "concerted voluntary unilateral liberalization," meaning, apparently, that APEC members could do what they liked but do it together. In November 1994, when Indonesia hosted the event, President Suharto stunned his counterparts by championing a plan to eliminate all trade and investment barriers in the region by the year 2010 for advanced industrial countries and 2020 for the developing ones. But the Osaka Action Agenda, which was meant to set out this plan in detail, instead offered a new escape clause—the principle of "flexibility"— allowing dissatisfied members of APEC to drop out anytime they pleased.

Even before the meeting ended, Malaysia became the first APEC member to resort to the flexibility principle. At a thirty-minute press conference following the ministerial meetings, Malaysia's brassy trade minister Rafideh Aziz created the day's major news story by declaring that Malaysia felt it could safely ignore any trade goals under APEC that it did not like. "There is no commitment on the part of any APEC member to liberalization by the year 2010 or by any date," she said. "These are indicative dates. . . . When we have difficulties we will go at the pace we feel comfortable with."[60]

U.S. president William J. Clinton's failure to attend the summit meeting the following weekend was a further disappointment. Clinton was home minding the budget debate and also, as it turned out, dallying with a young White House intern, Monica Lewinsky. The Japanese press claimed Clinton's no-show did not matter. APEC was an Asian affair, and the American president was a peripheral player. Still, for Japan, the biggest event on its 1995 diplomatic calendar was a wash in terms of the amount of attention it generated abroad. In U.S. papers, the APEC meeting was buried on the back pages. Clinton promised to make a separate trip to Japan, but almost immediately the date slipped from January to April 1996.

Thus, in the 1990s, the vision of Akamatsu, Okita, and Kojima became entrenched, even though it was shackled by the constraints of the U.S.-Japan relationship, which made Tokyo ever-sensitive to negative reactions from the United States. The ambiguity of APEC as an organization was not the only sign of the political limits of Japan's approach to regionalism. While APEC was taking root, a sideshow developed with almost comic dimensions, in which Japan played the role of the girl who could never quite say no, in a blighted courtship with Malaysian prime minister Mahathir playing the part of persistent suitor. In December 1990, in a meeting with Chinese premier Li Peng, Mahathir outlined his idea for an East Asian Economic Group, to include only Asian nations—grouping ASEAN with China, Japan, South Korea, Hong Kong, and Taiwan. The United States, Australia, New Zealand, and Canada were not to be members of the club. Mahathir apparently consulted neither his staff nor other Asian leaders beforehand, and the results were chaotic.[61] Carla Hills, the U.S. trade representative, said she could see nothing wrong with it, while Secretary of State James Baker thundered that Mahathir had drawn "a line down the Pacific." In April 1991, Japanese prime minister Kaifu Toshiki chided Mahathir, advising him to go back to his colleagues within the ASEAN and consult further.

In October, at the advice of Arifin Siregar, Indonesian trade and industry minister, Mahathir changed the word "group" to "caucus," and recast the body as a subcommittee within APEC. This failed to fly, either, when other ASEAN members bickered over the meaning of "caucus." Some argued that a "caucus" should remain independent of both the United States and APEC. Others saw it as an ASEAN clique within APEC. The U.S. ambassador to APEC, Sandra Kristoff, said that she didn't understand why APEC needed an EAEC or in what direction it would go.[62] Japan sat on its hands. U.S. opposition was explicit enough to suggest that Japan risked open confrontation with Washington if it went any farther, and in 1991, such conflict was still unimaginable. So Tokyo allowed Mahathir to dangle, neither firmly turning him down, or offering any strong encouragement.

In 1994, four years after Mahathir's initial proposal, Japan still wasn't ready to say yes or no. The indirection must have infuriated Mahathir. Tokyo defended itself by hinting that Washington was to blame. Japan's APEC ambassador, Endo Tetsuya declared, "Our official position was and still is, we have been studying it very seriously. Our position is that we don't want to offend anybody by taking any actions."[63] Indeed, Japan never formally refused Mahathir, and he continued to plug his concept in various forms for the next decade. As late as August 1998, Mahathir was still arguing that Asian countries should adopt EAEC in order to defend themselves against attacks on their economies. His education minister, Najib Tun Razak, was quoted saying, "The time is ripe for such a regional platform to emerge which will truly represent the interests of East Asia."[64]

There was at least some wisdom to Japan's position, however. Over time, as U.S. attention flagged, Mahathir's idea appeared in a new form in the ASEAN Plus Three summit sessions with the leaders of China, Japan, and Korea, begun in 1997. These summits followed closely the original Mahathir model. They excluded the "white" nations of the Asia-Pacific, the United States, Australia, and Canada, and gave ASEAN a link to the region's three top economies. The EAEG episode endured both as testimony to the practical constraints to which Japan's Asian strategy was subjected, as well as to the persistence of the vision.

Japan and Asia: A "Common Economic Logic"

In 1991, Yanagihara Toru, a Yale-trained development economist, was asked by the Mexican government to explain the emerging Asian regional trade bloc. He told the Mexicans, "The region has come to operate on a common economic logic (since the late 1980s). One can now speak of an economic zone defined functionally, not geographically, on the basis of a common logic."[65] Japan's vision of a new Asia, unfettered by Western preconceptions, was fast becoming reality. The vanguard made up of Japanese multinationals moved across the face of Asia, introducing company songs and calisthenics along with *kanban* (just-in-time) inventory control and quality circles, bringing Japanese technology and popular entertainment, transforming Asia's resource-based economies into manufacturers, and vastly increasing Japanese profits.

In earlier decades, the Japanese built simple electric products in Asia—electric irons, rice cookers, fans. They had looked to Asian markets to soak up items from the low end of Japanese industry, products they wanted to phase out of production in Japan either because margins were too low or too labor-intensive. South Koreans and Chinese, eager to move up the technology ladder, blamed the Japanese for withholding technology in joint ventures, and with good reason. Japan knew who its competitors in East Asia were, and in spite of its huge lead was unwilling to give them a head start.

Korea's giant conglomerates, the *chaebol*, aspired to build globally recognized brand names and spurned Japanese offers to serve as original equipment manufacturers (OEM) in which they would assemble products for sale under Japanese labels. Japan firmly closed its domestic market to Korean manufactures in response. Taiwanese manufacturers, more docile than the Koreans, accepted the Japanese bargain and gradually took over low-end production of Japanese goods such as calculators and cameras. Most of these flowed through Japan, for labeling and re-export. Taiwan proved the model of the future, in which Japanese multinationals would harness Asian energy and drive under Japanese brand names like modern-day equivalents of Japanese feudal crests.

In the 1960s and 1970s, during the heyday of Japan's export drive, one of the fundamental tenets of Japanese industrial policy was that the nation should husband its scarce capital resources for domestic reconstruction. Until the early 1980s, Japanese foreign investment was negligible. Between 1951 and 1981, Japanese worldwide investment was just $45.4 billion; between 1982 and 1992, its outward investment surged enormously, nearly doubling between 1985 and 1986. In 1988, 1989, and 1990, the outward flows in each year matched the entire pre-1981 stock of Japanese foreign investment.

At the same time, the pattern of Japanese investment underwent radical change. In the thirty years from 1951 to 1981, only one Southeast Asian country, Indonesia, was in the list of top ten countries for Japanese foreign investment. Thirty percent of Japanese foreign investment during this period went to Southeast Asia and the NIES of South Korea, Taiwan, Hong Kong, and Singapore, some $12.9 billion. But Southeast Asia as an investment target was not significantly more important to the Japanese economy than other parts of the world supplying raw materials or components to Japan's industrial machine.[66]

As late as the mid-1980s, Japanese manufacturers shaped their global manufacturing strategies around their home country as a principal base even if they engaged in subcontracting to take advantage of lower wage rates elsewhere. Offshore manufacturing was more likely to be a consequence of foreign market barriers than core strategy. Kojima implicitly acknowledged the Japan-centered strategy of Japanese multinationals in his hypothesis of a "kinder, gentler" Japanese foreign investment that responded to the comparative advantage of developing countries by focusing on resource extraction and low-technology manufacturing. In contrast, non-Japanese multinationals (according to Kojima) shifted production from country to country based on the whims of headquarters and market demand.

The change came dramatically, not so much as a shift to global production as a geographic expansion of strategies Japan had used successfully at home—moving rapidly through a product sequence and as rapidly flushing out obsolescent technologies, usually with government help. Suddenly, Japanese companies tailored such strategies to a regional map. Close behind them was a government that worked with its companies to weave the economic "zone" that so seized Yanagihara's imagination.

This shift in the investment patterns of Japanese companies went well beyond the bureaucratic stratagems of the Akamatsu clan and its allies in MOF, MITI, and OECF. From the mid-1980s through mid-1990s, the country experienced an economic realignment with Asia that followed the expansion of Japanese companies through the region, including thousands of small- and medium-sized investors to whom Asia was a first experience with foreign investment. The change in investment patterns developed complexity and momentum. Unexpectedly, Japan had a paradigm shift on its hands, one in which "fortress Japan" was replaced by an East Asian economic hinterland, mimicking the forced draft regional economy of the 1930s and 1940s. For a small number of liberal Japanese intellectuals, the shift was a moment of historic completion, proof that other countries would follow Japan as a non-Western model of economic success. Tokyo had shown that military power was irrelevant in a region so focused on economic growth. The country could emerge as regional leader by a process of eminent domain, or so the intellectuals and like-minded officials and businesspeople hoped.

Asia began to overtake the Japanese popular imagination in ways both subtle and profound. Dozens of official publications from internal white papers to MITI's annual yearbook on Japan's official aid celebrated its growing integration into the Asian economy. The development was presented as Japan's graduation from outlier status to Asian insider. With the huge disparity in size between the economies of Japan and the rest of the region, absorption might have been a more accurate expression of the process. In the 1990s, the Japanese economy was roughly twice that of the rest of Asia, and more than six times the size of China, its closest rival.[67] But the size discrepancy was never mentioned. Instead, Japan was portrayed as participating in a trend based on Asia's rising wealth. The larger the Asian market, by implication, the less dependent Japan would be on the United States for its survival.

About this time, Japanese officials and politicians began to break taboos of forty years' standing, addressing issues long dormant except among right-wing politicians and their friends in the black sound trucks. The death of Hirohito in January 1989 released one taboo, against delivering a formal apology to Japan's neighbors. As long as he had been alive, any apologies were considered disrespectful, because they raised questions about the ailing emperor's complicity in the war's atrocities. With his passing, Japan began the torturous process of delivering expressions of "regret"—satisfying China and Korea without offending the political right. At the same time, in the years after Hirohito's death, the mainstream Japanese media began a prolonged re-examination of the war period from a conservative Japanese point of view. In 1991, NHK, the government broadcast network, ran a documentary commemorating the fiftieth anniversary of Pearl Harbor in which it interviewed Southeast Asian alumni of the independence movements nurtured by Japan in the 1930s. Such accounts fostered a sense of closeness with an imagined Asia varying sharply with the conventional wisdom in Washington, which was that Asians feared and mistrusted Japan.

Socially, the Japanese became more conscious of Asians in their midst, as illegal workers from Southeast Asia, China, and Russia followed the high yen to jobs in Japanese service industries, from the "water trades" of prostitution and entertainment to manufacturing and construction. The numbers of Asian students climbed, particularly from China. Proprietors of Japanese language schools slyly acknowledged that many of the "students" spent most of their waking hours at jobs as short-order cooks or construction workers, despite the legal prohibition on foreign unskilled labor. Asian food followed illegal Asian workers and semilegal students, and Tokyo suddenly had a coterie of Malaysian, Thai, and Philippine restaurants. Japanese teenagers began listening to Asian pop music, albeit as part of the fashion for "world music." Discount stores displayed products with Korean and Taiwanese brand names such as Samsung and Acer. There were Asian celebrities as well, among them Malaysian prime minister Mahathir bin Mohamad, with a son at the Bank of Tokyo, his own regular newspaper column, and a series of books co-authored with the likes of economist Ohmae Kenichi and maverick politician Ishihara Shintaro.[68]

The Sasakawa Peace Foundation (SPF), whose ultranationalist founder had organized a citizens' brigade to fly supplies to Japanese troops in China in the 1930s, celebrated the 1990s by founding a "Commission for a New Asia" and an elite Asian Renaissance club modeled on the Club of Rome.[69] Inevitably, Okita Saburo presided over its first conference in 1992. "We believe that it is time for Asia to move to higher ground, to rise to its feet, to become a greater contributor to the advancement of human civilization, as great a contributor as we so often have been in the past," the group's manifesto stated. "This can only be done if in the years ahead we become the achieving continent, rapidly reforming ourselves and dramatically advancing on all fronts."[70]

Japan's rediscovery of Asia began on the other side of the world in an elegant Victorian hotel on Central Park South in New York City. In the third week of September 1985, finance ministers of the G5 industrial nations (the United States, Britain, France, Germany, and Japan) met at the Plaza Hotel to work out an agreement for coordinated market intervention by their central banks. The resulting accord became known as the "Plaza Agreement," and was intended to reduce the U.S. trade deficit by engineering a devaluation of the U.S. dollar on international currency markets. Specific targets were kept secret, but the meeting itself was public knowledge and an official press release was carefully timed for maximum impact on markets.[71] Takeshita Noboru, then finance minister, agreed to allow the yen to appreciate from Yen 239 to Yen 200 to the U.S. dollar. The yen began an ascent that would take it as high as Yen 79 to the dollar in 1995. The initial idea for coordinated currency intervention had, in fact, come from Tokyo. Prime Minister Nakasone Yasuhiro saw currency coordination as a way to ease tension in the U.S.-Japan relationship and perhaps deflect American pressure by expanding the circle to include the Europeans. Whatever the motive, both the Japanese trade surplus and Japanese foreign investment skyrocketed.

Among the reasons why the Plaza Accord had this effect was that Japanese leaders remained focused on placating Washington, with the result that they lurched from an expansive monetary policy through the exchange rate to an even more expansive fiscal policy through the discount rate. In Winter 1985–86 when U.S. Treasury Secretary James Baker found that the U.S. trade deficit remained high, he began to "arm twist" Germany and Japan to stimulate their economies to absorb more American imports. This effort, too, boomeranged. Finance Minister Takeshita decided that the way to satisfy Baker's demands was through discount rate cuts. This was enough to drive the real cost of capital into the negative zone, and Japanese companies responded with record high levels of capital investment at home and abroad. In 1986 and 1987, when the dollar's slide turned into a rout, Tokyo made further cuts in the discount rate as part of a broader policy of supporting the dollar.

The episode, writes R. Taggart Murphy, was one in which the Ministry of Finance and the Bank of Japan "threw the gasoline of more liquidity onto an already briskly burning fire of asset inflation."[72] The real cost of money in Japan, subtracting inflation, was negative or close to it for several years in the late 1980s and again in the mid-1990s. The condition created the "bubble economy" and also launched a new wave of Japanese investment in Asia. Japanese corporate borrowers could raise money on the cheap in Japan to invest anywhere in the world, and Japanese banks could make huge profits by rolling over low-interest Japanese funds into higher-earning local currency loans. The Asian economies, with the exception of China and Vietnam, pegged their currencies to the dollar, making them cheap and risk-free in yen terms. Japanese companies took a strategy they had pioneered in Taiwan—outsourcing whole product lines—and added a new wrinkle. They began integrating their Asian factories into a rapid-response network tied into the global market. Although Japanese factories claimed the highest value-added processes and latest technology, the Asian factories of Japanese multinationals were next in line in a production tier corresponding to the relative wealth of the host economy.

Akamatsu's flying geese, meanwhile, hovered close by. In December 1989, the head of the Asia-Oceania research division at JETRO described how Asian economies displayed the flying-geese pattern of development. "Countries soar and then level off, one flock after another," he said, displaying a chart with interlocking bell curves showing the emergence, peak, and maturing of the machinery industry in Japan, the newly industrializing economies (NIEs) of Northeast Asia, and ASEAN. On the chart, the NIEs were at the stage that Japan had been in 1966, while the ASEAN economies were just climbing the curve.[73] In the early 1990s, both MITI and MOFA published white papers on Asia, stressing the differences between the Asian pattern of development and those seen elsewhere. The MITI document referred explicitly to the flying-geese pattern:

> One of the main mechanisms for the deepening of interdependence in the Asia-Pacific region is the transfer of new industries, particularly manufacturing industries. In fact, there has been a shift in the countries which have international competitiveness in exports from mature industries such as textiles and steel, that is from the United States and Japan to the Asian NIEs, and from the Asian NIEs to ASEAN countries. This is known as the flying-geese pattern of industrial development, and has been a catalyst for the deepening interdependence. This pattern has already extended to the stage of developing the electronics and automobile industries in ASEAN countries. The continued success of industrial transfer in the future is the key to predicting the future success or failure of industrialization in ASEAN countries, and the probability of further deepening interdependence in the Asia-Pacific region.[74]

In terms no less grandiose, the Foreign Ministry's task force proclaimed:

> The economic relationship among the countries of Asia differs markedly from that among the countries of the EC [European Community] or North America. The factors and conditions of production in the various countries of Asia are many and diverse; the degree of industrialization differs; wage rates vary; and, by contrast with Europe with its European Monetary System, the region has seen a natural process of evolution toward the use of a

basket of currencies—which includes the dollar—as a medium for adjusting exchange rates among the various regional currencies. This has facilitated the growth of international investment, the transfer of production among countries and a steadily changing pattern of trade, all of which have had the effect of increasing the level of interdependence among the economies of the region. It is, moreover, precisely this growth of mutual dependence that has played a central role in maintaining the high levels of growth seen in almost all the countries of the East Asian region.[75]

Not surprisingly, chairing both the MITI and Foreign Ministry research teams was Yamazawa Ippei, the newly minted APEC EPG, student of Kojima Kiyoshi, and direct link with Akamatsu and the flying-geese tribe of economists.

In the decade after 1985, whole segments of the Japanese economy got into the act, from banks to trading companies to small businesses, exporting not only products but many of the practices that had made Japan rich—relational lending, equity-based project finance, and long-term supply relationships turning subcontractors into no-cost subsidiaries. As silent partner, the Japanese government used the cues and support systems honed to a fine art in the home islands, even exporting bureaucratic rivalry, particularly among the ministries of international trade, finance, and foreign affairs—MITI, MOF, and MOFA. One thing they could all agree upon: On this brand-new planet called Asia, countries that cooperated would get all the support they needed to create a welcome mat for Japanese business.

Why so much of Japan's post-1985 FDI flowed to Asia remains a question. Yanagihara argued that the phenomenon was based on market forces; others believed that Japan exported its growth formula once the costs became too great to bear at home, and that Asian countries were more receptive than those in the emerging economies of Eastern Europe and the Russian Federation.[76] Japanese executives said they were simply following the profit motive and making higher returns in Asia than elsewhere. Whatever the causes, the flood of Japanese money was as significant in its way as the U.S. Marshall Plan in Europe had been at the end of World War Two. It happened suddenly, and comprised threads both of opportunism and planning, politics and economics, historical reflection and spontaneity.

Market forces clearly played a role, and Japanese investment shifted from one part of the regional economy to another as wage rates rose or investment barriers disappeared or were created. Japanese investment itself became a growth indicator, triggering more investment in its path from South Korea, Taiwan, Hong Kong, and Singapore, where rising wage rates and strong currencies had been creating the same kinds of incentives as in Japan for a transfer of manufacturing offshore.

The leading edge of the Japanese investment boom just touched the Northeast Asian economies, then headed straight south to the developing economies of Southeast Asia, and finally north to China, following a course dictated partly by the pull factor of policy change within host economies, partly by the push factor of rapidly escalating wage rates. Wherever they landed, Japanese multinationals tended to dig in, deepening their position by importing more and more of the networks and institutions comprising Japan, Inc. This was not exploitation but a partnership within a hierarchical framework, as far as the Japanese were concerned. Asian host countries were offered the full benefit of Japanese industrial power, as long as they accepted being leashed to a system in which the most advanced manufacturing remained within Japan. Asian economies soared. Instead of creating islands of wealth in poor economies, Japanese investment brought with it a broad infusion of wealth across social classes, not only because of the payroll structure of its companies but because they traveled in industrial phalanxes planting vertical and horizontal production chains in their host countries.

For all the drama of the Plaza Accord and its aftermath, Asia's flying geese registered as little more than a faint honking to the international community of policy makers and their bureaucratic advisors. As late as the mid-1990s, senior economists in the UN Commission on Trade and Development were surprised when a Malaysian economist, Jomo Kwame Sundaram, proposed including the flying-geese theory in a report. Economists who had heard of the concept at all thought of it as a quaint Japanese notion, more haiku than economic theory.

Nonetheless, from the late 1980s, senior Japanese officials in MITI, MOF and MOFA attached a new ideological theme to the much-traveled flock. In all previous renditions—except, perhaps, that of the infamous wartime Ministry of Health and Welfare report—the geese had been associated with East Asia. The MITI vision was much more ambitious, considering the geese as emblematic of the Japanese model, a specific approach to development that could be "replicated" in any developing country and was associated as well with a particular market structure and relationship between business and government.

Tokyo's initial goal was to put an end to the interference in its lending policies in Asia from the multilateral lending agencies. In the late 1980s, the World Bank had pressured Japan to stop lending practices that had market-distorting effects by passing concessionary interest rates on to commercial borrowers. Japanese bureaucrats in MOF's coterie quickly realized that the only way to effectively combat the Bank and other multilateral lending institutions was philosophically and ideologically. Thus began an elaborate courtship with the global development community in which Japan led a counterrevolution against neoclassical economics and the flying-geese model took wing as a symbol of Asian values and Asian success.

This time the movement had no figure with the prestige of Akamatsu Kaname or Okita Saburo to lend it credibility. Instead, the flying-geese model was the product of a post–World War Two generation of bureaucrats committed to expanding Japan's global role and ending the era of junior partnership with the United States. Among them were Kubota Isao, head of the MOF Tax Bureau; Shiratori Masaki, former executive director for Japan at the World Bank and vice-chairman of OECF; and Sakakibara Eisuke, director-general of the International Finance Bureau of the MOF and later vice-minister of Finance. In the Foreign Ministry, influential figures included Ogura Kazuo, ambassador to Vietnam, and Okazaki Hisahiko, a China expert and ambassador to Thailand. All shared the view that Japan's role had been crucial to Asian economic growth. Okazaki declared bluntly, "Half of the prosperity of Southeast Asia is the achievement of Japan."[77]

Sakakibara—one of the rare Japanese officials with a Ph.D. in economics from an American university and a published author who argued that the Japanese economy had improved upon the basic Anglo-American model—was the intellectual flag bearer for the group within MOF. He argued that neoclassical economics, as well as policies for open, competitive global markets, had been a product of the Cold War and were as dead as communism. "Not universality but domination has produced the ascendance of the West," Sakakibara wrote. The twenty-first century will belong to an Asia in which the "coexistence of diverse civilizations" will replace the "progressivism" of neoclassical economics.[78]

As director of the MOF Institute of Fiscal and Monetary Policy in the mid-1990s, Sakakibara was in charge of a project comparing the "socioeconomic systems" of Japan, Germany, France, the United Kingdom, and the United States. The study challenged the convergence thesis and asserted that a "minority" of Japanese felt that Japan's structural transformation would direct it away from the American model: "If the majority in Japan (or Asia in general) accepts the universality of Western civilization—or the neoclassical socio-economic model—they will be in effect accepting the assumption that their own civilizations lag behind Western civilization, and will inevitably conclude that political and economic systems in Japan and Asia are at variance and awkward." The report found strong parallels between the "possessive individualism" of the United States and Great Britain on the one hand, and the "particularistic" cultures of Germany and France. Americans and Britons were more likely to put their companies first, while Germans, French and Japanese set community first.[79]

The work of Sakakibara and his fellow Asianists quickly translated into a new approach to the study of economic development in Japan. In the early 1990s, MITI, the Japanese MOFA, EPA, and a number of other government agencies busied themselves with policy studies designed to extract lessons from Japan's development experience for developing countries. The objective of these studies was to present Japan as an economic role model. Many of these study projects superficially resembled the World Bank's 1993 study on East Asian development, *The East Asian Miracle*, arguing similarly that Japan succeeded because of pragmatic, market-oriented policies. Their main agenda, however, was to build a new theoretical approach to development based on Japan's experience as a developmental state, to use the phrase of American political scientist Chalmers Johnson.[80] As such, they explicitly rejected the World Bank's view of industrial policy and claimed that government intervention was the source of East Asian success.

No visible or invisible hand orchestrated the studies. If anything, the agencies involved furiously duplicated each other's work programs—MITI, MOFA, MOF, the Economic Planning Agency (EPA), MITI's offshoots JETRO and the Institute for Developing Economies (IDE), the Foreign Ministry's Foundation for Advanced Studies of International Development (FASID), MOF's foreign-aid offshoots, the Oveseas Economic Cooperation Fund (OECF), and MITI's Japan International Cooperation Agency (JICA). MOF's Japan Center for International Finance was also deeply involved. The research output, driven by bureaucratic imperatives, was frequently mediocre. Practically, it was not always obvious where the Japanese would take this outpouring of theoretical research.

MOF and its allies, particularly the OECF, seemed to have the clearest objectives. Its brain trust hoped to come up with new lending conditions to counter those employed by the multilateral lending agencies. In the late 1980s and early 1990s, the World Bank and IMF had moved beyond simple macroeconomic "conditionality" to imposing sweeping institutional reforms on economies in trouble with their balance of payments. Behind the loans was an imposing array of policy research based on the revival of liberal or "classical" economics in the 1980s. The Japanese figured on using their own homegrown theory to justify official Japanese lending practices. If the World Bank had its small army of neoclassical economists, Japan would raise a militia of experts on its own brand of development.

By the mid-1990s, Tokyo increasingly used its connections with international organizations and its aid program to present its own prescriptions for growth. In 1995, in proposals to the United Nations, Japan hinted at what the criteria might be. Among other conditions, the proposal called on developing nations to set numerical targets for per capita GNP, literacy rates, infant-death rates, and other economic and social indicators over fifteen years. Such targets had been at the core of Japan's own "income-doubling" scheme of the 1960s and were in sharp contrast to the kind of macroeconomic house-keeping advocated by the World Bank and IMF. These institutions believed that if an economy got its macroeconomic "fundamentals" right, growth would just happen. Like Deng Xiaoping's famous adage about cats, to the Japanese it didn't matter how you reached the targets, as long as you caught the mouse.[81]

The Asian financial crisis in 1997 to 1998 interrupted these efforts but did not end them. If anything, the Asian crisis gave rise to a vigorous backlash within Japan against market liberalization. Sakakibara first championed an Asian Monetary Fund (AMF) to serve as a regional lender of last resort in 1997, as the Asian financial crisis was at its height. In the first round, the U.S. Treasury Department attacked the Asian Monetary Fund proposal as a violation of IMF precepts against creating "moral hazard" by rescuing economies from the results of their own bad decisions.

By 2000, the court of international public opinion shifted to the point of vindicating the strategies to arrest markets in free fall. Sakakibara was a candidate to replace Michel Camdessus as managing director of the IMF and had no less an ally than Mervyn King, deputy governor of the Bank of England, who was also proposing a "do-it-yourself" lending fund for economies in the throes of market panic. In February 2000, Sakakibara was still plugging the AMF, and the United States no longer complained as the ASEAN Plus Three summits began to cobble together an association of Asian central banks that was designed to perform many of the same functions.[82]

The Model Student: Vietnam

Perhaps the most outstanding product of MOF's brain trust was not the AMF, but Vietnam. Nowhere were Japan's efforts to shape the Asian economy more concentrated, direct, or successful. In the mid-1990s, to the fury of the World Bank and the U.S. Agency for International Development (USAID), Vietnam invited Japan to advise it on its five-year plan for 1996 to 2000. A delicious irony was embedded in this, which Japanese officials fully enjoyed. Vietnam had defeated not only the United States in the Vietnam War, but also driven back China in the 1979 Sino-Vietnamese border clash. Japan's alliance with Vietnam in economic policy thus teased both giants.

Vietnam was also a prime target for Japanese multinationals. It had the lowest labor costs in Asia, an economic system in transition from a command economy to a modified version of the free market, and access to major markets including China. By influencing Vietnam to follow the Japanese model, Japan could gain a commanding position for its multinationals in one of the key strategic economies of the Asian continent. Japan's strategy for Vietnam flouted the spirit if not the letter of OECD conventions against using foreign aid solely to benefit national companies of the donor country. The dispute set Japan openly, visibly, at odds with the World Bank and IMF and raised the stakes for the Japanese model by creating a test case in which Japan had a relatively free hand.

Money, clearly, was a big part of Japan's popularity with the Vietnamese. Tokyo first proposed conducting a study of Hanoi's development policy during a Japanese government mission to Vietnam in October 1994. The study was to be part of its official lending program to the country. Japan had been among the last of the industrialized nations to resume aid to Vietnam, after the Vietnamese government inaugurated the *doi moi* market liberalization reforms of 1986. From the early 1990s, however, Japan rapidly increased aid to Vietnam until by 1997 it was the leading donor, with $121 million in official aid—ahead of France, with $67 million, and Germany, with $53 million. By that year, Japan had given Vietnam nearly half a billion dollars in bilateral aid, far more than any other individual donor.[83] In 1996, when Hanoi endorsed Japanese proposals for its five-year plan, its acceptance was based in part on an understanding that the Japanese aid flow would continue.

Japanese advice to Vietnam ran sharply counter to that of the World Bank's in several important respects. In the first place, Japan advised Vietnam to proceed slowly with market opening measures, particularly in the financial and corporate sectors, until institutions were in place to handle them, warning against rapid privatization of state enterprises, especially. Secondly, the Japanese study advocated that Vietnam draw up a list of industries on which to practice industrial policy.[84] The latter was so far from World Bank norms or the U.S. Treasury Department's policy prescriptions of the time that the recommendation amounted to a declaration of independence.

In 1999, Vietnam became the first country to agree to a specific set of conditions to receive Japanese aid. The World Bank and IMF routinely applied "conditionality" to their loans, but Japan had merely talked about Japanese-style conditionality until then.[85] Japan approved a Yen 20 billion loan, about $161 million, while the IMF still quarreled with Hanoi about the terms of a $500 million emergency package for a balance-of-payments support. Japan's funding came from a Yen 600 billion special loan facility for public works tied to Japanese exports,[86] separate from the New Miyazawa Initiative, the Yen 1 trillion "emergency" package for Asia announced in November 1998. Loan terms under the special fund were 0.75 percent over forty years, with a ten-year grace period, almost unheard of even within the development-lending community.

So eager were the Vietnamese to get their hands on the money that they shared planning documents with Japan before showing them to the IMF.[87] Overall, the Japanese program was supposed to boost "corporate development," by forcing 100 state enterprises to undergo audits. The not-so-hidden agenda was to help Japanese companies such as Honda, which had entered the market in 1998 with a motorcycle operation based in a Hanoi suburb. The Vietnamese had failed to deliver on a promise to treat Honda as an infant industry, barring foreign competitors from the motorcycle market. Any such prohibitions would have cut into the profits of military and government-affiliated Vietnamese trading houses. The Vietnamese Industry Department, which controls foreign investment, had made the promises; its Commerce Department, in charge of the trading companies, blocked them. Japan's aid package, signed in Hanoi by Finance Minister Miyazawa Kiichi and Vietnamese prime minister Phan Van Khai, promised to convert nontariff barriers into tariffs and "introduce new instruments consistent with the WTO rules to protect domestic industries"—i.e., Honda.[88]

Few Japanese documents are as starkly critical of the World Bank as the 1995 country study of Vietnam with which Japan began its courtship of Hanoi. In a section on industrial policy, the study confronted the Bank head-on:

> Developing countries, and especially low-income ones, do not necessarily have to rely on market mechanisms in order to cultivate and strengthen market economies. Such countries should utilize state intervention in line with appropriately designed programs for action. . . . The World Bank, among other institutions, has strongly opposed government policies aimed at cultivating priority industries down to the sub-sectoral level as excessive market intervention by the state. That position has been based on the view that it is enough for governments to strive to expand infrastructure through public investment, strengthen macroeconomic fundamentals, and pursue structural adjustments that pave the way for the introduction of market-based systems, but to leave developments in the direct production sector or industrial structure up to the forces of the market. However, the structural problems Viet Nam faces are those of a country that until the start of the 1990s was a member of the former Soviet economic bloc, and that is currently striving to reorient its trade and industrial structure toward the West. As such, their solution will demand heavy investments, long-term planning, and deliberate design. This is the reason industrial policy is essential.[89]

Chairing the Vietnam research and advisory effort was perhaps the most profound intellect among the Akamatsu clan. This was Ishikawa Shigeru, a monetary economist with degrees from Hitotsubashi University in 1941 and, after the war, from Cornell. Taiwan's president Lee Teng-hui had been a classmate in Ithaca, New York. Ishikawa joined the Hitotsubashi economics

faculty after spending the war years in China, first with the South Manchurian Railway and later as a journalist with *Dohmei,* the official Japanese
propaganda organ, which survives today as the Kyodo News Service.
Ishikawa joined the economics faculty at Hitotsubashi in 1954, when
Akamatsu was dean. He was no toady to the bureaucracy. Over many years,
he says, his relationship with the government was "not good."[90]

From the early 1970s, however, Ishikawa became increasingly interested
in the philosophical underpinnings of Japanese aid, bringing him closer to
government circles. By the late 1980s, while in semiretirement at Aoyama
Gakuin University, Ishikawa chaired the most senior of the *benkyokai,* or
study groups, examining Japan's development experience and seeking ways
to promote a Japanese development model. This study group was convened
by MOF, and met from the late 1980s through the mid-1990s. The group was
by no means limited to MOF officials. Yanagihara was among the younger
participants, both in his capacity as a senior researcher at IDE and later, after
his move to Hosei University. This group began to plot the outlines of a
sweeping challenge to the World Bank and to Anglo-American economic
orthodoxy. Its most creative thinker, however, was Ishikawa, who had spent
many years on the outside contemplating the absurdity of Japan's huge aid
program. Ishikawa agreed with many of the foreign critics of Japanese aid.
As far as he was concerned, it was little more than a subsidy for Japanese
multinationals. Through the MOF *benkyokai,* he aimed to do better.

In Summer 1996, I met with Ishikawa in a JICA office in the Shinjuku
Mitsui Building, one among the massive array of office towers populating a
former reservoir west of Shinjuku Station in downtown Tokyo. Few settings
could seem farther from Vietnam, from Manchukuo in the war years, or from
the dark and striving Japan of the immediate post-war years. Efficient aides
with spreadsheets bustled about; others tapped away at laptop computers.

Ishikawa, too, seemed an unlikely member of Akamatsu's romantic flock.
He had survived the hard life of a post-war Japanese intellectual proving himself in a non-Japanese world. He had his American doctorate, had taught at
Harvard, and written extensively in English. The emotion that first drew him to
the subject of Japanese development aid was not nationalism but frustration.

Sitting ramrod straight, unbent at the age of seventy-eight, Ishikawa spoke
in clear, precise English, in long academic sentences laced with sarcasm. He
was among the first Japanese economists to be attracted to the field of development economics, and as Ishikawa began examining Japanese aid practices,
he found that its structure was carefully designed to eliminate any entangle-
ment with policy issues. Japanese aid was about promoting Japanese business.
It was supposedly based on the "request principle," meaning that recipient
countries had to request aid for specific projects. But this was a thin cover

for Japanese business and government to design, then fund, infrastructure projects in order to sell Japanese products and improve the environment for Japan's offshore manufacturers. Agencies such as MITI's JETRO offered free feasibility studies, tailored to the needs of Japanese industry. With careful shepherding from the Japanese embassy, and judicious amounts of foreign aid, these proposals would move up the ladder until the host country made its "requests." [91]

> Probably the motivation for this new field of study was the fact that the total amount of Japanese aid to developing countries was becoming larger and larger. It was obvious to me, however, that the basis of Japanese aid policy was nothing. What is called the "request principle" was a very poor thing, to be deplored. That's the reason I became more and more concerned about what really was behind these words, "request policy." At the same time I started teaching international development policy at Aoyama Gakuin, where I worked for more than ten years after retiring from Hitotsubashi. The course began in the 1982–83 school year. As I became aware of the components, the contents of the request policy, I also became concerned to utilize my knowledge of development economics to study the request policy. . . . When I came to consider the issue of the request policy and its later evolution, I came to recognize that the character of Japanese aid policy and aid practice could be explained very largely by the fact that Japanese policy is based implicitly upon their recognition of the underdeveloped framework of the market economy.
>
> There are a number of peculiar features in Japanese aid policy, and these often cause conflicts between Japanese aid organizations and the international aid organizations. But these differences may come from the ways that international aid organizations perceive developing economies. They perceive the same underdeveloped economies in different ways.
>
> Japan was providing aid, but this provision of aid was based on no policy. It was actually dictated by someone else's policy. What we can see quite often is the behavior of Japanese foreign policy itself. But as time goes on and experience is accumulated, the learning effect worked. Also, historically, Japanese aid organizations came to realize that there are a number of aspects where they can lay emphasis in providing aid, and in these points you can see a peculiar Japanese style emerging, a Japanese way of operating its economy, operating the firm, managing technology and business. In the end quite Japanese-style behavior is actually practiced and transferred.[92]

Ishikawa argued that it was, in fact, a good thing that the policy element in Japanese foreign aid was so meager. It allowed Japanese aid bureaucrats to learn from experience, rather than impose preconceived ideas.

The Japanese request policy has evolved. There are a number of aspects, which we could indicate. The major thing is that the application of the policy prescription is based upon very realistic perceptions of economic development and market developments . . . in Japanese economic policy, at least since the 1920s—before that the Japanese government was not inter-ventionist—the government is not prevented by any doctrinaire thinking from devising pragmatic policies. So they are very sensitive to reality. On the basis of a firm perception of real issues, they invented policy that could be effective, and those policies evolved as time went on. So we are now in a position to be able to look back at the process of policy evolution.[93]

It was also true that the more Japanese influence Asian economies ac-cepted, the more comfortable they would become for Japanese companies. Japanese investors in Vietnam complained endlessly about the country's weak bureaucracy and the absence of inside dealing in awarding foreign contracts. "The government doesn't have a unified window to authorize foreign com-panies to do business. There is no communication among the ministries you have to deal with. This is what a socialist country is," a Japanese executive from Mitsubishi Motors Corp. whined to a *Nikkei* reporter in 1995. The re-porter, Sumiya Fumio, commented: "Perhaps the biggest complaint [among Japanese companies] is that the [Vietnamese] government, in its eagerness to build an auto industry, is inviting too many foreign entities into the coun-try. That, it is feared, will lead to excessive competition—a special irritant to Japanese companies used to their own government controlling competition at home."[94]

The Japanese liked to picture themselves as producer, not director, of the East Asian miracle, offering advice but not calling all the shots. In a 1992 interview, Suzuki Yoshio, a former chairman of Nomura Research Institute (NRI) and opposition party politician, said:

The East Asian economy is now working for itself. Since the Plaza Accord, there have been so many direct investments, and the industries of ASEAN and the Chinese coastal zones have been stimulated so much. They have become capable of exporting finished goods, even technology-intensive items, to the United States, Europe, and Japan as well as to the Asian NIEs. So-called horizontal trade in the exchange of goods has developed for the first time in history.

In the past, Japan and the Asian NIEs have imported materials and ex-ported finished products to the United States and Europe, so we had only vertical trade. Now, horizontal trade has been established. The share of Japanese exports to East Asia is over forty percent, while the share of exports to the United States which once was over forty percent is now less than thirty percent. In my estimation, the share of exports to East Asia will exceed fifty percent sooner or later.[95]

Dreaming such dreams, of an autarkic Asia energized by growth, Japan entered the 1990s with its eyes firmly closed to the forces of globalization. These would tear the dream apart before the decade ended. Japan's Asian vision was based on the conviction that Asia had succeeded because it had done things differently from other regions of the world. Asians believed in the strength of the group, not the dazzling talents of individuals. The Asian financial crash would teach the lesson that global markets ignored such differences, and exacted a terrible price on economies systematically distorting the cost of capital. But for much of the decade, Japan could easily believe that its dream was coming true.

3

Second Invasion

In 1990, I was in Tokyo, working for the Toronto *Globe and Mail*. Japan loomed large in the global economy. It loomed even larger in Asia, as a result of five years of frenetic investment and lobbying, mostly of the checkbook diplomacy type. On top of billions in direct foreign investment, Japan had spent billions of dollars lending money on easy terms to Asian governments to build ports, roads, power lines, and other infrastructure needed to galvanize the region's economies. It was unclear how this massive wave of cash would affect the region. The smaller Southeast Asian economies were reeling under the influx of Japanese capital. Lingering Asian wariness toward Japan was reflected in *The Second Invasion*, a book published in 1989 and whose author, Renato Constantino, was a nationalist intellectual and political scientist at the University of the Philippines.

Constantino wrote: "Many Asians fear that a Japan-ASEAN partnership will be the contemporary version of the relationship of dominance-dependence which Japan sought to establish nearly four decades ago under the Greater East Asia Co-Prosperity Sphere. As the only Asian nation who is a member of the club of rich nations, Japan cannot but take the side of the developed countries. Her policies contradict the broad aspirations of the peoples of Asia who do not need foreign-dictated models of development that serve the needs of foreign corporations."[1]

The region had yet to experience the much greater onslaught of global capital that would come a few years later, peak, and collapse in the Asian financial crisis. I had yet to learn about flying geese, Mikhail Gorbachev had yet to fluster the Japanese by asking for tutorials in the Japanese model, and Japanese nationalists such as Ogura Kazuo and Okazaki Hisahiko had yet to begin their "Asian restoration." All that we had to look at were the numbers, and these on their own were arresting. In a few short years, Japan had carried out a transfer of wealth to its Asian neighbors that rivaled the U.S. Marshall Plan in its ambition and scope.

Between 1979 and 1989, Japan poured more than $100 billion into the region, including direct investment, foreign aid, and tourism. Official development assistance (ODA) multiplied the effect of private-sector investment. In the early 1990s, the combined outlay of Japanese government and private sector cash into Asia was surpassed only by the huge flows of overseas Chinese capital into China.

Moreover, attitudes on the part of Asians had undergone a sea change. One of the hints was the noticeable lack of hostility of many Asians to the incoming tide of Japanese money. Constantino was the exception, not the rule. If most Asians were silent, however, it was because they saw a miracle happening before their eyes. Besides, much of the population of Southeast Asia and China was still poor. Complaining about Japanese investment was a luxury many countries could ill-afford. "We fight our battles over smaller issues," said Jomo Kwame Sundaram, a development economist at the University of Malaya. "Do we have enough jobs for our people, are they healthy, are their babies dying?"[2]

The reception in Asia to Japan's growing economic importance in the 1980s starkly contrasted the attitudes and perceptions just a decade earlier. In the 1970s, Japan had used Southeast Asia as a dumping ground for industrial pollution and low-tech industries, and Southeast Asians did not like it. They knew all about the scandals surrounding Chisso Corp.—the poisoning of thousands of residents living in the sleepy fishing village of Minamata in southern Japan by mercury runoff from a Chisso plant. Most of the Japanese textile industry had moved to Asia in the 1970s and by the mid-1990s it still had among the highest ratios of overseas production of any Japanese industrial sector, 31.9 percent.[3]

In the late 1980s, however, Japanese companies and the government worked hard to counter potential backlash. They built cultural centers, stayed out of local politics, deferred to local sensitivities, and gave host governments what they asked for. In 1990, when Malaysia told Japan it wanted Japanese companies to move into new industries, Tokyo duly commissioned JETRO to prepare half-a-dozen elaborate studies on subjects ranging from rubber footwear to downstream chemical products. About the same time, Indonesia's leading business magazine, SWA Sembada, ran a cover story under the revealing caption, "Open the Door to Japan." "Right now we're in a phase where the role of Japanese capital is too important. We're not going to turn around to them and say, we don't want your managers," explained Sanjoy Chowdhury, the chief regional economist for Merrill Lynch in Singapore. "Here in Asia there are countries that are looking very hard for investment. And suddenly they turn around and see a gold mine."

It all seemed a little too good, or too ghastly, to be true. The Greater East Asia Co-Prosperity Sphere, like a legion of ghostly warriors, was springing up unheralded from the rubble of the Cold War as though during the long interregnum of American hegemony, they had not been vanquished but merely underground. I wanted to take a closer look. My editor, Peter Cook, a British journalist with twenty years of reporting experience in Asia, was intrigued as well. Together, we decided I would take a swing through the region, taking in Taiwan, Malaysia, Thailand, Singapore, and Indonesia. I would visit Japanese factories and offices, talk to workers and executives, and generally get close to the booming Japanese electronics, auto, retail, and financial industries in the region, trolling as well for signs of cultural influence.

My itinerary followed the outlines of Japan's old southern empire, absent Manchukuo and South Korea. And so, in the first few weeks of the Year of the Horse, aptly named for its skittishness and unpredictability, I went on the road. Starting in a gray Taipei, blustery with winter, I flew to Singapore and Bangkok, where I visited Japanese factories and offices soaked in perspiration after half an hour. In Kuala Lumpur, I visited the city-god temple to light joss sticks for the New Year, and wound up in Jakarta, riding in from Sukarno-Hatta International Airport on the first of the toll roads built by Suharto's daughter, Tutut. The children were still under control, Indonesia's wild speculative real-estate and financial bubble yet a few years away, and Suharto himself safely in his palace.

It was an odd time, a period of momentous and chaotic change. Asia was on the verge of an explosion of capital and growth that would ultimately prove fragile. Japan was just beginning its long tumble into the recession of the 1990s yet still rode the upswing of the 1980s in terms of chauvinistic rhetoric and national pride. I had chosen to make the trip during the dead lull over Japanese New Year, *oshogetsu*, when Tokyo empties out and business stops. During those days and weeks, the Nikkei began a precipitous crash that would last throughout the 1990s. While the bubble economy had just ended in Japan, it was just beginning in Japan's neighboring regions, as Tokyo attempted to replicate its model in Asia, using the levers of relational banking, negative domestic interest rates, and coordinated decision making within major industrial groups, or *keiretsu*.

Japanese investment was not just a matter of building factories and department stores. In the late 1980s and early 1990s, the whole Japanese industrial system seemed to be on the move, particularly the *keiretsu* companies with their tiers and networks of long-term subcontractors. Government support played a crucial role, although it was sometimes unclear whether MITI and its rival ministries were leading or following corporate Japan, trundling first to Korea and Taiwan in the early 1980s, then to Thailand, Malaysia, Indonesia, and Singapore in the mid-1980s, and finally to China and Vietnam in the early 1990s.

In the post-war period, Japanese manufacturing depended heavily on the output of small and medium enterprises. Within the *keiretsu*, large companies contracted out parts and some stages of the production process to smaller businesses. As late as 1987, MITI's basic survey of Japanese industry found that some 378,000 small- and medium-sized companies were engaged in *keiretsu* subcontracting, accounting for 55.9 percent of Japanese industrial production.[4] In the all-important electronics and auto industries, the figure was closer to 90 percent. Without their subcontractors, Japanese factories abroad would have been stranded, and so they followed.

The Japanese called this pattern "convoy" investment, and it was the organizing chord of Japanese investment in Asia in the 1980s and 1990s. The phrase reflected both the militant Japanese approach to executing the transfer of key industries offshore, and the determination to keep the Japanese export machine in Japanese hands, even when it was no longer in Japan. What distinguished Japanese investment from that of other foreign multinationals' was that the former brought with them huge chunks of industrial and institutional infrastructure.

Paul Summerville, a Canadian economist based in Tokyo from 1986 to 1994, told me that when Japanese companies moved abroad, they brought with them not only the economic structure but also their culture. "The Japanese are setting up companies now in Southeast Asia that are part of the fabric of the Japanese economy," Summerville said in 1990. "That means they will have to function as Japanese companies do."

Japanese investors had first employed the convoy pattern of investment, on a small scale, in Korea and Taiwan in the 1970s. In August 1971, when Nixon ended the system of fixed exchange rates by taking the U.S. dollar off the gold standard, the first yen "shock" hit Japanese export industries hard. They solved the problem by investing in assembly plants and joint ventures in their immediate neighbors, Korea and Taiwan, which had similar infrastructure to Japan, a legacy of the Japanese colonial period. Japanese subcontractors made the move along with their *keiretsu* parents, supporting their investments and helping to return profits home.

In the late 1980s, however, currency appreciation hit Taiwan and Korea much as it had hit Japan, as a direct result of the swollen current account surpluses created by their export successes. Wage and price inflation followed, and both countries quickly began to recycle their surpluses in the form of foreign investment. The Japanese government's economic bureaucrats, watching these developments, signaled Japanese business to re-direct investment to Southeast Asia. The signals came in the form of companion MITI and MOF support programs for Southeast Asian investment, both launched in 1987; the New Asian Industrial Development plan from MITI;

and MOF's Japan-ASEAN Fund. Since these cues were in the form of huge subsidized loans and other trade and investment support, Japanese companies merely applied the lessons of experience and common sense. The same year, Japanese investment shifted decisively toward Southeast Asia.

For a few years, Japanese investment literally swamped the market-based economies of Southeast Asia, particularly Thailand, Malaysia, and Indonesia. Between Japan's 1987 and 1988 fiscal years, Japanese investment in ASEAN countries nearly doubled, from $1 billion to $1.9 billion. In 1989 in Thailand, Japan accounted for nearly 70 percent of foreign investment, with $452 million in projects. The same year, Japanese companies had applications out for investments worth another $3.9 billion. Japanese investment swamped the Thai infrastructure. Problems with electricity and water shortages, traffic gridlock, and port congestion created a national crisis.

Tokyo-based economist Kenneth Courtis had a catchy way of describing the impact of Japanese investment in these years by relating it to the gross national product of Japan's target countries. By the late 1980s, Japanese investment in seven Asian countries—Thailand, Indonesia, the Philippines, Malaysia, South Korea, Hong Kong, and Singapore—was eight times its investment in Europe and four times its investment in North America, adjusting for the ratio of Japanese investment to GNP. "The Japanese want to get a hammer lock on these markets," said Courtis. "They're just pouring investment into the area like mad and will continue to do so over the next decade. They're positioning themselves to get a strategic hold on the market as it explodes." Perhaps a German investment promotion official with the Malaysian-German Industrial Cooperation Project based in Kuala Lumpur in the late 1980s said it best. "When you look at this part of the world," noted Guenther Piper, "everything is taken up by Japanese, Japanese, Japanese."

Among the first signs of Japan's influence on the regional economy was its effect on trade within Asia. In the mid-1980s as Japanese investment surged, its subsidiaries in Asia set up intricate manufacturing networks across the region, pumping intermediate goods back home to Japan. The country's Asian factories provided a captive market for Japanese capital goods—the machine tools and numeric processors, hydraulic presses, and earth-moving equipment—that went into the construction of Japan's new industrial outposts. As soon as the factories were up and running, they supplied a market for high value-added products that could not be manufactured locally, at least not initially, for example, the engine blocks and liquid-crystal displays that represented the highest concentration of value in products. The same factories sent back streams of subassemblies to Japan, where a few critical components might be inserted before they were packaged and brand labels applied.

When I packed my bags for Southeast Asia, the trend lines were already apparent. By the end of the 1980s, Japan's trade with Asia and trade among the Asian nations were both growing twice as fast as the region's trade with North America. As early as 1989, Asia surpassed the United States as Japan's major trading axis, at $140 billion in two-way trade. In the same year, Japan traded more with three Asian countries—Hong Kong, Taiwan, and South Korea—than with the countries of the EU.

Over the next few years, Asia as a whole replaced the United States as Japan's principal economic partner, a fact with enormous implications. By 1991, Japanese exports to Asia had outstripped its exports to the United States. By 1993, Asia provided more of Japan's trade surplus than did the United States.[5] By the mid-1990s, as industrialization projects took off and countries eased protectionist barriers, the trend had become entrenched. By 1995, Japan was exporting $186.5 billion to Asia and importing $115.5 billion. Exports to and imports from the United States in 1995 were $120.9 billion and $75.4 billion, respectively. Japan-Asia trade was 50 percent greater than Japan-U.S. trade.[6] By 1996, 42.8 percent of Japanese exports and 35.2 percent of import trade were with Asia.[7]

After a drastic falloff in interregional trade during the Asian financial crisis, Asian trade with Japan again skyrocketed, with imports and exports from ASEAN and the Asian NIES (South Korea, Taiwan, Hong Kong, and Singapore) rising faster than to any other region.[8] At the end of the decade, Japan's economic tilt to Asia was pronounced. By 1999, Japan was exporting $149.4 billion to Asia, 16 percent more than its $128 billion in exports to the United States. And, while its trade with Asia was far from balanced, Japan was importing almost twice as much from Asia as from the United States, $116.5 billion compared to $66.9 billion. This had political ramifications: Japan's trade surplus with its neighbors was only half that of its surplus with the United States, $32.9 billion compared to $61 billion. In 2000, Japan for the first time imported more from Asian countries than from North America and the EU combined. Imports from Asia totaled $145.8 billion, up 22.1 percent from 1999, while those from the EU and North America came to $117.9 billion, according to the Japanese Finance Ministry.[9]

The explosion in Japan's imports from Asia hung not on an opening of its clogged distribution system or a new enthusiasm for Asian brands. Rather, it reflected the degree to which Japanese multinationals had spread their net across Asia. Japanese companies were now using their Asian factories to produce goods for the domestic market, from the China-made textiles swamping discount chains such as Daiei to sports utility vehicles.[10] In 2000, Japanese imports from China rose more than 20 percent to $50.8 billion,[11] making that country the second-largest exporter to Japan after the United States. China alone surpassed the entire EU. Japanese clothing discounters such as the ubiquitous Uniqlo chain, operated by Fast Retailing, had come to rely heavily on China. Japan's textile imports from Asia in 2000, mostly from China, climbed 17.8 percent to $16 billion.[12] Imports of computers and other office equipment were also significant—growing by 34.3 percent, mostly from Taiwan—and semiconductors and other electronic parts from elsewhere in Asia surged 55.7 percent that year, a great deal of it delivered by Japanese electronics factories spread across the region.

The same trend away from the United States and toward Asia was apparent in Japan's foreign direct investment (FDI), although the United States continued as Japan's favorite investment target. In 1994, Japanese FDI in Asia, at $9.7 billion, surpassed Japanese FDI in Europe, at $6.2 billion. (The same year, Japanese investment in the United States was $17.8 billion.) In 1995, Japanese FDI in Asia, at $10 billion, was nearly double its investment in Europe, at $5.3 billion, if still only half of its $20.3 billion of direct investment in the United States. By this feat, Asia became Japan's second-largest venue for investment after the United States.[13]

On another scale, that of Japan's overseas manufacturing investment, Asia moved steadily ahead of both the United States and Europe. In 1994, Asia attracted $5.2 billion of Japanese manufacturing capital, compared to $4.8 billion for the United States. In 1995, the figure was up to $6.5 billion in Asia and $4.2 billion in the United States.[14]

Halfway through the 1990s, Japan crossed a practical, if not a psychological, divide. The nation was still dependent on the United States militarily, but its economy no longer relied on the tides of American growth and recession. On a late 1995 cruise through Tokyo bookstores, shelves groaned under the weight of rows and rows of handbooks for businesspeople on China, Vietnam, Laos, Cambodia, and Burma. *Imidas*, a telephone book-sized annual compendium of new words entering the Japanese lexicon, featured an entire section on Asia. "Yaohan's Strategy for Succeeding in China," a how-to manual by corporate executive Kazuo Wada, owner of Asia's largest department store in Shanghai, was prominently displayed. And *Chuo Koron*, a respected monthly magazine, ran a special issue on the "Era of Super-Competition in the China business."

Japan's leading intellectuals struggled to ring the changes. Funabashi Yoichi, diplomatic correspondent for the *Asahi Shimbun*, captured both Japan's excitement and its dilemma in a 1993 article for *Foreign Affairs*. Japan's role in Asia, whether as presumed leader or board director or silent partner, instantly invited comparison with its militarist past and raised a direct challenge to U.S. leadership in the region. Funabashi thus spent much of the article vigorously denying the possibility that Japan might act with the ferocious self-interest that it had displayed earlier in the century. "The emerging

Asian worldview is not one of imperialist pretensions, ideological fervor, totalitarian paranoia or superpower hubris—those ideas are viewed as retrogressive approaches that fractured the region for most of this century. The Asian consciousness is animated by workaday pragmatism, the social awakening of a flourishing middle class and the moxie of technocrats, although still tinged perhaps by anti-colonialist resentment, racism and indifference to civil liberties," he wrote.[15]

Japan, according to Funabashi, would lead Asia not in the direction of autarky but in the direction mapped out by its longtime Western mentor, the United States, toward liberal trade and investment models. "Whether Asia can play a constructive role in building a post–Cold War economic order depends on whether it can further strengthen the multilateral, free and non-discriminatory international trade system and open market economy. Japan's responsibility in this endeavor is considerable. It must reform its exclusive economic and social structure and revise the political and administrative structure that has sustained it. Accomplishing that would strengthen the economic and trade ties among Asian nations that lead to deepened global interdependence and facilitate worldwide economic development and growth. Japan's long-time obsession with an East-versus-West view of the world, and the definitions that worldview subsumes, will gradually fade with integration into the world economy." Memorably, Funabashi went on to herald Japan as the world's first "global civilian superpower."[16] He argued that Japan might provide global leadership as no power had done before, by the force of its economic rather than its military example.

Whether the readers of *Foreign Affairs* believed Funabashi may have depended on how committed they themselves were to the centrality of the U.S.-Japan alliance in Pacific affairs. U.S. policy-makers virtually ignored signs both that Tokyo was revising its alliance structure until late in the decade, despite a stream of official Japanese publications outlining the importance of its role within an integrated Asian economic community, and initiating less vocal efforts to begin the process of building an Asian security community as well. Asia was suddenly a popular topic in the Japanese Foreign Ministry. Okazaki Hisahiko, a China specialist and former Japanese ambassador to Thailand, wrote of a new enthusiasm for Japanese leadership among Asians worried by the increasing intensity of trade friction with the United States and the European Community.[17] Ogura Kazuo, another Foreign Ministry China specialist, shocked U.S. State Department Japan watchers by urging the "revival" of Asian values.

Ogura was a dashing figure in the ministry, author of books on U.S.-Japan friction and culture wars as well as a biography of Zhou Enlai's days in Paris in the 1920s. His article on Asian values, "For Asia's 'Reinstatement,'" was a manifesto urging Asians to shake off American and European cultural imperialism, and it fell just shy of advocating a break with the United States. Ogura said that the United States would have a role in Asia only to the extent that it "Asianized" itself, meaning "a process of Asian values being understood and accepted." He continued: "Asia has its own way of thinking about society and human beings. We can say that today, at long last, Asia as a result of cultural collision with Europe and America has secured its own political independence and economic prosperity, and will transmit its own messages in its own voice."[18] Ogura played, too, on Fukuzawa Yukichi's Meiji-era slogan, *Datsu A, Nyu Ou*, "Leave Asia Behind and Enter the West," signifying Japan's embrace of the West, and turned it into the reverse: *Datsu Ou, Nyu A*, "Reject the West; embrace Asia."

Prominent Japanese business leaders contributed to the dialogue as well. In April 1991, Kobayashi Yotaro, chairman and chief executive officer of Fuji-Xerox Corp., called upon Japan to share its leadership of Asia, not with the United States but Beijing. The tall, cosmopolitan Kobayashi was a regular on the Washington-Tokyo circuit, much cultivated by the American business community in Japan, a man with enormous prestige. He was as much at home chatting with a Wharton School business professor as with colleagues in Keidanren, Japan's powerful Federation of Economic Organizations.

The views he aired in an article in *Foresight* raised concerns not only because Kobayashi presented China as Japan's natural ally in Asia, but because the United States was nowhere in the picture: "It does not seem advisable or wise for Japan to be the sole leader in Asia," Kobayashi wrote. "China's immense presence in the region must not be overlooked. This nation was not only on the winning side of World War Two, but also is a permanent member of the United Nations Security Council. China commands special respect from a world, becoming only of mature nations [sic] perhaps by virtue of its history of having in the past once ruled the world, and by virtue of an enormous cultural heritage. I believe it prudent for Japan to cooperate with China, in particular as co-chairs, contributing to the development of Asia. By this means I am convinced also that Japan will be able to mitigate the distrust that Asian neighbors may continue to harbor."[19]

Similar exercises occurred in the gray area of study groups and advisory councils, chameleon-like bodies where Japan's iron triangle of business, politicians, and bureaucrats seek consensus, often with assistance from compliant academics. One such was undertaken by the Sasakawa Peace Foundation (SPF), an offshoot of the family fund set up by Sasakawa Ryoichi out of the vast profits of his motorboat-racing monopoly. In the 1930s, Sasakawa had helped organize airlifts of supplies for the Kwantung Army, Japan's occupying force in China. He was a fervent fascist and admirer of Mussolini who displayed a chameleon's aptitude for adapting to his times. In the last phase of his life—he died in 1995—Sasakawa worked to rehabilitate Japan's image in Asia by pouring his fortune into research and training programs for Asian elites.

In 1992, SPF set up a Commission for a New Asia in order to "provide a platform for Asians to define their own world for perhaps the first time in history, and, to consider the direction of their own collective course." Chaired by Noordin Sopiee, a Mahathir confidante and head of the Institute of Strategic and International Studies in Kuala Lumpur, the commission included Fuji-Xerox's Kobayashi Yotaro; Nukazawa Kazuo, executive director of Keidanren; Okazaki Hisahiko, the former ambassador; *Nihon Keizai Shimbun* Asia expert Ishizuka Masahiko; along with a score of prominent academics and bureaucrats. Two years later, the commission came up with two reports, the "Outlook for a New Asia and Japan's Response" and "Towards a New Asia."[20]

The documents were not in themselves revolutionary. They directed scathing yet predictable remarks at Western individualism ("we believe that the cult of selfish, self-centered individualism is repugnant, and in the end, self-defeating") and applauded Asian proclivities toward social harmony, community, and the "golden mean." More interesting than the recitation of homilies and conventional wisdom was the process of committee recruitment. Members included Russian and Australian academics but no Americans. The point was to draw a line in the sand—Asia on this side, America on the other. The exercise was in the fine Japanese art of building human networks, or *jinmyaku*, giving voice to an Asian sensibility free of Western—that is, American or European—interference. And however mild the opening salvos might be, they established a new reference point. SPF organizers talked expansively about setting up an Asian equivalent of the Club of Rome. With wealth came responsibility and opportunity.

It would be another decade before Japan's geopolitical stratagems resulted in making a substantial mark on regional institutions, embodied in the "ASEAN Plus Three" summits joined by China, Japan, and South Korea after 1997. In the early 1990s, Japan focused on the theme of regional economic integration. Confrontation was muted. The United States had long encouraged Japan to serve as the lead economy for the perimeter economies to China, using Japan's success in the international market to wean Asia's developing economies away from the seductions of socialism. Economic integration of Asia's market economies was consistent with Washington's commitment to forcing open the region's closed economies, as long as integration followed a free-market model. In Japanese eyes, however, "economic integration" was a rubric for a process moving in a very different direction.

When the Japanese looked at their neighbors in the first part of the 1990s, they saw economies sharing two characteristics—rocketing growth and a legacy of Japanese colonial rule. The case for economic integration was based on shared values, a common approach to economic growth, and a continuing relationship with Japanese industry, which had laid the basis for the Asian boom. Southeast Asian economies were a special point of pride. The surge in growth of the economies of Thailand, Malaysia, and Indonesia in the mid-1980s coincided with a huge "wave" of Japanese investment and an expansion by several orders of magnitude of Japan's aid flows to the region. Malaysia, the chief recipient of Japanese investment on a per capita basis, pursued an explicit "Look East" policy of modeling itself on Japan from the early 1980s. Singapore had also flirted with a direct emulation of Japan. Direct or indirect, the Southeast Asian economies all shared with Tokyo a deep involvement of their governments in the business world. The most successful of the Southeast Asian economies, Singapore, and to a lesser extent Thailand, also shared Japan's bureaucratic ideal. Even Indonesia had its bureaucratic technocracy steering the market toward success. "Economic integration" might not seem, at first glance, opposed to the Anglo-American model. But in fact, it posited a new-old model for Asia, one in which Japanese-style industrial policy and gradualism were strategic instruments in the hands of an Asian elite determined to build national strength based on exports and oppose premature market liberalization.

The boldest of Japan's claims, however, was that Japanese manufacturers had "broadened and deepened" the horizontal division of labor in Asia over the decade from the mid-1980s. Late in the decade, the regional production strategies of Japanese multinationals began to include the use of Asian factories as production platforms for export to Japan as well as to industrialized markets elsewhere, in itself a dramatic step. A few Japanese companies began to offer global mandates to their Asian subsidiaries. Matsushita Electric Industrial Co., for example, moved virtually all of its air-conditioning production to Malaysia. Malaysia in turn became the world's largest exporter of air-conditioning equipment, including the sophisticated, electronically controlled air conditioners that dominated the Japanese market.[21]

Japanese observers argued that Japan had played a key role organizing not only regional networks of production but also the rapid increase in levels of intraregional trade flows. According to Hosei University's Yanagihara Toru, "What was unique with the developments over the second half of the 1980s was increased product specialization among countries and formation of a tightly knit network of flows of parts and components, both strategically aligned on a regional scope. The Asia Pacific region has come to function as a conceptually separable regional module in the global strategy of Japanese corporations."[22]

In 1990, Japanese bureaucrats were still squeamish about using such phrases as "union" and "agreement" in connection with the region because it created false parallels, in their view, with the rules-driven European Union (EU) and North American Free Trade Agreement (NAFTA), both still in the process of being finalized. "Economic integration" represented a different concept, and from 1992, the Japanese government enshrined it as official policy. Unlike the EU and NAFTA, the Japanese shied away from rules and force-fed market liberalization. "Regional economic integration" was supposed to be led by the private sector exploiting the comparative advantage of a range of national production sites, from those providing only cheap labor to economies such as Singapore, offering advanced skills in software and finance. In theory, it might be any Asian multinational leading the charge. In fact, the list of Asia's Top 100 companies were almost all Japanese, and even MITI made little secret of the fact that Japanese corporations would be instrumental in the process. Government's role was to nurture, not obstruct. Again, in practice this meant that no country, let alone Japan, was under any obligation to open its markets or to mute in any way the success of its companies.

The intellectual premise was that of Akamatsu—technology and willpower drive growth, not open markets. In the early 1990s, both MITI and MOFA gave their blessing to the Akamatsu or flying-geese model of regional integration, advocating the expansion of transnational manufacturing industries in the Asia-Pacific region coupled with weak institutional development. For a few years, practically every white paper issued by MITI or its affiliate JETRO took note of trends toward the widening and deepening of regional manufacturing networks. An example of the argument comes from the English version of JETRO's 1995 White Paper on International Trade: "Backed up by such trends as deregulation in the direction of injecting foreign capital into East Asian countries and area, the increasing trend toward subdividing manufacturing processes [and] the advancement of information and communications technologies, enterprises are beginning to form a network of division of labor in all of East Asia."

The Japanese government was more than an equal partner in the transnational enterprise. In 1965, roughly 90 percent of Japanese ODA went to Asia. By 1970, the figure increased to 98.2 percent. As Japan's total aid budget grew, the relative share of Asian funding declined, but Asia was still the leading target. In 1992, the percentage figure had dropped to 65 percent, or $7.3 billion out of a total of $11.3 billion.[23] Nonetheless, Japan was still the major source of foreign aid flows in Asia, providing 52.3 percent of the region's total funding.[24] The same year, Japanese private-sector direct investment in Asia was $6.4 billion, about $1 billion less than public money.[25] In 1996, just before the massive influx of aid under the New

Miyazawa Initiative, Japanese aid to Asia as a percentage of its total aid budget had dropped to 46. 5 percent.[26] Nonetheless, Japan supplied 51.5 percent of official aid to China, 76.2 percent to Malaysia, 82 percent to Thailand, and 90.9 percent to Indonesia.[27]

Moreover, the official figures told only part of the story. MITI's Export Import Insurance Division ran the world's largest government trade and investment insurance program. In the 1994 fiscal year, MITI underwrote $70 billion worth of transactions in Asia, 37 percent of its total. The same year Asia accounted for more than 60 percent of MITI's outstanding liabilities.[28] The Japan Export-Import Bank (JEXIM), too, contributed substantial financial backing, through export financing, import finance (for buyers of Japanese capital goods), and loans and loan guarantees to support foreign direct investment (FDI). In FY 1995, cumulative JEXIM financings amounted to $330 billion.[29] One-third represented support for transactions in Asia. The OECF provided loans to Japanese companies in addition to official loans under the ODA program. According to its 1996 Annual Report, between 1961 and FY 1995, nearly half of its private-sector lending was to Asia, about $2.5 billion.[30]

To be sure, no matter how enthusiastic the Japanese bureaucracy was about mingling the Japanese and Asian economies, Tokyo was still a long way from the factories of Asia. The progress toward Asian regional production networks and horizontal division of labor, even among the largest of Japanese companies, was not nearly as swift as the official rhetoric suggested. Nonetheless, Japanese multinationals could bring enormous resources to bear, and when they did move, the effect was massive.

This was clearly what JETRO had in mind with its "network of division of labor in all of East Asia" formed by Japanese companies. The same year that Mitsubishi was launching its conquest of China, Kwan Chi Hung, a Taiwan-born economist who tracked Asian economies for Nomura Research Institute in Tokyo, wrote: "Direct investment has been a major factor driving changes in the industrial structure of Asian countries, and has contributed to a 'flying geese' pattern of economic development in the region. The newly industrialized economies . . . have seen the composition of their trade become more like that of the advanced industrial countries, while the trading structures of China and the ASEAN countries have become more like that of a NIE [newly industrialized economy]. Japan's trade with the developing countries of Asia is also moving away from a North-South pattern of manufactured exports and primary product imports, toward a more horizontal division of labor in manufacturing."[31] Mitchell Bernard and John Ravenhill made the same argument, writing in the journal, *World Politics,* that Japanese business practices led to triangular trade patterns in which "technology and components are sourced from Japan while the finished products are exported to third-country markets, principally to the United States and Japan."[32]

Sales of Japanese manufacturing companies in Asia rose quickly, from $29.7 billion in 1986 to $113 billion in 1994.[33] Far and away the lion's share of these sales went to customers within Asia, mainly other Japanese factories within the vast web of Japanese manufacturing that quickly sprang up in the region. By Japanese standards, their Asian factories were golden. According to a 1996 MITI survey, profits of Japanese manufacturing subsidiaries in Asia accounted for 52.2 percent of global profits of Japanese manufacturers, or $3.7 billion.[34] By the next year, sales of Japanese manufacturing subsidiaries in Asia reached $141 billion (Yen 15 trillion), just behind sales of Japanese subsidiaries in North America, at $148 billion.[35] Meanwhile, the Japanese government was a font of useful information and financial assistance for Japanese companies venturing into the region, with stacks of feasibility studies on new market sectors, government-funded infrastructure development, and direct subsidies for small- and medium-sized Japanese enterprises that wanted to relocate. These strategies, according to Japanese observers, made it possible for Japan to engineer new production networks in Asia that in turn sponsored a rapid increase in intraregional trade flows.

Even with this vast buildup, a signal feature of Japan's Asian factories was that they provided little competition in the markets that mattered most to Japan—Europe, the United States, or the domestic Japanese market. After a decade of massive Japanese investment in Asia, $58 billion between 1985 and 1994, it was 1995 before MITI first began to worry about the impact on domestic production as Japanese subsidiaries diversified their imports and accounted for an increasing volume of "Japanese" exports.[36] Immediately, hysterical articles appeared in the Japanese press decrying the *kudoka,* or hollowing out, of the Japanese economy.

The complaints were wildly exaggerated. Japanese exports to the world in 1994 were $405 billion.[37] In the 1994 fiscal year (ending in March 1995), Japan's Asian factories exported $7.5 billion[38] to the United States, $3.3 billion[39] to Europe, and $18.9 billion[40] back to Japan, mostly in the form of intermediate products, for a total of $29.7 billion[41]—7 percent of the Japanese total. In the same year, Japan sold $30.9 billion[42] in parts and components to its Asian factories. Thus, Japan's Asian factories were hardly stealing exports and jobs from Japan; instead, export sales of Japanese factories in Asia were neatly balanced by exports of Japanese parts and components to the same factories.

Japanese anxieties about *kudoka* were mirrored by U.S. critics such as Clyde Prestowitz who worried that Japan was using its Asian factories as export platforms to escape restrictions aimed at the country itself. Such criticism missed the intense paranoia within Japanese multinationals against allowing their Asian subsidiaries to compete in the rich U.S. and European markets with their own U.S. and European offshoots. But whether Japan was helplessly losing its core industries or shrewdly anticipating U.S. pressure, Asia was playing an increasingly important role in the global scheme of Japanese manufacturing. Japan's Asian manufacturing was leveraging Japanese industry in a way that Japanese manufacturing in North America and Europe did not.

In the early 1990s, the changes unleashed by Japan's economic tilt toward Asia seemed to have the inevitability of a force of nature. It was obvious that Japan's huge economy would overwhelm that of its neighbors: all one had to do was to extrapolate forward. Japan's economy represented three-quarters of all the wealth in Asia. At least in relative terms, it could nearly replace the role of the United States as market and knowledge source and would not compete with Asia's developing economies, as the United States did, in labor-intensive industries, agriculture, or raw materials. The notion of a Japan-centered economic zone began to take hold. In 1990, Sanjoy Chowdhury, the Merrill Lynch economist, said that "Japan is beginning to replace the United States as the center of capital and the market for the rest of the Asian countries."

This was not a casual insight. By the mid-1990s, Japan's economic power in Asia was pervasive. In Southeast Asia, Tokyo dominated the electronics, auto, and retail businesses; its banks, brokers, and insurance companies carpeted the region with their branches; and the *sogo shosha* conducted themselves like feudal baronies. By 1995, all of Asia except China, Brunei, and Indonesia were running huge trade deficits with Japan and all except Brunei were heavily indebted to Tokyo for its soft loans made in the name of development finance. Japan became Asia's most concentrated source of strategic capital, a growing market for intermediate products shipped from the Asian subsidiaries of Japanese multinationals and subcontractors, and a technological supplier of increasing importance.

Geese in Waves

Western economists scorned it, and the Asian crisis blew a hole through its center: Yet, from the mid-1980s to mid-1990s, if not earlier, the spectacular growth of East Asian economies followed very much along the lines of Akamatsu's, Kojima's, and Okita's vision. The patterns that emerged in this period had little to do with Asian values. They were based on the investment strategies of Japanese multinationals and their attendant flocks of subcontractors, evolving over time but always reflecting Japanese priorities and assumptions. By themselves, neither Japanese foreign investment strategies nor domestic industrial policy were adequate to explain the sudden concentration of Japanese resources in Asia. Both worked together. When market forces drove Japanese investors toward East Asia or Southeast Asia, the Japanese government was available to focus, amplify, and sometimes orchestrate their efforts. Government and private sector worked with the understanding that a developing Asia had roles to play as both manufacturing workshop and fast-emerging market for Japanese industry.

Rather than overwhelm Asia, however, Japan surfed on the region's growth wave. Japan attempted to turn circumstances in its favor. If Japanese companies were unable to impose a regional hierarchy of production along the lines suggested by Akamatsu, Okita, and Kojima, perhaps they could influence development in its favor another way—by the Japanese government working directly with governments in the region. As long as credit was free flowing, Japanese companies could put up with low returns and their own often foolish and speculative investments. When the crash came in 1997, however, Tokyo moved to the center of the drama, bailing out its Asian multinationals with massive infusions of cash.

Japanese perceived the outlines of three separate "waves" of Japanese investment between the 1970s and 1990s. To Westerners, the image calls to mind the famous Hokusai print with a tsunami poised over a fragile fishing boat. To the Japanese, it was pure Akamatsu. The "waves" reflected a building crescendo as Asian economies caught up with Japan in serried tiers.

The first "wave" was one in which Japan helped much poorer Asian economies begin to exploit international markets, with *sogo shosha* serving as brokers between Asian resource exporters and global commodity markets. Beginning in 1972, it was minuscule compared with the second and third ones. It was, however, attended by a tiny leap in Japan's total global FDI, from $858 million in 1971 to $2.3 billion in 1972, triggered by the collapse of the Bretton Woods fixed exchange rate system. The oil shocks and undervalued yen, along with capital controls, helped to restrain any greater outpouring, and Japanese global investment ranged from $2.3 billion to $3.8 billion until 1978, when it rose to $4.5 billion.[43] Meanwhile, Japanese investment in Asia rose from $401 million in 1972 (17 percent of the global total) to $1.4 billion in 1978, 23 percent of Japan's global FDI.

This first "wave," reflecting Japan's own rapid graduation from labor- and capital-intensive to knowledge-based industries, had a pronounced tilt toward Southeast Asia. The region no longer figured merely as a source of raw materials, but also as a source of cheap labor and a venue for industries that were so dirty that the Japanese no longer wanted to keep them. From 1973 to 1982, most of Japan's Asian investment went to four ASEAN countries—Indonesia, Malaysia, the Philippines, and Thailand. Cumulative investment in the "ASEAN Four" was nearly double Japanese investment in the Asian NIEs (South Korea, Hong Kong, Taiwan, and Singapore) between 1951 and 1981, $8.6 billion compared to $4.2 billion. Within ASEAN, the leading sectors for Japanese investment were chemicals, textile manufacturing, and mineral extraction. In both Northeast Asia and the ASEAN countries, import barriers forced Japanese investors to enter markets that were still negligible in size.[44] By the late 1970s, Japan was the leading investor in every ASEAN country, but its manufacturing investments were still concentrated in the NIEs. Then as now they were the most industrially sophisticated Asian economies after Japan. As early as the 1960s and 1970s, Japanese manufacturers were developing the NIEs as export platforms in order to avoid trade friction with the United States.[45]

The "second wave" was far more interesting, as Japan broadened its manufacturing investments to include all of Asia and began to engage in a much higher order of technology dispersion through Japanese subsidiaries. These subsidiaries, along with a myriad of subcontractors and Asian joint-venture partners, participated in a radically new process, for Japan, in which headquarters flushed technology through the system as soon as it became even modestly obsolete. The process left Japan as the technological leader, commanding ranks of Asian factories that were not very far behind.

These developments began with the Plaza Accord in 1985 and coincided with a vast surge in Japan's global investment. In 1989, Japanese investment outflows reached a peak of $67.5 billion, declining thereafter with the collapse of the bubble economy. As Japan's global investment spree tapered off, the decline in Japanese investments in Asia was much less than that in North America and Europe. From a high of $33.9 billion in 1989, Japanese investment in the United States dropped to $17.8 billion in 1994. Investment in Europe dropped over the same period from $14.8 billion to $6.2 billion. Investment in Asia, however, rose from $8.2 billion in 1989 to $9.7 billion in 1994. Northeast Asia, which had been on the periphery of the "first wave," was the major target of Japanese investment in the second, at least until the early 1990s. Japanese investment in the NIEs averaged $200–300 million annually in the 1970s. In 1986, it jumped to $1.5 billion (compared to $550 million for ASEAN), and hit $4.8 billion in 1989 (Japanese investment in the ASEAN Four was $2.7 billion that year). The reason for the bias in favor of the Asian NIEs was simply that they were ready with the infrastructure and the skills to augment Japan's drive to capture global markets in knowledge-intensive industries, ranging from flat-screen displays to luxury automobiles. Meanwhile, ASEAN was coming up fast. By 1990, Japanese investment in ASEAN and the NIEs was neck and neck—$3.2 billion and $3.3 billion. The next year, 1991, ASEAN was suddenly way ahead, with $3 billion in Japanese investment compared to $2.2 billion for the Asian NIEs.

The "second wave" of Japanese investment was different from the first in several other respects. For the first time, the panic effect driving Japanese companies to lower labor cost venues in Asia included a sizable number of small- and medium-sized companies. Many were encouraged to make the leap by their government or *keiretsu* patrons, but others simply fled bleak economic conditions at home. Despite Japanese government and corporate efforts to impose some order on the transfer, much of it was disorderly. Many of the smaller companies left behind little more than their administrative headquarters. Some companies moved those, too. One study found that during the 1980s, 60 percent of the "cases" of new Japanese investment in ASEAN was by small- and medium-sized companies.[46]

Kume Gorota, secretary-general of the Japan Institute for Overseas Investment (JOI) wrote that as many as two-thirds of Japanese investments in Asia were by small- and medium-sized enterprises, with 500 to 700 projects per year in the $2–3 million range.[47] With or without the brand-name giants behind the *keiretsu*, this influx of small- and medium-sized companies helped build a critical parts industry without which the Southeast Asian economies would have remained assembly lines for parts makers based in Japan and elsewhere. The birth of a Southeast Asian parts industry was among the most important legacies of the "second wave" and fueled a major expansion of intraregional trade that took off as the Japanese multinationals began trading intermediate parts and components among their Southeast Asian subsidiaries as well as back to their headquarters and home islands factories.

Finally, a "third wave" of Japanese investment that began in 1992–93 targeted the new frontiers for investment in Asia, particularly China. Japanese investment in China went from $349 million in 1990 to $1.7 billion in 1993, and both ASEAN and the NIEs feared the loss of investment to its giant neighbor as well as increased export competition. The "third wave" of Japanese investment coincided with the renewed bout of yen appreciation in the mid-1990s, peaking at 79 yen to the U.S. dollar in August 1995. By that time, Japanese multinationals were finally beginning to abandon the cherished ideal of maintaining employment at home. Blue-chip Japanese companies planned major retrenchments of a type not seen in the post-war era, closing whole factories and moving entire production lines out of the country. The destination for many of these was China.

At the same time, Asia's buoyant economy provided another rationale for moving production in order to gain access to markets. Japanese industry targeted China in this new wave. Japanese investment in China went from $349 million in 1990 to $2 billion in 1994, and ASEAN feared both loss of investment to its giant neighbor and increased export competition.[48] According to a 1995 Bank of Tokyo study of Japanese investment in East Asia, small and medium firms dominated the "third wave" of Japanese investment as they had the second, mainly in textiles but also in machinery, and 70 percent of the investment was directed at China.[49] In a survey of 250 companies conducted by the Nikkei Industry and Consumption Research Institute in February and March 1995, 48 percent said that China was their first choice as an investment location, 33.6 percent Thailand, 16 percent Malaysia, and 14 percent Indonesia. Taiwan and Singapore came in fifth and sixth place, with 11 percent and 10 percent, respectively.[50]

The Japanese saw investment in China as a natural move downstream in the hierarchy of Asian economies. The main motivation for Japanese investment in China, however, was to gain access to its domestic market. According to a 1994 survey by JEXIM, 73.2 percent of Japanese investors thought that the China market would be the most important one for any products they made there.[51] A 1996 Australian study predicted that China and Japan would become each other's most important trading partners in the following two decades.[52] By the mid-1990s, China had become the second-largest destination for Japanese manufacturing investment after the United States.[53]

Even with the shifting emphasis of each "wave," and Japan's heightened interest in China in the 1990s, nowhere was the impact of Japanese investment greater than in Southeast Asia. Japanese investment in manufacturing soared in each of the favored Southeast Asian economies—from $32.7 million in Malaysia in 1985 to $672 million in 1994; from $25.3 million in Thailand in 1985 to $2.55 billion in 1994; and from $66 million in Indonesia in 1985 to $1.56 billion nine years later. The true investment figures may have been much higher. According to MITI, if reinvestment by Japanese manufacturing subsidiaries in ASEAN were factored in, the total was at least double the figure of direct investment. In 1992, Japanese reinvested $4.2 billion compared to $1.8 billion in FDI. In 1993, the figure was $2.8 billion compared to $1.5 billion in FDI. In 1994, the reinvestment figure according to MITI was $2.4 billion compared to $2.2 billion in recorded FDI.[54]

Japan was not, of course, the only actor in this drama. The Thai economist, Pasuk Phongpaichit, observed that the policies of Southeast Asian governments shaped the Southeast Asian transformation as much as Japan did. Following the collapse of oil prices from the early to mid-1980s, Southeast Asia's resource-based economies were mired in a worldwide commodity slump. Many responded by radically overhauling foreign investment regimes that had become highly restrictive, especially during the long-lived commodity boom of the 1970s.[55]

In the early 1990s, host government policies in Southeast Asia shifted again, partly to put the brakes on runaway investment. Some countries, notably Thailand and Malaysia, attempted to tighten foreign investment rules in order to cope with infrastructure bottlenecks and a widespread impression that foreign investment was serving to overheat their economies. Other countries liberalized further, nervous that foreign investors might bypass them in favor of China. In June 1994, Indonesia launched a program to encourage foreign investment, abandoning decades of policies designed to keep foreign investment out of strategic areas of the economy.[56]

South Korea, Taiwan, Hong Kong and Singapore, the so-called Asian NIEs, quickly caught up with Japan in the race to capture Southeast Asia's runaway markets. As early as 1998, the NIEs were investing more in the ASEAN Four than Japan. By 1992, the NIEs' investment in the ASEAN Four was $6.8 billion, compared to $4.5 billion for Japan and $3.5 billion for the United States.[57] In 1993, as the Japanese yen entered another phase of rapid appreciation, Japan leapt ahead of its tiger rivals, with $4.2 billion to their $3.9 billion and $1.6 billion from the United States. Positions were reversed again in 1994, as the NIEs' investment in ASEAN soared to $15.9 billion, mainly due to a surge of Hong Kong investment in Indonesia, while Japan held steady at $4.8 billion.[58]

On the larger map of East Asia, investment by the Asian NIEs was even more frenetic because of a huge bulge of overseas Chinese investment in China in 1992–93, when Beijing accelerated its economic reforms after Deng Xiaoping's famous Southern Tour in Spring 1992. Japan had lagged behind in China, anyway, but by 1993 the Asian NIEs were investing $21.2 billion in China to Japan's $1.3 billion. By 1994, the NIEs were investing $24.9 billion in China to Japan's $2 billion.

Whatever the relationship with Japanese capital and investment, over the decade from the mid-1980s to mid-1990s, there was an explosion in the growth of manufactured exports from ASEAN. In 1995, the Japanese Economic Planning Agency (EPA) began an annual series of reviews of Asian economies. The first of these yearbooks made no secret of celebrating the export boom; it also took time out to castigate American economist Paul Krugman for casting doubt on the Asian miracle in a 1994 article in *Foreign Affairs*. The yearbook highlighted the share of manufacturing in exports of the "ASEAN Four" (Thailand, Malaysia, Indonesia, and the Philippines), which went from 37.4 percent in 1985 to 70.4 percent in 1993. Over the seven-year period from 1985 to 1992, the ratio of manufactured goods to total exports in Indonesia rose from 13.7 percent to 48.5 percent, in Thailand from 41.0 percent to 66.5 percent, and in Malaysia from 31.5 percent to 65.6 percent. Machinery exports over the same period accelerated from 8.8 percent to 26.6 percent of total exports for Thailand and from 18.6 percent to 43.9 percent for Malaysia. Among ASEAN countries, only Indonesia's ratio of machinery exports was paltry and declined, from 0.5 percent to 0.4 percent.[59]

Large as the size of Japanese investment was relative to the ASEAN economies, the strategic aspect of the investment resided not in the scale but the concentration on manufacturing. Japanese industry responded to a harshening manufacturing climate in Japan by choosing Southeast Asia and China as its principal offshore-manufacturing platforms. Since production costs in the NIEs were already prohibitive by the late 1980s, these became the principal focus of the expansion of Japanese manufacturing networks.

From Japan's perspective, too, the rising flow of manufacturing capital to Asia began to have an impact on Japan's domestic industrial structure. The "second" and "third" waves of Japanese investment inaugurated the first hints of internationalization in Japanese manufacturing. The most international of Japanese industries at the start of the 1990s was autos, which had begun exporting production in the 1970s. By 1994, the ratio of overseas production in the transport machinery industry was 20.3 percent (compared to 49.6 percent for the United States and 35.9 percent for Germany). The Japanese electrical equipment industry, concentrated in Asia, was less international than autos, but its ratio of overseas production in 1994 was still higher than the Japanese average, at 15 percent.[60] In 1984, the overseas manufacturing output of Japanese companies represented only 4.2 percent of Japanese gross domestic product. By 1995, the figure had risen to 8.7 percent and JETRO was predicting a rise to 31.3 percent "in the foreseeable future."[61]

To the Japanese, their role in East Asian success was not merely an accident of the market. Rather, the huge Japanese economy had begun to mold its neighborhood directly, and nowhere was this more evident—as far as the Japanese were concerned—than in Southeast Asia. By the early 1990s, the mainstream view in Japan held that Southeast Asia's runaway economic growth in the early 1990s was merely another example of Asian geese racing madly behind the regional leaders, Japan and the NIEs.

Implicit in Japanese thinking was the idea that foreign trade could be organized in two ways: one based on absolute advantage in which nations could only export products that their rivals didn't make, and another in which nations made the same goods but in different proportions based on global profit maximizing. The Japanese idea of "flying geese" was somewhere in-between. In the real world, the Japanese would say, developing economies strive to achieve the second case but never quite make it—by the time they are building television sets, the "leader" is making flat-panel displays. A static analysis would reveal a "vertical" division of labor, with Japan and the next tier of "geese" distributing obsolescent technology to the next-down tiers as they moved up the technological ladder.

Japan's relationship to Southeast Asia was, in fact, more complex than that between headquarters and offshore manufacturing workshops, resource bases, or markets. The influence of government was evident in a variety of ways. First, geopolitics played a major role sanctioning Japan's efforts. In the 1950s, Washington used the carrot of Southeast Asia to wean Japan from its long-established economic partnership with China. Encouraged by the United States, Japan used war reparations, foreign aid, and investment to secure a stable supply of resources for Japanese industry as well as to block the inroads of communism in Southeast Asia. All three "waves" of investment were triggered by sudden lurches in the foreign exchange markets that put pressure on Japanese producers to seek offshore production platforms. When such external shocks forced the transfer of Japanese industries abroad, Japanese government and industry alike sought to ease the pain by re-creating the domestic environment of government-business collaboration.

It made sense, from Tokyo's perspective, to work with other governments to support an orderly, sequential transfer of comparative advantage down through the ranks of developing countries in Asia. Japanese industry would cooperate by concentrating on selected industrial sectors in different countries. A logical political corollary was to present the extension of Japanese business networks in Asia in search of cheap labor in the most benign light possible in order to allay fears that this second invasion by Asia's largest economy would lead to political or military domination.

The late 1980s saw the emergence of an Asian manufacturing pyramid with Japan at the apex. Japan provided high-technology input, while South Korea, Taiwan, Hong Kong, and Singapore served as bases for high-quality manufacturing. Factories in less-developed countries provided the simpler components. Thailand had developed an electronics industry on this model, and Malaysia was fast becoming a center for production of televisions, videocassette recorders, facsimile transmission machines, and other high-tech consumer items. In Singapore, Japanese companies such as Matsushita and Sony were setting up research and design laboratories, helping to reverse the brain drain of local talent abroad. In resource-rich countries such as Thailand and Indonesia, Japanese companies had begun to build downstream petrochemical industries, increasing the value returned to the local economies.

By the mid-1990s, Japanese business leaders, such as Kaku Ryuzaburo, chairman and chief executive officer of Canon, Inc., were looking ahead to the next stage, when Asia's huge markets would be as important as those of the United States and Europe. In 1994, said Kaku in an interview, Canon was only getting 3 to 4 percent of sales from East Asia, out of total sales of $19 billion (Yen 1.933 trillion). But he predicted a huge and growing market for Canon's copiers, computer printers, fax machines, and cameras. By the year 2000, under a program called Asia 10, Kaku planned to raise Asian sales to 10 percent of total sales, a target requiring sales growth of 25 percent per year. "When I look at the future of Asia," the sixty-nine-year-old chairman said rather grandly, sitting in his penthouse boardroom in the silvery tower of Canon's suburban Tokyo headquarters, "its share will be much higher. Asia in the final stage will be equal in importance to North America. Canon will be giving equal play to the markets of North America, Europe, Japan, and East Asia."[62]

In a series of articles under the caption, "Eyes on Asia," Canon's English-language, in-house magazine framed its president, Mitarai Fujio, above a photo spread of Hong Kong harbor. "What excites me most about the Asian market is its diversity. It combines highly developed markets like Hong Kong and Singapore with many that are just emerging," he was quoted. Canon built its first factory in Asia in Taiwan in 1975. By 1995 it had five, which supplied more than half of its overseas manufacturing, or about 15 percent of the company's total output.[63]

Like Mitarai, Kawamoto Nobuhiko, the supercharged, charismatic president of Honda Motor Co., was thinking hard about the Asian consumer market. Honda, together with Toyota Motor Corp., Nissan Motor Co., and Mitsubishi Motors Corp., had announced projects to design and build "Asian cars" for the region. Nonetheless, he said, "If we ask ourselves, do we really know our fellows in Asia, the answer will be no. They are all different. Each is unique. We can't really group them as Asians. We have to learn from them, so that we will really know who they are." One implication, Kawamoto said, was that Honda would be manufacturing for Asians virtually the same cars that it sold in the United States and Europe. "This is an era in which there is excellent information flowing all around the world. The fact that Asians have less income doesn't mean that they will be satisfied with less quality. As long as we take that attitude we will not succeed in Asia. At least Honda will not take that approach." Kawamoto even rejected the term "Asian car," because, he said, it had a pejorative connotation. "It's like looking askance at someone, not looking at Asians as people."[64]

Meanwhile, in Thailand, Southeast Asia's fastest growing car market, Honda led the pack of Japanese companies that dominated the market in the mid-1990s. Of 400 new cars sold every day, the Japanese sold roughly 360. In 1995, total car sales were about 500,000. By the year 2000, the optimists predicted that sales would hit 1,000,000. Until September 21, 1995, Detroit had opted out of the market. That was when one of Thailand's twelve auto-assembly plants began manufacturing its first American car, the Chrysler

Jeep Cherokee. The American firms remained cautious. "I'm from Detroit. It's difficult for people there to imagine what's going on here," Timothy Dunne, an Asian auto industry consultant told the Associated Press. "I tell them about the great things happening in Thailand. But 500,000 units—that equals just two plants running at about full capacity in America. They're accustomed to enormous volumes." [65]

By the mid-1990s, Japanese capital would seem like a drop in the bucket. Early in the decade, Asia emerged as the favored destination for foreign investors worldwide. China and Southeast Asia were the darlings of global investors. In 1995, East Asia absorbed two-thirds of global capital flows— $54 billion of the $90 billion invested in developing countries. China was no. 1, with $38 billion of the total. Improbably, tiny Malaysia, with $6 billion, was no. 2.[66] If official development assistance was added in, that year East Asia accounted for a staggering $108.3 billion, or 47 percent of global "aggregate resource flows" to low- and middle-income countries. Japan sank into the mêlée of global capital, racing into the vortex of the Asian economy in hyperdrive—or, as it turned out, in the final stages of the bubble. Nonetheless, the Japanese would maintain, their investment was unique, because it was consistent with a dynamic momentum inherent in the Asian economies first perceived by Akamatsu and his colleagues. The regional economy was moving in directions unseen since the days of the rising sun's own empire. Only this time around, there would be no banzais or battle fleets, just money. It would be a "nicer" Co-Prosperity Sphere.

A "Nicer" Co-Prosperity Sphere

In 1991 Japan emerged as the world's leading supplier of official development assistance, a status it maintained virtually throughout the decade. Between 1993 and 1997, it spent about $55 billion on foreign aid. Much of this money went into a support program for regional economic integration in Japan's backyard. After the Asian financial crisis, Japan gave up any pretense of evenhandedness, devoting many more billions to shoring up the region's shattered economy.

In the 1990s, the annual budget for Japanese ODA averaged about $13 billion, compared to about $11 billion for the United States, the second largest donor. Japan became a major force in multilateral lending institutions through direct transfers, which made up about one-third of its aid budget. By the mid-1980s, it became the second-largest shareholder in both the World Bank and IMF, and to this one might add the Asian Development Bank (ADB), the principle multilateral lending agency under Japan's direct control. Japan and the United States are co-equal shareholders in the ADB, but the former takes precedence in management. In the 1990s, Japan began promoting its ideas about industrial policy through the Bank and the Fund, but it had never ceased doing so with the ADB. Meredith Woo-Cummings argues that Tokyo consistently used the latter to encourage development in the "flying-geese" mold.[67]

Japanese officials, particularly those of MITI, often spoke as though the nation had been extraordinarily prescient in devoting so much of its foreign aid program to Asia. The region's robust growth, they argued, was proof that Japan's money had been well spent. Through most of the 1990s, MITI's annual white papers on the economy urged that Japan continue to focus funds for "economic cooperation" on its immediate neighborhood. The 1994 MITI White Paper, for example, claimed that it was Japan's responsibility to support "ongoing self-help efforts" by the Asian economies to maintain their "growth dynamism." [68]

The strategic focus of Japanese aid shifted along with its increase in scale. In the 1970s, efforts had been made to package Japanese aid for Southeast Asia for political reasons, partly to quell resentment after the "first wave" of Japanese investment in the 1970s. The late 1980s saw the rise of a new approach, emphasizing the use of aid funds to pursue a master plan of regional development. In the early 1990s, the Japanese also began to urge host countries to study the methods of Japanese industrial policy. An early, controversial MITI paper had expressed Japan's role as an "Asian Brain." Japanese bureaucrats were evidently to play the role of "brain," as in the 1988 policy study from Japan's EPA, which first used the phrase in a document entitled *Promoting Comprehensive Economic Cooperation in an International Economic Environment Undergoing Upheaval: Toward the Construction of an Asian Network*. Describing the paper, the *Economist* observed in 1989, "The Japanese government is now committed to taking the initiative in promoting greater regional economic cooperation, starting in East and Southeast Asia. It would do so not on the basis of bilateral economic relations or even with ASEAN as a block, but by regarding Japan, the NICs [newly industrializing countries] and the new NICs as one economy."[69]

The spur for this new line of thinking was the 1985 Plaza Accord and the subsequent rise of the yen. Japanese business was thrown into considerable consternation by the "*endaka* shock." Companies realized that they would have to radically lower production costs in order to maintain market share and that the quickest way to do it was by moving offshore. This was the cue for MITI to step in with the New Asian Industries Development Plan (New AID Plan).

MITI described the Plan as "an aid program aimed at supporting economic development through industrialization in Asian countries, which these countries strongly desire. The basic concept of the Plan is the effective linkage of numerous measures, under close consultation with these countries, such as Japan's technical assistance, financial aid, investment promotion and import promotion in Japan."[70] From MITI's point of view, the New AID Plan attempted to create an industrial plan for Asia that would harmonize with the needs of Japanese industry as it made its bumpy, yen-induced exit from Japan. Modeled after Japan's own planning system, the New AID Plan prescribed phased industrial development over a period of five years from 1987 to 1992. In the first phase, MITI was to help each of the recipient countries formulate master plans for export development, beginning with Thailand and Malaysia in 1986, moving on to Indonesia and the Philippines, Pakistan, Bangladesh, and Sri Lanka.

In a second phase, Japanese advice would concentrate on development programs for specific industries. A MITI handout described this phase as a "transfer of industry promotion policy." Examples included, for Thailand, molds and dies, toys, textiles and garments, furniture, ceramics, and processed plastic goods. For Malaysia, the list was ceramics, molds and dies, office automation equipment, rubber footwear, personal computers, and foundries. For Indonesia, handicrafts, rubber-based products, electrical machinery, plastics, aluminum downstream products, and ceramics were listed. And for the Philippines, metal engineering, wooden furniture, computer software, oleochemical, fashion accessories, and toys were indicated. A third phase was to focus on the dispatch of experts and trainees, "project-type" technical cooperation, and the development of industrial estates and yen loans.

In 1990, when Bernard Wysocki, Jr., Tokyo bureau chief for the *Wall Street Journal*, paid a visit to the MITI office in charge of making up the master plans, he found a stack of documents with "blueprints for new industries ranging from rubber sneakers to color-television picture tubes." The most elaborate one was a seventy-page planning document for Malaysia that aimed to make it a major producer of word processors, answering machines, and facsimile devices. Seki Noboru, then section chief, told Wysocki, "We deeply hope that these will be the most important industries in Asia." In its headline, the *Wall Street Journal* referred to the Japanese scheme as a "nicer coprosperity sphere." Wysocki's offered a concise description of the way the New AID Plan worked:

> First, Japanese loans, mostly of government money, build up roads, bridges and such. Second, the Japanese government sends technical experts. Third, Japanese loans filter down to industry within the Asian country, to finance joint ventures and other business alliances. Fourth, Japan opens its doors to imports from these offshore strategies.
>
> More important than the amount of money is the methodical and so-

phisticated manner in which it is being spent. Far from using a case-by-case approach to foreign aid and investment, Japanese government and corporate strategists speak about shaping and even "coordinating" the economic development of the region. Implicit in this view is a division of labor. For example, as MITI sees it, Indonesia will pay special attention to textiles, forest products and plastics. Thailand will focus on furniture, toys and die-cast molds. And Malaysia will concentrate on sneakers, copiers and television picture tubes.[71]

How did the recipient countries react to Japanese advice under the New AID Plan? Not with unmixed enthusiasm. Liew Sew Yee, president of the Malaysian Plastic Manufacturers Association, told journalist Doug Tsuruoka of the *Far Eastern Economic Review* that Japanese assessments were often "colored by wholly Japanese views of Malaysia's productive capacity and resources." Others told Tsuruoka that they feared the "implied threat of not following Japanese advice." Saying no to Japan was "tantamount to committing suicide," they said.[72]

Bold though the New AID Plan was, it led a short and troubled existence. MITI Minister Tamura Hajime formally launched the program in January 1987 during a visit to Indonesia. Tamura told President Suharto that Japan was changing the focus of its aid program to the development of export industries.[73] His comment quickly drew fire from a number of sources. Washington suspected that Japan was attempting to shift its exports to third countries in order to avoid pressure to open its own market further. ASEAN, too, was uneasy with the program. Finally, MITI's venture ran into funding problems. In December 1987, the Japanese Foreign Ministry, which had its own Economic Cooperation Bureau, launched a $2 billion ASEAN-Japan Development Fund to foster joint ventures in high-technology fields. The MITI economic cooperation division and its Foreign Ministry counterpart had long been rivals, so the announcement of the parallel Foreign Ministry plan, together with its funding, signaled a triumph for the Foreign Ministry in the bureaucratic battle for control of the Asian program.

Funding for the New AID Plan was stymied as a result. No specific budget was ever associated with it. Danny Unger, an American political scientist who interviewed Japanese officials on the subject, claimed that the plan was "never formally endorsed" and Japanese foreign aid never achieved the high level of coordination suggested by early versions of the plan.[74] MITI officials themselves, including ones who worked on the original New AID Plan, were vague about what had become of it. In a 1995 interview, Kitayama Shigeru, an official in MITI's Economic Cooperation Division who had helped to draft the New AID Plan, described it as enjoying a bureaucratic afterlife. Elements of the plan, he said, were still in place even though the program itself was no longer in existence. In fact, the strategic concepts behind the New AID Plan had become ubiquitous. As an example of the way the New AID Plan philosophy colored Japanese pronouncements on Asia, Chino Tadao, then the administrative vice-minister for International Finance, told the *New York Times* that Japan would "increasingly use its aid . . . as seed money to attract Japanese manufacturers or other industrial concerns with an attractive investment environment." Edward Lincoln, a Brookings Institution economist, quotes a Japanese academic specialist on aid saying that the "easiest way to help other countries create export industries is for Japanese corporations to set up operations in them."[75] MITI seemed to identify so completely with the interests of Japanese industry in Asia that it included Asian economic cooperation in its budgetary request for "research and development" funds to promote industrial restructuring during this period.

There can be little doubt that Japan actively pursued an industrial policy in Asia. How much of an impact its policies had is open to question, however. Japanese business executives scoffed at the idea that their government had much to do with their own appetite for investing in Asia. The government's role, said some analysts, was merely to support decisions already made by business. Richard Doner, a political scientist at Emory University in Atlanta, argued that the Japanese government's role had been one of "promoting collective action toward goals already embraced by the private sector" rather than steering the show.

Indeed, Japanese investment in Southeast Asia was not monolithic, static, or even particularly loyal, all qualities that might be expected of a strategy to set up long-term manufacturing colonies in the region. The favorites of Japanese investors in Southeast Asia in the late 1980s did not remain favorites for long. Moreover, Japanese production networks went through fundamental changes once they moved offshore, even in developing countries where the Japanese had relatively strong leverage. The Canadian economist Wendy Dobson found that the behavior of Japanese electronics firms in Southeast Asia was less different than might be supposed from U.S. firms, which followed a similar cycle but with an earlier start. She writes: "Fierce global competition in the industry is forcing non-Japanese firms into network patterns to achieve efficiencies comparable to Japanese producers, while local governments are beginning to require more open procurement behavior which will open up the Japanese networks."

How deep, in fact, was the Japanese imprint? Did Japan actually shape regional development and forge a model of capitalism in its image? If so, one country after another should have used exports to climb a technological and productivity ladder. In fact, only South Korea was able to duplicate Japan's trajectory in technology, and none of the East Asian economies showed impressive gains in productivity. Japan's own protectionist habits inhibited East Asian growth.

Paradoxically, during a decade when Japan embraced a vision in which it was at the center of a regional transformation, trade statistics indicated that Japan was actually becoming less integrated into the regional Asian trading system, not more. As Asia boomed, the Japanese economy remained relatively closed to imports. Its exports to Asia soared, largely as a function of its shipment of plants and equipment. Naturally, governments in the region complained. While the region's total trade with Japan by the mid-1990s was 50 percent larger than its trade with the United States, exports were overwhelmingly in Japan's favor. Japan's trade surplus with Asia overtook its highly political trade surplus with the United States in 1991, and continued to increase steadily. By 1997, Japan's trade surplus with Asia, including China, was $75 billion; the same year, the United States was running a $54 billion deficit with Asia, excluding Japan.[76]

In 1990, 14.5 percent of the region's exports went to Japan, according to IMF figures. In 1993, the figure dropped to 12.3 percent. In 1997, as the Asian financial crisis was breaking, Japan absorbed 11.6 percent of the region's exports, compared to 19.6 percent for the United States.[77] This steady descent occurred despite continual proclamations by MITI and JETRO about opening of the domestic market and despite a substantial increase in intraregional trade. Intraregional exports excluding Japan grew from 31.7 percent to 34.9 percent between 1990 and 1993. Meanwhile, China was fast emerging as an important export market for the region—its share of regional exports went from 4.7 percent of total exports to 9 percent between 1993 and 1995.

Luck, too, played a significant role in Japanese investment patterns in East Asia, as well as the value of the yen. Southeast Asia, China, and Vietnam became enthusiastic participants in the global reform movement sweeping developing countries after the Latin American debt crisis of the early 1980s. Developing countries flocked to raise the free-market standard raised by the World Bank, among others, rejecting a wide range of policies lumped together under the banner of "import substitution."[78] For Japan, the reform movement coincided neatly with a major exchange-rate problem after the Plaza Accord.

Japanese companies might have ended up paying no more than lip service to their government's rah-rah if it had not been for the extraordinary success of those initial ventures. "Usually, Japanese companies are very cautious. They want to start their businesses small, and expand only once the market is proven. In the case of Malaysia, they planned their entry very cautiously. But then they found they were meeting their three- to four-year targets in two years.

They were very surprised. Headquarters found that they had better shift their operations here. This was the case of most Japanese companies here," Hayase Koichi, a former JETRO official in Kuala Lumpur, told me in 1992.[79]

Asia's strongest lure prior to the Asian currency crash was not easy money but profitability. Both MITI and the JEXIM minutely tracked the activities of Japanese companies abroad, which were published in annual surveys. One of the many criteria reviewed was the profitability of overseas ventures, and throughout the 1990s these studies were showing far higher profitability rates in Japan's Asian subsidiaries than anywhere else in the world. MITI's report for 1997, for example, showed profit ratios of 4.1 percent in the Asian manufacturing subsidiaries of Japanese companies versus 2 percent for North America and 1.3 percent for Europe.[80]

To give an idea of how closely MITI, in particular, tracked these numbers, take its 1997 "basic" survey of Japanese affiliates abroad. This massive tome (which had a price tag of Yen 23,800) was 751 pages long, with most of the text taken up by detailed answers to survey questions. The report was compiled by a statistical team in MITI's Industrial Policy Bureau, and for anyone who took the time to wade through it, the volume was a trove of information.[81] Particularly clear was the huge traffic in components trade between Japan and Asia, and the relatively large share of Asian manufactures leaving the region, compared to Europe and North America. Roughly a quarter of the output of Japanese factories based in Asia was exported, just under Yen 3 trillion in the 1995 fiscal year, compared to 7.2 percent of the output of Japanese factories in North America and 8.2 percent for Europe. Moreover, the total sales of Japan's Asian factories were getting ever closer to sales of Japan's North American factories. In 1995, Japan's Asian manufacturing sales had reached Yen 12 trillion compared to Yen 14.6 trillion in the United States.[82]

When all was said and done, the "waves" of Japanese investment might not have been a conclusive factor behind the Asian boom but had done an excellent job of shaping the Asian economy in ways serving the interests of Japanese multinationals. In the mid-1990s, Japanese companies dominated the Asian auto and electronics sectors as well as banking. Japanese trading companies served Asian economies as they had Japan a generation earlier— providing co-financing and technological support as well as global distribution for Asian products.

Prior to the financial crash of 1997, Asia's success provided ample proof to the Japanese that the geese were flying in unison. The theme of flying geese was a morality play in addition to all its other uses and celebrated Asian discipline and triumph in counterpoint to the sad blundering of that icon of individualism, the American eagle. In 1990, the United States seemed to be running on a suicidal track with its economy in disarray, financial mar-

kets prey to con artists on a grand scale, and citizens blindly spending despite it all. Japanese savings were bankrolling an Asian renaissance and propelling the country's economy to world leadership. True, U.S. imports
continued to power Asian growth, but they did so at the expense of the future
prosperity of its citizens. From a Japanese perspective, Americans were using tomorrow's dollars to purchase today's pleasure, a practice that would
inevitably pile debt upon debt and lead to financial ruin, while the Japanese
and other Asians saved their way to prosperity.

While Asians basked in the sun of Japanese largesse, Americans whim-
pered about the loss of such national icons as Columbia Pictures, Rockefeller
Center, and the Pebble Beach Golf Club, swept away by a tide of Japanese
money. Americans resented Japan, because it threatened their prestige and
hegemony. Asians welcomed it, with reservations, because they recognized
the promise Japan held out to share in the birth of a new regional economy,
fueled by the region's vast savings, inspired by traditional values of cooperation and discipline. The mantle of global economic power was about to pass
to a confederation of neighbors allied to the Japanese model. Tokyo's second
invasion, unlike the first, would engulf the region in spontaneous acclaim to
the splendor of Japan's vision.

This was the Japanese myth of the early 1990s. The reality, of course, was
far different. The United States was on its way to re-inventing itself, seizing
Japanese examples in outsourcing and inventory management and exploiting its early lead in information technology as well as the newest of new
things called the Internet. Asians indeed welcomed the astonishing influx of
capital, not only from Japan but from South Korea, Taiwan, Singapore, Europe, and the United States, but they would come to regret the burden it put
on their legal and financial systems.

In any event, Asians saw no point in worrying about a Japanese invasion.
The whole region was growing so rapidly that there was room enough for
everybody. Asian confidence was at a peak. The idea that Japan or any other
foreign entity could dominate and control such a huge, diverse area, with its
fast-expanding economies, was ludicrous. Even in the early days of the capital boom, when Japanese investment predominated, Asians seemed blasé.
"Japanese control? We worry about it, but not to the extent that we break out
in a rash," said Steven Wong, head of the Japanese program at the Institute of
Strategic and International Studies in Kuala Lumpur in a 1990 interview.
"The American monster created the whole sensitivity about control by
transnational corporations. Now we're dealing with a different kind of
transnational corporation. We haven't evolved what we think about the Japanese multinationals yet. But we think they are trying to make themselves
more accommodating. I think there are fewer problems between Japanese

and Southeast Asians than there are between Japanese and Caucasians," he mused. "Sometimes I wonder how much of this is driven by ethnicity."[83]

And yet, arguably, of all the varied pack of foreign investors, portfolio managers, investment bankers, and manufacturers buzzing around Asia like a swarm of voracious bees, none left an imprint as deep as the Japanese. Asians did not have to accept the eccentric Japanese vision of flying geese to be swept into it. A huge flotilla of Japanese multinationals, smaller enterprises, and their government had organized itself around the flying-geese model, placing investments and spending their cash in ways consonant with the vision of an Asia swooping in orderly tiers toward the heights of wealth and power. The cumulative effect was to shape Asian growth at a crucial stage, galvanizing a process of rapid industrialization that would turn Asian economies from commodity exporters to manufacturing powerhouses in the economic blink of an eye.

4

Tsunami

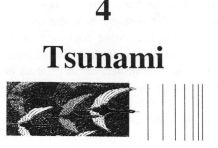

"Call me Eiko," Lin Hsiuying trills in Japanese as she bows a greeting to two distinctly non-Japanese customers. My friend Daniel Chang and I have dropped by the Volvo Club on a cold January night in 1990. Lin's greeting didn't bother my companion, who was Chinese, young, and male, as were most of the customers at the Volvo—a knockoff of a famous Hong Kong club located in a sleazy part of Taipei, crowded with ersatz barber parlors offering recreational massage. Daniel was so immersed in the craze for Japanese culture and business that a hostess speaking in Japanese at a Hong Kong–inspired club was perfectly normal to him. He worked for a Japanese company, Hotai Motor, an affiliate of Toyota, and claimed that the club was popular with expatriate Japanese businessmen. But the cacophony rising from the floor was distinctly Chinese, with hostesses providing most of the Japanese-language content in the form of honorifics and coy invitations to imbibe.

Eiko-san quickly organized a table, Daniel's private bottle of scotch, and bright conversation. As in most Japanese pubs, music was provided by the customers, crooning vocals to the tunes emanating from a *karaoke* machine, helped by a television monitor with the text of the lyrics and actors and actresses holding hands and loping along beaches in the sunset. Sometimes two or three singers would buoy each other's courage by standing up to the machine together. Concerned when I admitted my inexperience, Eiko hustled me to a tiny stage, where we sang "House of the Rising Sun," in English, drowned by the clamor of a boozy, happy crowd. This easy trilingualism was a trademark of the neighborhood. Every tiny bar and barber shop on the block had signs in Japanese and Chinese—most, like the Volvo, beckoning customers to revel in *karaoke;* the Chinese characters for the word "ka la" whimsically joined to the English letters, "OK."[1]

At the beginning of the 1990s, Eiko and Daniel were part of an extraordinary mosaic taking shape across Asia, members of a new subculture whose epicenter was Tokyo, not Washington or Paris or London. Working for a

Toyota affiliate was not just another job for Daniel. Eiko lit up when she learned that I lived in Tokyo and told me about her Japanese lessons and her hopes to work for a Japanese company. Young Asians were swamping Japanese-language schools. Signs for them were visible in every Asian capital, and in Tokyo, Asians made up 90 percent of the foreign student population, mostly enrolled in these establishments. Their number had grown nearly three-fold in a decade, from a scant 10,000 in the 1970s to 28,000 in the late 1980s.

After English, Japanese was the language of choice for upwardly mobile Asians willing to invest time in foreign language study. In a Korean street market, in department stores in Hong Kong's Causeway Bay, and along Orchard Road in Singapore, Koreans and Chinese and Southeast Asians could chat comfortably in Japanese, either as part of their livelihood or for pleasure. In 1990, "to be able to speak Japanese is regarded as very cosmopolitan," said Steven Wong, then an economist at the Center for Japanese Studies at the Institute of Strategic and International Studies in Kuala Lumpur. The mystique was based not only on perceptions of Japan's economic strength but also on the attractions of its popular culture, retail brands, television shows, and teenage music idols. Asian women followed the fashions of Tokyo office ladies. In Seoul and Taipei, tens of thousands of parabolic dishes were aimed at the NHK satellite, the Japanese government's broadcast network. Why were Asians so fascinated by Japan? Explained Rosano Barack, a Japanese-trained Indonesian entrepreneur: "They have the power." Japan had a buzz, the way a brand-new skyscraper might in the center of town. What had been in the background of everyone's minds was suddenly visible. Japan's immense resources were suddenly focused on Asia, and suddenly accessible to Asians too, in a way that they had not been before.

Of all the signs of a Japanese cultural invasion in the early 1990s, the most ubiquitous was *karaoke*. As in Taipei, in most parts of Asia the entertainment was not just a new type of electronic equipment or pastime; it maintained an association with Japan that enhanced its popularity. In Jakarta the *karaoke* scene had become localized to the extent that certain bars were identified as favored by the Batak, Sundanese, or Javanese ethnic groups. In Singapore, a Buddhist temple used *karaoke*, with Buddhist hymns and temple scenes on laser disks to keep the faithful happy. On Temple Hill in Suzhou, China, a sign advertised a local *karaoke* competition behind a guarded barrier at its base.

Karaoke has become "a marker of the modern Asian community," wrote Koh Buck Song, a columnist for Singapore's *Straits Times*. It "is so much a feature of the Asian community now, from Housing Board block parties to the Asia Bagus singing contest, that it explodes the myth of Eastern inscrutability." This was not the least of his claims—Koh considered *karaoke* as the harbinger of a new, collectivist "democracy" that Westerners did not understand. "*Karaoke*'s fascination lies in its democratic character," he argued. "It allows anyone to be the star of the moment. Anyone can use it to snap out of vicarious MTV-zombie mode to immerse self in microphone, musicality and mood. . . . *Karaoke* home sets have been introduced in such countries as the United States, but Westerners have yet to catch on. . . . Outside organized religion and mass spectator sports, there are few other small-group activities that bring people together like *karaoke* can. . . . *Karaoke* in Asia has contributed, however tenuously, to the building of community. And the public communion it represents could well make it the single most important unifier and leveler of our time."[2]

The reality was less dramatic than the rhetoric but astounding enough for what it was. An Asian community was coming together in the early 1990s as a spontaneous reaction to the influx of Japanese wealth. Other Asians eagerly soaked up the material culture of a country whose success they hoped to emulate. Much as the American dream had inspired their parents' generation, young Asians looked to Japan to build on its unfolding economic relationship with Asia. They looked to Japan to embrace them, as they were ready to embrace Japan. They were not to be requited, however. This was not the American dream of democracy for all, but one in which Japan assumed a technological and cultural superiority vis-à-vis its Asian neighborhood in which social leveling was not in the cards. Even in pondering Japan's Asian roots, Tokyo's intellectuals were far from considering an easy conviviality with living, breathing Chinese, Koreans, Malaysians, Filipinos, or Thais. In the late 1980s and early 1990s, Tokyo's perspective on the new Asian "zone of common logic" was that of a partnership for industrial growth, not a movement toward social or political rebalancing, and the view reflected one of Japan's basic strengths as well as a fundamental flaw. The warmth that the Japanese professed toward Asians was the kind one might have for a business partner, not a friend. These were the best kind of business friends, however, presiding over a strategic alliance to beat the world.

The partnership made its greatest impact in the developing countries of the Asia Pacific, in the region referred to by both Chinese and Japanese as the "Southern Seas." As the 1990s began, Japanese auto and electronics companies moved into Southeast Asia like elephants in a cane field, creating whole new industries as they tramped across economies specializing in labor-intensive assembly operations and agriculture. A single Japanese electronics company, Matsushita, set up so many factories in Malaysia that, by the early 1990s, it accounted for 3 percent of gross domestic product (GDP). Along with the manufacturers came retailers introducing to Asians a taste for luxury that the Japanese had only recently acquired for themselves during the late-1980s "bubble economy." Japanese banks followed their domestic clients to

Asia, helping to create a solid phalanx of *keiretsu*-driven business in the region. Leading the invasion were the trading companies that escorted their *keiretsu* partners through the unfamiliar maze of Asian family companies and family-run governments.

The circumstances of Japan's domestic economy helped trigger and sustain the tidal wave of Japanese investment during the decade and a half beginning in the early 1980s. The tsunami crested first in Hong Kong, Singapore, South Korea, and Taiwan, washed across the developing economies of Southeast Asia, and finally swept through China and Vietnam. Rapid yen appreciation meant that Japanese companies could no longer count on being bailed out of a tight spot by submissive subcontractors, docile unions, and consumers' blind acceptance of high prices. They had to move more and more production offshore, but as they did so they received a huge boost from the policy driving the speculative bubble, as the Japanese central bank attempted to use monetary expansion to ease pressure on the yen and soften the pain of higher export prices.

The high yen slashed the cost of imports, particularly fuel, and removed any threat of inflation. In the late 1980s, Japanese multinationals could borrow money at negative real interest rates—in other words, the banks were paying them to borrow money. Within Japan, this combination drove the creation of an asset bubble of staggering proportions. Japanese real estate and stock prices escalated so rapidly that in nearly every category except the real economy, its citizens suddenly had the biggest of everything—the largest companies and banks, the world's largest stock market, the most expensive land. Japanese exporters built up a huge balloon of dollar earnings.

The sudden cresting of Japanese investment in Southeast Asia came as Japanese business deployed cash from earnings as well as borrowed cash during the overheated speculative years. In mid-1989, the Bank of Japan changed course and gradually increased interest rates. The bubble ended in the first few trading days of 1990, when the stock market began a lengthy and precipitous decline, followed shortly by a real-estate crash. Thereafter, Japanese banks and investors helped to re-create the conditions of the domestic financial markets in Asia, leveraging off the difference between low domestic interest rates and much higher rates in most of Asia to invest in property and real estate.

If Japan's Asian empire had depended solely on a continuing outflow of Japanese capital, it would have come to an end in the early 1990s, when Japanese banks were faced with the spiraling debt created by the twin crashes of the domestic property and equity markets. Well before the Asian financial crisis, Japanese banks had retrenched from Asia in order to shore up their balance sheets at home. Instead of stopping, however, the transfer of

Japanese manufacturing to Asia accelerated in the early and mid-1990s. Much of the new investment was based on the re-invested earnings of Japanese subsidiaries. A renewed surge of yen appreciation in the mid-1990s sent new contingents to Asia from the vital Japanese parts industries as well as the flagship multinationals.

By late in the decade, Japan's Asian industrial colonies were a source of hidden strength to the domestic Japanese economy, sustaining profits at some of its premier companies and providing what little life existed in domestic consumption by filling the shelves of the discount retailers with inexpensive clothing and electronics. The Japanese distribution system continued to be biased against foreign imports. But the Japanese-branded products of Japanese companies based in Asia leapt over such barriers. When the Asian crisis struck in 1997, the sharp decline in both Japanese imports and exports to Asia reflected the degree to which trade with Asia was dominated by product flow within Japanese companies. The crisis made it much more expensive for manufacturers in Thailand, Indonesia, or South Korea to import Japanese components, which meant fewer products flowing back to Japan. For the first time, Japan recognized not only that it dominated the Asian economy but that the Asian economy dominated Japan. Interdependence engendered strength but also vulnerability.

Akamatsu's geese were never far behind the Japanese multinationals venturing into Asia in the 1980s and 1990s. The metaphor of the flying geese provided a blueprint for coordinated regional production that could be used even when the target was the domestic market, not exports. Japanese electronics companies, operating in policy environments that encouraged exports, employed strategies based on the Akamatsu notion of yoking competing economies to the international market. The big Japanese car companies, on the other hand, inverted the equation. They were determined to prevent Asian carmakers from following the path set by the Koreans, who had used Japanese technology to enter the North American and European markets. The individual Asian markets, however, were so tiny that it was nearly impossible to achieve efficient economies of scale, and technical levels were so low that it was a struggle to achieve sufficient quality to export components to Japan. So the carmakers used the Akamatsu model to create a regional components industry, based on competition among Asian host countries for investment as well as for export earnings. When the Asian crisis came along, Japanese auto manufacturers based in Asia suffered because they were tied to the local market. The lesson was learned, however, and the companies revised their strategies to accommodate the first exports of finished cars to the international market, albeit primarily to other developing countries. The Japanese electronics companies sailed through the financial crisis in 1997 and never looked back, stumbling only when global technology markets crashed in the year 2000.

Ten years earlier, around the time of Chinese New Year in 1990, it became my job to piece together a new map of Asia under the influence of Japan. I looked at Japanese electronics companies, carmakers, retailers, banks, and the trading companies. The picture that emerged was surprising. However wealthy Japanese multinationals might be, they were insecure in their Asian possessions. Their influence with governments was limited. It took hard work and was expensive to persuade Japanese subcontractors to follow their *oyagaisha* (their parent companies in *keiretsu* groupings), but once they made the move, the subcontractors more readily broke ranks and worked for rivals in ways that would have been unthinkable in Japan. Asia was a daunting environment for the Japanese. They were anything but masters of their Asian universe.

Japan's new role and presence in Asia abounded in paradox. The Japanese grew their offshore presence organically. Their patience—whether dealing with Asian governments or time horizons of their investments—was legendary. These advantages stemmed from domestic Japanese institutions and structures—the *keiretsu* system, cartels, and relational banking—that were already crumbling under the forces of globalization sweeping across Japan and Asia together. The same characteristics that made Japanese investors seemingly invincible juggernauts in their geographic neighborhood weakened their ability to respond quickly to market forces and upgrade their own economy to meet new challenges of the global marketplace.

In the developing economies of Asia, however, the strengths of the Japanese outweighed their weaknesses. The influx of Japanese investment coincided with host country strategies fostering rapid industrialization, almost by definition friendly to Japan because they were so closely modeled on the Japanese example. Meanwhile, the way Japanese investors played out their strategies reflected far more experiment than premeditation. If the flying-geese model was on the minds of Japanese managers—Tokyo cited it as a holy creed—in practice the investors did not always flock together or seem to expect others to do so. The fact that such patterns emerged over time perhaps owed as much to accident as to the nationalistic psychology that lay behind the metaphor. Yet, emerge they did, and even under the duress of the Asian financial crisis the vigor of the Japanese manufacturing networks in Asia proved that Akamatsu had caught on to something.

Electronics: "Just Behind Japan"

It is January 1990. Across the gleaming white factory floor—so spotless that a microbe would stand out like an oil spill—a robot car glides, gently beeping. Yokoo Kensuke, managing director of Matsushita Electric Industrial Co.'s brand-new Malaysian color television factory—the company's fortieth factory overseas—is bragging with a candor unusual in a Japanese: "We are just behind Japan here," he says. "We are a little ahead of the United States."[3]

In 1990, electronics made up 50 percent of Japanese merchandise exports, and Japan reigned supreme in the global electronics industry. Japanese electronics companies had taken over the markets for consumer electronics, followed by semiconductor chips, materials, and equipment. They were poised to repeat their success in information technology, office systems, and telecommunications.

The factory with the robots had only been open for two months. Along with its commissioning in November 1989 had come a global mandate to export color television sets, in the 14-inch to 21-inch range. Yokoo was getting ready to ship product to Japan the following September and talked about the prospect with all the nervous anxiety of a gallery owner trying to shop works of an unknown painter to the Louvre. As we walked, he pointed out the features making the Matsushita Television Co. plant the most advanced in Malaysia—printed circuit boards made by cauterized insertion machines to minimize defects, the robots, computer quality checks. This would be Matsushita's second offshore factory to make color TVs for the Japanese market. The first was in the United States, and according to Yokoo, very much behind the Malaysian facility.

Later, seated in a reception room, over iced coffee, Yokoo told me why Matsushita picked Malaysia for this plant. "This is the first time we have tried building a plant with this level of technology from scratch. We considered Malaysia, Singapore, and Thailand. There were four reasons why we chose Malaysia. First, the government is very, very aggressive. The prime minister has a 'Look East' policy, which favors Japan. Second, the infrastructure here is very healthy, compared with Thailand. Third, the language—most people speak English, as opposed to Thailand. Fourth, it's really easy here to collect the components and parts we need to make TVs. We began the feasibility study in January 1988, and made the decision in April. It was really quick."

Malaysia did not offer better treatment to Japanese investors than to those of other nationalities, although the government might tinker with the rules from time to time to favor specific projects, which might be Japanese. What the government did provide was a familiar, comfortable, operating environment for Japanese companies. As Japan was in the 1950s and 1960s, Malaysia became heaven for companies manufacturing goods for export. In the 1980s, Malaysia re-tuned its regulatory structure from the import-substitution model of the 1960s and 1970s to a policy of selective liberalization. The door remained closed to imports in industries Malaysia hoped to cultivate, such as autos, but wide open to virtually any company wishing to export. Thus, Malaysia allowed companies with high export ratios—the minimum was 80 percent of sales—to exercise 100 percent control of their subsidiaries. For any greater access to the domestic market, companies had to give up part of their equity to local partners. Malaysia's rule was lenient compared to Thailand's, for example, which required companies with 100 percent ownership to export 100 percent as well.

There were other boons for exporters, Yokoo said. Corporate tax was zero for five years, compared to the usual 30 to 35 percent. Matsushita could apply for another exemption after that, although it would have to show proof that the company was both generating exports and transferring technology to Malaysia. If the Malaysian government was displeased with Matsushita's performance, it could apply all sorts of corrective pressure—for example, by putting restrictions on the number of Japanese expatriates.

Dealing with the Malaysian government on this level was utterly familiar to the Matsushita organization, because the role was identical to the one that MITI had played during Japan's own salad days of double-digit growth. MITI, too, had rewarded successful exporters with tax incentives, subsidized loans, and grants of foreign exchange; it, also, had discretionary powers to punish companies that would get out of line. And in Malaysia, the interest in Japan started at the top, with a prime minister who was a frequent visitor to Tokyo and had a son working for a Japanese bank. "The difference between the attitude in the United States and here is that this government is trying to learn from Japan, which you certainly can't see in the United States. That's why we are saying we are proud to export from here," Yokoo said.

By 1990, Matsushita's industrial colony in Shah Alam was already close to the size of its headquarters in Kadoma City, a gritty industrial suburb on the outskirts of Osaka. I visited several other Matsushita factories that day, such as the largest air-conditioner factory in the world, and its story was interesting too. The original factory, commissioned in 1972, was designed to satisfy demand in the domestic market. In 1987, however, Matsushita added a second factory making rotary compressors and motors. The factory complex made everything locally except for raw materials such as oil, metal sheets, and plastic resins, according to J. Singam, the general manager. "We are really a manufacturing plant," Singam emphasized. "We are not an assembly plant."[4]

In 1990, production levels at the air-conditioner factory were just below 1,000,000 units annually, the output of the parent factory in Japan. The Malaysian factory exported its product to 120 countries, including the United States and Japan; in the United States, *Consumer Reports* had given the product high marks. Less than 5 percent of the factory's output stayed in Malaysia. Singam was getting ready to commission a third factory to make a "split" air conditioner mainly for the Japanese market. "The new Malaysian plant represents an expansion. The Japanese plant will concentrate on more high-tech products. We'll manufacture the normal split-unit models, but since we are exporting to Japan, they will be the most up-to-date models, because Japan is the most competitive market in the world. If we can sell to Japan, we can penetrate any market anywhere."

It wasn't just the level of technology and scale of production that made the factories unique, Singam argued. It was also the degree of decentralization. "The split-type air conditioner is mushrooming now. We have factories in Taipei, the Philippines, India, and Thailand, but mainly for the domestic markets. We supply them with CKD [completely knocked down] units and spare parts. We serve as an international service center, and send our own local people to analyze problems as far as the United States, the Middle East, and Hong Kong. Wherever there is a problem area, we send from here, not from Japan. This role is increasingly given to the company now. Until two years ago, the company was very Japan centered. Now, our managing director's vision is that the Malaysian companies should become fully localized operations. This company is in the forefront of that."

It stayed in the forefront, too. Two years later, I returned to Shah Alam, and the air-conditioner manufacturing complex had spawned a research center that would have been at home in the Hsinchu Science Park outside Taipei or in Silicon Valley. Early in 1994, under competitive pressure from Hitachi and Sharp, Matsushita instructed the center to come up with a cheap air conditioner for the Asian market. A year and a half later, Matsushita was shipping its new Asian model, called the "Eunos," to ten Asian countries. *Nikkei Business* quoted a Matsushita official in 1996 predicting that the research center would be fully independent by 1998.[5]

Finally, I went to see Akita Tadashi, who headed Matsushita in Malaysia. Akita explained how all this had come together. The story had an almost Biblical quality, the offshoots of Matsushita's original factory in the jungle propagating like tribes in a desert. In the beginning, that is 1965, there was MELCOM, a lonely rectangular building in a recently cleared rubber plantation, producing dry batteries for the Malaysian market. MELCOM eventually graduated to products such as electric irons, rice cookers, fans, and vacuum cleaners. It had an overwhelming market share in some of these products— rice cookers, for instance, which only 10 percent of Malaysians bought from anybody else. In 1972, MAICO was born, essentially as a distribution company but also to take charge of imports of components from Japan. A long time passed by. Then it was 1987, and in the next three years Matsushita set up six new companies one after the other—MEDEM, MTV, MACC, MMEC,

MAPREC, and MAEM. All were manufacturing companies, and 90 percent of their output was for export. "The nature of those companies," said Akita, "was to set up a production base for the worldwide market outside Japan." [6]

At the same time as its new export factories were put in place, the company kept careful track of the regional market. Matsushita predicted 10 to 15 percent annual growth in per capita incomes across Asia in the 1990s. "The stage of development is different from country to country, but the role of Asia will be prominent in the future because people are working so hard, and because it has such a big population," Akita said. "Asia is still at the developing stage, but within a decade, the Asian economy will be very great, and will become a very important region in the worldwide market. As long as we can provide products at a reasonable price and of good quality, we can grow together with Asian growth."

The Japanese themselves were overjoyed with the results of their efforts. Pausing in the course of a factory tour, Matsushita's managing director Yokoo gestured at a row of television sets moving down a testing line. "A U.S. manufacturer doesn't mind much if there's a millimeter or a half millimeter of space between the TV cabinet and the back panel. We do."

Matsushita's Asia strategy fit into the company's global plans as a preemptive response to the formation of regional trade blocs in the Americas and Europe. The Malaysian television factory was one element in a sweeping reorganization of Matsushita's global business operations in the early 1990s. The plan was for the company to set up parallel businesses for manufacturing and marketing in four world regions—Japan, North America, Europe, and Asia. Matsushita told its thirty-four Asian subsidiaries that they would operate independently from its other operations worldwide, in order to cope with an anticipated increase in global protectionism. Each unit would have to fend for itself in the new decentralized structure. "Over the long term, one of the ways for the Japanese economy to survive is to set up an economic bloc in the Asian region. Europe is already setting up a bloc, and so is North America. Just in order to come up to the same market level, we will need to do the same," said Yoshida Yasushi, an official with Matsushita's regional headquarters in Singapore.

The drift toward regionalism that began in the late 1980s also played a decisive role in the attitudes of host governments. The creation of the North American Free Trade Agreement (NAFTA) in 1994 and the European Union (EU) in 1995 worried Southeast Asians, who feared they might lose investment to Mexico and emerging East European economies. So they began working on their own investment codes and regulatory frameworks, finding ways to invite foreign companies in. They were more successful than they had dreamed possible.

More than any other Japanese company, Matsushita embodied what Japan was about in Southeast Asia and why Southeast Asians were more welcoming of Japan's presence this time around than in the 1970s. By 1990, Matsushita already had the infrastructure of a regional electronics empire in place, with 45 percent of its overseas production based in Asia. Matsushita had shifted its strategy to target Asian markets, which were then growing at double-digit rates, and by the mid-1990s, the company was selling 50 percent of the products of its Asian factories within the region. By 1996, 20 percent of Matsushita's global sales were in Asia, $14 billion out of $70.6 billion.[7] The same year, Matsushita exported $2.39 billion[8] worth of consumer electronic appliances and components from Malaysia alone, equivalent to 3.1 percent of total Malaysian exports.[9] By 1998, Matsushita had another ten factories in Malaysia, for a total of nineteen, and sixty-seven factories across the region. Sixty-five percent of Matsushita's non-Japanese production came from its factories in Southeast Asia, roughly $7.9 billion.[10]

The company had 79,000 employees in Southeast Asia and another 19,400 workers in China, and it remained Malaysia's largest employer, with 32,000 Malaysians on payroll. In the mid-1990s, Matsushita, as did other Japanese multinationals, turned its attention to the emerging economies of Asia—China, Vietnam, and India. Southeast Asia became one corner of a triangle that included Japan and Greater China. Matsushita set up its first factory in China in 1987, the Beijing-Matsushita Color CRT Company, to manufacture the Braun tubes for color television sets. By 1998, it had thirty-five factories in China, employing 25,000 people. China accounted for $1.4 billion[11] in annual sales. Before the Asia crisis, Matsushita was targeting an output level of $3 billion[12] for the year 2000 in China alone.[13]

The company's defects were obvious. Matsushita was slow and stodgy, tended to breed a rigid mind-set among its career managers, and considered it was moving quickly if it took four months to make a decision on a new plant site. Its internal culture was numbingly insular. Matsushita insisted that the only way locals could make it to the executive level was by following the Japanese path—recruitment straight out of college, followed by a slow progression through the ranks, with access to the next level based on age and gender. Matsushita was one of Malaysia's oldest Japanese companies. Yet, as late as 1996 none of its company presidents were Malaysians despite years of ostentatious grooming and promises.[14]

Matsushita's internal culture did not sit well with other Asians. Richard Chong, a Taiwanese businessman, described his experience in hiring a Matsushita executive to help run a start-up electronics company. The former executive insisted on wearing his Matsushita uniform to work. He fought endlessly with other managers and employees because they refused to go along with his ideas about company discipline, based on the Matsushita model—morning exercises, strict obedience to superiors, and long working hours. Eventually, he caused so much friction with other managers that Chong fired him.[15]

And yet, as one of the world's largest multinationals and the largest consumer electronics company, Matsushita had incomparable industrial depth and staying power. It brought to Malaysia a global distribution network for air conditioners and color TVs, which became major export products for the nation. It replicated its Japanese network of subcontractors. By 1998 there were 200 of them, some local, most joint ventures with Japanese businesses. These smaller companies created an industrial infrastructure of parts makers capable of selling their products to the world. Matsushita not only gave Malaysia its business, it created an industry. This pattern was repeated many times over, as Japan turned again to Asia in the late 1980s and found that the legacy of World War Two no longer mattered in a region eager for growth.

By 1995, most of the offshore production of Japanese electronics companies, 70 percent, was in Asia. Some $21 billion worth of Japanese electronics, from Sony Walkmans to compact disc players and printed circuit boards were made somewhere in the region.[16] It took just a few years for Thailand, Malaysia, and Singapore to become the fastest growing sources of Japanese exports outside Japan. U.S. congressmen fumed, while leaders of developing nations rubbed their hands with glee. The congressmen and women might say what they liked. Southeast Asian countries had gone overnight from resource exporters, vulnerable to the slightest shift in global commodities markets, to manufacturing exporters. For example, although most of Japanese electronics investment went to Malaysia and Singapore, Japanese companies in Thailand were among the only investors in the electronics sector in the late 1980s and early 1990s. In 1988, the United States was importing only $7 million of consumer electronics from Thailand. By 1990, U.S. imports from Thailand of electronic products, including microwave ovens, videocassette recorders, and color TVs, jumped to $310 million, an increase of more than 4,300 percent.[17]

All in the Family: Japan's New Asian Export Machine

Within the Japanese electronics industry, a fundamental change in thinking had occurred. Asia was no longer seen simply as a base for making cheap goods for domestic markets or simple parts and subassemblies for export to Japan. According to the new calculation, Asia would become an export platform for a much wider array of products. Japanese factories in Asia would supply the vast middle range of wares whose production Japan up until then had kept to itself—videocassette recorders, fax machines, stereo equipment, and automatic cameras. Japan would gradually lose production of standardized parts and components—with the emphasis on gradual—that would shift to Asian factories as regional trade barriers fell, another phenomenon expected to consume several decades. Meanwhile, Tokyo would support the marriage of Japanese parts makers and local affiliates, building up national industries with a certain amount of redundancy considered from a regional standpoint. Eventually, the Japanese planned to move their Asian factories several rungs up on the technological ladder—with Japan providing the research "brain" for new products and Asia the "brawn."[18]

This plan became strategic gospel for every big Japanese electronics company in the late 1980s—Matsushita, Sony Corp., Sharp Corp., Sanyo Electric Co. Ltd., Fujitsu Ltd., and Aiwa Ltd., to name a few. Between 1987 and 1990, Matsushita, the world's largest consumer electronics company, set up eleven new factories in Asia, at a cost of some $850 million. Sony, better known than Matsushita outside Japan but a latecomer in Asia, doubled its factories there about the same time. By the end of 1988, Japanese electronics companies operated 413 factories and employed 270,000 people in Asia.

More than any other industry, Japanese investment in consumer electronics in Asia exercised a visible transformation. Japanese investors brought not only the flashy side of high-technology production to their new Asian export platforms—robots, white rooms, and sanitized uniforms for workers—they also imported the guts of their factories from Japan, machines stamping out parts and shaping plastic or metal. In isolated sites just a few years away from jungle, molds and dies were built with their own machining centers and robots. As in a child's sketch of a factory, at one end of the building, nuggets of plastic and steel were trucked in. At the other end emerged computer disk drives and electronic keyboards.

Technology transfer, long a sore point among host countries for Japanese investment, gradually became a less-sensitive issue, at least in the electronics industry. Japanese companies shifted product design and ever more complex manufacturing to Asia. Matsushita's first robot-making factory in the world outside Japan, MASTEC, went to Singapore. At the site were regular training courses for engineering students in surface-mounted technology, a technique for constructing printed circuit boards. Sony also began to build and design robots at its Sony Precision Engineering Center in Singapore.

In Southeast Asia, where Japanese investment was concentrated in the early 1990s, its consumer electronics sector was clearly responsible for setting off an unprecedented boom in exports of manufactured goods. Malaysia became the world's biggest producer of semiconductors. Both Thailand and

Malaysia were on their way to becoming world leaders in consumer electronics manufacturing. Singapore seized the lead in providing computer software and product design for Japanese multinationals. Salaries in the city-state were about one-tenth the going rate in Japan for computer engineers, and Japan's top electronics companies began moving training and research facilities to the island.

Shipments between the offshoots of Japan's new electronic conglomerates in Asia generated a secondary trade boom among Asian countries. At MTV in Malaysia, in the early 1990s, 47 percent of components were supplied from within the region of which two-thirds came from other Matsushita factories in Singapore and Malaysia. Another 35 percent of the value of intraregional components came from cathode-ray tubes from a Matsushita factory in South Korea. Other components came from Japan. In short, roughly half the value of television exports that would have come from Japan a few years earlier was now sourced from two other Asian countries.

Getting Rich Is Hard Work

In the pioneer days of Japanese business in Asia, relations with governments were left to the Japanese trading companies. The chief executives of Mitsubishi Shoji and Mitsui Bussan divided up Asia like so many feudal fiefdoms, and their local representatives were showered with titles and other perks. By the late 1980s, the burdens of lobbying had become far more diffused. Even middle-sized Japanese companies spent so much time dealing with host governments that they needed their own expert lobbyists.

Consider Ikeda Makoto, director of Minebea Thai, the world's largest manufacturer of ball bearings. Ikeda led me on a tour when I visited the company in 1990. Tanned and good-natured, Ikeda had lived in Thailand for thirty-five years. He felt uncomfortable on his visits to Japan, with its ethnic and cultural homogeneity. Ikeda's children were born in Thailand, and he chattered fluently in Thai with employees as we cruised through the huge Minebea complex outside Bangkok, stopping here and there to admire displays of speakers, keyboards, and stepping motors—all products that used ball bearings.

"If we sell one million stepping motors, we sell two million ball bearings," Ikeda beamed. In 1990, Thailand represented 60 percent of Minebea's worldwide production. Its two ball bearings factories in Thailand comprised the largest such complex in the world, disgorging 40,000,000 ball bearings a month. Most were exported to Japan at Yen 100 each, paid in U.S. dollars so that Minebea Thai's profits rose in tandem with the strong yen. Export earnings for Thailand from Minebea products amounted to $414 million in 1989,[19] this was about 2 percent of Thailand's $20 billion in exports that year.[20]

At Pelmec Thai, the Minebea factory near Bangkok, we passed a room where sixteen people waited patiently for interviews, sitting under framed photographs of the Thai king and queen. Nearly all of Minebea's 14,000 employees were women. They made 3,000 Baht a month, less than $5 a day. Dressed in dove-gray uniforms, adorned with cloth caps, the women sat relaxed and confident. Each production line featured a Japanese manager who was, however, stationed in Japan, along with the presidents of Minebea's ten Thai companies. The company headquarters was in Kanda, an old district in Tokyo once famed for its bookstores, later a hive of discount ski equipment and adult comic book emporia. Ikeda described the home office as dirty and old. Gesturing out at the factory grounds, with its neat lawns fringed with trees, he asserted, "Our office here is much better. Thailand has made Minebea rich, but not without hard work." By this, he meant mainly working on the Thai government.

"The most difficult time was in eighty-one," he sighed. "We sent 200 Thai workers to Japan for a year, to our Karuizawa factory, from supervisors to line workers. Then we sent them back with all the machines from the factory to Thailand, and the factory opened in August 1982. Our initial investment was small, but we planned to get up to 2,000,000 ball bearings a month within three years. Ball bearings are used in videotape recorders, office machines, typewriters, copy machines, printers—all sorts of machines that need to be very quiet. We were the first ball bearing factory in Thailand. We had factories in Japan and Singapore, and by the early 1980s we had about ten years of experience from our factory in Singapore. Singapore was much the same as America. But there are all sorts of cultural differences between Japan and Thailand.

"When we started in Thailand, we faced so many problems, mainly due to the cultural differences. Simple things. If you imported goods, material, and machines from Japan, it would take a lot of time. The first time we tried, it took us one month to get Customs clearance. Later we learned how to do it properly. We contacted the government authorities and asked them to change the system. Now we can get Customs clearance within a week. It's not just me, anyone can do it," he added modestly. "It even took some people three months. But I talked with the government authorities to change the system."[21]

Minebea imported steel plate from Japan and plastic pellets from Singapore. Originally, the duty on such items was between 50 and 60 percent, Ikeda said. To get around that problem, Ikeda persuaded his Thai government friends to designate Minebea as a "promoted industry," which meant that the company could import machines and raw materials duty-free, as long as most of its product was exported. As a further sweetener, Bangkok offered Minebea a five-to-eight-year tax holiday. Unlike Matsushita, Minebea kept all of its manufacturing processes in house. However, it had to develop local sources for raw materials in order to satisfy Thai pressure for greater local content. Ikeda displayed a speaker cone that he described as "made-in-Thailand." Other products had as much as 80 percent local content. The steel plate Minebea used was simply unavailable in Thailand, Ikeda said apologetically. As to plastic, "We are waiting for the establishment of a petrochemical industry in Thailand."

During Ikeda's long years in the country, both Thailand and the Japanese community changed drastically. Minebea commissioned its first Asian factory in 1972, in Singapore, and began the stepping-stone process that characterized its experience in Thailand. By 1979, the Singapore job market was so tight that workers were difficult to find. Thailand's Board of Investment, sensing opportunity, invited Minebea executives to visit. It took Minebea two years to make a decision; the company was wary of Thailand because of the political chaos of its wild neighbors, Laos, Cambodia, and Burma. During the Vietnam War, Thailand was always seen as the country that would be the first domino to fall to communism, and investors remained skittish.

Minebea hired Ikeda from a Japanese construction company, Ohbayashi Gumi. When he first arrived in Thailand in 1955, a Japanese Chamber of Commerce (JCC) existed but with only a few members, mostly trading companies and banks. In 1990, JCC membership was up to 700 members, and growing. There were between 15,000 and 20,000 Japanese residents in Bangkok. Real-estate prices had escalated, and some Thais blamed the influx of Japanese expatriates. There was no doubt at all about the level of strain on Thai infrastructure, at least in Bangkok. I was advised to leave at dawn to reach the industrial estates on the outskirts of the city in order to avoid the traffic. Kojima Taijiro, Sanwa Bank's chief representative in Thailand, said "infrastructure is so poor at the moment, you have to wait a couple of months to receive goods from the ports."[22]

Thailand developed a mystique for Japanese investors in the early 1990s, as a country sharing Japan's Buddhist heritage and a willing collaborator with Japan during World War Two. Japanese businessmen had long sought out Thailand for its active sex trade, and an assignment there was considered posh. The main reason why Japanese companies flocked to Thailand in the early part of the decade, however, was because of Thai government policy to promote exports. "Newcomers are completely ignoring the local market," Kojima said. "Maybe in the first stage companies looked at it, but now they are mostly 100 percent exporters."

Crumbling Fortress

Until the Plaza Accord in 1985, the Japanese electronics industry was over-whelmingly Japan based. In 1985, just 3 percent of the value of Japanese manufacturing derived from Japanese-owned factories outside Japan.[23] Japanese investment in electronics abroad represented a negligible fraction of overseas investment, most of which went into financial businesses, real estate, and services.[24] When the Japanese electronics companies did invest abroad, it was invariably to service local markets, as was the case with Matsushita's first Malaysian company, MELCOM.

Meanwhile, in the 1980s, U.S. firms were already far along in decentralizing their output on a global map, a move that would leave them the clear market leaders in the new technologies of the 1990s. The initial attraction of Asia for U.S. firms was cheap labor, not local markets. They poured into Asia in the 1960s and 1970s, building assembly plants, particularly in the chip industry, followed by makers of electronic calculators, computers, and peripherals. In the early 1980s, American firms used the strong U.S. dollar to their advantage, upgrading the technical capabilities of what were originally assembly operations.

The strong dollar also provided an incentive to source more parts locally, and governments and business in Taiwan and elsewhere moved to fill the gap. Local firms sprang into the niche left by U.S. firms as they sold off their assets in the consumer electronics business in order to focus on information-processing technologies. By the early 1990s, according to Michael Borrus, a political scientist based at the University of California at Berkeley, American firms had created "an ever more elaborate and deepening technical division of labor between U.S. and Asian-based operations, bound together in production networks serving U.S. firms' advanced country markets."[25] U.S. companies concentrated on new product design and software, leaving mass production to their Asian affiliates and local producers. By the time the Japanese electronics companies arrived on the scene, they were playing catch-up in terms of discovering Southeast Asia as an export-manufacturing base. Not only did they have the Americans and Europeans to contend with but Taiwanese and Korean investors nipped at their heels, spurred by their own rising wage rates and production costs to transfer their export assets to cheaper platforms overseas.

Taiwanese investors rode the Japanese hard at the low end of the electronics industry, moving through overseas Chinese networks and melting into their supply arrangements with large U.S. and European customers. In the late 1980s, roughly half of Taiwan's foreign investment was in consumer electronics, with about one-third of the total in Asia, mainly in Thailand, Malaysia, and China.

Official Taiwanese capital outflow figures failed to capture the scale of some of the Taiwanese investments. Many smaller companies simply did not register with the authorities, hiding behind their local connections with ethnic Chinese companies. In 1988, for example, host country reports showed that Taiwanese companies were approved to invest $1.1 billion in Thailand, Malaysia, Indonesia, and the Philippines. According to Japanese sources, Taiwan's investments in those countries in 1988 amounted to $2.0 billion (up from $414 million in 1987). In contrast, the official Taiwanese statistics were just $52.4 million in 1988 and $14.6 million in 1987.[26] Most of the Taiwanese investors, though small, were already experienced in exporting to the high-income markets of Europe and North America by the time they arrived in Southeast Asia. In Southeast Asia, Taiwanese companies exported 67 percent of their output; in China 97.7 percent.[27]

In Korea's case, rising wage rates together with Korea's increasingly contentious labor force combined to send the *chaebol* conglomerates offshore, in the early days after the end of military rule in 1987. Like Japan, Korea was reluctant to lose its industrial base to foreign factories, even if they were Korean-owned, and it had gotten a slightly later start than Japan or Taiwan as investor in the region. Its total investments in Thailand, Malaysia, Indonesia, and the Philippines amounted to just $38 million in 1987 and $325 million in 1988. Japanese investment in the same countries was $1 billion in 1987 and $1.9 billion in 1988. Initially the Korean *chaebol* concentrated on Indonesia and resource extraction; in 1989, Samsung took the first plunge into offshore electronics manufacturing in Asia with a joint venture to make color TV sets and VCRs in Thailand. Lucky Goldstar was not far behind, with joint venture operations in Bangkok and Manila.

Korea was not at all happy to see its premier export industry drift offshore, and investment in the electronics sector was lukewarm up until 1992. Even so, the Koreans caused more trouble to Japanese multinationals than the Taiwanese. Like the Japanese, Koreans built large-scale, vertically integrated production complexes, rather than the assembly kitchens of the Taiwanese and overseas Chinese investors;[28] when they came to Asia, they brought their subcontractors with them, and by the early 1990s the major Korean electronics firms were no longer content to serve solely as original equipment manufacturers, making products under other companies' brand names.[29]

The Japanese worried about companies such as LG Electronics (as Lucky Goldstar was renamed) and Daewoo Electronics. "Like their Japanese counterparts, the Koreans are sharpening their cost-competitiveness by moving more production offshore in Asia, and are exporting products made at these offshore plants into the all-important North American market," wrote two top experts with Nomura Research Institute in 1995. "The competition between Japanese and Korean electronics companies is thus spreading from the same geographic markets to the same geographic centers of production."[30]

Notwithstanding the competition, in the mid-1990s, Japan emerged from a decade of intensive investment in the region with production networks stretching from Dalian in northeast China to Jakarta. The industrial zones that attracted Japanese business became, like Shah Alam, virtual Japanese villages. Besides Dalian, the Japanese clustered in the Beijing Airport Industrial Park between Beijing and Tianjin; the Pudong Development District outside Shanghai; the Suzhou and Wuxi industrial parks; the special economic zones (SEZs) surrounding Guangzhou and Hong Kong; Laguna Industrial Park near Manila; the vast industrial estates around Bangkok; Shah Alam in Malaysia; Jurong and Johore Bahru in Singapore; and Jakarta's MM2100 and East Jakarta industrial parks. Japan's top five electronics makers—Matsushita, Sony, Sharp, Sanyo Electric, and Pioneer Electronic—increased overseas production ratios from 20.1 percent in 1985 to 46 percent in 1995. The Nomura experts could observe that "the growing profitability of manufacturing operations in the region, driven by expanding economies of scale as production unit volumes rise, is now the single most important factor powering the renewed consolidated earnings growth of Japanese companies."[31]

Keiretsu Convoys

In one sense, the Japanese merely followed the model set by U.S. companies in the first half of the 1980s, when American companies massively shifted production offshore. U.S. multinationals had had their taste of the Japanese dilemma of the high yen era—a strong domestic currency, rising production costs, and competitors based in cheaper currency zones. In most other ways, the two were at opposite ends of the spectrum.

When they moved abroad, American multinationals established relatively porous production systems, sourcing from both local Asian producers as well as their own affiliates. In contrast, the Japanese kept overseas production strictly under Japanese control. In the first place, the Japanese insisted on keeping high-value-added, low-volume production at home in Japan. They did not insist on owning every stage of production but still preferred doing business with companies in their own *keiretsu* groupings. If there were none in an offshore location, second choice would be another Japanese company. In countries with strict limits on foreign ownership, they made do with Japanese local joint ventures whose local partners were often partners in name only. Such practices limited the developmental impact of Japanese investment on host countries, yet the investments were of such a scale that few host countries complained.

With ample help from the Japanese government, major Japanese manufacturers were often able to bring their *keiretsu* companies with them. Most of the big electronics companies belonged to one of the vast "horizontal" *keiretsu*, corporate assemblages centered on banks or insurance companies. Matsushita, for example, was part of the Sumitomo *keiretsu*; Sharp was part of the Sanwa *keiretsu*; Sony had its own *keiretsu* group consisting of subcontractors.[32]

Each of the big companies had a separate coterie of captive suppliers; captive in the sense that there were severe disincentives for doing business outside the *keiretsu* grouping, such as being cut off by their major customers. MITI helped out by putting together support programs to get these smaller companies offshore. In a 1996 interview, Tamagami Masaaki, MITI's director for International Policy Planning in the Small and Medium Enterprise Agency (SMEA), described this assistance: "Most of the big companies that go overseas have know-how for relocation abroad, but not the SMEs. So we provide them with information, guidance, and finance."[33] According to Tamagami, most of the *keiretsu* subcontractors made their moves in the 1980s. In the late 1980s and early 1990s, foreign investment by small- and medium-sized Japanese companies was dominated by the machinery sector.[34] Thus, Japan's most important export industry was able to preserve offshore much the same pattern that existed in Japan.

In the mid-1990s, MITI's SMEA helped this process along by extending loans and tax breaks to companies that made the jump and encouraging them to pay special attention to the merits of Asian locations.[35] A 1993 law promoting the entry of SMEs into new fields included overseas investment in its definition. Qualifying companies were eligible for grants of Yen 10 million per project.[36] MITI's 1996 White Paper on SMEs described Asian investment in terms of the "development and deepening of mutual dependence in the global division of labor in Asia including Japan" (*wagakuni wo fukumu Ajia no gurobaruna bungyo no shinten, fukamaru sogo yison kankei*).[37] Indeed, Japanese small business was almost preternaturally sensitive to the high yen, which peaked in 1986 and again in 1995. In both years, investments by small companies made up about 60 percent of the total number of Japanese companies investing abroad, with just under 1,625 companies making the jump in 1988 in the first panic. And of the 9,358 SMEs investing abroad in the ten years from 1985 to 1995, practically all of them went to Asia. By 1995, the ratio was as high as 91.6 percent.[38]

Hayase Koichi, a former official with the Japan External Trade Organization (JETRO), liked Malaysia so much that he stayed on after his government assignment ended. According to Hayase, the Japanese government worked hard to shape the transfer of Japanese manufacturing assets by making sure that subcontractors were part of the package; indeed, Hayase insisted that the most effective role played by the Japanese government was with small- and medium-sized businesses. MITI's Japan Overseas Development Corporation (ODC) provided them with low-interest loans. Instead of going directly to ODC, or through the still-loftier Overseas Economic Cooperation Fund (OECF) or the Japan International Cooperation Agency (JICA), small companies could get funds directly from JETRO, which operated a huge network of branches globally. In 1985, JETRO established a separate advisory agency for small- and medium-sized enterprises, the JETRO Overseas Investment scheme, known by the catchy acronym, "JOIN." By 1990, JOIN had brought some thirty projects to fruition in Malaysia alone.

Japanese aid projects normally began with a proposal made by Japanese interests, such as trading companies, to the host government. Smaller companies might not understand this process, however, so JOIN did it for them. JOIN also helped them save money by footing the bill for detailed feasibility studies tailored to their products and industries. It drafted specific proposals and delivered them to the Malaysian Industrial Development Authority (MIDA), which then passed them on to Japanese aid agencies under the MIDA imprimatur. Private companies handled the actual applications, but only after MITI had notified government departments. MITI got involved down to the level of helping companies with applications for industrial land. The JOIN scheme even paid part of the traveling expenses of small businesses to scope out business opportunities identified by JETRO. Finally, companies that participated in JOIN would be prime candidates for low-interest loans at close to prime rate, with ten-year repayment terms and lengthy grace periods.

This circular process flowed from Japanese government strictures that were designed to avoid any appearance that Japan imposed its aid programs on foreign governments; rather, Japanese money in theory would fund projects that were designed by the host countries operating independently of Japanese interests, whether strategic or commercial. In practice, the "request principle" simply provided a cover for Japanese interests to milk the system.

The government pull factor was not the only force at work in the exodus of Japanese small and medium business to Southeast Asia and China in the 1980s and 1990s. There were push factors too. As their cost structures in Japan rose ever higher, the *oyagaisha* companies pared down their lists of *keiretsu* suppliers in Japan, cutting off the more expensive or expendable ones. The trend was particularly marked in the auto sector. A 1996 survey by MITI's SMEA showed that between 1990 and 1995, *oyagaisha* with 100 or more subcontractors had shrunk from 75 percent of the survey sample to about 60 percent.[39] Domestically, major manufacturers began to take the radical step of sharing subcontractors with one other, although such instances were rare.

For their part, the subcontractors began muttering about "escaping" the subcontracting system and "divorcing" the *oyagaisha*. In many respects, small and medium enterprise represented the most market-oriented sector of the Japanese economy. Their long-term relationships with major companies were anything but comfortable. Large companies in the auto and electronics industries were essentially assembly operations. They readily shoved pricing pressures in foreign markets on to their affiliates, the *kogaisha* or "offspring" companies, in relationships that often noticeably liked familial warmth.

I went to talk with one such subcontractor on the outskirts of Tokyo. Fukata Kiroshi was managing director of the Asahi Group in Kawasaki City, a suburb packed with NEC factories and subcontractors. Asahi made the metal boxes housing NEC's mainframe computers and telephone-switching systems; it was a simple job of bending and pressing metal pieces, then slapping on some paint. Asahi had been making cases for NEC since 1919, when it was known as Nihon Denshi. "We developed along with NEC," said Fukata, whose father, uncle, brothers, and son all worked for the company.[40] Business was so good in the 1970s and 1980s that the company added a second factory in Yamagata Prefecture, in northern Honshu. The factory was finished in 1986, just as NEC demanded that all its suppliers reduce prices by 15 percent in order to help NEC cope with the implosion of its export markets caused by the strong yen.

Asahi survived, although not without difficulty. In 1992, however, NEC announced that its subcontractors would have to reduce prices by another 30 percent over the course of just a few months, again reacting to a sharp bout of yen appreciation. That hurt. In 1986, NEC had let them take a year to get their costs down. This time was different. For the first time in Asahi's history, Fukata had to cut staff. He took the drastic step of moving part of production overseas. In 1988, Asahi had taken a 17 percent equity stake in a Singapore company "as an experiment." In 1994, it built its first foreign factory, in Malaysia.

Fukata took pains to stress that he never actually laid anybody off. Instead, he stopped hiring new recruits and insisted that older employees retire at the official retirement age of sixty, rather than staying on for a few years as was Asahi's practice. But Asahi's foreign-manufacturing ventures were so successful that by 1996, Fukata was already talking about moving the company headquarters to Malaysia. Two years after breaking ground for the factory, it was producing 10 percent of Asahi's boxes, for 30 percent to 40 percent less than the cost in Japan. NEC's only complaint, Fukata said, was that it couldn't get enough of the steel boxes from the Malaysian factory. Fukata was making plans for a five-fold expansion that would leave Malaysia producing nearly half his total output. By law, the venture, located in Port Klang, had 30 percent Malaysian equity, but the money was all from Japan, Fukata said. He had no help either from the Japanese government or from NEC in making the move. All the managers but one in the Malaysian plant were local, mostly Chinese Malaysians.

The most unusual aspect of the Malaysian factory, however, was Asahi's 50–50 partner. Fukata had put together a deal with a subcontractor of Fujitsu, one of NEC's chief rivals in the telecommunications business. In Japan, such an arrangement would be unthinkable, Fukata admitted, partly because he could never keep it hidden. NEC engineers were constantly on the prowl in his factories in Yamagata and Kawasaki to check on the status of production, and would instantly spot the signs of collaboration with any of NEC's competitors. But in Malaysia, both companies knew about the joint venture and put up with it. The Fujitsu subcontractor took half the output and Asahi took half, shipping most of it straight back to Japan and NEC. Fukata said he was preparing for the day when most of his customers were abroad. "In Japan we have this major client called NEC," Fukata said. "But once we get out of Japan, we don't need to be addicted to NEC. We don't need to be controlled by them."

Whether it was Japanese entrepreneurs seeking new frontiers, or the Japanese government doing spadework to boost small-scale manufacturing, it all went down well with the Malaysian government. The Malaysians wanted to cut down on the flow of imported parts to Japanese manufacturers based in-country. They may have also figured on being able to apply pressure more effectively on small companies to share technology, even if the technology ultimately came from *keiretsu* giants. In any event, the arrival of Japanese small business along with the big multinationals did nothing to make Japan less popular with the Malaysian authorities, as long as it did not compete with Malaysian manufacturers. Because Malaysia was strongest in such resource-based industries as wood processing, rubber, and plastic products, the Japanese electronics industry, subcontractors and all, were breaking new ground.

Foreign ownership in the electronics industry in Malaysia rose from 50.7 percent in 1986 to 83.69 percent in 1991, after the rush of Japanese and Northeast Asian investment, but Malaysians were not complaining. Export earnings from electronics rocketed. They went from $2.5 billion in 1986[41] to $13.6 billion in 1992,[42] an annual growth rate of over 30 percent.[43]

The Cost of Money

Doing business with the Japanese had both short- and long-term costs that were never any secret. Integration into a Japanese industrial machine meant accepting the limitations of the machine as well as its benefits. Two of the most pressing problems for Asian manufacturers were Japanese hostility toward the emergence of rival Asian brands and continued protection of the Japanese domestic market against incursions by Asian manufacturers. When Japanese multinationals foresaw a wave of cheap imports buoyed by the strong yen, they determined early on to control it themselves by dominating the market for products imported from Asia, so that the ultimate source of the wares that made up Japan's rising imports from the region would be Japanese factories.

Indeed, Japan made it clear that its grand new adventure was about industrial collaboration, not competition. The deal that Tokyo offered its Asian neighbors was industrial development in exchange for global exports—under Japanese labels. If local companies reached the stage of wanting to develop their own brand names for global export, Japan was unlikely to welcome them into its markets. This was a story that had already played out in the 1980s, when Korea and Taiwan seemed likely to catch up with Japan in the global electronics industry. When they got close, Japan refused to give up its state-of-the-art technology. Meanwhile, both countries had become hooked on supplies of Japanese capital goods and industrial components, running steep deficits in their trade with Japan.[44]

There was, however, a difference between Korea and Taiwan. Korea's large *chaebol* conglomerates, consciously modeled after the Japanese *keiretsu* system, succeeded at becoming the world's fifth largest producers of electronic products by the early 1990s. The *chaebol* were increasingly determined to market products under their own brand names. As far as the Japanese were concerned, the proper role model for Southeast Asia was to be Taiwan. By the 1980s, Taiwan manufactured nearly all Japanese calculators and cameras under "original equipment" manufacturing (OEM) arrangements, assembling parts shipped from Japan. "It's true that effective technology transfer from Japan has not been realized in Korea," said Yamada Matsuhiko, an advisor to Nikko Research Center, in a 1992 interview.

> The reason for such problems is also very clear. First, according to Japanese engineers in Korea, the absorptive capacity of Koreans is not good because of their educational background, or their willingness to remain with the company. The turnover of Korean workers is higher than in the United States. Such high mobility prevents effective technology transfer.
>
> Second, managers of Korean companies do not honor intellectual property. They want to steal such trade or technological secrets without any charge. They assert that Japan should give everything to Korea for free, as compensation for past injustices. Another unique feature of Koreans is their Confucian ethics, which have also obstructed effective technology trans-

fer. There are people who say that Confucian morality is a factor in the economic progress of East Asia but I don't think so. High tech cannot grow in a feudal political or social system. Confucian mentality disappeared in Japan generations ago, but in Korea such a mentality exists and frustrates the younger generation.

And here's another thing. The competitiveness of Japanese goods is based on quality control in Japanese factories. But it's almost impossible to do much quality control in Korea. Japanese engineers say that Korean workers don't like such activities, which require devotion, effort, or sacrifice of their private life.

Japanese electronics and auto companies are not allowed to produce final goods in Korea, which are monopolized by Korean big business. Japanese are absolutely excluded from the production of final goods. All that Japanese companies can supply are parts and components only, because the *chaebol* make the finished products. As a result, Japan's role in the export of final goods from Korea has been very small, compared to ASEAN or Taiwan. And Japanese imports from Korea are very low for the same reason, because Japanese customers are very sensitive to brand names as well as to quality.[45]

Yamada merely expressed a mainstream Japanese view; when Koreans really began operating according to Akamatsu's principles, the Japanese did everything they could to block them. When Hyundai launched the first Korean-made car in the North American market in the mid-1980s, Japanese carmakers nearly succeeded in driving the company out of business through a destructive price war. If such tactics failed, the Japanese would resort to smears, doing their best to foster the image that Korean products were inferior.

A second major problem with Japanese investment, from the host country perspective, was Japan's desire to control the stream of products back to the homeland. Matsushita, for example, long anticipated that the high yen would eventually break down barriers to the Japanese market. Its solution was to dominate the market for imports as it already dominated exports. In 1996, Dick Greene, a professor at Kwansei Gakuin University's School of Policy Studies and a scholar with close ties to Matsushita, laid out the internal decision tree at the company.

The micro-level process works like this. MITI and Matsushita Electric executives in the early 1980s see an inevitable new relation to the United States vis-à-vis trade developing along with development of a WTO [World Trade Organization] infrastructure between trading nations. Without formal committees these people, who have been dealing with each other for years, sometimes decades, informally work to envision what a Japan that could not produce most of its manufacturing goods in Japan would do to maintain current long-term economic goals—first in the world economically at some future date, leverage through positive trade, currency, technology and service balances (i.e., negotiate away parts of the surplus to get concessions on other policy matters of interest to Japan) and so forth.

One conclusion that emerges in dozens of such casual and private conversations is that if Japan ends up importing *most* of its manufacturing goods, then it would be best if Japan were to import *most* of those imports from off-shore Japanese firms. This has employment implications that are unavoidably negative, but revenue and technology implications that are positive. Japan's domestic market can be open without foreign firms getting in. So, in the mid-1980s and late 1980s we see MITI and various industry associations training themselves in how to work as expatriates and import from Japanese expatriated facilities.[47]

Imports from Asia increased under Japanese labels and from Japanese factories in the region, many brand new. By the mid-1990s, only 21.9 percent of color televisions sold on the domestic Japanese market, and only 38.2 percent of VCRs, were made in Japan.[47] Nonetheless, nearly all the imports were sold under familiar Japanese brand names—Matsushita's National and Panasonic labels, Sony, NEC, Toshiba, and Hitachi.

Attempts to establish a market in Japan for Asian brand names failed miserably despite the efforts of some brave entrepreneurs. In 1988, I visited a discount store specializing in Asian-made electronics in a Tokyo suburb. Its owner, Mimura Michinori called his store the "NICs Shop," after an acronym for newly industrializing countries (NICs) that Japanese increasingly recognized from the business pages of *Nikkei* and other newspapers. It's like throwing a small stone into a big pond, he mused aloud to his visitor. As the ripples spread, Japan's yen-rich consumers might become not only the driving force of the Japanese market, but a growth machine for the global economy. "As long as the goods are cheap, I don't care if they're from the NICs or not," said a tourist from Osaka, who picked out a $20 stereo cassette recorder for his daughter.[48] Unfortunately for Mimura, it took at least another decade for most Japanese to start thinking that way. His store quickly disappeared, and although it left a legacy in the "100 Yen" discount stores of the mid-1990s, Asian brands remained invisible through most of Japanese retail.

Finally, over the long run, countries counting on the Japanese multinationals to deliver cutting-edge technology would almost certainly be disappointed. Critics such as Michael Borrus and Dieter Ernst, both associated with the Berkeley Roundtable on the International Economy (BRIE), argued that the closed production systems of Japanese electronics companies were a big part of the reason why Japanese multinationals had fallen behind in the key technologies of the 1990s. Ernst claimed that Japan's closed networks would "erode the capacity of Japanese firms to shape and benefit from the industrial development of the region . . . and find it very difficult to mobilize and harness the knowledge, ideas, and capabilities that exist today and that act as powerful sources of collective innovation and continuous improvement."[49] Such networks also, of course, made it that much more difficult for Japan's Asian flock to catch up unless they were on the inside.

Autos: Magic Market

When Matsushita and other Japanese consumer-electronics companies created their networks of horizontal production across Asia, they did so as an offshoot of strategies aimed at penetrating global markets. The Japanese auto companies pursued strategies that seemed to be the complete opposite. The electronics companies looked beyond Asia; the auto companies focused their attention within. In hindsight, the electronics companies seemed to have gambled right, particularly in the 1990s, when an expanding U.S. economy soaked up all the high-end audio equipment, television sets, laptop computers, and other toys that it could get. The Asian market for high-end luxury items such as cars, however, was based on a middle-class economy that was at best a fragile niche sector, easily imperiled by the vagaries of exchange rates and international capital markets.

The auto companies knew this—or had good reason to—but it was critical to their global market plans to keep an orderly separation between markets, so that competitors did not spawn their own factories or joint ventures in the world's major export markets. In North America, the Japanese companies were able to build huge, efficient factories geared to the continental market. Theoretically, the Chinese market offered opportunities on the scale of North America or grander. In Southeast Asia, however, the same approaches implied small, inefficient factories or assembly operations. The Japanese auto strategy in Southeast Asia was thus based almost entirely on calculations of rapid marginal growth, that is, where the number of car sales multiplied exponentially as whole sectors of the population bought cars for the first time.

Even so, the factories producing for these markets would remain small and highly dependent on imported parts. In order to succeed, the car manufacturers needed stable exchange rates and predictable growth rates, preferably steep. The global economy of the 1990s was to deny both. From the start, the Japanese odyssey in the Asian auto industry, particularly in Southeast Asia, was an exercise in the long shot, a belief in the magic of conspicuous consumption in a rapidly growing middle-class market. And yet, at the same time, the persistence and sheer vision of the Japanese auto companies reflected the most formidable qualities of Japanese business, as they doggedly looked ahead to a future when some of the world's most populous countries would graduate from bicycles to motorcycles to pickup trucks and finally sedans.

Another difference between the Japanese electronics and auto companies was the stark contrast in the policy and regulatory environments they confronted. Asian governments realistically viewed consumer electronics as a commodity business in which their comparative advantage was based on cheap labor. Capital requirements were relatively modest. Thus, in the 1980s and 1990s, Southeast Asian governments encouraged electronics companies to export and provided all sorts of incentives for exporters ranging from price breaks on the cost of imported goods to tax holidays and government-subsidized industrial parks.

The auto industry inspired entirely different emotions. Building up a car industry entailed huge amounts of capital and required support industries that were themselves capital intensive, from making tires to chiseling engine blocks. An auto industry brought with it not only employment but also skills, technology, and a raft of ancillary industries. Cars were anything but a commodity product. They were among the most expensive of consumer "durables"—most people might buy a car once every ten years—and brand names were important markers. Auto manufacturers, and not just the Japanese, tended to restrict licensing and joint-production agreements to specific markets. Each Asian government wanted to duplicate the Japanese and Korean successes with auto-manufacturing and exports. Each looked at the goal of a national auto industry with the same mixture of suspended disbelief and national chauvinism.

So, unlike the electronics industry, the Japanese and their host governments were inherently at odds. While the Japanese auto companies were doing everything they could to suppress exports from their Asian factories, their Southeast Asian hosts in the 1990s were working equally hard to induce domestic production of all but the most advanced products that could absolutely not be manufactured locally. In this improbable environment, the Southeast Asian auto industry struggled to its feet, nearly collapsed during the Asian crisis, but somehow persevered. This was a joint production between Japan and local governments; in a free market, it would have taken many more years and a completely different policy and regulatory environment to graduate from assembly plants to vertically integrated manufacturing. However wrongheaded the whole exercise might have been from the perspective of neoclassical economics or shareholder returns, the Japanese were instrumental in creating a regional auto industry that would soon entice other global manufacturers to build factories, and it was done at a time, in the late 1980s and early 1990s, when chances of success appeared to be minimal.

From a manufacturing standpoint, another difference between the Japanese auto and electronics industries was even more critical. Japanese electronics manufacturers could reasonably look to their Asian factories to provide sufficient quantity to dominate whole markets—air conditioners, for example. Many of the products were commodities, in the sense that consumers distinguished between different brands primarily on the basis of how much they cost. The Japanese auto companies found it impossible to produce to scale in the miniature markets of Southeast Asia. Nobody wanted to approach the car market as a commodity business. Perhaps only the Japanese were willing to buy into the unusual deal offered by Asian governments, which was to create vertically integrated auto-manufacturing industries for each tiny economy.

The size of factories appropriate to each domestic market was nowhere close to the scale required for efficient production, let alone export to a global market. Malaysians, Thais, and Indonesians regularly grumbled that the Japanese blocked them from exporting locally made cars to third markets. In fact, the Japanese auto factories were not large enough, or advanced enough, to provide a decent platform for third-country exports, unless it was to Pacific Islands or elsewhere lower down on the development ladder than Asia. This was also true of cars made in Mexico or other developing countries. These cars, Japanese executives explained tiredly, were more expensive to make than the cars from their big North American, European, or Japanese factories. They could not easily sell them to the high-end markets. They survived only with protection in the form of import barriers and luxury taxes on competing imports.

The Japanese electronics companies had few illusions about Southeast Asia as a consumer market in its own right. They looked on it as a fringe entity or ignored it entirely. The electronics companies could live with barriers to domestic markets because they did not much need to get around them. The Japanese automakers, on the other hand, saw Southeast Asia from the perspective of a global strategy in which dominant market share was the goal no matter how small the market. For them, domestic market barriers were significant, and the auto companies took an early and decisive interest in shaping domestic and regional market policy to their advantage. With a time lag of a few years, the Chinese market went in the same direction.

They had very different rides, these two groups of multinationals, during the heyday of Japanese investment in the region. The Japanese electronics industry functioned usually on the same frequency as local governments. They were petted, pampered, and lavished with subsidies. The Japanese auto sector was usually at odds with its hosts. Local governments wanted their own, fully independent auto sectors. The Japanese auto companies wanted sales. The cost of setting up shop, the so-called entry barrier was relatively cheap for the Japanese electronics industry, at least on the low end. Once beyond the stage of assembling vehicles from CKD kits, entry barriers were punishingly steep for the carmakers, primarily because of the small size of Asian markets. Electronics production was not limited by the size of local markets because, by mutual agreement, nearly all the output of Japanese factories was for export. Governments rewarded exporters with tariff reductions and tax exemptions. Aiming at domestic markets, the auto companies had to pay high tariff rates on imported parts and to meet stiff local content requirements. It was only in the context of the Malaysian and Indonesian national car programs that the foreign auto manufacturers got breaks similar to those accorded the electronics companies, but these also entailed the risk of creating new competitors in the global market, as the Japanese had in Korea.

In the 1980s, most electronics manufacturers were allowed to take 100 percent ownership of their Asian subsidiaries, as long as they exported all or most of the product. Car manufacturers had to accept local equity partners and faced constant pressure to export. To take two random examples, Toyota's first big engine plant in Southeast Asia was a 40 percent joint venture with Siam Cement, Thailand's largest industrial group with no history of auto production. This bore the marks of a forced marriage, although it was a lucrative engagement for Toyota—the engine plant, Siam Toyota, had 1993 sales of $150 million.[50] In the same year, Sharp was able to take 100 percent control of Sharp Appliances Thailand, which exported microwave ovens, air-conditioners, audio equipment, and fax machines.[51]

In general, because of their Asian market focus, the Japanese carmakers had less control and a smaller share of profits in their Asian operations than the electronics companies. When the Asia crisis hit in 1997, the carmakers were sideswiped with the iffy financing of some of these local affiliates. Even before the Asia crisis, observers wondered if the Japanese carmakers were wasting their time building relatively small, inefficient auto lines in Southeast Asia, existing in the gray zone between assembly and manufacturing. In 2003, ASEAN would drop tariffs on many products to 5 percent, when the ASEAN Free Trade Agreement came into effect. Cars were not on the list of products it covered, but they might be. The electronics makers did not have to worry about such things because their factories were already scaled to the global market.

The Japanese auto and electronics companies did have some things in common, of course. The continuous rise of the yen from 1985 to 1995 created pressures on both industries that led to a major overhaul of their Asian strategies. The electronics companies responded to the high yen by shifting from a local market strategy to an export focus. The Japanese auto companies coped by developing a low-cost parts industry that could be used either to develop competitive exports or to cement their hold over the emerging regional market.

Both industries relied heavily on the Japanese government, particularly government programs for small and medium industry. Government support made it possible for Japanese multinationals to bring the *keiretsu* subcontracting system with them to Asia, a move that had been difficult in Europe and North America because of public pressure and the existence of competing industries. Japan's premier economic agencies worked hard to shape the Asian business environment by controlling the pace of trade and investment liberalization and by supplying funds for projects that matched the Japanese vision of regional development or "economic cooperation." For the auto companies, the most significant assistance from the Japanese government was a program designed specifically to nurture the development of an Asian parts industry. The government program followed and built on efforts made by the companies themselves to create a favorable policy environment within ASEAN.

A direct link existed between the strategies of the Japanese electronics and auto companies, but it was subtle. The common denominator was the notion of regional coordination. The Japanese electronics companies had it easy. They could establish production hierarchies loosely tied to the developmental stage of different economies, yoked to the international market through exports. This was classic Akamatsu, with the Japanese supplying the capital, technology, and markets to the extent that the products of their Asian factories were shipped initially to Japan for branding and packaging before final export to third-country markets.

It was much harder to be a Japanese auto manufacturer in Asia and faithful to Akamatsu. The automakers had no intention of unleashing the finished products on the global market. Instead, they found another way to harness the competitive energy of developing Asia by setting up a trade in parts between their factories in the region. The objective of the parts trade was to build efficient scale production in critical upstream components. Thus, Toyota or Mitsubishi Motors would assign the regional production mandate for engine blocks or camshafts to one particular factory in their Asian constellation. Host countries initially complained and resisted but quickly shifted their attention to competing for production of the more technology-intensive components.

Slow and painful as the process was, it helped to build an Asian auto industry from the ground up. In the 1990s, the strategy gave the Japanese a dominant position in the fastest growing auto market in the world. As with the electronics companies, the underlying behavioral psychology was straight

Akamatsu. Through exports, even if only to neighboring countries, Southeast Asian governments hoped to raise the technological level of their domestic industries. In the process of selling intermediate parts to Japanese multinationals in the region, they would broaden and deepen secondary industries to serve as platforms for a range of industrial production. This is exactly what happened in Thailand, which by the late 1990s supported a thriving auto parts industry.

The approach used by the auto companies—principally Mitsubishi Motors, Toyota, and Nissan—was ingenious. First, they brokered deals with ASEAN governments to exempt parts trading from import duties and to count imported parts as local content as long as they were produced in approved factories. That made it possible to produce parts in one factory rather than five, six, or ten, which brought down costs through economies of scale. In the next stage, the automakers built "Asian" cars, using standardized parts and a common platform. By the mid-1990s, Nissan, Toyota, Honda, and Mitsubishi Motors each had begun marketing Asian cars based on regional production networks. Mazda was building common components but tailoring car bodies to local preferences.[52] Nissan, Toyota, Honda, Mitsubishi Motors, and Mazda, the Japanese "Big Five," were also exporting some of the Asian cars outside the region, typically to fringe markets in developing countries.

Gradually, the Japanese automakers followed the long-established pattern of the electronics companies, integrating the production of their Asian factories backward into the Japanese market. In late 1994, as the yen soared past 100 yen to the dollar, Japanese newspapers reported that Toyota and Nissan were thinking the unthinkable—importing cars from Southeast Asia.[53] Toyota was considering importing its 1.6 liter engine AD Resort pickup truck as a vehicle for the Japanese surfing crowd, while also eyeing its "Toyota utility vehicle" developed for the Indonesian market in the mid-1970s.

By the mid-1990s, Asian-made parts were also beginning to make inroads into Japan, a sign that larger-scale production was helping to bring costs down to a level where they were competitive with Japanese parts production. It was big news in 1994, when Nissan, Honda, and Mitsubishi Motors signed long-term contracts with Pohang Iron & Steel Co., South Korea's top steel maker, to import cold-rolled steel sheet, one of the main materials used in making auto bodies.[54] The same year, according to a Nissan executive, Japanese companies were getting 10 percent of their supply of wire harnesses from a Japanese parts company based in Taiwan, Yozaki Sogyo. Nissan had also begun importing labor-intensive parts, such as castings and rubber fittings, from Southeast Asia, and half of Nissan's parts suppliers had moved to

Taiwan or Southeast Asia by 1994. Parts made in Southeast Asia were as much as 35 percent cheaper than Japanese-made parts.[55]

By the end of 1995, however, the yen reversed course and weakened, allowing the manufacturers to put off such plans for the time being. Even with the weaker yen of the late 1990s, however, Southeast Asia continued to develop as a source of supply for auto parts for the Japanese industry. Japanese demand was fed principally by relocated Japanese parts makers in Southeast Asia, or by affiliates and subsidiaries of the Big Five. By 1998, Japan's largest automaker, Toyota, was importing engines and catalytic converters from a Thai subsidiary and transmissions from one of its companies in the Philippines.[56]

Selling the Japanese Dream Mobile

Sato Mitsuro is a tall man, clearly uncomfortable sitting behind a desk. With a visitor in tow, he paced around a tiny room papered with computer printouts and a large map studded with pins. Most of the graphs had lines vectoring up at forty-five-degree angles. The president of Honda Cars (Thailand), Sato refused to read too much into the figures, like a proud but anxious father. They showed a ten-fold increase in Honda's sales between 1987 and 1990.[57] In the late 1980s, Thailand's auto market doubled over a three-year period, and Thailand was not alone. All over Asia, sales of passenger cars, vans, and light trucks—often used by families in Asia—soared, as buoyant economies fed the region's first genuine consumption boom. Sato recognized, however, that the boom was still limited to a relatively small slice of the population. "It's a mushroom type of market," he said with understatement. "The total market is huge, but only a few people can buy."

What set the Japanese automakers apart in this period was that, rather than scale down their efforts, they lavished attention on each minuscule car market as if it were Japan or North America. They looked at the limitations of the market as sheer opportunity, because it had kept away their global rivals, the giant American and European car companies. The strategy was to establish dominant market share while the window lasted, and it was an article of faith that rocketing growth would expand the middle class whose first act would be to buy cars. In Sato's office at Honda Cars (Thailand), a colored pin on a map of Thailand marked every sale. Sato did virtually everything for his customers but chauffeur their cars. They received how-to manuals and video driving lessons, reminders when their licenses were about to expire, and home calls from technicians when they had problems. Sato boasted that his car showrooms had the amenities of "five-star hotels." Pretty Thai clerks wore different company costumes every day. Customers exhausted from the heat could reach into a refrigerator and wipe their faces with an ice-cold towel. Showrooms even had children's playrooms and libraries.

In 1986, when Sato had arrived in Bangkok, he decided that the way to sell cars to the new middle class was to give them the illusion of luxury. Thais might know that the cars they could afford were nothing extraordinary, but in many cases they were the first cars they had ever owned, and they wanted to feel special about their brand-new vehicles. So Sato took his mid-market Honda Civics and Accords and gave them a highbrow image to match the tax and tariff-inflated price tags of $35,000 to $50,000. The strategy worked so well that Thais were willing to pay cash and wait as long as six months for delivery because of the prestige of owning a Honda. The gregarious Sato gained a reputation as one of the most successful foreign businessman in Thailand. Yet, all this effort was to capture a dominant share in a market of a mere 47,000 vehicles in 1989. Even with a 22.4 percent share of the market, Honda sold just 10,470 cars that year. That did not bother Sato. "I want to be the most customer-oriented company in Thailand regardless of the type of business," he said.

An Asian middle class, still sparse, but with money to burn was just coming into its own. A sudden surge of first-time car buyers made Southeast Asia into one of the hottest auto markets in the world in the mid-1990s, and Japanese auto companies owned it. As of 1991, sales in the entire Asian auto market excluding China were only about 2.3 million, roughly a quarter of the motor vehicles turned out by Japanese factories in the same year. Two years later, Asian auto sales were up to 3 million, or 4.9 million counting other types of vehicles.[58] And nobody could see the end in sight, because many if not most Asians were buying cars for the first time. The next stage of affluence would see two-car families, where perhaps a decade earlier the same family might have had to make do with bicycles.

Including other types of vehicles than passenger cars, in 1990 Nissan Motor predicted that Asian demand would rise to 8.3 million by the end of the century, a little more than half the forecast levels of both the U.S. and European markets.[59] Toyota worked with similar numbers. Anyone could do the math in his or her head. By the year 2000, Asians would be buying as many cars, light trucks, and commercial vehicles as the entire Japanese auto industry produced. "The hottest area will be Asia for the next few years," Hasegawa Koji, general manager of Toyota Motor Corp.'s Asia Division, predicted in a 1990 interview. "We are looking for the market to double or even triple over the next ten years."[60]

In the late 1980s, the Japanese assigned some of their most talented executives to the region. Meanwhile, Americans and Europeans scorned Southeast Asia and even China, convinced the markets weren't worth the bother.

By the time American and European carmakers re-engaged, the Japanese had overwhelming market share and had built the beginnings of a manufacturing industry that was the first to attempt to ignore Asian borders and build "regional" cars.

From Assembly Kits to National Cars

Initially, Japanese carmakers used Southeast Asia as a testing ground for exports to industrial markets in the West, and in the 1970s Japanese auto sales in Southeast Asia were higher than sales in Europe and North America.[61] The problem was that each individual Asian market was too small to support manufacturing operations of 200,000 vehicles per year, the minimum size of an efficient auto factory, at least at the time the Japanese began selling cars to its Asian neighbors in the late 1950s. Like their European and U.S. counterparts, in the 1950s the Japanese set up local assembly operations, which offered the advantage of low costs and high margins. Such factories provided host economies with the illusion of a domestic auto industry but were almost completely dependent on technology and parts imported from Japan.

In nearly every Southeast Asian country, the Japanese carmakers quickly entered into alliances with local Chinese entrepreneurs; this was a comfortable match because ethnic Chinese made up the single largest chunk of middle-class buyers. In order to build up volume, the assembly factories frequently took on several different car companies as customers; the Japanese joint venture partners had no choice but to go along—governments kept strict limits on the number of companies in the business through licensing systems. Foreign companies faced local equity requirements not only on the manufacturing side but also in distribution. A Toyota executive in Malaysia complained bitterly about the requirement for local equity on the sales side. It forced Toyota to set up local dealerships, which were remarkably unproductive. Locally owned dealerships made up half the sales network in 1992 but provided only 10 percent of sales. "If we depended on our dealers, we would die," he said.[62]

For their part, Asian governments were only temporarily appeased by local assembly operations. They wanted the Japanese to build large, modern, efficient factories in Asia to produce cars for the local market and ultimately for export, particularly to the United States and Europe. With the exception of Singapore, each Asian economy hoped to use the auto industry as a building block for industrialization. They designed aggressive policies to make their dreams come true. In the 1970s, most Asian governments did their best to force foreign manufacturers to move beyond assembly operations. Typically, they used some combination of carrot and stick—the carrot was usually in the form of a ban or prohibitively high import tariffs on finished cars, and as sticks, they used requirements that companies source a certain percentage of the value of the cars locally.

Local content rules are never easy to implement, even when they are very precisely defined, but this was not the case in most of Southeast Asia in the 1970s. By the early 1980s, the Asian car industry was still an industry in name only, and governments became impatient. In the mid-1980s to early 1990s, about the same time that they were liberalizing rules for foreign investors in export industries, Southeast Asian governments looked at their auto industries in the opposite light. They offered tariff exemptions for imported parts, tax incentives, and other subsidies to induce foreign companies to set up large-scale factories while tightening barriers against imports. They re-created the classic Japanese and Korean environment for nurturing infant industries around their national car projects, with subsidies, strict limits on foreign competition, and huge investments of national ego. Unlike the Japanese and Korean auto industries in their babyhood, however, these were national car ventures without serious domestic rivals, which the markets were too small to support, or exports, which their Japanese partners stubbornly blocked. The results were predictable—swollen state industries mired in bureaucracy and inefficiency, churning out rust buckets to disgruntled local consumers unable to afford alternatives.

Malaysia did indeed have two national car projects, with Mitsubishi and Daihatsu, but imposed substantial tariff penalties on competing imported vehicles. Thailand enforced higher local content rules on pickup trucks than on other vehicles in order to spur a domestic industry. The Philippines insisted that carmakers come up with the foreign exchange to pay for imported parts through exports.[63] Indonesia, mimicking Malaysia, declared its own "national car" program in February 1996, under the stewardship of President Suharto's unpopular youngest son, Hutomo "Tommy" Suharto.

Tariff exemptions were the least of the privileges showered on the Indonesian deal. Tommy's partner, Korea's Kia Motors, was allowed to import its Sephia sedans without paying duties or Indonesia's stiff luxury tax until the factory's scheduled starting date in June 1998. Indonesia's state bank, PT Bank Dagang Negara, assembled a consortium of sixteen banks to lend $690 million to the project. The Sephia, renamed "Timor," sold for 60 percent less than the comparable 1,500 cc model. Japanese automakers were so incensed that they filed suit with the WTO against the deal; by the time its panel ruled in their favor in July 1998, after the fall of the Suharto government that May, the company was in ruins, with 15,000 unsold vehicles sitting in its parking lots.[64]

Foreign companies could become the beneficiaries of nationalistic policies by serving as lead contractor for domestic car-manufacturing projects, as Kia did with the Timor, Mitsubishi Motors with Malaysia's Proton Saga, and Toyota affiliate Daihatsu with Malaysia's second "national car," the Perodua. At some point, however, they would have to confront expectations on the part of their host countries to export their products. In the case of Mitsubishi Motors, this became a cat and mouse game between Mitsubishi and Prime Minister Mahathir, with the Malaysian taxpayers and consumers the ultimate losers.

Learning Experience: Korea and Taiwan

As in electronics, Japanese automakers used strategies in Southeast Asia that they had tested in Northeast Asia at an earlier stage. In both industries, Korea provided the negative example, from Japan's perspective, of allowing technological licensing arrangements and joint ventures to spring into full-blown competitors. Taiwan was the positive benchmark, Japan's apt pupil, accepting a hierarchy of production with Japan at the apex rather than breaking out of the mold. Arguably, the Koreans followed Akamatsu far more closely than the Taiwanese.

Japanese car companies began doing business in Northeast Asia in the late 1950s. In the 1970s, Korea made the automobile industry the centerpiece of its plan to "Koreanize" the machine-building industry, introducing stringent local content rules and import barriers. By the 1980s, Hyundai, the leading Korean automaker, was exporting cars to North America. By the mid-1990s, Hyundai, Daewoo, and Kia were major carmakers and exporters, with Samsung poised to leap into the business. Taiwan, on the other hand, waited until 1983 to launch its own industrial policy fostering a domestic auto industry, rocking back and forth on tariff rates and local content requirements. Its Japanese joint-venture car factories had some of the most sophisticated production lines in Asia, but the Taiwanese made no move to establish their own auto companies or move into competition with the Japanese.

Both Korean and Taiwanese industries relied heavily on Japanese parts, but Korea became a global export force while Taiwan remained bound to its island except for motorcycle and parts exports. In Korea, strong government support enabled the Korean *chaebol* to develop their own models and break free of restrictive technology agreements with Japan. Even so, Korea remained largely an assembly industry, dependent on Japan for both technology and parts.[65] By the time Taiwanese carmakers got similar support from their government, it was too late. The New Taiwan dollar had strengthened to a point at which exports were problematic.

The Korean experience strengthened Japanese resolve not to allow their Southeast Asian joint-venture partners to go their own way. Yet, the Taiwan model had its imperfections as well. Up until the early 1980s, the Taiwan government frowned on luxury car imports but did not go out of its way to promote a domestic industry. The government suppressed imports by allowing them only once a year. In Asian terms, this was a free market, and Japanese carmakers dipped in and out of it more or less at will. In the 1970s, when Toyota came under pressure from its original joint-venture partner to upgrade its assembly operations, it let its technical agreement lapse and simply exited the market. At the time, it had 30 percent of the market for passenger cars—although its total sales were only 2,800 units annually.

Toyota's local partner, Liu Ho, formed a new joint venture with Ford, which managed to last. Liu Ho had been dissatisfied with Toyota not only because the Japanese company refused to upgrade from assembly to manufacturing but because it insisted on using its own sales company, Hotai Motor. Even after Toyota's withdrawal from the market, it "supported" its distributor. When the Taiwan government allowed the import of trucks and buses in 1976, Hotai took over sales of Toyota's Hino subsidiary, which quickly took 38 percent of the market for trucks and 65 percent of the market for buses.[66] In 1978, it formed a new joint venture, Kuozui Motor Co., to assemble Hino trucks.

Not until 1987 did Toyota return to making passenger cars in Taiwan, this time under pressure from the strong yen as well as Taiwan's 1983 auto-industry development policy, which legislated a 70 percent local content rule. Toyota invested $13.8 million[67] in an assembly factory with a capacity of 40,000 units annually and a stamping and body-welding factory to supply local content. On paper, it owned just 22 percent of Kuozui Motor Co., but operationally Toyota was in charge and still reluctant to talk about exports, except of parts.

The language used in the Kuozui office was Japanese, although the chairman, vice-president, and senior directors were Chinese. In a 1990 interview, senior Chinese and Japanese executives at Kuozui explained how there were two problems in exporting from Taiwan—the high value of the New Taiwan Dollar and the lesser quality of Taiwan-made vehicles. Besides the stamping and body-welding factory, 80 percent owned by Toyota, thirty-five of Toyota's parts makers had moved to Taiwan to support the operation. Even so, only 10 percent of the welding line was automated at Feng Yong, the Toyota stamping and welding subsidiary, compared to 95 percent for comparable manufacturing in Japan.[68]

The Japanese parts companies in Taiwan were not quite as closed minded as the Japanese carmakers. Because of the smaller production volumes in the Taiwanese market, they regularly crossed *keiretsu* lines to sell to other customers, creating the foundations of a vigorous parts and after-market industry. In the end, it was the strength of the parts industry that enabled two motorcycle makers, Guangyang and Sanyang, to break free of their licenses with Honda and begin manufacturing vehicles of their own design for export. This created a second negative model for the Japanese carmakers in East Asia, one in which their own subcontractors led the revolution against them. Partly as a result, in Southeast Asia, the carmakers were to exercise strict supervision over their subcontractors, reproducing the subcontractor associations that helped enforce control over their suppliers in Japan.

In the case of Guangyang and Sanyang, Honda flatly refused to allow the companies to export Honda-designed motorcycles to any country where Honda already had a factory—a long list. Finally, the Taiwan government stepped in. "Both firms were in an awkward position," writes Greg Noble, a scholar at Australian National University (ANU):

> Sanyang because it was completely reliant upon Honda for car assembly, and Guangyang because a financial crisis in 1982 forced it to look to Honda for technical and managerial assistance, in the process giving Honda a 22.5 percent capital stake. Working with the government's Industrial Development Bureau the firms developed three-stage strategies.
>
> First, Sanyang and Guangyang decreased their reliance on Honda parts, investing in many of the more complex parts themselves. The last 10 percent of engine parts proved a challenge, but by the early 1990s the companies achieved virtually 100 percent self-sufficiency in parts. The next step was to develop an independent design capacity, in order to avoid paying the higher royalty fees for exports (reportedly 4 percent, compared to 2 percent for domestic sales). Sanyang developed a design and development center of 300 people; Guangyang soon followed with 200 employees and plans for a drastic expansion. Most models were completely designed in Taiwan.[69]

In the early 1990s, Guangyang emerged as a formidable competitor to Honda in China, while Sanyang concentrated on Vietnam. In mid-1995, Guangyang invested in three Chinese joint ventures, with a planned capacity of 1,000,000 motorcycles and 500,000 motorcycle engines annually. Sanyang leaped in ahead of Honda with Vietnam's first motorcycle assembly plant, then convinced the government to delay approval of Honda's application to set up a rival plant.

Proton in Malaysia

The Japanese were correct to worry about the potential of Southeast Asian competitors. Southeast Asians were alert to the examples of both Korea and

Taiwan, and understood the problems of technical cooperation with the Japanese. But understanding the problem did not automatically lead to the best solutions. Malaysia pursued a third course sandwiched between the Taiwanese and Korean model, its national car industry an ungainly hybrid of both. Malaysia ended up with not just one but two inefficient producers dependent on Japanese design and parts supply (three if you counted the model of Proton updated by the French automaker Citroën). Despite a vigorous industrial policy personally and enthusiastically directed by Prime Minister Mahathir, Malaysia's national car projects never managed to break free of Japanese control. His tactics included all the standard elements of industrial policy to nurture an infant industry—high local content requirements, punitive tariffs on imported cars and parts not associated with the national car projects, and direct subsidies from the government. Yet, primarily because of the huge rift in currency markets after the Plaza Accord, Malaysia was able to get much more out of its partnership with Japan, in terms of both technology transfer and exports, than Taiwan did. Its failure to match the success of the Korean auto industry can be blamed at least in part on Malaysia's small home market and obstacles posed by Japanese lead partners in reaching world export markets, making it difficult for any manufacturer to achieve economies of scale in auto production.

Economists warned Mahathir from the beginning that the Malaysian market was too small to justify building a factory of Proton's size. Against economic logic, Mahathir decided to go for annual production of 300,000 cars and three largish factories. He planned to use the excess capacity for exports. Malaysia ended up with two national cars, a national van, a national truck, and even a national motorcycle, but by 1998, the first of the national car projects, the Proton Saga, still relied for an estimated 45 percent of its parts on Japan.[70] Nor did Malaysia fulfill its promise on the export side, making only 22,000 sales abroad in 1996, mostly to the U.K. In 1996, the last peak of the auto market prior to the Asian financial crisis, Malaysia was still the third-ranking auto assembler in Southeast Asia, with a capacity of 297,000 vehicles, compared to 600,000 in Thailand and 378,800 in Indonesia.[71] Instead of spurring competition, the proliferation of state-sponsored auto companies turned into a dogfight among rather sleepy dogs.

From the moment he took office as prime minister in 1981, Mahathir was obsessed with the national car project. The history of the industry bears his personal mark, ranging from the vanity-inspired export campaign, heavily subsidized by the government, to the games he played with global investors, particularly the Japanese. The Malaysian government coddled the industry with protective tariffs and directed credit, stepping in whenever the industry seemed to be facing a rough patch. The Asian financial crisis virtually erased six years of growth in the Asian auto market, with an estimated loss of 2.35 million in car sales in 1997 to 1998. Overall demand fell by 7 percent in 1997 and 29 percent in 1998.[72] Yet, while neighboring Thailand progressively reduced barriers in a successful attempt to win foreign investment, Malaysia introduced yet more aggressive industrial policies to promote its national cars.

Malaysia's 1998 budget, introduced in October 1997, included provisions for tax hikes on foreign cars and mandatory use of the Proton Saga, a mid-sized, 1,300 to 1,500 cc sedan, by all government agencies. This act was merely the latest in a long series of measures designed to deliver between 70 and 80 percent of the auto market to Malaysian brands. In June 1998, Proton increased its stake in Britain's Lotus Group from 63.75 percent to 80 percent, and declared it would spend $1.4 billion[73] to put Lotus's 1,000 engineers to work designing an all-Malaysian car. Another $2.1 billion was to go toward boosting manufacturing capacity to 1,000,000 vehicles by 2010, and to the creation of a new town, "Proton City," to support the industry.[74]

Proton got its start as the centerpiece of a plan to restructure the Malaysian economy by reducing dependence on both imported products and ethnic Chinese capital, which dominated the Malaysian auto-assembly business in the 1970s.[75] When Mahathir, then trade and industry minister, looked for a partner for the project in 1980, Mitsubishi Motors won the contract by default—no other car company was even interested. Daihatsu broke off negotiations in 1981 when Mahathir made plain that he wanted a Malaysian car, not just a knockoff of a Japanese prototype. Mitsubishi alone had the imagination to see the factory as a permanent customer for Mitsubishi parts, a role it had pioneered with Korea's Hyundai Motors. In 1992, nearly a decade after the project started, a senior manager at Proton admitted that the company would continue to rely on Mitsubishi for engine parts "for some time."[76]

The Proton deal also built up political capital for other appendages of the Mitsubishi *keiretsu*. According to one account, Mitsubishi Motors was under orders from senior members of the giant Mitsubishi Group, which was then negotiating terms on the Malaysian liquefied national gas project in Sarawak with Petronas, the state oil company. The Mitsubishi chieftains knew the risks of the Proton venture but saw it as a reasonable trade-off for the LNG deal.[77] Moreover, Mitsubishi was smart enough to offer a design lacking key requirements for the United States and other export markets where the company already competed.[78] The original contract failed to mention a pre-existing government program for mandatory use of specific Malaysian parts, meaning that in the beginning, at least, Mitsubishi Motors would be free to use its own CKD assembly kits.[79]

At the beginning of the 1980s, Malaysia had the weakest car industry in Southeast Asia. For years, the government had been pressuring assembly companies based in Malaysia to upgrade, without visible results. Mahathir intended things to be different for Proton and stacked the deck in its favor in every way imaginable. First, he parked the project in the Heavy Industries Corporation of Malaysia (HICOM), a state holding company for heavy industries reporting directly to him. In 1985, when the first Malaysian Sagas rolled off the Proton production line, he exempted the "national car" from the 40 percent import duty on parts that foreign brands had to bear. Next, he raised duty on imported parts for auto-assembly plants three-fold. Non-Sagas ended up with a tax rate of almost 100 percent.

The early Sagas were a simple copy of the Mitsubishi Lancer. Mitsubishi Motors took a 15 percent stake in the venture, Proton Perusahaan Otomobil Nasional Berhad, arranged its $175 million[80] financing and implicitly barred exports of the Proton for the first five years of the project's life (the contract referred only to Mitsubishi's responsibility to help Proton build cars for the *domestic* market for five years).[81] Mitsubishi was in charge of building the plant, training workers, and supplying most of the components, including Mitsubishi's Malaysian stamping plant. Nonetheless, the Saga qualified as a domestic car, and with the duty exemptions, Proton was able to sell its 1,300 cc model for less than $8,500,[82] some 25 percent below competing brands. Within two years, the Saga had captured nearly three-quarters of the Malaysian market. Analysts estimated that the government's financial support amounted to $1,744 per vehicle[83] in 1986.[84]

Even so, the launch of the Proton was fraught with problems, some from just bad luck. Commissioned in 1983, by the time the factory produced its first car two years later, a full-blown recession was underway in global commodities markets, triggered by the collapse of the oil cartel. Malaysia depended heavily on resource exports, and its economy took a deep hit. At the same time, the yen began its historic surge, and Proton's yen-denominated debt soon doubled in terms of Malaysian dollars. In its first year of production, the company reported losses of $17.1 million,[85] and its unsecured debt had ballooned from $121 million[86] to $196.7 million.[87] Differences over the retail price of the Proton precipitated a huge fight between Proton and its independent sales company, EON, as the cost of imported Japanese components escalated sharply.[88]

With the domestic market in contraction and its domestic sales agent in a state of shock, Mahathir decided that the way out was to export the Saga, exploiting the ambiguity of the contract terms with Mitsubishi. Proton and HICOM announced that the first shipments would go to the U.K., because it used right-hand-drive vehicles. Mitsubishi screamed, partly because it was already shipping the Lancer to Britain from a factory in Australia. The Japanese argued that Proton lacked the marketing savvy to compete in Western markets. Mitsubishi protested even more when Mahathir signed a letter of intent with Yugo importer Malcolm Bricklin to bring the Saga into the United States, where it would compete with Mitsubishi models marketed by Chrysler.

The Bricklin deal, however, turned out to be a fiasco. A letter of intent was signed in December 1986 aiming at U.S. sales in the range of 100,000 to 250,000 vehicles per year. Bricklin promised to pick up the $10 million it would cost to modify the engine to meet U.S. emission control standards. Then Bricklin suddenly sold the franchise and disappeared. The ensuing scandal led to an equally strange turn of events in Malaysia. Mahathir became impatient with the Malaysian managers of Proton, blamed them for the company's mounting problems, and decided that the only way to rescue Proton was to bring back the Japanese.

While the Bricklin affair was playing out, Mahathir went back to the Japanese to refinance Proton's long-term loans, due to begin repayment in January 1989. In April 1987, Mitsubishi put together a syndicate of Japanese banks that extended both the grace and repayment periods for the debt.[89] In August 1987, the Mitsubishi syndicate put up a new, $89 million[90] loan.[91] Mahathir fired Proton's Malaysian deputy chairman and executive director, appointing two Mitsubishi men in their stead, Iwabuchi Kenji and Fujioka Kyo.[92] The final step was to buy out EON's Chinese partner and set up the new EON as a joint venture between Mitsubishi and Malaysia's Ministry of Finance.

Mitsubishi pushed for greater control from behind the scenes, both because it was anxious to block exports to third markets, and for reasons linked to the high yen. As the cost of imported parts went up, Mitsubishi faced the prospect of a future in which it would have to limit parts supply from Japan. The most efficient way to deal with the problem was to buy parts locally, but they were prohibitively expensive because they were made in tiny, inefficient factories. If Mitsubishi or any other company attempted to use Southeast Asia as an export production platform, the price of parts would first have to be brought down. The only way to do that, Mitsubishi reasoned, would be to develop facilities to serve the entire ASEAN region, with production at a high enough volume to reduce costs through economies of scale. In order to move such a plan along, Mitsubishi needed to control the region's first large-scale factory and its suppliers. In 1986, the Proton factory's output was 25,000 but was scheduled to expand to 80,000 units in 1988 and 120,000 units after 1994.[93]

Only after Mitsubishi got on board with Proton's export plans did things go more smoothly. Mitsubishi ruled out the U.S. market but otherwise promised its support. It sent the Proton to countries at the bottom end of the car market, including Bangladesh, Sri Lanka, Jamaica, Malta, and Nauru but also to the U.K., New Zealand, and Singapore, where it surprised both Mitsubishi and Malaysia with its success.[94] By 1992, 44,000 Protons were on the road in Britain. None of them retailed for more than $17,000, some $4,000 less than the nearest comparable model. Proton got a break on exports into the U.K. because it qualified for tariff exemptions under Europe's generalized system of preferences (GSP) for developing countries.[95]

Agents of Influence

On the way to the Proton factory in 1992, the taxi I hailed was a Proton, not that much of a coincidence—the brand had about 60 percent of the domestic market. The taxi driver was bitter about it. He claimed that the car had a soft body. He knew another Proton owner whose car's clutch fell out. An Indian, he said he had no choice but to buy a Proton because otherwise he would never have been able to get his taxi license. *Bumiputras* (ethnic Malays), were first in line for taxi licenses, but Proton owners were regarded with special favor even if they were not Malays.

The factory itself was huge, its production line spread over one and a quarter square miles. The manufacturing process was laid out on tracks. Parts and chassis came in at one end, finished cars rolled out the other. The Proton factory was on a different plane altogether than car factories in Japan. Toyota's Tahara plant, where the luxury Lexus line was made, had more robots than human workers. Vehicles moved from station to station where the robots responded to individual customer orders, fitting leather seats here, a sunroof there. The Tahara plant was difficult to take in visually. Choreographed and complex, its intense activity was confined to a small space. By comparison, the Proton plant had the look of a sprawling, highly simplified engineering flowchart, designed to serve as a learning tool as much as a factory.

As I made the rounds of Proton and its suppliers, talking to managers and engineers, government officials and rivals, it was not hard to see why Mahathir had given such short shrift to the economists and their warnings of economic inefficiency. What the prime minister had demanded from Mitsubishi, and got, was a huge vocational education project in the form of a car plant. Like Arthur Toynbee, Mahathir seemed to operate on the principle that civilization was a contagious disease, spread by means of cultural artifacts. The Proton factory was Mahathir's artifact. It would spread the contagion of Japanese business culture throughout the land, starting with the auto industry. Although technological transfer was among its objectives, cultural transfer was equally if not more important. Mahathir knew he was starting from scratch and may have figured that he would worry about technology transfer after he had an industry to transfer it to.

Cultural transfer seemed to be the main objective of Proton's subcontractors' association. Such associations were a pervasive feature of the Japanese auto industry. In theory, they served as mechanisms for technology transfer. In Japan, subcontractor associations were the main venue through which auto assemblers got parts makers to participate in the early stages of new model design. They helped reduce transaction costs by establishing a regular communications channel between the giant assemblers and their subcontractors, and by applying group pressure to observe exclusive ties with the manufacturer.

In the Malaysian context, the associations served to induce discipline but not to engage parts makers in the design process, because there was no indigenous design capability and R&D was carried out by the Japanese headquarters organizations, whether in final assembly of vehicles or parts production. Instead, the main policy justification of the subcontractors' association at Proton was to migrate technological learning from one government-led car project to the next, with dubious effect. From the perspective of the Japanese automakers, the usefulness of the parts association may also have been to prevent subcontractors following the Taiwan model and helping to build true domestic competitors. Proton's subcontractor association worked with the second national car project as well as Proton, the linkage supplied by HICOM, the government's heavy industry holding company. HICOM was an investor in Mitsubishi Motors' Proton, Daihatsu's Perodua, and key Proton subcontractors such as PHN. The various national car projects kept the subcontractors busy but also introduced Japanese-style cartelism, as well as providing an entrée for Japanese parts makers to dominate the nascent industry.

Although going along with the idea of a local stamping plant, Mitsubishi Motors Corp. (MMC) procrastinated in accepting expanded localization until more of its *keiretsu* parts makers arrived in Malaysia. One of its main strategies to fend off local parts vendors was to claim inferior quality. Because there were no indigenous testing labs in the early days of the project, MMC had to test the parts itself, giving it a free hand with the results.[96] In a notorious case involving sheet glass, MMC declared it would switch from the original supplier, Malaysian Sheet Glass, to another Japanese-Malaysian joint venture with ties to the Mitsubishi *keiretsu*. It introduced a new requirement for car windows, prohibiting any marks from handling equipment on the edges of the windows. Malaysian Sheet Glass spent $2.8 million[97] modifying its equipment so that it could meet this requirement, while the Mitsubishi-related company did not. Mitsubishi then relaxed the requirement and gave 40 percent of its business to the other company anyway.[98] Paul Low was cynical about it. Low was the president of Malaysian Sheet

Glass as well as the head of the Malaysian Automotive Component Parts Manufacturers. "It's a national car with the heart of Mitsubishi," he said. "Mitsubishi's reason for being here is to continue to sell its CKD packs."[99]

"If we look at the overall investment profile, there is sizable investment between Japan and Malaysia in component making," said Kisai Bin Rahmat, Proton's deputy managing director for manufacturing. "Mitsubishi provides instruction, in the sense of identifying vendors. It's only fair that they introduce us to the guy who actually produces the part. We believe they are the best ones to introduce that particular component. Why should MMC introduce anybody else?"[100]

On paper, the Proton subcontractors' association, Persatuan Pambekal Proton (PPP), was a joint project between the Malaysian government and Mitsubishi Motors. PPP was set up in July 1992, with 104 companies, 40 percent of which were Japanese affiliates, 30 percent from other countries, and 30 percent local. In practice, like the Proton factory itself, PPP was under Mitsubishi's control. "We were made aware of the environment of the motor industry in Japan," said Kisai. "One feature is that vendors have some sort of association. We liked the idea, and we sort of informed these features to our vendors. MMC gave us information on how to establish it, but we had to adapt it to our own environment. It is a vehicle to promote certain things. When we first started to introduce the concept, we did not know what was its real intention. [Before we introduced the association] if we had two or three suppliers, we would let them fight each other. Now we are saying, 'please group together and be strong so that it is easier for us to improve our business,' and it works."

The links between Mitsubishi's subcontractor association and PPP were direct. The lead company in the Proton subcontractors' association was called PHN Industry. Commissioned in July 1991, PHN was a stamping line for small- and medium-sized body parts, its capacity large enough to supply both national cars when it was in full production. HICOM Berhad, the government holding company, and Proton itself were the major shareholders, with 42.5 percent and 35 percent, respectively. Mitsubishi Corp. held 2.5 percent.[101] The fourth owner was Nagoya Oak Industries (NOI), with 20 percent. This was a company with fifteen employees, making dies for PHN's stamping press. NOI had been set up in November 1990 as a shell company for Mitsubishi Motors' twenty-five lead subcontractors, all Japanese companies. "The 25 member companies doing business with Mitsubishi Motors . . . joined hands to establish Nagoya Oak Industries Co., Ltd." reads a 1992 handout from the company. "All these 25 companies are located in and around Nagoya, and have been supplying parts and components for Mitsubishi vehicles."[102]

Khoriri H.J. Abu Sabri, PHN's manager of corporate affairs, who took me around the factory one day, described the joint venture with NOI as a "forced marriage." He said it with a laugh. But there was plenty of evidence showing the restrictive nature of the relationship. PHN's Malaysian shareholders wanted to take over die production as well as stamping, but as of my visit in 1992, Nagoya was stalling. It had allowed PHN to send workers for technical training in die repair and maintenance but not die design. The PHN factory was run as a training operation. At any given time, 3 percent of its 183 workers were in Japan, at a cost of $588 per day[103] to PHN, and it had two resident Japanese expatriates as well, one for five years, another for two. In order to ease communications problems, PHN sent people to a Japanese-language school in Kuala Lumpur, run by Japan's MITI. So far, said Khoriri, twenty-five people had completed the course. Machines and 100 percent of the steel coils that the factory used as raw material came from Japan.[104]

From Malaysia's perspective, such training was enormously valuable, enough so to warrant subsidized credit from the government to the tune of 5 percentage points lower than commercial interest rates, then running around 9.5 percent.[105] Khoriri's office was spacious. An interior decorator had worked on its white surfaces, blonde wood, and ergonomic chairs. The factory grounds held not only a tennis court but also a court for *sepak takraw*, a traditional game similar to basketball. The security guards had landscaped the manicured grounds on overtime, as "part of motivation," Khoriri said. There were trees, a waterfall, and a rock garden. Khoriri's Japanese vendors donated the carp in Khoriri's fishpond, and some of the plants came from Nagoya. Workers could expect to get a bonus of one month's pay.

There were a number of reasons why the Malaysian government lavished so much attention on the parts companies. Perhaps the most sensible one was that the Japanese model of auto manufacturing would not work without them. The major Japanese automakers—Toyota, Nissan, Honda, Mitsubishi Motors, and Mazda—were assembly companies. They were famous for lean management and innovative inventory-control systems, but these only worked because they rested on a pyramid of obedient, highly organized suppliers engaged in upstream processes of R&D as well as downstream work making subassemblies and, in some cases, an entire model.

Leaving aside Mahathir's "Look East" program and the Japanese model, the economic argument for using public funds to invest in a heavy industry like Proton was based on the externalities, or side effects, it would create. Principal among these was Mahathir's desire to create world-class multinationals that could compete on the same terms as the highly successful car companies created by Japan and South Korea, but at the same time the impact of the auto industry on any economy that succeeds in putting one together is profound. Neoclassical theory suggests that externalities magically "arise" in the form of supply industries and wealth effects (as they did in the relatively laissez-faire market environment of the Taiwanese auto industry). Mahathir surmised that the Malaysian parts industry would need some help, both because of the weakness of support systems and the demonstrated opposition of the Japanese and other multinationals to Malaysian ventures cannibalizing their own external sales, or using suppliers external to their *keiretsu*. Hence PHN and other auto parts companies were placed under HICOM's stewardship.

A third reason for making the development of an auto parts industry into a national cause was the assumption that parts companies by definition would be more Malaysian than the assembly companies. That this was a flawed assumption was all too evident from PHN's dependence on Japanese management as well as imported Japanese steel. Even so, Malaysian officials still appeared to view the concepts of parts makers, local content, and *bumiputra* control as the same thing. A major objective of Proton was to "spearhead supporting industries" in the Malaysian auto sector, said the senior Malaysian at Proton, Dato' Mohd. Nadzmi B. Mohd. Salleh.

"Proton has strategically developed itself," he declared proudly. "Even if protection is withdrawn [for the auto industry] most of the parts will be locally produced." Initially, Proton imported most of the bits and pieces that went into the car from Japan, in CKD kits. The only essential difference between Proton and the other car assemblers in Malaysia when it started out was that Proton had its own stamping line, Nadzmi said. So the arrival of Japanese auto parts companies in Proton's wake was not only welcome but essential to Malaysia's goals of developing a "local" auto industry, no matter if it was Malaysian in name only. Such things as the subcontractors' association represented an aspect of the learning experience. "This was the first time the Japanese concept was established in Malaysia," Nadzmi said. "We would like to learn as much as possible from the Japanese experience."[106]

PHN's training program was a mere shadow of the massive effort undertaken by Proton to school its workers in Japanese production skills. Nadzmi said that by 1992, Proton had sent some 500 to 600 people for training in Japan, out of 3,005 workers at the plant. In 1992, another 150 people were in Japan, working on "new projects," including a model adaptation and a new $157 million[107] castings plant. They came back to Malaysia from Japan with a little Japanese, enough to communicate with their Japanese "advisors," and hands-on knowledge of the production lines being introduced to Malaysia. This was not technology transfer in the strict sense of imparting proprietary designs and technical information, but it was transfer of manufacturing know-how. The Malaysians involved were well pleased.

"Technology transfer is a big word," Nadzmi said. "It means many things to many people. The fact is that we started from a zero base. Before I became involved in Proton, I had never been involved in the motor industry or anything like it. Mahathir saw that the world was shifting to the East because of the Japanese work ethic. A lot of people criticized him. Mahathir is one person who has never been trained in the West. Instead, he got his training in Singapore as a medical doctor. He saw that the Japanese were coming up. He decided to 'Look East,' to have fresh people. We had no people who were familiar with this industry. I had taught economic research and agri-business, and later worked at Petronas and in HICOM. We had nobody who was in the motor industry. I have gone through it from nothing. This has been some learning experience we have gone through. Over the short span of seven years, we Malaysians have acquired whatever technology we have today. I think that technology transfer is definitely there. We people associated with the project definitely feel it."

The Japanese executive actually in charge of the Proton factory in 1992 was Kawashima Yoshifumi. When I interviewed him, Kawashima had been in Malaysia just six months, after spending five years working on the Proton project from the Tokyo office of Mitsubishi Motors, as deputy general manager for ASEAN. "Proton was a major responsibility for me," Kawashima said. His first job in Malaysia was to supervise the construction of the new castings plant. He described this as "third-phase technology transfer." "Casting in general may be no big deal," he said. "A casting can be something like a manhole cover. But we are planning to produce cylinder blocks in-house. When we consider world-class auto manufacturers, none of them sources their cylinder blocks from outside. It's the heart of the engine, and engines are the heart of the car. Manufacturing production of cylinder blocks defines a company as a true auto manufacturer. To this extent, the technology is very high and difficult."[108]

The planning for the castings line was slow and deliberate. Proton spent a year in preparation, and development of the line was to take another two years. Mitsubishi Motors was fully engaged. "If we were just going to make casting parts, we might not need full involvement from Mitsubishi," Kawashima said. "But since we are going to produce the most difficult and important parts in-house, MMC is very much concerned with how to implement that, and a very basic concept is to train Malaysians in Japan." Twenty Malaysian trainees were already at work learning the ropes in a Mitsubishi Motors castings plant in Kyoto. They were to remain for six months, when another team would arrive. Eventually, 100 employees would spend between six months and a year and a half in Japan. "We were there two weeks ago, and both partners are enthusiastic," Nadzmi broke in. Kawashima continued, "To achieve a smooth and complete transfer, they are coming back here with

MMC engineers as teachers. Our trainees over there are undergoing training by Mitsubishi castings engineers. For that period they will be like students and teachers. By the time the castings plant is completed, the students will return home."

Kisai Bin Rahmat was a slender man of forty-two when I interviewed him, with a boyish face and gentle, refined manners. He held degrees from the University of Glasgow and Cranfield University and was among the "pioneers" on the management team, having joined Proton in 1983. He insisted that the Japanese had fully discharged their responsibilities as teachers. "The Japanese have been very good to us in technology transfer," says Kisai, who like most of his colleagues used the abbreviation "TT." "The thing for us to do is to learn as fast as possible. If things are printed in Japanese, we cannot say that they are not sharing with us. Previously all the books were written in English. We could not say that the material was inaccessible, before we learned English, just because the material was written in English. Of course, there's a great deal of expertise, a great deal of technology, in this business. Even if MMC opened the cupboard, we might not be able to digest it in one go."

Such defensiveness by Proton had several origins, including regular tirades by Mahathir himself against Japanese reticence in sharing technology. Another reason was the disorganization of the training programs themselves. It was unclear whether the chaos was intentional or simply a reflection of the difficulty the Japanese had in imparting production skills across linguistic and cultural barriers. In any event, despite the fact that Japanese companies such as MMC had spent most of their corporate lives on the receiving end of Western technology transfer, the challenge of exporting it seemed to befuddle them. By Japanese standards, Proton represented a full-blown technological partnership. This meant allowing Malaysian workers into Japanese factories and letting them work on the production line. It did not mean formal instruction, manuals, or access to engineering documents. The Malaysians were expected to learn by doing. Malaysian "trainees" who worked on Japanese production lines were allowed to observe but discouraged from asking questions. Few of them had the language ability to do so.

Japanese could argue that such inductive training was a Japanese tradition, and indeed sushi makers and students of Japanese pottery were encouraged to learn through observation for the initial years of their apprenticeships. They could also argue that language barriers prevented more direct training methods. The fact was that large Japanese industrial companies invested heavily in training for their Japanese employees but had difficulty translating such programs effectively for their foreign workers. To some degree, the Japanese clearly used language and cultural barriers as a pretext to maintain walls around core processes. Skilled engineers would be invited to study documents in Japanese, which they could not read. Unskilled workers would be invited to learn complex manufacturing processes without the aid of manuals, so that they could perform rote actions but not grasp the functions themselves. When challenged, the Japanese would fall back on the superiority of Japanese management, which in the late 1980s was regarded with almost mystical awe.

Later, I walked around the Proton factory floor with Muhammad Aris Anuar, a senior deputy manager in the body assembly section at Proton, who had gone through the MMC training program in Japan and shared his perspective on the experience. Aris had a degree in mechanical engineering and studied Japanese for five weeks in Osaka before beginning his formal training.

> I worked for four days in Mizushima, in each section—stamping, assembly, body, quality control, and just-in-time inventory. One week on the actual production line. If you don't know an area, that's where they put you first, after some small introduction. If you do that, any questions you might want to ask will be answered. People have all different interpretations of technology transfer. I think it depends on the individual. Before this, I wasn't exposed to an actual manufacturing line. In university, they did not teach these things. When you see them, you can learn a lot. Somehow these Japanese have the capacity to continue the learning process. They won't teach you unless you make the effort, I think. The most consistent Japanese thinking is, if you want to learn, you have to learn by yourself.

I asked him if the Japanese used written materials in their training programs. The answer was no. "When you are first exposed to all these things—JIT [just-in-time inventory control], QCC [quality control circles]—I thought it would have to be done with manuals. After you do your training, you know that the manuals are just for guidance. *Joshiki* or common sense is very important. You can learn from a manual but the knowledge is useful only for a short period of time. The first thing the Japanese will do with a new worker is ask them to sweep the factory. If they can't do sweeping properly, they won't be able to do the difficult work, either.

"I'm not sure what the real purpose of training is. Sometimes it's vague. They just tell you to follow orders. But you have to think for yourself when the situation advises." Aris spotted a Japanese walking down the line with a briefcase. The man stooped to pick up a piece of garbage. Aris nodded approvingly. "Once I was trained that way. The supervisor said to me, 'What's that?' I said, 'Rubbish.' He said to go pick it up. Then he pointed again. 'What's that?' 'It's rubbish, but it's outside my area,' I said. He said to pick it up anyway.

"Some say Japanese culture is too dictatorial. But it depends on the individual. If you're positive-minded and willing to learn, it's OK." Aris took me through an area where final preparations were being made for production of the Iswara, a model change that incorporated British design. Nonetheless, training for the line was conducted in the usual way, in Japan, and new equipment was Japanese. "If we do not bring the machines from Japan, the Japanese say they cannot teach. We bought the equipment on the advice of our technical advisor," Aris said. Five technical advisors had come from Japan to prepare for the launch, which would add 25,000 to 30,000 units in annual production, raising Proton's capacity to 100,000 vehicles annually.[109]

Meanwhile, Back in Detroit

While the Japanese delved ever deeper into the Asian auto industry and market, American automakers virtually ignored Asia. They dropped out of Southeast Asia in the 1970s and 1980s, paradoxically in part because of rising Asian demand.[110] Realizing that small-scale assembly operations, turning out 3,000 to 4,000 vehicles per year, were inadequate, they chose to quit rather than make larger investments to increase production. At the same time, the American companies were under heavy competitive pressure from Japanese carmakers in the all-important compact segment of the U.S. market. The decision was made to concentrate scarce resources at home. By the late 1980s, U.S. automakers were all but invisible in Asia. General Motors kept a bare minimum of exposure through its European affiliate, Opel; Ford worked through its equity relationship with Mazda; and Chrysler was represented by its disastrous AMC Jeep operation in China.

In the early 1990s, when the Big Three returned to Asia with substantial investments, they were thus entering enemy territory—markets dominated not only by the big Japanese assemblers but by their parts companies. All three picked Thailand as their production platform in a nod to Japan. In less than a decade, Japanese investment had turned Thailand into Asia's fourth-largest auto manufacturer, after Japan, China, and South Korea, with a production capacity of 1.1 million cars.[111] The Americans moved cautiously. Chrysler and Ford arrived in 1995 in joint ventures, Chrysler with the local Volvo assembler, assembling its right-hand-drive Cherokee sports-utility vehicle, and Ford in a $500 million deal with Mazda to produce pickup trucks.

The parts problem was clearly on their minds. Annual parts sales in Thailand topped $6 billion, and U.S. parts makers accounted for less than 2 percent.[112] Toyota alone had brought ninety-six of its Japanese subcontractors to the country.[113] Ford invested $53 million in automotive-components manufacturing operations at two factories, one a joint venture with Korean Mando Machinery Corporation. The splashiest deal was by GM, which decided to use Thailand as its Asian production base for a new, Opel-designed "Asian" car—another bow to the Japanese, who had been working on similar concepts for two decades. This was to be an export plant, and GM wanted to bring thirty of its parts suppliers to Thailand or nearby countries. Delphi Automotive, a GM parts subsidiary, was already in-country. In negotiating the $750 million factory with the Thai government, GM pushed for duty waivers. It got them but not without a parting jab by the Thai government at GM's latecomer status. Thailand finally agreed but explained it was only able to do so because Japanese producers had built up a viable parts industry; the waiver was extended to all Thai-based producers.[114]

A cascading waterfall cooled the lobby of UMW Toyota in Petaling Jaya, a suburb of Kuala Lumpur. Toyota Corollas were parked neatly on the marble under banners proclaiming "Toyota Lifestyle." Fountain pens and digital clocks with the Toyota emblem were on sale behind a glass counter. The air-conditioning was pleasantly frigid after the heat and exhaust fumes of Malaysia's heavily trafficked roads. In a corner of the sales floor, I asked the manager, Okabe Akira, why American and European auto companies had ignored the merits of the Asian market for so long.

"One reason," he opined, "is the nonmarket management style of the American auto companies. "Henry Ford II thought the Asian market was very important. He came here in 1970 to introduce an Asian car, the Ford Tierra, in the Philippines and Malaysia. That was a sign of interest, but after that, nothing. This is very much the way of American businessmen's thinking, and of American culture. They cannot survive on a long-term basis. Without short-term profits, they cannot continue. They don't know how to get down to the same eye level as their customers. The Americans just want to sell one product through their distributors to different-taste markets. They're very stupid, I want to say. They don't know about marketing."

Keiretsu Rivalry

Later, over drinks in the Concorde Hotel, Okabe tells me about himself and some of his business experiences in Malaysia. A middle-aged Japanese businessman, Okabe is a giggler, with a habit of leaning over and poking his Malaysian Chinese associate, Martin Wee, on the paunch. "He looks ugly on the outside, but he's smart inside!" Okabe wheezed. His career had been unconventional, for a Japanese company man. Before joining Toyota in 1971, he worked for ten months at a "private technical industry association" in Nepal. He was married there, to a Japanese woman, and insisted on a Hindu wedding ceremony. This made him a celebrity back in Japan. Okabe clearly liked attention. During a lull in the conversation, he opened his briefcase to pull out a copy of his "acceptance speech" for a ceremony conferring on him the title of Malaysian *dato*, or leader. The title was a gift from a rajah who loved antique cars and racing. Through the rajah, he heard that Mahathir, also a car enthusiast, wanted to add a Lexus to his official fleet. Mahathir bought and paid for the black Lexus ("duty-free because it was an official car"). Okabe brought a second vehicle into the country to serve as a backup, keeping it in the showroom headquarters. Two engineers were sent to Japan for two months of training and returned to Malaysia with $36,000[115] in tools. Okabe was vague about who paid for what.

The next round, however, was clearly on Toyota. "Delivery of the Lexus took six months, and Mahathir got impatient," Okabe recalled. "He sent his secretary over to look at the car when it finally came in. There was a big problem. The seats were covered with fabric, not leather! We had a Toyota executive bring leather seats with him as excess baggage from Tokyo. We set up backups all along the way. There was a car waiting in Singapore in case the flight was delayed past the time of the shuttle to KL. At the last minute, the engineers had trouble with a tiny spring inside the gear handle. Again, we had the part ferried from Tokyo. We took it out of a company Celsior, the Japanese version of the Lexus."

Okabe's unctuous ways may have helped Toyota affiliate Daihatsu Motor to land the Perodua contract and form its own joint venture, Perusahaan Otomobil Kedua Sdn. Bhd. The chairman of the new venture, Raja Tun Mohar, was Okabe's friend, of the antique cars and honorary *dato*ships. The rationale behind the Daihatsu deal was very much the same as Mitsubishi Motors and Proton. The Malaysian factory was to serve as a captive market for parts, initially from Japan, but over time as a participant in a regional parts market within the Toyota-Daihatsu group. By 1997, two Perodua models, the Kancil and an 850 cc minivan, the Rusa, were taking 40 percent of the Malaysian market, eating into the share of Mitsubishi's Proton. The Perodua factory, with a capacity of 120,000 vehicles per year, was half the size of Proton's 230,000 vehicle capacity, but moved through the launch of the Kancil and Rusa with far fewer problems than Proton's Saga. Much like the Proton vehicles, however, Perodua remained largely a Japanese car. By 1998, four years after it produced the first Kancil, the Perodua factory was still importing 40 percent of its parts from Japan. It produced Daihatsu mini-cars on the same line as the Kancils and Rusas.[116]

The rivalry between Mitsubishi Motors and Daihatsu was not just about cars and the future of the Asian auto market. On another level, it was a good example of how the *keiretsu* formed an important part of the backdrop to Japanese corporate rivalry outside Japan as well as domestically. Toyota was considered a *keiretsu* of the vertical type, the lead company of an army of subcontractors. Daihatsu nested in the Toyota *keiretsu* as an affiliate company, owned 16 percent by Toyota and cooperating closely with the much larger company. Toyota, in turn, was among the senior members of *Nigikai* (literally, Two Trees Club), the Mitsui *keiretsu*'s twenty-seven-company presidents' club. Mitsubishi Motors was among the twenty-eight members of the Mitsubishi *keiretsu*'s presidents' club, called the *Kinyobikai* (Friday club.)

Both Mitsubishi, the largest of the *keiretsu*, and Mitsui, the second largest, had been in Malaysia for several decades, represented by their trading houses, Mitsubishi Shoji and Mitsui Bussan. In Malaysia, Mitsui was considered the senior of the two. Many Malaysians viewed the Perodua deal, signed in February 1993, as a payoff to the Mitsui *keiretsu*. It would have made far more sense to park the second national car project under Proton as well, Steven Wong said in 1992. Wong, then working as a strategist with Zalik Securities in Kuala Lumpur, speculated that the Daihatsu deal was part of a subtle balancing act between Japan's two largest corporate empires in Malaysia and their networks of local "beneficiaries." "I have no evidence," Wong said. "But in this country, Mitsui and Co., are about as secretive as the mafia. They rarely surface. They don't have big projects. Every deal they've ever done, they have always paid big kickbacks. They have learned to work the system very well."[117]

Brand to Brand Complementation: Getting Regional Production Networks Aloft

The growth of regional production networks is among the more significant legacies of the expansion of Japanese car companies into Southeast Asia in the 1980s. It left the Japanese with a solid network of parts suppliers attached to locally based assembly companies. The latter anticipated the reduction of regional trade barriers the hard way, negotiating each trade of parts and subassemblies one by one. These networks were regional in scope but corporate in contour, working to the advantage of particular Japanese companies and their subcontractors. No matter how hard they were to put together, the networks gave the Japanese auto companies assurance that they would not be dependent in the long term on increasingly expensive imports from Japan, and provided a solid competitive foundation for their business in Asia. According to Nissan's general manager for Asia, Takabe Keisuke, production sharing reduced Nissan's costs by 20 to 30 percent.[118]

As they expanded their production networks in Asia, the Japanese auto companies maintained a production hierarchy based on the skills levels in each country, transferring more complex forms of manufacturing, up to a point, as the skills levels rose. Taiwan and South Korea were at the top of the ladder, with assembly plants producing standard Japanese cars, if not the luxury lines, indistinguishable from vehicles produced in Japan. At Toyota's joint venture in Taiwan, Kuozui Motors Ltd., local content had reached 70 percent by the late 1980s. Kuozui had its own stamping and welding facilities, and although there were not nearly as many robots on the production line as at a typical auto factory in Japan, the fact that it had robots at all set the company apart from labor-intensive operations elsewhere in Asia. In countries with less sophisticated infrastructures, such as Indonesia, more parts were imported and production was largely a matter of putting them together manually.

The idea of regional auto production in Southeast Asia dated back to the 1970s, and was originally pitched as a program to integrate industry within the six member countries of the ASEAN. Initially, the Japanese were cool to the idea, and it went nowhere until Mitsubishi Motors saw a way of using it to advantage. The original concept, called the ASEAN industrial complementation program, encouraged participating countries to share the production of ASEAN products through specialization. Under this approach, member countries would negotiate specific products to be included in the program, which would then receive preferential tariff rates.

Mitsubishi's proposal was quite different and seemed to come out of nowhere. In late 1987, it presented ASEAN with a variant on the ASEAN industrial complementation scheme in which individual companies would draw up a list of components for production sharing, then negotiate with each ASEAN member country to establish specific components they would manufacture. Each country would end up with the regional mandate for specific components, making it possible to set up larger factories that would supply Mitsubishi factories and assembly operations elsewhere. The strategy was to achieve economies of scale by decentralizing production. To political leaders, the deal offered the carrot of more concentrated investment than their countries would get if they insisted on an array of smaller factories; it also appealed to ASEAN's philosophy of moving toward a common market. Investment would be shared rather than fought over. Mitsubishi called the idea "brand to brand" complementation (BBC). Like the original ASEAN scheme, participating countries would get the benefits of larger, more efficient factories and foreign exchange earnings from exports of parts within the region. Under the BBC scheme, however, the initiative would come from the private sector, mostly multinationals with existing cross-border production facilities. Because the only multinationals with more than one auto assembly plants in ASEAN were Japanese, they would be the principal beneficiaries.

The inspiration for the BBC scheme came from Mitsubishi Motors' Thai joint venture, MMC Sittipol, which had just signed a six-year contract with Chrysler of Canada to sell 100,000 cars under the Dodge and Plymouth badges. The deal whetted Mitsubishi's appetite for direct U.S. sales, but there was a catch. In order to sell the Thai-assembled Colts directly to the United States, Mitsubishi would have to jack up local content to 51 percent to qualify as Thai-made cars under U.S. Customs rules. Local content of the cars assembled at the MMC Sittipol plant was only 30 percent.[119]

The price of parts imported from Japan was continually rising, along with the yen, and Mitsubishi had already begun shipping transmissions made by its Manila-based unit to MMC Sittipol, as well as stamped-metal parts and electrical components from the Proton plan in Malaysia. Local parts from the Philippines and Malaysia were cheaper than the parts imported from Japan, but by the time they got past Thai Customs the difference was minimal. As part of its BBC proposal, Mitsubishi proposed that participating countries cut tariffs by at least 50 percent for car components made by Mitsubishi in one of the other countries, and count the parts as local content.[120] This was similar to existing conventions under the U.S.-Canada auto pact, which offered such broad waivers that Japanese auto manufacturers based in Canada could take advantage of the duty exemptions for cars they shipped across the border into the United States, even if they were made largely with Japanese components. In the United States, domestic content definitions were tightened in the course of the negotiations over the U.S.-Canada Free Trade Agreement and its successor agreement, NAFTA. In Southeast Asia, however, the Japanese may have counted on more lenient treatment because of the intense ambition of each local government to establish its own auto industry.

Mitsubishi's first proposal went to ASEAN ministers at their annual summit meeting in Manila in December 1987, but it was brushed off. Mitsubishi then put together a high-powered mission with Gerald Greenwald, vice-chairman of Chrysler, and Mitsubishi Motors executive vice president, Ueda Masano, to call upon Thai prime minister Prem Tinsulananonda in February 1998. Mitsubishi promised to build an engine plant in Thailand under the scheme, and build cars locally with body panels imported from Malaysia and transmission blocks from the Philippines. Even with Thailand on board, still nearly two years passed before Thailand, Malaysia, and the Philippines signed a memorandum of understanding on BBC. Indonesia refused to participate until 1994.

In the end, however, BBC was about building up a parts industry for the Asian market, rather than exporting finished cars. Mitsubishi never shipped its Lancers to the United States, and reportedly fell well short of its planned export target to Canada.[121] Instead, the high yen forced the Japanese to move more and more production to ASEAN and get local costs down as quickly as possible. In 1993, when Honda got ready to manufacture a new "Asian" version of the Civic in Thailand, it first invited more than twenty of its parts makers to relocate to Thailand, offering capital infusions to help make the transfer easier.[122]

The parts makers did not need much encouragement. In the 1980s, the Japanese automakers and MITI provided substantial inducements to reluctant parts companies to relocate to Southeast Asia. Unlike their *oyagaisha*, the parts companies could not subsidize their Asian projects from the profits of a global business. Some were just a step away from family-owned machine shops. Few had experience in foreign markets. In 1994 to 1995, however, as the yen screeched past the psychological barrier of 100 yen to the dollar, the Japanese parts industry raced for cover. By 1995, according to the Japan Auto Parts Industries Association, some 700 Japanese auto-parts makers had established manufacturing in Asia.[123] According to the *Nikkei Sangyo Shimbun,* in 1995 more than half, or 58.3 percent, of the companies in a survey of the auto industry planned new production bases in Southeast Asia. Another 41.7 percent were planning new production bases in China.[124] These were not all *kogaisha* (captive or "child") subcontractors, following major customers to new markets. For Japan's global parts makers, and independent parts makers not tied to a single company, the motives were more entrepreneurial, as they attempted to meet demands from their big Japanese customers to lower prices.

As far as BBC schemes were concerned, China was a sideshow, attracting the bottom end of the parts industry as well as the largest parts makers. These saw China as a global production base; the smaller parts makers simply viewed it as a means to keep their customers in Japan. With labor costs in China one-twentieth of costs in Japan, the companies that relocated to China could afford to close down their Japanese factories. The output of the Chinese operations was entirely for export back to Japan. The same was not true of parts makers in Southeast Asia, which initially suffered under the same burdens of small-scale, inefficient production as the automakers. As regional auto production grew, so did the demands of their Japanese customers. By the mid-1990s, the automakers were pressuring locally based parts makers in Southeast Asia to meet domestic Japanese prices, instead of the domestic Japanese price plus transportation and taxes.[125]

The Japanese parts makers quickly staked out a control of the Southeast Asian industry that was as pervasive as that of the Japanese assemblers. In 1994, the Thai Board of Investment guessed that half the "important" auto-parts makers in Japan had commercial or technical cooperation agreements with Thai joint-venture partners. Such agreements gave the Japanese veto power over procurement by their affiliates.[126] On the demand side, nearly all the customers for auto parts were Japanese. In 1993, according to the U.S. embassy in Bangkok, 91.4 percent of all vehicles sold in Thailand were

Japanese, and the ratios were not much lower for the rest of ASEAN. U.S. parts makers found that the most efficient way to develop sales in Southeast Asia was to set up offices in Tokyo.[127]

Next to get into the BBC act was Toyota. In September 1988, Toyota applied to the Philippine Board of Investment to build a transmission plant with a capacity of 200,000 units per year, well beyond the ability of the Philippine market to absorb. In May 1990, Toyota formally commissioned three new entities to focus on complementary production—the transmission plant in the Philippines; a factory making steering links in Selangor, Malaysia, with a production capacity of 150,000 units annually; and a management company in Singapore. In Toyota's complex scheme, Thailand was to be the source of diesel engines and floor panels; the Philippines to supply transmissions; Malaysia, steering parts, radiators, and shock absorbers; and Indonesia, gasoline engines.

"We are starting small and going step by step," said Toyota's Hasegawa Koji in 1990, when the scheme was in its infancy. "We will split each product between several countries. Then, if the export market grows at a rate of 2.5 percent, we can try to push it to 10 percent. If it is 10 percent, we can push for 25 percent."[128] Toyota started shipping engines for its Kijang commercial van from Indonesia to Malaysia in May 1989. Within half a year it was exporting 500 engines a month, double its original target. Officially, Toyota gave October 1990 as the starting date for its complementary production scheme. By 1993, the value of components traded reached $58.4 million[129] and was projected to reach $83.6 million in 1994.[130] By 1996, annual turnover of Toyota's regional components trade had risen to $440 million.[131] In 1998, Toyota's Thai engine plant was exporting 20,000 engines per year, including some to Japan.[132]

Nissan handled BBC more gingerly than Toyota or Mitsubishi Motors. It began experimenting with BBC in 1991, trading trim and electrical parts for the Sunny between Thailand and Malaysia. Nissan's next move was more dramatic. In September 1993, the company introduced the first "regional" car, the AD Resort, a sports-utility vehicle with a 1.6 liter engine. Nissan initially launched the AD Resort in Thailand and Taiwan, with plans for later release in Malaysia and the Philippines. It shared parts production among all four countries. Taiwan provided the most sophisticated parts, such as connecting rods, rear suspension, and exterior trim; Thailand supplied major body panels, interior trim, camshafts, and other parts; Malaysia provided steering gears and medium-sized body panels; and the Philippines offered interior trim and medium-sized body panels. At the time the program was announced in 1992, Nissan said that it expected trade would amount to $15.7 million annually and involve more than two hundred parts.[133]

None of these deals was easy for the Japanese to cobble together, and they only got more difficult with time. When Malaysia, Thailand, and the Philippines first agreed to reduce tariffs for regional production sharing, they insisted that companies apply separately for each part involved in the schemes, rather than granting blanket reductions.[134] This by itself made the process a nightmare of red tape. But there was more. Under the BBC scheme, companies were supposed to get a 50 percent break on tariff rates. In practice, local customs officers had plenty of discretion in determining the rates. They could charge a flat rate on the value of the CKD kits, or they could take them apart and charge on the basis of individual parts, some of whose duty charges might be open to interpretation. The latter type of assessment would, of course, do the importing company much more damage than a flat rate on the kits. Different ministries might have different views of the best way to deal with foreign investors covered by the BBC scheme. In Thailand, it took a cabinet-level decision to break up a feud between the Ministry of Finance, in charge of Customs, and the Ministry of Industry, which had championed the BBC program. Even then, it did not quell complaints that the process was made for bribery and corruption.[135]

The Japanese company that had taken the first daring leap into auto production in Southeast Asia never seemed to get its strategy quite right. Through Proton, Mitsubishi Motors was a major name in the Southeast Asian auto industry generally. It had done yeoman's work in setting up the BBC scheme. Yet, by the mid-1990s, apart from Proton in Malaysia, its market share in the top four ASEAN markets was only 6.8 percent.[136]

In 1992, I met with a senior Mitsubishi Motors executive, Takeuchi Tohei, whose disappointment and cynicism were palpable. According to him, the BBC scheme was flawed from the start because the ASEAN market itself was too small to support a "hub and spoke" production-sharing scheme. Much of Takeuchi's long monologue aimed at justifying MMC's failures. Yet, it also was revealing in the degree to which he argued in favor of a more full-blown production hierarchy based on Akamatsu's flying-geese principle. MMC, in Takeuchi's view, had failed because the theory had been squeezed into an inappropriate strategy: building down from individual car models to parts rather than up from parts network to a regional car. I began the interview by asking him about the prospects for regional manufacturing in Southeast Asia.[137]

Some years ago, that was a very hot topic. But I don't know if it's a workable idea. Frankly, the complementation scheme or concept is not nearly as simple to work out as we originally planned. For example, Indonesia is virtually out of the scheme. I think the Government of Indonesia believes they are a little behind the others, and that these sort of transactions may have an adverse effect on their industry. They want to have an entire set of integrated manufacturing systems for auto products on their own. If some components, or major components start coming in from other countries before this integration is completed, Indonesia will have to give up developing that particular part.

If one country specialized in engine manufacturing, another in transmission, and a third in transmission axles, it might be O.K. if all three countries were manufacturing the same motor vehicle. But ordinarily, one country will need a bigger car, one a passenger vehicle. The market demand will vary. As a result, the complementation concept is a bit difficult to realize in the sense of a general concept. To an ordinary person, two vehicles may look much the same. Yet 80 to 90 percent of the parts of the vehicle are specific to it, even when it uses the same model name.

Another question is the difference in size of the markets involved. One country has, say, a demand of 300,000 per year. Another country only has 50,000. You need different equipment, and it's risky from a business point of view to invest in production equipment just to supply components to other countries. Only if all the conditions are met and economically justified is complementation viable.

Toyota has a very interesting motor vehicle, which could be called an Asian car. It's sold as the Kijang in Indonesia and the Tamaraw in the Philippines, and sold in Taiwan as well. If we could have that kind of car—I don't know if it was Toyota's intention—but if we could develop a car for the purpose of justifying a complementation scheme, perhaps it could be done. In our cars, we started with the opposite idea. First, we introduced cars that were best suited to the individual markets. Then we tried to find parts or components that could be shared among several countries. Less than 20 percent of the parts are involved in production sharing. We supply transmissions from the Philippines to Thailand and Japan and doors from Malaysia to Thailand. Thailand and Malaysia share the same base model, so we can share doors from Malaysian Protons and the Colts we make in Thailand. It's not the same model as the one we export, but the basic design is shared, with some parts of the body modified to suit individual markets. There are some other examples which I don't recall.

In each country, the government has some requirement for local production. Some countries nominate the components to be localized, and some increase the local content ratio. It varies from country to country, and the first thing we have to do is to comply with the local content requirements, then we can try to find out about the possibility of sharing components.

The basic requirement to be competitive in the auto industry is to find the most economical way to procure components and assemble in each location, then deliver the product to its final market. In that sense, we are always looking for ways to source and assemble locally. At the same time, you have to think about transportation costs and quality levels, because these enter into the equation for economic viability as well. You need to be able to adjust production capacity to market demand. In order to adjust these somehow complementary factors into systems, that is, in cases where complementation is workable, you have to have some kind of hub. You need to link local or overseas factories to a central hub. Japan has to be that hub, because production scale in Japan is the biggest in Asia. Mitsubishi alone makes 1.3 million vehicles a year in Japan, including trucks, cars, everything. Compared with that, the market size in ASEAN is very small. Indonesia is the biggest, but it has annual turnover of just 300,000, out of which our market share is only 10 to 15 percent.

If we try to find some common components to be shared among ASEAN markets only, you end up with a rather negligible volume. But if you can find out the commonalities between the hub and an outer ring of smaller production centers, that would be something else.

Originally everything came from Japan. MMC designed all the cars and supplied all the components. First we concentrated on local production that was suited to individual market requirements. We set up complementation in parts whenever it was economical. We were not doing this business for the purpose of complementation; this was just a secondary or rub-off effect. There were many restrictive conditions, and to meet them was not so easy or simple. We exported mainly in CKD kits or as production parts and components shipments.

As a concept, we may be able to arrange some sourcing from various countries. At the moment, we are importing cylinder blocks from Australia, and transmissions from the Philippines. These parts are not cheap. The cheapest parts are those we buy in Japan. To get the same part outside Japan at the same quality level, you have to pay 25 percent more, including transportation costs. If this type of production is to have a future, first, you have to open up these markets. Now they are basically closed. The complementation scheme was a very unique idea, a very beautiful idea, but the actual results have not been that fruitful.

With all its imperfections, the BBC program was still a tremendous success for the Japanese in the sense that they had shaped policy and outcomes in an important regional industry. The auto industry was growing faster than anywhere else in the world in Southeast Asia in the early 1990s. And the Japanese did not stop with BBC. In the mid-1990s, ASEAN began to worry that China's economic boom was sucking investment away from the region. The Japanese saw an opportunity to change some of the things they did not like about BBC by playing on ASEAN fears, and warned ASEAN that unless the region became more competitive it would lose incoming investment from the Japanese parts industry.[138] In 1996, ASEAN came up with the ASEAN Industrial Cooperation (AICO) program, which was to create a new flat tariff rate to replace BBC's 50 percent rule. However, AICO had its own problems. The new tariff rate became a serious political issue in most countries. In the Philippines, it took two years for Toyota to get a ruling on its AICO proposal, and it ended up with a higher tariff rate than under the original BBC scheme.[139]

North Americans and Europeans, meanwhile, rolled their eyes, viewing the ASEAN regional production schemes as a waste of time. But the Japanese had their eyes fixed firmly on the future. "We can afford to be patient with the government," said Sugimoto Kenji, Honda's representative in its joint venture in Indonesia, P.T. Imora Honda. "The auto markets will surely boom in these countries, and at that time we can enjoy good manufacturing volumes."[140]

Making an "Asian" Car

If plans to export Southeast Asian–made cars to rich country markets were fraught with difficulty, reverse imports of Japanese-made cars to the Japanese market were even unluckier. By 1998, Mitsubishi Motors had imported just 600 pickup trucks to Japan from its Thai factory, despite the fact that it had no domestic production of pickups.[141] The idea of an Asian car met a happier fate.

The original idea was simply to build the cheapest car possible adapted to "local conditions." Toyota was the first to develop an "Asian" car, called the Kijang (barking deer) in Indonesia and the Tamaraw (water buffalo) in the Philippines, to serve as both a commercial and passenger vehicle. The Kijang lacked side and rear windows and many other amenities, and had a low-budget image even in the developing countries for which it was intended. Nonetheless, the Kijang was the model for Japan's "Asian cars" of the 1990s. They drew upon regional production networks and were offered at retail prices considerably lower than anything that had previously been seen in these markets.

Unlike Mitsubishi Motors, Toyota had thought in terms of an "ASEAN car" for the Southeast Asian regional market since at least the 1970s. The specific vehicle, similar to the Ford Fiera, was a response to Indonesia's first industrial policy for the auto industry in 1976. Jakarta decided that the domestic industry would focus on one-ton commercial vehicles such as the Kijang and quickly introduced punitive tariffs on everything else. The Kijang could be sold as a station wagon, pickup truck, or as the chassis alone and, if not indestructible, was at least hardy and had few complicated parts to go wrong.

The first generation of Kijang was "simple to make, without a lot of pressed dies," Rudyanto Hardjanto, the president of Toyota-Astra Motor recalled when I visited the company in 1990. "In order to maintain a low cost, we kept the production system simple, until 1981. In the early second generation (of Kijangs), we used curtains instead of glass for windows. Later we used glass, and the body became less boxy. By 1985, we had to start manufacturing the engines and transmissions in order to get up to 70 percent local content in value terms. We still import components that we can't make here—electrical parts, some engine components, and crank shafts. In 1991, we will make the engine block here."[142] In Indonesia in 1990, total output of the Kijang was just 41,600 units. By 1994, however, the executive in charge of Toyota's Asian business was predicting sales of 300,000 units annually across Asia by the end of the century.[143]

The immediate catalyst for the birth of the ASEAN car or Asian car came from poaching by South Korean firms. Up until the Koreans entered the Southeast Asian market, Toyota seemed content to let the low end of the market drift. But when Hyundai launched its Excel sedan in Southeast Asia in 1993, followed swiftly by Kia, the Japanese realized that they had some serious competitors and would need to do more to maintain their 80 percent market share. The Korean cars were significantly lower in price than the Japanese-branded vehicles available in Southeast Asia at the time (other than the Malaysian Proton, whose price was heavily subsidized). The implication was that the Japanese would have to defend themselves in the lower price ranges by bringing their prices down. Toyota and Nissan thought that they saw another solution—dressing up low-cost vehicles to compete with the Koreans on the basis of brand image as well as price.

Thus, the Asian car was born.[144] Toyota upgraded the Kijang and positioned it as a sports-utility vehicle. Nissan quickly followed with its first Asian car, the 1.6 liter engine AD Resort pickup. Nissan AD Resorts began rolling off the line in the summer of 1994 in Thailand, Taiwan, Malaysia, and the Philippines, with an initial production target of 34,800 vehicles. Toyota was then producing about 114,000 per year of the Kijang, newly styled as the "Toyota Utility Vehicle." That same year, Mitsubishi Motors announced it would move its last remaining one-ton pickup factory from Japan to Thailand, and began construction of a $560 million factory on Thailand's eastern seaboard at Laem Chabang, with a planned capacity of 217,000 units per year.[145]

Nissan's AD Resort was an intermediate vehicle, closer to the Kijang in concept than Nissan would care to admit. But by 1997, both Toyota and

Honda brought out Asian cars far more in tune with the mind-set of Asia's nouveaux riche. In 1996, Honda unveiled a 1.3 liter compact known as the City, modeled on the Honda Civic. It was a runaway success. A year later, Toyota introduced its first Asian car, a 1.5 liter, four-door sedan called the Soluna, based on the Tercel. Both the City and the Soluna underpriced the comparable model from Kia. The Soluna sold for the equivalent of $12,700, the City for $15,500. Both carmakers were able to get prices down because of their extensive use of locally made components—which represented as much as 70 percent of the value of the cars, according to the chief engineer on the Soluna project, Ninnart Chaithirapinyo.[146]

Mitsubishi Motors waited until the eve of the Asia crisis to introduce its first "Asian" vehicle other than its nonproprietary Malaysian national cars. The new "Dynamic Family Wagon" (DFW) was designed to be manufactured and sold in three markets simultaneously, each with a different engine and "an equipment specification optimally tailored to the needs of each market."[147] The production target was 70,000 vehicles per year. For the first time, Mitsubishi designed parts for a project that had never been produced in Japan. Taiwan and Indonesia produced the chassis, trim parts, and stampings for the vehicle, while Mitsubishi's Philippine transmission factory supplied transmissions. The DFW debuted in Taiwan in September 1997 and in the Philippines in January 1998. Kyoda Toyoho, Mitsubishi Motors' corporate general manager for Southeast Asia, was visibly relieved that the deal had been structured to minimize parts shipped from Japan. "We were very lucky to be developing these new models when the crisis struck," he said. "The crisis had no impact on sales in Taiwan, and in the Philippines the DFW is doing quite well."[148]

The Invisible Hand: MITI

Unlike the more public support programs offered by MITI for the Japanese electronics industry as it moved to Asia, help for the auto sector was focused on the parts industry and submerged into broader programs to ease the relocation pains of small- and medium-sized enterprises (SMES). Up until the early 1990s, the number of auto parts makers transferring production to Southeast Asia and China was relatively small. An earlier wave of Japanese parts makers was already well established in Korea and Taiwan. In the mid-1990s, however, MITI stepped up its efforts as the parts companies themselves began moving in larger numbers. This was also part of a larger program directed at Japanese SMEs, in itself extraordinarily ambitious, with projects ranging from policy advice at the regional and governmental level to support programs tailored to specific companies.

In October 1994, MITI sponsored the first of several summit meetings of Southeast Asian officials in charge of SMEs. A special program was also set up with the Korean Ministry of International Trade and Industry to select model SMEs to receive special support in the form of technical exchanges between Korea and Japan. The same year, MITI began "policy dialogues" with Southeast Asian governments to "impress on them the importance of the parts industry and of implementing policies to develop the industry," according to *Nikkei Weekly*.[149] In the first six months of 1994, MITI held such "dialogues" with Thailand, Malaysia, the Philippines, and Singapore, and planned a similar exchange with Indonesia.

MITI paid three-quarters of the salaries of Japanese engineers delegated to provide technical advice to Asian parts makers, many of them created in joint ventures with Japanese companies and other "supporting industries." It gave offshore Japanese manufacturers and their local affiliates access to its new database, CALS (Continuous Acquisition Life Cycle Support), and provided information on design specifications of new products.[150] Another strategy was to hold conferences and road trips for parts makers. A July 1994 conference to promote Japan-China auto-parts manufacturing brought together some 300 government and manufacturing officials from the two countries.

The first ASEAN Auto Supporting Industries Conference met in Bangkok in March 1997. Japanese participants dominated the meeting—ninety-five Japanese parts makers and thirteen auto assemblers attended, accounting for more than half the audience.[151] JETRO, the Japan Automobile Manufacturers Association, and the Japan Auto Parts Industries Association were the sponsors, and they went to great lengths to dispel the notion that they might be trying to hijack American forays into the Southeast Asian market. "The conference is not limited to only Japanese companies," Nao Yoshiyasu, head of JETRO's Bangkok center, told *Jiji Press*. "The U.S. companies are also attending as visitors. Besides, we [Japanese firms] closely cooperated with Thailand to create strong supporting industries as a substitute for imports and to enhance the country's competitiveness."[152] The subtext was not difficult to read: We built this industry; we deserve our success.

Sadly for the Japanese, their work was about to be destroyed, not by American competition, but by ill winds blowing off the global capital markets. Less than a year after the big auto-parts exhibition in Bangkok, Thai workers burned the factory of Thai Summit Auto Parts in their rage at being laid off.[153] If the Japanese electronics industry was leading the region toward recovery, the automakers were limping in the years after the crisis. They had made their choice—rather than lead regional growth, they would follow, their fortunes dependent on the renewal of Asia's miracle.

Retail: "Birds in Winter"

While Japanese electronics and auto companies took the lead in exploiting the potential of East and Southeast Asia as a manufacturing base, Japanese retailers played a pioneering role expanding the boundaries of Asian consumer markets. To the tourist elbowing his or her way through the crowds on Orchard Road in the early 1990s, Singapore's premier shopping street was a tropical version of Shibuya or the Ginza, Tokyo's liveliest shopping areas.[154]

Japan's department store giants—Isetan, Sogo, Daimaru, Tokyu, Seibu, and Takashimaya—were each represented on Orchard Road, lining the broad, leafy avenue in a nearly unbroken procession from its beginning near the Istana Palace to the condominiums and hotels at the west end. If the tourists wanted to stock up on grocery items, chances were that a Japanese chain— Yaohan, Daiei, or Ito Yokado—owned the supermarket. By the early 1990s, Japanese retailers had squeezed out European and North American competitors in Southeast Asia; only some of the bigger local Asian retailers managed to hold their ground.

As early as 1990, the Japanese retail industry could boast an Asian network of some sixty stores and buying offices, controlling 80 percent of the retail market in Singapore and 60 percent in Hong Kong, the two most lucrative markets. Japanese market share in other Asian capitals ranged from 30 to 50 percent. Until the Asian financial crash, many of the stores were profitable, too. In 1995, the ten Japanese-affiliated department stores in Taiwan had sales of $1.42 billion,[155] nearly as much as the combined $1.7 billion in sales of the twenty-six local Chinese department stores in Taipei, Taichung, and Kaohsiung. Japanese department stores even had their own Taipei retail association, where the presidents of Mitsukoshi, Hankyu Department Stores, and Matsuya Co. met regularly.

In the early 1990s, as Asian economies exploded, the Japanese became shopkeepers to a new generation of affluent Asians. "Birds in the winter fly from north to south, not horizontally. So Japan and Asia conform to one territory, like Europe and Africa or the United States and Latin America," said Tsutsui Yoshio, executive manager for Planning and Development of International Operations at Isetan Co., Ltd. Isetan divided the retail world outside Japan into three main markets—Southeast Asia, Europe, and North America. With three-quarters of Isetan's total overseas activity, Southeast Asia was by far the most important of the regions. The same was true for most of the other Japanese department store and supermarket chains, which at the beginning of the 1990s opened up major new stores in Asia at the rate of two or three per year. In 1990, Takashimaya Co., owner of one of Tokyo's most prestigious department stores, opened a half-million square-foot store on Orchard Road, the biggest in Asia until Yaohan completed its Shanghai flagship store in 1995.

Yaohan, a supermarket chain that grew up in Japan's Shizuoka Prefecture, decided that its Asian business was so much more important than the domestic Japanese market that it needed to be closer to the action. In October 1989, it became the first Japanese company to establish its headquarters outside Japan. Yaohan's new headquarters was in Hong Kong, arguably Asia's shopping capital at the time. In 1990, Yaohan already operated fourteen stores in Asia and had plans on the books for a huge "resort store" complex in Penang, Malaysia, where condominiums and a playland were to be attached to its supermarket. A smaller version of the idea was launched in a posh residential area in Singapore called Ginza Plaza, which quickly revitalized the neighborhood around Singapore's old Bugis quarter and Arab Street. At its peak in the mid-1990s, Yaohan operated 450 stores in 15 countries.[156]

The Japanese retail drive in Asia began quietly. In the 1960s and 1970s, Japanese department stores moved into Hong Kong and Singapore. Then, starting in the early 1980s, operations were set up in Taipei, Seoul, Bangkok, and Kuala Lumpur. In the late 1980s, the same rapid expansion took place in Singapore, Indonesia, and Brunei. The mid-1990s saw a Japanese retail blitz in China. By 1992, according to one count, there were seven Japanese department stores in Taiwan, eight in Singapore, five in Malaysia, five in Thailand, fourteen in Hong Kong, and two in China.[157] Counting supermarkets and discount chains, by 1992 Japan had seventy-eight retail entities in Asia. Yaohan, the Hong Kong–based supermarket chain, was the overall leader, with nineteen stores across the region, followed closely by Jusco, a discount chain, with fifteen.[158]

When Japanese retailers first showed up in most of Asia's sprawling capitals, their main competition came from stores owned by overseas Chinese, bazaar-like emporiums providing bare-bones service and deep discounts. Outside of Hong Kong and Singapore, European and U.S. retailers were largely absent, discouraged by high costs of entry, low returns, and the foibles of Third World buying patterns. That gave the Japanese stores a straight shot for the luxury trade. They came from a retail culture in which the "customer is king," and knew how to lavish personal services on their "honored guests" in a way that Asians found all too seductive.

Invariably, the arrival of Japanese stores in a country triggered a revolution in shopping expectations. "Distribution channels as well as the retail business are at a primitive level" in Southeast Asia, according to Isetan's Tsutsui. "So there is ample room for us to go there and improve." And how. In Taipei, Taiwanese swarmed to the new Pacific Sogo department store when it opened in November 1987. Pretty young women in tight-fitting costumes bowed at the entrance and greeted shoppers. Clerks insisted on gift-wrapping ordinary parcels. Shoppers could use the store's own credit card. The main floor, Japanese-style, displayed a glittering array of the world's most expensive brands of clothes and cosmetics. Taiwanese loved it, partly because Sogo's arrival coincided with a surge in disposable incomes and the country's first big orgy of consumer spending.

Suddenly, the venerable Chinese *baihuo shangdian* (hundred-goods-stores), with their bargain bins and cheerful disorder, were history. The 377,000-square-foot Pacific Sogo, Taipei's largest store, was profitable within its first month, an extraordinary performance for any retail market. "We just got here at absolutely the right time," explained Nishiyama Suero, Pacific Sogo's general manager. The Taipei store also managed to tap a previously undiscovered Taiwanese passion for Japanese fashions, cosmetics, and accessories. Sogo imported 28 percent of its goods from Japan—about double the ratio of Sogo's other Asian stores. "The Taiwanese people knew the brand names already—they knew them better than the Japanese," Nishiyama explained. "They had been studying them."

The high cost of Japanese products was exacerbated by the strength of the Japanese yen relative to other Asian currencies. The expense prevented Japanese retailers from exporting more than a fraction of their merchandise directly from Japan. Most of the Japanese products sold in Japanese stores in Asia were made locally under license arrangements. When Japanese products did show up in Asia, they tended to be high-end, luxury wares—an about-face from the days when Japanese used their Asian shops as dumping grounds for products that failed to sell in Japan.

Through the mid-1990s, the Japanese had a clear field in Asian retail. It usually took between five and ten years to recover the initial investment of a department store in the region, and Europeans and Americans weren't interested. "Local developers have invited European and American retail chains to Southeast Asia, but they haven't come," said Tsutsui. "I feel that they are simply not willing to take the risk to invest." For the Japanese as well, Asia was a high-risk proposition. Rates of return were poor by Japanese retail standards—if only because the sales levels of Japanese stores in the late 1980s and early 1990s were so astronomically high. Sales volume ranged from $851 a square foot in smaller cities to $2,300 a square foot in Tokyo. In Asia, sales volumes averaged $1,160 a square foot, less than half the level of major urban areas in Japan and just above the level of rural towns and farm villages. At these levels, Asian store turnover was still two or three times the average of premier shopping malls in North America. Overhead costs were higher than in North America, however, if not as high as in Japan. In downtown Taipei, at the start of the 1990s land costs were already close to $4,400 per square foot. The Japanese took a philosophical view of such difficulties. "None of our shops has been open that long," said Ashida Terumori, executive director of Sogo's overseas enterprise office, in 1989. Sogo's first foreign venture was in 1984 in Bangkok. "We haven't caught up on our investment at all. But you have to look at it from a 10-year time frame."

In Hong Kong, the onslaught of Japanese retailers finally stumbled in 1997, not because of the Asian financial crisis, but because land prices skyrocketed as speculators sought to cash in prior to Hong Kong's handover to China in July. That year, the oldest of Hong Kong's Japanese department stores, Hong Kong Daimaru, moved out of the ground floor of its two-story lease in popular Causeway Bay. Daimaru had opened in Hong Kong in 1960.[159] Mitsukoshi, a relative newcomer, closed one of its two stores in Hong Kong in 1995, after the landlord tripled the rent. In 1996, Isetan pulled out of Hong Kong as well.[160] But even in Hong Kong, Japanese retailers on the way out tended to be replaced by Japanese retailers moving in. In 1998, in the midst of a post-handover slump in real-estate prices, Japanese discount king Jusco announced three new outlets, and Sogo Hong Kong talked about turning Causeway Bay into "Sogo Town," with two new stores and more planned.[161]

The retail industry had its own version of Akamatsu-inspired regional planning. Much the same way that the giant auto and electronics companies used Asia as a source of cheap components, the Japanese department stores and discount chains served as buying outposts for a range of Asian products that would find their way back to Japan under Japanese brand names. Even after the Japanese bubble economy folded in 1990, Japanese consumers turned up their noses at products with Asian labels, preferring to pay high prices rather than endure supposedly shoddy workmanship. Asian-made products with Japanese labels, however, were a different story. As Japanese consumers became more price conscious during the long recession of the 1990s, domestic Japanese stores were filled with Asian products.

The department stores helped the change along by investing in quality control and manufacturing. In the late 1980s, Daimaru, which set up the first Japanese department store in Bangkok in 1964, was involved with projects to set up a testing laboratory, a bakery and a factory for producing frozen food for export to Japan. "This is how we expand our operations here," said Tomitani Yasuo, managing director of Thai Daimaru Co. "We're not only a department store—we reinvest in all sorts of fields related to retailing." From the late 1980s, Japanese textile manufacturers had lobbied for restrictions on the sudden avalanche of imported clothes and fabrics, with little success. Japanese consumers wanted cheap stuff and flocked to stores such as Daiei and Jusco that had their own house brands of products imported from Asia.

There were pitfalls for Japanese retailers in Asia, however, because like the Japanese automakers their strategies were based on presumptions of continued growth. They were ill prepared for the steep dip represented by the Asian financial crisis in 1997 and 1998. Of all the Japanese retailers that planned, talked, and dreamed about Asia in the early 1990s, none had more faith than Wada Kazuo, proprietor of Yaohan. He rolled into Hong Kong in 1989, four months after the Tiananmen massacre and was greeted with open arms. This had something to do with the fact that Wada's wallet was wide open, too. When William Purvis, chairman of the Hong Kong and Shanghai Bank, invited Wada to join the prestigious Hong Kong Jockey Club, he returned the favor by cheerfully putting up $10.8 million[162] for Purvis's home on the Peak, which had been languishing on the market for months. Wada explained in an interview that he felt the property, with its spectacular view, deserved something "better" than the market price.[163]

His family business combined discount merchandising, fanatic dedication to a religious cult, and complete disregard for Japanese business conventions, including reliance on a "main bank." Wada did business with three banks, none related by *keiretsu* ties, and preferred the convertible bonds that eventually did his company in. Wada claimed that he modeled himself after Sony's Morita Akio, who had looked to the overseas market when the Japanese distribution system for electronic products shut him out early in his career. Wada, too, pointed his enterprise abroad from an early stage.

Yaohan began as a vegetable stand in the hot spring resort of Atami, squeezed around a tiny bay a few hours' drive from Tokyo. Wada's mother, Katsu, founded the company in 1930, the same year as she helped to set up *Seicho no Ie* (House of Growth), the religion that became the ticket for membership in Yaohan's inner circle. New employees were required to absorb the *Seicho no Ie* philosophy for three months before starting work and write three essays relating the philosophy to their prospective jobs.[164] The story of Wada Katsu's steely perseverance and rise from poverty to billionaire status inspired an enormously popular television series, *Oshin,* in the 1970s. The series was enough of a craze within Japan that the economic "boom" of 1983 was named after it as the *Oshin bumu.* A peasant child, Katsu struggled to make a living first as a peddler, then as the owner of Yaohan, a tiny grocery shop. By 1948, she had incorporated a thriving chain of supermarkets in Shizuoka and Aichi prefectures. Kazuo, the oldest son, was a student radical and Marxist at Nihon University. He wanted nothing to do with the grocery business, but Katsu managed to talk him into joining both her supermarket chain and *Seicho no Ie.*

The House of Growth was a throwback to the great proselytizing Buddhist sects of the Japanese medieval period. By the late 1980s, it had more than 1,000,000 disciples abroad, and Kazuo, by this time a dedicated businessman, made full use of the resources of the cult. Blocked at home by Japanese regulations favoring small stores, Wada's first big venture was in Brazil. He sent only his fellow *Seicho no Ie* members on the mission, with strict instructions to expect to live there as long as it took to make the venture a success. All of them acquired Brazilian residence cards. In 1980, as Brazil faced hyperinflation and economic collapse, Wada pulled out of South America and refocused on Asia. Shopping centers in Singapore, Kuala Lumpur, Brunei, and blue-collar districts of Hong Kong did much better than his Brazilian venture. By 1991, 117 Yaohan outlets in Japan, the United States, Hong Kong, Southeast Asia, and Latin America generated $2 billion in sales. In 1991, Wada told *Business Week* that in six years Yaohan would be a $7 billion empire "spanning Asia, Europe, and North America."[165]

Wada had a reputation as an iconoclast in his relations with Japanese banks. Unlike most of his retail counterparts, he refused to lock himself into a relationship with a single or "main" bank, and spread his business around. In another departure from standard Japanese practice, he tried to exploit capital markets, using convertible bonds as an alternative to bank financing. Consumer spending crashed in Japan in the mid-1990s, and the Japanese operations soon ran into trouble. In 1997, Wada's intricately leveraged empire fell apart, starting with Yaohan Japan, Yaohan's "core company." As problems began to mount in late 1996, Wada told the *Nihon Keizai Shimbun* that the group had total sales of $4.5 billion[166] and debt of $1.8 billion.[167] With interest rates skyrocketing, Wada's investors rushed to cash in their bonds—and like many other Asian kingpins, he did not have the funds to cover them at a time when local currencies were collapsing across the region.

In September 1997, Yaohan Japan announced that it was unable to meet payments on $1.2 billion in debt, including over $300 million[168] in convertible bonds. The debt was exactly equal to its sales for the year through March 1997.[169] The end came when Yaohan's three principal lenders, Tokai Bank, Sumitomo Trust and Banking Co., and the Long Term Credit Bank of Japan, refused a desperate plea to restructure his debt.[170] Two months later, Yaohan's Hong Kong stores were liquidated.[171] Within months, the problems at Yaohan Japan had swamped the rest of the company. In April 1998, Yaohan International admitted that it was under pressure from creditors and had a net asset deficit of $9.1 million.[172] Jusco, another retail giant, came to Wada's defense, combining its merchandise procurement and daily operations with Yaohan, and ending up with many of its stores in Japan and Hong Kong.[173] But Yaohan was finished. In 1999, Wada sold his share in Asia's largest department store, the "Nextage Shanghai," to his Chinese partner for $7.5 million, far less than the $127 million Wada had invested in it in 1995.[174]

The Shanghai store was the first foreign retail venture in China, part of the Chinese government's "Great Mall" program to introduce eleven to four-teen large-scale retail ventures with foreign capital.[175] It was to have been the flagship of a fleet of 1,060 Yaohan supermarkets in China, including Hong Kong. By 1996, Yaohan already had twenty-seven supermarkets in Shanghai and was set to expand the chain to the rest of the country. That same year, Wada moved the headquarters office of Yaohan International from Hong Kong to Shanghai, the better to oversee the project.[176] "Kazuo Wada is a visionary," a Hong Kong banker told the London *Financial Times*. "But like many vi-sionaries in business, it seems his ambitions got ahead of his balance sheet."[177]

In 1991, when I met him in Hong Kong, Wada's hardships were still a long ways off in the future. He bubbled with enthusiasm for China and his new home, Hong Kong. "I believe that China will be the biggest market of the twenty-first century," he said. He had moved up plans to enter the market by five years. Originally he had planned a venture in Shanghai in 2000. Now he wanted to begin in 1995. Wada loved Hong Kong. "When I was in Japan, I never enjoyed cruising in the harbor," he said. "I never would have ex-pected to join the Jockey Club. If I stayed in Japan, this would never have happened. Also I play golf more often than in Japan. On the weekend, I can go to my big home on the Peak, 'Sky High,' which I bought from Hong Kong and Shanghai Bank. I am enjoying the low tax rate in Hong Kong, too. In Japan, I have to pay as much as 60 percent. Here the average is 15 percent. That means that my income is three times what it would be in Japan."[178]

If Wada overplayed his hand in Asia, he also represented a strong new undercurrent in Japanese business. He rejected the cartels and incestuous qualities of the industry back in Japan. This may have been part of his undo-ing, because if he had been less of a radical, his Japanese bankers might have worked harder to keep him afloat. Wada saw Hong Kong and China as free-market playgrounds compared to Japan. In a grandly titled 1992 book, *Yaohan's Global Strategy: The Twenty-first Century in the Era of Asia*, Wada described Japanese retail restrictions on large stores as "evil." He wrote, "In fact, I even think it could be styled the worst law on earth. This law was established in 1974 and was intended for the protection of medium and small-scale stores. Today, however, the ones benefiting the most from it are Japan's larger stores."[179]

Although Wada dropped out of the picture, discount retailers like Yaohan would thrive while the luxury department store chains, the Seibus and Sogos, struggled and failed. The discounters' magic weapon, helping to break the logjam of Japan's protected domestic price structure, was the ability to use their Asian-store networks as sourcing operations. The inexpensive wares the discounters brought back to Japan to sell in their Japanese stores sparked a retail revolution. Thus, economic integration could work both ways. The legacy of the Japanese retail invasion of the 1980s and 1990s was, in some respects, less the crowded luxury shopping malls of Singapore or Jakarta and more the "100-yen" stores and high-volume suburban supermarkets popping up in Japan in the mid-1990s.

Exporting the Bubble: Japanese Banks

While Japanese manufacturers were going into overdrive, Japanese banks were doing their part, lending on a gargantuan scale. In the late 1980s, Japanese monetary authorities fought yen appreciation by creating a huge pool of virtually free money. Manufacturers took their cue by borrowing vast sums to enhance productivity and boost their market share abroad. Serving as intermediary for both domestic and foreign capital spending sprees were Japanese banks, working closely with the Japanese government and *keiretsu* circles. The result was to export the Japanese bubble economy to Asia, pumping up Asian stock and real-estate markets in much the same way Japan had experienced a few years earlier.

To be sure, Japanese money was not the only factor in the Asian bubble nor was the Asian boom all gangsters, stock speculators, and corrupt politicians. It rode on the back of an economic transformation that was solidly based on high local savings rates, investment in the real economy, and rising skills levels. At the onset of its bubble, in the mid-1980s, Japan was a mature economy with a slowing growth rate. In contrast, the developing economies of Southeast Asia and China were just beginning to experience the double-digit growth explosion that had been experienced earlier by Japan and its Northeast Asian confederates.

Nonetheless, there were elements in common. One was that both bubbles— Japan's in the late 1980s, and Southeast Asia's in the early to mid-1990s— depended on a combination of easy credit and export growth. According to Ron Bevacqua, senior economist at Commerz Securities in Tokyo, Japanese banks took advantage of rock-bottom Japanese interest rates to lend buckets of money to Japanese subsidiaries in Asia, ignoring indications of risk in favor of extending the relationships they had back in Japan.[180] Asia's bubble might have lasted longer if Japanese banks had continued their push into the region. But by 1995, five Japanese credit cooperatives, one regional bank, and seven housing-loan companies marked the first of many failures of major and minor financial institutions, and Japanese banks rapidly retreated, yanking $110 billion out of Asian markets in just two years.

In the mid-1990s, Japanese banks faced a series of disasters. First was a nonperforming loan problem in the range of $700 billion to $1 trillion, which was a closely kept secret within the Japanese financial community since at least 1990. In the first few years after the stock market crash, the banks clearly expected a short-term downturn and a quick return to the good times of the 1980s. Early on, the Japanese Ministry of Finance (MOF) publicly insisted that banking health was unimpaired, while privately engineering a few large-scale mergers, such as that between troubled Bank of Tokyo and Mitsubishi Bank.

Even when it entered a confessional mode, however, MOF continued to hide behind differences of accounting rules and definitions. In 1995, using an extremely narrow definition of nonperforming loans (the Japanese allowed nonpayment of interest charges to go on for at least six months before classifying the debt as problematic) the official estimate was $408 billion to $510 billion.[181] By 1998, after a change in bank disclosure rules, officials were admitting to $700 billion, but U.S. government and private-sector experts concluded that the Japanese were still understating the problem, and that the bad debt total came closer to $1 trillion.[182] It soon became abundantly clear that MOF and Japanese banks had colluded in a cover-up not only of the scale of the banking problems but also a series of financial crimes abroad.[183] One measure of distrust was that in the mid-1990s, foreign banks started charging a "Japan premium" for interbank loans. A few years later, credit-rating agencies challenged Japanese sovereign debt and large-scale banking failures loomed, while Japan's largest banks merged in four huge and unlikely alliances. The parlous state of the Japanese banking sector, by 2000–2001, was regarded as a major threat to the global economy.

For a few short years, however, Japanese banks reigned supreme, and they seemed just as powerful in Asia as Japanese manufacturers and retailers. Between 1993 and 1996, Japanese loans to Korea, Taiwan, and the ASEAN Four grew by 76 percent. Lending to Korea and Thailand doubled. Nearly all of it was in the form of direct lending to manufacturers—44 percent of Japanese lending went to Japanese subsidiaries, another 42 percent to large domestic firms.[184] The line between "domestic" firms and Japanese affiliates was often murky. For example, in March 1999, in a story on the nonperforming loans of Japanese banks in Asia, *Nihon Keizai Shimbun* reported that about half of the banks' $140 billion[185] exposure was to "non-Japanese firms." As an example, the paper gave the Indonesia's "auto assembler Astra," otherwise known as PT Toyota-Astra, a Toyota joint venture since 1991.[186]

At their peak, Japanese banks may have accounted for 50 percent of bank loans to Asia. In the financing of major infrastructure projects, traditionally dominated by the trading companies, the percentage may have been even higher. "Anything from 40 percent to 60 percent of the money for Asian project finance in the mid-'90s came from Japan," Frank Packard, managing director and head of project finance of Bank of America in Hong Kong, told the *Far Eastern Economic Review* in 1998.[187] In 1997, according to the Bank of International Settlements (BIS), Japanese banks accounted for 54 percent of lending in Thailand and 39 percent of loans to Indonesia. By mid-1997, Asians owed the Japanese banks $124 billion out of the $389.4 billion they owed to foreign banks overall.[188] Most of that, BIS noted, was lent to local subsidiaries of Japanese companies. Japan had by far the greatest exposure to the region's two offshore banking centers, Singapore and Hong Kong. In Hong Kong, Japanese banks accounted for 39 percent of foreign-banking assets, $87 billion out of $222 billion. In Singapore, the Japanese banks accounted for $65 billion, or 31 percent of $211 billion in foreign lending.[189]

Ironically, despite their huge presence, Japanese banks were latecomers in terms of the overall flow of Japanese capital. Although major Japanese city banks opened offices in Hong Kong and Singapore in the early 1970s, they only began building branch networks through the region in the mid-1980s. By the early 1990s, Japanese banks were in deep trouble from the stock and real-estate crashes that ended the bubble economy years.

The stock market crash came first. Listed Japanese companies lost $15.9 billion[190] in the value of listed assets in the first six months of 1990; ultimately the Nikkei Index fell by more than 60 percent, from 38,921 on opening day in 1990 to the 11,000 range in 2000 and 2001. Most of the loss came in the first year, and banks suddenly had to reckon with savage hits to their profit margins and capital reserves. BIS rules allowed banks to count 45 percent of their equity holdings toward their capital adequacy ratios, and Japanese rules allowed banks to invest in the stock market.

The banks had done both. They had also lent heavily to real estate, which crashed next, with about a year's delayed reaction to rising interest rates. Between 1991 and 1998, Japanese stocks lost $5.15 trillion, 28 percent of their peak value, and property values dropped by half, or $2.38 trillion.[191] Bank disclosure rules made it difficult for outsiders to estimate the true extent of the damage, but the banks knew. They began reining in credit almost immediately. As Japanese banks realized the implications of the stock market crash of 1990, asset growth fell from 14 percent in 1989 to 12 percent, 13 percent, and then 6 percent in the first three quarters of 1990.

Asia was the exception to the rule. In the early 1990s, the banks expanded their assets in Asia at a fast clip, while reining in lending overall.[192] By 1993, according to MOF, Asia accounted for about 25 percent of foreign loans by Japanese banks, up from 19 percent at the end of 1990.[193] Although Japanese banks virtually monopolized the financing needs of the Japanese multinationals pouring into Asia, they were in the business of servicing corporate debt of local businesses as well. They were clearly in close collaboration with the Ministry of Finance. Sometimes this meant being held in check; more often it seemed to entail encouragement and support. In 1994, despite the popularity of Vietnam with Japanese and foreign investors, MOF refused to allow Japanese banks to set up branches until Vietnamese borrowers made good on debt repayments suspended after Vietnam's invasion of Cambodia in 1979.[194] "Our financial sector isn't known for its creativity or entrepreneurship," Fujiwara Katsuhiro, director of the Asia department of Keidanren, Japan's major big business organization, told the *Far Eastern Economic Review* in 1994. "They depend on the Ministry of Finance to tell them what to do."[195]

By the mid-1990s, Japanese banks were beginning to retreat even in Asia. According to BIS data, Japanese banks slipped to second place after the European banks at the end of 1995, with 36.9 percent of loans to Asia versus 38.5 for the Europeans and 9.8 percent for North American banks. Between 1995 and 1996, Japanese loans to Asia (other than to Hong Kong and Singapore) grew a mere 0.9 percent, from $113 billion at the end of 1995 to $118 billion at the end of 1996.

Then came the big crunch, as banks began failing at home and the MOF, after a delay of eight years, finally began to pressure the banks to clear nonperforming loans from their books through write-offs and foreclosures. Japanese banks conducted a fire sale of their Asian assets, ripping $110 billion out of the region in two years. Hong Kong was particularly hard hit, because the loans were of higher quality than elsewhere, so the banks could dispose of them quickly. According to BIS statistics, by the end of 1998, Japanese banks had pulled $48.8 billion from Hong Kong, $29.9 billion from Singapore, and $32.1 billion from the rest of Asia.[196]

Ancestral Wave: The Japanese Trading Companies

If Japan exported its bubble, it wasn't just banks that were at fault. Trading companies had preceded the Japanese banks in the region by at least two decades and were active in trade finance, loans, and loan guarantees. Each of the trading firms was part of a "linked" *keiretsu*. By a tradition dating back to the Meiji Era, trading companies had an exclusive claim on the foreign business of their partners within the *keiretsu*. In post-war Japan, they developed expertise in merchant banking and project finance long before the banks ventured beyond the major world financial centers.

It was the trading companies that often served as lead banks in project finance involving their *keiretsu*, a formula that allowed the members of the syndicate to spread the risk of projects. Trading companies often became equity partners as well. When the Asian financial crisis struck, the difficulty of sorting out Japanese corporate debt was a major factor slowing down workouts in Indonesia and Thailand. Banks had lent recklessly because they were lending to Japanese entities, or had trading company guarantees. The tangle was so massive it would take years to sort out.

When entering a new market, the trading companies marched as invincibly as army ants. Working through the presidents' clubs of their *keiretsu* groupings, the trading companies could put together syndicates with the resources of small countries. When Mitsubishi Shoji, the largest of the trading companies, wanted China's attention, for example, its chief executive traveled with an entourage of sixteen of his ranking colleagues from other Mitsubishi Group companies, met with Chinese premier Li Peng, and generally conducted himself in a manner and style normally associated with heads of state.

Mitsubishi made its decision to pull out the stops in China shortly after celebrating its tenth anniversary in the market in 1994. By 1995, China was already Japan's second-largest trading partner after the United States. All nine of Japan's general trading companies, the *sogo shosha*, had caught "China fever" about the same time, according to the Japanese press, but Mitsubishi was considered a laggard despite the volume of its trade with China, $2.21 billion in 1993.[197] Its investments in China by the end of 1993 amounted to just $150 million.

Being last helped galvanize Mitsubishi into action, and in April 1994, its president, Makihara Minoru, started out by setting up an internal China policy council, cutting across the company's seven product and marketing divisions. Chaired by executive vice-president Hotta Yasushi, the group included three senior managing directors and five managing directors. The executives oversaw a China–Far East project team that coordinated with the marketing divisions involved in major projects. Makihara's idea was not only to energize Mitsubishi's China business but also to broker deals among China, the United States, and Japan.

The Mitsubishi policy council proceeded to launch several projects that easily caught the eye of the Chinese leadership. These included the first Japanese engine and auto parts manufacturing facility in China, a deal to set up a joint company to design steel mills in Shanghai, and, most important, a research and cooperation agreement with China's State Council. The latter involved thirty-one Mitsubishi group companies. Key players on the Mitsubishi side included Mitsubishi Motors Corp., Mitsubishi Bank, Tokio Marine and Fire Insurance Co., and Chiyoda Co. They were to set up training programs to teach Japanese approaches to economic and financial management, which had become hot topics for Chinese managers. In September 1994, when Mitsubishi Shoji chairman Morohashi Shinroku led a delegation of sixteen executives from Mitsubishi Group companies to Beijing for the tenth anniversary celebrations, they met with Chinese premier Li Peng, and would have met with President Jiang Zemin if the latter had not been on a trip to Europe.[198]

The trading companies could also make use of their regional networks to broker deals between governments. In June 1994, with help from Malaysia's prime minister, Mitsubishi Shoji cobbled together a triangular Japanese-Malaysian-Chinese deal to build auto engines and parts in China. The $1.5 billion deal brought together Mitsubishi Shoji; Mitsubishi Motors Co.; Edaran Otomobil Nasional (EON), the Malaysian government company that made the Proton; and three Chinese companies. Mitsubishi Motors and EON had been partners in Malaysia since the early 1980s, and the deal allowed Mitsubishi to leapfrog over such Japanese rivals as Toyota and Nissan Motor Co. by taking advantage of Prime Minister Mahathir's political influence in China. Mahathir was a signatory to the memorandum of understanding and got a foothold in the China market for EON. Shortly after the China deal was announced, EON and Mitsubishi Motors announced a similar agreement to make minibuses in Vietnam.

Indeed, if there was one thing that Japanese banks feared more than another bank failure, it was the failure of a trading company. In 1998 and 1999, the major trading companies hovered on the brink of disaster because of their deep exposure to Asia as well as to other emerging markets. Their *keiretsu* main banks gently led them back from the cliff edge. In September 1998, Nissho Iwai, the trading-firm component of the Sanwa Group, was foundering under a staggering $24.4 billion in bad loans.[199] Sanwa Bank came to the rescue. In May 1998, the little known trading company Kanematsu asked its main bank, Tokyo-Mitsubishi, to forgive more than $900 million[200] in loans. The bank complied, sending one of its senior managing directors, Kurachi Tadashi, to run the company. "I felt a chill down my spine," Kurachi said when he heard about his new appointment. The task was daunting, but he was certainly familiar with the company. The sixty-two-year-old executive had been at Kanematsu for three years in the early 1980s, as a result of a routine secondment within the Mitsubishi *keiretsu*. He had sold sports bags and shoes for the trading house.[201] This sort of interchange between mid-level executives of companies within *keiretsu* groups was so normal that the major Japanese publication that tracked *keiretsu* data, *Toyo Keizai*, included precise numbers for secondments to companies in the first section of the Tokyo Stock Exchange. In 1994, Mitsubishi led the others in such secondments with 789, including nineteen presidents or vice-presidents of *keiretsu* member companies.[202]

The foreign exposure of trading companies rarely showed up on balance sheets of the parent companies. Instead, it would be tucked away in accounts of subsidiaries and affiliates, and the trading companies were normally minority shareholders.[203] The Asian financial crisis hung out the dirty linen for public viewing. In Indonesia, for example, the exposure of trading companies was equal or greater than the $24 billion owed to Japanese banks. Each of the six largest Japanese trading firms had $1.5 billion to $4 billion in Indonesian exposure, ranging from equity to direct loans and loan guarantees, according to an estimate by Itochu.

"Any defaults could have a scary ripple effect on bankers," wrote Henny Sender, an expert on the Japanese financial system. "Trading firms are among Japan's largest bank borrowers, which means defaults could cause damage to Japan's already ailing lenders. That, in turn, would raise the banks' cost of funds and put further pressure on the yen, leading to a more intense credit crunch, which would hurt not only corporate Japan but all of Asia."[204] Anabuki Hiroyuki, a branch manager of Marubeni in Hong Kong, put it bluntly: "If Marubeni goes bankrupt, then Bank of Tokyo Mitsubishi goes bankrupt."[205]

There was another reason why trading companies couldn't fail. Even more than Japanese banks, they had a long history of close ties with the government. They got their start in the late nineteenth century, with the collaboration of government and industry in a plan to drive out foreign, mainly British, trading houses based in Yokohama and other port cities. In 1880, Western merchants controlled 86 percent of Japanese trade. They were driven to less than 50 percent by 1911, through introduction of a licensing system for trade called *shoken* (commercial rights). Mitsui Bussan and Mitsubishi Shoji, the trading houses for the Mitsui and Mitsubishi *zaibatsu* combines, got their start this way, as holders of coveted *shoken* licenses.

After the war, the huge financial conglomerates known as *zaibatsu,* or financial cliques, were broken up by the U.S. Occupation. After 1949, when American policy toward Japan reversed, the financial conglomerates were among the first beneficiaries. In the early 1950s, Mitsui Bussan and Mitsubishi Shoji were allowed to pick up the pieces of the disbanded *zaibatsu* through mergers and resume their old names. The era of the *sogo shosha* was born. Eventually the *zaibatsu* were reinstated as *keiretsu* groups, with cross shareholding taking the place of the holding companies that the U.S. Occupation authorities had banned. With steady encouragement from the reconstituted Japanese government in the form of subsidies and other incentives, the trading companies monopolized Japanese imports and most of Japan's exports during the 1960s and 1970s. By 1974, at their height, they furnished 32 percent of Japan's GNP.[206]

As Japanese manufacturers developed their own international marketing capabilities and Japanese labor costs rose, the *sogo shosha* developed a new area of expertise—project syndication in developing countries. As early as the 1960s, they urged Japanese manufacturers to establish ventures in low-labor-cost countries in Asia and began organizing syndicates within their *keiretsu* to invest in larger projects.[207] In this, the trading companies reflected views of the Okita Saburo "flying-geese" school within MITI and the EPA. Their vision of "sunset industries" involved moving obsolescent industries out of Japan with minimal destruction to companies and employment. Trading companies were useful to maintain control over the process. As manufacturers left Japan, they would control the flow of product and keep profits in Japanese hands. To encourage the process, the Japanese government included the trading companies in its foreign aid program. Japanese official aid statistics included projects with private-sector involvement in which the *sogo shosha* acted as lead developers and syndicators. The projects were underwritten by Japan's development lending bank, the Overseas Economic Cooperation Fund (OECF). The OECF became a partner in the projects, taking as much as a 30 to 40 percent stake, and giving the Japanese consortia a huge advantage over foreign rivals.

When the Paris-based Organization for Economic Cooperation and Development (OECD) asked Kojima Kiyoshi, Akamatsu's disciple and Okita's close associate, to assemble a profile of Japanese trading companies, he did his best to present them as "merchants of economic development." Even Kojima had trouble justifying OECF's close involvement with the trading companies, however. "This does not always produce a desirable result," he wrote, "for some huge long-term projects can be too eagerly pushed and too readily accepted without full consideration of all the future risks, partly because of government assistance and partly because of the nature of group investment."[208]

By the mid-1980s, when the great wave of Japanese investment began, the trading companies had established a pattern of business into which new entrants to the expatriate Japanese business fraternity readily fit. They participated in manufacturing and infrastructure projects through both equity and loans—the latter usually larger than the former, and had become deeply involved in manufacturing ventures, usually as minority shareholders with local partners. They had evolved into roles combining the functions of investment banks, intelligence gathering, and communication within the huge *keiretsu* of which they remained key players. Outside Japan, they were in many respects the most visible faces of the *keiretsu*, commanding resources several times the GDP of many of the economies in which they operated. When they trembled, it was not only Japanese bankers that turned pale but also the leaders of the countries where they played so large a role.

Akamatsu's Legacy

The wave of Japanese investment in Southeast Asia and China in the late 1980s to mid-1990s was so immense that its impact has taken at least a decade to register. Japanese money helped feed a speculative frenzy triggering the horrific financial collapse of 1997 and 1998. But it also helped to create an industrial landscape of tremendous depth and scope, in economies where palm oil and rubber plantations, oil wells and mines, had been the mainstays of wealth generation, and growth had been dependent on the ebb and flow of the global commodities markets. This was not just a financial investment on the part of the Japanese but a commitment of men and machinery, of countless people like Sato Mitsuro who zealously studied the quirks of markets that a Western executive might dismiss; of Yokoo Kensuke, creating a world-class factory from scratch; and of all the Japanese who shouldered the burdens of transplanting Japan, Inc., to the not-so-distant shores of Asia.

Much of what the Japanese did had an organic quality of trial and error as they attempted to escape the fortress-economy paradigm of post-war Japan. It represented an enormous break with the paradigm to move production outside Japan. Once beyond home shores, Japanese companies were automatically exposed to different standards and expectations. They knew this, and yet it was a measure of Japanese self-confidence that they assumed that they could use Asian aspirations for wealth and power to further Japanese objectives. The Japanese built their factories and ports and power stations in calm assurance that their Asian transplants would move along a common trajectory with their parents. They knew that this did not always happen— Korea in particular had shown the risks of technology partnership with a determined rival. Still, the Japanese plowed ahead, or sometimes blundered along, as in the various experiments with regional auto parts production. In a sense they were not creating specific strategies in response to new opportunities and challenges but operating under a belief system shaped by Akamatsu's vision of flying geese. At its most basic, Akamatsu's theory said that developing economies would do anything to catch up with a leader, even to the point of accepting the leader's standards, ways of dress, ways of managing factories, and certainly its money.

One theme emerging clearly from Japan's deep plunge into the Asian economy after 1985 was the extraordinary patience of the Japanese as investors. Tokyo's emphasis on long-range goals justified the perfectionism of Honda in its marketing exercise in Thailand or Matsushita with its robot-tended factories in Malaysia. Akamatsu assumed that companies and workers not only shared common nationalistic goals but also drove themselves in order to achieve benefits for their nations. In such a frame of reference, companies as well as workers might have to accept losses and other setbacks in the course of achieving their objectives. Shareholders' rights didn't enter into the equation. The dynamic was much closer to that of a politician, or an entrepreneur, who utilizes every resource available, whether it is friends or university classmates, or a *keiretsu* tie. The objectives were not just corporate growth but the success of whole economies. With such all-encompassing goals, organic methods were the only ones available to the strategist.

Even if Akamatsu and the Japanese were wrong, there is no question that Asian growth in the decade from the mid-1980s to mid-1990s owed much to Japan. Japanese investment was aimed not just at immediate returns but at preserving the core strengths of the Japanese economy, based on manufacturing. All of a sudden, the line between the Japanese and Asian economies was blurred. Faced with an implacable erosion of their productive capability in Japan, the Japanese looked to Asia as a second perimeter. Glancing around their neighborhood, perhaps viewing it still with the Meiji Era lens contrasting Asian primitivism with Japanese sophistication, the Japanese felt that they could succeed in transplanting the Japanese industrial machine and, of equal importance, maintain the collaboration with government that had been so successful at home. Instead of transferring the less valuable pieces of industrial production, the polluters and the stinkers, they shipped over what Matsushita Konosuke had once called "full set" production. Everything went. The Japanese weren't gearing their investments for maximum liquidity. They were ready to be illiquid. They were ready to stay. The consequence was that their host economies suddenly had, from companies such as Matsushita, a dozen manufacturers of related products and components, or, in the case of Toyota or Mitsubishi Motors, a replica of the production system, complete with subcontractors, that had made Japan the world's second largest auto manufacturer.

This was an incredible windfall for Southeast Asia, and only marginally less so for Northeast Asia and China. Aside from the fact that China's economy was much larger and therefore less easily influenced even by so large an economic power as Japan, China, South Korea, and Taiwan maintained much more severe restrictions against investment than Southeast Asia during the peak period of Japanese investment from 1985–95. Southeast Asia, by contrast, was in the mood to tear down barriers in the mid-1980s. The collapse in the price of oil in the early 1980s was followed by a general commodity price collapse that created havoc in the Southeast Asian economies. Their response was to become much friendlier to foreign investment, and the Japanese simply happened to be first in line.

The flip side of the coin was the deep-seated reluctance of Japanese companies to share technology with their host countries, reflected in their ineffective training programs and insistence on introducing and favoring Japanese suppliers, bankers, and trading companies. Such attitudes damaged the Japanese image and supported critics who argued that the benefits of Japanese investment were limited compared to those of Western companies, which tended to buy from the most efficient and least-cost provider, and offered clear training and promotion ladders to their Asian employees. Japanese companies were not good places for creative or ambitious individuals of whom there were very many in Southeast Asia, Korea, China, and Taiwan, not to mention Hong Kong and Singapore. By establishing internal barriers to sharing technology even with their employees, Japanese companies alienated the best and brightest Asian employees and doomed themselves to the same sort of institutionalized mediocrity they had at home.

So where, in the end, had Akamatsu and his flying geese taken Japan with this massive transfer of wealth to Southeast Asia, a region that Akamatsu himself had once supervised on behalf of the Japanese imperial government? Was Japan merely exporting the worst of its system to the countries in its economic backyard? Or was there something more to the Japanese model? Was its lesson one that could take developing economies through the most daunting challenges of globalization? In the mid-1990s, a crisis was brewing that would provide at least some of the answers. The results would be mixed. But they would show one thing clearly. The politics of export-led development did not end with the Cold War. In the era of globalization, markets had become a tool to build and preserve geopolitical alliances. The next round would go to the nation that could show, with its depth of investment, markets, and example, that it could lead the way out of disaster.

5

Crisis? What Crisis?

If Muhammad Azlan Bin Amran worried about the Asian financial crisis, he wasn't showing it. In May 1998, at a time when nearby Indonesia was self-detonating, Thailand and Korea were on the ropes, and Singapore was awash with overseas Chinese refugees from Jakarta, the thirty-two-year-old Malaysian engineer had no job problems. His company was on a roll. Trained in Japan, Azlan worked for Japanese electronics giant Canon, Inc., in a factory just outside Kuala Lumpur. Showing off a brand-new production line for new-format cameras that he helped design, Azlan bragged: "We picked up this production line from Japan because we wanted to learn how to do it. Compared to our parent factory in Oita [Japan], we're just a coffee shop. Oita is like a hotel. But we're the best coffee shop in the world, and our customers like coming to coffee shops."

There were a lot of electronic "coffee shops" in Azlan's neighborhood. Some 3,000 miles to the south of Tokyo and Beijing, between Kuala Lumpur and Port Klang, the giant industrial estate of Shah Alam sprawled like a city of its own, with tens of thousands of workers housed in neat compounds, sports complexes, and shopping malls. Thirty years earlier it was steamy jungle; by the late 1990s Shah Alam represented one of the largest assemblages of Japanese electronics companies on the planet. Out of 986 Japanese subsidiaries and affiliates based in Malaysia in 1998, 162 were electronics companies (nearly 16 percent), and most of them were in Shah Alam. Azlan's coffee shop was part of one the greatest concentrations of Japanese industrial firepower in the world.[1]

If U.S. and European multinationals dominated Penang to the north, Shah Alam was thoroughly Japanese. It even had a village-like quality. People knew their neighbors, many of them familiar from similar constellations of *keiretsu* companies and their subcontractors back home in Tokyo or Osaka. As in Japan, subcontractors tended to nestle close to their *oyagaisha,* the lead companies in the *keiretsu*. Unlike Japan, ample space was available around the sites, and many were neat and pretty. Their cafeterias sold the cuisines of Malaysia's three major ethnic groups, Malay, Chinese, and Indian, and provided prayer rooms for religious Muslims. The predominantly young, female workers seemed proud of their jobs; a male Malay manager cracked jokes as he led a visitor around his factory.

While the Malaysian economy was battered by the financial crisis like all its neighbors, there were exceptions to the rule. As long as you had deep pockets, an established global distribution system, and a hot product, your company might not feel the pain at all. The collapse of regional currencies, in fact, was an enormous windfall for some manufacturers, and the Japanese were at the head of the line.

Few Japanese companies had come to Malaysia to exploit the domestic market, and in the large group of Japanese electronics manufacturers based in Malaysia at the onset of the crisis, virtually all had just one purpose: to export. By the summer of 1998, a year into the Asian crisis, they were pumping. The Malaysian ringgit was 35 to 40 percent off its July 1997 peak, and the Japanese were adding production lines as fast as they could. The same was true elsewhere in Southeast Asia. Foreign multinationals that focused on the regional market were in trouble, as widespread banking failures forced Asia's high rollers into fire sales of their luxury cars, golf club memberships, and condos. Exporters were in trouble too, as banks refused to handle even the simplest of Letter of Credit transactions. But the big Japanese multinationals, like Canon, who could use internal financing for their export shipments, breezed through the crisis and played a crucial role in the preternaturally speedy recovery experienced by the Asian economies, except for Indonesia. For them, the crisis was no crisis, but a bonanza.

Before the Asian crisis, Japanese companies had already helped turn Malaysia into a world-class exporter of consumer electronics, building on its success as the world's premier semiconductor-manufacturing nation, in volume terms. Between 1992 and 1996, Malaysian exports doubled, from $40 billion to $78 billion.[2] In 1996, Japanese affiliates accounted for 19 percent of Malaysian exports,[3] and the largest Japanese company, Matsushita, accounted for 3.1 percent of Malaysian exports all by itself. Matsushita used Malaysia as a global production base for its air conditioners and color television sets, exporting 71 percent of its Malaysian output.[4]

In the midst of crisis, executives at companies like Matsushita, Sony, and Canon were talking easy street. Said Sakakibara Katsuro, Matsushita's board member for Asia and the Pacific: "If you look at our 43 production bases in Southeast Asia, there's a vast difference between those which target domestic markets and those which export to Japan, Europe, or North America. It's tough for the former, because the cost of imported parts has gone up with the currency crash, but it's basically smooth sailing for the exporters. If you look at it from a total profit perspective, we come out even.[5] Kawakyu Koichi, who directed Sony International's Asian business from an office overlooking Singapore's vast container port, echoed the sentiment. "Of course, the currency crisis is affecting domestic markets. On the other hand, exports are doing well."[6] Back in Tokyo, Canon president and CEO, Mitarai Fujio, was yet more positive: "If there are pluses and minuses to the Asia crisis, for Canon on balance it's a plus."[7]

The crisis was, of course, the antithesis of theories going back to Friedrich List and Akamatsu, that argued economies could insulate themselves from the storm of global competition. The currency collapse that began in July 1997 was like a giant vortex, sucking capital from the region and scattering the ambitious plans of a generation of strong leaders, corporate patriarchs, and immense corporate empires. The phenomenon raced through economies with cyclonic speed and force. It demonstrated with awesome effect that there was no hiding place from the global economy in the Age of the Internet. Yet there were more subtle lessons as well.

One of these was that the new global economy was itself a war zone. Individual economies might not be strong enough to weather it on their own. They would need allies. Around this simple idea, Japan began to re-assemble Akamatsu's flock, pouring on financial support to revive Asian exports, erecting emergency schemes in the event of another currency crisis, and renewing its ideological attack on market liberalization through the international financial institutions and the World Trade Organization (WTO). Its greatest source of leverage, however, was the skein of Japanese multinationals flung across the map of Southeast Asia and China. These multinationals represented large, fixed investments that contributed substantially to national economies. They gave some economies the means to export their way back to health. And they gave Japan a way to counterbalance its domestic problems by raising profits from its new economic perimeter, using the crisis to make new inroads into global markets.

The tsunami of Japanese investment in Asia in the 1980s and 1990s left Japan and Asia with a unique commonality of interests. In Thailand, exports of Japanese factories accounted for 45 percent of total Thai exports, an extraordinary figure. In the Philippines, the Japanese export share was 37.3 percent; in Indonesia, 23.2 percent; in Singapore, 11.6 percent; in Hong Kong, 5.7 percent; in China, 5.8 percent. Even in Korea, where Japanese companies were largely blocked from direct investment, the Japanese accounted for 9 percent of total exports. And in every country, despite the fact that most of them ran large deficits in their trade with Japan, the subsidiaries themselves were generating solid surpluses in the balance of exports against imports.[8]

Indeed, by 1996 Japan, Inc., had moved so much of its "Inc." to Asia that the sales, profits, and capital investment of Japan's Asian affiliates exceeded those of Japan's U.S. transplants. For the first time ever, in 1996 Japan's foreign manufacturing subsidiaries delivered more sales than the domestic export machine, Yen 53 trillion compared to Yen 51 trillion. Asia was extraordinarily important to this transformation. Japan's Asian manufacturing affiliates delivered Yen 594 billion in profits, compared to Yen 298 billion in profits from North America and Yen 988 billion from Europe. Manufactured goods from Japan's Asian factories accounted for 10 percent of total Japanese imports in 1996, some Yen 3.9 trillion.

Japanese exporters based in Asia weren't just benefiting from the collapse of Asian currencies, but also from the strength of the Japanese yen relative to Asian-currencies, which made Japanese multinationals better able to take advantage of asset fire sales and expanded terms for foreign investment in the Asian crisis countries. Even after Finance Minister Miyazawa Kiichi allowed the yen to depreciate freely after July 1998, Japanese manufacturers failed to abandon their Asian holdings.[9] Instead, they bought more of them, particularly in Southeast Asia. In yen terms, Japanese investment in Malaysia was up by 50 percent in 1997—from Yen 64 billion in 1996 to Yen 97 billion. Investment in Thailand was up by almost as much, 45 percent, from Yen 158 billion in 1996 to Yen 229 billion. In Asia overall, Japanese investment increased by 14.6 percent, to Yen 1.5 trillion, making Asia Japan's chief target for FDI in 1997 after the United States, despite a steep runup in Japanese investment in Europe and Latin America.[10]

In dollar terms, the increase in Japanese investment in Asia was less remarkable, with the yen slipping from Yen 103.38 to the dollar at the beginning of 1996 to Yen 130.15 to the dollar by the last trading day of 1997. In dollars, Asian investment in 1997 rose a mere 3.3 percent, from $12 billion in 1996 to $12.4 billion in 1997.[11] That was hardly a worry for Asia-based Japanese exporters whose repatriated profits would also be in inflated U.S. dollars.

Nor was the direct flow of capital from Japan the whole story. In fact, it was getting to be less and less of the story. According to MITI, by 1996–97, based on the Japanese fiscal year ending in March 1997, Japanese companies were drawing more than half of funds for new investment from local sources, either from profits or local debt markets. In a 1997 survey, MITI estimated total 1996 Japanese investment in manufacturing in Asia at Yen 1.4 trillion. The report, based on a survey of 12,806 companies, found that Japanese companies were raising 5.1 yen locally for every 4.9 yen coming from Japan. Thus, Japanese subsidiaries in Asia got Yen 694 billion in transfers from headquarters and raised Yen 747 billion from local sources in fiscal 1996.[12] In Northeast Asia, by 1995 to 1996 Japanese companies were raising up to 27 percent of funds from local sources, in ASEAN 30.9 percent of financing was local, and even in China the figure was up to 24.8 percent.[13]

According to the Japan Institute for Overseas Investment (JOI), most of the local funding was from retained earnings, although there was also substantial exposure to local debt markets. JOI's 1997 survey found that Japanese companies based in Northeast Asia were drawing 67.9 percent of funding from local sources. A further breakdown of the local funding showed that 60 percent overall came from retained earnings, with just under 40 percent from local debt markets. In Southeast Asia, 57 percent was from local sources, with 54 percent from local borrowing and 46 percent from retained earnings.[14]

As it turned out, the local borrowings were treacherous. Much of this local financing was in U.S. dollars, and Japanese borrowers did not bother to hedge more than a fraction of it, according to the Japan Export-Import Bank (JEXIM). In Thailand, for example, 70 percent of Japanese corporate borrowings were in U.S. dollars, and only 10 percent of the dollar-denominated funds were hedged.[15] Japanese banks were also in deep trouble, particularly in Korea, where they were the lead creditor by mid-1997, with $23.7 billion in outstanding loans.[16] The total exposure of Japanese banks at the start of the crisis was $275.2 billion, representing a 31.8 percent market share, well behind the European banks but an unwelcome addition to Japan's estimated $1 trillion in domestic bad debt. Japanese exports to Asia declined sharply, adding to Japan's domestic woes. A high proportion of Japanese exports to the region were capital goods, ordered by Japanese subsidiaries and affiliates. As Asian markets contracted, the yen appreciated in local currency terms, forcing plant closures and layoffs by Japanese companies selling primarily to local markets, such as the auto companies.

Even worse hit than the auto companies and the banks were trading companies, typically involved in large-scale infrastructure projects. Such deals might have survived a 10 to 15 percent currency devaluation but not 50 percent, as in Indonesia.[17] In May 1998, the *Wall Street Journal* reported that second-tier trading companies might face bankruptcy with "one more degree of meltdown in Indonesia."[18] Struggling in deep waters too were thousands of Japanese small and medium enterprises, whose real crisis was the sharp deceleration of the Japanese economy in 1997–98, which cut back orders from Japan. But they were also affected by the shutdowns and retrenchment that affected many Japanese subsidiaries in Asia in the first months of the regional currency collapse.

But then something happened; the hemorrhaging stopped, and companies began to expand. Wakamatsu Isamu, a young researcher at JETRO, combed Japanese newspapers between July 1997 and April 1998, looking for signs of a pullout by Japanese companies during the crisis. In an interview, he declared proudly that only one Japanese company had "retreated" from South-east Asia during the course of the crisis, a small-scale joint venture assembling trucks for Daihatsu Motors, a Toyota affiliate. Thailand had the densest concentration of Japanese automakers in Asia.[19]

By mid-year, conditions had started looking up even in the auto sector. More than any other group of Japanese companies in Asia, the carmakers had been quick to seize advantage of the rising Asian consumer culture of the 1990s, which translated readily into a surge of first-time car owners. By 1995, at the height of the consumer boom, Japanese car companies dominated the Asian auto market. They had 60 percent of the Thai market, 74,000 out of 163,000 new car sales; 95 percent of 223,000 new car sales in Malaysia (including the Japanese-designed "national cars" Proton and Perodua); 90 percent of the 69,000 cars sold in the Philippines; and 80 percent of the 36,000-vehicle Indonesian market.[20] Honda and Toyota battled for market supremacy without paying much attention to non-Japanese rivals; although Korea's Kia Motors gave them trouble in Indonesia and the Philippines, and Taiwanese motorcycle makers were successfully establishing themselves in China and Vietnam,[21] the Japanese had the rising middle class of Southeast Asia mostly to itself.

The Asian crash hit the car companies hard; a Mitsubishi Motors executive confessed his company had retrenched "1,500 percent" in Thailand.[22] And yet, many of the car companies closed production lines temporarily, only to reopen a few months later. Toyota, for example, closed its Hilux pickup in Thailand in November, only to reopen in January at one-quarter the capacity, according to Takemoto Motonobu, general manager of Toyota's Asia Division. Takemoto was planning to get the plant back up to at least half-capacity by exporting trucks to Australia and proceed "step by step" to improve production quality to the Japanese level. "We are in a survival mode," Takemoto said. "We are supported by our parent company in Japan. Likewise, we will support our subcontractors in Asia."[23]

In hard-struck Indonesia, Toyota applied a strategy of operating its assembly plant one week out of the month, and cutting assembly line temporary workers and contract workers to save costs. It also applied a favorable internal exchange rate of Rupiah 8,000 to the U.S. dollar, as opposed to the market rate of Rupiah 13,000, to components imported from Japan. But as late as August 1998 the company maintained its no lay-off policy for regular staff and still managed to squeeze 1,000 sales per month of its popular Kijang sport utility van, down from 7,000 before the currency crisis began. Considering that the Indonesian economy was in a state of double-digit contraction, such staying power was remarkable.[24]

The worst hit of the Japanese car companies was Mitsubishi Motors Corporation (MMC). The company took a $410 million dollar loss in its 1997 fiscal year, after writing off costs of its Thai subsidiary, MMC Sittipol, with net losses of $330 million.[25] But MMC also took advantage of the crisis to gain control of the subsidiary. In August 1997, it raised its stake in the Thai company from 48 percent to 98 percent, at a cost of $185 million. MMC also became the first Japanese automaker in Thailand to pump up exports, exporting about 41,000 small trucks to Europe in 1998 compared with 13,000 in 1997.[26] Added a colleague, Kyoda Toyoho, "We are thinking or hoping that within two years' time the situation in Asia will be back to the previous level. We are concentrating now on how to survive for two or three years."[27] "Japanese companies don't quit," said Ohkusa Tomoyuki, a spokesman for Mitsubishi Motors in Tokyo.[28]

In contrast to the general carnage in the Japanese auto sector, exports of auto parts took off quickly. In February 1998, the Bangkok *Nation* reported that the Japan External Trade Organization (JETRO) had dispatched seventy industrial experts to counsel local producers in the car parts, plastics, electronics, and metals industries. Toyota Motors simultaneously announced it would push car and car parts exports to 20,000 units, or $160 million, up from $90 million in 1997. Honda said its exports of cars and components would nearly double, to Baht 17 billion from Baht 9.2 billion in 1997.[29] Leading Japanese auto parts makers affiliated with Honda and Nissan, meanwhile, began raising their stakes in subsidiaries in Thailand and South Korea.[30] Retail showed signs of recovery as well. In September 1997, as Yaohan went under, seemingly confirming anxieties about the Japanese retail sector in Asia, Japanese discount stores based in Hong Kong were expanding to take advantage of lower rents.[31]

Japan's Asian empire was quickly getting back on its feet. One of the few major U.S. publications to notice was *Business Week*. The magazine reported in April 1998 that Japanese-controlled companies in Southeast Asia were planning to increase production of car parts and electronics by as much as 30 percent. Since Japanese-controlled companies already exported $70 billion worth of goods from the region, the "result could be a major change in global trade flows," *Business Week* predicted. One out of three products manufactured in Southeast Asia came from Japanese companies or affiliates, the magazine claimed. (According to MITI's own estimate, Japanese affiliates exported $57.5 billion from Singapore, Indonesia, Malaysia, Thailand, and the Philippines in 1996; when South Korea, Hong Kong, Taiwan, and China were added to the list, the figure jumped to $103.4 billion; the agency did not provide a breakdown on the destination of these exports, but the figures were still remarkable.)[32] Whatever the total value of exports, most of Japan's Southeast Asian subsidiaries were increasing their investments either by building new production lines or through buyouts of cash-strapped local partners. In

Thailand alone, the Thai Board of Investment had received 125 applications from Japanese companies to take larger stakes in their joint ventures.[33]

Yen depreciation was a big help, as well. "If you're a Toyota or a Honda or Matsushita or Canon, one of the big killer multinationals, the only thing better than 140 yen [to the U.S. dollar] is 145," said Kenneth Courtis, chief strategist for Deutsche Bank in Tokyo. "It hurts so much it's like, you've been skiing all day Sunday and every bone and muscle in your body hurts, you come back to your chalet and you slip into a nice warm, sudsy jacuzzi, and someone brings you caviar and champagne on a platter, that's how much it hurts. At 150, I guess it's a young lady who comes in to start massaging your shoulders; and 160 I'd blush if I told you what would happen. There's no sense of that in fact the very moment that some of the banks have been downgraded recently, the debt on Toyota and Sony has been upgraded to Triple A."[34]

So what happened? The answer is straightforward. In classic fashion, the Japanese government had jumped into action with a policy-based response to the crisis. Tokyo channeled more than half of Japanese emergency funding for the region into getting exports moving again, and that meant support for Japanese manufacturers. The Japanese did not see this as selfish; their assets in Asia were too big to lose. And if U.S. policy makers were disturbed by it, they showed no sign; Washington may have seen the Japanese support for its companies in Asia as parallel to the U.S. provision of trade and investment finance for U.S. multinationals.

It was not, either in terms of scale or intentions. By mid-year, the U.S. Export-Import Bank (EXIM) had offered $2.75 billion in short-term trade finance, together with $400 million in telecommunications-related loans from the Overseas Private Investment Corporation for American companies in trouble. The comparable figure from Japan, in terms of commitments, was $21 billion, nearly ten times as much. In August 1998, the *Nihon Keizai Shimbun* reported that Japan's EXIM had tripled lending to Southeast Asia in the first six months of the year, to Yen 699.2 billion, equivalent to $4.83 billion. Most of the money went to trade finance for Japanese companies based in Thailand and Indonesia, and included loans to 113 Asian companies. Counting loans to Korea and China, more than 70 percent of the government bank's lending had gone to Asia in the first half of the year, just under Yen 900 billion.[35]

To be sure, one side of Japanese support efforts was completely untied. Japan put $19 billion on the line for the IMF's balance-of-payments support programs for Asia, far ahead of the United States' $8 billion. Japan established its lead early on, organizing the initial $16 billion bailout for Thailand in August 1997, when the United States was still sitting on the sidelines. Japan and the IMF both contributed $4 billion to the package, with Australia,

Hong Kong, Malaysia, and Singapore offering $1 billion each and South Korea and Indonesia pledging $500 million. China subsequently joined the package as well. Sakakibara Eisuke, Japan's vice-minister for International Financial Affairs, called the pledges "a major step forward. What is important is that it shows that the Asian-Pacific region is approaching these issues with solidarity."[36]

What was interesting about Japanese emergency funding was not just the scale but also the philosophy behind it. There was nothing secret about what MITI did, but perhaps nobody bothered to read between the lines, look at it in historical perspective, or check back later. The Emergency Measures for the Economic Stabilization of Southeast Asia, a Japanese cabinet decision reached on February 20, 1998, spelled out support for Japanese companies in the form of investment finance and two-step loans to Asian governments to support "local export-related companies in Asia."[37] But in practice, such funds would go primarily to Japanese affiliates. The main import-related measure of the February document offered JEXIM financing for "Japanese companies whose imports are currently being affected by factors such as the credit crunch." Other provisions of this early document included technical training and the dispatch of Japanese "experts" and specific measures for Indonesia.

The philosophical backdrop to Japanese support consisted of a perspective on Japanese investment in the region that by 1997 had become official theology. MITI viewed Japanese companies as serving as the catalyst to industrialization on a regional scale. In a 1996 study of Japanese investment and technology transfer patterns, Yamamura Kozo, a distinguished economic historian at the University of Washington, and Walter Hatch, a former journalist and student of Yamamura's, came up with the phrase "embraced development."[38] The two argued that Japan had exported its developmental strategies to the rest of Asia once they became obsolescent at home, in the form of intracompany trade. Japanese companies moved production offshore, yet maintained tight control of the technology flow. Japanese government support, one way or another, primarily ended up in the pockets of their own multinationals. The authors quoted the marvelous analogy of a cormorant fisherman using his diving bird to capture fish.[39] The diving bird represented the energy and dynamism of developmental Asia. The government's role— not expressed in the parable—would be in financing the boat.

By the late 1990s, MITI had been actively promoting Asian economic integration for a decade, with Japan as the region's brain trust. This was precisely the idea behind MITI's package of trade and institutional support for the Asia crisis. By May 1998, MITI's non-IMF financial package comprised $13.5 billion in short-term trade credit (representing 90 percent of G7 contributions); $2.4 billion in two-step loans and loans to Japanese companies; and $2 billion each in export credits for Thailand and Indonesia.[40] MITI officials were not shy about explaining the rationale behind the Japanese program: "Of course there's a need to change the Asian financial system, and a need for short-term, blood transfusion type measures," said Ojimi Takato, an MITI official in charge of cooperation with developing countries, in an interview in May 1998.

> But such measures, while necessary, are not sufficient. These countries will have to pay back their debts sometime. They have to regain their export powers in order to pay back their debt. This brings us into MITI's area. MITI played an important role in bringing about a good division of labor between Asia and Japan.
>
> Fifteen years ago, when I was in charge of Asia, our prime minister was criticized for visiting Southeast Asia because of Japan's war-time aggression. ASEAN was just five countries, and its growth had just started. I was in Singapore to teach a course on increasing productivity. This was the beginning of Singapore's interest in learning from Japan, and they attached a lot of importance to Japanese strategy and industrial policy. Our interest was in fabricating industrial products using Japanese materials and re-exporting them to the United States. This was one of the ways out for Japan's difficulties with the United States at the time. We switched our surplus with the United States to Asia, and whenever the Asians complained about their deficit with us, we always said, because of their deficit, they could run huge surpluses with the rest of the world.
>
> I don't like to use the words, "Asian empire," but there is a division of labor. We have to grade up our own economy, and get rid of labor-intensive industries—this is very difficult—and replace them with infant industries. This is true not just for Japan, but for each of the Asian economies. Otherwise Asia will just continue on as a fabricator. We have to expand supporting industries and strengthen SMEs. Through the AFTA [ASEAN Free Trade Area] and AICO [ASEAN Industrial Cooperation] schemes, we want to have specific production bases in each area, for example, concentrating auto parts in Malaysia.[41]

If the IMF and liberal Western economists looked at the Asia crisis as an opportunity to restructure Asian economies along Western lines, Japanese bureaucrats such as Ojimi saw the crisis as a chance to accelerate "embraced" development in the spirit of Akamatsu. In some ways, MITI's institutional support program was more telling than the straight trade finance offers. On the surface it sounded innocuous. The MITI plan involved technical training to raise productivity of Southeast Asian workers; direct support for small and medium-sized industries as well as "foundation" industries; $1.8 billion in trade-related guarantees for infrastructure projects; and a program to strengthen economic "linkage" through the AICO scheme and AFTA.[42] Yet each of these programs either had a strong bias toward Japanese companies and their affiliates in Asia or developed it early on.

For example, according to Ojimi, MITI initially offered export credits from its $13.5 billion kitty directly to local exporters in Thailand, but found that approvals by the Thai government were taking too long. So MITI changed directions and offered the funds to Japanese affiliates. "By expanding exports even by Japanese affiliates, we can revive their economies through production linkage," he explained. "We have the idea that Japanese affiliates in Asia must contribute to the betterment of the economic situation in the area," the MITI official continued. "Of course, they have no special status, but their business is closely related to Japanese companies, in terms of exports back to Japan. So trade finance is more readily available to them. The exchange rate is a positive factor for them, but they may not be able to expand their exports due to credit scarcity. They need money to buy materials. So Japanese government will support them first. Even if insurance is available from the private sector, Japan has MITI, which can mobilize export credit and insurance for policy purposes."

MITI also spent massively on human resources development to train Asians working for Japanese companies to prepare for the expansion of Japanese investment. As early as March 1998, MITI detailed a director-level official to provide counseling to the Thai government, and invited hundreds of "enterprise people" to Japan for training programs with Japanese companies. According to a document outlining the program, in 1998 MITI would be sending more of its "old boys" to Asia for consultation and would recruit Japanese companies to provide "curricula" for its courses. One aimed at the Thai auto industry was to bring 400 trainees to Japan in 1997 and 1,000 in 1998. MITI also planned to designate particular regions in Thailand for intensive training programs.

Such training programs went right back to the beginnings of Japanese industrial strategy in Asia and its ties with Japanese ODA. Japan's grant aid arm, the Japan International Cooperation Agency (JICA), began its existence with the sole purpose of providing technical training. The idea was to provide skilled workers for Japanese companies. Until the mid-1980s, when it became more expensive, JICA would bring trainees to Japan; by 1994, according to one official, it had paid the way for more than 100,000 Asian workers to visit Japan, learn some Japanese, and undertake on-the-job training, often with Japanese companies. The first such program was in 1954, and involved sixteen Asian trainees. Even in the late 1990s, nearly half of JICA's trainees were from Asia. Each year the organization offered some 390 group training courses and 85 specialized courses, in such subjects as highway and bridge construction, maintenance of construction machinery, "machine condition diagnosis technique," plant-maintenance management, renovation of industrial equipment, and inspection and testing techniques for household electrical appliances.[43]

Most of the new arrangements for technical exchange were made in October 1997 at the sixth annual ministerial meeting between Japanese and ASEAN officials in charge of trade and industry, a conference framework initiated by MITI in the early 1990s. The session went unreported in the Western press, but from a regional perspective it was an early and aggressive attempt to deal with problems created by the currency crisis as it began to spill over into the real economy. By comparison, the APEC summit in Canada in November, and an ASEAN summit in December, produced only platitudes.

In connection with its SMEs program, MITI promised to send experts to review Japan's own growth experience and offered forty-year loans at 0.75 percent from Japan's own small- and medium-enterprise fund. Again, this seemingly benign provision was tailored to the thousands of smaller Japanese companies that had migrated to Asia to join their *keiretsu* groupings. (A 1997 follow-up study by Yamamura and Hatch asserted, "Japanese multinational enterprises have in the last few years redoubled their efforts to replicate *keiretsu* networks in Asia, extending their reach into and across the region. They are doing so, in part, by prodding their Japanese suppliers to follow them overseas.")[44] An infrastructure component similarly offered funding from sources usually reserved for domestic Japanese projects. Such funding, according to the MITI document, was to be directed toward projects promoting regional "linkage" and energy projects. In addition, MITI offered to help organize regional efforts to finance social infrastructure, and to develop common codes for financing long-term projects.

One item not in the MITI document despite months of preaching by senior U.S. officials was import promotion. Ojimi was not the least bit ashamed. "That's a tricky question," he said. "There are no strictly effective means to convince consumers to import Asian products, and we can't mobilize additional means to support the industries that might expand imports, because we run into both WTO [World Trade Organization] restrictions and our own political problems. Many of the items that we might expand, such as agricultural products, would run against Japanese interests and politics."

Why did the Japanese response to the Asia crisis fail to attract Washington's attention? There were several possible explanations, but the most persuasive was that outside observers had been conditioned to think of Japan as hopelessly weak. Evidence to the contrary dropped out of sight, lost in the white noise of cognitive dissonance. In Washington, Treasury Secretary Robert Rubin and his deputy, Larry Summers, were concentrating on pushing through IMF funding against tough congressional opposition.[45] Democrats on the Hill, led by David Bonior, the House Democratic Whip, insisted that the IMF open up new markets for American goods as well as expand democratic rights in Asia. Such pressures forced the administration to return to a posture adopted in Clinton's first term of forcing Japan to revive domestic demand, and, of course, imports. With some justification, the Japanese felt they were being scapegoated as U.S. rhetoric escalated. By the time of the yen panic in June 1998, U.S. officials blamed the regional crisis on Japan's weak economy and demanded structural change as the price of continued yen support. That month, Summers told the Senate Foreign Relations Committee that it was a "pivotal moment for Asia and the global economy. Weakness in Japan is now having a clear impact on the other troubled economies of Asia."[46]

Given the political dynamics, Summers needed to demonstrate to Congress that the United States would get something back for its money, and talking tough to Japan usually went down well on the Hill. At the same time, the administration was doing its best to fend off protectionists who predicted a huge runup in Asian exports to the United States. The last thing anybody needed to hear was that Japanese multinationals might be behind the expected surge in Asian exports.

Perhaps a third factor, in addition to politics and American stereotypes about Japan, was simple ignorance. Americans seemed oblivious of the scale of the Japanese presence in Asia or of the enormous buildup of that presence in the mid-1990s during the second post–Plaza Accord yen spike. By early 1998, Japanese companies had invested a cumulative total of $111 billion in Asia, most of it in a single decade. In 1995, Japanese companies based in Asia represented a market for components alone worth Yen 9.7 trillion, or $120 billion at Yen 79 to the dollar. In 1988, some 38 percent of the foreign subsidiaries and affiliates of Japanese companies were based in Asia, compared to 29 percent in North America, including Canada, and 18 percent in Europe. By 1997, the figures were 60 percent, 20 percent, and 13 percent, respectively.[47]

In Malaysia, for example, in 1988 there were 356 Japanese subsidiaries or affiliates. By 1997, the figure was three times as many. The story was much the same in the rest of Asia, with the most remarkable increase in China, where the population of Japanese companies grew from 159 in 1988 to 2,399 in 1997, a fifteen-fold increase. In Taiwan, the jump was from 633 companies in 1988 to 1,110 by 1997. In Korea, where Japanese companies were hardly welcome, the figure merely doubled, from 372 to 620. In Hong Kong, too, the number of Japanese companies doubled in ten years, from 680 to 1,480. In Singapore, the number went from 579 to 1,384. In Thailand, the number went from 512 to 1,396. In Indonesia, it went from 222 to 729. In the Philippines, the number rose from 142 to 464. The total count for Asia, by 1997, was 10,995 Japanese companies, double the 5,270 Japanese companies registered in the United States. By the mid-1990s, Japanese companies in East and Southeast Asia, excluding India, employed some 1.3 million people.[48]

Americans were also oblivious of the extent to which Japan's Asian multinationals operated as an expanded version of the domestic Japanese economy, lacking nothing but its high costs. Japanese companies, with government cooperation, virtually replicated the familiar *keiretsu* business structures of the domestic market. The pattern of trade that emerged between 1985 and 1995 was one in which Japanese companies created a vast, largely closed production loop across Asia, with Japanese intracompany trade as its predominant motif. The *keiretsu* system made the Japanese regional system virtually impervious to outside suppliers. According to Nagasaka Toshihisa, an analyst with the JETRO, the basic trade configuration was one in which "an eighty percent share of production by Japan-affiliated corporations is being supplied to Japan-affiliated corporations in East Asia and an eighty percent share of materials is being imported from Japan."[49]

To understand the magnitude of Japanese investment in Asia and how it survived the Asian financial crash, all it really takes is a walk in the park. Industrial park, that is. Consider Canon: The weak yen and strong sales of copiers helped boost group profits by 26.2 percent to Yen 118.8 billion (U.S.$914 million) and sales by 7.9 percent to Yen 2.716 trillion ($21.2 billion) in 1997. Then along came the Asian financial crisis. Once the crisis began, in July 1997, Canon decided to expand production by 50 percent in Thailand and 20 percent in Malaysia. Nearly all the output was shipped back to Canon factories in Japan, then abroad. In the first quarter of 1998, Asia's troubles helped boost Canon's foreign sales by 9 percent. Said Canon president Mitarai Fujio: "Even without the crisis, we would be increasing production, but as a result of the crisis, it has become cheaper to produce and we have tried to further production. We will continue to do so—unless there is strong political unrest, and I think any company would do so."[50]

Canon's dream was of an endless Asian spending boom. Mitarai himself launched the "Asia 10" project in 1995 to increase Asian sales from 5.2 percent of consolidated sales to 10 percent by the year 2000. The project was going so well up until 1997 that Mitarai upped the target to 15 percent—only to see Asian sales drop off 40 percent in the year of the crisis. Afterwards, Canon was left with a marketing network, a camera, and other products developed for Asian consumers, and not much to do with them until the Asian market recovered. Canon's board member in charge of Southeast Asia, Miyagi

Kohtaro, said that he would try to spend the time wisely until the market recovered. New hires, he said, were much cheaper than they were before the crisis.[51]

By the late 1990s, companies like Canon, Matsushita, and Sony had a depth of organization in Asia that allowed them to launch new products in their Asian manufacturing facilities soon after their Japanese debut. They were slowly decentralizing R&D as well, to allow them to tailor products to individual markets. The basic rule of thumb was, initial product launch in Japan, introduction of low-end models of the product in Asia, followed by introduction of the first-generation product as Japan moved to the second generation.

Canon's $1.8 billion camera business illustrated how this process worked. Two original Japanese factories, in Oita and Utsonomiya, made high-end cameras and optical lenses, at the top of the scale in value but lowest in terms of production volumes. Twenty-five years earlier, Canon built its first off-shore camera factory in Taiwan, which by 1998 not only made high-end cameras but served as a subsidiary R&D center for Asian production. It set up its second major offshore camera factory in Malaysia in 1988. The Malaysian factory had graduated from compact cameras to low-end APS [advanced photo system] cameras, and in 1998 was about to bring out its first camera designed entirely in Malaysia. In 1990, Canon built a fifth Asian camera factory in the SEZ in Zhuhai, China, which was its largest, churning out 300,000 low-end cameras per month, double the rate of Canon Opto Malaysia. Canon did not make cameras or optical equipment in Europe or North America—the Asian factories were it, a hefty 16.4 percent of Canon's global business.[52]

Canon Opto had an ideal production structure for the rocky times of 1997–98. Virtually all of its output was for the export market—one-third each to Japan, North America, and Europe, and it bought 90 percent of its inputs locally. Cameras and lenses were shipped first to Japan for repackaging, then exported to foreign markets. Canon staunchly claimed that it did not use the *keiretsu* subcontracting system, although it was part of the Fuyu Group, one of the largest and oldest so-called horizontal *keiretsu*, descendants of the prewar *zaibatsu*. Depending on the product, it might use non-Japanese suppliers. For leading-edge products such as APS, however, the Oita factory insisted on using its Japanese subcontractor list, and Mitarai, Canon's president, said that 80 percent of his subcontractors were Japanese. Forty percent of lenses went to the camera line, and the rest were exported to Japan. This set of production relationships meant that Canon got a double bang for its yen. It had the full benefit of the cheap Malaysian ringgit when it shipped its cameras and lenses to Japan, and another boost from the weak yen when it re-exported its products to global markets. The new production lines in Malaysia cost less because the yen was still relatively strong compared to the ringgit. Profits were in the stronger currencies of the United States and Europe.

On both floors of the factory, equipment had been moved around to make room for new production lines. It was planning to increase sales by 50 percent in 1998, from Ringgit 300 million in 1997, to Ringgit 400 million in 1998. It planned to increase production of cameras from 100,000 per month to 150,000 per month, and lenses from 3,000,000 units per month to 3.7 million units. "In that sense, the risk was minimal, from a market allocation point of view," said Fukuzawa Nobukazu, director and general manager for administration. Fukuzawa was a tall, slender man whose previous posting had been in France. "The Asian currency depreciation has been a rather positive factor for manufacturing companies in Asia. If they are export oriented, surely that means cost-competitiveness grows. Of course if they sell to the Asian domestic market, their position is totally different."

Touring Canon Opto with Muhammad Azlan Bin Amran, whose official title was assistant general manager of the Camera Engineering Division, it was hard to remember that the Japanese economy was in a state of utter ruin, according to its critics. The factory fairly hummed with energy and purpose. Canon seemed to have successfully transferred its cultural paradigm to its Malay, Indian, and Chinese workforce. Muhammad and Alias Bin Ban, another Malaysian manager, bantered in Japanese with Fukuzawa. Azlan was a graduate of the University of Electro-Communications in Tokyo and one of sixty Malaysian students sent to Japan in 1984–85 under Malaysia's "Look East" policy, supported by the Japanese and Malaysian governments. He joined Canon in March 1990, and one month later was in Oita to develop the first camera production line for the Malaysian factory.

Technical transfer at Canon Opto was in spurts, based on personal interaction rather than on manuals. Azlan learned mainly through observation. "Maybe this Japanese has done the job for ten to twenty years. What he knows is not written in books. You have to observe how he works," Azlan said. Other than Fukuzawa, no Japanese were in sight, hovering over shoulders, during a tour of the factory floor. According to Alias, who had visited Japan four times but never lived there, Canon introduced lens production through on-the-job instruction as well. "We had a lot of experts here in the beginning stage, more than fifty engineers," Alias said. "We learned from zero all the basics of lens manufacturing. Now we can handle everything with local people."[53] Local engineers designed a brand-new clean room for optical production, still under construction, which Alias said was faster than anything in Japan or Taiwan. Alias was proud of a new floor design to keep the production flow from second to third floor all in one direction, the brainstorm of the company's chief engineer, another Malaysian. Azlan said the new system used less space and increases productivity.

But what seemed to please Azlan and Alias most was the speed of the production cycle. They admitted that engineers in Oita were still doing most of R&D, yet new products were moving onto the line in Malaysia with increasing swiftness. For example, the new APS camera designed for the Malaysian market had taken six months from development to the mass market stage. "We picked up the production line from Oita, and brought it here," said Azlan. "It was the first model of APS, and we wanted to learn how to do it." Fourteen general engineers and five production engineers from the Malaysian factory spent a year in Japan, studying every aspect of the production line, then duplicating it in Malaysia.

When Canon Opto launched its first high-end camera in 1995, it began by supplying key components to the Oita factory. Its second luxury model, however, was never made anywhere else. Its third camera was a nonzoom APS, whose production it continues to share with Oita. It was in production by 1997, one year after Canon and other manufacturers launched the APS system in Japan. The fourth camera, launched in September 1998, was an APS designed for the Malaysian market, sturdier and cheaper than the Japanese export model.

Such short timespans between the release of a product in Japan and its production in Malaysia were a big change for Canon and other Japanese companies. Historically, it represented a major break with the pattern that existed up until the 1980s. Japan had considered itself a manufacturing fortress and used its foreign factories as assembly platforms or dumping grounds for low-end products. Japan produced its first color television set in 1960. It was thirty years before Matsushita began producing fourteen-inch television sets in Malaysia. It took seventeen years from the initial production of videocassette recorders in Japan in 1975 to the first offshore manufacturing of videocassette recorders (VCRs) by Sharp, also in Malaysia. Matsushita was the first to import compact-disc players from Singapore, ten years after their initial release in Japan. Even in the 1990s, it took three to four years for Japanese makers to move offshore with production of such new products as wide-angle TVs and mini-disc (MD) players.[54]

A short drive away from Canon Opto's sparkling white factory, with its gardens and cafeteria hung with cheerful banners, was one of the more ancient factories in Shah Alam, MELCOM, established in 1965. Matsushita preserved MELCOM the way some people keep old running shoes. It was dank, noisy, and antiquated. Its products were the cheap, low-end appliances that Japanese companies pumped into Southeast Asia during the Vietnam era, irons and rice cookers and electric kettles. This was my third visit since 1990, and the only change I could see was the removal of a set of cardboard figures that represented the Matsushita "family." These figures, four or five of them, used to be propped in a grassy plot near the visitors' entrance. Now they were gone, a victim perhaps of the tropical Malaysian climate.

MELCOM itself was still there, defiantly so. As the *senpai*, or eldest, among Matsushita's nineteen subsidiaries in Malaysia, MELCOM also served as headquarters for the managing director who oversaw Matsushita's Yen 360 billion per year Malaysian business. An experienced Asia hand, Yanagawa Masakazu probably spent more time thinking about air conditioners and color TVs than about MELCOM. Matsushita used Malaysia as a global production base for these two products. But tiny MELCOM, in some ways, was intellectually the most interesting of Matsushita's Malaysian companies, because it more fully captured Matsushita's problems in Asia and how the Asian financial crisis had exacerbated them.

Unlike Canon, Matsushita's production structure was less than ideal for the changed circumstances of the Asian market in the full flux of the crisis. As the world's largest consumer electronics company, its strategy had long reflected the principle of supplying all products to all the world's peoples. It was perfectly ready to leap over market barriers and build factories even when the local markets were poor and small, as Malaysia was in the 1960s. In 1968, Malaysia's per capita income was $285, compared to $4,628 in 1996.[55] And in each country, it applied the same kind of market logic that had inspired Matsushita Konosuke, the company founder, to attempt to manufacture every kind of appliance under the sun and sell it to consumers at the lowest possible cost.[56]

The Matsushita founder's inspiration was to create economies of scale so vast that electric products would become as cheap and abundant as tapwater, a project he reckoned would take 250 years. When Matsushita began to build its first factories abroad in the 1960s, it envisioned clones of itself, one per market. The result was a series of "mini-Matsushitas." Early on, Matsushita discovered that its foreign factories provided a captive market for key components made in Japan, and as long as the yen remained cheap, Matsushita did not bother to raise domestic content ratios. So, for example, in the MELCOM plant, its steam irons had a domestic content of 85 percent, but products like blenders had an imported content as high as 59 percent.

The Asia crisis hit while Matsushita was carrying out a cautious strategy of change. In Southeast Asia, the process was tailored to the slow reduction of trade barriers toward the year 2003, when ASEAN would enforce a common effective preferential tariff scheme. The Matsushita entities in Malaysia were at the forefront of the shift, mainly due to the efforts of Yanagawa's predecessor, Shohtoku Yukio, the Matsushita Group's regional representative in Malaysia from 1986 to 1993. Shohtoku had been head of Matsushita's air-conditioner business in Osaka and insisted on bringing it with him to Malaysia, especially after the first bout of *endaka* in 1986–87.[57]

By the early 1990s, Matsushita was producing all but the most sophisticated of Matsushita's room air conditioners in Malaysia for the global market. In 1996, the company finally closed down one last air-conditioner factory in Thailand, leaving the Malaysian factories as the world's major supplier of air conditioners since Matsushita also dominated the global market for air conditioners. Some nominal production remained in the Philippines and Indonesia. Matsushita exported 80 percent of its Malaysian-made air conditioners, 90 percent of audiovisual products, 80 percent of TV and audio components, and 100 percent of the color TVs and display monitors made by its MTV subsidiary. As a whole, the company exported 70 percent of its Malaysian output.

But this did not happen at MELCOM, whose original purpose was to supply Malaysian homes with all the wonderful products that made use of electricity. MELCOM shipped only 40 percent of its products beyond Malaysia's borders, and only as a result of considerable prodding. Ten years earlier, according to Yanagawa, the company began to put the screws on MELCOM. Before the crisis, MELCOM sold 85 percent of the rice cookers it made in Malaysia; by mid-1998, the ratio had dropped to 55 percent, and the company also brought in two new production lines. In blenders, too, MELCOM ratcheted up exports, from 16 percent in 1997 to 20 percent in 1998. In 1998, MELCOM exported 90 percent of its vacuum cleaners, 80 percent of its dry irons, and 70 percent of its electric fans. The Asia crisis turned up the pressure even more, however. Such victories may have been small, but the company needed each one. What else could Matsushita do with the 100,000 television sets it produced annually in Indonesia, or the small but unmarketable number of air conditioners made there?

In the early 1990s, Matsushita began an aggressive drive into China, still following the mini-Matsushita strategy. Unlike its strategy in East Asia in the 1980s, Matsushita's China strategy focused squarely on the domestic market. It worked out deals with Chinese partners to minimize the requisite export ratios. By the end of 1997, Matsushita had invested Yen 65 billion in its China operations and claimed to be the largest single Japanese investor in China. Its forty Chinese companies produced Yen 186 billion worth of goods annually, and Matsushita had plans to take sales up to 400 billion yen by the year 2000.[58] The company's main worry was that a Chinese devaluation, when it came, would force the company to divert a larger share of its China output to export markets, where it would inevitably compete with other Matsushita companies.

It did not take the Asia crisis to make Matsushita's fears come true. By mid-1998, Matsushita was already under pressure to export from China, not because of any slide in the currency but because of destructive pricing wars in the domestic economy. "Basically, every province and big city wants to maintain a complete line of manufacturing in its own territory and has encouraged state owned enterprises to boost production capacity," said Matsushita's Shohtoku, who took charge of the company's China business after he left Malaysia. "It's reminiscent of the old planning and state-controlled economy, where production capacity and actual production output are considered the strongest measure of competitiveness or success," he moaned. "So there is a very big production capacity which exceeds current demand in China, and as a result there is an oversupply to the market which leads to very strong price competition."

In 1996, Shohtoku boosted exports from China to Japan, the United States, and Southeast Asia as a "corrective action"—far different from Matsushita's original plan of concentrating on the Chinese domestic market. When the Asia crisis struck, suddenly products from Southeast Asia "were more competitive. At the same time exports from China became less competitive, making our operations in China much more difficult than before. Frankly speaking, we could be happier in China had there been no such oversupply."[59] As an example, Shohtoku offered air conditioners, where supply was three times the domestic market of 5,000,000 units per year. Matsushita made 500,000 units per year in its Chinese factory, but even with some exports the factory was running at just 50 to 60 percent of capacity in 1998.

Despite all its problems, Matsushita charged ahead, even taking measures to maintain its position in the shrinking Asian regional market. Yanagawa argued that Matsushita could maintain its Yen 1.3 trillion sales turnover in Asia by being more aggressive in introducing new products and "by eating another manufacturer's market share." To illustrate, he pointed to Matsushita's January 1998 performance in Malaysia. Matsushita's sales of household appliances doubled despite a contraction in household product demand by 20 percent. Customers would soon be deluged with new products tailored to the Malaysian sensibility. Yanagawa said that two years earlier, only 5 percent of his product lineup was new each year. In 1998, up to a quarter of the lineup was new, and a new "lifestyle R&D center" for Malaysia investigated adaptations of Matsushita products to the tropical climate and Islamic culture.

A year after the crisis started, Japan's Asian empire was shaken, but intact. Enough Japanese companies looked to East Asia primarily as an export platform to reverse the brief flirtation of the 1990s with the regional market. Only China had the potential to disrupt the pattern through currency devaluation, and Beijing had repeatedly assured markets that it wouldn't happen. The Japanese model might be discredited in theory, but in practice it was thriving, undaunted—just as Japanese economists had been predicting for the better part of a century—in the developing economies of Asia.

6

Miracle Makers

Sleeping with the Enemy

Among the outcomes of Japan's massive outpouring of investment and aid to Asia in the 1980s and 1990s was a quantum shift in the philosophy and outlook of one of the world's guiding institutions of financial management, the World Bank. One led to the other by way of personalities, connections, and more than a little bit of luck. Only a few insiders knew how the Japanese had manipulated bureaucratic politics and used the broader brush of money to shape a new orthodoxy within the Bank at odds with the liberal ideology of the 1980s. Retired Japanese bureaucrats told no tales. Those who did could rest easy that nobody would listen in the Washington of the 1990s, reveling in its status as the last remaining superpower, its economy in overdrive.

A whimsical title in the high-toned journal of a Washington think tank provided a rare clue to a process that was well underway by the mid-1990s. In 1994, the Harvard economist Dani Rodrik wrote an article for the Overseas Development Council (ODC) entitled "King Kong Meets Godzilla: The World Bank and the *East Asian Miracle*."[1] In it, he argued that the World Bank's 1993 report on East Asian growth had opened a serious wedge for Japan's economic philosophy, despite the Bank's "self-declared" victory in favor of liberal economics and the free market.[2]

"Godzilla" was Japan's Overseas Economic Cooperation Fund (OECF), its main loan agency for developing countries, while "King Kong" was supposed to be the World Bank. Six years later, what Rodrik called a "clash of celluloid titans" had become something more like a marriage of strange bedfellows. The World Bank had not only endorsed the East Asian and Japanese models but had also become Japan's strongest ally against the U.S.-inspired policies of the International Monetary Fund (IMF).

The mating dance lasted nearly a decade. It weathered the worst setback

238

in the Asian economy since World War Two, surviving even Japan's deepening economic and financial woes. Building on Japan's increasing prominence in the World Bank as its second-largest shareholder, Japan moved from defending its own economic practices to actively promoting them with the help of the Bank's legions of economists and privileged ties with presidents and prime ministers.

The courtship left Japan and the World Bank on the same side in a debate that would rock the intellectual foundations of the post-war economic order, strengthening Japan's hand in Asia even as its ability to project influence was challenged on other fronts by continuing disorder in the Japanese economy. The impact of the shift continued to unfold as the new century began, and it came together in a tight little waltz between two disparate but not altogether dissimilar cadres of officials, Japanese and the Washington-steeped international bureaucracy of the World Bank.

Another clue lay buried in news about the antiglobalization protests at the spring meeting of the World Bank and IMF in April 2000. Behind closed doors at the meeting, Japan was lobbying hard to expand its influence in both institutions. As protestors stormed the barricades outside, a senior Japanese official told the *New York Times*: "There's a sense that this has always been a white man's club, and that needs some rethinking."[3]

By the year 2000, Japan had sealed and delivered the World Bank, and was confident enough to extend its conquest to the IMF, the citadel of free-market philosophy, an institution far more doctrinaire than the World Bank had ever been. Indeed, at the dawn of the millennium, Tokyo came close to actually taking over the top management of the IMF. Leading up to the barricades and barbed wire that April, the world's senior finance officials had huddled in consultation to select a successor to Michel Camdessus, the IMF's managing director. Under attack for his role in handling the rolling global financial crisis of 1998–98, Camdessus had abruptly turned in his resignation in November 1999, well before the end of his third term in office. [4] Tokyo argued that it was high time to break with the pattern of U.S. and European dominance of the twin Bretton Woods institutions.

Traditionally, the United States and Europe shared control over the World Bank and IMF, by picking its leaders. The United States controlled the top job at the World Bank, also known as the International Bank for Reconstruction and Development, while the managing director of the IMF was picked through consultation among European governments and central banks. Thus, for Tokyo to field a candidate at all was audacious. Japan's improbable candidate was Sakakibara Eisuke, its most outspoken critic of free-market capitalism, an unabashed nationalist who took apparent joy in provoking the ideologues of the U.S. Treasury Department by coming up with schemes that challenged its intellectual predominance over the global financial community. Sakakibara had resigned as vice-minister of finance for international affairs in July 1999, but maintained high visibility in retirement by taking frequent shots at the Americans, whom he blamed for the Asian financial crisis. In keeping with Sakakibara's style were declarations that Japan should use its foreign aid to build up an Asian alliance to compete with the North American Free Trade Agreement (NAFTA) and the European Union (EU).[5] In March 2000, in time for him to preside over the spring Bank/Fund meeting, the IMF settled upon Horst Kohler as its new managing director. Kohler had been head of the European Bank for Reconstruction and Development, and his appointment was in keeping with tradition. Nonetheless, as the *New York Times* put it, "the world's second-largest economy was clearly laying down a marker that it no longer planned to acquiesce to the old order."

A few weeks earlier, on March 7, 2000, Reuters ran a brief story from its Tokyo bureau that, in its own way, was just as significant a measure of the changed relationship between Japan and the World Bank. Sakakibara and Joseph Stiglitz, the Bank's former chief economist and senior vice-president, were about to embark upon a joint research project into Asian economic growth and IMF reform.[6] Sakakibara invited Stiglitz to join the project in his capacity as newly anointed as head of the new Global Security Research Center at Keio University, Japan's first research institute specializing in crisis management, with a charter covering international conflicts and environmental problems as well as currency and financial meltdowns.[7] In terms of the philosophy of the institutions both men once represented, this was the equivalent of sleeping with the enemy.

To be sure, Stiglitz had left the World Bank in January, harried out of office by World Bank President James Wolfensohn; there were hints that the U.S. Treasury Department may have made Stiglitz's departure a quid pro quo for nominating Wolfensohn for a second term as World Bank president.[8] Nonetheless, such a pairing would have been inconceivable in the World Bank of the 1980s. In the World Bank of the 1990s, it was almost inevitable.

How did Japan and the World Bank manage to land on the same page? The short answer is, by degrees, beginning with a masterful stroke on the part of the Japanese Ministry of Finance (MOF) in providing substantial funding to the World Bank to explore the role of government in East Asian economic growth. The Japanese-financed research project produced the *East Asian Miracle* report. Japan's goal had been to fend off the international financial institutions' and the U.S. Treasury Department's imposition of free-market policies in Asia, and it succeeded brilliantly. By the end of the decade, Washington barely winced as Japan unveiled a succession of programs designed to shore up Asian economies without requiring American-style economic reforms. Over time, the United States simply opted out of a confrontation with Japan over its role in the Asian crisis and recovery.

The Japanese strategy succeeded, indeed, far beyond the imagining of the handful of officials who set it in motion in the late 1980s. The Asian financial crisis helped cement Japan's victory. As a result of Japan's massive aid to the stricken economies, Japanese multinationals were able to entrench themselves more deeply, and Japan could take credit for helping to prevent worse disaster. As a result of the World Bank's overblown portrayal of the success of Asian economies in the *East Asian Miracle*, it was forced into defending Asia's record, after the crisis. Independently of the Japanese and the Asian financial crises, the collapse of the Russian economy in the early 1990s had given rise to broad questioning of free-market-convergence theories by economists as well as policy makers. Japan became the champion of a new backlash against globalization, a role at strange odds with its own worsening economy.

The International Bank for Reconstruction and Development, otherwise known as the World Bank, is a large organization—one of Washington, D.C.'s biggest employers, with a Washington-based payroll of about 9,000 in the late 1990s. It was founded in 1944 to finance the rebuilding of Europe. Over the five decades since then, the World Bank had become the dominant institution overseeing policy lending to the world's poor countries.[9] It was certainly the world's largest repository of Ph.D. economists-turned-bureaucrats. Some 2,000 of them dominated the top jobs at the Bank, and a doctorate in economics was de rigueur for most high positions.

In April 2000, as antiglobalization protestors massed in Washington, the Bank and its next-door neighbor, the IMF, were besieged behind a ninety-block perimeter of yellow tape and barbed wire. On a mild and sunny day, demonstrators festively waved "Spank the World Bank" signs and staged mock battles with rubber sharks symbolizing the evils of capitalism. A papier-mâché image popular with crowds and photographers alike featured a pig stuffed with the world in its mouth like an apple.

Normally, the area around 18th Street and Pennsylvania Avenue, two blocks from the White House, has the atmosphere of an exclusive club; disdaining ostentation, its members comfortably rattle about with their coffee in Styrofoam cups and electronic identification cards dangling from their necks. Together with the IMF on 19th Street, and the International Financial Corporation a few blocks away, the whole community of international bureaucrats numbers 15,000. In this little township, the World Bank has pride of place. It populates sixteen buildings in the area around the headquarters site; many of them are identified by letters of the alphabet, and there are almost enough to rank them A through Z. In 1997, two of the older buildings were combined under a 178-foot atrium—an engineering feat reminiscent of the World Bank's heyday when it funded some of the developing world's largest infrastructure projects. The new building, designed by Kohn Pederson Fox of New York, ran $100 million over estimate and looks like an elegant ocean liner parked on the street.[10] Bureaucrats strolling through the neighborhood are greeted by cheery consultants seeking Bank contracts; colorfully clad officials from developing countries dash in and out of their limousines like so many tropical birds.

The atmosphere is particularly claustrophobic at the top, where an elite group of career economists are in charge. They have known each other for decades. The institutional culture has long been focused on internal hierarchy and how to rise through it. Although spending weeks and months in developing countries, bankers "on mission" limit their contacts to senior government officials, their own local office colleagues, and vigorously pursued sexual conquests. The World Bank's in-house newsletter, "Worldly Banker," has paid teasing tribute to the lifestyle. Back home in Washington from their "missions," Bank economists drop names of central bankers and burrow within their hermetic community. Perks include tax-free status and membership in exclusive country clubs operated by the "Bank" and the "Fund," as the World Bank and IMF were called by *cognoscenti*. Cloying, arrogant, and bloated, from an outside perspective the two cultures were distinguishable only in size—the Bank had ten times more economists, seconded government officials, and clerical staff of all nationalities than the more exclusive Fund.

When the Japanese began to court the Bank in the early 1990s, they were able to make good use of the intimacy of the Bank's structure at upper levels, where officials were linked closely with senior bureaucrats in the U.S. Treasury. Japan might just as well have picked the IMF for its courtship but did not for a number of reasons. Where the Bank was sprawling and somewhat permissive of dissent, the IMF had the reputation of being a cadré of uncompromising macroeconomists, loyal to an ideal. Moreover, the U.S. Treasury traditionally kept the Fund on a tighter leash than the Bank, tending to view the IMF as a beachhead of European influence. In the 1990s, as the U.S. administration regularly lost its battles with Congress to sponsor major international financial initiatives, it turned to the IMF as a primary mechanism for exerting influence on world monetary affairs.[11] These conditions would have made it more dangerous for the Japanese to work inside the IMF, promoting policies that ran counter to the IMF's purist, free-market stand and would have quickly generated U.S. opposition.

Another factor shaping the Japanese strategy was that Japan had a greater web of personal connections within the Bank than the Fund. The Japanese

MOF rotated a few bureaucrats into the Fund but nothing like the steady stream it sent to the World Bank. The IMF belatedly set up its Tokyo office in 1997, nearly three decades behind the Bank. By that time, the IMF was clearly on one side of the fence, with Japan and the World Bank on the other.

Between 1953 and 1966, Japan had been one of the Bank's chief client states, borrowing $862 million. The last of its loans were retired only in 1990.[12] World Bank loans had financed Japan's famous "bullet train," or *shinkansen,* and a long list of projects ranging from steel and power plants to a Toyota truck and bus factory. In 1970, Japan "graduated" to the status of a major lending country, and by late in the decade had become the principal co-financer of World Bank loans. In 1984, Japan's rank advanced from number five shareholder in the Bank to number two, after the United States.[13] By 1991, when the World Bank's Tokyo office published a commemorative volume for its twentieth anniversary, Japan had already emerged as the world's largest individual donor nation. Both the Bank and the Japanese government were aware that Japan's importance as a source of funding and its political, let alone philosophical, influence on the Bank were miles apart. Japanese officials could look back to a long history of relations with the institution, as well as their prestige as the world's largest donor country, and make a realistic calculation that they could at least begin to close this gap.

The relationship looked very different depending on which side of the Pacific you were on, however, and the Japanese were also able to take advantage of insecurities on the part of the Bank as the U.S. Congress tightened the screws on its financial backing. The Bank began to worry more about its communication channels with the Japanese. These, from the Bank's perspective, were dangerously weak. It was difficult to persuade midlevel officials in the Japanese Ministry of Finance, Bank of Japan OECF, or Japan Export-Import Bank to spend more than a few months at the Bank; not only did they lack the language skills, but time spent away from Tokyo was time lost in terms of bureaucratic promotion. That meant the Bank lacked the network of familiar faces that it had in the finance ministries and aid agencies of many of its member countries. Initially, the Bank's response amounted to no more than internal handwringing, but by the early 1990s, it was to have the financial resources, supplied by the Japanese, to start doing something more.

According to Lawrence MacDonald, a former *Asian Wall Street Journal* correspondent turned World Bank editor, "a recognition [exists], partly through the efforts of Mieko Nishimizu, and partly through trends in financing, that we have to make more efforts to see that the Japanese are involved." (Nishimizu was vice-president for South Asia at the Bank, her appointment in 1997 made her the first Japanese to be elevated to that rank.)

MacDonald said there was "an institution-wide effort to get rid of barriers that have impeded Japanese involvement. We can't treat the Japanese just the way we treat the Germans or the French. Japan is a special case, because of the size of the Japanese contribution and the declining U.S. contribution" to Bank funding.[14]

A final reason why Japan singled out the World Bank, however, was an accident of fate and personality. Each member country, also shareholder of the World Bank nominates an executive director, who is based in Washington and serves as shareholder's representative on the Bank's board. Shiratori Masaki was Japanese executive director in the late 1980s, and had been on the frontline of interventions by the World Bank in Japanese lending practices in the mid-1980s as vice-chairman of Japan's Overseas Economic Cooperation Fund. Shiratori brought a personal animus, as well as keen intelligence, to the job. He made it his mission to impress on the Bank Tokyo's impatience with the strict free-market philosophy holding sway, much as Sakakibara would try to do at the IMF a decade later.

As it evolved, the Japanese strategy not only made a friend of the World Bank but also introduced a schism between it and the U.S. Treasury Department, which had long considered the Bank its playground because of the Bretton Woods tradition giving the United States the right to appoint its president. The Treasury Department had moved closer to the IMF in the mid-1990s, partly because of harsh congressional reaction to the U.S. administration's $50 billion bailout of Mexico in 1994–95. But this was not because it perceived any wavering on the part of the Bank's principles. Rather, the Treasury considered the Bank its own impregnable preserve, and this fallacy helped drive the wedge deeper.

The drifting apart of the IMF and U.S. Treasury Department, on the one hand, and the World Bank on the other, predated by several years Japan's courtship of the World Bank. Rivalry between the IMF and World Bank dated back to the late 1980s when the IMF first involved itself with structural reforms in a second wave of Latin American debt crises. After 1991, this rivalry intensified as the IMF meddled (from the World Bank's perspective) with the Russian economy. The World Bank viewed reforms of institutions— so-called structural adjustment—as its own turf. The division of labor was supposed to be the Bank dealing with microeconomic issues, while the IMF supervised the macroeconomy. In any case, structural adjustment lending, whether from the Bank or the IMF, involved the lending institution's ordering fundamental alterations to an economy. From the Bank's point of view, the macroeconomists employed by the IMF did not have the skills for such work. From the IMF's seat, the World Bank did not have the religion to do the job right.

Starting in the late 1980s, the IMF ratcheted up the scope of reforms it demanded as well as their scale. In 1989, the IMF imposed sweeping economic reforms on Argentina, calling for the elimination of industrial promotion programs and "other subsidies," an end to import prohibitions and quotas, and a general reduction of import tariffs.[15] In a series of rescue packages for the Russian Federation between 1993 and 1996, the IMF demanded radical reforms that ran the gamut from liberalization of trade and energy to restructuring the banking sector, cutbacks in social spending, and agricultural reform.

The price tags kept getting bigger, too. Not counting other donors, the IMF paid out $3 billion for Russia in 1993, $18.9 billion for the U.S.-led Mexican bailout in 1995, another $16.8 billion for Russia in 1995 and 1996. Then came the Asian "stand-by" credits, that is, funds to meet balance-of-payments shortfalls resulting from the Asian currency crisis that began in July 1997—the first of which, $3.9 billion, the IMF offered to Thailand on August 20, 1997. This was the IMF's contribution to a total package of $17 billion. Next, on November 5, the IMF authorized $10.14 billion out of $40 billion for Indonesia and, in December, committed $21 billion out of a total package of $57 billion for Korea.

The Korean loan was nearly twenty times the IMF quota, or lending limit, for South Korea. The huge loans of late 1997 attached reforms that potentially would have reshaped the entire Asian economy, and the IMF had not even invited Bank officials to sit in on the negotiations. A team of five IMF officials negotiated the $57 billion Korea package (including other donors) over seven days in November and December 1997. The team's only Asian specialist was a young Japanese-speaking economist just a few years out of graduate school at Yale University, Robert Dekle.

Bureaucratic rivalry reinforced a sense at the Bank that the IMF was on the wrong track. Meanwhile, Japan had emerged as a hero within Asia during the early months of the crisis. When, on July 2, the Thai baht fell through the floor triggering a domino or "contagion" effect first in Southeast Asia, then Northeast Asia, South America, and Eastern Europe, the United States was distracted by its July 4 Independence Day holiday, and Deputy Treasury Secretary Lawrence Summers had to decide what to do on his own. He decided against providing financial support to Thailand, fearing a reprise of the storm of criticism that followed the U.S.-led Mexican bailout in 1995, which he and Rubin had engineered.

During that crisis, the Treasury drew from a pool of funds called the Exchange Stabilization Fund available to the executive branch to defend the dollar. Following the Mexican bailout, the then chairman of the Senate Banking Committee, Alfonse D'Amato, amended the Exchange Stabilization Fund

Act to prevent foreign countries from borrowing more than $1 billion during a six-month period. Summers used this restriction as his excuse for inaction, although he did play a role in shaping the IMF reforms for Thailand, insisting that the IMF raise its quota and take a tough line on Thai finance companies. He called for full disclosure of Thailand's forward foreign exchange positions.[16]

Nobody believed Summers's explanation, and the Thais fiercely resented the United States' standing aside while the IMF cobbled together a rescue package. Treasury officials grumbled that the Thais deserved what they got and had ignored warnings from the IMF that its current account deficit was in the danger zone.[17] In early negotiations with Bangkok, the IMF insisted it could lend no more than $3.9 billion, already 505 percent of the Thai quota. That left Thailand with a $10.5 billion gap for which it had to find financing.[18]

Japan saved the day by rounding up other Asian countries to help Thailand. At a meeting in Tokyo on August 11, 1997, the group came up with $10 billion, and Bangkok was able to meet its payments. Japan not only organized the bailout but put substantially more money on the table for Thailand than the United States did for the three crisis economies combined. Tokyo put $4 billion of its own funds into the Thai package and pressured twenty-one Japanese banks to roll over their Thai loans.[19]

When it came, the break between the Bank and the "Fund" was overshadowed by the drama of the Asian financial collapse. The final straw came amidst the debate over how to handle the unexpected spillover of the currency crisis into Korea, which up until October 1997 had been deemed immune. Korea was considered a model of macroeconomic management; the first of the high-growth Asian economies to gain entry to the Organization for Economic Cooperation and Development (OECD) in Paris, it was considered a member in good standing of the rich country club. When currency contagion spread to the Korean won, however, it quickly exposed the soft underbelly of the Korean financial system, based on leverage ratios that would make a loan shark blush.

By late November, the Korean economy was imploding. Beforehand, Stiglitz, as the Bank's chief economist, had begun lobbying the IMF to change its policy recommendations for fiscal austerity after observing the dramatic reactions to the Fund's emergency bailouts in Thailand and Indonesia, to no avail. Then, at a meeting of finance ministers and central bank governors in Kuala Lumpur, with the full backing of the World Bank, Stiglitz issued a "carefully prepared statement" suggesting that IMF austerity policies in Indonesia would lead to social and political turmoil. Camdessus responded by saying that Indonesia would end up all the stronger as a result of short-term pain.[20]

Meanwhile, the IMF, in concert with Treasury, decided to use the Korean catastrophe to further liberalize the Korean economy, insisting that Seoul accept a long list of conditions before any money would be put on the table. As of December 4, donors had pledged $57 billion, including $21 billion of the IMF's money. But after paying out an initial $5.51 billion in emergency balance-of-payments support, the IMF slammed on the brakes. A second payment of $3.58 billion was due December 18, and the Koreans pleaded with the IMF to accelerate disbursement in order to prevent a default. But the IMF stood firm.[21] Washington and the IMF told Seoul that they would go along only if the Koreans accelerated the reforms they had agreed to, reluctantly, at the beginning of the month.[22]

"There were about 10 days there where it's fair to say the Koreans were acting as if they were not going to do the program," a senior IMF official told the *Washington Post*. "Instead of getting on and doing the program, they kept asking us for more money publicly. . . . That helped destroy the confidence of the markets." U.S. Treasury Secretary Robert Rubin was in his "tough love" mode, according to the newspaper, refusing to "put more money into Korea unless [one can] make a judgment that it's going to work."[23] Only after the Korean elections on December 18 and a visit by Treasury Under-Secretary David Lipton to Seoul to meet with the newly elected president, Kim Dae Jung, did the administration's position turn around. On December 24, Christmas Eve, Rubin interrupted a bone-fishing vacation to announce a new $10 billion emergency package. One reason he acted was that the day before the World Bank had forced his hand by taking the radical step of providing its own $3 billion "economic construction loan" to South Korea, part of the $10 billion it had pledged to the Fund package three weeks earlier. The move was a snap decision by Wolfensohn, a former investment banker, based on his own reading of the markets. It was completely out of synch with the Bank's normal lending policies. There were no current off-the-shelf sectoral studies to draw upon, as there had been with Indonesia and Thailand, and Korea had graduated as a World Bank loan recipient in 1994.

The Bank did not even have an office in Korea; there was no staff dedicated to Korean matters within the East Asian vice-presidency, although it had a senior resident advisor on Korea, a former head of Hyundai Heavy Engineering. The decision to bail out Korea—and embarrass the Fund and U.S. Treasury— came from the top. Wolfensohn feared that U.S. and IMF stalling would send Korea into default, and he pulled Danny Leipziger, a career Bank economist who in the past had written extensively on Korea, from other work to take charge. The IMF finally paid out its second tranche at the end of the month. Rubin was widely credited with having prevented a Korean default, but the Bank package sent a reassuring signal to markets and helped the Koreans pay $20 billion in short-term debt due by the end of the year.

In the panicky mood of late 1997, the different positions staked out by the World Bank and IMF did not seem very important as the cost of the Asian financial crisis mounted ever higher. By October 1998, however, the split was so public and so extreme that during the annual Bank/Fund meeting in September 1998, Rubin virtually ordered the two institutions to settle their many differences. Wolfensohn delivered a public and blistering attack against the IMF at the meeting, telling an audience of finance ministers and central bankers from 182 countries that too much attention was being given to issues such as currency stabilization and economic reform. "The poor cannot wait on our deliberations," he said.[24]

Meanwhile, over the course of 1998, Stiglitz became more and more outspoken in his dismay over the IMF's policy recommendations for the economies at the center of the crisis: Thailand, Indonesia, and Korea. In January in its initial report on the clash between the two financial agencies, the *Wall Street Journal* commented, "Mr. Stiglitz's critique departs from the usual closed-door disagreements between the two institutions, which are aiding Asia jointly. Relations are so strained that Mr. Stiglitz and his team are to meet with the IMF to discuss them as early as next week. An exchange of views 'isn't unhealthy,' says IMF Treasurer David Williams, 'but we shouldn't have closely related institutions coming out with differing macro-economic analyses.' "[25]

Stiglitz and Wolfensohn ultimately prevailed. Slowly, gracelessly, the IMF changed course. By the fall, it was pushing reflationary policies in the crisis economies as earnestly as it had preached a combination of fiscal and monetary contraction a year earlier. The policy reversal humiliated the IMF as well as the U.S. Treasury Department, which had stood by the IMF during the dispute with the Bank and other critics. The Bank's advocacy of fiscal expansion very much accorded with Japanese prescriptions, but even more to Japan's advantage was the breakdown in the solid orthodoxy of a few years earlier. The world of development finance would never be quite the same. Japan did not have to confront the IMF itself. The World Bank was fighting Japan's battles for it.

Perhaps the strangest meeting of minds was that between Stiglitz—the amiable, bearded, former chief of the Council of Economic Advisors, one of the most creative economists of his generation—and Sakakibara—Japan's combative chief financial bureaucrat, nicknamed "Mr. Yen" because of his reputed ability to affect financial markets with his pronouncements. Sakakibara had long insisted on the "plurality" of capitalisms and for nearly as long had opposed structural adjustment lending by the IMF and World

Bank.[26] He argued that developing countries should try "alternative" paths, following models such as the Japanese "main bank" system, before launching full-scale privatization and deregulation along Western lines.

While serving as director-general of the International Finance Bureau at the Ministry of Finance in the mid-1990s, well before the Asian crisis, Sakakibara had raised the political ante by challenging the so-called Washington Consensus. This was tantamount to challenging U.S. management of the global economic system. The "Washington Consensus" was a set of views that in the narrow sense evolved out of the Latin American debt crisis of the early 1980s; it stressed privatization and market liberalization. The man who coined the phrase, John Williamson, a former chief economist for South Asia at the World Bank, argued that when he first aired the ten policy principles comprising the consensus at a conference on Latin American development in November 1989, he intended them only as a report on developments in Latin American economies, not as a neoliberal policy manifesto.[27]

A more trenchant definition comes from the Russian scholar and economist Steven Rosefielde, who wrote that the Washington Consensus "holds that Adam Smith's invisible hand, empowered by democracy, is the essence of the idea of the West; a 'natural law' destined to rule in developing, transitioning and advanced economic systems. Transitioning states like Russia and China it predicts Westernize to prosper, and 'illiberal' advanced nations like Japan will do so to avoid falling behind."[28]

The "consensus" reinforced Washington's view that with the fall of the Berlin Wall in 1989, capitalism had prevailed over all other economic ideologies. The consensus also lent credibility to the dominant philosophy reigning at the World Bank in the 1980s and for most of the 1990s; it argued that open markets and the free flow of capital were essential for growth. It became the IMF's credo as it engineered the huge Russian emergency support programs in 1993 and 1995. These were the IMF's first experiences with large-scale social and institutional engineering, and even the collapse of the Russian economy had failed to persuade the stalwarts of the Fund that there was anything wrong with their theory.

In September 1996, at a Japan-funded conference at the Inter-American Development Bank in Washington, Sakakibara argued that the neoclassical paradigm had "lost its luster." He used the occasion to rail against deregulation in general and of capital markets' liberalization in particular. "This neglect of different cultures and evolutionary processes of history is typical of neo-classical prescriptions and has often led to confusion and the collapse of the existing order rather than reform," he argued. "Does globalization imply that a universal model or uniform set of rules as envisaged in the 'Washington Consensus' will eventually spread to all parts of the world and that the world will become homogeneous, both economically and culturally? Definitely not."[29]

A year-and-a-half later, Sakakibara was pushing, albeit unsuccessfully, for APEC to adopt currency controls and hedge-fund restrictions.[30] At a conference in Melbourne in March 1999, he called on Asian finance ministers to enact prudential regulations to prevent "excessive exposure to foreign creditors and check surges in capital inflows."[31] By this time, at least in his advocacy of capital controls, Sakakibara had plenty of company.

The liberal Stiglitz was a pluralist by instinct. A full professor at Yale at twenty-six, Stiglitz had won the John Bates Clark Award, given every two years to the best American economist under the age of forty, an honor he shared with Summers, who had preceded him as chief economist at the Bank. In the early 1990s, Stiglitz began to view East Asia as a testing ground for his theories on the role of information in capital markets. By February 1997, when he became the World Bank's chief economist, Stiglitz was well versed in the literature on Japanese and East Asian growth and had already taken positions distinctly anti–Washington Consensus.

At Stanford, Stiglitz had invented a whole new branch of economics called "the economics of information." His theories contradicted a basic tenet of neoclassical economics that government has no role to play in the marketplace. In a seminal essay in 1986, Stiglitz, working with Bruce Greenwald, showed that government could make up for the imperfections of the market by filling in the gaps.[32] This made him one of the leaders of a counterrevolution against neoclassical economics gathering steam in the 1990s. He and his colleagues argued that endogenous factors in growth were important, such as social institutions that might help one society succeed where another failed.

While he was still at Stanford, Stiglitz was an enthusiastic member of the World Bank team that produced the *East Asian Miracle* report. This study, led by an experienced World Bank economist, John Page, was conducted during 1991–92. The project report was published in 1993 and became the basis for the Bank's enthusiasm for East Asian growth strategies right up to the time of the crash.[33] Afterward, the report was considered an embarrassment by many within the World Bank. Its title inspired innumerable op-ed pieces ridiculing the Bank for exaggerating a "miracle" that looked more like a con game, in the depths of the crisis of 1997–98. Stiglitz, however, regularly quoted from the *East Asian Miracle* in terms that became more passionate as time went on.

Stiglitz saw the case of high-speed growth in East Asia, starting with Japan, as evidence that government and market were not opposing forces but could indeed collaborate. From a development perspective, Stiglitz was a throwback to an earlier generation that assumed that markets were imperfect. The difference was that Stiglitz believed government could submit itself to market disciplines, unlike the *dirigiste* school that believed in the superiority of government. In any event, Stiglitz thought that the East Asian experience opened up new theoretical avenues for policy makers, particularly regarding the role of government in coping with market failure. In looking back at his role in the "Miracle" study, Stiglitz concluded, "In a way, my original motivation was in part the view by the Japanese that the most successful countries in the world had not followed the prescriptions the World Bank had been recommending to a lot of them."[34]

The most influential economist at the Bank, then, was ready to accept that the key to Asia's recovery might lie in some of the strategies that Asian economies had used in the past. The Asian financial crisis was a result of circumstance and human failure, not systemic problems. "The success of East Asia was in no small measure due to effective (and market-friendly) interventions by the government," Stiglitz told an audience in Bangkok in July 1999.[35] In an op-ed article for the *Wall Street Journal* earlier in the year, he wrote, "Many of the problems these countries face today arise not because governments did too much, but because they did too little—and because they themselves had deviated from the policies that had proved so successful over preceding decades."[36] Like Sakakibara, Stiglitz favored short-term capital controls in order to prevent speculative attacks such as the ones that had brought down the Asian economies. Temporary controls might give countries a "window of opportunity" to deal with economic turbulence, Stiglitz said.[37] Such views put Stiglitz at odds with strongly held positions by the IMF and the United States Treasury Department.[38]

During the two traumatic years following the Asian economic crisis, Stiglitz was not the only or the most outspoken critic of IMF/Treasury policies. Jeffrey Sachs, who had led a research team at the Asian Development Bank that produced a sunny book on the Asian regional economy just before the crash, made up for it afterward by asserting that the IMF, by pushing for reform too fast, had destroyed the Asian economies.[39] Paul Krugman, another winner of the John Bates Clark Award, argued that the globalization of financial markets made it too easy for investors to pull money in and out of emerging markets. He advocated both restricting the flow of capital and rules to block local banks and businesses from pulling money out of an economy suddenly.[40]

Within three years of the outbreak of the Asian crisis, in early 2000, the IMF had gone so far as gingerly supporting a revived Japanese effort to establish the Asian Monetary Fund (AMF). This was an extraordinary milestone, representing the degree to which the IMF had submitted, and indicative of the extent to which the interests of the Japanese were by now interwoven with those of the World Bank. Three years earlier, the U.S. Treasury Department had blasted the AMF proposal as a blatant exercise in "moral hazard" and easily scuttled its launch. The IMF had backed up the U.S. Treasury, warning the Japanese against setting up a rival franchise. There were no such protests when Japan finally began to put the structure in place.

In March 2000, Finance Minister Miyazawa Kiichi told the *Yomiuri* newspaper that he would propose a formal currency-swap agreement among Japan, China, South Korea, and the ASEAN countries, when the Asian Development Bank held its annual meeting the following May, as a preliminary step to establishing the AMF.[41] The IMF's regional director, Saito Kunio, purred, "If the AMF is ever to be established, the IMF is very happy to cooperate," although he added that the AMF needed to be consistent with IMF "activities." Even the hint of agreement would have been inconceivable three years earlier.[42] On May 6, when the finance ministers agreed on the "Chiang Mai Initiative," as it was called, the U.S. Treasury, too, seems to have accepted the inevitable. "We have long supported regional cooperation, in this region and others," Edwin M. Truman, assistant secretary for international affairs, told reporters. "We think this is a fine idea. But the nature of financial arrangements depends on the details."[43]

Indeed, details were not due until November, and the currency-swap plan was to be launched sometime afterward. Existing arrangements were relatively small—a $200 million swap facility within ASEAN, and bilateral deals between Japan and South Korea and Malaysia for $5 billion and $2.5 billion, respectively. It would take much more to influence global currency markets—Sakakibara, interviewed in Bangkok before the meetings, estimated the swap program would need at least $20 billion to be effective.[44] Nonetheless, the Chiang Mai Initiative was a start. Miyazawa described it as "something which will evolve naturally over time," and Chinese finance minister Xiang Huaicheng said that Beijing would support it in order "to ensure the financial and economic stability of this region."[45]

The history of the AMF captures many of the issues confronting the Japanese as they began the process of staking out a new Asian alternative for global economic management. Not only did they face opposition from the IMF and U.S. Treasury, but it was also no mean task to keep their fellow Asians from bolting. The AMF began as a proposal to assemble $100 billion in stand-by funds from Asian donors, serving as a quick-disbursing mechanism to head off future crises. Its model was to be the bailout fund assembled in such quick order for Thailand. Sakakibara was the principal mover behind the proposal, with its name clearly a slap at the IMF, suggesting that Asia had been treated so badly that it needed an IMF of its own.[46] Finance Minister Mitsuzuka Hiroshi tabled the proposal at the Bank/Fund annual meeting in September 1997, in Hong Kong, in the teeth of the crisis. Japan was not specific about its contribution but floated figures between $20 billion and $30 billion. The rest would come from other Asian countries.

Beforehand, Japanese officials had briefed their counterparts at a regular meeting of Asian central bankers that Japan had quietly started in 1995, and briefed Asian and European financial officials again before the Bank/Fund meeting at a separate gathering in Bangkok. The latter session, with Asian and EU finance ministers, was part of the Asia-Europe Ministeral process, called ASEM.[47] Sakakibara himself went on a tour of ASEAN countries before the Bank/Fund meetings in late September to quietly build support for the idea. Japan briefed China, too, a mistake, as it turned out. The Japanese spoke to virtually everybody, in fact, but the U.S. Treasury Department.[48] Treasury Secretary Robert Rubin and his deputy, Summers, were livid when they found out about it from the Chinese.[49] Japanese officials in Hong Kong tried unconvincingly to suggest that the original idea had come from the Thais and that they were simply offering their services to coordinate the process. Brushing off such explanations, Rubin and Summers saw the AMF as a clear challenge to the United States.[50]

The World Bank had decided years earlier to hold its 1997 annual meeting in Hong Kong, as a gesture of confidence in the reversion of Hong Kong to China, which would occur on July 1 of that year. Instead, the meetings became the occasion for what *New York Times* reporter David Sanger called "a nasty skirmish in the escalating war between nations and global markets."[51] Among the more bizarre incidents was a public spat, conducted on giant video-projection screens looming over the heads of assembled financial officials and businesspeople, between U.S. financier George Soros and Malaysian prime minister Mahathir. Mahathir described currency traders like Soros as "morons," while Soros got back by calling Mahathir a "danger to his country."[52]

The brawl over the AMF was just as brutal. Asians welcomed the idea, and economists who viewed the region's problems as stemming from currency speculation tended to agree that it would be helpful. They argued that it would make sense to have countries in the region, with their large holdings of U.S. dollar reserves, take some of the pressure off the international financial institutions. Earlier in the year, the IMF had even suggested the idea of closer monetary cooperation in East Asia.[53] Malaysian deputy prime minister Anwar Ibrahim endorsed the Japanese proposal, as did Hong Kong's financial secretary, David Tsang, who said wistfully, "I wish very much to see some form of standing arrangement whereby we will need to borrow, of course, with the discipline of the IMF, but with an Asian facility, to help any countries under economic attack."[54] Even Salomon Brothers, in its *Japan*

Daily comment for September 22, 1997, remarked that if the AMF were tied to IMF programs, it could serve as a "regional expansion of IMF resources."

It was not to be. The U.S. Treasury Department, led by Summers, harshly attacked the proposal, challenging it as a new source of "moral hazard," that is, the avoidance of risk, that would undermine IMF discipline in the region. Americans and Europeans were on the phones during the conference, persuading the Southeast Asians to back off. "Moral hazard" may have been part of the problem, but there was more to the Treasury's fierce opposition than that. China and Japan were the largest holders of U.S. Treasuries, and the AMF raised the specter of Asian financial coordination against the United States.

David Sanger, veteran *New York Times* correspondent, was on the plane with Rubin and Summers. "From the time the plane left Andrews Air Force Base and refueled and ultimately landed in Hong Kong, the whole discussion was about how the United States was going to kill the plan," he recalled in 2000. "The fear was that Japan would be interested in putting everything but conditionality into it, and that its real interest was in getting a diplomatic edge over the United States in Thailand, Indonesia, Korea, and the rest. The way it would work itself in was by offering cash without any conditions with regard to reform. The Japanese had given some quiet briefings to the Chinese who turned around and gave the information to the United States. We'll never know if conditionality was supposed to be there or not. The plan was in an infant stage when Rubin and Summers decided to blow it out of the water."[55]

The plan's failure wasn't just knee-jerk diplomacy on the part of the United States, however. China, too, was determined to block Japan from taking advantage of the Asian crisis to expand its influence. "The Chinese ratted on Japan because they did not like the idea either," said Sanger. "They did not want Japan to take the lead in settling the Asian crisis. They were determined to help Rubin blow it out of the water. Then comes the ego part. The United States had been doing a good job of playing the role of shadow IMF back in Washington. U.S. officials maintained that they stiffened the conditionality for Thailand, but they did not contribute any money. Their ability to do so in a regional structure would be greatly reduced. There was a much greater opportunity to influence these things through the IMF and World Bank. It was good cover."

At a meeting of finance and banking officials in Manila on November 18–19, 1997, Summers pushed successfully to replace the AMF with a proposal for increased regional surveillance, to be conducted by the new IMF office in Tokyo.[56] Southeast Asians looked at the dispute as windfall, hoping that it would prompt the United States to play a more active role in sorting out Asia's rapidly growing financial catastrophe.[57] This it did. As Indonesia's troubles mounted in September and October, the United States finally started digging into its pockets, contributing a modest $3 billion to the IMF's package for Indonesia.[58]

Asian monetary officials were deeply disappointed that Tokyo had failed to push harder. Teh Kok Peng, deputy managing director of Singapore's Monetary Authority, said Japan's timidity was unfortunate but it was even worse to have the two giants bickering while the rest of Asia faced financial collapse. "In the face of U.S. opposition, Japan backed down," he said. "In a sense they did not have a clearly articulated position. Japanese policy leadership is weak. Things were breaking out all over the region. [Under these circumstances] there's nothing worse you can do than have two major countries bickering with each other."[59]

At the Manila meeting, the Japanese formally dropped the idea of an AMF but went ahead and implemented it in other forms. They had never been specific about the amount of money they would contribute to the organization, which was supposed to be a multicountry fund. Japanese officials had initially floated the figure of $20 billion. A year and another $10 billion later, the same money turned up in the $30 billion New Miyazawa Initiative, a broad based emergency support fund to support the Asian recovery.

Simultaneously, Tokyo worked to weaken the dominance of the dollar over Asian currencies. The Japanese referred to the latter project as "internationalization of the yen," and it reflected Japan's frustration at the ease with which the United States could manipulate Japanese economic performance through the money markets. In 1998, the yen was by far the weakest of the currencies of major trading currencies. Only 15.7 percent of Japan's exports to the United States were denominated in yen, compared to 62.9 percent of German exports to the U.S. denominated in deutsche marks. Globally, 36 percent of Japanese exports, and 21.8 percent of imports, were yen based. In international financial markets, the yen accounted for a dismal 0.2 percent of loans in 1997, compared to 69.8 percent for the U.S. dollar, 15.6 percent for the British pound, 5.3 percent for the French franc, and 3.3 percent for the deutsche mark. As an official reserve currency, in 1997, central banks held only 4.9 percent in yen, compared to 57.1 percent for the dollar, and 12.8 percent for the deutsche mark. All of these ratios had sunk in the course of the 1990s. Japan's peak as a reserve currency, for instance, was in 1991, when it made up 8.1 percent of global reserve holdings.[60]

In 1995, matters became particularly difficult for Japan. U.S. policy helped drive the yen to an unprecedented 79 yen to the dollar. As the yen roared past the psychological barrier of 100 to the dollar, Asian currencies were blasted by financial contagion from the Mexican financial crisis. Sakakibara, then deputy director-general of the International Finance Bureau, thought he saw an opportunity to form a pressure group made up of Asian central banks, using their substantial dollar holdings as a bargaining chip.[61] Financial coordination with Asian central banks implied creating greater liquidity for Japanese government bonds. This was taboo among Sakakibara's colleagues in the Ministry of Finance, where many believed that greater liquidity in the Japanese debt market was tantamount to relinquishing control over monetary policy. Sakakibara had to somehow convince his colleagues that the risk was worth it. "Sakakibara realized that in his current position, he could do nothing without the help of his Asian counterparts," said Taniguchi Tomohiko, a correspondent for *Nikkei Business* in London. "He urged his counterparts to pay more attention to Asia."[62]

Sakakibara's trump card was the simple scale of reserves deployable by Asian central banks, if they acted in concert. In 1995, the combined foreign exchange reserves of Japan, Taiwan, China, Singapore, Thailand, Malaysia, South Korea, and Indonesia amounted to $566.5 billion, more than half of global reserves. Working with Vice-Minister for International Affairs Kato Takatoshi, and Katsu Eijiro, the director of the Foreign Exchange and Money Market Department, Sakakibara began a secret courtship of Asian central banks.[63]

Their first step was to ask the retired Vice-Minister of Finance Gyohten Toyoo to set up an informal conference of Asian central bankers, through his *amakudari* outpost at the Bank of Tokyo. Gyohten had the Bank set up a shell "International Monetary Institute" to host the meeting in Tokyo on April 8, 1996. Kato traveled around Asia putting the arm on central bankers and heads of monetary authorities to attend. Hong Kong, Singapore, Indonesia, Malaysia, Thailand, the Philippines, China, South Korea, and Australia sent representatives to the meeting. The United States was not invited.

According to Katsu, the Asian countries lobbied against including the U.S. Treasury or Federal Reserve Board. "They were afraid of the United States," Katsu said, particularly because of a U.S.-led effort to get a financial services agreement in the WTO.[64] Taniguchi said simply, "It was elaborately done, internally. It was about forming a sort of political pressure group against the United States that, hopefully, will be able to force some discussion on U.S. policy. There is a huge accumulation of U.S. dollar stockpiling in these countries. The MOF suddenly realized that if you put them all together they would make a useful bargaining chip."

The main result of the Tokyo meeting was to include Japan in a plan initially floated by Australia, China, and ASEAN to set up a network of dollar-repurchase agreements. "Repo" agreements come in handy when a government needs to intervene in foreign exchange markets but doesn't have sufficient foreign exchange reserves to do the job. By using U.S. Treasury bills as collateral, one central bank can borrow foreign exchange from another. Because of the huge size of Japan's U.S. dollar reserves, Tokyo had never felt the need to set up repo agreements. It had been reluctant to join the ASEAN plan, which involved short-term loans of dollar funds from other central banks in the event of a speculative attack.

Reluctance vanished with the yen spike of August 1995. In late 1995, Japan reached a "repo" agreement with Singapore, Hong Kong, and Australia; the Tokyo meeting expanded the list to ten countries. The Thai baht crisis blew right through the fragile agreement, but Japan persisted. It used the group to float the AMF idea and, when that crashed, came back in 1998 with something called a "yen funneling system," similar to the repo arrangement except based in yen. This idea was from the Bank of Japan and called for providing yen-denominated loans to Asian central banks to promote the use of Japanese currency in trade.[65] In 1999, Finance Minister Miyazawa upped the ante again, with his "new initiative" and the "resource mobilization plan for Asia" that went along with it. The new plan offered Yen 2 trillion in loan guarantees for yen-denominated government bonds issued by other Asian countries.[66]

The AMF proposal was testimony to Japan's dogged pursuit of a vision for Asia running counter to the Anglo-American free-market model. In most respects, the vision also ran counter to market realities. Malaysian prime minister Mahathir, too, had proposed greater use of regional currencies to reduce dependence on the dollar. Teh Kok Peng of the Monetary Authority of Singapore described the Malaysian and Japanese proposals as doomed. "I don't know whether Mahathir is a banker," Teh said in a 1996 interview. "His idea is that we should use more of regional currencies for transactions. My sense is that the idea will die a natural death. There is little interest on the part of banks or the private sector. Exporters are not seeking to receive payments in rupiah and so on. If you take Asia as a whole, three quarters of our trade is with countries outside Asia. There's no way you can get them to take Asian currencies. About 10 percent of the remaining 25 percent is intra-company trade. At the end of the day, real trade is only 15 percent."[67]

There was, indeed, a certain feigned naiveté to Japan's proclaimed intention of "internationalizing" the yen. Officials at the Bank of Japan and MOF had known what the problem was for years. Asian central banks, particularly those carrying large yen debt as part of Japan's foreign aid program, would have loved to hold more yen to protect against its violent swings post-1985. The reason they did not was largely inconvenience. For example, the Bank of Japan insisted on a ten-day rule for settling accounts, which made it largely impossible to purchase yen for the sake of currency-market interventions. There was a lack of short-term instruments and no equivalent of U.S. Treasury auctions in which government bonds were sold directly to the market. Inconvenience to other central banks meant preservation of control over monetary policy to Japanese finance officials.

Even when Japan moved to introduce changes to its government-bond market in December 1998 as part of the campaign to reduce "excessive" dependence of Asian currencies on the dollar, the Ministry of Finance failed to introduce the real-time settlement provisions recommended by its own advisory committee on the internationalization of the yen.[68] Miyazawa, in a speech to Asian finance ministers a few months later, delicately acknowledged the omission. "Another matter that requires quick resolution is settlement and clearance," he said. "Real-time gross settlement is a necessary ingredient in truly global transactions."[69]

Asians might be skeptical about Japan's efforts to solve Asia's problems through government-support mechanisms adapted from Japan's domestic experience, but in the context of the trauma of 1997–98, Japan was engaged, it put its money on the line, and did not hold the other Asian economies hostage to demands for policy reforms, in stark contrast to the United States and the IMF. American and European investors cruised the region, looking for cheap assets, while Japanese companies pumped money into existing joint ventures with local affiliates. The New Miyazawa Initiative further underlined the contrast.

The "old" Miyazawa Initiative had been a 1988 debt-relief plan for Latin America, proposed by Miyazawa Kiichi, then as in 1998, serving as Japanese finance minister. The Japanese had long claimed the initiative served as the model for Treasury Secretary Nicholas Brady's 1989 "Brady Plan" for repackaging debt into tradable bonds.[70] In the spirit of the failed AMF, the New Miyazawa Initiative loans offered below-market interest rates and few conditions. Japan launched a series of rescue vehicles for Asian economies and the thousands of Japanese multinationals based in them. A "second stage" of the New Miyazawa Initiative was designed to encourage wider use of the yen as a reserve currency. It set up a Yen 2 trillion fund to guarantee yen-denominated bond issues by Asia-Pacific economies.[71] The new Japan Bank for International Cooperation, established in October 1999 through the merger of the JEXIM and OECF, was to manage the fund.[72]

In addition to bilateral funding, Tokyo set up an emergency support agency at the Asian Development Bank (ADB), the Asian Currency Crisis Support Facility, providing it with Yen 367.5 billion in financing. Another add-on to the New Miyazawa Initiative, a Yen 600 billion "special yen facility"—later dubbed the "Obuchi Fund," offered unbelievably soft terms, including a ten-year grace period, forty-year repayment terms, and a 0.75 percent interest rate. The "special yen facility" was intended to sponsor public works projects in Asia, "in principle on a tied basis to Japanese exports," according to a Japan Export-Import Bank (JEXIM) press release.[73] Governments in the crisis economies promptly submitted loan requests for large pipeline and other infrastructure projects that normally would seek commercial funding.

Most Asians did not care that these special yen loans were tied aid, partly designed to assist the recovery of Japanese firms in Asia, because they depended on those same businesses for employment and exports. The Japanese, however, steered carefully. When Indonesia presented a long wish list of projects to be funded from the special yen facility, Tokyo turned down the requests for several billion dollars from the Indonesian government to buy two power plants from private investors including Sumitomo Corp. The U.S. Treasury Department showed little concern. The subject was merely raised in passing when the incoming financial minister at the Japanese embassy in Washington paid a courtesy call on Treasury Deputy Secretary Timothy Geithner in mid-July 1999. "We don't think the numbers add up," sniffed one Treasury official. "Why should we be concerned about an effort when it is obviously political?"

That month, Japanese officials briefed Asians on yet another project, aimed at reviving regional manufacturing and focusing on sectors dominated by the Japanese such as autos and electronics. In September, Toyota Chairman Okuda Hiroshi was appointed to lead the program. In November 1999 Prime Minister Obuchi Keizo went to Manila to explain its details to the third annual leaders' meeting of ASEAN Plus Three, the new summitry exercise that included China, Japan, and South Korea. The *Report of the Mission for the Revitalization of the Asian Economy* insisted on opening the Japanese economy to Asian imports and workers as well as engaging Japan more broadly in microinstitutional reforms and human resources development throughout the region. "The economic interdependency between Japan and Asia has reached the level that it should be termed an 'economic community,'" the authors declared. "Opening Japan will also enable us to be a true and trusted friend of Asia."[74]

Based on the report, the "Obuchi Plan" was to use some of the remaining New Miyazawa Initiative funds to launch human resources programs for small business and "marketization" in economies such as Vietnam and Thailand.[75] The Western press virtually ignored the ASEAN Plus Three summit exercise, despite its explicit exclusion of the United States. Prime Minister Hashimoto Ryutaro had first proposed the idea of such summits while visiting Southeast Asia in January 1997.[76] The Manila meeting marked the first time that the "Plus Three" heads of state—Japanese prime minister Obuchi, Chinese prime minister Zhu Rongji, and South Korean president Kim Dae Jung—held their own formal summit as well as a side meeting of finance ministers to encourage further discussion on both a common market and regional currency. "Let's face it, our future is intertwined with that of greater East Asia," host Philippine president Joseph Estrada declared to reporters.[77]

By March 2000, Japan was able to shut down the New Miyazawa Initiative.[78] The Asian economies had weathered the crisis, and even Indonesia experienced the early stages of recovery. Most of the funds had been drawn down by the previous July; Tokyo had disbursed the $26 billion associated with the New Miyazawa Initiative in addition to another $42 billion in support measures enacted earlier. JEXIM, which picked up about one-third of the Miyazawa Initiative financing, saw its loan volume shoot up by 80 percent, to a record Yen 3.8 trillion in the 1998 fiscal year, or about $30 billion (at Yen 128.05 to the dollar), through March 1999. In FY 1997, 64 percent of all JEXIM lending had been to Asia. The percentage in 1998 declined as the bank lent more funds directly to Japanese companies in Japan, which then supplied funds to their Asian subsidiaries.[79]

This was not funny money. JEXIM's funding to Asia alone was almost as much as the World Bank lent in a year. Tokyo's program in essence massively bailed out Japanese companies in Asia and was designed to replace almost exactly the funds yanked back to Japan by Japanese banks. The implications for non-Japanese companies in the region were unmistakable. When the Industrial Bank of Japan stepped in to jump start Thai exports in late 1997, it raised $500 million in capital for the Thai Export-Import Bank, which then lent it on to Thai businesses, many of them Japanese affiliates. The terms were so generous that U.S. and European banks were unable to join the syndicate because it violated prudential requirements for return on capital.[80]

Despite the fact that the majority of the New Miyazawa Initiative funds were technically untied, U.S. companies on the ground in Asia automatically inferred that most of the contracts for infrastructure development would go to Japanese companies. True or not, government money helped Japanese companies in the region to hold their ground. In Thailand, a government study found that Japan led all other countries in providing support for its local partners between November 1997 and January 1999. Of the 244 joint ventures in the study, 129, just over half, received help from their Japanese partners, compared to fourteen from U.S. firms. New Japanese investment of $390 billion represented 62.6 percent of all new foreign investment during the period.[81]

Japan's role as hero of the Asian recovery gave the World Bank another reason to want Japan in its corner. Both had taken credit for the boom era and both were tarnished by the sudden disaster overtaking regional economies. Both reacted by painting Asia as a victim of global capital flows and the IMF. Finally, both had an interest in presenting themselves as friends of the region—Japan in order to reduce its isolation and gain clout in its ongoing battles with the United States over its economic institutions and the Bank to restore its increasingly threadbare credibility in the age-old war against poverty.

In the era of James Wolfensohn, the World Bank exhorted its regulars to think in terms of "clients" rather than "loan recipients." Wolfensohn had founded his own Wall Street firm before coming to the Bank in June 1995. The crisis threatened to expose just how cozy some of the Bank's relationships with its clients had become. In February 1999, the Bank for the first time admitted to having made mistakes in Asia. It acknowledged that Indonesia's rapid growth had created a "halo effect" around Indonesian president Suharto; the Bank had been unwilling to deliver tough messages to him.[82] Earlier the Bank had made its split with the Fund formal, declaring in a 200-page report that the IMF/Treasury policy of forcing high interest rates in the early days of the crisis had led to ruin. The Bank laid the blame for the crisis not on Asia but on the changing nature of global capital markets. Stiglitz told reporters, "The heart of the current crisis is the surge of capital flows. The surge is followed by a precipitous flow out. Few countries, no matter how strong their financial institutions, could have withstood such a turnaround. But clearly the fact that the financial institutions were weak and their firms highly leveraged made these countries particularly vulnerable."[83]

Looking back, Stiglitz said that there were "moments of evolution" rather than a single event that influenced his thinking. One of the more significant of these, however, was the Japanese-funded research project on East Asian growth, the *East Asian Miracle,* in which he had been involved in the early 1990s. This project began the slow process by which the World Bank and Japan became true bedfellows. It may be, as the Japanese like to say, two can sleep in the same bed and yet have different dreams.

The Making of a Miracle

A chill wind blew through the haunts of the Japanese bureaucracy in 1987 and 1988. It was exhilarating to the nationalists at the Ministry of Finance, in its Spartan headquarters in Kasumigaseki, while next door in the chatty linoleum-tiled corridors of its more comfortable and plebian neighbor, the Foreign Ministry, diplomats fluttered. Across the street, in the MITI's ostentatiously contemporary office tower, officials were frantically busy micromanaging the first large-scale transfer of Japanese manufacturing abroad. The Japanese Diet, up the hill in its odd Masonic-looking tower, rumbled along, irrelevant as ever. In the OECF's stylish brick headquarters on the other side of the Imperial Palace in Takebashi and in the Japan International Cooperation Agency's posh digs in Akebonobashi and Shinjuku, the mandarins of Japan's foreign aid program fretted anxiously.

At the tail end of the 1980s, the neat progression that Japan's post-war leaders had desired—from economic superstar to respected global leader—suddenly fell apart, lurching into sudden confusion and disarray. The breakdown of Cold War geopolitics undermined the logic of U.S. intervention in the Pacific, just as it had in the North Atlantic, and however long U.S. troops might remain in Okinawa, South Korea, and the Philippines, Japan could no longer count on the United States to provide broad support for its economic aims, or shelter the interests of Japanese multinationals in Asia. In Geneva, the Cold War compact on free and open markets seemed to be in a terminal stage, as negotiators struggled to complete the Uruguay Round of negotiations on the General Agreement on Tariffs and Trade (GATT). The United States and Europe were closing ranks behind separate trade blocs—the United States in NAFTA and Europe in the long-planned EU. In Asia, without the United States, Japan had no cover. Economically, the rapid appreciation of the yen after 1985 had made Japan's Asian investments critical to the performance, even the survival, of some of its star multinationals. Out of this cauldron came the Japanese model of development.

Cynical and pragmatic, the Japanese bureaucracy had been little concerned with abstract theory up until this juncture, and the idea of direct proselytization was anathema to a generation schooled in the values of serving as a middle power under U.S. patronage. Somebody had to invent the Japanese model, and it was not going to be the Japanese themselves. To the rescue came an unlikely crew—the bearded academic Stiglitz; an idealistic and unconventional World Bank economist, Nancy Birdsall; and several on-the-make associates, including the superstar Lawrence Summers and a junior colleague, John Page. The Japanese wielded the magic wand of money. Serving as Merlin was a wiry, combative aristocrat of the Japanese financial bureaucracy, Shiratori Masaki. All he had to do was pull out his checkbook.

The check was for $200 million, and it was signed on July 30, 1990. At that time, Shiratori was Japan's executive director at the World Bank, a stature that gave him a powerful voting position on its board. Unlike the United Nations, the power of World Bank shareholders was based on their contribution to the Bank's capital fund, and Japan was the second largest shareholder after the United States. Shiratori's check created the Policy and Human Resource Development Fund (PHRDF), and his signature committed the Japanese government to contributing Yen 20 billion annually—which would translate into $200 million, more or less, depending on the exchange rate. This was on top of Japan's already large contributions to the international financial institutions (Yen 181 billion out of its Yen 1.38 trillion official development assistance budget in the 1998 fiscal year, for example, or in U.S. dollars, $1.3 billion out of $10.2 billion).[84] The bulk of the money under PHRD was to operate as a slush fund, identified as "technical assistance" in PHRD accounts.[85] In effect, the Bank gained a large, off-balance sheet grant for special projects. The unspoken understanding was that these would go to raise the stature of the Japanese within the institution.

Other countries had created such "trust funds" in the past but none on the scale of Japan's "PHRD." A part of the fund was explicitly linked to Japanese national interest, ranging from the so-called brain trust project supervised by the Bank's Economic Development Institute (EDI) to investigate Japan's approach to development to training programs for officials from the MOF, the Ministry of Foreign Affairs (MOFA), and the Bank of Japan. PHRD's 1997 annual report boasted that the World Bank or International Development Association projects supported by PHRD funds between 1991 and 1997 had attracted $90 billion in "follow-up" investment.

The EDI, which depended for half of its budget on outside donations, got $14 million per year from the PHRD. Another $11 million went toward a scholarship program that sent development economists from poor countries to the United States, Japan, France, and Australia.[86] The Brain Trust program, which began in 1991, identified two research projects per year that would reflect the "Asian experience," according to Farrukh Iqbal, who directed the project. "We try to engage Japanese experts and scholars in our activities so that they can speak from their experience," he said, describing the Brain Trust program.[87] Nobody noted the similarity between the program's name and Japan's own draft plan for regional economic coordination of a few years earlier.

The Brain Trust project produced a series of academic books, published by Oxford University Press, on subjects ranging from the role of government in East Asia, to such features of the Japanese political and economic landscape as the Japanese main bank system, local government development, and the civil service. Most of the books received scant distribution. "There's a suspicion around here that EDI served as a vanity press for the Japanese," said one Bank staffer conversant with the history of PHRD. "One reason why these projects went there may have been because they were rebuffed by the research core of the Bank. The fact is that EDI is not a research organization and not part of the intellectual process here."[88]

The most important of the PHRD offshoots by far, however, was the *East Asian Miracle*. The World Bank's eighty-person research department pushed out dozens of reports annually. Yet, few have had the stellar beginnings of the *East Asian Miracle* report. Japan put up its central bank governor, Mieno

Yasushi, to propose the idea at the most public forum the World Bank has—the lavish annual meeting of its board of governors. In October 1991, Mieno told the board that "experience in Asia has shown that although development strategies require a healthy respect for market mechanisms, the role of the government cannot be forgotten. I would like to see the World Bank and the IMF take the lead in a wide-ranging study that would define the theoretical underpinnings of this approach and clarify the areas in which it can be successfully applied to the other parts of the globe."[89]

Along with Mieno's pointed request came the money to carry it out. Lewis Preston, in his first month on the job as president of the World Bank, accepted Japan's offer. Tokyo would eventually shell out $3.5 million in research funds, drawn from the brand-new PHRD. The Japanese funding covered not only the principal *East Asian Miracle* study, with a research budget of $1.2 million, but an expanding list of companion studies on policy-based finance, East Asian civil services, Japanese tax administration, and savings and investment policies. The *East Asian Miracle* study itself was completed in a whirlwind eighteen months, but some of the companion studies would go on for years.

The *Miracle* volume was important because it marked the Bank's first major concession to the notion that government could play a constructive role in the global economy, after a decade of opposing precisely that idea. It was also stylish, well written, and had a good title. It represented a sharp departure from the traditional World Bank publications, packed densely with tables and mathematical formulas, written for specialists, and printed, frequently, on cheap paper and using mimeograph technology. In contrast, the *Miracle* book was on glossy paper, with short, sharp vignettes in "boxes" to give depth to the text without requiring lengthy exposition, and written in a simple, direct prose style. A professional graphics artist worked on its cover, which featured a medley of rice fields and the container port at Pusan, South Korea. It also had a remarkably catchy way with statistics. "Between 1960 and 1985, real income per capita increased more than four times in Japan and the Four Tigers and more than doubled in the Southeast Asian NIEs," it started out. "If growth were randomly distributed, there is roughly one chance in ten thousand that success would have been so regionally concentrated."[90]

The Bank went to extraordinary lengths to make sure that the project would make waves. In budget and design, it was the largest single publishing project the Bank had undertaken up until that point, ranking just below the scale of its flagship publication, annual *World Development Report* (WDR). Eventually it became a record bestseller (in Bank terms), with more than 100,000 copies sold. It was under the direct supervision of the chief economist, then Lawrence Summers, and Nancy Birdsall, director of the Policy Research

Department. Unlike the Brain Trust volumes, the *East Asian Miracle* was to go through a Bank-wide review as part of a process of "spreading the message within the Bank and to its clients," as one member of the research team put it. The Bank hired Lawrence MacDonald, Manila bureau chief for the *Asian Wall Street Journal*, as content editor, an unusual step for an organization that used journalists as freelance editors but rarely took them on full time except to handle public relations. In charge of graphics, design, and overall editing was Bruce Ross-Larson, an anthropologist and Southeast Asia hand turned ponytailed Washington consultant.

The mastermind, however, was John Page, a former Princeton associate professor and Rhodes scholar. The introduction merely lists Page as leader of the research team that put together the volume, but his actual role went far beyond research. Page put his own very individual stamp on the project. He aimed high—hoping to bridge the ideological gap between the Bank of the 1980s and the more government-friendly philosophy he perceived on its way up in the early 1990s. This meant, however, pacifying the strict neoclassical economists who continued to dominate the internal culture of the World Bank, while reaching out to the Japanese. Politically, it was an astute strategy. It was less successful as an intellectual approach. The result was a document so ambiguous and muddled that most people eventually remembered it by what the "miracle" in its title suggested rather than its interesting, if parsimonious, arguments.

"The fact is that Page is quite good at the politics of the Bank," said the Bank's MacDonald, a few years after *Miracle* was published. "Does that mean that he thinks politics is an end in itself? I think he would say no. His idea was that the report would come out somewhere in the middle and would please no one—and that the truth lay somewhere in the middle as well."[91]

Page was rare among Bank economists in attempting to continue publishing in academic periodicals after entering the bureaucracy as a "young professional" in 1980. As a member of the editorial board of the Bank's research journal, the *World Bank Economic Review*, Page mustered a certain cachet in academic circles. In 1995, his resume was ten pages long, including seven pages of his published works and "research in progress." Within the Bank, he had moved steadily up in the professional ranks, with stints in the Industrial Strategy and Policy Division and various subdivisions of the Latin American and Caribbean Region before moving to the Country Economics Department as senior advisor for private-sector development in 1992. A Rhodes scholar, with fluent Spanish and an Oxford Ph.D., Page longed for a higher profile both within the World Bank and the academic world outside, where he hoped to eventually return. His ambitions and background helped give the *East Asian Miracle* project a peculiar twist.

Robert Wade, a friend and critic, claimed that Page got the job of running the *Miracle* study because he lacked a hard ideological edge and would be sensitive to politics. "He could be expected not to go off the deep end ideologically," Wade said. "John says different things to different audiences. People at the Bank are divided into those who speak their minds and those who are on the way up."[92]

The research team that Page assembled included some of the foremost American academic economists, including Stiglitz, but no Japanese, and none of the American and European scholars, mostly political scientists and anthropologists, who had studied the institutions of East Asian development. It served Japan's interests to be excluded, since it would defray accusations that Tokyo had taken over the study. The Japanese and academic specialists were collateral, however, to the real target of Page's exclusion—the Asian experts within the Bank itself, who would almost certainly have used the project to air the orthodox view that East Asian success was based on "market-friendly" practices. This was partly Page's own choice, and partly a reflection of the premium the Bank placed on pleasing the Japanese.

"No one should think that the World Bank, Preston, or anybody else felt shoved into doing this," said Nancy Birdsall.[93] Nonetheless, her decision to assign Page to run the project reflected a deliberate decision to remove it from the jurisdiction of the Bank's East Asian experts. Under Vinod Thomas as the regional chief economist, the East Asian vice-presidency remained staunchly free market in orientation. Thomas had been the chief author of the Bank's 1991 World Development Report, which served as a summing up of neo-classical views that governments served best when they served least.

The term "market-friendly" was a slap at the many clients of the Bank, i.e., developing-country shareholders, for whom state planning and government control remained the order of the day. Page's chief rival for the job of managing the *Miracle* project was Danny Leipziger, who had spent more than a decade working on South Korea. He was rejected precisely because he came out of the East Asian vice-presidency and the Vinod Thomas mindset. "Danny had an ideological point of view which was very much the paradigm," recalled Birdsall. "Larry [Summers] and I both thought it was important to look at East Asia from a fresh point of view. In my opinion, John Page had the wherewithal to do it. He had the analytical capability, he had worked on the TFP (total factor productivity) stuff, and he had worked with Nishimizu Mieko [who had coauthored several papers with Page]. John was clearly interested, eager, ambitious, and intelligent."

While the core research team failed to include any prominent Asia specialists or Japanese, it was made up largely of Asian nationals—Filipinos Jose Edgardo Campos and Marilou Uy, as well as Korean Kim Chang Shik.

Campos was an accomplished institutional economist and responsible for some of the more creative work in the *East Asian Miracle* on consultative mechanisms used by East Asian governments to build constituencies for their growth policies. He later wrote his own book on the subject, *The Key to the Asian Miracle*.[94] Yet, Campos had spent his entire adulthood in the United States and was by no means an Asia specialist—just a highly competent Asian economist.

"It was my choice completely," Page said. "I'm not an Asian expert. I had eighteen months to get it done. First you have to get it formulated, then funded. In the beginning, it was just a gleam in the eye of Larry Summers. I needed to get people that I knew could turn out something sensible in fourteen months. I got people who were extremely good, and fresh to Asia. One of the things I think is wrong with Anglo-American analysis of East Asia is that it's done by Asia experts." As to the absence of Japanese on the team, Page says, "I did not know any Japanese whose English-language writing skills were good enough who were available."[95] The team of economists that he put together included a number of celebrity and semicelebrated economists, starting with Stiglitz and including W. Max Corden, Robert Z. Lawrence, Richard Sabot, Peter Petri, and Howard Pack. Most of them had only dabbled in work on East Asia, with the exception of Petri, who taught economic geography at Brandeis.

The absence of Japanese on the team was no handicap, given the Japanese government's understandings about the project. Page was savvy enough to provide the appearance of Japanese input, and the Japanese eagerly backed him up. Within the Bank, his key liaison was with Nishimizu, then a country manager in the Bank's South Asia vice-presidency, who was to become the South Asia vice-president in 1997. Nishimizu helped to organize a parallel exercise of seminars and papers by Japanese economists, supposedly helping to inform the report's conclusions. Nishimizu and Page were already good friends, and formed a tight little clique together with another former Princeton professor, Kemal Dervis, later finance minister of Turkey. All three had taught at Princeton in the late 1970s and early 1980s, and formed a support group helping each other on the long climb up through the Bank hierarchy. Nishimizu's husband was British, and she had left Japan in the early 1970s. Nonetheless, her connections in Japan were impeccable. Her family came from the old imperial aristocracy, and she commanded attention in the bureaucratic elite at MOF and OECF. She also had a personal tie with Ishikawa Shigeru, the leader of MOF's internal study group on Japanese development philosophy, and had gone to graduate school in the United States with Ishikawa's son, a Marxist economist at Tokyo University. The younger Ishikawa introduced Page to his father, who, unbeknownst to Page, was also a connection both to the Sakakibara crowd within the MOF and Akamatsu's lineage in policy circles.[96]

Another serendipitous connection to Ishikawa and the core thinkers within the Japanese financial bureaucracy came through Page's boss in the Policy Research Department at the Bank, Nancy Birdsall. Page and Birdsall, both microeconomists, joined the Bank about the same time, and had worked in the development economics vice-presidency during Hollis Chenery's tenure as chief economist. Chenery and his successors, Anne Krueger and Stanley Fischer, constructed the neoclassical regime that held sway in the Bank in the 1980s. Although not a member of the Princeton clique, Birdsall was well-liked by the neoclassicists, with whom she shared, in her own words, a "common vision." Birdsall had become friends in graduate school at Yale University with one of Ishikawa's disciples, Yanagihara Toru. Yanagihara and Nishimizu helped introduce what might be called the "Ishikawa control motif" in the *East Asian Miracle* project, an emphasis on the role of government in coordinating market failures. This was very much what Stiglitz had in mind, as well, with his notion of government filling in the "gaps" in imperfect markets.

Among the marvels of the *East Asian Miracle* project is that its chief patron within the World Bank, far above the trenches where Page and Birdsall labored, was Lawrence Summers, a hard-line advocate of the free-market model. It was largely through Summers's influence as deputy treasury secretary that the IMF plunged into full-bore restructuring of the Asian economies through its emergency packages for the Asian crisis economies. Yet, it was Summers who negotiated the *East Asian Miracle* project with Shiratori and ensured that it would get the high profile sought by Birdsall and Page. Summers cut the deal for the project immediately following the 1991 Bank/ Fund meetings in Bangkok, with support from Michael Walton, later chief economist for East Asia.

Like Stiglitz, Summers was a winner of the prestigious John Bates Clark Award for younger economists, and his career had rocketed nonstop since then. He became chief economist at the World Bank in 1990, at the age of 36, and left the Bank two years later, in November 1992, to work as an economic advisor to presidential candidate William J. Clinton. After Clinton was elected, Summers went to the U.S. Treasury, to work first under Lloyd Bentsen and then Robert Rubin as deputy treasury secretary, until he was nominated as treasury secretary after Rubin's departure in May 1999. After the Republican victory in 2000, he went on to become president of Harvard University. Summers's departure from the World Bank before the *East Asian Miracle* project was finished may have accounted for the way it staked a middle ground between Japan and the free market. The fact remains that Summers brokered the deal.

Summers considered himself a Japan expert by virtue of his preoccupation with the Japanese economy as deputy treasury secretary in the first Clinton term. He had written just one article on the Japanese economy, looking at Japanese savings patterns. His coauthor was Robert Dekle, an economist then still in graduate school, who later turned up as the sole East Asia specialist on the IMF team negotiating the huge Korea bailout in 1997. Dekle had grown up in Japan and spoke fluent Japanese, and did the research for the paper.[97] According to Dekle, the background to the paper was a debate current in the 1980s that Japanese national income accounting practices artificially inflated the Japanese savings rate. A lower actual savings rate would imply that Japan was managing its economy along more conventional lines. A higher actual savings rate meant that the Japanese were not playing by Western rules.

"Summers' view of Japan was that they did not listen to the United States or other advisors on their markets. They just did whatever they wanted to do," said Dekle, who went to work as a professor at the University of Southern California after leaving the IMF. "There was a debate in the late 1980s that the Japanese savings rate was not that high because their national income accounting standards were different. Summers thought that the argument did not make sense. How could their current account surplus be so huge and these people claim that the savings rate was low? We did the accounting and found that Japanese savings rates were still much higher."[98] Immediately after publishing this paper, Summers went to the World Bank.

In policy matters, his basic instinct with the Japanese was to get tough. He played tennis with Clyde Prestowitz, also on the advisory team to candidate Bill Clinton in 1992; Prestowitz had made a name for himself as a revisionist on Japan by arguing in a popular 1988 book that Japan was about to "trade places" with the United States to become the world's leading economic superpower.[99] In December 1989, just before he went to the Bank, Summers wrote in the policy magazine *International Economy*: "Today, Japan is the world's second largest economy. . . . Furthermore, an Asian economic bloc with Japan at its apex . . . is clearly in the making. This all raises the possibility that the majority of American people who now feel that Japan is a greater threat to the United States than the Soviet Union are right."[100] Of all people, he might least be expected to direct a sympathetic treatment of the role of Japanese-style industrial policy in Asian economic growth.

Five years after he left the World Bank, Summers seemed to have an unduly hard time putting himself back into the time period and mind-set that produced the *East Asian Miracle*. "It's been a long time, and there's been a lot of water over my bridge," he said in a 1997 interview, pulling on a Coke in his office in the Treasury Building. He recalled that the Japanese proposal dovetailed with one of his own pet projects, to develop a publications series for the World Bank that would be read by wider audiences than those of the traditional Bank publications, which were highly technical and written in the obscure language favored by economists. Summers never anticipated that the project would serve as a calling card for the Japanese model. His own convictions and credentials as a neoclassical economist were rock solid, although he may have lacked the fiery rhetoric of such predecessors as Chenery, Krueger, and Fischer, who had been his professor as an undergraduate at the Massachusetts Institute of Technology.

"To my recollection, it was not long after the Bangkok meetings, it could have been 10 days, it could have been three months [World Bank President] Lew Preston called me in, and said that it was important to address this set of issues, that it would be possible to learn something from them. This coincided with what had been an objective of mine, to commit the research area of the vice-presidency to produce more synthetic high profile studies on the model of the WDRs, mini-WDRs, drawing lessons for policy. I saw this as another area where a lot of questions had been raised and where the Bank could make a real contribution by doing this kind of synthesis. Basically, I thought this was a valuable exercise. I asked Nancy Birdsall, who was then director in charge of research—at some time after the Bangkok meetings, Johannes Linn left, and Nancy Birdsall came in, and I felt the study should be run out of her department."[101]

Summers exited the World Bank about the time the first draft of the *East Asian Miracle* was completed, which gave its authors leeway to move away from the Washington Consensus and neoclassical orthodoxy. The fact that they did annoyed Summers, who had been tracking the downturn of Southeast Asian economies in 1996 and early 1997, and was particularly concerned with Japan. The *East Asian Miracle*, made "an interesting report," Summers said in a 1997 interview, with noticeably faint praise.

"It suffered slightly from being a committee product. The message was a bit un-distilled and unclear. I think it missed; it should have surfaced the set of issues that were surfaced by Alwyn Young's work, on what the real total productivity contributions were. [Alwyn Young had written a series of articles arguing that East Asian growth came from "factor accumulation," or mobilizing resources, rather than productivity gains. Paul Krugman adopted the argument and made it famous in a 1994 article in *Foreign Affairs* magazine called "The Myth of Asia's Miracle"].[102] In fact, that was somehow avoided. Not all the consultants had the same set of initial views, and that tended to be reflected in the ultimate document. But I think that the basic conclusion that these economies had strong macroeconomic policies, strong education, strong central organizations, these areas were properly robust. [With regard to the *East Asian Miracle*'s endorsement of industrial policy], if I had been there toward the end, I would have been raising questions about that. But I think a great deal was learned in the process, and it was a worthwhile endeavor."

I asked, was the ambiguity intentional, to keep Japan happy? Summers answered: "Yes, I think a little bit of that, but I think also you find the Bank culture tends to be a little bit reluctant to draw things to sharp conclusions. The study probably contributed to a sense that many of the things behind the Asian success were conventional things that have been preached for a long time about strong institutions, education, strong macroeconomic policy and high savings. But it was a little bit Biblical in the sense that you can find things in it to support almost any point of view. If I had been there, frankly, I would have forced the thing to have a more sharply defined line. I think the need for consensus, and the difficulty of the issues, produced some lack of sharpness in the conclusions."

Like Birdsall, Summers was defensive about Japanese funding for the project. He said: "My guess is, they have, there's a Japanese fund at the Bank. I forget what it's called, but there's a fund the Japanese have to fund things, to co-finance things, to use the phrase of the Bank. My guess is that it came out of that fund, and they were, basically, volunteering, but I don't know for sure. I'd be surprised if I had any negotiations with the Japanese about the funding, because I'd expect to remember that, and I don't. Certainly there was none, but I want to emphasize that for better or for worse, there was no control or heavy continuing influence. I don't think that if you have an institution concerned with development, and you have an economy that had a phenomenal success, it's not rocket science to see that it'd be a good idea to study that, to understand that."

However hazy Summers's recollections may have been, he admitted that the *East Asian Miracle* was unusual. "My impression," he said cautiously, "is that this was one of the most important things the research vice-presidency was doing. The research vice-presidency was one, not insignificant, but not central pieces of the Bank, so you wouldn't want to build it as one of the most important things the Bank was doing. I was concerned that we got it right, and I was concerned that we actually reach some conclusions. My guess is that I was involved with it every several weeks over a period of a year or so. I read outlines and some of the drafts."

Later on in 1997, Summers would have plenty of reasons to distance himself from the *East Asian Miracle* book, as Asian economies crashed and burned. The book became an embarrassment within the Bank, even if Stiglitz continued to quote and defend it. The transition was amazingly abrupt. For most of the 1990s, within the Bank the book had iconic status, sponsoring endless seminars, spats with the IMF, alternately comforting and angering the Japanese, and attracting enthusiastic interest on the part of leaders in developing countries.

The politics that landed on Page's plate in working on the *East Asian Miracle* were, on one level, entirely local to 1818 H Street. At one extreme, he had to cope with Summers's hard line on market economics. Birdsall represented the other end of the spectrum. Her background in economics was unconventional, and she had a wide-ranging curiosity on issues that most neo-classical economists would be inclined to set aside as overly warm and fuzzy—the role of women in economies, the relationship between education and development, and human "capital" in general.

With her lank brown hair and ingenuous manner, Birdsall was anything but a typical Washington bureaucrat. Straight lines and square boxes were not part of the Birdsall style. In a city where many professional women sported hair and ensembles straight out of the Eisenhower era, Birdsall was a flower child— no jewels, no makeup, no hair color, no ersatz couture. Economics was by no means her first choice of profession. She did American Studies at Newton College of the Sacred Heart, then a master's degree in International Relations at the Paul H. Nitze School of Advanced International Studies in Washington, traditionally a breeding ground for diplomats. By the time she arrived at Yale as a graduate student in economics, Birdsall had lived for nearly a decade in Brazil and been through a divorce. While studying for her Ph.D., she was also a single mother. This made her unusual among her classmates there, too. At the World Bank, she was a breath of fresh air. Like Stiglitz, she disdained reading from scripts and comfortably dived into her thoughts.

"At Yale, I was a little bit of an oddball. I had to take boring things like calculus, and I was already thirty with a child," Birdsall said in an interview in 1996. "I did a Ph.D. in economics at Yale, but I came with an odd background. I was not already imbued with what was then becoming more and more mathematical and theoretical approaches to economics. My background was more in the subjective area."[103] She specialized at Yale in labor and human capital, issues on which she continued to work at the World Bank, while branching into education, health, and the environment. She also churned out academic papers, unlike many of her colleagues. Larry Summers picked her as head of the Policy Research Department, she said, because she combined a "quasi-academic" background with operational experience.

"Nancy is a risk taker. She is willing to jump into entirely new things," said Campos, who moved to the Policy Research Department of the Bank after working on the *East Asian Miracle* project team. "Nancy doesn't have to go through ten pages of equations and economic studies. She almost knows this is in the right direction. She has a knack for being able to say, well, I don't need someone to make 10,000 regressions to say this is heading in the right direction."[104]

It was Birdsall who provided the intuitive leap from the neoclassical orthodoxy of the 1980s to the government-friendly view of the Bank in the 1990s. According to Campos, she helped to "change the terms of the debate from less or more government to good government."[105] The methods of East Asian governments, Birdsall said, were something like running a children's birthday party. In order to prevent chaos, the adults would set up contests. This was a way of getting both competition—to keep the children busy— and cooperation. It also encompassed Stiglitz's view that East Asian governments had effectively addressed the coordination "failures" of imperfect markets.

Birdsall worked up "a little talk" for the World Bank's board of directors on her birthday-party concept, called the "Three C's and Three R's."

> The Three C's were cooperation, competition, and contests. You have to have cooperation and at the same time competition. Japan and Korea resolved the dilemma of having both by setting up contests. The Three R's were rules, rewards, and a referee. That's what you need for a good contest. In Japan, the reward was often subsidized credit, but the measure of performance was export success.
>
> The referee was usually the government, which was not subject to pressures from different interest groups. The rules of the game were based on competition. If the Japanese never came up with a theory, it was because their intellectual tradition was grounded in pragmatism and flexibility. In U.S. universities, the tendency is to focus on having a coherent theory, which is related to the development of economics as a discipline, and to the power of the neo-classical economic thing. That can be confining. I think the *East Asian Miracle* is very important. Of course, only time will tell if it affects the paradigm, but I believe it has really started a new round of debate on what is the right approach to development. [106]

Birdsall also took a very different tack from Summers on the issue of "factor accumulation." Summers agreed with Alwyn Young and Paul Krugman that East Asian governments had relied excessively on achieving gains in output through mobilizing resources, channeling high Asian savings into capital investment and repressing consumption. Writing in 1994, in a celebrated article in *Foreign Affairs*, Krugman predicted that, eventually, like the Soviet Union in the 1960s, East Asia would run out of gas unless it began to concentrate on improving productivity.[107]

Birdsall was less interested in theory and more interested in why the East

Asians had done such a good job of mobilizing resources, or "factor accumulation," in the first place. Governments in Latin America and Africa had tried similar strategies and failed.

> In other countries it was wasted. In some countries, rates of accumulation were higher than in East Asia [but they did not experience East Asian rates of growth]. What really distinguishes Japan and these other economies is that they had tremendous rates of investment and savings accumulation. There was a connection between that and the strategic role of the government. What was MITI doing? They were continually signaling, this is what we will support. If you go out into these areas, this is what we will support. This industry is going to get phased out, but we're going to take care of it. When you are looking at something like parents' investment in education for their children, the governments were very clear. They were saying, we're going to have lots of investment for primary education. So it was worth it for parents to invest in education. There's a sense of comfort of living in an economy where government seems to be leading things, and has a very transparent growth philosophy. My perception is that the success of coordination provided a sense of security.
>
> You need some coordination in poor economies. The returns to investment in a shoe factory will depend on the returns to the public sector in building a road. This was a fundamental concept in development economics in the 1950s and 1960s, that there can be a coordinating function [by government]. This is art of the justification for the idea that the state can take a commanding role in the economy. It's why governments in Africa took charge of the steel sector. It's much less of a factor in developing economies. Clearly, the need for coordination is greater in the earlier years when you are still in the process of accumulating investments.
>
> This was an old idea in development economics. In the 1980s, with the debt crisis, it became clear that the role of the state was too great in productive areas. What happened in the 1980s is that it became obvious that some adjustment was needed, and there was a lot of focus on the market. Japan is reminding us that there is a challenge in developing economies related to coordination, that they experience market failures, coordination failures, and government failures. Maybe we'll look back and see that this is the time when the whole concept of coordination got back on the agenda.

Unlike Summers and Birdsall, John Page had no pronounced ideological stripe, whether liberal or conservative. "John is trained in the straight neoclassical tradition—he grew up in that, and sees the world in those terms," said Campos. "But I would not see him as bound so tightly to that paradigm." The three administrators each attempted to give their own spin to the

East Asian Miracle, with Page having the most influence by the simple virtue of outlasting the other two. Birdsall left the Bank a month before the book was published to become executive vice president of the Inter-American Development Bank. By that time, Summers was long gone. Only Page stayed on at the Bank. The outcome, as Summers observed, was a committee product, with a chameleon quality that made it possible to read the study in different and contradictory ways. The lack of clarity in the report's conclusions was responsible, in part, for the confused debate that ensued after its publication in September 1993.

The *East Asian Miracle*'s argument went just far enough to establish that East Asian economies had done something different but not so far as to challenge the Bank's antipathy to industrial policy and government intervention generally. The intellectual hat trick to achieve this end was a simple timeline. There were two East Asian "miracles," not one. The Northeast Asian economies, led by Japan, represented one extreme of government intervention, reinforced by closed markets for capital, investment, and goods. At the other extreme were Southeast Asian economies that had secured their period of rapid growth by opening their markets to foreign capital and investment, within limits. Separating the two extremes were thirty years during which the United States had lost its tolerance of Asian protectionism. Page's central message was that the interventionist methods of Japan, South Korea, and Taiwan were history. They would no longer work in a post–Cold War global market that either swept such barriers aside or challenged them through global trade organizations.[108]

If there were two East Asian miracles, both the free-market and "coordination failure" views on the role of government might be right. At the same time, the report reflected the rising popularity of geography both as a discipline and an explanation for why some entire regions did well and others did badly. "Neighborhood effects" could account for the energizing or enervating effects of economic performance on a region. This was a serious breach of the neoclassic orthodoxy of the Bank in the 1980s, because it hinted that getting policy "fundamentals" right might not be enough; people made a difference too. The twist was that the bureaucrats of Northeast Asia were somehow capable of managing industrial policy while those elsewhere were not. Page and his team decided that it was more important to refrain from endorsing industrial policy than to deny the skills set of the Japanese, Korean, and Taiwanese bureaucracies. The introduction maintained that "more institutionally demanding strategies have often failed in other settings and they clearly are not compatible with economic environments where the fundamentals are not securely in place. . . . So the fact that interventions were an element of some East Asian economies' success does not mean that they

should be attempted everywhere, nor should it be taken as an excuse to postpone needed market-oriented reform."[109]

MacDonald recalled that this was among the more hotly debated points
within the research team. "We were reluctant to say that something was OK
for Japan but not for the Ghanaians, because that would have implied a negative judgment. The way we ended up was we said that there was some intervention, but governments got the macro policy right. Then the question
becomes why did they get the macro right—why were they able to implement these policies when people in other countries were not? Then the debate shifts away from industrial policy."[110]

Although analytically more precise than Akamatsu's flying geese, neighborhood effects were right at home with the concept. The *East Asian Miracle*
might repudiate Japanese-style industrial policy, but the net impact was to
assert three of Japan's key points—that Japan's role was crucial to East Asian
growth, that Japanese-style government intervention might provide a positive model for developing economies, and that it was better for markets to
liberalize in stages than all at once. Protection was necessary in the early
stages of growth.

Thus, the World Bank had not only endorsed the Japanese model, it invented it, with internal Bank politics serving as midwife. In 1993, except for
Ishikawa Shigeru, no Japanese policy maker or academic had successfully
delivered a general theory linking Japanese and East Asian patterns of development. Ishikawa's work was mostly conducted in policy seminars and
through papers with circulation limited to the MOF and seminar participants.
After the publication of the *East Asian Miracle*, however, the Japanese could,
in a sense, relax. They could disagree with the details, but the report had
made a point so basic that many of its authors might have been unaware of it.
The report had accepted that the Japanese model was different from the Anglo-
American model, and that other developing economies might learn from
Japan's experience. For the Japanese, this was a breakthrough. Suddenly,
Japan had the World Bank on its side arguing against convergence. It was an
extraordinary achievement for Japan, although it would take several years
and the Asian financial crisis for the implications to seep into the system.

On a cold December day in Washington, six months before the Asian
crisis began, I met Lawrence MacDonald in the World Bank cafeteria. He
was in a philosophical mood and mused, "My view is that there's sort of a
pendulum swing about these things. What is the proper role of the state? At
one point, the Bank was where the stereotypical view of Japan is. We were
involved in shoemaking factories in Africa. There was a shift away from
belief in the state to a belief in reliance on markets, which was espoused in
the Reagan years. I think the pendulum had reached its outermost point some-

time before the *East Asian Miracle*. We were ready to come back to a more sophisticated understanding. The pendulum goes back some distance but not to the same point it was before."[111] The metaphor was apt. People, however, set pendulums in motion.

In September 1993, building on eighteen months of conferences and forty-five background papers, the *East Asian Miracle* was published under the imprint of Oxford University Press. The 389-page report, subtitled *Economic Growth and Public Policy*, looked at the roles of government and markets in eight "high-performing" East Asian economies, adding its own acronym—HPAEs—to the crowded field of growth-theory abbreviations.

Between 1960 and 1985, the report argued, the eight HPAEs—Japan, Hong Kong, Korea, Singapore, Taiwan, Indonesia, Malaysia, and Thailand—were the stars of the global economy, outperforming not only the developing world but also the industrialized economies and the oil-rich Middle East. Among the book's most compelling illustrations were two charts, one on the performance of the HPAEs in terms of per capita output from 1965 to 1990, the other comparing growth rates and equity of the HPAEs and other parts of the developing world. The HPAEs were remarkable not only for their high growth rates but for the relative absence of wide gaps between rich and poor. Nonetheless, the report insisted that the East Asian economies largely fit into neoclassical explanations of economic growth. "There is little that is 'miraculous' about the HPAEs' superior record of growth; it is largely because of superior accumulation of physical and human capital," the authors wrote.[112]

The Bank advised economies not to look at Japan or the Northeast Asian economies as models but rather to the southern tier of East Asian "miracle" economies. Industrial policy was still a no-no. It said that the export promotion policies of East Asian economies succeeded because they occurred during a time of global economic expansion and that "global realities will limit developing economies' ability to adopt the more interventionist instruments of export promotion."[113] Indonesia, Malaysia, and Thailand were the appropriate models for "the next generation of developing economies to follow export-push strategies."[114] In the 1990s, the Bank explained, "Subsidies to exports and directed-credit programs linked to exports . . . may . . . invite retaliation from trading partners. Furthermore, like financial repression, these highly directed interventions require a high level of institutional capacity now lacking in most developing countries."[115]

Even though the *East Asian Miracle* operated from within the framework of neoclassical economics, its message was much more ambiguous than the 1991 WDR, as neoclassical economists quickly attested. It hinted that "state-led" policies might not be all bad, as long as the overall policy framework was correct. "Each of the HPAEs maintained macroeconomic stability and accomplished three functions of growth: accumulation, efficient allocation, and rapid technological catch-up," the report said. "They did this with a combination of policies, ranging from market-oriented to state-led, that varied both across economies and over time."[116] Birdsall, in an interview with *Institutional Investor*, nicely summed up the difference between the "market-friendly" view and the *East Asian Miracle* view of government intervention. "To some extent you might say that until now the World Bank has been viewed as putting the burden of proof on others; in other words, 'Show us that intervention works.' Now I think the burden of proof is on those [who want] to show intervention is clearly harmful."[117]

The *East Asian Miracle* gave Page a boost up the bureaucratic ladder within the World Bank, where unfortunately he remained to bear the brunt of public ridicule when the *East Asian Miracle* became a byword for the Bank's mistakes in East Asia. While it was underway, from 1992 to 1993, the *Miracle* project was the most glamorous thing going on in the Policy Research Department, traditionally a backwater operation. It put Page on the firing line and tested his considerable skills as a diplomat and tactician.

Page got his wish for increased fame and responsibility. He was rewarded with a coveted slot, as chief economist for the Middle East and North Africa Region (MENA), and summoned to brief such figures as Nelson Mandela in South Africa and Crown Prince Hassan of Jordan on the "lessons" from East Asia for other developing countries. He became a minor celebrity in development circles as the "miracle man," sporting a tie he received from Keidanren, Japan's major association of large companies, and making frequent trips to Japan.

Page's last hurrah as "miracle man" was at the Bank/Fund meetings in Hong Kong in September 1997, where he was listed on the program as the principal author of the *East Asian Miracle*. Subsequently, he faded from sight as an expert on East Asian success strategies. The job as chief economist for MENA, however, put Page among the top 100 officials at the World Bank, a significant distinction in the Bank's intensely hierarchical culture. The post of chief economist made him a key player in Middle East diplomacy, as well as speech writer and right-hand man to Kemal Dervis, his old friend and new boss as vice president for MENA. He eventually went on to become senior advisor to the development economics vice-presidency and director of poverty reduction strategies for the Bank.[118]

Birdsall's apotheosis was far more dramatic. She catapulted from relative obscurity into the policy limelight. At the Bank, she had been a mere research administrator, staff rather than line management. The *Miracle* project helped her into one of the premier executive spots among the international financial institutions. She went from being in charge of eighty-five economists in the Policy Research Department to running the major regional development bank for Latin America, with a staff of 1,798. In August 1993, Birdsall was appointed executive vice-president and chief operational officer at the Inter-American Development Bank (IDB), making her the second-ranking officer there after IDB President Enrique Iglesias. The United States had the right to nominate the IDB's No. 2, and Summers recommended her for the job over several other candidates. As emissary of the U.S. Treasury Department, Birdsall stood in for Iglesias when he was indisposed and articulated U.S. policy for aid to Latin America.[119]

At the IDB, Birdsall began running seminars and conferences on "lessons" of East Asia for Latin America. The conference series was introduced by Birdsall to provide "intellectual leadership" in Latin America, part of the "worldbankalization" of the IDB, according to *Institutional Investor,* and Page was an honored guest at many of them.[120] He remained close to Birdsall after she left the Bank. In 1994, Birdsall invited him to preside over a Japan-funded conference in Santiago, Chile, examining the topic, "The *East Asian Miracle* and the Latin American Consensus: Can the Twain Ever Meet?"[121] In 1996, she encouraged the Clinton team to consider Page as the U.S. nominee to head a proposed Middle East Development Bank (MEDB).[122]

The MEDB never got off the ground, yet the fact that Page was considered at all was certainly because of his involvement in the *Miracle* project, as well as his constant harping on the theme of the East Asian "lessons." In 1994, the World Economic Forum, working closely with the World Bank, launched a series of "Middle East/North Africa Economic Conferences" with the idea of reducing tension by holding out the carrot of economic growth. The East Asian model was a frequent topic. In 1997, at the fourth of the World Economic Forum conferences in Qatar, Dervis, obviously coached by Page, urged Middle Eastern policy makers to consider the way East Asian economies had built positive "neighborhood effects" by emulating Japan.[123] "Simply put, the idea behind the 'neighborhood effect' is that the consequences of good (or bad) policies and performance in one country can affect (or infect, hence the term 'contagion') the performance of neighboring countries to the point where a group of countries (an economic 'neighborhood') grows faster (or more slowly) than we would expect it to simply on the basis of individual countries' policies. . . . If one country adopts a given set of policies, neighbors follow suit leading to a regional multiplier effect."[124]

For the first few months after its publication, the Japanese publicly hissed and fumed. Initially, there was fury that the Bank had rejected industrial policy, despite the bone it had thrown to export promotion. Then, the *Miracle*'s possibilities seemed to dawn upon them. Though falling short of vindicating the Japanese-policy approach, it had done something equally important. The debate had been legitimized, and it opened the way for the Japanese to present their model as a work in progress.

The lack of a concrete outline made it possible to continuously add or subtract to it. Indeed, the invitation to debate the subject was even more useful as an open-ended construct than as a signed-and-sealed endorsement by the World Bank. Pragmatically, the Japanese considered the *East Asian Miracle* a success. It affirmed that the successful Asian economies had shared a common approach and followed strategies that were different from the Anglo-American economies. This was enough of a wedge for the Japanese to begin moving ahead with their own reports, conferences, and workshops, many conducted inside the international financial institutions. The *East Asian Miracle* had become Japan's entrée, and Tokyo pushed it mercilessly.

The Miracle Man

Japanese who met curly headed John Page when they encountered him in early 1992, on the first of many research trips to Japan, looked upon him as a typical World Bank apparatchik. His manner of wide-eyed, note-taking innocence reinforced the impression of malleability. At worst he would be a nuisance, more likely a pushover.

Page proved to be much more than that, shaping the *Miracle* report around a complex agenda that reflected more bureaucratic agility than intellectual courage, yet nonetheless had a powerful impact. As a study in ambiguity it has few equals. It was a statement for industrial policy yet not for industrial policy, twisting its basic assertions in knots so impenetrable that the Japanese initially took it as an insult. Only gradually did they catch on to the ways in which it would prove useful. In December 1993, senior Japanese officials who had sponsored the project shunned Page at the Japanese book launch in Tokyo, convinced that he had delivered a knockout punch to their aspirations. The Keidanren tie and invitations came much later.

Angriest of all was Shiratori Masaki, who had put his personal reputation on the line in sponsoring the *East Asian Miracle* project. It was not just the distinction between the "good" Southeast Asian and "bad" Northeast Asian models that incensed him; he had his eye on issues raised in the appendix to the volume that had sweeping implications. These were derived from a set of econometric proofs that Page had produced with Brown University economist Howard Pack.

This analysis, based on a concept called total factor productivity, invariably known by its acronym, TFP, focused on the "residual" or mysterious element in productivity growth left over after accounting for productivity gains from increased inputs of labor and capital. Page and Pack's analysis found that TFP had accounted for one-third of the growth of the HPAEs but there was little evidence of higher TFP in specific industrial sectors that had been subject to government promotion.

This was adding insult to the injury inflicted by the report's historical analysis. Privately, Shiratori told colleagues, the Japanese government had wasted its $10,000 consulting fee to Pack.[125] Mystifying a good number of his audience at the book launch, consisting largely of Japanese officials and businesspeople, Shiratori roundly attacked their conclusions. He said scathingly that the Bank's disregard for industrial policy "shows the limits" of its "functional" approach. The Bank "says that picking and nurturing specific industries are not only theoretically wrong but also beyond the ability of government. However, comparative advantage should be regarded as a dynamic notion rather than a static one as the neo-classicists argue. The trial and error inherent in current market-driven industrialization is too risky and expensive considering the scarcity of resources. Thus, Japan's industrial structure did not 'evolve largely in a manner consistent with market forces and factor intensity based upon comparative advantage,' as the Report claims. Rather, the government actively intervened to develop specific industries with high growth potential. We picked winners such as steel, shipbuilding, synthetic fiber, petrochemicals, automobiles, machinery and parts, electric appliances and electronics, and so forth, most of which were infant industries in Japan at that time. I totally disagree with the Report's statement that 'many infant industries have never grown up.'"[126]

Debates over TFP are esoteric even by economists' standards. Oddly, the controversy over Asian TFP eventually became one of the main levers forcing the Bank and the Japanese closer together. The Bank had to defend itself against critics who claimed that Asian success had nothing to do with productivity, a more extreme view than the World Bank had taken, and as a result the Bank ended up emphasizing the positive results of the Pack-Page regressions, rather than the negative tests showing low productivity growth for sectors targeted by industrial policy.

Development economists use total factor productivity analysis to measure the overall efficiency or productivity of economies, defined as the output per unit of all inputs.[127] TFP is the residual when increases in labor and capital inputs are subtracted from economic growth, and economists use regression analysis to isolate and quantify it, which is easier said than done. Economists could go on for hours about data sets and conclusions in a rarefied version of the old thesis, "garbage in, garbage out." Nonetheless, TFP analysis provided one of the few tools to screen for the impact on growth of factors that increase efficiency, such as technological innovation and education, and, more questionably, industrial policy.

Page was familiar with the work of Alwyn Young, who had written a highly regarded article claiming that TFP growth had made a "next to nil" contribution to Singapore's growth between 1960 and 1985, while TFP growth contributed "substantially" to the success of laissez-faire Hong Kong. Young concluded that Singapore's industrial policy was to blame. "I advance the notion that Singapore is a victim of its own targeting policies, which are increasingly driving the economy ahead of its learning maturity into the production of goods in which it has lower and lower productivity," Young wrote.[128]

Page and Pack's analysis of TFP essentially reflected the overall philosophy of the *East Asian Miracle* on industrial policy—that its benefits were limited to the export sector—although it did not go as far as Young in blaming industrial policy for undermining economic efficiency. Indeed, critics who sided with Young charged that the *East Asian Miracle* used an artificially low rate of return to capital in its growth calculations, effectively increasing the contribution of TFP.[129] The reason for this was the breadth of the Bank's data set, which used information from 133 developing economies, most considerably poorer than the East Asian group.

A year after publication of the *East Asian Miracle*, Young's TFP critique of East Asian growth hit the big time when Paul Krugman cited his work in an article in *Foreign Affairs* that gained wide attention.[130] Krugman compared East Asian growth to the growth record of the Soviet Union in the 1950s, arguing that it was similarly based on mobilizing labor and capital on a large scale: "Asian growth, like that of the Soviet Union in its high-growth era, seems to be driven by extraordinary growth in inputs like labor and capital rather than by gains in efficiency," Krugman wrote.[131] Meanwhile, Young had published several more essays in the same vein. These broadened his analysis to include South Korea and Taiwan.[132] Even the *Wall Street Journal* took up the theme, siding with Krugman and Young.[133]

The Japanese went ballistic after Krugman's article appeared, just as they were beginning preparations to host Asian leaders at the 1995 ministerial and summit meetings of the Asia Pacific Economic Cooperation grouping (APEC). In a Japanese-language publication prepared for Japan's APEC year by the Economic Planning Agency (EPA), an entire chapter was devoted to refuting the Krugman article.[134] Other economists complained about a "fundamental indeterminacy in measurement" of the TFP numbers.[135] It created questions even in the investment banking community, which then was engaged in promoting the Asian bull market.

Larry Hathaway, chief economist for East Asia at UBS Securities in Singapore, was asked by his senior management to investigate the Krugman-Young approach "to ask if Asian growth is sustainable—basically if this is where we should put our money."[136] UBS used the same mathematics as

Young but updated the data set to include another five years (Young's cut-off point was 1985, based on the Summers & Heston data series). The UBS economists found that the Asian economies had stronger productivity or TFP gains than Young's studies had indicated, with Hong Kong, Taiwan, Thailand, Singapore, and Korea ranking among the top twelve countries in productivity gains between 1970 and 1990. Echoing Young and Krugman, however, they admitted that most of Asian growth was because of extremely high levels of investment, or in Krugman's terms, "capital accumulation."[137]

For many years thereafter, Asia's critics would point to Krugman as an early prophet of Asia's demise. When the Asian financial crisis broke in July 1997, headline writers gleefully recycled the title of his 1994 article, the "Myth of Asia's Miracle." In August 1995, at a conference organized by the Korean Institute for Industrial Economics and Trade in Seoul, Krugman elaborated on his "Myth of Asia's Miracle" thesis. He distinguished among three "schools of thought" on East Asian growth: mainstream, revisionists, and cultural determinists. By mainstream, he meant "commentators who regard Asian growth essentially as a showcase for the power of the free market." He described the revisionists as those who saw a "consistent 'Asian system' of sophisticated government intervention that is the driving force behind rapid growth." The cultural determinists argued that "something about Asian culture—perhaps the Confucian legacy—provides the basis for high economic performance."[138] Krugman associated himself with a fourth way of looking at the East Asian economies, as failures of the free market, facing a limited future.

This was too much for Page to take. He had also spoken at the conference in Seoul, but been unable to engage in debate with Krugman, who delivered his remarks then rushed off to get on a plane. A few months later, an *Asian Wall Street Journal* correspondent asked Page for his response to the critique. He took sharp exception to Krugman's assertion that Asians had achieved their miracle through cheap and abundant labor supplies and captive capital. Krugman had said that the *East Asian Miracle* report even proved his point. Replied Page, "Careful reading of the report doesn't support his thesis, and it's a stretch to say that it does."[139]

Not quite as quickly as the Japanese, and from an entirely different perspective than Krugman, Asian experts went for the jugular, charging that the report displayed stunning ignorance of the pervasive role of government in East Asian economies. Within months, critiques of the *East Asian Miracle* had become a cottage industry.[140] Dani Rodrik, an institutional economist and one of the more balanced of the critics, described the Bank as a "self-declared victor" in its attempt to wrestle Japanese-style industrial policy to the ground. "Even as it acknowledges extensive government activism, the

Bank finds in the East Asian experience a confirmation of its market-friendly approach to policy, encompassing macroeconomic stability, human-capital formation, openness to international trade, and an environment that fosters private investment and competition. It also argues that most of the interventions that worked in the HPAEs are either too risky or too impractical in the 1990s for other developing countries to imitate."[141]

Alice Amsden, the author of a massive study on Korea's guided economy, wrote that "a step in the right direction would have been to begin to explore and analyze systematically which of East Asia's supporting institutions has served investment, education, and exports especially well with an eye toward what must be done to modify these institutions to make them work elsewhere. Instead, like Narcissus, all the Bank was capable of doing in its *Report* was seeing the image of its own 'market-friendly' policies in East Asia's fortunes."[142]

"All in all, the evidence is either unbelievably weak or altogether inadmissible to support the *Report*'s controversial conclusion that industrial policy in the world's industrial policy meccas was 'largely ineffective,'" Amsden wrote. "One comes away from the *East Asian Miracle* with a sense of just how powerful the Bank is. The contest between the revisionists and the orthodox is like a small firm confronting a multinational enterprise, or a guerrilla army engaging a nuclear power. . . . Whether top management will open the Bank's windows to empirically grounded ideas and try to make the East Asian model work elsewhere is another issue, and one that raises the question of whether it is possible to reform the Bank from within, as the Japan Delegation is trying to do." Amsden concluded with an ominous warning: "There are examples in history of guerrilla armies winning, and small firms trouncing the large ones, depending on the quality of the product. Time will tell about the power of the 'market-friendly' versus the East Asian approach."[143]

Joining Rodrik and Amsden was Robert Wade, an economic anthropologist who had worked at the Bank in the 1980s. Like them, Wade saw the *East Asian Miracle* as a cynical and hypocritical exercise, part of a sinister effort by rich countries to handicap poor countries interested in following Japan's highly successful example. In a 1994 paper with the amusing title, "The World Bank and the Art of Paradigm Maintenance," Wade argued that the *East Asian Miracle* served "to maximize commitment internally and authoritative reputation externally. It may not maximize truth."[144] At the 1993 launch of the Japanese edition, he aired his conspiracy theory: "I worry that the Bank's refusal to countenance selective industrial policies for other countries reflects an unwillingness on the part of the Bank to help countries in Southeast Asia and Latin America, an unwillingness to help them enter heavy and chemical industries or industries with relatively high entry barriers," he said. "One can imagine that the Bank may be unwilling to do this because it is governed by representatives from countries in the West that already have excess capacity in these industries and that are actually not very happy to see countries elsewhere develop these industries."[145]

Yet, Wade also was among the first to recognize the foothold that the report offered to the Japanese. Having worked at the Bank, he was intimately familiar with the committee process that lay behind the book, and had documented the intense negotiations behind the scenes. The project team had been under heavy pressure from management to produce a report that did not challenge what he called the Bank's "metapolicy." But the report was also "a compromise between the well-established World Bank view and the newly powerful Japanese view," he wrote. "The result is heavily weighted towards the Bank's established position, and legitimizes the Bank's continuing advice to low-income countries to follow the 'market-friendly' policies apparently vindicated by East Asia's success. But the document also contains enough pro-industrial policy statements to allow the Japanese to claim a measure of success."[146]

Wade offered numerous examples of what he meant by this in his 1994 article and a draft text of it circulated earlier. He said that Page and Birdsall had "grafted on" references to the "market-friendly" approach—instructing an editor to write a few paragraphs on it at the last minute—and eliminated references to "strategy" and "strategic." Any mention of strategy was associated with arguments in favor of industrial policy, and certainly within the Bank, some would view use of the words as a political statement. The original title of the book included the subtitle, *Public Policy and Strategic Growth*, which was changed to *Economic Growth and Public Policy*. Wade claimed that the changes were made after a heated meeting with Vinod Thomas and other economists from the East Asian vice-presidency, who demanded that Page and Birdsall provide "evidence" that strategic policies could be effective under some conditions.[147]

Page denied that there had been any change in message on the cutting-room floor. Wade "is entitled to his view of my personality and integrity—and that will make interesting reading—but he has a tendency to invent conspiracies even when they do not exist," Page wrote in an e-mail correspondence. "For example: in one of his papers he makes a meal out of the 'fact' that senior management removed the word 'strategic' from the title of the book. In fact the working title of the book and research project approved after all by the self-same senior management was 'Strategies for Rapid Growth—Public Policy and the East Asian Miracle.' It was changed because Al Imhoff my editor thought that it was dull and Bankese. I agreed; hence the EAM [*East Asian Miracle*] as published. No one in senior management gave a shit one way or the other." He added that less than 100 words had been changed to meet the objections.[148]

Page came under heavy personal criticism. He had done most of his field-work as a young economist in Latin America and Africa and had no serious claims to expertise on East Asia. He could startle South Americans with his Andes-accented Spanish, and he knew his way around Ghana, Egypt, and India, but like most economists of his generation, Page had disavowed re-gional expertise. Like certain types of foreign correspondent who are sup-posed to be able to parachute into a crisis unencumbered by local knowledge, the World Bank's ideal economist in the 1980s was versed in econometrics and price theory. Empirical knowledge was viewed as an impediment. The closest that Page came to Asian expertise was a 1987 book co-authored with British economist Ian Little, Page's teacher at Oxford, on the dangers of industrial policy as practiced in India. This was like throwing gasoline on the fire as far as his critics were concerned, because the South Asian expe-rience with government intervention was as disastrous as East Asia's was successful.[149]

Chalmers Johnson, who joined one of the early workshops that was part of the research project, was particularly disdainful. "With people like John Page making policy, the United States deserves what it is going to get," he wrote. "As John Page knows well, because I was present having been asked by the Asians and the Bank to make a presentation at one of his seminars leading up to the World Bank report, the charge to him and the other authors by his supervisors within the bank was to explain East Asian wealth in *any other terms* than political or differential capabilities of states, because that was destructive both to American theory and the American state. That is exactly what the Miracle Economies report does and why it has not impressed anyone who knows something about the East Asian economies," Johnson continued. "The lesson of East Asia's wealth is state-guided capitalism. The effectiveness of Japan's theoretical research may remain 'to be seen,' but the accuracy of the theoretical research of [Alice] Amsden, Wade, Woo Jung-en [Meredith Woo-Cumings] and other theorists who were ignored by the World Bank but who, differing from John Page, can do research in East Asia with-out hiring a guide dog is no longer in doubt."[150]

Helen Hughes, dean of development economics at Australia National University and a former World Bank official, sniffed that the *East Asian Miracle* was a "muddle" and said Page had bungled the job. Within the Bank, Vinod Thomas and his colleagues in the East Asian vice-presidency weighed in with papers that contradicted Page's findings. Thomas wrote that the high growth of East Asia was "rooted in low distortions and moderate interven-tions that are associated with better performance everywhere."[151]

The most stinging critique, however, came from Page's own teacher and mentor, Ian Little, at Oxford; he publicly lamented his failure, saying he obviously hadn't taught Page well enough. Although the remark was made jokingly, and the two men remained friends, one of the great names in neoclassic economics was calling Page incompetent. "Ian can attack hard, especially if he believes his opponent is talking or writing dangerous nonsense that could be influential," wrote two of his students, Maurice Scott and Deepak Lal, in the preface to a collection of essays in Little's honor.[152]

Scott and Lal described Little as an "Edwardian gentleman." He had flown as a test pilot for the Royal Air Force and worked in a series of economic policy jobs for the British government, United Nations, and World Bank, mounting one of the first serious critiques of the closely linked policies of import substitution and industrial strategy. These policies were favored by most developing countries in the 1960s, along with the United States and the major development lending agencies. Little helped popularize the application of business tools such as cost-benefit analysis to developing economies; Page's contribution to his festschrift was an essay using "total factor productivity analysis" to demonstrate that the main tools of rapid growth—protection from foreign competition, subsidized credit, and direct public investment in industry—had no measurable impact on productivity. Page's work on the *East Asian Miracle* ran directly counter to such ideas.[153]

Page had his own way of fending off criticism both from the Asia experts and the neoclassicists. He called the two groups, "mystics" and "fundamentalists." "As with those attempting to explain religious phenomena, economists analyzing the 'miracle' of East Asia's growth tend to fall into two camps," he told a Tokyo audience in 1994. "Fundamentalists argued that East Asian success was because of policies that allowed for efficient allocation of physical and human capital." Mystics gave credit to "activist government policies to alter industrial structure and promote technological learning, sometimes at the expense of static allocative efficiency."[154] Page called the Japanese "mystic fundamentalists" and said they were somewhere in-between. "A lot of Japan's success is because of better savings and investment behavior, but in addition, there is this effort to alter comparative advantage, to have stratagems for productivity improvement—things not recommended by neoclassical economists as completely kosher and desirable," he said in 1994.[155]

Indeed, Page's skin was thick enough to withstand criticism from the Japanese, Asia specialists, and even his old professor. The same narcissistic qualities that made it possible for him to ignore the critics also led him to view the *Miracle* as a vehicle through which to shape the Bank's relations with Japan, a principal client, and to advance his own career. The book reflects Page's vision of its mission, which was to tweak but not fundamentally change the

Bank's line on structural adjustment and minimal government intervention. It used statistics and case studies creatively without referencing the broader historical or institutional context of East Asia, and avoided detailed proofs of its basic assertions, which in any case were frequently ambiguous.

Page claimed that his appointment to the project was no more than coincidence.

> As nearly as I can figure out, I actually came to lead the *East Asian Miracle* by accident. I was recruited to the number two slot in the research department primarily to relieve the then director Johannes Linn (now a VP) of the burden of dealing with the major increase in emphasis on lending and developing the private sector. Johannes was spending so much of his time negotiating with the International Finance Corp. and various operational parts of the Bank that he had no time for managing research.
>
> Then, before I could take the job [World Bank President Lewis] Preston started making noises about creating a vice-presidency for the private sector (which we now have) so there was some question as to what I would do (to the point where at one time I was afraid that they would abolish the position before I got there). Larry Summers' solution was to say "he will do this private sector stuff as needed and can also work on the *East Asian Miracle*." I doubt that I was the first choice; he and I don't really get along that well. But when Nancy succeeded Johannes, she backed me with Larry to have full scope to do the job. I don't think either of them subsequently regretted it, but it casts some doubt on the finely drawn selection process that Robert [Wade] has produced.
>
> By the way, I frequently tell Robert that for those of us involved in the project, events to which he attaches great significance as evidence of the influence of the monolithic World Bank bureaucracy on the *East Asian Miracle* seemed much more random and chaotic at the time they were happening. There was never a sense that I was directed by the Japanese nor was I directed by Lew Preston or by any senior person in the World Bank. I was left alone for a year with the notion that if I hung myself that would be fine.[156]

Page described himself as "a pragmatic 'anti' on selective industrial policies, largely because I do not believe that most countries (the United States and contemporary Japan included) have the institutional integrity to avoid capture. But I am big on export-push and technology policies for LDCs (less developed economies)—there are high pay-offs and fewer institutional demands." When Page moved into the Bank's Industrial Strategy and Policy Division—whose role was to persuade governments such as India's to dismantle subsidies and other staples of industrial policy—his colleagues gave him a two-by-four with a plaque reading: "If Symptoms Persist, Call Dr. Page." The opposite side continued: "Warning: Do not use on perpetual infants." He kept it along with a hard hat on top of a bookcase in his office—the latter presumably to ward off rocks thrown by disgruntled employees of infant industries forced to shoulder the burdens of competition.[157]

As an individual, Page seemed more a product of the mixed-up liberalism of the 1970s than the black-and-white absolutes that characterized the intellectual climate of the 1960s, when he was an undergraduate. He had few firm convictions, other than an instinctive self-reliance. One college friend remembered Page as "always having a crew cut when everybody else had long hair. He sort of ran against the crowd."[158] Within the Bank, he was a quirky individualist, prone to the occasional outrageous remark, proud of his gifts with language in an organization that conducted most of its rational discourse in numbers and statistics.

Page grew up as the only child of a tight-knit family in a middle-class suburb in the Santa Clara Valley. His father worked for the Federal Bureau of Investigation, not a popular profession in the 1960s on a California campus. Graduating from high school in California, his mother wanted him to attend nearby Berkeley, part of the University of California system that waived tuition for residents. Page insisted on putting himself through Stanford instead, Berkeley's intellectual—and expensive—rival. In order to pay for Stanford, Page applied for a Reserve Officer's Training Corps Fellowship but that meant a four-year obligation to the U.S. Navy, which was deferred until after he returned from Oxford, where he was able to sit for the doctoral examination after his two years as a Rhodes scholar. He had done his undergraduate degree in economics; at Oxford he was at Nuffield College, where he met Ian Little. Eventually Page worked off his debt to the Navy by serving as a navigator on the USS *Kansas City*, a transport ship. The four years, though pleasant, came at the expense of a fast-track academic career.

In 1977, Page returned to Stanford to its innovative Food Research Institute. He then moved on to an untenured position as associate professor at the Woodrow Wilson School of Public and International Affairs at Princeton in 1978. Page was still under thirty, yet discouraged about his prospects for tenure. In 1980, he traded in his academic credentials and went to the World Bank. Meeting him by chance years later, Henry Bienan, former dean of the Woodrow Wilson School, later president of Northwestern University, recalled Page as "dripping with distinction" during his brief tenure at Princeton. In his mind's eye, however, Page was not doing as well as he had expected.

Page was not entirely devoid of knowledge of East Asia when he was tapped for the *Miracle* project. The region was for him a subject of romantic curiosity. As a young naval officer, he explored Japan during layovers at

U.S. naval bases in the islands. During one stay at Sasebo, on the west coast of Kyushu, Page took a slow local train across the island to visit Usuki Bay, the tiny coastal town in Oita Prefecture, where Will Adams, a British pilot known as "Miura Anjin," had washed ashore in the year 1600. Adams learned Japanese and became an advisor to Tokugawa Ieyasu, the first of the Tokugawa shoguns. His story had been popularized by James Clavell's novel and the television series, *Shogun*, and Page was fascinated by the story. He brought a little bit of Japan home with him by collecting modern Japanese prints, and by the time he started work on the *Miracle* project, his collection had become substantial. His friendship with Nishimizu, too, owed something to a naïve interest in Japan.

At age forty-five, Page retained the athlete's and naval officer's carriage; he had a nautical manner of squaring his shoulders and gazing at the horizon good-humoredly. A well-set man, tending to overweight, his sandy hair streaked with gray, Page had enormous physical energy. During the eighty-hour weeks of the *East Asian Miracle* project, he was undergoing chemotherapy for a cancer first detected in 1985. His vanity got the best of him at times; he left the Concorde baggage tags on an elegant handmade briefcase that looked like S.T. Dupont but was made in Argentina, and bragged shamelessly of his sexual exploits. For a while Page juggled women recklessly and conducted a bitter, contested divorce that, like the chemotherapy, was part of the background to the *Miracle* project. He liked joking and working with women, a rarity in the macho environment of the Bank. Birdsall's appreciation of him may have had something to do with his easy charm. He dismissed his critics but seemed without rancor toward them. Nor was Page shy about claiming that the intellectual line of the book was his.

The Japanese eventually dropped their pique with the miracle man. As early as the launch of the Japanese translation of the *East Asian Miracle* in December 1993, where Shiratori vented his spite, Ishikawa's student Yanagihara Toru expressed a differing point of view. To be sure, Yanagihara criticized the book as a rehash of the Bank's 1991 WDR, with its injunction to governments to behave in a "market-friendly" manner and follow the "three commandments": "Government intervention has to be applied reluctantly, cautiously, and openly." But Yanagihara, who had spent time at the World Bank in the early 1980s and understood its convoluted politics, was also among the first to sense the possibilities.

"The central question is whether there is anything new in the East Asian miracle report," he asked rhetorically. "The answer is yes, and no." He then went on to commend the Bank's research team for the concept of "contest-based competition" and its endorsement of "export-push" policies. However slender, these concepts provided a bridge to Japan's vision of government-led, market-based economic management.[159]

In the World Bank of the 1980s, at the height of free-market chauvinism, with Reagan in the White House a few blocks down Pennsylvania Avenue from the Bank's headquarters, nobody had dared to question the universality of the neoclassical economic model. The notion of competing models was taboo, except in the sense that other models were supposed to be dead. Page had given the Japanese a platform in the *East Asian Miracle*, and within a short time "lessons from East Asia" would become stock repertoire at the international financial institutions, from the IMF to the IDB. The "lessons" became the outline of a new East Asian model, a family of variants on Japan's economic experience.

Page argued that Shiratori was more pleased with the results of the study than he let on at first. "I think we actually went beyond his expectations," Page said in a 1994 interview. "My own sense is that it was part of broader Japanese government aspirations to have a piece that was endorsed by the World Bank, that got through the system and said something other than that there were all these lovely free market economies. That was why they were willing to accept that I would put together a team without a Japanese on it."[160]

In Page's published work, he stuck to the Bank's official line that government intervention was not a part of the East Asian success formula. In an article in the prestigious National Bureau of Economic Research journal in 1994, Page wrote that "export orientation rather than selective intervention played the dominant role in increasing economy-wide TFP growth rates."[161] As chief economist for the Middle East and North Africa, he enjoined Middle Eastern economies to learn from East Asia by "educating all the people, pushing exports, shrinking the state, and empowering the private sector."[162]

In speaking to Japanese audiences, however, Page gave considerably more credit to industrial policy, particularly in the context of export promotion. It was a change in emphasis, but an important one. At the launch of the Japanese edition in December 1993, Page finessed one of the central messages of the *Miracle*—that even if export promotion had worked for the Northeast Asian economies, times had changed and developing countries should anticipate resistance from the industrial markets of the West. "It really boils down to two questions," he told the audience. "Will markets be there if other developing countries want to try an export-push strategy, and even if they are there, will they have access to those markets? We looked very carefully at these issues and came to the conclusion that the answer was yes on both counts." Page went on to add that export-promotion strategies needed to be

"GATT-friendly," yet the nuance was quite different than in the *East Asian Miracle* itself.[163]

Most flattering of all, at that 1993 conference Page underlined a feature that the *East Asian Miracle* had not stressed—the role of Japan as model. "Relative geographical proximity is the most obvious shared characteristic of the successful Asian economies," he said. "East Asian economies have clearly benefited from the kind of non-formal economic linkages geographic proximity encourages, including in trade and investment flows. It is also likely that geography facilitated the adoption of imitative strategies, in both public and private sector activity. Policy imitation—specifically of Japan's industrial strategy—was an explicit objective in Korea, and Malaysia."[164]

Page borrowed his thoughts on geography from Peter Petri, at Brandeis University, who wrote one of the fifty-five background papers for the *East Asian Miracle*. Petri said that while South Korea, Malaysia, and Singapore took notes on Japanese industrial strategy, they took notes on different things: "Korea borrowed Japanese techniques for building large trading companies and directing the structure of industry, Malaysia focused on developing heavy industry, and Singapore on Japanese experience in penetrating foreign markets and shifting industry to knowledge-intensive branches," he wrote.[165] Petri argued that geographical proximity helped create economic linkages, both in trade within the region and in favorable "externalities" that came into play when the United States began to restrict Japanese products, opening up the U.S. market for fledgling Asian producers.

At an EPA conference in November 1994, a year after the *East Asian Miracle*'s publication, Page claimed that East Asia had adopted a "functional" approach to growth that attempted to accommodate both the "mystic" and the "fundamentalist" camps. "If industrial policy was not responsible for East Asia's unusual success in achieving productivity change, what was? The World Bank's answer is manufactured exports. Active promotion of manufactured exports was a key strategic objective of governments in East Asia."[166]

One sunny morning in 1995, Page and I shared a cab from the Colony Surf Hotel, in the shadow of Diamond Head, to the East-West Center in Honolulu. It was the last day of a Japanese government-funded conference on "lessons" from Japan for developing countries. Page had been the key speaker. I was in a giddy mood. "John," I said, "You know the Deming Prize? One of these days the Japanese are going to institute an annual prize for outstanding government interventions, and they will name it after you—the John Page Prize for Industrial Policy."

My companion laughed. The Deming Prize is Japan's most prestigious award for factory innovations, named for W. Edwards Deming, the Bell Labs consultant who popularized American quality-control strategies in Japan during the U.S. Occupation of Japan in the 1950s. By 1995, two years after publication of the *East Asian Miracle*, it was already becoming evident that the book, though controversial, had become the cornerstone of a debate in which the existence of a "Japanese model" was taken for granted.

If anyone had invented the Japanese model, in fact, it had been the plump little bureaucrat whom nobody took seriously at first. In the years between its publication and the onset of the financial crisis in 1997, the *East Asian Miracle* cemented the idea that the successful Asian economies had followed a similar pattern. This was part of the *Miracle*'s argument that the Asian economies had gotten their economic "fundamentals" right, but people remembered the conclusion without recalling all of the logic that went into it. So, for example, a 1995 *Economist* leader proclaimed, "to regard the booming economies of South-East Asia simply as pupils in a Japanese master class is to miss the point. The economic stars of the region—Singapore, Thailand, Malaysia, and Indonesia—have followed a distinctive path to development. As a result, they are now exporting not just goods, but ideas."[167]

Samurai Strategists

Compared to the Americans involved on the *Miracle* project, with their infighting and self-involvement, the Japanese knew exactly what they were after. Their side of the story began with two brilliant, irascible, and dedicated Japanese bureaucrats, Shiratori Masaki and Kubota Isao. Their game plan was to get the World Bank off Japan's back, and they succeeded. The rest of the project built on itself.

In the late 1980s, Shiratori was vice-president of Japan's Overseas Economic Cooperation Fund, which provides most of the soft loans that Japan extends to governments of developing countries. Kubota had been in charge of lending policy at OECF, as managing director of the Coordination Department from June 1989 to June 1992. Subsequently, he returned to the Ministry of Finance as a senior deputy director-general of MOF's International Finance Bureau, then became head of the powerful tax bureau in 1995.

Technically an independent agency, the OECF was considered an organ of MOF and its senior executives, such as Shiratori and Kubota, shuttled back and forth between the two agencies. From 1989 to 1992, the two used key positions—Kubota in the OECF and Shiratori as executive director for Japan at the World Bank in Washington, D.C.—to pressure the World Bank to open its gates to Japanese-style industrial policy. They shared a low opinion of World Bank economists. Kubota said dismissively, "Most are Ph.D.'s with no feel for the real side of the economy." Contempt, however, did not stop them from using the Bank's economists to make a point.

Kubota and Shiratori began their campaign in 1989, after several years of clashes between the World Bank and OECF over the latter's lending policy in Southeast Asia. In some respects, the disputes over Japan's Southeast Asian loans were more symbolic than real, and Japan usually ended up caving in and modifying its loan conditions. Nonetheless, they gave Kubota and Shiratori the excuse they were looking for to launch a fundamental attack on Bank policy.

The technical issues between the OECF and the World Bank went back to the late 1980s, when the Bank was in the full flush of enthusiasm for structural adjustment policies. Structural adjustment was both a reaction to the failure of Bank policies in the 1960s and 1970s and a reflection of the free-market ideological excesses of three Republican administrations in the United States. One way to visualize what the World Bank meant by structural adjustment in the 1980s is by looking at it as the mirror opposite of Japanese industrial policy. Developing countries were expected to tune their financial systems to global clearing rates for the value of currencies and interest rates, and the free market would take care of choosing "growth" sectors.

In contrast, Japanese lending tended to be for large-scale infrastructure projects that would create a favorable environment for industry. Japan did not attach conditions to its loans, although the process stacked the deck in the favor of Japanese contractors and consultants. Borrowers formally requested aid based on feasibility studies that were almost always carried out by Japanese companies who were plugged into the OECF network. Such manipulation, however, was a far cry from the Bank's habit of re-engineering monetary and fiscal policy of borrowing countries.

Japan's differences with the World Bank were partly because of the perception that the Bank represented American interests. The entire history of the Japanese aid program could be read as a series of moves to allay U.S. criticism or meet U.S. demands, starting with economic aid to Southeast Asia delivered as war reparations after the San Francisco Peace Treaty in 1952. In the late 1980s, however, the Japanese were in a mood to push back.

Said Edward Lincoln, a Brookings Institution economist and former advisor to the U.S. ambassador in Tokyo: "Japan started becoming a sizable aid donor in the late 1970s to mid-1980s. They felt under pressure to assume more of the burden of being an advanced country by coughing up more foreign aid money. If that's what it took to join the club, they would do it. If you're lending to lots of developing countries, who are you lending to? To governments. Then the Reagan administration comes along and says, we're encouraging socialism, and that's not good. The Reagan administration puts pressure on the World Bank to employ conditionality. But the Japanese couldn't give a damn what the countries were doing—whether they were socialist or free market. To be cynical, they were just as happy being involved with government control and all the sleaze that went with it. It was good for business. After the fall of Philippine president Ferdinand Marcos, when papers were taken out of the palace documenting kickbacks in foreign aid—five percent off the top—to the Marcoses, the Japanese were perfectly happy. They have no Foreign Corrupt Practices Act. The Japanese weren't interested in putting pressure on the system. They worried about American pressure, and a system dominated by the Americans." [168]

A graduate student at Columbia University, Anne Emig wrote her dissertation on Japan's efforts to develop an "alternative approach" to structural adjustment after several years at the JEXIM in the late 1980s. She argued that Kubota and Shiratori wanted only to get the Bank to let Japan alone in Asia, rather than introduce a fundamental change in Bank philosophy. "Japan aimed not to overthrow the prevailing neoclassical orthodoxy, but rather to get the Bank to adjust its lending approach at the margins," she wrote. "The Japanese needed the World Bank too much to divorce itself from structural adjustment lending totally; besides, Government of Japan officials understand the Third World realities enough to know that, despite its flaws, structural adjustment lending addresses important economic needs. In reality, the Government of Japan continued to be the number one source of structural adjustment lending cofinancing dollars throughout its critique of the Bank.

"Tokyo also sought tacit recognition of its leading role in promoting growth and development in Asia. In essence, Japanese officials wanted the World Bank to admit that Japan knows what it is doing in East Asia; that Japanese aid programs in the region may deviate from the approaches preferred by the Bank but that does not mean they stem from economic dim-wittedness; instead, Japan's approach to aid in Asia derives from a reasoned, pragmatic review of historical and empirical evidence (largely from Japan) of what works in stimulating lasting growth. The Government of Japan wanted greater appreciation (*hyoka*) for both its successful development performance and its extensive development financing programs."[169]

At the World Bank, structural adjustment became institutional gospel after a 1986 position paper by Bank economist Frank Levy advocated reform of a long-standing practice of the Bank to offer soft loans through government development banks, which would then turn over funds at concessional rates to the private sector. This, according to Levy, resulted in distortions of market interest rates that could interrupt efforts at macroeconomic reform instigated by multilateral agencies. The Japanese development community did not immediately react. According to Asanuma Shinji, the head of S.G. Warburg Securities (Japan) and a former World Bank official, lending through government credit institutions was "what OECF—and a lot of others—had been doing for years." Things only got nasty, Asanuma said, when an "over-zealous" Bank official began scrutinizing OECF loans to the Philippines under the $2 billion ASEAN-Japan Development Fund.[170] A bilateral loan offered by the OECF directly to the Philippine government conflicted with terms of another OECF loan cofinanced with the World Bank. In September 1989, the Bank formally demanded that Japan withdraw the bilateral loan and end its entire "two-step" loan program.[171] The phrase, "two-step loan" is unique to the Japanese ODA program, but the practice was clearly the one con-demned in the Levy paper.

The loans themselves were small beer by Japanese or Bank standards. One was a $125 million bilateral credit for small-business development to the Development Bank of the Philippines (DBP). The other was a $300 mil-lion World Bank financial sector adjustment loan cofinanced by the OECF. The bilateral loan allowed DBP to pass the subsidized interest rates of the OECF loan to small-business borrowers. The joint Bank-OECF loan stipu-lated the removal of all interest rate subsidies. An initial inquiry from the Bank asked Japan to remove the pass-along provision of its bilateral loan. The OECF compromised by adjusting the interest charge on the loan up-ward, though the final rate was still two percentage points below the six-month time deposit rates prevailing in the Philippines at the time. But the World Bank did not drop the matter there. In September 1989, a letter under the signature of Moeen A. Qureshi, a senior vice-president of the Bank, later to become prime minister of Pakistan, went to OECF President Nishigaki Akira, demanding that Japan shut down its entire "two-step" loan program.

Qureshi wrote that the OECF's below-market interest rates "could have an adverse impact on development of the financial sector" and "would create unnecessary distortions and set back the financial sector reforms" supported by the Bank's own Financial Sector Adjustment Loan and the IMF's Ex-tended Fund Facility. The Bank backed up its demand with a huge threat. Unless Japan removed the interest rate subsidies supported by the OECF, the World Bank would withdraw its support from the Philippines.

Shiratori had become executive director for Japan at the World Bank in June 1989. Qureshi's letter stunned him. Describing his reactions, Shiratori said, "I was quite upset at the contents. My first reaction was that it was interference with our domestic affairs. Secondly, and more fundamentally, I thought that it was not in the interest of developing nations." In that 1995 interview, Shiratori recalled: "At that time I was in the Finance Ministry. It was a relatively small loan. The World Bank said that if we were to provide subsidized loans to specific groups, it would jeopardize the World Bank's efforts to strengthen the financial sector in the Philippines. They mentioned two faults. One was that we shouldn't target specific groups. Two, we shouldn't provide loans at interest rates at below-market rates. These kinds of loans were quite popular in the sixties and seventies in the World Bank. But the World Bank had had too many failures. When the neo-classicists became dominant, they discarded the whole idea completely."[172]

A short, wiry man in his mid-fifties, Shiratori had once been seen as a fast-tracker in the Japanese Finance Ministry. He graduated from the Law Faculty of Tokyo University, which made him a member of an elite corps within the upper strata of the Japanese bureaucracy—in fact, an elite within an elite. He studied economics at Columbia University in the 1960s. By the mid-1980s, Shiratori was on his way to the Ministry's highest bureacratic office as administrative vice-minister when a loan scandal forced him to make a lateral transfer outside it, to the OECF. He doesn't take disappointments lightly, and Qureshi's high-handed letter brought out all his innate pugnacity.

From that moment on, Shiratori began to gather evidence that would shift the battleground from interest-rate policy to development philosophy. On his travels as executive director, Shiratori says, "Everywhere I went, I was asked to have a secret talk with high-ranking officials from the finance ministries and people. They complained about the diagnoses given by World Bank economists, and wanted to hear about the Japanese experience. They asked me to influence the Bank staff through the Board of Executive Directors."

At meetings of the board, Shiratori would regularly raise his hand and ask the Bank to do more research on industrial policy. He began lunching with Nancy Birdsall, then director of the Bank's Policy Research Department. Meanwhile, Kubota lobbied the MOF to supply funding for a series of studies to be carried out by the Bank's research department to analyze successful East Asian economies including Japan.[173]

Another factor worked to the advantage of Shiratori and Kubota—Japan's increasing prominence within the World Bank as a shareholder. As chief of the International Financial Institutions Division of the Finance Ministry's International Finance Bureau from 1981 to 1984, Shiratori lobbied successfully to raise Japan's shareholding in the World Bank from No. 5 to No. 2. Just as Shiratori moved into the job, in 1981, Japan had become the second-ranking subscriber to the International Development Agency (IDA), the Bank's main soft-loan facility. This gave Shiratori direct experience of the links within the Bank between influence and money.

After a stint at the World Bank in the mid-1980s, Robert Wade began to keep notes on Japan's evolving role within the multilateral financial institutions. Wade wrote that Japan first began to assert a distinct position within the World Bank at about the time that Shiratori assumed the portfolio for International Financial Institutions. Shiratori began to play politics with Japan's position in IDA and made Japan's pledges conditional upon gaining the right to increase its shareholding. Against strong British, French, and U.S. opposition, by 1984 Shiratori had achieved the objective of increasing Japan's shareholding in the larger institution.[174] In 1991, with the simultaneous launch of the PHRD and *East Asian Miracle* project, Shiratori succeeded in buying Japan's way into the all-important policy arena within the Bank.

Shiratori had accomplished his objective, which was to get the Bank's attention. Kubota had the next turn. Kubota's job was to put together a credible policy framework that was identifiably Japanese. He became the architect of an OECF backlash against the World Bank. Six years younger than Shiratori, Kubota was a member of the same elite club of graduates of Tokyo University's Law Faculty. He and Shiratori followed parallel tracks within the Finance Ministry. Kubota headed the International Organizations Division of the International Finance Bureau in the mid-1980s and occupied the same job that Shiratori held just before he became executive director at the World Bank—as senior deputy director-general of the International Finance Bureau. Kubota's precise English bears the mark of two years at Oxford from 1967 to 1969, where, like Shiratori, he studied economics.

Kubota hoped to push the World Bank off its philosophical pedestal by challenging its basic business—the way it lends money. As managing director of the OECF's Coordination Department, Kubota was in charge of the annual bilateral meetings between OECF and the World Bank and used them to begin introducing Japan's themes, first in Fall 1990, then in more formal sessions in May 1991 and April 1992.[175] In a 1991 paper entitled "The Case for Two Step Loans," Kubota laid out Japan's position succinctly. Two-step loans were the type that the World Bank had objected to in the Philippines, because subsidized interest rates were made available to private-sector borrowers. "There seem to be some specific sectors of the economy," Kubota wrote, "the special support for which tends to bring about faster growth. The specific sectors, or I should rather call strategic sectors, may be different according to countries with different human and natural resource endowments and with difference in the economic stage of development. If so, there is a strong case for a special support of the sector."[176]

The Japanese position as outlined by Kubota drew both from Japan's experience with industrial policy and the Akamatsu "flying-geese" school of development in which economies tackled the global market in stages, depending on their "level" of development. Such phased development had the corollary that the lifting of market controls and barriers should be gradual. In other papers, Kubota went on to argue that the Bank's structural adjustment programs forced change on too tight a timetable, failed to account for the diversity of economic circumstance, and put too little emphasis on what he called "balance-of-payments" issues.[177] Kubota described this last as the "central part" of the argument, arguing that the development banks would be left to prop up economies that were destabilized because of currency flight, overheating, and "too rapid" import liberalization.

In a 1992 interview, Kubota acknowledged that disagreements between Japan and the World Bank had been brewing for a "fairly long time." Japan's position was not new, he said; the Japanese government had simply not been "articulate enough." The World Bank tended "to apply the same policy mixes produced for Latin America to Asian countries." In particular, Kubota argued that the World Bank was rushing countries into liberalizing their financial markets before they had the financial institutions to cope. "The World Bank argued that liberalization of financial markets was important, and that the market should determine interest rates," he said. "This was a big difference in philosophy. We asked the World Bank where should the benefits of low interest rate loans go, and they said to making improvements in financial institutions. The OECF thought that was wrong."[178]

In the mid-1990s, as officials were still seething over the Qureshi letter, Nishigaki and Kubota put together a study group to prepare a critique of World Bank structural adjustment lending. Shimomura Yasutami led the team. Shimomura was director of the OECF's Economic Analysis Department and a professor at Saitama University. Coincidentally, Shimomura had a family tie with the "flying-geese" school of Akamatsu and Okita Saburo. His father, Shimomura Osamu, had worked under Okita on the income-doubling plan. Shimomura assembled a team of five outside economists, including Yanagihara Toru, the student of Ishikawa Shigeru and another link to the Akamatsu dynasty. Yanagihara was a member of a study group organized by Ishikawa at the MOF and served as a direct conduit for Ishikawa's ideas to Shimomura's team. Yanagihara also knew and revered Okita Saburo and had met with him frequently in the years before his death, as Okita became increasingly involved with realizing his dream of an Asia-Pacific regional organization. Both Ishikawa and Okita may have looked to the younger, attractive Yanagihara as an able lieutenant who could build on their ideas for the next generation.

It was in the OECF study group that Yanagihara first introduced the theme he would pursue for many years. Yanigihara tried to draw a contrast between the "framework" *(wakugumi)* approach of Anglo-American economics and the "ingredients," or *nakami,* approach of the Japanese. This became the philosophical foundation of the Japanese critique of structural adjustment lending. Anne Emig, who worked closely with Yanagihara while he was still at the Institute for Developing Economies (IDE), described his concept in these terms: "The former is based on rigid, universal theoretical framework for analysis, adopts a short-term macroeconomic focus, and trusts the nature of an economy's industrial structure to the market mechanism. The latter, by contrast, emphasizes flexible implementation of strategic performance targets based on a long-term vision of what type of economy a government would like to create."[179]

According to Robert Wade, the study group was under considerable pressure to wrap up its work in time for the annual World Bank/IMF meetings in Bangkok in October 1991. The group was unable to reach consensus, and in the end Shimomura wrote a draft and presented it to the OECF board even though some members were dissatisfied with his work. The English version of the paper was published in October 1991, five months before it was published in Japanese in the OECF's journal. There was a slapdash quality to both versions, with ambiguous language and poorly developed conclusions.[180]

The paper began with a bold promise to identify "problems" with the World Bank's approach to structural adjustment and to "propose some ideas" to solve them, followed by a statement of credentials—the OECF's Yen 450 billion ($4.5 billion) in funding for the World Bank's structural adjustment financing since the mid-1980s. In none-too-subtle fashion, the "Occasional Paper, no. 1" hammered the Bank for failing to offer safety nets for infant industries and developing-country markets and in general for putting economic efficiency before all other considerations. "Although efficiency and fairness are the major objectives to be pursued in economic policy, there is sometimes trade off between the two," the OECF paper concluded. "In the 1980s, economic theory as well as economic policy were heavily oriented toward the pursuit of efficiency. In this sense, it was a unique period. However, this period has come to an end. What is now needed is a policy well balanced between efficiency and fairness, in order to improve the welfare of the whole society."

The OECF document's tone ranged from the disingenuous ("we are afraid that the financial sector policy of the Bank is too much stressing market mechanism. Isn't it indispensable to have development finance institutions' lendings with subsidized interest rate [sic], under some circumstances, in order to maximize the social welfare?") to the obscure ("the World Bank's approach to structural adjustment may have to be changed reflecting the change of streams"). Even the sympathetic Wade complained, "The quality of argumentation leaves much to be desired." Nonetheless, he added, "The paper is important for what it signifies"—that is, a shot across the bows of free-market economics.[181]

Wade viewed the first OECF "Occasional Paper" (there was never an Occasional Paper, no. 2) as a manifesto for the role of government in markets. Wade summarized the paper's five main points as follows: first, "for a developing country to attain sustainable growth the government must adopt 'measures aiming directly at promoting investment.'" Second, "these measures should be part of an explicit industrial strategy designed to promote leading industries of the future." Third, "directed and subsidized credit has a key role in promoting these industries, because of extensive failures in developing country financial markets." Fourth, "decisions about ownership arrangements, including privatization, need to made in relation to actual economic, political, and social conditions in the country concerned, not with respect to an overriding rule about the universal desirability of privatizing public enterprises. For example, there are legitimate national sentiments about the desirability of foreign ownership." The fifth and last point was that "Japanese fiscal and monetary policies in the postwar era may be worthy of consideration. These were centered on preferential tax treatment and development finance institutions' lendings."[182]

Emig saw the OECF broadside somewhat differently. She argued that it was less an attack on structural adjustment lending than an argument for gradualism and policies leading to sustained growth. She also noticed the paper's emphasis on stages of development and matching policies to the level of institutional maturity. This became an enduring thread in the debate over the next decade, through the trauma of the Asian financial crisis and beyond. It was an argument that justified market protection and gradual liberalization, mirroring Japan's experience in development. In essence, the Japanese argued that market distortion was justified in order to promote growth. On one level, this was undiluted 1930s-era mercantilism. On another, the Japanese position was to match the growing backlash to globalization all too well.

The OECF formally presented its paper at the annual Japan–World Bank meeting in November 1991, attracting almost no attention. Several months later, however, Larry Summers visited Tokyo and met with Kubota and Shimomura. Summers was then chief economist at the World Bank and fresh from the Bank/IMF meeting in Bangkok at which Mieno had petitioned the Bank to conduct a study of the role of government in East Asian growth. Summers told Kubota that the ideas in the OECF paper "warranted further study," and, according to Emig, asked the Japanese to finance a project "to look more extensively into the causes of success in Japan and high-performing East Asian economies."[183] Kubota was able to direct Japan's

PHRD trust fund at the Bank to set aside the money for the *East Asian Miracle* study.

Meanwhile, Kubota and Shiratori had a Bank insider working with them to help make the *East Asian Miracle* project happen. Abe Yoshiaki had joined the Bank's Young Professional's Program in 1967, after finishing a Ph.D. in economics at Cornell, and spent his entire career at the Bank, retiring in 1995. Abe's dissertation had been on Japanese economic policy in the critical post-Occupation period, and he became the first Japanese economist at the Bank to work on Korea. "My God, this is the same as Japan," he remembered his initial reaction. From graduate school onward, Abe had found his professors and other Western economists ignoring basic parallels among the East Asian economies, such as the high savings rate. One professor told him that the data on Japanese savings rates simply had to be wrong. In the early 1980s, Abe had a particularly painful encounter with Anne Krueger, then chief economist at the Bank. At lunch, he boldly proposed that the Bank study the Japanese experience. "Why not the United States or United Kingdom?" Krueger responded coolly. "I don't take your point."[184]

Abe bided his time. In 1991, he became director of the Bank's Country Department III for Latin America and the Caribbean. Both Page and Nancy Birdsall had been division chiefs in the same department, and Birdsall was receptive to Abe's ideas. In 1991, when Larry Summers joined the Bank as chief economist and vice-president of development economics, "I thought, this guy might understand what I'm talking about," Abe said. "I felt very confident with this young man called Summers. He had the intellectual capacity to summarize everything in a simple way. I decided to tell him, how about this and that. He said, 'sounds interesting.' Nancy talked to him, and they formed a team."

Finally, in early 1992, Abe became the messenger once Summers and Birdsall had put a price tag on the project, which they did not want to come out of the Bank's program-resource budget. "I trotted myself into Shiratori's office, and told him, they need a substantial amount of money. He said, how much, roughly? I said, about $1.5 million." A few weeks later, at a lunch that included Summers, Shiratori, Birdsall, Nishimizu Mieko, Abe, and Page, the deal was done. "There was no formal agreement" on the money, Abe claimed. "But the Japanese government was acting together."

Of all the Japanese players, Abe was perhaps the loneliest and most disinterested. He felt it was a tragedy that the *East Asian Miracle* project was conducted without direct Japanese participation. "The saddest thing in my life was sitting in that room. Those two—Nancy and John—were going to do my dream book," he recalled several years later. "In spite of all my begging to quote unquote famous Japanese economists, nobody had the guts to publish our experience with any common themes that could be shared with

Western economies. They did not know how to think about or formulate this kind of book." Abe blamed both language problems and the lack of independent thinking in Japan. "There is no tradition of independent thinking in my country, and unless you belong to the MOF or research institute this or that, nobody listens to you," he said.

In fact, even though there were no Japanese on the core research team, some of the *East Asian Miracle* money went to fund papers by members of a study team under Ohkawa Kazushi, of the International Development Center of Japan. "We bought into that group by offering them a little bit of money as an excuse, to finish essays they were writing," Page said.[185] Ohkawa had been chief consultant to Henry Rosovsky on his 1961 book, *Capital Formation in Japan*, which introduced the thesis that Japan was a successful capitalist economy patterned after the United States. He was considered the leading free-market voice in Japanese economics.[186] Ohkawa could be expected to steer his group away from developmental-state explanations of Japanese and East Asian growth. But Page also solicited advice from Ishikawa Shigeru, who represented institutional economics, in Japan largely a Marxist discipline. Yanagihara Toru was a member both of the Ohkawa study team as well as Ishikawa's long-standing MOF *benkyokai* on Japanese development principles. Yanagihara became one of Page's main contacts in Japan, as well as the OECF's point man on the *East Asian Miracle* study. While the report was being written, Yanagihara played a key role monitoring its progress.

A brilliant, unconventional economist, Yanagihara had unique qualifications. Just a year older than Page, Yanagihara had gone to graduate school at Yale with Page's boss, Birdsall. Yanagihara was of the generation reaching maturity during the Vietnam Era. A mathematician by training, he was intimately involved in Tokyo University's radical student organization in the 1960s, and, like many in his year, never formally graduated. Yanagihara's foreign friends joked that he had the looks of an old-fashioned samurai. Short statured, with a lean, erect, broad-shouldered warrior's physique, he had the intellectual virtuosity of a Toshiro Mifune picking flies out of the air with his chopsticks. Japanese sometimes mistook him for a Korean because of his high cheekbones and narrow eyes. After manning the barricades during the student protests at Tokyo University in 1969, he worked for a few years as an instructor in a *yobiko*—a prep school for the college entrance exams—then joined the Institute for Developing Economies in 1971. IDE sent Yanagihara to do graduate work in economics at Yale University from 1976 to 1979, where he studied for his doctorate but failed to complete a thesis. A polyglot, Yanigihara spoke fluent English and Spanish, and was competent in French, Russian and Korean. He liked to make bilingual and even trilingual puns.

In a room of dour Japanese bureaucrats, Yanagihara would take off his jacket and work at stretching exercises while his companions sat primly with their arms at their sides. He liked to hold meetings standing up in order to get them over more quickly. On paper, his main credential for monitoring the *East Asian Miracle* project was a stint working in Washington at the World Bank in the early 1980s; he stuck close to the Bank's Tokyo office, sometimes doing yeoman's work as a translator. In 1989, Yanagihara left IDE to move to Hosei University, but he floated with ease among the premier Japanese government economic agencies. In the late 1980s, he was one of the few Japanese economists with formal training in development economics. He had originally encountered Ishikawa as an undergraduate at Tokyo University. As time went on, Yanagihara became increasingly obsessed with carrying on Ishikawa's mission, which he saw as establishing a new set of strategic prescriptions for developing countries, based on the Japanese model.

Yanagihara was given the role of delivering Japan's rebuttal to the *East Asian Miracle* study at the Tokyo launch of the book in 1993. The occasion was in a conference room of modest size at OECF headquarters. The Japanese sponsors of the project were all there—Nishigaki, Shiratori, and Kubota. The Bank sent John Page, Lyn Squire, who had replaced Nancy Birdsall as director of Policy Research, and one of Page's team, Jose Edgardo Campos, who had worked on institutional issues. Yanagihara used humor to cut the Bank down to size. His line, poking fun at the Bank, was "Where's the beef?" He dismissed the report for containing little that was new and claimed that it applied a "black box" methodology that obscured the "tangible, visible details" of economies as well as the social consensus that lies behind high levels of economic performance.

> The central philosophy that underpins the study is a neo-classical belief in the working of market mechanisms to achieve superior performance in growth functions. The *East Asian Miracle* essentially states that the most crucial task of development is determining the correct policy choices in a given institutional setting. In most cases, this boiled down to getting prices right and leaving the markets alone, possibly coupled with an export push. In that sense, I believe, the report repeats the same old policy conclusions.

The Bank's "framework" approach, according to Yanagihara, contrasted with the more atomistic, empirical approach to growth used by Japan. From the Bank's point of view, he said,

> If performance is distorted, it is bound to be inferior. If it is not distorted, then it promises to be good. That's the basic way of thinking. The economy

is, in itself, pretty much treated as a black box. You have policy input then you have performance output.

I happen to believe that Japanese views or mind-sets are different. Japanese tend to see economies as a bunch of ingredients, tangible visible details are important and so is an overall vision of the economy in the future. Thus, development is seen as adding more ingredients to an underdeveloped economy where the key components or ingredients of an advanced economy are still lacking

I suppose these different mind-sets sometimes make it difficult to realize meaningful dialogue and mutual understanding. In that light, I see dangers of an overly simple compromise in the sense that the Bank in the report emphasizes the pragmatic flexibility of East Asian governments and that most Japanese would probably say the same thing. Pragmatic flexibility is important; nobody would disagree with that. But I don't think we have reached a meaningful consensus.[187]

Yanagihara delivered his critique in a shaky voice. It was a difficult moment for him. Pressure was intense on Yanagihara to perform well, in this first public duel, and he showed it.

In temperament and outlook, he had more in common with senior bureaucrats such as Shiratori and Kubota, despite his cocky individualism. He was a doer, not a thinker. At IDE, he had maintained a breathtaking schedule of travel and conferences; one of his main jobs was organizing international meetings. In 1991, he had been on his way to become economic counselor at the Japanese embassy in Peru when the assassination of two Japanese aid workers by Shining Path guerrillas temporarily closed down the Japanese aid program. His arrangements with Hosei were cursory. He ran from classroom to administrative session to a brace of senior level "study groups" and then often onto a plane, usually to Washington or South America. His theoretical work had flashes of inspiration but was often murky. He simply lacked the time to turn out academic articles or build a case for his notion that Japanese development policy was strategic *and* pragmatic. Regardless, in the early 1990s, he was one of a small handful of Japanese economists with formal training in development as well as experience as a practitioner, in South Korea and Mexico. Among that handful, he was perhaps the only one with the credentials and the gift with languages to make Japan's case to a jury of senior Bank officials.

Yanagihara understood more clearly than most that Japan needed to move quickly to take advantage of the opportunity created by the ambiguities of the *East Asian Miracle* report. It was one thing to sit on the sidelines as a critic, another to enter into the debate with a position to argue and defend.

The World Bank might have conveniently invented the Japanese model, but Japan would have to provide the detail, or see the model die as its case attenuated.

Over the course of the next four years, Yanagihara attempted to refine his concept of *nakami,* or ingredients, that he argued was the foundation of Japanese economic policy and hence the Japanese model. His starting point was a schematic drawing that appeared in the *East Asian Miracle,* labeled "A Functional Approach to Growth." John Page originally had used the word "strategic" instead of "functional," but he had to throw it out for the same reason that "strategic" was stripped from the title of the book. The chart was intended to show how East Asian policy makers had embedded selective interventions in a solid framework of macroeconomic "fundamentals"— stability, rich human capital, sound financial institutions, openness to foreign technology, and policies to promote agricultural growth. Yanagihara, however, picked up another aspect of the "functional" approach. "This approach recognizes that policies, like tactics, can and should vary depending on the situation," the book explained. It added, "The central functions, which are crucial to development, must always be addressed."[188] Yanagihara ignored the latter, but was taken by the idea of policy and market institutions operating interactively in an organic framework.

About the same time that Page was organizing the research team for the *East Asian Miracle,* Yanagihara began working with Sambommatsu Susumu, an Economic Planning Agency official who was director of the Second Economic Cooperation Division and in charge of Japanese official development assistance policy. Sambommatsu had been in charge of an official white paper on the Japanese economic experience that predated the *East Asian Miracle.* It was part of EPA's five-year plan announced in June 1992, under the slogan of "Life Style Superpower." A career MITI official, Sambommatsu moved to EPA to assume command of the project. In 1993, after the completion of the first report, which seemed to have sunk without a trace, he took over a new, three-year project on the same theme. This one, however, was to be much more closely focused on ways to project the Japanese economic system through its foreign aid program.

A tall man with the unambiguous, down-to-earth manner of an engineer, Sambommatsu liked the "functional" chart in the *East Asian Miracle,* too, but from an entirely different perspective. Sambommatsu thought it would be neat to generate such charts for industry, so that if a developing country wanted to establish manufacturing in a particular sector, it could turn to MITI's charts to see how to do it. In his office, he displayed an elaborate diagram of policy relationships within the Japanese machine-building industry. "This is the main case for the Japanese machine industry," he said. "If any country would like to make machine industry products, this is the kind of network that will be useful for total quality control. The links between the components are bundles of contracts. In the neoclassical view, this kind of thing is unnecessary. It's just atomizing the economic system. But in Japan, we think this kind of network was good for East Asian economies. Based on this kind of idea, you can ask people in Korea or Taiwan, which kind of network did you make in each case? You can develop a global checklist." However mundane such checklists might appear, Sambommatsu argued that they were the basis not only of an alternative paradigm but of an entirely new approach to development economics. "We are finding a new approach to development economics," he said in a 1996 interview. "The problem is the lack of theory."[189]

Thus began the collaboration between Yanagihara, the maverick economist, and Sambommatsu, the visionary bureaucrat. In 1993, they set up a three-year study, which moved after the second year to the IDE, where Sambommatsu had gone on to another MITI secondment. The first year's theme was the Japanese development experience. In November 1994, EPA invited a small group of Japanese and Third World economists to Tokyo to discuss its report, *Possibility of the Application of Japanese Experience from the Standpoint of the Developing Countries*.[190] Page, who was the main guest and keynote speaker at the conference, called the report "an honest attempt to go beyond the war stories and pharmacology of how the Japanese economy works, and begin to put together an analytical framework. It's an important departure."[191] More grandly, the EPA claimed its study was "the first to take a comprehensive approach to Japan's development."

Through ninety-two turgid, poorly translated pages, the English-language report recapitulated the history of Japanese economic development from the Meiji Restoration to the present, explaining its version of the social and institutional keys to Japanese success. The EPA's basic argument—that policy "menus" would not work unless institutions were in place to serve them up—was similar to the *East Asian Miracle*'s argument that exceptionally strong bureaucracies were critical to industrial policy's positive track records in Japan, South Korea, and Taiwan. However, the EPA report attempted to go a step further and isolate the qualities that made Japanese institutions successful. It identified these as "self-help," "adaptive gradualism," an emphasis on building infrastructure at an early stage of development, "participatory interaction," and abundant "human capital." "Self-help" or "self-reliant" development (*jiritsuteki hatten*) was to become a particularly important theme because it represented a persistent feature of Japanese capitalism described in the *East Asian Miracle* in terms of government-organized "contests." Government might set the goalposts, but business was on its own in kicking the ball through. The government might offer bank credit to a protégé company, but woe to the firm that was unable to pay back its debts. The Japanese system preferred domestic savings over external sources of funds in order to avoid unexpected costs through the foreign exchange markets, as well as loss of control to foreigners. Japan had engineered its growth miracle from within, using foreign markets as a lever but carefully controlling their impact on the domestic economy.

The report contained two charts modeled after the *East Asian Miracle*'s "functional" approach. One was labeled "Schematic Drawing of the Relation between Policy Changes and Policy Acceptance Conditions," and asked rhetorically in a caption: "In the country concerned, are the government, enterprises, the above four markets and the infrastructure all developed, or when all elements are developed, operating organically as an integrated network?" The other showed the "self-help" Japanese model of "economic development based on adaptive gradualism."

The two charts were key to understanding the document, whose language was opaque. Essentially, they illustrated institutional networks rather than specific policies. The body of the report explained that "self-help" meant the ability of Japan to develop without foreign investment, based on a social consensus supporting government policy. Adaptive gradualism was the use of protection to nurture firms and market institutions, as well as the ability to abandon bad policies. Japan invested early both in human capital through widespread primary education and through the buildup of social infrastructure such as transportation and communications. Participatory interaction referred to cooperation between business and government. These were less policies, however, than institutional practices and preferences, particularly the last. The important thing, to the Japanese, was that policy was interactive and tactical rather than conforming to principles.

In other words, Japanese-style industrial policy was not based on a plan and had little predictive capability. According to Iwata Kazumasa, an international economist at Tokyo University who participated in the EPA study group, "participatory interaction" was the essence of Japanese-style industrial policy. "The government played the role of catalyst, giving incentives to a dynamic private sector," he told the small group of Japanese and Asian economists who attended the EPA conference in November 1994. "That function as catalyst means that in economic development one plus one equaled three or four instead of two."[192]

The next stage of the Sambommatsu-Yanagihara project was to examine the East Asian development experience. Sambommatsu put Yanagihara in charge. As Sambommatsu put it, this was the "same idea" as the first study, in a "new framework." It culminated in a conference in Tokyo on January 22, 1997, and its proceedings were published in a very thick book.[193] A third stage, interrupted by the Asian financial crisis, was to develop a formal critique of structural adjustment policies.

At the 1997 conference, Yanagihara presented a new version of his *nakami* theory, this time called the "economic system approach," dressed up with an acronym, ESA. Yanagihara described ESA as "an attempt to present an alternative paradigm for the understanding of the process of economic development and for the design of development policies." He said that the need for the new paradigm arose from the discontent of Japanese economists with the "functional" approach of neoclassical economics, because it failed to capture the "dynamic forces" driving East Asian growth. If the neoclassical view was based on the supremacy of markets, the Japanese perspective was based on the practical experience that markets were imperfect or nonexistent in the early stages of development. He defined "economic system" as the "way productive capacities exist embodied in cooperative relationships within and between firms and in relation to various factor markets,"[194] and produced a chart showing the linkages among economic agents and policies and development "mechanisms" adopted at the national and firm level.

The core of Yanagihara's argument directly assaulted the Adam Smith school and the theory of open, competitive markets. "Japanese criticisms center on the inadequacy of the market liberalization approach for the promotion of development process," he said. "Therefore, what is needed is to foster and develop firms and industries under government leadership and guidance; premature liberalization is likely to result in undesirable outcomes when viewed from a long-term developmental perspective."[195]

Economies required protection in order to build up institutional strength. Yanagihara waxed lyrical on the benefits of insulating fragile developing economies from the market. "Unlike the neo-classical school, ESA does not view stocks of productive resources comprising the productive capacity of an economy as perfectly malleable endowments. They exist in distinctive forms and contexts, embodying, and mediated and coordinated by, on-the-spot know-how and expertise acquired through learning by experience within specific organizational setups within a firm and particular arrangements between firms. From this perspective, an important function of a market economy is to provide opportunities for trial-and-error experiments aimed at enhancing organizational capabilities of firms and developing institutional arrangements between firms."[196]

Yanagihara's presentation was remarkable. It was much more forceful than the EPA paper of 1994, and included a clear statement in favor of a Japanese model of development. It assembled most of the themes promoted by Shiratori and Kubota (guided by Ishikawa) since the early 1990s—the need for government intervention in markets; the concept of gradualism, emphasizing timing and sequencing of reforms; and policy relativism, reflecting the "diversity" of economies rather than attempting to apply universal principles. Appropriately, Yanagihara gave credit to Ishikawa Shigeru, "the dean of development economics in Japan," as the major inspiration for ESA. Then, in a telling stroke that established ESA as the heir to Akamatsu and the flying-geese school, Yanagihara ended the paper with a review of the "evolving industrial configuration in East Asia."

Regional economic configuration is often captured by the flying geese metaphor. In fact, there are two versions to the flying geese metaphor. One is macroscopic relating to relative positions of national economies in the level of development (often measured by GNP per capita). The other is microscopic in the sense that attention is focused on a particular industry or even a product. In this microscopic approach the sequence of net exports of a certain product or a product group is traced over time for each economy and then superimposed to see a sequence and interrelation of events on a regional scope.

These two versions of the flying geese metaphor are logically interrelated. The theory of comparative advantage associates trade pattern with resource endowments, which in turn tends to be highly correlated with the level of per capita income. On the demand side, there are regularities between consumption pattern and income level. Thus, these underlying economic forces will tend to produce a similar pattern of sequence across economies as they move forward in the process of development. This logic may not be totally negated but could be significantly modified. Foreign direct investment could either accentuate or diminish production specialization. Policy intervention could either promote or hinder the realization of comparative advantage.

The paper concluded by noting that the East Asian economies had "come to form a closely connected layer in the web of region-wide corporate production networks."[197]

The strength of Yanagihara's paper was that it provided a snapshot of the Japanese model. It explained its differences from the neoclassical model as well as those of the Japanese "historical" school and the new "market-enhancing" approach of Stanford professor Aoki Masahiko, who viewed government as "an integral element of the market system."[198] The argument went well beyond the 1994 EPA paper and was laid out far more logically.

Its weaknesses, however, were readily apparent as well. Lyn Squire, head of the World Bank's Policy Research Department, attended the conference and provided formal comments. In his presentation, he criticized the paper's lack of an analytical framework or any empirical tests in support of the concept. Later, he said in private, "It was extremely difficult to understand what he was saying—to the point where it was difficult to frame my comments. I think the difficulty is when you have research that is not confronted by the data—research which may have some political motivation. If it's an attempt to capture in some sort of framework what people would like to believe about Japanese development, it's not a good starting point for research."[199]

Sambommatsu was comfortable with the politics. "Our ODA volume is the biggest in the world," he said in a 1995 interview. "Until now the World Bank has been the leading brain and Japan the follower. I, or we, want to cooperate with the World Bank rather than compete. We are studying our systems approach, hoping to shed new light on the development area, development strategy, or aid strategy. We can exchange information to cooperate. My intention is that Japan not be a follower. We don't want to be the leader, but a co-leader. We want to cooperate with the World Bank on a global basis. It's all based on good will. There's no hostility at all."[200]

Moreover, according to Sambommatsu, the project was about setting goals, not execution. There might be a Japanese model, but there was no blueprint, and Japan in the 1990s offered no answers. Sambommatsu advised developing countries to ignore Japan in the present and concentrate on its experience through the 1960s.

> Our way of development was rather different from the neo-classical model until the 1960s. But at this moment we have to behave based on a neo-classical way of thinking, because we are engaging in deregulation. I'm not saying, adopt the Japanese way of doing things, but one of the good results of 100 years of Japanese history is that we were able to shift our industrial structure from the export of raw materials to high tech industry. The sophistication of our industrial structure is one of the good points for modern developing countries.
>
> A second point is the way we moved from imports, to localization, then to export substitution. It's different now. For example, in Malaysia, some companies in the semiconductor business float from country to country, rather than conducting a successive shift. But this kind of export substitution is important.
>
> Third, how to sophisticate the economic system. The way how to do it is up to them, but this kind of level of formation of the economic system is the third good result of the Japanese economic experience. Also, we exercised "self-help" in basic commodities like rice. Those four items were the good results of Japan over 100 years. We haven't finalized a system of how to do it, but these results should be their goal, and they can find their own way to achieve them.

The Yanagihara-Sambommatsu project was one of many. The *East Asian Miracle* ultimately became godfather to a whole series of Japanese studies on the Japanese and East Asian models. It legitimized industrial policy as a research topic, after languishing for years in disrepute, and inaugurated a much higher level of dialogue between Japan and the international financial institutions.

The World Bank began holding annual "research fairs" in Japan at which Bank economists would stand next to kiosks displaying their work and be available for comment. According to Lyn Squire, after the first research fair, fourteen Japanese research institutes approached the Bank, asking it to "keep the group together." This provided a core group for the Bank to engage in "a lot more interaction with Japanese scholars." As head of the Bank's Policy Research Department, Squire designed several programs to increase interaction with Japan on a scholarly level. In one program, twenty to twenty-five Japanese would give presentations, followed by World Bank economists giving presentations on the same topics. There were also scholarly workshops, a series of joint conferences with OECF, and a blanket invitation to OECF representatives to be based in the department for stints of four to six months.

The Bank also took another pass at the subject of industrial policy and East Asian growth, this time in its annual flagship policy review, the *World Development Report*. The 1997 *WDR* was on the role of government in economies.[201] It presented East Asia as an example of the importance of "effective" states that encouraged business. In tone, *"The State in a Changing World"* was the mirror opposite of the 1991 *WDR* that had so incensed the Japanese. The 1991 *WDR* limited the positive role of government to "market-friendly" actions. The 1997 *WDR* said that effective states were essential to sustainable development. Stanford scholar Aoki Masahiko played a major role as consultant to the project, and the chief researcher, Ajay Chhibber, made several trips to Japan to consult with Shiratori and others as the report was under preparation.

"There's just a much bigger interaction between the Bank and Japan on a range of issues," Squire said in 1997. "Japan is now the world's largest provider of foreign aid. That's one factor. Another is that they've had a pretty striking economic performance since World War Two. If you put those two things together, why wouldn't Japan want to put a claim to the world? Their objective is to establish themselves as a really important player in thinking about development in general. I suspect that process would have continued with or without the *East Asian Miracle*. But the *East Asian Miracle* really highlighted the issue and gave it a lot of visibility and prominence."[202]

Mellowed, perhaps, by the passage of time, in 1995 Shiratori agreed. "The World Bank is still dominated by neoclassicists. But I see a very tiny change.

When I was at the Bank board, when young Japanese economists tried to talk about subjects such as directed credit or industrial policy, they were put down. Now they can openly talk about the replication or application of these policies."[203]

The Japanese studies used the *East Asian Miracle* both as a platform and a how-to manual. Each argued that the *Miracle* report was good enough in its way but failed to identify some crucial point that made East Asian industrial policy successful. Each was on the same scale or larger than the World Bank project. The Japanese Foreign Ministry funded a three-year, $3 million study through an affiliate, the Foundation for Advanced Studies of International Development (FASID). IDE had a second program on the same scale as the Sambommatsu-Yanagihara project. OECF and the Finance Ministry's Institute of Fiscal and Monetary Policy had each commissioned broad comparative studies on governance and privatization, seeking to demonstrate that the "Anglo-American" approach was not universal.

All five projects convened multiple conferences on East Asian lessons for developing countries, sponsored papers, and engaged large numbers of economists from developing economies in their work. In April 1995, FASID joined hands with the Washington, D.C.–based Institute for Policy Reform, with funding from the U.S. Agency for International Development as well as FASID to hold a closed workshop on the "East Asian Paradigm" in Honolulu. Those attending included John Page, Shiratori, and Henry Bienen, former dean of the Woodrow Wilson School at Princeton. In May of the same year, Shiratori and Yanagihara organized an OECF symposium in Tokyo on "Lessons of East Asia for Latin America" at which the principal guest was Nancy Birdsall, by then executive vice-president at the IDB. In September 1996, OECF helped fund a conference on "Development Thinking and Practice" at the IDB, at which Sakakibara Eisuke gave the keynote address and IDE president Yamada Katsuhisa and senior research fellow Kuchiki Akifumi presented their findings on the "growth mechanism of East Asia."[204]

There was a certain clumsy, tentative quality to many of the reports that emerged from the Japanese conferences and studies. Their detractors said they were based on wishful thinking and politics. The Japanese preferred to present themselves in the light of underdogs struggling with an oppressive global hegemony. "The neo-classical view is that the market always prevails despite government intervention," said Sakakibara, at the time director-general of the MOF's International Finance Bureau and its chief international negotiator, in a 1995 interview. "That made it difficult for our own scholars to confront the facts and build their own abstract model, based on empirical research. The neo-classical view is that there is only one framework. Our position is that both the economic and social frameworks are rooted in history and culture; that you have to be particularist. This neo-classical universalism to us is a problem." [205]

The Japanese may also have feared to be more explicit about their intentions because the implication of the studies—that Japan would run its foreign aid program at odds with the United States and the World Bank—was so provocative. Nonetheless, as time went on, Japanese officials seemed almost to embrace confrontation. So, for example, at FASID's conference in Hawaii in 1995, Ohtsuka Seiichi, director of the Evaluation Division of the Japanese Foreign Ministry's Economic Cooperation Bureau, described "selective government intervention" as the "paradigm for development in East Asian countries." Ohtsuka assured his audience that Japanese aid "matches practically and theoretically the developmental needs of the Asian countries." [206]

An important marker was the explicit introduction of an economic advisory role to Japan's foreign aid program. The Japanese Foreign Ministry set foreign aid policy together with the MITI and the Finance Ministry. In Fall 1994, for the first time it put macroeconomic advice on the agenda for foreign aid. This was a sharp departure from the traditional mix comprising financial and technical aid. In a 1995 interview, IDE president Yamada Katsuhisa asserted that Japan would apply "Japanese-style conditionality" in its lending program. A former official of MITI and OECF, Yamada argued that only by working with government could private firms "make maximum use of their initiative and entrepreneurship." [207]

Elfin and excitable, Yamada was career MITI but had spent two years, from 1986 to 1988, at the OECF. He had his own strong views about the nature of the Japanese model and was much blunter in his criticism of the *East Asian Miracle* than Yanagihara or Sambommatsu. "The market in reality is imperfect, unlike the market depicted by economic theories," Yamada had written in a 1984 article. [208] He was convinced that the key to the East Asian miracle was industrial policy and that the *East Asian Miracle* had been dead wrong in categorizing Southeast Asian economies as GATT-friendly or market-friendly. [209]

Working with IDE senior research fellow Kuchiki Akifumi, Yamada came up with his own solution to the East Asian "trick." [210] Kuchiki called it the EPZ (export processing zone) model. Economies adopting the EPZ model typically offered incentives to investors to export—the incentives went to domestic investors in Japan and Korea, foreign investors in the case of Southeast Asia. At the same time, EPZ policy tightly restricted access to domestic markets and made sure that special favors went to strategic export industries that offered high employment and access to foreign technology.

"In my judgment, Japan historically had more of a market mechanism than the present Asian developmental states," Yamada said. "But the World Bank concept—the market-friendly approach versus the developmental state—gives us the misunderstanding that Japan has been government-led and antimarket. That's quite 100 percent wrong." He continued:

> My explanation is pong, pong, pong, not so straight on. But, for example, look at the last ten years. Asian countries such as Malaysia, Thailand, and Indonesia showed high rates of growth—about 8 percent per annum. Such rates are very good and most of it came through the demand side, in the form of private fixed investment and exports. These two elements have led economic growth in the last ten years. Just under 50 percent of private fixed investment has been from foreign direct investment, which also played a role in exports. So the logic of the past ten years of high growth rates of these countries is based on FDI [foreign direct investment].
>
> I think this policy was correct. But the secret of this mechanism was that the governments have allowed FDI only with conditions for the ratio of exports and local content. If investors were interested in the domestic market, they would not be allowed. Only—for example—a joint venture or 100 percent FDI would be allowed if it exported 80 percent of its products and provided 60 percent local content. I contend that more than 80 percent exports, as an obligation, is an antimarket mechanism, a 100 percent antimarket mechanism. If the free market prevailed, any investment ought to be all right. The policy is correct but this is an antimarket friendly approach.[211]

Yamada's unlikely personal hero was Chalmers Johnson, the California-based political scientist who coined the terms "industrial policy" and "developmental state." Yamada had sought out Johnson in 1979 during a visit to San Francisco. He had heard that Johnson, then at Berkeley, was working on an article on MITI, and Yamada wanted to translate it. The article turned out to be a book, but Yamada went ahead with the translation project anyway, Johnson's landmark *MITI and the Japanese Miracle*.[212]

The book's thesis was that Japan's bureaucracy had played a crucial role in perfecting Japan's "plan-oriented market economy." Government and the private sector formed a nearly seamless whole with the common aim of success in international markets. "One clear lesson from the Japanese case," Johnson wrote, "is that the state needs the market and private enterprise needs the state; once both sides recognized this, cooperation was possible and high-speed growth occurred." Industrial policy was central to the process. Johnson himself became so attached to the idea that he advocated that countries competing with Japan set up industrial policies of their own. "Economic competitiveness does not result from picking winners but from a long-term strategy aimed at learning to win," he wrote in a 1993 article in the *California Management Review*.[213]

In the 1980s, Japanese officials trembled with indignation at the views of Johnson and others of the so-called revisionist school—a term first applied to Japan watchers by Robert Neff at *Business Week*. The revisionists included Johnson; trade consultant Clyde Prestowitz; the *Atlantic Monthly*'s Washington editor, James Fallows; Neff himself; and the Dutch journalist Karel van Wolferen. They argued that the Japanese economy, along with its political culture and society, was essentially a nationalistic shop aimed at creating wealth and power for Japan as a whole.[214]

As Johnson wryly commented in a 1992 paper written for a World Bank conference on governance and East Asian economic success, "There is considerable irony in this. My book is a virtual celebration of the post-war achievements of the Japanese economy and was translated into Japanese by a team of MITI officials headed by a former vice-minister who was subsequently elected to the upper house of the Diet. Nonetheless, my book does illustrate that the state can play an important role in market economies well beyond the roles envisioned in laissez-faire economics. Americans did not want to hear about this because it threatened vested interests (including intellectual vested interests) in their economy as constituted; and the Japanese decided, upon reflection, that if foreigners recognized Japan to be different, they might invent effective measures for dealing with it." [215]

Yamada simply saw the book as a celebration, and lamented that Johnson never updated the work with a "MITI, Mark II." Johnson characterized industrial policy, as practiced by MITI, as a fluid process, exercising power indirectly and through a network of relationships with industry. Yamada called this "soft administration" and couldn't see why the World Bank would look at "market-friendly" and government-friendly "developmental state" as opposites.

At IDE, Yamada presided over a Yen 300 million, three-year project that focused on "how to proceed with industrial policy" in developing countries. From his time at the OECF, he had picked up a healthy dislike of structural adjustment loans, which the OECF frequently co-financed with the World Bank. "The World Bank applied conditionality to those loans, but OECF did not have the capacity to suggest anything from the Japanese experience," Yamada sighed. "The OECF had always objected to the World Bank's conditionality. But there was no theory or positive analysis. I thought that was why we should have proof that government intervention was necessary for development." [216]

In the first stage of the project, launched in 1993, a small team under Kuchiki conducted fact finding on the introduction of industrial policy in

Japan, Korea, Thailand, and Malaysia. The second stage was to have researchers in India, Nigeria, Poland, and Thailand draw up reports on "how to proceed with industrial policy." In the third year, a different group of countries—China, Turkey, Brazil, and Malaysia—would do the same. Kuchiki was working with sixty researchers outside Japan, and expecting 300-page reports back from each country. In Poland alone, Kuchiki had twenty researchers on the project.

In addition to the three-year project on industrial policy, Yamada had commissioned three more studies. One was by Yanagihara and Sambommatsu on Asian financial markets. A second was the Yanagihara-Sambommatsu study on applications of the Japanese model to developing countries. Finally, Yamada hoped that "youngsters" in the institute would help him write a textbook on development economics. He wanted it to become an international standard, "like Samuelson's," the standard text for a generation of neoclassical economists written by Nobel Prize–winning Paul Samuelson.

At FASID, Director Fujimura Ken put the main emphasis on training Japanese aid administrators how to impart the Japanese experience to developing countries around the world. He had put 1,000 of them through his mill between 1990 and 1994. "We have few development economists in Japan, it's true," he said. "But we have thousands of development administrators."[217] A much larger project, however, was to put together a "Japanese version" of the *East Asian Miracle*. The Japanese Foreign Ministry had promised Yen 100 million annually for the project. Researcher Horikome Yumi expected it to last four or five years. "This initiative is from the Ministry of Foreign Affairs," she said, "because Japan would like to contribute something to the world. Different government ministries are in conflict about what to do, but the Foreign Ministry thinks it should be something more grand."

However nebulous, political, or misguided, these projects had a direct connection to the real world. Up until the late 1980s, Japan confined itself to a role as moneylender to developing countries. From the late 1980s on, Japan began to supply "master plans" for economic development. By the early 1990s, it had added programs to supply not only the hardware of economic development but the know-how, as well, in the form of elite training programs for government officials from developing countries. Such training programs represented Japan's first efforts to engage in direct propaganda for the "Japanese model." Up until the early 1990s, Japan had made no effort to train economic managers, as opposed to technicians, as part of its aid program, much less impose its model of economic development.

Most Americans ignored this example of Japanese hubris, especially because it coincided with a massive collapse in Japanese financial and real-estate markets. By the mid-1990s, Tokyo was no longer seen as taking over the world, but rather very rapidly backing out of the pieces it owned, usually at firesale prices. Japanese companies had sold off their high-profile investments of the 1980s—Rockefeller Center, Columbia Pictures, MCA, the Pebble Beach Golf Club—and instead of threatening the American house seemed to have lost control of their own economy. A spate of books and press reports reinforced a popular view that Japan was "finished." But the shift in Japan's official position on market economics did not go wholly unnoticed. It made a big impression among Japan's developing-country clients.

In Asia, Japanese government agencies and private foundations began a form of economic lobbying with China, Vietnam, Laos, Cambodia, Myanmar, and the Central Asian republics, weaning them away from free-market capitalism and courting them to adopt the Japanese model. The collapse of the Russian economy provided a powerful negative example. The Japanese—and many others—blamed the radical "shock therapy" recommendations of Harvard economist Jeffrey Sachs, which became the basis of the IMF reform programs in the 1990s. "We have been asked by many East Asian countries how we are running our economies," said the Finance Ministry's Sakakibara. "These countries are extremely conscious of what happened in Russia. They don't want that."

The reasons for Japan's policy shift were complex. One of its striking features was that the Japanese ministries involved—Finance, the Bank of Japan, MITI, the EPA, the OECF , and the IDE—each generated programs independently of each other. The policy shift evolved less as a formal plan than as a change in attitude on the part of the Japanese bureaucracy. As such, the causes were to be found in developments in Japan's broader political environment in the early 1990s, particularly in its critical relationship with the United States. Two external events threw these changes sharply into focus—the Gulf War and, as has been seen, the collapse of the Russian economy. Russia's problems, evident as soon as the policies were put into effect, sent Mikhail Gorbachev scurrying to Tokyo for advice. A third force came from within, in a new generation of officials moving up the ladder with no experience of war and defeat or the terrible poverty of the immediate post-war period.

In 1990 and 1991, the Gulf War shattered Japanese complacency about its supposed global partnership with the United States. In August 1991, Saddam Hussein's Iraq invaded Kuwait, and the United States immediately began to exert pressure on its allies to support a blockade against Baghdad. Japan demurred. When the United States pushed Tokyo for financial support, it gave, but stintingly. In the end, Japan's performance during the Gulf War reinforced the image of Japan as a selfish nation, dithering over matters that affected others while smoothly advancing its own borderless economic he-

gemony. This in turn launched a fierce debate within the Japanese bureaucracy about the relationship between money and influence, values and power.

In the early days of the blockade, in September, the *Asahi* ran an editorial
cartoon showing United States President George Bush (senior), dressed in
army fatigues, leading a camel through the desert with the face of Japanese
prime minister Kaifu Toshiki. The camel's hump was a big bag of cash, and
the goggle-eyed Kaifu looked worried. The cartoon reflected the role that
Washington had assigned to Japan in the crisis—an obedient follower with a
ready checkbook. But while Japan immediately offered $1 billion in aid to
the allies—a sum eventually reaching $13 billion—it entered into a clumsy
ballet that ultimately antagonized both Washington and Kuwait.

Japan's problem was that Iraq was a major oil supplier. Tokyo had fully
supported America's pre–Gulf War policy of supporting the Saddam Hussein
regime and had no desire to see it end. As a Japanese official in New York
testily complained, Iraq's invasion of Kuwait had no effect on the flow of oil
to Japan. Tokyo claimed that its Constitution prevented it from applying any
funding for military support. It agreed to charter commercial ships and aircraft to ferry supplies to the Gulf, as long as the supplies were nonmilitary.
But the United States had asked for help in carrying troops and weapons to
the region. When the first Japanese ship was due to leave port, carrying a
cargo of Japanese-made automobiles, the All-Japan Seaman's Union went
on strike, claiming it had not been told where the ship was headed. Japan Air
Lines refused to fly any of its aircraft into "danger zones." Bureaucrats
squabbled over Japan's existing aid commitments to Jordan, Egypt, and Turkey for refugee relief; they insisted that any Japanese funding go into a special trust fund administered by the six-nation Gulf Cooperation Council to
further distance Tokyo from the U.S. military effort. There were arguments
to deduct the funds from Japan's foreign aid budget and offer it in the form
of loans. At the start of the blockade, Japan called for civilian volunteers for
medical teams and refugee relief. Three months later, by October, only seventeen Japanese medical personnel had left for the Gulf.

Japanese politicians and diplomats claimed that they were stuck with a
painful dilemma—whether to abrogate the Japanese Constitution and send
troops into combat or restrict Japan's contributions to cash. But the pacifist
dilemma was phony, because none of the countries engaged in the confrontation had asked for Japanese combat troops. The supposed dilemma served
as a smokescreen for Japan's real problem—the political paralysis that set in
whenever it was confronted with an unexpected emergency. The first $9 bil-
lion of Japanese funds was approved in the lower house on February 28,
1991—just as the multinational forces suspended hostilities. The money let
the Japanese off the hook diplomatically. But suspicions lingered that Tokyo

had played to both sides in the conflict. After the end of the war, when the United States pushed its allies to come up with $50 billion in funds for the reconstruction of Kuwait, Tokyo made a point of sitting on the fence.

"If we started an aid program to the richest country in the world, with $300 billion in liquid assets, the poorer countries in Asia and Africa would scream," a Japanese Foreign Ministry official told reporters. He said that the Japanese government would supply aid for the repair of power stations and desalination plants in Kuwait City—many of which had been built by Japanese companies—but that the amounts would be modest. "We are not going to impose any particular policy framework or ideology on the region," the official said. By not taking sides, Japan argued that it was in a position to serve as a communications channel between the United States and Iraq. Most observers assumed that Japan merely was adopting a position allowing it to resume business with Iraq more quickly.

Ordinary Japanese were appalled that their politicians saw the Gulf War only as another exercise in smoothing out relations with the United States. Despite Japan's enormous potential influence in the conflict as a major customer for Middle Eastern oil, no proposals or attempts at mediation came from Tokyo. In the end, even Kuwait responded coolly to Japan's efforts, failing to list it in a public letter of thanks to the multilateral forces that drove the Iraqis out of their territory. Tokyo knew that its $13 billion had gone to waste. The view in the Japanese Foreign ministry was that the Gulf War had been an enormous public relations failure. The ministry wanted to get proper recognition at least for its financial support of the war effort. One possible answer was to take a cue from America's long-standing policy of attaching a value scheme to its spending initiatives. If American aid promoted American values around the world, why not have Japanese aid promote Japanese values? By 1991, Japan was pulling ahead of the United States as the world's largest source of bilateral financial aid for developing countries, and at least in theory Japan could use its ODA budget to better advantage, showcasing Japanese values and ideals.

But how? The post-war orthodoxy was that Japan was a democracy promoting free-market capitalism. If the reality deviated, nobody was prepared to examine it too closely. Japanese officials were uncomfortable with principles, and most instinctively felt that the distinguishing features of Japanese economic and social organization could not be transferred to foreigners, anyway. No other society had the social cohesion or racial homogeneity of Japan, and such factors were thought essential to the smooth functioning and collusive tendencies of its economic structure.

The first big clue came from Mikhail Gorbachev. In his last months as president of the Soviet Union, he paid a virtually sleepless, three-day trip to

Japan in mid-April 1991. His main mission was to squeeze some promise of financial support out of the Japanese for the struggling Soviet economy, and to do so he used every bit of flattery and larceny at his command. Gorbachev fanned Japanese hopes of a deal to return a few small islands in the southern Kurile archipelago seized by the Soviets in the days just before the Japanese surrender in World War Two. He walked Tokyo streets with his wife, Raisa, creating a storm of enthusiasm. An instant industry grew up in Gorbie and Raisa dolls. Japanese officials grew hopeful that they might actually get their "Northern Territories" back. As part of his high-energy courtship of the Japanese, Gorbachev asked Japan's EPA to train Soviet officials in Japanese-style economic management. Flustered, officials agreed despite the lack of textbooks, teachers, or even the concept of transferring the "know-how" of Japanese government-business cooperation in running the economy.

This was the beginning of formal efforts by the Japanese economic bureaucracy to offer training programs in Japanese-style "economic management" and industrial policy. Japanese companies had been providing technical training for clients from developing countries for years, and the Japanese government's earliest form of foreign aid was the provision of such training, in Japan, for workers from developing countries. None of the previously existing programs, however, had offered a systemic approach to Japanese-style industrial policy or economic development. Instead of an agreement on the Kuriles, Gorbachev came away with a handful of agreements on technical exchange. Thus, it was Gorbachev who unleashed the "Japanese model" on developing countries, including his own.

The technical exchange agreements presented Japan with both an opportunity and a problem. The opportunity was to show off Japan's allure as an alternative role model for "transitional" states seeking to acquire market economies. The problem was that the Japanese had nothing to say. Despite the existence of a vast literature on Japanese industrial policy and its "economic miracle," no one had attempted to put together a how-to policy manual on Japanese-style economic development.

The Russian technical agreements came just as U.S.- and World Bank–inspired economic reform programs were leading the newly formed Commonwealth of Independent States (CIS) to the brink of economic disaster. Said the IDE's Yamada, "The World Bank insisted on severe conditionality from the standpoint of neo-classical thinking" in its prescriptions for Russia. "It was short-sighted and completely based on market-oriented mechanisms. This history is a history of failure. Now, five years' experience has told us that the World Bank style is not appropriate to Russia, Eastern Europe, or other developing economies. We had always had objections to World Bank conditionality. But we had no theory or positive analysis. I thought that was why we should have proof that government intervention was necessary for development."

In April 1992, a year after the Gorbachev visit, MITI was ready to present its own blueprint for economic reconstruction and development in Russia, based on Japanese-style industrial policy. This document, from the MITI Research Institute, said that "market mechanisms cannot be almighty" and stated that "the worst choice would be to diversify investment in an all out manner, because . . . what is now most needed is focus on specific sectors of particular importance as a way to increase overall production."[218]

Over the next few years, hundreds of officials from the former Soviet Union and Central Europe visited Tokyo to study Japanese economic policy. Yasuda Osamu, a counselor to Nomura Research Institute (NRI), was in charge of technical cooperation with the Soviet Union at the EPA at the time of the Gorbachev's visit. He described the trip as a watershed in the attitude of government agencies toward economic policy. "Frankly, a few years back, we did not think economic policy was a form of technology that could be transferred to other countries," he said.[219]

After Gorbachev's visit, every major Japanese economic agency jumped into the policy trainee business. They only discovered after they had committed themselves to accepting several hundred students a year that training materials were nonexistent. At the EPA, the solution was to dragoon agency "old boys"—retired senior officials like Yasuda—to lecture and write textbooks. Four years after the training department was set up, its core curriculum listed thirty-two print titles and two videos. The EPA training literature was frank propaganda for industrial policy. One training video, on "Main Features of the Market Economy in Japan," began with montages of fireworks and the collapse of the Berlin Wall, implying a revolution. A voice-over intoned, "As a result of the reforms in the former Soviet Union and Eastern Europe, the tendency throughout the world is toward the market economy. But the market economy has taken on different forms in Japan, the United States and Europe, and each has their own special features."

The video then dealt with "harmonious competitive" ties among Japanese businesses—cartels, that is—the "cooperative relationship between government and the general public," and harmony between owners and employees because of the lifetime-employment system in which employees pledged their allegiance to the company, "in sharp contrast to the standard practice in America." "The essence of Japanese supply-side policies was that the government emphasized the vitality and entrepreneurial spirit of business and pushed it in the desired direction. This helps explain the growing dynamism of the Japanese economy," the EPA video concluded. "From this Japanese-style market economy, Japan has achieved remarkable growth in the past half century, so that the noninterventionist market economy is not omnipotent."

Among the ironies of the EPA's new effort to crank out material on the Japanese model was that the Japanese maintained one of the world's largest technical training programs for foreign factory workers and mid-level managers from developing countries. Several courses on policy and government had been developed but these were little more than walkthroughs of Japanese government agencies. By the mid-1990s, the Japan International Cooperation Agency was handling 5,000 to 6,000 trainees per year, enrolled in courses ranging from industrial pollution control engineering to information processing and customs techniques. Between 1954, when its program began, and 1992, JICA trained some 93,883 workers and officials, the vast majority from neighboring countries in Asia. The private sector conducted even more such training programs, many of which verged on full-time jobs as Japanese workers began rejecting less desirable manual labor. Here the government lent a helping hand as well, by establishing screening organizations such as the Japan International Training Cooperation Organization, set up in October 1991 by four ministries. Between 1987 and 1991, according to Labor Ministry sources, the number of foreign trainees in Japan jumped from 17,100 to 43,600, and the government projected eventual enrollment in officially endorsed trainee programs would be 100,000 per year.[220]

Japanese officials themselves guessed that the absence of programs on Japanese economic management or governance reflected in part the absence of any need on the part of Japanese companies for high-level, non-Japanese managers. "The managerial level in Japanese companies is always occupied by Japanese people," said Kuwajima Kyoko, a Harvard-trained administrator at the Institute for International Cooperation in Tokyo, run by JICA. "Sometimes I feel that the Japanese managerial side thinks that managerial ideas are things that only Japanese people can understand or make operational." The dearth was also incurred by a lack of imagination on the part of Japanese officials. They were not theoreticians, and did not think of their work in abstract terms. "My private idea," said Kuwajima, "is that these were ideas used by officials in their own jobs. They never gave them theoretical expression. As far as JICA is concerned, we never noticed that economic management was a very strong point of the Japanese bureaucracy. What we thought we could sell was the kind of working philosophy that exists in Japanese companies, and the only way you could get at them was through very technical subjects, in courses run by the private sector."[221]

Added Sugita Nobuki, an EPA official involved in training programs, "In terms of transferring Japanese technology or capital to foreign countries, the first thing is just to set up a factory using less expensive labor. It did not matter if there was any transfer of economic thinking. Japanese business all around the world is very practical. Japanese businessmen don't give much thought to the idea of transferring economic thinking or values. The first thing was to set up a factory and produce something, then export, so that the company could survive. That's what they thought."[222]

The third force behind Japan's new policy activism was the growing ascendancy of Japanese bureaucrats who, in the late 1980s, were reaching their forties. These were mostly men who had been in university during the Vietnam War era. By virtue of the Japanese seniority system, Japanese officials typically reached the height of their bureaucratic careers by their late forties and early fifties. Unlike their elders who actually fought the Americans and proceeded to adopt their business management style and technology, the elite bureaucrats of the 1990s came of age in the 1960s, a decade that began with the "Ampo" riots against the U.S.-Japan security treaty and ended with Japan's own student paroxysms against the government and its support for the Vietnam War.

This generation group retained a visceral resentment against the United States into middle age. "We grew up thinking of America as the enemy," said Yanagihara Toru, the development economist. "When Japan caught up with the United States in the late 1970s, we had no one left to hate." In the early 1990s, as the 1960s-generation bureaucrats hit their stride, a period of political confusion and collapse in Japan coincided with attempts by the U.S. government to break with its tradition of achieving incremental gains in favor of a "results-oriented" trade strategy with Japan. The younger generation of Japanese bureaucrats viewed the latter as a welcome invitation to do battle.

In its evolution, the bureaucratic campaign to develop and propagate the Japanese model may have originally been motivated by a desire to preserve Japanese autonomy in its economic activities in Asia, but over time, the scope of the bureaucrats' ambitions widened. Many of the tactics and strategies used in the campaign to promote the Japanese model were also used to attack U.S. hegemony over the rules of international trade. The same argument came into play—that the diversity of economic systems required different rules and gradual approaches. In March 1996, one of the younger-generation bureaucrats, Sakamoto Yoshihiro, MITI's vice-minister for International trade declared, "The era of bilateralism is over." He told a group of foreign correspondents in Tokyo that from then onwards, the World Trade Organization (WTO) would serve as the "constitution" of international trade. "Considering the globalization of industrial activities, it is no longer relevant to negotiate and have an agreement on issues related to global industries in a limited bilateral context such as between Japan and the United States," Sakamoto said.[223]

The announcement was startling because it came weeks before a summit meeting between President William J. Clinton and Japanese prime minister Hashimoto Ryutaro that otherwise focused on security matters. The economic relationship with the United States seemed relatively calm. Sakamoto and his colleagues at MITI, however, were concentrating on an issue just over the horizon—the anticipated U.S. strategy in the WTO, due to be launched at the end of the year in December 1996 in Singapore.

The U.S. media treated Sakamoto's speech as a diversion, a delay tactic designed to tie up the United States in clumsy, multilateral trade machinery.[224] Few recognized the depth of his threat. Edward Lincoln, then special advisor to U.S. ambassador Walter Mondale, saw the remarks as an example of familiar disinformation tactics. He wrote, "Sakamoto is preying upon public ignorance of the WTO. . . . I have argued for the past two years that little has changed in the Japanese government negotiating patterns. Denial of problems, rigid resistance, strong rhetoric, vigorous PR efforts abroad, minimal concessions, weak implementation are all familiar patterns for the past thirty years. The advent of a non-LDP government in 1993 raised hopes among some journalists and others that the pattern would change with the Japanese government embracing open markets more enthusiastically. This speech by Sakamoto provides public testimony to the lack of change in a more open direction. Indeed, the concepts expressed in the speech move Japan backward. The underlying message is that not only will Japan resist change, it may even refuse to talk about moving toward more open markets."[225]

Sakamoto wasn't just moving backward, however. He was in charge of the study group that eight years earlier, in 1988, had advised the government to form an Asian trade bloc to defend itself from rival economic blocs in Europe and North America. Now, Sakamoto was equally alarmed about prospects that the United States would use WTO to pursue an enlarged agenda encompassing competition and regulatory barriers as well as the conventional terrain of tariff barriers to trade and investment.

Battle lines were drawn months before the first WTO meeting in December 1996. In April, Sylvia Ostry, a Canadian economist, told a small audience at the Monetary Authority of Singapore, "In a world of deepening internationalization, the new agenda is to focus more on domestic policies, or systems differences as I call them, rather than border barriers." Up until now, Ostry said, the international trade regime of the Uruguay Round of the GATT had concentrated on "border barriers." While GATT implied "an acceptance of systems diversity," the WTO would move toward harmonization of systems. "This is focused on Japan, this question of moving beyond trade. The new terminology will be 'effective access.' "[226]

The old antagonists of GATT had managed to beat back previous U.S. initiatives infringing on national sovereignty. Although the Uruguay Round concluded agreements on intellectual property rights and trade-related investment measures, they were narrow in scope and provided substantial caveats for developing countries. The new U.S. initiative went back to the Havana Charter of 1948, which created the GATT to safeguard tariff concessions already negotiated in bilateral trade agreements in the pre-war years. The Havana Charter included prohibitions against restrictive business practices including cartels, market access barriers, and trade monopolies. It also proposed an International Trade Organization (ITO) that was fifty years ahead of its time. But the U.S. Congress killed the ITO, and competition and regulatory policy had so far escaped the GATT arena. For the United States to include either on the WTO agenda or to call for systems harmonization directly attacked the type of economic ideology Japan had been fostering as an "alternative paradigm" to Western capitalism, based on industrial policy, gradualism, and export-push policies. Developing economies immediately recognized the challenge, and so did Japan.

This was natural because Washington had first tried out systematic pressure against the business practices of another country with Japan; the Bush administration's (senior) 1989 Structural Impediments Initiative had similarly made use of convergence and harmonization arguments, attacking Japanese exceptionalism. Early on, the Japanese had blunted, SII by insisting that it be a "two-way street," with the U.S. doing something to fix its macroeconomic policy (then sufferening from twin budget and balance of payments deficits) and poor savings habits. The discussions had meandered on under different names through two terms of the Clinton administration, first as the "framework talks," later as the "enhanced framework initiative."

Washington was aware of the background of its push to even out the differences between economic systems and remembered all too well the failure of the SII talks. At a preparatory conference for the WTO in Singapore in April 1996, Peter Watson, chairman of the U.S. International Trade Commission, admitted that "the reality is we got nowhere with those talks." He recounted his own experience when visiting Japan in February 1990, in company with then Defense Secretary Dick Cheney. Meetings at the Japanese Defence Agency were "all harmony, sweetness and light." When he met with Japanese diplomats on SII, however, the result was "verbal pugilism." Nonetheless, Watson insisted that something had to be done to redress the omissions of the Uruguay Round. "The Uruguay Round agreements still do not address to any meaningful degree many sources of recent worldwide trade friction such as cartel activities, restrictive business practices, and informal government–private sector arrangements." He went on to talk about a new standard to measure the relative openness of economies—"contestability." "In the international arena," he said, "contestability is becoming the all-encompassing term for market access."[227]

The last place the Japanese wanted to see structural negotiations re-emerge was in WTO. Tokyo hoped that the WTO would become a large, mushy organization that it could use to sidestep future trade pressure. Between 1996 and 1999, Tokyo lobbied successfully to postpone substantive discussions on competition policy and investment rules until after the formal completion of the Uruguay Round agenda early in the next century. Japan sought to prevent the launching of another broad "round" of economic negotiations, pressing instead for loose conventions within the private sector. Finally, it argued that WTO rules should supersede national trade legislation, but that the WTO itself should tolerate diverse institutional and rules structures. Thus, "diversity" and "pluralism" became code words for preserving the status quo.

Sano Tadakatsu, director-general of MITI's International Economic Affairs Department, presaged each of these themes at the Singapore conference in 1996. Sano described Japan's version of the global economic order of the future: "What I perceive as the future international society is not one which is thoroughly harmonized under a single international framework, but a multi-layered society, where various systems coexist, including multilateral systems, plurilateral systems based on specific issues, regional trade agreements, and bilateral relationships, whether comprehensive or issue-specific. From another perspective, there will also coexist various frameworks with regard to issues, i.e., not only trade but also security, politics, economy, labor, and so on. The trade framework alone is not almighty, and its coverage should not be stretched beyond its capacity."[228]

There were many reasons for the failure of the WTO meeting in Seattle in November and December 1999. To start out with, the United States and EU even fought over the name of the round. The Europeans called for a "Millennium Round" that would cover a wide swathe of issues, while the United States insisted on "manageable" talks focusing on the "built-in" agenda of services and agriculture, and wanted to call it "GATS 2000" (standing for General Agreement on Trade in Services, which the United States hoped to update in the session). Japan allied itself with the EU in its call for a comprehensive round; with developing countries, in supporting their push for gradual implementation of Uruguay Round commitments; and with its farmers, on agriculture. Japan's pitch for agriculture included a new concept called "multifunctionality," defending agricultural subsidies as multiple-use policy tools that also protected the environment and advanced the cause of sustainable development. On the public relations front, Japan came fully armed.

Officials distributed Japan's WTO proposals on agriculture, genetically altered foods, and forestry and fishery products in a handout in six languages—Japanese, English, French, Spanish, Chinese, and Korean. Another pamphlet called for the "establishment of trade rules for the twenty-first century that contribute to the era of diversity and coexistence."[229]

Tokyo did not need its elaborate preparations. The emotions in Seattle ran in Japan's favor—against globalization. In the streets, demonstrators from a host of causes shut down the city on November 30, charging WTO with sins ranging from environmental destruction to child abuse. Many were particularly angry with the organization for its infringements against national sovereignty, real and imagined. "When did we ever elect the WTO?" read placards. Finally, the delegates let the moment go, each suspicious of the other's motives, tired of battling their way into meetings. In one episode, MITI Vice-Minister Arai Hisamitsu had just begun a speech to an audience of economists, businesspeople, and officials. He was skeptical about the meeting's chances to successfully launch the next round. "What is going to happen?" Arai asked rhetorically. "If I were to make a prediction about the outcome, I would say it would be either a resounding success or a total failure."[230] At that very moment, police announced a "lockdown" of the hotel, providing an abrupt end to the session.

At 11:00 P.M. on December 3, delegates streamed with their umbrellas from the Seattle Convention Center. Emotions ranged from outrage to exhaustion. Inside, WTO Director-General Michael Moore and U.S. Special Trade Representative Charlene Barshefsky, like the band playing on the deck of a sinking *Titanic,* were conducting the final plenary session with nervous aplomb. Journalists gathered around a TV in the media center, laughing as Moore made lame jokes about Seattle hospitality and vowed to resist pressure to step down. "I intend to fulfill my contract," said Moore, a former prime minister of New Zealand and head of its Labor Party. "I have a background of fulfilling contracts in the labor movement." After the plenary, Moore and Barshefsy held a press conference. At 1:00 A.M. on December 4, the last of the journalists, officials, and NGO observers straggled out. The "Battle of Seattle" was over, and the negotiating round that was supposed to lay the groundwork for the international trade system in the next century was postponed indefinitely.

Barshefsky claimed that the Seattle conference failed because "issues that had been intractable remained intractable," and blamed the process, not substance. She said, "What I think happened—this was the fourth in a series of episodes—was that the delegations came, they proceeded to work exceptionally hard, and in good faith, but were not quite willing to make political decisions." Her EU counterpart, however, saw a much deeper failure. At the same midnight press conference, EU Trade Commissioner Pascal Lamy said, "The process has to be reassessed, reinvigorated, refurbished, and maybe rebuilt. The WTO does not have the institutional strength, the culture, or procedures to do this right."

Apprentices

Sun slants through the plate-glass windows of an overheated conference room. Outside, the magenta and gold of Japanese maples and gingko trees in full autumnal bloom light a corner of the East Garden of Tokyo's Imperial Palace. Swans trace desultory trails across the jade-green imperial moat. Inside the room, two-dozen finance officials, most in their thirties, all from developing countries, listen attentively to a tall, patrician Japanese.

Kinoshita Toshihiko sits back in his chair, easing into his subject, speaking in slow but polished English. A former treasurer of the Japan Export-Import Bank (JEXIM), Kinoshita has lectured at Harvard and many other universities. In 1994, he was in charge of the bank's research institute, a retirement job thrown his way after losing a power struggle as part of the bank's upper management. Kinoshita was not old, but he had been suddenly relegated to the ranks of teacher and explainer. He had the leisure now to think about such abstractions as Japanese industrial policy. His manner was confident and relaxed. He had given this lecture before. He would give it again.[231]

It was history seen through the eyes of an insider and a nationalist. The lecture has a single theme: How Japan got rich. For any Japanese, the subject is a source of powerful pride. He is courteous to the visiting officials. Perhaps, they have forgotten that Japan was ever poor. He hands around a chart, comparing the Japanese and U.S. economies in 1870, when Japan began its modernization spurt. Its baseline is the U.S. GNP per capita in 1973, set at 100. The chart shows that 125 years earlier, Americans were ten times as wealthy as Japanese. The gap closed slowly. In 1870, the U.S. per capita income was at 13 on Kinoshita's index; Japan was at 1.4. A hundred years later, in 1970, Japanese incomes were just slightly higher than U.S. incomes in the year 1900. In 1973, Japanese incomes were just under one-half of U.S. incomes. It was only in the preceding twenty years that the Japanese had become the wealthiest people in the world, after the Swiss.

Patience may be the first lesson for those who wish to learn from the Japanese model. Kinoshita picked up his thread four centuries earlier. The scene was the island of Tanegashima, off Kyushu, now one of Japan's main satellite launching centers; the subject was Japanese aptitude for technology absorption. In 1543, the Lord of Tanegashima acquired two samples of a primitive shoulder gun, the arquebus, from a shipwrecked Portuguese sailor. "Japanese artisans learned how to manufacture guns within one year," Kinoshita said, "at almost the same level of quality. This shows the high level of craftsmanship of artisans at the time. By the end of the sixteenth century, wars were going on all over Japan to integrate the country, and they were fought with guns. It was the gun that integrated Japan."

Another subject: How high levels of literacy in premodern Japan helped to propel its industrial revolution around the time of the beginning of World War One. Kinoshita turned to education. "Although schools of the modern type were established in the nineteenth century, even the children of farmers went to temples and learned how to read, how to write, and do arithmetic. In the sixteenth to eighteenth centuries, the children of farmers could read, write, and use the abacus. Without that background, even if new technology had been introduced, it would not have spread throughout the nation."

The visiting officials fidgeted. This sounded like a familiar argument— that Japan was beyond compare; it was never an underdeveloped country really, and therefore nobody could emulate it. Its people were simply waiting for the right moment to put their craft and management skills to work. The officials are grateful when the story livens up a bit. In 1853, American gunships forcibly ended Japan's two centuries of self-imposed exile under the *sakoku* policy that began in 1639; the term means a country that is locked away. According to Kinoshita, Japan had all the ingredients for rapid development—a highly educated people and craft tradition—but it had no idea what to do with them. There was no game plan. Japan was in a quandary. It solved its problem by deciding to model itself after the West. "When Japan looked at neighboring Asian countries, Japan found that most of them were colonies. So when Japan opened its doors to the West in 1868, at the time of the Meiji Restoration, the leitmotif of the Japanese government was not to be colonized," said Kinoshita. To learn how to preserve sovereignty in an aggressive, imperial age, the Meiji government sent some of its most senior members on a two-year odyssey to the industrial center of the world, Europe and North America.

The Iwakura Mission was not Japan's first embassy abroad, but it became the most influential. Led by Iwakura Tomomi, the delegation left late in 1871, with fifty "young leaders" and fifty-nine students on their way to study in the United States and Europe. Landing in San Francisco on January 15, 1872, the Japanese spent seven months in the United States, then went on to England for four months, finally spending seven months on the continent. In the United States, they learned about the pioneer spirit, education for the masses, and practical protectionism. In Europe, they learned about industrial policy. "Japan was really very poor. Japanese were very much shocked when they visited the United States for the first time and saw how well people lived," Kinoshita said. This shock translated into urgent action upon their return.

Kinoshita dates the beginning of Japanese industrial policy to German chancellor Otto Bismarck's welcome speech to the Iwakura group in 1887. Bismarck "contended that laissez faire is the logic of the strongest. The governments of less developed countries must protect their own industries first." Bismarck drew on the theories of Friedrich List, the German economist who was much in vogue in the 1870s and 1880s. List argued that the state should play a role in guiding trade and industry in order to preserve national independence. England had done it and was the dominant nation of the age.

"By accepting or excluding the import of their raw materials and other products, England—all powerful as a manufacturing and commercial country—can confer great benefits or inflict great injuries upon nations with relatively backward economies," List wrote. The economist provided a German alternative to the free-market theories of Adam Smith and others who crafted liberal economics of the Anglo-American type. The Japanese got the point instantly. The industrial revolution was not about machines. It was about power. Industrial strategy was a variant of military strategy. Fukuzawa Yukichi, a Japanese intellectual who accompanied the Iwakura mission, coined the phrase, *fukoku kyohei*, "rich country, strong army." The two went together. The samurai of the Tokugawa Era, schooled in war, were ready to learn how to do business.

The Iwakura mission put its stamp on Japanese industrial policy for the next century. Japan virtually banned foreign investment and fostered national enterprises in textiles, shipbuilding, steel and rubber manufacture and the railways—before turning them over to the favored conglomerates that formed the pre-war *zaibatsu*, or big business cliques. This elaborate system crumpled with Japan's defeat in World War Two, only to be reborn with United States help.

"The United States thought that to strengthen Japan was the thing to do to prevent the rise of leftists," Kinoshita continued. "Spurred by the United States, the bureaucrats again began to build up a very strong Japanese economy. Most of the technocrats were not purged. With their knowledge of the Japanese economy, accumulated in wartime, they knew which companies could produce good steel or cement. For them to deploy a new industrial policy was not so difficult. Thus the industrial policy of the post-war period began. And it was justified," said Kinoshita. "If the government had not done anything, Japan would not have had coal, steel, electricity, or shipping. Our ideas did not come from economic textbooks. They came from people's sentiments that we should have big industries, industries that would make Japan grow strong."

Kinoshita ends his lecture. There are a few minutes left for questions. Hands go up. Amarananda Abeygunasekara, from Sri Lanka's Ministry of Finance, asks, "Was there one person that really changed your thinking? One of your leaders who said, 'This is the way to go?'" Kinoshita is stunned; this is not a question that he was expecting. "I have no idea," he replies lamely. "Like Lee Kuan Yew," says Abeygunasekara, coaching, trying to help him out. "I don't think we had a Lee Kuan Yew in Japan," replies Kinoshita, referring to Singapore's former prime minister. "There were so many people who began to change their ideas. They were unknown, faceless. "What about MITI?" asks a young African official. "Did not it have a great influence on Japan's success?" "Well, yes," Kinoshita prevaricates. "Particularly in the post-war period. Its influence was so great, but there were so many exceptions. MITI was very successful at retreating bad industries, declining industries. Sometimes MITI contributed, sometimes it intervened too much. Now MITI people, with few exceptions, think they should keep permanent power for emergencies, but that the private sector should handle most things."

As treasurer of JEXIM, Kinoshita spent much of his career advancing the interests of Japanese business in Southeast Asia. The aim of his lecture was simple: construct a new mythology of development based on the Japanese experience. This was the message: get the power, adopt Japanese-style industrial policy.

Kinoshita's lecture provided a snapshot of Japanese thinking about its "model." The lecture was, first of all, a form of mythmaking. It left out a great deal, but that is the way of myths. The heroes and icons of Japanese nationalism were all there. Japanese believed that they created their powerful economy through a combination of patriotic zeal, bureaucratic brainpower, human resources in the form of a sophisticated—though preindustrial culture—and native pragmatism. The toolkit for Japanese development was by nature eclectic; its goals of policy were not so much economic as political. The Meiji state understood power and accurately recognized that military strength in an industrial age was based on industry.

As the "class" streamed out of the red-brick office tower that JEXIM shared with the OECF, the comments get more personal. "It's all supply side," scoffed a brash Egyptian, Ashraf Attia Hassannien Nofal, a Japan specialist in Egypt's Ministry of International Cooperation. Others complained they had heard too much of it before. The twenty officials were close to the end of a two-month "seminar on economic development policies," sponsored by the JICA, Japan's major humanitarian aid organization, and the EPA.

The "students" said that Kinoshita's presentation was among the best they had heard, and were impressed by his charm and command of the material. But they seemed far from convinced. Their questions reflected the fundamental ambiguity of Japan's efforts to propagate the Japanese economic model. The objective of Japanese industrial policy was to foster national strength, not to nurture rivals.

The officials had gone to lectures on "Japanese Society and People," "Japanese History and Culture," "Japan's Economy" (twice), "Politics and Administration System in Japan," "Education in Japan" (twice), the "World Economy"; seen a video on "Japan's Economy and Enterprises in the Post-war Rehabilitation Period"; and experienced a single Japanese conversation lesson. They had gone to programs on Japanese economic planning, fiscal policy, aid policy, "deregulation," labor policy, the Export-Import Bank of Japan, OECF and the Japanese central bank, and visited the Tokyo Stock Exchange and Kyoto and a handful of companies, including Toto, the toilet maker. Before leaving Japan, each was supposed to submit a report on their "studies." Not one of them felt that they had been able to engage in significant debate with their Japanese hosts—and all were very tired of the history lessons.

A frustrated Maria Judith Guabloche, an analyst with the Central Reserve Bank of Peru, said: "We heard a lot of this in the first week we were here. When we heard about agricultural policy, first we got the history of Japan. When they told us about industrial policy, we also got the history of Japan. It's not to say I haven't enjoyed myself, but I feel exasperated." Lamented Misran Basir, an official with Malaysia's Economic Planning Unit, "Every single lecture started with the Meiji Era. Every lecture. All of them. This was quite different from similar courses I have gone through in the United States and U.K. I attended one on infrastructure and industrial development in the U.K., for example, where they gave us lots and lots of theory and then case examples. Here, there was no theory. What they wanted to tell us was how Japan developed, but the methodology they used was totally different from the Western concept. Once they start lectures, it's difficult to interrupt. In terms of discussion, there is none."

Miguel Herrera, an economist with the Philippines's National Economic and Development Authority, thought he understood the Japanese approach. "During the years when Japan was engaged in high-speed growth, Japanese bureaucrats did not have this global view of their role. It's only in the last few years, in the last decade, that they began to realize they had to put more emphasis on their role as a global power, because they have so much power economically today. They thought they were obligated to act responsibly instead of just growing their economy. This kind of policy has something to do with these training programs they are doing now. They are just trying to do their perceived duty. That's why suddenly they are doing training [in] all fields."

"In my case," said Guabloche, "it was very, very elementary. I supposed that it would be more technical. I'm not asking about theory, but a little more technical analysis of the economic situation, not only on the history of Japanese economic development, but using theory for analysis." "We're all here to look at what Japan did in the last few decades that we might apply to our own economies," said Herrera. "At the end of the day, you realize that there's nothing here that these countries that we represent can adapt, because the answer is always historical and all countries have different histories. While a few of our countries have parallel histories, Japan is something different. You really have to isolate Japan and then there's nothing we can get out of it."

I asked Herrera if he thought the training program was designed to influence him to model the Philippines after Japan. Yes, he said. "The way the training was structured, I think that was a major objective. But the system was simply not delivering." Herrera continued: "Based on my experience before coming here, I knew this course was supposed to be about Japan's experience, how they got here. So they're trying to influence our economies into probably adopting some of the success stories. The big disappointment—as I said—is that anything about Japan's development was historical. There was nothing scientific."

The students had other complaints. Their reading materials were outdated, their Japanese tutors unhelpful. No attempt was made, for example, to put the students—after all, midranking officials in their nations' main economic ministries—together with Japanese specialists in their areas. The Peruvian central banker, for one, searched without success during her two months for a Japanese economist who specialized in the Latin American economy. She wanted to explore possible applications of the Japanese development experience to the Peruvian economy. The JICA official who served as her tutor had nothing to say.

I tried to help. I phoned Yanagihara, the development specialist, who had a special connection with Peru, and was fluent in Spanish. I told him about Guabloche's problem and her search for a Latin American specialist. But Yanagihara failed to get in touch with Guabloche, and she left Tokyo no wiser.[232]

Part Two
Japan's Lost Decade

Determined to fall
A weather-exposed skeleton
I cannot help the sore wind
Blowing through my heart

—Basho Matsuo, *The Narrow Road to the Deep North*

7
Legacy

American Dreams

Time and events are a kind of music. I can hear Akamatsu and his flying geese set to the tune of "Sakura," the Asian crisis as a snatch of Kitaro, shimmering, emotive, irresolute. Woven between the two, if you listen closely, are the strains of big band music, an electric guitar riff, a line from "America, the Beautiful."

I look down the long slope of Aoyama Dori and into my past. The leafy Togugosho, the imperial family compound, is to the left. To the right, a column of nondescript office towers marches downhill. The Canadian embassy is on this block, parked like an errant iceberg. Passersby take the escalator to its broad public plaza, decorated with stone and metal sculpture, one of the few spots in central Tokyo from which the entire skyline is visible, peeking above the forest of the Togugosho.

To the west are the ghostly towers of Shinjuku. North is the sixty-story "Sunshine City," marking the big train station at Ikebukuro; to the east, musty 1950s office blocks intermingle with vanity buildings dating from the "bubble" era. The Tokyo skyline is defined not so much by height as by the course of the Yamanote Sen, a light-rail line that encircles the Imperial Palace in an irregular loop with the shape of a tooth yanked out of a jaw. It separates Tokyo's densely packed downtown from the more tranquil suburbs. Yet, even this view across serried concrete has its charms—an old garden adjacent to the embassy, trees and an ancient wall across the street, a glimpse of serried lanterns at an imperial shrine down the hill.

If I look hard, I can see the same landscape in the 1950s, dusty, without tall buildings, a flat sea of black-tiled roofs. I first gazed out across the city in 1959, a few weeks after my seventh birthday. We were on our way to Southeast Asia; an average American family, naïve, confident, owners of a single family home and a blue Chevrolet station wagon, which came behind us on a freighter. We left behind an America basking in the security of an economy so huge it left the rest of the world as paupers, armed to the teeth, with a victorious general as president. We entered Asia, at the front lines of the Cold War. It was a deep plunge; I never recovered.

Asia is a mythical region, its name and boundaries artificial. In Chinese and Japanese, the words *Yazhou* and *Ajia* have a foreign ring. To an American child of the 1950s, Asia was a huge new house with servants, an *ayah*, stares of street children, curious adults noting the hair on our arms and the color of our skin. It was a flood of colors, piercing scents, noise, dust, chaos; and most of all, brilliant sunshine that made the sun of North America seem thin and pallid. The tidy neighborhoods of North America, warehouse-sized supermarkets, empty streets and traffic lights, television, theme parks, people speaking in a language we could understand, were 6,000 miles away. We huddled like damp kittens in a storm.

There is a spider, velvet black and chrome yellow, hanging over a cool current of water. It flows down the side of a volcano to the Java Sea, an inlet of a luminous Pacific, buoying up islands and majestic continents. I am eight, and wearing a sarong. It has a pattern of green and brown leaves and butterflies. I dip myself in the cool water; I get out and walk down a smooth dirt path. Villagers greet me; it is my village. The road leads to a great temple mound, an emblem of Mount Meru, the cosmic mountain. I stand on the upper platform, survey the sacred rivers Elo and Progo, the hill Tidar, and see that I am at the center of the universe. The great Boddhisatvas silently wait inside their bell-shaped stupas, impervious to time. This is where I begin.

My father arranges us on the lawn for a last photograph before our departure. The backdrop is our little house, a cottage on a quiet cul de sac. We are pale and pudgy. My infant brothers wear beanie caps and Buster Brown suits; my twelve-year-old sister, Mary Ellen, kneels behind us, looking queenly and mischievous in a rhinestone tiara. I have on something white and frilly, and prop up a big red umbrella. The light is soft and luminous, as it often is in Salem, Oregon, where misty rain can fall from a cloudless sky. We had no idea where we were going or why we were going there. We knew about the Soviet Union and Sputnik. In my first-grade class in the school at the top of the hill there were nuclear attack drills. We would crouch beneath our desks until we got the all clear. We had never heard of Indonesia. It was as mysterious as a star.

Collecting the shards of a memory so scattered across time and place is no easy task. Even the mementos are haphazard. Above my desk is a "proclamation" signed by Captain Robert Judd of Japan Airlines, attesting to the fact that Miss Edith Buchanan Terry has crossed the international dateline on February 19 of *inoshishi*, the year of the pig, 1959. It was a drama, back then, to cross the dateline. The flight, by propeller plane, was interminably long. We flew to San Francisco, then Honolulu, from Honolulu to Guam and Tokyo. From Tokyo, according to my mother, we flew in a huge zigzag to Hong Kong, Singapore, back up to Manila, and finally south to Jakarta, by way of Garuda Airlines, Indonesia's official carrier. I remember long waits in airports, excursions to a teahouse and to Tokyo Tower, to Tiger Balm Gardens in Singapore. I was homely and bookish, with brown bangs and pointy eyeglasses like exclamation points. I explained primly to a stewardess that I would be unable to eat anything because I was on a diet.

Scenes from that trip are like ancient postcards. In Tokyo, we stayed in the old Imperial Hotel, designed by Frank Lloyd Wright, with its narrow corridors engineered from volcanic blocks, which survived the Great Kanto Earthquake of 1923 only to be knocked down in the name of progress in the 1970s. Not far away were the former headquarters of the Supreme Command of Allied Forces, SCAP, and the green lawns and tooled pines of the Imperial Palace. We surveyed the city from the viewing platform of Tokyo Tower, just completed, a garish orange-and-white replica of the Eiffel Tower in Paris, painted in those colors for reasons of "airline safety" according to its owners. We saw the landscape as a fighter pilot might as he swooped down for a bomb run. The tower was a needle stuck in a gritty industrial landscape that stretched to the horizon, Mount Fuji a smudge to the southwest. The city, stretched out beneath us, was a warren of wooden buildings that, looking old, were mostly new.

Our journey ended. Dangerous herds of geese roamed the muddy streets, chasing us away screaming. We moved into a big, red-tiled mansion fronted by an open sewer, then a dirt road; beyond these were ramshackle houses on stilts. Farther still were rice fields, a wall of jungle, and volcanoes. I dreamed of Krakatoa, of oceans filled with strange fish, glittering water, and sand like a harsh mirror, reflecting nightmares. I dreamed of poisonous snakes that came up through the sewers and into the bath and toilets, creeping across the tiles, and chickens running headless from the cook, with her bloody knife. I dreamed of slender young girls, wearing gilt crowns and lipstick, fingers bent back to the wrist, performing solemn, emblematic Javanese court dances to wailing flutes and the cascading percussion of *gamelan* music.

With other children, I learned how to explore the neighborhood. We walked high walls laced with glass shards to keep out thieves. I ran barefoot down the road, and up ladders into the homes of rice farmers; sometimes we were invited. Poverty was a person, tapping at the window glass, clutching at your shoe as it trundled past, legless, on a wheeled cart. Shantytowns puffed over canals, walked on stilts over the flowing garbage. There were no stray pieces of tin, plywood, or cardboard. They went into the construction of subdivisions of the poor. I learned how to look away.

There are moments that rearrange the stray filings of consciousness like a magnet. I was anguished and waiting to go home. The next moment, I despaired at the thought of leaving. It happened during a family vacation in 1960. In the States, we had regularly taken the car across the country to visit relatives in Alabama and Georgia. Traveling across Indonesia was a far different proposition. There were splinter army groups in the mountains, and roads were unreliable.

We drove the blue Chevy through the forest, fearful of mercenaries hiding in the mountains, spooked by bands of monkeys racing wildly across the road, dark with overhanging trees. We drove up through Puncak, past the Dutch resort of Cibulan, past Bogor and the palace full of Sukarno's mistresses, past the leafy, cool town of Bandung, and into central Java and the high plains. We stopped in Jogjakarta, famous for its *batik* textiles, its *wayang* puppet theater, and its temples. At night, in the downtown plaza, vendors would spread mats and sell food and music. Tourists would sit down next to tired shopkeepers, chatting and watching the flickering *wayang* dramas.

Not far outside the city are the great temple cities of Borobodur and Prambanan, built by the Sailendra and Mataram kings. We went first to Borobodur. I remember looking very carefully at the friezes. On the lower levels, there are lively scenes of villages and palace ceremonies; the scenes become more abstract as one climbs the step-shaped pyramid to the summit. I looked out to the valley ringed by hills and realized that the temple organized a space consisting of the valley, the angle of the sun, and the hills beyond. The broad dome of the temple echoed the shape of the hills and the dome of the sky. I was shaken and excited.

There was a thriving village market at the base of the monument, but no glossy pamphlets explaining who built it or what it meant. My parents' knowledge of Indonesia was based on a U.S. embassy post report, a few books, and word of mouth. They had not come to Indonesia as scholars. Their intellectual horizons were narrow, and they assumed that countries like Indonesia were moving toward a take-off stage in which they would fly into an American universe. Borobodur receded into memory like a star. As a college freshman, I crept into the stacks at Yale's Sterling Library and was rocked to discover a crumbling, oversized volume in French, Paul Mus's monumental *Barabudur* published in Hanoi in 1935, with silvery photographs and precise architectural drawings. I pored over the illustrations as though they contained clues to my stranded self.

In 1960, Borobodur had called me out of the place where I had been in hiding, a juvenile American in shades of gray. At Yale, my excitement in the stacks was part of a lengthy progress into an expatriate adulthood, the beginning of a dive into scholarship. I studied China, Japan, and India, as well as

Southeast Asia, recreating in my own mind the people and inventions that wrapped around central Java in the ninth century, which made possible but did not sufficiently explain the miracle. I became a journalist, and went on, and did other things. My next visit was not until 1989, in the company of Didiek Samsu, an Indonesian archeologist and friend. We admired together a frieze depicting merchants, serving women, holy men, and warriors of a thousand years ago, part of a sculptural narrative of the life of Buddha, 1.8 miles long. "No Indonesian ever went to India," Didiek told me. "We read books and imagined how it should look by ourselves. This was an Indonesian invention, not a copy." [1]

Old photographs. My father strides across a room in a checkered Indonesian sarong, clutching his flash camera. My mother has jasmine in her hair; she is wearing a *batik* sarong and the tight-fitting, lace *kebaya* of an Indonesian woman of means. The setting is lushly tropical, the faces white, American. My mother, Sarah, Mississippi-bred, product of a delta plantation, a Southern sorority girl, smiles brilliantly. My father, Charles, looks rumpled and uncomfortable, and is clearly in a hurry. He carries the faintly worried features of a white man in the tropics. He seems to be muttering to himself, so much to do, so little time. The photograph hides a joke. A moment later, my mother's sarong came undone, to her consternation; a maid had wrapped it the Indonesian way, without safety pins.

More photographs from the family album: A street peddler offers a melon for sale, comically balanced on his head. A handsome woman swings down the road, clad in a Playtex brassiere and *batik*. One picture shows in cameo the white columns and cupola of the presidential summer palace at Bogor, shaded by palms and acacia. Lotus pads drift on its lakes like fleets of flying saucers. My father in a white Panama suit lectures officials at Indonesia's Bank Negara, the central bank. In another photograph, a few years later, in Taiwan, he is seated with elderly Chinese bureaucrats in silk gowns, their wispy white beards like those of scholars in a Chinese painting. There are more photos, of the Philippines, all of parties, of long tables laden with platters of *lechon*, or suckling pig; the men in filmy *barong Tagalog*, their undershirts showing, the women in embroidered dresses with butterfly sleeves.

The snapshots, yellowed with age, have the calm remoteness of museum pieces. The Jakarta, the Taipei, the Manila of the late 1990s have razed their shantytowns, or hidden them behind high-rises. The old American School in Makati has shrunk behind a fence of apartment buildings, its soccer field a tiny square of green. In Taipei, the ranch-style homes of U.S. military and State Department families filled the slopes and valleys of Yangmingshan, a hill north of the city. Now it is one of Taipei's most exclusive suburbs, and wealthy Chinese enjoy its cool temperatures and the sulfurous fumes from its hot springs. Our old neighborhood in Jakarta, Kabayoran Baru, is an area of expensive boutiques and shopping malls.

On a visit to Jakarta in 1998, the contemporary city seems like a mirage. From the back of a motorcycle, the long line of blue skyscrapers flickers in and out of view. Behind each row are dirt roads and slums. The rice paddies, squares of green velvet neatly packaged with mud dikes, sprouts placed delicately by hand, have gone. You see few women in the downtown wearing sarongs or *kebaya*. Gone too are the vendors of fighting fish, carried in jars on racks suspended from a carrying pole. They would set them down to demonstrate the viciousness of their wares. The *betchaks*, tricycle taxis, have long since been banished. What happened to my village?

Family Album

Not long ago, my cousin came across another old photograph as she was cleaning out drawers after her mother's death. They lived in a pleasant Victorian house with a wraparound porch, now a bit unsteady, unlikely to be repaired. Uniontown is one of the fading Southern towns that are just off every highway in West Alabama, a victim of nostalgia, resentment, and the absence of work. In the late nineteenth century, one rhapsodist declared: "There are only two places on earth worth living, Paris and Uniontown!" The mansions lining Franklin Street echo with stories; they are senile but elegantly dressed, their columns missing a capstone or two.

There was my father in the photograph, leaning so close to his younger brother that they look like Siamese twins. He is dark haired, tall and lean; he wears a Confederate belt buckle that must have been a prize for a man without means. My uncle, sweet and affable, looks square at the camera's eye. Neither man is out of his twenties. Both brothers married women from the wealthy families of Uniontown, college roommates, in fact. One left this part of the country where both had grown up and joined the Air Force, went to Europe as an intelligence officer, came back and married, and went west, eventually as far west as Indonesia, Taiwan, the Philippines, and Vietnam. My uncle stayed behind, raising children and hunting dogs. He was a good old country boy, living in a landscape that changed little from the time of that photograph to the present. I am astonished at the contrast between these two worlds, united only by my family's experience—the Asian cities where I grew up, each scrambling through generations of change, and Uniontown, slumbering in its memories.

If I was a hybrid character, tentative and uncertain, my parents were American originals. Like high-wire artists, they walked out boldly over the abyss, offering no sign of anxiety, not just believing the American dream, but living it. Their long sojourn in Southeast Asia was a logical extension of this belief. One night, my mother was with a crowd of expatriates, at a dinner party or over a game of bridge. "You're here for the money, aren't you?" a woman asked. My mother was shocked. "Certainly not," she said. "We are here as government missionaries."

Many years after my father's death, he remains a mystery. There was no connection between his upbringing and his work in Asia. I, who have always been so concerned with continuity and identity, found this difficult to understand. Deserted by their parents at an early age, he and his brother were handed off to be raised by their older sisters, themselves little more than children. It was a family of small landholders in West Alabama, in a county that still ranks among the poorest in the nation. The women stayed in their houses and grew immensely fat. The men hunted, traded stories, and sometimes ran off when they were frightened by life, as my grandfather had after his wife's sudden death.

The Terrys immigrated to Virginia and the Carolinas in the eighteenth century and worked their way down to the vast pine forests of Alabama. My father was born in Greensboro, Alabama, in 1913, a region where kinship relationships are as dense as the material culture is thin. Even by the standards of West Alabama, my father was a disadvantaged child. He was unlucky; graduating from high school just as the Great Depression began, he borrowed money to start university from an uncle who quickly thought better of it. He dropped out from the University of Alabama, later enrolling in night classes at a law school, paying for it with a job as chief clerk for the state government. World War Two transformed him. I have a photograph of my father in his Air Force uniform, when he was in his early thirties. His look is serious and composed, his uniform well tailored. He came back from the war with stories of night flights and England during the blitz; stories, always stories, my father, strong narratives, entertaining and to the point.

My father had the grace and assurance of a full-blooded member of the Camelot generation. It was a time when Americans were confident that they had a message for the world, blatant in their arrogance, earnest to the point of fanaticism. Charles Terry, Cholly to his friends, with his black hair and Southern charm, was one such, making his way through receptions in Merdeka Palace or Malacanang and embassies as though they had been family barbecues back in Uniontown or Greensboro. He was a good diplomat; people confided in him. Imelda Marcos used to order him to the palace to complain about Ferdinand's infidelities. I have sat for hours listening to my father talk politics with Benigno "Ninoy" Aquino, Cory bustling about, at their spacious plantation in Tarlac Province in the Philippines. His friends were ministers, even presidents. He was known for his integrity and acumen.

I like to think of my father as an advocate of "good governance" before that awkward phrase was coined. Like many Americans of his time, he believed in big government. Government could absorb the best and brightest minds. It could sort out the mistakes made by the market, as many had learned during the depression years. By no means bureaucratic in mind-set—he was neither political nor fussy—he became an expert in public administration. In Alabama, he was associated with reform projects under Governor Frank Dixon; Alabama still uses a civil service examination that he helped design, replacing an older system of patronage.

It is a matter of strict family lore that my father did not seek out the assignment to Indonesia. The federal government came to him, in a nationwide talent scout for technical and management specialists to go overseas to work in the brand-new foreign aid program. At the time, he was head of personnel for Oregon. My father had left Alabama in 1952 with a political cloud over his head, the mood having changed from the reforms of the 1940s. We lived in a tiny, one-bedroom house in a suburb of Salem, the capital. My bedroom was in the attic, where my grandmother would sleep beside me when she came to visit. I walked up a hill to school, and had a teacher named Miss World, or so I remember. I loved her name, and would repeat it to myself, dreaming of the unknown.

My mother and I sit on a couch crowded with pillows in her comfortable home in Marion, the "Athens" of Alabama, so called because of a women's college and a military school. She turns the pages of the 1945 *Corolla,* the University of Alabama yearbook. This was her class, although, like my father, she failed to graduate. After her second year, she moved to Converse College, a finishing school for young Southern women of means. She knows her class at the University, though, pointing out the popular ones and the women who were pretty but not "that pretty." They are almost all women, and solidly white. Male professors wear military uniforms, as though ready to head for the front after the bell sounds for the end of class.

In a formal yearbook picture, Sarah Davis stands in a three-quarters pose, hands draped across the back of an antique straight-backed chair. She is wearing black lace, her light-brown hair in an incongruous puff of innocence around her face, her mouth in a half smile. Her family came from one of the grander Uniontown mansions, a classic Greek Revival house with six columns striding across the front, known as Indian Camp. The Glasses presided as well over a splendid Regency mansion, called Westwood, still standing on its hill at the end of a winding driveway, dominating the approach from Water Street, lived in by an elderly cousin who nurtures it like a weathered old camellia tree.

My grandmother, Mae Glass, was the second wife of a Mississippi Delta banker, mistress of her own plantation house, Mae Day. Both Indian Camp and Mae Day are gone, destroyed by fire. Flamboyant, wealthy, a world traveler, Miss Mae was no lightweight—she took her master's degree at Columbia, in child psychology, and was teaching school in Tennessee when she met my grandfather. One sister wrote novels; the other was in China for ten years as a missionary, returning to become the first female fellow of the American Psychiatric Association; another sister died young. In their teens, the four sisters gaze with serious intent from a family portrait, proud, chin first.

My mother was the youngest Davis child, a spoiled tomboy. In a photograph at the age of three or four, with white blonde hair in a blunt cut, she looks like she can barely sit still. She was lucky, missing the Great Depression. Within the family, she got things that her older sisters and brothers did not, a finishing school, a horse, attention. She was vivacious, physically strong and tall, and beautiful, with poor skin and teeth that nobody noticed but herself. She has deep blue eyes that could stop a bus, and in her seventies, she catches the eye with her erect carriage, flamboyant clothes, and vivid manner.

After college, she planned to go to graduate school to study Spanish but dropped the plans when she met my father. Instead, she ended up learning an array of exotic languages—Bahasa Indonesia, Mandarin Chinese, Tagalog. My mother spent her childhood "burying her nose in the sunshiney smell of cotton bolls"; riding "Buck," her thoroughbred Tennessee-gaited stallion; swinging on the grapevines hanging from tall trees near the banks of the Yalobusha in summertime; and hand-turning ice cream, made from "tree-ripened Elberta peaches, cream and custard."[2] Perhaps plantation living made my mother adaptable. Some years after my father's death, she remarried and moved to the little town of Marion, Alabama, not far from Greensboro and Uniontown. She compared her new environment to Jakarta in the 1950s. What she meant was that she could handle the isolation and find ways to enjoy it. It was also, in many ways, nearly as primitive as Jakarta had been in the 1950s. Coming back to America, my mother seemed to go back in time, to a place resembling her childhood.

Little Sarah was about six when somebody snapped a picture of her with her brother John and a young black man, James, in a flat-bottomed canoe on the Yazoo River. Her head is turned coquettishly toward the camera, half-hidden by hair. She is in the bow position, in a ballooning dress, directing the two boys, poling. In the distance, across the water, is a ragged tree line; the girl is fearless, exultant. This little child, so carefree and bold, became in many respects the ideal diplomat's wife. She loved the work. In later years, as she discarded the wonderful gowns she had worn to endless parties and receptions, I collected them. They are locked away now in a warehouse with other possessions, in a plastic container, folded, gleaming, a *cheong sam* in raised silver brocade; a slinky cocktail dress in a gilded red batik; a creamy, luxurious mink stole from a boutique in Hong Kong. She was glamorous, athletic, and nonchalant. Our yards were always infested with cobras; my mother would go out and kill them with a six iron. Well into her forties, she could do a headstand on a bicycle, gripping the handlebars.

In Asia, my mother's life was governed by a rigid protocol. Her rank in the wives' association depended entirely on her husband. This bothered her not at all. She was luxuriantly happy in the exotic, sociable, gilded high life of Southeast Asia in the middle part of the century, from the 1950s to 1970s. She loved people, she loved learning languages, and the hardships of life in Indonesia were hardly more than those on a delta plantation in the 1930s. She glittered, played bridge and golf, hosted receptions and dinner parties.

There are few photographs of me as a child. Part of the reason may be that I spent the toddler stage hiding in boxes. Later I would take a pile of books into a field and find a corner, against a wall, where I could read unseen. One picture has my blurred outline against a trace of hills, the Dutch resort of Cibulan in the foreground. I am squat and fat, with stringy brown hair and thick spectacles, wearing a sweater that is several sizes too small. In another photo, I am at an Embassy costume party, at age nine. I am wearing a red voile princess outfit, looking hot and miserable, with a Balinese dancer's gilt tiara on my head. Perhaps it took a child who thought she could be invisible, with an instinct for eclectic combinations, to feel so drawn to Asia, and later to Japan. When I was a child, Americans were new to Asia. I carried the weight of my American identity like a curse.

At the age of eleven or twelve, we were in Baguio on a family vacation when I picked up *The Ugly American* in the base library at Camp John Hay. My parents loved to take us there, for the golf as well as the cool air. A resort town dating from the American colonial period, with beautiful old hotels, Baguio was dominated by the American base. The book is a Cold War parable, whose principal characters are American diplomats. Bad guy Tom Knox is seduced by the luxuries of Paris. Good guy Homer Atkins invents a water pump that transforms his tropical host country and wins the hearts and minds of the Sarkhanese against Viet Minh and Soviet agents. The idea of winning "hearts and minds" away from communism fascinated America. John F. Kennedy loved this book, by William Lederer and Eugene Burdick, along with 4,000,000 other readers. Kennedy sent a copy of the book to every senator. There was a 1963 movie with Marlon Brando. I hardly remember the plot, but the title affected me, offering a clue to a new mythology, not a happy one, in which Americans were not automatically loved and admired. I put down the book and wondered why my parents were so blind.

Kennedy and the Camelot generation had created the myth of a civilizing mission in Asia, to spread democracy and the free market. I thought they had gotten things backwards, and fell in love with a dream of an Asian society building upon its own set of traditions. My manner was apologetic and halting, like a student in the first few lessons of a foreign language. I affected a Filipino accent, and sprinkled my sentences with bits of Taglish, an urban hybrid of Tagalog, Spanish, and English. I studied Philippine art and literature, poked around archeological sites on the outskirts of Manila, collecting Ming and Qing Dynasty pottery shards in shoeboxes, and swooned over provincial architecture, with its capiz shell windows, Philippine mahogany construction, and deep shadows.

My friends were artists, poets, and revolutionaries. I read the accounts in *Time* and *Newsweek* of Haight-Ashbury and the riots in Washington, Paris, and Tokyo; in my imagination, I was part of an underground movement whose currents were rippling around the world. I joined demonstrations outside the American embassy against the Vietnam War. Enrolling in a Philippine university, Ateneo de Loyola, I reveled in the sensation of leaving America behind. I was flattered when a classmate, Emman Lacaba, told me I looked like a Russian. He was a poet, tall and handsome, with constantly changing girlfriends; a few years later, he would be ambushed and killed by the Philippine constabulary in his New People's Army camp in Mindanao. By this time I was in a mode of high Germanic gloom, struggling through Hegel and Marx, reading Thomas Mann and Günter Grass. I dipped into Baudelaire and Rimbaud. The sunny self-mockery of the Philippine sensibility was lost on me. I swam laps in a local pool to the point of exhaustion. A friend remembers me as a fashion model. This was an aberration, an inside joke against the establishment. In a photograph, a group picture with my sister and brothers, I am lithe and brown and have an odd look on my face, squinting at the camera, dazed with the sun.

To my grief, I had no staying power; I also had a suspicion that I was acting out a caricature of rebellion and self-discovery, rather than the real thing, and that I could no more become a Philippine revolutionary than I could strip away the other places that I had been and known, the multiple layers of identity that had already stuck in my psyche like coral polyps, and begun to grow. In 1969 and 1970, I was unnerved by the increasing violence of the country. Marcos was in the process of declaring martial law and joining the ranks of former Asian democrats turned dictators. The New People's Army gathered strength in the Cordilleras and elsewhere in the islands. At the University of the Philippines, not far from Ateneo, Marcos sent tanks to confront the students.

In Spring 1970, I suddenly dropped out of Ateneo and applied to university in the United States, picking Yale from among a small stack of admission letters. It was no more than a distant image of books and libraries, ever in short supply in the countries where I had grown up. Once there, the soft shades of Connecticut reminded me of a black-and-white photograph, color leached away. The university won me over by sound, not sight—the spume of piano music and electric guitars drifting from windows onto the street, enthralling rhetoric, concerts heard from the choir seats of Woolsey Hall, great volumes of music washing over my head. In a photograph, I am in Bloomsbury mode, owl-eyed and impish, seated on an antique armchair, a thick, leather-bound volume resting on my lap. And yet, I was awkward, out of place, an Asian in disguise inhabiting a New England paradise that was far too cold, and dismal in its grays and beige. When I think of the Japanese, caught between the worlds of Asia and the West, I remember myself at age eighteen or nineteen, frustrated with my ambiguous position somewhere in the middle. I thought if there was a door, I would walk through it, into certainty, into Asia.

And then, between my freshman and sophomore years, like magic, a door appeared, together with a guide. Manuel Elizalde Jr., known by his nickname, Manda, sought escape. His Shangri-la was an image of a less complicated time, before Americans or Spaniards had touched the Philippine archipelago. Manda, however, was a billionaire, and had the resources to bring his myth to life.

Blit, July 13, 1971, 8:35 A.M.

The Tasaday waited for us outside the forest, in an encampment that Dafal, the Bird, had taught them how to build, bamboo shelters of a common type. They were shy and graceful [I have scratched these words out], disturbed but brave before the onslaught of helicopters and aliens. Manda and Mai Tuan went immediately down into the forest, about half a mile, to a stream where the group stopped. The Tasaday build nothing of their own. They carry with them on their backs mats of pounded bark. These were placed on the ground and most of the group—they have no leaders—gathered around Mai Tuan and Igna, the translator. The people were far more at ease inside the forest than in the clearing. A fire was made. The rest of the party—Ching, myself, and what baggage there was, had followed, slipping and sliding in the soft mud. Occasionally, Manda would cry, "Tasaday," the name of the people. To bring them from the forest, Dafal told them that God, and his disciple Mai, had called them. Manda brought a smile from one boy by the gift of a whistle. He told Mai to tell them to ask whatever they wanted from him; as usual they had no answer. The Tasaday say they have all they need. Manda said to say he would think of nice things.

All the cloth and the brass wire earrings they wear, men and women alike, were brought by Dafal who has been in contact with them for over eight years. Some wore their hair tied back with bits of rag, these Manda thought ugly and told Mai to ask them to remove and replace it with natural material. One man brought down from a hiding place the stone tools they used until Dafal came. The Tasaday have no word for iron. Before brass was brought to them, they used a type of vine for earrings. The largest implements shown were pounding instruments for the pith of the wild palm, their staple food. Dafal, when he first came to them, brought them *bolos*, long knives—these were obviously used in the construction of the pounding instruments.

People walked off down the stream somewhat inexplicably. If we made a wrong move, if for instance someone fell and convinced them that our bad spirits were at fault, the Tasaday would all disappear instantly into the jungle, impossible to bring back. After about fifteen minutes, those who had gone upstream returned, with the rags removed from their hair and the imported cloths gone from their waists. Now, their hair was dressed with fresh palm and bamboo. The men wore girdles of braided bamboo, a bamboo leaf tied on it, to cover their genitals. The women turned the leaves out over the girdle all around their waist, in skirt fashion. Their hair was loose. There is a range of skin coloring and hair types, from one dusky and charming boy (who made the front page of the *Chronicle* report on the "Lost Tribe of Cotabato") to a woman with yellow tones in her skin, a boy with powdery white infected (a fungus of some kind) skin, and the albino.

When the photographers and newsmen arrived, the people seemed only a bit more nervous. They were reserved and shy but not coy. It seemed to me they showed admirable courage in the face of the strangely dressed newsmen, not to mention the rest of the party. A few would accept objects Manda handed them; a few timidly smiled. When the Panamin team made their first encounter, they would not even accept cooked rice, eating it raw instead.[3]

I wrote this account in a plastic covered notebook, sitting on an embankment on a mountainside deep in the tropical rainforest that then covered much of southern Mindanao. I was nineteen. The ink has faded, first with the damp of the hill side, then with age.

I was restless that summer, after my first year at Yale. The State Department paid for two round trips for dependents studying abroad, and I elected to take one of them even though my parents were on their way back to the States, on home leave. The idea was to get out of Manila, somehow. At Yale I was studying anthropology, and my professor, Harold Conklin, famous for his work on the Hanunoo tribe of Mindoro, introduced me to Bob Fox, chief anthropologist at the National Science Museum in Manila. Bob was a gruff, genial alcoholic in his sixties who had made his name by tracing the prehistoric traffic across long-disappeared land bridges from the Asian continent. He was an expert on stone tools and prehistoric campsites on the island of Palawan, dating from the time of the earliest human migrations to the Philippines. He knew Manda slightly. Manda had then been tracking the Tasaday for a little over a month, based on field reports, a helicopter survey, and a single encounter. About the time I called Bob, Manda wanted him to come over to talk about the Tasaday, and Bob invited me along.

Manda was thirty-five at the time, good-looking, arrogant, detested by others in his social class, adored by a ragtag "staff" of tribal and family retainers. He was the scion of one of the six wealthiest families in the Philippines. An uncle had been a foreign minister; his father opened the season each year at the Manila Polo Club, riding on a white horse; and he was related to most of the other top five families. At Harvard, Manda had roomed with Michael Rockefeller, who shared his interest in anthropology and adventure and later died on an expedition to New Guinea. The Rockefellers liked Manda and tried to involve him in some of their Asian projects. Manda's bush attire consisted of a beat-up yachting cap, leather flight jacket, and dark glasses. In some ways he was highly disciplined, abstaining from alcohol, cigarettes, and women.

He was called "Soda," for the cases of club soda he took everywhere. Manda hated Manila society and got out of the city as much as possible, to the big family haciendas and to company property here and there. John Nance, one of the first journalists to cover the Tasaday story, was his friend until Manda's death from cancer in 1996. Nance wrote that Manda began spending time in the Philippine outback in 1964, when he was twenty-seven, also the year he married. In 1966, he set up an old fishing boat as a hospital ship and started sending out medical missions. In 1967, Panamin was founded, and the next year, he began a lengthy relationship with the Tboli, a tribe of 100,000 in Cotabato Province. Christian homesteaders pressing up from the lowlands were driving them off their land, raping and murdering those who resisted. [4]

Manda brought lawyers, doctors, and guns to the tribes. His message was direct. Manda told the tribes to be proud of their heritage and customs, to fight back when outsiders tried to take advantage. "You must remember your Tboli greatness," Manda told the Tboli at an initial meeting. "Remember it or you die!" The crowd, according to Nance, jumped to its feet and began shouting "Tboli, Tboli, Tboli." [5] Since one of the family companies manufactured guns under license, he was able to keep his movement well armed. After this, Manda became almost totally absorbed in Panamin and began to attract wider attention—Charles Lindbergh enlisted his support in a quest to save the Philippine monkey eagle; the *New York Times* wrote a story about him; Imelda Marcos called him frequently, both in Manila and in the bush. In Spring and Summer 1971, a *National Geographic* film crew camped out in Tboli to work on a special documentary about Manda's tribes.

We met in Manda's turn-of-the-century mansion in Quezon City, a huge place with mahogany floors, antique Spanish furniture, and paintings by the turn-of-the-century Philippine artist Fernando Amorsolo on the walls. Manda lived here with his three children and a rotating group of "tribal scholars." By this time, Panamin had twelve settlements, an administrative office in Manila, and maintained an extensive radio network in tribal territory. Manda wanted Fox to come south to look at the Tasaday, together with whoever else was available. He had arranged for the press to come down as well but wanted the anthropologists in first. I was to go along as an assistant to Fox.

A typhoon was blowing across northern Luzon, and Manda decided to catch his helicopter in Legaspi City, southeast of Manila. To get there, he took his own train. I was invited along for the ride. We talked about Harvard and Yale, dumb stuff he'd got up to as a student, even dumber stuff he'd gotten into as an adult, searching for lost Japanese gold and the fabled "white" tribe of Palawan. When I followed Manda down to Mindanao—the train ended in Legaspi and we went the rest of the way by helicopter—I became part of the household, a kind of bumbling white mascot. We flew down the long chain of islands to the artificial settlement of Tboli, then deep into the rainforest to Manobo Blit, a village where women blackened their teeth and the only motorized vehicle anyone had ever seen was Manda's helicopter. In a photograph of that time, my face is in profile, chin buried in a tape recorder, my legs awkwardly drawn up beneath me. I am wearing a velveteen pullover and corduroys; from my posture I might be sleeping. Dulak, a young, beautiful Tasaday woman, has thrown her arm affectionately around my shoulder, and looks down quizzically. Dulak is wearing copper bangles and little else. She has the manner of an accomplished hostess faced with guests from Mars. I remember her touch as light and gentle as a leaf.

A few days later, I came down with a fever in the middle of one of Manda's gun battles. The Tboli had called over the Panamin radio network, asking for help with a land dispute. A tribal boy had been murdered while fishing at a disputed lake; the assassins had tortured him first with boiling water, and his skin had peeled off in places. Manda's idea of arbitration was to buzz the Christian village with his helicopter and bring in federal agents to document the murdered boy. I took pictures of the corpse for the National Bureau of Investigation, and immediately fell ill. I had to be taken out while the shooting match was still underway.

Manda had enemies. He bricked up the wall of his bedroom and kept a pistol ready. In the field, a lean killer named Felix was commander of a dozen or so bodyguards. Manda would send Felix with me when I went out on walks in the hills behind Tboli. Manda was involved in a political environment that in 1970 was becoming increasingly treacherous. He was in the early stages of a relationship with Marcos that left him a pariah in post-Marcos society and the bane of anthropologists and human rights groups.

From the beginning, Manda kept tight control over access to the Tasaday, and within a year or two of their discovery, barred outside contacts. Left alone, they intermarried with local Manobo Blit people and began to shed their Stone Age ways. In 1986, after the fall of Marcos, Osvald Iten, a Swiss freelance journalist, walked into Tasaday country and came back saying that the Tasaday were imposters from a neighboring tribe.

Thus ensued a Rashomon-like exchange of accounts and interviews that confused the issue further. Much of the controversy centered on Manda, who, as cabinet minister for "cultural minorities," had been a de facto warlord in charge of hill tribes and counterinsurgency schemes. Marcos had used Manda to help build a personality cult based on himself as "father" of all of the Philippines's diverse ethnic and linguistic groups, including tribes that lived in the same remote areas used by the New People's Army and Islamic separatists to hide from government troops. Marcos would bring tribal delegations to Manila to participate in huge parades in his honor. My father filmed one of these, and I have talked to tribal friends who participated in these marches, laughing about it as though it were a comedy.

As correspondent for the *Globe and Mail*, I came back to Manila several times in the late 1980s and retraced my steps, wondering if I had been tricked. I looked up Manda, who had fled the country shortly after Benigno Aquino's assassination in 1983. Until 1986, when Marcos fell, he had wandered, living in Spain and Costa Rica. A presidential pardon from Corazon Aquino brought him back. In 1989, Manda lived alone in his big mansion in White Plains, whose grounds were planted to resemble a rainforest.

Malarial and prone to screaming fits, he was engrossed in a project to buy his way back into society through a business venture with Cardinal Jaime Sin, the hero of the People Power movement. He was no longer careful about his women. At the same time, he was working to salvage the Tasaday's reputation, backing a libel case against their detractors. I never doubted that the Tasaday were real. But I had failed in my second attempt to lose my American self, and was too old to try again.

Boulder Boys

Growing up, my brothers, Charles and Hilliard, used to pore over scrapbooks of war photographs collected on the job by my father, an aerial intelligence officer. Bomb bursts appeared like roses over the distant landscape of France and Germany. In some photos, my father poses with his flight mates in sheepskin jackets against the backdrop of their B-17 bombers.

About the same time that my father was making midnight passes over the darkened cities of Western Europe, another group of junior officers engaged in decidedly less glamorous work in classrooms at the University of Colorado in Boulder. No rugged farm boys here. This bunch was geeky. Most came straight out of the classics departments at Harvard, Yale, Columbia, Berkeley, and other major universities. They had thick glasses, the women, too. Their mission was to master the Japanese language at battle speed, with a curriculum designed to blast out graduates in fourteen months. This was the U.S. Navy Japanese Language School, a wartime institution that later became the Monterey Language Institute. By the end of the war, one thousand men and one hundred women graduates served as field interrogators and translators.

The Navy, Army, and Army Signal Corps each had similar institutes, different in their approaches to the task, but reflecting the same dire need. When Japan attacked Pearl Harbor, the Navy had only twelve officers who were competent in the Japanese language. It did not take advantage of native speakers of Japanese because, in the early days of the war, the Navy had expelled its 3,500 Nisei (second-generation) Japanese-Americans as "unfit" to serve. The Navy even moved its language school from Berkeley to Boulder, because it wanted its fifteen Nisei instructors well away from the Pacific coastline where they were thought to be at greater risk of aiding the Japanese war effort. In contrast, when the Army lifted a similar ban on Japanese-Americans in the military in 1943, its Niseis were sent to Europe in the celebrated 442nd Infantry Regiment.

Although racial prejudice may have been behind their creation, the military language schools were seedbeds for talent. The geeks, diverted from their Ivory Tower ambitions, shaped America's Cold War image of Asia. They brought passion, brilliance, and a sense of personal mission to the task. But they were also sensitive to the uses of propaganda and intelligence and determined to hold back the forces of communism from an Asia they had grown to love.

For many of the "Boulder Boys and Girls," the Navy Language School was their first introduction to Japan. Frank Gibney, one of the youngest in the group, had been majoring in Greek classics at Yale when the Navy's recruiter, Commander Al Hindmarsh, a former assistant dean at Harvard, visited the campus. Hindmarsh figured that "anybody who was studying Latin and Greek—some knew Sanskrit—would be able to study Japanese. It was very primitive reasoning," Gibney said.[6] Like many of the recruits, he had no interest in Japan per se—the Navy Language School was a shortcut to the battlefront. Gibney had tried to sneak into the Marine Corps' platoon-leaders program by memorizing the eye chart but flunked the exam when the eye test was changed.

Gibney entered the program in December 1942, and by March 1943 had shipped out to Honolulu, to the Joint Intelligence Center Pacific Operations Area (JICPOA). There, he was selected to do interrogation work with Japanese prisoners of war at a secret prison camp at Iroquois Point in Pearl Harbor. Over the next two years, Gibney served as a field interrogator in some of the Pacific War's bloodiest battlefronts, at Peleliu in Palau and in Okinawa. In the Battle of Okinawa, he landed on the second day and helped the Navy's capital ships offshore locate hidden Japanese artillery emplacements by interviewing people used as laborers by the Japanese army. "Inescapably, we were given a view of the Japanese quite different from the stereotypes," Gibney said. "The reason why people who went into Japanese studies after the war were so affected is because they had this direct experience."

Donald Keene was barely nineteen when he wrote Commander Hindmarsh begging to be admitted to the program. Keene had been majoring in French literature at Columbia but switched to comparative literature to study Chinese and Japanese just before the Pearl Harbor attack. Keene sped through the Boulder program in eleven months and spent the next three years in the Pacific, initially in the Aleutian Islands. The Navy noticed that Keene was adept at reading handwritten Japanese, a challenge for most students, and set him to translating diaries of slain Japanese soldiers. He was immediately struck by the literary quality of some and later wrote movingly about them in his 1994 memoir, *On Familiar Terms: A Journey across Cultures.* "I had the funny feeling that the authors of these diaries did not know themselves as well as I did," he says. "They were my first Japanese friends, except they were all dead."[7]

The alumni of the Navy Japanese Language School broke all the laws of averages. Out of its 1,100 graduates, a dozen, including some of the Japanese instructors, would become the most influential teachers, writers, and translators of their generation. A Library of Congress search of the seven most prolific authors in the group, including Gibney, turns up an astonishing 228 book titles. Keene, emeritus professor at the East Asian Institute at Columbia, is the leader of the pack, with sixty-six Library of Congress "hits." Keene's anthologies of Chinese and Japanese literature, translations and appreciations of Japanese theater, and books on Japanese intellectual history are staples of comparative literature and Japanese area studies. Runner-up Robert A. Scalapino, emeritus director of the Institute of East Asian Studies at the University of California at Berkeley, with forty-eight titles, was by any account the single most influential political economist of East Asia in his generation. Third-ranking Edward Seidensticker, with twenty-eight, translated the monumental *Genji Monogotari* (Tale of Genji). The Library of Congress average for the group was thirty-two.

When I was studying Chinese and Japanese history at Yale and Stanford in the early 1970s, Keene, Scalapino, Seidensticker, and other Boulder Boys were already the grand old men of the profession, and it never occurred to me that they might have had personal lives. My first inkling of the real men and women behind the enterprise was in a photograph on the wall of the Foreign Correspondents' Club (FCCJ) in Tokyo, where I arrived as a new correspondent in 1988. It is one of the older photos in the FCCJ collection, dating from a time when Tokyo was a staging ground for reporters heading for action in Korea.

A young, very blonde, very handsome and swaggering Frank Gibney is in the middle of the group, together with half-a-dozen other well-known Korean War correspondents. I knew Gibney as the author of *Japan, the Fragile Superpower* and *Five Gentlemen of Japan*, both readings from my undergraduate and graduate school days. Gibney was among those who had helped present Japan in a favorable light to American readers; so much so that he was awarded an imperial honor, the Order of the Chrysanthemum. This made him beloved of one school of Japanese studies, suspect to another. Through most of the 1990s, Japanese scholarship was highly politicized. The 1950s generation was labeled the "Chrysanthemum Club," after the Japanese imperial crest. Their critics were styled the "revisionists" and argued that the Japanese were in fact very complicated friends, with an economic vision and goals radically at odds with those of the United States. The revisionists accused their predecessors as having falsified Japan's past. "Silly us, we thought the Soviet Union was out to destroy us," said Gibney. "We tended to downplay Japanese atrocities, and did not say anything about American atrocities because we did not know about them."

One has to reach back into the history of the U.S. Occupation of Japan from 1945 to 1952, the year of my birth, to understand the thinking of the Boulder Boys, the "Chrysanthemum Club" academics with whom they overlapped, the American policy makers who sought to strengthen Asia economically in order to resist communism, and, indeed, my father. In the early years of the Occupation, the United States was preoccupied with changing the Japanese system and building on America's pre-war experience in the Philippines, its sole Asian colony. America's policy in the Philippines was one of "benevolent assimilation," to use the phrase of the U.S. president who had seized the islands as spoils of the Spanish-American War. William Howard Taft, the first American governor-general of the Philippines, called Filipinos his "little brown brothers" and saw himself as their "missionary, steering them into the pastures of righteousness."[8] Americans bent on whitewashing the bloody suppression of the Philippine revolution emphasized the contrast between the generosity of the U.S. regime and the brutal ways of the Spanish. An essential part of the myth was the concept of tutelage. Over time, Filipinos would become more like us.

"Benevolent assimilation" in the Philippines was not mere rhetoric. It involved social engineering on a grand scale. As in Japan under the Occupation, the United States experimented with introducing American institutions and values, from its public schools to the two houses of the Congress and presidential system. By the time of Philippine independence on July 4, 1946, Americans and Filipinos alike looked at the country as an American-style democracy, although its democracy was only skin deep. As the Philippines's economy strengthened through the 1960s, Washington touted it not only as a "showcase of democracy" but as a model of American-style capitalism.

In the 1960s, in the Manila of my childhood, Enrique Zobel y Ayala developed the cane fields of Makati into a gleaming urban center, the envy of Asia. The Philippines was the second most successful economy in the region, after Japan. Economic success had clear-cut political rewards. In the mid-1960s, President Lyndon Johnson's aide Jack Valenti described Philippine president Ferdinand Marcos as "enormously intelligent" and "tough"; on a state visit to the United States in September 1966, Imelda was toasted as a combination of Jackie Kennedy and Eleanor Roosevelt.[9]

In Japan, SCAP had the same idea of transplanting both American values and the American way of making money. It drafted a new Japanese constitution, legalized political parties and the vote for women, changed the status of the emperor, and introduced a new civil code and an American-style public school system. On the economic front, SCAP planned to tear up the Japanese economic system and rebuild it from the ground up. It started out by attacking the pre-war industrial conglomerates known as the *zaibatsu*, declaring that the holding companies at the core of the groups were illegal.

By the time of the Japanese defeat, the four top *zaibatsu*—Mitsui, Mitsubishi, Sumitomo, and Yasuda—accounted for one-quarter of Japan's paid-in capital.[10] SCAP's commander, General Douglas MacArthur, had a visceral dislike of them—"the record is one of economic oppression and exploitation at home, aggression and spoliation abroad," he wrote.[11] The big four *zaibatsu* submitted plans for self-dissolution, but before a more radical scheme to "de-concentrate" Japanese industry could get under way, Washington put an end to the reforms and instituted the "reverse course" to rebuild the country as its chief ally against communism in the Pacific. The reformers were accused of imposing socialism on Japan, and the *zaibatsu* continued working together as they had in the past, knitting together new structures through cross-shareholdings and cross-directorships rather than holding companies, which quixotically remained illegal.[12]

On October 1, 1949, Mao Zedong stood on a balcony overlooking Tiananmen Square in Beijing and exhorted a vast crowd to "stand up" and reclaim its national identity. Not long after, Edwin Reischauer, the son of missionaries in Japan and the State Department's leading academic advisor on East Asia, complained in a State Department policy conference on China that the people of Asia "are asking for an ideology. We have in many ways failed to give it to them. There is a crying need for people to have our ideology. We aren't in the habit of giving it. We have the ideology but we aren't presenting it to other people."[13]

Reischauer believed that in order to combat Chinese ideological warfare, the United States would need a sophisticated program of its own. He published his own prescriptions for U.S. ideological warfare in 1955, in a tract entitled *Wanted: An Asian Policy*. In it, Reischauer argued that the United States represented "true radicalism" because it had created the world's first working democracy; communism was the "counter-revolution of the democratic revolution in Asia." America could not represent itself directly in this complex battlefield, Reischauer said. "To the extent that we identify democracy exclusively with the United States, we are actually undermining our cause in Asia, for then we make democracy seem hopelessly unattainable."[14] He did not think Japan was ready for the role of proxy and suggested France.

Despite Reischauer's caution, however, Japan had emerged as the chief representative of American-style capitalism, anointed by academics and policy makers as the most successful of the "late modernizers."[15] It was one of the Boulder Boys, Marius Jansen, who declared that Japan was the "model for Asia" and urged American scholars to present Japan's successes positively. "Most of us, for instance, think of Japan's modern wars as turning points, and find it convenient to arrange our material—for economic growth, for thought, for politics—accordingly," he wrote. "But we ought to remember that this may be partly responsible for the interpretation of modern Japan's history as dominated by wars and rumors of wars, and we ought to be prepared to try something else."[16]

The scholars' views lent credibility to the policy of using a former enemy to enlarge the zone of American influence in Asia, directing Japanese money away from China (where it wanted to go in the early 1950s) and instead toward Southeast Asia, Taiwan, Hong Kong, and Korea. The strangeness of the policy reflected its original expediency, designed as a quick fix to counter a sudden and unexpected threat from the Soviet bloc, represented by China. China's entry into the Korean conflict in October 1950, just a year after Mao and his battle-worn forces marched into Beijing, caught the Central Intelligence Agency, U.S. media, and the Truman administration by complete and utter surprise.[17] This became the trigger for SCAP to revive Japanese military production and the pre-war *zaibatsu* oligopolies, whose dissolution had been ordered by General Douglas MacArthur just a few years earlier. The SCAP plan was to reconstitute Japan's wartime Greater East Asia Co-Prosperity Sphere and use it to contain China.[18] The first leg of the strategy was Southeast Asia, later to be extended to South Korea and Taiwan. Washington needed Japan and Southeast Asia to serve as American strongholds, with Japan acting as U.S. subcontractor for the reconstruction of the Southeast Asian economies. Japan was threadbare, the cities of Southeast Asia gutted and filled with beggars and revolutionaries.

In mid-1951, a year before the U.S. Occupation of Japan ended in April 1952, SCAP organized the first Japanese economic mission to Southeast Asia.[19] Washington envisioned a triangular policy, involving itself, Japan, and Southeast Asia in a mutual support scheme to encircle and contain the Chinese. The Japanese were hard to bring along in this scheme; it meant an abandonment of China's rich resources and huge market for the relatively primitive economies of Southeast Asia. But Tokyo finally agreed, and the Asia policy became part of Prime Minister Yoshida Shigeru's larger Cold War bargain with the United States, trading Japanese sovereignty over defense and foreign policy for economic growth. The relationship was a "dual hegemony," according to Meredith Woo-Cumings, a political scientist at Northwestern University. Japan footed the bills; the United States provided the security mantle.[20]

Washington's Cold War stratagems turned out to be an enormous bonanza for Japan. As the first step toward dominating the economies of its neighbors and erstwhile colonies, Tokyo used war reparations mandated by the 1952 San Francisco Peace Treaty.[21] The language of the Japanese reparations programs bore Washington's clear imprint. The Japanese referred to the aid programs in their former colonies as *keizai kyoryoku,* or economic cooperation. By "cooperation," Japan's leaders at the time meant cooperation between the United States and Japan in Southeast Asia, Taiwan, and Korea. George Kennan and Dean Acheson literally plotted Korea's subordination to a revived Japanese superpower. "From the standpoint of our interest it is preferable that Japan should dominate Korea than that Russia should do so," Kennan wrote Acheson in 1950. "We must hope that with the revival of her normal strength and prestige, Japan will regain her influence there. . . . It is important that the nominal independence of Korea be preserved, for it provides a flexible vehicle through which Japanese influence may someday gradually replace Soviet influence without creating undue international repercussions."[22]

Tokyo was aware that feelings were too raw in Southeast Asia and Korea for any direct assertion of political power. For the next three decades, Japan kept strictly to the blueprint of U.S. diplomacy in the region.[23] In economic matters, however, Washington gave Tokyo a blank check, and Japan's politicians, bureaucrats, and big business proceeded to use it enthusiastically. It never seemed to have entered the mind of John Foster Dulles, Eisenhower's secretary of state, that a defeated Japan might challenge the United States on grounds of its economic system. For Dulles, the fight was between Communism and capitalist democracy. His only fear was that Japan would drift into China's sphere of influence.[24]

In Washington, convergence became an article of faith. Japan was to evolve gradually into a democracy and free market economy in the American image. In a celebrated essay written in 1950, Reischauer made two observations that would be carried over into U.S. policy for a generation. One was that the predominant U.S. concern in Asia was to maintain security, rather than to exploit the region for commercial advantage; this meant adopting tolerance toward Asian governments desperate for industrial growth. The other was that Japan should be viewed as a "special case" because democracy was already deeply rooted. "In many ways Japan differs sharply from its neighbors, resembling the nations of Europe in these respects more than the other lands of the Far East," Reischauer wrote. "Because of these differences, our policies in Japan have inevitably differed from those we have followed elsewhere in the Far East and have tended to parallel our European policies."[25]

As the Cold War progressed, the notion that U.S. economic favors to Japan would keep it from falling to Communism segued into a much larger concept—that modernization itself constituted a defense against China and the Soviet Union, which by the mid-1950s were actively proselytizing their economic systems to the developing world. Reischauer had advocated launching an aid offensive to counter the Soviet aid program. "Russia is already embarked on large-scale programs which will teach Asians to do things the Communist way," he wrote in his 1950 article. "Such programs can only be countered by an even larger and better organized effort on our part to give Asians the skills and knowledge they need."[26]

It was the end of the decade, however, before the White House shared such views, with the advent of Kennedy in the White House. Kennedy had begun thinking along these lines as early as 1952, as a junior senator, after a visit to the Middle East and Asia. "The Communists have a chance of seizing all of Asia in the next five or six years. What weapons do we have that will stop them? The most effective is technical assistance," he told the House of Representatives on June 28, 1952.[27] Over the next few years, Kennedy advocated a technical aid program for South Asia and compared the "economic gap" between developing and developed countries to the nuclear missile gap with the Soviet Union. "It is this gap [the economic gap] which presents us with our most critical challenge today," Kennedy told the House in 1959. "It is this gap which is altering the face of the globe, our strategy, our security and our alliances, more than any current military challenge."[28]

The tactic was opposite in spirit to the strategies prevailing in the Eisenhower administration, which favored military but not economic or social aid. As president, Kennedy launched the Peace Corps and the "Decade of Development," both initiatives premised on an economic and institutional struggle with communism. Kennedy was as determined to use ideology to win the economic battle as any of his advisors could have desired. He sent Reischauer to Tokyo as ambassador in 1960. In Washington, Walt W. Rostow supplied the intellectual muscle for the cause. He argued that development proceeded in identifiable stages, from traditional society to a takeoff to the "age of high mass consumption."[29] For Rostow, modernization was more than just an alternative to communism; the two systems were incompatible. U.S. foreign aid escalated rapidly, reaching a high of $10 billion in 1965.

Along with efforts to promote American values and American-style capitalism, during the Cold War years Washington steadily built up its military presence in the Pacific. After the Korean War, U.S. troops withdrew only to return with the gradual scaling up of the Vietnam conflict. Through the 1960s, American military commitment to the region rose quickly. U.S. troops, battleships, and fighter planes policed the region from a ring of bases in South Korea, Japan, Okinawa, Taiwan, Guam, and the Philippines; force levels rose from 55,800 in 1960 to 816,500 in 1965 to 1.1 million in 1970.[30]

In 1957, Kennedy's views were reinforced by the launch of the Sputnik satellite. Its success achieved a tremendous propaganda victory for the Soviet Union, which was then achieving growth rates of between 8 or 9 percent annually. Fears mounted that developing countries would adopt the Soviet model, further expanding Soviet political influence. The Soviet economy appeared to be growing so rapidly that it might outstrip the United States within a matter of years. Such fears were based on straight-line projections derived from faulty numbers, but the impact was profound. Serious economists argued that "a collectivist, authoritarian state" was probably better than free-market democracies at stimulating economic growth, based on the Soviet evidence. In 1959, *Newsweek* proclaimed that the Soviet Union was on its way to "economic domination of the world."[31]

This was not just an abstract fear. Moscow was literally paying poor countries to adopt the Soviet system. It had spent much of the 1950s developing a formidable program of strategic aid to support noncommunist governments in Afghanistan, Egypt, India, Indonesia, and Syria. It poured money into China. Washington might be able to write off China as a lost cause, but not the powder-keg buffer states in the Middle East and Asia. In the 1950s, the United States and the Soviet Union were neck and neck in the foreign aid wars. In dollar terms, between 1955 and 1958, the Soviet Union spent $1.092 billion on economic aid to a short list of strategic allies, slightly more than the $1.047 billion spent by the United States on the same countries, excluding agricultural sales and private-sector investment.

Even more than the dollar amounts, it was the style with which the Soviets executed their aid program that jangled nerves. For the Soviets, aid to "underdeveloped areas" was part of a total package aimed at demonstrating Soviet success. Moscow confidently played the economic and military realms against each other. "It was altogether typical of this strategy that when Krushchev and Nikolai A. Bulganin barnstormed through India in 1955, a fusion weapon was test-exploded in Central Asia," Rostow wrote.[32] Economic aid flowed in order to woo countries to the model of Soviet planning and national mobilization. For the first time, economic success was linked both to an ideology and a growth strategy. The Soviets seemed to be proving that communism actually worked.

Deep in the Republican 1950s, the idea of spending taxpayers' money to promote capitalism was unnatural, even repugnant to many in Washington, starting with the president. This was the private sector's job, not that of government. U.S. foreign policy was preoccupied with building military alliances, and until 1957, aid to developing countries was overwhelmingly focused on military assistance. Rostow recalled Dwight Eisenhower's bias against foreign aid, reminiscent of Ronald Reagan's presidency three decades later, expressed in a terse Eisenhower message to Congress in 1954: "Aid—which we wish to curtail; Investment which we wish to encourage; Convertibility—which we wish to facilitate; Trade— which we wish to expand."[33]

Attitudes had begun to shift before Sputnik, although the launch engendered a new anxiety about Soviet propaganda successes. The International Cooperation Administration was set up in 1955, and in May 1957, Eisenhower launched the Development Loan Fund, a soft-loan agency entirely dedicated to foreign economic aid. But it was not until 1959, when Kennedy, still a senator, was able to push through a bill to send a group of "wise men" to India to design an international aid effort to help design India's third Five-Year Plan, that foreign aid became an explicit part of U.S. policy. The wise men were sent, an international aid consortium was organized for India, and Kennedy, as president, was able to see the first pledging session through. In March 1961, Kennedy announced the "Development Decade" in a speech to

Congress, shortly after creating the Peace Corps and the Alliance for Progress with Latin America. He told Congress:

> The economic collapse of those free but less-developed nations which now stand poised between sustained growth and economic chaos would be disastrous to our national security, harmful to our comparative prosperity and offensive to our conscience. There exists, in the 1960s, an historic opportunity for a major economic assistance effort by the free industrialized nations to move more than half the people of the less-developed nations into self-sustained economic growth, while the rest move substantially closer to the day when they, too, will no longer have to depend on outside assistance. . .
>
> Without regard to party lines, we shall take this step not as Republicans or as Democrats but as leaders of the Free World. It will both befit and benefit us to take this step boldly. For we are launching a Decade of Development on which will depend, substantially, the kind of world in which we and our children shall live.[34]

Thus, in the 1950s and 1960s, America acquired roles in Asia as model and guardian that remained central tenets of U.S. diplomacy in the region, with Japan as its chief protégé and protectorate. Both roles demanded high levels of commitment. With the end of the Vietnam War came a prolonged period of relative stability. As Asian nations clambered out of poverty, U.S. foreign aid went to needier regions. Congress and the American public grew weary of picking up the bill for the world's poor and paying for wars in strange places. On the ground as well, exhaustion set in. We won the war against communism, but the battle for hearts and minds was another matter.

In 1959, the International Cooperation Agency sent my father to Indonesia, which was well on its way to becoming a Soviet and Chinese client state. A year earlier, Washington had blundered by lending support to a rebel movement in Sumatra. U.S. intervention was among the excuses that Sukarno used to declare martial law and impose a new constitution with broader powers for the president. We were settling into temporary quarters off a muddy lane filled with honking geese while this episode played out in June 1959. Our arrival coincided not only with a new wave of anti-Americanism but with the beginning of a frightening new episode of political and economic chaos.

Sukarno used his new powers to launch "guided democracy," a concept he had first developed as an engineering student at Bandung Technical Institute in the 1920s. His ideas were eclectic, drawing upon the Koran as well as revolutionary philosophers from Thomas Jefferson to Marx, Engels, and Lenin. He proposed uniting the forces of nationalism, Islam, and communism, and wanted to establish communes after the Chinese model.[35] Sukarno kept the army happy by handing over assets he had seized from the Dutch, and became increasingly demonstrative in his courtship of the Indonesian Communist Party, the PKI. By the time of the Bandung Conference in 1955, when he proclaimed the birth of "New Asia and Africa" and set up the Conference of Non-Aligned Nations, Sukarno viewed himself as the leader of a new coalition of post-colonial states that would reject Western models and create their own.

Not surprisingly, the antiquated Dutch export machine sputtered and ground to a halt. Inflation mounted and by the mid-1960s had turned into hyperinflation. With help from the Soviets, Sukarno diverted the public's attention by staging military confrontations with Holland and Malaysia. In Jakarta, Sukarno created a different kind of diversion by organizing a building campaign on a grand scale. Sukarno filled Jakarta with statues of wildly gesticulating heroes of the revolution; he built Monas, a huge obelisk with a viewing tower; the Hotel Indonesia, the country's first high-rise hotel; its first department store, the Sarinah; the Jakarta bypass and the Senayan clover-leaf interchange, Indonesia's first modern highways.[36] Monuments and architecture alike were hideously ugly, reflecting both Sukarno's egomania and his contempt for economic realities.

My family left Indonesia in 1961, moving on to Taiwan, and, in 1963, the Philippines. The International Cooperation Agency became the U.S. Agency for International Development (USAID). The American investment was a write-off. Over the next few years, Sukarno embarked on a new campaign of "living dangerously," whipping up frenzies of antiforeign sentiment against the United States, Dutch, British, and Malayan governments. By the mid-1960s, the army routinely used the downtown as a staging ground for military exercises. Maslyn Williams, an Australian visitor to Jakarta, recalls being trapped in traffic while soldiers used vehicles as cover. The objective was to take the telephone exchange. Her Indonesian companions were unfazed. They viewed it as they might a sporting event. One, an official, snorted, "They are crazy. This telephone exchange is a very inefficient installation. Whoever holds it will be handicapped and lose the battle."[37]

President Sukarno alarmed even the army with his ideological harangues and intrigues with Beijing and Moscow. The army probably was behind the attempted coup of October 1, 1965, and launched the bloody anti-Chinese pogroms that followed, killing perhaps 1,000,000 Chinese. General Suharto, then a brand-new face in Indonesian politics, was a key figure in the sweep against ethnic Chinese; by March 1966 he was in effective control of the country. Over the next thirty years, Suharto created Asia's most successful, democracy-free developmental state. America was not his model.

The Asia that I knew as a child was an extraordinary region, desperately poor, culturally rich, and violent. Gunnar Myrdal, the Nobel Prize–winning economist, speculated that Asia's huge population, deep corruption, and traditional culture would keep it mired in poverty for generations, and that democracy would be more hindrance than help.[38] International donors viewed Asia much the way they viewed Africa in the 1990s, as a region of intractable problems, in desperate need of external assistance. Reading through Myrdal's classic *Asian Drama*, published in 1968, there is a curious foreshadowing of the commentary that would become popular with the Asian financial crisis. Like the 1990s critics, he focused on Asian corruption and the social and cultural sources of Asian poverty. Like them also, he put the blame for Asian poverty on its institutions. In the mid-1960s, South Asia had uncontrollable population problems; Southeast Asia was a political quagmire; Northeast Asia was growing fast but was still poor. All of these countries, according to Myrdal, lacked the "initial conditions" for modernization.[39]

The "economic gap" between Asia and the industrialized West was extreme. In the 1960s, Indonesia's per capita income was $62; the Philippines's was $213; Taiwan's was $230. Taiwan and the Philippines were considered stars. U.S. aid had made headway in both countries, through land reform in Taiwan and massive cash infusion in the Philippines. Nonetheless, Taiwan and the Philippines were both poor by world standards. The basic task of foreign aid was to ensure that these countries could produce enough food to meet their growing populations. Those who predicted modest growth were considered wild optimists. An Asian Development Bank (ADB) publication predicted that, in the 1970s and 1980s, noncommunist Southeast Asian economies would experience "high variant" growth rates of between 6 and 7 percent. The "low variant" range was between 4.3 and 6 percent.[40] The forecast was off by half.

Something happened. If I could take a freeze-frame movie of the Asian cities I lived in over the years since I first saw them, skyscrapers would grow out of rice fields and giant department stores would suddenly replace bazaars and street vendors. The "miracle" that began in Japan in the early 1960s spread first to Northeast Asia, then southward. Northeast Asia reached its peak in the 1970s, with growth rates of 9.3 percent for South Korea, 10.2 percent in Taiwan, and 8.9 percent in Hong Kong.[41] The 1970s saw phenomenal growth in Southeast Asia, where the two oil shocks translated into higher prices for basic commodities. The Philippines defined the low end of the range with a growth rate of 6.1 percent. Other Southeast Asian economies did much better, ranging from Thailand's 7.3 percent to 9.4 percent for Singapore. This feverish pace slowed in the 1980s, only to resume in the first half of the 1990s.

By 1995, on a per capita income basis, the three countries in which my family had lived were doing remarkably well. Indonesia and the Philippines, the low performers, both had per capita incomes above $1,000, higher than the average for Japan in the 1960s. Taiwan's per capita income of $12,490 in 1995 put it roughly between Portugal and Spain. The Indonesian economy was growing at 8.1 percent per year, Taiwan at 6.1 percent, and the Philippines at 4.8 percent. In the 1960s, U.S. incomes had been six times those of Southeast and Northeast Asia, excluding Japan. By 1995, they were only about double. "The region is unrecognizable compared with only a generation ago," a 1997 report from the ADB proclaimed.[42] History proved Myrdal to be wrong. But he was clearheaded enough in his political predictions. Writing about Indonesia at the time of the 1965 coup, Myrdal predicted an army takeover. "Any future government in Indonesia that wants to come to grips with its grave problems will have to be a dictatorship," he wrote in *Asian Drama*. "Only the army could conceivably carry out this type of relentless but benevolent and enlightened dictatorship."[43]

The Asia of my childhood was not only an Asia of miraculous growth but of generals and dictators. This was not at all contradictory with the policies of the United States or Japan, America's silent partner in regional development. Like Sukarno, Asia's quasi-democrats—leaders such as Syngman Rhee and Diosdado Macapagal—were either disastrous or corrupt. The strong men, generals or not, did a far better job of mobilizing their economies in the fight against communism, and Washington supported them—Park Chung Hee in Korea, Chiang Kai-shek in Taiwan, various governors-general in Hong Kong, Ferdinand Marcos in the Philippines, Lee Kuan Yew in Singapore, Suharto in Indonesia, the generals who ran Thailand, and the monolithic political parties holding power in Japan and Malaysia.

The war in Vietnam began with a steady stream of U.S. advisors to the government of Ngo Dinh Diem in the mid-1950s, escalated as Hanoi deployed the southern branch of the anti-French Viet Minh in 1960, bumped up again with American support for Diem's assassination in 1963, and took off in earnest as the United States gradually increased its forces in an undeclared war to 525,000 troops. Americans were vividly conscious of the war as it played out on the evening news. For a young American in Asia, deprived of American television, it loomed just beyond the horizon. You could sense the increased air pressure of an impending storm.

In Asia, the war was on our doorsteps, in the tens of thousands of American troops on their way to or from the battlegrounds, in the droves of investors who gathered around the fringes like bees to honey, in the anxieties and posturing of leaders who looked to the war to secure their own hold on power. The Vietnam War inspired a generation of student radicals in Asia who viewed the United States as a neo-colonial power siding with the worst elements in their own governments. Some of these student radicals would go on to become advocates of the Asian model of development, updating the older conflict between Communism and the free market to a new tension between different forms of capitalism.

Vietnam left its mark on my family. The undeclared war became a real one about the time I was a high school junior. In the terrible years from 1967 to 1969, my father worked in Vietnam, while the family stayed in Manila. My father would fly close to the war zone in open-backed transport planes, returning to a Saigon that was in many ways more frightening than the front line. His job was building hospitals and carrying out land reform. The hospitals were in dangerous forward zones and the North Vietnamese army would blow them up as soon as they were finished. Land reform was in the safer southern delta areas. My father was in Saigon for the Tet offensive and the bombing of churches and movie theaters, and he was a great churchgoer and loved any type of theater. I remember his account of the bombing of a Catholic church in downtown Saigon, which he visited shortly after he heard the sirens. He grieved for the Vietnamese and complained at home about the chaos and disorganization of the massive USAID mission in Saigon, the largest in the world at the time. The agency played a principal role in the hearts and minds campaign. Its failures shook him deeply.

As the era of U.S. dominance faded, Asia asserted itself more forcefully, buoyed by self-evident economic success. Developing countries and emerging economies were eager to learn from the Japanese model. Asians had achieved miracles and were convinced that they had done so by managing their economies differently than Americans or Europeans. Like my father, a generation earlier, they had dreams they thought would change the world.

Elusive Paradigm

Americans ignored Japan's efforts to seed its alternative paradigm and missed entirely the extent to which Japan had built its campaign along familiar lines. But the Japanese were excellent students of history. They remembered that Asian growth had been a joint production between Japan and the United States, and in promoting a Japanese economic model, Tokyo was merely following the American example.

During the Cold War, the United States had used economic ideology to build an alliance structure, and Japan attempted to do so as well, building on geographical relationships originally endorsed by the United States. The latter had encouraged Japan's economic penetration of South Korea, Taiwan, and Southeast Asia as part of its Cold War strategy, sanctioning the overwhelming focus of Japanese foreign aid on Asia and urging Japan and its Asian flock to rely on exports to the U.S. market as an engine of growth. In associating itself with Southeast Asia as an area of common economic interest, Japan capitalized on existing assets as well as its investments after 1985. When the Cold War was at its height, Washington assumed that Japan was a willing proxy for American interests in the region and advanced the fiction that Japan had adopted American-style capitalism. In the 1990s, the United States seemed to shrug off the debate with Japan over forms of capitalism, convinced that it had won.

Japan did not have to tweak the U.S. legacy by much to have it serve a purpose adapted to Japanese national interests. The 1950s and 1960s, a period celebrated by a generation of U.S. historians and political scientists as the era of Japan's Americanization, became the belle époque of Japanese industrial policy and business-government cooperation. "High exports through hard work" was the phrase that George Kennan used to characterize his plans for the Japanese economy in 1947 in his National Security Council memorandum 13/2.[44] A generation of American scholarship depicted noncommunist Asia as a region striving to establish capitalist economies and democracies in the American image. For the Japanese, it was only a small step to assert that they were converging not toward the United States but toward each other.

By the end of the 1990s, Japan had achieved many of the bold objectives it had set a decade earlier in its relations with Asia. A busy schedule of regional meetings and organizations existed and provided Tokyo with the platform it needed for a diplomacy focused more on Asia and less on the United States. Relations with China remained touchy but increasingly civil. In May 2000, in a small but significant gesture, China succumbed to Japanese pleas for consultations before the Nago G-8 summit, sending Chinese foreign minister Tang Jiaxuan to Tokyo.[45] That year, in addition to the G8 summit in Okinawa, three more were planned—the regular APEC summit in Brunei in November, the fourth ASEAN Plus Three meeting in Brunei in December, and the third biannual ASEM (Asia-Europe Meeting) in Seoul. The ASEAN Plus Three summit meetings had started to percolate downward to the workaday level as well. In May 2000, ASEAN organized the first "Plus Three" meeting of economic ministers in Rangoon, Myanmar.

At a closed conference in Washington in March 2000, Tanaka Akihiko, a leading Japanese political scientist, argued that the four summits were preparing the region for a new geopolitical regime. "Japanese diplomacy should seize the opportunity to solidify coordination among East Asian countries," he said. "ASEAN Plus Three is a summit meeting without the United States. This is important for the East Asian region, to invite a mechanism for coordination even if it doesn't involve the United States or Australia. The challenge for Japan is to create a new consensus that includes China and East Asia but is compatible with strong ties with the United States."[46]

However, as Shiratori, Kubota, Yamada, Sambommatsu, and other officials were struggling to identify the Japanese paradigm in order to identify its "applicability" to developing countries, the Japanese political, economic, and social structure was unraveling. Their campaign to promote the Japanese model abroad was at odds with the direction in which the Japanese economy itself was evolving.

Japan's Cold War role as U.S. satellite had left ordinary Japanese as isolated from policy and strategic issues as though they had been denizens of North Korea. The slow disintegration of the Cold War framework pressured Tokyo's leaders and policy makers to come up with new ideas, which they also needed to market to a populace that had been told for five decades not to concern itself with issues of international security, diplomacy, or economics. Those who tried to make a difference, like the politician Ozawa Ichiro, found it extraordinarily difficult to accomplish the objectives that seemed so rational and obvious on paper.[47]

Ozawa wanted Japan to become a "normal" nation; and recognized that to do so would require extensive revamping of its domestic and foreign affairs. A protégé of Tanaka Kakuei, Ozawa argued that it was critical for Japan to develop a relationship with Asia similar to the role Germany had with the rest of Europe. He called on Japan first to address the still-unresolved grievances of its Asian neighbors from Japanese military adventures of the first half of the century, then to get on with the job of constructing a new "multilateral" diplomacy in the Asia-Pacific region, based on Foreign Minister Nakayama Taro's 1991 proposal for an Asia-Pacific "ministerial conference." Nakayama's proposed conference had included all the APEC countries except the United States, Canada, Australia, and New Zealand.[48] It was Japan's obligation to support regional growth, Ozawa said. "The engine driving this development is Japan," he wrote. "Along with America, it supplies the capital and technology that has enabled the Asian NIEs and now ASEAN to develop as Japan has, in a process that has been called development in 'flying-geese formation.' . . . Japan must redouble its efforts to maintain and spread this development."[49]

In order to play these new roles, Japan would need an equivalent to the American dream, a "Japanese dream" that foreigners could share. It made a difference, he said, that Asian laborers who came to Japan to earn money had no desire to stay on, building lives in the islands. Ozawa thought it was mainly a matter of low Japanese living standards. It was more than that. In the early 1990s, the Japanese public had shown itself altogether unhappy with an influx of Asians in their midst, among the side effects of Japan's new regional prominence. Ordinary Japanese were unready to take on a larger security role; moreover, many assumed that China would simply replace the United States as the leading regional power, despite the huge disparity between China and Japan in the scale of their economies, technological prowess, and military power.

Worried about unemployment, the falling value of their homes, detached from the political process, the Japanese of the 1990s simply wished for the rest of the world to go away. Leadership, whether regional or global, was the last thing on their minds. Japanese politics was in shambles. Japanese companies were beginning to abandon policies of seniority and lifetime employment that workers in blue-chip companies had come to expect. Unemployment was suddenly higher than that of the United States and Britain.

Through this time of ferment and malaise, in harsh counterpoint to the official embrace, ordinary Japanese seemed to vent their anger and frustration with particular force on resident Asians, who occupied the bottom rung of the social and economic ladder in Japan. In April 2000, the governor of Tokyo, Ishihara Shintaro, who had once called Asia "Japan's backyard," caused a stir when he warned Japanese soldiers that Asians in Tokyo might riot in the wake of a major earthquake. At the time of the Great Kanto Earthquake in 1923, rumors had spread that resident Koreans were poisoning wells, and vigilante groups killed thousands of them.[50] Not long after Ishihara's blunder, Japanese newspapers carried reports of a foreign "crime wave." Analysis showed that the majority of foreign crimes were visa violations, but few Japanese read the fine print. Right-wing sound trucks frequently surrounded the Tokyo office of software entrepreneur Son Masayoshi, who founded one of the world's most successful software companies, Softbank. His offense was that he was Korean-Japanese.[51]

Such contradictions, between a recalcitrant Japanese public and the machinations of the elite, between an aggressive international policy and a failing domestic economy, were profound. In order for Japan to succeed in its policy of re-Asianization, it would need to re-invent itself. It would need to become Ozawa's "normal" nation. In the listless, angry Japan of the 1990s, success was elusive on both fronts.

8

Sphere of the Sun

The Bubble

Japan's economic bubble was at its zenith, round and full as the emblem of the sun on the national flag, the *hinomaru*. Nobody foresaw its dramatic end. By the time realization sank in, it was far too late. Between the late 1980s and mid-1990s, Japan went from a mood of giddy extravagance to frozen anger, as ordinary Japanese assessed the impact of a miracle gone wrong. It was like listening to a long sigh of disbelief.

I arrived in Japan in September 1988, so close to the end that I almost missed it. My work as a correspondent for the *Globe and Mail* newspaper gave me a privileged front row seat on the excesses and the distress. Living in Tokyo through early 1996, I would see firsthand how Japan and the Japanese struggled to grasp the concept that their paradigm was failing in its apogee. The brutal national transition was in harsh counterpoint to the hyperbole and frenzy of the boom times in the rest of Asia, then in full swing.

As Japan came to end of its postwar cycle, there were daily lessons in the shortcomings of the developmental state it had pioneered. Between the fall of 1988 and the following summer, Japan would see the death of an emperor, the resignation of a prime minister caught in an enveloping financial scandal, and secret decisions that would indelibly tarnish the government's pristine image when they came to light a few years later. The bureaucracy was playing out the last act of a style of administration rooted in medieval Japan. Major corporations held up a façade of collective harmony while small- and medium-sized companies fled the high yen and eroded the foundation of the *keiretsu* subcontracting system.

Between mid-1989 and the end of the year, the Bank of Japan, fearing inflation, would begin sopping up liquidity through the discount rate, and by the first few weeks of 1990, Japan's crash would begin in earnest. The Japanese model was exposed as an unholy mix of sleazy politicians, carnivorous conglomerates, and corrupt bureaucrats. Stock speculators and gangsters had greased the wheels. Propping up the system, complacent Japanese consumers toiled in a producer-oriented economy, their loyalty guaranteed by a system that made job hopping impossible, kept women in their place, and maintained sturdy barriers against foreign competition. An "iron triangle" of business, bureaucrats, and politicians remained invisible as long as the economy was in overdrive, with consumers willing to forego present consumption for the promise of future wealth, and corruption soaking up the surplus. After the bursting of the bubble, it lay exposed like the guts of an obsolete computer, operational, but prone to inexplicable crashes and circuit failures.

One could still admire the purpose the old machine had served, in its time. Single-party politics maintained stability by providing a safety valve and communication channel among industry, regions, and the central government. Giant conglomerates helped shape a business-friendly environment by greasing the political wheels and working closely with the bureaucracy, which drafted legislation and deftly served business by serving as venture capitalist for the nation, backing winners and easing out losers. The real key to the system lay in the bureaucracy, arguably the world's most selective civil service. It was up to the bureaucracy to balance the claims of competing sectors of the economy, protect public goods such as health and the environment, and keep the politicians from doing too much damage. Their role was much more than that, however. In the classic model, the bureaucracy played the role of modern-day samurai, guiding and managing the larger society, leading it through the example they set of stern self-sacrifice.

As long as the Japanese economy expanded, the iron triangle served the function of maintaining a consensus around strategies and objectives. Once the economy slowed down, the easygoing corruption at the top and the personal sacrifices required at the bottom could no longer be sustained. Without knowing it, in those first days and months after my arrival, I was able to watch as the mask fell, revealing the stagecraft behind the magic.

The "Japanese model" was thus beginning to come apart, even before the "lost decade" of the 1990s. But for a brief while, Japan basked in a golden age, when you could walk into a supermarket and quite literally buy gold flakes, or *kinpaku*, to sprinkle in your sake or your bath. I have a vial of gold flakes still, slowly crumbling into dust, a keepsake from my early days as a correspondent.

My apartment in Tokyo overlooked the Mitsui Club, a massive granite building in the style of an English country manor. Cascading down a steep hill was its classic Japanese garden, carefully planted to produce a harmonious tableau with each changing season. An emblem of wealth and privilege, six acres of expensive and exclusive nature in downtown Tokyo, surrounded by steep walls, the garden was like the flawless mask of a Noh actor, revealing little of the machinations within.

The corporation that owned the grounds traced its ancestry to the beginnings of Japan's drive for wealth and power; the men who built Japan into the world's second-greatest economic power had walked these grounds, paused to admire the carp or long-necked crane, resting from its travels. For most of the years I lived next door, in the late 1980s through early 1990s, the Mitsui Club might easily have bought a small U.S. state or Caribbean nation. It was a popular venue for the weddings of Mitsui men, and now and then a gaggle of family members would pause by the orange, half-moon bridge and waterfall, the women in kimonos, the men in cutaways, the bride in a white wedding gown with a bell-shaped skirt, as though Scarlett O'Hara had taken a wrong turn from Tara. Otherwise, it was empty except for diligent gardeners dressed in baggy *mompei*, crouching like peasants in a samurai movie. As I walked out onto the balcony for the first time, the hum of cicadas drowned out traffic, past and future.

Gold Dust

In the middle of the avenue, a rocker with hair pomaded in a rippling crest pumps his hips and belts out an Elvis Presley tune through a microphone attached to a boom box. He is lost in the pulsing crowd on a Sunday afternoon in Tokyo's Yoyogi Park, where Japanese teenagers came every weekend to dance under a sound blanket as fierce as a couple of jet engines in full crescendo.

Not far away, tucked into a corner of the park, a young American spreads handmade jewelry on a grass mat and waits for customers. Billy Fenster, like thousands of other foreigners, has been drawn to Japan by the lure of the strong yen. Selling trinkets is just a sideline, he says. Soon he will begin teaching English at a Japanese company. The pay is about $60 an hour, and he expects to save $1,200 a month. "Japan is just about the center of the world, economically anyway," he says without a hint of exaggeration. On the other side of the planet, at a conference at the London School of Economics, Gyohten Toyoo, vice-minister of finance, tells an audience to start thinking about the yen replacing the U.S. dollar as the world's leading currency.

It is 1988. Each in his own way, Gyohten and Fenster are convinced that the age of Japan is about to begin. Japan was rising. Over at the Bank of Japan, in its sleek building like a modern version of a castle keep, Governor Mieno Yasushi seemed content with the effects of flooding the economy with liquidity to counteract the strong yen. He had not yet begun tightening interest rates; real interest rates, factoring in inflation, were negative. The banks were virtually paying Japanese companies to borrow money, and the economy was in the midst of its longest post-war expansion. New college graduates had dozens of offers to choose from, and unemployment was the lowest among the major industrial economies. Investors reaped mountains of wealth from a record-making bull run on the stock market. Retailers rejoiced at the free spending habits of new stock market billionaires. Property values soared, yet inflation remained low or nonexistent. There was talk in Washington and Tokyo about the emergence of a new economic paradigm. Japan was as giddy with its achievements as the United States would be a decade later and as unconscious that it might not be on top forever.

In 1936, *Fortune* magazine had invented the term "Japan, Inc.," in an article declaring: "The industrial hierarchy of Japan is so compact that you can almost think of its works as the products of a single beautifully integrated and highly diversified corporation."[1] On February 26, 1990, the magazine ran the story "Fear and Loathing of Japan." Its cover featured Japan viewed from the East Coast of the United States, a giant mass overshadowing the Pacific Ocean and everything in-between.

In the Fukiage Palace, in the heart of downtown Tokyo, Emperor Hirohito was dying of cancer, his vital signs monitored by teams of doctors and broadcasted on special newsbreaks. The Nikkei Index bumped up against 30,000, with no sign of retreat. The turnover of stocks on the Tokyo Stock Exchange regularly exceeded that of New York, and land values were galloping in tandem with the stock index. Japanese liked to joke that if you folded a 10,000 yen note into the tiniest possible square, you might be able to buy the land underneath it, in one of the cheaper parts of town.

The grounds of the Imperial Palace, where the emperor lay on his deathbed, were said to be worth more than the state of California. Japanese investors were piling off planes in Honolulu, New York, and Los Angeles, with wads of cash to buy up American landmarks. As the United States began to slip behind Japan economically, the mood grew vicious. There were random attacks on Asian-Americans and more selective assaults on Japanese cars. Two American professors warned of a "coming war" between the United States and Japan.[2] Japanese words like "*keiretsu*" and "*dango*"—slang for cartel, after a Japanese sweet in which rice balls are skewered on a stake—became battle cries as U.S. trade officials and Congress begin pressuring Japan to change its rigged economy. Visiting Tokyo, Assistant Treasury Secretary Charles Dallara dropped warnings that the United States would block Japanese investment unless Japan agreed to change its ways.[3]

As a correspondent fresh to Japan, I watched for signs of transformation and found them on all sides. Japan was growing at unheard-of rates for a mature industrial economy. Its economy was supposed to be on the verge of a "third miracle." The "Izanami Boom"—named for the ancestral goddess of Japan who created the Japanese islands by dipping her spear into the ocean— began in November 1986 and ended in November 1991, with an average growth of 5.3 percent annually. The boom would later be renamed Heisei and come to be identified as a bubble, but in 1988 and 1989 serious analysts were predicting that the Japanese economy would soon catch up with that of the United States.

Memories of the "yen crisis" of 1985 and 1986 were fading. The economy had weathered the crisis and come out stronger than before. The high yen slashed prices for fuel and raw materials for domestic manufacturers, generating a spending boom of historic proportions. Japanese industry, far from falling prey to competition from cheap imports, had solved the problem by moving its own factories offshore and participating in the import boom. Japan's Byzantine distribution system gave domestic manufacturers a favored position, allowing them to capitalize on the spurt in domestic demand. At the same time, most big corporations pared production costs, enabling them to maintain their position in export markets.

In the first year of the new Heisei Era, beginning in 1989, Japanese companies swarmed into the U.S. market, snapping up American properties. After Sony's purchase of Columbia Pictures, *Newsweek* conducted a poll that indicated Americans feared Japan even more than the Soviet Union. "This time the Japanese hadn't just snapped up another building; they had bought a piece of America's soul," the magazine wailed. In response, Sony chairman Morita Akio observed, "Americans harbor some resentment when their business is bought by a Japanese group. The feeling is different when the buyers are European."[4] Less diplomatically a Japanese reporter snapped, "It is as if a kabuki troupe was bought by someone considered to be an inferior people."

Low-cost raw material and fuel imports took the heat off the economy. It "quieted down out of respect for Hirohito, and due to inflation fears," said Hugh Simon, a Tokyo-based fund manager, in Fall 1988, when the emperor lay ill. "But inflation has ceased to be a worry. When the new era does start, the economy will start out with a bang." The Nikkei Index was trading around 30,000 in late 1988 and would come close to 40,000 a year later. Capital investment soared. In 1988, Japanese companies invested more money in new factory buildings and equipment than did the United States. Kenneth Courtis, a Canadian economist working for Deutsche Bank Capital Markets in Tokyo, was among the most buoyant in his predictions. He estimated that the Nikkei Index would hit 65,000 and the 1990s would be an era of phenomenal growth. The Japanese economy would nearly double in size over the course of the decade, Courtis said, and Japan would become the "new product laboratory for the world."[5]

Dripping with cash, Japanese politicians enjoyed throwing it around. Prime Minister Takeshita Noboru, fighting for his job as scandal lapped at his feet, organized a giant giveaway to 3,100 Japanese villages. Each one got a one-time payment of $1 million. The ostensible purpose was to promote *furusato,* or village spirit. The villagers did not know what to do with the windfall. The community of Tsuna, on a small island in Japan's inland sea, decided simply to buy a lump of gold and put it on display as a tourist attraction. Another town faced with the same problem put a facsimile machine in every household. Japan's $457 billion budget for 1989 was so lavish that it was dubbed the "*matsuri,*" or "festival" budget. It also made Japan the world's largest foreign aid donor for the first time, with $8.9 billion compared to $7.7 billion for the United States.[6]

Not unlike the gift to villagers, Japan's foreign aid budget reflected more pride than common sense. "Japanese aid has been a slow-moving process until the recent past," said Inoguchi Takashi, a political scientist at Tokyo University. "This recent rush is a result of U.S. and other industrialized countries' pressure—plus internal pressure to do more for the world." To administer a program equivalent in size to that of the United States, Japan utilized one-third of the personnel. Experts were discouraged in its bureaucracy, with the result that there was little expertise on development issues among the 1,500 people who made up the aid establishment. Yanagihara Toru, then at the Institute for Developing Economies (IDE), guessed that there were only five development specialists in the entire country, including himself. "It's not only a matter of the number of people, but a certain type of person which is lacking," he said. "Unlike the Anglo-American orthodoxy, we are not very articulate. The Japanese don't operate through concepts. We somehow feel our way through, but we're not good at making ourselves clear."[7]

Before Tokyo, I had lived in great cities—New York, Washington, Toronto, and Beijing, as well as the Asian capitals of my childhood, Manila, Taipei, and Jakarta. None compared in its opulence and bravado, however, to Tokyo in the late 1980s. Each November, its restaurants vied to be the first in the world—not just the first in Japan—to serve the earliest bottles of Beaujolais Nouveau. The Japanese *shinjinrui,* the "new" men and women of the 1980s, spent their vacations touring the Australian outback in motorbike cavalcades or scuba diving in a legion of Japanese-built resorts across the Pacific. The metropolitan government of Tokyo, presiding over an economy roughly the size of China's, busied itself concocting outrageously expensive plans for urban renewal. Suzuki Shunichi, Tokyo's octogenarian governor, built the world's most expensive city hall and dreamed of a new "Technopolis" to rise on garbage fill in Tokyo Bay. There was even a proposal to build a mammoth underground cavern to take some of the pressure off the chaotic urban environment on the surface.

Japan's myth of invincibility was not built by Japan alone. In the heady atmosphere of the bubble economy, some of the most heated hyperbole came from *gaijin* economists in Tokyo. Some made their names that way. In the late 1980s, Kenneth Courtis, the Deutsche Bank economist, was the acknowledged master of the "Japan story." His critics called him a showman, while his admirers said he was eloquent. Either way, his superstar status was undisputed and made him a lightning rod for criticism and controversy. Despite frequent mistakes, his reputation grew in exponential leaps. By the mid-1990s, he had switched from optimistic predictions of recovery to dire warnings of Japan's potential to wreck the global economy through its nonperforming-loans problem. To Courtis, nothing associated with Japan was ever less than colossal.

Tall and reedy, with a hushed voice and receding chin, Courtis had a genius for sound bites, an obsession with the media, and a genuine fascination with Japan. He joined Deutsche Bank's investment-banking arm in Tokyo in 1987. The timing was perfect—Japan's bubble economy was just taking off and massive spending abroad was building the myth of the Japanese juggernaut. Up until then, the Toronto native had been teaching Canadian politics and economics as a visiting professor at Tokyo and Keio universities. Previously, while on the faculty of Laval University in Quebec, he had made a mark as a specialist in the politics of Quebec nationalism, and was the author of two books in French on the political motivations of Quebecois teenagers.

In Tokyo, Courtis's German colleagues grumbled that he got the attention of the press by running up a huge fax bill, sending out pronouncements with every twitch of the Japanese economy. When *Fortune* published a story describing Courtis as "one of the few strategists who correctly called the Nikkei's tumble from the very beginning," fellow Canadian Paul Summerville faxed journalists a copy of Courtis's 1989 prediction that the Nikkei would go to 65,000. Academic economists regarded him with some disdain. "My understanding is that Ken Courtis is not an economist," sniffed Edward Lincoln, an advisor to the U.S. ambassador. "But he has made the transition gracefully. In many ways the Japanese economy is an incredibly boring subject. It helps to have people like him around who make it sound livelier—as long as they don't treat it as gospel truth but as part of a debate."

Courtis modestly referred to himself as "an international economist looking at the world from Asia, centered in Japan." He enjoyed telling people how he breakfasted in Tokyo with Bill Clinton, hobnobbed in New York with Henry Kissinger and in Paris with François Mitterrand. He was on familiar terms with Deng Xiaoping's daughter in Beijing. In 1994, well into the Japanese recession, Courtis was still arguing that "once the economy is brought down again to its rock-hard, competitive core, Japan will be poised for another powerful leap ahead through the end of the decade."[8] The same year, he published a book in Japanese called *Invisible Empire* in which he argued that Japan needed only to make the right choices to cement its preeminence.

For every Kenneth Courtis, there was a Paul Kennedy, predicting that Japan's destiny would follow the path of commercial empires of the past that faded into obscurity because they lacked strategic vision. Hubris, in the golden era, was intermingled with anxiety. In every bookstore, customers lined up for copies of the Japanese translation of Kennedy's *The Rise and Fall of the Great Powers*.[9] In the book, Kennedy discussed the many obstacles that stood in the way of Japan's assuming the role of a first-class world power. Kennedy wrote:

> There is no doubt that with its economic power expanding, [Japan] could become a second Venice, in the sense not just of extensive trading, but also of protecting its maritime sea lanes and of creating quasi-dependencies overseas; yet the internal and external objections to a strong Japan are such that not only will it avoid any move toward territorial acquisitions along old-fashioned imperialist lines, but it is also unlikely to increase its defense forces very much. . . . This suggests, once again, a Japanese preference for as little change as possible in the military and political affairs of East Asia, even as the pace of economic growth quickens. . . . As other nations have discovered in the past, commercial expertise and financial wealth sometimes no longer suffice in the anarchic world of international power politics.[10]

Japanese were fascinated by this thesis. They were on top, but, like a gymnast balancing on a ball, seemed to feel that time and gravity weighed against them. Meanwhile, they would have some fun.

The New Era: Peace, Achievement, and *Mugicho*

All through the month, a thick haze hid Mt. Fuji, and the rain never stopped. On Thursday, September 22, 1988, the deathwatch began for Emperor Hirohito. Under heavy skies and a fine soft rain, long lines snaked up to the Imperial Palace and other royal shrines as thousands of Japanese assembled to pay last respects. The mood was somber as the nation counted the remaining moments of the emperor, invisible in his villa behind the massive palace walls and moat, whose sixty-three-year reign had carried Japan through extraordinary changes. His health took a bad turn just as the country was preparing to mark the autumn equinox, when Japanese traditionally visit family graves to remember their own dead. The death would belong to the whole country.

At eighty-seven, Tenno Heika, the formal title of address for an emperor and the phrase most Japanese used when they referred to him, had been a figure of controversy all his life. The emperor had been a symbol of Japan's imperial ambitions, an emblem of its supple adjustment to post-war geopolitics dominated by the United States, and finally a benign old man nodding and smiling as Japan ascended to economic superpower status. His life had spanned an era when the country embraced radically different ways of addressing the world, and many hoped that his death would reconcile the extremes of the Japanese political spectrum.

Many citizens, indeed, appeared to be eager to put the Hirohito Era behind them as quickly as possible. For them, his death was more a beginning than an ending, a chance to shed the psychological baggage encumbering Hirohito's interminable reign. "At last we may say, it is time for Japan to try something more positive instead of remaining inwards and passive," said Sato Hideo, dean of the school of International Relations at Tsukuba University. "I hope that Japan will take a more active international role, and that the new emperor will create an atmosphere in which people will be encouraged to try new things."[11]

Four decades earlier, on January 1, 1946, Hirohito had renounced his divine status and officially joined the human race. During his final illness, that did not stop Japanese from treating him like a god. Festive events from chamber of commerce fairs to theater parties and weddings were canceled. In his room in the Fukiage Palace, the emperor lay hidden behind two screens to ensure his privacy from the nurses who attended him. If they needed to ask him a question, they did so, on their knees.

Hirohito's illness lasted for three-and-a-half months. When he died on January 6, 1989, great pains were taken to ensure that the reign name of his son, Akihito, reflected the secularization of the institution. The new *gengo*, or reign name, was "Heisei," meaning "peace and achievement." For the first time, the committee choosing the name of a new reign included members of the public. In 1926 Hirohito had chosen the name "Showa" himself after the death of his father the Taisho emperor, in a fit of imperial pique, when the Imperial Household Agency prematurely leaked its own choice of reign name, Kobun or "light and literary attainments."[12] Showa meant "enlightenment and peace." The contrast in the way the reign names were selected was meant to underline the strict restraints under which the post-war institution of the emperor had operated, despite the lingering effects of the emperor system and the obvious veneration for Hirohito. Akihito's first official address marked the debut of a new official style. Presiding over an antiquated ceremony known as *Sokuigo-cho-ken-no-gi,* in which government ministers meet a new emperor, Akihito used ordinary Japanese speech rather than the court dialect spoken by his father even on routine occasions. In a three-minute speech that he wrote himself, Akihito pledged to uphold the Constitution in a Japan that had "achieved an honorable place in international society as a nation of peace."[13]

About this time, Yoshioka Shinobu, a well-known writer, canvassed the population on their opinions of Akihito. One thirty-seven-year-old engineer said: "The Crown Prince? Isn't he just an ordinary guy?" Japanese seemed to like that about him. After the emperor's death, on a Saturday, commentators predicted that the Japanese stock market would rest quietly for a week out of respect. During two days of public mourning on the weekend, the lights were turned out on Tokyo Tower and in the Ginza nightlife district. Japanese television networks yanked advertising and most regular programs and ran hours of documentary footage from the Showa Era, including scenes from the bombed out Japan of the 1940s. For many Japanese born after the war, this was their first direct exposure to the searing poverty of the period. Many more Japanese, however, rented videos for the weekend, and on the following Monday, the Nikkei Index soared to record highs. Tokyo was back to normal. If you had slept through the weekend, or gone out of the country, it would be hard to believe that anything had happened at all.

The event capturing the national imagination was not so much Hirohito's death as his funeral, which was designed as a national coming out party despite the somber occasion. Part ceremonial, part summit, Hirohito's funeral was intended to mark a milestone, projecting an image of a Japan at peace with its past and enormously proud of its present. Among 10,000 guests, there were 55 heads of state, 14 members of royal families, 11 prime ministers, and another 74 officials representing 163 countries. The Tokyo Metropolitan Police force mobilized 32,000 officers and blocked 70 percent of traffic on February 24, 1989, the day of the funeral.

The city park where the event was held, Shinjuku Gyoen, was closed to the public from January 9. Organizers did their best to achieve a theatrical statement of the country's continued attachment to its roots, embodied by the emperor. Attendants wore white linen and black silk in the style of the medieval Heian Era, from 794–1185. Guests froze in open-air pavilions while the thirteen-and-a-half-hour ceremony dragged on and on behind filmy curtains in the *sojoden,* or funeral hall, carved from massive wooden beams. In two huge tents adjacent to the formal seating areas, the nation's elite warmed themselves over tea and goggled. Chiyonofuji, the brilliant sumo *yokozuna* known as "The Wolf," swaggered by with his attendants. Eda Satsuki, the liberal politician, stopped to chat. If you were Japanese, to be invited to

Hirohito's funeral was to walk into history. We journalists froze and wrote and rewrote our stories several times over, restricted from leaving the grounds until the ceremony ended.

Immediately after the funeral, the assembled leaders raced to a frenetic round of summit meetings, many of which were significant. Indonesia's Suharto met with Chinese foreign minister Qian Qichen, in the first high-level contact between the two countries since 1967. Israel and Egypt held their first presidential summit since Anwar Sadat's visit to Jerusalem in 1977. Japanese prime minister Takeshita had the toughest slate of all, meeting with forty foreign leaders over the course of a few days. In a Japanese custom of long standing, he offered gifts to his guests from developing countries—a $1.5 billion mixed fund of yen credits and Export-Import Bank loans for Brazil, and assurances of aid to come for many others.

It was a sign of the times that the nation tuned into the new era as though it was yet another novelty. Teenage girls complained about being typecast as "Showa" because it made them seem old. Heisei, on the other hand, was amusing and fresh. Clearly, the Japanese wanted to erase the dour aftertaste of the immediate past, and it was not long before enterprising marketers discovered the commercial value of "peace and achievement."

In the deep peace of a mountain afternoon, two elderly mushroom farmers wandered outside their front doors to take in the sunshine. They found themselves facing a waiting posse of reporters. Within minutes, a television crew's Toyota screeched to a halt in front of the farmers. By the time the car arrived, one farmer was already deep in an interview with a reporter from the *Nagoya Times*. Two more Japanese reporters and a foreign reporter lined up waiting to talk to the second farmer, who was busy conferring with a member of his village assembly. Meanwhile, tourists in cars with license plates from Osaka, Tokyo, and other far-off places drove up and down Henari's main, and only, street.

The only previous time that anyone had taken notice of Henari was in 1580. That year, a local geographer climbed into the foothills of the Japanese Alps and recorded its name. It also happened to be the name of the new imperial reign, Heisei, with a different pronunciation for the same Japanese *kanji*. A Japanese wire service reporter made the discovery, and instantly anointed the settlement the "village of the new era." On January 8, 1989, when the Heisei Era officially began, five television stations, five newspapers, and two weekly magazines were on hand to capture the initial reaction of Henari's residents—all thirty-seven of them. Henari wasn't alone in being exploited as a symbol of the new era. TV crews invaded dozens of hospital wards in the early hours of January 8, searching for "Heisei babies." They even rounded up two Japanese with the characters for Heisei in their names.

Henari was the only one of the Heisei celebrities to instantly perceive the marketing possibilities in its name. "I was really surprised when I saw the characters of Henari's name on TV," Tsuchiya Kiyoshi, mayor of Mugicho, the district that incorporates Henari, told one of the first Japanese reporters to pounce on the story. "It was terrific luck. We can really use this to promote the community." Within two days of the emperor's death, the mayor had planted signs along Mugicho's main highway reading "Mugicho, Town of Mushrooms and the *Gengo*," "Heisei District Starts from Here," and "Place Linked with the New Reign Name." By the third day, Henari and Mugicho had come up with a business plan. The community decided to start selling its mushrooms under a new Henari label, set aside a patch of forests to be known as the Heisei Forest for tourists, and create a monument to be set up somewhere along Henari's half-mile stretch of roadway. "Even now, it feels like I'm dreaming," said Sato Yoshihiro, one of the mushroom farmers. "This could be as big as Mt. Fuji. Like Mt. Fuji, there's only one Henari."

Orchids and *Ochakumi*

When I began my assignment in Japan, I looked first at my own gender. Surely, I thought, the reality of Japanese women must be very different from their image as docile, tea-serving dolls. In 1991, Mitsui Mariko was one of eight women among 136 members elected to the Tokyo metropolitan assembly. An outspoken feminist, Mitsui had taken up causes ranging from battling Asian sex tours organized by the tour-bus subsidiary of the Tokyo government to sexual harassment in the workplace, the lack of benefits for female temporary workers, and the practice of setting lower quotas in Tokyo public high schools for girls than for boys. Her crusade of the moment, however, was the fight against *ochakumi*, or serving tea.

Women in Japanese offices were obliged to serve tea, regardless of their job description. This included elected politicians, and *ochakumi* went far beyond the concept of the Western coffee break. Every business meeting in Japan began with tea, offered by a demure young woman with downcast eyes (or, as the case may be, a fuming older woman, like Mitsui). Like the classic Japanese tea ceremony, which has religious connotations, the presentation of tea in the Japanese office was formal and precise.

The idea was to honor the visitor—and elevate their status—by casting the tea lady in the role of inferior. Mitsui argued that the practice was symbolic of women's work and the way that sexist stereotyping works in Japan. A survey conducted by the group found that tea service took from forty minutes to an hour of the women's day.

"It may be abstract," she said, "but it's something everybody understands."

So much so, that when Mitsui organized sixteen female legislators from lo-cal assemblies around Japan to introduce resolutions to stop the practice, their male colleagues howled with laughter.

In the 1990s, despite three decades of Japanese feminism and a 1985 law upholding the ideal of equal employment opportunity, few young Japanese women took up the challenge to enter the professional ranks of the male-dominated work world. One who did, Kanai Rieko, was the second woman hired by the Bank of Japan in 1982. She majored in economics at Tokyo University, graduating among the top ten in her class. At the Bank of Japan, she placed fourth on its entrance exam. As a woman, Kanai faced two sets of rules: one for the bank's female clerical staff, and another for professionals. She was expected to wear the same uniform as the female clerical staff; men wore suits. Her male colleagues could expect to circulate through a range of departments in the course of their careers; women were restricted to back office functions, where they would not have to deal with the public. "Any little mistake you make is magnified," Kanai said. "I'm not that sensitive but anyone who is would have trouble." When she first entered the central bank, Kanai used ordinary Japanese language to address her fellow "freshmen," many of them college friends. A supervisor quickly dressed her down. It did not matter that she was on the bank's professional track, he said. She still had to use the "appropriate" language for women addressing men—language which emphasized the lower status of the woman. Any other practice would be disruptive.

Symbols of women's second-class status in Japan were plentiful. Banks decorated the screens of automated teller machines with cartoon figures of bowing women. Most government agencies and companies required all women to wear clerical uniforms, whether they were clerical staff or not. A card game called *Ningen no Kuzu* (Human Trash), based on buying and sell-ing women, was wildly successful before the license holder, Tahara, finally withdrew it from the shelves. In the game, playing cards showed a woman's photograph, name, blood type, job description, number of sexual experi-ences, and male come-on lines, such as "Something is missing from my life." Virgins were rated zero, and the object was to clear the player's hand of all other cards through such means as selling them off to Hong Kong flesh bro-kers. The game was sold in toy stores, along with plastic models of Ultraman, "Kitty" dolls, and Nintendo games.

If women were forced to serve tea, Japanese men were held to super-human standards of loyalty and self-sacrifice for their companies. Most Japa-nese women felt they got the better bargain. Lifetime employees were, by definition, men. The practice reduced the costs to companies of hiring and retraining, but the men were held in place by the virtual absence of lateral job mobility. The lack of outside prospects meant that workers could improve their chances only by working harder at their existing positions. It also bred conservative spending habits and risk aversion, because to rebel against the system was to risk permanent unemployment.

The classic way for a Japanese company to phase out a business or production line was not to lay off workers, but to redeploy them in new businesses. Viewed close up, however, even the most benevolent job transfers left something to be desired. In Spring 1989, Japan's Foreign Press Center—a wholly subsidized offshoot of the Foreign Ministry that organizes interviews for visiting foreign journalists—put together a press tour of restructuring efforts in the Japanese steel industry. In the mid-1980s, competition from lower-cost producers in Korea and Taiwan put pressure on the Japanese steel industry, which then became a focus of industrial policy to diversify from heavy industry to high technology. MITI launched a "sunset industry" plan designed to help phase out capital-intensive production, replacing it with specialty steels and products. Industry, meanwhile, had to find something to do with tens of thousands of former steelworkers.

The showpiece of the Foreign Press Center tour was the Yawata Works of Nippon Steel. The world's largest steel company, Nippon Steel was originally founded by the Japanese government in 1901 and privatized during the Occupation. For many years, the company had its Tokyo sales office within the headquarters of the Ministry of Commerce and Industry, the predecessor to MITI. In 1988, Nippon Steel had shut down nine of the ten blast furnaces at the Yawata Works. In the previous three years, its workforce had been slashed by 3,000 people, or 20 percent, and the object of the press tour was to demonstrate how this had been done without firing anyone.

We went to visit a "biotechnology project," on the grounds of one of the dismantled blast furnaces, now overgrown with brush. At the end of a winding dirt road there was a tiny clearing with four greenhouses. Inside one of them, Koyauemura Yoshimasu, former steelworker, was tending orchids. Two years previously, slumping oil prices had forced Nippon Steel to close part of a big seamless pipe plant where Koyauemura worked. He was given a choice—he could tend orchids in the company greenhouse, or he could retire. He chose to tend orchids, even though it meant a 20 percent pay cut. At the age of forty-eight, he could have expected another eleven years of work at full salary. With reporters and senior company managers around, Koyauemura was diplomatic. "I really don't bear any resentment towards the company," he said. "Gardening was my hobby before. It wasn't just a question of asking for the job versus being told to do it. The company recommended that I take it, but I was interested, too."[14]

The orchid project was part of a larger program at Nippon Steel to explore biotechnology, one of the new technologies flagged by the Japanese government at the time. Typically, big companies created subsidiaries to handle such businesses, using them to accommodate workers from redundant business lines in transfers called *shuko*. In theory such transfers were temporary, but in many cases they might be permanent. Over time, the parent company then gradually reduced its equity in the *shuko* company. Once the subsidiary was independent, it might go bankrupt and fire all its workers with impunity. After the orchid farm, several Nippon Steel managers drove the foreign reporters to another of its new projects, a $270 million theme park called Space World, built on the site of a defunct blast furnace. Space World had employed 200 steel workers to build and maintain its facilities. No one seemed to question that families would want to drive an hour from the nearby twin cities of Kitakyushu and Fukuoka into an industrial park to put their kids on the rides. On a return visit to Space World in 1993, the grounds were nearly deserted. Attendants admitted that the theme park was unpopular. They were clearly worried about its survival. "Sometimes it does happen that the employee is not too happy about the transfer," admitted Sato Tadafumi, the general affairs manager at the Yawata Works. "When that happens, we talk with them. Ultimately they accept the job that they are advised to move to."

Deeply conservative consumers were the flip side of captive workers. In the era of high-speed growth in the 1950s and 1960s, forced savings, high domestic prices, and long working hours became part of the fabric of Japanese life. By 1995, according to the World Bank, at $39,640, Japan had the world's highest per capita income after Switzerland, compared to $26,980 for the United States.[15] On a purchasing power parity basis, the Japanese per capita rate was lower, at $22,110, but even so Japan ranked ahead of all of its G7 industrial nation partners except the United States Japanese consumers spent lavishly on relatively minor consumer items, such as clothes and electronics equipment. Big-ticket items, however, were another matter.

Kiuchi Mikio, a thirty-nine-year-old executive with Nissan Motor Co., and his wife, Kazuko, were unhappy with life in Japan. "I think living conditions here are outrageously bad," he protested. His wife worked, and together they made about $100,000 a year. After paying taxes, housing payments, day-care fees for their two toddlers, and grocery bills, they had just $1,300 a month left over. Their $300,000 two-story house was a mere 1,000 square feet, and while they had a backyard, it was too small for the children to play in or even to grow a tree.[16]

To earn his $65,000-a-year salary, Kiuchi worked twelve hours a day, five days a week, seldom returning to his home in a Yokohama suburb before midnight. The only time he took off was when his children were sick or the company shut down—which it only did on weekends and during the annual five-day "Golden Week" holiday. The Kiuchis paid $1,500 a month for groceries, spending $20 on an eleven-pound sack of rice, $2 for a single Golden Delicious apple, $2 for an onion, and up to $15 for a bunch of grapes. Instead of being rebellious, Kiuchi was resigned—even proud. When I asked if he would consider leaving Japan to work for a foreign company, he recoiled. The pain, he said, was worth it—for the company's sake. "I think, as most other Japanese workers, that it is inevitable to experience such sacrifices in order for our company"—that is, Nissan, with $60 billion in sales— "to survive." According to Takahashi Johsen, an economist with Mitsubishi Research Institute, "Strangely enough, people don't feel miserable under the current circumstances. To the extent people can feel they are no worse off than the next man, they can live with it. Japanese are good at adapting themselves to extreme conditions."

Under pressure from abroad to stimulate consumer demand, the Japanese Labor Ministry mounted a public campaign to get people to take the twenty days of paid leave to which they were constitutionally entitled. The ministry even published a handbook to give workers ideas about how to spend their leisure time, entitled *Try Your Best: Salaryman's Guide to Relaxation.* "Try your best," "*ganbatte,*" has the connotation of struggling against odds. You've got your job cut out for you, but "*ganbatte*"!

The Seagull and the Politicians

A Japanese proverb goes, "It's cheaper to buy than receive a gift," and in the late 1980s, Japanese had occasion to think of it often.[17] It was a time when popular culture offered primers in the inner workings of the Japanese political system with an exuberance that belied the sliminess of the subject matter.

Toy stores were selling a board game called "Za Kuromaku" that was like a twisted version of Monopoly. The literal translation of *kuromaku* was "black curtain" and referred to the politics of feudal Japan, when the chief advisor to the *daimyo* whispered into his ear from behind a curtain. The game offered a devastatingly accurate portrayal of Japanese political culture at work. Playing cards represented politicians, *yakuza* (the Japanese mafia), the CIA, Japanese companies, and other sharp manipulators. Each card assigned points based on money, politics, violence, information, or connections. The way the game worked, a player with money could easily buy the card of a politician. Politicians, in Za Kuromaku, had good connections, lots of political influence, and gobs of greed.

The game conflicted with the squeaky-clean images of Japan prevailing at the time—as one of Asia's few working democracies, with its hardworking *sarariman*, honest officials, and technological wizardry. So it was all the more ironic that a company whose corporate logo was a seagull was the inspiration behind Za Kuromaku. The seagull could be taken for an emblem of sublime purity—or a mere garbage scavenger.

The logo belonged to Recruit, a company that sold information about new college graduates to companies hungry to draft the best possible candidates for lifetime employment. It was a new concept in Japan and took off in an ever-expanding economy where young, male college graduates were in perpetual short supply. Recruit built the process of advertising employers to new college graduates into a $4 billion business. Precisely because Recruit was an outsider, a new company in a world of giant conglomerates, it poured a great deal of energy into setting up its own web of connections. The company played the *kuromaku* game to the hilt.

Eventually, it got caught. Recruit's chairman, Ezoe Hiromasa, offered cheap stocks in a subsidiary, prior to its public listing, to no fewer than 160 of his close associates, including more than 50 leading politicians of all parties and members of their staff. The politicians made $4 million in total on the stock deals when the stock went public and predictably shot up by more than 400 percent in value. Prosecutors claimed that Recruit received political favors in return.

In the beginning, everyone implicated in the affair denied any wrongdoing. By Spring 1989, the scandal had engulfed three cabinet ministers, the former head of one of the world's largest companies, Nippon Telegraph and Telephone (NTT), the editor in chief of Japan's prestigious financial newspaper, the *Nihon Keizai Shimbun,* and scores of lesser bureaucrats, company officials, and politicians. By the time Emperor Hirohito was buried in February, political pundits had begun a deathwatch on the government of Prime Minister Takeshita, who resigned in April. No comparable scandal had so rocked Japan since the 1976 Lockheed bribery affair in which then-Prime Minister Tanaka Kakuei had lost his job and received a four-year prison sentence (which remained on permanent appeal until his death in 1993) for accepting a bribe from the U.S. company. Most people assumed that the Recruit scandal would bring down not only Takeshita but also his predecessor, Nakasone Yasuhiro, a member of the Japanese Diet, former prime minister, and senior advisor to the Liberal Democratic Party (LDP). It was under Nakasone's government that Recruit's alleged influence peddling reached epic proportions.

For many Japanese, the Recruit affair was a disquieting exposition of the obvious, as if the newspapers had suddenly decided to hone in on middle-class tax evasion or the extracurricular sex lives of businessmen. To foreigners, it came as a shock; they were used to a fictional Japan that successfully kept corruption under wraps. After Recruit, the Japanese "model" became unstrung, its inner workings exposed to unwelcome view. It had been founded on a wartime system of total economic mobilization and included extensive laws and regulations supporting domestic manufacturers at the expense of consumers and foreigners. These were designed to nurture Japanese infant industries while protecting the domestic market, and it was no accident that they lasted years after Japan had reached parity with the industrial West. Under this system, the politicians' role was to represent producers, not consumers, because it was large Japanese companies that kept them in office. Political contributions were one method, but large companies also controlled the vote of their employees. Consumers never had a chance.

Nonetheless, the corrupt political system exposed by the Recruit scandal proved remarkably resilient. Frank Gibney, writing in the *Los Angeles Times* more than a decade later, described Japan's politics as the main obstacle to the much needed "third opening" of the country, after the Meiji Restoration of 1868 and MacArthur's democratization reforms after 1945. "The trouble is, to deregulate and restructure the economy, with all the temporary pains that would cause, would strike at the heart of most of the ruling Liberal Democratic Party's special-interest constituencies," he wrote.[18] Between 1988 and 2000, Japanese prime ministers came and went frequently, with political parties forming and disappearing around them. Recruit was responsible for the turbulence, but beneath the surface the LDP continued to dominate politics. All but one of the ten prime ministers between 1988 and 2000, Gibney observed, were LDP products, and the only exception, Murayama Tomiichi, who served from June 1994 to January 1996, represented an LDP-led coalition.

As paper-white plum blossoms gave way to popcorn clusters of cherry blossoms in Spring 1989, the Tokyo Public Prosecutor's Office began making arrests on bribery charges. The dominoes began to fall in the direction of Nakasone and Takeshita. As the stakes grew higher, the Recruit scandal raised another question. Japan's domestic politics were beginning to have an impact on world affairs, and the LDP's competence to deal with international issues had never been tested. The post-war system had effectively exempted Japan's legislative arm from foreign policy and defense, and when politicians did unburden themselves of views—often indistinguishable from the nationalistic and xenophobic demagoguery of the 1930s—most citizens shrugged them off. It was becoming harder for the bureaucrats to control the damage created by such remarks, and the more exposure Japanese politics received, the worse it got.

The LDP had been in power since 1956. The only important elections were those held within the party, and they took place behind closed doors in elaborate negotiations between LDP factions. When the Recruit scandal first broke, most of the Western press assumed it was a minor brushfire. The authoritative *Wall Street Journal* ran an op-ed piece explaining that Japanese politics were no more or less than the "money politics" back in the United States. "Indeed, an American viewing the Recruit scandal notices pronounced similarities between the Japanese political fund-raising system and his own," wrote Urban Lehner, Tokyo Bureau chief. "American politicians, like Japanese, rely for their money on business and other special-interest groups, which clearly hope that their contributions will be remembered. In both countries, politics is so expensive that there is hardly any alternative."[19]

In fact, far fewer constraints on influence peddling were present in Japan than in the United States, and the "iron triangle" allowed politicians to operate with near total impunity. The difference between the Tanaka bribery scandal and Recruit was one of scale. Recruit implicated nearly the entire political establishment, but the practices were similar, and Takeshita had grown up politically under Tanaka's tutelage.[20] In the next decade, it would become conventional wisdom that Japanese politics were corrupt, but in 1989 the concept still had shock value. The Japanese were acutely aware that Recruit was bad for public relations, so much so that newspaper editorials questioned if the United States had planted the scandal in order to advance its own interests. According to this line of reasoning, if the United States could discredit the LDP, it would become easier to insist on further opening of the Japanese market. Such irrational charges only underlined the anxieties that the Japanese themselves felt as their powerful economy dragged them toward a more central role in world affairs. One Japanese newspaper reported indignantly, "A single step inside Nagatacho [Japan's Parliament Hill], primitive boss politics prevail with impunity." The money trail from Recruit crisscrossed politics, business, and the bureaucracy. Even worse, when senior officials, politicians, and businesspeople were found out, they acted as though nothing was particularly unusual.

Picture this: the prime minister, his immediate predecessor, the finance minister, top officials of the governing party, and about six-dozen friends outside politics are caught in a major stock scandal.[21] A huge, legendarily successful conglomerate has offered inside trading information and a chance to buy shares before its first public listing on the stock market. The investors make profits of 400 percent. The press finds out, and makes a fuss. The prime minister and finance minister are caught lying about their involvement. There is evidence of open bribery. And nothing happens. The governing party makes apologies—and promptly moves on to other matters. That was supposed to be the blueprint for the Recruit scandal. The LDP had been able to sweep aside such troubles previously. Instead of subsiding, however, Recruit rocked the LDP to the core. In October 1988, the first charges were filed, and the narrowing net of the investigation squeezed a public confession out of Finance Minister Miyazawa Kiichi, who had previously denied involvement. Up until then, the LDP successfully resisted efforts by the opposition parties to haul the case before the Diet, a mistake. As public attorneys uncovered additional evidence, it became increasingly clear that Takeshita himself had been engaged in a massive cover-up. "If this happened in a foreign country, all the cabinet ministers would have to resign," said Murobushi Tetsuro, a political critic.

To cheerful melodies played by the Central Musical Band of Japan's Ground Self-Defense Forces on a fine spring day in 1989, Japan enacted one of its annual rites of spring in a downtown Tokyo park—the prime minister's cherry blossom party, or *hanami*.[22] Thousands of Japan's elite and the foreign diplomatic corps admired the park's late-blooming cherry blossoms, waved at friends, and raised glasses of sake in square wooden flasks to celebrate the season. Some joined a long, snaking line to shake hands with a smiling Takeshita, the host. Others, cognizant of Takeshita's troubles, held back. "How do I know who's going to be prime minister by the time I get to the front?" joked a diplomat who shunned the reception line. His jest summed up the mood in the Japanese capital. Foreign residents dubbed the prime minister's *hanami*, "Takeshita's farewell party." He resigned a few days later, on April 25, after the suicide of a trusted aide, Aoki Ihei.

Even while Takeshita remained in office, he paid so little attention to anything other than the Recruit scandal that he might as well have gone earlier, observers said. Foreshadowing international criticism for a decade to come, Japan's diplomatic and trading partners complained that the political gridlock affected the country's ability to handle major issues. A visit to Washington that spring by Japan's deputy minister of Foreign Affairs, Kunihiro Michihiko, ended glumly because of confusion in Tokyo. Kunihiro was trying to advance troubled negotiations with the United States over the joint development of a new fighter support aircraft, the FSX. But Takeshita's lack of engagement made it impossible to resolve the issue. The dilemma presaged a decade of communications glitches and diplomatic jams. "If he has to spend his days and nights wondering when the next shoe is going to drop, he simply can't be effective," said a diplomat. "Japan can muddle along very, very well without political leadership for a while, but not forever."

Nearly the entire LDP inner circle had received financial favors in one form or another, including Takeshita. The politicians under investigation, however, benefited from stock transactions under Recruit's tutelage that were particularly lucrative and easy to hide. The politicians and some of their close associates received heavily discounted shares in an unlisted Recruit subsidiary and were counseled when to sell them for maximum profit. In most cases, a Recruit subsidiary also financed the purchases. Under Japanese law, such transactions did not have to be registered as political donations. In addition, the politicians and others who received the unlisted shares did not have to pay any capital gains tax. In the case of Nakasone and his associates, profits from Recruit stock exceeded $1 million. Nakasone's inner circle acknowledged that it had received 29,000 shares of the Recruit real-estate subsidiary, Recruit Cosmos, more than any other set of beneficiaries.

Normally, when the LDP suffered setbacks and a prime minister resigned, the party's five major factions conferred to come up with a replacement. This time, there were no obvious successors to Takeshita, because Recruit had tainted so many senior LDP members. Among other undercurrents, one was a battle of leaks between politicians and the Tokyo Public Prosecutor's Office, whose special investigation team was in charge of the Recruit case. In news conferences, the prosecutors confined their statements to terse reports of indictments and arrests. So reporters trooped to the homes of the investigators in a nightly ritual called *yomawari*, where they waited for the officials at their front gates. If the officials invited them in, reporters were kept up to date with subtle and often cryptic hints. But the hints were sufficient to generate a flood of detail in the press, such as speculation about the next politicians to be arrested. In retaliation, politicians accused the Prosecutor's Office of police state tactics. The prosecutors, they claimed, used intimidation to wring confessions from those under suspicion.

During the ten months between the time that the scandal first broke and Takeshita's resignation, Japanese had the chance to take a long, hard look at the pervasive relationship between politicians and big business in Japan. They called it *kinken seiji* or "money politics." The phrase was coined in the 1970s, when former Prime Minister Tanaka put together a formidable political machine based on streams of cash from the private sector. Reforms launched after Tanaka's arrest only made things worse. In the aftermath of the Lockheed scandal, corporations found ways to get around limits on individual contributions. The post–Lockheed Political Funds Control Regulations became a national joke. The Japanese call the law *zaruho*—"leaky as a bamboo sieve."

The Japanese political scandals of the 1980s and 1990s, however, made Tanaka's shenanigans look like small change. The Lockheed scandal began and ended with Tanaka, and the $1.4 million bribe he had accepted. With the Recruit scandal, literally hundreds of politicians, bureaucrats, and big businessmen were directly involved, having received money directly from Recruit. Together, they made up one of the most powerful elites in the world, and they were in the pocket of a company that was virtually unknown outside Japan. According to a calculation published in *Asahi Weekly*, Recruit lavished upwards of $23 million on its powerful associates. The politicians excused themselves by saying that the money they received from Recruit was for necessary political expenses, not fancy shoes, Swiss bank accounts, or expensive automobiles. Recruit, too, contended that its donations were legal. For example, it spent heavily on tickets to political fund-raising events, on which there were no set limits. At one 1986 party for Takeshita, before he became prime minister, Recruit purchased 1,500 tickets at a cost of about $300,000. No Recruit executive attended the party. Much more of Recruit's largesse was in the form of offers to purchase stock at a steep discount to the anticipated market price. Those who took the offer saw the stock soar from the pre-listing price of $12 a share to as high as $52. In return, Recruit's flamboyant chairman, Ezoe, received favors galore from his friends in politics and the bureaucracy.

The roots of the Recruit affair went back thirty years. Ezoe, while a student at Tokyo University, started an executive recruitment agency aimed at university graduates—a new concept at the time, even though Japan's system of lifetime employment created enormous competition among employers for the best of the graduating crop. Ezoe built the Recruit Group into a conglomerate with twenty-six subsidiaries, spanning employment services, real estate, publishing, and computer databases. In 1984, he decided to take public a real-estate subsidiary, Recruit Cosmos.

Under Japanese law, a company had to have a certain number of shareholders prior to listing. So, Ezoe offered shares of Recruit Cosmos to seventy-six friends of the company, ranging from Takeshita and Nakasone to Miyazawa and two of the most senior LDP officials, Secretary-General Abe Shintaro, and Watanabe Michio, chairman of the LDP's policy coordinating committee. Ezoe offered the shares not to the men directly but to their political secretaries, yet few observers perceived any real difference. "A politician may use his secretary's name without asking for the secretary's approval, but there is no way a secretary is going to receive stocks without telling the politicians," said one political secretary, quoted anonymously in the Tokyo weekly *Shukan Shincho*. "It is simply unthinkable." Ostensibly, they were employed to keep track of the affairs of constituents but routinely served as their boss's bagmen as well. One editorialist compared them to *kuroko*, the black-clothed artists who manipulate the puppets in Bunraku theater. They were supposed to be invisible, "but as soon as anything bad is disclosed, the Dietmen blame it on their secretaries."

The system was no mystery, explained one stockbroker, requesting anonymity. Initial listings, he said, usually made a profit of between $45 million and $90 million. Brokers regarded them as a low-risk type of investment. Companies sold the shares to their personal associates at a discount from the first market price of as much as 50 percent or even more, so the profits were generally high. "The Recruit affair is an absolutely typical example of the way politicians make money," he said. "When companies do their first listings, they set aside 30 percent of the shares, which will go to politicians or to companies with which they have ties. It's a bribe when the politician promises a favor in exchange. But here it's rarely that clear. The politician who needs money now may be ready at some point in the future to execute a favor." Ordinary shareholders did not object to this cozy system, said Murobushi, the political critic, because individuals accounted for less than 10 percent of market activity. Moreover, he claimed, "The Japanese simply don't go up against authority."

So pervasive was the network tying companies to politicians that each of the major factions within the LDP was associated with a particular stock. Besides actual political favors, the politicians often helped to sell their "brand-name" stocks. For example, Nakasone's name was linked with a pharmaceutical company. Shortly after it was listed in 1985, the stock went from Yen 2,000 to Yen 16,600. "This is a society of exchange," said Kenneth Courtis, the economist. "With the dynamism of the Tokyo market, new listings go up quickly in price. So to make for future pleasant business relations, I will make sure those shares are in good, strong and stable hands. And if I help you, you would expect at some point, to return the service."

Some of the more progressive LDP members admitted that the system itself was flawed. "The required amount of money being used by politicians has reached enormous proportions," explained Aichi Kazuo, a member of the lower house. "The need for this flow of funds arises from the present structure of the election system. Under this system it could probably be said that the more powerful a politician becomes, the more money flows to him." According to Aichi, the problem arose partly because of the low pay of Diet members. He calculated that his own overhead ran to just under $1 million annually, but his salary and bonuses were only about $95,000. The difference had to be made up out of political contributions. In 1988, there was no tax required on capital gains, so the stock market offered an ideal source of funds.

If Recruit did not know where to draw the line, neither did the politicians. The nine opposition parties tried to make headway with the Recruit affair, said Okano Kaoru, dean of the faculty of political science and economics at Meiji University. But their hands were tied because many of them raised money in the same manner. "If they threaten to present their evidence, the LDP can threaten right back," he said. Fukuoka Masayuki, a political scientist at Komazawa University, said political donations by Japanese companies in 1988 amounted to about $3 billion a year. When under-the-counter contributions such as stock market deals were added, he said, the figure could be as high as $10 billion. Not all politicians were created equal in the world of money politics. A leader of a powerful faction within the LDP, such as Takeshita, needed enough funds to support weaker members. Money that a faction leader received trickled down to faction lieutenants and junior members. Fukuoka said that Takeshita collected about $10 million annually from his supporters. Corporate donations, he said, made up at least 70 percent of political financing.[23]

Even a junior Diet member needed between $650,000 and $1.8 million just to run his office, according to Ishiba Shigeru, a thirty-two-year-old Diet member. That was because Diet members were expected to spread largesse to their constituents, showering endless favors on them in return for votes. Nearly 40 percent of Ishiba's operating budget of $700,000 in 1988 went to expenses in his prefecture, Tottori, the smallest electoral district in Japan. "If someone builds a new house, we have to send them a gift," he said. "That happens maybe ten times a year. If someone has a first grandchild, that's another gift." The most expensive events were funerals, which could cost Ishiba as much as $10,000 for the funeral of a key supporter. "If I don't send cash or flowers to them, that sort of attitude would go against the social code. I would be considered inhuman, a man with no emotions."

Ishiba's total pay from the government amounted to about $160,000, including the salaries of two secretaries. He made up the difference partly through regular "allowances" from his party, the LDP, of $40,000 a year. His faction gave him another $40,000, and his personal mentor, Watanabe Michio, secretary-general of the LDP, provided another $40,000. The rest came from political fund-raising parties of the type that got Takeshita in hot water. The popularity of such parties grew after the 1976 Lockhheed scandal. The government subsequently set a $1 million limit on direct political donations and required politicians to report all donations over $1,000. Such restraints did not apply to tickets to attend parties, however, and they became a major source of funds for politicians. At one megaparty, Amano Mitsuhari, a former minister of construction, collected $2.1 million, for a net value of $2 million. Because of a loophole in Japan's regulations governing political financing, Takeshita did not have to report the purchases. It took ten months of hard questioning about Recruit before the purchases were admitted, and only after a Japanese wire service reported it.

For months, Ezoe's gaunt, unshaven face hung over the Japanese consciousness like some evil omen of disaster.[24] In the course of clawing his way to the top, Ezoe spread his favors far and wide among the elite circles of politics, business, and the press. It made him popular. Until mid-1988, Ezoe was the darling of the Japanese media. Prime ministers took him into their confidence. Shinto Hisashi, former chairman of NTT, personally helped him to set up a lucrative new business leasing high-speed digital telephone lines from NTT. At the age of fifty-two, Ezoe was frequently described as the greatest entrepreneur produced by prestigious Tokyo University in the post-war generation. According to documents seized from Recruit by the Tokyo Public Prosecutor's Office, he had personally launched a campaign in January 1983 to systematically target politicians and bureaucrats, charging his executives to "establish pipelines in a positive way." In September 1988, the Japanese public got a taste of Ezoe's business tactics when a videotape of a Recruit official offering a bagful of money to an opposition politician was aired on national television. The politician, Narasaki Yanosuke, had been demanding more information on the case. Up until that point, the Recruit case appeared to be a local scandal. After the Narasaki incident, however, it exploded.

The irony was that the *zaikai*, or big business circles, regarded Ezoe's methods as standard operating procedure. Far larger transactions were routine. Succeeding in Japanese business meant building intricate networks by all means available. Cash, stocks, sake, and sex were all fair game, and Ezoe tried them all. In the basement of his headquarters in the Ginza, Tokyo's longtime pleasure district, he maintained a nightclub called "Passionata" in which to entertain clients. He could take his guests out of town, too, to a posh ski resort in Iwate Prefecture. His company was known for its bevy of beautiful young female employees, and more than once he seems to have taken them as lovers and then shared them with his associates.

Indeed, when the elite struck back at Ezoe, it was to blame him for getting caught, not for his connections or sharp practices. He was seen as a pushy overachiever who stretched the rules of the system past a reasonable limit. "The weak point of this society is that if somebody does not observe traditional self-control and self-constraint, the whole system will collapse," said Shiratori Rei, dean of the department of political science at Tokai University. "Recruit's problem was that it did not know where to draw the line," said Takehara Takanobu, a lawyer with the law firm of Nishimura Sanada. "It's not that they were doing anything different, but that they did too much. It's a kind of extreme symbol of Japanese society."

There was plenty of evidence to support the notion that Ezoe was an erratic character, who finally spun out of control once he came close to the pinnacle of the Japanese establishment. Ezoe's father, a high school math teacher, was a restless womanizer who drove his first wife out of the house, settled down temporarily with an entertainer, then dumped her for a third woman who served as Ezoe's stepmother. Through his teenage and college years, Ezoe was a quiet loner, cagey, and antisocial in manner. His high school classmates called him *"ojin"* (old man). Sometimes his behavior was eccentric. At his fifty-second-birthday party in 1988, he suddenly took an umbrella that had been given to him by his staff as a gift, opened it up, and lay prone on the floor for photographs.

No matter how oddly he behaved in his private life, however, Ezoe was bright enough to get into Tokyo University—which he did by selecting the unpopular education faculty. He once told a classmate that his only ambition was to be an executive, a *keieisha*. Ezoe joined the student newspaper as an ad salesman—unusual at the time because the university normally hired full-time professionals to do the job. He got the idea for his own business after he observed the bottomless appetite Japanese advertisers had for reaching the student market.

When he started out, associates say, Ezoe was a considerate boss who would fry up fish and rice for his employees on an electric burner. From 1960, when he served as company cook and still lived in a student dormitory, Ezoe traveled the length of Japan's corporate hierarchy. In December 1988, Recruit's profits jumped 30 percent to $160 million on sales of $2.7 billion. But after the scandal broke, the company was cut off by its bankers and shunned by the stock market. Shares of Recruit Cosmos were put under a one-year moratorium on the Tokyo over-the-counter market. Major government agencies pulled their advertising from Recruit's housing and employment magazines. Competitors in the student employment information market moved fast to grab its market share.

Kirin, *Keiretsu*, and Kotani

Among the rituals of humid summer nights in Tokyo was the corporate beer raid. It might be any side street in the Ginza or Shinjuku neighborhoods, where the bars were stacked in skinny high-rise buildings, ablaze with neon. A group of *sarariman*, clad in dark suits, would plunge into a doorway. *"Biru!"* they shouted. "Beer!" If the bartender offered Asahi Beer, a popular brand, they scowled. "We're Kirin men," one might say. The tactic was to crowd other customers out of the bar. The Kirin men were not necessarily employees of Kirin Beer itself but one of any of 148 companies associated with the Mitsubishi *keiretsu* that controlled Kirin, Japan's most popular brand.[25]

Mitsubishi and other *keiretsu* had the power to order their employees to wage personal warfare on the commercial brands of a rival combine. A foreign businessman in Tokyo told of a Japanese friend who was scolded by his boss for buying a set of golf balls from a rival *keiretsu* company. "How do you know which golf balls to buy?" asked the astonished foreigner. "Is there a manual?" "No," was the reply. "You just know. It's part of the social acclimatization process."

The *keiretsu*'s influence did not stop with brand wars. On a corporate level, they could dictate who sat on executive boards of group members, select the stock portfolios of individual companies, and even choose which company in their ranks would take a loss or gain a profit. They effectively blocked foreigners from participating in their supply chains or investing in their companies. And their view of capital markets was fundamentally opposed to that of Western companies. While managers in Western firms might be tossed out after a quarter of bad stock performance, Japanese executives could comfortably ignore such performance measures as the company's share price or returns on investment. Cross-shareholding relationships with other *keiretsu* members meant that the market price of shares was illusory, reflecting churning at the margins of a company's equity stock. Because Japanese banks ignored returns, the companies could ignore them, too. In the bubble economy, asset values escalated so rapidly that the paper wealth of Japanese companies rose immensely. Paying back the banks was no problem, and with negative real interest rates all the normal prudential measures flew out the window.

Oddly, given General MacArthur's vendetta against the *zaibatsu*, it became a mantra among Western experts and policy makers in the post-war period that *keiretsu* exerted a benign influence on the Japanese economy, with only mildly distorting effects. Part of the reason was that after MacArthur disbanded the holding companies in 1946, a new generation took charge of major Japanese enterprises and was celebrated for its radical views. When these same young executives began recruiting their former colleagues from the *zaibatsu*, they did so quietly. The early meetings of the "presidents' clubs" for the *keiretsu* took place secretly, shortly after the dissolution of the *zaibatsu* holding companies. The gatherings served as steering groups for the conglomerates and were illegal under rules of the U.S. Occupation. The clubs exchanged information on U.S. activities and various means of obtaining scarce supplies. Over time, their functions became much broader.[26]

Meanwhile, the Cold War presented a wide-open window of opportunity for the *zaibatsu* to regroup and encouraged a generation of American scholars and policy makers to overlook past exclusionary practices associated with them, once they were reborn as *keiretsu*. *Keiretsu* and the presidents' clubs barely got a mention in the first broad study of the Japanese "miracle," *Asia's New Giant* published by the Brookings Institution in 1976. The editors of the volume, Hugh Patrick at Yale and Henry Rosovsky at Harvard adopted the Cold War perspective that Japanese economic institutions, however different in origin they might be from those of the United States, were gradually converging on a free-market model. They viewed *keiretsu* as a transitional institution helping Japan get on its feet again after the destruction of its economy in World War Two.

In one of the essays in *Asia's New Giant*, Richard Caves and Uekusa Masu acknowledged that the three leading *zaibatsu*—Mitsubishi, Mitsui, and Sumitomo—had quickly reassembled after the end of the Occupation in 1952. Nonetheless, they argued, "The presidents' clubs and interlocking directorates provide no effective means of continuing coordination, and contemporary accounts of the groups' behavior suggest no more than sporadic mutual aid and collaboration in joint ventures. Fraternal battles over shares in specific products even break out occasionally."[27] In another essay on the Japanese main bank system, Henry and Mable Wallich acknowledged that there were indeed some differences, but ascribed them to culture, not economic strategy. They wrote that the reappearance of the *zaibatsu* in the "less tightly structured" form of *keiretsu* indicated a reassertion of the "group principle" in Japan. "Since the phenomenon appears to repeat itself frequently under very different circumstances, one is bound to conclude that in the Japanese environment the group principle offers important advantages."

In banking, this amounted to unconditional access to funds from the main banks of the *keiretsu* organization. "Group membership means both more or less than does a bank line of credit in the United States," they wrote. "It means a commitment by the bank to protect the enterprise in all but the direst circumstances by lending or otherwise finding money for it." However, they added, it was not exactly as firm or as formal as a bank credit line. "If the Bank of Japan orders a cutback or slowdown in credit expansion, the group bank must cut credit or slow it down. Firm credit lines of the U.S. variety do not exist in Japan."[28]

The Wallichs weren't the only outsiders to have trouble getting a grasp on these entities. In 1990, when Robert Z. Lawrence, an economist at the Brookings Institution, accepted a dare to conduct a study of *keiretsu*, he claimed that he couldn't find any data that he could use for an academically respectable study. When he finally got his numbers together, Lawrence found extensive evidence of collusion, including a distinct correlation between *keiretsu* and industries in which imports were abnormally low. He found that the *keiretsu* displaced about $30 billion in imports.[29]

Japanese economists and experts retorted that the trade-distorting impact of the six major *keiretsu* groups was modest and only 10 to 12 percent of their business went to other members of their groups. Another aspect of Lawrence's study was even more inflammatory to the Japanese. Lawrence argued that *keiretsu* practices did little to improve Japanese competitiveness except in the auto sector. Japan had already staked out a position that the entities were crucial to Japan's economic success; thus U.S. criticism was little more than sour grapes. The Japanese scoffed Lawrence for his ignorance. "As compared with the U.S. system, which emphasizes price, *keiretsu* emphasizes quality and delivery," Yoshitomi Masaru, a senior official with the Economic Planning Agency (EPA), told a Washington conference in 1991 at which Lawrence presented his findings. "And this is an era favoring quality and delivery." Yoshitomi went on to suggest that U.S. industry should try to embrace the *keiretsu* system and seek to penetrate the Japanese market by joining the conglomerates.[30]

That was not the least of Japanese claims for *keiretsu*. In a 1990 interview, Professor Imai Ken'ichi of Tokyo's Hitotsubashi University laid out the Japanese view at its most apocalyptic: "An age of competition between variant systems of capitalism has begun," he said. "Ultimately, it will involve a struggle for leadership in shaping the economic systems of the century to come." Imai claimed that Japan's *keiretsu* would be at the center of a struggle for dominance among competing forms of capitalism and argued that the huge alliances provided the ideal template for corporate organization in a high-technology age. "Today, technological advances are moving forward in a process of systemic innovation propelled not by top-down commands but by lateral exchanges among companies and individuals. In line with this shift, *keiretsu* are being transformed from organizations that restrict corporate activities to ones that utilize their linkages to enhance the exchange of information."

Another economist, Nakatani Iwao, described *keiretsu* ties between firms as "the very foundation of Japanese corporate operations." He added, "These relations do not stop with simple short-term transactions in the marketplace. Rather, they are wide-ranging cooperative relations which stretch out over a long period of time. They comprise one of the most important factors behind the Japanese economic 'miracle' in the post-war era." Nakatani, however, acknowledged that *keiretsu* represented a substantial market barrier. "Japan's industrial mechanisms, with *keiretsu* relations at the fulcrum, become extremely closed and exclusionary if left to themselves. Foreigners have no chance of breaking in," Nakatani said.[31] The bias against shareholders was no secret. According to another Japanese academic, Okumura Hiroshi of Ryukoku University, the *keiretsu* system was "bad from the viewpoint of economic democracy," because it virtually eliminated the rights of shareholders other than the *keiretsu* companies.

Historically, the leading *keiretsu* could trace their identity back to the nineteenth-century merchant clans of Osaka and Edo that turned against the Tokugawa *bakufu* and bankrolled the Meiji Restoration. Their reward was rich. The Meiji government sold to its business friends the mines and factories seized from supporters of the defunct shogunate, usually at steeply discounted prices. Meiji leaders then provided subsidies to strategic industries needed to support their military buildup, and oversaw the formation of financial companies, which were gradually incorporated into the merchant conglomerates. The resulting entities were called *zaibatsu*, or "financial cliques."

By the end of the nineteenth century, the largest *zaibatsu* had aligned themselves so closely with the government that they could manipulate Japan's fledgling political parties virtually at will. In 1898, Ozaki Yukio, the minister of education, remarked cynically, "Suppose that you dreamed Japan had adopted a Republican system of government, a Mitsui or Mitsubishi would immediately become the presidential candidate."[32] After the U.S. Occupation abolished holding companies in 1946, the *zaibatsu* retained their identity through cross-shareholdings and interlocking directorates. The new organizational model was called *keiretsu*, and implied outsourcing and management through contractual relationships rather than ownership.

The term *keiretsu* simply means "series" or affiliated companies, but the ties that bound them together were intense, and through the 1990s and the vicissitudes of the Japanese recession the *keiretsu* remained among the world's largest corporate groupings. In addition to the three *zaibatsu*-related *keiretsu*, another three combines centered on banks: Dai-Ichi Kangyo Bank; Sanwa Bank; and Fuji Bank. Anchors for another forty *keiretsu* were generally the largest companies in their industries, such as Toyota, Nissan, or NTT. All had a huge impact on the Japanese economy.

In 1990, the six largest *keiretsu* accounted for a staggering 61 percent of the Tokyo stock market's capitalization, with corporate assets of Yen 684 trillion, or $5.1 trillion, while some forty smaller groupings made up 17 percent of market capitalization and accounted for Yen 56.4 trillion, or $423 billion, in corporate assets. In all, *keiretsu* assets represented at least double Japan's $2.5 trillion gross national product in 1990. The six big conglomerates by themselves represented 4 percent of Japanese employment, with 1.4 million workers, 15 percent of sales, and 13.7 percent of profits. Cross-shareholdings of the six in 1990 were about 25.7 percent of total share ownership, and while these figures declined through the end of the decade, by 1998 their piece of total share ownership was still close to 16 percent. The largest decline was in the first few years after the stock and real estate crash, as short selling hit even *keiretsu* shares. During the bubble years, easy money encouraged a rapid expansion of cross-shareholdings, which peaked and subsequently declined. The ratio in 1998 of around 15 percent was about the same as the figure in 1983.

In 1998, the big six continued to account for 3.2 percent of employment, 11.2 percent of corporate assets, 11.5 percent of sales, and 9.9 percent of gross profits. The only number that dropped like a stone was net profits, which fell from 15 percent of the national total in 1990 to nothing in 1998, when Japanese industrial companies in the aggregate were deeply in the red.[33]

By the end of the decade, bank mergers that crossed *keiretsu* lines seemed to point to a breakdown of the system, but, as Douglas Ostrom has observed, the big Mitsui, Mitsubishi, and Fuyo groups were all busy aligning their financial companies to become financial supermarkets. Meanwhile, Japanese Internet companies, such as Softbank Corp., were beginning to form their own *keiretsu*-like structures.[34]

To some extent, the scale of such numbers was vastly inflated because of the overlapping between *keiretsu* groups, which were defined both by their equity and funding relationships with main banks and by equity relationships with subcontractors. Toyota, for example, was one of the most prominent of the subcontracting type of *keiretsu* but also belonged to the Mitsui *keiretsu*, a banking *keiretsu* with Sakura Bank at its core. There was no easy way to identify a *keiretsu*, because cross-shareholdings were spread across members of a group of companies. It was not possible to check *keiretsu* membership just by looking at a list of major stockholders, because not every one belonged to the *keiretsu*, as Texas oilman T. Boone Pickens found in his struggles in 1989 and 1990 to join the board of directors of Toyota *keiretsu* member, Koito Manufacturing. Professor Okumura offered six criteria that defined *keiretsu*: the existence of cross-shareholding; a presidents' club in which top executives met regularly to exchange information; joint investment among member companies; the provision of financing to *keiretsu* member companies by *keiretsu* banks; extensive buying and selling among member companies, often brokered by a *keiretsu* trading company, the *sogo shosha*; and a "densely networked industrial structure, particularly in the field of chemical industries."

If you were Japanese, however, none of this intricacy seemed particularly confusing. One way to identify *keiretsu* was by going to the business section of any Japanese bookstore and investing in one of several massive directories, such as the one published at regular intervals by Toyo Keizai Shinposha, a major business publisher. Its directories broke down each of the *keiretsu* by members of the presidents' clubs and provided detailed information on when and where they met, as well as how many and what level of executives each of the *keiretsu* seconded to its member companies. Smaller, more topical handbooks identified hot new areas of *keiretsu* formation, giving thumbnail sketches of the corporate strategies and current fortunes of existing *keiretsu*.[35]

However enigmatic the *keiretsu* may have seemed to foreigners, Japanese saw them as a key factor in analyzing corporate and market behavior, and followed their every move. Like most such manuals, Toyo Keizai's *Kigyo Keiretsu Soran* (Survey of Industrial *Keiretsu*), about the size of a telephone book, covered two main types of *keiretsu*: those centered on banks—"horizontal" *keiretsu*, such as Mitsui and Mitsubishi—and those that coalesced around tiered subcontracting relationships in specific industries—"vertical" *keiretsu*, such as Toyota and Nissan. Banks, trading companies, and the presidents' clubs played key roles in organizing the *keiretsu,* making them more than just collections of profit-making enterprises. The trading companies put members of their *keiretsu* together in package deals—brokering supply against demand and bringing together corporate resources spread across the group for specific projects. In many cases, such arrangements included reciprocal purchasing—if one *keiretsu* member company bought goods from another, it could demand that the other company buy its products. The banks not only provided financing but also encouraged such mutual back scratching through their "*keiretsu* management" divisions. The presidents' clubs, with names such as the Friday Club and the White Water Society, provided information channels at a senior corporate level among key members of each *keiretsu.*

Among the most remarkable aspects of the system was its ability to tie up large amounts of the stock of member companies in rock-solid holdings that buffered the entire group during times of financial shock. In one case study, Asahi Glass, a Mitsubishi *keiretsu* company, held on to virtually all of its *keiretsu* shares during the high-yen crisis after 1985, while dumping shares of Matsushita and Hitachi companies, which were not related to Mitsubishi. Aaron Martin Cohen, a senior analyst with Daiwa Securities, said his study showed that Asahi Glass kept its *keiretsu* shares even when economics suggested it should give them up. "Their portfolio was one, Mitsubishi; two, their suppliers; three, their customers, and very little else," he said.

In a 1990 interview, Robert Zielinski, a financial analyst with Jardine Fleming Securities in Tokyo, called the *keiretsu* "the single most important characteristic of the Tokyo Stock Exchange." Out of 1,612 companies listed on the Tokyo Exchange, he identified 1,100 that belonged to *keiretsu*—a fact that he said influenced the cheap cost of money, the generally low dividends paid by Japanese corporations, and the paradox of an often wildly fluctuating stock market and robust companies. Japanese banks were able to restrain profit and offer cheap credit, according to Zielenski, because their major customers were also their chief shareholders. Corporate dividends were low for the same reasons—the owners were not anxious to dilute their own profit by paying out dividends. So many of the shares were owned by *keiretsu* companies—which rarely released them to the marketplace—that the public float in the stock market was kept small. These "independent" shares were subject to volatile price changes. All the pain in *keiretsu*, said Zielinski, was reserved for outsiders. "There is no reason to buy those shares. You have to treat the entire entity as a single company, and it's like you're buying someone's house. You can buy a 10 percent stake, but that doesn't mean you'll be able to move in tomorrow."

Like Western corporations, the *keiretsu* competed with one another. But within each conglomerate, which might encompass hundreds of publicly listed companies, an elite group of core companies established broad channels for collaboration and control. "A *keiretsu* is a cartel, and a cartel is a cartel is a cartel," T. Boone Pickens declared in 1989, after being heckled out the door at the annual meeting of Koito Manufacturing, a company in which he was the largest shareholder with 26 percent. However, Pickens's influence was negligible compared with Toyota, which held just 19 percent of Koito's stock but was the leader of the *keiretsu* group to which Koito belonged.[36]

In the early 1990s, the clash between Japanese *keiretsu* and Western-style corporations brought the economic rivalry between Japan and the United States to a new level. For four decades, an economically expansive United States had set the standards for multinational business, spawning a corporate culture in which profits were king and shareholders held unrivaled power. Japanese business, although forcibly restructured along U.S. lines after Japan's defeat in the Second World War, had been able to evolve a radically different set of standards in which profits and shareholders' interests were subordinated to long-range national and corporate goals. During a period of economic expansion, the *keiretsu* supplied bottomless pockets for new ventures. In times of crisis, they helped to dilute the pain and establish an order of priority for rescue operations. The only practical difference between the *zaibatsu* and the *keiretsu* was in size. The scope of the *keiretsu* was much larger.

Until the early 1990s, Japan's economic success was attributed mainly to Japanese management techniques, such as the "just-in-time" inventory control developed by Toyota, or, as some analysts believe, to Japanese industrial policy. But the outflow of Japanese foreign direct investment (FDI) between 1985 and 1989—$182.5 billion according to Japanese government statistics —brought new owners and new rules to companies around the world. Along with the heightened Japanese presence came recognition that its management practices were indivisible from the large-scale groupings to which most Japanese companies belonged. "It has become more and more evident that *keiretsu* is what makes Japan different" said Jardine Fleming's Zielinski. He described *keiretsu* as incompatible with Western-style capitalism. *Keiretsu* "takes the capitalists out of capitalism," he said. "The basic problem with *keiretsu* is this: It was designed to take ownership away from outside shareholders. It's the means by which Japanese companies stole ownership from the Japanese people. Japanese companies are answerable to no one."

The administration of George Bush Senior, responding in part to the outbursts of Pickens, took its first shot at *keiretsu* in the Structural Impediments

Initiative (SII), a year-long philosophical jousting match that ended in June 1990. The effort was a dismal failure. The United States attacked *keiretsu* as a barrier to foreign investment in Japan, but negotiators shied away from demanding specific changes, partly because of the vastness of the subject. U.S. officials said that Japanese disclosure requirements were inadequate, but the discussion bogged down as it became evident that virtually every corner of the *keiretsu* system operated on the basis of habitual relationships, rather than contractual ones. Most Japanese viewed the push for better disclosure as an attack on the foundations of the system. "There were some people in the U.S. administration who were so ignorant of Japan as to believe that *keiretsu* could somehow be monitored for more transparency" said one observer who was close to the negotiations. "But Japanese government officials were ultimately successful in persuading the United States to lower its expectations."

The SII negotiations backfired so badly that many Japanese read the results as an endorsement of the *keiretsu* system. Just a month after the SII agreement was signed, the EPA praised the *keiretsu* in its 1990 economic white paper. "The aforementioned intra- and inter-company systems often seen in Japan are relatively superior in the fact that they have a tendency to raise technological development capability, improve production efficiency, and maximize long-term business profits in the recent economic environment," the agency reported. "Such systems are not necessarily incompatible with a free market economy." "The EPA paper doesn't say the American way of doing things is bad," said Nukuzawa Kazuo, managing director of Keidanren, the Japanese Federation of Economic Organizations. "What they say is that this is our way of doing things."

The Pickens story had all the elements of old-fashioned vaudeville—a hero, a villain, and a damsel tied to the tracks.[37] The spectacle crystallized American anxieties of the 1980s, presaged the first cracks in the *keiretsu* system, and demonstrated its formidable resilience, in a drama with an unhappy ending for the American protagonist. Playing the part of American-style capitalist hero was T. Boone Pickens, Texas oilman, corporate raider, and guru. The villain was Toyota, tyrannical overlord of Koito Manufacturing, which supplied lighting fixtures to its giant master. Koito had the role of damsel. Pickens's declared aim was nothing less than to force Toyota to break with ironclad practice and accede to the demands of a single shareholder—himself. Toyota said, "No way." Japanese saw Toyota as the aggrieved party, a benevolent manager trying to protect a member of its large family of subcontractors from outside aggression. Few observers who looked closely could approve of Pickens's tactics. He allied himself with a notorious Japanese speculator in order to acquire the stock, which he later summarily dumped, and conducted his bid for a director's seat with a full-fledged media assault.

Even so, the fight came to symbolize the extraordinary ease with which Japanese business blocked attempts by outsiders to change it, and showed how effectively the *keiretsu* could ward off attempts at manipulation from outside. Pickens first broke into the Japanese consciousness in early 1989 when he announced that he had bought one-fifth of Koito's stock and made the unheard of declaration that he was interested in a seat on Koito's board. Koito ignored him. When Pickens stepped up the pressure by buying even more stock, he found himself heckled at Koito's annual meeting by hired thugs called *sokaiya*. Pickens's next move was to run a full-page advertisement telling Americans, "It's Time to Fight Back" against Japan. "Japan's Cartels Are Taking Us to the Cleaners and Laughing All the Way to the Bank" and "Now, They're Even Doing It under the Protection of Our Aircraft in the Middle East."

Pickens had a strong case, in non-Japanese terms. He was the largest single shareholder in Koito, with 26.4 percent, against Toyota's 19 percent. Individual shareholders held just 2.5 percent of Koito shares. The rest of the shares—52.1 percent—were under the control of so-called stable shareholders, including Nissan, Matsushita Electric, Nippon Life Insurance, Dai-Ichi Life Insurance, and Mitsubishi Bank. Toyota's closest connections outside its own *keiretsu* were with the two *keiretsu* anchored on Mitsui Bank and Tokai Bank. Nonetheless, Toyota was able to count on its fellow Koito shareholders to keep Pickens out. The Pickens-versus-Toyota saga played interminably in Washington. "I'm not at all sympathetic to Boone Pickens," said Charles Stevens, a lawyer who had been based in Tokyo, on and off, for two decades. "But I think that if any large business had tried to take over Koito—let's say a highly respected company like Bosch—it would have run into the same kind of resistance."

Foreign companies had difficulty with the sheer intensity of the *keiretsu* system, Professor Imai said. "Foreign companies lose their incentive to join the fray." The demands on subordinate members of a *keiretsu* could be even more ferocious. The lesser members were expected to take losses—sometimes years of them—in order to sustain the profitability of the core companies. Douglas Kennedy, a Tokyo-based investment banker who made a study of automobile subcontractors, compared the relationship between a core *keiretsu* company and its suppliers with that between a remora and a shark. "As long as it's attached to the shark, the remora doesn't get eaten. Meanwhile, it can scoop up the little shreds of nourishment that fall out of the shark's mouth."

While the *keiretsu* established rigid internal rules, externally they were remarkably adaptable. The original three large groups that survived the destruction of the pre–Second World War *zaibatsu*—Mitsui, Mitsubishi, and Sumitomo—came back together partly because the larger groupings proved to be efficient at raising capital at a time when banks had little money to lend. The *keiretsu* were each originally formed around a core bank. The *keiretsu* banks were able to provide preferential terms to group members, because as shareholders they participated in their profits. In the 1980s, as equity markets spiraled in the asset bubble, bank-centered *keiretsu* became less prominent, while *keiretsu* occupying vertical slices of industries multiplied. According to the handbook *Kigyo Keiretsu Soran*, however, even such vertical groupings often formed around powerful individual companies within an existing "horizontal" or banking *keiretsu*. Instead of hiving off, the vertical *keiretsu* retained their relationship within the original grouping, like a centipede growing new feet. "While retaining their membership in horizontal business groups, some influential individuals will have to endeavor to create business groups of their own along vertical lines. The future trend will be the new importance of vertical unity and the role of vertical corporate groups," the handbook observed in its 1995 edition.[38]

One of the anomalies of the *keiretsu* system in Japan was that Japan's antimonopoly law was modeled closely on U.S. statutes, generally acknowledged to be the world's most Draconian when it comes to manifestations of cartel-like behavior. Well before the end of the U.S. Occupation, however, the Japanese had managed to take the teeth out of their law. In the four decades after it was set up in 1949, the Japan Fair Trade Commission (JFTC) filed criminal suit on antitrust grounds just five times. Cumulative fines exacted by the JFTC in 1990 amounted to less than Yen 23 million, or $180,000.

Nothing was more likely to undermine confidence in the Japanese government's earnestness about reforming *keiretsu* than a visit to the agency that was in charge of antimonopoly actions. Stuck in a corner of the Science and Technology Agency, the JFTC reeked of neglect. Officers sat at tables languidly flipping through documents. When one of them needed to consult corporate data banks, the officers were forced to apply to the EPA, which had quarters across the street. The JFTC's main sources of intelligence were the daily newspapers and the wholesale price index, according to Hosoda Koichi, in the First Detection Department. Most of the JFTC's work consisted of responding to complaints from shop owners that another store owner had slashed prices, violated the rules against dumping, or charged below the manufacturer's cost.

After 1990, the JFTC struggled to become more aggressive. The Japanese government allowed it a budget for another 25 officers, increasing its total head count to 154. The JFTC made threatening noises. In 1990, it announced that it would review the legitimacy of 260 cartels that up until then were officially sanctioned. A government-organized committee made recommendations on a code of conduct for companies that would require them to account for themselves if they rejected a reasonable foreign bid. It also threatened to step up its regular reviews of the structure and internal trade relationships within *keiretsu*. Previously, such reviews were based on general estimates provided by each *keiretsu*. The JFTC continued to gradually build up its staff and sporadically went after liquor-price discounting and other recession phenomena. Complaints that went to the JFTC had a way of disappearing into the bureaucracy, however. Foreign companies preferred taking their problems to MITI, which at least had industry specialists, and the U.S. government continued to raise questions about JFTC's independence and authority. In the 1990s, improvements in the Japanese antitrust regime were largely cosmetic.

The flip side of *keiretsu* stability was stock market volatility. The market was thoroughly rigged. In the late 1980s, stock speculation was a type of boutique specialty, highly prized by politicians, gangsters, and others who turned to the market for a sure killing. Individual investors never had a chance. They kept most of their assets—$12 trillion in 2000—in the postal savings system, and stocks accounted for only 6 percent of the average Japanese family's household income.[39]

In an antiquated office building next to the Tokyo Stock Exchange, Watanabe Shigeo mused on a favorite subject, the Japanese stock market. The Japanese entity was different from other stock markets, he maintained. Watanabe was a veteran stock analyst with one of the oldest brokerages in Tokyo, Yamani Securities. He compared the Japanese stock market to Noh, Japan's stately medieval drama.[40] "In Noh, even when a player remains silent, he is accumulating energy to move—just as in the stock market, when there is no movement, some fluctuation is about to begin." The stock market was "a mythical world, a wonderful world."

When the stock market crashed, however, on the first trading day of 1990, ending the bubble economy, the debacle revealed a nasty secret at the heart of the Japanese market. Insider trading, greenmail, and real-estate speculation had accounted for all too much of the wonder and the mystery. Playing a central role were shadowy, often gangster-related groups called *shite shudan*, whose main function was to flush stock profits out of a market that was structurally biased against individual shareholders in favor of stable, corporate investors.

While Japan's Big Four mainstream brokers—Nomura Securities, Daiwa, Yamaichi, and Nikko—as well as the top banks focused largely on corporate investors, many of them kept backdoor ties with the speculator groups for the sake of the unusual profits they made. Far from looking down on stock speculators, Japanese investors flocked to them during Japan's seven-year bull market in the 1980s. Even the term for stock speculators in Japanese, *shite shudan*, echoed their popularity. The word refers to the leading actors on the Noh stage.

Most outsiders found Noh and Japanese stocks equally incomprehensible. Japanese stocks came at such towering multiples to their earnings per share that they made all other equities' seem cheap. The movement of share prices seemed to defy logic as well. Whole groups of stocks might begin to climb after long inaction without giving any warning. The reason for such arbitrary phenomena was, in part, that speculators were at work pushing stocks to stratospheric levels in order to make a quick profit. Because they had free run of the Japanese market, they often met with spectacular success. The *shite shudan* helped to keep smaller companies terrorized, often sending them in desperation into protective relationships with *keiretsu* companies that maintained huge networks of cross-shareholdings to fend off takeovers. Once firmly planted in a *keiretsu*, too few of their shares would be available to make a raid worthwhile.

The *shite shudan*'s usual gambit was greenmail. They cornered the shares of a company, driving up the price, and then demanded that the company pay the higher price to get its shares back. They often increased the pressure by calling on the services of *yakuza*. Although the sinister side of the *shite shudan* rarely came to light, foreigners were not immune. Charles Stevens, the Tokyo-based lawyer, kept a baseball bat in his office as added insurance against a speculator group he prosecuted on behalf of a non-Japanese client.

The money for the speculators' ventures came from a variety of sources, including investors close to them, members of cults forming around a lead speculator, subscribers to phony "investment magazines," and respectable brokers. The latter typically funneled their funds through third parties, usually smaller brokerages. But mostly, over the course of the 1980s, the money came from real estate, both from profits on property sales, and huge loans based on the expectation that Japanese real-estate assets would continue to multiply in value at the exponential rates of the late 1980s. Real estate was behind most of the 350 speculator groups active at the peak of the market in 1989. The speculator groups included landlords, owners of resort hotels in Hawaii and Australia, bus service operators, golf course owners, and guitar makers. The common link was land, and bankers were ready to shovel money in their direction as long as real estate was the collateral.

Stable corporate shareholders, many of them grouped in *keiretsu*, tied up 70 percent of Japanese stocks. The *shite shudan* dominated the rest. In the 1980s, from 10 to 20 percent of the annual trading volume of the Tokyo market was generated by the *shite shudan*, estimated Nakamori Takakazu, a specialist with Teikoku Data Bank in Tokyo, at about $700 billion annually. In 1989, speculative trading probably amounted to more than $1 trillion. According to Nakamori, ordinary investors helped to multiply the impact of the *shite shudan* by racing to join in once they spotted a speculative rise. Stocks that attracted a speculator's attention were put on analysts' lists and watched closely for any sign of renewed movement. The reason for the success of the speculative stocks with ordinary investors was simple. They were one of the few sources of substantial gains in an otherwise slow-moving market. "The *shite* groups are a necessary evil," Nakamori said. "They are what ordinary investors dream about. . . . Even if the money handled by the *shite* groups has not been that large, investors have been excited by the knowledge that they exist." "They provide the action," explained Yamani's Watanabe, more simply.

The speculator groups also engaged in tactics that were illegal even in Japan, such as insider trading, although the rules were barely enforced. In 1990, Japan's law restricting insider trading was only a year old, and its first year on the books drew only one conviction. Stock manipulation was also illegal. Penalties, however, were minimal. The maximum fine was about $27,000 or three years in jail. Only a handful of investors were ever charged.

The cozy world of the speculators, according to economist Atsuyuki Suzuta, was given another boost, paradoxically, by plans to liberalize Japanese financial markets. Japanese banks began throwing their best people into retail positions in the domestic market. Smart executives saw the real-estate price spiral as an opportunity to advance their own careers as well as to expand their loan portfolios. Many ended up working with speculators. None of this would have come to light or even mattered in the eyes of most Japanese if the bubble had somehow kept going. As long as real-estate and stock prices continued to rise, speculative stocks might double in value in a week, or run to five times their original value in a few months. The Ministry of Finance and Bank of Japan, the chief regulatory authorities, looked the other way.

But when share prices crumbled, Japanese financial authorities began to worry that the carnage might undercut the pillars of the Japanese financial system, especially if it washed into the real-estate market. As part of an effort to prevent a greater collapse, MOF set out to cut the ties between the speculator groups and the mainstream. "This is not a moralistic crackdown, the way the Americans have moved against insider trading," said Charles Lambert, a salesman with Jardine Fleming Securities in Tokyo. "They want to set an example, to show that flagrant violations will not be allowed, and that others will get the message from that."

The chosen scapegoat was a flashy real-estate broker named Kotani

Mitsuhiro, whose Koshin Group led some of the most ambitious speculative ventures of the 1980s. The Japanese press covered Kotani's trial in 1990 with huge headlines and lurid details about him and his associates. There was a lurking sympathy with Kotani, however. Many Japanese viewed him as a dupe of greedy banks and big stockbrokers, who were his principal sources of funds. They, too, were punished, though not ruined. In October, Sumitomo Bank chairman Isoda Ichiro resigned to accept responsibility for the bank's loans to Kotani, sending shudders through the banking world. Less noisily, MOF reprimanded four branch offices of major securities firms for their dealings with Kotani, including Daiwa Securities, National Securities, Ace Securities, and Citicorp Scrimgeour Vickers International.

Kotani was the "emperor" of the stock speculators, a "Yen 200 billion man" who built a money machine out of the crumbs swept aside by conventional brokers. He could turn obscure companies into the darlings of the Tokyo Stock Exchange just by dropping word that he had invested in them. A vast network of friends and clients made fortunes acting on his advice.[41] He thrived on the stock and real-estate bubble that turned Japan into the world's largest equities market in the late 1980s, then became the preeminent symbol of the bubble's collapse. When he was charged with stock fraud and placed under arrest in July 1990, the first question in the minds of Japanese observers was, "Who's next?" The answer was not long in coming. In October, the Tokyo Public Prosecutors Office moved against present and former executives of Sumitomo Bank, then the world's second-largest bank, and Mitsui Trust & Banking. All of the arrests were traced to connections between the bankers and Kotani or his close associates. The two banks reportedly lent Kotani hundreds of millions of dollars to bolster his stock-rigging schemes.

The Kotani case cast a chill on stock and real-estate speculation, which had been the driving forces behind the Japanese market. After the market crash, there were few investors eager to take part in schemes such as the ones he had invented. Warned by MOF, banks and brokers cut their ties to speculators. "The future of the speculator groups is dark. They can't expect to recover," said Yamani's Watanabe. Japanese authorities pitched the Kotani case as a step along the way toward the internationalization of Japanese financial markets. "Japan used to be known as a heaven for insider trading," said Kamikawa Shinryo, an official in the Finance Ministry's market-investigation unit, established in 1990. "But now, both the ministry and the stock exchange are making efforts to prevent irregularities."

Among other reforms, starting in April 1991, MOF imposed a requirement for full disclosure of any stock holdings above 5 percent in a company. About the same time, Japan began to impose a small but uniform capital gains tax designed to reduce the attraction of stock speculation. Even with the improvements, however, Japan remained a country where greenmail was legal, and market surveillance was almost entirely in the hands of the industry. In the early 1990s, MOF's entire stock market monitoring staff consisted of 17 people, compared with 2,000 in the U.S. Securities and Exchange Commission. This was a big improvement: As of May 1990, the ministry's surveillance staff had numbered just seven people.

In few previous instances were the inner workings of the Japanese stock market so clearly exposed as in the Kotani case: It underscored the connections between stock speculators, big business, and politicians in Japan. Stock manipulation offered big gains to dedicated investors, provided that they could raise enough capital and manage to keep investigators off their backs. As a result, successful speculators in Japan were measured partly by the stature of their allies. When a powerful speculative group went after an individual stock, droves of smaller investors followed in its wake hoping to catch windfall profits. "It's one of the reasons the Tokyo securities market is so unclear," said Nishimura Nobukatsu, branch manager of Wood Gundy Japan, a Canadian brokerage. "In Canada, people trade based on fundamentals. But in Japan, most investors don't even look at financial statements. Instead they look for rumors."

Like Recruit's Ezoe, Kotani was a maverick who upset people by moving up the ranks too fast. In December 1988, he broke an unstated but nonetheless potent taboo against hostile takeovers in Japan when he acquired a majority share in Kokusai Kogyo, an aerial survey company. While other stock speculators in Japan tried to keep out of the limelight, Kotani seemed to dare regulators to take notice of his activities. His problems began after he dipped into Kokusai Kogyo's till to finance further market ventures. When the stock market crashed in Spring 1990, Kotani suddenly found himself in a bind, owing $170 million. He quickly came up with a plan to corner shares of Fujita Tourist Enterprises, Japan's largest travel agency, and netted $270 million in profit by driving up the share price, then selling the shares to a third company with which he maintained friendly connections. Kotani was able to repay Kokusai Kogyo on time, but the flurry of activity made a target too big for the investigators to miss. At the height of his glory, Japan's corporate and political elite flocked to Kotani for his legendary investment advice. His style was a mixture of glitz and the gutter. At the private golf club where he brought his powerful clients, he would take to the fairways elegantly outfitted in a cutaway and pinstripes.

After July 1990, when he was arrested, the activities of the *shite shudan* went into a deep freeze. Only a dozen or so speculative groups remained active, including one group that was little more than a *yakuza* front organization. "Those were dream times in the 1980s, with 2.5 percent interest rates, declining oil prices, and a rising market," said Jardine Fleming's Lambert, who predicted that the *shite shudan* would gradually fade from the Japanese scene. "Without those unusually ideal conditions, the speculators can't expect to see the same kind of growth in the future." But most Japanese observers had faith in the tenacity of the *shite shudan*. "They're learning a lesson now, but if there was no more stock manipulation, there probably would be no more trading," Yamani Securities' Watanabe said.

The Last Samurai

I am on the back of a motorcycle, it is 2:00 in the morning, and a cold wind whips my face. The driver, Takahashi Shuji, is crazy. He keeps shouting over his shoulder, "This is not my normal personality," as he takes his Honda over road dividers, along sidewalks, through the wreckage of the ruined city of Kobe. Refugees push shopping carts full of household goods, moving slowly in the direction of Osaka. For twelve miles in both directions, traffic is stalled in a dead gridlock. Only pedestrians and smaller vehicles, such as Takahashi's bike, can get through. We pass a stone-sculpture shop. A life-sized plaster statue of a woman lies on its back, arms outstretched as though calling for help. Stone lions are tumbled about like kittens at play.

Heisei Seven, 1995, began with the most devastating earthquake since the Great Kanto earthquake of 1923. The city I am leaving behind in the dark will eventually count 6,425 among the dead from the temblor. Another 121 people died of exposure in shelters for the homeless. The deaths were tragic. They were not, however, the worst of the earthquake's legacies. It brought to a crux the feelings among ordinary Japanese that the nation had taken a serious wrong turn. "I feel strongly that since the earthquake, things are going in the wrong direction," Ei Rokusuke, a songwriter, told a Japanese concert audience in early 1997.[42]

These feelings had been growing for years, but Kobe's nightmare symbolized to many Japanese everything that was wrong with their society in the 1990s. Japanese pride had prevented the government from immediately accepting foreign offers of help. Japanese politicians, starting with the prime minister, passed the buck to bureaucrats, who then fought with each other. People followed rules that made no sense in a time of emergency. Riot police ringed the sites where bodies were being removed to prevent television cameras from capturing the scene but ignored calls for help if they were outside their sectors. Local Japanese officials even discouraged offers of help from other parts of Japan, fearing invasion of their jurisdictional turf. Said Nakauchi Isao, chairman of the Daiei retail empire based in Kobe, "In emergencies like this quake, someone must exert leadership, but today's Japan is a country where no one dares to take responsibility."

The greatest fury of all was reserved for the bureaucracy. It had mismanaged nearly every aspect of the tragedy. Glen Fukushima, president of the American Chamber of Commerce in Japan, wrote that the earthquake showed the practice of *tatewari gyosei*, or "vertical" administration—the caste system—at its worst.[43] Examples of *tatewari gyosei* included the adamant refusal of foreign help by authorities, excessive respect for bureaucratic protocol in situations that clearly demanded risk taking, and local jurisdictional conflicts, particularly between local police and the national Self-Defense Forces, whose training in earthquake disaster prevention was largely wasted. A new command structure for disaster relief that included the prime minister was among the positive results of the crisis, but its effectiveness was questionable. There were replays of the tragic confusion of Kobe in the Sarin poisoning attack on the Tokyo subway system a few months later, the Tokaimura nuclear incident in 1999, and the collapse of Prime Minister Obuchi Keizo in 2000. Prime Minister Obuchi's sudden death in May 2000 revealed that nobody had any idea what to do in the event of the sudden death of the nominal head of government.

Of all the institutions of postwar Japan, none was more august than the bureaucracy. It cultivated a mystique of service, self-sacrifice, and reserve. The ideal bureaucrat was faceless, like Magritte's image of the invisible gentleman in his bowler and suit. Even the architecture of the Japanese bureaucracy was conspicuously inconspicuous. In Tokyo's government district, Kasumigaseki, the nondescript buildings of the "misty gate" melted into each other. Entrances even to major agencies were poorly marked. A *koban,* or police booth, at the border between Kasumigaseki and Toranomon, the neighboring business district, posted a large map with lights, but somehow it did not help. The subway exits list agencies at each stairwell in Japanese and English, but even so, I would emerge unable to get my bearings, fooled by the absence of visual clues.

The Japanese Ministry of Finance, the most powerful of Japan's economic bureaucracies, occupies an ancient, sooty building ringed by unkempt garden plots. Offices inside are dusty, with aging light fixtures and peeling paint. The only sign of the agency's importance are the black limousines outside, regularly rolling past the security checkpoint into an inner courtyard. Until the mid-1990s, security was nominal, and virtually anyone could enter and roam the dark and murky halls. Its neighbor, the Ministry of Foreign Affairs (MOFA), had a busy front reception desk but none of the public sculpture, symbolic fountains, or gilded emblems of state, common to its counterparts in other nations. MITI, a newer, high-rise building across the street from them, lacked even the checkpoint. Visitors breezed in and out with a brief wave of an identification tag or passport.

The world inside the bureaucracy was as cozy and comfortable as an old shoe. At night, young officials slumped at their steel desks in felt slippers, jackets off, beer and cigarettes at hand. Futons were always available if they needed to pull an all-nighter, as they frequently did. The section chiefs and their deputies sat at the back of the room, facing out across the gray steel desks of their subordinates. Only the most senior officials had their own offices, and these, too, seemed curiously anonymous. Décor was limited to official gifts and calendars. Stacks of memos and reports covered desks and file cabinets. Day faded into night, summer into winter. The fluorescent lights were always on, the room temperature set to a constant seventy degrees. Periodically, the noise of right-wing sound trucks, ideologues screaming slogans or chanting patriotic songs, drowned out conversation. The bureaucrats cultivated a mildly mournful look, like country parsons in a nineteenth-century novel. They were among the most powerful people on earth, these minions of the world's second largest economy, and they guarded their anonymity as fiercely as though it were a belt of distinction, which in their strange world, it was.

In the early part of the century, Omori Shoichi, an official at the former Ministry of Internal Affairs, the Naimusho, wrote a letter to his son who was entering the bureaucracy. The agency published the letter in 1934 in order to educate the public on the high moral aims of its employees. Omori described the role of the bureaucrat as a form of priesthood, ubiquitous yet detached from the common life. Implicit in the "code" was an assumption of superiority; the prejudice reflected in the saying *kanson minpu*, "revere the bureaucrats, despise the people." Yet, the bureaucrat was expected to be able to tap into the soul of the people as well, "not shun sweat or labor," and assiduously apply himself to the mundane details of his job, which included the entire machinery of the Japanese economy. Omori told his son:

> Bureaucrats must be pure and above any form of criticism. Bureaucrats must conduct their affairs without the entanglement of private sentiments and retain their impartiality. Bureaucrats must nourish common sense and respect the middle of the road. Bureaucrats must listen to others and not assert themselves exceedingly. Bureaucrats must take utmost care and not shun sweat or labor. Bureaucrats must be discreet in words and conduct.
>
> Bureaucrats must keep their promises. Bureaucrats must live a humble life. Bureaucrats must not be ashamed of asking questions and must not mind teaching others. Bureaucrats must not fawn upon senior bureaucrats and must be faithful to their colleagues. Bureaucrats must not be addicted

to hobbies. Bureaucrats must be prepared to devote their physical persons to the state.

Bureaucrats must not speak about their official duties. Bureaucrats must content themselves with their official duties and not hope for matters outside their duties. Bureaucrats must revere the emperor and Buddha and respect the elderly in the spirit of filial piety. Bureaucrats must know the history of the jurisdiction with which they are concerned, whether it is an institution or a region. Bureaucrats must be calm in handling matters. Bureaucrats must study their official duties and acquire higher learning. Bureaucrats must refrain from partisan strife. [44]

The long litany was intentionally reminiscent of *bushido*, the "way" of the samurai. Bureaucrats were the direct heirs of the warrior class of premodern Japanese society. Like the samurai, Japanese bureaucrats ranked at the top. In the premodern era, for most of the three centuries of Tokugawa rule, actual samurai spent very little time practicing martial arts. Most of their energy was focused on administrative tasks. When the Tokugawa *bakufu* collapsed in 1868, former samurai made up the ranks of a bureaucracy modeled along European lines.

In some ways, Japanese bureaucrats in the 1990s were remarkably close not only in philosophy but even in their operating style to the Tokugawa samurai. Under the Tokugawa system, the shogun forced the *daimyo* and their key retainers to rotate their domains frequently. The retainers that accompanied the *daimyo* to each new domain were a small, exclusive group, selected on merit. According to Inoguchi Takashi, the political scientist, they were the most highly educated group of officials in the world in the seventeenth and eighteenth centuries. Their allegiance was to the family code of the *daimyo* rather than to the *daimyo* themselves, and if a lord violated the canon, they would quietly remove him from public life.[45] The bureaucrats of the "iron triangle" system similarly disdained the politicians and at times treated them with outright disrespect. In 1995, when Prime Minister Murayama instructed the bureaucracy to turn in a list of superfluous government agencies as part of a three-year deregulation campaign, the bureaucrats calmly responded with a blank sheet of paper. They saw themselves—not the people's elected representatives—as the final arbiters of public welfare.

In the first part of the twentieth century, as Japan's Imperial Army and Navy fanned through Asia, the bureaucracy followed, carrying out the economic experiments that became the basis for post-war industrial policy. During the war, the entire Japanese and colonial economy was effectively nationalized, starting with foreign exchange control measures enacted in January 1937 and culminating with the New Economic System of 1940–41, which established control associations called *toseikai* in each industry. These entities became the levers by which the bureaucracy engaged directly in management of business. In 1938, the military government decreed the Total Mobilization Act, the Kokka Sodoin Ho, as the basis for wage and price controls and the beginning of the wartime policy of "total mobilization." A government Planning Board, established in 1939, allocated resources and set production targets. It used the *toseikai* to gather information for its economic plans in an iterative process familiar to any student of planned economies.[46]

According to the economist Noguchi Yukio, the bureaucracy's powers under the total mobilization policy were preserved in the post-war period. The classic Meiji bureaucracy aimed to nurture and support the private sector, Noguchi argued. The merchant clans of Osaka had given strong support to the Meiji Restoration, and in the late Tokugawa disorder, wealthy merchants seized the opportunity to enhance their prestige by marrying into samurai families, eroding the traditional boundaries between the two Tokugawa-era classes. During World War Two, however, the bureaucracy established much stricter controls, including security controls over economic intelligence. This "1940s system" became the basis of the post-war bureaucratic system, including the practice of *gyosei shido,* or administrative guidance.[47] *Gyosei seido* grew up out of discretionary powers given to the bureaucracy by law, which became the basis for a system of private communiqués between officials and individual companies. Noguchi thought that its lack of transparency was based on the military practice of imposing secrecy conventions on instructions to battalions in the field.

Noguchi also argued that the war government intentionally undermined the influence of corporate shareholders by encouraging banking finance, particularly through long-term credit banks such as the Industrial Bank of Japan, and by undermining the expansion of capital markets. Even in the 1990s, Japanese bond and equity markets were rigged in ways that made them relatively illiquid and investor-unfriendly. Because MOF could control the supply of credit to commercial banks through the central bank, it retained substantial influence over the Japanese economy long after MITI had lost its direct management role in Japanese industry, Noguchi said. "MITI was very powerful up to 1955, as long as foreign exchange was under the direct control of the government," he explained. "If you were a steel company and wanted to buy something from abroad, you had to go to MITI. That ended, but if you look at MOF rather than MITI, you see real continuity."[48]

After a brief interregnum of New Deal–inspired reforms, the "1940s system" was restored in 1949, with the imposition of a Foreign Currency Control Law (not lifted completely until the 1960s) and the resurrection of the *toseikai* as trade associations. The trade associations, established under the

Businessmen's Group Act of 1948, became among the principal instruments of post-war industrial policy and cartel formation. Representatives of the trade associations joined a new Industrial Rationalization Screening Association, or deliberation council, under MITI, which during the war had been the Munitions Ministry. Both trade associations and deliberation councils, or *shingikai,* put business under the direct supervision of MITI.

The World Bank's 1993 report on the *East Asian Miracle* described the *shingikai as* "an institutionalized form of wealth sharing aimed primarily at winning the support and cooperation of business elites," and they were among the more widely copied aspects of the Japanese model. South Korea, Malaysia, Thailand, and Singapore each had entities more or less modeled on Japanese deliberation councils.[49] In Japan, at least, it was clear who was in charge in this collaboration. A MITI vice-minister, Sahashi Shigeru, asserted, as far as he was concerned, "deliberation councils were important primarily as a device to silence in advance any criticism of the bureaucracy."[50]

The bureaucracy thus rested at the calm apex of Japanese society, and one measure of its power was that in the increasingly turbulent political climate of the 1990s it stood apart, the last bastion of the iron triangle to crumble. Its esprit de corps was formidable; it was linked to the Japanese corporate world in ways that reinforced its ability to manage the economy; and its power and prestige were accompanied by a reputation for incorruptibility. Hired out of the nation's best universities at the age of twenty-two, a typical entering class in a government agency would number about twenty-five; these twenty-five freshmen would know their exact ranking from the agency entrance exam and stay in close contact throughout their careers at each ministry. As they moved up the bureaucratic pyramid, they would be winnowed out—not enough positions existed for each class—and beginning at the age of fifty, the National Personnel Authority would take over their careers.

After retirement, some went into politics, but after a two-year mandatory waiting period most entered the private sector under the system known as "descent from heaven," *amakudari.* Officials who left would keep in close touch with their former colleagues in the ministries through formal "old boys' clubs" (these were called *OB-kai* in Japanese). In 1991, according to research by Ulrike Schaede at the University of California, 5 percent of the boards of directors in Japan were made up of ministry "old boys." In 1992, there were 1,111 ex-bureaucrats at the 2,000 largest Japanese companies.[51]

The economist Nakatani Iwao described this "intimate" relationship between government and business as one of the mainstays of the post-war economy. Japan in its high-growth phase was essentially a socialist, not a market, economy, he believed. The ties the bureaucracy maintained with business helped it implement industrial policy, particularly the "catch-up" strategies associated with Japan's flying-geese approach to economic growth.[52] "The Japanese system was very well adapted to a developing-type economy," Nakatani said.

> When I was young, I worked for Nissan for five years. We were exporting to the United States and Canadian markets. At that time, the quality of Japanese cars was very bad, very inferior to U.S. cars, but our prices were low, because our production costs were low. This was thirty years ago, in the late 1960s, when the wage differential between the United States and Japan was about six times.
>
> Engineers from the Japanese car makers visited Detroit frequently to learn auto technology, how to make transmissions and so forth. The Americans were very generous about teaching their technology. They did not think that the Japanese would ever become competitive. Once we absorbed American technology, the cars we could produce were about 70 percent of the quality of American cars but 50 percent of the cost. That was the typical pattern of industrial development of the catch up type.
>
> Meanwhile, in the late 1950s and early 1960s MITI had begun focusing on autos as a strategic industry, and offered carmakers preferential tax treatment and credit allocation, at a time when Japan's stock of foreign exchange reserves was small and highly controlled. Preferential allocation of foreign exchange allowed the manufacturers to import parts.
>
> All sorts of industrial policies were set to have economic resources concentrated on a certain industry. After the auto industry, the government shifted its target to electronics and computers. We were able to do this because we had a leader, mainly the United States. If the bureaucracy studied closely, what is the essence of a particular industry, they could accelerate the development of that industry by setting appropriate regulations. Of course we had some failures, but autos, electronics, and computers were our successes. But this regulatory policy is effective only when there is a leader going ahead, and now, in autos and electronics, Japan itself has become the front runner, and there is no room for MITI to do effectively their old fashioned industrial policy.[53]

Even before the collapse of the bubble economy in 1990, the other two legs of Japan's iron triangle, the politicians and big business, had been in trouble, but the bureaucracy seemed relatively immune. Officials manifestly made no money for themselves outside their modest government salaries and were not caught on public golf courses with their gangster friends. There were routine dinner and drinking invitations from supplicants of various sorts, but although the amounts spent were scandalously large there was still something acceptably impersonal about the practice.

When the bureaucrats did begin to lose their mantle of perfection and invulnerability, it was far more shocking than the exposed peccadilloes of politicians and financial executives. Nakatani argued that when the bureaucracy lacked a model to work from, it went haywire. At a time when Japan desperately needed new initiative and creativity, the bureaucrats did not have the resources to supply either.

9
Japan Adrift

Guardian

A zone of constantly moving air, brilliant blue skies, and misty squalls, rainbows stacked like incoming waves blurs the spiny outline of interior ranges while the overbuilt plains and foothills bask in sunshine. Like a dream of a perfect summer's day, Hawaii is sweet and easy. Nobody irons their clothes. Few places could be farther from images of war, death, or the brutal language of geopolitics. Yet, for all its laziness and languor, Hawaii is the preeminent symbol of American power in Asia, the command center for 354,000 American sailors, soldiers, and civilians who keep the region's peace; one-fifth of all U.S. forces; and the only American territory in the twentieth century to suffer enemy attack. It wields terrible power, like one of Hawaii's ancient goddesses, and like them, lies dormant most of the time.

More than fifty years after Hawaii forcibly gripped the American consciousness by calling the nation to war, the symbolism remains. Here, America first encountered the fury of Imperial Japan, in fighter planes flying low against the Pali, in the battleships lining the shallow bottom of Pearl Harbor. In the present, Hawaii symbolizes as well the post-war military relationship between Japan and the United States, asymmetrical yet resilient. Among the picturesque white bungalows and plumeria trees of Camp H.M. Smith lies the command and control center for the Seventh Fleet and U.S. forces from Alaska to Madagascar. Camp Smith is the base of the Commander in Chief, Pacific Command (CINCPAC), the highest-ranking U.S. Navy admiral. In the shimmering light, it hardly seems like the terrible hammer it is, to be capable of keeping peace across a region that comprises 50 percent of the earth's surface. Perched on a crenellated hill above Honolulu, white against green, it might be the nineteenth-century summer home of a sugar baron.

Nonetheless, the bungalows cast their nuclear shadow over 100 million square miles, guarding America and its allies against potential adversaries that include the world's largest military forces, ranging from Russia and

China to India and North Korea. It takes thirty-nine hours to conduct an airlift from one side of this vast region to the other, and thirty-five days for a battle group to steam from the west coast of the United States to the Arabian Sea. Of the 354,000 soldiers, sailors, and marines under its jurisdiction, more than 100,000 are "forward deployed"—based outside the U.S. mainland in Hawaii, Japan, South Korea, Guam, Singapore, Diego Garcia in the Indian Ocean, Kwajalein, and Majuro, a huge archipelago of personnel, ships, and weaponry. Camp Smith, as pretty up close as it is from a distance, makes this vast exercise seem as neat and nice as lawn tennis, no more taxing than a walk on the beach.

Because of Camp Smith, for five long decades, Japan and its surrounding seas were among the safest, most secure places on earth, troubled only by the occasional earthquake, tidal wave, or volcanic eruption. In other parts of Asia, there were wars, skirmishes, armies of refugees, and domestic insurgencies. Japan was an immaculate testimony to the awesome benefits of American military protection. It had security without sacrifice, nuclear deterrence without the mess and fuss. Wars could sweep across the sea lanes of the South China Sea, send armies through Southeast Asia and battle fleets into the Straits of Taiwan, and Japan would remain untouched. Under terms of the 1960 Mutual Security Treaty, it had no reciprocal obligation to defend the United States, despite large, domestic "self-defense" forces held in readiness for a communist invasion. Instead, it picked up the bills for U.S. bases and soldiers in Japan, spinning enormous wealth from the safety of its cocoon. No other nation has done so little or so much in exchange for U.S. protection; Japan willingly sacrificed its autonomy in defense and foreign affairs for the opportunity to grow rich. It was worth the trade.

The payoff for the United States was the containment of Russian and Chinese communism. Japan served as a check to both powers, and even as the Cold War waned, the Japan-U.S. alliance held China back as it attempted to lure Japan into a new economic partnership. Under the Cold War military framework, Japan prospered, the U.S. Defense Department saved money on overhead, and the Japanese public was able to conduct its daily business in blithe ignorance of the enormous military superstructure that supported their endeavors.

In 1989, when the Cold War abruptly ended, Japan faced a harsh dilemma. Without an active threat from Asian communism, the United States was likely to conclude that it was no longer necessary to keep such massive forces deployed around the region. Without the protective umbrella of the United States, Japan would suddenly be alone, pitted against a potentially hostile China, nuclear-armed rogue states in the Russian Far East, and an easily predictable increase in tensions among traditional rivals in Southeast Asia. The scenario demanded that Japan begin to think more actively about crisis and response; any active movement in this direction, however, might be self-fulfilling, forcing the United States to abandon its protective role just when Japan might need it most.

This was not the only or the worst of the problems that Japan faced. A U.S. withdrawal was hypothetical; meanwhile, Japan had demographics to worry about. By the 1990s, a third generation of Japanese was reaching maturity with no direct experience of war, conditioned to the constitutional status of Japan as a pacifist nation. Japanese leaders could not persuade its people of the need to engage in security matters without encountering fierce opposition. In 1990 and 1991, Iraq's invasion of Kuwait and the Gulf War had launched a fierce public debate over the propriety of providing any support to the U.S.-led multinational forces. The Japanese public made known that it still believed in the pacifist clause in the Japanese Constitution, Article 9, which limited Japan's military to territorial defense. The first clause of Article 9 was that Japan would "renounce war as a sovereign right of the nation and the threat or use of force as a means of settling international disputes," officially designating Japan as a pacifist nation. The second clause insisted, "land, sea, and air forces, as well as other war potential, will never be maintained." Japan's support operations for the Gulf War were so politically charged that the Japanese government had to hire commercial aircraft to conduct its airlifts of refugees and medical supplies.

In 1992, a senior Japanese career official at the United Nations, Akashi Yasushi, was appointed as leader of the UN Transitional Authority in Cambodia, monitoring the Cambodian elections in June 1993; however, Japanese peacekeepers were not allowed to carry weapons and the two men that died led to a furious public outcry. Efforts to modify the Constitution moved ahead with tortured delicacy. In 1994, a government commission chaired by Higuchi Hirotaro, chairman of Asahi Breweries, proposed that Japan should revise its defense policy around the principle of collective security, allowing Japan to participate in the defense of its allies as well as in peacekeeping operations. In 2000 and 2001, new parliamentary commissions and new prime ministers were still haggling over the terms of this new regime and how to adapt Article Nine to broader standards of international security.

In the Japanese Foreign Ministry, two camps emerged, one dedicated to keeping the U.S. alliance intact, building on U.S. fears of a Sino-Japanese axis, and a second faction that was intent on gradually transforming Japan's security ties with its neighbors and re-educating its public. The difference between the two positions, however, was one of emphasis rather than fundamental principle. They shared a common strategy of preserving the U.S. alliance at least as long as it took to build a new web of relationships in which U.S. withdrawal from the region would be less disastrous.

Thus began an elaborate and convoluted odyssey, as warring factions within the bureaucracy helped to blunt each of Japan's bolder initiatives to recast its security model. All through the 1990s, Japan had faced the possibility that a major regional conflict would force its hand, precipitating a fast resolution of its internal dilemma. Instead, the debate limped along. By the end of the decade, both camps of diplomats had made both gains and losses. The internationalists succeeded in upgrading the Mutual Security Treaty and U.S. ties but antagonized China in the debate over Theater Missile Defense (TMD); the change "radicals" had succeeded in fostering a new network of security organizations and military dialogue in the region, but these were far from responding exclusively to Japanese interests. Meanwhile, the Japanese public was no closer to being convinced on the need for a larger military role either within the context of the Mutual Security Treaty or outside it. Almost as soon as Japan set out to redefine its security needs, its policy was adrift, buffeted by the crosswinds of conflicting bureaucratic interests. In the new post–Cold War environment, Japan needed strong political leaders to cut through the thicket of confusion; instead, it got Kaifu, Uno, Hosokawa, Murayama, Hashimoto, Obuchi, Mori, and Koizumi, none of whom was capable of stepping out of the traditional mold and do more than simply rubber stamp policies delivered by the bureaucrats.

For their part, the bureaucrats talked tough but did little. "The biggest risk is to lose the alliance," said Okazaki Hisahiko, a former ambassador to Saudi Arabia and Thailand, and the leader of the pro-U.S., internationalist camp within the bureaucracy. "Japan will not fight wars to save lives of the South Koreans or Taiwanese. But we may have to fight to save the alliance."[1]

As far as Okazaki was concerned, radical change would simply play into China's hands. To Okazaki, the U.S.-Japan alliance was an effective counter to the expansion of Chinese influence. "What China wants is for Japan to keep its distance from the Americans," Okazaki said. "If you read between the lines, look at every statement that China makes, in all their recent meetings the Chinese have been saying two things. Japan should make independent decisions—which is a subtle way of saying, Japan should not follow the Americans. The Chinese also say they are not opposed to Japan having an alliance with the Americans, but that they should not use it against China. China is not a threat now, but it will be in ten years if the U.S.-Japan alliance is not solid."[2]

A change hawk, Kikuchi Kiyoaki, former Japanese ambassador to the UN, Canada, and Mexico, argued that Japanese leadership would emerge gradually, as a consequence of its growing economic role in the Asia Pacific.

"The countries of Southeast Asia look to Japan as a leader, whether they profess it or not. One morning we will wake up to a political grouping with Japan as head. We would like to see it emerge gradually and without doing a lot. This will come about gradually, through the formation of new institutions and through economic cooperation. By and by, Japan will take its place as a huge import market replacing the United States. It will be a natural evolution, not a result of conscious planning."[3] Yet, Kikuchi could not foresee the financial turmoil of the late 1990s, or supply a more persuasive logic than economics to keep Japan's Asian flock together.

The change radicals suffered more than the internationalists in the course of the decade, but neither side was a clear victor. In the early 1990s, Satoh Yukio, the former consul general in Hong Kong, subsequently ambassador to the Netherlands, staked out the "change" position in a controversial article published in a Foreign Ministry gazette. Satoh advocated moving away from the "bipolar" diplomacy of the Cold War toward a "multiplex" security framework for Asia in which existing subregional organizations would begin to replace the "hub-and-spoke" doctrine advocated by the United States, as the ultimate arbiter of disputes.[4] The article raised hackles because it mounted a clear challenge to the United States, but through most of the 1990s Satoh's ideas seemed to lie fallow, and Satoh himself was tossed out of Asia, where he could make trouble, to an ambassadorship in The Hague.

Satoh's eclipse was matched by the vindication of the pro-U.S. internationalists, who made the most of relatively minor confrontations between the United States and North Korea and China. These convinced Washington to change its plans of the early 1990s to draw down forces in the region and, instead, shore up its relationship with Japan.

By the late 1990s, however, the balance shifted again, as regional conflicts came closer to home, alarming the public and strengthening the hand of the group seeking a new security paradigm, represented by Kikuchi, Satoh Yukio, and others. To some extent, this phase represented a coming together of the two strands in Japanese security policy, since it satisfied both the requirements of the internationalists for re-armament and the change radicals for greater independence from the United States. In August 1998, North Korea stunned the Japanese by launching a *Taepodong* ballistic missile— Pyongyang claimed it was merely a "rocket"—over Japanese territory. By March 1999, when the Maritime Self-Defense Force chased two North Korean speedboats out of Japanese waters, Tokyo was beginning to craft a new euphemism for re-armament under the rubric of "crisis management."

The Japanese Defense Agency began work on a $1.7 billion surveillance satellite, and pledged $10 million for joint research with the United States on Theater Missile Defense, despite protests from China. In July 1999, Japanese officials announced plans to seek $660 million in funding from the Diet for four midair refueling planes, which would extend the range of Japanese fighter planes.[5] In August, the Japanese Diet quietly resurrected use of the rising sun flag and Kimigayo, a hymn to the emperor, as official symbols of the nation. By the fall of 2000, the Japanese Maritime Safety Agency, renamed the Coast Guard, was able to seek a budget for two unarmed long-range jets to patrol the Malacca Straits, without visible reaction from Southeast Asian or the Japanese public.[6]

The most significant success of the change radicals, however, was the creation of a new regional security apparatus, the ASEAN Regional Forum, or ARF as it was called from its acronym, in which the activist Satoh played an energetic role. To the credit of the radicals, this was the first successful attempt to draw the major powers of the Asia Pacific into a security dialogue since the ill-fated Southeast Asia Treaty Organization (SEATO) of the 1960s, and far broader in its membership and objectives. Even so, in its ambiguous mission and wooden response to various crises, it mimicked all too faithfully the shortcomings of Tokyo as its mentor.

ARF began with creative shuttle diplomacy on the part of Satoh, backed by more senior diplomats. In June 1991, with the blessings of Policy Planning Division chief Yanai Shunji (a former Japanese prisoner of war who became ambassador to the United States in the late 1990s), Satoh had visited Jakarta in advance of the annual "roundtable" meeting of the leading security think tanks of Indonesia, Malaysia, Singapore, and Thailand, held that year in Kuala Lumpur. He told the Indonesians that Japan was prepared to support a new departure on the part of ASEAN to engage in security affairs.[7] When it was established in 1967, during the height of the Vietnam War, ASEAN had studiously avoided security issues, but Satoh argued that times had changed and ASEAN needed to build a political dialogue on "matters of mutual concern." In the wake of its annual ministerial meetings, ASEAN already conducted a "post-ministerial conference," dubbed the PMC, to brief its major trading partners on ASEAN policy. Why not use the PMC meetings to begin a regional dialogue on security? The Indonesians agreed, and Satoh brought word back to Tokyo that a deal was in the making.

Its implications were profound. Satoh had written, "The question of how far the United States will withdraw from the region and how far Japan will expand her political, and possibly, military role in the region are now the two major points of concern to many Asian countries. . . . For the United States and Japan to engage themselves in a process of dialogue with these countries is critically important for the sake of mutual reassurance." Up until the 1990s, Japan would not have dared to initiate such a process for fear of angering the United States. Now the inclusion of the United States was more for cosmetic value than substance; the initiative had come from Japan, not Washington. Japanese officials now told reporters that Japan felt a need to "fill the void" created by the closure of U.S. bases in the Philippines.[8]

Taking his cue from Jakarta, Satoh urged Japanese foreign minister Nakayama Taro to make a statement on Asian security at the twenty-fourth ASEAN Ministerial Meeting in Kuala Lumpur in 1991. The intention was to declare indirectly that Japan was ready to take steps into this formerly forbidden terrain. Unfortunately, Nakayama lacked Satoh's subtlety, misunderstood his directions, and spontaneously declared that Japan would take a more visible role in Asian security. Japan's Indonesian support fell away, and there was embarrassment in Tokyo.

Nonetheless, at the twenty-fifth annual meeting of ASEAN foreign ministers in Manila in July 1992, ASEAN followed Satoh's recommendations by holding an elaborate council on security at the PMC, involving twenty-one foreign ministers. At the meeting, Blas Ople, chairman of the Foreign Relations Committee of the Philippine Senate, proposed a new "ASEAN Security Forum." This would "prevent [its members] from a premature and dangerous arms race," and act as a "tacit guarantee that the balance of power will work," Ople said.[9] Two years later, ASEAN held the first meeting of ARF in Bangkok. By 2000 the organization was attracting international attention with the attendance of North Korea at the seventh ARF ministerial, once again in Bangkok. According to the *Los Angeles Times*, North Korean foreign minister Paek Nam Sun met "for the first time in fifty years" with the foreign ministers of South Korea and Japan, and agreed to resume normalization talks with South Korea.[10]

Critics complained that ARF was affected by the same sense of drift that had dogged ASEAN for most of its three decades and had failed to play a major role resolving the conflict in East Timor. Even so, ARF had a clear enough rationale to keep it going. Writing in 2000, Singaporean analyst Chienpeng Chung suggested that the underlying logic was fear. Southeast Asian nations "are worried that either a collapse or expansion of the North Korean state, or any conflict between North and South Korea, China and Taiwan, or China and Southeast Asia, would divide the Asia-Pacific into two mutually antagonistic blocs, drawing in the United States and Japan on one side, against China, with perhaps Russia, on the other, with small and weak Southeast Asian states caught helplessly in the middle."[11]

Paul Evans, a Canadian specialist on Asian security matters, argued that ARF "wouldn't have gone a foot outside Southeast Asia if Japan hadn't set up carefully the idea of what this was about. It's not a matter of Japanese confidence but whether it wants to play a quiet but expanding leadership role. There is no better way to do it than from the center. Let others be the yappers. This is leadership from the middle, and they have done a subtle job of holding together both the Americans and ASEAN. They operate from the middle, but are going where they want to go."[12]

Within a few years, however, Japan's role in initiating ARF was forgotten, and Southeast Asians had ceased to badger Japan to exercise greater leadership for fear of offending China and the two Koreas. ASEAN had embraced ARF, and meanwhile the confrontation in North Korea over its attempts to develop nuclear capability had given ascendance to the pro-U.S. faction in the Japanese Foreign Ministry. The Southeast Asians were blasé. According to Chan Heng Chee, director of the Institute of Southeast Asian Studies in Singapore, and later Singaporean ambassador to the United States, "The United States disapproved, and (Secretary of State James) Baker put it down. The Japanese floated the idea and the idea fell down hard. But a year later it became an ASEAN initiative. Now, some ASEAN countries will say, this idea began with Japan. But who really remembers? Even the Japanese will tell you, Japan doesn't know how to be a leader. It's a consensus society. Nobody knows how to take the initiative."[13]

Nonetheless, Japan was amassing diplomatic dividends from ARF in such developments as the three-way meeting with the Koreas and the launch of the "ASEAN Plus Three" summits. The meetings and summits, like ARF, were tacked onto the platform of the ASEAN post-ministerial conference. "ASEAN Plus Three," a three-way summit meeting among the leaders of Japan, China, and South Korea, became a regular feature of the ASEAN PMC after 1997.

The internationalists got their boost as a result of a sharp shift in U.S. policy, from gradual troop withdrawal to upgrading the force structure in East Asia. The turnaround in U.S. policy came after a visit to Beijing by Defense Secretary William J. Perry in October 1994. Stanley Roth, Clinton's national security advisor on Asia, and Winston Lord, under-secretary of state for East Asian affairs, accompanied Perry, along with Harvard professor and East Asian expert Joseph Nye. On the way home, they spent a week in Tokyo, where Perry decided to task Nye as his "point man" on Japan. Nye then conducted a review of the entire U.S.-Japan security relationship and tried to develop a "deeper dialogue" with Japan in order to decide new directions in the security relationship.[14]

The result was the "Nye Initiative," which reinstated the traditional primacy of security matters in U.S.-Japan relations and reversed the Bush senior policy of holding the security relationship with Japan hostage to its acceptance of U.S. trade and economic demands. The new security deal became the centerpiece of the Clinton-Hashimoto Summit in Tokyo from April 16–18, 1996, and the hard line in trade that characterized the early years of the first Clinton administration disappeared. Notwithstanding the sudden show of attention from the United States, Prime Minister Hashimoto Ryutaro put the new defense guidelines on a slow cycle of a joint study commission and parliamentary review. It was May 1999 before the Japanese Diet finally enacted the modest changes agreed upon at the 1996 summit.

Politically, the new guidelines were aimed squarely at North Korea and China. In 1999, the Pentagon would formally elevate China to the status of "potential adversary" and designate Asia as the most likely zone for military conflict in the new century. Over the course of the decade, the United States had come close to writing off its security relationship with Japan, but by its end, Japan had again assumed primary importance in U.S. security calculations.[15]

Objectively, the defense guidelines hardly seemed worth a lengthy debate. The real surprise was that they exposed gaping loopholes in a security pact that Washington had described as the foundation of its Asian security policy since at least the 1960s. This foundation was built on sand. Before the guidelines came into effect, it was not even certain that the United States would be able to use Japan as a staging ground for operations elsewhere, and receive logistical support for its 40,000 troops stationed in Japan in the event of a crisis. This had become an irritant during the 1994 Korean Peninsula affair when North Korea's plans to operate a nuclear power plant that produced enriched plutonium nearly provoked a military clash. While the United States threatened air strikes unless North Korea allowed inspection by the International Atomic Energy Agency, Japanese officials dithered for weeks over whether or not to allow transit rights for U.S. troops in the event of a confrontation.[16]

The process by which the internationalists had adopted the idea of rearmament went back to the early 1990s. Re-armament had long been associated with the conservative core of the LDP, and part of the raison d'être of the Foreign Ministry internationalists was to keep the politicians from hijacking the U.S. alliance. According to Peter Ennis, editor of *The Oriental Economist* in New York, "The review process really began after the Gulf War, when Japan was caught flat-footed, with no clear policy. A band of officials within Boeicho (the Defense Agency) and the Jieitai (Self-Defense Forces), as well as some within Gaimusho (Foreign Ministry) got together around the idea that Japan should never be caught off-guard again. Japan needed to consider crisis scenarios."[17]

These concerns led to the discussions with Nye on a three- to four-year program to "significantly upgrade Japan's ability to act in a crisis and to upgrade the ability of the United States and Japan to work together in a crisis." Ennis credited the Japanese with devising the Nye Initiative. It was to be a five-part process, starting with a joint security declaration. Japan would then draft its new National Defense Program Outline, the bilateral defense guidelines would be reviewed and rewritten, crisis management legislation would be introduced in the Diet, and Japan and the United States would engage in detailed military planning.

By the end of the Clinton administration in 2000, Japan had pushed through the first three of the five stages, but just barely. Public opposition to any expansion of Japan's military role remained formidable. The 1999 defense guidelines made clear that U.S. forces would be able to use commercial airports, local harbors, and roads in a regional crisis, as well as draw on "rear support" from the Japanese. More dramatically, they committed Japan to provide certain types of support for U.S. forces during a crisis in regions "surrounding Japan," and allowed Japanese ships to conduct rescue and minesweeping operations in international waters. This nuance was strong enough to make the guidelines debate "the single most important problem of Japanese foreign policy," said Inoguchi Kuniko, a specialist in international relations at Sophia University. "How can we provide support for 'areas around Japan' and be consistent with our Constitution?"[18]

Indeed, many Japanese shared Inoguchi's passionate attachment to the peace clause in the Japanese Constitution and feared that any small step away from it would unleash dark currents lurking in the national psyche of militarism and nationalism. Unlike Inoguchi, most of them paid little attention to such arcane matters as ARF and the new defense guidelines. Of all the pieces of unfinished business as Japan muddled into the twenty-first century, the most poisonous was this disconnect between the bureaucracy driving Japan incrementally toward re-armament, and the Japanese public burrowing ever deeper into its postwar cocoon. No other policy had so much potential to create havoc in the event of an actual crisis. The bureaucracy might have prepared itself for machinations of war and peace, but the minds of the Japanese people were locked contentedly in the past.

Thus, the 1990s saw only gradual erosion, a faint ripple of change in the myth that Japan had adopted during the Cold War, with U.S. encouragement. The myth proposed that the world's second-largest economy could maintain the world's second-largest military force in budgetary terms without ever having to use it. In its 1998 to 1999 fiscal year, Japan spent $42.9 billion on its military, four times more than China's $12.6 billion and well ahead of France and the United Kingdom.[19] Japan's military spending was roughly one-fifth that of the United States, but it was still a remarkable anomaly given the explicit mission of mere readiness for an assault on the homeland. Although possessing no ballistic missiles, aircraft carriers, or long-range heavy transports to move troops and equipment, in the 1990s it had added such high-tech military assets as Aegis-class destroyers and Patriot-missile defenses. Japan's Self-Defense Forces were indeed among the world's smallest military establishments in terms of personnel, but in terms of high-technology weaponry and potential nuclear capability they were formidable.

Every year, the Ground Self-Defense Forces invited foreign journalists to a demonstration of the firing capability of Japanese tanks, designed to confront a land invasion. There were few such invitations issued to the Japanese public, however, and in any event they were not much interested. They rarely caught a glimpse of their military, whose officers were required to doff their uniforms before leaving the front gates. The Japanese military was elaborately fenced off from public view, ostensibly to prevent a resurgence of 1930s militarism. Recruitment literature focused on the public service nature of military careers, and throughout the 1990s, military bureaucrats fretted over the persistent decline in new enlistments.

So circumscribed were the powers of the Japanese armed forces that during the Kobe earthquake the governor of Hyogo Prefecture initially declined help from the Self-Defense Forces and prevented units from entering the city to help. Both Governor Kaihara Toshitami and the mayor of Kobe, Sasayama Yukitoshi, had been antagonistic toward the Self-Defense Forces long before the disaster. In contrast to the political complexion of the federal government, the Japan Communist Party and the Japan Socialist Party frequently controlled municipal and local governments. Both regarded any intrusion of the Japanese military as an affront to their prestige, even during times of crisis, and painted the Self-Defense Agency as a gang of ravening militarists longing for the good old days of secret police and emperor worship. In Kobe, roads were jammed, further impeding rescue efforts, because of a long-standing ban on the use of sirens. Sirens were also associated with the militarist era of the 1930s, and had been proscribed by the municipal government along with military uniforms and language referring to the military.

Japanese military officers faced suspicion and distrust even within their own families. In May 1993, a group of American journalists called upon the commandant of the Maritime Self-Defense Forces base in Sasebo, Japan. The journalists asked how families coped with military life. The answer was that they did not. Hayashizaki Chiaki, the officer conducting the briefing was young, polished, and one of the highest-ranking officials in the Maritime Self-Defense Forces, the post–World War Two equivalent of the Japanese Imperial Navy. When I translated *kaijo jietai* as "navy" in English, Vice-Admiral Hayashizaki winced, saying that if he used the direct Japanese translation of navy, *haigun*, "People would look at me like a ghost." The ghosts of Japan's military past left a cold imprint on family life. He had two daughters in their twenties. Neither was aware of their father's rank nor what he did at work. "Even my wife doesn't know what kind of work I do. It makes me quite uncomfortable that they don't know. I explain to them, but they don't understand," he said. "Since 1945, there has been no education, or discussion within any family about military matters. If even my own family doesn't understand, how can others?"[20]

Hayashizaki was no mere military factotum. Sasebo was the naval station that had launched the armada that defeated Russia in 1905, marking Japan's transition to a major military power. Since 1945, the U.S. Navy had taken over the old Imperial Navy headquarters at the waterfront, but the Japanese base was just behind it. Hayashizaki's fleet included nine destroyers and two support ships, with a helicopter squadron and an air wing.

"The purpose of our forces is to stabilize northwest Asia," he said proudly. "The Americans may think that there is no more threat in the Pacific because Russia is weak. But we think the region is unstable for Japan, and if American forces left, the situation would become even worse. Even now, in the East China Sea, Japanese merchant ships and fishing ships are being attacked. Both the Chinese and Koreans have ballistic missiles, and the Chinese have submarines. These are no direct threat to Japan so far, but they are deployed in this area, and that's a fact. What Asian countries fear the most is that U.S. military power in the region will decline and that China will rush in to fill the vacuum." This brief lecture would have been a deep embarrassment to his children.

In Kumamoto, an ancient castle town, we asked a high school student what he thought of Japan's role in the United Nations operation supervising the Cambodian elections. The United States and Japan were among forty countries sending some 22,000 troops to monitor the Cambodian elections, but for Japan the troop dispatch was unique—it was the first time since Japan's defeat in 1945 that it had sent soldiers abroad. The 1,200 Ground Self-Defence Forces troops served mainly as road-building crews.

It was quite unfair, the student replied. The United States had pressured Japan into violating its Constitution. Why should Japanese have to put themselves in harm's way in Cambodia? He believed that Japan was the only foreign country with troops there. Even without such a misconception, opposition was intense to the first dispatch of Japanese troops into a foreign war zone. For most Japanese, enlisting or being wounded in battle was a direct challenge to their constitutional rights. The two Japanese deaths in the U.N. peacekeeping mission in Cambodia drew such ferocious criticism that parliamentary debate became hung up much smaller efforts in Mozambique and the Golan Heights. Japanese troops finally joined both operations in 1994 and 1995, but only after significant delays.

For half a century, the centerpiece of Japan's Cold War defense policy was the U.S.-Japan Security Treaty, drafted in 1952 and revised in 1960.

After disbanding and neutralizing the Japanese Imperial Army and Navy, Washington persuaded Japan to set up the tactically circumscribed but powerful Self-Defense Forces. Clark Field and Subic Bay in the Philippines and the U.S. military installations in South Korea, Okinawa, and the Japanese main islands were the front line of the Cold War policy of containing Asian communism. Until 1994, the South Korean military was technically under U.S. command. Washington visualized itself as the "hub" of regional security arrangements. Its allies—Japan, South Korea, the Philippines, and the noncommunist developing countries of the region—were "spokes." Apart from China itself, Washington saw Southeast Asia as the central theater of Cold War aggression.

The critical problem of the 1990s for Japanese military thinkers was how to prepare for an anticipated new security environment without actually appearing to do so. In Fall 1995, Japan revised its national defense program outline for the first time since 1976. It scrupulously avoided listing threats that might require specific military responses, such as the closing of sea lanes or missile launches in nearby waters, instead concentrating on nebulous changes in the global security environment. The charade went so far as to preclude contingency planning for emergencies. In questioning in the Japanese Diet in 1997, the opposition Shinshinto Party grilled the government on its contingency plans for regional conflicts. A reluctant Defense Agency official admitted that there were none.

And yet, beneath the official veneer and the elaborate denial mechanisms, with the end of the Cold War, the strategic outlook had changed fundamentally. Much as with the debates over Japan's war crimes, Japanese began to wonder what it might be like to be alone in the Pacific, without the U.S. security umbrella, and experiment with new ideas. In private, Japanese strategists vented their frustration with the government's determination to preserve the status quo ante of the Cold War relationship with the United States.

"Security is a dirty word in Japan," said Mamoi Makoto, a retired Defence Agency official who joined the editorial staff of a conservative Japanese monthly magazine, *This Is*.[21] Mamoi blamed the taboo against the word on post–World War Two paranoia within the Japanese Foreign Ministry. In the 1930s and 1940s, the Japanese military crushed the independence of the Foreign Office; after the defeat, Mamoi said, the Foreign Office took its revenge. "No defense attaché abroad could send a cable or a letter without it being checked by the ambassador," he said. "It was forbidden to send a cable to the Defense Agency. When Nakasone [Yasuhiro] became defense minister in the early 1970s, he insisted that attachés could at least send letters if not cables. It was all due to the phobia Foreign Ministry officials had about military affairs.

"For a long time, the National Security Affairs Section in the Foreign Ministry was in the North American Bureau. In other words, it was part of American Affairs. In the last few years, it has moved to the United Nations Section. But for a long time, any discussion on security went through the U.S. section. Whenever the Defense Agency did a study, it was done in terms of U.S. policy, not in terms of an Asian policy, and much less global policy. When the Gulf War started nobody had any answers. 'Crisis' is a funny word in Japanese. It implies something like a typhoon or an earthquake. It's something you can't predict. Eventually it goes away. Nothing can be done about it. The attitude was to wait and see what the Americans would do. Now we have a problem. The problem we have today is that we cannot wait and see what the Americans will do. Maybe the Americans will do nothing."

Earlier in this conversation, conducted on a brisk fall day in 1992 in a cozy sushi bar near Tokyo's Ebisu Station, Mamoi said that nobody in the Japanese security community believed that the United States would come to Japan's rescue in an attack despite the 47,000 troops stationed in Okinawa and the main islands under terms of the U.S.-Japan Security Agreement. "There's no reason why the United States would come," he said. "I would even agree if someone said we could not defend our country by any means."

In Hawaii, the tens of thousands of Japanese who vacationed there every year relaxed into a milieu in which the relationship with the United States as military protector seemed as light and natural as the pure air they breathed. They seemed to become imaginary citizens of a hybrid nation, one rich, the other strong, as though the two countries could embody the old dream of *fukoku kyohei*, "Rich Nation, Strong Army" by combining their resources.

Part of the illusion came from Hawaii's demographic mix. Ethnic Japanese make up some 22 percent of the population, and the Japanese joke about *"Hawaii ken,"* or Hawaii as a Japanese prefecture. Japanese nationals easily fit in among the mélange of ethnic Japanese, Chinese, Koreans, and Filipinos. The Hawaii Department of Business, Economic Development, and Tourism, is headed by a Japanese-American economist, Seiji Naya, who spends at least as much time worrying about the Japanese economy as he does about the ups and downs of Silicon Valley. California and Japan are Hawaii's two main sources of tourism and investment. When both economies are strong together, real estate values in Honolulu soar and the hotels have waiting lists.

Tour groups descend by the busload at Pearl Harbor, waiting for the water ferries that take them to the ark-like memorial to the USS *Arizona*, sunk in the Japanese attack. The memorial blazes white in the sun, and the brief trip to Battleship Row is made solemn by U.S. Navy ritual and the neatly uniformed midshipmen who run the ferry. The climax is always the same. Stepping onto the marble platform of the memorial, the crowds go silent.

They look for familiar names engraved in stone, for the bubble of oil from the hold of the *Arizona*, still trickling half a century after the Japanese attack. To most Americans, the casualty list still chills: 13 capital vessels sunk, 8 heavily damaged, 328 aircraft damaged or destroyed, 2,403 dead, 1,178 wounded.

In December 1993, on a Hawaii-perfect day, all blue sky and cumulus clouds, a group of two-dozen Japanese college juniors and seniors waits in line for the documentary film that visitors are required to see before boarding the water shuttle to the *Arizona*. One student wielded the latest palm-sized video camera, with a digital screen for instant picture display. Others just looked. Relaxed, curious, personable, with their cotton sweaters, polo shirts and tennis shoes, they had much the same style and manner as a group of American Ivy Leaguers their age. Several were the children of diplomats or multinational executives, and most had spent at least some years abroad. Inside the darkened theater, one young woman breaks into tears, not from shame but because the film was so fair, she said. It made a hero of Yamamoto Isoroku, the brilliant admiral who led the attack. Yamamoto argued strenuously against luring the United States into the war, which the film points out, along with the strategic daring of the Pearl Harbor raid. "In the first six to twelve months of a war with the United States and Great Britain I will run wild and win victory upon victory. But then, if the war continues after that, I have no expectation of success," the admiral had said in 1940.[22]

The Japanese students studying the sunken coral-encrusted hulks in Battleship Row, half a century after Pearl Harbor and the Battle of Midway, can hardly imagine Japan at war. It is easier for them to think of the United States as part of a Third World of chaos and poverty than to imagine Japan in such a light. Even their parents would be hard put to remember when Japan was poor, most of them born after Japan entered its double-digit drive for superpower status. In 1993, Japan's per capita income was $33,903, compared to $25,009 for an American and $458 for a Chinese. Japan, with its population of 124 million, had a gross domestic product of $4.2 trillion—two-thirds that of the United States, with its population of 255 million, and nearly eight times the output of fast-growing China, with a population of 1.18 billion. Japan's wealth was double the $2 trillion produced in the rest of Asia in the same year.[23]

Members of a special two-year seminar on international relations at Keio University, the students were well versed in the geopolitics of Japan's relationship with the United States and Asia. Keio is Japan's Yale, ranked second only to Waseda among private universities. Their professor, Soeya Yoshihide, had arranged a week's excursion to Hawaii as an information-gathering exercise. Soeya, a quietly humorous, energetic, young scholar with a Ph.D. in political science from the University of Michigan, was a visiting fellow at Honolulu's East-West Center, a U.S. government-funded research institute. He had been there for two years with his wife, Kazuko, an English teacher. The tour showed a side of Hawaii that most Japanese visitors blithely ignored—as the strategic command center of U.S. forces that provides Japan's first line of defense.

A yellow school bus ferried the "Soeya Seminar" around town; after Pearl Harbor and the *Arizona* memorial, it pulled next into the U.S. Pacific Command at Camp Smith, with its palm trees and aura of tropical indolence, and then circled down the drive into the crater into Punchbowl, an extinct volcanic caldera where 25,000 U.S. soldiers are buried, half from actions in the Pacific in World War Two. The seminar's home base was the East-West Center, one of the front-line institutions used by Washington during the Cold War to build a Pacific constituency. With the brashness of youth, Soeya's students were ready to dismiss such Cold War relics as CINCPAC's nuclear umbrella and start from scratch.

At a briefing at U.S. Pacific Command headquarters at Camp Smith, Kiyoshige Kazuhiro, one of Soeya's graduate students, took on the briefer, Colonel Peterman. "A sense of readiness is not so common with us," he said. "We've been living in a peaceful world. We never thought about why we might have to be ready for anything. I understand that you guys have to be prepared, but how should we balance it since we are a totally civilian country?" Colonel Peterman answered the question carefully, ponderously, speaking slowly in order to make sure the students understood.

"Do any of you have mothers or fathers in the military?" he asked. A chorus of no's comes from the Soeya Seminar. "So, you are not close to the military. My children ask me the same question. My answer is that history shows us it is important to be ready. Your country has gained tremendously in economic influence. It's incredible when I think that in 1960 your trade with my country amounted to a few million dollars. I feel that responsibility comes with that economic power, the responsibility to protect yourselves internally and externally out to a certain radius. The question is how far should that go? Should your Constitution be amended to permit that expansion? It's a tough question. But we think because of your economic power we would like to see you increase your burden sharing. Things are peaceful now, but if you've heard the news from Russia, one individual on the scene with radical views said he would not hesitate to use nuclear power. All of a sudden, we're drawing our forces away from Europe. Maybe we shouldn't be, because things can change so quickly based on one individual. These are the tough questions. Maybe you'll have to answer them one day when you move into positions of leadership."[24]

The Keio students, so confident in the CINCPAC briefing room, recoiled at the suggestion of entering a Japanese military base and exploring strategic issues with members of their own country's military. Yamasaki Goro cringed when asked if he would consider a military career in Japan. "People like me, we never thought about joining the military. Never, never, never!" The only people who signed up were those whose family insisted they join, because their fathers or grandfathers were in the military, he said. What would it be like if he regularly saw Japanese officers in uniform on the streets of Tokyo, I asked. Should the Japanese military become more visible as Japan broadened its role in international peacekeeping? "It's good to have a framework for discussion," he admitted cautiously. "But nothing more. Not yet." Did he feel uneasy visiting CINCPAC? "No, here, never," Yamasaki said. "But in Japan, no, I couldn't do it."

Later in the week, the students put on a public forum at the East-West Center, examining Japan's post–Cold War role in Asia.[25] They did not foresee an expanded security role for Japan. While they agreed that the end of the Cold War had made it possible for Japan to exercise an "autonomous diplomacy," the students spun the most cautious of scenarios. There were no crises or confrontations in their vision of the future; no military clashes in which Japanese national interests might be at risk. Instead, they portrayed Japan gradually easing into the role of regional economic leadership and handling security matters multilaterally. How this was supposed to work was unclear. "Economic integration is easy," said Kiyoshige, the graduate student. "Political integration is problematic."

The students had something they called a "dual-track" approach to guide the process of political integration within Asia. Disputes and conflicts were to be settled by subregional entities, such as ASEAN. They saw Japan working to build political dialogue through the region's new multilateral organizations, the Asia Pacific Economic Cooperation grouping (APEC) and ARF, which was about to hold its first formal meeting the next year, 1994. The key relationship remained that between Japan and the United States. They could not explain what would happen if U.S. and Japanese interests failed to coincide with the regional organizations in which Japan was to play so large a role. Perhaps innocently, the students were merely parroting Foreign Ministry doctrine—implying that Japan was to serve in the role of Asian branch manager for the U.S. State Department and Armed Forces.

Japan as branch manager was a faithful representation of Japan's security policy in the 1990s. The official position—separate from the machinations of the factions within the Foreign Ministry—changed little through the decade, and charted a quiescent course quite different from the energetic policies emanating from MITI and the Ministry of Finance, promoting economic integration with Asia and the Japanese model. Among the consequences of Japan's muddled security message was a formal Asian diplomacy that was equally if not more incoherent.

In July 1992, Prime Minister Miyazawa Kiichi made a tentative attempt to outline the new thinking, describing Japan's Asia policy in terms that were a single cautious step beyond the "hub-and-spoke" approach of the senior Bush administration. This, as it turned out, would be the last and most ambitious effort by the Japanese government to spell out its policy toward the region in the 1990s.

Internally, the policy represented a compromise between advocates of the radical change and pro-U.S. factions in the Foreign Ministry, between the Kikuchis and the Okazakis. Miyazawa's compromise, however, preserved the tensions of the rivalry. Externally, the policy charted a new multilateral regime for post–Cold War Asia, subsuming big power rivalries. Satoh Yuko's "multiplex mechanisms" would be available to policy makers to solve regional problems. Existing subregional organizations, such as ASEAN, would be at the forefront in resolving disputes, while the new regional organizations would foster wider political dialogue. Miyazawa called this a "two-track" approach (the Soeya students had borrowed the phrase). In fact, it involved an unacknowledged third track, which was to embrace the United States at all levels. The United States was a key member of APEC and had a relationship as a so-called dialogue partner with ASEAN. Instead of a single hub, Japan envisioned a web of relationships, all of them including the United States as the region's dominant power.

The problem with the formula was that it defined no specific role for Japan, other than as cheerleader for a process in which it remained invisible. The students were aware of Japan's role in launching ARF, and believed that the strategy behind Japan's reticent posture within the organization was to forestall U.S. opposition. Memories were still fresh of the way that Washington had slammed the East Asian Economic Group proposed by Malaysian prime minister Mahathir in 1990. Japan was content to let ASEAN shepherd the ARF. By adopting a low profile, Tokyo limited its own maneuverability but such limits were more acceptable than an open breach with the United States.

The Keio professor, Soeya, put Tokyo's hesitation in the context of history and identity. Explained Soeya: "There is a strong school of thought within the Japanese Foreign Ministry that Japan will not be driven in the wrong direction as long as it maintains relations with the Anglo-Saxons. Okazaki Hisahiko [Japan's former ambassador to Thailand] has been saying that the Anglo-Saxon relationship is key. The golden period of the Japanese empire was the time of the British alliance. Japan strayed into the wrong course when it strayed away from its relationship with the Anglo-Saxons. The overall dilemma of Japanese foreign policy is that it's sandwiched between East and West.

"Japan's search for identity is a long-term quest. Maybe it's Japan's mission forever. We are demonstrably located that way and our history since the Meiji Restoration has been that way. Our accumulation of civilization came first from China, then received a great impact from the West after the Meiji Restoration. This is the source of the Japanese enigma. It's also the source of the difficulties the Foreign Ministry has in charting its Asia policy."[26] Kikuchi, the former diplomat, had said the same thing more bluntly: "As long as the U.S.-Japan security treaty is in existence, we can't articulate our positions on Asia-Pacific affairs with any precision. We can only wait to see how things evolve. As our economic bloc takes on political characteristics, we will still only be able to discuss security matters on an ad hoc basis. I think this is what Miyazawa had in mind with his two-track approach."[27]

A few years later, I was strolling along the Singapore waterfront at night, admiring the reflections of city lights against the dusky black of the water and pushing through the crowds of young investment bankers mobbing the bars along Boat Quay. My companion was Tanaka Akihiko, a specialist in international relations at the Institute of Oriental Culture at Tokyo University, a China expert and trusted government advisor. Tanaka is funny and literate. On this particular humid evening, he claimed to be suffering as a result of his recent transition from the good life at Oxford University, on sabbatical, back to a pressure-cooker existence in Japan. It was March 22, 1996, the night before Taiwan's elections. Two U.S. aircraft carriers, the *Nimitz* and the *Independence*, were patrolling the South China Sea at the head of battle groups; during the day, the *Nimitz* steamed past Singapore on its way north. Tensions were high. In the preceding weeks various Chinese officials had threatened to invade Taiwan, lob nuclear bombs at Los Angeles, and, at a minimum, blockade its ports at the first motion toward independence.

For fifteen days, Beijing had been holding military exercises off the Taiwan coast to put muscle behind its threats. It had fielded 150,000 troops, forty vessels including submarines and landing craft, and shot off ten expensive M-9 surface-to-surface missiles because of the cost, most armies restricted such launches to one per regiment annually. The United States had responded by sending the two battle groups; Japan's intervention had consisted of a faint warning that it might suspend the next round of negotiations with China on development loans. Discussing these events with Professor Tanaka, I maintained that the Chinese military exercises represented a watershed moment in history when China's potential for disruption lay in stark view. I wanted to know if Tanaka was worried, how the event had affected strategic planning in Tokyo, and what Japan might do if the United States failed to provide a show of force.

Tanaka dismissed the threat. According to Tanaka, Japan was not in danger. Japan could ignore even a full-scale naval blockade by the Chinese in the Taiwan Strait. "Our oil tankers don't have to sail through the South China Sea. We can choose another route. We can sail around Taiwan." The presence of the *Nimitz* and *Independence* battle groups was a mixed blessing. "If the United States overreacts, the region will condemn it."

I was astonished. The shipping channel that leads north from Singapore to Yokohama and Tokyo Bay is among the busiest in the world. Steaming up it is like being on an expressway. Huge tankers and container ships pass within scant miles of each other. Beijing, by a determined grab at the Spratly Islands, or a siege of the Taiwan Straits, could bring it to a halt. Tanaka's insouciance, however, accurately reflected the steamy undercurrents of the 1990s, a sense of mounting pressure to readjust the framework of Japan's defense policy to match the increasing depth of its economic relationships with Asia, yet without concrete ideas about how to do so. To this way of thinking, the U.S. alliance was a psychological barrier to reinventing Japan, and however practical it might be, Japan would be better off without it.

Perhaps the strongest statement in favor of radical change came from former Prime Minister Hosokawa Morihiro, who in many ways embodied the aspirations of Japan's first post-war generation of bureaucrats and intellectuals. Although his tenure in office lasted only eight months, from August 1993 to April 1994, Hosokawa's unlikely coalition government broke the fifty-six-year LDP monopoly of power, and it pushed reform along the lines advocated by Ozawa Ichiro, whose sudden exit from the LDP camp led to the coalition victory. Ozawa had called for a more "active" military role for Japan in the context of United Nations peacekeeping operations, but argued that the U.S.-Japan Security Treaty should remain intact as a guarantee of continued alliance between the region's major two powers.[28]

Hosokawa, however, focused on the critical question of what would happen if Japan were suddenly engulfed in a regional crisis. In a speech in Seattle in March 1996, two years after his resignation, Hosokawa asserted that the Japanese public would no longer tolerate the Cold War arrangement of "no questions asked, no answers given." Hosokawa charged that the treaty was "really about military bases," and that it failed to reflect fundamental changes in the nature of the U.S.-Japan relationship; it was "misguided" for the United States to try to put the U.S.-Japan security relationship back on track with a few minor adjustments, and that any review must include the Japanese public. "One can flatly say that there has been practically no dialogue from the Japanese side with America in the last fifty years," Hosokawa said. "Although a bilateral security agreement has been in effect during this time, there's been no dialogue about the level of troops stationed in Japan and their necessity from a national security standpoint. At least, there has been no dialogue with the Japanese public about these issues."[29]

Like Okazaki, the internationalist, Hosokawa was preoccupied with China. His family, after all, had been feudal lords of Kumamoto Prefecture, long a center of trade and contact with the mainland. The logic of history suggested to Hosokawa a different solution than Okazaki's *realpolitik*—something closer to the old adage, if you can't beat them, join them. Lurking beneath the political science jargon of the change radicals was a vision of a partnership between China and Japan that would mirror the geopolitics of China's Middle Kingdom, the principal organizing glue of the Sinified states of East Asia for a millennium. "Until World War Two, Japan's destiny of course was largely determined by our relations with China," he said. "In fact, the most serious issues Japan may confront in the future may well be those related to China." Others felt the same way. In April 1996, Japan's Keizai Doyukai, the powerful Federation of Employers, called on the Japanese Diet to review the U.S.-Japan security alliance. In a report, the federation argued that the continued expansion of Japanese business interests overseas "no longer allows the business community to remain indifferent to security affairs . . . Business relations cannot go smoothly unless Japan plays its due role in the international community."

History seemed to be on the side of the change radicals. Quietly, without any formal reckoning, the Japanese public began to desert the Cold War status quo. The rape of a twelve-year-old Okinawan girl by two American service men in 1995 threw into sharp exposure the issue of U.S. troops stationed in Japan. Until the rape few Japanese understood why. Okinawans bitterly resented that 50 percent of U.S. troops were in their prefecture, or why Okinawa governor Ota Masahide led a movement to reduce the burden. Although the public protests failed to move the Japanese central government to action, they were a factor in Tokyo's decision to hold the G8 summit in Okinawa in 2000. Outside observers began to notice a sudden shift in the political chemistry, as greater public attention collided with the pressures for change from within the bureaucracy, like hot and cold streams of water.

"The intellectual ferment over security policy in Japan is stunning to long-time observers of this pacifist nation," wrote Michael Green, a senior fellow at the Council on Foreign Relations in Washington, D.C, later the National Security Council advisor on Japan in the administration of George W. Bush.[30] Over 60 percent of the Japanese public supported changing the Peace Constitution, according to Green; among Diet members, 90 percent wanted change. Over 50 percent viewed China "in a negative light." Eight percent supported legislation to respond to security crises. A Japanese major general, Yamaguchi Noboru, speaking to a Washington audience in March 2000, claimed that "the Japanese public has become more willing to utilize the capabilities of self-defense forces in non- or semi-combat operations such as UN peacekeeping operations, humanitarian or disaster-relief operations in or outside Japan." He added, "This became very prominent when the Maritime Self-Defense Force was ordered to conduct a maritime security operation for the first time in its history, to chase two North Korean speedboats violating Japan's territorial waters."[31]

Very gradually, with little fanfare, Japan began to find its way toward an independent strategic role in Asia. The absence of mechanisms to inform and engage the Japanese public continued to be a severe impediment, but over time even ordinary Japanese might get the idea that Japanese and U.S. interests would not always converge. If there was anything to convince the Japanese public that things had changed since the end of the Cold War, it was China.

Neighbor

It is a hot July day in 1991. I am in Beijing on holiday and awash in nostalgia for the city of ten years earlier. Beijing was a far different place in the early 1980s, when I worked there as a business consultant. It had a certain funky charm with its back alleys, or *hutong*, many with their own long histories. Foreign businesspeople and journalists were confined to a handful of hotels, and the only place in town open after 8:30 P.M. was the coffee shop in the "new" 1974 wing of the Peking Hotel, built by Zhou Enlai as a symbol of national pride. By the early 1990s, dozens if not hundreds of new hotels and luxury high-rise apartment buildings cluttered the horizon, and the Peking Hotel was a relic, even with the addition of several new wings. The high-rises housed China's newly rich entrepreneurial class and a vastly expanded expatriate community.

The International Club, where I used to have my office, was much the same, however. The Guoji Zhuluobu had served as a country club for the foreign community, with a beautiful Olympic-sized pool and tennis courts where George Bush Senior had played when he was head of the unofficial U.S. mission to Beijing. In 1980, the club made some of its former game rooms available for rent to the first batch of legally resident foreign companies. There was no air conditioning, and the windows overlooked the grand expanse of Chang An Jie, the Avenue of Everlasting Peace. Dust coated everything—our desks, the telex machines, and any glass or plastic surfaces.

"Private enterprise" was illegal, or at least highly circumscribed, when I arrived in China in 1981. The first markets were for vegetables and birds. Ten years later, just outside the diplomatic quarter, vendors hawked silk clothes with designer labels. In 1980, foreign garment companies struggled to get their Chinese partners to understand concepts like "size" and "style." People stuck to their uniforms of blue and khaki Mao suits. It could cost your career to be seen with a foreigner.

I cycled on. The accents hadn't changed, with their thick "ers" on final consonants. I hear offers for *waihuizhuar*—foreign exchange scrip—on the streets and even in hotels. Street vendors uttered long, emotive cries, hawking *binguar*, or frozen popsicles. Prices had gone way up in Gugong, the Forbidden City. In 1981, the cost of admission for foreigners was RMB 2.00, and the ticket got you free run of the grounds. Ten years later, the price was RMB 20.00, and another 20 for a tape of Peter Ustinov narrating the palace's ancient glories. In 1991, thankfully, the old lanes of Beijing, with their four-cornered houses, were still intact. In another ten years, this would no longer be true. The smell of garlic drifted out from behind spirit gates. The tiled roofs provided just enough foothold for weeds to sprout.

A turn of the handlebars and I am in Tiananmen, the vast plaza identified by the monumental "Gate of Heavenly Peace" that guards the Forbidden City. A summer haze weighs heavily on the vast square with its monument to heroes of the revolution and outsized buildings. Mothers held their babies in split pants over the sidewalks for a pee; young women were still wearing knee stockings with their dresses, a daring fashion a decade earlier. A comfortable dowdiness hung about the scene, the terror of the great demonstrations and killings of 1989 all but forgotten.

I am with a Malaysian companion, Jomo, who is visiting Beijing for the first time, and am showing him the sights. We wander up the stairs to the Museum of Revolutionary History. This monster of academic Marxism-Leninism-Maoism sits dourly in a key position on the square, opposite the Great Hall of the People, and built for eternity. The exhibits inside, however, are put together in such a slapdash way that the museum curators evidently learned their craft at the feet of workers and peasants. The displays, consisting mainly of plaster of Paris dioramas and photographs mounted on cardboard, would have been at home in the average American high school.

The museum has a rather simple organization, starting at the beginning of Chinese history and moving through the important highlights—from a Marxist-Leninist-Maoist perspective—through peasant rebellions and the incursions of imperialist powers through to the downfall of the Qing Empire in 1911. It made a narrative, and its protagonist was Japan. View this exhibit, and you could not possibly fail to notice which foreign power most inspired, annoyed, and changed China over the fifty years from 1895 to 1945. Japan was an enormous distraction. Forget Britain and the Opium Wars; the United States does not even get a mention.

In the mid-nineteenth century, China and Japan were equally weak, and foreign powers treated them with common contempt, demanding concessions and trampling on their sovereign powers, which both were equally helpless to protect. Both countries sent out boatloads of students to Europe and North America, seeking the keys to the Industrial Revolution that so clearly underlay the technology of Western gunboats and weaponry. Intellectuals in both countries used the phrase "Rich Country, Strong Army" as a national slogan. Senior government bureaucrats pondered ways to develop modern factories, railroads, and ports. Both countries were obsessively concerned with building a modern army. Only one of them succeeded.

Before the turn of the century, Japan had subjected China to more humiliations and indignities than any of the other colonial powers. The Sino-Japanese War of 1894–95 triggered the first great wave of industrialization in Japan and made it a great power. "The Meiji Japanese learned from China's disastrous wars with the European nations, made war on China in turn, and established their country as a colonial power by snatching territory away from China," writes Iriye Akira, the great Japanese historian of modern East Asia.[32] With the Treaty of Shimonoseki in 1895, Japan became the only foreign nation to acquire Chinese territory—albeit, just Taiwan and the Pescadores, since European intervention forced Japan to give back southern Manchuria and the port of Dalian.

Meanwhile, China languished. But out of the depths of its national frustration, China roared to life, ever more fiercely resisting as Japanese demands grew and threatened to annihilate the Middle Kingdom. In one last furious contest, communist forces under Mao Zedong rallied China to push the Japanese out, and the People's Republic was born. This, at least, is the orthodox Chinese view of events; as one might expect in the museum of the nation, there is no effort to provide balance or exonerate Japan in any way for its transgressions. The exhibits are frankly calculated to rouse hostile emotions. There are photographs of Japanese atrocities during the long 1931–45 Sino-Japanese War—piles of bodies in Nanjing, Japanese soldiers grinning over a contest to see who can decapitate the most Chinese, Japanese soldiers marching through Chinese cities.

The atrocities are less striking, however, than the compelling evidence of the psychic pull the two countries had for each other. Each spurred the other toward triumphs and mistakes. Japan's modern army and navy got their first test in an attempt to eliminate Chinese dominance of the Korean Peninsula. The tariff concessions it won in the Treaty of Shimonoseki gave Japan its first trade surplus, and the territorial claims became the nucleus of its modern empire. For its part, the Qing Dynasty suffered a huge loss of prestige because of the defeat. Its chief negotiator, Li Hongzhang, who had presided over the construction of China's first steam engine and telegraph lines, as well as factories for guns and textiles, was shot in the face at point-blank range by a Japanese fanatic. Li survived, and even won better terms on the treaty as a result, but it was a personal humiliation for the man who had championed the development of Western-style institutions to defend China against the West. At that point, the Qing Dynasty seemed to heave a sigh and give up after 300 years.

Japan's advances came at China's expense, as Japan became ever more deeply involved in intrigues to upset the last imperial dynasty and extend Japanese control as the empire disintegrated. The early twentieth century poses a problem for China's official historians. Japan was a haven for anti-Qing revolutionaries, and the radical Westernization of the Meiji government was a major source of inspiration to the Chinese reform movement. In the period between Japan's defeat of Russia in 1896 and before its annexation of Korea in 1910, many both inside and outside Japan saw it as a legitimate model for Asian modernization.

Kang Youwei and Liang Qichao both took refuge in Japan after the Empress Dowager Zi Xi deposed the young emperor Huang Xu and scuttled their hundred-day reform movement. Sun Yat-sen, leader of the anti-Qing radicals, escaped to Japan in 1895 after authorities discovered his plot to seize the government in Guangzhou and assumed the Japanese name Nakayama. The Revolution of 1911 was "largely made in Japan," according to John K. Fairbank and Edwin Reischauer, in their classic *East Asia: The Modern Transformation.*[33] At the same time, Japanese Pan-Asianism was inextricably linked with Japanese territorial aims. The first whiff of the Greater East Asian Co-Prosperity Sphere came with the establishment of Toa Dobun Kai, the "East Asia Common Culture Society," in 1898, which aimed at political and economic modernization of China. In 1901, Japanese activists who felt the Manchus needed more of a push established the Black Dragon Society. The Society was a clandestine organization that sent Japanese students, travelers, and businessmen into China on missions to foment revolution and prepare the way for Japanese territorial expansion "beyond Korea and against Russia."[34]

The Museum of Revolutionary History skips over this tangled era to focus on the dramatic birth of Chinese communism and the anti-Japanese movement that swept it to victory. One of the lengthiest series of documents and photographs is of Japan's seizure of the Shandong Peninsula in 1914 and its imposition of the infamous Twenty-one Demands in 1915. These initially contained clauses that would have placed Japanese advisors in the Chinese central government and police force. Other "demands" included the virtual cession to Japan of the provinces of Shandong and Manchuria, where Japanese interests were already entrenched. The protests that ensued gave birth to Chinese nationalism, reflected both in the student-led May Fourth Movement of 1919 and in Chinese military modernization.

The display puts me in mind of a *xiangshuo,* or "crosstalk," act I saw in Beijing in the early 1980s. *Xiangshuo* is a type of stand-up comedy involving punning jokes and slapstick, beloved by Beijingers, at least in the days when alternative forms of entertainment were hard to come by. The skit involved a succession of various wily foreign businessmen tricking an innocent Chinese. Worst of the lot was the Japanese businessman who tried to sell his Chinese dupe something like a Chinese equivalent of the Brooklyn Bridge. Naturally, when the Chinese yokel sees through the scheme, the audience roared in appreciation.

The act portrayed Americans as dumb but honest, and Hong Kong Chinese as wily and obsessed with money. It represented Japanese as voracious, lying, and licentious. I had my first exposure to Japanese business when I was in Beijing in 1980 and 1981. Foreign companies rented hotel rooms to serve as offices. Americans might put five or six people in one of the larger suites. The Japanese trading companies would stuff twenty people into the same space, and their lights would be on all night. They had the reputation of knowing more about China than anybody.

The Chinese complained bitterly that when the Japanese finally did build factories, they refused to share their technology. Beijing would occasionally punish Tokyo, as it did in 1995 when it left Japanese companies out of the final draw for companies that would participate in its "family car" manufacturing program. It was part of a centuries-old dialogue conducted partly in code, partly with genuine emotion. Like brothers whose competitive instincts are always at work and who keep mental scorecards that span decades, China and Japan continued to shape each other in ways that were not always obvious to outsiders.

In terms of statistics, the trend was unambiguous. The countries, so often at each others' throats politically, economically sank in and out of a profound embrace. Japan emerged as China's leading trading partner in the 1920s, eclipsing Britain, and endowed its puppet state of Manchukuo and the Taiwan colony with efficient industrial infrastructure, rail systems, and ports. These were designed to provide raw materials for the Japanese war machine, but after the war they provided the foundation for Chinese industrial growth. In 1900, 44 percent of Japanese exports went to China; by 1920, the figure had fallen to 27 percent but the value had multiplied six-fold from Yen 85 million in 1900, to Yen 524 million in 1920. By 1940, Japanese exports to

China tripled again to Yen 1.8 billion, and the Chinese and Japanese economies had reached a state of integration matched only, in a later era, by the continental economies of North America and Western Europe. In 1940, China took 74 percent of Japan's exports, and provided 22 percent of imports. At a time when the yen was worth roughly two to the dollar, Japan ran a surplus in its trade with China of Yen 1.1 billion. The China trade literally bankrolled Japan's war effort.[35]

During the Cold War, U.S. policy successfully diverted Japan's exports to the rest of Asia and the U.S. market. By 1960, at the beginning of Japan's growth spurt, China accounted for only a tiny fraction of Japanese exports, while Asia, excluding China, was Japan's leading market, absorbing 36 percent. The United States ranked second, with 30 percent. Japan never quite let go its ties with China, however, and as the U.S.-led trade embargo tightened, Japan became one of China's only sources for capital goods and equipment outside the Soviet bloc. In 1955, just three years after the end of the U.S. Occupation, a Chinese trade delegation visited Japan and reestablished ties, despite the fact that the two nations formally remained in a state of war.[36] After the Shanghai Communiqué in February 1972, the United States resumed trade with China and opened an unofficial embassy in Beijing. Japanese business took this as a cue to rush feverishly back into China. Between 1960 and 1980, Japanese exports to China grew more than 1,000-fold, from Yen one billion in 1960 to Yen one trillion in 1980.

There were, of course, some glitches along the way even with the business love-in. When China first proclaimed its *kaifang,* or "open door," economic policy in 1978, the Japanese seemed determined to lock China into its economic orbit. "China fever" swept the Japanese business community at the prospect of China turning to the West for billions upon billions of dollars worth of new factories and infrastructure. In February 1978, at the very beginning of the reforms, Beijing signed a long-term trade agreement with Tokyo that promised Japan $7–8 billion in plant contracts and $20 billion in trade by 1985. China would sell its oil and coal to Japan; Japan would supply China with technology. In the first few years of *kaifang*, Japanese firms took nearly 60 percent of all Chinese plant contracts.

Within three years, however, the 1978 agreement was in shambles. In early 1981, after meetings of the Politburo and a Central Work Conference in November and December 1980, the big projects were abruptly cancelled, including a huge steel complex at Baoshan, near Shanghai, and petrochemical factories in Nanjing, Shandong, and Beijing. Japanese firms were left holding cancellations worth $1.6 billion. The cancellations affected other nations as well—the nearest runner-up was West Germany, with cancelled contracts worth $783.2 million. The United States was left with a mere

$88.1 million in bad deals.[37] Before the year was out, Japan had revived the projects by offering $1.3 billion in government loans, but its embarrassment was intense.

According to the scholar Kokubun Ryosei, among the key players in the abrupt cancellations was Vice-Premier Chen Yun, an ideologue who took a dim view of capitalists. "We must see clearly that foreign capitalists are capitalists; they do business in order to make profits," he said, presenting his views on economic reform. Wounded, Japanese investors shunned China for a decade after the Baoshan fiasco, concentrating instead on the rich, if smaller-scale opportunities offered by Southeast Asia. In 1990, Japan-China trade was only half that of Hong Kong with Japan. Japan's direct investment in China in the same year amounted to only 1 percent of its foreign direct investment total. Shuichi Ono, a World Bank economist, commented that it was "somewhat surprising that Japan has failed to strengthen its economic relationship with China to the extent it should have over the past decade or so."

The mood began to shift in the early 1990s. Japanese companies were among the first to send their managers back to China after the Tiananmen massacre in 1989. But it was not until Emperor Akihito's trip to China, from October 23–28, 1992, that the *endaka*-inspired freeze ended and a new "China boom" began in earnest. Between 1991 and 1994, Japanese exports to China more than doubled, from $8.5 billion to $18.6 billion, while imports went from $22.8 billion to $46.2 billion. According to Chinese figures, Japanese investment increased over the same period from $812 million to $3.5 billion. Japanese statistics provide a lower estimate, with investment in China going from $579 million in 1991 to $1.1 billion in 1994; nonetheless, it was enough of a leap to make China Japan's leading investment target in Asia.

By 1996, Japan had become China's leading trading partner, and was running a trade deficit of $18.5 billion with its neighbor. The only other Asian countries that had a trade surplus with Japan were oil exporters Indonesia and Brunei. Japan imported $40.4 billion in goods from China in 1996, mostly textiles and industrial components, and exported $21.8 billion, mostly capital goods and high-technology components.[38] According to Chinese statistics, in 1996 Japan accounted for the largest share of Chinese imports, at 21 percent, compared to 11.6 percent for the United States.[39] Four years later, in 2000, total trade with China topped $80 billion, and Japan's trade deficit had risen to $23 billion. Two-way trade was growing at rates over 20 percent. China had also emerged as the leading target for Japanese investment in Asia. Cumulative Japanese investment in China and Hong Kong through 1996 came to $32.2 billion; China's closest Asian rival was Indonesia, with $20 billion.[40] Although Japanese investment in China had slowed substantially in the aftermath of the Asian financial crisis by the end of 1999 the official figure was $37 billion; cumulative Japanese official aid amounted to $26.3 billion.[41]

This tightening web of trade and investment had its own momentum, reducing options for open conflict and enhancing the stability of the region. China's *kaifang* policy of economic reforms in 1978 led to a decade of extraordinary growth. In 1979, restoration of diplomatic relations with the United States ended three decades of political isolation. Yet as China's economic and political horizons widened, Beijing also sought to resume its traditional role as the preeminent power in Asia. While the United States began to envision a "coming war" with China, Japan wondered which side it would be on. Okazaki, the diplomat, argued that China would not be satisfied until it regained all the territory lost by the Qing Dynasty, which collapsed in 1911. "What does China want?" Okazaki asked rhetorically. "In one word, China wants to reassert its national prestige. China has had a history of overwhelming humiliation in the last century. It was a celestial empire, worshipped by all its neighbors. But once it was invaded, its people were treated like animals. Its desire to regain its national prestige takes many forms, but at the moment China wants to regain the territory of the former Qing Empire, especially Taiwan."[42] Okazaki's own fascination with China was highly personal; he was born in Dalian and lived there as a child.

From the perspective of the United States, China's rise and Japan's decline seemed like complementary trends defining a future in which China would become the preeminent Asian power after a period of time. For Japan, the picture was more complex. Far more than Americans, the Japanese could envision multiple scenarios for Asia's future. Clearly, one scenario was for the restoration of Chinese supremacy. In 1800, China was the richest and most productive country in the world, accounting for one-third of global manufacturing.[43] In the 1990s, as growth moved to double-digit levels, China could dream of resuming its status as the world's largest economy, surpassing the United States and Japan. Chinese growth averaged 10.2 percent between 1985 and 1994, comparable to Japan's performance during its "miracle" years, the "Izanagi Boom" from 1965 to 1970, when its economy grew by more than 12 percent per year.[44]

Unlike Japan, China faced few constraints in its external policy. It had one of the world's largest standing armies, however dilapidated its equipment might be, and a daring style of diplomacy that was long on bluff and short on tact and finesse. In foreign affairs, the Chinese were like tigers to Japan's mice; the communist leadership had almost made a fetish of brandishing China's big power status despite its distinctly Third World assets. Its membership as one of the Permanent Five of the United Nations Security Council was a club that it freely used to block U.S. initiatives on human rights, Middle East policy, and other matters. The Japanese, who desperately wanted and felt they deserved a seat on the P5, by virtue of their role in UN funding, could only gnash their teeth.

The Japanese could easily envision a future in which competition between China and Japan became the defining political relationship of Asia in the twenty-first century. They were fairly sure that they would be the losers. In the late 1980s and early 1990s, Beijing had put together a vigorous new Asian diplomacy, partly in reaction to its perception that Japan was doing the same. From Beijing's perspective, Japan had clearly set out to knit a web of alliances to contain China, using ASEAN as a platform. Given the legacy of Japanese militarism and its protectorate status with the United States, Japan was constrained from moving aggressively on its own, but with its vastly superior economic power, it could use Asian multilateralism as a proxy for its interests. Beijing also kept close watch as Japan began regular summit meetings with South Korea, elevated ties with Taiwan, set up regional gatherings on security matters, and established an annual round of meetings with ASEAN economic ministers. MITI heralded the creation of the latter in 1992 as an "epoch-making event"; it was at least a step in the direction of organizing an Asian economic union under Japanese direction.

Japan's networking moved into the sub-official level as well. In November 1993, the Japanese Foreign Ministry launched a program of cultural exchange visits with Asian nations. In 1994, a Defense Agency think tank, the National Institute for Defense Studies, inaugurated meetings of military officials from the region. At the same time, Japan inaugurated an aggressive new China policy, sending Emperor Akihito to China and putting pressure on Beijing to soothe regional fears by providing more information on its military buildup.[45]

China's regional diplomacy, in contrast, had been squarely based on bilateral ties, using its vast market as leverage in much the same style as U.S. policy. By the late 1980s, Beijing had already begun its own initiatives in Southeast Asia and South Korea. In the late 1980s and early 1990s, Beijing began military cooperation with Thailand, established a high-level political dialogue with Singapore despite the absence of formal diplomatic ties, and participated in the Cambodian peace settlement despite lingering ill feelings toward both France and Indonesia. After establishing diplomatic relations with Malaysia, China improved ties with Thailand and the Philippines.

The Chinese diplomatic onslaught of the late 1980s made an immediate impact in encouraging a stronger and less fragmented ASEAN, which ultimately was able to incorporate the communist transitional states that had kept Southeast Asia on edge for a quarter century. Beijing played a key role in Vietnam's withdrawal of troops from Cambodia in 1989 by distancing itself from the Khmer Rouge, opening the way for the Paris talks that led to the Cambodian peace settlement in 1991. In 1990, Beijing restored diplomatic relations with Jakarta, which had been frozen since the anti-Communist massacres of 1965. In 1991, it renewed ties with Brunei and Singapore. In July 1991, China attended the ASEAN conference of foreign ministers for the first time. In November, it pushed its way into APEC, at the third APEC ministerial meeting in Seoul. With the collapse of the Soviet Union that year, Vietnam became isolated and China re-entered Southeast Asia as a key player.[46]

In 1992, a series of visits by Chinese leaders to Singapore, Malaysia, Indonesia, and Vietnam heralded a warming of ties throughout the region; the Southeast Asians went along despite the ominous declaration by the Fourteenth Communist Party Congress in October that China would defend its rights on "the high seas," implying that it might apply its own version of gunboat diplomacy in the Spratly Islands. In April, border crossings between Vietnam and China were reopened for the first time in thirteen years, preceding Chinese premier Li Peng's visit to Vietnam in November. In August, China restored full diplomatic relations with South Korea, triggering a wave of South Korean investment and dramatically altering the strategic balance with Japan.[47] In the mid-1990s, China further expanded its ties with ASEAN, joining the PMC and ARF meetings, and working to dispel fears that it would use military force to take the Spratly Islands as it had seized the Paracels from Vietnam in 1975. China had been a major critic of ASEAN when it was established in 1967. By the late 1990s, it had become an enthusiastic cheerleader, and when ASEAN celebrated its thirtieth anniversary in 1997, the *People's Daily* dedicated a whole page to the celebration.[48]

Cementing the new diplomacy, in November 1994, President Jiang Zemin made a triumphal visit to Singapore, Malaysia, Indonesia, and Vietnam. A welcome mat for Asian investors accompanied the diplomatic offensive. By 1996, Singapore was the fifth largest source of foreign direct investment in China after Japan, the United States, Taiwan, and the European Union. Korea was sixth. About one-fifth of ASEAN investment in East Asia went to China in the mid-1990s. Hong Kong and Taiwan, which together in 1996 accounted for $31.2 billion of Chinese FDI, also served as conduits for investment from ethnic Chinese businesses in Southeast Asia.[49] By the mid-1990s, the prominent Japanese economist Nakatani Iwao could describe the Chinese economy as "more open" than Japan. "If and when a big economic power that could take the place of Japan comes into being in Asia, and if its market is more open than the Japanese market and its future market scale is inexhaustible," Nakatani wrote, "China will bypass Japan."[50]

China actively played on anti-Japanese sentiments lingering throughout

Asia. In December 1994, South Korea was quietly seething after the United States worked out a nuclear accord with North Korea that left Seoul largely outside the decision-making process. China chose the moment to stage its first summit meeting with South Korea. Together with forty-seven Chinese industrialists, Premier Li Peng arrived in the South Korean capital, visiting factories, admiring Korean technology, and proposing a grand industrial partnership between the two countries. Li also reassured the Koreans that Beijing would keep up pressure on the North to scrap its nuclear processing plants—a gesture that helped to restore wounded Korean sensibilities. Washington had been unsuccessful in its attempt to wring such a pledge from Beijing.

In a subtle but pointed slap that was particularly upsetting to Tokyo, Premier Li simultaneously dropped a plum in South Korean president Kim Young Sam's lap—an agreement for direct flights between Seoul and Beijing. The Japanese fumed over the agreement, which gave the Koreans a route to Beijing over the Yellow Sea that was shorter than the longer paths that Japanese airlines took. The *Asahi* newspaper called the Korean summit "a moment of historic consequence for the international politics of East Asia." By this it meant that China had started to give Japan real trouble.

At a conference in Singapore in 1996, a top French government expert on China, Nicolas Chapuis, deputy director for East Asia in the French Foreign Ministry, outlined the terms of the game. "For China, Japan is the enemy in the long-term perspective," he said. "The United States presence in Asia is acceptable as keeping the reins on Japan. China puts itself on the same level as the United States and puts Japan a little lower. Japan is a tributary state in terms of culture. The United States is the real equal and can help tame the little fishermen. Beijing and Tokyo will never be reconciled in my lifetime."[51] Chapuis argued that Beijing's belligerent behavior in the South China Sea in the late 1980s and early 1990s was a direct response to its perception of growing Japanese control in Southeast Asia. China aimed at the resumption of its imperial role as "paterfamilias" of the Asian family, he said. It wanted obedience from Southeast Asian states, and containment of U.S. and Japanese influence. Chinese pressure would inevitably break the security triangle of Japan, the United States, and ASEAN as China "came of age."[52]

A 1994 incident illustrated his point. When Japanese prime minister Hosokawa Morihiro visited Beijing in March 1994, hoping to make an impression as a new type of Japanese statesman, he earnestly raised the subject of human rights in a meeting with Chinese president Jiang Zemin and Premier Li Peng. In a press briefing after the meeting, Japanese officials said that Hosokawa had described human rights as a "universal value" and urged the Chinese leaders to be more scrupulous about protecting them. Chinese

Foreign Ministry officials did not hesitate to supply a different version of the conversation, to Hosokawa's embarrassment. They told the press that Hosokawa had agreed with China that it was unwise for any country to impose its values on another.

The version that stuck was the Chinese one. Washington responded angrily. At the time of Hosokawa's visit, U.S. president William J. Clinton was threatening to withdraw China's most-favored-nation status unless it improved its human rights record. China's account of what Hosokawa had said was a setback for Clinton and a gain for China. The American business community argued that Japan's soft approach on human rights was aimed at getting a better position in the China market. Pressure from the business lobby helped to force Clinton off his attempt to couple trade and human rights, and by 1996, he was actually fighting the congressional proponents of such linkage. Hosokawa's mangled statement had been only one of many dominoes to fall, but it showed how vulnerable the U.S.-Japan relationship was to Beijing's manipulation.

There was a third scenario as well, based on an economic partnership and a common approach to economic management, lying in the gray area between the market economy and central planning. In this role, China played off Japanese egotism by suggesting it would return to the century-old motif of modeling itself after Japan. This was the theme of the first visit to Japan by China's economic czar, Vice-Premier Zhu Rongji, in February to March 1994. The nine-day trip was an unashamed exercise in public relations of a type that would have been impossible to imagine a decade earlier. Zhu threw out the first baseball at a Daiei Hawks game in Fukuoka, visited Osaka in western Japan, hobnobbed with auto and electronics company executives, made the usual rounds in Tokyo, and blithely predicted that bilateral trade would soar by 1,000 percent by the end of the decade.[53] Most beguiling of all, Zhu dangled the prospect to his hosts that China might shun Western models of economic reform in favor of Japan's. China wished to adapt Japan's gradual approach to liberalizing equity markets as well as its *keiretsu* system of business conglomerates, Zhu said, and he lived up to his word.

With Zhu's blessing, later that year China created a state development bank, an agricultural bank, and an export-import bank based on Japanese models.[54] In October 1992, Jiang Zemin, then general secretary of the Chinese Communist Party, had called for a "new revolution" to launch a market economy. Japanese observers instantly noticed the resemblance of his proposals to Japan's system. "The idea is for the central government to oversee the economy through macro-economic measures but to give corporations the responsibility to run their own operations. That concept resembles Japan's economic management style and is at least partly a result of China's close examination of the Japanese system," the *Nikkei Weekly* commented.[55]

The same article reported that China was planning to revamp its State Planning Commission and Economic and Trade Ministry to more closely resemble Japan's EPA and MITI. "Basically, we are aiming at a free economy but we are also interested in ways to control corporations through administrative guidance when necessary," an unnamed translator told the Japanese newspaper. (He was the same man who had translated the official history of MITI into Chinese.) In fact, the thread went back to the very beginnings of the Chinese *kaifang* policy, in 1978. That year, Deng Xiaoping had lectured that "from the Meiji Restoration on, Japan established its power by emphasizing science and technology and by emphasizing education. Even though we are the proletariat, and the Meiji Restoration was conducted by the bourgeoisie, still we must go one step beyond them in our achievements."[56]

Kong Fanjing, an economist with China's State Planning Commission, argued that China and Japan shared a common economic model in a 1983 book, *Japan's Strategy of Economic Development*.[57] China could learn from Japan's export-led growth strategies because they shared certain basics. First, Kong argued, both governments gave economic development priority in both external and domestic affairs. Secondly, both countries engaged in planning, shifting their targets in accordance with the stage of economic development. Third, Beijing and Tokyo alike believed in the virtue of keeping consumption in check in order to promote the level of savings necessary to develop heavy industry. Fourth, they realized that they could achieve faster results by importing technology than by trying to re-invent the Industrial Revolution on their own. Finally, Kong admired the way that Japan had adapted American management techniques to its own domestic conditions, and its focus on education.[58]

In 1982 and again in 1988, Beijing modeled two major economic programs directly after the Japanese experience. In 1982, China launched an income-quadrupling campaign mimicking the Japanese income-doubling program of the 1960s. In 1988, it launched a program for rapid development of China's coastal zones based on another Japanese precedent. In the 1990s, as China slowly began the process of privatizing its state enterprises, it studied the Japanese *keiretsu* and Korean *chaebol* as possible models for mixed government and private enterprise, and crafted industrial policies, notably for the auto and electronics industries, with Japan in mind. It also began to shape its domestic banking system in the Japanese image in an effort to foster a system of channeling domestic savings toward strategic industries, in the Japanese and Korean manner.

China paid particular attention to Japan's MITI, reshaping some of its own institutions in the Japanese image. The Office of Trade and Economics, headed by Vice-Premier Zhu Rongji, was closely modeled after MITI, and Beijing had Japan's Economic Planning Agency in mind when it expanded powers of the State Planning Commission in the early 1980s. Japan's EPA, although much diminished in stature by the late 1990s, had been the lead agency for the income-doubling plan in the 1960s.[59] In March 1994, the Chinese State Council approved the *Outline for Industrial Policy in the 1990s*, with distinct echoes of Japanese industrial targeting. The plan set priority sectors, designated as "pillar industries": electronics, machinery, petrochemicals, automobiles, and construction.[60]

The Asia crisis provoked some backpedaling on China's part; Chinese intellectuals began to point out the flaws of the Japanese model, often in the context of Beijing's more eclectic approach. Shen Caibin, a Chinese economist associated with the Nomura Research Institute in Tokyo, echoed such Japanese economists as Nakatani Iwao in arguing that the Japanese model was fine as long as Japan was catching up with the West but was ill-adapted for an economic superpower. "As long as Japan was in the era of catching up [with the West] it was undoubtedly an excellent student. But once Japan achieved its goal, it had no model to follow, and both its economy and political system drifted aimlessly," Shen wrote.[61]

This did not stop the Chinese from continuing to hammer away at projects to transform state owned enterprises into flagship multinationals; one major difference from the classic Japanese industrial policy, however, was China's enthusiasm for capital markets. The mid- to late 1990s saw a series of huge public listings of Chinese multinationals that raised billions of dollars, despite murky accounting and majority government control of virtually all such entities.

Within the Japanese business community, Kobayashi Yotaro, chief executive of Fuji-Xerox, took up the theme of economic partnership. Few Japanese, however, believed that a genuine partnership with China was possible, not out of any objective analysis of Chinese strengths and weaknesses but because of profound intimidation.

In the course of the 1990s, a sensibility emerged in Japan that can only be described as China phobia. In 1994, it was big news in Japan when the World Bank estimated that the Chinese economy was already 20 percent larger than the Japanese economy, using a method of estimating prices called purchasing power parity (PPP).[62] The method linked the nominal value of currencies to what money would actually buy, in the manner of *The Economist*'s Big Mac index, which is based on PPP modeling. By 1995, according to PPP measures, the Chinese economy was 25 percent larger than Japan's, at $3.5 trillion compared to $2.8 trillion for Japan (the corresponding figures in nominal terms were $697 billion and $5.1 trillion). Although Japanese per capita income remained ten times Chinese per capita income even using the PPP approach, Japanese confidence sagged as the country's economic woes deepened. An *Asahi* newspaper poll in August 1994 asked the Japanese which nation they felt would have the greatest influence on Asia in the twenty-first century: 44 percent said China; 30 percent said the United States. Only 16 percent said Japan.[63]

After the Asian Games in Hiroshima in 1994, when Chinese athletes competed in Japan for the first time, one Japanese reporter was so overcome with China's athletic successes that he read into them a metaphor for its ascent to superpower status. "What is significant was the opportunity the games presented for the Japanese to witness the real strength of the Chinese athletes firsthand—a strength that before they knew of only indirectly. Many were overwhelmed by the power of the Chinese. Beyond such immediate feelings, we perceived China's depth and diversity, and experienced a sense of awe, feeling that it may be impossible to predict what extraordinary things may come out of China next. I consider the Hiroshima Asian Games to have been significant because during them the Japanese had to face this question: What is Japan's position in Asia in the context of this new awe of China?"[64]

According to the writer, Asami Tamotsu, "a considerable number of Japanese" thought, "it is only natural for Japan to lose to China, as China is so powerful. This is essentially giving up, yet it is a quite common response. China's vastness, its long history, and its cultural depth are well known. There is also the Chinese people's legendary fearlessness and stubbornness in achieving goals. This is represented, at least in Japanese eyes, by Beijing's tenacious opposition to Taiwan president Lee Teng-hui's attendance at the (Asian) games and its total disregard of what the reaction might be. All things considered, it is only a matter of time before China overtakes Japan in every field."

"There is no possibility for Japan to provide the kind of leadership in Asia that the United States can provide," argued Keio University's Soeya Yoshihide. Added Yoshibumi Wakamiya, an editorial writer for *Asahi*, "Japan's history suggests that it will not easily become a political leader in Asia. It is not just a matter of the wartime invasions; the Asian outlook in Japanese politics is still confused."

Meanwhile, as Japanese self-esteem sagged, one prominent economist urged Japan to consider following the Chinese model. "Japan is a socialist country, in substance if not in name. China is the other way around," said Kwan Chi Hung, a longtime resident of Japan who headed Nomura Research Institute's Asian research unit. Kwan argued that China achieved a more deep-seated revolution in its economy than Japan through a strategy of gradual reform. "Japan is altogether too backwards," Kwan said. "It spends most of its energy protecting vested interests, while China respects its vested interests, but does not protect them."[65]

The growing national inferiority complex seemed partly responsible for the timidity of Japan's responses to China in the 1990s. For example, Japan was sharply critical of renewed French nuclear testing in contravention of international bans. But in the summer of 1995, when China conducted nuclear tests just days after it had joined 169 other countries in voting to indefinitely extend the global Nuclear Non-Proliferation Treaty, Japan merely suspended its grant aid. Grant aid was minuscule compared to the much larger yen loan program, amounting in 1994 to just Yen 7.8 billion (about $78 million) compared to Yen 140.3 billion, or $1.4 billion, in yen loans. The effect, of course, was a wrist slap.

During 1995, Taiwan lobbied hard to send its President Lee Teng-hui to the APEC leaders' summit in Osaka, Japan, an act that would have offended China. Japan made it clear that it would not allow a visit by Lee under any circumstances. "It would undermine the foundation of Japan-China relations," a Japanese Foreign Ministry official said unambiguously. Yet, when Prime Minister Murayama visited China in May 1995, such instances of Japanese tact did not stop Beijing from using the occasion to embarrass Tokyo by joining the chorus of demands to compensate Japan's wartime sex slaves. China ran its own program during 1995, the fiftieth anniversary year of Japan's defeat to remind its citizens of Japanese perfidy.

Japan ended the twentieth century much as it had begun, obsessed with China. Unlike the 1890s, however, Tokyo had no distinct strategy; it harbored a sense of vulnerability despite overwhelming superiority in terms of teeth, claws, and economic bulk. The fear was irrational, but stretched from the grass roots to the elite, trapping Japan in its own psyche and hobbling it from pursuing the obvious strategy of playing Beijing and Washington against one other. This would have required boldness and clarity, and a willingness to accept a high risk of failure, all of which Japan lacked in the 1990s. Instead, Tokyo held tight to the façade of the diplomatic paradigm of the Cold War, in which the U.S.-Japan security alliance was all that Japan needed to protect itself against the future.

With its beautiful garden laid across a hillside in one of Tokyo's most fashionable districts, the International House of Japan is a natural magnet for foreign scholars unable or unwilling to pay the high rates in Tokyo hotels, policy advisors brushing up their contacts, and for Japanese intellectuals seeking a Western academic ambiance. The little coffee shop bristles with Ph.D.s, and conversations are rich with inside-the-Beltway Washington gossip. Outside in the garden, family groups, foreign and Japanese, help their children feed the carp and explore the pathways. Most days a Japanese wedding is in progress, making use of the stone lanterns and waterfall as a backdrop for photographs.

In addition to serving as an academic hostel, the I-House also provides shelter for various *benkyokai,* or study groups, that ubiquitous feature of

Japanese intellectual life, serving as part of the process of national consensus building as well as providing social relief for teetotalers. The East-West *benkyokai* met once every few weeks. The membership was mostly Japanese, the sort of international businessmen or junior scholars who felt the need to keep up their English. The English-only rule seemed to unleash a talkative streak among the normally reticent Japanese. This week the subject was Japan and Asia. The group seethed with anxiety and frustration.

Shibuya Tadashi, a former trading company executive, leads the conversation. There are eight in the group, and at least one is an executive with experience in Asia. Shibuya worked in China for many years with Nichimen, a trading company. "What is Asia?" Shibuya asks rhetorically, then answers his own question:

> Asia is one-third of the world's landmass, and half of the world's population. There are six subregions in Asia, and twenty-three languages across the region. The feeling about Japan varies from nation to nation. Malaysian prime minister Mahathir asks why does Japan keep on apologizing? Singapore's president supported Japan to join the United Nations Security Council, in order to balance power among Asian countries. But Prime Minister Murayama failed to give Mahathir a clear response on his proposal for Japan to lead an East Asian Economic Caucus, which would include Japan but exclude the United States. Japan's problem is how to balance between the United States and Asia. Japan, as a nation at the edge of Asia may be driven into isolation in the international community once again.
>
> China is booming economically but has problems. It has double-digit inflation, there is a widening gap between the rich and the poor, and government offices are filled with corrupt officials. They lack technocrats. Even so, Asians are looking for ways to co-exist with the Greater China Economic Zone, because of its massive capability to absorb exports and its military strength. Japan has no unified approach to China. It has lagged behind in advancing into China. Now Japanese manufacturers are rushing into China, attracted by the huge market. The number of Japanese manufacturers there has increased in geometric progression. We're afraid Japan will drop very far behind the United States and China, in economic as well as political power. We're already very far behind politically, but we might fall behind economically as well.
>
> South Korea still takes a very severe attitude toward Japan. Even now, there is an official ban on singing Japanese songs. Korean students are educated about the cruelty of the Japanese military during the war. According to the newspapers, there is a movement in Korea to stop pro-Japanese Koreans. Koreans are the most similar to Japanese in personality among Asians. All they want to do is catch up with Japan.[66]

The Japanese government, Shibuya noted, was seeking to expand its role in Asia. Visits to Asia by Japanese prime ministers had been rare; now they were at least annual events. Japan was seeking a place among the Permanent Five members of the United Nations Security Council, and was engaged in UN peacekeeping. Japan had claimed to represent Asia at the annual meetings of the G7 industrial nations. At least one Asian leader, Malaysian prime minister Mahathir, had asked Japan to formally lead a new economic grouping, the East Asian Economic Group or Caucus. Was Japan ready?

The group is tentative at first, then increasingly scornful. The first comment is a question. "Asian students in Japan mostly become anti-Japanese after they have lived here. Is that true?" Takeuchi Tetsuo, a high school teacher, asks. "Yes," answers Shibuya. "Japanese have the bad habit or custom of mistreating them. The students have difficulty finding lodging, and have to look hard for someone to provide guarantees for them. Japanese families offering homestays will reject them even if they speak English, because they are not white. The Japanese mentality is to focus only on Americans and Europeans, so they don't think about Asians or consider their circumstances."

One of the younger members of the *benkyokai*, resentful of the way the conversation is drifting toward criticism of Japan, bursts out, "Maybe the reason that Asians won't let Japan forget the past is because they think they can get more compensation from Japan that way." Kawamura, a retired executive who has lived in India and Malaysia, looks at him thoughtfully. "I visited a small Malaysian village once, a *kampong*, and found an old man, a gardener who spoke Japanese and could sing Japanese military songs. He asked me, Did you bring your Japanese flag, the *Hinomaru*? When he was young he was told that the flag was the most important thing in the world to Japanese. This is the way Asians look at us. They would say to me, I will do business with you, but you must understand that the Japanese killed my father and raped my mother. If they are Chinese, they will tell you how the Japanese killed people unnecessarily *after* the surrender."

Mahathir has just told Prime Minister Murayama that apologies will be unnecessary when he visits Malaysia. The younger man wonders whether others in Asia share his willingness to move on and forget the past. "Is Mahathir isolated?" he asks. "Unless you have this kind of future-oriented idea, how can things develop?" Kawamura replies, "Mahathir is a smart, strong, cunning politician, the most important politician in Southeast Asia, telling Americans to go and Japan to come in. But his statement has two meanings. One is that he doesn't believe in lip service. He's tired of Japanese politicians coming to him with meaningless apologies. Second, he's trying to carve out a niche against the power of China and the United States. He gives good lip service to China but knows that if China comes in as a big power, ASEAN will be isolated." The overtures to Japan are designed to keep China off-balance, not to draw Japan closer, he says.

"Before Murayama's visit to Southeast Asia, a Japanese political critic went around asking Asian leaders about the visit," Kawamura says. "They told him Japan is great, but we can see China's face, and we can't see Japan's. Japanese politicians want Japan to be a great power, to join the UN Security Council. But Japan is too indecisive for that. We don't know which way to go. We may blame Murayama now. But all those prime ministers in the past never showed their true colors either. Japan is stuck in between America and Asian countries. It wants to be able to watch what's going on without participating, and to look elsewhere if anybody wants our help. So no country respects us. If we really want to be on the UN Security Council, the system will have to be changed [to increase the number of seats of the Permanent Council from five to six]. We have to change the system, but no one knows if Japan really wants the slot or not. We are waiting for others to support us, and that's ridiculous."

Saito Katsuyo, a researcher, contends: "If the government doesn't define its policy vis-à-vis the United States and Asia, Japan will be the orphan of Asia, without friends. Japan's ties with the United States are for the sake of security, but Japan should make a more concrete, deeper policy—how we go with Asia, whether we are even an Asian country. This concept is absent. Shibuya adds, "I always wonder whether young people think that they are real Asians. In order to think of ourselves as Asians, we need to break out of our old conceptions. We may be, technically, part of Asia, but we don't really think we are. Western countries may think that Japan has an Oriental face, but not Asians. They think that our face is always to Europe or the United States."

The thoughts are confused, the emotions incoherent, but the answer to Shibuya's question is clear. Far from wishing to compete with China, most Japanese quailed at the thought. Within Asia, they felt vulnerable and isolated. China could reach down to the bedrock of Chinese nationalism to draw public support for its bold and inventive diplomacy. Japanese leaders might reach down, but they would be grasping at air. Japan might think it was ready to lead Asia, but the Japanese were not. Something more must change. The paradigm must be broken.

History Lessons

What Japan saw looking at China was a tiger lusting for vengeance, no longer constrained by the geopolitics of the Cold War. Japan, in contrast, had drifted in the U.S. embrace, accepting Washington's friends and sharing its enemies.

Asia seemed far away, so much so that Japanese remembered themselves in the war as victims rather than aggressors, an illusion promoted first by the Occupation regime in the 1940s. History had been allowed to lapse, in the minds of the Japanese. As the Cold War ended, Japan found itself newly vulnerable on all fronts. One of these was the neglected battleground of history.

In the early 1990s, Japan used the most powerful symbolism at its disposal to underline the new trajectory of its relationships, by sending its new emperor on twin trips to China and Southeast Asia. This was something Akihito's father had never been able to do, although he managed two visits to Europe—one as a twenty-year-old prince and later in his seventies—and one to the United States. But Asia, with its searing memories of World War Two, was deemed unsafe for Hirohito, no matter how carefully crafted his post-war image was as a kindly, peace-loving marine biologist. Sending the newly enthroned Akihito abroad tested the dimensions of Japan's role within Asia as lead investor and creditor and exploring possible new roles as an intermediary between Asia and the United States, or even replacing the United States as guarantor of regional security. These were bold experiments. But the real significance of the visits, immediately comprehensible to all Asians, was that Japan had dared to revisit a past in which it played the role of aggressor, not victim. This was a necessary act of closure to Japan's role as U.S. protectorate, but just as Japan failed to decisively shed that role in the 1990s, its attempts to come to grips with history were equally tentative and disappointing.

Akihito's first trip abroad as emperor was to Thailand, Malaysia, and Indonesia in late September and early October 1991. It was a carefully orchestrated love fest and culminated a decade in which Japan, as the world's second largest economy, had ignited Southeast Asia's explosive growth by its investment and example. Just as the emperor and Empress Michiko left on their trip on September 26, Japan's longest post-war expansion, the "Heisei Boom" entered its fifty-eighth month and became official.[67] Japanese diplomats wrung commitments from each of the three countries on the itinerary not to raise such painful subjects as Japan's wartime atrocities or complaints by citizens' groups that Japan's war reparations were inadequate.[68]

The visit was serene. The *Jakarta Post* remarked suavely that Japan was Indonesia's largest source of foreign aid and investment, and, following a twenty-one gun salute to his visitors, President Suharto tiptoed around the subject of history, saying cagily that remembering the past could "make people somewhat emotional" but that the lessons of history should provide "strength to develop the future with a new spirit and with new objectives."[69] In Malaysia, Sultan Azlan Shah told the emperor he hoped that Tokyo would "recognize its natural leadership role in the region."[70] In Thailand, Prime Minister

Anand Panyarachun told Akihito that it was time for Japan to move beyond the economic sphere to take the role of regional policeman. Akihito himself raised the subject at a state dinner in Thailand. It was the mildest of references, using an expression that was the late Emperor Hirohito's standard reference to the events of the war: "unfortunate." Akihito told his host, King Bhumibol Adulyadej, that Japan hoped never to repeat the horrors of "that most unfortunate war."[71] It seemed, however, to be enough for Southeast Asia, then reveling in a flood tide of Japanese aid and investment, in the midst of an unparalleled economic boom.

Thirteen months later, in October 1992, Akihito visited China. This was a far more complicated dance. Unlike Southeast Asia, China gave no points for building factories or opening department stores, although a flood of Japanese investment followed the visit, and China quickly replaced Indonesia as the leading target of Japanese aid. The Chinese had much broader aims. While continuing to apply pressure on Japan to supply moral restitution, they also put a lid on emotional protests by individuals during the visit. Police were stationed every thirty yards along the route followed by Akihito's sixty-seven-car motorcade.[72] Bao Ge, a researcher at Shanghai Medical School, threatened to immolate himself to protest the visit, and was placed under house arrest until the Japanese delegation returned home.[73] Beijing University warned its students to stay off the streets, and authorities reportedly refused to allow the publication of a poll that showed 95 percent of Chinese wanted an apology from Akihito.[74]

For his part, Akihito took a step beyond the bland pronouncements of his Southeast Asian trip, acknowledging at a banquet in his honor that Japan had "inflicted severe suffering upon the Chinese people" and that he felt "deep sorrow" for it.[75] Conservative Japanese politicians had bitterly opposed the trip ostensibly to celebrate the twentieth anniversary of the normalization of Sino-Japanese relations, on grounds that it might lead to just such an embarrassing admission of guilt, and at several points the Japanese seemed ready to cancel.

However much the trip may have raked popular sensibilities in both China and Japan, the two governments approached it with the deliberateness of the opening moves of a deeply serious chess game. In 1990, the United States announced a new "East Asia Strategy Initiative" to reduce forces in the Asia-Pacific as Cold War tensions eased. The policy, which was not implemented, would have blown up the geopolitical framework under which Japan had operated since the end of World War Two. For Beijing, it looked like an opportunity to drive a wedge between the United States and Japan; Japan had little choice but to play along, while internal fights raged within the bureaucracy about what to do.

This was the geopolitical environment as Japan re-opened questions of history that had remained under wraps for a generation. Japanese officials hoped that the process would be smooth and that their old adversaries would be satisfied with gestures. So, for the most part, the Malaysians, Singaporeans, Thais, and Taiwanese were indeed satisfied. The Koreans and Chinese could operate from positions of greater strength than the Southeast Asians, and were more difficult to please. Yet all sides recognized that the series of vague pronouncements from the Japanese served to symbolize a new set of political offerings on the table.

Far less predictable than the kabuki drama of Japanese formal policy was the popular response to the apologies. In China and the rest of Asia, most of the old prejudices prevailed at street level, some waning with the passage of time. In Japan it was a different story, both much better and much worse.

On the positive side of the ledger, the 1990s precipitated national soul searching that entered the mainstream and began to foster a genuine change of sentiment toward the pain suffered by the rest of Asia as a result of Japanese military aggression. Aging soldiers sat before the cameras with horrific confessionals, perhaps feeling that their time was short to make amends. While the Japanese government may have played a subtle role in making such activity acceptable by virtue of the round of official apologies, most of the public activity, in the form of investigations by citizens' groups, seemed to be spontaneous, mainstream, and non-ideological.

Less attractive was the way in which this ferment was constantly undercut by a government determined to set the pace and tone of the confrontation with history. Failing to recognize the opportunity presented by the citizens' movements, Tokyo either tried to block them or let them peter out through a process of attrition. In either case, a gap appeared between a Japanese public eager to connect with Japan's past in new ways, and a bureaucracy more comfortable with the symbolism than the substance of its efforts to address history.

In 1991 and 1995, two anniversaries provided a focus for popular contemplation of the past—the fiftieth anniversary of the Pearl Harbor attack on December 7, 1941, and, four years later, the anniversary of Japan's surrender on August 15, 1945. The two anniversaries were far different in terms of the events that they commemorated—the audacious Japanese attacks on Hawaii and Southeast Asia in 1941, the stunning defeat in August 1945. The Japan that remembered was also in starkly different moods. Despite the collapse of the bubble economy in 1990, for the next few years Japan remained in the throes of hubris, and the anniversary of the Pearl Harbor attack was observed with a smugness that would be absent four years later.

In December 1991, the Japanese magazine *Sapio* could illustrate a cover essay by Eto Jun on "The Japanese 50 Years after Pearl Harbor" with a montage of a Mitsubishi Zero aircraft bombing the White House.[76] Japanese networks rambunctiously delegated reporters to cover the Pearl Harbor ceremonies underwater, taking their cameras down with scuba diving gear. The tone was set, perhaps, by a tightlipped fighter pilot interviewed on an NHK program who recalled his state of mind as he guided his plane toward the target on December 7, 1941. "I had no feelings at all," he said.[77]

The fiftieth anniversary of Japan's defeat came as the political cycle returned from reform to reaction, and Japan's 1995 "official apology" for the war dissolved into a pathetic tussle between the first elected Socialist Prime Minister Murayama Tomiichi, who faithfully represented the old Japan Socialist Party's critique of Japan's war crimes, and his LDP backers.

After a long and embarrassing public battle, Murayama's coalition government finally dropped plans to deliver a strongly worded apology for Japanese wartime aggression; Murayama modified initial, bolder language so that a reference to "mistaken national policy" was left vague and ambiguous. Under pressure from conservatives within the coalition, Murayama also dropped references to specific countries that Japan invaded, such as China and South Korea, and to the *ianfu*, or "comfort women," the estimated 200,000 women who were forcibly drafted as prostitutes for the Japanese Imperial Army. The final statement, released on August 15, 1995, had a certain dreamlike quality. "During a certain period in the not too distant past, Japan, following a mistaken national policy, advanced along the road to war, only to ensnare the Japanese people in a fateful crisis, and, through its colonial rule and aggression, caused tremendous damage and suffering to the people of many countries, particularly to those of Asian nations."[78]

Nonetheless, truth telling was at its height in the years between 1991 and 1995, while the diplomatic push toward reconciliation with Asia was also at its height. The prospect of a new partnership between Japan and Asia coincided with a breakdown in the political monopoly of the LDP, which defanged its more ardent nationalists, often referred to as the LDP "right" wing. The right wing of the LDP represented continuity with Japan's wartime leadership, anticommunism, and economic expansion in Asia, and it had actively suppressed efforts by Japanese academics and others to hold Japan accountable for its war crimes.

The right wing could trace its ideological roots back to the activist Kwantung Army faction in Manchuria in the 1930s, which, once it had established control of northeast China, focused its attention on the border threat to the north and was defeated by Soviet troops in August 1945. To refer to such views as right-wing missed the point—similar attitudes were diffused through the LDP's core membership, exerting broad influence. They were also tolerated, if not actively supported, by Japan's Cold War ally, the United

States. As George Hicks pointed out in the introduction to his book on Japan's post-war policy on war crimes, this was a joint effort. It was more than fifty years after the war before the United States put sixteen Japanese war veterans on its immigration watch list for war criminals, on December 3, 1996. By that time, the list was up to 60,000 Germans and others.[79]

The LDP traditionally linked the denial of war guilt with its Cold War bargain with the United States. Paradoxically, admitting guilt threatened Japan's post-war myth of a free-market democracy and the reality of its close ties with the United States. The ten-month interregnum of reform politics, from August 1993 to June 1994, with its bizarre aftermath of a Socialist-LDP coalition government, also marked the high point of experiments with the politics of history. Reform Prime Minister Hosokawa enraged Japanese conservatives by using his very first policy address, on August 23, 1993, to declare that Japan's military aggression in the 1930s and 1940s had been "a wrong war and an aggressive war." Hosokawa said that Japan "realized the great mistake we made and vowed to start anew, determined never to repeat the wrongs of the past." About the same time, Ishihara Shintaro, a maverick LDP legislator collaborated with Malaysian prime minister Mahathir bin Mohamad on *"No" to ieru Ajia* (The Asia That Can Say "No"). He subtitled the book, *A Card against Europe and the United States,* and made it plain that the "end of the East-West ideological conflict has finally enabled Japan to start to disengage from the West."[80]

By 1995, however, Japan's effort to redress history in a hurry had gone awry, in part due to the magnitude of the public relations problem that Japan had created for itself. Although its neighbor states seemed ready to forget the past in exchange for a continuing stream of official aid and private Japanese investment, individual claims against the Japanese government mounted. Bureaucrats struggled to deal with a long line of Japanese war victims demanding compensation, from Korean *ianfu* to British and Dutch prisoners of war.

Foreign critics also chose this moment to examine the reasons why Japan had done so little to confront the evils associated with the war and the aggressive military adventures of the first half of the century, compared to Germany, with its dark soul-searching and publicly repentant politicians. By the end of the decade, critics ranging from the elegant Ian Buruma (*The Wages of Guilt*) to the scholarly George Hicks (*Japan's War Memories; The Comfort Women*) and strident Iris Chang (*The Rape of Nanking: The Forgotten Holocaust of World War II*), had weighed in on Japan's neglect of its conscience. But by the time their books were published, the debate within Japan had come to a halt, at least on an official level.[81]

Meanwhile, the conservative mainstream reconstituted itself and by January 1996 had resumed its hold on power under Prime Minister Hashimoto

Ryutaro, a nationalist who denied the evidence of the Nanjing Massacre and sought to strengthen Japan's security alliance with the United States. After the near brush with a nuclear clash with North Korea in 1994, and increasingly aggressive moves by China in the South China Sea and Taiwan, the United States, too, had changed its mind about a troop drawdown in the Pacific. In February 1995, the United States released a new East Asia Strategy Report, outlining its commitment to continued forward deployment and maintenance of the U.S. force level at 100,000 troops. The Japanese political establishment reverted not only to its long-standing arrangements with business, government, and the United States, but also to its post-war posture of denying Japanese war crimes.

Ironically, the new regional security context made it possible for Japan to resume its efforts to develop a web of bilateral and multilateral ties in Asia that excluded the United States without antagonizing it. Washington showed displeasure only erratically, much of the time seeming to find Japan as an acceptable proxy, as long as it cooperated within its strategy of containing China. The issue of formal apologies faded away. When Chinese president Jiang Zemin visited Japan in November 1998, Prime Minister Obuchi Keizo offered a perfunctory apology but refused to put anything in writing. A government spokesman, Nonaka Hiromu, was studiously nonchalant. "Isn't this a finished problem?" he said in a briefing with foreign journalists. "There is a school of thought that Japan has already reflected on its past and apologized to China any number of times before."[82]

Jiang was so incensed that he refused to sign a summit declaration of "partnership for the twenty-first century." With Obuchi at his side, he told students at Waseda University that Japanese aggression in China had cost the lives of thirty-five million soldiers and civilians and caused economic losses of "more than" $600 billion. At his parting press conference, he told reporters in scathing language that Japan had not "properly laid to rest" its conduct in the war. "In Japan, there are still certain people, and people in high positions, who constantly distort history and try to beautify aggression," Jiang said. "It is important that you squarely face that history and learn a lesson from it." Yet, Jiang was clearly the exception among Asian leaders. Just a month before Jiang's visit, South Korean president Kim Dae Jung visited Tokyo and brushed aside Obuchi's formal apology for the Japanese annexation of Korea as unnecessary for Korea-Japan relations in the twenty-first century. Malaysia's Prime Minister Mahathir had been saying as much for years. Thailand and the Philippines had also made it clear that they were ready to ignore, if not forget the past.

The Cold War view of history was thus resurrected. Inoguchi Takashi, a political scientist at Tokyo University, and senior vice-rector of the United Nations University in Tokyo, in a 1996 speech in Adelaide, Australia, explained that among Japanese, there were "universally accepted" premises that ran counter to any notion of unique crime or evil committed by Japan during the war:

> The Japanese version of history is roughly as follows. World War Two should be called, at best, a complex war. From the very beginning of Japan's encounter with the West, Japan felt itself to be under attack, militarily, economically and culturally. The intensity of Japanese modernization was linked directly to the desire to avoid the experience of China and Southeast Asia—China with its Western treaty ports, "no dogs or Chinese" public parks, extra-territoriality and opium trade, Southeast Asia with its colonies and resident populations of white rulers. Japan excelled at the games of the industrializing West. It built modern armies, industries and a government modeled after Bismarck's Prussia. By the turn of the century, it had won victories both over China, in 1895, and Russia, in 1905. By the beginning of World War I, Japan had become the first modern economy in the world outside Europe and North America. In the late nineteenth century, it became the first non-Western government to introduce parliamentary democracy.
>
> In the buildup to Japan's confrontation with the West, it was Japanese success at imperial gamesmanship that led it into trouble. When the Western powers tried to limit the expansion of Japanese influence by putting barriers first on its military growth, and later on its trade, Japan was forced to react. Its response took the form of military occupation of adjacent areas. This was in order to defend itself in the event of a future confrontation with the Western powers. Japan faced a Hobson's choice—to accede to Western demands by giving up its territorial acquisitions, or stand and fight. Japan chose the latter.
>
> Japan's war against the West is widely seen as an evil war. But the West, in its colonial and imperialist phases, was no less evil. Japan's war against its Asian neighbors was plainly wrong. But it was the West that first victimized Asia, not Japan. Asia's tragedy was that it became an arena for imperial competition between Japan and the West. Thus, in the Japanese version of history, it becomes impossible to clearly assign guilt in the conflict. Japan is guilty, but no more guilty than the West. But if the international community condemns Japan only, something is wrong. Or so the Japanese argument goes.[83]

Inoguchi admitted that this view of history ruled out any sense of common identity between Japan and the rest of Asia. The rest of Asia was experiencing "re-Asianization" by celebrating its newfound economic strength and the beginnings of geopolitical influence, he said. Japan, by contrast, was merely "re-associating" itself with Asia. "Psychologically speaking, juxtaposing Japan and Asia [as separate entities] seems more comfortable for many Japanese than placing it within Asia." In the same paper, Inoguchi captured neatly the change in atmosphere from a few years previously. Rather than disengage from the West, Inoguchi said, "It is still abundantly clear that Japan's ties with Asia are not going to become predominant in relation to its bonds with the United States."

Beyond the geopolitical calculations of leaders in Washington, Tokyo, and other Asian capitals, the human calculus followed a different and less orderly metric. However diligently Japanese bureaucrats and politicians tried to set back the clock, activity at the grassroots level had a way of building on itself. The Cold War pact between the United States and Japan had indeed been successful in robbing the post-war generation of its memory, and thereby its conscience. Yet the officially sanctioned truth telling of the 1991–95 period was not without impact. In the early 1990s, there were enough survivors left to make the stories real to the young. Those who opened the closet door found skeletons tumbling out.

There had always been a few maverick intellectuals—mostly academics and journalists—who kept alive the issue of Japan's war responsibility, much to the annoyance of the Japanese Foreign Ministry and other officials. But in the early 1990s, as official Japan went through the motions of formal apology to its neighbors, gradually, cautiously, the mainstream media and citizens' groups began probing the war legacy closer to home. Prior to the first of the World War Two anniversaries, virtually all the Japanese networks had seized the occasion of Hirohito's death in January 1989 to run hours of documentaries on the era of his reign, from 1926 to 1989, as well as his father's and grandfather's reigns. These exposed many younger Japanese for the first time to the visual evidence of Japanese imperialism in China and Southeast Asia, as well as to the hardships of the immediate post-war era. For the film buff, they were a field day; for the cultural historian, they were evidence that Japan had definitively awakened from collective amnesia with regard to its war legacy. Popular magazines followed the lead of the networks.

The public exorcism of war ghosts may have seemed barely to scratch the surface of events to some Japanese, while to yet others the events were too far in the past to register as anything more than ancient history. Yet, clearly the replaying of the events of the war were deeply troubling to some, and had far greater impact than the activities of left-wing intellectuals who had worked furiously but for the most part, futilely, to focus public attention on the problems of history. Japanese support groups began forming around octogenarian victims of the Japanese military machine. In the 1990s, often with the help of Japanese lawyers, some of these former victims demanded and won compensation for the first time.

Among the die-hard liberals who had pursued issues of Japanese war guilt long before it became popular or permissible was Nakahara Michiko, a cultural historian at Waseda University. A tall, elegant woman in her fifties, Professor Nakahara wore a purple streak in her hair and spoke bluntly. She had done research on Asian laborers along the Burma-Thailand Railroad in World War Two that exposed the suffering of Asian draft laborers; more than six times as many Asians had died on the infamous "death railroad" than Western prisoners of war.

"The Japanese never passed judgment on their own war crimes," Nakahara wrote in one of many essays. "Therefore the Japanese have not brought the war to an end by their own hands."[84] In 1993, she was invited to join a newly established research center—all male, she noted wryly—with funding from Toyota Foundation, the Senso Sekinin Senta (War Responsibility Center). She had been conducting interviews with former soldiers and victims from the Philippines, Indonesia, and Malaysia. In 1991, when she put a small advertisement in two Tamil newspapers in Malaysia for Asian survivors of the "death railway," she was overwhelmed by the response. "I thought if I could get five or six responses I would be lucky," she wrote. "The result was surprising. I listened almost every day for an entire month to stories of the Indian Malaysians. They did not bother to make appointments. They came and waited for me in front of my flat."[85]

In 1993 and 1994, Nakahara's research for the War Responsibility Center assumed a life of its own. She met with an ex-*Kempeitai* commander based in Singapore, who later had a long career with the Japan Self-Defense Force, as well as high-ranking officers from the Japanese Imperial Army in Malaysia. In the classically pretty island of Miyajima, with its ancient Heian shrine and sacred deer, Nakahara interviewed a man who had been a driver for the army in Malaysia. In Japan, the old man made his living by carving wooden rice spatulas.

"One day he was ordered to bring Chinese people in his truck to a plantation site," Nakahara recounted. "There were four trucks, with 100 Chinese, all from a jail in Kuala Lumpur. Japanese soldiers surrounded them. The head—the *taicho*—shouted an order, 'Kill them.' The driver said that he was thinking, how could he kill them? It was the first time he had ever seen any Chinese people. The soldiers were shrinking back. Then the *taicho* shouted again, 'This is the emperor's order!' The *taicho* cut off the head of one Chinese man, and blood spurted out. The old man imitated the sound of the blood gushing out. Then the soldiers became infuriated and killed the rest of the Chinese. It was the man's first experience with killing another human being."[86]

At the start of the decade, the Japanese government made a practice of tolerating and even tacitly encouraging such investigations—up to a point. It was one thing for earnest individual Japanese and even the media to explore Japan's war record and demonstrate by their sensitivity and emotions that Japan had a human side. It was a different matter when such efforts interfered with larger Japanese goals or when the citizens' investigations contradicted the official line.

Nakahara claimed that the Japanese government had put a stop to matters when Malaysia and other countries attempted to put the *ianfu* on the agenda of the UN Human Rights Commission. In Malaysia, Mustapha, the head of the international youth bureau of UMNO, the Malaysian governing party, had called for survivors of draft labor or prostitution for the Japanese military to come forward and was planning to submit a report to the UN. The Japanese ambassador got on the phone to the Malaysian defense minister, Najib, and told him to stop, since "everything had been settled between Japan and Malaysia and we have already paid compensation" (in the form of war reparations under the 1952 San Francisco Peace Treaty).

Despite such conflicts between broad policy and the specific calculus of Japanese diplomacy, long-established taboos were lifted on a host of issues relating to Japan's war legacy. The Japanese government was clearly unprepared for all the ramifications of this wave of truth telling. Among the more tragic and intractable issues was compensation due to Asians and to others forced into draft labor or prostitution during the war. Despite ample evidence that the Japanese Imperial Army had played a large role in organizing sex services for its soldiers—including official army manuals for the maintenance of brothels—Tokyo denied their actual existence as late as 1993. In 1994, when Prime Minister Murayama finally acknowledged the existence of the "comfort women," he did so as part of a public relations campaign during a tour of Southeast Asia; he seemed to think that he could satisfy claims without directly admitting government responsibility or involvement.

In August 1994, Murayama pledged Yen 100 billion over ten years to support educational and cultural projects for Asian women, to include the aging comfort women. The plan infuriated both Japanese conservatives and the comfort women. After a year's debate in the Japanese Diet, the government pledge was withdrawn and in its place was a plan to set up a fund entirely dependent on private sector contributions. It had a target of collecting Yen 1 billion, or about $10 million. In its first four months, the fund had collected less than $700,000 and had yet to identify any potential beneficiaries. In November 1995, Korean comfort women demonstrated in front of the Japanese Diet in order to protest the structure of the fund, which they complained allowed the Japanese government to shirk its responsibility for its wartime military brothels.

The fumbling and backtracking of the Japanese government continued to attract criticism and undermine the public relations benefits of official apologies. Yet, the apologies, however tardy or ambiguous, had an impact. Perhaps the clearest sign of change was simply the redrawing of the line separating the taboo from the routine. By the mid-1990s, the history of Japanese aggression in Asia was no longer a fringe subject. There was a new curiosity about the war era, less passionate but also more objective than in the past. The war had become acceptable, in a neat, tidy, Japanese way. Even if it lacked the drama of public acts of contrition, there was a palpable shift.

The conflicting threads of curiosity and defensiveness came together most poignantly in the 1991 commemorations. Americans looked back at Pearl Harbor with a mixture of grief and soul-searching. Japanese were quizzical, curious, and defensive—but far from guilt stricken.

Defensiveness, perhaps, was foremost. "To say we've done wrong—we've done that many times," said Kikuchi Kiyoaki, a one-time lieutenant in the Japanese Imperial Navy who became a diplomat and later served as Japanese ambassador to Mexico, Canada, and the UN. "What more do the Americans want?"[87]

In 1991, analysts such as Kikuchi argued that Japan should give up the pretense of endless apologies for the war and present its point of view in a more straightforward manner. The post-war alliance between Japan and the United States in which Japan played the role of junior partner was collapsing, he said, and would be replaced by a more testy relationship between equals. One consequence should be to give up caviling over which was the guilty party when the two countries were at war. "By competing with each other in a blunt, natural way, both economies will become more efficient," Kikuchi argued. When Frank Fasi, the mayor of Honolulu, suggested in August 1991 that Japan send representatives to Hawaii to deliver a formal apology, a Japanese government spokesman, Ishihara Nobuo, replied: "It will take tens of hundreds of years before the correct judgment is delivered on who is responsible for the war."

While official Japan was busy soothing Asians, Japanese revisionists were hard at work portraying Japan as the benefactor of its erstwhile colonies. Much as the United States saw Pearl Harbor as the end of a period of U.S. isolationism, the revisionists harked back to Japan's pre-war empire as they urged a bigger role for contemporary Japan in Asia and the world. They said that while the war ended in tragic failure, its original intent was to expel white colonialists from Asia and to assert Asian values. The argument concluded that Japan went to war with the United States only because the United States threatened Japan's Asian interests.

"Japanese policy has always been clear when it waged war," wrote Eto Jun, an emeritus professor at Tokyo Institute of Technology. "In the declaration of war against the United States . . . the Japanese intention was clearly expressed—to secure stability in East Asia and contribute to world peace."

In contrast to saturation coverage of the Pearl Harbor anniversary in the United States, the Japanese press approached the actual events of the Pearl Harbor attack with an almost palpable distaste. The anniversary was, in fact, the very first time that the subject had been covered in detail on Japanese television, according to Hayashi Yoshihisa, an NHK official who was executive producer of its Pearl Harbor documentary. "We had more interesting things to cover—Hiroshima, Nagasaki, the Japanese invasion of China and other countries," he said. The war with the Allied Powers, for all the moral outrage of Westerners who argued that it was conducted in barbaric fashion, was portrayed by Japanese as a textbook conflict waged by European rules and paid for in defeat.

Popular magazines and television networks concentrated on the Japanese role in Asian independence movements. A lead story in the weekly magazine *Aera* in December 1991 examined the Japanese invasion of British colonial Malaya, launched at Kota Bahru eighty minutes before the Pearl Harbor attack.[88] The story quoted villagers who witnessed Indian soldiers chained to their guns by British officers. Abdul Malik, a former Malaysian ambassador to Singapore who was eight years old at the time, was quoted saying that when the Japanese came, "I thought, now Asian people can stand on the same footing as Westerners. The Japanese are also Asians, like the Malays—not white Caucasians."

The coverage of Southeast Asia was not recycled jingoism, however. There were efforts to cover the dark side of Japanese colonial rule in Asia, as well. To NHK's credit, it weighed in with a documentary on "Asia and the Asia-Pacific War" that covered some of the same ground as the *Aera* story, that is, Japan's role in Southeast Asian anticolonial movements but with an entirely different slant. Breaking faith with the mainstream conservative view that Japan had been a savior to the anticolonial movements, NHK presented Japan's role as harsh and manipulative. The three-hour documentary, aired in August 1991, showed how Japan initially supported Asian revolutionaries in order to undermine their European and American colonial overlords, only to snatch independence back as their empire expanded.

In one poignant episode, a Japanese radio orchestra records and broadcasts the Indonesian national anthem, *Asiaraya*; a few years later, the Japanese Occupation government banned the song. The documentary visits the graves of Islamic protestors against emperor worship and shows scenes of Indonesian schoolgirls being taught Japanese songs. The most interesting part of the film lays out the ambiguities of the relationship between Sukarno, the charismatic Indonesian revolutionary leader, and the Japanese naval command in Jakarta, which kept Sukarno and his co-revolutionary Hatta on a tight rein. In one scene, Sukarno leads a throng of schoolchildren in shouts of *banzai* in honor of the visit to Jakarta of Tojo Hideki, Japan's wartime prime minister. According to the film, the Japanese had a hand even in the Indonesian declaration of independence in 1945; naval authorities insisted that the document indicate that the Japanese "transferred" control of the nation to the Indonesian people rather than the Indonesians wresting independence for themselves.

The strongest currents of guilt roiled around Japan's territorial expansion into China, which antedated Pearl Harbor by ten years and still haunted the Japanese imagination. The anniversary became an occasion for a look back at the wrenching events of the Japanese invasion and occupation. From the Japanese perspective, the attack on Pearl Harbor was an event that came late in a wider fifteen-year war. That conflict began with the Mukden Incident on September 18, 1931—a rigged explosion along a railway line that gave Japan the pretext to invade Manchuria. Japanese attitudes toward the Asian conflict were layered and complex. For four decades, the Japanese government had glossed over the experience of what it called the Pacific War, suppressing accounts of it in textbooks and shying away from any public reckoning. A sense of guilt about the colonial period in Asia ran like a muddy subterranean current through all of Japan's contemporary dealings with its neighbors.

Media investigations dug deep into Japan's guilty conscience. Among the more shocking episodes of the war in China had been the use of live prisoners in experiments with deadly bacteriological agents conducted by the infamous "Unit 731," operating in North China in the 1930s. In September 1991, Tokyo Broadcasting System aired the first-ever Japanese documentary on Unit 731. A reporter tracked down the former commandant at his home in a quiet, wealthy Tokyo suburb. Gaunt and ghost-like, the man came to the door but refused to speak, scuttling down the street and back into his hole in history. The news team found another man, who as a sixteen-year-old had been a member of the "youth brigade" at the Unit 731 headquarters near Harbin, China. He sat with a reporter on the beach, overlooking a gray Pacific, talking in a calm and matter-of-fact manner about his role.

"We had no choice" but to carry out orders, he said. He saw women and children in cells undergoing experiments, and was entirely familiar with the terminology in which the prisoners were called "logs," or *maruta*. In China, the TBS film showed the scanty remains of the prison incinerator alongside aerial photos of what was once a huge complex, including the railway line that brought prisoners in but not out. The team found a Chinese woman whose husband had been dragged away by the *Kempeitai*, the secret police, probably to the medical experimentation lab. She took them on a tour of the old *Kempeitai* building in Harbin, breaking down in tears.

Behind the TBS special was the grisly incident of the Shinjuku bones. In July 1989, construction workers at a site in the busy Shinjuku District of downtown Tokyo stumbled across a cache of human skulls and thighbones.[89] When local police asked the Japanese Ministry of Health and Welfare, owner of the land, what to do with the bones, word came back, "Burn them." For years, the bones rested untouched in cardboard boxes in a Tokyo funeral parlor until finally they were incinerated. But the controversy surrounding them did not dissipate as easily.

The bones had been located on the grounds of the former Japanese Imperial Army Medical College, now the National Institute of Nutrition, near what was once the office of General Ishii Shiro. Ishii masterminded an ambitious program of bacteriological warfare from a secret base in northeast China from 1936 to 1945; its arsenal of biological weaponry was large enough to kill the world's population several times over. The code name for this deadly enterprise was Unit 731. U.S. and Soviet archives showed that Unit 731 used some 3,000 prisoners of war as guinea pigs in lethal experiments on chemical and bacteriological weapons. Their bodies were cremated, with the exception of a few samples that were sent back to General Ishii and his staff of doctors at the Army Medical College in Tokyo. The Japanese government dismissed such accounts, and said that Unit 731 merely conducted disease prevention and control programs.

The discovery of the bones put this official representation in a new perspective. The bureaucratic stonewalling at higher levels was so dramatic that the Shinjuku municipal government finally sought an independent analysis of the bones. With a considerable degree of understatement, Negishi Koichi, who headed the Health and Welfare Division of the municipal government, said: "There has been a difference of opinion on the matter between the Health and Welfare Ministry and the Shinjuku government." Even after the results of the analysis were published in March 1992, the controversy simmered. But in one sense, it was nothing new. The contest of wills between Shinjuku and the health ministry was part of a decades-old cover-up.

After World War Two, stories had circulated about Japanese Army medical experiments on human beings in China. At a Soviet war-crimes trial in 1949, former Japanese officers spoke of the experiments. The U.S. Occupation, and later the Japanese government, dismissed the claims as fantastic. The first independent evidence of human experiments came in 1980, after a lengthy investigation by an American journalist and China expert, John Powell. In 1954, the U.S. government charged him with treason and sedition. Powell was accused of helping the Chinese communists by reporting that the United States had engaged in bacteriological warfare during the Korean War. More than twenty years later, he picked up the thread again, using the Freedom of Information Act to gain access to U.S. Army archives. That put him on the trail of Unit 731. The documents he found clearly described experiments involving human beings. Another of Powell's findings was even more explosive—that the United States and Japan together had engineered the cover-up so the United States could obtain an edge over the Soviets in the race for bacteriological-warfare supremacy.

The U.S. Occupation authorities gave amnesty to officers and men of Unit 731. As explained in an internal War Department memorandum, dated June 23, 1947: "Since it is believed that the U.S.S.R. possesses only a small portion of the technical information, and since any war-crimes action would completely reveal such data to all nations, it is felt that such publicity must be avoided in the interests of defense and security of the United States. It is believed also that the war-crimes prosecution of General Ishii and his associates would serve to stop the flow of much additional information of a technical and scientific nature."

General Ishii lived on the outskirts of Tokyo until his death in 1959. Other "graduates" of Unit 731 included the former governor of Tokyo, Suzuki Shunichi; the former president of the Japan Medical Association; the former director of the health ministry's preventive health research center; the former chairman and president of Green Cross Corp.; and the past heads of a number of prestigious Japanese medical schools. At its height, more than 9,000 people were imprisoned in Unit 731's headquarters at Pingfang, near Harbin in northeast China. Until Powell's exposé, the only confirmation of the stories about Unit 731 was in a few wartime medical journals with references and records of the Soviet trial. In 1981, journalist Morimura Seiichi published a fictional account of Unit 731, called *Gluttonous Devils*, which was based in part on interviews with surviving Japanese who worked at the laboratory. It was filled with accounts of victims being subjected to freezing, high pressure, and vivisection. But the book was derivative and written in a sensational style that undermined its credibility. The story remained in the realm of left-wing doggerel, as far as most Japanese were concerned.

That changed in 1984, when a graduate student at Keio Medical University in Tokyo found records of human experiments in a bookstore. The pages described the effects of massive dosages of tetanus vaccine. There were tables describing the length of time it took victims to die and recording the muscle spasms in their bodies. Subsequently, researchers were able to locate additional documents on experiments. "The government has so far tried to keep this matter as a kind of secret," said Koshida Takashi, headmaster of Tokyo's prestigious Gakushuin High School and a member of a group pressing the

Shinjuku ward government to investigate the bones. "But we want to disclose the facts and hand them down to the next generation so that such things will never be repeated."

In an effort to focus more attention on the victims, Tsuneishi Keiichi, a science historian, led a group to the site of the former Unit 731 complex in the summer of 1991. They were able to locate a few Chinese who had worked as day laborers at the camp, as well as the widow of a prisoner. When the group returned to Japan, they presented letters from four Chinese asking the Japanese Foreign Ministry for clarification on the matter of the bones. Professor Tsuneishi argued that by ignoring the history of Unit 731, Japan glossed over the fact that they had benefited from the accelerated research done in the human-experiment program. Unit 731 formulated a vaccine against typhoid fever, for example.

Even more dangerous than historical amnesia, he said, was that without an airing of the background of Unit 731, Japanese might fail to recognize the cultural traits—obedience and authoritarianism—that led doctors to perform human experiments without experiencing remorse. In the early 1980s, Tsuneishi interviewed surviving doctors who had worked in Unit 731. Most were graduate students at the time of the experiments. "They did not feel guilty because their teachers would get the credit—and the victims were said to have been sentenced to death," Tsuneishi said. "Some doctors even thought the victims would be happy to contribute to the advancement of medical science."

While Tsuneishi and his colleagues focused their efforts on the Foreign Ministry, another citizens' group was involved in a parallel effort to force the Ministry of Education (MOE) to allow mention of Unit 731 in high school textbooks. Ienaga Saburo, one of Japan's foremost Marxist historians, launched his first lawsuit against the Japanese government in 1965 to protest MOE's censorship of virtually all mention of Japanese wartime atrocities. In the hearings on Unit 731 in the late 1980s, the government continued to maintain that there was insufficient evidence to prove that atrocities had taken place.

In 1989, the district court ruled against Ienaga. The case then went on appeal to the Tokyo High Court. Members of Ienaga's group of activists said that the government was able to find only one historian in Japan willing to agree with its position—and even this key witness recanted his views in a professional journal. When the witness, Hata Ikuchiko, showed up in court, he appeared to suffer an attack of amnesia and claimed that he could remember neither the contents of his article nor his testimony at earlier hearings.

Public interest in the second anniversary, commemorating Japan's defeat, was far more muted. In the spring of 1995, a major Tokyo museum exhibition demonstrated both the limitations, and extent, of the changes that had taken place in the national psyche.

The exhibit, sanctioned by the Tokyo city government, marked the fiftieth anniversary of the devastating bombing raids launched against the Japanese capital in March 1945.[90] A single Allied war raid in the predawn hours of March 10 hurled thousands of tons of bombs on Tokyo, killing 100,000 people—almost as many as died in the two atomic bombs dropped on Hiroshima and Nagasaki five months later. The bombing ranked with the 1923 Great Kanto Earthquake in the scale of tragedy. The exhibition included twisted pieces of metal, fused in the firestorms sweeping the city, and videotapes of interviews with survivors. A casualty chart showed the headcount of dead and injured in the raids, which began in Fall 1944 and kept on until nearly the close of the war. Besides the horrific air raids, many of the exhibits were devoted to scenes and articles of daily life from the war years. These showed how the militarist regime gradually sucked the life and color from the vibrant metropolis. In the final days, citizens wore drab uniforms, made cardboard shoes, improvised daily implements from materials that came to hand, covered their light bulbs with black light shades, and kept water buckets at hand for the inevitable fire brigade.

But that was not all. In one corner, a video screen showed documentary films on Japan's conquests of China and Southeast Asia. Like permanent exhibitions in Hiroshima and Nagasaki, the Edo-Tokyo Museum's exhibit condemned the bombing of noncombatants and portrayed the Japanese as victims. But the inclusion of Japan's air raids on the civilian populations of Chinese cities in the 1930s put the show in a rare new category of attempts to provide a balanced view of Japan's war experience. The Edo-Tokyo Museum show began a few months after the Smithsonian Institution decided to scrap a large part of its own anniversary exhibition, originally intended to highlight the sufferings of the Japanese population in wartime. The Smithsonian planned to display objects from the Hiroshima and Nagasaki museums, as well as the fuselage of the *Enola Gay*, the B-52 long-range bomber that dropped "Fat Boy," the bomb obliterating much of Hiroshima. Objections by war veterans led to the revamping of the Smithsonian show to exclude such objects. Compared with such references, the Edo-Tokyo Museum's effort to present Japanese war guilt was highly nuanced, relying on a four-minute videotape that a casual viewer might easily have missed.

"The show did not go far enough," fumed Saotome Kasumoto, a writer who headed a group of private citizens who had worked for twenty years to collect information on the air raids. But others understood the significance of including the video. Said Nakahara Michiko, the historian, "This is wonderful, especially compared with the Smithsonian's backtracking. I'm amazed that a Japanese institution would do this much." Quietly, without fanfare, Japan had taken another step toward accepting, if not embracing, the history that bothered its neighbors so deeply.

Tribe

Against a clear winter sky, the undulating hills of Fukushima and Tochigi prefectures race past under a full moon, piebald with snow. On a weekday night, the Yamabiko Shinkansen heads down the main northeastern trunk line from Sendai to Tokyo Station. Businessmen idly read comic books under the harsh fluorescent lights. Before going home tonight, they may stop in an *akachokin*, a "red lantern" bar, for some noodles or *oden*—bits of turnip and fish paste stewed almost beyond recognition. They may sing sentimental Japanese *enka* to an old and scratchy *karaoke* set, encouraged by the brassy, overage surrogate mother or girlfriend behind the bar.

Sometime in the early hours of the morning, they will stumble home, pink-faced, to a sleeping household, then sink gratefully into the family bathtub. The routine represents comfort and predictability. Even the deep tub, with its tepid, gritty water under a plastic cover to retain the heat, symbolizes domestic order and the down-home Japanese values of frugality and togetherness. The water is recycled as long as possible to save on the water bill, and despite the Japanese practice of showering before bathing, the water is also a family soup. After a few hours of sleep, the men rise, often before their spouse and children stir. Back to the train, subway, or *shinkansen*, back to the working world, to the section chief and serried ranks of underlings at their neatly arranged desks just so, a pattern as fixed as the geometries of a snowflake, and as fragile in its way.

So went the good life in Japan in the 1990s, cozy, insular, a model of adaptation to an age already past, when rapid industrialization depended on the loyalty and long work hours of the men, strict separation of roles by gender, and intense, almost unbearable, discipline. In the century's last decade, change was in the air, yet the psychology of the time was more insidious than urgent. The Japanese were like passengers on a ship in a calm sea with bad weather on the way, disinclined to interrupt their day in the sun until the impending storm washed over the decks.

Politicians, executives, and the Japanese press ranted about Japan's lost decade and warned of structural changes overtaking its economy. Some citizens, enraged at the disarray of postwar institutions, took to the streets. But the dominant view of the *sarariman*, office ladies, bureaucrats, and part-time working housewives who conducted the daily business of the world's second-largest economy was *shikata ga nai,* "there is nothing I can do about it," with regard to the complexities of the national economy or international relations. Torpor warred with complacence, and the physical and spiritual exhaustion left over from Japan's fifty-year race for global preeminence seemed to drag Japanese public life into yet greater depths of paralysis and inaction.

Indeed, Japan in the 1990s reflected perhaps the deepest ambivalence of any major industrialized nation toward the costs of globalization, the first of them being change in the sheltered habits of everyday life. By the mid-1990s, Japan had been open to the outside world for more than 100 years, but the habits of the previous 200 years of self-imposed isolation, the *sakoku* policy of the Tokugawa Era, remained strong.[91] The domestic economy remained protected by dense thickets of regulation even as its flagship multinationals were beating a retreat to cheaper, less stifling climes. But the real barrier to globalization was in the Japanese heart and hearth, in the stubborn tribalism of the society. Few other nations laid so much emphasis on the importance of maintaining racial, ethnic, and linguistic integrity as Japan, on preserving Japanese communalism against the various encroachments of immigration, multiculturalism, and the Internet. However global the Japanese might be in their tastes and interests, they remained stubbornly convinced that the world stopped where the Japanese shoreline began. Of all the obstacles to Japan's search for a new paradigm, this was the most intractable.

Through most of the twentieth century, Japanese military leaders, politicians, and business leaders were able to exact extraordinary sacrifices from the Japanese people by cultivating the image of Japan as a tribe, reducing the global landscape to a flat horizon of primitive competition in which the Japanese were always visible and vulnerable as a unit. The brilliant cultural historian Nakahara Michiko complained about the inability of the Japanese to view the world in any but hierarchical terms. This led to "an almost hysterical adulation of the West and a feeling of inferiority toward the West that remain strong in many groups today," she wrote.

Tribalism helped the Japanese cope with the stresses of rapid modernization by compartmentalizing, by establishing a core of unchanging Japanese values against the hectic flurries of Western material culture and institutions. It also laid the basis for a racial and ethnic exclusiveness so strong it could easily subvert the best intentions. Nakahara quoted Ito Hitoshi, a novelist who was among Japan's most outspoken liberals until he abruptly transmogrified into a foaming supernationalist in 1941.

In his diary, Ito wrote, "We Japanese have been given a fate that dictates that there is only one way for us to realize that we belong to the highest race in the world. That is to go to war with the Caucasians, who are now the world's highest race." In the 1940s, Asians were seen as dark-skinned primitives at the opposite end of the spectrum from Japanese and whites; in nationalistic cartoons, they were portrayed as thick-lipped bongos with vacant eyes. In the pre-war years, a comic strip called "Dankichi, the Adventurer" "won unprecedented popularity." Dankichi, a young boy, falls asleep while fishing off the coast of Japan. His boat drifts to the South Seas, where the natives make him their king. Dankichi, who always wears a watch, gives each of his subjects a number—written on their chests—so that he can tell them apart. The tribe was called simply, "Nameless," or Mujirushiban. "This was the commonly held image of Southeast Asia" by the Japanese, wrote Nakahara.[92]

In the 1990s, such prejudices collided with the aims of Japan's leaders to build a new relationship with Asia. At the end of the century, the country needed to rearrange its mental boxes, in order to include itself in a broader regional community within Asia, and a favorite neologism among the Japanese elite was *kokusaika* (internationalization). The phrase conveyed a lofty notion of abandoning tribal insularity and embracing international norms, whatever they might be. If it meant taking Asians home to dinner, however, *kokusaika* went out the window. Whatever Japan's political and intellectual elite might say about common Asian values and an Asian renaissance, down in the *shotengai*, the shopping lanes, and on the commuter trains, ordinary Japanese expected certain things to remain constant, and their expectations were self-fulfilling.

So I muse on the train south from Sendai to Tokyo on an early December evening in 1995. I have two companions, one imaginary and one real. My imaginary companion is Basho. The *haiku* master visited the barbarian wilds of northeastern Honshu in the seventeenth century on foot, as an exercise in spiritual rebirth. The Yamabiko Shinkansen follows his route, and the ragged line of hills has an untamed look that it must have had in his time as well. The small towns along the tracks are crowded now with factories and *pachinko* parlors, however, not much different than the towns to the south and west of Tokyo, but fewer of them.

I am reminded of Basho not only because of the route but as a symbol of all that is adventurous, creative, and bold in Japanese culture. Surely, the civilization that produced the master poet must have extraordinary regenerative powers. The materialism, self-absorption, and paralysis of Japan at the end of the twentieth century must be a pause, a mere phase. Basho also brings to mind journeys of self-discovery and the pain that they often bring. The latter is the theme of my actual companion, Chiang Shu-ling.

Pert and attractive, Chiang was the daughter of a civil servant in Taiwan. She enrolled as a graduate student in international economics at Tohoku University in the city of Sendai. Her litany of woe was as old as the century. Back home in Taiwan, Chiang dreamed of Japan as the progenitor of a bold, new Asian civilization, able to compete with the West on its own terms. She came to Japan in order to try to find out what gave the country its head start in the race to catch up with the West, assuming that these lessons would be there for the taking. Like generations of Asians before her, Chiang assumed that Japan would gladly share its secrets with its neighbors. Instead, she learned the hard way that Japan didn't think much of the neighborhood. In the strict divisions of the Japanese sensibility, Asians are neither *uchi*, insiders, nor *soto*, outsiders. They float in a netherworld in which they have to try harder, accept more abuse, and be satisfied with fewer rewards than their European or North American counterparts in Japan.

Beginning in the late 1980s, Tokyo officially encouraged Asians to study in Japan, offering scholarships and a variety of other supports. By the mid-1990s, they made up 90 percent of a foreign-student population of some 80,000, including 30,000 Japanese-language students. In 1983, when the total number of foreign students in Japan hovered at a mere 10,000, Prime Minister Nakasone set a target of attracting 100,000 foreign university students to Japan by the year 2000. In the early 1990s, the number of foreign students was growing by 20 to 30 percent per year.[93]

The policy encouraging Asian students was part of a broader one of fostering better relations with the rest of the region. But many of these students returned home with a far different image than Japanese authorities intended, so disillusioned that, like Chiang, they simply wanted nothing more to do with Japan. "I'd say 95 percent of the Chinese students here hate Japan," Guo Peiyu, a Chinese artist, told a visiting reporter in 1996.[94] Japan's unwelcoming reputation was at least a partial factor in the slump in foreign students in the country after 1995. Excluding Japanese-language students, most of whom were not affiliated with universities, the number of foreign students peaked at 53,847 in 1995, then declined to about 51,000 annually.

Chiang, at twenty-three, was animated and opinionated in contrast to the studied coyness of many Japanese women her age. "I first fell in love with Japan as a child, when my father brought me here on a trip," she said, chatting in *putonghua* on the long train ride to Tokyo. "I was always interested in being a *liu xuesheng* (foreign exchange student). But I was never interested in going to America, never. I wanted to go to Japan. I studied business management in college. I already had a master's degree. I thought that once I had the language, I could go to work for one of the big Japanese trading companies, like Marubeni or Mitsubishi."

Chiang started out at Hitotsubashi University in Tokyo, moving after a year to Tohoku University in Sendai, where an advisor said it would be easier for her to get her Japanese up to speed. Meanwhile, she leaned on a friend from Hitotsubashi who had joined Marubeni to arrange an interview for her.

Japanese companies hold recruitment drives simultaneously in the fall to catch the seniors who will graduate the following March.

The rules are strict at these job fairs. For the most part, companies recruit only graduating college seniors. The interviews themselves are usually the tail end of a process that begins nearly a year earlier, when employers put out feelers to promising juniors. Chiang thought she might have a chance, despite being overage and a graduate student, because of her business training and fluent Chinese and Japanese. So, she caught the train down to Tokyo, a $200 roundtrip from Sendai. But when Chiang called her friend, he claimed that she had missed the time of her appointment. Chiang says he never gave her a specific appointment time. "It was unforgivable," she said. "But none of the big companies are hiring women now. Maybe if I were a Western woman, they would be polite. But for an Asian like me, no way."

If Japanese looked down on Asians generally, many Japanese automatically assumed that any Asian woman in Japan had come to the country as a prostitute. Among the largest categories of legal immigrants in the 1980s and 1990s were Asian women, who entered Japan as "entertainers" or on short-term visas, often without realizing that they would be working in the sex trade. In 1994, for example, 136,000 Asian women in the twenty to twenty-four-year-old age category entered Japan, almost two-and-a-half times the number of Asian men in the same age group, according to the Japanese Ministry of Justice (MOJ). Most of the women were from Taiwan, South Korea, and the Philippines.[95] The prostitutes' stories were often horrific; the flesh traffickers kept the women in small rooms, forcing them to pay off the expenses of their travel and lodging without recourse to legal or any other form of counsel.[96]

The experiences of educated, middle-class Asian women such as Chiang were distasteful rather than life threatening. They were subjected to breaches of civility rather than violations of their human rights. Even so, they did not make for happy memories. In her graduate study room, Chiang was the only female among a group of Japanese males. They expected her to pour tea and clean up after them. One day, after a colleague instructed her to clean the windows in the room, the petite Chiang rebelled. "Why don't you do it yourself," she cried. "Look at me! I'm short! That work would be much easier for one of you men. Why do I have to do all the cleaning here?" The men were stunned. Another time, accepting a casual lift from two Japanese male friends, Chiang happened to refer to herself as a *gaijin*. "What? You're not a foreigner!" snorted one of her Japanese male colleagues. "You're an Asian. Western people are *gaijin*! You're just *soto*, outside." Drawing a circle, the man said, "Look, Japanese people are here, inside. You're out there. You can't call an Asian a *gaijin*."

Chiang's academic advisor, Hakogi Masumi, pasted MIT and Harvard stickers on his car windows, and affected a Western-style handshake rather than a bow. He was sensitive and cosmopolitan. But even the affable Hakogi betrayed attitudes relegating Asians to a second-class status. Once, Hakogi sharply reprimanded Chiang for using a slightly casual Japanese verb form in talking with him. In hierarchical Japan, language is coded for superiors and inferiors. Women are expected to use honorific language to men, as are students to teachers. Hakogi sighed, Chiang recalls, and said that he would probably have forgiven her if she was a Westerner, but as an "Easterner," it was impossible. She had to get it right. After two-and-a-half-years, Chiang had had enough. She planned to move to Seattle to join a brother, a computer scientist. "There's no point in staying here," she said. "There are no opportunities for women. Japanese women can't find jobs in the recession. What can I expect?"

Early in the twentieth century, Japan had been a magnet for Asian, anticolonial revolutionaries who came to Japan looking for inspiration—among them Sun Yat-sen, Lu Xun, Jose Rizal, Ba Maw of Burma, and Subas Chandra Bose. Most quickly realized that Japanese colonial aims in the region were far more sweeping than anything the Europeans or Americans had attempted. The first experiments were with Japan's northern island of Hokkaido. Well into the nineteenth century, Japan exercised loose control over Hokkaido through fortified ports that managed a sparse commercial traffic with Russia as well as serving as collection points for the island's resources. The interior, with its aboriginal Ainu tribes, was left to its own devices. The Meiji government began a program to extend control over Hokkaido by banning the Ainu language and moving poor farmers from the southern Japanese islands to Hokkaido through land grants.

With the formal annexation of Taiwan in 1895 and Korea in 1910, Japan became a colonial power on a large scale, reshaping economies and forcing indigenous populations to adopt Japanese language and institutions. Unlike European and American colonialism, resettlement by ethnic Japanese was a core part of Japanese colonial strategy. The Japanese intended not only to replace urban elites with their own nationals but also to repopulate the countryside with Japanese. Although there was some diversity in colonial administration, in many of its colonies Japan banned the use of local languages, including Chinese and Korean, ripped up historic landmarks that might become a focus of nationalist sentiment, and replaced local temples with Shinto shrines. By 1945, Japan developed a style of colonialism so harsh that its legacy continued to be a major theme in relations with its neighbors.

Nowhere was this legacy more poignant than in the struggles of the ethnic Korean community in Japan to define itself and seek a legal basis for equality. Since the end of World War Two, it had constituted the largest single group of non-Japanese residents in Japan. Many Korean-Japanese were third or fourth generation. According to one estimate, by the late 1990s, 90 percent of Japan's ethnic Koreans were born in Japan and spoke little or no Korean. But less than 30 percent had been naturalized over the forty years since the San Francisco Peace Treaty had taken away the Japanese citizenship of former colonials who chose to remain in Japan after Japan's defeat.[97] For some Koreans, it was a matter of pride to remain apart and refuse to go through the tedious, lengthy, and uncertain process of naturalization. Many others, however, were left in limbo, their status reflecting a combination of Draconian Japanese immigration laws and direct and indirect discrimination.

In 1932, when Shimizu Hideo arrived in Japan from the Japanese colony in Korea, the Korean teenager fell instantly in love. "I was so moved by the affluence of this country," recalled Shimizu at age seventy-eight. "I had been living in a very remote village in Korea, and I dreamed all the time about eating rice. That dream came true in Japan." Shimizu never looked back after leaving his native country. He acquired his Japanese name in 1939, when the Japanese colonial government ordered all Koreans to adopt Japanese surnames. During an interview, he stumbled pronouncing his Korean name, Ben San-Seou, as he spelled it in Roman letters, in a language he had largely forgotten. To the younger generation of Shimizus, Korea was a foreign country. Shimizu's thirty-eight-year-old son, Mitsuo, who visited South Korea for the first time in 1981 to honor the family's ancestral graves, explained his preference for Japan: "In this country, even people at the bottom have some kind of living, while in Korea the people at the bottom are desperately poor."[98]

For Shimizu Hideo, and hundreds of thousands of ethnic Koreans who moved to Japan on their own or as draft labor during World War Two, the good life in Japan meant an escape from poverty and a stake in Asia's most modern economy. In classical immigrant fashion, Shimizu started out working as a pig farmer and day laborer, trading up to factory jobs and his own small business. His son Mitsuo also had his own business, making concrete blocks. Even so, living in Japan meant adapting to permanent second-class status in a society that sometimes took extreme measures to cordon off non-Japanese and prevent assimilation. Officially, Japan insisted that there were no minorities in Japan—hence, there was no need to protect minority rights. As a result, non-Japanese faced a myriad of social and legal barriers.

The dilemma was especially acute for Japan's pre–Second World War colonial subjects, conservatively estimated at 860,000 Koreans and 50,000 Chinese. Under Japanese rule, their second-class status was part of colonial policy. During the Second World War, millions of Koreans and Chinese were drafted as soldiers, workers, and prostitutes—the latter euphemistically called *ianfu,* or "comfort women"—for the Japanese Imperial Army. After World War Two ended, 1.7 million Koreans returned to the Korean Peninsula. Some 600,000 chose to remain in Japan, among them the Shimizus.

Japan's ethnic Koreans worked hard, kept their expectations low, and did their best to fit in. Only in the last decades of the century did they begin to ratchet up their social and legal expectations. Encouraged partly by the civil rights movements in the United States and other countries, in the late 1980s Korean-Japanese began to bang on the doors of the Japanese establishment. In response, the Japanese government grudgingly adopted a more generous standard of minority rights. In 1991, Tokyo created a category for "special permanent residents" to cover former colonial subjects and their descendants. In 1993, the government finally abolished the practice of fingerprinting foreign residents. But Koreans continued to face subtle restrictions. In 1998, Kim Kyu Il, founder of a nonprofit ethnic Korean think tank, told one researcher, "Some people contend that Japan has changed considerably in this era of so-called internationalization. . . . But despite the changes on the outside, the inside hasn't changed very much at all."[99]

In the early 1990s, the Korean civil rights movement broadened to include even such middle-of-the-road Korean-Japanese as the Shimizus. In the early 1990s, the Shimizus joined other residents of their village in a campaign against Nissan, the auto manufacturing giant and their former landlord. The movement reached deep into the tragic history of Koreans in Japan. Until 1987, Nissan owned the land under the Shimizu house in Utoro Village, a Korean enclave twelve miles south of Kyoto. Shimizu and most of his neighbors first moved there during the Second World War, as laborers building a huge military airport. Although the Kyoto prefectural government originally owned the property, in the 1950s Nissan gradually took it over. In 1987, as land prices rose rapidly in the Kyoto area, Nissan sold the property to a real-estate developer. A year-and-a-half later, the developer sent eviction notices to Utoro's 380 mostly elderly residents.

Instead of moving off the property, the Utoro community mounted a fierce media campaign to get Nissan to disavow the deal with the developer. Although the company had not been in charge of the airport project that was responsible for bringing the Koreans to Utoro in the first place, the campaign used the big automaker as a symbol of the systematic deprivation of the rights of Korean-Japanese. The residents argued that if they had been ethnic Japanese, Nissan would never have sold their property so cavalierly. "You have to look at history," said Moon Kwan-ja, a diminutive, seventy-two-year-old who was among the original residents of Utoro. "Nissan forced us to do very hard labor, and to live in shabby houses. We endured that situation. We thought the land was owned by the government. I want to know why Nissan would let things go on for so long and then suddenly sell off the land without telling us."

The "Save Utoro" campaign was only one example of a variety of movements to uphold Korean-Japanese rights in Japan that appeared in the 1970s and 1980s. They were led by second-generation Korean-Japanese such as Shimizu's son Mitsuo. "I am regarded as a Korean but in my mind I am a Japanese," Mitsuo said. While their parents were content to work at jobs that Japanese did not want, younger Koreans began to challenge hiring barriers in the Japanese private sector, the professions, and some public service and teaching jobs—most of which legally or informally barred Koreans from entry. In a landmark 1974 case, Pak Chong Suk, a second-generation Korean, sued Hitachi for job discrimination and won. Pak passed an entrance examination for company employment but was refused a job once Hitachi learned he was an ethnic Korean. Four years later, Kim Kyong Duk, a graduate of Waseda University, fought and won the right to practice law after passing the notoriously difficult national legal examination. Until Kim challenged the rule, only Japanese nationals were allowed to become lawyers.

Between 1978 and the mid-1990s, a total of thirty-three ethnic Koreans followed in Kim Kyong-duk's footsteps, passed the bar exam and became attorneys, thirteen of them after changing their nationalities to Japanese. Over the same period, about thirty Koreans managed to get jobs as public school teachers, mostly because local school jurisdictions flouted MOE guidelines against hiring non-Japanese. The rule against offering teaching positions only to Japanese was finally abandoned in 1991.

While the number of Korean-Japanese professionals was still small by the late 1990s, the breakthroughs had a profound psychological effect. "I think the court battles had a great impact on Korean residents," said Tanaka Hiroshi, a civil rights activist and professor at Aichi Prefectural University. "It gave them the confidence that if they challenged social barriers they were likely to win." The plight of the Korean-Japanese was complicated by the fact that most of them—640,000 out of 860,000—were unable or unwilling to obtain Japanese citizenship. Thus, Tokyo could argue that it was only applying the normal restrictions of noncitizenship to Korean-Japanese, such as those on teaching in public schools or a blanket requirement for fingerprinting. Foes of the fingerprinting system charged that it represented a form of "Japanese apartheid" similar to South Africa's notorious erstwhile requirement that blacks carry passbooks. All foreigners living in Japan had to carry identification cards that included their thumbprints. Korean-Japanese argued that the system was particularly onerous for their community because it reinforced a common stereotype of close ties between Korean-Japanese and organized crime. In 1991, when Japan finally created an exemption to the rule for Korean residents in Japan, the decision was triggered not by a concern for minority rights but as part of a process of strengthening diplomatic ties with South Korea.

Even with the emergence of Korean professionals and elimination of some of the cruder forms of legal discrimination, Korean-Japanese said that there was much left to be done, particularly in the areas of Korean language education, equal employment, and recognition of the concept of minority rights. The Japanese government ratified the International Convention on Human Rights in 1979 but failed to approve its codicil against racism. Japan's 1980 letter to the United Nations Human Rights Commission stated baldly, "Minorities . . . do not exist in Japan," a position still not revised by the late 1990s.

Koreans remaining in Japan after World War Two fell under the intense scrutiny of Japanese immigration authorities, fearful of infiltration from communist North Korea. Japanese immigration policy discouraged Korean-Japanese residents from applying for citizenship. Even for non-Koreans, Japanese naturalization procedures are tedious and opaque. Citizenship in Japan is based on descent, or *jus sanguinis*, and for those not of Japanese descent the naturalization process can take twenty years. For Koreans, the wait could last forever, and even if they did obtain citizenship, they would continue to face severe discrimination. It made more sense to many Korean-Japanese to retain their Korean citizenship, which at least gave them theoretical recourse to governments in South and North Korea that cared about Korean welfare.

Korean-Japanese were also swept up in a rising wave of post-war Korean nationalism. Japan figured as South Korea's chief capitalist rival and North Korea's main capitalist villain, and a cardinal tenet of Korean nationalism was that Japan's colonial agenda—to crush Korea—was alive and well in post-war Japan. Both nations bitterly decried Japanese cultural policies during the colonial period from 1910 to 1945. In the early years of Japanese colonialism, the Japanese merely confiscated or destroyed cultural antiquities in the Korean peninsula, observing a long tradition in which Japanese despised Koreans but prized their ceramics, furniture, and sculpture. By the 1940s, the Japanese colonial administration banned the use of the Korean language and even personal names. Following the Nazi lead, Tokyo was moving toward a genocide program toward the end of the war. Wartime Justice Minister Yanagawa Heisuke had this to say about Koreans: "Outwardly, they appear to be submissive, but inwardly, they resist. All the lawless Koreans should be banished to an island and castrated."

Kim Kyong Duk, who ran a law office in Tokyo that catered mainly to Koreans, contended that the first step was for the Japanese government to recognize the rights of the 110,000 Korean-Japanese who had obtained Japanese citizenship by 1991. Once their rights were assured, other Korean-

Japanese would be more willing to naturalize, he argued. "I believe that Japan will become a multicultural society," Kim said. "Our movement is in line with the future of Japanese society. Japan cannot avoid this course." Indeed, after the reforms of the early 1990s, the naturalization rate for Korean nationals in Japan jumped from about 5,000 per year in the 1980s to 10,000 per year in the 1990s.

Kim's own struggle for recognition reflected both how far Korean-Japanese had come in the 1970s and 1980s and how much further they had yet to go. Until he graduated from college in 1972, he went by his Japanese name, Kanazawa Keitoku. "It was for self-preservation," Kim said. "I was defeated by the discrimination that exists in Japanese society." After graduation, he decided that he could no longer put up with the pretense and began using his Korean name and studying the Korean language. But when he passed the national legal examination, the Japanese Supreme Court refused to admit him to its Legal Training and Research Institute, where Japanese lawyers are required to carry out an apprenticeship. The pass ratio of the national legal exam is about 2 percent. In 1978, when Kim sued the government and won, he became the first Korean-Japanese to practice law under a Korean name and passport. Eighteen years after Kim's legal victory, three to four Korean-Japanese lawyers passed the exam every year and became lawyers without having to renounce their Korean names or nationalities. "I am fighting for the benefits of Korean residents," Kim said. "At the same time, I want to make this country better."

The flip side of the tortured experience of Koreans in Japan was the welcome held out to ethnic Japanese immigrants, mostly from Latin America, who poured into Japan starting in the late 1980s. They arrived in Japan at a time when the Japanese economy was booming and its industry faced a severe labor shortage, particularly for workers at the bottom end of the scale. These were jobs that the Japanese were no longer willing to do and the country's immigration rules barred foreigners from unskilled labor.

On a cool December evening in 1991, the warm yellow glow of the Restaurante e Pastelaria São Paolo lit a dingy side street in Hamamatsu, Japan, a blue-collar city situated between Tokyo and Nagoya. Mery and Mario Mizumoto greeted friends in Portuguese and scanned the racks of *feijoada*, *café cacique*, and other Brazilian groceries for sale. Posters advertised cheap airfares to São Paulo and Rio de Janeiro and explained how to tune in to Portuguese programs on local radio stations.[100]

The air was thick with nostalgia. But despite such reminders of home, the Mizumotos weren't thinking of returning to Brazil anytime soon. Both their parents had moved to Brazil as teenagers, part of an exodus of Japanese labor to South America that began in the 1860s and peaked again after World

War Two. In the early 1990s, the Mizumotos joined the exodus back to Japan. In São Paulo, they had scraped by with a small company making plastic bags. In Japan, Mario, forty, assembled elevators and escalators for Mitsubishi Electrical Corporation, one of Japan's premier companies. Mery, his wife had a job teaching Portuguese to Japanese executives. In Brazil, the Mizumotos had to cope with runaway inflation and nurse along an old car; in Japan, the Mizumoto's yen-based salaries keep getting bigger and bigger in terms of *cruzeiros* or any other foreign currency. In Japan, they became a two-car family. After three years, their son, Ricardo, aged nine, refused to speak Portuguese at all. "I don't really know about the future," Mery said. "We may just go back to Brazil as tourists."

The Mizumotos—and tens of thousands of other Latin Americans of Japanese descent—were part of a twentieth-century immigration gold rush focused on Japan. It reached its height in 1990, when the Japanese government introduced three-year work visas for all foreigners of Japanese descent. Afterward, the volume abated with the collapse of Japan's bubble economy in the early 1990s. Also in 1990, the Japanese government introduced harsh new penalties against illegal foreign workers not of Japanese descent and their employers. Under Japanese immigration law, unskilled workers were banned altogether. The only exemption was for unskilled workers of Japanese descent.

The first easing of such rules came only in 1999, after the UN pointed out that Japan would need to take in 600,000 immigrants a year in order to maintain its rapidly declining workforce. According to UN projections, by 2050 the Japanese population would shrink from 127 million to 105 million. By the end of the 1990s, public concern about the shrinking of the Japanese population had risen to such a point that private groups were researching and recruiting overseas Japanese to come back to fill service jobs. The *Washington Post* interviewed one such entrepreneur, Saito Toru of the Ajia Nikkeijin Relief Center (Relief Center for Overseas Japanese in Asia). He was busy contacting the children of Japanese soldiers who had remained in a remote part of Thailand after the war and had succeeded in persuading twenty Thai Japanese to enter a training program at a Bangkok hospital to become "Level 2 Home Helpers" in Japanese nursing homes.

Even if all 2.5 million estimated overseas Japanese returned to Japan, it would not be enough to fill the gap. The Japanese Justice Ministry responded by urging Japanese to "aggressively carry out the smooth acceptance" of foreigners, and formulated new, slightly looser rules governing the categories of jobs that foreigners could hold in Japan. Even so, the head of the Asian People's Friendship Society told the *New York Times*, "Japanese society still has fantasies about our pure blood, and about the ability of Japanese people to understand each other better than others. Even if the government or the business community accepts more foreigners, without much more effort on our side, these feelings of rejection toward foreigners will remain strong."[101]

The aggressive asymmetry of Japanese immigration rules was certainly not unique to Japan. In the 1920s, both the United States and Canada accepted white European immigrants while limiting Asian immigration to males or banning it altogether. Australia prohibited Asian immigration well into the 1970s. Japanese politicians and nationalist intellectuals frequently made reference to the anti-Japanese immigration laws in the United States, reminding their audiences of the long history of American prejudice against them. In Germany, which also granted citizenship based on descent, resident Turks faced similar discrimination to Koreans in Japan. "Japanese are not confident about opening up, but this is because of historical factors," said Yamazaki Masakazu, a playwright who looked at immigration policy as a member of a prime minister's commission in the late 1990s. "Japan was effectively closed until the 1970s or 1980s."[102]

Similar to the White-only policies in North America seventy years earlier, Japan's immigration strategy in the 1990s was to deny entry to unskilled labor from developing countries, mostly those nearby in Asia, while welcoming ethnic Japanese "returning" after several generations from abroad. One million citizens had left Japan earlier in the century, many as part of official resettlement programs. After World War Two, the government again encouraged demobilized soldiers and Japanese settlers of Manchuria, China, and Korea to emigrate. The main targets were Brazil, Paraguay, Argentina, and Bolivia, which already had resident ethnic Japanese populations, and welcomed new Japanese emigrants; they brought Japanese money with them in the form of official grants and, much later, corporate investment.

In all, about 262,000 Japanese left to live abroad after the war.[103] Japanese officials saw these ethnic Japanese communities as the answer to Japan's low birthrate and worsening demographics. In Latin America, the impact of the Japanese recruitment drive was extraordinary. In the first two years after the initial easing of rules, 150,000 *nikkeijin* ("ethnic Japanese") moved back to Japan seeking jobs. The number included 120,000 Brazilians, an incredible 10 percent of Brazil's entire Japanese population. The other 30,000 immigrants came from Peru and other countries, where a thriving black market sprang up selling false Japanese family registers, which were used to obtain *nikkei* visas. In Hamamatsu, where the Mizumotos lived, the Brazilian-Japanese community grew tenfold between 1989 and 1991, when immigration was at its highest, from 520 to 5,400.

The policy of banning immigration by unskilled workers of Asian origin while encouraging ethnic-Japanese workers angered Japan's neighbors, but there was little they could do about it. "This is nothing new," said the Reverend Watanabe Hidetoshi, who ran a Yokohama-based counseling service for foreign workers. "It is in line with Japanese policy for the past half-century. They want the homogeneity of Japanese society to be kept by blood." If Japanese society gave a big welcome to overseas Japanese, its treatment of job-hungry Asians arriving on its shores in the late 1980s was callous and brutal, Watanabe said. He described the increasingly abusive treatment of non-Japanese foreign workers as the flip side of its generous behavior toward the *nikkeijin* job seekers.

Around the same time that Chiang Shu-ling was laying plans for graduate school in Japan, the Shimizus were agitating for expanded civil rights, and the Mizumotos starting their new life in Hamamatsu, Japan began to face powerful new pressures on its immigration policy from an unexpected source—upwardly mobile economic migrants from the developing countries of Asia. These immigrants swarmed into Japan on short-term visas for tourists or Japanese-language study and immediately found service-sector jobs as cooks, janitors, construction workers, and maids. By the end of the decade, despite numerous crackdowns, illegal aliens made up nearly 20 percent of the 1.3 million foreign population in Japan.

The previous large-scale inflow had occurred before World War Two, when Koreans and Taiwanese flooded into Japan to fill the economic niche left vacant as blue-collar Japanese were siphoned into the war effort in China and Southeast Asia. After the war, Japanese immigration policy was to encourage the natives of former Japanese colonies, especially Koreans, to go home. In 1947, the U.S. Occupation drafted an Alien Registration Law that denationalized Koreans in Japan and required them to carry alien registration cards identifying themselves as Chosen, the Japanese term for Koreans as an ethnic group. The policy of banning immigration of unskilled foreign workers was set during this period, part of SCAP's strategy to screen out potential communist agitators. The 1950 Nationality Làw, also enacted by SCAP, preserved the principle of citizenship by descent established by the Meiji government in 1899. Both Americans and Japanese assumed that Japan was a racially homogeneous nation, whoever else might happen to live in the country.

What happened in the 1980s was almost purely a function of the sudden appreciation of the Japanese yen after 1985. Although large Japanese manufacturers were able to move production abroad, where they could find cheap labor, thousands of small subcontractors at the bottom of Japan's industrial hierarchy were unable to afford the move, at last initially. The small companies eagerly hired Asians without checking their visa status. As word got around, Filipinos, Chinese, Thais, Koreans, Pakistanis, and Bangladeshis rushed to Japan, entering on short-term tourist visas and quickly disappearing into the factory workshop enclaves of Osaka, Yokohama, and Nagoya.

At the same time, the bubble economy created an enormous demand for workers. Japanese graduates of elite universities could choose from dozens of job offers, and companies worked out elaborate gimmicks to compete for new recruits, from paid trips to resorts where they conducted job interviews to luxury housing for freshmen employees. The Japanese press made much of the fact that Japanese had become unwilling to perform "Three K" jobs, standing for *kitsui*, *kitanai*, and *kurai*—difficult, dirty, and dangerous. For many employers, illegal foreign workers were the only solution.

It is late afternoon, and the lights are coming on in Ikebukuro. In this neighborhood in northwestern Tokyo, the department stores loom like megaliths over a swirl of honky-tonk bars, Asian discount stores, and noodle restaurants. Most Tokyo dwellers see little more of Ikebukuro than its train station, but about 11,000 Chinese, Koreans, Filipinos, and other Asians called it home in the early 1990s. Tiny though that number was, it gave Ikebukuro one of the densest concentrations of non-Japanese in the country, and made it a focus of the government's efforts to block Asian immigration.[104]

Zhou Yi, a twenty-six-year-old from China's Guangdong Province who drove trucks until he arrived in Ikebukuro in March 1988, said he "would never have had an opportunity like this in China." By day, Zhou studied Japanese at the Tokyo Language School, one of hundreds of quickie language schools advertising their services from billboards and canvas banners throughout the neighborhood. By night, he waited on tables at the Genya Ramen Shop, just a few blocks away from the school.

Like many of his fellow students, he entered Japan on a student visa, which limited his part-time work to a maximum of twenty hours per week. Zhou claimed only to work up to the approved limit, but many other students said that they worked forty hours a week and more, for a monthly income of about $375.[105] Guo Gang, another student at the Tokyo Language School, said that was about four times what he made in China as a full-time clerical employee of the Shanghai Customs Bureau, even though his job was considered privileged and desirable. Guo took Japanese classes four hours a day and swept floors as a janitor for another four hours. "Before I came to Tokyo," he said, "I never did this kind of work. But if I had stayed in China, I would never have seen the world. At home, you may think you're satisfied, but once you're outside it seems very inadequate."

Such starry-eyed optimism and persistence on the part of foreign workers was new to the Japanese labor market. It had Japanese immigration authorities tied in knots. In the late 1980s, Japan was the target country of choice for

Asian migrant workers, whether they were looking for maximum returns from low-level labor, or, like Guo Gang and Zhou Yi, pursuing dreams of self-fulfillment. The fact that the rise of the yen was accompanied by the collapse of oil prices and a weak U.S. dollar intensified the trend, undercutting the attractions of the Middle East and North America for transient workers. Moreover, Japanese business quickly saw the benefits of some form of controlled immigration of cheap labor from Asia. "We can't stop the flow and we shouldn't," said Kurosawa Yoh in 1988, when he was deputy president of the Industrial Bank of Japan. "We should allow such workers to get into Japan legally and control how they work. To shut off opportunity for foreign workers is unfair."

Employers were often initially reluctant to hire non-Japanese, but exposure tended to change their minds. Kawanabe Takeshi, personnel manager of Nihon Building Service, a janitorial services agency with about 2,300 employees, admitted to hiring four Chinese on student visas. He sent them to work at City Hall—the Tokyo Municipal Government Building. "Look," Kawanabe said, "I don't think it's a good idea to publish it abroad that Japanese workers have become lazy. The Japanese work hard, but let's just say that the Chinese work a lot harder than I expected." The hiring attracted the attention of newspapers since it appeared to imply government approval of unskilled foreign labor. In fact, the opposite was the case. The Japanese Ministry of Justice and Labor Ministry were in charge of immigration and labor policy. Their officials dearly wanted to slam the door shut but didn't know how. An official report on illegal immigration in 1988 condemned the "malign" influence of unskilled foreign workers and called for a system in which employers would have to seek government approval prior to any such hires.

"The reason why Asian people hope to get jobs in Japan is that they see Japan as economically a big country," said Kitaura Masayuki, a Labor Ministry official. "Perhaps their governments will ask us to expand job opportunities here. But if Japan gives them jobs, it doesn't lead to any resolution of their domestic problems. Japan would prefer to provide technical and financial aid to help the job problem in their home countries." As to the shortage of service-sector workers, Kitaura insisted that it was preferable to use elderly Japanese to plug the gap than to open the gate to unskilled workers.

During the bubble economy years, however, the flow of Asian workers was virtually unstoppable. Officials at Tokyo's Narita International Airport said that the numbers of Asians entering the country increased dramatically in the late 1980s, along with the numbers of detentions of illegal aliens. The officials estimated that they caught only one-fifth of the offenders. It was particularly difficult to check such gray areas as the growing army of Japanese-language students. Visa requirements for students provided a loophole for would-be unskilled workers. The government regarded the language schools with large Asian clienteles as little more than facades. This was particularly true in Ikebukuro, where not a single Japanese-language school was accredited with the Education Ministry. There, classrooms that were packed with students at 4:20 P.M. were deserted by 4:32 P.M., as students left in a rush to get to their part-time jobs.

Officially, the Japanese government decried the influx of illegal foreign workers, estimated at between 200,000 and 300,000 at the height of the inflow, and tried hard to turn them back. Unofficially, according to Watanabe, the Christian minister and activist, the government allowed the hiring to continue but kept pressure on foreigners to leave by denying them access to basic medical and legal services. The result was that Japanese employers were left free to abuse their foreign workers. They were routinely paid less and worked longer hours than Japanese co-workers. Employers denied their salaries at will and generally refused sick leave and medical insurance.

Watanabe made it his business to arouse international concern for the plight of foreign workers in Japan. In August 1991, representing the World Council of Churches, he went to Geneva to testify before a subcommittee of the UNHCR. He told the UN that he had tracked thousands of human-rights violations among foreign workers in Japan, ranging from unpaid wages to forced prostitution and traffic in women. "No one was aware that Japan has this problem," recalled Watanabe, a thin, intense man in his fifties. "In other countries, there are channels to accept legal migrant workers. But in Japan the door is *de jure* closed to foreign workers, leading to much suffering. The reason why the problem becomes more serious in Japan is due to the total illegality of the workers."

Unlike the ethnic Japanese Mizumotos, the Asians who come to Japan seeking work told stories of hostile bosses, unsafe working conditions, and narrow opportunities. Equipped with a degree in mechanical engineering from Punjab University, Arif Azeem came to Japan in 1988 hoping to land a white-collar office job. Instead, the young Pakistani fell into a succession of factory jobs. "I had high expectations," he said. "If I had been in the United States or Canada, I would have a master's degree by now. All I got in Japan was frustration. Among the most difficult things for many of the illegal immigrants to accept were Japanese stereotypes of Asians as illiterate, backward people with loud and dirty habits. Every Japanese thinks foreigners are third-class citizens," Azeem said. "In each of the factories I have worked in for the last three and a half years, the thinking has been the same." He said his bosses routinely applied a double standard to foreign and Japanese workers. At one factory, Azeem says, he had to load 11,000 to 15,000 lbs. per day onto trucks, twice the amount handled by Japanese workers, for lower wages.

Not all foreign workers were bitter. Celso Sahagun, a former clerk for the Philippine Congress, went to work on the night shift for a subcontractor to Nissan, which helped him obtain a valid working visa. "It's really strange, but the work is not as hard as I expected," he said. "My job is exactly the same as the Japanese. We respect each other. So long as you don't bother them, they don't bother you."

As the Japanese economy went into recession in the early 1990s, illegal aliens ceased to cause consternation, both because control was tightened and because the influx slacked off. Japanese immigration authorities began methodically rounding up and deporting the foreigners. By the mid-1990s, the more visible communities of illegal workers—the Iranian men who once flocked to Ueno Park and later Yoyogi Park, the Chinese "students" who once packed the ersatz language schools in Ikebukuro, even the Filipina and Thai hostesses—largely vanished.

Many Japanese heaved a sigh of relief. Some, however, were concerned about the apparent return of homogeneity to Japanese society. Okuda Michihiro, a sociology professor at Rikkyo Univesity, argued that Japan had lost a "precious opportunity" to establish the foundations of a multicultural society. He conducted the first-ever academic study of a community of new immigrants in Ikebukuro. Okuda's study looked at the social structure and attitudes of both the immigrants and Japanese there. Ikebukuro had first become a magnet for Chinese students in the late 1980s. They flocked to its language schools and worked in the thousands of tiny restaurants around the train station. By the early 1990s, non-Japanese made up 12 percent of the population of Ikebukuro, compared to an average of 1 percent of the population nationwide. Okuda's findings flew in the face of common Japanese stereotypes about Asians. Far from lacking skills, he found that 37.5 percent of Ikebukuro's foreign residents had college degrees. Nor did they seek out Japan merely for economic reasons. Most listed the United States or Europe as other places they had considered before coming to Japan.

Much to Okuda's surprise, he also found that with time, the Japanese grew to accept the Asians next door. After an initial coolness, landlords and shopkeepers in the area gradually became more respectful. Okuda chalked this up to the Asians' diligent efforts to get along. Still, there was a trend toward greater tolerance and understanding, he said. When the Asians first began to move in, local authorities predicted that crime levels would rise. No such thing happened. Okuda found few instances of conflict or confrontation among the immigrants and local residents.

The warm feelings of locals for the immigrants did not extend to the Japanese police, however. The police looked at the survey as an interesting way to monitor the foreign community and were among the first to make inquiries about Okuda's work. They quickly began using phony surveys to trap illegals. In one incident, police arrested fifteen foreigners after they completed forms passed out by plainclothes officers in Yoyogi Park, a popular weekend haunt of foreign workers.

Some of the ugliest incidents involving illegal Asian immigrants were in 1989 and 1990, when the arrival of ships carrying Chinese seeking refuge in Japan led to an anti-Chinese panic and communal manhunts.

Omura, a modest town on the craggy Kyushu coast had long been considered a little different. Four hundred years ago, it was the stronghold of one of the country's first Christian *daimyo*s. At a time when it was a capital offense for a Japanese to even talk to a foreigner, Portuguese and Chinese merchants were allowed to maintain small trading posts there. In the early 1990s, Omura once again played host to outsiders. It was the site of Japan's largest refugee camp, set up in the early 1980s. At the time, Vietnamese and Cambodian refugees were pouring out of war-torn Indochina, and the camp gave the community considerable pride.[106]

Such pride made the events of the late 1980s and early 1990s all the more painful. Omura became a symbol of Japanese xenophobia at its worst. The controversy stemmed in part from the fact that located immediately adjacent to the Omura Refugees Reception Center was a far more sinister facility. Past the Baw Baw Pachinko Parlor, a batting range, and a Budget Rent-a-Car outpost, the watchtowers and gray concrete of the maximum security Omura Intruders' Holding Center loomed over the cheerful, cluttered detritus of the town. Japanese authorities described the center as a place where illegal foreigners waited peacefully until arrangements could be made for their departure. But it had all the appurtenances of a maximum-security prison. No visitors were allowed, including members of the press. Even staff workers were not supposed to go inside the walls, and they monitored activities inside through closed-circuit television.

Until 1990, the refugee center and the deportation facility operated separately despite their physical proximity. Then, for the first time since the Indochinese exodus, a large number of new boat people began arriving in Japanese waters, in large, well-equipped vessels. The initial reaction on the part of Japanese authorities was confused. Since the boat people were Asians speaking unknown languages in boats, immigration officials assumed they were Vietnamese. But when the officials discovered that the boats carried Chinese rather than Vietnamese or Cambodian refugees, there was national indignation. Newspaper headlines fanned anxieties by proclaiming "mass arrivals" of refugees from China. Citizens' groups put together voluntary manhunts to track down escapees. Arriving at the height of the speculative frenzy of the bubble years, Japanese condemned the Chinese refugees as economic opportunists. According to the Japanese government, not one of the 2,084 "fake boat people" made a formal claim for political asylum. Most had paid huge fees to brokers to board the boats, which left from ports in southern China for their voyage to Japan.

The boats began arriving in May 1989 and continued through the fall. Nonetheless, Tokyo was adamant about the absence of any connection between the Chinese refugees and the Chinese democracy movement or the Tiananmen massacre of dissidents in June. Human rights activists said that at least some of the Chinese refugees tried to present petitions for political asylum but were ignored. The activists were not allowed to meet with the refugees, and the government quickly worked out a face-saving and economical deal with Beijing to deport the Chinese using Chinese ships. China sent the first one in December 1989, and by the end of the year the "fake" boat people were gone.

On the Japanese side, the operation began to get out of hand when immigration officials decided to use the opportunity to deport all recent Chinese arrivals. This meant screening the Indochinese refugee centers, ostensibly to catch Chinese nationals who had managed to slip in with the Vietnamese and Cambodians. Omura and eleven other refugee centers were plunged into confusion.

Residents of the refugee centers were naturally terrified. At Omura, they rioted twice and tried to escape when word spread that some would be transferred to the deportation center next door. During the second riot, police had to call in reserves from Nagasaki, the largest city in the area. Townspeople who once held sporting matches and parties for the refugees began to shun the center. The uproar left many of those sympathetic to the refugees' plight deeply perplexed. Observers said that the crux of the matter was that Japan still had no general policy on refugees and that racist attitudes predominated. Although Japan gave in to international pressure and set a permanent quota of 10,000 for Indochinese refugees in the early 1980s, critics said that refugees of other nationalities were virtually excluded. Because of the Japanese ban on visas for unskilled labor, by definition an "economic refugee" was also an illegal alien.

"Many Japanese think other Asians are coming to steal the wealth which Japan worked so hard for," said Inyaku Tomoya, a staff member of the Pacific-Asia Resources Center in Tokyo. "I think they are afraid of them. In Asia, only Japan has become an economic giant. The other nations are still poor." When Inyaku's organization put out a tiny newspaper advertisement pleading against deporting the Chinese, the office was bombarded with angry phone calls complaining that they behaved in an "un-Japanese" manner. Inyaku and others at the time noted the contrast between Japan's skyrocketing prosperity and its efforts to exclude disadvantaged foreigners. In 1990, the Justice Ministry moved to introduce new and more stringent rules against foreign workers. Amendments to the Immigration Control and Refugee Recognition Law included fines of up to two million yen, about $20,000, and three years in prison for anyone employing illegal foreign workers. The reasoning, said Tanaka Minoru, a spokesman for the Tokyo Regional Immigration Bureau, was that "if unskilled foreign laborers are allowed into Japan, it will lead to total chaos."

In the late 1980s, Rey Ventura, a young Filipino journalist, went undercover in Japan to write about the lives of illegal foreign workers. "There is no Japanese Dream," he wrote plaintively. "And yet Japan, for the Filipino, has become a second America. There is no Statue of Liberty in Yokohama—why should there be? A statue of the Yen would be more appropriate. We do not dream of becoming Japanese citizens—even for brides who achieve this, it is a secondary consideration. We do not imagine that we will settle there forever. We know that we will not be accepted, and anyway we cannot imagine submitting to the extreme discipline of Japanese life. Still, more and more, we see Japan as part of our future."[107]

One category of unskilled Asian workers, however, was greeted with open arms. While Japan's urban areas and factories were running short of Japanese men in the late 1980s, rural areas had the opposite problem—no women. The solution was found in a brisk business in mail-order brides, exclusively from Asia.

Kajimoto Kenji, an aging groom at thirty-six, had a hard time getting married. But he had an even harder time living with his bride, Dolores, a sweet twenty-two-year-old Filipina. She spoke no Japanese, and Kajimoto spoke no Tagalog, his wife's native language. So they tried to get by in English, which neither of them knew well enough to put together a complete sentence. "We spend a lot of time with dictionaries," grumbled Kajimoto, a construction worker. "She carries around a Tagalog-English dictionary and an English-Japanese dictionary and I carry a Japanese-English dictionary." Asked how she liked this arrangement, Dolores replied in faltering English, "Good. I like. Nice people. Very kind."[108]

Kenji and Dolores, together with their two-month-old son, Tetsuya, were part of a roaring business in mail-order brides that ran counter to centuries of prejudice against marriage to foreigners. Were it not for the servant status of wives in traditional Japanese households, the trade might be seen as a beacon of tolerance. As things stood, many of the women found themselves virtual captives of their husbands and mothers-in-law in remote villages, far from any source of help. As long as they bore sons, however, their role was valued. Dealing mainly in poor Asian women from the Philippines, Thailand, and South Korea, the mail-order bride business rankled Japanese feminists, worried traditionalists, and produced some very confused couples.

Kenji and Dolores met in July 1987 through Kajimoto's village council in the tiny town of Higayashi Iyayama on the southern Japanese island of Shikoku. A second son, Kajimoto had twice failed in his courtship of Japanese women and was ready to pay about $15,000[109] to cover the village council's costs, including the services of marriage brokers. "I would rather have married a Japanese woman, but I had no choice," he said. Kajimoto claimed that his wife was adjusting despite the constant struggle to master the cultural niceties of living in a Japanese farming village and coping with his many relations. For his part, Kajimoto had curbed a drinking habit to please his wife.

Although Japan's boom in Asian marriages started in the countryside, where there was a desperate shortage of marriageable women, it gradually took hold in the cities as well. In 1988, between 100 and 200 marriage brokers were active in the Tokyo-Osaka area, according to Itamoto Yoko, who tracked the Asian bride business for Nippon Seinenkan, a national youth organization that formerly ran its own marriage agency. "I get dozens of phone calls from Japanese men asking about Asian women," she said. "If you ask them, why not get married to an American or a Canadian woman, they'll say no, we don't want independent women. The Asians come from disadvantaged backgrounds relative to their husbands, so they are much more dependent." Itamoto and other observers worried about the women, who had few resources if the marriages failed to work out. At least the *yakuza* seemed to have kept out of the business, unlike the traffic in Asian prostitutes.

In the late 1980s, the numbers of such marriages were small—about 4,000 couples in 1987—but the strength of the yen slashed costs for prospective grooms to the point that a bride might cost less than a new car. Marriage brokers bombarded Japanese village offices with direct mail advertising. In Tokyo and other cities, they advertised in popular sports magazines. "I've got marriage catalogs all over my office," said Kawakami Yukio, a village headman in Aichi Prefecture. Mostly, however, the brokers worked through personal contacts and the mail even in cities, said Ochiai Kazuaki, who described himself as the Japanese liaison of a Manila-based marriage broker and doubled as the agent for a Philippine scuba diving club. "At first I felt like an arrogant Japanese, throwing my money around in poor countries and choosing anyone I liked," he said in his office in a fourth-floor walkup, strewn with diving equipment. "But now I've met couples where both members are happy."

Ochiai sent prospective clients pages of photographs with basic data including the name, date of birth, height, weight, and hobbies of each woman. For the men, Ochiai said, the only requirement from the company was that they have a proper job. Education, age, and appearance did not matter. For women, there was an age limit of thirty. Women who spoke Japanese were ruled out on grounds that they might have worked as entertainers or prostitutes in Japan. Finally, the agency looked for women from rural areas, who would want to make their families happy through marriage, according to Ochiai. The brokers' fees bought an introduction and paid for four- or five-day trips to Manila. That was time enough for a trial introduction, or *omiai,* with two or three women, a date or two, and a church wedding.

At least for the Kajimotos, money seemed to have bought an adequate measure of affection. "Dolores is quite obedient and respects our parents and neighbors," Kajimoto said. "In general, she treats my parents, older brother, and two elder sisters pretty well." He planned for his son to learn both Japanese and Tagalog.

Inevitably, Japanese prejudices against Asians followed Japanese multinationals as they rocketed into Asia in the 1980s and 1990s. Unlike mail-order brides and illegal Asian workers in Japan, the Asian employees of Japanese companies had high expectations. Many grew up hooked on Japanese products and as adults had developed a certain reverence for Japanese management and technology. Most quickly learned the limitations of their employers, and if their objective was fast-track promotion, moved on. Nonetheless, friction between Japanese companies and their Asian employees was a subtle but significant factor undermining Japan's grander Asianization schemes of the late 1980s and early 1990s.

Robert Solodow, a Tokyo-based management consultant, told a story about a Japanese manager in Malaysia. He frequently did work for the company, and its president came to him and said that things were going wrong and nobody could understand why. "Well, we sent a consultant down to talk to the guy," said Solodow. "He communicated with his staff in English. It turned out, for reasons of family background or whatever, that he insisted on addressing his Malaysian staff, in English, as 'colonial scum.' We had our consultant virtually move in with him for six months, trying to persuade him that regardless of what his personal opinions were, there were some things it was wrong to project." Sato Mitsuhiro, the president of Honda Motors, Thailand, solved this sort of problem by making sure his Japanese staff did not get close to the Thai elite. He described his staff's manners as "barbaric." "They simply don't know what to do," he said. "They don't know how to eat, how to talk or what role the big Thai families play in business."

In the mid-1990s, Japanese companies routinely expressed dismay about the quick turnover of their white-collar workforce in Asia, particularly in the overheated Thai and Malaysian economies. Local engineers were in such short supply that they could leave jobs virtually at will for higher salaries or better perks. Japanese companies, used to feudal loyalty from employees and passive company unions, found such job mobility subversive. At the same time, they exacerbated the problem by refusing to promote local employees into senior management. The standard explanation was that it took time to cycle local employees through the Japanese seniority system—in which the company hired high school or college graduates and moved them up salary grades at the same time as others in their age group. "Time" for many Japanese companies seemed to translate into a generation, starting from the point when they first made the commitment to opening up their executive suites. This practice did not endear the Japanese to governments such as Singapore, which obsessively tracked the number of Singaporeans in senior management in foreign-owned companies and subsidiaries.

In 1990, the Malaysian government pressured Matsushita Electric, Malaysia's largest foreign employer, to promote more Malaysian managers. Matsushita complied, promising to groom two of its employees for top management at one of its thirteen subsidiaries. At a huge Matsushita training facility near its Osaka headquarters, I watched the reaction as one of Matsushita's Malaysian employees, Gan Wee Feng, described his ambitions within the company. "I'd like to be top man of MELCOM [Matsushita's electric appliances subsidiary in Malaysia]," he said. "If not, I'll be top man of my own company."[110] His boss, Fukuda Shin, was sitting next to him during the interview, and laughed nervously at the comment, cringing at the young man's brashness.

Gan was part of a new program designed to give promising foreign workers closer exposure to Japanese culture as well as Matsushita's management style and values. Seventy percent of the 61 foreigners in the program were from Asia, a tiny minority among the 76,000 Japanese trainees. Another 728 foreigners were enrolled in technical programs in Osaka, 64.7 percent from Asia, and 3,346 trainees toiled at regional centers in the United States, Singapore, and Europe. Set in rolling hills outside Osaka, with low-rise white buildings, the center had the look and feel of a university campus. The grounds included a traditional tea garden, and signs in Japanese and English proclaiming *manabu shin* ("a studious heart" in Japanese) and "Attitude of Learning" (in English).

Gan was thirty-one, and in 1992, had been with the company for more than a decade. Matsushita had just selected him to participate in the "working in Japan program" whose graduates were meant to begin moving up the ranks as Matsushita "globalized" its operations. It was his second training stint in the country. From an ethnic Chinese family on the backward east coast of the Malay Peninsula, Gan joined Matsushita in 1981, right after graduating from Kuantan Polytechnic in the state of Pahang. Gan had a degree in electrical engineering. There were a lot of offers. He decided on Matsushita because he saw it as a "company that wanted people to grow." After a year on the job in Malaysia, he eagerly accepted the company's invitation to spend time in Osaka as a trainee at Matsushita headquarters.

When Gan first visited Japan in 1983, Malaysia was in the full throes of its "Look East" policy of following the Japanese model as an alternative to free-market capitalism in the Anglo-American mode. With funding from the Japanese government, Malaysia sent between 400 and 500 technical trainees per year to Japan, for language training followed by placement with companies. Gan was one of an elite group sponsored by MITI's Association for Overseas Technical Scholarship. He was sent first to Tokyo for three weeks of language training, then to Osaka to carry on his training in the corporate production engineering division, where research engineers designed ways to make products such as rice cookers faster and more efficiently.

When Gan arrived in Osaka, he was promptly shown to a desk piled high with technical papers—in Japanese. At the time, the young Malaysian could barely manage a word of the language, let alone read its written script. "It was very difficult," he said. "Everything we did was through our own observations. We had to try to catch up with what we needed to do. If they took a step back, so did we." Gan shyly asked if he might spend time in the factory, taking notes on the actual machines, rather than sitting in an office trying to decipher documents written in *kanji*, which he couldn't read. No, he was told. *Ganbatte*. So Gan stayed in the office, taking notes on mechanical drawings and charts. When he went back to Malaysia, Gan took with him a set of worksheets describing processes the Japanese used in developing new machines, and how jobs were structured.

I asked Gan's current boss, the executive director of the training institute, what he thought about Gan's experience. "Excellent," the manager said. "Very Japanese." He commended Gan's diligence. "By having key Matsushita personnel in Japan they can further understand the Japanese management style and system," he said. Gan wasn't so sure. He was not convinced on the practicality of learning production processes without the benefit of manuals or instruction. "Some of the methods of Japanese management would not be applicable in my country directly," Gan said. "You can learn from them, but it's very difficult to apply. The culture is different, the people are different, and the behavior is different." Yet, ten years after the first experience, Gan returned to Japan for a two-year stint in a rice cooker factory in the Japanese countryside. By the time of the second visit, Gan's Japanese was not much better, although he had seized opportunities to chat in Japanese with Japanese engineers assigned to his factory in Malaysia. "It's going to be quite tough," he admitted.

Japanese companies had particularly severe problems in China. "The ways Japanese and Chinese think about business clash head on," wrote Sonoda Shigeto, a sociologist at Chuo University.[111] The *JETRO China Newsletter*, an English-language publication of the Japan External Trade Organization, routinely carried articles about the problems of Japanese companies in China. In 1996, Japan's government television network, NHK, ran a sympathetic documentary on the woes of Japanese joint ventures.[112] So bad were the problems that the documentary created a reaction of "culture shock" when it aired in Japan, according to one observer. The Chinese went ballistic and took out their ire on the Japanese companies that had cooperated with NHK. In order to appease their Chinese hosts, the Japanese companies had to formally complain to the network.[113]

Japanese were dumbfounded when their Chinese partners walked out on contracts and shut down joint venture factories without warning. When the Japanese attempted to take their former business partners to court, the Chinese government took a hands-off stance. "Despite the Chinese government's frequent intervention in the normal activities of business enterprises, when there is a problem, it seems unable to help," fumed Sugita Toshiaki, a Japanese consultant. "Although the business has been conducted for over ten years, the Chinese partner still insists on bargaining over everything."[114]

According to Sonoda, the problems came down to the diametrically opposed working styles of the Chinese and Japanese, from shop floor to management suite. In the first place, the Chinese viewed their business relationships with the Japanese as fundamentally exploitative, "and in extreme cases take the attitude of grabbing everything possible from the Japanese." Senior Chinese managers were in the habit of making their own decisions, rather than farming them out for "bottom up" consensus in the time-consuming Japanese style.

If the actions of their Chinese managers were maddening, the Japanese found the behavior of Chinese workers simply "unfathomable." Unlike the passive and cooperative Japanese factory worker, the Chinese openly flouted company rules and were aggressive in demanding special perks, such as training trips to Japan. They commandeered company property at will and showed no loyalty to the enterprise. The processes of hiring and firing were fraught with pitfalls. Chinese were accustomed to getting jobs through personal relationships, or *guanxi*, and frustrated the attempts of Japanese managers to introduce objective criteria for promotion. Once the Chinese had advanced through the ranks, whether by education or on-the-job training, they refused to go back down to the factory floor. To the Japanese, this was the worst form of snobbery, and created barriers to technical transfer within the enterprise. Wrote Sonoda: "Furthermore, even if the Japanese side gives technical guidance, there is no system of communication between the engineers and the line workers. The engineers tend to consider the technical expertise they have acquired to be their own 'personal property,' and are loathe to teach it to others. As a result, it is difficult to spread technology throughout the entire factory."

For their part, the Chinese balked at the overbearing manners of the Japanese managers, and at being forced to observe rules that reflected Japanese cultural values and norms. "When one or another trouble surfaces, there are all the ingredients for a conflict of 'Japan versus China' or 'capitalists versus workers,'" Sonoda sighed. A strike at a Canon factory in Zhuhai in Guangzhou Province in Spring 1994 was caused partly by friction over a requirement that workers and managers had to eat in the same dining room, something encouraged in Japan to promote shop-floor harmony. The Chinese also objected to Canon's strict rules for such things as toilet breaks and personal phone calls. In the end, in order to smooth things over, Canon had to agree to a 30 percent wage hike.[115] When Chinese themselves were in charge, such rules got short shrift.

There were ironies to the friction between Chinese and Japanese work styles, since some of the worst problems arose from institutions shared by both economies, such as the seniority-based wage system and lifetime employment. These were alike, yet different, and the nuances could drive the Japanese crazy. The Chinese insisted on employing a wage system modeled after the eight-tiered wage structure of state enterprises, but worker groups, not management, were in charge of evaluation based on "collective assessment." Japanese were amazed that workers could improve their score simply by showing up for work on time; they took attendance for granted.

The Chinese system of lifetime employment also bothered the Japanese, despite its resemblance to the much-touted Japanese institution, associated almost exclusively with blue-chip companies. Unlike elsewhere in Asia, in China, firing was virtually impossible, and Japanese and other foreign employers were obliged to find new jobs for dismissed or redundant workers. This could take several years.[116] Maruyama Nobuo, an economist at the Institute of Developing Economies in Tokyo, explained, "Since China has an almost infinite supply of labor, it might be thought both possible and important to select workers strictly on the basis of merit. And yet, since enterprises also serve as quasi-communities for their workers, the contractual relationship with the enterprises becomes unclear and it becomes hard to fire or even lay off workers."[117]

One solution was to work through overseas Chinese entities, continuing a long-established Japanese tradition in East Asia. In the pre-war years, Japanese manufacturers and investors were heavily dependent on overseas Chinese networks in their business in Southeast Asia.[118] According to Sonoda, who conducted a survey, all the Japanese companies that succeeded in establishing full control over personnel issues worked through overseas Chinese affiliates or partners, particularly from Hong Kong. "The Hong Kong Chinese play an important role as intermediaries between the Chinese and Japanese sides in matters of the communications of ideas and collection of information," Sonoda wrote.[119] The Japanese magazine *Ekonomisuto* devoted a cover story to the "keys" to using "human relations" in Hong Kong to break into the China market.

The use of such go-betweens reflected Japanese insecurities. Like other foreigners, they were excluded from the dense web of *guanxi* ties based on clan, village, and education. They could and did make up some of the difference through gift-giving, another institution common to Japanese and Chinese cultures. Over the years, Japanese business "gifts" in China escalated from air conditioners and mini-refrigerators to luxury cars.

When all was said and done the Japanese were unable to grasp that the Chinese operated along very much the same assumptions of superiority that they did. The Chinese were aggressive, tribal, nationalistic, and would stop at nothing to defend the nation from perceived threats. China had, of course, invented many of the basic cultural paradigms within which the Japanese operated. So perhaps it was no surprise that, as the twentieth century ended, Japan would be looking over its shoulder not at the United States, or Europe, or even Russia, but at China as its most formidable potential foe.

Unable to bridge the gap of understanding between themselves and other Asians, Japan forgot one of the most basic tenets of the creed that had guided it from early in the century. The reason why Akamatsu's geese had flown together was that they had shared a common dream. If the dreams were different, no amount of money or persuasion could get them to fly again.

10

Vortex

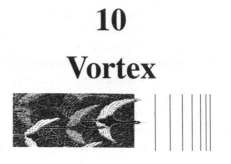

There are times when the laws of economics become as immediate as a broken window, broken doors, and charred bodies. In the Asian crisis of 1997 and 1998, it was like this: The machinery stopped for an agonizing moment, and when it coughed back to life, it was to a different world. Emerging from this vortex, the whole panoply of the Asian economy would crystallize along new lines. Japan would shift its axis of diplomacy decisively to Asia. The choice that nations had between embrace of the free market, with all its costs, and the even greater costs of retreat from globalization, would appear more starkly. It was a turning point for some; for others, a vindication. For Japan, it was a warning and a promise.

As a warning, the crisis pointed to the risks of Japan's exposure to the Asian economy. Japan had experienced a modest economic rebound in 1996, the year before the crisis. In 1997, it slumped into negative growth as a direct result of the sudden contraction of its Asian markets. Japan felt for the first time its dependency on the Asian economy, as its Asian factories shut down and shipments of intermediate goods came to a halt. In terms of the fallout from the crisis, Japan had so much at stake it simply could not walk away. From this point onward, Japan and Asia were more intertwined than either party understood or was prepared to admit.

The promise was subtle. Japan's new vulnerability within Asia had the potential to deepen the fissures that had already appeared within Japan's old fortress economy, including the habits and attitudes that went with it. This was positive for Japan in the way that a grand *yokozuna*, upon retiring, might extend his glory as head of his own stable of aspiring sumo wrestlers. Japan would no longer be the outlier as far as Asia was concerned, but lie somewhere in the middle, perhaps even struggling to keep up.

Japan's strengthened relationship with Asia after the crisis would enter into the ferment that was rearranging the Japanese paradigm from within. It would leave Japan more responsive to pressures from its neighbors not only to accept their products, services, and labor but also to accept an order in which Japan was no longer the first of its flock but simply an equal. Together they would need to collaborate in managing Asia's new giant, China. This lesson was not new, but the crisis underlined Japan's new role within Asia as well as its fragility.

For Indonesia, Thailand, and South Korea, the countries most affected by the crisis, the effects were less abstract. They were swept helplessly into new postures, victims of the newly powerful backdraft from global capital markets. None had the luxury of Japan to ease into new paradigms, to pick and choose among alternatives. The old order simply vanished. Over time, they would be able to salvage some of the old patterns, but in the midst of crisis, globalization clearly meant only abrupt loss and catastrophic change.

Jakarta, Tuesday, May 19, 1998

At midnight, the fragrant courtyards and lanais of Sukarno-Hatta International Airport are ablaze with light. Jumbo jets laden with foreigners and ethnic Chinese lumber down the runways, bound for nearby Singapore. Three-quarters of Indonesia's 18,000-resident Japanese nationals have left the country. The U.S. embassy ordered out its 12,000 Americans. Taiwan sent chartered planes and hired guards for seventeen shelters in Jakarta, Surabaya, Medan, and Bandung to protect its 30,000 nationals. A hotel room in Singapore is not to be had for love or money.

The Cathay Pacific flight into Jakarta at this hour is almost empty. Friends in Tokyo have warned me to cancel my trip. A female British journalist snaps edgily at the stewardess as the aircraft taxis toward the gate; a small band of Indonesians is singing and keeps it up as they march off the plane. At the immigration counter, a military officer barely glances at my U.S. passport. Customs and immigration officials have stayed home from work these past few days to avoid the airport chaos. Roving bandits have stopped drivers on the airport toll road, shaking down refugees fleeing with their prize possessions. These are desperate times. Five days earlier, Jakarta burned and hundreds died as looters poured out of the Jakarta slums to exercise three decades worth of pent-up resentment of Indonesia's privileged few.

The grounds of Sukarno-Hatta are choked with refugees, mostly ethnic Chinese, waiting for a flight, any flight. Many expect the next day to be bloody. Some 30,000 students have taken control of the saddle-backed parliament buildings in the central Jakarta district of Senayan, and are calling for reinforcements. News reports say that the 30,000 will become 1,000,000 in a demonstration scheduled to begin at dawn. The tension grows by the minute. General Wiranto, head of Indonesia's powerful armed forces, has announced grimly that he will back President Suharto's decision not to resign. Hundreds of foreign journalists have converged on the city, with digital cameras, cell phones, and portable earth stations. I am visiting Indonesia on my own, and have no editors back home to monitor my safe arrival or departure. It is a frightening moment; I have been watching the Asian crisis from a comfortable distance, in Washington, D.C. Now it is time to see it up close.

Among other minor inconveniences that Tuesday night, there were no taxis. A cheerful man in a Toyota offers to take me into the city, for U.S. dollars, at ten times the commercial rate, and I gladly accept. He assures me that the rioting and looting of the previous week are largely over. His optimism appears to be unfounded; from the air, I could see fires in the southern part of the city. The driver takes me downtown along what he calls the "scenic" route, past mile after mile of gutted and burnt-out buildings. Most of the damage has been the work of gangs of men with rocks and matches. Once the situation stabilizes, I think, there will be good business here for plate-glass companies. They will be standing in line after the plywood manufacturers, who will soon be sealing up the hundreds of ruined car dealerships, shopping malls, and banks. In one day, the gangs destroyed 6,000 buildings. Five hundred people have died. Many of the dead were looters in shopping mall fires that they themselves had set.

There is almost nobody on the streets. The airport toll road is empty except for military trucks parked here and there and the odd knot of men around camp fires. No troops are visible. In the early hours of the morning, the haunting strains of *mullahs* will wake me, over amped-up sound systems, calling the Islamic faithful to prayer.

Jakarta, Wednesday, May 20, 1998

The next day, waking up in the Cemara Hotel, a low-budget establishment in downtown Jakarta, there is no sign of chaos. Motorcycles put-put outside the window; the coffee shop is full of reporters and the electronic tinkle of cell phones. My friend the newspaper publisher, Aristides Katoppo, made the reservation for me. The Cemara has become a journalists' hangout of the type that always springs up in times of war and crisis; the hotels compete for their business because nobody else is in town. The Cemara attracts the low end and is popular with still photographers and free-lance journalists; Australians predominate. From a budget-travel perspective, the collapse of the rupiah has created some terrific deals. The rate at the Cemara is only $15 a day, down from $75 before the crisis, and includes marble bathrooms, air-conditioning, international phone lines, and breakfast. At the Mandarin Hotel, favored by staff correspondents, a delicious brunch buffet goes for just $2.50; it was $12.50 six months ago.

By the time I come down for breakfast, the photographers have long since departed, seeking images of carnage and revolution—if they can find any. The city is still and quiet; it has the feel of the eye of a typhoon before the wind changes direction, an atmosphere simultaneously calm and stressful. Overnight, the convoy trucks have disgorged some 40,000 troops and police. The streets are dead. Barbed wire and light tanks block major intersections. The only way to get around the city is on foot or by motorcycle. Commando units have locked down Monas—a monument known as "Sukarno's last erection," after the founder of the Indonesian republic. The demonstration has been called off. Amien Rais, the charismatic leader of Muhammadiyah, went on the radio at 6:00 A.M. to tell the students to stay home. This decision has saved the city from massive bloodshed.

Early in the morning, my friend Cameron Barr, a Tokyo-based journalist for the *Christian Science Monitor*, walked past barbed wire barricades on foot to Monas, looking for students. On his cell phone, while walking, Cameron complains of the heat and total lack of activity. The students are nowhere to be seen. "I haven't seen anyone under thirty," he says. The day's major gathering has moved to Jogjakarta, he learns from his wife, Nicole Gaouette, also a correspondent for the *Monitor*. Sultan Hamengkubuwono X has told 600,000 students in the ancient seat of the Javanese sultanate that "the government's power has ended. I am ready to be present among you, to be in the front row and will not retreat. The people have long suffered. It is time for them to get their rights back." The sultan has no political power and little money but enormous prestige. His grandfather helped organize resistance against the Dutch. The demonstrations in Jogjakarta and elsewhere are being carried out on National Awakening Day, which commemorates the anti-Dutch movement. The symbolism is intense.

An hour later, on the back of a motorcycle, I get as close as I can to Monas, which I estimate is at least a mile distant. I can see the bronze flame that caps the monument above the trees. A squadron of commandos, wearing maroon berets, makes it clear that I am to go no further. I ask the motorcycle driver, Gantar, to head for the Parliament grounds, where the students are still holed up.

The back of a 50 cc motorcycle has exactly one thing to recommend it, a wide-angle view. Gantar and I zip along streets cleared of traffic, past boarded-up shop windows and storefronts hung with signs that read, *"Allahu Akbar! Milik Pribumi Muslim"* (God is great! Property of Native Indonesian Muslims). The message is intended to deter looters who have targeted Chinese shops, playing off assumptions that ethnic Chinese—many who have been in Indonesia for generations—are foreigners who own shops. It is true that few Chinese are wealthy as a group, and this has made them a target of fundamentalist rage.

On a normal day, we would be weaving through streets lined with traffic; this day the roads are empty and Gantar keeps his bike at cruising speed. We zoom past office buildings hung with "reformasi" banners and flags at half mast in honor of the six Trisakti University students who were shot on May 12, triggering the riots and confrontation between students and military on the parliament grounds. We fly along roads lined with old Dutch bungalows and shopping malls in the Kebayoran Baru neighborhood, past faint memories of rice paddies and villages that were there forty years ago, when I was a child, Sukarno was president of Indonesia and Suharto a junior officer on his staff. Since then, Kebayoran Baru has become a tangle of overpasses and shopping malls, a swank part of the city favored by the *nouveaux riches.* In my childhood, I remember big open spaces; behind the International School was a large field, with a gleaming marble mosque. Our teachers sometimes took us there, and we would take off our shoes and walk silently across the cool stone floor. I think I spot the minaret, squeezed between shops and apartment buildings.

There are few interruptions, but when they occur, we are reminded of the danger that hangs over the city, like an unspoken warning. There are barricades at every major intersection, neat professional jobs made with barbed wire and flanked by light tanks. The soldiers are studiously relaxed. This people's revolution would not be happening at all without the consent and support of ABRI, Indonesia's military. They make a party out of it; according to a report in the *Jakarta Post*, a group of soldiers assigned to guard Monas arranged an "impromptu song and dance performance, lampooning the hardships of their job."[1] Soldiers have been giving students the high five. Of the commando units I encounter, one is singing, as though the soldiers were around a campfire; others snooze. Maroon and orange berets give them a festive air. At one barricade, I start to worry. The head of a unit speaks sternly to Gantar in *Bahasa.* To emphasize a point, the man leans close and brutally yanks a stray hair from the young man's cheek. Gantar sheepishly dons his crash helmet as he drives off. It has been a lecture on motorcycle safety principles. Once out of sight, Gantar offers me the helmet. I decline.

Gantar is good at threading his bike through crowds and manages to get all the way to the front entrance of the Parliament, which is jammed with a cavalcade of buses filing slowly past, with students perched on top waving banners and shouting slogans. "The Army Belongs to the People!" reads one. The gates are guarded by officious groups of commandos and students, each forming a separate gauntlet yelling for ID. Provocateurs from the youth wing of Golkar, the government party, got into the grounds on Tuesday and tried to start a fight. They were persuaded to leave, but the admissions committee has become doubly cautious. The students know it is only a matter of time before the military pushes them off the grounds. There are perhaps 15,000 students, half the number reported yesterday. The number of students camping out on the roof of the parliamentary building has also thinned. Its architect warned on television this morning that the structure was in danger of caving in.

Meanwhile, the atmosphere is determined and festive. An inter-university support group drives a pickup around the grounds, passing out food and water. The area in front of the main entrance is densely populated with burly Caucasian and Japanese cameramen, street vendors selling water and *satay*, sympathizers, and layabouts.

Suddenly the entire surreal scene goes underwater as a stray rainstorm bears down. Standing under a tree with a newspaper over his head, Arif Bekasi, an engineer, complains about price hikes, the slumping rupiah, and his inability to benefit from Indonesia's economic boom. The juxtaposition of topics is typical; Arif's anger is felt by many, fed by sudden shortages and price hikes of electricity, fuel, and imported commodities, and has translated into physical attacks on the wealthy Chinese minority. "We feel resentment because of the different social conditions between ourselves and the Chinese," Arif says. "The downtown area is almost all Chinese people, not Indonesian people. We call it Chinatown."

Back in the heart of "Chinatown," President Suharto has been hiding out all day at his residence on Jalan Cendana, down the street from my hotel. On Monday and Tuesday, rumors flew of his impending resignation. But Suharto apparently changed his mind. On Tuesday, he called for a cabinet reshuffle and the appointment of a reform committee to oversee new elections, but without saying when. The entire Indonesian elite has boycotted Suharto's latest gambit, however. There are no takers for positions on either council. The papers that night hint broadly that Suharto will resign on Thursday morning.

This is the nadir. The world's fifth most populous nation is at a standstill. No factories run. The banks are boarded up. The streets, normally in gridlock, are empty. The city evokes images of a tropical Los Angeles, with its broad expressways, tree-lined avenues, and flamboyant contemporary office towers and condos, but this is a Los Angeles emptied of cars and shoppers, its thoroughfares blocked by light tanks and barbed wire. Only a few enterprising vendors have pulled their carts along the sidewalks and through the barricades to catch whatever stray customers they may find.

It is the last day of Suharto's reign, although nobody knows it yet, apparently least of all the seventy-one-year-old autocrat. Back from my morning ride with Gantar, one of the first calls I make is to Mari Pangestu, an economist and ethnic Chinese who heads the Center for Strategic and International Studies (CSIS) in Jakarta, a prestigious think tank. Mari is a short, bold, energetic woman. She gives the impression of talking at twice normal speed. The week before, Mari shut down CSIS and sent its researchers and staff home. I reach her on her cell phone; she is feeding lunch to her two small children, issuing instructions to her *amah* as we talk. The riots targeted Chinese women, and there were a number of rapes. I ask if she is making plans to leave Indonesia because of the violence. "I'm not going anywhere," Mari says. "This is history in the making." A few months later, she quietly moved her family to Houston after her husband accepted a transfer with the oil multinational where he was employed.

The economy is imploding fast. Mari has been trying to get a handle on the scale of damage. The IMF has called off meetings on Indonesia's next emergency loan disbursement. Everything is going wrong at once. In 1996, the Indonesian economy produced goods and services worth $225 billion. That was when the rupiah was at 3,000 to the U.S. dollar. At mid-week, it was bumping up against 14,000 to the dollar and ended the week at 16,000. "The longer they wait, the worse things will get. As an economist, I want the good guys to come in as soon as possible," Mari says. She scoffs at the notion that Indonesia is in the throes of a Philippine-style "people power" movement, a line that some of the international media has taken under the influence of the student extravaganza. As far as Mari is concerned, ABRI is pulling the strings. "Even in the Philippines, at the end of the day it was the power brokers who brought change. The army still has the key."

Jakarta, Thursday, May 21, 1998

Mari has been prophetic. Together with Cameron and Nicole, the husband-and-wife reporting team, I watch Suharto's resignation on CNN in their room at the Mandarin Hotel. Suharto gives an emotional speech, while an ashen-faced B.J. Habibie, his vice-president and titular successor, looks on with folded hands. Clutching the Koran, Habibie is sworn in with the most casual of nods to due process. Under the Constitution, Parliament was supposed to approve the succession. Supposedly, the "unusual situation" with the students occupying the buildings has made this impossible.

Aides hustle Suharto and Habibie away from the cameras, and Wiranto steps to the mike. His hatred for Habibie is palpable. With a grimace of distaste, Wiranto outlines ABRI's position: It supports the resignation, will support Suharto's successor "within the Constitution," and will protect Suharto and his family. It is all too clear where the power in this "revolution" has come from. Later in the day, I revisit Parliament, where the number of students is now down to 500. On Friday, the last remaining students—the ones who have ignored ABRI's warnings—will finally be thrown out. Today, however, they are performing for the foreign and domestic press. A group of about twenty links arms and jumps into a shallow decorative pool, marching back and forth for the benefit of half-a-dozen news photographers and cameramen. They keep it up for several hours, and the wet students become one of the principal images of the day, seen in newspapers and television broadcasts around the world.

I spend a few hours watching the scene and chatting with Primdas Suhandra, a University of Indonesia alumnus who works for a German telecommunications firm. Business is down. A few days later, when I am in Singapore, he sends me a giddy e-mail. "How is your 'investigation' report on Indonesia so far? Enjoy the Indonesian style!"

On Thursday, the clarity of Suharto's resignation the day before is replaced by endless and confusing rumors. "This is round one—other rounds are coming up," Aristides Katoppo said later in the day, over a glass of cold lime juice in his high-ceilinged, nineteenth-century home, crammed with antiques including a Balinese temple gate. Aristides, a veteran Indonesian journalist, is publisher of *Sinar Harapan*, Jakarta's third-largest daily newspaper. He has been putting together the inner history of the past two days. Suharto, the master strategist, finally ran out of strategems, he says.

> On Tuesday, most of the academics at the University of Indonesia pledged not to join Suharto's cabinet, and the word spread. It was the same when he was trying to seek members for the national reform committee. He put together forty or fifty names, but most of the people he approached, declined. It was almost a solid boycott. In Parliament, the presidential faction had three hundred signatures on a resolution supporting a demand for Suharto's resignation. It was couched in terms of an ultimatum. Unless Suharto resigned, the party would call for a special session of Parliament. This is something of which Suharto had an irrational fear, because it's the way he ousted Sukarno in 1967. He also realized that military support was waning. During the riots, it was clear that some of his cronies were targeted —men like Lim Sioe Liong but also House Speaker Harmoko. Their houses were attacked at almost the same time, like a surgical strike. At Lim's house, the guards mounted a counterattack for the first few moments, then stopped. Maybe they radioed for help but instead got an order to evacuate. His house was guarded by red berets.
>
> Then there was a great show of protecting Suharto's house. The joke is going around town that you had to look at which way the turrets of the cannons were aimed—in the direction of the house rather than outside.

Lots of the soldiers were marines. In the end the navy and air force sided with Wiranto, tipping the balance against Suharto. Even after the military took control, there were signs on the streets criticizing Suharto. I myself saw one the size of a door, right in the middle of the street that said, "Down with Suharto." There were a lot of signals and scary moments. Whatever their differences, the military agreed not to shoot at each other and especially not to shoot at the students. Wiranto's group was essentially in control.

The whole thing snowballed and accelerated when Suharto's henchman Harmoko caved in. He was chairman both of Parliament and Golkar, the government party. The president was livid and very angry when Harmoko made the statement calling for his resignation. Then Wiranto called the armed forces' chiefs of staff together and said they each had their own individual opinions but would announce them collectively. I thought it was masterly. If I compare it with 1967, the fairly strange thing was, there was no counterplay from the president. Here ABRI's strategy was, look, if you're the supreme commander, if you give us a direct order we will do something but unless you give a direct order, we don't understand. Then there's a crescendo of statements from all over Indonesia. By the time they started to counter it, he was just drowned.

It's a breathing spell, but I don't think it will last too long—maybe a couple of days. The most important thing is that it happened without bloodshed. We passed the first stage without that. There was a lot of danger but we passed it. Suharto is gone and he's gone without a shot being fired. That's a great achievement. OK, you have a new president and he's from a corrupt system, but we have at least avoided armed conflict, violence, and bloodshed. In one day, 6,000 buildings and 500 lives were lost—with no armies shooting at each other and only a minority of looters. Can you imagine what would have happened with a real civil war? Jakarta would be in flames. We would have lost not 6,000 buildings but 60,000 buildings.

The BBC and the World Bank distract Aristides with phone calls and requests for interviews. Meanwhile, his elegant wife, Mismis, takes me to a garden house, where the carved temple façade is used as a doorway, to give Aristides some quiet. Mismis's eyes are wide and piercing. Her family comes from the inner court in Jogjakarta, and like the aristocrat she is Mismis takes great interest in Javanese traditions. She describes the political events in terms of Javanese shadow theater, *wayang kulit*, where puppets act out the stories of the Hindu epics, the *Ramayana* and *Mahabharata,* behind a backlit screen. The dramas go on all night, as people eat and talk and sleep while the images flicker on.

Mismis laughs. "Suharto liked to compare himself to the last surviving member of the Bharata family in the *Mahabharata.* He would call himself

Arjuna Vijaya, who killed Karna, his own brother, although of a different father." "Karna," which means ear, stood for Sukarno, who always identified himself as listening to the people. Habibie has his place among the Hindu gods and goddesses, as well, although not a very reverential one. According to Mismis Katoppo, most people compare Habibie to the brother of Krishna whose chief task was to take care of the grandchildren. Clearly he was a minor character.

That evening, I am invited to a family dinner with Arifin Siregar, who ' returned to Indonesia at the height of the crisis the previous November, after four years as Indonesian ambassador to the United States. Arifin has been trade minister, central bank governor, and executive director for Indonesia at both the IMF and World Bank. In retirement from government work, he advises Goldman Sachs on its Indonesian business. Arifin's opinion of Habibie is low. He is busy trying to figure out the minimum amount of time it will take to get Habibie out of office, using constitutional means. He estimates one month.

Arifin ridicules Habibie's inaugural speech, broadcast live on Indonesian television. His contempt for the man is based on familiarity; Arifin was studying for his doctorate in economics in Germany about the same time that Habibie was a student in engineering there. "I have known Habibie for forty years," said Arifin. "All he knows about is planes. He's a zero in politics, a zero in economics. All he has is that he was close to the president. He has no grassroots support." The phone rings every few minutes—the IMF, Newport Mining, other elite Indonesians wondering what is going on. Soemitro Djojohadiksumo calls. Not only is the respected economist considered the father of Indonesian growth strategy, he is also the father of Lieutenant General Prabowo Subianto, Suharto's son-in-law, and widely viewed as presidential material when Suharto was in power. Arifin claims there is no individual strong enough to replace Suharto: "Until this morning, it was the president who decided everything, a one-man show." Arifin's solution is to put together a triumvirate, with a technocrat, Islamic leader, and military man sharing power.

Arifin is an advisor to a committee of fourteen retired generals, formed to convince Suharto to resign. It is encouraging Wiranto to keep Habibie in place temporarily. The committee is proposing a three-person transitional leadership, with Wiranto, Emil Salim—one of the original Berkeley technocrats who ran an unsuccessful presidential campaign during the recent mock elections—and Amien Rais. The idea is to have a transition team while preparing for genuine elections two years later, an alternative to yanking Habibie and holding immediate elections, The group fears that Indonesia isn't ready for democratic process in its current weakened state, thirty years out of practice in democracy and with the economy at rock bottom.

The power-sharing concept sounds appealing but unlikely. The unacknowledged problem is that ABRI is unwilling to relinquish control. I say my farewells. I have a plane to catch at dawn. After six months of turmoil, justice has been served and Indonesia is back in business. It is stunned and limping, but has made the essential break with the past. Suharto was the old paradigm. Habibie, reluctantly perhaps, will drag Indonesia toward reform. The question was how deep the reforms would go. In a country whose elites operated in the manner of a village council, the concept of democratic rule has little meaning. ABRI, the military, is a vast commercial enterprise with its own complex political chemistry, and will put up a bitter fight against any diminution of its influence. Islamic fundamentalism is on a slow boil. Habibie and his successors will have to deal with these; in the end, the new paradigm may not look much different from the old.

Aftermath

Three weeks after the fall of Suharto, Mari Pangestu is in Washington. "I have been playing my economic song and dance everywhere," she sighs. But the message is not amusing. "During the political crisis, we all forgot that we had an economic crisis going on which got worse," Mari tells a small group gathered around an oval conference table at the Overseas Development Council, a research organization.

Nobody can forget now. The rupiah has dropped again, rattling like a rock in a tin can in the range of 13,000 to 14,000 to the U.S. dollar. "Nothing can work if the exchange rate continues to go south," Mari says. There is very little to stop the slide, however. The central bank has been pumping out money—Rupiah 8 trillion in three weeks, she estimates—and she and other economists are predicting inflation rates between 80 and 100 percent. Before the political crisis, she was forecasting that the Indonesian economy would shrink by 5 percent. Now the range of estimates is for a contraction of the economy between 10 to 20 percent. Unemployment is running at 25 percent—16 million Indonesians have lost their jobs, out of a workforce of 90 million and a total population of 193 million.

The statistics are numbing, but this was not the worst news. Indonesia's economy was running in reverse, back to square one, where it was when I was a child. The vision is horrific; four decades of progress lost in a sudden paroxysm of financial markets. Indonesia in the 1950s was an immense scar, squalid, desperately poor, and chronically violent. The streets of Jakarta were filled with stunted children, skin diseases, and the legless veterans of nameless civil wars begging for scraps. Indonesia had left this world behind. Now, it was returning before our eyes, hideously. At 100 percent inflation, 100,000,000 people, or 50 percent of the population, would fall below the official "poverty line," Mari said. Three years earlier, according to the World Bank, the number of officially poor was just 21.5 million.

A World Bank report released in August 1997 praised Indonesia for managing to reduce poverty in absolute terms by three-quarters between 1975 and 1995.[2] The praise and the achievements were genuine. Now both are gone. Granted, the concept of a "poverty line" is absurd if exchange rates are bouncing off the wall. The World Bank uses $1 per day as the dividing line separating the "poor" from those relatively well off in developing countries. This can only be a rough benchmark. Nonetheless, it offers a crude measure for the scale of the tragedy. In less than a year, 80 million Indonesians, 40 percent of the population, went from relative security—no matter how dubious the calculation—to penury. "It will take us five years to get back to the real level of income of 1997," Mari predicts. It sounds like desperate optimism.

Mari's audience included development economists, policy makers, and the retired officials who haunt Washington policy seminars and conferences as though they crave even the secondhand scent of power. There is John Sewell, ODC's genial, lanky, longtime president; Robert McNamara, former chief of the World Bank, and architect of the Vietnam War before he invented the Bank's "war against poverty"; Karin Lissakers, the U.S. delegate to the IMF; Katherine Marshall, a senior official from the World Bank's East Asia and Pacific department; and a few others. ODC does its best to maintain ties with research institutes in the developing world, such as Mari's CSIS. Some of the people sitting around the table have followed Indonesia for thirty years or more. Yet, the events that Mari describes, like the Asia crisis itself, have taken them by utter surprise.

June is a languorous month in the nation's capital. Washington eases back at this time of year, waiting for the congressional recess, already under the heel of tourists. It is not an impressive city, away from the mall and its monuments. The view from ODC headquarters, in Kalorama Heights, looks down a broad sweep across former swampland toward the Potomac. The brick dome of St. Matthews and a toy-like Capitol and Washington Monument are visible beyond the drab low-rise office towers of K Street. This is no city to compare to Jakarta, with its population of 9,000,000, steamy haze and acacia trees, and the skyscrapers marching to the horizon. Yet, it is here, in the capital of the world's last remaining superpower, where much of the drama of the Asian crisis will continue to play out.

Mari's presence in Washington, so soon after the political crisis, is testimony to the power the United States wields. She is one of hundreds of Asia's elite who have come here in the course of the crisis, seeking help. "We don't want political conditionality to be linked to assistance," she says. "But neither do we think you should play a low-key role. We want you to keep up the pressure on our domestic process."

Clever Mari, with her singing and dancing. Pressure is exactly what the United States has not applied, until very recently and far too late. The history of the Asian crisis was one in which Washington dropped the ball at crucial times in crucial ways. This was obvious to most Asians in June 1998, a year into the crisis. "What do you think about Larry Summers?" asks McNamara. The deputy secretary of the Treasury Department was patently skeptical of the need for intervention in the crisis; he had kept the United States out of the Thai bailout and backed the IMF's program of stiff conditionality even through the Indonesian fiasco. Mari flashes back, "He did not come across at all sympathetically to anyone in the region during the Thai crisis. Even now we don't see the U.S. Treasury Department in a sympathetic light."

In its first year, the Asian catastrophe polished off the governments of Indonesia's Suharto, Thailand's prime minister Chavalit Yongchaiyudh, and South Korea's president Kim Young Sam. None of them were saints, and yet the political convulsions triggered by the financial crisis seemed far out of proportion to their sins. These were no "small glitches along the road," as U.S. president William J. Clinton called the crisis at a summit meeting of Asia-Pacific leaders in Vancouver in November 1997. It was Armageddon. By August 20, Thailand had gone to the IMF for $3.9 billion; Thailand's Asian trading partners, led by Japan, brought the total to $17.2 billion. Two months later, Indonesia had its hand out for $43 billion. In early December, the Fund put together a $57 billion package for South Korea, the largest ever organized for any country, surpassing the $50 billion Mexican bailout of 1995. All told, by early 1998, the international community had pledged $117 billion to help the three worst-hit economies meet their balance of payments shortfalls, and the crisis had barely begun.

Like Indonesia, the economies of Thailand and South Korea collapsed suddenly after years of seemingly endless growth. Economic prosperity had eased social tensions in a rising tide of wealth. Trouble threatened to bring old tensions to the surface and create new ones, such as the riots breaking out among Acehnese migrant workers from Sumatra in March and April 1998 when Malaysian authorities began carrying out mass deportations. The demonstrations that brought about Suharto's fall were fueled by tensions between mostly rich ethnic Chinese and mostly poor *bumiputras*. South Korea, Thailand, and many of its Southeast Asian neighbors introduced national campaigns to reduce imports, reversing years of progress in trade liberalization. Financially weak Asian nations began canceling arms orders, tipping the balance, some analysts believed, in favor of Chinese hegemony in the region.[3]

In Summer and Fall 1997, the Asian financial crisis tore through the Asian economy like a financial version of the Ebola virus. It spread destruction so quickly that its victims hardly knew what hit them. For months afterward, the world's financial and business press kept up a steady fusillade, blaming the victims for bringing on the crisis through excessive greed and corruption. Books quickly appeared as well, with titles like *Asia Falling?; Tigers Tamed;* and *Meltdown.*[4] Questions raised by the Asian crisis went to the heart of the post–Cold War debate about the nature of capitalism and culture. Did the Cold War disguise fundamental tensions among competing civilizations, which would now explode, as Samuel Huntington argued, or was the globalization of capital markets raising a new and inexorable standard of convergence?[5]

For many of the critics, Asian capitalism was the disease. The cure would lie in adopting the neoliberal standard of free markets and minimal government intervention, held together by rational self-interest, maximizing the welfare of consumers. Summers believed this; so did many others.

Some of the most influential thinkers and policy makers in the West joined the chorus, urging Asian economies to junk the Japanese and Asian models in favor of open markets and liberal trade regimes based on strong legal institutions. Ranging from Alan Greenspan, governor of the Federal Reserve Board, to London *Financial Times* columnist Martin Wolf, they proclaimed the end of the "Asian miracle" and denounced Asian "crony capitalism." Lawrence Lindsey, later President George W. Bush's economic advisor, represented an extreme: Dismissing, on the one hand, the cultural explanation ("excesses are human nature"), Lindsey argued that the only way to solve Asia's problem was through a financial markets variant of Harvard economist Jeffrey Sach's "shock therapy"—open global capital markets everywhere.

"The greater the volume of capital markets, the more stable the situation," he told a Washington audience in February 1998. "You should be able to invest wherever you want; there cannot be a global economy where only goods move freely. The capital markets must be opened, and on the debt side, you need bankruptcy provisions." From Lindsey's perspective, the IMF was "irrelevant," because it allowed policy makers to postpone reform rather than allowing the market to force change. "This is the worst of all worlds," he said. "The IMF is seen as a pawn of the U.S., but it is not there bankrupting companies responsible for the default, but making all of society pay."[6] Lindsey's views were popular with the U.S. Congress, which was deeply suspicious of the IMF and its huge bailout packages, with or without "conditionality." On Capitol Hill, the dominant sentiment was that any financial help to Asia would merely line the pockets of corrupt dictators. As long as the Asian banking crisis did not spill over into the United States, Congress could wash its hands of the crisis.

Many of the same people who became Asia's harshest critics had been its fans a few years earlier. So, for example, Clyde Prestowitz, former advisor to Secretary of Commerce Malcolm Baldrige who had once described Japan as the "undisputed world economic champion," described the Japanese model as the fatal flaw causing Asia's crash. Writing in the *Washington Post* in late 1997, Prestowitz argued that China's devaluation of the renminbi in 1994 and 1995's yen depreciation pushed the Asian export machine into overdrive and finally into cardiac arrest. "It was in 1964 that the Japanese miracle was first proclaimed," he wrote in the *Post* article. "In the next three decades, this phenomenon spread through much of Asia as the smaller economies there, imitating and adapting Japan's methods, created the world's most economically dynamic region. It was an unprecedented achievement, but the force always had a dark side. With much of Asia now on life support it is time to recognize that the Asian brand of capitalism is dangerous to the world economy's health and that it must be abandoned, particularly by Japan."[7]

The opposing camp was a loose coalition, united more in their dislike of the IMF than admiration for the East Asian economies. Economists led by Dani Rodrik and Jeffrey Sachs of Harvard University, and Joseph Stiglitz of the World Bank, took issue with the doctor, not the patient. They argued that the IMF had turned a currency run into an economic collapse by issuing the wrong prescriptions. But they laid emphasis on the role of the IMF itself, and took issue with it for reasons going back in part to a strand of development theory originating in Marxism, viewing the IMF as an instrument of rich countries. For such critics, it was reasonable and even desirable for developing economies to adopt national strategies. The tools of industrial policy—fiscal expansion, government control of the capital account, and export promotion—were reasonable, and the IMF's strictures against them reflected a global economy that was biased against poor countries.

From Asia, views of the crisis were more complex. People in a typhoon are less likely to conduct arguments about why the wind is blowing than people elsewhere. Once the immediate danger was over, however, they occupied a middle ground that was both pragmatic and conservative. On the one hand, most Asians understood that they would lose their wealth forever if they failed to respond to demands for reform. On the other, they were disinclined to interpret the financial crisis as a metaphysical rebuke.

Instead, Asians saw the crisis as part of a historical pattern of global economic upheavals in which their main mission was to survive—like the oil crisis of the 1970s, the commodity price crash of the 1980s, the semiconductor wars of the 1990s that presaged the crash with a global slump in chip prices. The earlier crises had taught Asia how to go with the flow. This one taught them that they would need to reach further, to do more. But it also was a resounding lesson in the risks of liberalizing too quickly, and the benefits of easing into globalization rather than leaping headlong.

With each of the crises of the 1970s and 1980s, Asians had stretched to accommodate a little more of the free market, whether by opening their economies to foreign investors for the purpose of developing export-manufacturing industries or by allowing their own companies and investors to make use of global markets. The last great assimilation of global standards and global institutions had begun in the mid-1980s, as a direct result of quarrels between the United States and Japan over the latter's artificially low exchange rate, which had boosted Japanese exports to stratospheric levels. Post-1985 volatility in the U.S. dollar–Japanese yen exchange rate was one of the principal reasons why Asian economies had opened up a wedge of their equity and capital markets; in an environment of where interest rates were volatile, they needed to diversify away from debt finance with its exposure to interest rate swings.

Decisions made in the mid-1980s to early 1980s to liberalize financial markets in Indonesia, South Korea, and Thailand led directly to crash of 1997, by way of chaotic banking sectors, real estate, and stock markets. In this sense, the crash was not a failure of the Japanese model, but actually vindicated an aspect of it. Japan, and later China, had pioneered policies of liberalizing their economies piecemeal. The lesson Asians could take from 1997 was that they had not been piecemeal enough, liberalizing too much rather than too little.

Gradualism, or sequencing, which meant one thing to the international financial institutions, provided brigades of lawyers and accountants to advise the crisis economies how to set up bankruptcy courts, establish independent regulatory agencies, and conduct asset sales of distressed conglomerates. It meant something else within Asia—a chance to conserve and build upon existing institutions. Asians had retained their version of capitalism through several previous throws of the global dice. Their success was built on a different kind of bargain between business and government, and between companies and workers, than prevailed in North America or, for the most part, in Western Europe. That bargain could change over time, but it was by no means clear to Asians that they would have to change it all at once.

Asian interpreters of the crisis had a very different approach to explaining and analyzing the events of 1997 and 1998 than did the legions of Western analysts. Rather than the apocalyptic generalization, one often heard them break down the events of the crisis into their separate parts. Viewed in its fragments, the story was often one of bad timing, advice, and leaders; a clash between one generation of Westernized technocrats and the next; the failure of monitoring systems to cope with a phenomenon that had ensued so rapidly it had left the major Western institutions gaping.

Even the way the crisis began seemed almost a matter of chance. It started with a marginal currency in a country better known for its silks, prostitutes, and pristine beaches than its financial markets. Before dawn on July 2, 1997, Thailand's top bankers scrambled into their limousines to attend an emergency meeting in a low-rise building facing Bankhumpron Palace, head office of the Thai central bank.[8] At the 6:30 A.M. meeting, the bankers learned that the Bank of Thailand was abandoning the dollar peg, that is, its longstanding policy of keeping the Thai baht at a fixed ratio to the U.S. dollar. The move spelled disaster for the banks, which by early 1997 had accumulated bad debt amounting to 25 percent of their total assets, much of it in U.S. dollars. Between late 1996 and early 1997, the Bank of Thailand had spent nearly Baht 1,000,000,000,000 to prop up the currency and thereby keep the banks in business.

Devaluation would be disastrous because the banks, relying on the government's continuing patronage, had plunged into the booming business in short-term lending through the newly created Bangkok International Banking Facility, which had allowed the banks to run up a $31 billion debt in just four years; the BIBF offered a window for short-term borrowing in U.S. dollars. Prior to its creation, only the Thai government was able to borrow money in foreign currencies; Bangkok had grand plans about serving as banker to the transitional states of former Indochina that were in the process of creating a "Mekong Delta" economic zone. Its idea in creating the BIBF was to create an international financial center where this could happen; instead, the difference between the high interest rates charged to domestic Thai borrowers and much lower international rates attracted foreign banks like bees.

Meanwhile, currency traders, sniffing the winds, began a series of speculative attacks against the Thai currency, stoutly resisted by the central bank until that July morning. Unknown to any but a handful of mid-level bureaucrats and the central bank governor, the Bank of Thailand had spent down virtually all of its $40 billion in foreign reserves. Just a few weeks before the devaluation, the central bank had announced that it still held reserves of $34 billion. It lied.[9] In May, the Foreign Exchange Department of the bank pledged $30 billion in a forward transaction to shore up the baht—meaning that it would buy baht and sell dollars at a specific rate later. The dollars were still in the Thai treasury. But for all practical purposes, the Thai government was broke. Within hours of the announcement of the devaluation, the baht plunged by 15 percent against the dollar.

Looking back at these events, Anek Laothammatas, an advisor to the Thai Finance Ministry, traced the process of the Thai collapse. The moral of the story was that the Thai central bank, renowned for its incorruptibility, had simply screwed up, and failed to tell anybody, not even the prime minister. Anek had been there:

When Prime Minister Chavalit came to power in December 1996, Thailand was apparently in good shape. It had growth of 7–8 percent, and low inflation, of 4–5 percent, for a decade. The savings rate was 20–30 percent, and interest rates were reasonable for a developing country, at 13–14 percent. We had a decade of fiscal surpluses, and very low public international debt. Our international reserves were close to $40 billion. We were very proud. Underlying our success was export growth of 15–20 percent for half a decade.

Of course, we had weaknesses. There were increasing signs of uneven income distribution, and the agricultural sector had been neglected for over a decade. But Thailand was one of the most successful LDCs [least developed economies] in agricultural terms. It was a food exporter. We had the feeling that we were lacking in human resources development, and that education was not good enough. We worried that the boom in real estate development was excessive—we saw high rise buildings all over Bangkok and provincial cities too. Real estate was like a bubble that was ready to burst. We had a feeling that it would burst soon. We also had a feeling about our volatile stock exchange. Investors treated the stock exchange like gambling. And we had a worry that our trade and current account deficits would keep growing. At one point the current account deficit amounted to 8 percent of GDP, double half a decade ago.

But in the main, we were upbeat about globalization. The integration of the Thai economy into the world would be a good thing. This was the subject of coffee talk conversation. We looked at it in a good light. We talked about Thailand as a center in Southeast Asia for financial and monetary integration, following the Singaporean model.

What we lost sight of at that time was that the international debt incurred by the private sector had increased rapidly, to $60 billion, half of it with duration of less than a year. In 1994–95 it had grown rapidly as a result of the government's opening of the Bangkok International Banking Facility. If you added the government's debt of $27 billion, it came to a total of $90 billion, more than three times Thailand's international reserves. In hindsight, we should have been very cautious, but this was lost at the time.

There was a heavy inflow of capital because of the U.S. dollar peg, of Baht 25 to the dollar in relatively fixed terms. This facilitated the inflow of international capital. Most of the loans from Japan, for instance, were made in U.S. dollars, mostly unhedged, and these had accumulated very rapidly over three years. Private-sector debt went from about zero to $60 billion, because of the baht peg. If not for the peg, people would have been less enthusiastic about foreign borrowing.

The Bank of Thailand had also issued hundreds of billions of baht in order to shore up the banking and financial sectors, which were suffering from nonperforming loans in the declining stock and real estate markets. The Bank of Thailand traditionally would not allow banks to fail.

Finally, the baht came under attack by foreign speculators, with a first wave in November 1996, followed by a second and third attack in the first half of 1997. The Bank of Thailand defended the baht with commitments of over $30 billion. The central bank kept the figure secret. Plus, there was another $8 billion that BOT had to hold as priority money, as a guarantee of the value of the Thai currency. When BOT unpegged the baht, it had no international reserves at all. Amidst the crisis, there was no economic or political leadership to reverse things or create a plan to tackle the problem. The problem was left in the hands of the BOT.

Between 1995 and 1996, Thailand had two prime ministers, and neither was that sophisticated or had capable economic advisors. The Ministry of Finance had six ministers in two years, each of them in office for only about two months. It was a mess, especially compared with the previous government, in which there was only one finance minister, Tarrin, from 1992–95.

Amid this crisis in the making, between late 1996 to June 1997, I can attest to the fact that Prime Minister Chavalit was not informed at all. The minister of finance, Amnoi Binawan, followed the policy of the BOT in trying not to unpeg the baht. The economic ministers of Chavalit's cabinet were not unified—they did not work as a team. Chavalit's government was a coalition government made up of five or six parties. The minister of finance was from one party, the minister of industry from another, and the minister of agriculture from a third. All except minister Amnoi knew what was happening. He was a non-party man, a technocrat, and had been the economic czar of Thailand. He had been good in the 1970s and 1980s, but I don't think he lived up to expectations. In the 1990s, in the era of globalization, he lacked sophistication in economic management.[10]

Similarly, Han Seung Soo, a member of Korea's National Assembly who had been deputy prime minister of Korea in 1996–97, blamed Korea's collapse on the Korean government's dogged defense of the currency; like Thailand, the bureaucrats had kept the government's insolvency from President Kim Young Sam until the last minute. The ensuing banking crisis caught most people unawares. Even the IMF had given Korea a clean bill of health about the time that Indonesia was going under. An IMF mission to Korea in mid-October 1997 had concluded that its situation was different from Southeast Asia, and that its macroeconomic fundamentals remained strong. This gave the Koreans a sense of false confidence.

"By mid-autumn, we thought we had escaped the worst of the financial contagion," Han told an audience at the Carnegie Endowment for International Peace in Washington in January 1998, while the crisis was still in full swing. "The real shock was in late October, after the plunge in the Hong

Kong stock market. Foreign banks stopped rolling over. We had discussed the weaknesses of the financial system from the mid-1980s, but were blinded by the dramatic success of the real sector. For too many policy makers, the last war was the war for industrial development. At the end of 1997, short-term liabilities made up 58.8 percent of debt. By attempting to defend the currency, the government prolonged the pain."

Thus began a wild ride for global high rollers and a nightmare for Asia. The baht was the first of the Asian currencies to collapse; the rupiah, the ringgit, and peso quickly followed suit. A few months later, the Korean won dropped through the floor. The Singapore, Hong Kong, and New Taiwan dollars wobbled under speculative pressures, stabilized, but remained sensitive to each new warning signal. Asians watched appalled as wealth built up over a generation suddenly evaporated. In November and December, the Indonesian and Korean governments joined Thailand in seeking emergency funding from the IMF. As currencies plunged across the region, every unsound business practice and reckless investment was exposed, like rotting seaweed left behind by an ebbing tide.

As early as 1995, signs of impending trouble were there for anyone to read—a sharp slowdown in the region's key exports, a speculative free-for-all in property prices across the region, the growing gap between rich and poor in some countries, labor scarcities in highly skilled sectors, and labor gluts in unskilled trades. The signs were ignored. The biggest sign of all, a sharp runup in short-term bank lending, was viewed as an indicator of the attractions of Asian assets, not their risks. "There were no crisis meetings, and certainly no sense that this was the start of an economic crisis that would roll around the world," Clinton's top economic advisor, Dennis Tarullo, told the *New York Times* in 1998.[11]

By 1998, the predominant view in the United States was that the Asian crisis was a moment of reckoning for economies that had become greedy and complacent. Wrote Michael Zielenziger, a veteran correspondent based in Tokyo for Knight Ridder, "Remember the fateful moment when Detroit's autoworkers first learned the name 'Toyota'? Or when Pittsburgh discovered that Koreans made steel, too? In those fearful flashes of insight, Americans found out they were no longer unchallenged in the world, but were facing fierce new competitors. A painful era of layoffs, mergers, economic restructuring and rethinking quickly followed. In its simplest form, that's what has happened to Asia."[12]

The difference between Asia and Detroit was the absence of such "fearful flashes" of insight. In fact, there was no reckoning, in the sense of a widespread consensus on the best way to respond to the crisis. East Asians behaved as they had in the past when faced with severe economic pressure.

They adapted to the new international environment in ways that would solve their immediate problems while conserving their underlying economic and political models. With the IMF reforms, they coped rather than believed, waiting for the Fund to relax its conditionality following the prescribed quarterly reviews. Even the most ardent reformers within the crisis economies admitted that the IMF had gone too far.

Said the National Assembly's Han Seung Soo: "The Korean financial crisis arrived so suddenly, within a matter of days. We found our foreign reserves had been depleted completely. Without the IMF package, we would have had to declare a moratorium. We had to restore international confidence, and Koreans could not do it alone. We were not in a position to reject conditionality at the time. As the economy progresses, we will be in a position to reverse the terms."

Indeed, one measure of East Asian conservatism was the contrast between the rapid execution of certain IMF reforms compared to the sluggish course of others. Thailand, Indonesia, and Korea each quickly dropped barriers to foreign investment and closed wildcat credit institutions under the IMF whip. IMF pressure was markedly less successful, however, in encouraging corporate restructuring or reductions of the public sector through privatization and deregulation. Indeed, East Asian governments addressed the banking crisis by reclaiming large parts of the financial sector, reversing the process of privatization that had begun in the early 1990s. Although a true paradigm shift occurred, it was one in which the crisis economies played a conservative and evolutionary rather than a revolutionary game.

From a cynical perspective, the aftermath of the crisis was one in which two mutually exclusive, equally conservative ideologies managed to survive each other. Asians were not alone in responding to the crisis in fundamentally conservative ways. The IMF and the World Bank were just as intensely focused on preserving paradigms as the East Asians. If it took a few lies, so much the worse, but the end would justify the means. Self-delusion was also at work. Many of those who insisted that the situation was manageable simply could not believe that things could have gone so wrong. For its part, the IMF identified East Asian success with its prescriptions, so applying them in the midst of crisis ought only to bring them back to where they began.

In the self-justification department, none was more meretricious than the World Bank. It had spent the better part of the 1990s promoting East Asia as its preeminent success story, even as its own menu of policy prescriptions was changing. The crisis boiled up just as the World Bank and IMF were preparing to take their annual fall conference of governors to Asia, for the first time since the Bangkok meeting in 1991 that had been the genesis of the Bank's *East Asian Miracle* report. In 1997, the Bank planned to hold the meetings in Hong Kong, in order to please China, by highlighting the economic achievements of "Greater China" a few months after Britain had returned the lease territory of Hong Kong. China was the Bank's largest single borrower. In 1995, when the decision was made, the Bank had also been in the full swing of recommending East Asia as a model, based on the argument that East Asia had adopted the Bank's macroeconomic philosophy of the 1980s.

East Asian economies had been at the center of a huge surge in private-capital flows to developing economies, a trend endorsed by both the Bank and the IMF. The Bank published most of the background study papers for the *East Asian Miracle*, then focused four consecutive annual development reports on East Asia–related topics—transitional economies in 1996; the role of the state in 1997; the role of information in development in 1998; and, finally, China in 1999.

In August 1997, a month before the meetings in Hong Kong, the Bank's chief of public relations, Mark Malloch-Brown, sent his boss a briefing book on Asia and its leading issues to prep him for interviews with some of the thousands of journalists who would attend the meetings. "Jim," Malloch-Brown wrote, "This is an historic early opportunity for the international community to see the 'one country, two systems' arrangements close up." The "flagship feature" of the meetings was to be a program of seminars entitled "Asia and the World: Capital, Competitiveness, and Community."

After listing the "many noteworthy speakers" for this grand event, Brown added, apologetically, "There are also a few hot-button issues that you should be prepared to respond to in case they come up." These included the crisis in Thailand "and its spillover in East Asia." Malloch-Brown's instructions were explicit. "Here you should emphasize that the short-term crisis has been stabilized, thanks to rapid and effective international action in which the Bank played an active part. Disciplined implementation of the adjustment program will now be absolutely key to Thailand's early resumption of strong growth, and to ensuring this crisis only has an effect in the short term. The same holds true for the other countries in the region that have been affected by the currency crisis."[13]

Such optimism was entirely in keeping with views held by the World Bank and IMF over the course of the 1990s. In late 1996, as economic warning signals flashed through the region, the World Bank had put out a press release insisting that "high growth in East Asia is set to continue into the next century. The fundamentals remain in place for the world's fastest growing countries to sustain their economic success. Much of the recent bad news, from the export slowdown to high current account deficits and price falls in some markets, reflects temporary phenomena and does not signal an economic decline."[14] The Bank's chief economist for East Asia at the time, Michael Walton, was engrossed with indicators that showed that income inequality was growing in key economies such as China, Hong Kong, and Thailand, a sign that the East Asian "miracle" paradigm was deteriorating.[15] Yet, although Walton was concerned with the lack of "robust" banking systems and capital markets in East Asia, he offered no indication that they were a threat to growth. In the atmosphere of the Bank at the time, it would have been heresy.

About the same time, the IMF's in-house magazine, *IMF Survey*, featured Indonesia as one of the outstanding economies in the developing world in terms of rapid growth in per capita income, poverty reduction, and improvement in social indicators. The challenge for Indonesia was "to sustain the successes of recent years."[16] In 1997, Malloch-Brown's main worry was that journalists might nag his boss about charges by Northwestern University scholar Jeffrey Winters that up to 30 percent of Bank loans to Indonesia had been siphoned off by the Suharto family and its many cronies. Between 1991 and 1997, the Bank had lent $8.9 billion to Indonesia, second only in Asia to China.

In a follow-up note to Wolfensohn, the Bank's vice-president for East Asia, Jean-Michel Severino, added, "We have never had any evidence that it [the siphoning off of Bank funds] happens, despite repeated controls and audits, but we are aware of the wide corruption of the Indonesian society— and so is the government. Therefore, it is not impossible that some of the procurement procedures under our funds are biased without us having any possibility to prove it or even see it. While making these points, you could mention that we are discussing with the Indonesian government ways to increase, if possible, our controls on our projects, and to develop more thorough actions against corruption."[17]

If the world's major development institutions minimized the problems even after the carnage had begun in Asian currency markets, banks and brokerage analysts were even worse, touting Asian investment opportunities and predicting a quick end to the crisis well into Fall 1997. Capital markets aside, Indonesia and Thailand were among the favorites of global investors, second only to China. In 1996, the year before the crash, Indonesia attracted $29.9 billion dollars in foreign-capital flows, while Thailand got $13.1 billion. Both were darlings of Japanese investors in particular, who put $7.6 billion into Indonesia and $6.1 billion into Thailand that year.[18] Korea had emerged as one of the region's major investors in its own right, with $3.7 billion in investments in East Asia in 1996.

To be sure, up until the eve of the crisis, there was ample reason for enthusiasm, whether from the IMF or the private sector. Neither the Bank nor the

IMF thought they were propagandists for East Asia; it was just that East Asia had brilliantly proved the wisdom of their counsel and advice. Thailand, as a 1995 *IMF Survey* article noted, had increased its per capita income five-fold between 1965 and 1995. "Resilient and pragmatic, the Thai economy has relied on a vigorous private sector and enduring commitment to macroeconomic stability," the IMF purred.[19] In 1994, Michel Camdessus, the IMF's managing director, hailed Korea as standing "at the threshold of the group of advanced industrial countries," and praised it for its "structural policies" that encouraged "efficient and competitive private enterprises."[20] The IMF also lavished praise on "Indonesian authorities." They "have persistently addressed poverty and income distribution problems through targeted measures," proclaimed the Fund house organ.[21]

By 1998, the markets had gone stone cold on Asia and emerging markets generally. Most observers agreed that the crisis had fallen just short of provoking a global economic collapse. Major brokerages such as Merrill Lynch simply shut down their emerging markets businesses, and the high-rolling hedge fund traders of the mid-1990s were on the street looking for jobs. Allen Sinai, chief global economist for Primark Decision Systems, an investment advisory firm, told the *New York Times* that the Asian crisis was "off the radar screens in terms of severity. It is the single most negative economic event since the Great Depression in the United States. But what makes this problem so distinct is that it is not just an economic bust. It is laced with every type of financial crisis and instability that has ever shown up in the real world or any textbook. And while there are some brilliant minds working on it, no one can deal with it—not [Robert] Rubin, not [Larry] Summers, not any single country, not the IMF."[22]

For each of the crisis economies, the events of 1997 to 1998 were shattering. None, however, was so steeped in denial, fell as far, or had as much difficulty in managing the aftermath of crisis, as Indonesia. Before the financial crisis, the country was seen as a megastar of the developing world. Over a quarter century, the number of Indonesians living below the officially defined "poverty line" had decreased from 60 percent in 1970 to 11 percent in 1996—despite the fact that the population had grown from 117 million to 200 million. Political corruption was so open and widespread that people joked about it. Foreign investors simply factored corruption in as a cost of doing business. Suharto's wife, sons, and daughters were all deeply involved in business and an assortment of shadowy foundations.

After the crisis, Indonesia became the leading evidence for those who argued that the Asian model had always been based on cronyism and corruption. Indonesia's downfall was seen as proof that Indonesia's rapid growth had been a bubble, lining mainly the pockets of the rich and the military. Its slow recovery demonstrated the fate of economies that failed to embrace democracy and the free market. The U.S. Congress tried to block the IMF's emergency bailout fund for Indonesia, arguing that it would go straight into the pockets of the Suharto family. Stapleton Roy, the American ambassador, publicly derided Habibie, Suharto's successor, and helped organize an effective vote-monitoring scheme for the June 1999 parliamentary elections, which prepared the way for the presidential election the following October. The World Bank finally admitted the truth of Jeffrey Winters's assertions about the divergence of Bank funds to the Suhartos, and published a self-flagellating report.

From October 1997 to October 1999, nobody had a kind word for Indonesia, when a shaky, but democratic government under President Abdurrahman Wahid, chairman of the Islamic Nahdlatul Ulama, finally replaced Habibie. The real question was why so many discovered Indonesia's defects so late. The answer would be the same as to the question, why did it take so long for the world to notice Asia's problems? In fact, the problems had been well known, and the major change was the new velocity of global capital markets. Nobody had a clue how to organize a defense, and it was easier to blame immature markets and corrupt politicians than it was to understand how to manage the forces that had been unleashed by the rapid expansion of capital markets in the mid-1990s.

Indonesia became the emblem of everything that was supposed to have been wrong with Asia and had everything in spades that the critics argued would impede Asia's recovery. Yet, a close chronology of events fails to support the thesis that Indonesia was institutionally hardwired to precipitate an economic collapse; like Thailand, mistakes were made that compounded structural problems, but structural defects were not enough to explain the crisis.

More than anything else, the Indonesian crisis was a forceful example of the damage that can flow from bad decisions, in this case the decisions of two stubborn personalities insistent on preserving turf and paradigm, Suharto and his nemesis, Michel Camdessus, managing director of the IMF.

Suharto, unlike his colleagues in Thailand and Korea, lacked the means and desire to make a quick exit and helped turn Indonesia's currency crisis into a conflagration through his public battles with the IMF. For its part, the IMF applied the same formula as it had used in Thailand and would soon apply in Korea, which was to impose fiscal discipline and monetary tightening simultaneously. In terms of population if not per capita income, however, Thailand and Korea were midgets compared to Indonesia.[23] Indonesia's swift and devastating economic contraction opened up huge ethnic and religious fissures and jeopardized the security of the crucial Malacca Straits and submarine passageways through the Java Sea. It raised the specter of new waves of economic refugees across Southeast Asia and the breakdown of the delicate consensus between military and government that had sustained the Suharto regime since 1967. In short, Indonesia was nothing to play around with. A meltdown in Indonesia was big time in terms of regional and global stability.

Initially, like Korea, Indonesia seemed immune to the financial contagion triggered by the float and subsequent collapse of the baht. Dennis De Tray, the former country director for Indonesia at the World Bank, ruefully recalled that on July 8, 1997, he had told the Bank's directors, "Indonesia would not be affected by contagion."[24] Nonetheless, the Indonesian economy crashed with a magnitude that set two post–World War Two records—one for GDP contraction, a second for currency devaluation.[25] In 1998, Indonesia's 1998 GDP fell by 13.7 percent on an annual basis.[26] Most of the fall in output was concentrated in the latter half of the year, after a period of political confusion, capital flight, and wrangling with the international financial institutions. Foreign and domestic investment began to collapse in the second quarter as anti-Chinese riots swept Jakarta and other cities. In the fourth quarter of 1998, GDP contraction reached 19.5 percent.[27]

Up until July 1997, the rupiah was stable within a range of Rupiah 1,900 to the dollar—the average exchange rate in 1991—to Rupiah 2,450 to the dollar. In June 1998, the rupiah reached an all-time low of 17,000, at a time when the IMF was refusing to disburse funds from the $43 billion "rescue package" it had signed more than eight months earlier. For the next year and a half, between the resignation of President Suharto and the installment of Wahid as Indonesia's first democratically elected president in October 1999, Indonesia was the most troubled of the Asian economies. Ethnic Chinese took an estimated $80 billion out of the country in the weeks and months following the 1998 riots, and most of it stayed out, at least through 1999.[28]

Indonesia's moves during the early stages of the Asian crisis were by the book. No economist could have disapproved. The Indonesian central bank not only followed the advice of the international financial institutions—it anticipated the advice. Monetary and banking officials kept a wary eye on speculators as baht contagion rippled through the region's currencies. After floating the rupiah on August 14, 1997, the Bank of Indonesia quickly imposed a severe liquidity squeeze, pushing overnight rates as high as 81 percent.[29] These rates were not nearly as high as the 200 percent overnight rates that Hong Kong saw a few months later, during the speculative attack on the Hong Kong dollar of October 22 to 24, but they were extreme by Indonesian standards.

Officials of the central bank were familiar with emergency measures. They had used tight monetary policy successfully on at least three previous occasions when speculators attacked the rupiah in 1984, 1987, and 1991.[30] Anticipating the strategy that would later be imposed by the IMF, in September 1997 the government announced a belt-tightening program that included postponement or cancellation of a number of major infrastructure projects. Yet, within a few weeks, on October 13, the government was forced to call in the IMF for the first of six emergency balance-of-payment support agreements. From this point on, the economy was basically in the hands of an ailing and inept President Suharto, floundering since the death of his wife in 1996, and the IMF. Neither proved to be up to the task.

The year 1998 was dire for Indonesia, with inflation hitting 77.63 percent,[31] money market rates reaching as high as 81 percent in August, some 4.2 million people laid off as a direct result of the crisis,[32] and an external debt ballooning to $73 billion in private-sector and $66 billion in public debt. Foreign direct investment, measured by approvals, fell by 60 percent; domestic investment by half.[33] The budget deficit reached Rupiah 135 trillion,[34] including Rupiah 114 trillion in foreign loans—a painful experience for a nation that had boasted of its "balanced budget" policy before the crisis (although the Indonesian government defined a "balanced" budget as one in which total expenditures equaled domestic revenues plus foreign borrowing). This was not as bad as some forecasts—many believed unemployment would reach 20,000,000, for example. It was bad enough, however, and even though by 1999 there were signs of improvement, Indonesia's recovery was far more sluggish than in Thailand or South Korea, the other two major crisis economies.

The reasons for this were not complex. Both Thailand and Korea floundered under the initial onslaught of the crisis, but quickly introduced new leaders and new governments that could justify bold actions as correcting the mistakes of their predecessors. Indonesia, by contrast, limped through the crisis under discredited leaders whose every move was hemmed in by institutions—both cronies and policies—they themselves had created. In Indonesia, a political convulsion boiled up in the wake of the economic crisis. This was, in part, a lesson in the virtues of democracy, however inept or constrained by bad leaders.

As Aristides Katoppo argued in a compelling essay, once Suharto resigned, Indonesians swiftly formed a consensus around the need for political reform. "The amazing thing was that the old hardware embraced the new software smoothly without a hitch," Katoppo wrote. "Was this a political miracle? How was it possible that consensus could be forged during tense days of high uncertainty, severe turbulence and political turmoil? If compared with the strained negotiations between the Indonesian government with the IMF over the conditions for the rescue package, which had to be renegotiated several times, the conflict resolution amongst the Indonesian political actors could arrive at a core consensus about the direction in a less formal way, but yet not less binding."[35] Unfortunately, Habibie, following in Suharto's footsteps, was equally incompetent to deliver clear and unambiguous decisions.

In the years leading up to the crisis, like its neighbors, Indonesia pegged its currency to the U.S. dollar. Like its neighbors as well, Indonesia experienced a sharp deterioration in the growth rate of its merchandise exports, which led to an increase in the current account deficit, and large capital account surpluses created by an influx of FDI and portfolio investment. Finally, just as Thailand and Korea, Indonesia maintained relatively high domestic interest rates in order to sustain its policy of linking the rupiah to the U.S. dollar. The official discount rate, the rate charged on funds lent to banks by Bank of Indonesia, was 13.99 percent in 1995, 12.80 percent in 1996, and 20 percent in 1997. But Indonesia was not on anybody's watch list until Fall 1997. Its macroeconomic management was considered sound. The government budget was consistently in surplus. Inflation was on a downward trend between 1995 and 1997, despite supercharged growth rates—8.2 percent in 1995, 8 percent in 1996, even 4.6 percent in 1997, the year the crisis hit.

Of the three danger signs, the most significant was the high-interest-rate policy. Devaluations in the Chinese renminbi in 1994 and Japanese yen in 1995 triggered the deterioration of Indonesia's trade account. Both devaluations eroded the competitiveness of Indonesian exports. A glut in semiconductor supplies and consequent price collapse also affected regional exporters. But these were temporary effects, and the trade account deficit was more than covered by the inflow of portfolio and direct investment.

High domestic interest rates were another story, however, particularly as discount rates on the yen and deutsche mark sank dramatically. The yen discount rate went from 1.75 percentage points in 1994 to 0.50 in 1995–97, while the deutsche mark slid from 4.5 in 1994 to 2.5 in 1997. The result was that European, Japanese, and domestic banks piled into short-term lending, rolling over low-interest funds from offshore deposits into domestic loans at the high domestic market rates. U.S. banks ended up with less exposure to Indonesia because the U.S. discount rate was rising over the same time period that yen and Eurorates were sinking.

By December, the average maturity rate on commercial bank loans in Indonesia was eighteen months, and $20.8 billion was due within one year or less.[36] Most such loans went unhedged, because of the security blanket provided by the fixed exchange rate, at least until August 14, and because of the implicit assumption that the government would act to prevent bank failures. According to the Indonesian central bank, lenders could make as much as a 10 percent spread on unhedged borrowing offshore;[37] depending on market arbitrage rates the transaction cost of hedging might actually erase any advantage of borrowing abroad. Naturally, domestic and many foreign borrowers preferred to take their profits.

A drive through downtown Jakarta in 1999 was a tour of gleaming but empty bank towers. Financial liberalization had played a major role in expanding the scope of the disaster that occurred when lenders began to call in their loans and credit vanished. Two banking reforms in 1983 and 1988 created a boisterous domestic banking sector. By 1997, there were 240 domestic commercial banks, most of which had been aggressively expanding their branch networks in the previous two years. Total branches rose from 4,888 in 1994 to 6,308 in 1997.[38] Prudential supervision was nearly absent, and many of the banks behaved with radical indiscretion. They lent to their shareholders, conducted money laundering for the Suharto family foundations, and funded their own ill-considered investments.[39]

The Indonesian banks were sitting ducks for the huge increase in private capital flows to developing countries.[40] When the rupiah collapsed and interest rates skyrocketed, the domestic banks crumpled; by March 1999 only seventy-three commercial banks were left in the government's "Category A" for banks meeting minimum capital adequacy standards. Of the other fifty-five that remained independent by that time, thirty-eight were closed and the rest were recapitalized with government funds, making the government the major shareholder.[41]

Poor prudential supervision and wildcat credit expansion helped turn the crisis into a catastrophe once the currency run was in full swing. At its trough in June 1998, the rupiah's decline reached 85 percent. A third factor, however, predisposed the market to assume that the rupiah was likely to weaken dramatically. This was because it was significantly overvalued to start out with. The rupiah had long been pegged to the U.S. dollar; formally until 1978, virtually thereafter. In 1978, the government announced that it would adopt a managed exchange rate based on a basket of trading partner currencies, but in practice the U.S. dollar had a weight of 100 percent against the "basket."[42]

The Indonesian central bank, Bank Negara, then pursued a policy of slow but steady rupiah depreciation against the dollar, punctuated with large devaluations when oil prices fell in 1983 and 1986. Beginning in the 1990s, however, the combination of growth in output and growth in investment put pressure on the rupiah to appreciate to which the government responded by steadily widening its trading "band"—beyond this band the central bank would intervene. This tendency toward rupiah appreciation was the source of the currency's vulnerability in October 1997, when speculators attacked it. The motive behind the Indonesian government's policy was to sustain its export drive, first in oil then in merchandise exports. But it also served as a signal that the rupiah was significantly overvalued. Policy intervention helped relieve upward pressure on the rupiah but also set the conditions for a drastic devaluation.

If the rupiah had floated freely, as long as Indonesia maintained high growth and low inflation, increasing real money demand would have driven both interest rates and the currency upward. Instead, under a fixed-exchange-rate regime, the government had few tools other than expanding the money supply to keep the exchange and interest rates constant. This is just what the Indonesian central bank did throughout its high-growth period. M1 steadily increased from Rupiah 22.1 trillion in the first quarter of 1990 to Rupiah 78.3 trillion in the fourth quarter of 1997.[43] Because money supply consistently ran slightly ahead of growth (over the same period, from 1990 to 1997, the GDP grew from Rupiah 195.5 trillion to Rupiah 624.3 trillion), a move to a free float would automatically imply a snapback of the exchange rate to a lower level if demand or interest rates showed signs of weakening. The government moved immediately to raise interest rates and contract the money supply, but it also made the crucial mistake of fiscal retrenchment at a time when foreign investment was beginning to pull back as well. The market paid attention to the signal of demand contraction, and ignored the tight money policy, which was in any case short lived.

Until November 1997, however, the central bank's mistakes were largely technical errors, reflecting its anxieties when faced with a degree of financial market turbulence outside the range of its experience. After November, the issues and mistakes were increasingly political in nature. In one of the many tragic moments of the crisis, financial markets plummeted after the IMF entered the picture, ostensibly to shore up the Indonesian balance of payments with emergency stabilization funds. In the two agreements that created the Indonesian bailout package, on November 5 and January 15, 1998, the IMF insisted upon fiscal restraint measures that went well beyond anything the Indonesians had considered and proved to be disastrous.

The November agreement called for the immediate shutdown of sixteen banks, which triggered a general run on banks; the second agreement, in January, called for tax increases, more cancellations of projects, and the gradual elimination of subsidies. The January agreement allowed for a deficit target of 1 percent, but the message of fiscal austerity was clear. The markets, correctly assuming demand would contract under the circumstances and that inflation would erode any efforts to stabilize the currency through manipulating the money supply, simply abandoned ship.[44]

The Bank and the IMF had both chided Indonesia on its monetary policy, saying that it was using the wrong set of tools to ward off inflation and overheating. As early as 1993, the World Bank had warned Indonesia that it should shift to fiscal measures "for ensuring that excess demand pressures do not arise, causing inflation to accelerate or the current account deficit to become unsustainable."[45] So the IMF may have seen itself as taking advantage of an opportunity to strongarm Indonesia into the adoption of fiscal tools for macro-economic management, rather than promoting demand contraction per se. This was the approach that the IMF had taken during the Latin American sovereign debt crisis of the early 1980s, when the issue was public-sector debt. Indonesia's problems, however, were related to private-sector debt. Between 1992 and July 1997, according to the World Bank, 85 percent of the increase in Indonesia's external debt was due to private-sector borrowing.[46] Fiscal restraint would do little to fix the problems of private-sector debt, yet in the early stages of the crisis, both the IMF and the Indonesian government moved in this direction, with disastrous consequences.

Meanwhile, Suharto was growing more delusionary all the time. During the critical period between November 1997 and May 1998, when he resigned, Suharto gave every indication of being on a completely different track from his advisors. To start out with, he made exceptions to the IMF programs for his notoriously corrupt children. One of his sons, Bambang Trihatmodjo, filed suit against the government when asked to close down his Bank Andromeda. Eventually he backed down, only to transfer Bank Andromeda's assets to a new bank.[47] Against explicit warnings from the World Bank to pull back in the power sector, the state electricity company, PLN, approved a power purchase deal for a project partly owned by his eldest daughter, Siti Hardiyanti Rukmana.[48] Instead of scrapping tax privileges for the car company owned by his son, Hutomo Mandala Putra, known as "Tommy," the government merely agreed to wait for the decision of the World Trade Organization, which was considering a complaint filed by Japanese automakers. The tax privileges, tailored to Tommy's "Timor" car, based on South Korean technology, were only scrapped with the January IMF agreement.[49]

Finally, Suharto delivered a 1998 budget that left analysts gaping. Released on January 6, the budget called for deficit spending of 2.5 percent of GDP, the continuation of fuel subsidies, and a current account deficit of 2.5 percent, half a percentage point above the IMF's recommendation. Basic assumptions included an exchange rate of 4,000 rupiah to the dollar, 4 percent growth in GDP, and 9 percent inflation.[50]

Within two days, markets panicked. The rupiah dropped below 10,000 rupiah to the dollar, and capital flight began on a massive scale. Indonesians snatched food off the shelves of grocery stores, fearful that prices would spiral out of control, as they soon did. IMF officials were in Jakarta within days, and Suharto humbly promised IMF managing director Stanley Fischer and U.S. Deputy Treasury Secretary Summers that he would "commit his country to vigorous enforcement of economic reforms that it has failed to enact."[51] According to Dennis De Tray, Suharto told Fischer, "He would personally negotiate the program. In effect, there would be no negotiations. You tell me what to do. It was clever. It put the burden of proof on the IMF and the World Bank. But he did what he said he would do. He signed off on the reforms."[52]

The next six months featured unrelieved turmoil in Indonesia, both inside the Merdeka Palace in Jakarta and on the streets. Suharto's faithful finally deserted him, and he was forced to step down on May 21. Vice-President Habibie, an erratic industrialist who had been raised as Suharto's foster son, took over as president. But Indonesia's economic slide did not stop, and the prospects of an economic and political implosion were so visible and frightening that investment, and to a large extent economic production, simply halted. Even the IMF stood on the sidelines, fearing to disburse funds while the economy was so clearly out of control. Only in June, with the Frankfurt debt agreement, did the IMF feel sufficiently confident to begin offering balance-of-payments support again, out of the $43 billion agreement negotiated the previous year.

Suharto and the IMF were a poisonous combination. The IMF continued to insist upon fiscal contraction while Indonesians were panicking about issues of basic food supply, driving Indonesians onto the streets. Suharto's peculiar monetary strategy led to a further collapse of the rupiah, ensuring that Indonesians would find it virtually impossible to purchase any imported goods, including pharmaceuticals and rice. Although Suharto had initially listened to his advisors who advocated tight money after the floating of the rupiah, he changed his mind after the first IMF agreement and for two months flooded the economy with money. Base money increased by 36 percent over the previous month in December 1997, and by 22 percent in January 1998. Broad money increased by 8 percent in December and by 27 percent in January.

Having fired his central bank governor, Suharto seems to have made up his mind that he could manage the rupiah just as he had in the days of the fixed exchange rate—by manipulating money supply. With the floating rate, however, the outcome was disastrous. He followed this performance with a prolonged flirtation with Johns Hopkins University economist Steve Hanke, an advocate of currency boards. The problem with currency boards is that they are premised on a central bank that is able to fully back the foreign-currency value assigned to the domestic-currency unit out of reserves. Bank of Indonesia was simply not up to the task. The rupiah continued to plunge until July, before beginning a gradual appreciation. This followed six months of contraction or slow growth in money supply, and was mirrored by a gradual easing in interest rates and inflation.

In March, April, and May 1999, Indonesia experienced zero or negative inflation, convincing many analysts that the Indonesian economy had bottomed out. After the disastrous agricultural harvest of 1997–98, a successful one in 1998–99 helped bring prices down for food, and prices for clothing, education, and transport fell as well. Sjahril Sabirin, the central bank governor, predicted that interest rates would fall to 17 to 20 percent by the end of the year, down from 26 percent in June.[53] In March and April, for the first time exports showed signs of life, although they were still down by 14 percent for the first four months of the year compared to 1998. The current account was in surplus, however, mainly due to a 20 percent slide in imports.

With higher oil prices, the president of Pertamina was quoted saying that if current prices persisted, government oil and gas revenues would increase by 50 percent by the end of 1999.[54] According to the Central Bureau of Statistics, real GDP expanded by a nearly invisible 1.34 percent, mainly due to the strong agricultural performance. The government continued to predict an economic contraction for the year, but a relatively mild one, of 1.02 percent.[55] Indonesians reacted euphorically to the June 7 parliamentary election, and the victory of the PDI-P (Indonesian Democratic Party of Struggle), led by the daughter of former President Sukarno, Megawati Sukarnoputri. Both the stock market and rupiah celebrated with significant upturns.

Finally, over the course of 1998, the IMF gradually revised its fiscal targets for Indonesia until the policy was expansive, a turn of 180 degrees. In November, an IMF memorandum of understanding actually called for a budget deficit of 6 percent of GDP.[56] The rupiah eased from 14,900 to the dollar in June to 8,025 in December; interest rates also declined substantially, from 70.7 percent for one-month central bank certificates of deposit, called SBIs, at the end of August, to 38.4 percent at the end of December.

Politics, rather than policies, were responsible for the modest upturn. The IMF's exchange-rate strategy, based on its experience with Latin America in the early 1980s, was to use currency depreciation to simultaneously encourage domestic demand and bring the current account into balance. Pre-crisis, Indonesia's current account deficit had not mattered, because it was covered by an ample capital inflow. But capital flooded out of Indonesia during and after the crisis, and the current account deficit, as well as the slump in exports, had become a serious issue. IMF funds were running out, and international donors were unable to cover the deficit in both current and capital accounts indefinitely.

According to a study by the Asian Development Bank, most exporters had not been affected by the credit squeeze due to widespread bank failure.

Instead, their main problem was the collapse of domestic demand, and the increased cost of imported inputs. Exporters of products in the food sector showed no reduction or an increase in production in 1998. Firms in the electronics sector, by contrast, were hard hit, due to their heavy dependence on imported components.[57]

These results implied that Indonesia's best hope for recovery was through the revival of domestic demand, led by agriculture. Given the unpredictability of agricultural returns, that was cold comfort, yet it underlined that the East Asian financial crisis was not the stark clash of competing systems that had been portrayed by Western analysts and the Japanese—the command economies of East Asia versus the free-market practices of the global economy. Indeed, to most Asian observers, the key issues were politics and the inadequacy of Asian financial institutions, particularly those with a supervisory role, to handle rapid fluctuations in the global capital markets. These suggested that globalization had gone too fast for these economies to handle; the obvious implication was to slow the process down.

Scattered Flock

In the gray 1990s, Japan was like the child prodigy stumbling on his or her way to middle age; its friends, never wholly friendly, skipped Tokyo on their way to Beijing and Hanoi. One could almost hear the scraping of chairs as global investors dropped their seats on the huge Tokyo Stock Exchange.

A gaggle of editorialists breezily dismissed Japan: "Making Sashimi of the Experts' Predictions: Why Japan Did Not Turn Out to Be the World Power Everyone Feared," cleverly explained the *Washington Post*, pored over by America's political elite.[58] Japan practices "Mainframe Economics in a PC World," wrote Richard Katz, New York correspondent for a Japanese business magazine, about the same time.[59] Japan is losing its "Inc.," said Michael Hirsh and Keith Henry, writing in *Foreign Affairs*, the prestigious journal of the Council on Foreign Relations.[60] "Today no sensible person would consider Japan as a model," Steve Hanke, Suharto's advisor, wrote in *Forbes* in the winter of 1996.[61]

"Japan passing," then "Japan nothing" became the bywords of the 1990s, as foreign multinationals, impatient with the high cost and exasperating difficulties of doing business in Japan, headed for the deal-making frenzy of China, Vietnam, the Southeast Asian "tigers," and the Northeast Asian "dragons." The downturn of sentiment began in 1989 with a prescient book by Bill Emmott, former Tokyo correspondent for *The Economist*. The book was entitled *The Sun Also Sets*, a mocking allusion to Hemingway.[62] Emmott argued that demographics—particularly the swelling numbers of the elderly—would undermine the Japanese miracle, a counterbalancing view to what was then the conventional wisdom. But by the late 1990s, Emmot's favorite shibboleth, the view of Japan as juggernaut, was as dead as a beached whale. It took a brave counter-cyclical voice and a good publicist to contest that Japan had any bottom-line virtues or oomph left in its model. In December 1996, organizers of a Washington conference on Asian technology quixotically entitled one panel, "Don't Forget Japan," and scheduled it for the end of the day when many of the audience would be on their way home.

On a visit to Tokyo's Yoyogi Park on a spring day in 1998, things were much the same on the surface as they were a decade earlier. Life bustled on in the Japanese capital. In nearby Omotesando, young Japanese women experimented with platform shoes, long narrow skirts, and porkpie hats that were part of a new fad for Afro-American style. Hip-hop was all the rage, along with a new beer called "Dunk," and the coffee shops and street cafés seemed no less crowded than before.[63]

In the newspaper headlines and television talk shows, however, the Japan of the 1990s was the reverse image of Japan in the 1980s. The difference was reflected on factory floors and in corporate boardrooms as well. Instead of arrogance, there was self-flagellation. Rather than inspiring fear abroad, Japan evoked something close to contempt. President Clinton created consternation in Tokyo by failing to stop by on a visit to Beijing. On June 17, 1998, Treasury Secretary Robert Rubin directed a massive Fed intervention to support the floundering yen, and a *New York Times* reporter argued the only reason he did so was to defend U.S. prosperity, as though Japan's prosperity and the forty-six-year-old alliance were no longer reason enough.[64] The intellectual tone was set by a book by two former China hands, warning of an impending great-power confrontation between the United States and Beijing.[65] U.S. policy consultants and government officials alike heaped scorn on Japan. Its economy was sliding into outright depression, after years of stagnation. Led by Rubin, American officials blamed Tokyo for failing to lead an Asian recovery. In a region and a world looking for scapegoats, Japan was a favored target.

Edward Lincoln, a Brookings Institution economist and one-time advisor to the American ambassador to Tokyo, recommended that the United States signal its displeasure with Japan "through canceled meetings, unreturned telephone calls, and a lack of advance notice of American policy moves."[66] Japan's old friends and allies railed at Japanese dithering. A disgusted Japanese public joined in, forcing Prime Minister Hashimoto Ryutaro to step down, to be replaced with a politician described as having all the flair of "cold pizza." The new prime minister, Obuchi Keizo, responded in kind by delivering hot pizza to the Japanese press corps gathered at the door of his family home.

We are sitting across from each other in the coffee shop of the International House of Japan, overlooking its lovely garden. Another wedding is in progress, and a large, merry party chases children and waves victory signs at the photographer, tirelessly grouping and regrouping for the camera. It is a bit beyond iris season, but the rain has deepened the garden's hues of green to the startling emerald of a Genji scroll by Sotatsu, the seventeenth-century painter.

Japan does not seem to be in any kind of crisis. My lunch companion is not fretting. Another appointment has been unexpectedly canceled, so Kinoshita Toshihiko has time to spare. The interview goes on for four hours. Kinoshita, once treasurer of JEXIM an advisor to the central bank of Indonesia, has become an "*amakudari*," a bureaucrat "descended" from heaven to the private sector. He advises A.T. Kearny, an American management consulting firm, and keeps his contacts warm with the Indonesian central bank governor and other old friends. I ask him what he thinks of Washington's insistent criticism of Japan's handling of the Asian crisis. A few weeks earlier at the annual spring meetings of the World Bank and IMF in Washington, U.S. Treasury Secretary Rubin had publicly pinned the blame on Japan for the region's continued slide. He declared that the key to Asia's recovery lay in revamping the Japanese economy: "A sustained global expansion and recovery in Asia cannot be achieved when the second largest economy in the world . . . is in recession and has a weakened financial system," Rubin told the IMF's policy-making Interim Committee.[67] Nor was Washington to let up on this theme. A month after my conversation with Kinoshita, U.S. Trade Representative Charlene Barshefsky was telling Asian trade ministers in Kuching, Malaysia, that "Japan must be the engine of growth for Asia," ignoring the markets, in which the yen was falling precipitously.[68]

Kinoshita's response is angry and distraught. "Japan brought so much money to the troubled countries," he says, with feeling.

The U.S. refused to do anything to support Thailand, and unwillingly approved $3 billion for Korea, but only in second-tier financing. In Korea, the U.S. approved the same amount as Japan, but in most of the countries, Japan is assuming most of the risk, and not for export but for balance-of-payment support. So why is the Asia problem a Japan problem? Americans invest more than Japan in China, Hong Kong, Singapore, Malaysia, and India. The Europeans as a whole, their commercial banks lend more than Japanese banks in Asia. Forty percent of outstanding credits in the region last year were from Europe. Japan is spending so much on official development assistance while the Americans and Europeans have cut back. Thinking of the whole picture, of course Japan is responsible, but maybe for 50 percent, because America wants to be the biggest partner of the Asia-Pacific region. The United States has kept pressure on Japan not to create a special zone in Asia, and the Japanese government has followed this line.

Considering all the facts, why do Americans and Europeans criticize Japan? They don't think of their own responsibility, or propose to join Japan in supporting Asian countries. And Japan is stuck because the economy is bad. The best economists in Japan couldn't do much to improve Japan in less than a year. It's the same situation as the United States in the 1970s and 1980s. The people of the world laughed at the United States, and Americans lost their confidence. When U.S. interest rates went to 20 percent, it created the Latin American debt problem. So in that situation, even a country like great America was unable to improve its situation overnight. But did Japan refuse to back America? Or refuse to join the United States in the Latin American bailout? In fact the biggest money to support Latin America came from Japan. The World Bank and IMF know this fact quite well. The United States made the program, and got Japanese support for it. I don't criticize the U.S., but any country has that kind of period.

Moreover, any suggestions from Japan are rejected by the U.S. because of the hegemonic problem. The U.S. says why don't you take leadership? But when Japan tries to take leadership, the U.S. says don't lead; follow us. The U.S. policy on Japan is actually against Japan taking any kind of lead, which frustrates many Japanese. They tell the government, why doesn't Japan show to the world that we are doing such things, while the U.S. is doing nothing? But basically the Japanese government as a whole had tended to think that no matter how big the Asian crisis is, it is much more important to keep good relations with the United States. So, if we oppose any aspect of U.S. policy toward the Asia crisis, we should do it in private, and not expose our criticism to the rest of Asia.

There is strong criticism of U.S. policy behind the scenes—people saying, let's kick out the U.S. proposals and set out our plans to the Asian region. This is what many leaders, many rightists are asking of the Japanese government. But the Japanese government doesn't want to do anything that will invite repercussions from the U.S., which might lead to a vicious circle between the two countries and drive our relations in a threatening direction. That is why we are keeping a low profile, because U.S.-Japan relations are more important. Because if something happens—if there is a big mess in China, the United States will suddenly recall that Japan is more important than China. This year, the United States is having its big dream of China, but it's only for the moment, for one or two years. Inevitably, there will be a problem, with balance of payments, or something, I don't know. Suddenly the Americans will recognize, we have a good friend in Japan.

It may be frustrating to us now, but true courage is to hold back. If you show up your courage today, you will lose forever. Maybe you don't want to be humiliated, and so you show your courage today. But now the United States sees itself as the only remaining superpower. Any action against the U.S. will be construed as threatening. If Japan takes real leadership in Asia without the United States, the American people will get angry and journalists will write that Japan has taken a very risky road.[69]

Listening to Kinoshita's monologue was frightening, like the sound of a piece of fabric slowly ripped in two. Japan was leaning ever closer to an open break with the old regime in which U.S.-Japan relations indeed came first. A sense of anxiety and frustration was growing, and Asia as an ally looking better and better.

Nine months later, I am back in Jakarta again. Habibie is still in power, though not for long. Indonesia's post-Suharto nightmare continues, with daily massacres in the outer islands, riots in Jakarta and other big cities, tens of thousands of people out of jobs and hungry. I am traveling with a group of American businesspeople, feeling the pulse of Indonesia in the months before the general election. One of our invitations is from the Japan Club of Jakarta. There are 1,600 Japanese companies in Indonesia, with 9,600 Japanese expatriates in Jakarta alone. In a darkened banquet room in the basement of a fine hotel, the elite of the Japanese business community gathers, to tell us, one by one, why they are still here.[70]

A man from Honda tells us he has just signed a $70 million joint venture, despite the fact that sales have dropped like a stone. "That is Honda's commitment to Indonesia. We have no intention at all to withdraw," he says. None of the other companies are leaving either; their exposure is too huge. "This country is changing little by little, but it doesn't have the power to revive by itself," says an executive from Itochu, the trading company. "We call it a transition period. They don't know what to do. After the election, they will be able to see what to do." A third man adds, "Japan understands very well about legally oriented countries, but we are also experienced in Asia. We can easily understand the Indonesian people's way of thinking. We are always in between. But in principle we believe in the future of our companies here. We are patient when we negotiate with the people of this country. We don't expect anything from the legal system here, so we must solve problems by ourselves."

Finally, a man from Marubeni tries once more to explain why he feels comfortable. "It's important to understand the difference between the Indonesian way and the Western way. There's a big mental difference. Let me give you two examples. I'm a member of an Indonesian golf club, and was asked to translate the club rules into Japanese. I saw a couple of clauses about a policy warning slow players—Indonesians can be very slow—and was excited. I thought it was a sign that Indonesia was changing. But in the end they told me to translate, if players are slow, please be understanding."

"Here's the other example. I hold a bank account in Texas, and was overdue on a check and got a letter from a collection agency. I paid the amount but the account was cut anyway. Such haircuts are not the way here. We settle 65 percent of our debt. To us, if you take a haircut it means the end of the relationship. We don't want it and the Indonesians don't want it. Rescheduling doesn't work here because the idea doesn't fit. In our case, most of our clients are not one-time clients. We have long business relationships with them. If we give them time, we believe we can get our money back."

Muddled, a tad masochistic, a little drunk, the Japan Club was here to stay. It was the end of a long trajectory, of an idea that began with the young Akamatsu and a calculator, marched through China, was remodeled under the U.S. Occupation, brandished by gimlet-eyed bureaucrats, and finally landed here, as Asia seemed to be sinking back into poverty and degradation. The bad times would not last forever, and Japan would soar again, perhaps next time as follower, not leader. Its idea remained.

11

Paradigm Lost

Rage

Stepping off the ledge of her *genkan*, or entryway, Iwase Fusako slides deftly into a sturdy pair of walking shoes. The seventy-three-year-old grandmother and former schoolteacher normally walks three miles a day to stay in shape. This day, though, Iwase was not walking for her health. Outside, it was a cold, drizzly June morning. Ignoring the rain, Iwase clapped on a soft-brimmed hat, unfolded an umbrella, and headed for the train station at the center of Jujo, an old-fashioned neighborhood in northwestern Tokyo.

In another hour, Iwase would join two-dozen fellow demonstrators in front of Japan's National Diet Building on a hilltop that Japanese call Nagatacho. Some held signs that read *ikari* ("rage") in Japanese. Others wore tall, pointed, orange hats in the shape of *oni*, or devil's horns, a traditional Japanese symbol for ire. Iwase and her colleagues stood in the rain, which was pelting hard. "I'm angry," Iwase shouts into a hand-held mike. "I will never forget this anger."[1]

On a cold February morning in another corner of Tokyo, Tanigawa Toshimitsu, the fifty-seven-year-old owner of an electrical repair shop, draped his Toyota Mark II in placards and set out for the MOF building, not far from the Diet. For six weeks, Tanigawa kept up a one-man protest movement using a loudspeaker to air his complaints against some of Japan's most powerful financial mandarins. "Onlookers said *ganbatte*, or keep up the good work," Tanigawa recalled. "These were unprecedented financial crimes. I had to stand up, and I felt very right to do so."[2]

The object of their anger was the Ministry of Finance, the charge, abuse of power. MOF was intimately involved in a housing-loan scandal that riveted the nation for the better part of 1996. Although the case was one of many examples of bureaucratic mismanagement that year, when MOF officials engaged in a clumsy cover-up of their role in the housing-loan company mess, Japanese felt especially betrayed. From Winter 1995 through early Summer 1996, the Japanese public poured out its sense of outrage. While the Japanese Diet debated the housing-loan issue, demonstrators laid siege to MOF. Private citizens like Tanigawa vented their anger singly and in groups. Caravans of gray-and-black sound trucks operated by right-wing patriotic associations daily circled the ministry, which was guarded by riot police wearing shields and visors. Citizens' groups marched from nearby Hibiya Park. Iwase joined a party of 800 in March; other groups of demonstrators numbered in the thousands.

Call it malaise or revolution, like a wind-up toy missing a spring, Japan, Inc., was badly out of kilter. In the mid-1990s, for the first time in recent memory, Japanese white-collar workers, the celebrated *sarariman,* endured the loss of jobs they expected to hold for a lifetime. Young female university graduates joined the ranks of the unemployed as Japanese companies cut back on new hiring overall but cut jobs for women first. Homeless people became a new and visible feature of life in Japan's big cities. The government's handling of the nation's banking and housing loan crisis had cost Japanese taxpayers billions of dollars, and would cost billions more.

In the cozy world of Japan, Inc., benign and incorruptible officials were supposed to steer less farsighted business executives and the public toward clear goals. The reward for self-sacrifice was always a better life. "In our experience, economic growth of three to five percent was normal," said Mizutani Kenji, an economist who had written in 1995 a book entitled *Japan's Economy on the Downslope.*[3] "During the recession, we have been dealing with stagnant or negative growth. As a mature economy, we cannot expect high growth rates to returns, and on top of that, we have structural problems that may take ten or twenty years to resolve."[4] The crisis in Japanese values was no less severe. Bureaucrats had been among the most revered of figures in Japanese society, and their downfall in public esteem was similar to the trauma of the American presidency after Watergate.

Every recession has its victims, but in Japan's case, the casualties struck at the heart of Japan's post-war economic system—faith in the bureaucracy, an egalitarian society, and the institution of lifetime employment. Suddenly fissures of inequality appeared in Japanese society where before the surface had been smooth. When these cracks opened, people had few resources to relieve their pain. There was no system of checks and balances to restrain the bureaucracy when it made mistakes and no social safety net to tide over the bad times for those at the bottom end of the work ladder, day laborers and women.

A family of six raccoons lives in a bamboo grove on the hillside behind the Yamada's small, neat house. Until 1993, Kazuhiro was rarely home. That was before he lost his job as an executive with an auto parts machinery company. Hiroko and Kazuhiro had time for the raccoons' antics after that, and for each other. "For the first time since we got married, we have been able to eat dinner together," said Hiroko, a lively, animated woman. Hiroko spent a lonely twenty-six years, until the day her husband, Kazuhiro, came home unexpectedly in mid-afternoon. Up until then, Kazuhiro had routinely worked a ten- to twelve-hour day, including Saturdays and some Sundays. Suddenly, at the age of forty-five, Kazuhiro was unemployed.[5]

Layoffs are a routine, if unfortunate occurrence in most industrialized nations, but they had been rare in Japan in the postwar period. When Kazuhiro joined Japan Automatic in 1963, he was twenty-two. He told his chief that he intended to "bury his bones" in the company, and the company responded by setting him on a management track. Kazuhiro was unusual for a future *sarariman*. A farm boy with no more than a high school education, he was recruited with other farm boys in his native village on the Oga Peninsula, famous for its wind-carved rocks. Kazuhiro worked first for a company making 8-mm movie cameras, then one that made fluorescent lamps for trains and traffic signals, before settling on Japan Automatic. His 1967 marriage to Hiroko was one reason for the move; "I was aiming at moving up," he said in 1996. And move up he did.

"The economy was good in those years. Our work was very successful," Kazuhiro recalled. Japan Automatic's parent company went bankrupt in the early 1980s, but the subsidiary did a booming business on its own. It was a time when the American auto industry was reeling under the impact of Japanese exports. Japan Automatic, which had moved into design and development as well as machine building, built new factories in Yokohama and Fukushima prefectures. It exported its machines to the United States, Thailand, and Singapore. "I gradually moved upstairs, from worker to supervisor to section chief and finally, to the top of the manufacturing department." In 1990, at the age of forty-three, Kazuhiro's salary, with an annual bonus, came to about $57,000 per year. Many nights, he never came home at all, sleeping on a pad in his office before starting back to work the next day. He went to work even when he was sick. Encounters with his family were limited to one or two days a month. Most weekends he worked as well.

When the end came, it was sudden. "I was called to the president's office. Three of the senior company officers were there. It was the first thing in the afternoon. I just got a call to go in. They did not tell me to quit. The general affairs manager said, 'Our company is not making profits because of the recession. Our situation is very bad.' Then the factory director suggested that I transfer to one of our company's subcontractors. They did not say, resign from this company and go to the subcontractor. But I knew what it meant— that I was fired, or something close to it." Stunned, Kazuhiro did something out of character—he took leave and went home. "I lost my voice," he recalls. "I was puzzled. How could this be happening to me?" Kazuhiro never went back to the factory. Two weeks later, he received formal notice of termination, as part of a plan to cut eighteen employees from the payroll.

In 1996, at age forty-nine, Kazuhiro was working on the factory line again, his third job since leaving Japan Automatic. His salary had been cut in half, and he had to quit at least one of his recent jobs because his back could no longer take the strain. A lanky, taciturn man, he admitted that it was hard to start over again. Hiroko, however, was more upbeat. "When it happened," she said, "I was very pessimistic. Life was dark. But now I feel more free and light and easy."

Japan's "lifetime" employment system grew out of wage control and labor mobilization schemes of the late 1930s and was designed to focus national resources on strategic industries. After the war, labor was scarce, and companies used guarantees of lifetime employment to compete for the best male workers. Under that system, Japanese companies hired men straight out of college or high school and expected them to stay for life. In the half-century since the end of the war, Japanese had come to view such "lifetime" jobs as not only a privilege but also as a right. To fire a white-collar worker hired under such expectations was to tamper with a fundamental social contract. Yet, the crisis of the early 1990s left Japanese employers with little choice. Bit by bit, a basic Japanese social institution expired.

The fact that lifetime employment was threatened was a measure of the severity of the recession. Besides stocks and real estate, in the late 1980s Japanese investors were also pouring funds into capital expansion. When the bubble collapsed, they were stuck with huge holding costs for new factories and infrastructure. The slowdown of the early 1990s was, in fact, a double whammy—a sharp slowdown in domestic demand was followed by a renewed spike in the value of the yen, hurting exports. In August 1995, the yen briefly hit seventy-nine cents to the dollar, and Japanese manufacturers panicked. In previous slowdowns, companies would go to almost any extremes to avoid layoffs of full-time employees. Workers might be asked to do unusual jobs—cleaning, for example—while production lines stood quiet.

This time around, corporate planners understood all too well that the entire labor system was in the throes of change. They would have to make ruthless and permanent cuts, including even some of the workers at the apex of Japan's corporate system, the vaunted *sarariman*. Yet, companies were reluctant to admit to downsizing. Instead, they resorted to a variety of tricks to force employees to leave. This gave to a whole new social ill in Japan— corporate *ijime*, or bullying.

Ijime leans heavily on psychological tactics. In the summer of 1992, NJK, a computer software company, sent groups of unwanted employees to a semirural "training camp" in Hokuriku, northeast of Tokyo. The employees were treated to equal doses of hard manual labor and intimidation. "A company representative would tell them, 'We're not going to give you any work to do when you go back—why don't you resign?'" said Otsuka Tatsujo, a labor lawyer who represented some of the former NJK employees. About 400 of them took the suggestion—before a media outcry forced NJK to close the operation down.[6]

Shitara Kiyotsugu, general secretary of the Tokyo Manager's Union, said that Japanese companies "know they need to change, but they can't do it smoothly. They want to keep both the old system of lifetime employment and make some changes. It means that no change comes quickly, and that we still maintain the illusion of lifetime employment."[7] Executives who ignored hints to leave might be subjected to tormenting demotions. One senior researcher was put in charge of the corporate library when he refused to resign. Four years later, at the age of fifty-two, the company tried to fire him again. This time, it took away his office, and ordered the man to write a report every two weeks entitled "My Second Life." Stumped, the man began to write children's stories with animal characters.

Shitara counseled white-collar workers in trouble, advertising his "*ijime* hot line" through newspapers and word of mouth. His union, founded in 1993 with 15 members, had 400 members by 1996. Coached by Shitara, Otsuka, and other activists, disgruntled managers began to fight back—another extraordinary departure in a corporate culture that favored the metaphor of a "big family."

Kikawada Hiroshi, a forty-eight-year-old manager with a telephone maintenance company, was among those who were using bargaining tactics traditionally associated with labor unions in order to keep their jobs. The company claimed just cause in pressuring him to resign—three years earlier, Kikawada had run up high entertainment expenses. Kikawada claimed that the expenses had been authorized. When Kikawada refused to budge, management demoted him from section chief to supervisor, cut his salary by $630 a month, banned him from sales meetings, and set him on the company's lowest rung— answering customer calls for maintenance and repair. Shitara helped Kikawada negotiate a compromise with the company in which he accepted a somewhat smaller pay cut and demotion. It was not a happy ending, but Kikawada was proud that he hadn't given up. He said he stayed in the company "to appeal to them to recognize my existence as a human being, not just an employee."[8]

There was a Tokyo "women's union" too, but not for managers. Until the early 1980s, women graduates were unable to apply for professional jobs. Japan's post-war labor system was based on a ready pool of short-term and part-time female workers to fill clerical posts. When the recession hit in the early 1990s, Japanese employers made such deep cuts in the clerical work force that the Japanese press labeled it the "super ice age" for women. But the real tragedy was that the job freeze arrived just as women were beginning to have modest expectations of equal treatment.

Muto Emiko, thirty-seven, had wanted it all. Like many of her contemporaries, Muto thought that learning English would be a ticket to a better career. After graduating from a two-year junior college, Muto worked for a few years, and then went to the United States for a year of language training. Returning to Japan in 1988, Muto had no inhibitions against job-hopping as a way to move up. After her first position with the Japanese subsidiary of Peugeot, in 1991 Muto went to work in the sales department of a Japanese advertising company. "It was challenging and exciting," Muto recalled. "Of course, the men in the company were old-fashioned in their way of thinking. But compared to major Japanese companies, my small company was relatively liberal."[9]

Then the recession hit. By the mid-1990s, the advertising business was in a free fall, and in April 1994 Muto's ambitions received a rude jolt. The company demanded that she go from permanent to contract status and take a pay cut of 30 percent, amounting to about $11,700 on an annual basis. At the same time, the company introduced an incentive pay scheme in which it promised to distribute half of net profits to employees. The pay cuts and the new bonus were supposed to balance out. "They targeted an impossible figure" for profits, said Muto. "The idea was to establish a base salary plus profit sharing. The reality was that the company was cutting personnel costs."

For a year, Muto struggled to live on $1,350 a month, working as a manager for a friend who taught Chinese martial arts. She also thought of marriage as a way to make ends meet, and paid $2,700 to a marriage broker to come up with a mate, to no avail. Her best move, however, was to call up the Tokyo Women's Union, which put her on television and offered to help her re-negotiate her contract with the company. Two years later, Muto had most of her old salary back, if not the permanent status, and a job in the international marketing department. "They don't say anything directly, but the attitude of the company is that they don't care as much about women as they do about men," Muto said. "They targeted women for restructuring because their idea is that men have to feed their wives and children—but women can do anything because they will still get married in the end."

Ito Midori, executive chairman of the Tokyo Women's Union, said that the recession had taken a disproportionate toll of working women, many of whom began their careers after the Japanese parliament passed the Equal Employment Opportunity Law for Men and Women in 1985. Although the law imposed no penalties and merely urged employers to "endeavor" to provide equal treatment for women, it coincided with the heady early days of the "bubble," when labor demand, especially for graduates of elite universities, ran well ahead of supply. "Women who entered in the professional track in those days, in the same category as men, are now in their early thirties," said Ito. "They are now targets—they are the ones receiving demotions, reductions in income, and suggestions to get married and leave the company. If it was in the United States, you would be fired and that would be it. But in Japan, the methods are darker and more cynical."[10]

If white-collar workers and older Japanese women were being forced out of their jobs, women just entering the workforce had the hardest time of all. In Spring 1996, six years after the stock market and real-estate crash that triggered the recession, new college graduates faced unemployment levels higher than 30 percent—the worst job market since 1950. Among new women graduates, 36.5 percent failed to find jobs, according to a Ministry of Education survey published later that year. For young men, the figure was 32.9 percent. Baba Hiroshi, former head of the career-planning section of Waseda University in Tokyo, recalled that the first sign of active discrimination in college recruiting came in 1992. "Japan is a male society," he said. "There are lots of people who think that when women get married, they should stay at home. They graduate from university when they are twenty-two or twenty-three, work for five or six years, marry at twenty-nine, then leave the company. So the companies think it's a waste to spend money on training women, only to have them leave at the age when men are just starting to work really hard."[11]

Japanese companies formally hire new college graduates in April at the end of the school year. Until 1993, they would usually announce hiring "quotas" by gender. When companies stopped hiring women, the Ministry of Education moved in and banned the use of separate quotas for men and women. But this only made things worse, according to Baba. "Companies may not have any intention of hiring women, but the students don't know that. They interview women without any intention of hiring them."

Ito Aya, twenty-two, and Hamanaka Akiko, twenty-one, were among the nervous seniors who would graduate in April 1997 from Tsuda Women's College, Japan's most prestigious women-only university. They knew it would not be easy. In one job interview, Ito and two young men were asked to come in together. On the company side, there were also two men and one woman. Ito said the recruiters, including the lone woman, concentrated almost entirely on the men. At the end of the interview, they asked if there were questions. "Yes," said Ito. "What are you proudest of, working at this company?" The woman quickly answered, "The fact that there is no sexual discrimination." Hamanaka, who wanted to work at a travel agency, attended a company recruitment session where the president of the company sent the women to another room when he began to talk about assignments outside Tokyo.

"Only men can go to our branch offices or outside Japan," he told the group. "You women will have to stay in Tokyo." Hamanaka decided not to apply.[12]

Twenty-year-old Sugiyama Keiko's business card listed her as a representative of a group called "The Association of Women Students Who Definitely Will Not Cry Themselves to Sleep No Matter How Hard It Is to Find a Job." Its slogan: "I Want To Work, Too!" A junior at Hokkaido Education University, Sugiyama took a year off to work for the group when she began hearing from graduating seniors about their experiences at job interviews. Company recruiters routinely pried into the sex lives of female candidates and made rude personal observations, said Sugiyama. Sexual harassment was considered part of the job, for women. "They do this to let women know that this is the way life will be once they enter the company," she said.[13] When three women got together to form the group in 1993, the only recourse women had against abusive recruiters was to take their complaints to the "women and juveniles" department of the Labor Ministry, which duly recorded them and reprimanded companies.

Unfortunately, the ministry rarely intervened directly. According to Hayashi Masahiko, an official in the Women's Bureau of the Ministry of Labor, between 1985 and 1995 the ministry became directly involved in only twenty-one cases—involving all types of complaints, not just about hiring. In 1995, a year when Hayashi said 90,000 women sought advice on labor situations, the ministry stepped in once. Hayashi argued that Japanese women themselves were in part to blame for their job difficulties.

"The reason why women are in a difficult situation now is not just because companies are cutting back hiring but because women insist on doing clerical work," he said. Japanese women ought to consider manual labor as well, according to Hayashi. The Labor Ministry was encouraging them to sign up for vocational training programs to equip them for a more "diverse" range of occupations. "We want high school and college graduates to think about going out to construction sites—not just sit in an office—to broaden their image of management."[14] Few young Japanese women appeared eager to act on such suggestions, however. For one thing, they would have had to take their place behind a long line of men whom the recession had put out of work. The giant construction projects and feverish factory shifts of the bubble era were long gone. Tokyo residents needed only to glance in alleyways and cubbyholes as they hurried to board their homebound trains to see the human evidence of an economy gone sour.

Tokyo's Shinjuku Station has a geography all its own. Seven train lines and two subways converge on its jumble of ramps, department stores, underground shopping centers, and entry and exit gates. To the east lies Japan's largest retail district and the sleazy nightlife of Kabukicho. To the west is the

"Shinjuku Desert"—a new district of sleek skyscrapers built over a former city reservoir. In the depths below the skyscrapers, in a half-mile-long underground walkway known as "Corridor No. 4," was Japan's first village of the homeless.

The Tokyo Metropolitan government built the walkway to connect Shinjuku Station when it built its new headquarters in the early 1990s, a billion-dollar edifice that looks like a giant transformer toy. Homeless men started sleeping there almost as soon as it was completed in 1991, despite Tokyo's efforts to get them out. Instead of leaving, more and more homeless came. By 1996, 600 to 700 men and women made their home there in cardboard shelters. Activists decorated the more central structures with graffiti. The shelters had an air of solid domesticity. Some had battery-run television sets, futons, and small wardrobes. Calendars hung on the walls. Postmen delivered mail to residents.

Like many other problems brought on by the recession, Japanese society was ill-prepared to cope with the growing numbers of homeless. Homeless people were not supposed to exist. For most of the century, except in times of national disaster, Japan's economy had always grown fast enough to provide jobs somewhere. There was, in fact, no word in Japanese for homeless people. They were called, instead, "workers who sleep outside" *(nojoku rodosha)*. But even this was a new term and concept. For most of the postwar period, the problem had not been too few jobs but too few workers. Young men who drifted in from the countryside were quickly sucked into the labor hierarchy, working as day laborers. Such men were at the bottom of the social ladder. The government used police and labor brokers to nudge them into areas where they could be monitored and remain far from view. They lived in cheap boarding houses and were trucked to construction sites or shipping terminals each morning by labor brokers who would show up in assigned places.

The day laborers' area in the Sanya District of Tokyo is just blocks from the temple grounds of Asakusa, a popular tourist haunt, yet so self-contained that only a determined visitor can find it. Within its borders, men lie slumped on the sidewalk, reeking of cheap *shochu*, a vodka-like liquor made from rice and molasses, traditionally used as a disinfectant. Others warm their hands at open bonfires, or wait their turn at soup kitchens run by ten local Christian and Buddhist missions. Japan's new homeless were a different breed from the Sanya day laborers, however. They were people who had once had jobs and now could not find work. Some had been construction workers. Some had been clerks. Some worked in factories or *pachinko* parlors, or were cooks and waiters. Nationwide, estimates of the homeless population ran as high as 20,000 in the late 1990s, with half to a quarter of that number in Tokyo. And the government had no idea what to do. In January 1996, Tokyo brought in bulldozers to clear out the cardboard village in Corridor No. 4, amid shouts and protest. By March, the village was back.

Sasaki Toshiya, the unofficial historian of Tokyo's dispossessed, arrived in Sanya in 1991 as pastor of the Nihon-Dutsumi Church. In college, he was fascinated by Martin Luther King, Jr., and the civil rights struggle of African-Americans. In 1990, he became a frequent visitor to the southern Philippines, where he worked with tribal minorities. Only then did Sasaki begin to think of leaving his well-to-do parish for Sanya. "I thought I should try to solve the problems of my own country before working on those of the Philippines," he said.[15]

In 1996, Sasaki had already been bringing his soup kitchens to the Shinjuku homeless village for several years. The Shinjuku village had asked to negotiate directly with the metropolitan government for jobs and places to live. But the government refused to talk. "From the government's point of view, the homeless have no rights," Sasaki said. "We want them to take measures to create jobs for these people, or provide welfare for those who can't work. But all they say is, 'We don't have to listen to people just because they are occupying public space.'" Things would get worse, predicted Sasaki. Gangs of junior high school boys were attacking homeless people; several had been killed. "If people don't realize that homelessness is a social problem, caused by the recession, these kinds of attacks will increase. There may be tens of thousands of homeless now. The potential is in the hundreds of thousands. But in Tokyo, the government just says, 'You can't sleep there.' They don't look into the situation or ask why the homeless exist."

Japanese were not affected equally by the collapse of the bubble and the recession that followed. "It depends on whom you look at," said Fujiwara Mariko, a Stanford-trained social anthropologist who directed the Hakuhodo Institute of Life and Living. "Many suffered, but others did not, and some even gained."[16] The recession had its winners—investors who pulled out at the right time, companies that exploited niches in Japan's changing industrial structure. Discount stores had soared in popularity as Japanese consumers became ever more cautious with their money. But for every success story, there were a dozen more of the walking wounded. Just when Japan most needed new ideas and businesses, its bureaucratic and regulatory maze choked them off. Much the same as foreign companies that attempted to introduce new products or services in Japan, Japanese entrepreneurs faced a bewildering array of rules designed to protect obscure vested interests or industries that had long since grown obsolete.

One executive in open revolt against Japan's over-regulated, bureaucracy-dominated economy was Nambu Yasuyuki. One month before graduating from Kansai University in 1976, Nambu had founded a temporary job placement agency. His theme was: "The right person at the right time," a subversive concept in a society that valued job stability in the form of lifetime employment. Business soared during the recession, as Japanese companies cut back on permanent office staff, and by the mid-1990s, Nambu's $1.1 billion Pasona Group was Japan's largest. Nambu did not mince words. "I believe the role of the people should be to change bad laws," he said.[17]

A few days after the Kobe earthquake on January 17, 1995, Nambu visited the city and stayed for ten days. Then he came up with an idea. He would use temporary workers to help clean up the city and run its shattered businesses. By February 3, Nambu had put together a formal proposal to the Ministry of Labor. The answer came on April 6. "They said, 'Absolutely not,'" recalled Nambu, in his sleek office overlooking Tokyo's fashionable Hiroo neighborhood. "They said the government could solve everything. But the government doesn't work weekends. They spend all their time gathering information, while Pasona has people all over and could act instantly. Being what they are, the government doesn't understand real people or their sufferings." Nambu went ahead with his plan despite the Labor Ministry's opposition, organizing job fairs and dispatching recruitment personnel to Kobe as volunteers. "Government officials came to us and said, 'You're not doing this are you? It's against the law.' Imagine saying that to the people of Kobe. These officials are not human beings. As a Japanese citizen, I cannot forgive them."

In Nambu's main line of business, government regulations defined the types of work his temporary workers could do and for how long. Of sixteen permissible work categories, the majority were for office work. Employers were banned from using temporary nurses, maids, waiters, handymen, or salespeople. "There is a mismatch in Japan, with a lot of college graduates who can't get jobs," said Nambu. "The labor market needs restructuring, and we could help to fill that gap. But the reality is that we are allowed to provide only certain types of service workers. Anything more would threaten the ethos of lifetime employment."

Compared to Nakauchi Isao, chairman of the giant Daiei supermarket group, Nambu was a mere stripling in the battle against the bureaucratic society. Nakauchi, born in 1922, took his family grocery store and turned it into a $27.2 billion business, with 7,171 retail outlets, ranging from convenience stores to Walmart-like "Hyper-Marts." He pioneered the concept of high-volume, low-priced retailing in Japan despite a regulatory regime biased against it. Rules protecting Japan's 1.5 million mom-and-pop stores required the consent of neighborhood retailers to open stores over a certain size. Other rules made it difficult to sell imported products that compete with anything grown, manufactured, or packaged domestically.

In 1993, Nakauchi was appointed to a government commission charged with sifting through Japan's 40,000 federal regulations to eliminate rules that were obsolete or served as trade barriers. Three years later, he laughed at the suggestion that deregulation had taken root in Japan. "We only did it under pressure from foreign countries," he said. "The bureaucrats are in charge in this country. Look at this," he added, writing the words "bureaucrats," "industry," and "politicians" on a piece of paper and drawing a triangle between them. "Industry puts pressure on politicians to protect industry. Politicians put pressure on bureaucrats to make regulations. Consumers exist outside the triangle. They have no influence. They are just an entity to consume," Nakauchi said.[18]

Indeed, while the Japanese government introduced deregulation bills in 1994 and 1995, critics said the lists included only easy targets. The Japanese phrase usually translated as "deregulation," *kisei kanwa*, actually means regulatory easing or streamlining, words with far less punch. Moreover, bureaucrats drafted nearly all legislation in Japan's parliamentary system. The prime minister could instruct officials to produce a law, but neither he nor his party determined the contents. Long before a bill hit the Japanese Diet, officials made sure to cut out anything that would limit their powers.

Ironically, Japan's political reform movement served only to strengthen the power of the bureaucracy. When the LDP government collapsed in 1993, the election defeat was seen as a referendum on the bureaucracy as well. LDP rule had created the "iron triangle" of bureaucrats, politicians, and industry, and many Japanese hoped that the end of the LDP's monopoly on power would also break the power of officials. Instead, a succession of coalition governments proved unable either to steer policy in any firm direction or to retain a grip on power. The resulting vacuum made it easy for powerful ministries such as finance to deflect attempts at reform.

Japanese had been used to the high-handed ways of officials for more than a thousand years. Anger and resentment of the bureaucracy rarely came to the surface in a society that placed a premium on harmony. Something seemed to have snapped, however, over the course of the 1990s, as more and more evidence emerged of bureaucratic bungling and even crime. Yet another example surfaced during the murder trial of Aum Shinrikyo cult leader Asahara Shoko in Fall 1996—an elaborate cover-up engineered by the National Police Agency to hide its own involvement in the cult's activities. In March 1995, a thirty-one-year-old policeman who was a member of Aum Shinrikyo shot and wounded the head of the National Police

Agency, Kunimatsu Takaji, in order to disrupt the agency's investigations of cult members. According to court transcripts, officials of the police agency kept the fact hidden for nineteen months in order to save the police force from embarrassment.

But the most riveting saga of bureaucratic mismanagement of the mid-1990s was the housing-loan scandal. The housing-loan mess embodied the central themes of the bubble era and its aftermath—unchecked greed, aloof and irresponsible officials, and astronomic cost to the Japanese public. Sitting at the dining room table in her neat house in Jujo, Iwase Fusako's white cat rubbed against her leg. It was June 18, 1996. Later that day, the Japanese House of Councilors would approve a bill to spend $6.2 billion in public money to pay off a small part of the estimated $57.7 billion in bad loans of the seven housing-loan companies.

For six months, Iwase had been picketing government offices in protest. On June 14, she paid a visit to the Ministry of Finance herself to deliver a petition with 2,500 signatures against the legislation. Four days later, Iwase was still seething. Unlike the U.S. Treasury building, people could enter MOF freely. "I went inside the building and tried to get the attention of a young bureaucrat. I gave him my business card, but he refused to return the favor. Now, wasn't that rude? I told him, 'Young man, you are a civil servant, and I am a taxpayer. I paid for my business card on my own, while my tax money paid for yours. What kind of behavior is that?' Finally, he went back to his office and got his section chief, who was a little more polite. The section chief accepted our petition. But they never did invite us into their office. All this took place in a corridor. That young man was about to brush me off, but I was too angry to let him."

Such arrogance stemmed from feudal days, according to Iwase. Officials then were openly contemptuous of the common people. "The attitude of bureaucrats is, 'On no account let the public come near or know anything,'" Iwase said, citing a Japanese proverb. She added: "MOF is the source of evil. They can do anything. Their powers must be limited somehow."

The *jusen* scandal was a story of industrial policy gone sour. The eight *jusen* companies were set up in the early 1970s to provide individual home mortgages at a time when the big Japanese banks found such business unprofitable. In the mid-1980s, as financial deregulation increased competition in the banking industry, the banks piled into the home mortgage business, squeezing the *jusen*, which typically charged a premium for their services. The *jusen* lenders responded to competition from Japanese commercial banks by moving into new areas of business. In the high-rolling climate of the late 1980s, they poured funds originally intended for homeowners into luxury condos, golf courses, and office projects. Their ties with MOF, meanwhile, remained close. For one thing, the *jusen* companies were considered prime targets for the practice of *amakudari* in which ex-MOF bureaucrats landed cushy jobs after "retirement" from the ministry.

At MOF and other agencies, entering classes of bureaucrats moved up through the ranks until they reached the coveted post of administrative vice-minister. The agency then assigned the also-rans to senior positions in private industry or government-affiliated organizations. At least ten ex-MOF bureaucrats were in the top ranks of the *jusen* companies. This was not in itself offensive. But the *jusen* were not deposit-taking institutions. The funds they lent came from elsewhere. As the *jusen* became more deeply involved in speculative real estate, they attracted funds not only from Japan's big national or "city" banks but also from Japan's 2,400 cash-rich, poorly supervised agricultural cooperatives.

The agricultural coops ultimately lent as much as $50.4 billion to the *jusen*. In early 1990, as the Japanese stock market went into free fall and property prices began slipping, MOF got nervous. It slapped a ceiling on bank lending to real estate developers. Unaccountably, MOF ignored lending by the agricultural coops. Later, MOF officials explained that the coops were under the jurisdiction of the Agriculture Ministry, not MOF. The result was that the agricultural coops poured money into the *jusen* even though real-estate prices were collapsing. By 1993, even the coops were nervous. They put pressure on the Agriculture Ministry to guarantee their debt, which in turn secured a note from MOF, which administers the national budget. MOF, conducting its own review in 1993, found that the *jusen* were in dangerous waters and launched a program to restructure the *jusen* debt, without ever disclosing the scale of the problem to the Japanese public.

The stage was thus set for crisis, when the *jusen* debt finally became uncontrollable in Spring 1995. A MOF study in August found that bad debt levels were as high as 80 percent of total lending. At the same time, suspicions were growing that Japan's larger banks might be imperiled as well, as MOF bit by bit revealed the scope of the total nonperforming loans of Japanese banks. That same month, for the first time a publicly held Japanese bank, Hyogo Bank, failed. The *jusen* problem was sensitive not only because of the scale of lending by the housing loan companies but also because of their connection with the politically powerful farm sector. MOF, under pressure to come up with a solution, decided to shift responsibility for the debacle from the agricultural coops to the banks and general public. The banks grudgingly agreed to write off their $46.8 billion in loans to the *jusen*, but the agricultural coops ended up making only a "contribution" of $4.7 billion. The *jusen* even continued to make interest payments to the coops. According to one estimate, between 1993 and early 1996, the *jusen* paid the coops $6.7 billion. Meanwhile, MOF's plan put little pressure on those who had actually borrowed the money—many of them con artists with underworld connections, who simply refused to pay up on their loans.

They may have had trouble understanding the details, but the Japanese public easily comprehended the general outline of the bailout plan. MOF's mistakes were costing them $6.2 billion—about $50 per taxpayer—while the guilty parties were getting off lightly. Tanigawa, the small businessman who carried out the one man and a Honda protest, deducted $50 from his own income taxes and encouraged others to do likewise. He said, "These *jusen* were terrible companies, with terrible management. When I learned that they were trying to use our tax money to pay off their debts, I was furious. Normally, when a company goes bankrupt, the owner expects to lose his house and his land, his family may break up, and they experience all kinds of troubles. With the *jusen*, on the other hand, even though it was their fault, they have lost nothing themselves and are even turning to the public for money. It's always the honest people who end up taking the rap. The MOF bureaucrats are just like gangsters."

Reinventing Japan

Historical markers lead from the Kunitachi train station, a little more than an hour by train from downtown Tokyo, to the birthplace of Japan's industrial revolution. Hitotsubashi University, the former Imperial University of Economics, was the brain bank for Japan's race to catch up with the West. Its economists had invented the flying-geese theory and kept it aloft for nearly a century. Nakatani Iwao, a successor to Akamatsu as dean of the economics faculty at Hitotsubashi, devoted his days to dreaming up the shape of Japan's economy to come.

In Nakatani's view, Japan's economic problems went much deeper than the 1990s recession. The bubble era postponed an inevitable process of industrial hollowing out that would transform the Japanese economy. Within a few short years, he predicted, the export superpower of the late twentieth century would be obsolete. "We are seeing the contraction of the trade surplus at a very constant and rapid speed," Nakatani said. "If this trend continues, although Japan has been a country with a trade surplus for over thirty years, within a few years it may be running a trade deficit. Japanese export industries are moving out, particularly to China, as it has become more and more difficult for industry to operate competitively within Japan. Electronics and autos—the engines of Japanese economic growth for twenty years—have been hit particularly hard."[19]

"A close relationship between government and business is no longer viable," said Nakatani. "Once people's consciousness is more mature, and the economy is more globalized, you can no longer keep the door closed, revealing nothing to outsiders."

Japan in the late 1990s, facing the twenty-first century, was timorous and indecisive, its economy stagnant, its basic values in question. "In previous recessions, we always had answers," said Kikuchi Tetsuro, a columnist and former London correspondent for the *Mainichi*.[20] "This time, the Japanese system cannot find answers, and that is very serious. Five or six years ago, when I would go out drinking with my friends, the talk was all about their dreams for the future, what they would do to make Japan Number One. We would stay out until 2:00 or 3:00 A.M. Now people just make small talk, or discuss their retirement plans, and we get home before midnight. We know that the high-growth era will never come again. But 2 percent growth is enough. People go home earlier. My wife doesn't talk about buying a bigger house anymore. But we are happy."

At mid-decade, the national mood was captured in a hit movie, "Supermarket Woman," directed by the independent producer Itami Juzo. It told the story of a rivalry between two local supermarkets. The first supermarket slashes prices, sells low quality imported items, and employs lighting tricks to make food look fresher than it is. It is a success. The other, "Honest Supermarket," languishes. The butcher is stealing meat, register clerks are rude, and the owner has taken to drink. Enter the heroine, an old college classmate of the owner, played by the perky actress Miyamoto Nobuko, Itami's real-life wife.

She starts by rebuilding team spirit among the supermarket employees, enjoining them to remember the old Japanese adage that the customer is "king." She goes after the butcher despite his threatening knife. And when there are problems with spoilage, she follows the food chain all the way down to the sweatshops where the store's stuffed dumplings are prepared to upbraid the cooks. In the end, "Honest Supermarket" gets its customers back, and its rival is foiled. It was not just a matter of one supermarket selling better products than the other. "Honest Supermarket" was presented as an idealized version of a traditional Japanese village. The company was a "big family," in which the workers and their bosses were part of a focused, caring community—committed to each other as well as to success in business.

Japan in the 1990s was like a traveler who comes to a crossroads in a dense fog. The way ahead was murky. Each step forward entailed risk. Most Japanese were forced to lower their expectations for the future. Yet people had grown tired of the self-sacrifice that relentless growth required. They were ready to go home and meet their families. Turning inward, they turned away from the bureaucracy and the "iron triangle," with its grand and futile designs.

Conclusion

Was there a Japanese idea, then, that would survive Japan's rise and fall, migrating into a yet unknown matrix? Had this idea changed Asia? Or was it so compromised by Japan's slow decline that, like emperor worship or Maoism, it would survive only in caricature, a collectible in the intellectual flea markets of university departments and editorial pages? Like a Zen *koan*, the Japanese legacy was easier to describe in terms of what it was not than of what it might become.

It was not, for instance, a credible basis for empire. Twice in a century, Japan had taken a run at building an imperial system and overrun much weaker surrounding states, first militarily, later economically. Both attempts failed. Much as Japan's military adventures ended in defeat by a stronger, better organized enemy, so Japan's attempt to restructure the Asian economy in its own image was overwhelmed by the emergence of a highly motivated competitor with infinitely greater resources and a long-established pattern of thinking and behaving as a global power.

At dinner in a Hong Kong apartment crowded with antique stone sculptures, Hirao Koji, a retired Japanese banker, picks delicately at his roast lamb and string beans. Japan's economy is awash in Chinese imports, he says. Soon China will overtake Japan, if only because Japan has proved incapable of making the changes it needs to make. Across the table, the American director of one of Asia's vast, Chinese family conglomerates holds forth. An imposing man whose life and career have traversed New York, London, Tokyo, and Hong Kong, he is vigorous in his opinions, celebrated for his skill in the capital markets. If Japan insists on using yen depreciation to export its way out of its problems at the expense of China, he says, the two could go to war. He reasons that China will let nothing stand in the way of growth and that Beijing will hold Tokyo accountable for the millions of Chinese who would be put out of work in the event of a yen squeeze and a resulting set of disastrous economic figures. How would China feed and employ its citizens? How long would it be before China took advantage of Japan's weakness, as Japan had once trampled on China? How much restraint would Beijing show, given the weight of history and the urgency of its economic mission?

The conversation flows on. Few take seriously the proposal that China and Japan might become enemies again soon. The stakes are too great. The big American does not, himself, believe that this will happen, and although he has offered his thesis in a provocative vein, he is later indignant that I might take him seriously. Yet I and my temporary companions across the table are left wondering what it will mean, as a new wave begins to build.

A few months earlier, China had stunned the Association of Southeast Asian Nations (ASEAN) by offering to establish a free trade agreement with the region. ASEAN had enthusiastically accepted Beijing's offer, which had included a broad timetable. "In a sense, it shows a signal of a fundamental shift of mind of the ASEAN from being nervous and defensive (about China) to being able to say that we will find some ways to cooperate," Simon Tay, the chairman of the Singapore Institute of International Affairs, had said to an audience in Tokyo in November 2001. "So the decision is a strong political signal about the nature of China-ASEAN relations for the future."[1]

'About the time of the dinner party, Prime Minister Koizumi Junichiro embarked on a trip to Southeast Asia. The popular Liberal Democratic Party politician had taken over after the short, unhappy government of Mori Yoshiro, vowing bold actions to reform the Japanese economy, politics, and international relations. Hopes for the visit were high. In early January 2002, Koizumi intimated that he would propose an East Asian community stretching from Japan, Korea, and China in the north to Australia and New Zealand in the south. The trip was widely seen as a chance for Tokyo to make a comeback to Beijing's similar initiative, although it was uncertain how this would be accomplished or if either proposal would advance beyond public relations. In terms of public relations, however, Tokyo did as badly as Beijing had done well. The Japanese provided no details about what they had in mind, nor was ASEAN in a receptive mood, despite more than a decade of Japanese financial support culminating in the huge financial injections of the Asian financial crisis.

Philippine President Gloria Macapagal-Arroyo briskly informed Koizumi that he should get his own economy back in shape before launching any grandiose, new schemes.[2] Japanese newspapers had also expressed doubts about the practicality of a free trade area, which would be bitterly opposed by Japan's politically powerful farm bloc.[3] In the end, Koizumi merely called for establishment of a "comprehensive economic partnership" with ASEAN at a speech in Singapore, after signing a limited free trade pact with the city state that retained tariff exemptions for tuna and other farm products on the

Japanese side. "Japan wants to cooperate not only with Singapore, but with members of ASEAN in as wide-ranging a way as possible," Koizumi told Singaporeans. "Rather than trying to conclude pacts within a deadline, I think it is important to deepen cooperation in that direction."[4]

Its overtures rebuffed, Japan replaced hard outlines with ambiguity. Tokyo had long used ambiguity as a strategic tool in its diplomacy, to enlarge its scope of action and to temporize, but this time around, it seemed little more than a face saving façade. The contrasting Chinese and Japanese offers of regional linkage, as well as ASEAN's responses, summed up the decade. Japan had dithered with globalization and reform while Beijing embraced both. Asians could take Japan's past seriously, as represented by the history of its high-growth era and theories of its economic model, but not its present. By comparison, China was compelling in the here and now. China's exports soared despite a global economic downturn, and its robust economic performance, as well as its clarity and decisiveness, were irresistible. As Simon Pritchard, a columnist for the *South China Morning Post* put it: "The magnet of cheap labor, strong domestic demand and a pro-reform government create a compounding effect of expanding inward investment, supplier networks, and trading channels. Growth creates its own dynamics and Beijing is reaping the benefit in the shape of regional diplomatic muscle."[5]

Around the same time, U.S. policy makers began to notice the gravitational effects an increasingly powerful and assertive Beijing was having on Tokyo and the rest of Asia, bringing them into its orbit. The tributary system of the Middle Kingdom was re-emerging in a new form. In this version, as yet incomplete, Tokyo needed Beijing as much or more than China needed Japanese capital, technology, and markets. Both Beijing and Tokyo seemed to be aiming at some form of pragmatic symbiosis, rather than conflict or dependence. This remarkable turnaround was premised on China's rapid ascent up the value chain from basic manufacturing to high value-added technology and services. In an article published in an online journal in January 2002, Michael H. Armacost, president of the Brookings Institution and former ambassador to Japan, and the scholar Kenneth Pyle wrote:

> A number of forces encourage Beijing and Tokyo to pursue closer collaboration. Their economic interests are complementary. China needs capital; Japan needs markets; both depend on trade and require secure lines of communication to key trading partners—most importantly their suppliers of oil. China still accords top priority to the modernization of its economy, and it needs outside help to accomplish this objective. Japan is a prime source of assistance through its overseas development assistance (ODA), exports of capital equipment, flows of investment funds, technology trans-

fers, technical assistance, and help in educating China's human capital. Japan, struggling with a prolonged bout of economic sluggishness, is counting on exports to China to help rekindle its growth and on imports from China to lower its cost structure. [6]

In Hong Kong, over dinner, the evening's Manchester-born host is in a thoughtful mood. He reminisces about his own experience as finance director for Hong Kong's largest public transport company. In the early 1980s, nobody thought of the Japanese as a source of capital. Hong Kong's *taipans* and tycoons—British and Chinese money—both thought that the Japanese had an odd way of doing business, with their clannish ways and stumbling English. They seemed to stick together. It took a leap of faith for an outsider to go to Tokyo looking for money. Even so, when Hong Kong's Mass Transit Railway asked, Japan gave. The Japanese had been more alert than others to the long-term prospects of infrastructure, our host recalled. They envisioned railways, ports and power lines as building blocks for the Asian economy to come. Japanese capital became a flood, washing over Hong Kong and the region like a tidal wave, now receding.

Three different men, each with long histories in Asian financial markets, each a witness to the brief era of Japan's dominance in Asia, in their separate ways looking beyond it, to an era of Chinese preeminence, restoring an ancient pattern. Behind them, jumbled together on a raised table, headless bodhisattvas preside over the dinner-party chatter, serving as silent and impartial witnesses. Among them is the slender torso of a young woman, her robes a delicate filigree of stone creases. She was crafted about the time that Japanese courtiers were first losing their heads—in enthusiasm, that is— over Chinese verses, Buddhism, and statuary. The moment has more than a hint of déjà vu. "It is unprecedented in our history for another nation to catch up with us," says Hirao. "China will become the workshop of the world, and I hope that Japan can bite its bullets and become closer to it."

Hirao represents two extremes of Japan's encounter with the century just past. In the 1950s, Akamatsu Kaname, the author of the flying geese theory and patriarch of Japanese industrial policy, had been one of his professors at Hitotsubashi University. Hirao spent most of his career as a strategic lender working for one of the classic instruments of directed credit, the Long-Term Credit Bank. He is well couched in the logic and principles of industrial policy. By the end of his career, as managing director of LTCB, he was there to see it fail and be taken over by the Japanese government, as part of the general collapse of Japan's post-war economic model. It was under Hirao's watch, in 1999, when LTCB became the first Japanese bank to be bought by a foreign entity, Ripplewood Holdings, a U.S. private equity group that paid

$1 billion for the assets. These changes were, no doubt, wrenching. Hirao's gentle manner belies the pain.

Our host interrupts the conversation and requests that his guests join him in remembering a dead friend, Nakajima Hiroshi, a colleague of Hirao's at LTCB. Nakajima had been a renowned mountain climber. A photograph pictures him, tanned and smiling, on Everest. We view other photographs of a posthumous expedition to Ma On Shan, Hong Kong's highest peak, green and precipitous, where our host has constructed a stone memorial, carrying the rocks up on his back. Each of us writes a brief epigraph on the overleaf of a commemorative volume in Japanese, of which Hirao is the author. Somehow, the moment seems like the closing of a chapter.

The idea of Japan is not, as it turns out, an economic theory. The concept of flying geese, for all its elaborate hierarchy and talk of "dynamic" comparative advantage, worked best as a motivational tool, rather than as a set of principles for organizing economies or conducting business with net returns or public shareholders in mind. Logically, it always offered the possibility that an energetic competitor might soar beyond Japan as the "lead" goose. Once this happened, Japan abandoned the game.

In May 2001, after a year in which the Nikkei Index had slumped to new lows and the Japanese economy was hopelessly stalled, Japan's Ministry of Economy, Trade and Industry (METI) declared an end to the flying-geese pattern of development. "No paradigm currently exists which is able to replace the market economy system," a METI white paper noted, going on to bemoan the rigidity that had crept over Japan's post-war institutions, undermining its ability to transform itself anew in an era of globalization.

The dry language of the official publication did little to dramatize METI's change of heart, but the numbers spoke loudly. In the 1990s, China had set the pace and changed the rules by demonstrating that a still-developing economy could compete with the giants, right up and down the technology scale, based on a more open economy and through entrepreneurial effort. Deng Xiaoping had said, "To get rich is glorious." Where Japan had made a religion of "self-help" and abjured foreign capital, China had successfully pressured foreign money into the service of national goals.

Using foreign direct investment to drive growth, China quadrupled its exports over the decade. Foreign companies accounted for 46 percent of Chinese exports and 52 percent of imports. Moreover, competition for China's market had done more to drive Asian regional growth than Japan's billions of dollars in manufacturing investments in the region. In the 1990s, China had contributed 40 percent of Asian growth, according to METI's own calculation. Despite all of Japan's planning and stratagems, the decade had gone to China, and the new century, METI said, would foster a "fiercely competitive environment" in contrast to the organically soft collaborative strategies exercised by Japan.[7]

Thus METI, the architect of Japan's postwar miracle, conceded defeat to China, the last of the Asian tigers, whose protean ability to manage change and ride the even bigger tiger of the global economy outshone Japan's in the shaky years after the Cold War ended. Japan, which had gained so much by virtue of the Cold War regime, now became one of its biggest losers. Unable to muster enough will or energy to move on to the next stage, the nation seemed ready to accept a humbler future, in which its nineteenth-century vision of wealth and power might give way to an ambition of mere survival.

If the idea of Japan was neither political nor economic in nature, still less might one suppose it to be cultural. Few Japanese would argue that the world could or would share its tribal and exacting identity. Japan's insularity, the brusque way in which Japanese treated non-Japanese in its midst, the elaborate hierarchies embedded in its language and social system, all argued against the possibility of universal appeal or an ability to accept and integrate outside influences.

That *karaoke* bars became ubiquitous in Asia from the late 1980s and that in Hong Kong supermarkets prominently displayed prepared sushi and that Japanese television game shows were widely emulated were examples of cultural froth, not penetration. Japanese culture attracted Asians much the way it attracted Americans or Europeans. Its extremes of experimentation are juxtaposed with equal extremes of conservatism. It appealed to both the adventurous and the nostalgic spirit among Asians as it did to others. The attraction had little to do with the bedrock society or its conventions. The adventurer and the sentimentalist alike could sample their sushi or play at karaoke without changing the way they thought about the world or conducted their business. The appeal had implications for policy and for global culture, but of a highly specific kind.

To the global middle class of a technologically sophisticated era, Japan represents a certain retro charm, of a country that preserves quaint institutions such as cultivating rice by hand and an emperor who communicates with divine ancestors, while forging the world's second largest modern economy. Conservatives approve of such things as the strict discipline and second-class status of women; liberals cite the preservation of innumerable rituals and crafts. To the leaders and policy makers of poor countries anxious about social change, Japan's message is it is possible to conduct economic growth behind walls that leave social and political institutions intact. Reassuring to one based on a seductive image of tradition, to the other based on an apparent alternative to the risks of rapid social and economic change, Japan's cultural model was to both an illusion of an intermediate world in which ordinary rules did not apply. It was not the idea of participating in Japanese culture that appealed, but rather its eclectic style and underlying inertia, its ability to mix economic dynamism with social conservatism. When the economy began to unravel, however, all that was left was the inertia.

China's allure, on the other hand, as it emerged from its long flirtation with autarky and authoritarian rule, was more direct, operating on the level of politics and economics as well as culture. The habits of empire were deeply ingrained even at China's weakest moments. It knew how to rally support, to use greed as a lever, and to employ weapons of style as well as those of substance in the global market of ideas. The examples were legion.

In February 2002, just before U.S. president George W. Bush was to arrive in Beijing for a visit on the way from Tokyo, China was busy plying its magic in the erstwhile colonial fortress of Hong Kong, whose once-pampered elite was awash in anxiety about the future. Over dinner for 650 in a cavernous ballroom at the Hong Kong Convention and Exhibition Center, Dai Xianglong, governor of the People's Bank of China, held Hong Kong's top business people spellbound, weaving a dream of a Greater China in which Hong Kong was to be Beijing's favored protégée. China, in short, would hover over Hong Kong as protectively as Britain once had.

One of Dai's proposals was to make Hong Kong's Special Autonomous Region a testing ground for convertibility of the Renminbi, a promise that in theory would put Hong Kong on the front lines of Beijing's monetary experiments as it continued to relax restraints on its controlled economy. Three days later, Beijing declared a fifty basis point interest rate cut, a move widely interpreted as another gift to Hong Kong and the regional economy, because it would further stoke Chinese growth. There was more theater than substance to both gestures. China remained largely outside globalization, behind the walls of its closed capital account, semi-closed current account, and state-owned industry. The convertibility proposal, like many such proclamations, was vague in terms of details, and the interest rate cut was unlikely to do much to stimulate the Chinese economy other than provide temporary relief to debt-burdened, inefficient state enterprises.

In terms of symbolism and timing, however, both statements were profound. China was telling Hong Kong and a visiting United States president, we are not Japan. We do something about our problems. We do not allow debt, deflation, or scandals to drag us down. We lead. And we will soon lead Asia.

In Japan the same week, despite President Bush's attempt to stress the U.S.-Japan military alliance, a slip of the tongue when he substituted "devaluation" for "deflation" in the course of urging Japan to solve its economic problems told the real story. Financial markets panicked momentarily. Japanese officials had been talking down the yen for months; the yen had lost about 40 per cent of its value against the U.S. dollar since 1995; and Sakakibara Eisuke, Japan's perennially chatty "Mr. Yen", had said he wished for the yen to go to 150 to the dollar, a decline of almost half relative to its 1995 peak. It looked as though the yen might go into free fall, with both Japan and the United States tipping it over the edge.

Jesper Koll, Merrill Lynch's chief economist in Tokyo, said: "It's very simple and straightforward. The Bank of Japan is going to continue to lower the value of the yen by pumping up liquidity. The Japan that grows because of exports is better than the Japan that loses employment because of restructuring." Japan had long since passed the point where rate cuts or fiscal stimulus would have any impact. Interest rates hovered around zero. Its restructuring efforts were feeble. Andy Xie, Morgan Stanley's chief economist in Hong Kong, noted that while Japan invested 26 percent of gross domestic product every year, the "impact on Gross Domestic Product is virtually nil."

There was little difference between the thinking of the Chinese and Japanese governments, Xie added. Both economies were centrally managed. "The difference between China and Japan is that China can grow while Japan cannot. In Japan, you have Sony and Honda who are capitalists, and the rest of the economy is socialist. The export economy is 15 percent of GDP. In China, 40 per cent is socialist and 60 per cent is capitalist. They are closer to each other than to anybody else." Within ten years the Chinese and Japanese economies would be so closely integrated that they would have to deal with political and security issues in new ways, he thought.

The reasons for Japan's inability to face up to restructuring were multiple and complex, but there was nothing mysterious about China's mastery of the message. Simply put, this message was that China was doing the right thing for the Asian economy and the world and, despite its problems with deflation and export slowdown, was shifting to domestic demand as the basis for growth from exports. Japan was nationalizing banks to solve its problems; in contrast, China was privatizing banks to make them accountable. Beijing had moved swiftly to crush corruption at the Bank of China. Japan's Ministry of Finance remained mired in scandals. Beijing's rate cut represented an implied threat as well as a bargaining chip in its relationship with Washington. If the U.S. failed to force Japan to keep the yen firm, Beijing might devalue the Renminbi, a move that would create incalculable tensions with Tokyo and Washington. Thus Japan's fragility had become a means for Beijing to strengthen the U.S.-China relationship at Japan's expense.

In 1994, the economist Nicholas Lardy argued that China had a more open economy than Japan.[8] What seemed then like a radical concept had become almost conventional wisdom, despite the huge size of the Chinese state sector with its even bigger problems. In fact, Beijing's interest rate cut was similar to the bad economic practices that had plagued Japan over the previous decade. By relieving the debt burden of state enterprises, it risked encouraging them to postpone their own restructuring. Yet, partly because the impact was expected to be modest and even more because the Chinese leadership projected toughness and focus, the rate cut had been an effective piece of stagecraft for the Bush visit and beyond.

A gap between symbolism and substance remained, and China's economy, at $1.1 trillion, was still far smaller than Japan's $4.6 trillion economy, however much one might seem to be tethered to the other. China might run into serious problems if it failed to carry through with restructuring of the state firms. It had no multinationals as yet to rival the Sonys and the Hondas. But for showmanship, one had to look no further than Governor Dai's performance that evening in the convention center. In the question-and-answer session following his speech, a student from Hong Kong University of Science and Technology got up and asked in fluent *putonghua* about the job market in China for Hong Kong finance graduates. "Come on," the governor responded, to applause. "We have jobs. We need you. Our door is open."[9]

About the same time, Earl Kinmonth, a long-time foreign resident in Tokyo observed: "One cannot go even a day without an article in *Nihon Keizai Shimbun* noting this or that corporation has decided to cease production and move everything to China."[10] Books with titles such as *The Day China Passes Japan* had moved onto the bestseller lists, and NHK, the government broadcast network, had aired several specials on Chinese competition, "the basic tone of which has been a mixture of surprise, admiration, and fear."

To see how derelict the Japanese idea had become, yet how persistent, one needed to look no further than the Japan Club in Jakarta. In 1999, its members were still talking the language of ten years earlier, when the structures that permitted the "long view" of industrial policy were still intact. These men had no intention of going home. Some of them were doing well. Much as they might have viewed the aftermath of a typhoon or an earthquake in the home islands of Japan, they had survived by hunkering down and waiting out the storm. Profitability was not the issue. These things happened. In March 2002, Takeuchi Akio, the new managing executive officer for Mizuho Corporate Bank's Asian regional headquarters in Hong Kong, chatted with one of the most successful Japanese joint venture companies in Indonesia.

"It has been increasing production as well as profitability since 1997," he said. "This year, it is expecting a record new production level. But they are still not making any new investment because of the political risk." This was the Japanese approach that had once been so celebrated. Stick it out. Ignore shareholders and rates of return and keep your eye fixed on the horizon.

Mizuho had taken huge write-offs in Indonesia after the Asian financial crisis, yet Takeuchi described Mizuho's approach to debt restructuring as patient and constructive in contrast to the imperious ways of European and North American banks.[11]

Indeed, that spring Mizuho itself seemed to shrug off the lessons of the Asian crisis, METI's self-reckoning, and all the other signs of tailspin to seize anew the promise and prospect of Japan's Asian dream. In an interview a few days before Mizuho, the world's largest bank, formally opened its Asian regional headquarters on April 1, 2002, Takeuchi, declared proudly a "dramatic expansion" of the bank's Asian network and a new focus on China. "Japan has to become more globalized," Takeuchi said. "In the Asian region, Japanese companies, banks, and the economy itself should have more two-way commerce and traffic."[12]

For anyone with a sense of history, Takeuchi's comments were troubling. In the early 1990s, Japanese banks helped ignite the Asian bubble by pumping cheap credit into the region. In 1997 and 1998, their rapid exit exacerbated the credit crunch that sent regional economies to the wall. Yet in 2002, Japan's largest bank was preparing for a new onslaught. "Japanese investment peaked in 1996 and drew back in 1997," admitted Takeuchi. "Even at this stage, it is still waiting." Yet he took issue with the suggestion that Japanese banks had made things worse by their retreat. "I can't understand that kind of feeling," he said. "Asian countries are very important to us and growing more so. Even in Indonesia, we didn't withdraw our lending. Of course we had some write-offs, but we were patient enough to discuss and negotiate with our borrowers."

Nonetheless, between September 30, 2000, and September 30, 2001, Mizuho itself reduced its Asian assets by $2.3 billion[13]to $19.29 billion[14], out of $99.8 billion[15]in overseas lending. On a percentage basis, Mizuho drew down Asian lending by 11 percent. Japanese banks overall reduced Asian lending by 9 percent over the same period. During the financial crisis, Hong Kong had been a particular target for asset sales by Japanese banks, because its borrowers were of higher quality than those elsewhere in the region and thus the assets were easier to get rid of. Once again, in the year ending September 30, 2001, Mizuho's asset reductions hit Hong Kong particularly hard, with Hong Kong providing 43 percent of the overall contraction in Mizuho's Asian loans.

But even if Mizuho's optimism was feigned, the picture was far from simple. Hong Kong and China had become a regenerative center for Mizuho, providing the largest reductions in Mizuho's nonperforming loans, compared to elsewhere in the region in 2000 and 2001. Indeed, from a Japanese perspective Mizuho's buildup in Asia was a natural corollary of the increasingly rapid migration of Japanese industry to China. Mizuho's newly established Asian network of fifteen branch offices, ten representative offices, and six subsidiaries was concentrated in China, where it had five representative offices, branches in Beijing, Dalian, Shenzhen, and Shanghai, and conducted Renminbi business in Shanghai and Shenzhen. Mizuho was getting ready for a watershed shift in the relationship between Asia's two largest economies, and its presence would be one of the largest of any foreign banks in China.

"China is booming," said Takeuchi. "Most new Japanese investment is there. Since coming to Hong Kong, I have visited a lot of the Japanese factories in China. They are very state of the art and cost effective. I was amazed by their size as well as the technology. Factories like these mean that the companies are shifting entire production lines to China."

In the half-year from April to September 2001, Japanese investment in China more than doubled, to $771 million,[16] well below the peak of $4.4 billion[17]in 1995, but clearly rebounding. The week before I met with Takeuchi, for example, camera maker Minolta Co. announced that it would stop making photocopiers, cameras, and other equipment in Japan. It was moving nearly all its information technology-related products to two factories in Guangdong and Hubei Provinces.

The relocation of Japanese companies to China had become so pervasive that it had become a factor in the continuing decline of Japanese real estate prices, which had fallen for eleven straight years.[18] With prices for factory sites one-tenth the cost in Japan, it was not only METI that had given up on the flying geese strategy. Japanese companies as well had abandoned the priorities of the 1980s and 1990s, when they took care to keep jobs in Japan by leaving higher value-added manufacturing in the home islands. After Minolta has completed its move to China in 2006, it will have left in Japan manufacturing equivalent to just five percent of sales.

Such economics were driving Japanese banks to China, as well. "We can no longer survive on the domestic market alone," said Takeuchi, who became Mizuho's chief man in Asia after three decades with Fuji Bank, one of the three merged banks. Mizuho, with $1.4 trillion[19] in assets through September 30, 2001, obtained 30 percent of its international profits from Asian business, compared to 50 percent from the U.S. and 20 percent from Europe. Unlike Mizuho's business in Europe and North America, where a large part of its portfolio was non-Japanese, just over 50 percent of its business in Asia came from Japanese companies. This was down from 80 percent at the beginning of the 1990s, Takeuchi said, yet still "quite different from our portfolio in the U.S. or Europe."

In Tokyo, analysts greeted Mizuho's plans for China with more than a touch of derision. "Japanese banks should be taking care of business at home," said James Fiorillo, senior banking analyst with ING Financial Markets. "Give me a reason why they should be more successful now than in the past. Being the world's largest bank has zero meaning if your return on assets is as bad as Mizuho and the other banks."

The brashness of Japanese banks in the 1980s and 1990s—when they accounted for more than one-third of Asian loans and a healthy 39 percent of foreign banking assets in Hong Kong—had disappeared. But with loans in Japan falling and deposits continuing to grow, Japanese banks were hungry for investment opportunities abroad. Asian customers were not likely to worry about Mizuho's returns as long as loans were forthcoming.

And so the cycle began again, but with a new objective and a new trajectory, this time to link Japan's economy with that of its larger neighbor. The old paradigm had failed, and the seeds of failure lay incontrovertibly in Japan. As Chalmers Johnson observed, Japan's problem in the 1990s was not that crony capitalism prevailed but that the discipline and autonomy of bureaucratic rule had broken down.[20] Without either that discipline or effective political leadership, Japanese multinationals in Asia were subject to the ordinary pressures of the market. The deep pockets and convoy system of the *keiretsu* would no longer suffice. The *keiretsu* depended for survival on lending ultimately directed by the Japanese government, and with that government in disarray, it had no longevity.

So the long enterprise, to harness Asia's energy to a Japanese design, had failed. Failure and extinction are two different things, however. The splinters of an idea can be as influential as the core. There was a Japanese idea that survived the 1990s, seeping into global institutions where its influence was likely to be preserved. The idea, put simply, was that globalization must live with economies that are moving up the scale through non-liberal means. Globalization has to make room for newcomers; convergence is not automatic. The Japanese were unsuccessful in creating a global model based on the closed, highly managed Japanese economy. Yet, Japan's example of rapid growth through industrial policy remained powerful despite Japan's own ills.

China became its foremost student in the art of embracing globalization by degrees. Japan lost its way once it reached its apogee, still encumbered with the legacy of gradualism. In the early years of the new century, China was still far from the point of exhausting the deep well of labor and capital resources firing its incredible growth. From the Hong Kong border north to Dongguan, weekenders with their golf clubs drove through 70 kilometers of factories, in land that had been farms two decades before. The traveler might be amazed, not least at the similarity to the Tokyo-Osaka corridor, its plains and inlets clogged with smokestacks created by the same dream, the same strategies, and with the same pell-mell rush.

Moreover, even if Japan's empire and its economic model did fail, the sheer flamboyant drama of its quest continued to intrigue the historian, the businessman and woman, the economist, the policy maker, the armchair traveler, and perhaps the romantic.

To what extent may nations or individuals simply choose their personalities by picking through the hodgepodge of global culture? At the outset of its drive for modernization, Japan cut its ties with Asia and with China at great cost to any sense of continuity and at the expense of access to fields of knowledge once considered supreme. It adopted an eclectic identity, invented a national cult of emperor worship and promoted the use of Western dress and technology. Even if Japan fell short of adopting the Western soul—its democratic and philosophical foundations—and imposed a hierarchical, tribal screen on every imported institution, it was still an extraordinary transformation.

Japan thus became the first nation to identify globalization with an interruption and overhaul of its cultural traditions and collective psyche. A century later, Japan seemed ready to reinvent itself as an "Asian" nation, this time based on an Asian economic model that, like the "hearts and minds" rhetoric of the United States during the Cold War, linked economic ideology with so-called Asian values at the zenith of Asian prosperity in the mid-1990s. Japan aimed at becoming the first to carve out an alternative to Anglo-American capitalism, with its associated legal and political institutions. In its place, the East Asian model of capitalism offered a strong bureaucratic state focused on national growth, with publics that were docile at least as long as they continued to grow wealthier by the decade, if not by the day.

Both efforts were deeply flawed. Japan proved unable to shift easily from one identity to the other and was left with bitter feelings on the part of Westerners and Asians alike. Japan's self-imposed alienation from Asia left the Japanese imagining that they were a nation apart, neither Western nor Asian. In the 1980s and 1990s, other Asians remembered the values they had demonstrated in World War II, and viewed Japanese attempts to assume an Asian identity as a public relations gimmick imposed by the Japanese Foreign Ministry. It was all too clear that ordinary Japanese felt no compulsion to get closer to ordinary Asians.

Not long ago, at another dinner party in Hong Kong, Edith Kuruneru, a Sri Lankan-Chinese-Peruvian friend, voiced an old complaint: Japanese are considered whites when traveling abroad, unlike Chinese, she said. It was so unfair. The ethnic indeterminateness of the Japanese was a result both of Japan's economic success, and its determined avocation of Western institutions and ideas. Fukuzawa's exhortation to embrace the West had succeeded in making Japanese seem different from other Asians in the eyes of Westerners. But Japanese themselves frequently express unease in being surrounded by Caucasians. A Japanese acquaintance, Fumiko Halloran, once wrote about Hawaii, where she lived with her husband Richard Halloran, a former *New York Times* correspondent, that it was the only U.S. state where she felt comfortable, because it was not dominated by whites or by the tension between African Americans and Caucasian Americans. And yet the same Japanese who felt threatened in white-dominated countries readily discriminated against Chinese, Koreans, Filipinos, Thais, Malaysians, Singaporeans and other Asians resident in Japan. Japan had changed the geographical orientation of its identity without changing the hierarchies of its soul.

In a globalized world, all of us must be more nimble—whether we have somehow found ourselves in culturally intermediate zones, or as economic migrants, or simply imbued with a desire to take advantage of technologies and social constructs that erase political and social boundaries. We must be willing to adopt what seems to work no matter where it comes from. Even so, Japan's experience should give us pause. The cost of treating national and personal identity as malleable can be substantial. Nonetheless, this particular form of eclecticism will remain with us almost by definition, as globalization accelerates in speed and intensity. Japan's lesson is thus two-sided, reflecting both the economic imperative and the psychological risks associated with globalization.

If Japan's radical eclecticism was problematic, what happens when the question is reversed? To what extent can nations or individuals deny convergence? From the mid-1980s to the late 1990s, Japan insisted that economic pluralism was the wave of the future, not globalization along an Anglo-American model. The defense of pluralism, however plausible, was associated with a resistance to structural change in the domestic Japanese economy that was led by fossilized political and vested interests. Was it a matter of the particular model that Japan defended—the fortress economy unable to abandon its protections even after it had caught up with the world leaders—or the indefensibility of pluralism itself?

On a rainy Easter weekend in 2002, almost ten years after I first began to think about the subject of Japan and Asia, I check myself into the Island Shangri-La Hotel in Hong Kong to finish writing. The hotel rooms begin on the fortieth floor, and I look down on soaring kites and a Brueghelian scene of winding streets and densely packed highrises. On one side of the hotel's convex tower is a view of Victoria Harbor, the clamshell-shaped convention center, and green and white ferries busily plying waters dimmed by an overcast sky. On the other side, a verdant swathe begins with the lakes and gardens of Hong Kong Park far below, and rises through Mid-Levels and the Peak. Villas and apartment towers hang from the cliffs like the improbable constructions of some rare insect. On this day, fog rolls down the green pitch, and tiny figures below hoist their umbrellas, greeting the start of the rainy season.

In childhood, I had dreamed of being able to adopt at will constituencies different from those of my own upbringing. I had lost any sense of attachment to a home culture and wanted desperately to become part of Asia, a villager, an Asian nationalist liberating the region from the shackles of Western cultural dominance. I was a lost child who was also a champion of lost tribes. I had tried to reinvent myself along the lines of an imagined model and in so doing found each model dissolving the closer I came. The village disappeared, to be replaced by skyscrapers. My nationalist friends became absorbed in personal agendas. The people of the rainforest, the Tasaday, adapted as quickly as they could to acquire the rudiments of wealth and power as defined by their immediate neighbors, and in doing so became far different from the gentle band of hunter gatherers they had been on the first encounter, with no word for moon or stars.

In their way, the Tasaday moved toward convergence as resolutely as Japan had in the Meiji period, when the Japanese abandoned their writing brushes for fountain pens and samurai swords for field artillery, or as China had done after the economic reforms of 1978 and 1979. I had wanted to become part of Asia; Asians wanted to join the world. The goals were incompatible, and thus I failed but also succeeded in becoming something new, a person in transition to a global culture.

Japan was at its apogee when it was at its most global, as it transformed itself in the late nineteenth and mid-twentieth centuries. Autarky is weakness. Why then, do we continue to long for antidotes to the homogenization of global culture, for diversity rather than convergence? The question may be unanswerable. In an average world, convergence is the order of the day.

Acknowledgments

In writing *How Asia Got Rich*, I went through several manuscripts, three laptop computers, and five countries before the project was done. In 1997, I abandoned a nearly completed manuscript when the Asian financial crisis threw my original thesis into serious doubt. The book became in some senses a personal rite of passage. It is part of my life, its plot twists and ambiguities mirroring changes in my own perspective. I was persistent, but persistency can be a curse. I fought against the hyperbole associated with Japan whenever that country's society, politics, or economic system was raised as a topic. Yet my own starting point was a fascination with the problem of Japan's greatness and its quest for a legacy. Japan was so clearly flawed, and yet, the miracle was real.

Research for the book was exhausting, and required frequent relocations. I moved from Tokyo to Honolulu, from Honolulu back to Tokyo, from Tokyo to Singapore, Singapore to Alabama, Alabama to Washington, D.C., and finally from Washington to Hong Kong. While working on the book, I was also making a living in a variety of ways. As I went, I transited from journalism to think tanks, from think tanks to the corporate world, and finally back to journalism again, as I attempted to preserve the thread of my interest in contemporary Asia while pursuing a research project that accumulated ever more bulk, in terms of files, subject matter, and the people and lives that intersected with my own.

Work on the book started in 1992 when I was Journalist in Residence at the East-West Center in Honolulu. This was the first of six substantial fellowships that supported my project. As I became more deeply engrossed in the material, an Abe Fellowship from the Japan Foundation's Center for Global Partnership made it possible to extend my efforts for another year. After a few more months at the East-West Center as Visiting Fellow in the Program on International Politics and Economics, I moved back to Tokyo in early 1994. There, I maintained affiliations with Keio University, as Visiting Fellow in the Law Faculty, and the Foreign Ministry's Japan Institute of International Affairs.

When funds from the Abe Fellowship ran low, I extended my stay in Japan for another year and a half as Researcher and Visiting Fellow at the Sasakawa

Peace Foundation. Feeling that I had not seen enough of Japan's industrial and diplomatic projects in Southeast Asia, I applied for and won a Pacific Rim Fulbright Fellowship to spend six months in Singapore at the Institute of Southeast Asian Studies. In the fall of 1996, I returned to the United States, moving a few months later to Washington, D.C., where for another year I was Senior Adjunct Fellow at the Economic Strategy Institute. The Hong Kong–based Kearny Foundation provided me with a grant to conduct research on Japanese investment in Southeast Asia, funding a monthlong trip to Hong Kong, Japan, Indonesia, Singapore, and Malaysia in May 1998, during the height of the Indonesian political crisis that followed the collapse of the rupiah in late 1997. For the next three years, I was in the corporate sector, working in strategic and intelligence roles for large U.S. corporations.

In October 2000, for one of these companies, I moved to Hong Kong. Thus, as I was finishing the final chapters of *How Asia Got Rich*, the newspapers I read, my colleagues, and my work, for the most part, were engaged with China to a degree that made Japan seem almost irrelevant. Like the classic *New Yorker* cover, the view of Asia from Hong Kong is one in which China and the United States loom large; Japan is not much more than a misty island in the middle ground. Perhaps this is one direction to which Asia's future points, with China as the rising regional superpower eclipsing Japan's shrinking giant. But to my mind, the obsession with China in Hong Kong was only another indication of how separate the worlds of China and Japan remained, how much they continued to compete for the same stakes within Asia and on the world stage.

One aspect of my rite of passage was a need to be close to the events I chronicled. I conceived the project as essentially an empirical and journalistic task, requiring extensive field observation and hundreds of interviews. If I had been able to finish it in six months or a year, the story might have remained succinct. Instead, it went through dramatic reversals. Japan went from being a paragon of Asian success in the late 1980s to a paradigm for social and economic exhaustion in the mid- to late 1990s. Meanwhile, I accumulated more and more files. By the time I returned to the United States in late 1996, I was carrying with me nearly a ton of them. Like Coleridge's ancient mariner, I was unable to escape the weight. My mother came to the rescue.

Living in a tiny, rural village in West Alabama, Sarah, my mother, entertained me with lively e-mail accounts of local life, wired money when I most needed it, and provided a temporary platform of respite when I returned to the United States, broke, after my Fulbright in Singapore. I like to think of my mother and grandmother, Mae, as having taken a personal interest in the completion of the manuscript.

My mother was marked by her experience in Asia as the wife of a U.S. Foreign Service officer. As an adult, I was marked in my own way. So, this book is in part a memoir as well as a description and analysis of a particular time, place, and context. Asia's muddles as well as its successes were affected by the intense relationship that arose across the Pacific, beginning with Pearl Harbor and continuing into the twenty-first century. Those of us who have lived in Asia feel this instinctively. Many other Americans, with no direct personal experience of the region, may find it difficult to read the history of late-twentieth-century Asia as, in part, a by-product of U.S. policy. The point is not that the United States was able to inflict its vision on Asia unilaterally but that the magnitude of U.S. power led to a concatenation of effects.

Many people provided intellectual support and comfort over the course of the decade that I worked on the book. I would start with Frank Gibney, president of the Pacific Basin Institute, who introduced me to his agent and lobbied M.E. Sharpe to accept the manuscript. A snapshot of Frank in his twenties hangs on the wall of the Foreign Correspondents' Club in Tokyo. He slouches glamorously with some of Asia's most famous correspondents, men and women with serious attitude, breathtaking in their youth and style. Frank landed with U.S. troops in the Battle of Okinawa as a young naval officer, covered the Korean War for *Time* magazine, and spent much of the rest of his life engaged with Japan. He is one of the few foreigners to have received the Japanese emperor's Order of the Chrysanthemum. Now in his eighties, Frank has the vigor and charm of a man who has lived life fully several times over. May he never slow down.

Some of the protagonists of the book were also close friends, and I am not sure that I have written about them with complete objectivity. Among these are Yanagihara Toru and John Page. At different times, in different ways, they took me inside their worlds and helped my endeavors in many practical ways. If it had not been for Yanagihara and Page, I would have had little sense of the ambition and scope of Japan's effort to promote its model of capitalism. In many ways, these men provided the heart of the book, at least in the sections dealing with the history of the Japanese model.

Among the academic experts who took an interest in my work, Chalmers Johnson, president of the Japan Policy Research Institute and one of the most eminent scholars of post-war Japan, was kind enough to publish several excerpts of my earlier material in his institute's influential newsletter. Charles Morrison, president of the East-West Center in Honolulu, offered his guidance and friendship during my year and a half in Hawaii from 1992 to 1994 and for many years thereafter. I am grateful to Ralph Cossa, also of Honolulu, at the Pacific Forum of the Center for Strategic and International Studies, for his insights on Asia-Pacific security matters, exchanged often under delightful circumstances in Honolulu, Tokyo, or Washington, D.C. My friend Steven Rosefielde, an economist at the University of North Carolina, kept up with my book and travels for years by e-mail, providing valuable advice and intellectual stimulation, as well as commenting on various drafts. Meredith Woo-Cumings, Professor of Political Science at Northwestern University, one of the leading thinkers on Asian development, provided ideas and guidance at several key junctures.

In Japan, much of my original education in Japanese political and economic affairs came from Oguchi Toshiko, a former television journalist who taught Japanese to a number of foreign correspondents. Along with her language exercises went gentle, humorous, and wide-ranging lessons on the way Japan worked. Oguchi was unfailingly generous with her insights. Because of unusual circumstances, a premier journalistic mind became available to coach neophytes such as myself. I deeply appreciated the opportunity to learn from such an extraordinary teacher.

My news assistants at the *Globe and Mail* newspaper in Tokyo, Hasegawa Miharu and Uchida Tamaki, helped me gather intelligence from a much wider range of sources than I could have handled on my own, and they added their sharp critical abilities to analyses of the news in ways that considerably expanded my range. Their contributions were essential to maintaining the high quality of the Tokyo Bureau's output and are reflected as well in this book. I would also thank Miharu and Tamaki for their friendship. As I bumbled around Japan in the early days, I must have been an exasperating boss, but both were invariably tolerant and kind.

Iriyama Akira, president of the Sasakawa Peace Foundation, was unfailingly generous during a particularly difficult stretch of my stay in Japan and, among other things, introduced me to Frank Gibney. Iriyama-san thus bears indirectly a shared responsibility for the publication of *How Asia Got Rich*. Although it does not reflect his views in any way, my book project was sustained by his interest, and I remain grateful for his help and that of the Sasakawa Peace Foundation. At Keio, my friends Soeya Yoshihide and Banno Kazuko were the gentlest and most sympathetic of counselors. Ambassador Kikuchi Kiyoaki, who had represented his country at the United Nations, in Canada and Mexico, as well as numerous Asian posts before rising to his present rank, shared his bracing views on Japanese foreign policy and the world. Imanishi Shojiro, Japan's ambassador to the Asia Pacific Economic Cooperation group in 1995, later ambassador to Luxembourg, was similarly generous with his opinions and friendship. Thanks also go to Ron Morse, for his counsel and the T-shirt, urging me to "just do it," a lasting inspiration. I am grateful to my *gaijin* colleagues with whom I organized the Global Benkyokai, a political economy seminar that operated for about a year from my teahouse-style Tokyo residence—John Neuffer of the Mitsui Marine Research Institute, more recently serving on the Japan Desk of the United States Trade Representative Office, and Brad Glosserman of the *Japan Times,* now research director at the Pacific Forum in Honolulu.

In Southeast Asia, Mari Pangestu, executive director of the Center for Strategic and International Studies in Jakarta; Aristides Katoppo, publisher of *Sinar Harapan,* Jakarta's largest daily newspaper; and Arifin Siregar, former Indonesian ambassador to the United States and former central bank govenor, were enormously helpful. So was Chan Heng-Chee, ambassador from Singapore to the United States and executive director of the Institute for Southeast Asian Studies in Singapore, during my tenure there in 1996.

In Washington, D.C., Edward J. Lincoln and Mike Mochizuki of The Brookings Institution, Nathaniel Thayer of the Paul H. Nitze School of Advanced International Studies at the Johns Hopkins University, James Clad of Georgetown University, and Clyde Prestowitz of the Economic Strategy Institute offered useful advice and were helpful in many ways beyond their own published work on Japan and Asia. Bruce Stokes of the Council on Foreign Relations, Steve Clemons of the New America Foundation, and Mindy Kotler of the Japan Information Access Project were interested and supportive. Clyde Prestowitz and Tom Koppel read and commented on early drafts of the manuscript. My friend and Yale classmate, the economist Constance Dunham, provided a close reading of several chapters of the text that helped me to revise key sections. In Hong Kong, in the last stages of the project, Tad Beczak, deputy chairman of the *South China Morning Post,* became my mainstay as friend and gadfly, encouraging me through to the end.

A number of friends and colleagues generously provided places to stay during low-budget research trips to Japan and Southeast Asia. These included Michael Zielenziger, Tokyo Bureau chief for Knight Ridder newspapers, and his wife, Diane Abt; Cameron Barr and Nicole Gaouette of the *Christian Science Monitor*; Clay Jones, also of the *Christian Science Monitor,* and Gladys Montgomery-Jones; Yoka Makkink and the late Otto Smith of Singapore; and Jomo Kwame Sundaram of the University of Malaya in Kuala Lumpur. As foreign editor of the *Monitor,* Clay Jones published a number of my freelance stories, as did Richard Kirkland of *Fortune* magazine. Michael Zielenziger was my lifeline through several difficult years in Washington, D.C., providing e-mail bulletins on East Asia and helping to offset the parochial obsessions of the nation's capital.

Many of those who shaped my development as a journalist have, like me, moved on to other employers and occupations since we worked together. At *Business Week,* Bob Neff and Bill Javetski helped teach me the craft. At the *Globe and Mail,* foreign editor Gene Allen and business editor Peter Cook encouraged me to push the envelope, to understand and convey as much as possible about Japan and Asia in the late 1980s and early 1990s. After 1992, when I was no longer subject to the rigors of daily journalism, I relied heavily on the works of several correspondents, especially the dispatches of David Sanger, international economics correspondent for the *New York Times* in Washington, D.C.; Henny Sender, Hong Kong–based finance editor of the *Far Eastern Economic Review*; and Michael Zielenziger in Tokyo. I also leaned on the work of Awanohara Susumu, one of Asia's most seasoned financial correspondents. For several years, Awanohara edited an emerging markets newsletter for Nikko Research Center (America), Inc., based in Washington, D.C. Until Nikko closed its U.S. operations in Fall 1998, *Nikko Capital Trends* was among the best sources of informed commentary on Asian economies anywhere. Its coverage on the Asian financial crisis was superb.

I would especially thank Doug Merwin, Asian editor at M.E. Sharpe, my publisher, and Patricia Loo, his successor, for their patience while waiting for the delivery of my manuscript. Finally, I would thank Leona Schecter, my agent, for her suggestions on the first three or four versions of the manuscript and kindness during my dreadful first year back in the United States. Leona and her husband, Jerrold Schecter, knew Japan well from their experience with the *Time* magazine bureau in Tokyo in the 1960s. They encouraged the addition of two major themes to the book—the decline of the domestic Japanese economy and Japan's growing rivalry with China. Expanding the book in this way was not easy, but the effort added depth to the project. To the extent that I have added to the already vast literature on these topics, my contribution owes much to Leona's advice and counsel.

Most of these friends have long since given up hope that I would bring the book to completion. Now, I can say to them: I could not have managed the book without your help but in no way do I lay its shortcomings at your feet.

Notes

Notes to Chapter 1

1. Funabashi Yoichi, *Nihon no taigai koso—Reisigo no bijion o kaku* (Japan's idea for the world—An essay on a post–Cold War vision) (Tokyo: Iwanami shoten, 1993).

2. Doug Struck, "Japanese Leader Trips over Tongue," *Washington Post*, May 17, 2000.

3. Michael Zielenziger, "Japan's Premier Lays Out Agenda—Military, Eventual Armed Role Proposed," *Mercury News* (San Jose), April 8, 2000.

4. John Dower, "E.H. Norman, Japan, and the Uses of History," in *Origins of the Modern Japanese States: Selected Writings of E.H. Norman*, ed. John Dower (New York: Pantheon, 1975), p. 77.

5. *Nihon no Hyaku Nen: Shuji de Miru* (One hundred years of Japan as seen in statistics), 3rd. print. (Tokyo: Kokusei sha, 1991), p. 25.

6. Bank of Japan, International Department, *Comparative Economic and Financial Statistics of Japan and Other Major Countries, 1995*, vol. 32 (Tokyo: Bank of Japan, 1995), p. 145.

7. MOF, *Trade Statistics: Value of Exports and Imports [FY] 1998*, at ·www.mof.go.jp/english/trade-st/199838ce.htm, April 28, 1999.

8. Ito Takatoshi, "Asian Currency Crisis: The 'Mai Thai' Hangover," *Nikko Capital Trends* 2, n0. 11 (September 1997) (Washington, D.C.: Nikko Research Center [America], Inc., 1997), p. 10.

9. Japan's cumulative stock of investment through the end of FY 1996 (March 1997) was $100.094 billion; see JETRO, *Sekai to Kaigai Chokusetsu Toshi, 1998 JETRO Hakusho* (Foreign Investment of Japan and the World) (Tokyo: Nihon beokei shinkokai, 1998), p. 527. In FY 1997 and 1998 according to the MOF, Japan invested another Yen 2.3 trillion, the equivalent of $11.5 billion in 1997 and $6.179 billion in 1998; see MOF, International Finance Division, www.mof.go.jp, May 27, 1999. The U.S. stock of direct investment in Asia was $142.704 billion in 1997, the latest year available of which $26.125 billion represented the U.S. amount in Australia and $35.569 billion in Japan; see *Survey of Current Business*, June 1999, Table G.2. Note, throughout book, all references for values of yen to the dollar are in U.S. dollars.

10. Figures on reinvested earnings are from MITI, Enterprise Statistics Division, Research and Statistics Department, Minister's Secretariat, International Business Affairs Division, Industrial Policy Bureau, *Summary of the Twenty-eighth Survey of Overseas Business Activities (Gist) (1998 Survey—Fiscal '97 Results*, May 1999. FDI figures are from the Japanese MOF at www.mof.go.jp.

11. Akio Mikuni, "Why Japan Cannot Deregulate Its Financial System," Working Paper, no. 68, Japan Policy Research Institute (JPRI) (Cardiff, Calif.: JPRI, June 2000).

12. Akio Mikuni, "Japan's Big Bang: Illusion and Reality," no. 39 (October 1997).

13. Pasuk Phongpaichit, *The New Wave of Japanese Investment in ASEAN* (Singapore: Institute of Southeast Asian Studies, 1990), p. 10.

14. "U.S. Multinational Companies: Operations in 1996," *Survey of Current Business*, September 1998.

15. Yen 115.2:$1. Total Japanese multinational sales were Yen 16.7 trillion, with Yen 7.7 trillion from Northeast Asia and Singapore, and the same for the ASEAN Four. China-based Japanese multinationals sold Yen 1.3 trillion in 1996.

16. Yen 116:$1. The yen figure for profits of Japanese multinationals is Yen 594 billion.

17. MITI, *Summary of the Twenty-eighth Survey of Overseas Business Activities.*

18. Ibid.

19. Yen 121.7:$1. Yen 1.4 trillion; Yen 137:$1. Yen 835.7 billion; and the MOF, "Foreign Direct Investment," May 27, 1999, at www.mof.go.jp.

20. Yen 121.4:$1. Yen 498 billion.

21. Ayako Doi, "After Two Down Years, Japanese Investments in Asia Bounce Back," *Japan Digest*, May 21, 1999.

22. Yen 109:$1. Exports of Yen 18.5 trillion and imports of Yen 14.7 trillion.

23. "Japan's Trade with Asia Surges in March," Agence France-Presse (Tokyo), April 24, 2000.

24. Diane Francis, "Playing a Cunning Postwar Game," *Maclean's*, July 4, 1988.

25. Tom Spears, "Japanese Leader Says He Got the Job Done," *Toronto Star*, June 22, 1988.

26. The part of the declaration relating to Asia reads: "Certain newly industrializing economies in the Asia-Pacific region have become increasingly important in world trade. Although these economies differ in many important respects, they are all characterized by dynamic, export-led growth which has allowed them to treble their share of world trade since 1960. Other outward-oriented Asian countries are also beginning to emerge as rapidly growing exporters of manufacturers. With increased economic importance comes greater international responsibilities and a strong mutual interest in improved constructive dialogue and co-operative efforts in the near term between the industrialized countries and the Asian NIEs, as well as the other outward-oriented countries in the region." In "Leaders Pledge to Help the World's Poor," ibid.

27. ASEAN, "Speech of HE President Kim Dae Jung of the Republic of Korea, ASEAN + 3 Summit," at www.aseansec.org/summit/inf3rd.

28. Yang Razali Kassim, "ASEAN Post-Ministerial Conferences: The Quiet Rise of the East Asian Economic Forum," *Business Times* (Singapore) July 29, 1999.

29. "Southeast Asia Welcomes Japan Efforts in G8 Summit Next Year," Agence France-Presse (Singapore) July 28, 1999.

30. NIC, "Japan's Evolving Strategic Calculus," NIC 508–99, Washington, D.C., June 16, 1999.

31. Presentation by Ambassador Hyun Hong-Choo, Korean ambassador to the United States, 1991–93, Center for Strategic and International Studies, Washington, D.C., June 22, 2000.

32. William R. Cline and Kevin J.S. Barnes, "Spreads and Risk in Emerging Markets Lending," Institute of International Finance (IIF) *Research Papers*, no. 97–1 (November 1997), rev. one (Washington, D.C.: IIF, 1997).

33. World Bank, *Managing Capital Flows in East Asia*, principal authors John D. Shilling and Yan Wang (Washington, D.C.: World Bank, 1996), p. 133.

34. IIF, "Capital Flows to Emerging Market Economies: Update" (September 11, 1997) (Washington, D.C.: IIF, 1997).

35. Interview with John D. Shilling, World Bank, Washington, D.C., January 27, 1998.

36. Cline and Barnes, "Spreads and Risks."

37. EPA, *Keizai Keikakucho, Heisei Roku Nenban, Keizai Hakusho* (White paper on the economy, 1994 edition) (Tokyo: EPA, 1994), p. 7.

38. Figures are from Japanese MOF at www.mof.go.jp.

39. "Japan Vows to Aid Asia, but Shows No Cure for Domestic Slump," Agence France-Presse, October 6, 1998.

40. Michael Zielenziger, "Asian Economies Shrug Off Japan," *Mercury News* (San Jose), June 13, 1999.

41. MOFA, *Report of the Mission for Revitalization of Asian Economy: Living in Harmony with Asia in the Twenty-first Century*, November 1999 at www.mofa.go.jp/policy/economy/asia/mission999/report.

42. Zielenziger, "Asian Economies Shrug Off Japan."

43. World Bank, *The East Asian Miracle: Economic Growth and Public Policy* (New York: Oxford University Press, 1993).

44. MOFA, *Report of the Mission for Revitalization of Asian Economy, Part Two, Section Three: Assessment of Japanese Aid Programs.*

45. Interview with Kishore Mabubhani, permanent secretary, MOFA, Singapore, July 7, 1996.

46. Ibid.

47. Edith Terry, "Invisible Japan: A View from Singapore," *NIRA Review*, Autumn 1996.

48. JETRO, *Sekai to Nihon no Kaigai Chokusetsu Toshi, 1998* (Tokyo: JETRO, 1998), p. 17.

49. Fukuzawa Yukichi, *The Autobiography of Fukuzawa Yukichi, with Preface to the Collected Works of Fukuzawa*, trans. Eiichi Kiyooku (Tokyo: Hokuseido Press, 1981).

50. Marius B. Jansen, *China in the Tokugawa World* (Cambridge, Mass.: Harvard University Press, 1992), p. 86.

51. The photograph is in Fukada Yusuke, frontispiece, *Reimei no Seiki: Dai Toa Kaigi to sono shuyakutachi* (Daybreak of the century: The Greater East Asian Conference and its stars) (Tokyo: Bungei shunju, 1991).

52. Ibid., p. 6.

53. Edith Terry, "Prince's Three Bows Fuel Funeral Debate," *Globe and Mail*, February 27, 1989.

54. Bill Tarrant, "Japan Seeks to Broaden Ties with Southeast Asia," Reuters, Kuala Lumpur, Malaysia, January 14, 1997.

55. Yamaguchi Yoshiko and Fujiwara Sakuya, *Ri Koran: Watashi no Hansei* (Ri Ko Ran: Half a lifetime) (Tokyo: Shincho bunka, 1987).

56. The musical *Ri Koran*, by Asari Keita 1991, adapted from the biography, *Rikoran Watashi no Hansei.*

Notes to Chapter 2

1. Yamaguchi Masahito, ed., *Kinyu-Keizai-Waei Sho Jiten* (Japanese-English dictionary of finance and economics) (Tokyo: Taishukan shoten, 1995), p. 39.

2. World Bank, *The East Asian Miracle: Economic Growth and Public Policy* (New York: Oxford University Press, 1993), p. 2.

3. Daniel Yergin and Joseph Stanislaw, *The Commanding Heights: The Battle between Government and the Marketplace That Is Remaking the Modern World* (New York: Simon & Schuster, 1998).

4. The definition follows "traditional" or neoclassical economics as given by Michael P. Todaro, in *Economic Development* (Reading, Mass.: Addison-Wesley, 1997), p. 7.

5. Lady Thatcher's lecture fee was Yen 100 million (at Yen 132.95:$).

6. Edith Terry, "Iron Lady Preaches Ethics to Unprepared," *Globe and Mail*, September 7, 1991.

7. Friedrich List lived from 1789 to 1846. James Fallows writes extensively about List's influence on Japanese economic thinking in Fallows, *Looking at the Sun: The Rise of the New East Asian Economic and Political System* (New York, Pantheon Books, 1994).

8. Tessa Morris-Suzuki, *A History of Japanese Economic Thought* (London: Routledge, 1989), pp. 59–61.

9. Pekka Korhonen, "The Theory of the Flying Geese Pattern of Development and Its Interpretations," *Journal of Peace Research* 31, no. 1 (1991).

10. See W. Edward Deming Institute's home page at www.caes.mit.edu/products.

11. John Dower, *War without Mercy: Race and Power in the Pacific War* (New York: Pantheon, 1986), p. 263.

12. Ibid., p. 274.

13. Ibid., p. 266.

14. W.G. Beasley, *Japanese Imperialism, 1994–1945* (Oxford, U.K.: Clarendon Press, 1987), p. 200.

15. Ibid., pp. 204–5.

16. Ibid., p. 47.

17. Ramon H. Meyers, *The Japanese Economic Development of Manchuria: 1932 to 1945* (New York: Garland Publishing, 1982), p. 4.

18. Ibid, p. 4.

19. Mehmet Sami Denker, "The Ties That Bind: Malayan-Japanese Economic Relations up to the Japanese Occupation," unpublished paper; see also "The Evolution of Japanese Investment in Malaysia," in *Japan and Malaysian Development: In the Shadow of the Rising Sun*, ed. K.S. Jomo (London: Routledge, 1994).

20. Dower, *War without Mercy*, p. 273.

21. Morris-Suzuki, *A History of Japanese Economic Thought*, pp. 150–52.

22. These characterizations are drawn from Korhonen, "The Theory of the Flying Geese Pattern of Development and Its Interpretations," pp. 93–108.

23. Ibid., p. 94.

24. Akamatsu Kaname, "Gakumon Henro" (Learning as pilgrimage), in *Akamatsu Kaname sensei tsuitoo ronshuu* (Festschrift in honor of Dr. Akamatsu Kaname), ed. Monkasei (Tokyo: Sekai keizai kenkyu kyokai, 1975), pp. 9–68.

25. Myers, *The Japanese Economic Development of Manchuria*, p. 4.

26. Ronald A. Morse, "Dr. Okita Saburo," Appendix 1, in *Tightrope: Balancing Economics and Responsibility in Japanese Diplomacy, 1979–1980*, by Okita Saburo (Tokyo: Institute for Domestic and International Policy Studies, 1992).

27. Korhonen, "The Theory of the Flying Geese Pattern," pp. 102–3.

28. Okita Saburo, "Pacific Development and Its Implications for the World Economy," in *Japan in the World Economy of the 1980s* (Tokyo: University of Tokyo Press, 1989), pp. 208–9.

29. Ibid., p. 210.

30. Pasuk Phongpaichit, "Kojima and a 'Japanese' Model of Investment," in *The New Wave of Japanese Investment in ASEAN: Determinants and Prospects* (Singapore: Institute of Southeast Asian Studies, 1990), pp. 9–14

31. Friedemann Bartu, *The Ugly Japanese: Nippon's Economic Empire in Asia* (Singapore: Longman, 1992), p. 49.

32. Dennis T. Yasutomo, *The Manner of Giving: Strategic Aid and Japanese Foreign Policy* (Lexington, Mass.: Lexington Books, 1986), pp. 94–95.

33. Pasuk Phongpaichit, "Kojima and a 'Japanese' Model of Investment," in *The New Wave of Japanese Investment in ASEAN: Determinants and Prospects* (Singapore: Institute of Southeast Asian Studies, 1990), pp. 9–14.

34. Watanabe Toshio, *Asia: Its Growth and Agony* (Honolulu: East-West Center, 1992).

35. Ozawa Terutomo, "The 'Flying Geese' Paradigm of Foreign Direct Investment, Economic Development, and Shifts in Competitiveness," unpublished manuscript, revised April 5, 1995, pp. 1, 34.

36. Ibid., pp. 27, 42.

37. Cited in Richard Child Hill and Kuniko Fujita, "Flying Geese, Swarming Sparrows or Preying Hawks? Perspectives on East Asian Industrialization: Competition and Change," *Journal of Global Economy*, no. 3, 1996.

38. Ibid.

39. E-mail correspondence with Bruce Cumings, December 8, 2001.

40. Kit G. Machado, "Japanese Foreign Direct Investment in East Asia: The Expanding Division of Labor and the Future of Regionalism," in *Foreign Direct Investment in a Changing World: Empirical Studies in National and Regional Development*, ed. Steve Chan (New York: Macmillan/St. Martin's Press, 1995).

41. Quoted in Hill and Fujita, "Flying Geese, Swarming Sparrows." The analysis of the "flying-geese critics," Cumings, Bello, and Amsden, is drawn from their work.

42. Richard F. Doner, "Japanese Foreign Investment and the Creation of a Pacific Asian Region," in *Regionalism and Rivalry: Japan and the United States in Pacific Asia*, ed. J. Frankel and M. Kaplan (Chicago: University of Chicago Press, 1993), p. 173.

43. Leon Hollerman, *Japan's Economic Strategy in Brazil: Challenges for the United States* (Lexington, Mass.: Lexington Books, 1988), p. 8.

44. Korhonen, "The Theory of the Flying Geese Pattern," p. 106.

45. Pekka Korhonen, *Japan and Asia Pacific Integration: Pacific Romances, 1968–1996* (London: Routledge, 1998), p. 3.

46. Edith Terry, "Trade Bloc Taking Shape in Anxious Asian Minds," *Globe and Mail*, February 18, 1989.

47. CRS, Library of Congress (LOC), "An Asian-Pacific Regional Economic Organization: An Exploratory Concept Paper" (Washington, D.C.: U.S. Government Printing Office [GPO], 1979), p. 18 .

48. J.G. Crawford, Saburo Okita et al., *Australia, Japan and Western Pacific Economic Relations: A Report to the Governments of Australia and Japan* (Canberra: Australian Government Publisher, 1976).

49. Esme Marris and Malcolm Overland, *The History of the Pacific Basin Economic Council, 1967 to 1997* (Wellington and Honolulu: Pacific Basin Economic Council, May 1997), pp. 6–7.

50. C. Fred Bergsten, "Preface," in *Pacific Dynamis and the International System*, ed. C. Fred Bergsten and Marcus Noland (Washington, D.C.: IIE, 1993), p. x.

51. CRS, LOC, "An Asian-Pacific Regional Economic Organization."

52. Kiyoshi Kojima, *Trade, Investment, and Economic Integration: Selected Essays of Kiyoshi Kojima* (Tokyo: Bunshindo, 1996), p. 200.

53. James A. Baker, III, "America in Asia: Emerging Architecture for a Pacific Community," *Foreign Affairs*, Winter 1991/92. "To visualize the architecture of U.S. engagement in the region, imagine a fan spread wide, with its base in North America and radiating west across the Pacific. The central support is the U.S.-Japan alliance, the key connection for the security structure and the new Pacific partnership we are seeking. To the north, one spoke represents our alliance with the Republic of Korea. To the south, others extend to our treaty allies—the Association of Southeast Asian . . . countries of the Philippines and Thailand. Further south a spoke extends to Australia—an important, staunch economic, political and security partner. Connecting these spokes is the fabric of shared economic interests now given form by the Asia-Pacific Economic Cooperation . . . process. Within this construct, new political and economic relationships offer additional support for a system of cooperative action by groups of Pacific nations to address both residual problems and emerging challenges."

54. Yoichi Funabashi, *Asia Pacific Fusion: Japan's Role in APEC* (Washington, D.C.: IIE, 1995), p. 59.

55. Ibid., p. 59.

56. Ibid., p. 58.

57. Ibid., p. 60.

58. Ibid., p. 55.

59. MOFA, "Partners for Progress," SPR-182 (paper submitted to the Second Senior Officials Meeting in Sapporo for the Seventh Ministerial Meeting, July 6, 1995).

60. Concluding press conference, APEC ministerial meeting, Osaka, Japan, November 17, 1995.

61. Funabashi, *Asia Pacific Fusion*, pp. 68–69.

62. Interview with Furukawa Eiichi, executive director, Japan Center for International Strategies, February 21, 1994.

63. Interview with Endo Tetsuya, special ambassador to APEC, MOFA, Tokyo, April 13, 1994.

64. "Mahathir Hopes for Creation of East Asian Caucus," Agence France-Presse, Kuala Lumpur, Malaysia, August 21, 1998.

65. Yanagihara Toru, "Outline of the Development of the Asia-Pacific Zone and Its Relations with Latin America, Especially with Mexico" (discussion paper prepared for the Second Plenary Meeting of the Japan-Mexico Commission for the Twenty-first Century, Mexico City, November 1–2, 1992), p. 16, 13; see also id., ed., "Ajia Taiheiyo no Keizai Haten to Chiiki Kyoryoku" (Economic development and regional cooperation in Asia-Pacific) (Tokyo: IDE, 1992).

66. Source for these numbers is the Ministry of Finance, International Finance Bureau, various years, spreadsheets in binders from the MOF library.

67. Based on Table 2 in *Keizai Keikakucho chosakyoku hen, Ajia Keizai, 1999* (Asian economies, 1999, edited by Economic Planning Agency) (Tokyo: Okurasho insatsukyoku, 1999).

68. Ohmae Keniichi, *Ajiajin to Nihonjin* (Asians and Japanese) (Tokyo: Shogakukan, 1994); Mahathir and Ishihara Shintaro, "No to ieru Ajia" (The Asia that can say no) (Tokyo: Kobunsha, 1994).

69. SPF, *Towards a New Asia: A Report of the Commission for a New Asia* (Tokyo: SPF, 1994).

70. Ibid., p. 2.

71. R. Taggart Murphy, *The Weight of the Yen: How Denial Imperils America's Future and Ruins an Alliance* (New York: W.W. Norton, 1996), pp. 167–94.

72. Ibid., p. 231.

73. Interview with C. Kikutani, director, Asia-Oceania Division, Overseas Research Department, JETRO, Tokyo, December 18, 1989.

74. Japan MITI, *APEC Vision for the Economy of the Asia-Pacific Region in the Year 2000 and Tasks Ahead: Ad Hoc Economic Group Meeting, August 10–11, 1992* (Tokyo: MITI, 1992), p. vi.

75. Japan MOFA, *The Group on Asia-Pacific Economic Integration toward Twenty-first Century, Economic Integration in the Asia-Pacific Region and the Options for Japan* (Tokyo: MOFA, April 1993), p. 26.

76. Kozo Yamamura and Walter Hatch, "A Looming Entry Barrier: Japan's Production Networks in Asia," National Bureau of Asian Research (Seattle), *NBR Analysis* 8, no. 1 (February 1997), p. 7; see also p. 6, n. 5, for a review of market-force analyses of Japanese investment in Asia.

77. Quoted in Sam Jameson, "Japan's New Sphere of Power," reprinted from the *Los Angeles Times* in the *Daily Yomiuri*, August 5, 1995.

78. Sakakibara Eisuke, "The End of Progressivism—A Search for New Goals," *Foreign Affairs*, September/October 1995, p. 13.

79. MOF Study Group of the Institute of Fiscal and Monetary Policy, "Socio-Economic Systems of Japan, the United States, the United Kingdom, Germany and France" (Tokyo: MOF, February 1996) (English version based on Japanese original of July 1995).

80. Chalmers Johnson, "Capitalism: East Asian Style" (paper prepared for the World Bank Conference on Governance and East Asian Economic Success, East-West Center, Honolulu, Hawaii, November 19–21, 1991), pp. 22–23. Johnson used the term "developmental state," citing the definition of Manuel Castells: "A state is developmental when it establishes as its principle of legitimacy its ability to promote and sustain development, understanding by development the combination of steady high rates of economic growth and structural change in the productive system, both domestically and in relationship to the international economy."

81. "Japan Offers Development Strategy," *Japan Times*, August 28, 1995.

82. Louis Beckerling, "Asia Needs Home-Grown Defence Fund," *South China Morning Post*, February 15, 2000.

83. MOFA, *ODA Annual Report, 1998* (Tokyo: Association for Promotion of International Cooperation, 1999), p. 158.

84. JICA and the Ministry of Planning and Development, Republic of Vietnam, *Study on Economic Development Policies in the Transition toward a Market-Oriented Economy in Vietnam (Phase I): Opinions on the Draft New Five-Year Plan for Social and Economic Development in Vietnam*, June 1996.

85. Ishizuka Masahiko, "Vietnam Exerts Strong Pull on Japanese," *Nikkei Weekly*, May 24, 1999.

86. Interview with Okazaki Katsuhiko, deputy chief representative, Export-Import Bank of Japan, Washington, D.C., August 6, 1999.

87. "Miyazawa Initiative (1): Doubts Weaken Japanese Leadership," *Nikkei Interactive*, July 21, 1999.

88. MOF, "Japan-Vietnam Joint Press Release: Japan's Financial Support for Vietnam's Economic Reforms," Hanoi, May 16, 1999; provisional trans. at www.mof.go.jp.

89. JICA, *Country Study Committee for Japan's Development Assistance to Viet Nam* (Tokyo: JICA, April 1995), pp. 12, 20.

90. Interview with Ishikawa Shigeru, advisor to JICA, in Tokyo, June 27, 1996.

91. Until 1991, when Japan introduced an ODA Charter, the only formal principle of Japanese foreign aid was the "request principle," when recipient countries formally requested aid for specific projects from Japan. The phrase was intended to contrast with Western aid programs that offered funding only for projects of interest to the donor country. In fact, Japanese trading companies and consultants usually initiated the "request" process, drawing up plans and advising recipient countries on the means of applying for Japanese aid.

92. Ishikawa Shigeru interview.

93. Ibid.

94. Sumiya Fumio, "Vietnam's Red-Tape Maze Snarls Auto Investors," *Nikkei Weekly*, June 15, 1995.

95. Interview with Suzuki Yoshio, counselor, NRI, Tokyo, December 1, 1992.

Notes to Chapter 3

1. Renato Constantino, *The Second Invasion: Japan in the Philippines*, updated ed. (Quezon City, Philippines: Karrel Inc., 1989), p. 39.

2. Edith Terry, "Popular Culture Follows in Wake of Investments," *Globe and Mail*, February 27, 1990.

3. JOI, "Trends in Japanese Foreign Direct Investment," *Highlights of JOI Review*, no. 37 (January 1998) (Tokyo: JOI, 1998), fig. 3–1.

4. MITI, Small and Medium Enterprise Agency, *Heisei Hachin Nenban Chusho kigyo hakusho* (1996 white paper on small and medium enterprises) (Tokyo: MOF Press, 1996), pp. 144–46.

5. Jonathan Friedland, "The Regional Challenge," *Far Eastern Economic Review*, June 9, 1994, p. 40.

6. MITI, *Tsusan Sangyosho hen, Heisei Hachinen Bank Tsusan Hakusho* (1996 white paper) (Tokyo: MITI, 1997), pp. 98, 100.

7. JETRO, *Sekai to Nihon no Boeki: 1998 JETRO Hakusho* (Japan and world trade: 1998 JETRO white paper) (Tokyo: JETRO, 1998), p. 51.

8. Ibid., p. 7.

9. Yen 17.06 trillion, at Yen 117:$; Yen 13.8 trillion, at Yen 117:$; *Japan Digest*, February 5, 2001.

10. JETRO, *JETRO Boeki Hakuzho, 2000 Nenpan* (JETRO trade white paper, 2000 edition) (Tokyo: JETRO, 2000), pp. 69–70.

11. Yen 5.94 trillion, at Yen 117:$.

12. Yen 1.88 trillion, at Yen 117:$.

13. "Japan Placed Big Bets on Asia Last Year," *International Herald Tribune*, May 17, 1995.

14. MITI, *Tsusan Sangyosho hen*, p. 142.

15. Yoichi Funabashi, "The Asianization of Japan," *Foreign Affairs* 72:5 (November/December 1993), p. 84.

16. Yoichi Funabashi, *Nihon no Taigai Koso—Reisengo no Bijiyon o Kaku* (Japan toward the world—A post–Cold War vision) (Tokyo: Iwanami shoten, 1993).

17. Okazaki Hisahiko, "'Ajia Chotaien' e no Shin Senryaku" (A new strategy for an "Asian super-zone"), *This Is Yomiuri*, August 1992.

18. Ogura Kazuo, "Ajia no Fukuken no tame ni," (For the restoration of Asia), *Chuo koron*, no. 7 (July 1993).

19. Kobayashi Yotaro, "Japan on the Road to Re-Asianization," *Foresight*, April 1991 (translation by Fuji-Xerox Publicity Section, fax, July 1, 1992).

20. SPF, "Outlook for a New Asia and Japan's Response—A Report of the Japanese Committee on Outlook for a New Asia to the Commission for a New Asia" and "Towards a New Asia—A Report of the Commission for a New Asia" (Tokyo: Sasakawa Peace Foundation, 1994).

21. Interviews with Matsushita Electric Industrial Co., Selangor, Malaysia, January 1990 and December 1992.

22. Yanagihara Toru, "Outline of the Development of the Asia-Pacific Zone and Its Relations with Latin America, Especially with Mexico" (discussion paper prepared for the Second Plenary Meeting of the Japan-Mexico Commission for the Twenty-first Century, Mexico, November 1–2, 1992), pp. 41–42.

23. MOFA, Economic Cooperation Bureau (ECB), *ODA Annual Report, 1993* (Tokyo: Association for Promotion of International Cooperation [APIC], 1994), p. 43.

24. MOFA, ECB, *ODA Annual Report, 1994* (Tokyo: APIC, 1995), pp. 18, 25.

25. JETRO, *Sekai to Nihon no Kaigai Chokusetsu Toshi: 1995 JETRO Hakusho* (Foreign direct investment in Japan and the world: 1995 JETRO white paper (Tokyo: JETRO, 1995), p. 511.

26. MOFA, ECB, *ODA Annual Report, 1998* (Tokyo: APIC, 1999).

27. Ibid., statistical appendix.

28. Christopher B. Johnstone, "How Much Bang for the Buck? Japan's Commercial Diplomacy in Asia," *Japan Economic Institute Report*, no. 13A, April 4, 1997.

29. Yen 33 trillion.

30. Yen 250 billion; ibid.

31. Chi Hung Kwan, "Asia's New Wave of Foreign Direct Investment," *NRI Quarterly* (Winter 1994).

32. Mitchell Bernard and John Ravenhill, "Beyond Product Cycles and Flying Geese: Regionalization, Hierarchy, and the Industrialization of East Asia," *World Politics* 47 (January 1995), p. 178.

33. Yen 3.15 trillion in 1986 to Yen 12 trillion in 1994; conversions are based on a rate of Yen 106 to the dollar.

34. Yen 400 billion, at 106 yen to the dollar; MITI, International Business Affairs Division, *Summary of the Twenty-fifth Survey*, p. 32.

35. Yen 15 trillion.

36. MITI, *Summary of the Twenty-fifth Survey*, pp. 58–59.

37. Yen 44.4 trillion.

38. Yen 800 billion.

39. Yen 350 billion.

40. Yen 2 trillion.

41. Yen 3.15 trillion.

42. Yen 3.28 trillion.

43. Wendy Dobson, *Japan in East Asia: Trading and Investment Strategies* (Singapore: Institute of Southeast Asian Studies, 1993), p. 10.

44. Pasuk Phongpaichit, *The New Wave of Japanese Investment in ASEAN* (Singapore: Institute of Southeast Asian Studies, 1990), p. 31.

45. Yanagihara Toru, "Outline of the Development of the Asia-Pacific Zone," p. 41.

46. Takeuchi Junko, "Foreign Direct Investment in ASEAN by Small- and

Medium-sized Japanese Companies and Its Effects on Local Supporting Industries," in *RIM: Pacific Business and Industries* 4 (1993), p. 37.

47. Kume Gorota, "Trends and Prospects of Japanese Direct Investment in Asia: Increased Contribution to Economic Development of Asian Countries," *JOI*, no. 1 (May 1992), p. 4.

48. Takeuchi Junko, "Trends and Prospects for Foreign Investment in ASEAN Counties in the 1980s," *Pacific Business and Industries* 1, no. 27 (1995), pp. 37–39.

49. Bank of Tokyo, "Kakudai suru Nihon tai Higashi Ajia Boeki" (Japan's expanding trade with East Asia) *Togin Shuho* (Bank of Tokyo weekly report), August 24, 1995, p. 3.

50. Cited by Ron Bevacqua, economist, Merrill Lynch, Tokyo, in newsletter dated April 13, 1995.

51. Cited in Chi Hung Kwan, "The Emergence of China and Its Implications for the Asian Economies," *Nomura Asian Perspectives* 12, no. 1 (February 1995), p. 19.

52. Australian Department of Foreign Affairs and Trade, *Asia's Global Powers: China-Japan Relations in the Twenty-first Century* (Department of Foreign Affairs and Trade, East Asia Analytical Unit, Parkes, Australia, 1996).

53. Chi Hung Kwan, "The Emergence of China," p. 17.

54. MITI, *Summary of the Twenty-fifth Survey*, p. 43.

55. Phongpaichit, *The New Wave of Japanese Investment in ASEAN*.

56. Takeuchi, "Trends and Prospects," p. 29.

57. JETRO, *White Paper on International Trade, 1995* (Tokyo: JETRO, 1995), p. 35.

58. JETRO, *1996 JETRO Hakusho: Sekai to Nihon no Kaigai Chokusetsu Toushins* (1996 JETRO white paper: Japan and the world's foreign direct investment), p. 19.

59. EPA, *Ajia Keizai, 1995* (The Asian economy, 1995) (Tokyo: EPA, Research Department, July 1995), p. 23.

60. MITI, *Summary of the Twenty-fifth Survey*, p. 26.

61. JETRO, "JETRO to Release Its Annual White Paper on International Trade," press release, Tokyo, July 31, 1995.

62. Interview with Kaku Ryuzaburo, chairman, Canon Co., Tokyo, December 15, 1995.

63. Drew Gibson, "Eyes on Asia," *Canon Chronicle*, July-August 1995, p. 13.

64. Interview with Kawamoto Nobuhiko, chief executive officer, Honda Motor Co., Tokyo, December 7, 1995.

65. Grant Peck, "Big Three U.S. Automakers Finding Themselves Way Behind in Thailand," *Japan Times*, November 6, 1995.

66. World Bank, *Private Capital Flows to Developing Counties: The Road to Financial Integrations* (Washington, D.C.: Oxford University Press, 1997).

67. Meredith Woo-Cumings, "The Asian Development Bank and the Politics of Development in East Asia" (paper presented at the International Conference on U.S.-Japan Relations and International Institutes after the Cold War, International House, Tokyo, April 8–11, 1994).

68. "White Paper Stresses Aid to Asia," *Mainichi Daily News*, June 4, 1994.

69. "Together in the Sun: The Yen Block Survey," *The Economist*, July 15, 1989.

70. Interview with Hayafuji Masahiro, Industrial Policy Bureau, MITI, Tokyo, July 10, 1995, typed manuscript, n.d.

71. Bernard Wysocki, Jr., "Guiding Hand: In Asia, the Japanese Hope to 'Coordinate' What Nations Produce—They Use Investment and Aid to Determine Who Makes

TVs and Who Makes Toys—Nicer Co-Prosperity Sphere," *Asian Wall Street Journal*, August 21, 1990.

72. Doug Tsuruoka, "Look East—and Up," in *Japan and Asia: The Economic Impact on the Region*, ed. Nigel Holloway (Hong Kong: Review, 1991), p. 131.

73. Robert M. Orr, Jr., *The Emergence of Japan's Foreign Aid Power* (New York: Columbia University Press, 1990), pp. 77–78.

74. Danny Unger, "Japan's Capital Exports: Molding East Asia," in *Japan's Emerging Global Role*, ed. Danny Unger and Paul Blackburn (Boulder, Colo.: Lynne Rienner, 1993), pp. 161–62.

75. Quoted in Edward J. Lincoln, *Japan's New Global Role* (Washington, D.C.: Brookings Institution, 1993), p. 124.

76. *Ajia Keizai, 1999* (The Asian economy, 1999), Keizai Kikakucho Chosakyoku hen (edited by Economic Planning Agency Research Department) (Tokyo: Okurasho insatsukyoku, 1999), p. 358–59.

77. Ibid.

78. Dani Rodrik, "Understanding Economic Policy Reform," *Journal of Economic Literature* 34 (March 1996), pp. 10–11.

79. Interview with Hayase Koichi, Japanese advisor, Deloitte Touche Tohmatsu Tax Services, Kuala Lumpur, Malaysia, December 18, 1992.

80. MITI, *Dai Roku Kaigai Jigyo Katsudo Kihon Chosa "kakuho" no pointo* (Highlights of "the sixth basic survey" of overseas business activities of Japanese companies, definite report) (Tokyo: MITI Industrial Policy Bureau, International Enterprise Division, November 1997).

81. MITI, *Dai nijuroku kai, Wagakuni Kigyo no Kaigai Jigyo Katsudo, Heisei hachi nen kaigai jigyo katsudo kihon chosa (dai roku kai)* (Twenty-sixth overseas business activities of our national enterprises, heisei 8 basic survey of overseas business activities, no. 6) (Tokyo: MITI, 1998).

82. Ibid., pp. 59–61.

83. Terry, "Popular Culture Follows in Wake of Investments."

Notes to Chapter 4

1. Edith Terry, "Popular Culture Follows in Wake of Investments," *Globe and Mail*, February 27, 1990.

2. Koh Buck Song, "Karaoke in Asia Helps to Foster a Sense of Community," *Straits Times* (Singapore), May 20, 1996.

3. Interview with Yokoo Kensuke, managing director, Matsushita Television Co. (Malaysia), Shah Alam Industrial Site, Selangor, Malaysia, January 24, 1990.

4. Interview with J. Singam, general manager of legal, corporate, industrial relations, and compensation, Matsushita Industrial Corp., Sungei Way Free Trade Zone, Selangor, Malaysia, January 24, 1990.

5. "Nihonjin Resu de sekai e senpatsu no tsuyomi hito de ikasu" (Without any Japanese around, they bring to life a pioneering hit that puts them in the lead in the world), *Nikkei Business*, April 29, 1996.

6. Interview with Akita Tadashi, regional representative, Matsushita Group in Malaysia, Shah Alam Industrial Site, Selangor, Malaysia, January 24, 1990.

7. Yen 7.6 trillion, at Yen 108.7:$.

8. Yen 260 billion, at Yen 108.7:$.

9. "Matsushita's Business in Asia," international publicity group circular, Matsushita Electric Industrial Co., July 1997.

10. Yen 1.1 trillion, at Yen 140:$.

11. Yen 186 billion, at Yen 130.9:$.

12. Yen 400 billion, at Yen 130.9:$.

13. "Matsushita's Business in China."

14. "Nihonjin Resu de sekai e senpatsu no tsuyomi hito de ikasu."

15. Edith Terry, "Asians Balk at Japanese Corporate Culture," *Christian Science Monitor*, January 26, 1995.

16. Yen 2 trillion, at Yen 94.1:$.

17. Letter correspondence, John Stern, vice-president, Asian Operations, American Electronics Association, Tokyo, Japan, December 15, 1992.

18. Edith Terry, "Electronics Empire Is Shifting Its Focus," *Globe and Mail*, February 28, 1990.

19. Yen 57.2 billion, at Yen 137.9:$.

20. Exchange rates are taken from line "ae" (representing exchange rates at the end of a given period) of the exchange rates section for Japan, in *International Financial Statistics* (Washington, D.C.: IMF, various issues).

21. Ikeda Makoto interview.

22. Interview with Kojima Taijiro, chief representative, Sanwa Bank, Bangkok, Thailand, January 26, 1990.

23. MITI, *Highlights of the Sixth Basic Survey of Overseas Business Activities of Japanese Companies*," fig. 3–1 (Tokyo: Okurasho insatsukyoku, 1997).

24. Tejima Shigeki, "Japanese Foreign Direct Investment in the 1980s and Its Prospect for the 1990s," *EXIM Review* 11, no. 2 (1992), chart 1, p. 30.

25. Michael Borrus, "Left for Dead: Asian Production Networks and the Revival of U.S. Electronics," BRIE, University of California, Berkeley, draft, May 1995.

26. Twu Jaw-yuan, "Overseas Investments of Asian NIEs in ASEAN—Among Taiwan, South Korea, and Japan Relationship with the Pacific Triangular Contexts" (paper prepared for the Waseda International Conference, Tokyo, Japan, June 12, 1991).

27. Tain-Jy Chen, Yi-Ping Chen, and Ying-Hua Ku, "Taiwan's Outward Direct Investment: Has the Domestic Industry Been Hollowed Out?" in *The New Wave of Foreign Direct Investment in Asia*, comp. NRI and the Institute of Southeast Asian Studies (Singapore: Institute of Southeast Asian Studies, 1995), p. 94.

28. Twu Jaw-yuan, "Overseas Investments."

29. Honggue Lee, "Globalization, Foreign Direct Investment, and Competitive Strategies of Korean Electronics Firms," in ibid., p. 71.

30. Teranishi Kiyotaka and Yamasaki Masaya, "Going Offshore: Japan's Electronics Industry in Asia," *NRI Quarterly* (Autumn 1995), p. 38.

31. Ibid., p. 23.

32. *Kigyo keiretsu to gyokai chizu* (Map of *keiretsu* enterprise and industrial groups) (Tokyo: Nihon jitsugyo chuppansha, 1997).

33. Interview with Tamagami Masaaki, director, International Policy Planning, SMEA, MITI, Tokyo, Japan, June 18, 1996.

34. JETRO, "Chusho kigyo no chiiki betsu gyoshu betsu kaigai toushi kenshu" (Instances of investment by small and medium-sized enterprises broken down by region and industrial sector), in *Sekai to Nihon kaigai chokusetsu toushi: 1993 JETRO*

Hakusho (Foreign direct investment of Japan and the world: 1993 JETRO white paper) (Tokyo: JETRO, 1993), p. 74.

35. Interview with Ashikawa Toshikazu, senior specialist, International Affairs, SMEA, MITI, Tokyo, June 18, 1996; SMEA handout (in Japanese).

36. Interview with Tamagami Masaaki, director, International Policy Planning, SMEA, MITI, Tokyo, June 18, 1996.

37. *Chusho Kigyocho* (Small and medium enterprises agency); *Heisei Hachi Nenban—Chusho Kigyo Hakusho* (Small and medium enterprises white paper, 1996) (Tokyo: MOF, 1996).

38. Ibid., p. 207.

39. MITI, SMEA, *Heisei Hachin Nenban Chusho kigyo hakusho* (1996 white paper on SMEs) (Tokyo: MOF Press, 1996), pp. 182–97.

40. Interview with Fukata Kiroshi, managing director, Asahi Group, Kawasaki City, Japan, June 24, 1996.

41. 6.6 billion Malaysian ringgit, at Ringgit 2.58:$.

42. 34.7 billion Malaysian ringgit, at Ringgit 2.54:$.

43. Ismail Md. Salleh, "Foreign Direct Investment and Technology Transfer in the Malaysian Electronics Industry," in *The New Wave of Foreign Direct Investment in Asia*, pp. 136, 142.

44. Ted Holden, Laxmi Nakarmi, and Bruce Einhorn, "How Japan Keeps the Tigers in a Cage," *Business Week*, August 17, 1992.

45. Interview with Yamada Matsuhiko, advisor, Nikko Research Center, Tokyo, Japan, December 3, 1992.

46. E-mail to Dead Fukuzawa Society list, March 17, 1996, reprinted with permission of the author, Dick Greene, professor, School of Policy Studies, Kwansei Gakuin University, Japan.

47. Nakatani Iwao, *Nihon Keizai no Rekishiteki Tenkan* (The historical transformation of the Japanese economy), pp. 88–89.

48. Edith Terry, "Yen-Rich Japanese Start to Snap Up Imports," *Globe and Mail*, October 6, 1988.

49. Borrus, "Left for Dead"; Dieter Ernst, "Mobilizing the Region's Capabilities? The East Asian Production Networks of Japanese Electronics Firms," in *Japanese Investment in Asia: International Production Strategies in a Rapidly Changing World*, ed. Eileen M. Doherty (prepared for The Asia Foundation and BRIE Conference, San Francisco, California, September 26–27, 1994).

50. 3.8 billion baht, at 25.3 Baht:$.

51. Toyo Keizai, *ASEAN Shinshutsu kigyo soran, 1996* (Survey of overseas industrial advances into ASEAN, 1996) (Tokyo: Toyo keizai, 1995).

52. Richard Doner, "Japanese Automotive Networks in Asia," in *Japanese Investment in Asia*, p. 108.

53. "Toyota, Nissan: Tonan a kara gyakuyunyu, shoyosha, hikuikakaku de" (Toyota and Nissan considering reverse imports of low-priced commercial vehicles from Southeast Asia), *Yomiuri shimbun*, December 5, 1994.

54. Sumiya Fumio, "Automakers Sign Korean Steel Pacts," *Nikkei Weekly*, December 12, 1994.

55. Interview with Takebe Keisuke, general manager for Asia, Nissan Motor, Tokyo, Japan, December 16, 1994.

56. "Toyota Announces 1997 Progress Report on Its New Global Business Plan," Public Affairs Division, Toyota Motor Corp., March 25, 1998.

57. Edith Terry, "Japan's Automakers Eye Future Market," *Globe and Mail*, March 1, 1990.

58. Management Research and Consulting Section, "Going Offshore: Asian Strategies of Mid-Sized Japanese Companies," *NRI Quarterly* (Summer 1995).

59. Nissan Motor Co., Asia & Oceania Operations Division, "Forecast of Total Asian Vehicle Demand," undated printout, ca. December 1994.

60. Interview with Hasegawa Koji, general manager, Asia Division, Toyota Motor Corp., Tokyo, January 11, 1990.

61. Nagata Osamu, "The Automotive Industry and Toyota's Operations within Southeast Asia," in *Can Asia Recover Its Vitality?: Globalization and the Roles of Japanese and U.S. Corporations*, ed. IDE and JETRO (Tokyo: IDE, 1998).

62. Interview with Okabe Akira, executive coordinator, UMW Toyota Motor Sdn. Bhd., Federal Highway, Petaling Jaya, Malaysia, December 10, 1992.

63. Kuniko Fujita and Richard Child Hill, "Auto Industrialization in Southeast Asia: National Strategies and Local Development," *ASEAN Economic Bulletin* 13, no. 3 (March 1997); Doner, "Japanese Automotive Production Networks in Asia."

64. "Indonesia's Automotive Industry on the Brink of Collapse," *Indonesian Commercial Newsletter*, June 15, 1998.

65. Gregory W. Noble, "Trojan Horse or Boomerang? Two-Tiered Investment in the Asian Auto Complex," Working Paper 90, BRIE, University of California, Berkeley, November 1996.

66. Interview with Daniel Chang, manager, Sales Department of Toyota Vehicle Division, Hotai Motor Co., Taipei, Taiwan, January 12, 1990.

67. Yen 2 billion yen, at Yen 144.64:$.

68. Interview with Su Yuanhuei, chairman, Kuozui Motor; vice-chairman, Hotai Motor; and Hiroshi Kano, manager, Business Operations Department, Kuozui Motors, Taipei, January 12, 1990.

69. Gregory W. Noble, "Trojan Horse," p. 20.

70. Oon Yeoh, "Proton Hoping for Car to Call Its Own," *Nikkei Weekly*, October 27, 1997.

71. Numbers attributed to the ASEAN Automotive Federation, in "Japanese Carmakers Eager to Expand ASEAN Biz," *Jiji Press*, January 17, 1997.

72. "Asia Industry: Crisis Erases Six Years of Auto Growth," EIU Views Wire, *Economist Intelligence Unit (EIU)*, February 20, 1998.

73. M$ 4 billion, at M$ 2.815:$.

74. Oon Yeoh, "Proton Hoping for Car to Call Its Own."

75. Richard F. Doner, *Driving a Bargain: Automobile Industrialization and Japanese Firms in Southeast Asia* (Berkeley: University of California Press, 1991), pp. 96–125.

76. Interview with Kisai Bin Rahmat, deputy managing director, Manufacturing, Proton, HICOM Industrial Estate, Shah Alam, Selangor, Malaysia, December 18, 1992.

77. Kit G. Machado, "ASEAN State Industrial Policies and Japanese Regional Production Strategies: The Case of Malaysia's Motor Vehicle Industry," in *The Evolving Pacific Basin in the Global Political Economy*, ed. Cal Clark and Steve Chan (Boulder, Co.: Lynne Rienner, 1992), pp. 181–82.

78. Interview with Paul Low Seng Kuan, president, Malaysian Automotive Component Parts Manufacturers, Kuala Lumpur, Malaysia, December 21, 1992.

79. Doner, *Driving a Bargain*, p. 113.

80. Yen 33 billion, at Yen 189:$.

81. Doner, *Driving a Bargain*, p. 121.

82. M$ 21,000, at M$ 2.48:$ (1985).

83. M$ 4,500, at M$ 2.58:$ (1986).

84. S. Jayasankaran, "Made-in-Malaysia: The Proton Project," in *Industrializing Malaysia: Policy, Performance, Prospects*, ed. K.S. Jomo (London: Routledge, 1993).

85. M$ 42.5 million, at M$ 2.48:$ (1985).

86. M$ 280.9 million, at M$ 2.32:$ (1983).

87. M$ 487.9 million, at M$ 2.48:$ (1985).

88. Machado, "ASEAN State Industrial Policies," p. 182.

89. "Mitsubishi Corp. and Mitsubishi Motors Corp., the Two Japanese Companies That Have a 30 Percent Share in Perusahaan Otomobil Nasional, Agreed to Help the Malaysian Car Maker with Its Marketing, Plant, and Debt Problems." *Business Times* (Malaysia), April 8, 1987.

90. Yen 12 billion, at Yen 144.6:$.

91. "Car Sales Constant; Proton Project News," *Country Report, Economist Publications*, no. 3, August 20, 1987.

92. Ibid., pp. 182–85; Goldstein, "Saga of Recovery," *FEER*, August 3, 1989.

93. Shiode Hirokazu, *Japanese Investment in Southeast Asia: Three Malaysian Case Studies* (Kowloon: Center for the Progress of Peoples, 1989), p. 31.

94. Jayasankaran, "Made-in-Malaysia."

95. Jonathan Miller, "Road Warrior: Malaysia's Proton Is a Surprise Hit with U.K. Buyers," *Asia, Inc.*, December 1992.

95. Doner, *Driving a Bargain*, p. 115.

97. M$ 7 million, at M$ 2.48:$ (1985).

98. Machado, "ASEAN State Industrial Policies," p. 189.

99. Low Seng Kuan interview.

100. Kisai Bin Rahmat interview.

101. PHN Industry Sdn. Bhd., company profile (1992).

102. NOI Co., Ltd., handout (1992).

103. M$ 1,500, at M$ 2.55:$ (1992).

104. Interview with Khoriri H.J. Abu Sabri, corporate affairs manager, PHN Industry Sdn. Bhd., Shah Alam, Selangor, Malaysia, December 9, 1992.

105. Ibid.

106. Interview with Dato' Mohd. Nadzmi B. Mohd. Salleh, deputy managing director, Corporate Services, Proton, HICOM Industrial Estate, Shah Alam, Selangor, Malaysia, December 17, 1992.

107. M$ 400 million, at M$ 2.55:$ (1992).

108. Interview with Kawashima Yoshifumi, executive director, Corporate Planning Division, Proton, HICOM Industrial Estate, Shah Alam, Selangor, Malaysia, December 18, 1992.

109. Interview with Muhammad Aris Anuar, senior deputy manager, Body Assembly Section, Production Department I, Proton, HICOM Industrial Estate, Shah Alam, Selangor, Malaysia, December 18, 1992.

110. David Fernandez and James Riedel, "U.S. Companies' Business Operations in Asia: Automobiles and Automotive Parts Industry," in *Can Asia Recover Its Vitality?*

111. Ted Bardacke, "GM to Open Asian Base in Thailand," *Financial Times*, May 30, 1996.

112. Ibid.

113. Hill and Fujita, "Indonesia's Automotive Industry."

114. Fernandez and Riedel, "U.S. Companies' Business Operations in Asia."

115. Yen 5 million, at Yen 137.96:$ (1989).

116. T.L. Khoo, "Perodua Optimistic of Sales Picking up Later This Year," *New Straits Times* (Malaysia), January 21, 1998.

117. Interview with Steven C.M. Wong, strategist, Zalik Securities, Kuala Lumpur, Malaysia, December 18, 1992.

118. Interview with Takabe Keisuke, general manager, Asia, Nissan Motor Co., Tokyo, December 16, 1994.

119. Peter Ungphakorn, "Japanese Eye Thailand Investments," *Tokyo Business Today*, April 1988.

120. Carl Goldstein, "Steering Committee: Japanese Carmakers Forge ASEAN Component Links," *FEER*, February 15, 1990.

121. "Subject: Thai Automotive Industry," American embassy, Bangkok, August 27, 1994.

122. "Toyota tai Honda, hake arasou" (Toyota and Honda battle for supremacy), *Nikkei Business*, June 17, 1996.

123. "Japanese Auto Parts Makers Expanding into Asia," Kyodo News, August 19, 1996.

124. "Tomaranu kudoka" (Hollowing out isn't stopping), *Nikkei sangyo shimbun*, August 10, 1995.

125. Management Research and Consulting Section, "Going Offshore: Asian Strategies of Mid-Sized Japanese Companies," *NRI Quarterly* (Summer 1990), pp. 49–51.

126. Ibid.

127. "The Motor Vehicles and Automotive Component Parts Market in Thailand" (prepared by the Brooker Group Ltd., American embassy, Bangkok, Thailand, September 1994).

128. Interview with Hasegawa Koji, general manager, Asia Division, Toyota Motor Corp., Tokyo, January 11, 1990.

129. Yen 6.5 billion, at Yen 111.2:$.

130. Yen 9 billion, at Yen 107.6:$; "Toyota Moves Ahead with Complementary Auto Parts Scheme for ASEAN Region," in *News from Toyota*, International Public Affairs, Toyota Motor Corp., May 29, 1990.

131. Nagata Osamu, "The Automotive Industry and Toyota's Operations within Southeast Asia," in *Can Asia Recover Its Vitality?*

132. Interview with Takemoto Motonobu, general manager, Asia Division, Toyota Motor Corp., May 15, 1998.

133. Yen 2 billion, at Yen 126.65:$; "Nissan Develops a New Model for Southeast Asia and Plans to Establish a Full-Scale System of Mutual Parts Complementation in the Region," *Nissan News*, Corporate Communications Department, Nissan Motor Co., December 22, 1992.

134. Goldstein, "Steering Committee."

135. "The Motor Vehicles and Automotive Component Parts Market in Thailand."

136. "Toyota tai Honda, hake arasou."

137. Interview with Takeuchi Tohei, director, deputy corporate general manager, Office of International Business, Mitsubishi Motors Corp., Tokyo, October 16, 1992.

138. Achara Ashayagachat, "Auto Parts Agreement," *Bangkok Post*, October 8, 1997.

139. "Toyota Bid for Preferential Tariffs Gains Government Approval," *Businessworld* (Philippines), May 19, 1998.

140. Interview with Sugimoto Kenji, advisor, PT Imora Honda Inc., Jakarta, Indonesia, January 29, 1990.

141. Interview with Kyoda Toyoho, director, corporate general manager, Office of International Business C, Mitsubishi Motors Corp., Tokyo, May 18, 1998.

142. Interview with Rudyanto Hardjanto, president director, Toyota-Astra Motor, Jakarta, Indonesia, January 30, 1990.

143. Interview with Hasegawa Koji, general manager, Asia Division, Toyota Motor Corp., Tokyo, December 22, 1994.

144. "Toyota tai Honda, hake arasou."

145. "Subject: Thai Automotive Industry," American embassy, Bangkok, Thailand.

146. Matthew Fletcher, "Here Comes the Asian Car; It Is Cheap and Designed for the Region, but Will People Buy?" *Asiaweek*, February 7, 1997.

147. "Mitsubishi Motors Introduces Strategic New Concept Multi-purpose Model in Asia-ASEAN Markets," *News from Mitsubishi Motors*, May 23, 1997.

148. Kyoda Toyoho interview.

149. Oishi Nobuyuki, "MITI Aims to Boost Parts Industry in Asia," *Nikkei Weekly*, July 25, 1994.

150. Oishi Nobuyuki, "High-Tech Requests Big in Small-Growth Budget," ibid., August 29, 1994.

151. "Japanese Carmakers Eager to Expand ASEAN Biz," *Jiji Press*, January 17, 1997.

152. "ASEAN Auto Industry Meeting Opens in Bangkok," *Jiji Press*, March 5, 1997.

153. Harish Mehta, "Thai Workers' Bid to Torch Plant Raises Spectre of More Violence," *Business Times* (Singapore), January 22, 1998.

154. Edith Terry, "Stores Set to Catch Tidal Wave of Wealth," *Globe and Mail*, March 2, 1990.

155. Yen 146 billion, at Yen 102.83:$; Yen 180 billion, at Yen 102.83:$; and Shimoharaguchi Toru, "Japan's Retail Giants Rattle Local Rivals," *Nikkei Weekly*, February 3, 1997.

156. Yamamoto Yuri, "Yaohan's Storied Expansion Now Clouded," *Nikkei Weekly*, December 23, 1996.

157. Osono Tomokazu, *Ajia o Yomu Chizu* (An Asian Reader with map) (Tokyo: Kodansha, 1993), p. 71.

158. "Ryutsu gyokai, Ajia de gekisen," *Nihon keizai shimbun*, November 19, 1992.

159. Ishibashi Asako, "Territory Keeps Booming as Financial Hub, but High Costs Diminish Role as Factory Site," *Nikkei Weekly*, May 19, 1997.

160. Amy Tong, "Japanese Retailers in Hong Kong Defy Slump; Some Companies Adapting, Expanding Despite Tough Conditions in Territory," ibid., February 16, 1998.

161. Ibid.

162. HK$ 85 million, at HK$ 7.8:$.

163. "Pearl Report: The Yaohan Dream," TVB Pearl, Hong Kong, videotape, broadcast on September 3, 1990, 8:00 to 8:30 P.M.

164. Pete Engardio in Hong Kong and Peter Finch in Edgewater, New Jersey, "Kazuo Wada's Answered Prayers," *Business Week*, August 26, 1991.

165. Ibid.

166. Yen 500 billion, at Yen 108.8:$.

167. Yen 200 billion at Yen 108.8:$; Yamamoto Yuri, "Yaohan's Storied Expansion Now Clouded: Company Denies Cash Crunch but Plans Broad Cutbacks," *Nikkei Weekly*, December 23, 1996.

168. Yen 161.3 billion, at Yen 129.95:$; Yen 40 billion, at Yen 129.95:$.

169. Yen 161.9 billion, at Yen 129.95:$.

170. "Yaohan Japan Goes Under with Largest Debt for Retailer," Tokyo, Kyodo News Service, September 18, 1997.

171. "Yaohan Shuts Department Stores," *Financial Times*, November 24, 1997.

172. HK$ 71 million, at HK$ 7.75:$.

173. "Jusco to Help Ailing Retailer," *Financial Times*, October 7, 1997.

174. "Yaohan in Shanghai Sale," ibid., June 3, 1999.

175. Akita Hiroyuki, "China Takes First Step to 'Great Mall': Beijing Selects Foreign Partners for Retail Ventures," *Nikkei Weekly*, October 10, 1994.

176. "Yaohan Transfers Headquarters from HK to Shanghai," Kyodo News Service (Shanghai), July 1, 1996.

177. "Ambition the Undoing of Yaohan Visionary," *Financial Times*, September 20, 1997.

178. Interview with Wada Kazuo, chairman, Yaohan International, Hong Kong, May 22, 1991.

179. Wada Kazuo, *Yaohan's Global Strategy: The Twenty-first Century in the Era of Asia* (Hong Kong: Capital Communications Corp., 1992), p. 49.

180. This thesis is explored by Ron Bevacqua, in "Whither the Japanese Model? The Asian Economic Crisis and the Continuation of Cold War Politics in the Pacific Rim," *Review of International Political Economy* 5, no. 3 (Autumn 1998), pp. 410–23.

181. Yen 40 trillion to 50 trillion, at Yen 98:$; Edith Terry, "'Bubble Economy' Froth Still Troubling Japanese Banks," *Christian Science Monitor*, September 1, 1995.

182. David E. Sanger, "Bad Debt Held by Japan's Banks Now Estimated Near $1 Trillion," *New York Times*, July 30, 1998.

183. Ulrike Schaede, "MOF, Money, and the Japanese Banking Crisis of 1995," *Mitteilungen des Instituts fur Asienkunde Hamburg*, no. 286 (1998), pp. 95–128.

184. Bevacqua, "Whither the Japanese Model?"

185. Yen 16 trillion, at Yen 113.9:$.

186. "Japanese Banks Are Taking Another Hit on Their Loans to Asia," *Japan Digest*, March 1, 1999.

187. Henny Sender in Tokyo and Hong Kong, "Out of Asia: Japanese Banks and Companies Head Home," *FEER*, April 16, 1998.

188. Peter Nielson, "Banks Ignored Asia Crisis Warnings in Early 97—BIS," Reuters (Zurich), January 4, 1998.

189. BIS, *The Maturity, Sectoral, and Nationality Distribution of International Bank Lending, First Half 1997* (Basle, Switzerland: BIS, Monetary and Economic Department, January 1998) at www.bis.org.

190. Yen 21 trillion, at Yen 125.20:$.

191. Ito Hiro and Andrew Z. Szamosszegi, *A Cure for Japan's Sick Banks* (Washington, D.C.: Economic Strategy Institute, June 1998).

192. Edith Terry, "Japan Bowing Out As Creditor," *Globe and Mail*, October 8, 1990.

193. Jonathan Friedland in Tokyo and Henny Sender in Hong Kong, "Faulty Finance: Japan's Big Manufacturers May Play a Significant Role in Asia, but the Country's Banks and Brokers Are Having a Hard Time Competing with American Firms," *FEER*, June 9, 1994.

194. Maeyama Atsuki, "Banks Play Catch-up with Global Rivals in Asia," *Nikkei Weekly*, August 8, 1994.

195. Friedland and Sender, "Faulty Finance."

196. BIS, "BIS Consolidated International Banking Statistics for End-1998," press release, May 31, 1999; idem., *The Maturity, Sectoral and Nationality Distribution of International Bank Lending: First Half 1996*, ibid., January 1997.

197. "Seibi Susumu Boeki—Toushi Kankyo" (Setting up the environment for trade and investment), *Nihon kogyo shimbun,* February 14, 1994.

198. Interview with Kamezaki Hidetoshi, general manager, Regional Coordination Department II, Mitsubishi Corp., September 21, 1994; "Mitsubishi Grupu Ote," (The head of Mitsubishi group), *Zaikai,* November 8, 1994.

199. Yen 3.3 trillion, at Yen 135.25:$.

200. Yen 120 billion, at Yen 130.9:$.

201. "New Kanematsu Head Has His Own Restructuring Plan," *Nikkei Interactive,* July 15, 1999.

202. Toyo Keizai, *Kigyo keiretsu soran,* 1996 (Survey of industrial keiretsu, 1996) (Tokyo: Toyo keizai shukan, 1995), p. 36.

203. Kiyoshi Kojima and Terutomo Ozawa, *Japan's General Trading Companies: Merchants of Economic Development* (Paris: OECD, Development Center Studies, 1984), p. 45.

204. Henny Sender, "Hidden Exposure: Japan's Trading Companies Have Vast Indonesia Risk," *Asian Wall Street Journal,* May 27, 1998.

205. Ibid.

206. Kojima and Ozawa, *Japan's General Trading Companies,* pp. 18–21.

207. Ibid., p. 83.

208. Ibid., p. 49.

Notes to Chapter 5

1. Toyo Keizai, *Kaigai shinshutsu kigyo soran, 1998* (Survey of overseas Japanese affiliates, 1998) (Tokyo: Toyo keizai shinposha, 1998).

2. JETRO, *ASEAN in Figures* (Tokyo: JETRO, 1998).

3. MITI, *Highlights of the Twenty-seventh Survey, May 1998* (English version); figures are based on the Japanese FY ending March 31, 1997.

4. Interview with Yanagawa Masakazu, regional representative, Matsushita Group in Malaysia, Shah Alam Industrial Site, Selangor, Malaysia, May 26, 1998.

5. "Ajia Kei'ei Shin Senryaku: Tantoyaku ni Kiku—Matsushita Denki Torishimariyaku" (New strategies for Asian management: Executive interviews—chairman of Matsushita Electric Industrial Co.) (*Nihon keizai shimbun,* February 10, 1998).

6. Interview with Kawakyu Koichi, managing director, Sony International (Singapore) Ltd., Singapore, May 25, 1998.

7. Interview with Mitarai Fujio, president and CEO, Canon Inc., Tokyo, May 18, 1998.

8. MITI, *Highlights of the Twenty-seventh Survey, May 1998.*

9. Simon Kuper, "Japan to End Support of Yen," *Financial Times,* July 31, 1998.

10. FDI in FY 1997, MOF, Japan, May 28, 1998, at www.mof.go.jp.

11. Author's calculation, based on 1996 average exchange rate of 108.7 yen: U.S.$ and 1997 average of 120.96 yen:U.S.$. 366-day averages from historical currency-exchange-rate service at www.oanda.com.

12. MITI, *Dai Roku Kaigai Jigyo Katsudo Kihon Chosa "kakuho" no pointo* (Highlights of "the sixth basic survey" of overseas business activities of Japanese companies, definite report) (Tokyo: MITI Industrial Policy Bureau, International Enterprise Division, November 1997).

13. "Trends in Japanese Foreign Direct Investment," *Highlights of JOI Review,* no. 37 (January 1998), fig. 2–1.

14. Ibid.

15. Jin Shinichi, "Trends in Japanese Foreign Direct Investment, Part I: Investment in Asia and Associated Problems in Investment Countries," *Highlights of JOI Review*, no. 37 (January 1998) (Tokyo: JOI, 1998), p. 3.

16. "Japan Banks Largest S. Korea Creditors—BIS," Reuters, January 4, 1998.

17. Charles Smith, "Japan, Inc., Hangs on in Asia," *EIU Business Asia*, April 6, 1998.

18. Henny Sender, "Japan's Trading Companies Have a Vast Indonesia Risk," *Wall Street Journal*, May 27, 1998.

19. Interview with Wakamatsu Isamu, assistant director, Asia-Oceania Division, Overseas Research Department, JETRO, May 14, 1998.

20. "Toyota tai Honda, hake arasou" (Toyota and Honda battle for supremacy), *Nikkei Business*, June 17, 1996.

21. Gregory W. Noble, "Trojan Horse or Boomerang: Two-Tiered Investment in the Asian Auto Complex," working paper 90, Berkeley Round Table on the International Economy, University of California, Berkeley, November 1996.

22. Interview with Kyoda Toyoho, director, corporate general manager, Office of International Business C, MMC, Tokyo, May 18, 1998.

23. Interview with Takemoto Motonobu, general manager, Asia Division, Toyota Motor Corp., Tokyo, May 15, 1998.

24. "Toyota's Indonesian Assembler Astra Cuts 1,000 Temporaries," *Japan Digest*, August 6, 1998.

25. "Japan's Mitsubishi Motors Hit by Heavy Losses," Agence France-Presse, May 28, 1998.

26. Inoue Tatsuya, "Companies Struggle to Recoup Abroad: Many Recovery Efforts in Thailand and Indonesia Falter; Japanese Manufacturers Lose Numerous Sales Channels," *Nikkei Weekly*, May 11, 1998.

27. Interview with Kyoda Toyoho, director, corporate general manager, Office of International Business C, Mitsubishi Motors Corp., Tokyo, May 18, 1998.

28. Interview with Ohkusa Tomoyuki, deputy general manager, External and Government Affairs Department, MMC, Tokyo, May 18, 1998.

29. Watcharapong Thongrung, "Exporters to Receive Japanese Help," *The Nation*, February 26, 1998.

30. "Japanese Auto Parts Makers to Raise Stakes in Asian Units," Agence France-Presse, June 7, 1998.

31. Amy Tong, "Japanese Retailers in Hong Kong Defy Slump," *Nikkei Weekly*, February 16, 1998.

32. MITI, *Highlights of the Twenty-seventh Survey*, fig. 8; *International Financial Statistics*, December 1997 (Washington, D.C.: IMF, 1997); JETRO, *Sekai to Nihon no Boeki: 1997 JETRO Hakusho* (Trade of Japan and the world: 1997 JETRO white paper) (Tokyo: JETRO, 1997). Estimates for Malaysia and Thailand are based on 1995 exports; all others are for 1996.

33. Emily Thornton in Tokyo, with Ron Corben in Bangkok; Hugh Filman in Manila; and Moon Ihlwan in Seoul, "Bagging More Tigers: Japan Sees Opportunity in Asia's Crisis," *Business Week*, April 20, 1998.

34. Transcript of phone interview with Kenneth Courtis, provided by Deutsche Bank Capital Markets (Asia), June 19, 1998.

35. "Ex-Im Bank Tripled Lending to Southeast Asia in First Half," *Japan Digest*, August 7, 1998.

36. Gillian Tett, "Thai Bail-Out: Asian Neighbours Queue Up to Help," *Financial Times*, August 12, 1997.

37. MITI, web site at www.miti.go.jp.

38. Walter Hatch and Kozo Yamamura, *Asia in Japan's Embrace: Building a Regional Production Alliance* (Cambridge, U.K.: Cambridge University Press, 1996).

39. Ibid., p. 30.

40. MITI handout (in Japanese), ca. May 1998, provided by Ojimi Takato, MITI, May 15, 1998.

41. Interview with Ojimi Takato, deputy director-general for development cooperation, MITI, Tokyo, May 15, 1998.

42. MITI handout, provided by Ojimi Takato on May 15, 1998.

43. Interview with Yutaka Noshiro, deputy director, Operations Division, Institute for International Cooperation, JICA , October 17, 1994.

44. Kozo Yamamura and Walter Hatch, "A Looming Entry Barrier: Japan's Production Networks in Asia," National Bureau of Asian Research (Seattle), *NBR Analysis* 8, no. 1 (February 1997), p. 12.

45. Nancy Dunne, "White House in IMF Financing Offensive," *Financial Times*, January 26, 1998.

46. "World Economy Faces 'Pivotal' Moment in Wake of Japan Crisis: Summers," Agence France-Presse, June 24, 1998.

47. "Shinshutsu Buumu ni kyu breeki" (A sudden halt to overseas expansion), in Toyo Keizai, *Kaigai shinshutsu soran, 1998* (Survey of overseas affiliates, 1998) (Tokyo: Toyo keizai shinposha, 1998).

48. Data are from Toyo Keizai.

49. Nagasaka Toshihisa, "The Industrial Networks of Japanese Corporations," in *Can Asia Recover Its Vitality?* p. 23.

50. Interview with Mitarai Fujio, president and chief executive officer, Canon, Inc., Tokyo, May 18, 1996.

51. Interview with Miyagi Kohtaro, managing director, Canon Singapore, Singapore, May 25, 1998.

52. Canon Group financial data are from Canon's web site at www.canon.co.jp.

53. Ibid.

54. Gomi Norio, "The Current Status and Problems of Asia's Electrical Machinery Industry," in *Globalization and the Roles of Japanese and U.S. Corporations*, ed. Institute of Developing Economies and Japan External Trade Organization (Tokyo: Institute of Developing Economies, 1998), p. 124.

55. ADB, *Southeast Asia's Economy in the 1970s* (New York: Praeger, 1971), p. 248; and JETRO, *ASEAN in Figures* (Tokyo: JETRO, 1998).

56. Edith Terry, "Smarter Than Ever," *Report on Business Magazine*, March 1989.

57. Interview with Shohtoku Yukio, director, member of the board, Matsushita Electric Industrial Co., Tokyo, May 13, 1998.

58. "A Brief Profile of Matsushita Electric's Business in China," handout in English, undated, from Matsushita Electric Industrial Co., international publicity group, faxed May 11, 1998.

59. Interview with Shohtoku Yukio, director, member of the board, Corporate Management Division for China, Matsushita Electric Industrial Co., Tokyo, May 13, 1998.

Notes to Chapter 6

1. Dani Rodrik, "King Kong Meets Godzilla: The World Bank and the East Asian Miracle," in *Miracle or Design? Lessons from the East Asian Experience, Policy Es-*

say, no. 11, by Albert Fishlow, Catherine Gwin, Stephan Haggard, Dani Rodrik, and Robert Wade (Washington, D.C.: ODC, 1994).

2. World Bank, *The East Asian Miracle: Economic Growth and Public Policy* (New York: Oxford University Press, 1993).

3. John Kifner and David E. Sanger, "Financial Leaders Meet as Protests Clog Washington," *New York Times,* April 17, 2000.

4. David E. Sanger, "Longtime IMF Director Resigns in Midterm," ibid., November 10, 1999.

5. Sakakibara Eisuke, "Mr. Yen Looking Back: 'Cybercapitalism' World Needs a Roadmap," *Yomiuri Shimbun,* January 28, 2000; Hasegawa Mina, "Mr. Yen Defends Aggressive Approach to Market: Sakakibara Advocates Asian Trade Alliance to Vie with NAFTA, EU," *Nikkei Weekly,* July 19, 1999.

6. "IMF Critics to Join in Asia Research," Reuters (Tokyo), March 7, 2000.

7. "Sakakibara to Head New Research Center at Keio University," *Japan Digest,* August 26, 1999.

8. Anthony Rowley, "A Changing of the Guard? The Buzz: Camdessus, Wolfensohn Positions Threatened," *Emerging Markets: IMF/World Bank Annual Meeting Daily,* Washington, September 25, 1999.

9. Paul Blustein, "Missionary Work; One of the Least Examined Institutions of Its Size in Washington, the World Bank Has Grown into a Huge Bureaucracy, Too Often Ineffective in Its Mission to Help Poor Countries Grow Rich. Can Renaissance Man James D. Wolfensohn Turn the Bank Around?" *Washington Post,* November 10, 1996.

10. Benjamin Forgey, "World Bank's Capital Gains: HQ Investment Pays Off Grandly," *Washington Post,* February 8, 1997.

11. Eric Altbach, "The AMF Proposal: A Case Study of Japanese Regional Leadership," *JEI Report,* no. 47A, December 19, 1997 (Washington, D.C.: JEI, 1997).

12. World Bank, Tokyo Office, *Segin Tokyo Jimusho 20 Nen Shi* (Twenty years of the World Bank's Tokyo office) (Tokyo: Sekai ginko tokyo jimusho, 1991).

13. Robert Wade, "The World Bank and the Art of Paradigm Maintenance: *The East Asian Miracle* as a Response to Japan's Challenge to the Development Consensus" (Institute of Development Studies, Sussex University, draft, October 28, 1994).

14. Interview with Lawrence MacDonald, Economic Development Institute, World Bank, Washington, D.C., December 5, 1996.

15. IMF, press release, no. 89/48, November 13, 1989.

16. Kevin Muehring, "It's Summers' Time," *Institutional Investor,* December 1997; Awanohara Susumu, "Asian Crisis Impact: Treasury's Change of Heart," *Nikko Capital Trends* 3, no. 3 (February 1998).

17. Ibid.

18. Anthony Rowley, "Asian Fund Special:'The Battle of Hong Kong," ibid., 2, no. 13 (November 1997).

19. Hamamoto Takahiro, "Asian Financial Crisis: Just the Beginning," ibid. (August 1997).

20. Joseph Stiglitz, "The Insider: What I Learned at the World Economic Crisis," *New Republic,* April 17, 2000.

21. John Burton in Seoul and Gerard Baker in Washington, "S. Korea Asks IMF to Speed Rescue Deal," *Financial Times* (London), December 12, 1997.

22. Michael Zielenziger, "Seoul Balks at Harsh Terms of IMF's Financial Bailout Plan," San Jose *Mercury News* (Seoul), December 3, 1997.

23. Paul Blustein and Clay Chandler, "Behind the S. Korea Bailout: Speed, Stealth, Consensus," *Washington Post*, December 28, 1997.

24. David Sanger, "Dissension Erupts at Talks on World Financial Crisis," *New York Times*, October 7, 1998.

25. Bob Davis and David Wessel, "World Bank, IMF at Odds over Asian Austerity: Some Economists Contend That Harsh Measures Could Worsen the Crisis," *Wall Street Journal* (Washington, D.C.), January 8, 1998.

26. Sakakibara Eisuke, *Beyond Capitalism: The Japanese Model of Market Economics* (Lanham, Md.: University Press of America, 1993).

27. John Williamson, "The Washington Consensus Revisited," in *Economic and Social Development into the XXI Century*, ed. by Louis Emmerij (Washington, D.C., Inter-American Development Bank, 1998). From a paper originally presented at the Development Thinking and Practice Conference [hereafter DTP Conference], Washington, D.C., September 3–5, 1996.

28. Steven Rosefielde, "Economic Liberalization in Russia, China and Japan: Reconciling Culture and Free Competition" (paper presented at the annual meeting of the AAASS, Crystal City, Virginia, November 2001).

29. Sakakibara Eisuke, "Globalization and Diversity," *Inaugural Address*, ibid.

30. "Japan Raises Aid to Asia under 'New Miyazawa Initiative,'" *Nikkei Interactive*, May 18, 1999.

31. Sakakibara Eisuke, "Reform of the International Financial System" (speech at the Manila Framework Meeting in Melbourne, Australia, March 26, 1999, draft).

32. Bruce Greenwald and Joseph E. Stiglitz, "Externalities in Economies with Imperfect Information and Incomplete Markets," *Quarterly Journal of Economics* 101 (May 1986), pp. 229–64.

33. World Bank, *The East Asian Miracle: Economic Growth and Public Policy* (New York: Oxford University Press, 1993).

34. Interview with Joseph Stiglitz, chief economist, World Bank, Washington, D.C., August 15, 1997.

35. Joseph Stiglitz, "Back to Basics: Policies and Strategies for Enhanced Growth and Equity in Post-Crisis East Asia" (presented at the Shangri-La Hotel Conference [hereafter Shangri-La Conference], Bangkok, Thailand, July 29, 1999).

36. Joseph Stiglitz, "Asia's Reckoning: What Caused Asia's Crash?—Bad Private-Sector Decisions," *Wall Street Journal*, February 4, 1998.

37. "World Bank's Stiglitz Sees Benefits of Limits on Flows of Capital," ibid., Washington (D.C.), April 28, 1999.

38. David Wessel and Bob Davis, "Markets under Siege—Crisis Crusaders: Would-Be Keyneses Vie over How to Fight Globe's Financial Woes," ibid., September 25, 1998.

39. ADB, *Emerging Asia: Changes and Challenges*, principal authors David Bloom and Jeffrey Sachs, Harvard Institute of Development Studies (Manila: ADB , May 1997).

40. Wessel and Davis, "Markets under Siege."

41. "Miyazawa Will Propose Formal Currency Swap Agreement for Asia," *Japan Digest*, March 30, 2000.

42. "AMF Must Complement Not Counter IMF: IMF Official," Agence France-Presse (Bandar Seri Begawan), March 23, 2000.

43. Patrick McDowell, "Asian Nations Back Currency Plan," Associated Press (Chiang Mai, Thailand), May 7, 2000.

44. "Sakakibara: ASEAN Currency Swap Plan Needs $20B," Dow Jones (Bangkok), May 3, 2000.

45. "ASEAN + 3 Agree in Principle to Expand Currency Swap, Leave Details for Later," *Japan Digest*, May 8, 2000.

46. Altbach, "The AMF Proposal."

47. Gillian Tett, John Ridding, and Ted Bardacke, "Idea Whose Time Has Come Closer: Proposals for an Asian Currency Support Fund May Now Be Even More Popular," *Financial Times* (London), October 9, 1997.

48. Nicholas D. Kristof and Sheryl Wudunn, "Of World Markets, None an Island," *New York Times*, February 17, 1999.

49. David Sanger, *New York Times* (presentation at a Conference on the New Global Financial Architecture, sponsored by the New America Foundation and Council on Foreign Relations, Cosmos Club [hereafter Cosmos Club Conference], Washington, D.C., June 14, 2000).

50. Ishizawa Masato, "Asia Bailout Fund Gets Key Ally in Finance Minister," *Nikkei Weekly*, September 29, 1997.

51. David Sanger, "Asia's Economic Tigers Growl at World Monetary Conference," *New York Times* (Hong Kong), September 22, 1997.

52. Edward A. Gargan, "Premier of Malaysia Spars with Currency Dealer," ibid.; Loh Hui Yin, "Soros: Dr M a Menace to Malaysia," *Business Times* (Singapore), Hong Kong, September 22, 1997.

53. Tett, Ridding, and Bardacke, "Idea Whose Time Has Come."

54. Ibid.

55. Sanger, Cosmos Club Conference.

56. Anthony Rowley, "International Finance: AMF, RIP," *Nikko Capital Trends* 2:14 (December 1997).

57. Muehring, "It's Summers' Time."

58. Awanohara Susumu, "Asian Crisis Impact: Treasury's Change of Heart," *Nikko Capital Trends* 3, no. 3 (February 1998).

59. Interview with Teh Kok Peng, deputy managing director, Monetary Authority of Singapore, Singapore, May 25, 1998.

60. MOF, "Internationalization of the Yen," at www.mof.go.jp.

61. IMF, *International Financial Statistics, December 1997* (Washington, D.C.: IMF, 1997); EPA, *Ajia Keizai, 1998.*

62. Interview with Taniguchi Tomohiko, correspondent, *Nikkei Business*, Tokyo, June 6, 1996.

63. Taniguchi Tomohiko, "Okurasho no 'En Gaiko' hisoka ni hatsu do tai doru 'atsuryoku dantai' no kessei e" (How the MOF aimed to form a dollar "pressure group" through secret yen diplomacy), ibid., April 22, 1996.

64. Interview with Katsu Eijiro, director, Foreign Exchange and Money Market Division, MOF, Tokyo, Japan, June 26, 1996.

65. "BOJ Will Propose Funneling More Yen to Asia for Use in Trade," *Japan Digest*, July 13, 1998.

66. "Japan to Provide 2 Trln Yen in Debt Guarantees for Asia: Miyazawa," *Nikkei Interactive* (Langkawi, Malaysia), May 15, 1999.

67. Interview with Teh Kok Peng, deputy managing director, Monetary Authority of Singapore, Singapore, May 25, 1996.

68. MOF, "Measures to Facilitate the Internationalization of the Yen," provisional trans., December 22, 1998, at www.mof.go.jp.

69. Miyazawa Kiichi, "Beyond the Asia Crisis" (speech by Mr. Kiichi Miyazawa on the Occasion of the APEC Finance Ministers Meeting, Langkawi, Malaysia, May 15, 1999).

70. Walter S. Mossberg, "Japan Pledges New Lending, Readies Plan, Leading Policy Role Sought with Proposals on Debt for Third World Nations," *Wall Street Journal* (West Berlin), September 27, 1988.

71. "Japan Raises Aid to Asia under 'New Miyazawa Initiative,'" *Nikkei Interactive*, May 18, 1999.

72. "Japan Will Offer to Guarantee Sovereign Debt of Its Asian Neighbors," *Japan Digest*, May 14, 1999, quoting *Nihon keizai shimbun*.

73. "JEXIM's Role in Japanese Assistance for the Asian Economy: Status Report," rev. ed. (Tokyo, JEXIM press release, June 1999).

74. Anthony Rowley, "Japan Plans New ASEAN Aid Initiative," *Business Times* (Singapore), July 24, 1999.

75. "Press Statement by Prime Minister Keizo Obuchi," Manila, The Philippines, November 28, 1999, at www.aseansec.org/summit/inf3rd.

76. Michael Battye, "Hashimoto Calls for Annual Japan-ASEAN Summits," Reuters (Singapore), January 13, 1997.

77. Ayako Doi, "ASEAN Plus Three: Asian Togetherness, Western Inattention," *Japan Digest Forum*, November 30, 1999.

78. "Japan Winding Down Miyazawa Plan Due to Low Demand," Dow Jones Newswires, March 1, 2000.

79. "Ex-Im Bank Lends Record 3.8 Trillion Yen in FY 98," *Nikkei Interactive*, April 16, 2000.

80. Henny Sender, "Out of Asia: Japanese Banks and Companies Head Home," *FEER*, April 16, 1998.

81. "Japanese Firms Supported Thai Partners Better Than Firms of Other Countries," *Japan Digest*, June 10, 1999.

82. David E. Sanger, "World Bank Beats Breast for Failures in Indonesia," *New York Times*, February 11, 1999.

83. David E. Sanger, "Decisions by United States and IMF Worsened Asia's Problems, the World Bank Finds," ibid., December 3, 1998.

84. MOFA, Economic Cooperation Bureau, *ODA Annual Report, 1998* (Tokyo: Association for Promotion of International Cooperation, 1998), p. 98.

85. World Bank, *Seisaku Jinteki Shigen Kaihatsu (PHRD) Kikin: 1997 Nendo Nenji Hokaku, Dai Ichi Bu* (PHRD fund: 1997 Annual report, part one) (Washington, D.C.: Resource Mobilization and Co-Financing, World Bank, 1997).

86. Telephone interview with Oyama Keiko, office of the executive director for Japan, World Bank, Washington, D.C., June 18, 1997.

87. Telephone interview with Farrukh Iqbal, ibid.

88. Interview with World Bank staffer, ibid., December 5, 1996.

89. World Bank, press release, no. 16, October 15, 1991, p. 6.

90. World Bank, *The East Asian Miracle*, p. 2.

91. MacDonald interview.

92. Interview with Robert Wade, Sussex University, Tokyo, Japan, February 10, 1995.

93. Interview with Nancy Birdsall, executive vice-president, Inter-American Development Bank, Washington, D.C., December 6, 1996.

94. Jose Edgardo Campos and Hilton L. Root, *The Key to the Asian Miracle: Making Shared Growth Credible* (Washington, D.C.: The Brookings Institution, 1996).

95. Interview with John Page, chief economist for the Middle East and North Africa, World Bank, Tokyo, November 14, 1994.

96. Interview with John Page, chief economist, Middle East and North Africa Region, World Bank, Washington, D.C., December 10, 1996.

97. Robert Dekle and Lawrence H. Summers, "Japan's High Savings Rate Re-Affirmed," *Monetary and Economic Studies* 9, no. 2 (September 1991), pp. 63–78.

98. Interview with Robert Dekle, University of Southern California, Los Angeles, Calif., May 19, 2000.

99. Clyde V. Prestowitz, Jr., *Trading Places: How We Are Giving Our Future to Japan and How to Reclaim It* (New York: Basic Books, 1989).

100. Lawrence Summers, "The Ishihara-Morita Brouhaha," *International Economy*, December 1989, quoted in Richard Katz, *Japan: The System That Soured: The Rise and Fall of the Japanese Economic Miracle* (Armonk, N. Y.: M.E. Sharpe, 1998), p. 9.

101. Summers interview.

102. Alwyn Young, "A Tale of Two Cities: Factor Accumulation and Technical Change in Hong Kong and Singapore," *NBER Macroeconomics Annual 1992*, ed. Olivier Jean Blanchard and Stanley Fischer (Cambridge, Mass.: MIT Press, 1992); Paul Krugman, "The Myth of Asia's Miracle," *Foreign Affairs* 73, no. 4 (November/December 1994).

103. Birdsall interview.

104. Interview with Jose Edgardo Campos, economist, Policy Research Department, World Bank, Washington, D.C., December 5, 1996.

105. Ibid.

106. Birdsall interview.

107. Krugman, "The Myth of Asia's Miracle."

108. World Bank, *The East Asian Miracle*, pp. 24–25.

109. Ibid., p. 26.

110. MacDonald interview.

111. Ibid.

112. World Bank, *East Asian Miracle,* p. 5.

113. Ibid., p. 360.

114. Ibid., p. 25.

115. Ibid.

116. Ibid., p. 10.

117. Michael Hirsh, "The State Strikes Back," *Institutional Investor*, September 1993, p. 88.

118. World Bank, press release, "World Bank Announces Three New Appointments," no. 99/2280/S, June 23, 1999.

119. Steven Irvine, "Inter-American Development Bank: The Edict of Nancy," *Euromoney*, March 1996.

120. Ibid.

121. John Page, "The East Asian Miracle and the Latin American Consensus: Can the Twain Ever Meet?" in *Pathways to Growth: Comparing East Asia and Latin America*, ed. Nancy Birdsall and Frederick Jasperson (Washington, D.C.: IDB, 1997).

122. E-mail correspondence with John Page, February 11, 1996.

123. Kemal Dervis, "Growing Together: Why the Regional Neighborhood Matters for the Middle East and North Africa" (speech by Mr. Kemal Dervis, the Middle East/North Africa Economic Conference, November 16–18, 1997).

124. Ibid.

125. Conversation with Shiratori Masaki, IPR/FASID Workshop on Development Policy, Governance, and the Asian Miracles Lessons, Honolulu, Hawaii, April 7, 1995.

126. OECF Proceedings, pp. 33–35.

127. Michael P. Todaro, *Economic Development* (Reading, Mass.: Addison-Wesley, 1996), p. 112.

128. Young, "A Tale of Two Cities," p. 16.

129. Urban C. Lehner, "Is the Vaunted 'Asian Miracle' Really Just an Illusion?" *Wall Street Journal*, October 20, 1995.

130. Krugman, "The Myth of Asia's Miracle."

131. Ibid., p. 70.

132. Alwyn Young, "Lessons from the East Asian NICS: A Contrarian View," *European Economic Review* 38 (1994); Alwyn Young, "The Tyranny of Numbers: Confronting the Statistical Realities of the East Asian Growth Experience," *Quarterly Journal of Economics* 10, no. 3 (August 1995).

133. Lehner, "Is the Vaunted 'Asian Miracle' Really Just an Illusion?"

134. "Dai San Cho: Higashi Ajia no seicho ryoku" (An examination of East Asia's capacity for growth), *Ajia Keizai 1995*, pp. 175–222.

135. Dani Rodrik, "TFP Controversies, Institutions, and Economic Performance in East Asia," Centre for Economic Policy Research Discussion Paper Series (London), no. 1587, March 1997, abstract and nontechnical summary.

136. Interview with Larry Hathaway, chief economist for East Asia, UBS Securities (Singapore), June 27, 1997.

137. "The Asian Economic Miracle," UBS International Finance (Zurich), no. 29 (Autumn 1996).

138. Paul Krugman, "What Are the Lessons of Asian Growth?" (paper submitted to the Conference on "Political Economics of Korea's Industrial Revolution," Korea Institute for Industrial Economics and Trade, Seoul, Korea, August 22, 1995).

139. Urban C. Lehner, "Dismal Science vs. the Dragons," in Asian Economic Survey 1995, *Asian Wall Street Journal*, October 9, 1995 (a shorter version of this article appeared the next day in the *Wall Street Journal* domestic ed.).

140. A short bibliography of *East Asian Miracle* critiques is in Robert Wade, "Selective Industrial Policies in East Asia: Is the *East Asian Miracle* Right?" in *Miracle or Design? Lessons from the East Asian Experience*, Policy Essay, no. 11 (Washington, D.C.: ODC, 1994), p. 77, n. 1.

141. Dani Rodrik, "King Kong Meets Godzilla," p. 14.

142. Alice H. Amsden, "Why Isn't the Whole World Experimenting with the East Asian Model to Develop? Review of the *East Asian Miracle*," in *World Development* 22, no. 4 (1994), p. 628.

143. Ibid., pp. 630–33.

144. Robert Wade, "The World Bank and the Art of Paradigm Maintenance: *The East Asian Miracle* as a Response to Japan's Challenge to the Development Establishment," unpublished manuscript, October 28, 1994, p. 32.

145. Symposium Proceedings, p. 38.

146. Wade, "The World Bank and the Art of Paradigm Maintenance," p. 5.

147. Ibid.

148. E-mail from John Page, January 26, 1996.

149. I.M.D. Little, D. Mazumdar, and John Page, *Small Manufacturing Enterprises: A Comparative Study of India and Other Countries* (New York: Oxford University Press, 1987).

150. E-mail correspondence from Chalmers Johnson, March 21, 1995.

151. Vinod Thomas and Yan Wang, "Government Policies and Productivity Growth: Is East Asia an Exception?" (paper prepared for the World Bank Workshop on the

Role of Government and East Asian Success, East-West Center, Honolulu, Hawaii, November 19–21, 1992).

152. Scott and Lal, *Public Policy and Economic Development*, p. xi.

153. John M. Page, Jr., "The Pursuit of Industrial Growth: Policy Initiatives and Economic Consequences," in ibid.

154. John Page, "The East Asian Miracle One Year Later: Are Its Lessons Relevant to Other Countries?" Paper presented to the Conference on the Possibility of the Application of Japanese Experience from the Standpoint of the Developing Countries. EPA, Tokyo, November 14 and 15, 1994, p. 218.

155. Page interview.

156. E-mail from John Page, February 11, 1995.

157. E-mail from John Page, February 10, 1996.

158. Telephone interview with Brooke Shearer, Washington, D.C., April 27, 1997.

159. Yanagihara Toru (presentation, *The East Asian Miracle* Proceedings of a Symposium, Jointly Sponsored by the World Bank and OECF [hereafter Symposium Proceedings], Tokyo, December 3, 1993).

160. Page interview.

161. John Page, "The East Asian Miracle: Four Lessons for Development Policy," in *NBER Macroeconomics Annual*, ed. Stanley Fisher and Julio J. Rotemberg (Cambridge, Mass.: MIT, 1994), p. 220.

162. John Page, "A Middle Eastern Miracle: Lessons for Development Policy from East Asia," June 1996 (rev. October 1996). Presented at the Conference on How Can Egypt Benefit from a Trade Agreement with the EU, sponsored by the Egyptian Center for Economic Studies, Cairo, Egypt, June 26–27, 1996, p. 6.

163. OECF Proceedings.

164. Page, "The East Asian Miracle One Year Later," p. 225.

165. Peter A. Petri, "Government and the East Asian Miracle: One Model or Many" (paper prepared for the World Bank Conference on Governance and East Asian Economic Success, East-West Center, Honolulu, Hawaii, November 19–21, 1992).

166. John Page, "The East Asian Miracle One Year Later," p. 222.

167. "Asia's Competing Capitalisms," *The Economist*, June 24, 1995, p. 13.

168. Interview with Edward J. Lincoln, U.S. Embassy, Tokyo, February 9, 1995.

169. Anne L. Emig, "Japan's Challenge to the World Bank: An Attempt at Intellectual Leadership," unpublished manuscript, December 10, 1996, pp. 4–5.

170. Interview with Asanuma Shinji, S.G. Warburg Securities, Tokyo, Japan, February 10, 1995.

171. Emig, "Japan's Challenge to the World Bank," p. 29.

172. Interview with Shiratori Masaki, vice-chairman, OECF, Tokyo, Japan, March 6, 1995.

173. Interview with Kubota Isao, MOF, Tokyo, Japan, December 3, 1992.

174. Wade, "The World Bank and the Art of Paradigm Maintenance: The East Asian Miracle as a Response to Japan's Challenge to the Development Consensus," unpublished paper, October 28, 1994. This paper was revised and published two years later as "Japan, the World Bank, and the Art of Paradigm Maintenance: The *East Asian Miracle* in Political Perspective," *New Left*, no. 217 (May-June 1996).

175. Interview with Kubota Isao, MOF, Tokyo, Japan, December 3, 1992.

176. Kubota Isao, "The Case for Two Step Loans (Private Note)" (paper read at the Workshop on Financial Sector Issues on the Occasion of Bi-Annual Consultation between the World Bank and the OECF and JEXIM, May 15, 1991).

177. Kubota Isao, "Reflections on Recent Trends in Development Aid Policy," unpublished paper, November 5, 1991; and "The Role of Domestic Saving and Macroeconomic Stability in the Development Process," *Economic Society of Australia* 10, no. 2 (June 1991).

178. Kubota interview.

179. Emig, "Japan's Challenge to the World Bank," p. 34.

180. "OECF Occasional Paper, no. 1: Issues Related to the World Bank's Approach to Structural Adjustment—Proposal from a Major Partner" (English version), OECF, October 1991; (Japanese version, with English trans., published under the title, "Sakai Ginko no kozo chosei aprochi no mondaiten ni tsuite" (Issues related to the World Bank's approach to structural adjustment), *Kikin chosa kiho*, no. 73 (February 1992), pp. 4–18.

181. Wade, "Japan, the World Bank, and the Art of Paradigm Maintenance," p. 10.

182. Ibid.

183. Emig, "Japan's Challenge to the World Bank," p. 39.

184. Interview with Abe Yoshiaki, Tokyo, June 28, 1996.

185. Page interview.

186. Dower, "E.H. Norman, Japan and the Uses of History," p. 52.

187. OECF Proceedings, pp. 26–28.

188. World Bank, *The East Asian Miracle*, pp. 88, 86.

189. Interview with Sambommatsu Susumu, EPA, Tokyo, June 21, 1996.

190. EPA, *Possibility of the Application of the Japanese Experience from the Standpoint of the Developing Countries*, November 14–15, 1994, Tokyo, Japan.

191. Page interview.

192. Iwata Kazumasa (presentation at the Fifth Economic Cooperation Symposium, Tokyo, Japan, EPA, November 14, 1995).

193. Toru Yanagihara and Susumu Sambommatsu, eds., *East Asian Development Experience: Economic System Approach and Its Applicability* (Tokyo: IDE Symposium, January 22, 1997).

194. Ibid., pp. 10–11.

195. Ibid., p. 9.

196. Ibid., pp. 11, 13.

197. Ibid., pp. 32–33.

198. Masahiko Aoki, Kevin Murdoch, and Masahiro Okuno-Fujiwara, "Behind the East Asian Miracle: Introducing the Market-Enhancing View," Center for Economic Policy Research (Stanford University), DEPR Publication, no. 442 (October 1995).

199. Interview with Lyn Squire, director, Policy Research, World Bank, Washington, D.C., May 9, 1997.

200. Interview with Sambommatsu Susumu, EPA, Tokyo, February 8, 1995.

201. *WDR 1997: The State in a Changing World* (Washington, D.C.: University Press Books, 1997).

202. Squire interview.

203. Shiratori interview.

204. Yamada Katsuhisa and Kuchiki Akifumi, "Lessons from Japan: Industrial Policy Approach and East Asian Trial" (main paper, DTP Conference).

205. Interview with Sakakibara Eisuke, MOF, Tokyo, March 2, 1995.

206. Ohtsuka Seiichi, "Contributions of Japan's ODA to the East Asian Development" (typescript notes presented at the Evaluation Division, Economic Cooperation Bureau, Japan MOFA, Hawaii, April 6, 1995).

207. Interview with Yamada Katsuhisa, president, IDE, Tokyo, February 20, 1995.

208. Yamada Katsuhisa, "Government-Business Interface," typescript, 1984.

209. Yamada Katsuhisa, "Lessons from Japan: Industrial Policy Approach and East Asian Trial," DTP Conference.

210. Kuchiki Akifumi, "The East Asian Trick: A Theoretical Approach to EPZ" (prepared for the Session, Further Research on the *East Asian Miracle*, the World Bank–Japan Research Fair/Workshop, TEPIA, Tokyo, Japan, December 13, 1995).

211. Interview with Yamada Katsuhisa, president, IDE, Tokyo, June 21, 1996.

212. Chalmers Johnson, *MITI and the Japanese Miracle: The Growth of Industrial Policy, 1925–1975* (Stanford, Calif.: Stanford University Press, 1982).

213. Chalmers Johnson, "Comparative Capitalism: The Japanese Difference," *California Management Review* 35, no. 4 (Summer 1993), pp. 51–67.

214. Chalmers Johnson, "Comparative Capitalism: The Japanese Difference," in *Japan: Who Governs? The Rise of the Developmental State* (New York: W.W. Norton, 1995), p. 64.

215. Chalmers Johnson, "Capitalism East Asian Style" (manuscript for limited distribution, World Bank Conference on Government and East Asian Economic Success, East-West Center, Honolulu, Hawaii, November 19–21, 1992), p. 7.

216. Yamada interview.

217. Interview with Fujimura Ken, director, FASID, Tokyo, September 28, 1994.

218. Ota Fusae, Tanikawa Hiroya, and Otani Tasuke, "Russia's Economic Reform and Japan's Industrial Policy," MITI Research Institute, typescript, ca. April 1992.

219. Interview with Yasuda Osamu, NRI, Tokyo, Japan, September 16, 1994.

220. Itoh Yoshiaki, "More Unskilled Workers May Find Welcome," *Nikkei Weekly*, November 30, 1992.

221. Interview with Kuwajima Kyoko, Japan Center for International Cooperation, Tokyo, Japan, September 30, 1995.

222. Interview with Sugita Nobuki, Research Cooperation Department, EPA, Tokyo, Japan, September 20, 1994.

223. Sheryl WuDunn, "In Summit Silences, a Truce in United States–Japanese Trade Wars," *New York Times*, April 18, 1996.

224. Andrew Pollack, "Japan's Tack on Trade: No More 1–on-1," ibid., July 30, 1996.

225. Edward J. Lincoln, special economic advisor, U.S. embassy, Tokyo, e-mail to Dead Fukuzawa Society, April 9, 1996.

226. Sylvia Ostry, chair, Centre for International Studies at the University of Toronto, Monetary Authority of Singapore, April 23, 1996.

227. Peter Watson, "Practical Implications of the Post-GATT Order: Consideration for the Future Multilateral Agenda" (presentation by Peter Watson, Singapore Congress on World Trade, Singapore, April 24–26, 1996).

228. Sano Tadakatsu, "Trade and Investment Liberalization in the Twenty-first Century" (paper delivered at the Singapore Congress on World Trade, Singapore, April 24–26, 1996).

229. *WTO kosho ni mukete no Nihon no teian: Proposal of Japan on the WTO Negotiations—Nogyo/GMO/Rinsanbutsu, Suisanbutsu—Agriculture/GMOs/Forestry and Fishery Products* (n.d., bound pamphlet); and *Toward the Establishment of Trade Rules for the Twenty-first Century That Contribute to the Era of "Diversity and Coexistence"—Japan's Proposal for the WTO Negotiations—(Agriculture, GMOs, Forestry/Fishery Products)* (n.d., bound pamphlet).

230. "Speech Note for Vice Minister Hisamitsu Arai, MITI" (prepared for the IIE Symposium on the World Trading System—Seattle and Beyond, Seattle, Washington, November 30, 1999).

231. Presentation by Kinoshita Toshihiko, JEXIM, Tokyo, Japan, October 19, 1994.

232. Interview with Maria Judith Guabloche, Tokyo, October 25, 1995.

Notes to Chapter 7

1. Edith Terry, "Indonesian Archaeologists Hard-Pressed to Keep Dreams Alive," *Globe and Mail*, December 7, 1989.

2. Sarah Anderson, electronic file, n.d., ca. 1996.

3. Edith Terry, *Tasaday Notebook*, unpublished, July 1971.

4. John Nance, *The Gentle Tasaday: A Stone Age People in the Philippine Rain Forest* (New York: Harcourt Brace Jovanovich, 1975), pp. 79–81.

5. Ibid., p. 82.

6. Interview with Frank Gibney, president, Pacific Basin Institute, May 5, 2000.

7. Interview with Donald Keene, Columbia University, May 6, 2000.

8. Stanley Karnow, *In Our Image: America's Empire in the Philippines* (New York: Random House, 1989), p. 173.

9. Ibid., pp. 375–76.

10. Robert H. Hsu, "Zaibatsu," in *MIT Encyclopedia of the Japanese Economy* (Cambridge, Mass.: MIT Press, 1994).

11. Theodore Cohen, *Remaking Japan: The American Occupation as New Deal*, ed. Herbert Passin (New York: Free Press, 1987), p. 354.

12. Ibid., p. 373.

13. Quoted in John W. Dower, "E.H. Norman, Japan, and the Uses of History," in *Origins of the Modern Japanese State: Selected Writings of E.H. Norman* (New York: Pantheon, 1975), p. 44.

14. Edwin O. Reischauer, *Wanted: An Asian Policy* (New York: Knopf, 1955).

15. Dower, "E.H. Norman, Japan, and the Uses of History," p. 48.

16. Ibid., p. 59.

17. Bruce Cumings, *Korea's Place in the Sun: A Modern History* (New York: W.W. Norton, 1997), p. 283.

18. John Dower, *Empire and Aftermath: Yoshida Shigeru and the Japanese Experience, 1878–1954* (Cambridge, Mass.: Harvard University Press, 1988), p. 305.

19. Ibid., p. 425.

20. Jung-en Woo (Meredith Woo-Cumings), *Race to the Swift: State and Finance in Korean Industrialization* (New York: Columbia University Press, 1991), p. 92.

21. Dower, *Empire and Aftermath*, p. 457.

22. Quoted in Dower, *Empire and Aftermath*, p. 54.

23. Soeya Yoshihide, "Japan's Policy towards Southeast Asia: Anatomy of 'Autonomous Diplomacy' and the American Factor, in *China, India, Japan, and the Security of Southeast Asia*," ed. Chandran Jeshurun (Singapore: Institute of Southeast Asian Studies, 1993).

24. Ibid., p. 97.

25. Edwin O. Reischauer, "Toward a New Far Eastern Policy," Headline Series, no. 84 (November-December 1950) (New York: Foreign Policy Association, 1950), p. 26.

26. Ibid., p. 52.

27. W.W. Rostow, *Eisenhower, Kennedy, and Foreign Aid* (Austin: University of Texas Press, 1985), p. 59.

28. Ibid., p. 157.

29. Walt W. Rostow, *The Stages of Economic Growth: A Non-Communist Manifesto* (London: Cambridge University Press, 1960), p. 3.

30. Pacific Command, *Command Digest* 3, no. 1; 7, no. 4; 13, no. 1.

31. Paul Krugman, "The Myth of Asia's Miracle," *Foreign Affairs* (November/December 1994), p. 65.

32. Rostow, *Eisenhower, Kennedy, and Foreign Aid*, pp. 18–20; 89–90.

33. Ibid., p. 92.

34. Ibid., p. 171.

35. Brian May, *The Indonesian Tragedy* (Singapore: Graham Brash, 1978), p. 82.

36. Susan Abeyasekere, *Jakarta: A History* (Singapore: Oxford University Press, 1989), p. 207.

37. Ibid., p. 167.

38. Gunnar Myrdal, *Asian Drama: An Inquiry into the Poverty of Nations*, vol. 1 (New York: Pantheon, 1968), p. 65.

39. Ibid., pp. 673–705.

40. ADB, *Southeast Asia's Economy in the 1970s* (New York: Praeger, 1971), p. 129.

41. Data are from Table 1. EPA, Research Department, "Keizai seicho ritsu" (Economic growth rates) in *Ajia Keizai, 1996* (Asian economy, 1996) (Tokyo: MOF, 1996), p. 294.

42. ADB, *Emerging Asia: Changes and Challenges,* principal authors David Bloom and Jeffrey Sachs, Harvard Institute of Development Studies (Manila: ADB, 1997), p. 1.

43. Myrdal, *Asian Drama*, p. 380.

44. Kennan is quoted in Patrick Smith in *Japan: A Reinterpretation* (New York: Vintage Books, 1998), p. 25.

45. Ben Goldberg, *Intellibridge Global Outlook*, May 8–12, 2000.

46. Tanaka Akihiko, presentation at the Center for Strategic and International Studies, Washington, D.C., March 2, 2000.

47. Ozawa Ichiro, *Blueprint for a New Japan: The Rethinking of a Nation* (New York: Kodansha, 1994).

48. Ibid., p. 135.

49. Ibid., p. 131.

50. "Tokyo Governor Expects Riot," Associated Press, Tokyo, April 9, 2000.

51. Peter McKillop, "Letter from Japan: Achilles' Heel—Japan's Entrenched Xenophobia Is Its Downfall in the New Economy," *Time* (Asian ed.), May 5, 2000.

Notes to Chapter 8

1. Michael Williams and Peter Landers, "When Keiretsu Lose Their Way, It's Time for a Change," *Wall Street Journal*, April 27, 2000.

2. George Friedman and Meredith LeBard, *The Coming War with Japan* (New York: St. Martin's Press, 1991).

3. Bill Powell and Rich Thomas, "Japan: All in the Family," *Newsweek*, June 10, 1991.

4. Edith Terry, "Sony Chairman Says He Will Try to Soothe U.S. Irritation over Columbia Purchase," *Globe and Mail*, October 4, 1989.

5. Edith Terry, "Japan Enters '90s Set to Lead World," *Globe and Mail*, December 27, 1989.

6. MOFA, "Japan's *ODA*, 1992" (Tokyo: MOFA, 1992), p. 61.

7. Edith Terry, "Learning to Spend, Spend, Spend," *Globe and Mail*, January 28, 1989.

8. Edith Terry, "Stalking the Japanese Juggernaut with Ken Courtis," *Institutional Investor*, September 1994.

9. Paul Kennedy, *The Rise and Fall of the Great Powers: Economic Change and Military Conflict from 1500 to 2000* (New York: Random House, 1987).

10. Ibid., pp. 470–71.

11. Edith Terry, "Showa," *Globe and Mail*, September 24, 1988.

12. Edward Behr, *Hirohito: Behind the Myth* (New York: Villard Books, 1989), pp. 52–53.

13. Edith Terry, "Sparse Ritual Confirms Akihito's Reputation as a Non-Conformist," *Globe and Mail*, January 10, 1989.

14. Ronald Dore, *Flexible Rigidities: Industrial Policy and Structural Adjustment in the Japanese Economy, 1970–1980* (London: The Athlone Press, 1986).

15. World Bank, *WDR, 1997* (New York: Oxford University Press, 1997), p. 215.

16. Edith Terry, "Letter from Tokyo: Why the Japanese Can't Relax," *Report on Business Magazine*, August 1989.

17. Edith Terry, "Letter from Tokyo: Friends in High Places," *Report on Business Magazine*, April 21, 1989.

18. Frank Gibney, "Why Tokyo Can't Get the Economy Going: One-Party Rule," *Los Angeles Times*, May 7, 2000.

19. Urban C. Lehner, "Japan's Political Structure Recruits Scandal," *Wall Street Journal*, December 14, 1988.

20. Jacob M. Schlesinger, *Shadow Shoguns: The Rise and Fall of Japan's Postwar Political Machine* (Stanford, Calif.: Stanford University Press, 1999).

21. Edith Terry, "Stock Scandal Shakes Japan's Unshakable LDP," *Globe and Mail*, October 22, 1988.

22. Edith Terry, "Japan's Politics Paralyzed by Corruption Case," *Globe and Mail*, April 21, 1989.

23. Edith Terry, "Japanese Prime Minister Ignores Calls for His Early Resignation," *Globe and Mail*, April 19, 1989.

24. Edith Terry, "Scandal at Recruit Firm Could Trigger Collapse of Japan's Government," *Globe and Mail*, April 17, 1989.

25. Edith Terry, "Japan's New Capitalism: Corporate Groups Hold Japan's Business Community Together," *Globe and Mail*, September 24, 1990.

26. Douglas Ostrom, "The Keiretsu System: Cracking or Crumbling?" *JEI Report*, no. 14A, April 7, 2000, p. 3.

27. Richard E. Caves, with the collaboration of Masu Uekusa, "Industrial Organization," in *Asia's New Giant: How the Japanese Economy Works* (Washington, D.C.: The Brookings Institution, 1976), pp. 499–500.

28. Henry C. Wallich and Mable I. Wallich, "Banking and Finance," in *Asia's New Giant: How the Japanese Economy Works*, ed. Hugh Patrick (Washington, D.C.: The Brookings Institution Press, 1976). pp. 294–95.

29. Paul Blustein, "A New Study Fuels the Clash over Keiretsu," *Washington Post*, April 26, 1991.

30. Ibid.

31. Nakatani Iwao, "Opening 'Keiretsu' System to Scrutiny Is Crucial Task for Japan's Prosperity," *Japan Economic Journal*, May 26, 1990.

32. Dower, *Origins of the Modern Japanese States*, p. 299.

33. Shukan toyo keizai, *Kigyo Keiretsu Soran 2000* (Survey of industrial keiretsu, 2000) (Tokyo: Shukan toyo keizai, 1999), p. 24.

34. Ostrom, "The Keiretsu System."

35. A representative example is in Ohsono Tomokazu, *Kigyo Keiretsu to Gyokai Chizu* (A map of industrial keiretsu and business circles) (Tokyo: Nihon jitsugyo shuppansha, 1997).

36. Edith Terry, "Japan's New Capitalism: Huge Alliances Called Keiretsu Have Become the Main Channel for Japanese Business Abroad," *Globe and Mail*, September 22, 1990.

37. Edith Terry, "Japan's New Capitalism: Japanese Business Has Put Up a Wall that Keeps Out the Rest of the World," *Globe and Mail*, September 25, 1990.

38. Toyo keizai, *Kigyo Keiretsu Soran*, 1996 (Survey of industrial keiretsu, 1996) (Tokyo: Toyo keizai shukan, 1995).

39. Clay Chandler and Kathryn Tolbert, "In Japan, Reviving an Ailing Economy: Old Ways Fade, New Voices Heard," *Washington Post*, January 3, 2000.

40. Edith Terry, "Shady Stock Deals: Japan's Market Slump Revealed a Cozy World Where Insider Trading, Greenmailing, and Real Estate Speculation Ran Rampant, with the Shite Shudan Playing a Central Role," *Globe and Mail*, November 13, 1990.

41. Edith Terry, "Kotani Connection: A Structure Is Unraveling of Insider Trading Reaching Japan's Elite," ibid., November 12, 1990.

42. Edith Terry, "Two Years after the Kobe Earthquake," in *Unlocking the Bureaucrat's Kingdom*, ed. Frank Gibney (Washington, D.C.: The Brookings Institution Press, 1998), p. 233.

43. Glen Fukushima, "The Great Hanshin Earthquake," *JPRI Occasional Paper*, no. 2 (Santa Monica, Calif.: JPRI, March 1995).

44. Inoguchi Takashi, "Kanryo: The Japanese Bureaucracy in History's Eye." Paper for Conference on "Crisis and Change in Japan Today," Seattle, Washington, October 20–21.

45. Ibid.

46. Okazaki Tetsuji, "From Wartime Controls to Post-War Recovery," in *Unlocking the Bureaucrat's Kingdom*, pp. 21–24.

47. Noguchi Yukio, *1940 Nen Taisei* (The 1940s system) (Tokyo: Toyo keizai shimbunsha, 1995), pp. 37–39.

48. Interview with Noguchi Yukio, University of Tokyo, Tokyo, Japan, June 20, 1996.

49. World Bank, *The East Asian Miracle*, p. 14.

50. Johnson, *MITI and the Japanese Miracle*.

51. Ulrike Schaede, "Bureaucrats in Business," in *Unlocking the Bureaucrat's Kingdom*, pp. 161–63.

52. Nakatani Iwao, *Nihon Keizai no Rekishiteki Tenkan* (The historical transformation of the Japanese economy) (Tokyo: Toyo keizai shimbunsha, 1996), ch. 4, pp. 125–60.

53. Interview with Nakatani Iwao, dean, faculty of economics department, Hitotsubashi University, Tokyo, Japan, June 13, 1996.

Notes to Chapter 9

1. Interview with Okazaki Hisahiko, Okazaki Institute, Tokyo, Japan, June 19, 1996.

2. Ibid.

3. Interview with Kikuchi Kiyoaki, senior advisor, Matsushita Electrical Corp., Tokyo, Japan, October 7, 1992.

4. Satoh Yukio, "Asian-Pacific Process for Stability and Security," in *Japan's Post Gulf International Initiatives*, August 1991, MOFA, Japan (bound manuscript in English).

5. Mary Jordan and Kevin Sullivan, "Tensions Heat Up in Asia: Security Concerns Replace Financial Crisis," *Washington Post*, July 24, 1999.

6. "Coast Guard Seeks Long-Range Jets to Help It Deal with Piracy in Southeast Asia," *Japan Digest*, August 21, 2000.

7. Interview with Paul Evans, University of Toronto/York University, Tokyo, Japan, May 30, 1994.

8. Abby Tan, "ASEAN Moves to Consider Security Issues," *Japan Times*, (Manila,) July 16, 1992.

9. Ibid.

10. Sonni Efron, "Historic Meeting Joins Japan, Koreas," *Los Angeles Times*, July 27, 2000.

11. Chien-peng Chung, "Southeast Asian Perceptions of Major Power Relations in Northeast Asia," *PacNet* 30 (July 28, 2000).

12. Evans interview.

13. Interview with Chan Heng Chee, Institute of Southeast Asian Studies, Singapore, April 8, 1996.

14. Ezra Vogel, Harvard University (presentation sponsored by the American Chamber of Commerce in Japan, Tokyo, August 14, 1995).

15. Thomas E. Ricks, "For Pentagon, Asia Moving to Forefront, Shift Has Implications for Strategy, Forces, Weapons," *Washington Post*, May 26, 2000.

16. "Tai Nichibeigun kaiji hatten o dashin" (U.S. military in Japan sounds out Tokyo on dispatching Maritime Self-Defence Forces) *Asahi shimbun*, November 26, 1995.

17. Peter Ennis, e-mail posted to the Dead Fukuzawa Society, October 14, 1997.

18. Michael Zielenziger, "The U.S.-Japanese Military Alliance Is Under Scrutiny," *Mercury News* (San Jose), March 20, 1999.

19. CIA, *The World Factbook 2000*, at www.cia.gov/cia/publications/factbook.

20. Interview with Vice-Admiral Hayashizaki Chiaki, Marine Self-Defence Force, Sasebo, Japan, May 31, 1993.

21. Interview with Mamoi Makoto, National Defense University, Tokyo, Japan, October 15, 1992.

22. Edwin P. Hoyt, *Yamamoto: The Man Who Planned Pearl Harbor* (New York: Warner Books, 1991), p. 1.

23. Keizai Koho Center, *APEC: A Statistical Compendium* (Tokyo: Keizai Koho Center, 1995), pp. 4–6.

24. Briefing, CINCPAC, Honolulu, Hawaii, December 16, 1993.

25. "Student Seminar: Japan between U.S. and Asia—Presentation 2," in *Japanese Diplomacy toward Asia in a Post–Cold War Era* (Honolulu, Hawaii: East-West Center , 1993).

26. Interview with Soeya Yoshihide, visiting fellow, East-West Center, Honolulu, Hawaii, October 22, 1993.

27. Interview with Kikuchi Kiyoaki, senior advisor, Matsushita Electric Industrial Corp., October 7, 1992.

28. Ozawa Ichiro, *Blueprint for a New Japan: The Rethinking of a Nation.* Translated by Louisa Rubenfein, edited by Eric Gower (New York: Kodansha, 1994), pp. 105–6.

29. Hosokawa Morihiro, "Rebuilding the U.S.-Japan Security Structure" (keynote address at the Japan-America Society of the State of Washington, Seattle, Washington, March 12, 1996).

30. Michael Green, "Why Tokyo Will Be a Larger Player in Asia," Foreign Policy Research Institute E-Notes, distributed exclusively via fax and e-mail, July 27, 2000, at <e-mail address: fpri@fpri.org>.

31. Major General Yamaguchi Noboru (presentation at a Conference on the United States and Japan: Strategic and Economic Partners, Center for Strategic and International Studies, Washington, D.C., March 2, 2000).

32. Akira Iriye, *China and Japan in the Global Setting* (Cambridge, Mass.: Harvard University Press, 1992), p. 18.

33. John K. Fairbank, Edwin O. Reischauer, and Albert M. Craig, *East Asia: The Modern Transformation* (Boston: Houghton Mifflin, 1965), p. 631.

34. Ibid., p. 632.

35. *Nihon no Hyaku Nen: Shuji de Miru* (One hundred years of Japan as seen in statistics), 3rd pr. (Tokyo: Kokusei sha, 1991), pp. 323–24.

36. Iriye, *China and Japan in the Global Setting*, pp. 106–7.

37. Kokubun Ryosei, "The Politics of Foreign Economic Policymaking in China: The Case of Plant Cancellations with Japan," *China Quarterly*, no. 3 (1986).

38. Yen 3,382.363 billion in exports; Yen 4,399.676 in imports; for a deficit of Yen 2,017.313. Exchange rate of Yen 108.8:$; Japanese MOF, *Value of Exports and Imports by Area (Country) 1996* (calendar year) www.mof.go.jp/english/trade-st/199628ce.htm.

39. JETRO, *Sekai to Nihon no boeki: 1997 JETRO Hakusho*, p. 173.

40. JETRO, *Kaigai Chokusetsu Toushi: 1998 JETRO Hakusho*, p. 527.

41. Yen 3 trillion; US$ figure is based on the 1999 average exchange rate of Yen 113.7:$.

42. Okazaki Hisahiko interview.

43. Iriye, *China and Japan in the Global Setting*, p. 19.

44. World Bank, *The Chinese Economy: Fighting Inflation, Deepening Reforms* (Washington, D.C.: World Bank, 1996), p. 13.

45. Edith Terry, "China Checks Japan's Power in Asia," *Christian Science Monitor*, January 10, 1995.

46. Nicholas Chapuis, "China and Southeast Asia: Integration and Multipolarity." Paper prepared for Conference on the New Geopolitical Order in Southeast Asia and Europe-Asia Relations, Institute of Southeast Asian Studies, Singapore, July 4–5, 1996.

47. Kotake Kazuaki, "Beijing's Diplomatic Offensive in Asia," *JETRO China Newsletter*, no. 4. (May-June 1993).

48. Abe, Jun-Ichi, "China's Eye Toward the Expanding ASEAN," *JETRO China Newsletter* 6:131 (1997).

49. JETRO, *Sekai to Nihon no Kaigai chokusetsu Toushi: 1998 JETRO Hakusho*, p. 17.

50. Nakatani Iwao, "Possibility of United States and China By-Passing 'Closed Japan': Is Rapidly Growing China a Threat to Japan? How Japan's Economy Should Respond," *Asuteion* (Quarterly magazine) (Tokyo), Summer 1994; trans. U.S. Embassy.

51. Interview with Nicholas Chapuis, deputy director, East Asia, Asia Department, French Ministry of *Foreign Affairs*, Singapore, July 5, 1996.

52. Ibid.

53. "Zhu Hints Japan Firms Could Aid China Reforms," *Yomiuri*, February 26, 1994.

54. "The New Nationalists," *The Economist*, January 14, 1995.

55. *Nikkei Weekly*, October 19, 1992

56. Quoted in Shen Caibin, "Nihon moderu to Chugoku" (The Japanese model and China) in *Seiron: Chugoku keiai* (The Chinese economy: An argument), ed. Guan Zhixiong and the Chinese Expatriate Researchers Assoc. in Japan (Tokyo: Toyo keizai shinposha, 1998).

57. Kong Fanjing, *Riben jingji fazhan zhanlue* (Beijing: Zhongguo shehui kexue chubanshe, 1983).

58. Paraphrased by Shen, "Nihon moderu to Chugoku."

59. Robert Taylor, *Greater China and Japan: Prospects for an Economic Partnership in East Asia* (London: Routledge, 1996), pp. 27–28.

60. Ibid., p. 39.

61. Shen, "Nihon moderu to Chugoku."

62. World Bank, "China: GNP Per Capita," report no. 13580–CHA (Washington, D.C.: World Bank, China and Mongolia Department, 1994).

63. Terry, "China Checks Japan's Power in Asia."

64. Asami Tamotsu, "A Case of Mixed Feelings over Behemoth Next Door Neighbor," *Yomiuri*, November 1, 1994.

65. Interview with Chi Hung Kwan, senior economist, NRI, Tokyo, May 14, 1998.

66. East-West Discussion Group, International House of Japan, Tokyo, July 8, 1994.

67. Rick Tetzeli, "Japan, Inc.'s New Growth Record," *Fortune,* October 7, 1991.

68. Edith Terry, "Japanese Imperial Visit Symbolic: Southeast Asia Draws Attention," *Globe and Mail*, September 30, 1991.

69. Ian Stewart, "Emperor's Tour Buries Memories of Hirohito," *Daily Telegraph* (London), October 5, 1991.

70. Ibid.

71. Alison Clements, "War Horror Pledge by Akihito," *Daily Telegraph* (London), September 27, 1991.

72. James McGregor, "Cautious Steps during Emperor's Trip Show Fragility of Tokyo-Beijing Ties," *Wall Street Journal*, October 28, 1992.

73. Kent Chen, "Activist to Continue Fight for Apology," *South China Morning Post*, November 5, 1992.

74. Susan V. Lawrence, "The Emperor's New Clothes," *U.S. News and World Report*, November 2, 1992.

75. McGregor, "Cautious Steps."

76. Eto Jun, "Shinju Wan go 50 nen no Nihonjin" (The Japanese, 50 years after Pearl Harbor), Weekly Business *Sapio*, December 12, 1991.

77. Edith Terry, "The War That Haunts Japan," *Globe and Mail*, December 6, 1991.

78. Ian Buruma, *The Wages of Guilt: Memories of War in Germany and Japan* (New York: Farrar Strauss & Giroux, 1994); George Hicks, *The Comfort Women: Japan's Brutal Regime of Enforced Prostitution in the Second World War* (New York: W.W. Norton, 1994); George Hicks, *Japan's War Memories: Amnesia or Concealment?* (Aldershot, U.K.:. Ashgate, 1977); Iris Chang, *The Rape of Nanking: The Forgotten Holocaust of World War Two* (New York: Basic Books, 1997).

79. Hicks, *Japan's War Memories: Amnesia or Concealment?* p. vii.

80. Mahathir Mohamad and Shintaro Ishihara, *The Voice of Asia: Two Leaders Discuss the Coming Century*, trans. Frank Baldwin (Tokyo: Kodansha, 1995), p. 31; trans. from *Mahatiru to Ishihara Shintaro, No to ieru Ajia: Tai oubei e no hosaku* (Mahathir and Ishihara Shintaro: The Asia that can say no) (Tokyo: Kobunsha, 1994).

81. Buruma, *The Wages of Guilt*; Hicks, *The Comfort Women*; idem, *Japan's War Memories*; Chang, *The Rape of Nanking*.

82. Michael Zielenziger, "Jiang Insists Japan Atone for War Role," *Mercury News* (San Jose), November 29, 1998.

83. Inoguchi Takashi, "Asia's Impact on Japan." Paper presented at the Conference on Economic Change, Political Pluralism, and Democratic Reform in the Asian Region, University of Adelaide, Adelaide, Australia, April 20–21, 1996.

84. Nakahara Michiko, "Asian Laborers along the Burma-Thailand Railroad," *Waseda Journal of Asian Studies* 15 (1993), p. 106.

85. Ibid., p. 104.

86. Interview with Nakahara Michiko, Waseda University, Tokyo, Japan, September 21, 1994.

87. Eto Jun, "Shinju Wan go 50 nen no Nihonjin."

88. "Taiheiyo Senso Kaisen 50 nen Tokushu: Ajia de Nihon gun ga shita koto" (Special issue on the 50th anniversary of the Pacific War: Where the Japanese army was in Asia," *Aera* 4, no. 52 (December 10, 1991).

89. Edith Terry, "The Awful Secret of Unit 731," *Globe and Mail*, February 1, 1992.

90. Edith Terry, "Japan's Take on '45 Raid Shifts in a New Exhibit," *Christian Science Monitor*, February 10, 1995.

91. The period of *sakoku*, or national seclusion, lasted from 1639 to 1854 and was adopted by the Tokugawa shogunate to strengthen its authority against the incursions of Western missionaries and military and commercial domination.

92. Nakahara Michiko, "Japanese Intellectuals and Southeast Asia during the Great East Asian War," *Waseda Journal of Asian Studies* 5 (1983), p. 89.

94. Jesse Wong, "Asian Students Learn to Dislike Japan," *Asian Wall Street Journal*, February 13, 1996.

93. "International Exchange and Cooperation: Student Exchange," English-language page, MOE, at www.monbu.go.jp/aramashi/1999eng/e09/e09–2.htm.

95. MOJ, *Dai 34 Shutsunyukuni Kanri Tokei Nenpo, Heisei Shichinenban* (Annual report of statistics on legal migrants, ed. 1995), ed. Judicial System and Research Department, Minister's Secretariat, MOJ (Tokyo: Okurasho insatsukyoku, 1996).

96. Abigail Haworth, "Flesh and Blood, Part One," *Tokyo Journal* (July 1994); and "Flesh and Blood, Part Two," ibid. (August 1994).

97. Erin Aeran Chung, "Korean Voluntary Associations in Japanese Civil Society," *JPRI Working Paper*, no. 69 (July 2000).

98. Edith Terry, "Japan's 'Apartheid' Establishment in Battle over Minority Rights: Ethnic Koreans Are Challenging the Systematic Discrimination of a Society That Has Been Reluctant to Recognize Them," *Globe and Mail*, December 12, 1991.

99. Ibid.

100. Edith Terry, "Open Door—As the Government Greets People of Japanese Descent with Jobs and Visas, Critics See a Bid to Maintain Racial Purity," *Globe and Mail*, December 13, 1991.

101. Howard French, "Still Wary of Outsiders, Japan Expects Immigration Boom," *New York Times*, March 14, 2000.

102. Ibid.

103. Kathryn Tolbert, "Japan Opens a Door to Emigrants' Descendants," *Washington Post*, March 7, 2000.

104. Edith Terry, "Japanese Find Eager Migrants Hard to Replace," *Globe and Mail*, October 19, 1988.

105. Yen 40,000.

106. Edith Terry, "Refugee Policy: In Omura, Illegal Foreigners Are Kept in a Sinister Looking Center before Being Deported," *Globe and Mail*, June 16, 1990.

107. Rey Ventura, *Underground in Japan* (London: Jonathan Cape, 1992), p. 165.

108. Edith Terry, "Japan's Brisk Marriage Trade Creates Strange Bedfellows," *Globe and Mail*, September 23, 1988.

109. Yen 1,650,000.

110. Interview with Fukuda Shin and Gan Wee Feng, Matsushita Training Center, Osaka, December 4, 1992.

111. Sonoda Shigeto, "Growth Process of Japanese Ventures in China," *JETRO China Newsletter*, no. 111 (July-August 1994).

112. NHK TV, March 10, 1996.

113. Sugita Toshiaki, "Foreign Direct Investment and Its Subsequent Withdrawal—Investigation of Chinese Business," *JETRO China Newsletter* 3, no. 28 (1997).

114. Ibid., p. 22.

115. "Season of Discontent," *Business China, Fortnightly Report to Managers of China Operations*, EIU, June 28, 1993.

116. Zhang Jixun, "Problems in Direct Investment in China," *JETRO China Newsletter*, no. 103 (March-April 1993).

117. Maruyama Nobuo, "Current Problems Facing China-Japan Joint Ventures," ibid., no. 95 (November-December 1991).

118. Fukuda Shozo, *With Sweat and Abacus: Economic Roles of Southeast Asian Chinese on the Eve of World War Two*, ed. George Hicks (Singapore: Select Books, 1995), p. 229.

119. Sonoda Shigeto, "Growth Process of Japanese Ventures in China."

Notes to Chapter 10

1. "Tension Reigns over Jakarta's Monas Square," *Jakarta Post*, May 21, 1998.

2. Vinod Ahuja, Benu Bidani, Francisco Ferreira, and Michael Walton, *Everyone's Miracle? Revisiting Poverty and Inequality in East Asia* (Washington, D.C.: World Bank, 1997), pp. 9–10.

3. Richard P. Cronin, *Asian Financial Crisis: An Analysis of U.S. Foreign Policy Interests and Options*. CRS Report 98–74F, updated April 23, 1998 (Washington, D.C.: CRS), p. 22.

4. Selected major books published on the East Asian financial crisis include *Meltdown: Asia's Boom, Bust, and Beyond*, Mark Clifford and Pete Engardio (New York: Prentice-Hall, Inc., 2000); *Asia in Crisis: The Implosion of the Banking and Finance Systems*, Philippe F. Delhaise (Singapore: John Wiley & Sons, 1998); *Tigers Tamed: The End of the Asian Miracle*, Robert Garran (Honolulu: University of Hawaii Press, 1998); *Asia Falling? Making Sense of the Asian Currency Crisis and Its Aftermath*,

Callum Henderson (Singapore: McGraw-Hill, 1998); *Asian Contagion: The Causes and Consequences of a Financial Crisis*, ed. Karl D. Jackson (Boulder, Colo.: Westview Press, 1999); and *Tigers in Trouble: Financial Governance, Liberalization and Crises in East Asia*, ed. K.S. Jomo (London: Zed Books, 1998). *Thailand's Boom and Bust*, by Pasuk Phongpaichit and Chris Baker, is the best analysis of the crisis in the Thai economy (Chiangmai, Thailand: Silkworm Books, 1998). The *FEER* published two collections of articles on the crisis, *Crash of '97: How the Financial Crisis Is Shaping Asia*, ed. Dan Biers (Hong Kong: Review Publishing, 1998) and *The Aftershock: How an Economic Earthquake Is Rattling Southeast Asian Politics*, ed. Faith Keenan (idem., 1998).

5. Samuel P. Huntington, *The Clash of Civilizations and the Remaking of World Order* (New York: Simon & Schuster, 1996).

6. Presentation by Larry Lindsey, American Enterprise Institute, at The Brookings Institution, Washington, D.C., February 18, 1998.

7. The first quotation is from Clyde V. Prestowitz, Jr., *Trading Places: How We Are Giving Our Future to Japan and How to Reclaim It* (New York, Basic Books, 1988). The second quotation is from Clyde Prestowitz, "Retooling Japan Is the Only Way to Rescue Asia Now," *Washington Post*, December 14, 1997.

8. This account is taken from an article by Nayan Chanda, "Rebuilding Asia," *FEER*, February 7, 1998.

9. Anek Laothamatas, a political scientist at Thammasat University, Thailand's second-oldest university. Professor Anek was an advisor to the deputy finance minister, Chaturon Chaisaeng, at the time of the devaluation.

10. Lecture by Anek Laothammatas, vice rector, Thammasat University, Paul H. Nitze School for Advanced International Studies, Washington, D.C., February 4, 1998

11. David Sanger, "After a Year, No Letup in Asia's Economic Crisis," *New York Times*, July 6, 1998.

12. Michael Zielenziger, "No End in Sight for Asia Crisis," *Mercury News* (San Jose) June 28, 1998.

13. Mark Malloch Brown, vice-president, External Affairs, World Bank, letter to Mr. James D. Wolfensohn, August 26, 1997.

14. "Is the East Asian 'Miracle' Over?" World Bank Group, press statement, Washington, D.C., December 16, 1996.

15. Ahuja et al., *Everyone's Miracle*.

16. "Indonesian Economic Growth Accompanied by Improved Social Indicators," *IMF Survey* 26, no. 16 (August 18, 1997).

17. Jean-Michel Severino, office memorandum, World Bank/IFC/MIGA, to James D. Wolfensohn, August 26, 1997.

18. JETRO, *Sekai to Nihon no Kaigai Chokusetsu Toushi: 1998 JETRO Hakusho*, p. 17.

19. "Thailand's Rapid Growth Linked to Prudent Policies," *IMF Survey* (December 11, 1995).

20. "Korea Poised to Join Advanced Industrial Countries, Says Camdessus," ibid. (November 14, 1994).

21. "Indonesian Economic Growth."

22. Sanger, "After a Year."

23. In 1997, Korea's per capita GDP was $9,511; Thailand's was $2,535; and Indonesia's was $1,055. In terms of population, there were 45.5 million Koreans, 60.1

million Thais, and 193.7 million Indonesians. Data are from *Ajia Keizai 1998*, ed. EPA, Research Department (Tokyo: MOF, Publications Department, 1998).

24. Dennis De Tray, speech to the U.S.-Indonesia Society, Cosmos Club, Washington, D.C., June 3, 1998.

25. Ibid.

26. Asian Development Bank, from the web site of Bank of Indonesia, at www.bi.go.id.

27. "IMI: Dreary Economic Projections for 1999," *Recent Economic Reports (RER)* (Embassy of the United States of America, Jakarta, Indonesia), 1998.

28. *International Financial Statistics (November)* (Washington, D.C.: IMF, 1998).

29. "Indonesia in Crisis: A Macroeconomic Update" (Washington, D.C.: World Bank, July 16, 1998), p. 1.4.

30. Ross H. McLeod, "Indonesia," in *East Asia in Crisis: From Being a Miracle to Needing One?* ed. Ross H. McLeod and Ross Garnaut (London: Routledge, 1998), pp. 38–39.

31. "IMI: Dreary Economic Projections for 1999."

32. "IMI: Signs of the Times: Indonesian Economic Highlights and Lowlights: April 1999," *RER* (Embassy of the United States of America, Jakarta, Indonesia, May 2, 1999), citing a labor-force survey of the Central Bureau of Statistics.

33. "April 1, 1999: IMI: There Is No Safety in Numbers: Indonesian Investment Statistics, 1998," *RER* (Embassy of the United States of America, Jakarta, Indonesia).

34. $4.9 billion.

35. Aristides Katoppo, "Indonesia's Torturous Road to Reform" (paper presented at the National Defense University's Annual Pacific Symposium on U.S. Engagement Policy in a Changing Asia: A Time for Reassessment? Honolulu, Hawaii, March 2, 1999).

36. "Indonesia in Crisis," p. 1.8.

37. Ibid., p. 1.6.

38. Central Bureau of Statistics, from Bank of Indonesia web site, at www.bi.go.id.

39. Interview with Arifin Siregar, former finance minister, Jakarta, Indonesia, May 21, 1998.

40. Between 1990 and 1997, private-sector capital flows to developing countries increased six-fold, from about $40 billion in 1990 to $247 billion in 1996 and $256 billion in 1997, and by the mid-1990s, East Asia was absorbing roughly half of them. John D. Shilling and Yan Wang, *Managing Capital Flows in East Asia* (Washington, D.C.: World Bank, 1996), p. 6.

41. "Government of Indonesia Announces Sweeping Reforms of the Banking System," press release, Jakarta, March 13, 1999.

42. Ross H. McLeod, "Indonesia," p. 32.

43. Bank of Indonesia, "Money Supply (M1), 1990–1997," in "Indonesia in Crisis," table 20.

44. "Indonesia—Memorandum of Economic and Financial Policies," IMF, Jakarta, Indonesia, January 15, 1998, from its web site, at www.imf.org/external/np/loi/011598.htm.

45. Cited in William H. Branson, "Financial Sector Reforms in the ASEAN Countries," in *Contemporary Problems of the Financial System and Policy Options in ASEAN 4* (Tokyo: MOF, 1998), p. 179.

46. "Indonesia in Crisis," p. 1.8.

47. "Suharto's Son Files Suit against Finance Minister over Bank Closure," Agence France-Presse (Jakarta), November 4, 1997.

48. Greg Earl, "Jakarta Ignores World Bank on Power Project," *Australian Financial Review* (December 29, 1997).

49. Bhimanto Suwastoyo, "Indonesian Car Program Loses Tax Edge in IMF-Supported Reforms," Agence France-Presse (Jakarta), January 15, 1998.

50. Sander Thoenes, "Indonesian Budget Ignores Rescue Targets Set by the IMF," *Financial Times* (London), January 7, 1998.

51. David E. Sanger, "Indonesian Leader Yielding to Pleas to Mend Economy," *New York Times*, December 13, 1998.

52. Dennis De Tray, World Bank (presentation at the Cosmos Club, Washington, D.C., June 3, 1999).

53. "Bank Indonesia Gov Sees Interest Rates at 17–20% Yr End," Dow Jones newswire, June 1, 1999.

54. "RI Sees 50 Percent Jump in Oil/Gas Revenues," *Indonesian Observer*, June 1, 1999.

55. "May 11, 1999: Indonesia's Economy by the Numbers, May 1999," *RER* (Embassy of the United States, Jakarta, Indonesia).

56. Letter of Intent, Government of Indonesia, Jakarta, Indonesia, November 13, 1998, from the IMF web site, at www.imf.org/external/np/loi/1113a98.htm.

57. Bambang Widianto and A. Choesni, "Indonesia: The Impact of the Economic Crisis on Industry Performance" (Jakarta, BAPPENAS and the World Bank, 1999).

58. Kotkin, "Making Sashimi of the Experts' Predictions: Why Japan Did Not Turn Out to Be the World Power Everyone Feared," *Washington Post*, March 30, 1997.

59. Richard Katz, "Japan's Self-Defeating Trade Policy: Mainframe Economics in a PC World," *Washington Quarterly* 20, no. 2 (Spring 1997).

60. Michael Hirsh and E. Keith Henry, "The Unraveling of Japan, Inc.: Multinationals as Agents of Change," *Foreign Affairs* 76, no. 2 (March/April 1997).

61. Steve W. Hanke, "Anything in Asia but Japan," *Forbes*, December 16, 1996.

62. Bill Emmott, *The Sun Also Sets* (New York: Times Books, 1989).

63. Michael Zielenziger, "Black Chic: Young Japanese Say Hip-Hop and Jazz Are Exciting Escapes from a Nation of Conformity," *Mercury News* (San Jose), May 28, 1998.

64. Jacob Weisberg, "Keeping the Boom from Busting," *New York Times Magazine*, July 19, 1998.

65. Richard Bernstein and Ross Munro, *The Coming Conflict with China* (New York: Knopf, 1997).

66. Edward J. Lincoln, "Japan's Financial Mess," *Foreign Affairs* 77, no. 3 (May/June 1998), p. 66.

67. Knut Engelmann, "World Economic Leaders Agree to Disagree on Japan," Reuters, April 17, 1998.

68. "Barshefsky Says Japan Must Open Up Economy," Agence France-Presse, June 22, 1998.

69. Interview with Kinoshita Toshihiko, visiting research fellow, Japan Center for Economic Research, Tokyo, May 16, 1998.

70. Dinner between Japan Club and visiting delegation of the U.S.-ASEAN Business Council, Jakarta, February 25, 1999.

Notes to Chapter 11

1. Interview with Iwase Fusako, Tokyo, June 18, 1996.

2. Interview with Tanigawa Toshimitsu, Shimoura, Nakayama, Chiba Prefecture, June 12, 1996.

3. Mizutani Kenji, *Migigata kudari no Nihon keizai* (Japan's economy on the downslope) (Tokyo: PHP Institute, 1996).

4. Interview with Mizutani Kenji, president, Tokai Research and Consulting, Inc., Tokyo, June 19, 1996.

5. Interview with Yamada Kazuhiro and Yamada Hiroko, Futokumachi, Kanagawa Prefecture, June 22, 1996.

6. Interview with Otsuka Tatsujo, attorney, Yokohama, June 19, 1996.

7. Interview with Shitara Kiyotsugu, general manager, Tokyo Managers' Union, Tokyo, June 8, 1996.

8. Interview with Kikawada Hiroshi, Tokyo Managers' Union, Tokyo, June 15, 1996.

9. Interview with Muto Emiko, Tokyo Women's Union, Tokyo, June 24, 1996.

10. Interview with Ito Midori, executive chairman, Tokyo Women's Union, Tokyo, June 15, 1996.

11. Interview with Baba Hiroshi, director, Careers Planning Section, Waseda University, Tokyo, June 26, 1996.

12. Interview with Ito Aya and Hamanaka Akiko, Tsuda Women's College, Tokyo, June 27, 1996.

13. Interview with Sugiyama Keiko, Hokkaido Education University, June 27, 1996.

14. Interview with Hayashi Masahiko, deputy director, Policy Planning Division, Women's Bureau, MOE, June 17, 1996.

15. Interview with Reverend Sasaki Toshiya, Sanya Welfare Center for Workers, Nihon-Dutsumi Church UCCI, Sanya District, Tokyo, June 23, 1996.

16. Interview with Fujiwara Mariko, director, Hakuhodo Institute of Life and Living, Tokyo, June 14, 1996.

17. Interview with Nambu Yasuyuki, CEO, Pasona, Tokyo, June 24, 1996.

18. Interview with Nakauchi Isao, chairman, The Daiei, Inc., Tokyo, June 20, 1996.

19. Interview with Nakatani Iwao, Hitotsubashi University, June 13, 1996.

20. Interview with Kikuchi Tetsuro, columnist, *Mainichi*, June 7, 1996.

Notes to Conclusion

1. "Japan May Wane as China's Star Rises," *Japan Times,* November 22, 2001.

2. "Koizumi Opens Southeast Asia Trip with Vague Cooperation Proposal," *Japan Digest,* January 10, 2002.

3. "Tokyo, Bested by China, Will Scramble for Free Trade Pact with ASEAN," *Japan Digest,* January 8, 2002.

4. "Instead of FTA with ASEAN, Koizumi Offers Vague 'Comprehensive Partnership,' " *Japan Digest*, January 15, 2002.

5. Simon Pritchard, "Emerging Mainland May Eclipse Land of Setting Sun," *South China Morning Post,* January 11, 2002.

6. Michael H. Armacost and Kenneth B. Pyle, "Japan and the Engagement of

China: Challenges for U.S. Policy Coordination," *NBR Analysis* 12, no. 5.

7. Ministry of Economy, Trade, and Industry, "External Economic Policy Challenges in the 21st Century," in *White Paper on International Trade 2001: Key Points* (Tokyo: METI, May 18, 2001).

8. Nicholas R. Lardy, *China in the World Economy* (Washington, DC, Institute for International Economics, 1994).

9. Edith Terry, "Dai Rolls Rate Cut Dice," *South China Morning Post*, February 22, 2002.

10. Earl H. Kinmonth, "NBR's Japan Forum (Econ), Land Prices in Japan—The Chinese Connection," email sent March 28, 2002.

11. Interview with Takeuchi Akio, managing executive officer, Mizuho Corporate Bank, Hong Kong, March 28, 2002.

12. Edith Terry, "Mizuho Moves on Asia," *South China Morning Post,* April 4, 2002.

13. Yen 268 billion at US$1:Yen 119.23.

14. Yen 2.3 trillion.

15. Yen 11.9 trillion.

16. Yen 91.9 billion.

17. Yen 432 billion, at US$:Yen 99.1.

18. "Land Prices: Structural Problems Exert Downward Pressure," *Nikkei Interactive,* March 27, 2002 (http://www.nni.nikkei.co.jp).

19. Yen 163.4 trillion.

20. Chalmers Johnson, "Japanese 'Capitalism' Revisited," JPRI Occasional Paper no. 22, August 2001 (Cardiff, CA: Japan Policy Research Institute, 2001).

Glossary:
Acronyms and Terms

Ajia Fukuken (Asian reinstatement or restoration). From the title of an influential article by Japanese Foreign Ministry Asia expert Ogura Kazuo, "Ajia no Fukuken no tame ni" (For the restoration of Asia), *Chuo koron*, no. 7 (July 1993).

APEC. Asia Pacific Economic Cooperation. Grouping of Asian and other Pacific Rim nations (North and South American countries bordering on the Pacific, as well as Australia, New Zealand, and Pacific Island states) established in 1989. Although originally focusing exclusively on trade and investment issues, APEC has included since 1993 an annual summit of regional heads of government. In 2000, its twenty-one economies represented a GNP of $18 trillion, accounting for 43.85 percent of world trade. For current details, see APEC's web site at www.apecsec.org.sg.

ARF. ASEAN Regional Forum. Founded in 1994, ARF was the first regionwide governmental organization for consultation on security issues, including the Northeast Asian economies of China, Japan, and South Korea. In 2000, North Korea joined as an observer. See ARF's web site at www.asean.or.id.

ASEAN. Association for Southeast Asian Nations. Founded in 1967 by Indonesia, Malaysia, the Philippines, Singapore, and Thailand to address economic and trade issues, ASEAN had created by the late 1990s a free trade zone (FTZ) and expanded its membership to include Brunei, Cambodia, Laos, Myanmar, and Vietnam. By the late 1990s, the economic grouping developed a significant security dimension, through ARF, and dialogue with China, Korea and Japan through the ASEAN Plus Three meetings. Its members represent a GNP of $685 billion and a population of 500 million. See ASEAN's web site at www.asean.or.id.

ASEM. Asia Europe Meeting. France and Singapore initiated these biannual meetings of heads of government of ten Asian and fifteen European countries. See ASEM's web site at www.asemconnect.com.sg/welcome.html.

bakufu (historically, literally, "tent government"). The word originally referred to the residence of the commander of the Inner Palace Guards. The Japanese military governments that prevailed from 1192 to 1867 were presided over by military dictators called *shoguns*. The Tokugawa *bakufu* from 1603 to 1867 was the third such government, following the Kamakura and Muromachi shogunates.

CINCPAC. Commander in Chief, Pacific Command. The commander of the U.S. Pacific forces, including the California-based Third Fleet and Japan-based Seventh Fleet, is in charge of 100,000 forward-deployed troops and reports directly to the secretary of defense and the president of the United States. CINCPAC headquarters is at Camp H.M. Smith in Honolulu, Hawaii. See CINCPAC's web site at www.pacom.mil.

daimyo (historically, literally, "large landholders"). The *daimyo* were military lords commanding the allegiance of *samurai* warriors, who were in turn vassals of the *shogun*, the military overlord. During the Tokugawa period, from 1603 to 1867, the *daimyo* were required to live for six months or one year every two years in Edo, as a means of enforcing greater control over their activities. The *daimyo* had broad powers in administering their domains as long as they kept the peace, refrained from building ocean-going vessels, and suppressed Christianity.

Dai Toa Kaigi (Greater East Asian assembly). This assembly launched the Greater East Asia Co-Prosperity Sphere in Tokyo in November 1943.

Dai Toa Kyoeiken (Greater East Asia co-prosperity sphere). Proclaimed by Japanese foreign minister Matsuoka Yosuke in August 1940, the "co-prosperity sphere" was to encompass the countries originally included in Prince Konoe Fumimaro's "New Order in East Asia"—Japan, China, and the puppet state of Manchukuo—as well as the Dutch East Indies and French Indochina.

Dai Toa Senso (Greater East Asian war). The war began with Sino-Japanese hostilities in 1937 and continued through the entry of the Allied Powers in December 1941. Tokyo officially announced the term—signifying an expansion of the China conflict—shortly after the Pearl Harbor attack.

Dai Toa Sho (Greater East Asia ministry). The Japanese imperial government established the ministry to run its new Asian colonies. The *Dai Toa Sho* took over responsibilities of the Asia Development Board, which was created in 1938 to manage the economic affairs of China and Manchukuo.

Datsu A, Nyu Ou (Reject Asia, embrace Europe). The slogan originally derived from the title of an influential essay written by Fukuzawa Yukichi.

Datsu Ou, Nyu A (Reject Europe, embrace Asia). This slogan was an inversion of the Fukuzawa theme and became popular in the 1990s.

EAEC. East Asian Economic Caucus. This was the second iteration of a proposal by Malaysian prime minister Mahathir bin Mohamad to form an Asian economic grouping excluding Anglo-American members, specifically the United States, Canada, Australia, and New Zealand. In its watered-down version, also proposed by Mahathir in April 1991, the EAEC would form a caucus or subgrouping within APEC.

EAEG. East Asian Economic Group. This was to be an exclusive economic grouping of Asian nations proposed by Malaysian prime minister Mahathir in December 1990, serving as a counterpoint to the newly organized APEC. He argued that APEC would be dominated by the United States and thus incapable of representing Asian interests. Mahathir frequently and unsuccessfully solicited Japan to organize the entity, and maintained pressure on the issue well into the late 1990s.

endaka (high-yen). The phrase generally refers to instances of rapid yen appreciation as a result of coordinated currency intervention and signaling by the Group of Seven industrial economies, beginning with the Plaza Accord in 1985.

endaka fukyo (high-yen recession). This recession followed the September 1985 Plaza Accord, lasting from June 1985 to November 1986.

EPA. Economic Planning Agency. The Japanese government agency responsible for the income-doubling growth plan of the 1960s.

EU. European Union.

FASID. Foundation for Advanced Studies on International Development. Founded in 1990 as a joint subagency of the Ministry of Foreign Affairs and the Ministry of Education, FASID's mission is to train Japanese development professionals. See FASID's web site at www.fasid.or.jp.

Fukoku kyohei (rich nation, strong army). A slogan taken up by anti-Tokugawa forces of the mid-nineteenth century and used by the Meiji government (1868–1912) to support industrial strategy to catch up with the West, economically and militarily.

ganko keitai (flying in formation) as geese do. The figurative image was used to describe a model of dynamic hierarchy of economies in various stages of "catch-up" development.

gankoteki keizai hattenron (literally, "theory of formation-like economic development"). The phrase is generally translated into English as the "flying-geese" theory of economic development.

GATT. General Agreement on Tariffs and Trade.

Greater East Asia Co-Prosperity Sphere. See above, Dai Toa Kyoeiken.

IDE. Institute of Developing Economies. It is known in Japanese as the *Ajia Keizai Kenkyujo* (Institute of Asian Economies) and is now based in Makuhari, outside Tokyo, after a 1998 merger with the Japan External Trade Organization. IDE was established in 1958 as a dependency of the Ministry of International Trade and Industry; its principal mission is to gather data on Asian and Middle Eastern economies, Japan's main sources of raw materials and energy. IDE maintains a huge database on Asian economies and it is partially accessible through the United Nations Development Program, which maintains an office inside the institute. See IDE's web site at www.ide.go.jp.

IMF. International Monetary Fund.

izakaya. Traditional Japanese pubs, serving beer, sake, *shochu*, and a variety of hors d'oeuvres.

JBIC. Japan Bank for International Cooperation. A bank for new development established in October 1999, JBIC merged the former Japan Export-Import Bank and the Overseas Economic Cooperation Fund. See JBIC's web site at www.jbic.go.jp.

JETRO. A subagency of the Ministry for International Cooperation and Development. JETRO performs intelligence gathering as well as trade and investment support activities. In the early 1990s, JETRO became the principal government agency providing support for foreign investors and importers to Japan. See JETRO's web site at www.jetro.go.jp.

JEXIM. Japan Export-Import Bank. JEXIM is Japan's leading project finance institution, providing long-term loans and guarantees for Japanese infrastructure and manufacturing projects in high-risk developing countries. It merged in 1999 with the Overseas Economic Cooperation Fund; the two long shared a headquarters building near the Otemachi section of Tokyo.

Jomon Era. A Neolithic hunting and fishing culture in Japan. It existed from 10,000 B.C. to A.D. 300 and was named for its distinctive cord-marked pottery.

kakaku hakai (price destruction). The phrase marked the introduction of discount pricing in Japan in the early 1990s.

Kamigami no kuni (country of the gods). The phrase became associated with emperor worship. In the spring of 2000, newly minted Prime Minister Mori Yoshiro created ripples of alarm across Asia by declaring to a Shinto political organization that Japan was the *Kamigami no kuni*, a "divine country with the emperor at its center."

karaoke (literally, "empty orchestra"). Outrageously popular form of entertainment in which the participants sing to an orchestral recording, usually with a monitor providing lyrics, visuals, and a "dancing dot" to help participants follow the tune.

keiretsu ("linked" companies, or companies arrayed in a "series"). These are giant conglomerates that duplicated the assets and functions of the pre–World War Two *zaibatsu* (financial cliques) outlawed by the U.S. Occupation government. The *keiretsu* are fundamental to the corporatism of Japan, Inc. Unlike the *zaibatsu*, *keiretsu* are linked through cross-shareholdings, informal organizations of their chief executive officers, and noncontractual agreements that guide the corporate practices of entities controlling hundreds of billions of dollars in assets. *Keiretsu* are such a familiar feature of corporate Japan that they have become the subject of numerous popular handbooks as well as the encyclopedic data compilations by Toyo Keizai and other publishing houses. The older *keiretsu* are described as "horizontal" organizations and centered on banks or insurance companies. Newer *keiretsu* are vertical organizations of manufacturers and subcontractors, such as Toyota or NEC. Both types have survived remarkably intact through the stagnant economy of Japan in the 1990s but are said to be increasingly less relevant to the economy overall.

kendo (traditional Japanese fencing), usually practiced with wooden swords.

Kimigayo. Japan's national anthem. Unofficial before it was officially adopted, Kimigayo was resurrected together with the Japanese "rising sun" flag in 1999.

kodo (the Japanese "imperial way"). The term is associated with emperor worship and the militarist regime of the 1930s.

kokutai ("national polity" or "national essence"). The term usually is associated with the concept of the emperor descending in an unbroken imperial line, thus linking Japan and the Japanese with the gods.

Kwantung Army. The Kwantung (Guandong) Army. The army was commissioned in 1906 to guard parts of Chinese territory ceded to Japan after the Russo-Japanese War of 1904–5. The Kwantung Army later intrigued to seize all of Manchuria, moved into Inner Mongolia, and confronted the Soviet Union, which was perceived as its chief enemy after 1931.

Manchukuo. The puppet state established by the Kwantung Army in Manchuria and part of Inner Mongolia in 1931.

Meiji Ishin. Meiji Restoration of 1868.

Meiji Restoration. A political coup in January 1868. It occurred when the *daimyo* of Satsuma and Choshu seized the Imperial Palace in Kyoto and proclaimed the "restoration" of the Meiji emperor as head of government as well as titular head of state. The coup marked the toppling of the Tokugawa shogunate and the birth of modern Japan.

METI. The Japanese Ministry of Economy, Trade and Industry, formerly MITI.

MITI. The Japanese Ministry of International Trade and Industry.

MOF. The Japanese Ministry of Finance.

Nihon Keizai Shimbun (Japan economic journal). Japan's leading business and financial newspaper, headquartered in the Otemachi District of Tokyo.

Nikkan kogyo (Japan industrial daily). Published by the same publishing company as the *Nihon keizai shimbun.*

Nikkei. Short form of the *Nihon Keizai Shimbun.*

nio (benevolent kings). The word refers often to a pair of sculptures, depicting burly, grimacing warriors flanking a temple gate.

OECF. Overseas Economic Cooperation Fund. Japan's premier soft-loan agency for developing countries, which in 1999 merged with the Japan Export-Import Bank to form the Japan Bank for International Cooperation.

oyagaisha. Lead company in a *keiretsu* grouping.

PBEC. Pacific Basin Economic Council. A government, academic, and business forum founded by Japan and Australia in 1967. For details, see PBEC's web site at www.pbec.org/home.

PECC. The Pacific Economic Cooperation Council. The first Asia-Pacific government-to-government forum on economic cooperation issues, designed and launched by Japan in 1980. For details, see PECC's web site (under US. Committee) at www.pecc.org/ie.html.

Pia. A weekly magazine featuring Tokyo events.

rikishi. An aspiring sumo wrestler.

ristora (corporate restructuring).

ryotei. Elegant traditional drinking houses, with an exclusive clientele, where business is conducted with the assistance of discreet women trained in traditional dance and conversational arts.

sento. (Japanese communal bathhouses).

shogun (formally, the *seii tai shogun,* or literally, "barbarian subduing commander in chief"). Head of the military governments that ruled Japan from the twelfth to the nineteenth centuries.

Sumo. Japan's national sport of wrestling, a 2,000-year-old game in which the object is to force one's opponent out of the ring (*dohyo*), or to touch the outside with some part of the body other than the feet.

Toa Shinchitsujo (New Order in East Asia). Proclaimed by the government of Prime Minister Konoe Fumimaro in 1930, the New Order established a joint Sino-Japanese government in China.

tojin (person of the Tang Dynasty), synonymous with foreigner in nineteenth-century Japanese.

Tojin Orai. (A primer on foreigners), an essay written by Fukuzawa Yukichi between 1861 and 1863.

uji (clans). They formed the basic unit of governance in Japan at the time of initial contact with Chinese civilization and culture.

WTO. World Trade Organization. For details, see the WTO's web site at www.wto.org.

Yayoi Era. The period from 300 B.C. to A.D. 300, associated with the first use of bronze and iron and intensive agriculture in Japan.

yokozuna (*Sumo* grand champion).

A Note on Japanese Names

I have followed the Japanese order for names, giving surname first, followed by the personal name—just the opposite of the normal Western convention in presenting Japanese names, with personal name first followed by surname. This is also the Japanese practice when presenting their names for foreign consumption. I have used the domestic Japanese norm in order to retain a quality that otherwise might become lost in translation, reflecting both the rhythm of the language and a subtle element of identity. Names are special. Changes in order and orthography are almost always deliberate. The order of names may confuse those from other cultures, speaking other languages, and it was in this spirit that Chinese, Japanese, and many others adopted Anglo-American formats for their names when traveling abroad. The Japanese have carried the practice further than others, however, to the extent that it has become one more way of magnifying the differences between Japan and other countries.

The order of names becomes a way of distinguishing levels of Japaneseness. Long-term Japanese expatriates often find that their countrymen and women refer to them as they would to foreigners, using the *katakana* alphabet to transcribe their names instead of the original Chinese-Japanese characters. One of two Japanese phonetic scripts, *katakana* was originally developed to transcribe the phonetics of Chinese texts. A small matter, but Japan ought to abandon the duality of names that are presented one way at home, another way when dealing with foreigners.

The "norm," it should be emphasized, is Japanese. Japanese officials and executives often keep two sets of name cards. Their Japanese name cards are in Japanese order and their foreign business cards follow Western order. Thus, Morita Akio, the late chairman of Sony, became Akio Morita when meeting foreigners or traveling abroad. There was a certain pride in this—Japanese mastering a Western game—but also a deep insecurity, in mastering the game on Western terms, not Japanese.

By contrast, the Chinese have rarely fiddled around with the order of their names, except when living or traveling abroad, and Western publications abide by their rules. Since the early 1980s, the West has adopted not only

Chinese word order in names but also the strained, Russian language–filtered pinyin script. This was by no means a casual decision. The normalization of diplomatic relations between China and the United States in 1979 triggered the use. Afterwards, Peking suddenly became Beijing and Deng Xiaoping was never again Teng Hsiao-p'ing. Spelling is hardly among the most profound of political markers. Nonetheless, it was one of the ironies of the late twentieth century that Japan remained stranded in the formal devices underlining its historical quest for equality with the West, while China set its own terms, in language as in big-power politics.

Bibliography

Books

Akranasee, Narongchai. *ASEAN-Japan Relations: Trade and Development.* Workshop and conference proceedings sponsored by the Japan Center for International Exchange and the ASEAN Economic Research Unit, Institute for Southeast Asian Studies, December 5–6, 1981, and May 20–23, 1982, Singapore and Oiso, Japan, respectively.

Akyuz, Yilmaz. *East Asian Development: New Perspectives.* London: Frank Cass, 1999.

Anderson, Benedict R. O'G. *Some Aspects of Indonesian Politics under the Japanese Occupation, 1944–1945.* Ithaca, N.Y.: Cornell University, Department of Far Eastern Studies, Southeast Asia Program, Modern Indonesia Project, 1961.

Aoki, Masahiko, Kim Hyung-ki, and Okuno-Fujiwara Masahiro, eds. *The Role of Government in East Asian Economic Development: Comparative Institutional Analysis.* Oxford: Clarendon Press, 1997.

Ariff, Mohamed. *The Malaysian Economy: Pacific Connections.* New York: Oxford University Press, 1991.

Asia Society and Japan Society. *Japan's Economic Role in East Asia: Implications for U.S. Business.* New York: The Asia Society and Japan Society, 1983.

Asian Development Bank (ADB). *Emerging Asia: Changes and Challenges.* Principal authors, David Bloom and Jeffrey Sachs. Manila, Philippines: ADB, 1997.

Barnhart, Michael A. *Japan Prepares for Total War: The Search for Economic Security, 1919–1941.* Ithaca, N. Y.: Cornell University Press, 1987.

Bartu, Friedemann. *The Ugly Japanese: Nippon's Economic Empire in Asia.* Singapore: Longman Singapore, 1992.

Beasley, W.G. *Japanese Imperialism, 1894–1945.* New York: Oxford University Press, 1987.

Biers, Dan. *Crash of '97: How the Financial Crisis Is Reshaping Asia.* Hong Kong: Review Publishing, 1998.

Bridges, Brian. *Japan and Korea in the 1990s: From Antagonism to Adjustment.* Aldershot: Edward Elgar, 1993.

Buruma, Ian. *God's Dust: A Modern Asian Journey.* London: Jonathan Cape, 1989.

———. *The Wages of Guilt: Memories of War in Germany and Japan.* New York: Farrar, Straus & Giroux, 1994.

Campos, Jose Edgardo, and Hilton L. Root. *The Key to the Asian Miracle: Making Shared Growth Credible.* Washington, D.C.: The Brookings Institution, 1996.

Chang, Iris. *The Rape of Nanking: The Forgotten Holocaust of World War II.* New York: Basic Books, 1997.

Chung, Il Yung, ed. *The Asian-Pacific Community in the Year 2000: Challenges and Prospects*. Seoul: Sejong Institute, 1991.

Clark, Cal, and Steve Chan, eds. *The Evolving Pacific Basin in the Global Political Economy*. Boulder, Colo.: Lynne Rienner, 1992.

Clifford, Mark L. *Troubled Tiger: Businessmen, Bureaucrats, and Generals in South Korea*. Armonk, N.Y.: M.E. Sharpe, 1998.

Clifford, Mark L., and Pete Engardio. *Meltdown: Asia's Boom, Bust, and Beyond*. Paramus, N.J.: Prentice-Hall, 1999.

Congressional Research Service (CRS). *An Asian-Pacific Regional Economic Organization: An Exploratory Concept Paper*. Prepared for the U.S. Senate, Committee on Foreign Relations, Washington, D.C.: Government Printing Office (GPO), July 1979.

———. *East Asia: Challenges for U.S. Economic and Security Interests in the 1990s*. Workshop sponsored by the CRS of the Library of Congress (LOC), the Woodrow Wilson International Center for Scholars, and the Committee on Ways and Means, June 29, 1988. Washington, D.C.: GPO, September 1988.

Constantino, Renato. *The Second Invasion: Japan in the Philippines*. Quezon City, Philippines: Karrel, Inc., 1989.

Crawford, Sir John, and Saburo Okita, eds. *Raw Materials and Pacific Economic Integration*. Vancouver: University of British Columbia Press, 1978.

Cronin, Richard P. *Asian Financial Crisis: An Analysis of U.S. Foreign Policy Interests and Options*. CRS Report for Congress, updated April 23, 1998. Washington, D.C.: CRS, LOC, 1998.

———. *Japan, the United States and Prospects for the Asia-Pacific Century: Three Scenarios for the Future*. Singapore: Institute for Southeast Asian Studies, 1992.

Curtis, Gerald L., ed. *The United States, Japan, and Asia: Challenges for U.S. Policy*. New York: W.W. Norton, 1994.

Delhaise, Philippe F. *Asia in Crisis: The Implosion of the Banking and Finance Systems*. Singapore: John Wiley & Sons, 1998.

Dobson, Wendy. *Japan in East Asia: Trading and Investment Strategies*. Singapore: Institute of Southeast Asian Studies, 1993.

Doherty, Eileen M., ed. *Japanese Investment in Asia: International Production Strategies in a Rapidly Changing World: A Conference*. San Francisco: Asia Foundation, September 26–27, 1995.

Doner, Richard F. *Driving a Bargain: Automobile Industrialization and Japanese Firms in Southeast Asia*. Berkeley: University of California Press, 1991.

Dore, Ronald. *Flexible Rigidities: Industrial Policy and Structural Adjustment in the Japanese Economy, 1970–1980*. London: The Athlone Press, 1986.

———. *Taking Japan Seriously: A Confucian Perspective on Leading Economic Issues*. London: Athlone Press, 1987.

Dower, John W. *Embracing Defeat: Japan in the Wake of World War II*. New York: W.W. Norton, 1999.

———. *Empire and Aftermath: Yoshida Shigeru and the Japanese Experience, 1878–1954*. Cambridge, Mass.: Harvard University Press, 1988.

———. *Japan in War and Peace: Selected Essays*. New York: New Press, 1993.

———. *War without Mercy: Race and Power in the Pacific War*. New York: Pantheon Books, 1986.

———, ed. Introduction, "E.H. Norman, Japan, and the Uses of History." In *Origins of the Modern Japanese State: Selected Writings of E.H. Norman*. New York: Pantheon Books, 1975.

Duus, Peter, Ramon H. Myers, and Mark R. Peattie, eds. *The Japanese Wartime Empire, 1931–1945.* Princeton, N.J.: Princeton University Press, 1996.

Economic Cooperation Bureau, Ministry of Foreign Affairs (MOFA). *Japan's Official Development Assistance (ODA) Annual Report, 1998.* Tokyo: Association for Promotion of International Cooperation, 1999.

Economic Planning Agency (EPA), Research Department. *Ajia Keizai, 1995* (The Asian economy, 1995). Tokyo: Okurasho insatsukyoku, 1995, also 1996, 1998.

———. *Possibility of the Application of Japanese Experience from the Standpoint of the Developing Countries.* Conference report, Tokyo, November 14–15, 1994.

Ellison, Herbert J., ed. *Japan and the Pacific Quadrille: The Major Powers in East Asia.* Boulder, Colo.: Westview, 1987.

Emmott, Bill. *Japan's Global Reach: The Influences, Strategies, and Weaknesses of Japan's Multinational Companies.* London: Century Business, 1992.

———. *The Sun Also Sets: The Limits to Japan's Economic Power.* New York: Times Books, 1989.

Encarnation, Dennis J. *Rivals beyond Trade: America Versus Japan in Global Competition.* Ithaca, N.Y.: Cornell University Press, 1992.

Ensign, Margee M. *Doing Good or Doing Well? Japan's Foreign Aid Program.* New York: Columbia University Press, 1992.

Fallows, James. *Looking at the Sun: The Rise of the New East Asian Economic and Political System.* New York: Pantheon Books, 1994.

Francks, Penelope. *Japanese Economic Development, Theory and Practice.* London: Routledge, 1992.

Fujiwara, Hiro, and Tsuneo Tanaka. *Ajia no Zaibatsu to Kigyo Chizu A* (Map of Asian financial cliques and industrial groups). Tokyo: Nohon jitsugyosha, 1996.

Fukada, Yusuke. *Reimei no Seiki: Dai Toa Kaigi to sono shuyakutachi* (Daybreak of the century: The Greater East Asian Conference and its stars). Tokyo: Bungei shunju, 1991.

Fukuda, Shozo. *With Sweat and Abacus: Economic Roles of Southeast Asian Chinese on the Eve of World War II.* Translated by Les Oates; edited by George Hicks. Singapore: Select Books, 1994.

Fukuzawa, Yukichi. *The Autobiography of Fukuzawa Yukichi, with Preface to the Collected Works of Fukuzawa.* Translated by Eiichi Kiyooka. Tokyo: Hokuseido Press, 1981.

Funabashi, Yoichi. *Asia Pacific Fusion: Japan's Role in APEC.* Washington, D.C.: Institute for International Economics (IIE), 1995.

———. *Nihon no taigai koso: Reisigo no bijion o kaku* (Japan's idea for the world: An essay on a post–Cold War vision). Tokyo: Iwanami shoten, 1993.

Gao, Bai. *Economic Ideology and Japanese Industrial Policy: Developmentalism from 1931 to 1965.* Cambridge, U.K.: Cambridge University Press, 1997.

Garran, Robert. *Tigers Tamed: The End of the Asian Miracle.* Honolulu: University of Hawaii Press, 1998.

Gerlach, Michael. *Alliance Capitalism: The Social Organization of Japanese Business.* Berkeley: University of California Press, 1993.

Goldstein, Morris. *The Asian Financial Crisis: Causes, Cures, and Systemic Implications, Policy Analyses in International Economics.* IIE, no. 55. Washington, D.C.: June 1998.

Green, Michael J., and Patrick M. Cronin, eds. *The U.S.-Japan Alliance: Past, Present, and Future.* New York: Council on Foreign Relations, 1999.

Harrison, Selig, and Clyde V. Prestowitz, Jr., eds. *Asia after the Miracle: Redefining U.S. Economic and Security Priorities.* Washington, D.C.: Economic Strategy Institute, 1998.

Hatch, Walter, and Kozo Yamamura. *Asia in Japan's Embrace: Building a Regional Production Alliance.* Cambridge, U.K.: Cambridge University Press, 1996.

Healey, Derek. *Japanese Capital Exports and Asian Economic Development.* Paris: Development Centre of the Organization for Economic Cooperation and Development (OECD), 1991.

Henderson, Callum. *Asia Falling? Making Sense of the Asian Currency Crisis and Its Aftermath.* Singapore: McGraw-Hill, 1998.

Hicks, George. *The Comfort Women: Japan's Brutal Regime of Enforced Prostitution in the Second World War.* New York: W.W. Norton, 1994.

———. *Japan's War Memories: Amnesia or Concealment?* Aldershot: England: Ashgate, 1997.

Hill, Hal. *Foreign Investment and Industrialization in Indonesia.* Singapore: Oxford University Press, 1989.

Ho, Samuel P.S. *Economic Development of Taiwan, 1860–1970.* New Haven, Conn.: Yale University Press, 1978.

Hollerman, Leon. *Japan, Disincorporated: The Economic Liberalization Process.* Stanford, Calif.: Hoover Institution Press, 1988.

———. *Japan's Economic Strategy in Brazil: Challenges for the United States.* Lexington, Mass.: Lexington Books, 1988.

Holloway, Nigel, ed. *Japan in Asia: The Economic Impact on the Region.* Hong Kong: Review Publishing, 1991.

Ienaga, Saburo. *The Pacific War, 1931–1945: A Critical Perspective on Japan's Role in World War II.* New York: Pantheon Books, 1978. Translation of *Taiheiyo Senso* (Tokyo: Iwanami shoten, 1968).

Ikeido, Jun. *Hitome de wakaru Kigyo Guruupu no Renketsu Kakazu* (Understanding the linkages within the industrial groups at a glance). Tokyo: Nihon jitsugyo shupansha, 1998.

Imada, Pearl, Manuel Montes, and Seiji Naya. *A Free Trade Area: Implications for ASEAN.* Singapore: Institute of Southeast Asian Studies, ASEAN Economic Research Unit, 1991.

Inoue, Ryuichiro, Hirohasa Kohama, and Shujiro Urata. *Industrial Policy in East Asia.* Tokyo: Japan External Trade Organization (JETRO), 1993.

Institute of Developing Economies (IDE) and JETRO. *Can Asia Recover Its Vitality? Globalization and the Roles of Japanese and U.S. Corporations.* Proceedings of the JETRO-IDE Joint Symposium, Tokyo. Tokyo: IDE, 1998.

Institute of Fiscal and Monetary Policy, Ministry of Finance (MOF). *Contemporary Problems of the Financial System and Policy Options in ASEAN 4.* Tokyo: MOF, Printing Bureau, 1998.

International Monetary Fund (IMF). *International Financial Statistics, December 1997.* Washington, D.C.: 1997.

Iriye, Akira. *China and Japan in the Global Setting.* Cambridge, Mass.: Harvard University Press, 1992.

———. *The Origins of the Second World War in Asia and the Pacific.* London: Longman, 1987.

Iriye, Akira, and Warren Cohen, eds. *American, Chinese, and Japanese Perspectives on Wartime Asia, 1931–1949.* Wilmington, Del.: Scholarly Resources, 1990.

Islam, Shafiqul. *Yen for Development: Japanese Foreign Aid and the Politics of Burden-Sharing.* New York: Council on Foreign Relations, 1991.

Ito, Hiro, and Andrew Z. Szamosszegi. *A Cure for Japan's Sick Banks.* Washington, D.C.: Economic Strategy Institute, June 1998.

Jackson, Karl D., ed. *Asian Contagion: The Causes and Consequences of a Financial Crisis.* Boulder, Colo.: Westview, 1999.

James, William E., Seiji Naya, and Gerald M. Meier. *Asian Development: Economic Success and Policy Lessons.* Madison: University of Wisconsin Press, 1989.

Jansen, Marius B. *China in the Tokugawa World.* Cambridge, Mass.: Harvard University Press, 1992.

Japan Committee for Pacific Economic Outlook. *Changing Patterns of Foreign Direct Investment in the Pacific Region.* Background Papers for the Final Report 1: Orientation Papers, prepared for the Pacific Economic Cooperation Conference, Tokyo, March 1992.

Japan Society and Asia Society. *Summary Report: Global Implications of Japan's Changing Financial Structure and an International Yen: What's Ahead for Asia—A Two Conference Series.* New York: Japan Society and Asia Society.

Jeshurun, Chandran, ed. *China, India, Japan and the Security of Southeast Asia.* Singapore: Institute of Southeast Asian Studies, 1993.

JETRO. *China: A Business Guide—The Japanese Perspective on China's Opening Economy.* Tokyo: JETRO, 1979.

———. *Sekai to Nihon no Boeki, Boeki Hen, 1994 JETRO Hakusho* (Trade of Japan and the world, 1994 JETRO white paper). Trade edition. Tokyo: JETRO, 1994, also 1995, 1996, 1997, and 1998 editions.

———. *Sekai to Nihon no Kaigai Chokusetsu Toushi, 1993 JETRO Hakusho—Toushi Hen* (Foreign investment of Japan and the world—1993 JETRO white paper). Investment edition. Tokyo: JETRO, 1993, also 1995, 1996, 1998 editions.

———. *White Paper on International Trade, 1995.* Tokyo: JETRO, 1995.

Johnson, Chalmers. *Blowback: The Costs and Consequences of American Empire.* New York: Metropolitan Books, 2000.

———. *Japan: Who Governs? The Rise of the Developmental State.* New York: W.W. Norton, 1995.

———. *MITI and the Japanese Miracle: The Growth of Industrial Policy, 1925–1975.* Tokyo: Charles E. Tuttle, 1982.

Joint Economic Committee. *Japan's Economic Challenge: Study Papers Submitted to the Congress of the United States, Joint Economic Committee.* Washington, D.C.: GPO, 1990.

Jomo, K.S. et al. *Southeast Asia's Misunderstood Miracle: Industrial Policy and Economic Development in Thailand, Malaysia, and Indonesia.* Boulder, Colo.: Westview, 1997.

Jomo, K.S., ed. *Japan and Malaysian Development: In the Shadow of the Rising Sun.* London: Routledge, 1994.

———. *The Sun Also Sets: Lessons in "Looking East."* Kuala Lumpur: Institut Analisa Sosial Malaysia, 1985.

———. *Tigers in Trouble: Financial Governance, Liberalisation, and Crises in East Asia.* London: Zed Books, 1998.

Katz, Richard. *Japan: The System That Soured—The Rise and Fall of the Japanese Economic Miracle.* Armonk, N.Y.: M.E. Sharpe, 1998.

Katzenstein, Peter J., and Takashi Shiraishi, eds. *Network Power: Japan and Asia.* Ithaca, N.Y.: Cornell University Press, 1997.

Keenan, Faith, ed. *The Aftershock: How an Economic Earthquake Is Rattling Southeast Asian Politics.* Hong Kong: Review Publishing, 1998.

Kendall, Harry H., and Clara Joewono. *Japan, ASEAN, and the United States.* Berkeley: Institute of Southeast Asian Studies, University of California at Berkeley, 1991.

Kodama, Toshihiro, Hideshi Udea, and Toru Sunada. *Agenda for Industrial Policy in East Asian Countries.* Tokyo: MITI, Research Institute of International Trade and Industry, March 1994.

Koh, Tommy T.B. *The United States and East Asia: Conflict and Cooperation.* Singapore: Institute of Policy Studies, 1995.

Kojima Kiyoshi. *Japanese Direct Investment Abroad.* Mitaka, Tokyo: International Christian University, 1990.

Kojima, Kiyoshi, and Terutomo Ozawa. *Japan's General Trading Companies: Merchants of Economic Development.* Paris: OECD Development Center, 1984.

Komai, Hiroshi. *Japanese Management Overseas: Experiences in the United States and Thailand.* Tokyo: Asian Productivity Organization, 1989.

Komiya, Ryutaro, and Keiichi Yokobori. *Japan's Industrial Policies in the 1980s.* Tokyo: MITI, Research Institute of International Trade and Industry, March 1991.

Koppel, Bruce M., and Robert M. Orr, Jr., eds. *Japan's Foreign Aid: Power and Policy in a New Era.* Boulder Colo.: Westview, 1993.

Korhonnen, Pekka. *Japan and Asia Pacific Integration: Pacific Romances, 1968–1996.* London: Routledge, 1998.

Kunio, Yoshihara. *The Rise of Ersatz Capitalism in South-East Asia.* Quezon City, Philippines: Ateneo de Manila University Press, 1988.

Lebra, Joyce C. *Japanese-Trained Armies in Southeast Asia.* Hong Kong: Heinemann, 1977.

————, ed. *Japan's Greater East Asia Co-Prosperity Sphere in World War II: Selected Readings and Documents.* Kuala Lumpur: Oxford University Press, 1975.

Lim, Chee Peng, and Lee Poh Ping. *The Role of Japanese Direct Investment in Malaysia.* Occasional Paper, no. 60. Singapore: Institute of Southeast Asian Studies, 1979.

Lim, Linda Y.C., and Pang Eng Fong. *Foreign Direct Investment and Industrialisation in Malaysia, Singapore, Taiwan, and Thailand.* Paris: OECD Development Center, 1992.

Lincoln, Edward J. *Japan's Economic Role in Northeast Asia.* Lanham, Md.: University Press of America, 1987.

Little, I.M.D., D. Mazumdar, and John Page. *Small Manufacturing Enterprises: A Comparative Study of India and Other Countries.* New York: Oxford University Press, 1987.

McKenzie, Colin, and Michael Stutchbury. *Japanese Financial Markets and the Role of the Yen.* North Sydney, Australia: Allen & Unwin, 1992.

McLeod, Ross H., and Ross Garnaut, eds. *East Asia in Crisis: From Being a Miracle to Needing One?* London: Routledge, 1998.

McNamara, Dennis L. *The Colonial Origins of Korean Enterprise, 1910–1945.* Cambridge, U.K.: Cambridge University Press, 1990.

————. *Japan's New Global Role.* Washington, D.C.: The Brookings Institution, 1993.

————. *Japan's Rapidly Emerging Strategy toward Asia.* Paris: OECD, April 1992.

Mahathir, Mohamad, and Shintaro Ishihara. *No to Ieru Ajia* (The Asia that can say no). Tokyo: Kobunsha, 1994.

————. *The Voice of Asia: Two Leaders Discuss the Coming Century.* Translated by Frank Baldwin. Tokyo: Kodansha International, 1995.

Makino, Noboru. *Ajia 1995: Zen Yosoku* (Asia 1995: Comprehensive forecast). Compiled by Mitsubishi Research Institute. Tokyo: Daiyamondo sha, 1994.

Manglapus, Raul S. *Japan in Southeast Asia: Collision Course.* Washington, D.C.: Carnegie Endowment for International Peace, 1976.

Maswood, Syed Javed. *Japan and Protection: The Growth of Protectionist Sentiment and the Japanese Response.* London: Routledge, 1989.

Mendl, Wolf. *Japan's Asia Policy: Regional Security and Global Interests.* London: Routledge, 1995.

Ministry of Foreign Affairs (MOFA). *Economic Integration in the Asia-Pacific Region and the Options for Japan.* Tokyo: MOFA, Group on Asia-Pacific Economic Integration towards the Twenty-first Century, April 1993.

————, Economic Cooperation Bureau. *Japan's Official Development Assistance: Annual Report, 1993.* Tokyo: Association for Promotion of International Cooperation, 1994; also 1994, 1996, 1998.

————. *Outlook of Japan's Economic Cooperation.* Tokyo: MOFA, April 1992.

Ministry of International Trade and Industry (MITI). *Chusho Kigyo Hakusho, Heisei 8 Nenpan* (White paper on small and medium enterprise, heisei 8 edition). Tokyo: Okurasho insatsukyoku, 1996.

————. *Keizai Kyoryoku no Gencho to Mondaiten, Heisei 5 Nenpan.* (Economic cooperation: Current conditions and issues, heisei 5 edition). Tokyo: Tsusho sangyo chosakai chuppanbu, 1993; also heisei 6 edition, 1994.

————. *Vision for the Economy of the Asia-Pacific Region in the Year 2000* and *Tasks Ahead.* Proceedings of the APEC Ad Hoc Economic Group Meeting, August 10–11, 1992. Tokyo: MITI, 1992.

————, Industrial Policy Division, International Enterprises Section. *Waga Kuni Kigyo no Kaigai Jigyo Katsudo*, Dai 24 Kai (Overseas business activities of our national enterprises, no. 24). Tokyo: Okurasho insatsukyoku, 1995.

————, International Enterprises Section. *Waga Kuni Kigyo no Kaigai Jigyo Katsudo*, Dai 25 Kai (Overseas business activities of our national enterprises, no. 25). Tokyo: Okurasho insatsukyoku, 1996.

————. *Waga Kuni Kigyo no Kaigai Jigyo Katsudo*, Dai 26 Kai, Heisei 8 Nen Kaigai Jigo Katsudo Kihon Chosa, Dai 6 Kai (Overseas business activities of our national enterprises, no. 26, sixth basic survey of overseas business activities, heisei 8). Tokyo: Okurasho insatsukyoku, 1997.

Mitsubishi Research Institute. *Zen Yosoku Ajia, 1995* (All-Asia forecast, 1995). Tokyo: Diamond Publishers, 1994.

Miyoshi, Masao. *As We Saw Them: The First Japanese Embassy to the United States.* New York: Kodansha, 1994.

Mizutani, Kenji. *Migigata kudari no Nihon keizai (Japan's economy on the downslope).* Tokyo: PHP Institute, 1996.

Mochizuki, Mike. *Japan Reorients: The Quest for Wealth and Power in East Asia.* Washington, D.C.: The Brookings Institution, 2002.

Morley, James W., ed. *Driven by Growth: Political Change in the Asia-Pacific Region.* Armonk, N.Y.: M.E. Sharpe, 1993.

Morris-Suzuki, Tessa. *A History of Japanese Economic Thought.* London: Routledge, 1989.

Murphy, R. Taggart. *The Weight of the Yen.* New York: W.W. Norton, 1996.

Muscat, Robert J. *The Fifth Tiger: A Study of Thai Development Policy.* Armonk, N.Y.: M.E. Sharpe, 1994.

Myers, Ramon H. *The Japanese Economic Development of Manchuria.* New York: Garland Publishing, 1982.

Myers, Ramon H., and Mark R. Peattie. *The Japanese Colonial Empire, 1895–1945.* Princeton, N.J.: Princeton University Press, 1984.

Nakatani, Iwao. *Nihon Keizai no Rekishiteki Tenkan* (The historical transformation of the Japanese economy). Tokyo: Toyo keizai shinposha, 1996.

Naya, Seiji. *Is the United States Missing the Boat in ASEAN? A Comparison of U.S. and Japanese Trade and Investment Experience.* Economic Brief, no. 1. Honolulu: Institute for Economic Development and Policy, East-West Center, 1989.

Naya, Seiji, with the assistance of Pearl Imada. *Towards an ASEAN Trade Area.* Kuala Lumpur: Institute of Strategic and International Studies, Malaysia, in collaboration with the Resource Systems Institute, East-West Center, Hawaii, 1987.

Nester, William R. *The Foundation of Japanese Power: Continuities, Changes, Challenges.* London: MacMillan, 1990.

———. *Japan and the Third World: Patterns, Power, Prospects.* London: MacMillan, 1992.

———. *Japan's Growing Power over East Asia and the World Economy: Ends and Means.* Hondmils: MacMillan, 1990.

Nishihara, Masashi. *The Japanese and Sukarno's Indonesia: Tokyo-Jakarta Relations, 1951–1966.* Monographs of the Center for Southeast Asian Studies, Kyoto University. Honolulu: East-West Center Books, 1976.

Noble, Gregory W. *Trojan Horse or Boomerang? Two-Tiered Investment in the Asian Auto Complex.* Berkeley Roundtable on the International Economy (BRIE) Working Paper 90, November 1996. Berkeley: University of California at Berkeley, 1996.

Noguchi, Yukio. *1940 Nen Taisei Sareba "Senji Keizai"* (The 1940s system, or the wartime economy). Tokyo: Toyo keizai shinposha, 1995.

Nolan, Peter. *China and the Global Economy.* Houndsmills, Palgrave, 2001.

Noland, Marcus *Pacific Basin Developing Countries: Prospects for the Future.* Washington, D.C.: IDE, 1990.

Noland, Marcus, et al. *Global Economic Effects of the Asian Currency Devaluations, Policy Analyses in International Economics.* Institute for International Economics (IIE), no. 56 (July 1998). Washington, D.C.: IIE, 1998.

Nomura Research Institute (NRI) and the Institute of Southeast Asian Studies. *The New Wave of Foreign Direct Investment in Asia.* Singapore: Institute of Southeast Asian Studies, 1995.

Numnonda, Thamsook. *Thailand and the Japanese Presence, 1941–1945.* Singapore: Institute of Southeast Asian Studies, 1977.

OECD. *OECD Economic Surveys: Japan.* Paris: OECD, 1991.

———. *Trade with Asia: A Reference Aid.* McLean, Va.: Central Intelligence Agency, Directorate of Intelligence, February 1992.

———, Development Assistance Committee. *Aid Review 1990/1991: Report by the Secretariat and Questions for the Review of Japan.* Paris: OECD, 1991.

Ohmae, Kenichi. *Ajiajin to Nihonjin* (Asians and Japanese; subtitled: *Japan in Asia's new map: A dialogue with Dr. Mahathir Mohamad*). Tokyo: Shogakkan, 1994.

Ohno, Izumi. *Sekai Ginko: Kaihatsu Enjo Senryaku no Henkaku* (The World Bank: A revolution in development aid strategy). Tokyo: NTT shuppan kabukushigaisha, October 2000.

Ohno, Kenichi. *Tojo Kuni no Gurobarizeshon: Jiretsuteki Hatten wa Kanoka* (The globalization of developing countries: Is self-reliant development possible?). Tokyo: Toyo keizai shinposha, October 2000.

Ohno, Kenichi, and Ohno Izumi, eds. *Japanese Views on Economic Development: Diverse Paths to the Market*. Studies in Growth Economies of Asia, 15. London: Routledge, 1998.

Ohsono, Tomokazu. *Ajia o Yomu Chizu (A Reading Map of Asia): "Asian Dynamism"– Latest Data on the Changing Economy, Government, Nation, and Military*. Tokyo: Kodansha, 1994.

Okita, Saburo. *Japan in the World Economy of the 1980s*. Tokyo: University of Tokyo Press, 1989.

———. *Steps to the Twenty-first Century*. Tokyo: *Japan Times*, 1993.

———. *Tightrope: Balancing Economics and Responsibility in Japanese Diplomacy, 1979–1980*. Tokyo: Toyo keizai shinposha, 1992.

Ono, Shuichi. *Sino-Japanese Economic Relationships*. World Bank Discussion Papers, 146, China and Mongolia Department Series. Washington, D.C.: World Bank, 1992.

Orr, Robert M. *The Emergence of Japan's Foreign Aid Power*. New York: Columbia University Press, 1990.

Oshima, Harry T. *Economic Growth in Monsoon Asia: A Comparative Survey*. Tokyo: University of Tokyo Press, 1987.

———. *Strategic Process in Monsoon Asia's Economic Development*. Hitotsubashi University, Discussion Paper Series B, no. 9. Tokyo: Institute of Economic Research, August 1991.

Overseas Economic Cooperation Fund Japan (OECF). *Japanese Contribution to Economic Development of Malaysia through OECF Loans*. Tokyo: OECF, March 1989.

———. *Japan's Contribution to Economic Development in Indonesia through OECF Loans*. Tokyo: OECF, March 1992.

———. *OECF Economic Report Malaysia: Growing Economy and Anticipated Bottlenecks of Infrastructure and Manpower in Comparison with the Case of Thailand*. Kuala Lumpur: OECF Kuala Lumpur Office, March 1990.

———. *Outline of OECF's Economic Cooperation in Malaysia*. Kuala Lumpur: OECF Kuala Lumpur Office, March 1991.

———. *Thirtieth Anniversary Symposium: Experience of East Asian Economic Development, Proceedings*. Tokyo: OECF, March 4–5, 1992.

Ozawa, Ichiro. *Blueprint for a New Japan: The Rethinking of a Nation*. Translated by Louisa Rubenfein; edited by Eric Gower. New York: Kodansha, 1994.

Ozawa, Terutomo. *Recycling Japan's Surpluses for Developing Countries*. Paris: OECD Development Center, 1989.

Palat, Ravi Arvind, ed. *Pacific-Asia and the Future of the World-System*. Westport, Conn.: Greenwood Press, 1993.

Patrick, Hugh. *Asia's New Giant: How the Japanese Economy Works*. Washington, D.C.: The Brookings Institution, 1976.

Phongpaichit, Pasuk. *The New Wave of Japanese Investment in ASEAN: Determinants and Prospects*. Singapore: Institute of Southeast Asian Studies, 1990.

Prestowitz, Clyde V., Jr. *Trading Places: How We Are Giving Our Future to Japan and How to Reclaim It*. New York: Basic Books, 1989.

Pyle, Kenneth B. *The Japanese Question: Power and Purpose in a New Era*. Washington, D.C.: American Enterprise Institute Press, 1992.

Reischauer, Edwin O. *Wanted: An Asian Policy.* New York, Knopf, 1955.

Reischauer, Edwin O., and John K. Fairbank. *East Asia: The Great Tradition.* Boston, Mass.: Houghton Mifflin, 1960.

Research Project Team for Japanese Systems. *Masuda Foundation, Japanese Systems: An Alternative Civilization?* Yokohama: SEKOTAC, 1992.

Rix, Alan. *Japan's Foreign Aid Challenge: Policy Reform and Aid Leadership.* London: Routledge, 1993.

Rohwer, Jim. *Asia Rising: Why America Will Prosper As Asia's Economies Boom.* New York: Simon & Schuster, 1995.

Rostow, W.W. *Eisenhower, Kennedy, and Foreign Aid.* Austin: University of Texas Press, 1985.

Round Table on Japan and the Asia-Pacific Region in the Twenty-first Century. *Japan and the Asia-Pacific Region in the Century-Promotion of Openness and Respect for Plurality.* Typed manuscript. Tokyo: Office of the Prime Minister, December 25, 1992.

Rutter, Owen. *Through Formosa: An Account of Japan's Island Colony.* Original edition. London: T. Fisher Unwin, 1923; Taipei: SMC, 1990.

Sakakibara, Eisuke. *Beyond Capitalism: The Japanese Model of Market Economics.* Lanham, Md.: University Press of America, 1993.

Sandhu, Kernial Singh, and Eileen P.T. Tang, eds. *Japan As an Economic Power and Its Implications for Southeast Asia.* Singapore: Singapore University Press for the Institute of Southeast Asian Studies, June 1974.

Sasakawa Peace Foundation (SPF). *Outlook for a New Asia and Japan's Response: A Report of the Japanese Committee on the Outlook for a New Asia to the Commission for a New Asia.* Tokyo: SPF, 1994.

———. *Towards a New Asia: Report of the Commission for a New Asia.* Tokyo: SPF, 1994.

Sazanami, Yoko et al. *The Global Trend toward Regional Integration.* Tokyo: Foreign Press Center, Japan, 1993.

Scalapino, Robert A., and Masataka Kosaka, eds. *Peace, Politics and Economics in Asia: The Challenge to Cooperate.* McLean, Va.: Pergamon-Brassey's International Defense Publishers, 1988.

Scalapino, Robert A., and Lewis Coleman. *America's Role in Asia: Interests and Policies: Report of a Working Group Convened by the Asia Foundation's Center for Asian Pacific Studies.* San Francisco: Asia Foundation, Center for Asian Pacific Affairs.

Schlesinger, Jacob M. *Shadow Shoguns: The Rise and Fall of Japan's Postwar Machine.* Stanford, Calif.: Stanford University Press, 1999.

Sekiguchi, Sueo, ed. *ASEAN-Japan Relations: Investment.* Workshop and Conference Proceedings Organized by the Japan Center for International Exchange and the ASEAN Economic Research Unit of the Institute for Southeast Asian Studies, December 5–6, 1981, and May 20–23, 1982, Singapore and Oiso, Japan, respectively.

Shibusawa, Masahide et al. *Pacific Asia in the 1990s.* London: Routledge, 1992.

Shiode, Hirokazu. *Japanese Investment in Southeast Asia: Three Malaysian Case Studies.* Kowloon and Hong Kong: Center for the Progress of Peoples, 1989.

Smith, Patrick. *Japan: A Reinterpretation.* New York: Vintage Books, 1998.

Stephan, John J. *Hawaii Under the Rising Sun: Japan's Plans for Conquest after Pearl Harbor.* Honolulu: University of Hawaii Press, 1984.

Steven, Rob. *Japan's New Imperialism.* Armonk, N.Y.: M.E. Sharpe, 1990.

Stokes, Bruce. *The Inevitability of Managed Trade: The Future Strategic Trade Policy Debate.* New York: Japan Society, 1990.

Sunada, Toru, Michiko Kiji, and Makoto Chigira. *Japan's Direct Investment in East Asia: Changing Division of Labor and Technology Transfer in the Household Electric Appliance Industry.* Tokyo: MITI, Research Institute of International Trade and Industry, March 1993.

Sung Yun-Wing. *The China–Hong Kong Connection: The Key to China's Open-Door Policy.* New York: Cambridge University Press, 1991.

Takahashi, Tadashi. *Ajia Zen Yosoku* (Asia: A comprehensive forecast). Compiled with Mitsubishi Research Institute, Asian Markets Research Department. Tokyo: Daiyamondo sha, 1998.

Taylor, Robert. *Greater China and Japan: Prospects for an Economic Partnership in East Asia.* London: Routledge, 1996.

Terashima Shunsei. *Te ni toru yo ni Ajia no koto ga wakaru hon* (A handbook for understanding Asian affairs). Revised edition. Compiled by Sanwa Research Institute, Discussion Room of Overseas Management. Tokyo: Kanki shupan, 1998.

————, ed. *Te ni toru yo ni Ajia no koto ga wakaru hon* (A handbook for understanding Asian affairs). Compiled by the Sanwa Research Institute, International Department, Head Office. Tokyo: Kanki shupan, 1995.

Thorn, Richard S. *The Rising Yen: The Impact of Japanese Financial Liberalization on World Capital Markets.* Singapore: Institute of Southeast Asian Studies, ASEAN Economic Research Unit, 1987.

Todaro, Michael P. *Economic Development.* Sixth edition. Reading, Mass.: Addison-Wesley, 1996.

Tokunaga, Shojiro, ed. *Japan's Foreign Investment and Asian Economic Interdependence: Production, Trade, and Financial Systems.* Tokyo: University of Tokyo Press, 1992.

Toyo Keizai. *ASEAN Shinshutsu Kigyo Soran, 1996* (Survey of overseas industrial advances into ASEAN, 1996). Tokyo: Toyo keizai shukan, 1995.

————. *Chugoku Shinshutsu Kigyo Soran, 1995* (Survey of overseas industrial advances into China, 1995). Tokyo: Toyo keizai shukan, 1994.

———— *Kaigai Shinshutsu Kigyo Soran, 1992* (Survey of overseas industrial advances, 1992). Tokyo: Toyo keizai shukan, 1992.

————. *Kigyo Keiretsu Soran, 1996* (Survey of industrial keiretsu, 1996). Tokyo: Toyo keizai shukan, 1995.

————. *Nihon Kigyo no Ajia Shinshutsu Mappu* (A map of Japanese overseas advances into Asia). Tokyo: Toyo keizai shinposha, 1995.

Tsuda, Mamoru, and Leo A. Deocadiz. *RP-Japan Relations and ADB: In Search of a New Horizon.* Metro Manila: National Book Store, 1986.

Unger, Danny, and Paul Blackburn, eds. *Japan's Emerging Global Role.* Boulder, Colo.: Lynne Rienner, 1993.

U.S. Congress. House of Representatives, Hearings before the Subcommittee on Asian and Pacific Affairs Jointly with the Committee on Foreign Affairs, Subcommittee on International Economic Policy and Trade, April 2 and 29, 1992. *U.S.-Asia Economic Relations.* Washington, D.C.: GPO, 1993.

————. House of Representatives, Hearings and Markup before the Committee on Foreign Affairs, Subcommittee on Asian and Pacific Affairs. *U.S.-Japan: A Looming Crisis?* Washington, D.C.: GPO, 1992.

————. Congress of the United States, Hearings before the Joint Economic Committee, December 17 and 18, 1991. *U.S.-Japan Interdependencies*. Washington, D.C.: GPO, 1992.

U.S. International Trade Commission (USITC). *East Asia: Regional Economic Integration and Implications for the United States*. Washington, D.C.: USITC Publication 2621, May 1993.

Valencia, Mark J., ed. *The Russian Far East and the North Pacific Region: Emerging Issues in International Relations*. Selected papers presented at the East-West Center Conference, Honolulu, Hawaii. Honolulu: International Relations Program, East-West Center, 1992.

Vogel, Ezra F. *The Four Little Dragons: The Spread of Industrialization in East Asia*. Cambridge, Mass.: Harvard University Press, 1991.

Wada, Kazuo. *Yaohan's Global Strategy: The Twenty-first Century Is the Era of Asia*. Hong Kong: Capital Communications Corp., 1992.

Watanabe, Toshio. *Asia: Its Growth and Agony*. Honolulu: East-West Center, 1992.

Whiting, Allen S. *China Eyes Japan*. Berkeley: University of California Press, 1989.

Wilson, Dick. *China: The Big Tiger: A Nation Awakes*. London: Little, Brown, 1996.

Woo-Cumings, Meredith, ed. (Woo Jung-en). *The Developmental State*. Ithaca, N.Y.: Cornell University Press, 1999.

Woo, Jung-En. *Race to the Swift: State and Finance in Korean Industrialization*. New York: Columbia University, 1991.

Wood, Christopher. *The Bubble Economy: The Japanese Economic Collapse*. London: Sidgwick & Jackson, 1992.

World Bank. *East Asia: The Road to Recovery*. Washington, D.C.: World Bank, 1998.

————. *The East Asian Miracle: Economic Growth and Public Policy*. New York: Oxford University Press, 1993.

————. *Indonesia in Crisis: A Macroeconomic Update*. Washington, D.C.: World Bank, 1998.

————. *Managing Capital Flows in East Asia*. Principal authors John D. Shilling, and Yan Wang. Washington, D.C.: World Bank, 1996.

————. *Seigin Tokyo Jimusho 20 Nen Shi* (Twenty years of the World Bank's Tokyo office). Tokyo: Sekai ginko tokyo jimusho, 1991.

————. *Seisaku Jinteki Shigen Kaihatsu PHRD. Kikin: 1997 Nendo Nenji Hokaku, Dai Ichi Bu* (Policy and Human Resource Development Fund: 1997 Annual Report, Part One). Washington, D.C.: World Bank, Resource Mobilization and Co-Financing, 1997.

————. *World Development Report 1997: The State in a Changing World*. Washington, D.C.: University Press Books, 1997.

World Bank/OECF. *The East Asian Miracle*. Symposium Proceedings jointly hosted by the World Bank and the OECF, Tokyo, December 3, 1993. Tokyo: OECF, Research Institute of Development Assistance, 1993.

Yamada, Bundo. *Internationalization Strategies of Japanese Electronics Companies: Implications for Asian Newly Industrializing Economies*. Paris: OECD, October 1990.

Yamashita, Shoichi, ed. *Transfer of Japanese Technology and Management to the ASEAN Countries*. Tokyo: University of Tokyo Press, 1991.

Yamazawa, Ippei. *Economic Development and International Trade: The Japanese Model*. Honolulu: Resource Systems Institute, East-West Center, 1990.

Yanagihara, Toru, ed. *Ajia Taiheiyo no Keizai Haten to Chiiki Kyoryoku* (Economic Development and Regional Cooperation in Asia Pacific). Tokyo: IDE, 1992.

Yanagihara, Toru, and Sambommatsu, Susumu, eds. *East Asian Development Experience: Economic System Approach and Its Applicability*. Tokyo: IDE, 1997.
Yasutomo, Dennis T. *Japan and the Asian Development Bank*. New York: Praeger Publishers, 1983.
―――. *The Manner of Giving: Strategic Aid and Japanese Foreign Policy*. Lexington, Mass.: Lexington Books and D.C. Heath, 1986.
Yoshihara, Kunio. *Japan in Thailand*. Kuala Lumpur: Kyoto University, Center for Southeast Asian Studies, in association with Falcon Press Sdn. Bhd., 1990.
―――. *The Rise of Ersatz Capitalism in South-East Asia*. Quezon City, Philippines: Ateneo de Manila University Press, 1988.
―――, ed. *Thai Perceptions of Japanese Modernization*. Kuala Lumpur: Kyoto University, Center for Southeast Asian Studies, in association with Falcon Press Sdn. Bhd., 1989.
Yoshino, M.Y., and Thomas B. Lifson. *The Invisible Link: Japan's Sogo Shosha and the Organization of Trade*. Cambridge, Mass.: MIT Press, 1989.

Articles

Abe, Jun-Ichi. "China's Eye towards the Expanding ASEAN." *JETRO China Newsletter* 6, no. 131 (1997).
Abe, Motoo. "Foreign Aid: A Dissenter's View." *Japan Echo* 16, no. 1 (Spring 1989).
Ahn, Choong Yong. "Economic Integration in Asia: With Emphasis on Northeast Asia." Paper presented at the Third Convention of the East Asian Economic Association, Seoul, Korea, August 20–21, 1992.
Akeneya, Tatsuo. "The Development of Post-War Japan–Australia Relations and the Impact of Declining American Hegemony." Australia-Japan Research Centre, Pacific Economic Paper, no. 153 (November 1987).
Alburo, F.A., C.C. Bautista, and M.S.H. Gochoco. "Pacific Direct Investment Flows into ASEAN." *ASEAN Economic Bulletin* 8, no. 3 (March 1992).
Altbach, Eric. "The Asian Monetary Fund Proposal: A Case Study in Japanese Regional Leadership." *Japan Economic Institute (JEI) Report* (Washington, D.C.), no. 47A (December 19, 1997).
―――. "Japan-China Relations: Challenges and Prospects." *JEI Report*, no. 11A (March 20, 1998).
―――. "Weathering the Storm? Japan's Production Networks in Asia and the Regional Crisis." *JEI Report*, no. 35A (September 18, 1998).
Amsden, Alice. "Post-Industrial Policy in East Asia." Paper presented at the Conference on Political Economics of Korea's Industrial Development, Korea Institute for Industrial Economics and Trade, Seoul, Korea, August 22, 1995.
―――. "Why Isn't the Whole World Experimenting with the East Asian Model to Develop? Review of *The East Asian Miracle*." In *World Development* 22, no. 4 (1994), p. 628, from Special Section: The World Bank's *East Asian Miracle*: Economic Growth and Public Policy; edited by Alice H. Amsden.
Aoki, Masahiko, Kevin Murdoch, and Masahiro Okuno-Fujiwara. "Behind the East Asian Miracle: Introducing the Market-Enhancing View." Stanford University, Center for Economic Policy Research, DEPR Publication, no. 442 (October 1995).
Arai, Hisamitsu. "Speech Note for Vice-Minister Hisamitsu Arai, MITI." IIE Symposium on the World Trading System—Seattle and Beyond, November 30, 1999.
Arase, David. "Economic Cooperation in the Region Where China, Russia, and North

Korea Meet." Japan Policy Research Institute (JPRI) Working Paper, no. 53. Cardiff, Calif.: JPRI, 1999.

Ariff, Mohamed. "ASEAN Free Trade Area: Problems and Prospects." Paper prepared for the National Outlook Conference, Shangri-La Hotel (hereafter, Shangri-La Hotel Conference), Kuala Lumpur, Malaysia, December 8–9, 1992.

Ariff, Mohamed, and Chye Tan Eu. "ASEAN-Pacific Trade Relations." *ASEAN Economic Bulletin* 8, no. 3 (March 1992).

"Asia's Competing Capitalisms." *The Economist*, June 24, 1995.

"The Asian Economic Miracle." Union Bank of Switzerland (Zurich), *International Finance* 29 (Autumn 1996).

Awanohara, Susumu. "Asian Crisis Impact: Treasury's Change of Heart." *Nikko Capital Trends (NDC)* 3, no. 3 (February 1998).

———. "Japan and East Asia: Towards a New Division of Labour." *Pacific Review* 2, no. 3 (1989).

———. "Japan and East Asia: Towards a New Division of Labor: A View from Japan." East-West Center, International Relations Program, Occasional Paper, no. 1.

———. "The U.S. and Japan at the World Bank." Paper presented at the International Conference on U.S.-Japan Relations and International Institutions after the Cold War, International House, Tokyo, Japan, April 8–11, 1994.

Baker, Gerard. "Japanese Banking: The Fallen Samurai?" *Accountancy* (June 26, 1996).

Baker, James A., III. "The United States and Japan: Global Partners in a Pacific Community." Special Issue on Asia-Pacific Partnerships. *Japan Review of International Affairs* 6 (1992).

Bank for International Settlements (BIS). "Press Release: BIS Consolidated International Banking Statistics for End-1998." *Basle*, May 31, 1999.

———. "The Maturity, Sectoral, and Nationality Distribution of International Bank Lending: First Half 1996." *Basle*, January 1997.

———. "The Maturity, Sectoral, and Nationality Distribution of International Bank Lending: First Half 1997." *Basle*, January 1998.

Battat, J. "FDI in China in the 1980s and Prospects for the 1990s within the Asian Context." FIAS/EWC/UNDP Roundtable (hereafter, FIAS/EWC/UNDP Roundtable) on Foreign Direct Investment in Asia and the Pacific in the 1990s, East-West Center, Honolulu, Hawaii, March 26–28, 1991.

Beechler, Schon. "International Management Control in Multinational Corporations: The Case of Japanese Consumer Electronics Firms in Asia." *ASEAN Economic Bulletin* 9, no. 2 (November 1992).

Belchere, William. "Can Asia Now Go Mexico's Way?" Merrill Lynch, Economics Brief. *Asian Strategy Monthly* (April 1998).

Bello, Walden. "Inviting Another Catastrophe." *Far Eastern Economic Review (FEER)*, August 12, 1999.

Bernard, Mitchell, and John Ravenhill. "Beyond Product Cycles and Flying Geese: Regionalization, Hierarchy, and the Industrialization of East Asia." *World Politics* 47 (January 1995).

Bevacqua, Ron. "Whither the Japanese Model? The Asian Economic Crisis and the Continuation of Cold War Politics in the Pacific Rim." *Review of International Political Economy* 5, no. 3 (Autumn 1998), pp. 410–23.

Bhongmakapat, Teerana. "Structural Adjustment: Experience of Thailand." Paper prepared for the UNESCO Regional Expert Meeting on Coping with the Effect of Structural Adjustment: Asia-Pacific Experiences, Korean National Commission for UNESCO, Korean Social Science Research Council, Seoul, Korea, June 25–28, 1991.

Brandt, Christopher, and K. S. Jomo. "Malaysian Forests, Japanese Wood: Japanese Involvement in Malaysia's Deforestation." Typed manuscript. Kuala Lumpur: December 1992.

Burton, John, and Gerard Baker. "S. Korea Asks IMF to Speed Rescue Deal." *Financial Times*, Seoul and Washington, D.C., respectively), December 12, 1997.

"The Call for a New Asian Identity: An Examination of the Cultural Arguments and Their Implications." Carnegie Council, Japan Programs Occasional Papers, no. 5 (1994).

"Capital Flows to Emerging Market Economies: Update." Institute of International Finance (Washington, D.C.), September 11, 1997.

Chalmers, Ian. "International and Regional Integration: The Political Economy of the Electronics Industry in ASEAN." *ASEAN Economic Bulletin* 8, no. 2 (November 1991).

Chan, Heng Chee. "Democracy: Its Evolution and Implementation." Conference organized by the Asia Society, Institute of Policy Studies, Institute of Southeast Asian Studies, and Singapore International Foundation on Asian and American Perspectives on Capitalism and Democracy (hereafter, Capitalism and Democracy Conference), Singapore, January 28–30, 1993.

Chen, Tain-Jy. "Taiwan's Direct Foreign Investment: Patterns and Effects on Trade." Kyushu University International Symposium on Intra-Pacific Economic Competitiveness and Cooperation—Which Direction Is Asia-Pacific Moving Towards? Hotel "Fukuoka Garden Palace" (hereafter, Fukuoka Garden Palace Conference), Fukuoka, Japan, July 27–28, 1992.

Chintayarangsan, Rachain, Nattapong Thongpakdee, and Pruttipohn Nakornchai. "ASEAN Economies: Macro-Economic Perspective." *ASEAN Economic Bulletin* 8, no. 3 (March 1992).

Chirathivat, Suthhiphand. "Managing Thai Trade Policy to Better Access Developed Countries' Markets." *ASEAN Economic Bulletin* 8, no. 1 (July 1991).

———. "Perspectives on Economic Development and the Role of the State: Industrial Policy and Government-Business Relations." Capitalism and Democracy Conference, 1993.

Cho, Dong-Sung, and Hyeon-Deog Cho. "Comparison of Competitiveness between Jonghap-Sangsa and Sogo-Shosha in the Korean Market." Typed manuscript. Seoul National University, Seoul, June 1991.

Chowdhury, Sanjoy. "Intra-Asian Investment Drops As Outflows from Japan Fall." *Asian Economic Commentary—A Monthly Review.* Merrill Lynch, New York, May 1992.

———. "Intra-Asian Trade Stood Larger Than Trans-Pacific Trade in 1991." *Asian Economic Commentary—A Monthly Review.* Merrill Lynch, New York, October 1992.

———. "Japanese Investment in Asia: Growth (ex-China) Remains Strong." *Asian Economic Commentary—A Monthly Review*. New York, Merrill Lynch, 1992, August 1989.

Chung, Chien-pung. "Southeast Asian Perceptions of Major Power Relations in Northeast Asia." *PacNet* 30. CSIS Pacific Forum 2000, Honolulu, Hawaii, July 28, 2000.

Chung, Erin Aeran. "Korean Voluntary Associations in Japanese Civil Society." JPRI Working Paper, no. 69 (July 2000).

Clark, William, Jr. "The Asia-Pacific Area Needs a Stronger Sense of Community."

ASEAN Economic Bulletin 9, no. 3 (March 1993). Address by William Clark, Jr., at the Mid-America Committee, Chicago, December 4, 1992.

Cline, William R., and Kevin J.S. Barnes. "Spreads and Risks in Emerging Markets Lending. IIF Research Paper, no. 97–1 (November 1997). Rev. 1. IIF, Washington, D.C., 1997.

Craib, B. Anne. "Prospects for Japan's Foreign Aid Program: Quality versus Quantity?" *JEI Report*, no. 44A (November 1994).

Cronin, Patrick M. "Pacific Rim Security: Beyond Bilateralism?" *Pacific Review* 5, no. 3 (1992).

———. "A Japan Dominated Asia-Pacific Region?" Japan's Economic Challenge: Study Paper Submitted to the Congress of the United States, Joint Economic Committee. Washington, D.C.: GPO, 1990.

———. "Asian Financial Crisis: U.S. Foreign Policy Interests and Options." Typescript, 1998.

Danaraj, N. et al. "Industrial Niches for Malaysia: Is Globalisation the Next Frontier?" Shangri-La Hotel Conference, 1992.

Das, Dilip K. "The Challenge of the Appreciating Yen and Japanese Corporate Response." Australia-Japan Research Centre Pacific Economic Paper, no. 217 (March 1993).

Dekle, Robert, and Lawrence H. Summers. "Japan's High Savings Rate Re-Affirmed." *Monetary and Economic Studies* 9, no. 2 (September 1991), pp. 63–78.

Denker, Mahmet Sami. "The Evolution of Japanese Investment in Malaysia." University of Malaya, Faculty of Economics and Administration, typescript, n.d.

———. "Internationalization of the Malaysian Economy: The Role of Japan." Ph.D. dissertation, University of Malaya, Kuala Lumpur, Malaysia, 1990, typed manuscript.

———. "Ties That Bind: Malayan-Japanese Economic Relations up to the Japanese Occupation." University of Malaya, Kuala Lumpur, Faculty of Economics and Administration, typescript paper, n.d.

Dervis, Kemal. "Growing Together: Why the Regional Neighborhood Matters for the Middle East and North Africa." Speech by Mr. Kemal Dervis, vice-president, World Bank, Middle East and North Africa Region, Middle East/North Africa Economic Conference, November 16–18, 1997.

Doner, Richard F. "Japanese Automotive Production Networks in Asia." In *Japanese Investment in Asia: International Production Strategies in a Rapidly Changing World*, edited by Eileen M. Doherty. Conference proceedings, sponsored by The Asia Foundation, San Francisco, and BRIE, the University of California at Berkeley, September 26–27, 1994.

———. "Japanese Foreign Investment and the Creation of a Pacific Asian Region." In *Regionalism and Rivalry: Japan and the United States in Pacific Asia*, edited by J. Frankel and M. Kahlan. Chicago: University of Chicago Press, 1993.

Drobnick, Richard L. "Economic Integration in the Pacific Region." OECD Research Program on Globalisation and Regionalisation (Paris), Technical Papers, no. 65 (1992).

Drysdale, Peter. "Japan As a Pacific and World Economic Power." Australia-Japan Research Centre Pacific Economic Paper, no. 166 (December 1988).

———. "Japan's Trade Diplomacy: Yesterday, Today, Tomorrow." Australia-Japan Research Centre Pacific Economic Paper, no. 178 (December 1989).

———. "Japan's Worst Nightmare." *International Economy* (March/April 1992).

―――. "Open Regionalism: A Key to East Asia's Economic Future." Australia-Japan Research Centre Pacific Economic Paper, no. 197 (July 1991).

―――. "A Pacific Free Trade Area?" Australia-Japan Research Centre Pacific Economic Paper, no. 171 (May 1989).

―――. "Regional Economic Cooperation and International Trade Policy in Asia and the Pacific." Fukuoka Garden Palace Conference, 1992.

Economic Planning Agency (EPA). "Dai San Cho: Higashi Ajia no seicho ryoku" (An examination of East Asia's capacity for growth). In *Ajia Keizai, 1995* (Asian economy, 1995). Tokyo: Keizai keikakucho, July 1995.

"Economic Reform and Trade Expansion in the Western Hemisphere." Transcript of Conference Proceedings on Citizens' Network for International Affairs, Tokyo, October 23, 1991.

Ellison, Herbert J. "Political Transformation of Communist States: Impact on the International Order in East Asia." Paper prepared for a Conference on Asia in Transition: Toward a New Regional Order, Program on International Economics and Politics, East-West Center, Honolulu, Hawaii, January 4–7, 1993.

Emig, Anne L. "Japan's Challenge to the World Bank: An Attempt at Intellectual Leadership." New York: Columbia University, December 10, 1996, typescript draft.

Emmerson, Donald K. "Slouching toward Symmetry? Notes on the Idea of Indonesia As a Rising Power." Paper prepared for a Conference on Asia in Transition: Toward a New Regional Order, Program on International Economics and Politics, East-West Center, Honolulu, Hawaii, January 4–7, 1993.

Eto, Shinkichi. "China and Sino-Japanese Relations in the Coming Decades." *Japan Review of International Affairs* (Winter 1996).

―――. "Japan's Asian Identity: Past, Present, and Future." Special Issue on Japan and East Asia. *Economic Eye* 13, no. 2 (Summer 1992) Tokyo: Keizai Koho Center, 1992.

Fallows, James. "Containing Japan." *Atlantic Monthly* (May 1989).

―――. "Getting Along with Japan." *Atlantic Monthly* (December 1989).

―――. "Perspectives on Political Development and the Nature of the Democratic Process: Human Rights and the Freedom of the Press." Capitalism and Democracy Conference, 1993.

Fingleton, Eamonn. "Eastern Economics." *Atlantic Monthly* (October 1990).

Flamm, Kenneth. "Perspectives on Economic Development and the Role of the State: Industrial Policy and Government-Business Relations." Capitalism and Democracy Conference, 1993.

Flatters, Frank. "After NAFTA: Implications for ASEAN/NAFTA." Shangri-La Hotel Conference, 1992.

Friedland, Jonathan. "The Regional Challenge." *FEER*, June 9, 1994.

Friedland, Jonathan, and Henny Sender. "Faulty Finance: Japan's Big Manufacturers May Play a Significant Role in Asia, but the Country's Banks and Brokers Are Having a Hard Time Competing with American Firms." *FEER*, June 9, 1994.

Fries, Steven M. "Japanese Banks and the Asset Price 'Bubble.'" IMF, Research Department (Washington, D.C.) (1993).

Fuentes-Berain, Rossana. "Afta NAFTA." *International Economy* (July/August 1992).

Fujita, Kuniko, and Richard Child Hill. "Auto Industrialization in Southeast Asia: National Strategies and Local Development." *ASEAN Economic Bulletin* 13, no. 3 (March 1997).

Fukasaku, Kiichiro. "Economic Regionalization and Intra-Industry Trade: Pacific-

Asian Perspectives." OECD, Research Program on Globalisation and Regionalisation Technical Papers, no. 53 (1992).

Fukuda, Shin-ichi. "The 'Big Push' in ASEAN Countries and the Role of Japan." Japan Center for International Exchange, ASEAN-Japan Dialogue 6: Oiso Conference (hereafter, Oiso Conference), Tokyo, June 20–21, 1992.

Funabashi, Yoichi. "The Asianization of Asia." *Foreign Affairs* 72, no. 5 (November/December 1993).

Funabashi, Yoichi, and Hisashi Owada. "Dialogues: How to Push Japanese Diplomacy." *Sekai* (December 1991). Translation by the United States Embassy, Tokyo.

Garnaut, Ross. "China's Growth in Northeast Asian Perspective." Australia-Japan Research Centre Pacific Economic Paper , no. 167 (January 1989).

Gerlach, Michael. "Trust Is Not Enough: Cooperation and Conflict in Kikkoman's American Development." *Journal of Japanese Studies* 16, no. 2 (Summer 1990).

———. "Twilight of the *Keiretsu*? A Critical Assessment." *Journal of Japanese Studies* 18, no. 1 (Winter 1992).

Gilpin, Robert. "Economic Change and the Challenge of Uncertainty." Paper prepared for a Conference on Asia in Transition: Toward a New Regional Order, East-West Center, Program on International Economics and Politics, Honolulu, Hawaii, January 4–7, 1993.

Gordon, Bernard K. "Japan: Searching Once Again." University of New Hampshire; Visiting Professor, Kobe University, 1991–92," typed manuscript, n.d.

Goto, Kazumi. "The Main Issues of the East Asian Miracle: The World Bank Report As Assessed by U.K. Critics." *Journal of Development Assistance* (OECF) 1, no. 1 (July 1995).

Gourevitch, Peter. "Competition and Cooperation in the Post Cold War Era." Fukuoka Garden Palace Conference, 1992.

Gree, Michael. "Why Tokyo Will Be a Larger Player in Asia." *Foreign Policy Research Institute E-Notes* (July 27, 2000).

Greenwald, Bruce, and Joseph E. Stiglitz. "Externalities in Economies with Imperfect Information and Incomplete Markets." *Quarterly Journal of Economics* 101 (May 1986), pp. 229–64.

Guisinger, Stephen. "Foreign Direct Investment Flows in East and Southeast Asia." *ASEAN Economic Bulletin* 8, no. 1 (July 1991).

Gyohten, Toyoo. "Regionalism in a Converging World." Paper presented at Plenary Session 2 on the Role of East Asian Economies in an Emerging New World Order: Globalism Versus Regionalism, the Third Convention of the East Asian Economic Association, Seoul, Korea, August 20–21, 1992.

Hall, Ivan P. "Japan's Asia Card." *National Interest*, no. 39 (Winter 1994/95).

Hamamoto, Takahiro. "Asian Financial Crisis: Just the Beginning." *Nikko Capital Trends* 2, no. 10 (August 1997).

Hasegawa, Mina. "Mr. Yen Defends Aggressive Approach to Market: Sakakibara Advocates Asian Trade Alliance to Vie with NAFTA, EU." *Nikkei Weekly*, July 19, 1999.

Hayashi, Takashi. "Intrafirm Transfer of Production of Japanese Multinational Enterprises: A Case Study in Electric Machinery Industry," n.d.

Hebner, Kevin J., and Stephen J. Turnbull. "Sogoshosha As Overseas Project Intermediaries." York University, North York, Ontario, 1993.

Henry, E. Keith, and Ken Okamura. "A New Era of Restructuring: Corporate Japan Leads the Way." *American Chamber of Ccommerce in Japan Journal* 4, no. 7 (July 1997).

Herschede, Fred. "Competition among ASEAN, China, and the East Asian NICs: A Shift-Share Analysis." *ASEAN Economic Bulletin* 7, no. 3 (March 1991).

Hiemenz, Ulrich. "FDI Flows to Asia and Economic Events in Europe." FIAS/EWC/UNDP Roundtable, 1991.

Hill, Hal. "The Emperor's Clothes Can Now Be Made in Indonesia." *Bulletin of Indonesian Economic Studies* 27, no. 3 (December 1991).

———. "Foreign Direct Investment Flows in the Asia-Pacific Region: Trends and Issues." Paper presented to the Roundtable on Foreign Direct Investment in Asia and the Pacific in the 1990s, East-West Center, Honolulu, Hawaii, March 26–28, 1991.

———. "Past Trends in FDI Flows to Asia and the Pacific: Economic and Policy Factors." FIAS/EWC/UNDP Roundtable, 1991.

Hill, Richard Child, and Kuniko Fujita. "Flying Geese, Swarming Sparrows, or Preying Hawks? Perspectives on East Asian Industrialization." *Competition and Change: Journal of Global Economy*, no. 3 (1996).

Hirsh, Michael. "The State Strikes Back." *Institutional Investor* (September 1993).

Hufbauer, Gary. "Perspectives on Economic Development and the Role of the State: Economic Development Strategies and Trade Relations." Capitalism and Democracy Conference, 1993.

Hughes, Helen. "Does APEC Make Sense?" *ASEAN Economic Bulletin* 8, no. 2 (November 1991).

Huntington, Samuel. "Democracy: Its Evolution and Implementation." Capitalism and Democracy Conference, 1993.

Imai, Satoshi. "Comparison of Western, Overseas Chinese, and Japanese Ventures." *JETRO China Newsletter*, no. 119 (November-December 1995).

Imaoka, Hideki. "Structures of Trade Interdependence in Asia." Report of the Special Research Project on the New International System. Tsukuba University, Tsukuba, Ibaragi Prefecture, 1992.

"The Impact of Yen Appreciation on Automobile Manufacturers." *Nikko Monthly Bulletin* (November 1992).

Inoguchi, Takashi. "Japan in Search of a Normal Role." The Thirty-fourth Annual Conference of the International Institute for Strategic Studies, Seoul, Korea, September 9–12, 1992; Institute of Oriental Culture, Tokyo, 1992, typed manuscript.

———. "Japan's Foreign Policy in a Time of Global Uncertainty." *International Journal* 46, no. 4 (Autumn 1991).

———. "Japan's Foreign Policy in East Asia." *Current History* (December 1992).

———. "Japan's Role in International Affairs." *Survival* 34, no. 3 (Summer 1992).

Inoue, Shozo. "Human Resource Management and Industrial Relations Issues at Japanese Transplants Abroad." Paper presented at the Third Convention of the East Asian Economic Association, Seoul, Korea, August 20–21, 1992.

"Internationalization of the Yen." MOF, at <http://www.mof.go.jp>.

Iokibe, Makoto, and Shin'ichi Kitaoka. "The Persistence of the Post-War Setup." Special Issue: Japanese Views of Asia. *Japan Echo* 20 (1993).

Irvine, Steven. "Inter-American Development Bank: The Edict of Nancy." *Euromoney* (March 1996).

Ishiyama, Yoshihide. "Regional Routes to a New World Order." *Japan Echo* 19, no. 1 (Spring 1992).

Ishizawa, Masato. "Asia Bailout Fund Gets Key Ally in Finance Minister." *Nikkei Weekly*, September 29, 1997.

Itoh, Yoshiaki. "More Unskilled Workers May Find Welcome." *Nikkei Weekly*, November 30, 1992.

James, William E., and Robert McCleary. "Trade Liberalization in Asia in Theory and Practice." Paper presented at the Third Convention of the East Asian Economic Association, Seoul, Korea, August 20–21, 1992.

"Japan-ASEAN Symposium." Asian Affairs Research Council (Tokyo), Special Issue. *Asia Quarterly* (1979).

"Japanese Direct Investment in Asia and Its Impact on Trade-Formation of a Network." Typed manuscript, n.d.

Japan International Cooperation Agency (JICA), Country Study Committee. "Country Study for Japan's Official Development Assistance to Viet Nam." Tokyo: JICA, 1995.

Jawhar, Mohamed. "Pacific-Asian Regional Security Structures and Their Potentials." Institute of Strategic and International Studies, Kuala Lumpur, Malaysia, typed manuscript, n.d.

Jayasankaran, S. "Made-in-Malaysia: The Proton Project." In *Industrializing Malaysia*. London: Routledge, 1993.

JEXIM. Japan's Symposium on Economic Cooperation and Overseas Direct Investment, Export-Import Bank of Japan, Tokyo, December 12, 1991.

"JEXIM's Role in Japanese Assistance for the Asian Economy: Status Report." Revised edition, June 1999. Tokyo: Japan Export-Import Bank, 1999.

Johnson, Chalmers. "Capitalism: East Asian Style." World Bank Conference on Government and East Asian Economic Success, East-West Center, Honolulu, Hawaii, November 19–21, 1992.

———. "Comparative Capitalism: The Japanese Difference." In *Japan: Who Governs? The Rise of the Developmental State*. New York: W.W. Norton, 1995, published originally in *California Management Review* 35, no. 4 (Summer 1993).

———. "Japan in Search of a 'Normal' Role." Paper presented to the Conference on Pacific Security Relations After the Cold War, sponsored by the Institute on Global Conflict and Cooperation, University of California, held in Hong Kong, June 15–18, 1992, typed manuscript.

———. "Nationalism and the Market: China As a Superpower." JPRI Working Paper, no. 22 (July 1996).

Johnstone, Christopher B. "How Much Bang for the Buck: Japan's Commercial Diplomacy in Asia." *JEI Report*, no. 13A (April 4, 1997).

———. "'Managing' China: American and Japanese Policies and Prospects for Cooperation." *JEI Report*, no. 13A (April 5, 1996).

Johnstone, Christopher B., and Atsushi Yamakoshi. "Strength without Dominance: Japanese Investment in Southeast Asia." *JEI Report*, no. 19A (May 16, 1997).

Jun, Nishikawa. "Tri-polarization of the World Economy and Asian Economic Development." Fukuoka Garden Palace Conference, 1992.

Kaifu, Toshiki. "Japan and ASEAN: Seeking a Mature Partnership for the New Age." Policy Speech by Prime Minister Toshiki Kaifu, Singapore, 3 May 1991. In *ASEAN Economic Bulletin* 8, no. 1 (July 1991).

Kaifu, Toshiki. Policy Speech by Prime Minister Toshiki Kaifu to the Nineteenth Session of the National Diet, October 12, 1990. Provisional and unofficial translation, Foreign Press Center, Tokyo, Japan, 1990, typed manuscript.

Kakizawa, Koji. "A New Stage in Sino-Japanese Ties." Special Issue, Japanese Views of Asia. *Japan Echo* 20 (1993).

———. "Sino-Japanese Relations after Emperor's Visit to China—Not As Rivals but As Partners." *Chuo koron* (December 1992). Full translation by United States Embassy, Tokyo.

Kan, Hideki. "International Relationships in East Asia and Economic Cooperation in the Yellow Sea Area." Paper presented at the Conference on the Newly Emerging Structure of East Asia and Japan, International Centre for the Study of East Asian Development, Round Table on East Asia (hereafter, Round Table on East Asia Conference), Tokyo, September 25–26, 1991.

Kanamori, Hisao. "Vietnam Revs Up for Economic Takeoff." Special Issue, Japan and East Asia. *Economic Eye* 13, no. 2 (Summer 1992).

Kaneko, Fumio. "Japanese ODA: Politics of Strategic Assistance." AMPO Japan. *Asia Quarterly Review* 20, nos. 1 and 2 (1989).

Kangwanpornsiri, Kanjanee. "Thailand's Major Problems, Issues and Challenges in the 1990s: Implication for Its Relation with Japan and ASEAN." Oiso Conference, 1992.

Kasai, Nobuyaki. "The Age of Japan–South Korea Cooperative Coexistence and the Yellow Sea and Japan Sea Economic Zones." Paper presented at the Round Table on East Asia Conference, 1991.

Katsuhara, Takeshi. "Formation of AFTA and Its Impact on Regional Trade and Development." International Center for the Study of East Asian Development, Kitakyushu, 1993, typed manuscript.

———. "Rapidly Developing Economies of East Asia and the Role of Kyushu Area." International Center for the Study of East Asian Development, Kitakyushu, 1993, typed manuscript.

Katz, Richard. "Japan's Role in the Asian Financial Crisis." U.S. Joint Hearing, Statement Before the Subcommittees on Asia and the Pacific and International Economic Policy and Trade, April 23, 1998, typescript.

Kawakami, Takao. "Japan's Aid Policy toward the Twenty-first Century: Toward Aid with a 'Face.'" Translated by Gaiko Forum, Tokyo, March 1993, typed manuscript.

Keidanren Japan Federation of Economic Organizations. "Economic Cooperation for International Causes: A Proposal for Formulation of Basic Rules of Official Development Assistance." Tokyo: Keidanren, March 24, 1992, typed manuscript.

———. "Japan's ODA: Its Philosophy and Future Development." Provisional translation. Tokyo: Keidanren, June 26, 1990, typed manuscript.

Kim, Han Soo, and Ann Weston. "A North American Free Trade Agreement and East Asian Developing Countries." *ASEAN Economic Bulletin* 9, no. 3 (March 1993).

Kim, Won Bae. "Korean Peninsula and the Future of Northeast Asia." Workshop on the Prospects of Economic Interactions among Countries in East Asia, sponsored by the Ushiba Memorial Foundation (hereafter, Ushiba Memorial Foundation Workshop), Odawara, Japan, November 28–29, 1992.

Kinoshita, Toshihiko. "Decision Making Process of Japanese Firms in Foreign Direct Investment." Essence of speech (entitled "Decision Making Process of Japanese Firms and Prospect of Japan's Investment in Laos") made to Lao government officials et al., Vientiane, October 30, 1990. Tokyo: Export-Import Bank, April 1991, typed manuscript.

———. "Deregulation Policy and Foreign Debt Management in Indonesia toward the Twenty-first Century: A Personal View." For Indonesian Economists Association, Jakarta, and Bank Dagang Negara. Typed manuscript, Export-Import Bank of Japan, September 5, 1990.

————. "Developments in the International Debt Strategy and Japan's Response." *Exim Review* (January 1991).

————. "Japanese Investment in Indonesia: Problems and Prospects." *Bulletin of Indonesian Economic Studies* 22, no. 1 (April 1986).

————. "An Open Asia." *Look Japan* (March 1992).

Kitaoka, Shin'ichi. "From the Editor: Japanese Views of Asia." Special Issue, Japanese Views of Asia. *Japan Echo* 22 (1993).

Kobayashi, Yotaro. "Japan on the Road to 'Re-Asianization.'" Tokyo, n.d.

Koo, Bon Ho. "The Emerging Structure of Northeast Asia and the Prospect of Regional Cooperation." Paper presented at the Round Table on East Asia Conference, 1991.

Korhonen, Pekka. "The Theory of the Flying Geese Pattern of Development and Its Interpretations." *Journal of Peace Research* 31, no. 1 (1991), pp. 93–108,

Kotake, Kazuaki. "Beijing's Diplomatic Offensive in Asia." *JETRO China Newsletter*, no. 104 (May-June 1993).

Krause, Lawrence B. "The North American Free Trade Area and Asia-Pacific Economic Cooperation." Fukuoka Garden Palace Conference, 1992.

Krugman, Paul. "The Myth of Asia's Miracle." *Foreign Affairs* 73, no. 4 (November-December 1994).

————. "What Are the Lessons of Asian Growth?" Paper submitted to the Conference on Political Economics of Korea's Industrial Development. Korea Institute for Industrial Economics and Trade, Seoul, Korea, August 22, 1995.

Kubota, Isao. "The Case for Two Step Loans: A Private Note." Paper read at the Workshop on Financial Sector Issues on the Occasion of Bi-Annual Consultation between the World Bank and the OECF and J-EXIM, Tokyo, May 15, 1991.

————. "Reflections on Recent Trends in Development Aid Policy." Unpublished paper, November 5, 1991.

————. "The Role of Domestic Saving and Macroeconomic Stability in the Development Process." *Economic Society of Australia* 10, no. 2 (June 1991).

Kuchiki, Akifumi. "The East Asian Trick: A Theoretical Approach to EPZ." For the Session on Further Research on the East Asian Miracle, the World Bank–Japan Research Fair/Workshop, *TEPIA*, Tokyo, Japan, December 13, 1995.

Kume, Gorota. "Trends and Prospects of Japanese Direct Investment in Asia: Increased Contribution to Economic Development of Asian Countries." *Japanese Institute for Overseas Investment* (May 1992).

Kuribayashi, Sei. "Appraising the Ties among East Asian Countries." Special Issue, Japan and East Asia. *Economic Eye* 13, no. 2 (Summer 1992).

Kwan, Chi Hung. "The Rise of Asia and Japan's 'Hollowing Out' Problem." Nomura Research Institute (NRI) (Tokyo), *NRI Quarterly* 6, no. 1 (Spring 1997).

————. "Towards a Yen Bloc in Asia." *Look Japan* (May 1993).

Lai, Francis F. "Prospects of Economic Interactions in the Asian Pacific: The Case of Hong Kong." Ushiba Memorial Foundation Workshop, 1992.

Lall, Sanjaya. "Emerging Sources of FDI in Asia and the Pacific." FIAS/EWC/UNDP Roundtable, 1991.

Langhammer, Rolf J. "ASEAN Economic Co-operation: A Stock-Taking from a Political Economy Point of View." *ASEAN Economic Bulletin* 8, no. 2 (November 1991).

————. "Financing of Foreign Direct Investment and Trade Flows: The Case of Indonesia." *Bulletin of Indonesian Economic Studies* 24, no. 1 (April 1988).

———. "Towards Regional Entities in Asia-Pacific: The Role of Japanese Foreign Investment in Service Industries." *ASEAN Economic Bulletin* 7, no. 3 (March 1991).

———. "Trade in Manufactures between Asian Pacific Rim Countries: Trends and Determinants." *ASEAN Economic Bulletin* 6, no. 1 (July 1989).

Lee, Chung H. "Direct Foreign Investment, Structural Adjustment, and International Division of Labor: A Dynamic Macroeconomic Theory of Direct Foreign Investment." *Hitotsubashi Journal of Economics* 31, n.d.

Lee, Chung H., and Manuel Montes. "When Intangible Private Assets Meet Inconstant National Comparative Advantage: Structural Change and Direct Foreign Investment." Presented at the Conference on the Role of Direct Foreign Investment in Structural Change in East and Southeast Asia, East-West Center, Honolulu, Hawaii, September 18, 1992.

Lee, Poh Ping. "Asia and the Future." Oiso Conference, 1992.

———. "Japanese Official Assistance to Malaysia." Paper presented at the Seminar on Japanese Official Development Assistance to ASEAN, organized by the United Nations University, Tokyo, November 1990.

———. "U.S.-Japan Relations and Their Impact on the Asia-Pacific Region." Special Issue on Asia-Pacific Partnerships. *Japan Review of International Affairs* 6 (1992).

Liefer, Michael. "Vietnam's Foreign Policy in the Post-Soviet Era: The Imperatives of Development and Independence." Paper prepared for a Conference on Asia in Transition: Toward a New Regional Order, East-West Center, Program on International Economics and Politics, Honolulu, Hawaii, January 4–7, 1993.

Lim, Chee Peng. "ASEAN-Indochinese Relations: From Confrontation to Cooperation." Ushiba Memorial Foundation Workshop, 1992.

———. "Asia-Pacific Economic Development and Transnational Corporations." Fukuoka Garden Palace Conference, 1992.

Lim, Linda. "The Emergence of a Chinese Economic Zone in Asia?" *Journal of Southeast Asia Business* 8, no. 1 (Winter 1992).

———. "The U.S., Japan and Other East Asia Economies: The Emergence of a Pacific Economic Triangle." *Journal of Southeast Asia Business* 7, no. 4 (Fall 1991).

Lin, Tzong-biau. "Economic Cooperation and Integration in the Southern Part of China: Implications for Taiwan." Ushiba Memorial Foundation Workshop, 1992.

Lincoln, Edward J. "Japan's Financial Mess." *Foreign Affairs* 77, no. 3, (May/June 1998).

———. "Whither Trade Policy with Japan?" JPRI Working Paper, no. 56 (April 1999).

Lo, Fu-chen. "East Asian Economic Integration: A Basis for EAEC?" Shangri-La Hotel Conference, 1992.

Loh, Hui Yin. "Soros: Dr M a Menace to Malaysia." *Business Times* (Singapore and Hong Kong), September 22, 1997.

Machado, Kit G. "ASEAN State Industrial Policies and Japanese Regional Production Strategies: The Case of Malaysia's Motor Vehicle Industry." In *The Evolving Pacific Basin in the Global Political Economy: Domestic and International Linkages*, edited by Cal Clark and Steve Chan. Boulder, Colo.: Lynne Rienner, 1992.

———. "Japanese Foreign Direct Investment in East Asia: The Expanding Division of Labor and the Future of Regionalism." In *Foreign Direct Investment in a Changing World: Empirical Studies in National and Regional Development*, edited by Steve Chan. New York: Macmillan/St. Martin's Press, 1995.

———. "Japanese Transnational Corporations in Malaysia's State Sponsored Heavy

Industrialization Drive: The HICOM Automobile and Steel Projects." *Pacific Affairs* 62, no. 4.

Maeyama, Atsuki. "Banks Play Catch-up with Global Rivals in Asia." *Nikkei Weekly*, August 8, 1994.

Mahubhani, Kishore. "Japan Adrift." *Foreign Policy Magazine*, no. 88 (Fall 1992).

Management Research and Consulting Section. "Going Offshore: Asian Strategies of Mid-Sized Japanese Companies." *NRI Quarterly* (Summer 1995).

Mardon, Russell. "The State, Foreign Investment, and Sustaining Industrial Growth in South Korea and Thailand." California State University, Department of Political Science, Fresno, Calif, n.d..

Maruyama, Nobuo. "Current Problems Facing China-Japan Joint Ventures." *JETRO China Newsletter*, no. 95 (November-December 1991).

Mathews, John A. "High Technology Industrialization in East Asia." *Journal of Industry Studies* 3, no. 2 (December 1996).

Mathews, John A., and Linda Weiss. "The Case for an Asian Monetary Fund." JPRI Working Paper, no. 55 (March 1999).

Matsui, Noriatsu. "The New Roles of Japan in the Global Political Economy." *Asian Economic Journal* 5, no. 1 (1991).

Matsunaga, Nobuo. "A Japanese Perspective on the Pacific Rim in the 1990s." Special Issue on Asia-Pacific Partnerships. *Japan Review of International Affairs* 6 (1992).

"Measures to Facilitate the Internationalization of the Yen." Provisional translation. MOF, December 22, 1998, at www.mof.go.jp.

Merá, Koichi. "Problems in Aid Program." *Japan Echo* 16, no. 1 (Spring 1989).

Meyer, Cornelia. "Japan's Capital Flows to East Asia." UBS Securities, Ltd., Japanese Research (Tokyo), May 6, 1993.

Mikuni, Akio. "Japan's Big Bank: Illusion and Reality." JPRI Working Paper, no. 39 (October 1997).

———. "Why Japan Cannot Deregulate Its Financial System." JPRI Working Paper, no. 68 (June 2000).

———. "Why Japan Can't Reform Its Economy." JPRI Working Paper, no. 44 (April 1998).

Miller, Jonathan. "Road Warrior: Malaysia's Proton Is a Surprise Hit with U.K. Buyers." *Asia, Inc.* (December 1992).

Ministry of Foreign Affairs (MOFA). "Japan's ODA, 1992." Tokyo: MOFA, 1992, typed manuscript.

———. "Japan's Official Development Assistance Charter." Tokyo: MOFA, June 30, 1992, typed manuscript.

———. "Partners for Progress." SPR-182. Paper submitted to the APEC Second Senior Officials Meeting in Sapporo for the Seventh Ministerial Meeting, July 6, 1995, typescript.

Miyazaki, Isamu. "The Asian Economy at a Turning Point." Paper presented at the Round Table on East Asia Conference, 1991.

Miyazawa, Kiichi. "Beyond the Asia Crisis." Speech by Mr. Kiichi Miyazawa on the Occasion of the APEC Finance Ministers Meeting in Langkawi, Malaysia, May 15, 1999.

———. Policy speech by Prime Minister Miyazawa on the New Era of the Asia-Pacific and Japan-ASEAN Cooperation, January 16, 1993. Provisional translation. Bangkok: MOFA, 1993.

Mochizuki, Mike M. "Japan As an Asia-Pacific Power, December 1992." Paper prepared for the Conference on Asia in Transition: Toward a New Regional Order, sponsored by the Jackson School of International Studies, University of Washington, and the Department of Political Science, Boston College, at the East-West Center, Honolulu, Hawaii, January 4–7, 1993, typed manuscript.

———. "The U.S.-Japan Alliance: Beyond the Guidelines." CSIS Pacific Forum, 2000 (Honolulu). *PacNet* 35 (September 1, 2000).

Montes, Manuel F. "Macroeconomic Models for Interdependent Economies." East-West Center, Honolulu, Hawaii, October 15, 1990, typed manuscript.

Morino, Tomozo. "The Development of Pudong in Shanghai and the Changjiang Yangzi River Economic Zone." *East Asian Economic Perpectives* 4, no. 1 (March 1993).

Morrison, Charles E. "Japan As a Non-Military Global and Regional Power." East-West Center, Honolulu, Hawaii, January 1993, typed manuscript.

———. "The United States and East Asia: New Directions in a Clinton Administration?" Paper prepared for the Ushiba Memorial Foundation Conference, 1992.

———. "The United States in Post–Cold War Asia." Presentation for the Sixth Asia-Pacific Roundtable, Kuala Lumpur, Malaysia, June 21–25, 1992, typed manuscript.

Muehring, Kevin. "It's Summers' Time." *Institutional Investor* (December 1997).

Muto, Kabun. "Keynote Speech by HE Kabun Muto, Minister for Foreign Affairs at the Asia Society's Fourth Annual Conference, 14 May 1993." Provisional translation. Tokyo: MOFA, 1993.

Nakahara, Michiko. "Asian Laborers along the Burma-Thailand Railroad." *Waseda Journal of Asian Studies* 15 (1993).

———. "The Japanese in Chop Suey—Singapore under the Japanese Occupation." *Waseda Journal of Asian Studies* 11 (1989).

———. "Japanese Intellectuals and Southeast Asia during the Great East Asian War." *Waseda Journal of Asian Studies* 5 (1983).

Nakajima, Mineo. "Roadblocks to a New Regional Order." Special Issue, Japan and East Asia. *Economic Eye* 13, no. 2 (Summer 1992).

———. "The Three Chinas in Asia's New Order." Special Issue, Japanese Views of Asia. *Japan Echo* 20 (1993).

Nanto, Dick K. "Japan's Industrial Groups, the *Keiretsu.*" Japan's Economic Challenge: Study Papers Submitted to the Congress of the United States, Joint Economic Committee, Washington, D.C.: GPO, 1990.

Naya, Seiji, and Michael G. Plummer. "ASEAN Economic Co-operation in the New International Economic Environment." *ASEAN Economic Bulletin* 7, no. 3 (March 1991).

Naya, Seiji, and Narongchai Akrasanee. "Thailand's International Economic Relations with Japan and the U.S.: A Study of Trade and Investment Interactions." Discussion Paper Series (Bangkok), Thammasat University, Faculty of Economics, n.d.

Neff, Robert, with Michael Shari, Joyce Barnathan, and Edith Updike. "Japan's New Identity." *Business Week*, April 10, 1995.

Neff, Robert, with Paul Magnusson and William Holstein. "Rethinking Japan." *Business Week*, August 7, 1989.

Nishimura, Akira. "Economic Development in Shandong and the Yellow Sea Economic Zone." Paper presented at the Round Table on East Asia, 1991.

Nomura Research Institute. "Application of the IMF Prescription throughout the World." *Nomura Asia Focus* (Autumn 1998).

———. "The ASEAN Automobile Industry, Now and in the Future." *Nomura Asia Focus*, no. 1 (1999).

———. "The ASEAN Electronics Industry and Japanese Direct Investment." *Nomura Asia Focus*, no. 1 (1999).

———. "Asia's Bubble Crisis: No Instant Cure." Nomura Research Institute, Asia Pacific Research Group (January 19, 1999).

———. "Japan's Direct Investment in Asia at the Crossroads." *Nomura Asia Focus* (Winter 1997/98).

———. "Verifying the IMF Prescription: Suggested Improvements to the International Financial Assistance Policy." *Nomura Asia Focus* (Autumn 1998).

Nowels, Larry Q. "Japan's Foreign Aid Program: Adjusting to the Role of the World's Leading Donor." Japan's Economic Challenge: Study Paper Submitted to the Congress of the United States, Joint Economic Committee. Washington, D.C.: GPO, 1990.

Nye, Joseph S., Jr. "Coping with Japan." *Foreign Policy Magazine*, no. 89 (Winter 1992–93).

O, Sonfa. "The Cultural Roots of Japanese-Korean Friction." Special Issue, Japanese Views of Asia. *Japan Echo* 20.

Ogata, Shijuro. "Capitalism, the Market Mechanism, and the State in Economic Development: A Conceptual Overview." Capitalism and Democracy Conference, 1993.

Ogawa, Yuhei. "Development of Inter-Regional Economic Cooperation and the Yellow Sea and Japan Sea Economic Zones." Paper presented at the Round Table on East Asia Conference, 1991.

Ogura, Kazuo. "Ajia no fukuken no tame ni" (For the restoration of Asia). *Chuo Koron*, no. 7 (1993).

———. "Japan's Asia Policy, Past and Future." *Japan Review of International Affairs* (Winter 1996).

———. "Regional Integration, Japan's Options." Translated by Gaiko Forum, December 1992, typed manuscript.

Ohno, Izumi. "Beyond the East Asian Miracle—How the Asian Commentators See the Phenomenon and the Future." OECF, *Journal of Development Assistance* 1, no. 1 (July 1995).

Ohta, Hajime. "Prospects for Japanese FDI in Asia and the Pacific." FIAS/EWC/UNDP Roundtable, 1991.

Ohtsuka, Seiichi. "Contributions of Japan's ODA to the East Asian Development." Notes for presentation, Japanese MOFA, Evaluation Division, Economic Cooperation Bureau, Honolulu, Hawaii, April 6, 1995, typescript.

Oishi, Nobuyuki. "Japan's Trade in Asia: More Becomes Less." *Nikkei Weekly*, February 13, 1995.

Okazaki Hisahihko. "A National Strategy for the Twenty-first Century." *Japan Echo* (October 1999).

———. "Southeast Asia in Japan's National Strategy." Special Issue, Japanese Views of Asia. *Japan Echo* 20 (1993).

Onozawa, Jun. "Japan and Malaysia: The EAEC Test of Commitment." *Japan Quarterly* (July-September 1993).

Orr, Robert M., Jr. "Collaboration or Conflict? Foreign Aid and U.S.-Japan Relations." *Pacific Affairs* (Winter 1989–90).

Ostrom, Douglas. "Complementarity and Competition: Japan–South Korea Trade." *JEI Report*, no. 12A (March 27, 1998).

———. "Japan and the Asian Economic Crisis: Part of the Solution or Part of the Problem." *JEI Report*, no. 8A (February 27, 1998).

———. "The *Keiretsu* System: Cracking or Crumbling?" *JEI Report*, no. 14A (April 7, 2000).

———. "Limping toward the Millennium: Japan's Economy in the Late 1990s." *JEI Report*, no. 14A (April 10, 1998).

Ota, Fusae et al. "Russia's Economic Reform and Japan's Industrial Policy." MITI Research Institute, n.d, ca. April 1992.

Otsuka, Jiro. "The Yen's New Role." *FEER* , January 1992.

Overseas Economic Cooperation Fund (OECF). "Issues Related to the World Bank's Approach to Structural Adjustment—Proposal from a Major Partner." OECF Occasional Paper, no. 1 (October 1991).

———. "Sekai Ginko no kozo chosei aprochi no mondaiten ni tsuite" (Issues related to the World Bank's approach to structural adjustment). *Kikin chosa kiho*, no. 73 (February 1992), pp. 4–18.

Owada, Hisashi. "New Year Special Interview—Hearing the Views of Administrative Foreign Vice-Minister Hisashi Owada, Should Play Positive Role in Creation of New International Order." Interview by Professor Nobutoshi Nagano, Tokai University, Kankai, February 1992. Translation by the United States Embassy, Tokyo.

Ozawa, Terutomo. "The Flying Geese Paradigm of Foreign Direct Investment, Economic Development and Shifts in Competitiveness." Revised April 5, 1995, unpublished manuscript.

Packard, George R. "Japan's Role in the World Following the End of Communism." Paper presented at the Round Table on East Asia Conference, 1991.

Page, John. "The East Asian Miracle and the Latin American Consensus: Can the Twain Ever Meet?" In *Pathways to Growth: Comparing East Asia and Latin America*, edited by Nancy Birdsall and Frederick Jasperson. Washington, D.C.: Inter-American Development Bank, 1997.

———. "The East Asian Miracle: Four Lessons for Development Policy." Edited by Stanley Fischer and Julio J. Rotemberg. MIR Press, *NBER Macroeconomics Annual* (1994).

———. "The East Asian Miracle One Year Later: Are Its Lessons Relevant to Other Countries?" Paper presented to the Conference on the Possibility of the Application of Japanese Experience from the Standpoint of the Developing Countries. EPA, Tokyo, November 14–15, 1994.

———. "A Middle Eastern Miracle: Lessons for Development Policy from East Asia." Revised October 1996. Presented at the Conference sponsored by the Egyptian Center for Economic Studies on How Can Egypt Benefit from a Trade Agreement with the European Union? Cairo, Egypt, June 26–27, 1996.

———. "The Pursuit of Industrial Growth: Policy Initiatives and Economic Consequences." In *Public Policy and Economic Development: Essays in Honor of Ian Little*, edited by Maurice Scott and Lal Deepak. Oxford: Clarendon Press, 1990.

Pangestu, Mari, Hadi Soestrato, and Mubariq Ahmad. "A New Look at Intra-ASEAN Economic Co-operation." *ASEAN Economic Bulletin* 8, no. 3 (March 1992).

Parrenas, Julius Caesar. "Step by Step, Asians Are Finally Getting Together." *PacNet* 27 (July 7, 2000).

Petri, Peter A. "Government and the East Asian Miracle: One Model or Many?" World Bank Conference on Government and East Asian Economic Success, East-West Center, Honolulu, November 19–21, 1992.

Phongpaichit, Pasuk. "The New Wave of Foreign Direct Investment in ASEAN." Fukuoka Garden Palace Conference, 1992.

Pollack, Andrew. "Japan's Tack on Trade: No More 1–on-1." *New York Times*, July 30, 1996.

Powell, Bill. "The Yen Bloc: Asia's Message to Washington: Sayonara, America." *Newsweek*, August 5, 1991.

Prasartset, Suthy. "An Emerging Trade Pattern since the New Wave of Japanese Direct Investment in Thailand." In *Japan in Thailand*, edited by Kunio Yoshihara. Kuala Lumpur: Kyoto University in association with Falcon Press, 1990.

Pratomo, Andre Surya. "Recent Developments in Indonesia and Their Implications for Japan-Indonesia Relations." Oiso Conference, 1992.

Pyle, Kenneth B. "The Japanese Question." *International House of Japan Bulletin* 10, no. 3 (Summer 1990).

Ramstetter, Eric D., and Michael G. Plummer. "Motives and Policies Affecting U.S. Direct Investment in ASEAN." *Development & South-South Co-operation, Development Experience of Asia* 5, no. 9 (December 1989).

———. "An Overview of Multinational Firms in Asia-Pacific Developing Economies: An Introduction to the Commonplace Ignorance." Paper prepared for the Asian Productivity Organization and Institute for Economic Development and Policy Seminar on the Role of Foreign Direct Investment in Development, Seoul, Korea, September 16–20, 1991.

"Reaching Out: Japan's Global Initiatives." Tokyo: MOFA, July 1992.

"Report on Japan's Overseas Investment: Japanese Corporations Become Selective; Efficiency May Be the Best Strategy to Survive the Transition Period." Press release, Japan Institute for Overseas Development, Tokyo, September 1992.

Rix, Alan. "Japan's Foreign Aid Policy: A Capacity for Leadership?" *Pacific Affairs*, (Winter 1989–90).

———. "Ushiba Nobuhiko: A Japanese `Economic Diplomat.'" Australia-Japan Research Centre Pacific Economic Paper, no. 170 (April 1989).

Rodrik, Dani. "King Kong Meets Godzilla: The World Bank and the East Asian Miracle." In *Miracle or Design? Lessons from the East Asian Experience, Policy Essay*, no. 11, by Albert Fishlow, Catherine Gwin, Stephan Haggard, Dani Rodrik, and Robert Wade. Washington, D.C.: Overseas Development Council, 1994.

———. "TFPG Controversies, Institutions, and Economic Performance in East Asia." Abstract and Non-Technical Summary. Centre for Economic Policy Research Discussion Paper Series, no. 1587 (March 1997).

Rosefielde, Steven. "Economic Liberalization in Russia, China and Japan: Reconciling Culture and Free Competition." Paper prepared for the AAASS Meetings, Crystal City, Va., November 2001.

Ross, Robert S. "China and the Stability of East Asia." Paper prepared for a Conference on Asia in Transition: Toward a New Regional Order, East-West Center, Program on International Economics and Politics, Honolulu, Hawaii, January 4–7, 1993.

Round Table on Japan and the Asia-Pacific Region in the Twenty-first Century. "Japan and the Asia-Pacific Region in the Twenty-first Century—Promotion of Openness and Respect for Plurality." Office of the Prime Minister, Tokyo, December 25, 1992, typed manuscript.

Rowley, Anthony. "Asian Fund Special: The Battle of Hong Kong." *Nikko Capital Trends* 2, no. 13 (November 1997).

———. "Generosity Has Its Limits." *FEER*, June 20, 1991.

————. "International Finance: Asian Monetary Fund, RIP." *Nikko Capital Trends* 2, no. 14 (December 1997).

————. "Japanese Aid-Bonus for Reform." *FEER*, October 16, 1990.

————. "Yen for a Model." *FEER*, July 4, 1991.

Saito, Shiro. "Building a New Order in a Region of Diversity: Japan's Crucial Role." Special Issue on Asia-Pacific Partnerships. *Japan Review of International Affairs* 6 (1992).

Sakakibara, Eisuke. "The End of Progressivism—A Search for New Goals." *Foreign Affairs* (September-October 1995).

————. "Globalization and Diversity." Inaugural Address at the Development Thinking and Practice Conference, 1996, typescript.

————. "Mr. Yen Looking Back: 'Cybercapitalism' World Needs a Roadmap." *Yomiuri shimbun*, January 28, 2000.

————. "Reform of the International Financial System." Speech by Dr. Eisuke Sakakibara at the Manila Framework Meeting, Melbourne, Australia, March 26, 1999, draft.

Salih, Kamal, Ho Ting Seng, and Chua Chin Pen. "World Capital and Direct Foreign Investment in Malaysia: What Is the Outlook?" Shangri-La Hotel Conference, 1992.

Sano Tadakatsu. "Trade and Investment Liberalization in the Twenty-first Century." Speech delivered at the Singapore Congress on World Trade, Singapore, April 24–26, 1996, typescript.

Sasaki, Takeshi, and Daizaburo Yui. "Special Report: Japan-U.S. Relations without Prospects; Bush's Visit to Japan Full of Miscalculations; Difficulty of 'New Japan-U.S. Age' Symbolized." *The Economist* (January 28, 1992). Full translation by the United States Embassy, Tokyo.

Sasaki, Yoshitaka. "Japan's Undue International Contribution." *Japan Quarterly* (July-September 1993).

Sato, Hideo. "The Demise of the Cold-War Order: Regional Cooperation on the Rise." Special Issue on Asia-Pacific Partnerships. *Japan Review of International Affairs* 6 (1992).

————. "The Emerging Role of Japan in the World Economy." *International Spectator* 26, no. 3 (July-September 1991).

————. "Japan As an Emerging Power in the World Economy." Report of the Special Research Project on the New International System, Tsukuba University, Tsukuba, Ibaragi Prefecture, 1992.

Satoh, Yukio. "Asian-Pacific Process for Stability and Security." In *Japan's Post-Gulf International Initiatives*. Tokyo: MOFA, August 1991.

Sayle, Murray. "How Rich Japan Misled Poor Asia." JPRI Working Paper, no. 43 (March 1998).

Scalapino, Robert. "Perspectives on Political Development and the Nature of the Democratic Process: Leadership and the Institutionalization of Democratic Structures." Paper prepared for the Capitalism and Democracy Conference, January 1993.

Schaede, Ulrike. "MOF, Money, and the Japanese Banking Crisis of 1995." Mitteilungen des Instituts fur Asienkunde (Hamburg), no. 286 (1998).

Scott, Maurice, and Deepak Lal. "Preface." In *Public Policy and Economic Development: Essays in Honor of Ian Little*. Oxford: Clarendon Press, 1990.

Seki, Mitsuhiro. "Japanese Ventures in China—A Status Report." *JETRO China Newsletter*, no. 111 (July-August 1994).

Sekiguchi, Sueo, and Makito Noda. "An Overview of East Asia." Ushiba Memorial Foundation Workshop, 1992.

———. "Japan in East Asia." Ushiba Memorial Foundation Workshop, 1992.

Sender, Henny. "Out of Asia: Japanese Banks and Companies Head Home." *FEER*, April 16, 1998.

———. "Rethinking Asia: Don't Look to Japan." *FEER*, October 15, 1998.

Sheard, Paul. "The Economics of Japanese Corporate Organization and the 'Structural Impediments' Debate: A Critical Review." Australia-Japan Research Centre Pacific Economic Paper, no. 205 (March 1992).

Shiina, Motoo. "At A Foggy Mountain Pass: The World in Search of a New Order." *Japan Review of International Affairs* (Fall/Winter 1990).

Shinohara, Miyohei, and Toru Yanagihara, Kwang Suk Kim, and Ramgopal Agarwala, eds. "The Japanese and Korean Experiences in Managing Development." World Bank Staff Working Papers, no. 574; Management and Development Series, no. 1 (1983).

Shukan Daiyamondo. "Spheres of Development in a Regional Renaissance." Special Issue on Japan and East Asia. *Economic Eye* 13, no. 2 (Summer 1992).

Shukan Toyo Keizai. "Going Global through Offshore Production in Asia." Special Issue on Japan and East Asia. *Economic Eye* 13, no. 2 (Summer 1992).

Siamwalla, Ammar. "Can a Developing Democracy Manage Its Macroeconomy? The Case of Thailand." J. Douglas Gibson Lecture, Queens' University, School of Policy Studies, Kingston, Ontario, Canada, and Thailand Development Research Institute (Bangkok), October 15, 1997.

Simandjuntak, Djisman S. "The Roles of Japan in Asian Economies." *Asian Economic Journal* 5, no. 1 (1991).

Sjahrir. "Perspectives on Economic Development and the Role of the State: Economic Development Strategies and Trade Relations." Capitalism and Democracy Conference, 1993.

Skully, Michael T. "Financial Deepening in the East Asian Region." Fukuoka Garden Palace Conference, 1992.

Smitka, Michael J. "Business-Business Relations: Auto Parts Sourcing in Japan." In *Japan's Economic Challenge: Study Papers Submitted to the Congress of the United States, Joint Economic Committee.* Washington, D.C.: GPO, 1990.

———. "The Decline of the Japanese Auto Industry—Domestic and International Implications." Fukuoka Garden Palace Conference, 1992.

Soeya, Yoshihide. "Japanese Attitudes and Policies towards Indochina in a Regional Context: An Overview." Paper presented at a panel on the Asia Pacific Region in Transition, Symposium of the Abe Fellows Conference, Tokyo, Japan, July 26, 1993.

———. "Japan's Policy towards Southeast Asia: Anatomy of 'Autonomous Diplomacy' and the American Factor." In *China, India, Japan, and the Security of Southeast Asia*, edited by Chandran Jeshurun. Singapore: Institute for Southeast Asian Studies, 1993.

———. "Japan's Post-War Economic Diplomacy with China: Three Decades of Non-Governmental Experiences." Ph.D. dissertation, University of Michigan, Department of Political Science, 1987.

Sonoda, Shigeto. "Growth Process of Japanese Ventures in China." *JETRO China Newsletter*, no. 111 (July-August 1994).

"Special Discussion: Outlook of Japan's Direct Investment in China in the Present and Future." *JOI Review*, no. 4 (September 1992).

Standing, Jonathan. "Asian Ambitions." *Business Tokyo* (July 1992).

Steven, Rob. "Japanese Foreign Direct Investment in Southeast Asia: From ASEAN to J-ASEAN." *Bulletin of Concerned Asian Scholars* 20, no. 4 (October 1988).

Stevenson, Richard W. "Europeans Challenge U.S. in Economic Crisis." *New York Times*, October 7, 1998.

Stiglitz, Joseph E. "Asian Model: Critics Are Too Harsh." *Nikko Capital Trends* 3, no. 5 (April 1998).

———. "Asia's Reckoning: What Caused Asia's Crash?—Bad Private-Sector Decisions." *Wall Street Journal*, February 4, 1998.

———. "Back to Basics: Policies and Strategies for Enhanced Growth and Equity in Post-Crisis East Asia." Shangri-La Hotel Conference, 1992.

———. "The Insider: What I Learned at the World Economic Crisis." *New Republic*, April 17, 2000.

———. "Some Lessons from the East Asian Miracle." *World Bank Research Observer* 11, no. 2 (August 1996), pp. 151–77.

"A Strategic Framework for the Asian Pacific Rim: Report to Congress," 1992.

Sudo, Sueo. "The Road to Becoming a Regional Leader: Japanese Attempts in Southeast Asia, 1975–1980." *Pacific Affairs* (Spring 1988).

Sugita, Toshiaki. "Foreign Direct Investment and Its Subsequent Withdrawal—Investigation of Chinese Business." *JETRO China Newsletter* 3, no. 128 (1997).

Sumiya, Fumio. "Vietnam's Red-Tape Maze Snarls Investors." *Nikkei Weekly*, June 15, 1995.

Summers, Lawrence. "The Ishihara-Morita Brouhaha." *International Economy* (December 1989).

Suphachalasai, Suphat. "Economic Dimension of Indochina and ASEAN Relations." Oiso Conference, 1992.

Surakanvit, Banyat. "Japanese Direct Investment and Its Impact on Thai Economic Development." typescript, n.d.

Takagaki, Tasuku. "Facilitating the Recycling of Japanese Capital to the Developing Countries." Bank of Tokyo, Tokyo, May 1993, typescript.

———. "Dynamic Growth As an Antidote for Trading Blocs." Special Issue on Japan and East Asia. *Economic Eye* 13, no. 2 (Summer 1992).

Takeda, Isami. "A New Dialogue for Japan, ASEAN, and Oceania." Special Issue, Japanese Views of Asia. *Japan Echo* 20, Special Issue, 1993.

Takeshita, Noboru. "Address by Prime Minister Noboru Takeshita, Japan and ASEAN: Thinking Together and Advancing Together, Jakarta, 5 May 1989." *ASEAN Economic Bulletin* 6, no. 1 (July 1989).

Takeuchi, Junko. "Foreign Direct Investment in ASEAN by Small- and Medium-Sized Japanese Companies and Its Effects on Local Supporting Industries." *Pacific Business and Industries* 4 (1993).

———. "Trends and Prospects for Foreign Investment in ASEAN Countries in the 1990s." *Pacific Business and Industries* 1, no. 27 (1995).

Takeuchi, Kenji. "Does Japanese Foreign Direct Investment Promote Japanese Imports of Manufactures from Developing Economies?" *Asian Economic Journal* 5, no.1 (1991).

Tanahashi, T. Keisei. "Modalities for East Asian Cooperation and Japan's Initiatives." Presentation paper at the Second Annual Conference on Japan and East Asia: Attitudes and Policies of the Past, Present, and Future, Kuala Lumpur, Malaysia, January 20–21, 1993. Typescript manuscript, East-West Center, Program on International Economics and Politics, 1993.

Taniguchi, Koji. "The Role of Foreign Capital in the Manufactures Market Development in Thailand." Paper presented at the Conference on the Role of Direct Foreign Investment in Structural Change in East and Southeast Asia, East-West Center, Honolulu, Hawaii, September 18, 1992.

Taniguchi, Tomohiko. "Okurasho no 'En Gaiko' hisoka ni hatsu do tai doru 'atsuryoku dantai' no kessei e" (How the Ministry of Finance aimed to form a dollar "pressure group" through secret yen diplomacy). *Nikkei Business*, April 22, 1996.

Tecson, Gwendolyn R. "Comparative Advantage and Direct Foreign Investment in the Philippines." Typed manuscript, n.p.

Tejima, Shigeki. "Japanese MNCs' Overseas Business Operations in the Asia-Pacific Region—Foreign Direct Investment by Japanese Firms in Asia-Pacific Region, 1980s and 1990s." Fukuoka Garden Palace Conference, 1992.

Than, Mya. "ASEAN, Indo-China, and Myanmar: Towards Economic Cooperation?" *ASEAN Economic Bulletin* 8, no. 2 (November 1991).

Tho, Tran Van. "Comments on Professor Pasuk Phongpaichit's Paper, 'The New Wave of Foreign Investment in ASEAN.'" Fukuoka Garden Palace Conference, 1992.

———. "Vietnam and the East Asian Economy." Ushiba Memorial Foundation Workshop, 1992.

Thomas, Vinod, and Yan Wang. "Government Policies and Productivity Growth: Is East Asia an Exception?" World Bank Conference on Government and East Asian Economic Success, East-West Center, Honolulu, Hawaii, November 19–21, 1992.

"Toward the Establishment of Trade Rules for the Twenty-first Century That Contribute to the Era of 'Diversity and Coexistence'—Japan's Proposal for the WTO Negotiations—Agriculture, GMOs, Forestry/Fishery Products." Bound pamphlet, n.d.

Toyoda, Shoichiro. "World Trade and East Asia." Paper presented at the Asia Society's Corporate Conference, Tokyo, May 13, 1993.

Tsay, Ching-lung. "Taiwan and Prospects of Economic Interaction in East Asia." Ushiba Memorial Foundation Workshop, 1992.

Tsuruoka, Doug. "Look East—and Up." In *Japan and Asia: The Economic Impact on the Region*. Hong Kong: Review Publishing, 1991.

Unger, Danny. "Japan's Capital Exports: Molding East Asia." In *Japan's Emerging Global Role*, edited by Danny Unger and Paul Blackburn. Boulder, Colo.: Lynne Rienner, 1993.

Ungphakorn, Peter. "Japanese Eye Thailand Investments." *Tokyo Business Today* (April 1988).

Wade, Robert. "East Asia's Economic Success: Conflicting Perspectives, Partial Insights, Shaky Evidence." *Quarterly Journal of International Relations* 44, no. 2 (January 1992).

———. "Japan, the World Bank, and the Art of Paradigm Maintenance: The East Asian Miracle in Political Perspective." *New Left*, no. 217 (May-June 1996).

———. "The Role of Government in Overcoming Market Failure: Taiwan, Republic of Korea, and Japan." In *Achieving Industrialization in East Asia*, edited by Helen Hughes. Cambridge, U.K.: Cambridge University Press, 1988.

———. "Selective Industrial Policies in East Asia: Is the East Asian Miracle Right?" In *Miracle or Design? Lessons from the East Asian Experience*, Policy Essay, no. 11. Washington, D.C.: Overseas Development Council, 1994.

———. "The World Bank and the Art of Paradigm Maintenance: *The East Asian Miracle* As a Response to Japan's Challenge to the Development Consensus." Sussex University, Institute of Development Studies, n.p., October 28, 1994.

Wai, Peng Teck. "Malaysia-Japan Trade Interdependence: Implications for Long-Term Growth." Shangri-La Hotel Conference, 1992.

Wain, Barry. "Leaning on Asia's Keeper." *Asian Wall Street Journal*, May 29, 1993.

Watanabe, Michio, and Sumiko Iwao. "How to Push Japanese Diplomacy in the Fluidly Moving World." *Bungei Shunju* (March 1992). Full translation by the United States Embassy, Tokyo, Japan.

Watanabe, Toshio. "Age of Localized Economic Zones—Dissolution of the Cold War and the New Map of Asia's Economy." Paper presented at the Round Table on East Asia Conference, 1991.

Watanabe, Toshio, and Hisahiko Okazaki. "Asia's Changing Political Landscape." *Japan Echo* 19, no. 1 (Spring 1992).

Watson, Peter. "Practical Implications of the Post-GATT Order: Consideration for the Future Multilateral Agenda." Presentation at the U.S. International Trade Commission, Singapore Congress on World Trade, Singapore, April 24–26, 1996.

Weisberg, Jacob. "Keeping the Boom from Busting." *New York Times Magazine*, July 19, 1998.

Wie, Thee Kim. "The Surge of Asian NIC Investment into Indonesia." *Bulletin of Indonesian Economic Studies* 27, no. 3 (December 1991).

Williamson, John. "The Washington Consensus Revisited," in Economic and Social Development into the XXI Century, edited by Louis Emmerij (Washington, D.C., Inter-American Development Bank, 1998), from a paper originally presented at the Development Thinking and Practice Conference, Washington, D.C., September 3–5, 1996.

Woo-Cummings, Meredith. "The Asian Development Bank and the Politics of Development in East Asia." Paper presented to the International Conference on U.S.-Japan Relations and International Institutions after the Cold War. International House, Tokyo, April 8–11, 1994.

Wood, Bernard et al. "Japan Ascendant: Wealth, Power, Reponsibility in a Turbulent World." Roundtable discussion, Tokyo, February 1992. *Peace & Security* 7, no. 1 (Spring 1992).

"WTO kosho ni mukete no Nihon no teian: Proposal of Japan on the WTO Negotiations—Nogyo/GMO/Rinsanbutsu, Suisanbutsu—Agriculture/GMOs/Forestry and Fishery Products," bound pamphlet, n.d.

Wu, Jiapei. "China's Development and Prosperity of Economy in Asia and the Pacific." Paper presented at the Round Table on East Asia Conference, 1991.

Yam, Tan Kong, Toh Mun Heng, and Linda Low. "ASEAN and Pacific Economic Cooperation." *ASEAN Economic Bulletin* 8, no. 3 (March 1992).

Yamada, Katsuhisa. "Government-Business Interface." Typescript, 1984.

Yamada, Katsuhisa, and Akifumi Kuchiki. "Lessons from Japan: Industrial Policy Approach and East Asian Trial." Keynote paper for the Development Thinking and Practice Conference, 1996.

Yamagata, Yuichiro. "The Role of Japan's Aid in Asia's Development." Special Issue, Japan and East Asia. *Economic Eye* 13, no. 2 (Summer 1992).

Yamakoshi, Atsushi. "Japan in Asia: Perceptions and Realities." *JEI Report*, no. 17A, May 3, 1996.

Yamamura, Kozo, and Walter Hatch. "A Looming Entry Barrier: Japan's Production Networks in Asia." National Bureau of Asian Research (Seattle), *NBR Analysis* 8, no. 1 (February 1997).

Yanagihara, Toru. "Economic System Approach and Its Applicability." In *East Asian Development Experience: Economic System Approach and Its Applicability*, edited by Toru Yanagihara and Susumu Sambommatsu. Tokyo: IDE, 1997.

———. "Japan's Official Aid." Revised paper, originally prepared for presentation at the Council on Foreign Relations, New York, June 28, 1988; Tokyo, IDE, typed manuscript.

———. "Outline of the Development of the Asia-Pacific Economic Zone, and Its Relations with Latin America, Especially with Mexico." Discussion paper prepared for the Second Plenary Meeting of the Japan-Mexico Commission for the Twenty-first Century, Mexico, November 1–2, 1991, typed manuscript.

———, ed. "Ajia Taiheiyo no Keizai Haten to Chiiki Kyoryoku" (Economic development and regional cooperation in Asia-Pacific). Tokyo: IDE, 1992.

Yanagihara, Toru, and Miyohei Shinohara. "Japan As a Newly Industrializing Country: Mechanism of Growth and Structural Change in the Post-War Period." Paper prepared for the Conference on Patterns of Growth and Structural Change in Asia's Newly Industrializing Countries (NICs) and Near-NICs in the Context of Economic Interdependence, East-West Center, Honolulu, Hawaii, April 3–8, 1983.

Yanagiya, Kensuke. "Directing Japan's Aid Efforts." *Japan Echo* 6, no. 1 (Spring 1989).

Yasutomo, Dennis T. "Between a Rock and a Hard Place: The Foreign Policy Context of Japan's Strategic Aid." Paper prepared for the Workshop on Japan as No. One Donor: Japan's Foreign Assistance, Missoula, Montana, and the Conference on Japan and the United States in Third World Development: Looking to the Future, sponsored jointly by the Maureen and Mike Mansfield Foundation and the Center for Strategic and International Studies, Washington, D.C., May 14–17 and May 19, 1987.

Yb Tan Sri Dato' Jamil bin Mohd. jan. "Heavy Industries in Malaysia—Lessons from the 1980s and Challenges for the 1990s, HICOM's Experience and Views." INTAN Economic Lecture Series. Kuala Lumpur, Malaysia, February 21, 1990, typed manuscript.

———. "Why Aid? Japan As an 'Aid Great Power.'" *Pacific Affairs*, (Winter 1989–90).

Yochelson, John. "Letter from Japan: Nippon's Re-Asianization." *International Economy* (July/August 1992).

Young, Alwyn. "Lessons from the East Asian NICS: A Contrarian View." *European Economic Review* 38 (1994).

———. "A Tale of Two Cities: Factor Accumulation and Technical Change in Hong Kong and Singapore." In NBER (National Bureau of Economics Research) *Macroeconomics Annual, 1992*. Cambridge, Mass.: MIT Press, 1992.

———. "The Tyranny of Nos: Confronting the Statistical Realities of the East Asian Growth Experience." *Quarterly Journal of Economics* 110, no. 3 (August 1995).

Young, Soogil. "Economic Development of East Asia: Its Impact on Asia-Pacific." Fukuoka Garden Palace Conference, 1992.

———. "Regionalism in a Converging World: Comments on the Presentation by Mr. Toyoo Gyohten, Bank of Tokyo." Paper presented at the Third Convention of the East Asian Economic Association, Seoul, Korea, August 20–21, 1992.

Yue, Chia Siow. "Developments in the Singapore-Johor-Riau Growth Triangle." Ushiba Memorial Foundation Workshop, 1992.

Yuen, Ng Chee, Sueo Sudo, and Donald Crone. "The Strategic Dimension of the 'East Asian Developmental States.'" *ASEAN Economic Bulletin* 9, no. 2 (November 1992).

Zagoria, Donald S. "The United States and East Asia in the Post–Cold War Era: Time for New Thinking?" Paper prepared for the Conference on Asia in Transition: Toward a New Regional Order, East-West Center, Program on International Economics and Politics, Honolulu, Hawaii, January 4–7, 1993.

Zhang Jixun. "Problems in Direct Investment in China." *JETRO China Newsletter*, no. 103 (March-April 1993).

Index

Abe Shintaro, 391
Abe Yoshiaki, 302–303
Abeygunasekara, Amarananda, 332
Acheson, Dean, 358
Adams, Will, 290
Aichi Kazuo, 392
Aiwa Ltd., 146
Ajay Chhibber, 312
Akamatsu Kaname, 31–32, 55, 57, 58,
    63–67, 68, 72, 113, 164, 215–217, 562
Akashi Yasushi, 421
Akihito, Emperor, 83, 378–379, 446, 448,
    459–460
Akita Tadashi, 142–143
Alias Bin Ban, 233–234
Amano Mitsuhari, 393
Amorsolo, Fernando, 351
Amsden, Alice, 73, 284, 286
Anabuki Hiroyuki, 213
Anek, Laothammatas, 520
Anwar, Dewi Fortuna, 42
Anwar Ibrahim, 253
Aoki Ihei, 389
Aoki Masahiko, 310, 312
APEC. *See* Asia Pacific Economic
    Cooperation
Apology for war crimes, xxvi, 17, 88, 457,
    459–461, 462, 463, 464
Aquino, Benigno, 343, 352
Aquino, Corazon, 352
Arai Hisamitsu, 328
Arifin Siregar, 84, 513
Aris Anuar, Muhammad, 184–185
Armacost, Michael H., 561–562
Armed forces. *See* Military
Asahara Shoko, 554–555
Asahi Glass, 401
Asahi Group, 155–156
Asami Tamotsu, 454
Asanuma Shinji, 296
ASEAN. *See* Association of Southeast
    Asian Nations

ASEAN Industrial Cooperation (AICO)
    program, 196
ASEAN-Japan Development Fund, 128
ASEAN Regional Forum (ARF), 424,
    425–426, 435, 436
ASEM (Asia-Europe Meeting), 253, 367
Ashida Terumori, 203
Asia Development Board, 62
Asian Development Bank (ADB), 258, 364,
    365
Asian Drama (Myrdal), 364
Asian Economics Research Institute, 56
Asian economy
    Bretton Woods institutions and, xiv, 52
    "crony capitalism" and, 51
    free market and, 48–51
    growth of, xiii, xvii–xviii, 47–48,
        364–365
    Japanese investment and, 116–117, 122
    productivity of, 280–283
    recovery of, xxi–xxii, 22, 29, 32, 37
    See also Asian financial crisis of 1997–98;
        East Asian Miracle project; Japanese
        model of development
Asian financial crisis of 1997–98, xvi,
    xviii–xix, 13, 23, 37
    Asian model blamed for, xix–xx, 517–518
    Asian Monetary Fund (AMF) plan, 95,
        251–254
    Asian view of, 518–519
    critics of IMF policy, 248–251, 517, 518
    crony capitalism blamed for, 527–528
    globalization blamed for, xx–xxi, 260–261
    IMF response to, 14, 15, 29, 95, 245–248,
        516, 523, 524, 525, 526, 528,
        533–535
    indicators of, 523, 526, 531
    in Indonesia, 515–516, 527–537
    Japanese economy and, xxv, 504–505
    Japanese support efforts in, 15, 21–22,
        219–237, 255, 258–260, 539–540
    Japanese *vs* Western view of, xix–xxi

669

Asian financial crisis of 1997–98
    (*continued*)
  private sector response to, 526, 527
  in South Korea, 522–523
  in Thailand, 516, 519–522
  World Bank response to, 524–526,
    533–534
Asian-Japanese relations
  Akihito's visit and, 459–460
  balance of power and, 25–26
  China and, 447–450, 454
  cultural influences and, 134–136,
    564–565
  desire for reconciliation, 43–45
  East Asian economic model and, xiii–xvi,
    5, 7, 13–14
  economic integration policy, 111–113
  foreign aid. *See* Foreign aid to Asia
  foreign investment. *See* Foreign
    investment in Asia
  foreign trade. *See* Foreign trade with Asia
  G7/G8 summits and, 22–24, 367
  historical background, 16, 38–41
  Japanese economic model and, 93–106
  Okuda Report on, 31
  Ozawa Ichiro on, 368–369
  pre-1990, 6–7, 36
  public attitude toward Asianization policy,
    15–16
  regional currency, 255–257
  regional policeman role and, 15
  regional security apparatus, 424–426
  regional summits, xxvi, 24, 42, 85, 111,
    259–260, 367, 426
  shifts in direction, 36–37
  tilt to Asia, 7, 9–11, 12–13, 18, 22, 29,
    87–89, 107–110
  under U.S. Occupation, 358–359
  war guilt and, xxvi, 17, 88, 457, 460, 461,
    462, 463, 464, 465–466
  See also Asia Pacific Economic
    Cooperation (APEC); Colonialism;
    Ethnic prejudice; Flying-geese
    concept; *specific countries*
Asian Monetary Fund (AMF) plan, 95,
    251–254, 257
Asians in Japan
  ban on unskilled workers, 488–489, 496
  with Japanese companies, 498–503
  Korean community, xxvi, 369, 481–486,
    489
  in labor force, 88, 489–493
  mail-order brides, 496–498
  students, 17–18, 88, 457, 479–481

Asia Pacific Economic Cooperation
    (APEC), 14, 33, 57, 282, 367
  creation of, 75–78
  DAC limits on aid, 80
  EAEC proposal and, 84–85
  Eminent Persons Group (EPG), 76, 79
  Kuala Lumpur meeting, 80, 82
  membership of, 78–79
  naming of, 78
  Osaka meeting, 42, 80–84
  Partners for Progress plan, 80, 82
  south-south economic cooperation and, 79
  United States and, 78, 82, 84
Asia's New Giant (Patrick and Rosovsky),
    396–397
Asia That Can Say No, The (Ishihara and
    Mahathir), 463
Association of Southeast Asian Nations
    (ASEAN), xxvi, 4, 90, 435
  ASEAN Plus Three summits, 24, 42, 85,
    111, 259–260, 367, 368, 426
  Auto Supporting Industries Conference,
    199
  China relations, 448, 449, 560
  EAEC proposal and, 84
  economic partnership proposal, 560–561
  Free Trade Agreement, 163
  Fukuda Doctrine, 71
  post-ministerial conference (PMC) of,
    424, 425
  regional production programs of, 189–196
  See also Southeast Asia
A.T. Kearny, 539
Atsuyuki Suzuta, 408
Aum Shinrikyo, 554–555
Australia, in APEC, 75, 78
Automobile industry in Asia
  "Asian" car of, 194, 196–198
  assembly operations, 168, 174–175
  brand-to-brand complementation (BBC)
    in, 189–196
  comparison with electronics industry,
    160–164
  domestic market focus of, 124, 160–161,
    162, 163
  domestic sales, 166–168
  exports, 138, 170, 172, 175–177
  financial crisis of 1997–98 and, 223–224
  goal of national industry, 161
  Japanese imports from, 165–166, 196
  keiretsu rivalry in, 187–188
  Korean model, 170
  local content rules, 168–169, 174, 178, 190
  MITI support and, 198–199, 417

Automobile industry in Asia *(continued)*
   origins of regional production, 189–190
   parts trade, 164–166, 171–172, 180–181,
      188, 190–192, 198–199, 224
   production companies, 105, 122, 136
   production hierarchy in, 188–189
   Taiwanese model, 170–172
   technology transfer in, 178, 181–185
   U.S. companies and, 124–125, 185–186
Azeem, Arif, 492
Aziz, Rafideh, 83
Azlan Bin Amran, Muhammad, 218, 233,
   234

Ba Maw, 41
Baba Hiroshi, 549
Baker, James, 24, 77, 84, 89, 426
Bakufu system, 11
Balance-of-payments support program,
   225–226, 245
Baldrige, Malcolm, 518
Bandung Conference of 1955, 363
Bank for International Settlements (BIS), 26
Bank of International Settlements (BIS),
   209
Bank of Japan, 19, 137, 257, 372–373, 382
Banks
   Asian assets of, 209–210, 568
   in China, 569–570
   credit expansion and, 19, 568
   failure of, 207, 210
   keiretsu, 397, 399, 400, 405
   loans to Asia, 114, 207, 208–209
   nonperforming loans, 207–208, 210, 222
   regional currency and, 257
   in stock speculation case, 409
   trading companies and, 210–211,
      212–213
Bao Ge, 460
Baoshan steel project, 445–446
Barabudur (Mus), 340
Barr, Cameron, 507, 510
Barshefsky, Charlene, 328, 539
Basir, Misran, 333
Beasley, W.G., 59–60
Bellow, Walden, 73
Bentsen, Lloyd, 268
Bergsten, C. Fred, 76
Berkeley Roundtable on the International
      Economy (BRIE), 159
Bernard, Mitchell, 114–115
Bevacqua, Ron, xxii, 207
Bienan, Henry, 289, 313
Binawan, Amnoi, 522

Birdsall, Nancy
   background of, 272
   birthday party concept of, 273
   characterized, 272–273
   in *East Asian Miracle* project, 264–265,
      266, 268, 270, 275, 288, 290, 302
   on factor accumulation, 273–274
   at Inter-American Development Bank,
      278–279, 313
Bismarck, Otto von, 331
Black Dragon Society, 443
Blaker, Michael, 325
Bogor declaration, 82
Bonior, David, 230
Borrus, Michael, 150, 159
Bose, Subas Chandra, 41
Brady, Nicholas, 258
Brain Trust program, 263
Brand-to-brand complementation (BBC),
   189–196
Brand wars, 395
Bricklin, Malcolm, 176
Burdick, Eugene, 346
Bureaucracy
   Asian alliance and, 18, 22, 77, 78, 81, 87, 91
   deregulation efforts and, 554
   disaster relief failure of, 411–412, 553
   faceless image of, 412–413
   flying-geese concept and, 92, 113
   foreign aid and, 20, 32, 126–129,
      226–228, 229, 314
   foreign investment and, 105–106, 114, 131,
      141, 153–154, 198–199
   foreign policy camps, 421–422
   housing-loan scandal, 543–544, 555–557
   invulnerability of, 417–418, 555
   Japanese model and, 92, 94, 318
   mismanagement, 554–555
   moral aims of, 413–414
   postwar system, 415–416
   private sector ties of, 315–316, 416–417
   rivalries in, 91
   training programs of, 228–229
   war government, 414–415
Buruma, Ian, 463
Bush, George H.W. (senior), 319, 326,
   402–403, 440
Bush, George W., 439, 565
Bushido, 55, 414
Business Week, 224, 316

Cambodia, 430, 448–449
Camdessus, Michel, 37, 52, 95, 239, 246,
   527, 528

Campos, Jose Edgardo, 266, 267, 273, 274, 304
Canada, in APEC, 75, 78
Canon, Inc., 123–124, 218, 220, 231–234
Capital Formation in Japan (Rosovsky), 303
Caves, Richard, 397
Center for Strategic and International Studies (CSIS), 510
Chang, Iris, 463
Chapuis, Nicolas, 450
Chavalit Yongchaiyudh, 521, 522
Chen, Edward K.Y., 73
Chen Yun, 446
Chenery, Hollis, 268
Cheney, Dick, 326
Cheong Mun Kun, 30
Chiang Kai-shek, 365
Chiang Mai Initiative, 252
Chiang Shu-ling, 478–481
China
    Akihito's visit to, 460
    in APEC, 82, 449
    ASEAN and, 448, 449, 560
    Asian NIEs investment in, 121, 449
    automobile production in, 191
    economy of, 453–454, 456, 561, 563–567
    foreign investment in, 125, 563
    influence on Japan, 37–38
    Japanese model in, 451–453
    Japanese multinationals in, 501–502
    Japanese popular culture in, 135
    Japanese retailers in, 201
    Japanese trading companies in, 211–212
    in Korean War, 358
    nuclear tests of, 455
    -U.S. relations, 25, 447
China-Japan relations, xiv–xv, 13, 33, 422, 442–455
    aid, 114, 460
    collaboration, 562–563
    colonial rule and, 6, 58–61, 68, 471–476
    competition in Asia, 447–450, 454
    fear of China, 453–355
    human rights and, 450–451
    investment, 119–120, 144, 152, 236–237, 444, 445–447, 456, 568–570
    Ryukyu Islands dispute, 24–25
    security concerns and, 437–438, 439, 447, 455
    trade, 107–108, 444–445, 446
Chinese in Japan, 478–481, 490, 493, 494–496
Ching, Frank, 83
Chino Tadao, 129

Chisso Corp., 203
Chiyoda Co., 211
Chong, Richard, 144–145
Chowdhury, Sanjoy, 103, 116
"Chrysanthemum Club," 355
Chrysler, 185, 189–190
Chuan Leekpai, xxi
Chung, Chien-peng, 425
Clavell, James, 290
Clifford, Mark, xvii
Cline, William R., 27
Clinton, William J., 84, 230, 268, 269, 325, 326, 426–427, 451, 516, 538
Cohen, Aaron Martin, 401
Cold War, 359–362, 367, 368, 419–420
Colonialism, 16–17
    in China, 6, 58–61, 68, 471–476
    comfort women and, 468, 482–483
    in Korea, 42–43, 485
    language policy and, 481
    public knowledge of, 41, 466–468, 471–474
    in Southeast Asia, 61–62
Comfort women, 468, 482–483
Commission for a New Asia, 88, 111
Comparative advantage, 122–123
Conference of Non-Aligned Nations, 363
Congressional Research Service (CRS), 76
Conklin, Harold, 349
Constantino, Renato, 102, 103
Consumer spending, 384–385
Convergence theory, xiv, 93, 276, 359
Convoy investment, 105
Cook, Peter, 104
Corden, W. Max, 267
Corruption scandals. *See* Japanese corruption scandals
Council of Rome, xvi
Courtis, Kenneth, 106, 225, 374, 376–377
Crawford, John, 75
Cultural influence of Japan, 134–136, 564–565
Currency
    dollar dominance, 255
    yen appreciation, 23, 27–28, 29, 89, 121, 126, 137, 163–164, 374
    yen depreciation, 225, 255, 565–566
    yen internationalization, 255–258
Daewoo Electronics, 151
Dai Toa Kaigi, 41–42
Dai Xianglong, 565, 567
Daihatsu Motor, 187–188
Daimaru department store, 203
Daimyo, 11, 414

Dallara, Charles, 373
D'Amato, Alfonse, 245–246
"Dankichi the Adventurer," 478
Datsu-A ron (Fukuzawa), 39
Datsu Ou Nyu A, 12
Dekle, Robert, 245, 269
Deliberation councils (*shingikai*), 416
Delphi Automotive, 186
Deming, W. Edwards, 56–57, 292–293
Deming Prize, 292–293
Deng Xiaoping, 95, 121, 452, 563
Department stores, 200–207
Dependencia theory, 49, 70
Dervis, Kemal, 267, 278
De Tray, Dennis, 529, 535
Development Assistance Committee (DAC),
    of OECD, 79–80
Development Loan Fund, 361
Diem, Ngo Dinh, 365
Djojohadiksumo, Soemitro, 513
Dobson, Wendy, 129
Doner, Richard F., 73–74, 129
Doronila, Amando, 83
Dower, John, 57–58
Drysdale, George, 76
Dulles, John Foster, 359
Dunne, Timothy, 125
Dynamic Family Wagon (DFW), 198

EAEC. *See* East Asia Economic Caucus
Earthquake disaster relief, 411–412
East Asia: The Modern Transformation
    (Fairbank and Reischauer), 443
East Asia Economic Caucus (EAEC), 84
East Asia Common Culture Society, 443
East Asia Economic Group (EAEG), 24,
    84–85
East Asian Miracle project, 94, 240, 241,
    250, 416
  background papers for, 292
  criticism of, 282–287
  endorsement of Japanese model, 276,
    292–293
  financial crisis and, 524–525
  flying geese concept in, 32
  "functional" chart in, 306–307
  Japanese input and, 267–268, 302–303
  Japanese view of, 279–280, 281, 290–291,
    304–305, 313, 314
  Northeast/Southeast Asian models in,
    275–278
  origins of, 261–265, 301–303
  Page's leadership of, 265–266, 274–275,
    280, 282, 287–288

East Asian Miracle project *(continued)*
  publication of report, 277
  research team for, 266–267
  Summers' role in, 268–271
  total factor productivity (TFP) analysis in,
    280–282
Economic Development Institute (EDI), 263
Economic integration policy, 111–113
Economic Planning Agency (EPA), 30, 69,
    94, 121, 126, 282, 306, 307–308,
    322–324, 403
Economics
  anti-globalization and, 51–52
  of information, 250
  neoclassical model, 48–51, 291
Economic and Social Council for Asia and
    the Pacific (ESCAP), 76–77
Economic Stabilization Board, 69
Economy. *See* Asian economy; Japanese
    economy
Edaran Otomobil Nasional (EON), 212
Eda Satsuki, 379
Edo-Tokyo Museum exhibit on bombing
    raids, 474–476
Education policy
  history curriculum and, 40–41, 474
  non-Japanese teachers and, 484
Ei Rokusuke, 411
Eisenhower, Dwight D., 360, 361
Electronics industry in Asia, 105, 122, 123,
    136
  China, 152
  comparison with automobile industry,
    160–164
  costs of Japanese investment, 156–160
  decentralized structure of, 143–144
  as export platform, 145–147, 163
  financial crisis and, 220–221, 231–237
  keiretsu groupings, 104–105, 137, 139,
    152–156
  Korean investment in, 151–152, 157
  Malaysia, 139–144, 146, 147, 155–156,
    218, 219
  production of, 145
  Taiwanese investment in, 150–151, 157
  technology transfer and, 146, 157–160, 233
  Thailand, 146–149
  U.S. companies, 150
Elizalde, Manuel, Jr. "Manda," 348–349,
    350–352
Emergency Measures for the Economic
    Stabilization of Southeast Asia, 226
Emig, Anne, xviii, 295, 300, 301
Emmott, Bill, 537–538

Employment
  Asians in Japanese multinationals,
    498–503
  day laborers, 551
  discrimination, 480, 484, 547–548,
    549–550
  illegal foreign workers, 88, 486–493, 496
  immigration policy and, 487, 491
  labor shortage and, 487, 549
  lifetime system, 382–384, 546
  temporary workers, 553
  white-collar job loss, 544–549
Ennis, Peter, 427
Enola Gay exhibit, 475
EPA. *See* Economic Planning Agency
EPZ (export processing zone) model, 314
Ernst, Dieter, 159, 160
Estrada, Joseph, 260
Ethnic prejudice against Asians, xxv–xxvi,
    572
  foreign students, 17–18, 88, 457, 477–481
  foreign workers, 486–493
  in Japanese multinationals, 498–503
  Korean-Japanese, xxvi, 481–486
  Omura refugees and, 494–496
Eto Jun, 461, 469–470
European Union (EU), 78, 113, 143, 240,
    262
Evans, Paul, 425–426
Exchange rate realignment, 14, 27–28
Exchange Stabilization Fund, 245–246
Export-Import Bank (EXIM), 225
Export promotion policy, 291–292
Ezoe Hiromasa, 386, 391, 393–395

Fairbank, John K., 443
Fallows, James, 316
FASID. *See* Foundation for Advanced
    Studies of International Development
Fasi, Frank, 469
Fenster, Billy, 372
Financial crisis. *See* Asian financial crisis of
    1997–98
Fiorillo, James, 570
Fischer, Stanley, 268, 534–535
Flying-geese concept
  abandonment of, 563
  Akamatsu and, 63–67
  Asian economic model and, 14, 46, 47–
    48, 57, 92–93
  in Asian occupied territories, 58–63, 68
  data collection in, 55–56
  defined, 47
  economic integration and, 113

Flying-geese concept *(continued)*
  of foreign investment, 68, 71–72, 79, 90,
    92, 114
  of foreign trade, 122–123
  industrial policy and, 31–32, 56–57,
    60–62, 66–67
  Kojima and, 67, 71–72, 74
  newly industrializing economies (NIEs)
    and, 90
  Okita and, 67–70, 74
  origins of, 52–55
  Ozawa and, 72–73
  pyramidal structure of, 46, 55
  Western analysts on, 73–74
  World Bank policy and, 298–299
Ford, Henry II, 186
Ford Motor Co., 171, 185, 186
Foreign aid to Asia
  budget for, 23, 113–114, 125, 375
  as Cold War strategy, 359–362, 367
  conditionality and, 96
  conflict with international agencies,
    96–97, 99
  economic advisory role in, 96, 314
  JOIN (JETRO Overseas Investment), 154
  New Aid Plan, 126–129
  New Miyazawa Initiative, 29–30, 255,
    257, 258–259, 260
  Obuchi Plan, 259–260
  request principle in, 98–99
  shift in focus, 126
  south-south cooperation and, 79
  World Bank-OECF loan policy dispute,
    294–297
Foreign Currency Control Law of 1949, 415
Foreign investment in Asia, 15, 18, 566
  Akamatsu's legacy and, 215–217
  "bubble economy" and, 19–20, 89–90
  change in patterns of, 20, 85–87
  China, 119–120, 144, 152, 236–237, 444,
    445–447, 568–570
  convoy pattern of, 105, 152–153
  cumulative total, 230–231
  financial crisis support efforts and, 15,
    21–22, 219–237, 260
  financing of, 114, 207, 208–209
  flying-geese model, 68, 71–72, 79, 90, 92,
    114, 139
  global, 125
  impact on domestic production, 115–116,
    122
  impact on regional economy, 106–107,
    129–130, 216
  Japanese control and, 132–133

Foreign investment in Asia *(continued)*
  keiretsu subcontracting system, 104–105,
    137, 139, 152–156, 164
  manufacturing pyramid and, 123
  mutual funds, 26–27
  objectives of, 20
  production strategies, 87, 105, 112
  profitability of, 21, 91, 115, 130–131
  reception of, 103
  reduction in, 568
  of re-invested subsidiary earnings, 138
  retail stores, 200–207
  Sakamoto Report, 77–78
  shift from U.S. to, 108
  of Singapore, 34–35
  by small-and medium-sized companies,
    105, 119, 120, 153–155, 164,
    198–199
  in Southeast Asia, 28, 86, 91, 105–106,
    112, 117–118, 122, 129
  trading companies and, 210–214, 222
  vs U.S. investment, 19, 20–21
  waves of, 117–119
  See also Automobile industry in Asia;
    Electronics industry in Asia
Foreign policy
  change radical position, 422–423, 424,
    438–440, 458
  factionalism, 421–422
  internationalist position, 422, 423, 426
  multilateral approach, 8, 436–437
  regional security and, 424–426
  security concerns in, 420–421, 423–424,
    425
  See also Asian-Japan relations;
    China-Japan relations; Military;
    United States-Japan relations
Foreign trade
  export promotion policy, 291–292
  import substitution policy, 49, 130
  See also World Trade Organization
    (WTO)
Foreign trade with Asia
  China-Japan, 107–108, 444–445, 446
  comparative advantage in, 122–123
  deficits, 116
  growth of, 18, 107–108
  import promotion and, 229
  invoiced in yen, 18–19
  Japan's surplus, 116, 130
  product flow within Japanese companies,
    138
  triangular patterns of, 114–115
Fortune magazine, 373, 376

Foundation for Advanced Studies of
    International Development (FASID),
    94, 313, 314, 317
Fox, Bob, 349–350, 351
Fujimura Ken, 317
Fujioka Kyo, 176
Fujita Tourist Enterprises, 410
Fujitsu Ltd., 146
Fujiwara Katsuhiro, 210
Fujiwara Mariko, 552
Fukata Kiroshi, 155, 156
Fukuda Doctrine, 71
Fukuda Takeo, 71
Fukuken, 12, 13
Fukuoka Masayuki, 392–393
Fukuzawa Nobukazu, 233
Fukuzawa Yukichi, 39, 40, 110, 331
Funabashi Yoichi, 8, 78, 108–109

Gan Wee Feng, 499–501
Gaouette, Nicole, 507, 510
Garran, Robert, xvii
GATT. *See* General Agreement on Tariffs
    and Trade
G8 (Group of Eight) summits, 24
Geithner, Timothy, 259
Gender discrimination, 381–382, 480,
    547–548, 549–550
General Agreement on Tariffs and Trade
    (GATT), 77, 262, 325–326
General Motors, 185–186
Gibney, Frank, 353–354, 355, 387
Gluttonous Devils (Morimura), 473
Gorbachev, Mikhail, 318, 320–321, 322
Greater East Asia Co-Prosperity Sphere,
    xiii, xxvi, 13, 14, 47, 57, 58, 62, 64,
    82–83, 102, 103–104, 443
Greater East Asia Assembly, 41–42
Greater East Asia Ministry, 62–63
Green, Michael, 439
Greene, Dick, 158–159
Greenspan, Alan, 517
Greenwald, Bruce, 250
Greenwald, Gerald, 190
G7 (Group of Seven) summits, 22–24
Guabloche, Maria Judith, 333, 334
Guangyang motorcycle company, 172
Gulf War, 318–320
Guo Gang, 490
Gyohten Toyoo, 256, 372

Habibie, B.J., 510, 513, 514, 528, 531, 535,
    541
Hakogi Masumi, 481

Halloran, Fumiko, 572
Hamanaka Akiko, 549–550
Han Seung Soo, 522–523
Hanke, Steve, 535, 537
Harris, Townsend, 40
Harvard Bureau of Economic Statistics, 65
Hasegawa Koji, 192
Hashimoto Ryutaro, 42, 259, 325, 427,
    463–464, 538
Hata Ikuchiko, 474
Hatch, Walter, xxiii, 226, 229
Hathaway, Larry, 282
Havana Charter of 1948, 326
Hawaii
    as command center, 419–420
    Pearl Harbor memorial, 432–433
Hawke, Robert, 75, 78
Hayase Koichi, 131, 153–154
Hayashizaki Chiaki, 429, 430
Heavy Industries Corporation of Malaysia
    (HICOM), 175, 178, 181
Heckscher, Eli, 64
Heisei Era, 380–381
Herrera, Miguel, 333–334
Hicks, George, 463
High-performing East Asian economies
    (HPAEs), 277–278
Higuchi Hirotaro, 421
Hills, Carla, 84
Hindmarsh, Al, 353, 354
Hirao Koji, 559, 562
Hirohito
    Emperor, 42, 59, 83, 87–88, 459
    funeral of, 379–380
    illness and death of, 373, 374, 377–378,
        466
Hiroshima Asian Games, 454
Hiroshima bombing, 475
Hirsh, Michael, 537
History, view of, 458–476
    anticolonial movements, 470–471
    apology for war crimes, xxvi, 17, 88,
        457, 459–461, 462, 463, 464, 469
    commemorations of war, 461–462, 469,
        470, 474–476
    denial of war guilt, 461, 464–465
    public examination of war crimes,
        466–468, 471–474
    textbook censorship and, 40–41, 474
    war responsibility and, 469–470
Hitotsubashi University, 65, 67, 74, 97–98
Hollerman, Leon, 74
Homelessness. See Japanese
    homelessness

Honda Motor Co.
    Asian car of, 198
    Asian consumer market of, 124–125, 165
    Asian financial crisis and, 223
    in Indonesia, 541
    in Taiwan, 172
    in Thailand, 166–167, 190–191
    in Vietnam, 97
Hong Kong
    Beijing and, 565
    economic growth of, 364
    free market and, 50
    investment in Southeast Asia, 121
    Japanese investment in, 28, 86, 106, 220,
        230
    Japanese retailers in, 201, 203, 205
    World Bank meeting in, 253
Horikome Yumi, 317
Hosoda Koichi, 405
Hosokawa Morihiro, 438–439, 450–451,
    463
Hotai Motor, 171
Hotta Yasushi, 211
Housing-loan scandal, 543–544, 555–557
Huang Xu, 443
Hughes, Helen, 286
Human experiment program, 471–474
Human rights, 450–451
Hussein, Saddam, 318, 319
Hyundai Motors, 170, 174

IDE. See Institute for Developing
    Economies
Ienaga Saburo, 474
Iglesias, Enrique, 279
Ikeda Hayato, 69
Ikeda Makoto, 147–148, 149
Imai Ken'ichi, 398
Imanishi Shojiro, 55, 81
IMF. See International Monetary Fund
IMF Survey, 526
Imhoff, Al, 285
Immigration policy
    ethnic Japanese immigrants and, 486–487
    foreign workers and, 487–489, 496
    illegal immigrants and, 489–493
    Omura refugees and, 494–496
    postwar, 489
Imperialism ideology, 59
Import substitution policy, 49, 130
Income, per capita, 384
Indonesia
    Akihito's visit to, 459
    in APEC, 82, 83

Indonesia *(continued)*
automobile production in, 169, 223
colonial rule of, 470–471
economic collapse of, 514–515, 516,
    527–537
economic recovery of, xxi, 32, 530,
    541–542
export growth of, 121, 365
IMF loans to, 255, 526, 528, 530
investment rules in, 121
Japanese aid to, 114, 127, 128, 259
Japanese investment in, 28, 86, 106, 112,
    118, 231
Japanese trading companies in, 212–213
Korean investment in, 151
overthrow of Sukarno, 365, 505–514
political unrest in, 541
regional security and, 424
Suharto regime, 363–364, 534–535
Sukarno regime, 362–363
Taiwanese investment in, 151
Inoguchi Kuniko, 428
Inoguchi Takashi, 375, 464–466
Institute for Developing Economies (IDE),
    55–56, 94, 305, 308, 313, 316, 375
Institute for Policy Reform, 313
Inter-American Development Bank (IDB),
    279
Interest rates, 137
International Bank for Reconstruction and
    Development. *See* World Bank
International Cooperation Administration,
    361, 362, 363
    See also U.S. Agency for International
    Development (USAID)
International Development Agency (IDA),
    297, 298
International Financial Corporation, 241
International House of Japan, 455–456
International Monetary Fund (IMF), xiv,
    xviii, xxi, 37, 52, 125
antiglobalization protests at, 239, 241
in Asian financial crisis, 14, 15, 29, 95,
    245–248, 516, 517, 518, 524, 528,
    530, 533–535
Asian Monetary Fund (AMF) proposal
    and, 251–254
balance-of-payments support program,
    225–226, 245
critics of financial crisis policy, 248–251,
    517, 518
Japan's influence on, 239, 242, 251–252
rivalry with World Bank, 244, 245,
    246–248, 261

International Monetary Fund (IMF)
    (continued)
Washington Consensus at, 249
International Trade Organization (ITO), 326
"Investigation of Global Policy with the
    Yamato Race as Nucleus, An," 57–58
Invisible Empire (Courtis), 377
Inyaku Tomoya, 495–496
Iriye Akira, 442
Isetan Co., 200
Ishiba Shigeru, 393
Ishihara Nobuo, 469
Ishihara Shintaro, xxvi, 88, 369, 463
Ishii Shiro, 472, 473
Ishikawa Shigeru, 74, 97–100, 267–268,
    276, 310
Ishizuka Masahiko, 111
Isoda Ichiro, 409
Isolationism, 39
Itami Juzo, 558
Itamoto Yoko, 497
Iten, Osvald, 352
Ito Hitoshi, 477–478
Ito Midori, 548–549
Iwabuchi Kenji, 176
Iwakura Mission, 330–331
Iwakura Tomomi, 330
Iwase Fusako, 543, 555
Iwata Kazumasa, 307

Jansen, Marius, 357
Japan-Australia Business Cooperation
    Committee, 76
Japan Auto Parts Industries Association,
    191, 199
Japan Bank for International Cooperation,
    258
Japan Center for International Finance, 94
Japanese-Asian relations. *See* Asian-Japan
    relations
Japanese Chamber of Commerce (JCC), 149
Japanese Constitution, pacifist clause of, 8,
    9, 421, 428, 439
Japanese corruption scandals, 386–395
Japanese economy
    Asian financial crisis and, xxv, 29,
        504–505
    "bubble economy," 19, 89, 372–377, 490
    collapse of "bubble economy," 7–8, 137,
        370–371, 537–538
    comparison with China, 453–454,
        563–567
    exchange rate realignment and, 14, 27–28
    future of, 557–558

Japanese economy *(continued)*
  government role in, 10, 315–316
  interdependence with Asia, 138
  Meiji Restoration and, 11
  in recession, 543–552, 565–566
  reform and restructuring of, 8, 30
  stock market crash of 1990, 137, 209
  under U.S. Occupation, 356–357
  See also Currency; Employment;
      Flying-geese concept; Japanese
      model of development; *Keiretsu*
      system
Japanese homelessness, 550–552
Japanese language schools
  in Asia, 135
  for immigrants, 490, 492, 493
  U.S. Navy, 353–355
Japanese model of development
  challenge to convergence thesis, 93
  China and, 451–453
  corruption scandals in, 386–395
  East Asian Miracle report and, 276,
      292–293, 302–303
  flying-geese concept and, 92
  history of, 329–334
  Japanese studies of, 94–95, 307–314,
      316–317
  management training programs in, 317,
      321, 322–324, 334
  promotion of, 318, 324
  in Russia, 321–322
  U.S. *vs* Japanese versions of, 10
  in Vietnam, 95–97
Japan Export-Import Bank (JEXIM), 114,
      120, 131, 222, 258, 259, 260
Japan External Trade Organization
      (JETRO), 32, 90, 94, 99, 113, 114,
      130, 131, 153, 154, 199, 224, 231, 501
Japan Fair Trade Commission (JFTC),
      405–406
Japan Institute for Overseas Development
      (JOI), 222
Japan International Cooperation Agency
      (JICA), 80, 94, 154, 228, 262, 323, 332
Japan International Training Cooperation
      Organization, 323
Japan Overseas Development Corporation
      (ODC), 154, 238
Japan's Economy on the Downslope
      (Mizutani), 544
Japan's Strategy of Economic Development
      (Kong), 452
JETRO. *See* Japan External Trade
      Organization

JETRO China Newsletter, 501
JEXIM. *See* Japan Export-Import Bank
Jiang Zemin, 212, 450, 451, 464
JICA. *See* Japan International Cooperation
      Agency
Job discrimination
  Korean-Japanese, 484
  women, 480, 547–548, 549–550
Job loss, white collar, 544–548
John Bates Clark Award, 250, 268
Johnson, Chalmers, 94, 286, 315–316
JOIN (JETRO Overseas Investment), 154
Jomo, Kwame Sundaram, xvii, 92, 103
Jusco, 205

Kaifu Toshiki, 84
Kaihara Toshitami, 429
Kajimoto Keni, 496
Kaku Ryuzaburo, 123–124
Kanai Rieko, 382
Kanematsu (trading company), 212
Kang Youwei, 443
Kantor, Mickey, 81
Karaoke, 134, 135–136, 564
Kato Kakatoshi, 256
Katoppo, Aristides, 506, 511–512, 530
Katoppo, Mismis, 512–513
Katsu Eijiro, 256
Katz, Richard, 537
Kawakami Yukio, 497
Kawakyu Koichi, 220
Kawamoto Nobuhiko, 124
Kawanabe Takeshi, 491
Kawashima Yoshifumi, 182–183
Keene, Donald, 354
Keidanren, 210
Keio University
  Global Security Research Center at, 240
  international relations seminar at, 433–435
Keiretsu system
  anti-monopoly law and, 405–406
  bias against shareholders, 398, 401
  brand wars and, 395
  clash with Western-style corporations,
      402–404
  defined, 400
  economic influence of, 396, 397
  expansion of, 399–400
  history of, 396–397, 398–399
  horizontal and vertical types, 400–401, 405
  Japanese defense of, 397–398
  in offshore production, 86, 104–105, 137,
      139, 152–156, 164, 187–188, 210,
      211, 231

Keiretsu system *(continued)*
  speculator groups and, 407
Kcizai Doyukai, 439
Kennan, George, 358, 367
Kennedy, Douglas, 404
Kennedy, John F., 346–347, 359–360,
  361–362
Kennedy, Paul, 377
Key to the Asian Miracle, The (Campos),
  267
Khoriri H.J. Abu Sabri, 179–180
Kia Motors, 169, 223
Kigyo Keiretsu Soran, 400, 405
Kijang (automobile), 194, 196–197
Kikawada Hiroshi, 547
Kikuchi Kiyoaki, 422–423, 469
Kikuchi Tetsuro, 558
Kikutani, C., 90
Kim Chang Shik, 266
Kim Dae Jung, xxi, xxvi, 16, 26, 247, 259,
  464
Kim Jong Il, 26
Kim Kyong Duk, 484, 485–486
Kim Kyu Il, 483
Kim Young Sam, 450, 516, 522
King, Mervyn, 95
"King Kong Meets Godzilla: The World
  Bank and the *East Asian Miracle*"
  (Rodrik), 238
Kinmonth, Earl, 567
Kinoshita Toshihiko, 31, 329–332,
  539–541
Kisai Bin Rahmat, 179, 183
Kitaura Masayuki, 491
Kitayama Shigeru, 128
Kiuchi Mikio, 384–385
Kiyoshige Kazuhiro, 434, 435
Kobayashi Yotaro, 110, 111, 453
Kobe earthquake, 411–412, 429, 553
Koh Buck Song, 135–136
Kohler, Horst, 240
Koito Manufacturing, 400, 402,
  403–404
Koizumi Junichiro, 560–561
Kojima Kiyoshi
  APEC and, 75, 76, 77
  flying-geese concept of, 64, 67, 74, 75
  on foreign investment, 20, 71–72
  on trading companies, 214
Kojima Taijiro, 149
Kokubun Ryosei, 446
Kokusai Kogyo, 410
Koll, Jesper, 566
Komura Masahiko, 25

Kong Fanjing, 452
Konoe Fumimaro, 59, 62
Korea
  colonial administration of, 42–43, 485
  influence on Japan, 40
  See also South Korea
Koreans in Japan, xxvi, 369, 481–486
Korean War, 357–358
Korhonen, Pekka, 74, 77
Koshida Takashi, 473–474
Kotani Mitsuhiro, 408–409, 410
Koyauemura Yoshimasu, 383–384
Kozo Yamamura, xxiii
Kristoff, Sandra, 84
Krueger, Anne, 268, 302
Krugman, Paul, 121, 251, 270, 273,
  282–283
Kubota Isao, 93, 293–294, 295,
  298–299, 301–302
Kuchiki Akifumi, 313, 314,
  316–317
Kunihiro Michihiko, 389
Kuozui Motors, 189
Kurachi Tadashi, 212
Kurile Islands dispute, 321
Kurosawa Yoh, 491
Kuruneru, Edith, 571
Kuwajima Kyoko, 323
Kwan Chi Hung, 114, 454
Kyoda Toyoho, 198

Labor force. *See* Employment
Lal, Deepak, 287
Lambert, Charles, 408, 411
Lamy, Pascal, 329
Language schools. *See* Japanese
  language schools
Lardy, Nicholas, 566
Latin America, ethnic Japanese
  immigration from, 486–488
Laurel, Jose Paciano, 41
Lawrence, Robert Z., 267, 397
Lederer, William, 346
Lee Kuan Yew, 365
Lee Teng-hui, 17, 97, 454, 455
Lehner, Urban, 388
Leipziger, Danny, 247, 266
Levy, Frank, 295
LG Electronics, 151
Li, Richard, 13
Li Hongzhang, 443
Li Jichun, 41
Li Peng, 84, 211, 449, 450
Liang Qichao, 443

Liberal Democratic Party (LDP)
  bureaucracy and, 554
  corruption scandals and, 387–395
  right wing of, 462–463
Liew Sew Yee, 128
Lifetime employment system, 382–384, 546
Lincoln, Ed, 129, 294, 325, 376, 538
Lindbergh, Charles, 350
Lindsey, Lawrence, 517
Linn, Johannes, 288
Lipton, David, 247
Lissakers, Karin, 515
List, Friedrich, 53–54, 64, 65, 331
Little, Ian, 286, 287
Liu Ho, 171
Lockhead scandal, 386, 390, 393
Lotus Group, 174
Low, Paul, 178–179
Lytton Commission, 59

Macapagal-Arroyo, Gloria, 560–561
MacArthur, Douglas, 356, 358, 396
MacDonald, Lawrence, 243–244, 265,
    276–277
Machado, Kit, 73
McNamara, Robert, 515
Mahathir bin Mohamad, 24, 88, 456, 457,
    463
  automobile industry and, 170, 173, 174,
    175, 176, 177, 180, 182, 183, 212
  EAEG proposal of, 84–85
  regional currency and, 257
  Soros and, 253
Mahbubani, Kishore, 33–34
MAICO, 142
Mail-order brides, 496–498
Makihara Minoru, 211
Malaysia
  Akihito's visit to, 459
  in APEC, 82, 83
  automobile production in, 169–170,
    172–185, 186–188, 192
  EAEG proposal of, 84–85
  economic recovery of, xxi
  electronics production in, 139–144, 146,
    147, 151, 155–156, 218, 219,
    231–236
  export growth, 121, 122
  financial crisis in, 219–220, 234–237
  global investments in, 125
  investment rules in, 121
  Japanese aid to, 114, 127, 128
  Japanese investment in, 28, 106, 112, 118,
    123, 131, 230

Malaysia (continued)
  Japanese retailers in, 201
  Korean investment in, 151
  Taiwanese investment in, 151
Malaysian-German Industrial Cooperation
    Project, 106
Malaysian Industrial Development
    Authority (MIDA), 154
Malaysian Sheet Glass, 178–179
Malik, Abdul, 470
Malloch-Brown, Mark, 525, 526
Mamoi Makoto, 431–432
Manchukuo, 59–62, 68, 471
Manchurian Electric Co., 60
Manchurian Mining Development
    Company, 60
Mao Zedong, 357, 442
Marcos, Ferdinand, 295, 343, 347, 352,
    356, 365
Marcos, Imelda, 343, 356
Marshall, Katherine, 515
Maruyama Nobuo, 502
Matsuoka Yosuke, 62
Matsushita Electric Industrial Co., 136,
    140–145, 147, 152, 153, 158–159,
    219, 234–237, 499–500
Megawati Sukarnoputri, 536
Meiji Restoration, 11, 12, 40, 55, 65, 330,
    398–399, 415, 452
MELCOM, 142, 150, 234–235, 236
Middle East Development Bank (MEDB)
    plan, 279
Middle East and North Africa Region
    (MENA) of the World Bank, 278
Mieno Yasushi, 263–264, 301, 372–373
Miki Takeo, 71, 75
Mikuni Akio, 19–20
Military
  budget, 23, 428–429
  constitutional peace clause and, 8, 9, 421,
    428
  Gulf War and, 319
  lack of contingency planning, 431
  in peacekeeping operations, 421, 430
  rearmament of, 25, 422–423, 427, 428
  security policy of, 435–436
  security taboo, 431–432
  suspicion and distrust of, 429–430, 434–435
  U.S. alliance and, 25–26
Military bases, U.S., 360, 419–420
Minebea Thai, 147–149
Ministry of Economy, Trade and Industry
    (METI), 563–564
Ministry of Education (MOE), 41, 474, 484

Ministry of Finance (MOF), 19, 22, 32, 91, 92, 93, 94, 98, 106, 208, 240, 243, 256, 261, 263, 293, 303, 313, 412, 415
housing-loan scandal, 543–544, 555–557
Ministry of Foreign Affairs (MOFA), 18, 22, 32, 81, 91, 92, 94, 113, 263, 267, 412–413, 421–423, 431–432, 436, 448
Ministry of International Trade and Industry (MITI), 20, 91, 130, 318, 412–413, 415, 416, 448, 452
Asian alliance and, 18, 22, 32, 77, 78, 81, 87
automobile industry and, 191, 198–199, 417
foreign aid and, 126–129, 226–228, 314
foreign companies and, 406
on foreign investment, 120, 131, 221, 224
foreign investment and, 105–106, 113, 114, 141, 153, 261
foreign trade and, 324
influence on economic growth, 332
private sector ties of, 315–316
on Russian reconstruction, 322
training program of, 228, 500
See also Japan External Trade Organization (JETRO)
Ministry of Labor, 550, 553
Miroku Bosatsu, 40
Mitarai Fujio, 124, 220, 231
MITI. See Ministry of International Trade and Industry
MITI and the Japanese Miracle (Johnson), 315–316
Mitsubishi Bank, 211
Mitsubishi Motors, 62, 124, 165, 211, 212
Asian car of, 197, 198
Asian financial crisis and, 223–224
Asian imports of, 196
brand-to-brand complementation (BBC) and, 189–190
keiretsu of, 174, 395
in Malaysia, 169, 170, 174, 175–176, 178– 179, 182, 187–188
Mitsubishi Shoji, 211–212, 213
Mitsui Club, 371–372
Mitsui and Co., 188
Mitsui Mariko, 381–382
Mitsui Trust & Banking, 409
Mitsuzuka Hiroshi, 252
Miyagi Kohtaro, 231–232
Miyamoto Nobuko, 558
Miyazawa Kiichi, 29–30, 97, 114, 221, 252, 257, 258, 389, 391, 436
Mizuho Corporate Bank, 567–568, 569

Mizumoto, Mery and Mario, 486–487
Mizutani Kenji, 544
MMC Sittipol, 189–190
Mochizuki, Mike, xxiii
MOF. See Ministry of Finance
MOFA. See Ministry of Foreign Affairs
Mondale, Walter, 325
Moon Chung-In, 73
Moon Kwan-ja, 483
Moore, Michael, 328
Mori Yoshiro, 8
Morimura Seiichi, 473
Morita Akio, 204, 374
Morohashi Shinroku, 211
Mukden Incident, 471
Multinationals. See Automobile industry in Asia; Electronics industry in Asia; Foreign investment in Asia
Muraoka Shigeo, 78
Murayama Tomiichi, 387, 414, 455, 456, 463
Murobushi Tetsuro, 389, 392
Murphy, R. Taggart, 89
Mus, Paul, 340
Muscat, Robert, xvii
Museum of Revolutionary History, Beijing, 441–442, 443
Muto Emiko, 548
Mutual fund investment in Asia, 26–27
Mutual Security Treaty, 422
Myers, Ramon H., 60–61
Myrdal, Gunnar, 364, 365
"Myth of Asia's Miracle, The" (Krugman), 270, 283

Nadzmi B. Mohd. Salleh, 181–182
NAFTA. See North American Free Trade Agreement
Nagasaka Toshihisa, 231
Nagasaki bombing, 475
Nagoya Oak Industries (NOI), 179
Nagoya University, 65
Nakahara Michiko, 467–468, 475–476, 477, 478
Nakajima Hiroshi, 563
Nakama (ingredients) theory, 299–300, 306, 309
Nakamori Takakazu, 408
Nakasone Yasuhiro, 33, 386, 390, 391, 392, 431
Nakatani Iwao, 398, 416–417, 418, 449, 557–558
Nakauchi Isao, 411–412, 553–554
Nakayama Taro, 425

Nambu Yasuyuki, 553
Nance, John, 350
Nanjing massacre, 41, 442
Nao Yoshiyasu, 199
Narasaki Yanosuke, 394
Naruhito, Crown Prince, 42, 83
National Institute for Defense Studies, 448
National Intelligence Council (NIC), 25
Nationalism, 8, 12–13
National Police Agency, 554–555
National System of Political Economy
(List), 54
Navy (U.S.) Japanese Language School,
353–355
Naya Seiji, 432
Neff, Robert, 316
Negishi Koichi, 472
Neoclassical economics, 48–51, 268, 291
New Asian Industries Development Plan
(New Aid Plan), 126–129
New Economic System, 414–415
New Miyazawa Initiative, 29–30, 250, 257,
258–259, 260
New Order in East Asia, 57, 62
Newsweek, 374
New Zealand, in APEC, 75, 78
Nichiman Jidosha Kaisha, 60
Nikkei Industry and Consumption Research
Institute, 120
Ninnart Chaithirapinyo, 198
Nippon Steel, 62, 383–384
Nippon Steel Tube Manufacturing, 62
Nippon Telegraph and Telephone (NTT),
386
Nishigaki Akira, 296
Nishimizu Mieko, 243, 266, 267, 268, 290,
302
Nishimura Nobukatsu, 410
Nissan Motor Co.
Asian car of, 124, 192, 197–198
Asian market and, 165, 167
Korean-Japanese campaign against,
483–484
regional production network, 188
Nissho Iwai, 212
Nixon, Richard, 105
Noble, Greg, 172
Nofal, Ashraf Attia Hassannien, 332
Noguchi, Isamu, 44
Noguchi Yukio, 415
Nomura Research Institute (NRI), 151–152,
322
Nonaka Hiromu, 464
Noordin Sopiee, 111

Norman, E.H., xxvii–xxviii, 9
North American Free Trade Agreement
(NAFTA), 78, 113, 143, 190, 240, 262
North Korea
at ASEAN Forum (ARF) meeting, 425
nuclear capability of, 423, 427
Nukazawa Kazuo, 111, 403
Nye, Joseph, 426
Nye Initiative, 426–428

Obuchi Keizo, xxvi, 25, 259, 412, 464, 538
Obuchi Plan, 259–260
Occupation, U.S.
benevolent assimilation policy, 355–356
conglomerates and, 356–357, 396
immigration policy, 489
Ochiai Kazuaki, 497–498
OECD. *See* Organization of Economic
Cooperation and Development
OECF. *See* Overseas Economic Cooperation
Fund
Ogura Kazuo, 93, 102, 109–110
Ohira Masayoshi, 71, 75
Ohkawa Kazushi, 303
Ohlin, Bertil, 64
Ohmae Kenichi, 88
Ohno Izumi, xxiii
Ohno Kenichi, xxiii
Ohtsuka Seiichi, 314
Ojimi Takato, 227, 228, 229
Okabe Akira, 186–187
Okano Kaoru, 392
Okazaki Hisahiko, 93, 102, 109, 111, 422, 436
Okita Saburo, 88, 214, 299
APEC and, 75, 76
flying-geese theory of, 64, 67–70, 74
Okuda Hiroshi, 31, 259
Okuda Michihiro, 493–494
Okumura Hirokzu, 77
Okumura Hiroshi, 398, 400
Omori Shoichi, 413–414
Omura refugees, 494–496
*On Familiar Terms: A Journey Across
Cultures* (Keene), 354
Opium Wars, 38
Ople, Blas, 425
Organization of Economic Cooperation and
Development (OECD), 214, 246
Development Assistance Committee
(DAC) of, 79–80
Organization for Pacific Trade and
Development (OPTAD), 75
Osaka meeting of APEC, 42, 80–84
Osaka Special Steel Co., 162

Osaka strategy, 80
Oshima Sadamasu, 53–54
Oshin, 204
Ostrom, Douglas, 400
Ostry, Sylvia, 325
Ota Masahide, 439
Overseas Development Council (ODC), 238, 514, 515
Overseas Economic Cooperation Fund (OECF), 69, 154, 214, 238, 258, 261–262, 293, 313
-World Bank loan policy dispute, 94, 294–301
Ozawa Ichiro, 368
Ozawa Terutomo, 72–73

Pacific-Asia Resources Center, 495–496
Pacific Basin Economic Council (PBEC), 76
Pacific Economic Cooperation Conference (PECC), 75, 76
Pacific Trade and Development Conferences (PAFTAD), 75
Pack, Howard, 267, 280–281, 282
Packard, Frank, 208–209
Paek Nam Sun, 425
Page, John, 250, 262, 302, 303, 304, 306, 313
  background of, 289
  characterized, 289, 290
  connection to Ishikawa, 267–268
  criticism of *East Asian Miracle* leadership, 286–287
  on export promotion, 291–292
  on Japanese model, 292
  knowledge of East Asia, 289–290
  leadership of *East Asian Miracle*, 265–266, 275, 280, 282, 287–288
  response to critics, 283, 285–286, 287
  World Bank career of, 265, 278, 288–289
Pangestu, Mari, 510, 514, 515–516
Panyarachun, Anand, 460
Park Chung Hee, 365
Partners for Progress plan, 80, 82
Pasona Group, 553
Pasuk Phongpaichit, 71–72, 120
Patrick, Hugh, 76, 396
Pearl Harbor attack
  anniversary of, 461–462, 469, 470, 471
  memorial, 432–433
Perry, Matthew, 11
Perry, William J., 426
Persatuan Pambekal Proton (PPP), 179
Perusahaan Otomobil Kedua Sdn. Bhd., 187

Petri, Peter, 267, 292
Phan Van Khai, 97
Philip, Prince (Duke of Edinburgh), 42
Philippines, 343, 347, 348–352
  automobile production in, 192
  economic growth of, 364–365
  Japanese aid to, 127, 296–297
  Japanese investment in, 28, 106, 118, 231
  Korean investment in, 151
  mail-order brides from, 496–498
  Taiwanese investment in, 151
  U.S. Occupation, 355–356
PHN Industry, 179–180, 181
Pickens, T. Boone, 400, 402, 403–404
Pioneer Electronic, 152
Piper, Guenther, 106
Plaza Accord, 14, 27, 89, 118, 126
Pohang Iron & Steel co., 165
Policy and Human Resource Development Fund (PHRDF), 262–263
Possibility of the Application of Japanese Experience from the Standpoint of the Developing Countries, 307
Post-ministerial conference (PMC), 424, 425
Powell, John, 472–473
Prejudice. *See* Ethnic prejudice
Prem Tinsulanonda, 190
Preston, Lewis, 264, 270, 288
Prestowitz, Clyde, 115–116, 269, 316, 518
Primas Suhandra, 511
Pritchard, Simon, 561
Proton Saga, 173–185
Public goods, 49
Purvis, William, 204
Pyle, Kenneth, 561–562

Qian Qichen, 380
Qureshi, Moeen A., 296

Radius, Prawiro, 78
Rais, Amien, 513
Raja Tun Mohar, 187
Ravenhill, John, 114–115
Razak, Najib Tun, 85
Reagan, Ronald, 294–295, 361
Recruit scandal, 386–395
Reifman, Alfred, 76–77
Reischauer, Edwin, 357, 359, 360, 443
Report of the Mission for the Revitalization of the Asian Economy, 259
Retail stores in Asia, 200–207
Ri Koran, 43–45
Ricardo, David, 54

Ripplewood Holdings, 562–563
Rise and Fall of the Great Powers, The
    (Kennedy), 377
Rockefeller, Michael, 350
Rodrik, Dani, 238, 283, 518
Rosefielde, Steven, 249
Rosovsky, Henry, 303, 396
Ross-Larson, Bruce, 265
Rostow, Walt W., 360, 361
Roth, Stanley, 426
Roy, Stapleton, 528
Rubin, Robert, 230, 245, 247, 248, 253,
    254, 268, 527, 538, 539
Rudyanto Hardjanto, 197
Russia
    foreign aid to Asia, 360–361
    Japanese model in, 321–322
    Kurile Islands dipute, 321
Ryukyu Islands dispute, 24–25

Sabot, Richard, 267
Sachs, Jeffrey, 251, 517, 518
Sahashi Shigeru, 416
Saito Katsuyo, 458
Saito Kunio, 252
Saito Toru, 487
Sakakibara Eisuke, 93, 95, 239–240,
    248–250, 252, 253, 255–256, 313,
    566
Sakakibara Katsuro, 219
Sakamoto Report, 77–78
Sakamoto Yoshihiro, 77, 324–325
Sakura Bank, 401
Salim, Emil, 513
Salomon Brothers, 253–254
Sambommatsu Susumu, 306–307, 311, 317
Samsu, Didiek, 341
Samuelson, Paul, 64, 317
San Francisco Peace Treaty, 358, 482
Sanger, David, 253, 254
Sano Tadakatsu, 327
Sanwa Bank, 212
Sanwa Group, 212
Sanyang motorcycle company, 172
Sanyo Electric Co., Ltd., 146, 152
Saotome Kasumoto, 475
Sasakawa Peace Foundation (SPF), 88, 110,
    111
Sasakawa Ryoichi, 110–111
Sasaki Toshiya, 552
Sasayama Yukitoshi, 429
Sassa Atsuyuki, 7
Satoh Yukio, 423, 424, 425, 436
Sato Mitsuhiro, 498

Sato Mitsuro, 166–167, 215
Sato Tadafumi, 384
"Save Utoro" campaign, 483–484
Scalapino, Robert A., 354–355
Scott, Maurice, 287
Seattle Round, xix, 52, 327–329
Second Invasion, The (Constantino), 102
Seidensticker, Edward, 355
Seki Noboru, 127
Self-Defense Forces. *See* Military
Sender, Henny, 213
Severino, Jean-Michel, 526
Sewell, John, 515
Sharp Corp., 146, 152, 153, 163, 234
Shen Caibin, 453
Shibuya Tadashi, 456–457
Shilling, John, 26, 27
Shimizu Hideo, 482, 483
Shimomura Osamu, 299
Shimomura Yasutami, 299
Shimuzu Mitsuo, 482, 484
Shinjuku bones incident, 471–474
Shinto Hisashi, 393–394
Shiratori Masaki, 93, 262, 302 on *East
    Asian Miracle* report, 280, 281, 290,
    291
    in OECF-World Bank loan policy dispute,
        293–294, 296–297
    on World Bank change, 312–313
    World Bank development policy and,
        297–298, 300
Shiratori Rei, 394
Shitara Kiyotsugu, 547
Shite shudan, 406–408, 410–411
Shohtoku Yukio, 235–236, 237
Showa Kenkyukai, 59
Shuichi Ono, 446
Simon, Hugh, 374
Sin, Jaime, 352
Sinai, Allen, 527
Singam, J., 141–142
Singapore
    China relations, 449
    economic growth of, 365
    foreign aid of, 79
    foreign lending in, 209
    free market and, 50
    investment in Southeast Asia, 121
    Japanese electronics production in,
        147
    Japanese investment in, 86, 106, 123
    Japanese model and, 34–35, 112
    Japanese popular culture in, 135
    Japanese retailers in, 200, 201

Sino-Japanese War of 1894–95, 442
Sjahirl Sabirin, 536
Small and Medium Enterprise Agency
    (SMEA), 153
Smith, Adam, 54, 331
Smithsonian Institution, *Enola Gay* exhibit
    at, 475
Soeya Yoshihide, 433–434, 436–437, 454
Sokaiya, 404
Solodow, Robert, 498
Sone Kenko, 81–82
Sonoda Shigeto, 501, 502, 503
Sony Corp., 146, 152, 153, 220
Soros, George, 253
Southeast Asia
    Asian NIEs' investment in, 121
    automobile production in, 160, 161, 163,
        165, 166–170, 172–185, 189,
        190–193, 197
    export growth, 121–122
    Japanese aid to, 126
    Japanese investment in, 28, 86, 91,
        105–106, 112, 117–118, 122, 129,
        136
    See also Association of Southeast Asian
        Nations (ASEAN); *specific countries*
Southeast Asia Treaty Organization
    (SEATO), 424
South Korea
    in APEC, 78
    automobile production in, 170
    China relations, 449, 450
    economic collapse of, 516
    economic growth of, 364
    economic recovery of, xxi, 32
    electronics production in Asia, 151–152,
        157
    IMF loan, 245, 246, 247
    investment in Southeast Asia, 121
    Japanese investment in, 28, 86, 105, 106,
        220, 230
    -Japan relations, xxvi–xxvii, 17, 42–43,
        56, 358–359
    regional economic cooperation and, 24
    World Bank loan, 247–248
South Manchurian Railway, 60
Soviet Union
    foreign aid to Asia, 360–361
    See also Russia
Special export zones (SEZs), 28
Speculators, stock market, 406–409,
    410–411
Squire, Lyn, 304, 310–311, 312
"State in a Changing World" report, 312

Steel industry, 383–384
Stiglitz, Joseph, 52, 240, 246, 248, 262, 518
    on East Asian growth, 250–251
    in *East Asian Miracle* project, 250, 261,
        266, 267, 268, 271
Stock market
    in "bubble economy," 373, 374, 379
    crash of 1990, 137, 209, 406
    keiretsu and, 401
    Recruit scandal and, 391–392
    reforms, 409–410
    speculation, 406–409, 410–411
Structural adjustment policy, 294–295,
    299–301, 316
Structural Impediments Initiative (SII), 326,
    402–403
Subcontracting system, 86, 104–105, 153,
    155
Subianto, Prabowo, 513
Sugimoto Kenji, 196
Sugita Nobuki, 323–324
Sugita Toshiaki, 501
Suharto, 15, 42, 128, 169, 363–364
    APEC and, 83
    China meeting, 380
    corrupt children of, 534
    IMF and, 528, 534–535
    resignation of, 505–514, 535
    World Bank and, 261
Suharto, Hutomo Mandala Putra "Tommy,"
    169, 534
Sukarno, 362–363, 470–471, 508
Sumitomo Corp., 259
Sumitomo Trust and Banking Co., 205, 409
Sumiya Fumio, 100
Summers, Larry, 51, 230, 250, 262, 272,
    279, 527, 535
    Asian Monetary Fund plan and, 253, 254
    East Asian Miracle project and, 264–265,
        266, 268, 269–271, 275, 288,
        301–302
    as Japan expert, 269
    Thai aid and, 245, 246
Summerville, Paul, 105, 376
Sun Also Sets, The (Emmott), 537–538
Sun Yat-sen, 443
Supreme Command of Allied Powers
    (SCAP), 8
Surin Pitsuwan, 25
Suzuki Shunichi, 375–376, 473
Suzuki Yoshio, 100–101
Suzuki Zenko, 71

Taft, William Howard, 355–356

Taisho Era, 64
Taiwan
  automobile production in, 170–172
  economic growth of, 364, 365
  electronics production in, 150–151, 157
  investment in Southeast Asia, 121
  Japanese investment in, 28, 86, 105, 230
  Japanese popular culture in, 134–135
  Japanese retailers in, 201–202
Takabe Keisuke, 188
Takahashi Johsen, 385
Takashimaya Co., 200–201
Takehara Takanobu, 394
Takeshita Noboru, 22–24, 51, 77, 89, 374,
    380, 386, 388, 389, 390, 391, 393
Takeuchi Akio, 567, 568
Takeuchi Tetsuo, 457
Takeuchi Tohei, 193–195
Tamagami Masaaki, 153
Tanaka Akihiko, 368, 437–438
Tanaka Hiroshi, 484
Tanaka Kakuei, 71, 368, 386, 388, 390
Tanigawa Toshimitsu, 543
Taniguchi Tomohiko, 256
Tarullo, Dennis, 523
Tay, Simon, 560
Technology transfer
  in automobile industry, 178, 181–185
  barriers to, 216–217
  in electronics industry, 146, 157–160,
    233, 500
  in financial crisis support effort, 228, 229
  JICA programs, 228–229, 323
Teh Kok Peng, 254, 257
Terry, Charles, 338, 341, 342–344,
    352–353, 366
Terry, Sarah, 341, 343, 344–346
Thailand
  Akihito's visit to, 459–460
  automobile production in, 124–125, 163,
    166–167, 169, 185–186, 190–192
  China relations, 448
  economic collapse of, 516, 519–522
  economic growth of, 365
  economic recovery of, xxi, 32
  electronics production in, 145, 146–149,
    151
  export growth, 121, 122
  IMF loan and, 245, 246
  investment rules in, 121
  Japanese aid to, 114, 127
  Japanese investment in, 28, 106, 112,
    118, 123, 145, 146–149, 220,
    230–231

Thailand (continued)
  Japanese retailers in, 201
  Korean investment in, 151
  Taiwanese investment in, 151
Thatcher, Margaret, 51
Theater Missile Defense (TMD), 25, 422,
    423
Theories of Foreign Investment (Kojima),
    71
This Is magazine, 431
Thomas, Vinod, 266, 285, 286
Tojo Hideki, 41
Tokio Marine and Fire Insurance Co., 211
Tokugawa Ieyasu, 39, 290
Tokugawa system, 11, 414
Tokyo School of Economics, 65
Tokyo Stock Exchange. See Stock market
Total factor productivity (TFP), 280–282
Total Mobilization Act of 1938, 415
Toyoda Masakazu, 78
Toyo Keizai Shinposha, 400
Toyota Motor Corp., 124, 163, 165, 166
  Asian car of, 194, 196–197
  Asian financial crisis and, 223, 224
  brand-to-brand complementation (BBC),
    192
  Daihatsu-Mitsubishi rivalry, 187–188
  Pickens' clash with, 400, 402, 403–404
  in Taiwan, 171
Trade associations, 415–416
Trade. See Foreign trade with Asia
Trading companies, 210–214, 222
Training programs
  economic management and policy, 317,
    321, 322–324
  See also Technology transfer
Treaty of Shimonoseki, 442–443
Tribalism, 477–478
Truman, Edwin M., 252
Tsang, David, 253
Tsuchiya Kiyoshi, 381
Tsuneishi Keiichi, 474
Tsuruoka, Doug, 128
Tsutsui Yoshio, 200, 201, 202

Ueda Masano, 190
Uekusa Masu, 397
Ugly American, The (Lederer and Burdick),
    346
Unger, Danny, 74, 128
Unit 731, 471–474
United States
  in APEC, 75, 78, 80, 81, 82, 84, 436
  ASEAN and, 436

United States *(continued)*
Asian automobile industry and, 124–125,
185–186
Asian financial crisis and, 230, 516, 517,
523, 528
Asian Monetary Fund (AMF) plan and,
253, 254
Asia-Pacific alliances and, 76–77
-China relations, 25, 447, 451
competition from Japan, 131–132
East Asia Strategy Initiative and, 460,
464
foreign aid to Asia, 359–360, 361–362
foreign investment in Asia, 19, 20–21,
150
Gulf War and, 318–319
IMF and, 242, 255
Japanese bureaucrats' resentment of, 324
Japanese immigration and, 488
Japanese investment in, 108, 118
keiretsu system and, 402–403
military bases of, 360, 419–420
money markets and, 255
Navy Japanese Language School,
353–355
offshore production of, 152
in Philippines, 355–356
in Plaza Accord, 89
in Vietnam War, 365–366
World Bank and, 239, 240, 244, 248
World Trade Organization (WTO) and,
325, 326–327
United States-Japan relations, 8, 9, 18, 25,
33–34, 84, 109, 110, 464
Asian financial crisis and, 538–541
Cold War strategy, 359, 367, 368,
419–420, 431
defense guidelines, 428
Nye Initiative, 426–428
pro-U.S. *vs* radical change factions,
421–423, 436–440, 458
Security Treaty, 422, 427, 430–431
See also Occupation, U.S.
Uruguay Round agreements, 326–327
U.S. Agency for International Development
(USAID), 95, 363, 366
Uy, Marilou, 266

Valenti, Jack, 356
Ventura, Rey, 496
Vernon, Raymond, 73
Vietnam, Japanese economic model in,
95–97
Vietnam War, 365–366

Wada Katsu, 204
Wada Kazuo, 204–205, 206
Wade, Robert, 266, 284–285, 286, 288,
297–298, 300–301
Wahid, Abdurrahman, 528
Wakamatsu Isamu, 222–223
Wallich, Henry and Mable, 397
Wall Street Journal, 222, 251, 388
Walton, Michael, 268, 526
Wang Jingwei, 41
Wan Waithayakon, 41
Wanted: An Asian Policy (Reischauer), 357
War commemoration, 461–462
War crimes, 6, 8
apology for, xxvi, 17, 88, 457, 459–461,
462, 463, 464, 469
compensation of victims, 463, 466, 468
denial of, 461, 464
Jiang on, 464
public examination of, 466–468, 471–474
textbook censorship on, 41, 474
U.S. Occupation and, 472–473
War reparations, xxvi, 358, 468
War responsibility, 469–470
War Responsibility Center, 467
Washington Consensus, 249
Watanabe Hidetoshi, 489, 492
Watanabe Michio, 391, 393
Watanabe Shigeo, 406, 408, 409, 411
Watanabe Toshio, 72
Watson, Peter, 326–327
Williams, David, 248
Williams, Maslyn, 363
Williamson, John, 249
Wilson, Dick, xvii
Winters, Jeffrey, 526, 528
Wiranto, General, 506, 510, 512
Wolf, Martin, 517
Wolfensohn, James, 240, 247, 248, 261, 526
Wolferen, Karel von, 316
Women
foreign students, 479–481
job discrimination, 480, 547–548,
549–550
job loss, 548–549
mail-order brides, 496–498
second-class status of, 381–382, 480
Wong, Steven, 132–133, 135, 188
Woo-Cummings, Meredith, 126, 286
World Bank, xviii, xxi, 26, 47, 95, 96, 125,
126, 384, 515
anti-globalization protests at, 239, 241
Asian financial crisis and, 524–527,
533–534

World Bank *(continued)*
changeover from neoclassical economics, 52, 92–93
conditionality and, 96, 321
conflicts with Japanese aid policy, 96–97, 99
founding of, 241
Hong Kong meeting of, 253
institutional culture of, 241–242
Japanese model and, 276, 292
Japan research fairs of, 312
Japan's courtship of, 238–239, 242–244, 293–298
Japan's influence on, xiv, xxiii, 239–240, 260–261
Japan's shareholder status in, 243, 262–263, 294, 297–298
neoclassical economic model and, 268, 291
-OECF loan policy dispute, 294–301
PHRD fund, 263
rivalry with IMF, 244, 245, 246–248, 261
Russian reform programs and, 321–322
"State in a Changing World" report of, 312
structural adjustment policies of, 294–295, 299–301, 316
Suharto and, 528
Washington Consensus in, 249
See also East Asian Miracle project
World Bank Economic Review, 265
World Council of Churches, 492
World Development Report (WDR), 264, 266, 312
World Economic Forum, 279
World Trade Organization (WTO), xiv, 220, 229, 256, 324
Chinese entry, 4
Japanese agenda for, 324–325, 327–328
Seattle Round failure, xix, 52, 327–39
Uruguay Round agreements and, 325–326
WTO. *See* World Trade Organization
Wysocki, Bernard, Jr., 127–128

Xiang Huaicheng, 252
Xie, Andy, 566

Yamada Katsuhisa, 313, 314–315, 316–317, 321–322
Yamada Kazuhiro, 544–546

Yamada Matsuhiko, 157–158
Yamaguchi Fumio, 44
Yamaguchi Noboru, 440
Yamaguchi Yoshiko, 44–45
Yamamura Kozo, 226, 229
Yamasaki Goro, 435
Yamazaki Masakazu, 488
Yamazawa Ippei, 74, 79, 91
Yanagawa Masakazu, 235
Yanagihara Toru, 45, 85, 91, 98, 268, 334, 375
background of, 303
characterized, 303–304
on *East Asia Miracle* report, 290, 304–305
Japanese model study of, 307–311, 317
link to flying-geese school, 299
nakama (ingredients) concept of, 299–300, 306, 309
on regional trade, 85, 112
on United States, 324
on war record, 43–44
Yaohan's Global Strategy (Wada), 206
Yaohan supermarket chain, 201, 204–206
Yasuda Osamu, 322
Yen
appreciation, 23, 27–28, 29, 89, 121, 126, 137, 163–164, 374
depreciation, 225, 255, 565–566
internationalization, 255–258
Yergin, Daniel, 48
Yokoo Kensuke, 140, 141, 143, 215
Yoshida Shigeru, 358
Yoshida Yasushi, 143
Yoshioka Shinobu, 379
Yoshitomi Masaru, 398
Young, Alwyn, 270, 273, 282–283

Za Kuromaku game, 385, 386
Zaibatsu, 356–357, 396–397, 399
Zhang Jinghui, 41
Zhou Yi, 490
Zhu Rongji, 259, 451, 452
Zi Xi, Empress, 443
Zielenziger, Michael, xxii, 31, 523
Zielinski, Robert, 401, 402
Zobel y Ayala, Enrique, 356

Edith Terry is a writer and journalist based in Hong Kong. She has been a correspondent for the *South China Morning Post*, the *Globe and Mail Newspaper*, and *Business Week*, and has lived and worked in Indonesia, Taiwan, the Philippines, the People's Republic of China, Canada, Japan, Singapore, and Hong Kong, in that order, as well as New York, Washington, DC, and Honolulu in the United States. Her family on both sides immigrated to the United States from England in the eighteenth century, settling in the Carolinas and Alabama. In 1959, she moved with her parents Sarah and Charles to Jakarta, Indonesia, beginning a life-long fascination with Asia.